Civilization Past & Present
SINGLE VOLUME • FIFTH EDITION

T. WALTER WALLBANK
Emeritus Professor of History, University of Southern California

ALASTAIR M. TAYLOR
Professor of Political Studies and Geography, Queen's University

NELS M. BAILKEY
Professor of History, Tulane University

GEORGE F. JEWSBURY
Associate Professor of History, Oklahoma State University

Cover: A 1974 exhibition of sculpture by Henry Moore, held on the roof of the Pitti Palace in Florence, Italy, is viewed by spectators. Moore's abstract figures provide a stark contrast to the Renaissance splendor of the Florence Cathedral with its Brunelleschi dome (center) and campanile (left), and to the tower (right) of the Piazza Della Signoria. G. Tortoli, Photo Researchers.

1. (frontispiece) "The Hunt of the Unicorn II, The Unicorn at the Fountain" (fifteenth century). This tapestry of French or Flemish origin is an example of the courtly aspect of late Gothic art. The scene is a wood where a group of hunters have confronted the unicorn, a fabulous animal whose symbolic meaning varies in history, but which is here represented as a gentle, kindly beast. Courtesy of the Metropolitan Museum of Art, The Cloisters Collection, Gift of John D. Rockefeller Jr., 1937.

Civilization Past & Present
SINGLE VOLUME • FIFTH EDITION

Scott, Foresman and Company • Glenview, Illinois

Dallas, Tex. • Oakland, N.J. • Palo Alto, Cal. • Tucker, Ga. • London, England

Preface

Originally published in 1942, *Civilization Past and Present* was the first text of its kind. Its objective was to present a survey of world cultural history, treating the development and growth of civilization not as a unique European experience but as a global one through which all great culture systems have interacted to produce the present-day world.

This Fifth Single-Volume Edition of *Civilization Past and Present* continues to present a global survey of humanity's experiences and accomplishments. It maintains the various strengths that have made *Civilization Past and Present* a widely popular introductory textbook. Fifteen chapters of the text have been completely reorganized and rewritten for this major revision.

In Part Three, for example, coverage of the nonwestern world has been expanded. In Chapter 16, "Old Worlds Beyond the Horizon," the treatment of China during the Ming dynasty and Japan during the Ashikaga and Tokugawa periods covers both political development and social and cultural emphasis. Chapter 17, "Before the European Impact," now includes a detailed treatment of sub-Saharan Africa from the rise of the early great kingdoms beginning in 3000 B.C., through the intrusion of the Europeans and the development of the slave trade to 1800 A.D.

The authors of the Fifth Single-Volume Edition have also completely rewritten and expanded Part Five, "The European Primacy," and Part Six, "The Interdependent Planet." Chapter 22 now includes a detailed discussion of the causes and the repercussions of the first Industrial Revolution. Chapters 23 and 24 contain a more effective presentation of romanticism, nationalism, and Marxian theories. The political history of each major European state has been restructured in Chapters 25

and 26 to provide a clearer chronological progression. The concluding segment and climax to Part Six is Chapter 30, "The Waning of European Primacy: World War I" which traces the many factors leading to this tragic event.

Another section to undergo a complete revision is Part Eight, "Toward a New World," which contains totally reorganized and augmented coverage of world events since the end of World War II and has been expanded into four chapters. In addition, the revised Epilogue focuses on future studies and features an in-depth presentation of three world-views for the future. Other chapters in Parts One, Two, Four, and Seven have been updated for this new edition.

This Fifth Single-Volume Edition introduces a new feature for students — the Family Profiles. Each of the nine Family Profiles describes the daily life of individuals in a different historical period in order to provide an extra dimension of relevance to social history.

Finally, there are over 150 new black-and-white photographs pertaining to topics covered in the text, and 23 new full-color reproductions, carefully selected for their importance to the history of world art. The text also contains updated chronological tables and a more thorough index.

The Fifth Single-Volume Edition places particular emphasis on the fundamental forces that are speeding up change as we enter the final two decades of the twentieth century. The need is greater than ever to understand these changes in their historical perspective. The authors and publisher wish to express their appreciation to Donna Maier, Carolly Erickson, and Charles P. Ridley, and to gratefully acknowledge their contributions to this edition.

Library of Congress Cataloging in Publication Data
Main entry under title:

Civilization past & present.

Single volume 4th ed. by T. W. Wallbank, A. M. Taylor, and N. M. Bailkey.
Includes bibliographical references and index.
1. Civilization. I. Wallbank, Thomas Walter, 1901-   Civilization past & present.
CB57.W35   1977   909   77-12590
ISBN 0-673-07951-1

5 6 7 8 9 10 -VHJ- 85 84 83 82 81 80

Acknowledgments for quoted matter and illustrations are included in the Footnotes and the List of Illustrations beginning on page 899. The Footnotes and List of Illustrations pages are an extension of the copyright page.

Note to the Student

This book has been developed with the dual purpose of helping you acquire a solid knowledge of past events and, equally important, of helping you think more constructively about the significance of those events for the difficult times in which we live. In the Prologue you will learn more about studying the meaning of history. This note is intended to acquaint you with the principal features of the text.

THE INTERCHAPTERS

Aid in the organization and review of your reading will be provided by the interchapters, which outline the material to be covered in each unit.

THE FAMILY PROFILES

Appearing at the end of each Part (with an additional one following Chapter 17), are nine Family Profiles. These concisely-written descriptions look into the world of individuals living during the period of history covered in the preceding section. Each Family Profile tells about living conditions, social activities, occupations, religious attitudes, political loyalties, aspirations, and constraints of the family members depicted. We get a good insight into the lives of a working-class Roman family; a medieval Chinese family; an Aztec family; English families in the Tudor period and during the Restoration; a Parisian family in 1815 and their descendants in 1914; and a peasant family living in India during the early 1930's updated by the next generation of this same family during contemporary times.

THE COLOR PLATES

Seven folios of full-color art reproductions appear throughout the book. The works of art have been carefully selected and faithfully reproduced to illustrate, in every case, some facet of a culture pattern discussed in the text. These reproductions, with the accompanying commentary, constitute a capsule history of world art.

SUGGESTIONS FOR READING

At the conclusion of each chapter, you will find an annotated bibliography, pertaining especially to what was covered. The readings list special historical studies, biographies, reputable historical fiction, and some collections of source materials. As indicated in the listings, many of these works can be purchased in less expensive paperbound editions. These bibliographies will provide you with ample readings from which to develop special reports or with which to improve your understanding of a given subject.

THE CHRONOLOGICAL CHARTS

At the end of the book is a series of eight chronological charts showing the sequence of events discussed within the eight units of the text. By studying these charts, you can fix in your mind the relationship of events in the various parts of the world.

THE MAPS

Two-color maps are liberally distributed throughout this book. Some are designed to make clear the nature of a single distinctive event or idea discussed in the text; others illustrate larger trends, as, for example, the map showing trade and cultural interchange in the ancient world (see p. 116). At the end of the book are sixteen pages of full-color reference maps, showing all the major areas of the world and virtually every town, political subdivision, and geographic feature mentioned in the text. Most of the reference maps and several of the two-color maps appear in relief.

THE PRONUNCIATION KEY

In the index the correct pronunciation is given for many proper names. Thus you will find it easy, as well as extremely helpful, to look up the correct pronunciation of the names of persons and places referred to in the text.

Contents

PROLOGUE

Perspective on Humanity

If the time span of our planet — now estimated at some five billion years — were telescoped into a single year, the first eight months would be devoid of any life. The next two months would be taken up with plant and very primitive animal forms, and not until well into December would any mammals appear. In this "year" members of *Homo erectus*, our ancient predecessors, would mount the global stage only between 10 and 11 P.M. on December 31. And how has the human species spent that brief allotment? Most of it — the equivalent of more than half a million years — has been given over to making tools out of stone. The revolutionary changeover from a food-hunting nomad to a farmer who raised grain and domesticated animals would occur in the last sixty seconds. And into that final minute would be crowded all of humanity's other accomplishments: the use of metal, the creation of civilizations, the mastery of the oceans, the harnessing of steam, then gas, electricity, oil, and, finally, in our lifetime, atomic energy. And now humankind's technological genius has enabled it to escape from age-old bondage to the earth and to initiate an interplanetary age. Brief though it has been, man's time on the globe reveals a rich tapestry of science, industry, religion, and art. This accumulated experience of the human species is available for study. We call it *history*.

THE PAST AS PAST

The Koster site. The Koster family farms its land in the lower Illinois River valley, some forty-five miles north of St. Louis. A neighbor with an interest in archaeology had been impressed by large numbers of artifacts lying about in the Kosters' fields, and reported his finds to an archaeologist at Northwestern University. Dr. Stuart Struever investigated and, in 1969, began to excavate in a cornfield close to a stream which runs all year and to 150-foot-high bluffs that would protect the site from severe weather. Since then, the "dig" has yielded fifteen distinct "horizons" (the archaeologist's term for strata bearing traces of human habitation), each excellently preserved, together with thousands of items that have been washed, analyzed, and catalogued (with the aid of a computer). The Koster site — possessing the greatest potential yet found for unfolding the story of ancient human existence in North America — has shown that prehistoric humans lived in this valley for more than 8000 years, and further excavation may uncover signs of the Paleo-Indian, who inhabited this continent from 10,000 to 8000 B.C.

It may be asked: what is the "use" of all this painstaking effort? The Koster site has unearthed no sarcophagus, gold mask, or jeweled scarab deemed worthy to grace a museum of art. Yet its seemingly prosaic evidence can yield something no less exciting: information about the lives and environmental challenges of men and women who lived at Koster on fifteen different occasions during eight millennia. Thus at Horizon 11 were found the remains of structures believed to have been houses containing hearths and food-storage pits — so that, dating back to 4200 B.C., these dwellings are the earliest habitations yet discovered in North America. Found, too, were the skeletons — placed by radiocarbon dating at 5100

B.C. — of a small, evidently domesticated dog, and a human infant whose body had been covered for burial with powdered hematite, a yellowish-red ore of iron. Evidence also shows that the Indians at Koster had knowledge of squash, pumpkins, and gourds by 800 B.C., and domesticated corn by 200 B.C., yet they did not become agriculturists until 800 to 1000 A.D. Why did this shift take so long to occur, compared with societal transformations in other parts of the world? The archaeologists have determined, too, that for thousands of years — from the periods of Horizons 11 through 2 — the population remained at zero growth, yet before and after Horizon 1 came into existence (100 B.C.), a large population increase occurred. The Horizon 1 years also initiated organized violence, which means collective conflict against other peoples in the environment.

Thus, the scientists at the Koster site are augmenting and altering our knowledge of North American preliterate history. The interest displayed by the thousands of visitors to the site, and the enthusiasm of students working in the archaeological field program, attest to the curiosity which we all share to learn more about our past. Our resulting satisfaction is enhanced, moreover, when we use this knowledge as a yardstick to measure our own age and experiences within a global time-space perspective.

PAST AND PRESENT

"The more things change . . ." Obviously, the cultural horizons being revealed by the archaeologist's spade are very different from our own. The Koster farm possesses electricity and modern agricultural implements; it is near a state-highway system and within an hour's drive of a metropolis, itself a microcosm of twentieth-century science, technology, education, soaring buildings, and complex institutions. From their autos and trailers parked near the diggings, visitors disgorge cameras, transistor radios, and camping equipment which would have mystified the original inhabitants. These present-day nomads breakfast on Florida grapefruit, Brazilian coffee, and meats and cereals of a variety and quality far beyond the capability of the Archaic hunters and farmers. Those differences in technology, societal structure, and world-view are further demonstrated as the campers' radios report news from all parts of the globe.

". . . the more they remain the same." And yet, we are linked by more than mere curiosity to these archaic Illinois River valley inhabitants. Why? Because we are of the same species, and we share a fundamental invariance which connects present with past: the man-environment nexus. Ultimately speaking, it is the dynamic interplay of environmental factors and human activities that accounts for the terrestrial process known as history. Because of the biological continuity of our species, coupled with mankind's unflagging inventiveness, each generation has been able to build upon the experiences and contributions of its predecessors — so that continuity and change in human affairs proceed together. Hence, the two groups of *Homo sapiens* at the Koster site — ancient and modern — are at once dissimilar and similar.

The universal culture pattern. In this interplay of men and women with their environment and fellow-beings, they have always expressed certain fundamental needs. These form the basis of a "universal culture pattern" and deserve to be enumerated.

1. *The need to make a living.* Men and women must have food, shelter, clothing, and the means to provide for their offsprings' survival.

2. *The need for law and order.* From earliest times, communities have had to keep peace among their members, defend themselves against external attack, and protect community assets.

3. *The need for social organization.* For people to make a living, raise families, and maintain law and order, a social structure is essential. Ideologies may hold different views about the relative importance of the group and the individual within any such social structure.

4. *The need for knowledge and learning.* Since earliest times, humankind has transmitted the knowledge acquired from experience, first orally and then by means of writing systems. As societies grow more complex, there is increasing need to preserve knowledge and transmit it through education to as many people as possible.

5. *The need for self-expression.* People have responded creatively to their environment even before the days when they decorated the walls of Paleolithic caves with paintings of the animals they hunted. The arts appear to have a lineage as old as man himself.

6. *The need for religious expression.* Equally old is humanity's attempt to answer the "why" of its existence. What primitive peoples considered supernatural in their environment could at a later time often be explained by science in terms of natural phenomena. Yet today, no less than in archaic times, men and women continue to search for answers to the ultimate questions of existence.

These six needs have been common to people at all times and in all places. They apply equally to

7000 YEARS OF KOSTER LIFE

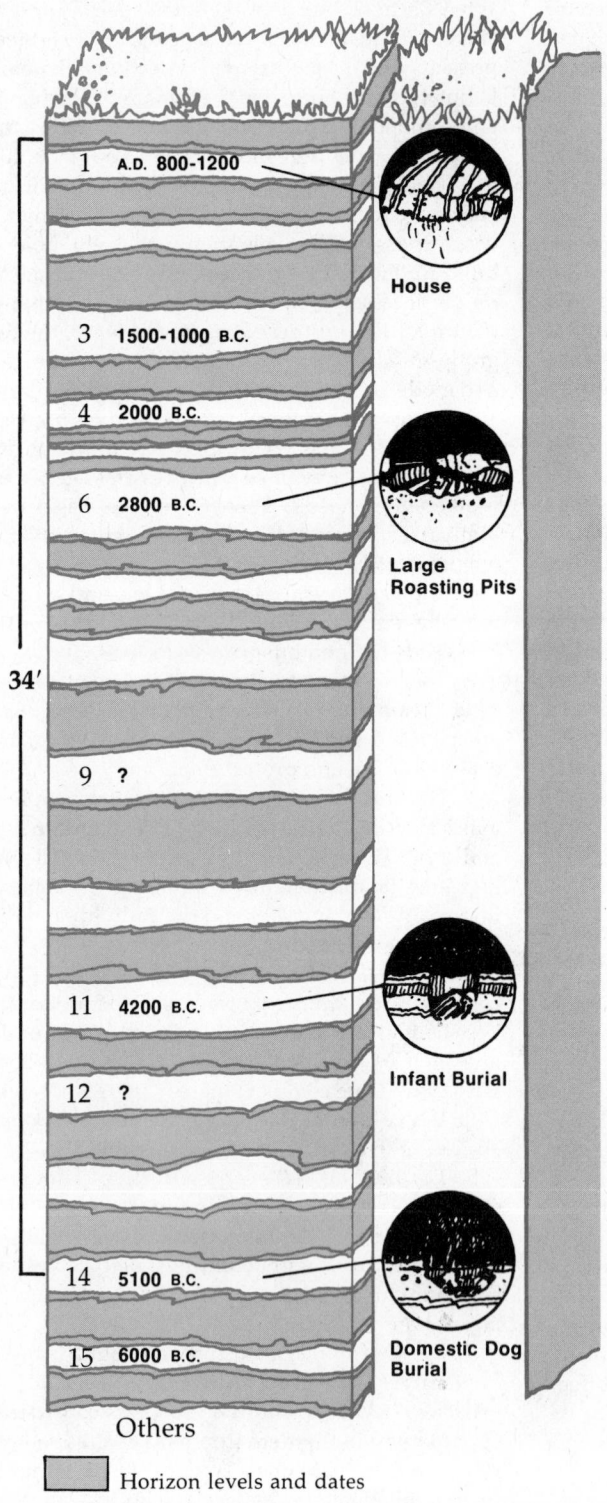

1 A.D. 800-1200

House

3 1500-1000 B.C.

4 2000 B.C.

6 2800 B.C.

Large Roasting Pits

34'

9 ?

11 4200 B.C.

Infant Burial

12 ?

14 5100 B.C.

15 6000 B.C.

Domestic Dog Burial

Others

⬛ Horizon levels and dates
   Sterile levels

the ancient and present-day inhabitants at the Koster site. Thus, the archaeologists have discovered stone tools, postholes for dwellings, and foodstuffs as part of the response to the need to make a living. Again, examination of the 15 horizons attests both to peaceful continuity and, eventually, recourse to collective conflict, either to defend the site against external aggressors or, again, to attack other communities. The presence of ancient villages underscores the organization of the species at a level more complex than the primary family unit—while the phenomenon of a stable population for millennia suggests societal behavior patterns and perhaps even regulations of some kind. Knowledge of how to make tools, weapons, and pottery had to be acquired, systematized as learning, and transmitted from one generation to the next. The designs found on pottery fragments did not serve any "practical" purpose, but satisfied the potter's aesthetic sense; while the elaborate burial rite for the infant found at Horizon 11 can hardly be divorced from a religious significance.

Culture traits and diffusion. Carrying the concept of a universal culture pattern one step further: when a group of people behave similarly and share the same institutions and ways of life, they can be said to have a common culture. Each person born into that group will derive from it his basic way of life. It follows that the basic differences between the archaic Indians at the Koster site and those of the present-day Koster family are due mainly to the fact that their culture traits are at different stages of development or that they worked out different methods of solving the same problems of existence. In the succeeding chapters, we shall be looking at a number of different cultures, some of which are designated as *civilizations*. (If *all* tribes or societies have culture, then civilization is a particular *kind* of culture.) "A culture is the way of life of a human group; it includes all the learned and standardized forms of behavior which one uses and others in one's group expect and recognize. . . . Civilization is that kind of culture which includes the use of writing, the presence of cities and of wide political organization, and the development of occupational specialization."[1]

Cultures are never static or wholly isolated. A particular culture may have an individuality which sets it off sharply from other cultures, but invariably it has been influenced by external contacts—and this process would have applied to every "horizon" at the Koster site. Such contacts may be either peaceful or warlike, and they meet with varying degrees of acceptance or resistance. The early American colonists took from the Indians the use of corn and tobacco, while the latter obtained the horse and firearms from the new-comers. On the other hand, the Second World War saw the Nazis and Japanese force their cultures upon subjugated peoples with little or no permanent result.

Environment and invention in culture change. Geography has profoundly influenced the development of cultures, but we should not exaggerate its importance. Although riverine civilizations evolved along the Nile and the Tigris-Euphrates, for example, none emerged in the physically comparable valleys of the Jordan and Rio Grande.[2] Moreover, environmental influences tend to become less marked as people gain increasing technological skill, as shown by the transformation of arid regions in southwestern United States into rich citrus areas and the extension of the grain-growing belt in the Canadian prairies further north through the development of frost- and rust-resistant types of wheat.

Invention is therefore another important source of culture change. The domestication of animals and cereals, for example, took place in both the old and new worlds, albeit the animals and grains were different because of dissimilar ecological factors—yet so far as we know, there was no physical contact at the time between the two cultural heartlands. To what extent, then, is physical contact required in the process of invention? Or, is it possible for men and women in different times and places to hit upon similar solutions to the challenges posed by their respective environments—resulting in the phenomenon known as "parallel invention"?

Culture lag. Some parts of a culture pattern change more rapidly than others, so that one institution sometimes becomes outmoded in relation to others in a society. When different parts of a society fail to mesh harmoniously, the condition is often called *culture lag.* Numerous examples of this lag could be cited: the failure to give women the vote until this century; the tragedy of hunger in the midst of plenty during the 1930's; in our own day, the repeated inability of the United Nations to limit atomic energy to peaceful uses because of the insistence by national states to arm themselves as they please.

PAST AND PRESENT AS PROLOGUE

Toward tomorrow's world. While time can be regarded as a continuum, we experience it only in a single direction. The Koster "dig" is an excavation from yesterday, but our "present" must become tomorrow's "past" in turn. And thus is "history" created. Past and present conjoin to become prologue for tomorrow's world, precisely because human and environmental processes must bring about continued transformations within societies and culture patterns alike.

What can the past and present—as history—suggest to us for tomorrow's world? In the first place, changes in the physical and social environments will probably accelerate as a result of continued technological invention. These changes can result in increased disequilibrium and tensions among the various segments comprising the universal culture pattern—in other words, in increased culture lag. To some observers, this culture lag has assumed dangerous proportions in the apparently widening gap in communications and outlook between science and the technological sector on the one hand and our traditional humanistic culture and value system on the other. These two major segments of our culture pattern appear to be advancing, and changing, at the speeds of a supersonic jet and of a horse-and-buggy respectively.

Just what dynamic factors are at work which bring about different rates of speed in the processes of change? Owing to the fact that our modern age derives its particular world outlook in ever growing measure to the discoveries of science and the changes wrought by technology, we shall have greater need than ever before to understand the dynamics involved and how they are already shaping the pattern of our culture for the decades ahead.

The 1970's are now having to pay the price of environmental and societal disequilibrium—as evidenced by an energy crisis, the rapid depletion of many nonreplenishable minerals and fossil fuels, physical environment deteriorating from pollution, and a population explosion in the underdeveloped regions of the world. Throughout its long planetary experience, mankind has had to endure shortages. Today, however, those shortages result from causes very different from anything that has happened hitherto in history. Our scarcities stem not from a traditional inability to do much more than scratch the earth's riches, but from our technological genius to convert and consume those resources on a scale both prodigious and prodigal.

From exponential growth to steady-state? Has the past anything to tell the future about the consequences of cultural disequilibrium—anything which we might profitably utilize in present-day planning for the decades ahead? The evidence found in the Koster horizons is relevant. It tells us that for 8000 years or more, men and women were able to lead what Dr. Struever terms the "good life." Archaic man "had plenty of leisure time in which to domesticate pets. It's sheer folklore that primitive people had to struggle from dawn to dusk simply to survive. How hard a man works depends a lot on what he considers necessary goals in life, and there was no environmental imperative in the valley requiring man to work hard. . . . Man lived in a land of milk and honey, with tremendous food resources all around him in this valley, and the taking was easy."[3] During that long period of successive habitations, the Indians at Koster maintained a stable equilibrium with an environment which in turn underwent no apparent deterioration.

Again, for much the longest part of that time, when the economy was still at the food-collecting stage, the Indians maintained their numbers with little change. True, prior to Horizon 1, there occurred a large increase in population, and this increase may either have occasioned, or in turn been occasioned by, a shift to agriculture. Yet in any case, it would appear that a new overall balance was struck between environmental factors and societal processes—a balance that would have eventuated sometime in zero growth, or steady-state.

The experience at the Koster site is far from unique. The historical record shows that all societies, previous to the present, have tended to shift from open-ended increase of physical size, population, and social complexity toward steady-state. Because our planet and its resources are finite, at some point, too, our society in turn must expect to shift from exponential growth to no-growth. By that term, we mean the setting of maximal levels upon the numbers of humans who can inhabit this planet with an assured minimal standard of life, and upon the exploitation of the earth's resources required to provide that standard. Otherwise, environmental disaster on an unprecedented scale could result in the decades ahead. But here we are talking about quantitative, not qualitative, no-growth. Too often, we have confused mere size and expansion with quality of life— which is about as logical as comparing a lump of coal with a diamond (though they both derive from carbon). Past and present conjoin to alert us to the need not only to engage in new forms of planning for the years ahead, but no less to rethink our existing social goals and value system. We shall require as long and accurate a perspective as possible from our global experience in order to make realistic analyses and take the right kinds of action to improve our quality of life.

THE "HOW" OF HISTORY

Definition of history. History is the record of the past actions of humankind, based upon surviving evidence. The historian uses this evidence to reach conclusions which he believes are valid. In this way he becomes an interpreter of the development of humanity. History shows that all patterns and problems in human affairs are the products of a complex process of growth. By throwing light on that process, history provides a means for profiting from human experience. In this connection it is salutary to recall the words of the philosopher George Santayana when he declared, "Those who cannot remember the past are condemned to repeat it."

Is history a science? There is more than one way of treating the past. In dealing with the American Revolution, for example, the historian may describe its events in narrative form. Again, he may prefer to analyze its general causes or perhaps compare its stages with the patterns of revolutions in other countries. But the historian does not aim for the same kind of results as the scientist. The latter can verify his conclusions by repeating his experiment under controlled conditions in his laboratory, and he also seeks to classify the phenomenon in a general group or category. For his part, the historian has to pay special attention to the *uniqueness* of his data, because each event takes place at a particular time and in a particular place. And since that time is now past, he cannot verify his conclusions by duplicating the circumstances in which the event occurred. Moreover, since history is concerned fundamentally with the lives and actions of men and women, the causes involved are bound to be relatively subjective.

Nevertheless, historians insist that history be written as scientifically as possible and that evidence be analyzed with the same objective attitude employed by the scientist when he examines natural phenomena. This scientific spirit requires the historian to handle his evidence according to established rules of historical analysis, to recognize his own biases and attempt to eliminate their effects from his work, and to draw only such conclusions as the evidence seems to warrant.

Historical method. To meet these requirements, historians have evolved the "historical method." The first step is the search for *sources*, without which there can be no history. They may consist of material remains—such as the bones, tools, weapons, and pottery found at the Koster site; oral traditions such as myths, legends, and songs; pictorial data such as drawings and maps; and, of course, written records ranging from ancient manuscripts to treaties, diaries, books, and yesterday's newspaper.

Having acquired his sources, the historian must next infer from them the facts. This process has two parts. *External criticism* tests the genuineness of the source. Its importance was demonstrated dramatically in recent years by the unmasking of a hoax—Piltdown Man—which had long duped scientists. For the most part however, the historian has to deal with less spectacular problems, such as checking ancient documents for errors that have crept into the text through faulty copying or translating.

The second step in the analytical process is called *internal criticism*. In evaluating written materials, the historian must ascertain the author's meaning and the accuracy of his work. To do so may require study of the language of the era or the circumstances in which the author's statement was made. A politician's memoirs may be suspect because of an almost universal tendency to present oneself in the most favorable light, while official documents must in turn be examined for what they may conceal as well as what a government wishes to reveal.

The final step in historical method is *synthesis*. Here the historian must determine which factors in a given situation are most relevant to his purpose, since obviously he cannot include everything that occurred. This delicate process of selection underscores the role that subjectivity plays in the writing of history. Furthermore, the more complex the events involved, the more crucial becomes the historian's judgment.[4]

The problem of periodization. Can we really categorize history as "ancient," "medieval," and "modern"? When we reflect upon this question, it becomes clear that what is "modern" in the twentieth century could conceivably be considered "medieval" in the twenty-fifth century, and eventually "ancient" in the thirty-fifth century A.D. Yet not to break up the account would be akin to reading this book without the benefit of parts, chapters, paragraphs, or even separate sentences. Like time itself, history would then become a ceaseless flow of consciousness and events. To simplify his task and to manage his materials more easily, the historian divides time into periods. The divisions he chooses, the lines he draws, reveal the distinctive way in which he regards the past—namely, in terms of patterns which appear to him logical and meaningful. Needless to add, no two historians see the past in an identical pattern; thus the division of the past into periods is necessarily arbitrary—and, like airline schedules subject to change without prior notice.

THE "WHY" OF HISTORY

Historical analysis. The historian seeks to describe not only *what* has happened and *how* it happened, but also *why* society undergoes change. Any search of this kind raises a number of fundamental questions: the roles of Providence, the individual, and the group in history; the extent to which events are unique or, conversely, can fit into patterns; and the problem of progress in human affairs. The answers vary with different philosophical views of the universe and man's role therein.

Providence or the individual. Those who hold the teleological view see in history the guidance of a Divine Will, directing human destinies according to a cosmic purpose. This concept was accepted as self-evident in ancient theocratic societies and medieval times, but lost ground after the Renaissance, when the spread of rationalistic doctrines and scientific triumphs seemed to forecast unlimited progress in human affairs. Other thinkers have exalted the role of the individual in the historical process—such as Thomas Carlyle, who contended that major figures, or "Great Men," chiefly determined the course of human events. In our own day, there has been a reaction against the nineteenth century's comfortable assumption that man is virtually a free agent.

"Laws" and "forces" in history. Opponents of Carlyle's thesis often contend that history is determined by "forces" and "laws" and by the actions of entire societies. Sociologists approach history primarily by analyzing the origins, institutions, and functions of groups. Like the sociologist, the economist tends to look at the historical record from the standpoint of group action and especially the impact of economic forces such as that of, say, supply and demand or diminishing returns.

The most explosive interpretation of history in modern times was made by Karl Marx. To him, irresistible economic forces governed human beings and determined the trend of events. Marx contended that the shift from one economic stage to another—such as from feudalism to capitalism—is attained by upheavals, or revolutions, which occur because the class controlling the methods of production eventually resists further progress in order to maintain its vested interests. He predicted that the proletariat would overthrow the exploiting capitalists and that the end result would be a classless society, followed by a gradual withering away of the state itself. These predictions, however, have proved considerably less than "scientific" in their accuracy.

Theories of civilization. Numerous other attempts have been made to explain societal processes according to a set of principles. Oswald Spengler, a disillusioned German, maintained that civilizations were like organisms; each grew with the "superb aimlessness" of a flower and passed through a cycle of spring, summer, autumn, and winter. He declared that western civilization was in its winter period and had already entered into a state of rapid decline. Like Spengler, other thinkers have sought to explain societal behavior in terms of biological growth and decay. Charles Darwin's evolutionary hypothesis made a strong impact upon nineteenth-century thought and gave rise to the concept that the principle of "survival of the fittest" must also apply to human societies. This line of thought—known as social Darwinism—raises social and ethical questions of major importance.

Does history obey impersonal laws and forces so that its course is inevitable? Or, at the other extreme, since every event is a unique act, is history simply the record of unforeseen and unrelated episodes? Can this apparent dilemma be avoided? We believe it can. Though all events are in various respects unique, they also contain elements which invite comparison—as in the case of the origin and course of revolutions in different countries. The comparative approach permits us to seek relationships between historical phenomena and to group them into movements or patterns or civilizations. For our part, we eschew any single "theory" of history, preferring to see merit in a number of basic concepts. These include the effects of physical environment on social organization and institutions; the roles played by economic, political, and religious factors; and the impact exerted by men and women occupying key positions in various societies.

Progress and growth is a continuous factor. It depends on, and contributes to, the maintenance of peace and security, the peaceful settlement of international disputes, and worldwide improvement in economic and social standards.

THE CHALLENGE

The role of history today. The archaeologists at the Koster site are adding to our understanding about humanity's life on this planet, its challenges and creative responses. The evidence at Koster shows that there is no single, predetermined road along which humanity must travel, or a set pattern of responses to its environmental problems and opportunities. Societal development is a creative, open-ended process, whether at Koster or any other location on this planet. The archaeologists as they sift and evaluate the unearthed evidence from the ancient past, the historians as they analyze the written records of classical civilizations, and the social scientists as they investigate present-day societal phenomena—all share a common interest and concern: to learn more about the human condition.

And we shall need to know all we can about that condition. While human technology is at present moving ahead at supersonic speed, there has been no corresponding increase in man's own mental or physical capacity. He has probably no more native intelligence than his predecessors at the Koster horizons—and just as probably less muscle. So we come to a fundamental challenge: how is twentieth-century man to cope with the ever widening disparity between what he *is* and what he *has?* How can he control and utilize his tremendous technological powers for happiness and not for nuclear self-annihilation? Today he seeks to conquer other planets before he has learned to govern his own.

Surely an indispensable step toward solving contemporary humanity's dilemma—technology without the requisite control, and power without commensurate wisdom—must be a better understanding of how man and all his works became what they are today. Only by understanding the past can we assess both the perils and the opportunities of the present—and move courageously and compassionately into the uncharted future.

PART ONE
The Ancient World

■ How old the universe is and how the planet earth came into being may never be known precisely, but modern scientists believe that our world has been circling the sun for four and one-half to five billion years. During that incredibly long time, the earth changed from a gaseous to a liquid state and finally solidified; waters formed on the earth's shell, and in their depths life took form. As one geological epoch succeeded another, first single-celled and then multicelled organisms evolved, and some of them learned to live on land. Eventually this ceaseless process of adaptation to environment brought forth the mammal class, of which man is a member.

Remains of early manlike creatures unearthed in Africa may be nearly three to four million years old. The time span from those remote days to about 3500 B.C. is usually referred to as prehistoric, or preliterate, times. By far the greater part of that time span was taken up by man's relentless struggle for survival—a struggle in which he learned to shape crude weapons and tools from stone, make fire, and domesticate certain plants and animals. The latter achievement was of revolutionary consequence, for it freed man of the necessity to hunt the migrant beasts. And a measure of control over plants and animals meant that he could settle down in one place and become a farmer and herdsman.

The stage was now set for a progressively rapid extension of man's control over his environment. Life became more complex and more rewarding. The discovery of metallurgy, progress in arts and crafts, the organization of larger social and political units, and the invention of writing heralded a new era of existence. These momentous advances did not occur over the entire earth but were concentrated in a few great river valleys. There the well-watered, fertile soil produced abundant harvests and food surpluses supported increased populations. Cities sprang up, inhabited by men with diverse talents: priests, potters, basket weavers, tool makers, and merchants.

Along the banks of rivers, then, we must look for the first civilizations. We shall find them widely scattered: Mesopotamia straddled the Tigris and the Euphrates; Egypt stretched along the Nile; India arose along the Indus and the Ganges; and China expanded eastward from the region of the Wei and the Huang Ho. Prolific in their gifts to mankind and so dynamic that two of them have retained unbroken continuity to our own day, these civilizations possessed similarities at least as arresting as their differences. In all four, political systems were developed, crafts flourished and commerce expanded, calendars and systems of writing were invented, art and literature of extraordinary beauty were created, and religions and philosophies came into being to satisfy men's inner yearnings.

Indebted to the Egyptians and Mesopotamians, the inhabitants of Crete and Mycenaean Greece fashioned a wealthy, sophisticated, commercial culture. Much of this Aegean civilization —the first advanced culture to appear in Europe —was destroyed by the end of the second millennium B.C., but enough remained to serve as the foundation for Greek civilization. Insatiably curious about man and man's world, the Greeks enjoyed a freedom of thought and expression unknown in earlier societies. Their fierce passion to remain untrammeled, however, was too often unrestrained. The failure of the Greek city-states to find a workable basis for cooperation doomed them to political disaster. Although the conquest of the city-states by King Philip of Macedonia ended the Hellenic Age, the influence of the Greeks was destined to increase. The establishment of a vast empire in the Near East by Philip's talented son, Alexander the Great, ushered in the Hellenistic Age and the widespread diffusion of Greek culture.

Meanwhile, a new power—Rome—had been evolving on the Italian peninsula. After five centuries of modest growth, this city-state embarked upon a career of unprecedented expansion. The splendor of Roman arms was matched by skill in administration, wisdom in law, and ingenuity in the practical arts of engineering and communication. These talents and abilities enabled the Romans to erect a Mediterranean empire which survived until the fifth century A.D. Probably the greatest achievement of the Roman Empire was the skillful maintenance of a diversity of cultures within a political unity. To the Romans we owe a debt for preserving and disseminating classical culture, for the legacy of Graeco-Roman culture is the foundation of western civilization.

In the first centuries of the Christian era we enter a brief but fascinating period in which the principal civilizations of West and East were in contact, engaged in a mutually beneficial exchange of wares and ideas. Unhappily, this process of culture contact and diffusion—which, had it been allowed to continue, might have had incalculable effects for good on world history— was brought to an untimely halt, largely as a result of a crisis in the West. The Graeco-Roman world was subjected to a series of shattering invasions which will be described in the next unit. The present unit surveys the classical age of civilization in both the West and the East—a period which must always remain one of the glorious epochs in human achievement.

CHAPTER 1

The Civilizations of the Ancient Near East

Along the Banks of Rivers

INTRODUCTION. As early as three million years ago or more, man's ancestors appeared on earth, naked in a world of enemies. The story of man's journey out of the darkness of ignorance and fear covers a period of hundreds of thousands of years during which he mastered the skills necessary for survival. Early man's most important achievements concern agriculture and the ways of life it engendered. Wild beasts were tamed as work animals or kept for their meat and hides. The first farmers scattered kernels of grain on the earth and waited patiently for harvest time. Because their fields and flocks could supply most of their wants, a settled existence became possible; men were no longer compelled to move on endlessly in search of food, as their food-gathering ancestors had done for countless generations. Where conditions were favorable, these ancient farmers were able to acquire more food than they needed for survival—surpluses to tide them over seasons of cold and drought. Thus, in green oases and on fertile plateaus, farming villages sprang up.

It was along the banks of great rivers that villages first grew into towns and cities. In early Egyptian picture writing a town is shown as a cross within a circle—the intersection of two pathways enclosed by a wall. The symbol is an appropriate one, for in the history of mankind the town—⊗—marks the spot where civilization as we know it began.

Within the towns the business of living took new turns. While the majority still farmed, there were now more craftsmen turning out specialized wares, merchants trading for metals and other needed raw materials, priests conducting religious ceremonies, and administrators planning and supervising the necessary cooperative effort for the common good. Time could be found also for intellectual and artistic pursuits that enriched the lives of the participants and developed a cultural heritage.

A culture can endure only if the knowledge necessary for its survival is passed on from generation to generation. Early peoples relied on information transmitted by word of mouth. But as towns and cities grew up and cultures became increasingly complex, methods for keeping records were devised and systems of writing were created. To most authorities, the development of writing is a prerequisite to civilization.

The four earliest civilizations—the Sumerian, the Egyptian, the Indian, and the Chinese—arose between c. 3500 B.C. and c. 1500 B.C., in each case in the valley of a great river system. In this chapter we shall trace the progress of civilization, including man's earliest advances in technology and his creation of written languages, in Mesopotamia and Egypt. In Chapter 4 we shall see the stirrings of civilization far to the east, in India and in China.

TOOLS AND ART OF EARLY MAN

The development of early man. Benjamin Franklin is credited with first defining man as a "tool-making animal." The making and using of tools is the first evidence of man's ability to use reason to solve problems. Since the use of stone implements was the most distinctive feature of early man's culture, this first cultural stage is known as the Paleolithic or Old Stone Age. The Paleolithic is a food-collecting stage, when men hunted, fished, and collected wild fruits, nuts, and berries. (Paleolithic culture survives among a few primitive peoples today.)

Who the ancestors of early man were and when and where tools were first made are much debated questions in scholarly circles. An important point in the development of early man occurred when the ape family became differentiated into the tree-dwelling apes and the ground-dwelling types known as *hominids*, "prehumans" or "protohumans." The Australopithecines, the earliest known hominids, were discovered in 1924 in Africa. *Australopithecus* had a fully erect posture but an apelike brain; his cranial volume measured no more than 500 cubic centimeters, as compared to 1300 to 1600 cubic centimeters in modern man. Now extinct, this genus may not be in man's line of descent.

In 1964 at Olduvai Gorge in Tanzania, L. S. B. Leakey discovered *Homo habilis* (mentally skillful man) in a site about 1.75 million years old. *Homo habilis* possessed a cranial capacity of 656 cubic centimeters, was about four feet tall, walked erect, had a well-developed thumb, and was found in association with crude tools.

In 1975 Mary Leakey (widow of L. S. B. Leakey) announced the oldest reliably dated remains of early man—fossil jaws and teeth of eight adults and three children, dated between 3.35 and 3.75 million years old.

In 1974 in Ethiopia, Dr. C. D. Johanson discovered four human leg bones which he believed were "in excess of three million years" old. Dr. Johanson has also constructed a composite hand, working with bones from humanlike creatures whose fossils, found in Ethiopia, have been dated at least 3 million years old. It is the most complete hand of such great age, which indicates that this early relative of modern man did not walk on his knuckles as well as his legs, as some apes do.

In 1972 at a site in Kenya, Leakey's son Richard found a skull and two intact thigh bones similar to bones of modern man and indicating that their owner walked erect. The skull, for which "available evidence points to a probable date of 2.9 million years," has been labeled KNM-ER 1470. Though further work is necessary, "it seems certain that a volume greater than 800 cubic centimeters for KNM-ER 1470 can be expected."[1] Although over a million years older and possessing a larger cranial capacity, KNM-ER 1470 bears some morphological resemblances to the more primitive *Homo habilis*. Because of the skull's comparatively large size and certain morphological features, Leakey and other scientists have attributed KNM-ER 1470 to the genus *Homo*. KNM-ER 1470 strongly indicates that *Homo* coexisted in East Africa with *Australopithecus*. Additional evidence for this theory has been provided by Leakey's discovery of another skull dated from 2.5 to 3 million years old and of the same type as KNM-ER 1470.

Richard Leakey believes that his finds and those of his mother and Dr. Johanson suggest that man's direct ancestor was a separate line of creatures which developed side by side with *Australopithecus* from a common ancestor.

A phylogeny of Plio-Pleistocene hominids. Can we sort out these various finds in order to understand the evolutionary relationship of the hominids during the Pliocene and Pleistocene epochs, and thereby develop a sequence that led eventually to *Homo sapiens,* namely, to ourselves? Professor P. V. Tobias, writing in the British journal *Nature,* has adopted a bigeneric classification because the recognition of two hominid genera "enjoys the greatest consensus at the present time." He divides *Australopithecus* into *A. africanus*, *A. robustus*, and *A. boisei*, the last two forming one superspecies. His phylogenetic tree shows that *Homo* was a distinct genus by between 3 and 4 million years ago (a date that would be compatible with the recent Ethiopian finds). Impressed by the morphological resemblances between KNM-ER 1470 and *Homo habilis,* Tobias concludes, as a "provisional judgment," that the East African find "may even extend our concept of the range, in time and morphology, of

H. habilis." On this basis, *Homo habilis* existed from at least 2.9 to around 1.5 million years ago, *Homo erectus* (see below) for a subsequent million years, while *Homo sapiens*—with its subdivisions or "races"—has been inhabiting the planet only within the relatively recent past.

Homo erectus. The first evidence of the group *Homo erectus*, which appears later than *Homo habilis*, was discovered in Java in 1891. Peking man and other members of this group have been discovered in Asia, Africa, and Europe. *Homo erectus* had a cranial volume larger than *Homo habilis* but smaller than modern man. He was about five feet tall, had heavy brows, and a receding forehead. *Homo erectus* knew the use of fire and produced tools, including the first true handax. He became extinct about 300,000 years ago, well before the end of the Pleistocene epoch.

Neanderthal man. Until after the middle of the fourth glaciation, *Homo neanderthalensis* was the principal inhabitant of Europe and adjacent parts of Asia and Africa. About five feet tall, Neanderthal man possessed a thick-set body, short forearms, and a slouching posture. He invented tools of advanced design, was an able hunter, and adapted to extreme cold by using fire and living in caves and rock shelters.

The culminating stage in the development of the genus *Homo* occurred in the later Upper Pleistocene, when Neanderthal man in Europe was displaced by *Homo sapiens*, the immediate forerunner of modern man. *Homo sapiens* may have been living in western Europe as early as 70,000 years ago, probably as a contemporary of Neanderthal man. By 20,000 B.C. *Homo sapiens* inhabited Europe, Asia, Africa, and Australia—and had begun to move across the Bering Strait to America. Today, *Homo sapiens* is the only existing member of the genus *Homo*.

The dawn of Paleolithic culture. Australopithecine sites in South Africa indicate that although *Australopithecus* did not fashion tools, he at least occasionally made use of objects as improvised tools and weapons. This simple *utilization* has been described as the first of three major steps in the formative history of toolmaking. "The second step would have been *fashioning* — the haphazard preparation of a tool when there was a need for it. The third step would have been *standardization*. Here, men began to make tools according to certain set traditions."[2]

The haphazard fashioning of tools is associated with pebble tools, the earliest of which are made of split pebbles or shattered chunks of stone about the size of one's fist or a bit larger. Such occasional toolmaking is found in early Pleistocene geological beds in Africa, including the Olduvai Gorge. Standardized toolmaking includes the later and better made pebble tools having sharp edges. Richard Leakey's finds in Kenya indicate that *Homo*'s toolmaking capability is older and more sophisticated than previous evidence had suggested. Some 600 knifelike tools unearthed by Leakey had been carefully fashioned from smooth volcanic rock, had edges that were still sharp, and have been dated as 2.6 million years old.

Hand-axes were the first major standardized, all-purpose implement. They were equipped with a sharp cutting edge on both sides and were probably used both for hunting and for chopping, cutting, scraping, and digging up grubs and roots. Hand-axes are associated with *Homo erectus* and possess such uniformity of design that specimens from Madras, Kenya, and London are nearly identical as regards form.

Homo sapiens developed a technique of pressure flaking to produce a long, slender, sharp-edged blade which made an excellent projectile point and a useful chisel, the burin. The invention of the spearthrower made hunting more efficient.

To withstand the cold, late Paleolithic peoples made garments from skins and erected buildings in areas where natural caves did not exist. The reindeer and mammoth hunters of present-day Czechoslovakia and Russia lived in tents and huts made of hides and brush or in communal houses partially sunk into the ground with mammoth's ribs for roof supports. There is evidence that they used coal for fuel.

The first artists. One of the highest achievements of late Paleolithic culture was art. Man was an artist endeavoring to give expression to his creative imagination long before he could write or fashion a metal knife. Animated, realistic paintings of animals, colored in shades of black, red, yellow, and brown, have been found in caves in Spain and France (see Color Plate 2). Paleolithic people also modeled clay and chiseled pictures on rock and bone. Cave art rivals that of civilized man both stylistically and as an expression of significant human experience. It represents Paleolithic man's dependence on an abundance of game animals and success in hunting them.

Mesolithic or Transitional cultures. With the final retreat of the glaciers about 10,000 B.C., Europe became covered with dense forests. Because of their highly specialized adaptation to cold weather, many animals hunted by late Paleolithic peoples became extinct. Man, however, adjusted to postglacial conditions by developing new cultures called Mesolithic or Transitional. Many of these Mesolithic groups lived along the coast, fishing and gathering shellfish. Others lived inland, where they made bows and arrows for hunting and devised skis, sleds, and dugout canoes. Our Mesolithic forebears also domesticated the dog.

The Neolithic revolution. By 7000 B.C. the people in the Near East, north of the area called the Fertile Crescent (see map, p. 17), had shifted from food gathering to food producing. Men in this region had domesticated wheat, barley, sheep, goats, and pigs and lived in village communities near their herds and fields. This was the most important breakthrough in the relationship of man to his environment and ushered in the Neolithic or New Stone Age.

One of the oldest Neolithic village sites to be excavated is Jarmo in northern Iraq. The 150 people of the village lived in twenty mud-walled houses, reaped their grain with stone sickles, stored their food in stone bowls, and possessed domesticated goats, sheep, and dogs. The later levels of settlement contain evidence of domesticated pigs and clay pottery. Since many tools were made of obsidian, a volcanic rock from beds 300 miles away, a primitive form of commerce must have existed.

The best preserved early village so far uncovered is Catal Hüyük in southern Turkey, excavated in 1961. The large, 32-acre site, first occupied shortly before 6000 B.C., contains some of the most advanced features of Neolithic culture: pottery, woven textiles, mudbrick houses, shrines honoring a mother goddess, and plastered walls decorated with murals and carved reliefs.

The Neolithic revolution spread to the Balkan Peninsula by 5000 B.C., Egypt and central Europe by 4000 B.C., and Britain and northwest India by 3000 B.C. The Neolithic cultures of Middle America and the Andes are independent developments, while a possible relationship between China and the Near East remains an open question.

PRIMITIVE THOUGHT AND CUSTOM

Analysis of primitive societies. Perhaps it is natural for most of us, living as we do in a highly complex machine-age society, to assume that primitive men, prehistoric or modern, would possess few laws, little education, and only the simplest codes of conduct. But this is far from true. The organization of a primitive society may be as complex as our own. Rules regarding the role of parents, the treatment of children, the punishment of the evildoer, the conduct of business, the worship of the gods, and the conventions of eating and recreation have existed for thousands of years, along with methods to compel the individual to do "the correct thing."

How can we know about those features of early man's culture which are not apparent from the remains of tools and other objects? The early myths and epics which originated in prehistoric times reflect the ideas and customs of early peoples. Studies of present-day primitive societies have given scholars hints about the culture of prehistoric man, but caution must be used in applying the findings of such studies to prehistoric primitive societies: the fact that the general level of technological development appears to be similar in both groups does not mean that all aspects of the two societies are comparable. Further-

more, it is difficult to measure the impact of advanced civilization on modern primitive societies.

Forms of social organization. Among all peoples, the basic social unit appears to be the elementary family group—parents and their offspring. Anthropologists do not know what marriage customs were prevalent in the earliest societies, but monogamy was probably most common. Other social groupings found in primitive societies include the extended family, the clan, and the tribe.

The extended family is an individual family together with a circle of related persons who usually trace their descent through their mothers and are bound together by mutual loyalty. The extended family strengthens the elementary unit in obtaining food and in protecting its members against other groups. Land is communally owned but allocated to separate families. Weapons, tools, and utensils are individually owned.

A clan is a group of individuals within a community who believe that they have a common ancestor. A clan is patrilineal if its members trace their relationship through the male line and matrilineal if through the female. Many primitive peoples identify their clans by a totem—an animal or other natural object—which is revered and made the subject for amulets of various sorts. Totemism exists today in military insignia and the emblems of fraternal organizations.

The term *tribe* lacks a precise definition but may be thought of as a community characterized by a common speech or distinctive dialect, a common cultural heritage, and a specific inhabited territory. Group loyalty is strong and is often accompanied by a contempt for the peoples and customs of other communities.

Collective responsibility in law and government. In primitive societies ethical behavior consists in not violating custom. The close relationships that exist in extended families and clans encourage conformity. Justice in a primitive group operates to maintain equilibrium. Theft disturbs economic equilibrium, and justice is achieved by a settlement between the injured man and the thief. The victim is satisfied and the

The Venus of Laussel is a stone seat from the Laussel shelter in Dordogne, France. Like many similar statuettes of the Paleolithic period, it is visibly a fertility symbol with obvious female characteristics.

thief is not punished. Murder and wounding are also private matters to be avenged by the next of kin. On the other hand, certain acts, such as treason, witchcraft, and incest, are considered dangerous to the whole group and require punishment by the entire community. If a member of a clan gets into trouble too often, his fellows may outlaw or execute him.

As a general rule, government in primitive societies is of a democratic character. The older tribal members—the council of elders—play a dominant role in decision making because of their greater experience and knowledge of the group's customs and lore. Serious decisions, such as going to war or electing a chief, require the consent of a general assembly of all adult males. The elected chief of the tribe is pledged to rule in accordance with custom and in consultation with the council of elders. Due to the strong element of representation present, this early form of government has been called "primitive democracy."

Religion, magic, and science. Religion is a strong force in the lives of primitive people. One form of religious belief among primitive peoples was animism, the belief that all things in nature—wind, stones, trees, animals, and man—were inhabited by spirits. Many spirits became objects of reverence, with man's own spirit being one of the first. Neanderthal man placed food and implements alongside his carefully buried dead, an indication that he believed in an afterlife and held his ancestors in awe. We know also that late Paleolithic man revered the spirits of the animals he hunted for food as well as the spirit of fertility upon which both human and animal life depended. This led to totemism and to the worship of a fertility goddess who is known to us from many carved and modeled female figures with exaggerated sexual features.

Closely associated with primitive religion is the practice of magic. In addition to revering the spirits, primitive man wants to compel them to favor him. For his purpose he employs magic to ward off droughts, famines, floods, and plagues. There may have been an element of magic in the paintings of primitive peoples, who may have believed that through their paintings they could wield power over the spirits of animals.

Traditionally, magic has been regarded as diametrically opposed to science. Magic claims supernatural powers over natural forces, whereas science rejects any such determinism and studies natural phenomena by open-ended methods in its search for general laws. Yet, as scholars are increasingly recognizing, both primitive man and the scientist believe that nature is orderly and that what is immediately apprehended by the senses can be systematically classified. The great contributions of Stone Age men and women—domestication of plants and animals, invention of tools, pottery, and weaving—involved centuries of methodical observation and oft-repeated experiments, few of which could have yielded immediate results. Early man must therefore be credited with a desire for knowledge for its own sake.

Further indications of this desire have been provided by studies of the large stone monuments (megaliths) constructed by Neolithic peoples. An engineering professor, Alexander Thom, surveyed 300 megalithic sites in Britain; he discovered a widespread use of a uniform measure of length, the "megalithic yard," which is 2.72 feet. Some sites were set out with an accuracy approaching 1 in 1000, and the builders of the sites had knowledge of practical geometry. The megalithic complex of Stonehenge had traditionally been considered a religious structure. However, an American astronomer, Professor Gerald Hawkins, using a computer, found an "astonishing" number of correlations between the alignments of recognized Stonehenge positions—stones, stone holes, mounds—and the solar and lunar declinations as of 1500 B.C. when Stonehenge was built.[3] The alignments made possible an accurate calendar and the prediction of the rising and setting of the sun and moon. Hawkins also saw in these Neolithic structures the joy of achievement by man the problem-solver as he searches for order in the cosmos.

MESOPOTAMIA: THE FIRST CIVILIZATION

Prelude to civilization. About 5000 B.C., after the agricultural revolution had begun to spread from its place of origin on the northern fringes of the Fertile Crescent, Neolithic farmers started filtering into the Fertile Crescent itself. Although this broad plain received insufficient rainfall to support agriculture, it was watered by the Tigris and Euphrates rivers. Known in ancient days as Mesopotamia (Greek for "between the rivers"), the lower reaches of this plain, beginning near the point where the two rivers nearly converge, was called Babylonia. Babylonia in turn encompassed two geographical areas—Akkad in the north and Sumer, the delta of this river system, in the south.

Broken by river channels teeming with fish and refertilized every year by alluvial silt laid down by uncontrolled floods, Sumer had a splendid agricultural potential—provided the environmental problems were solved. "Arable land had literally to be created out of a chaos of swamps and sandbanks by a 'separation' of land from water; the swamps . . . drained; the floods controlled; and lifegiving waters led to the rainless desert by artificial canals."[4] In the course of the several successive cultural phases that followed the arrival of the first Neolithic farmers, these and other related problems were solved by large-scale cooperative effort. By 3500 B.C. the foundations had been laid for a type of economy and social order markedly different from anything previously known. This far more complex culture, based on large urban centers rather than simple villages, is what we associate with the term *civilization*.

Authorities do not all agree about the definition of *civilization*. Most would accept the view that "a civilization is a culture which has attained a degree of complexity usually characterized by urban life"[5]—that it is capable, in other words, of sustaining a substantial number of specialists to cope with the economic, social, political, and religious needs of a populous society. Other characteristics usually present in a civilization include a system of writing to keep records, monumental architecture in place of simple buildings, and an art that is no longer merely decorative but representational of man and his activities. Moreover, an urban environment is important because of the self-consciousness and pride which it generates.

During the millennium preceding 3500 B.C. some of the most significant discoveries and inventions in human history were achieved. By discovering how to use metals to make tools and weapons, Neolithic man effected a revolution nearly as far-reaching as that wrought in agriculture. By 4500 B.C. Neolithic artisans had discovered how to extract copper from oxide ores by heating them with charcoal. Unlike those made of stone or bone, copper implements could be formed into any desired shape, and they were less likely to break. Moreover, a stone tool had to be discarded when broken; a damaged copper implement could be recast. Soon after 3000 B.C. metalworkers discovered that copper was improved by the addition of tin. The resulting alloy, bronze, was more fusible than copper and therefore could be cast more easily; also, bronze was harder and provided a sharper cutting edge.

The farmer's first plow was probably a stick which he pulled through the soil with a rope. In time, however, the cattle that his forebears had domesticated for food and milk were harnessed to drag the hoe in place of his mate or himself. Yoked, harnessed animals pulled plows in the Mesopotamian alluvium by 3000 B.C. As a result, farming advanced from the cultivation of small plots to the tilling of extensive fields. "By harnessing the ox man began to control and use a motive power other than that furnished by his own muscular energy. The ox was the first step to the steam engine and gasoline motor."[6]

Since the Mesopotamian plain had no stone, no metals, and no timber except its soft and inadequate palm trees, there was great need of an economical means of transporting these materials from Syria and Asia Minor. Water transport down the Tigris and Euphrates solved the problem. The oldest sailing boat known is represented by a model found in a Sumerian grave of about 3500 B.C. Soon after this date wheeled vehicles appear in the form of ass-drawn war chariots. For the transport of goods overland, however, men continued to rely on the pack ass.

Another important invention was the potter's wheel, first used in Sumer soon after 3500 B.C. Earlier, men had fashioned pots by molding or coiling clay by hand, but now a symmetrical product could be produced in a much shorter time. A pivoted clay disk heavy enough to revolve of its own momentum, the potter's wheel has been called "the first really mechanical device."

The emergence of civilization in Sumer. By 3500 B.C. the population of Sumer had increased to the point where people were living in small cities and had developed a preponderance of those elements previously noted as constituting civilization. Since these included the first evidence of writing, this first phase of Sumerian civilization, to about 2800 B.C., is called the Protoliterate period.[7]

New settlers appeared in Sumer at the beginning of the Protoliterate period, and another migration occurred shortly before 3000 B.C. Scholars cannot agree on which, if either, of these newcomers were the Sumerians, whose language is not related to those major language families of mankind that later appear in the Near East—Semites and Indo-Europeans. (The original home of the Semitic-speaking peoples is thought to have been the Arabian peninsula, while the Indo-Euro-

peans migrated from the region north of the Black and Caspian seas. A third, much smaller language family is the Hamitic, which included the Egyptians and other peoples of northeastern Africa.)

How would life in Protoliterate Sumer have appeared to a visitor seeing it for the first time? As he approached Ur, one of about a dozen Sumerian cities, he would pass farmers working in their fields with ox-drawn plows. He might see some of the workers using bronze sickles. The river would be dotted by boats carrying produce to and from the city. Dominating the flat countryside would be a ziggurat, a platform (later a lofty terrace, built in the shape of a pyramid) crowned by a sanctuary, or "high place." This was the "holy of holies," sacred to the local god. Upon entering the city, the visitor would see a large number of specialists pursuing their appointed tasks as agents of the community —some craftsmen casting bronze tools and weapons, others fashioning their wares on the potter's wheel, and still others, merchants, arranging to trade grain and manufactures for the metals, stone, lumber, and other essentials not available in Sumer. Scribes would be at work incising thin tablets of clay with picture signs. Some tablets might bear the impressions of cylinder seals, small stone cylinders engraved with a design. Examining the clay tablets, the visitor would find that they were memoranda used in administering the temple, which was at once the warehouse and workshop of the entire community. Some of the scribes might be making an inventory of the goats and sheep received that day for sacrificial use; others might be drawing up wage lists. They would be using a system of counting based on the unit 60, still used today, over five thousand years later, in computing divisions of time and angles.

Certain technical inventions of Protoliterate Sumer eventually made their way to both the Nile and the Indus valleys. Chief among these were the wheeled vehicle and the potter's wheel. The discovery in Egypt of cylinder seals similar in shape to those used in Sumer attests to contact between the two areas toward the end of the fourth millennium B.C. Certain early Egyptian art motifs and

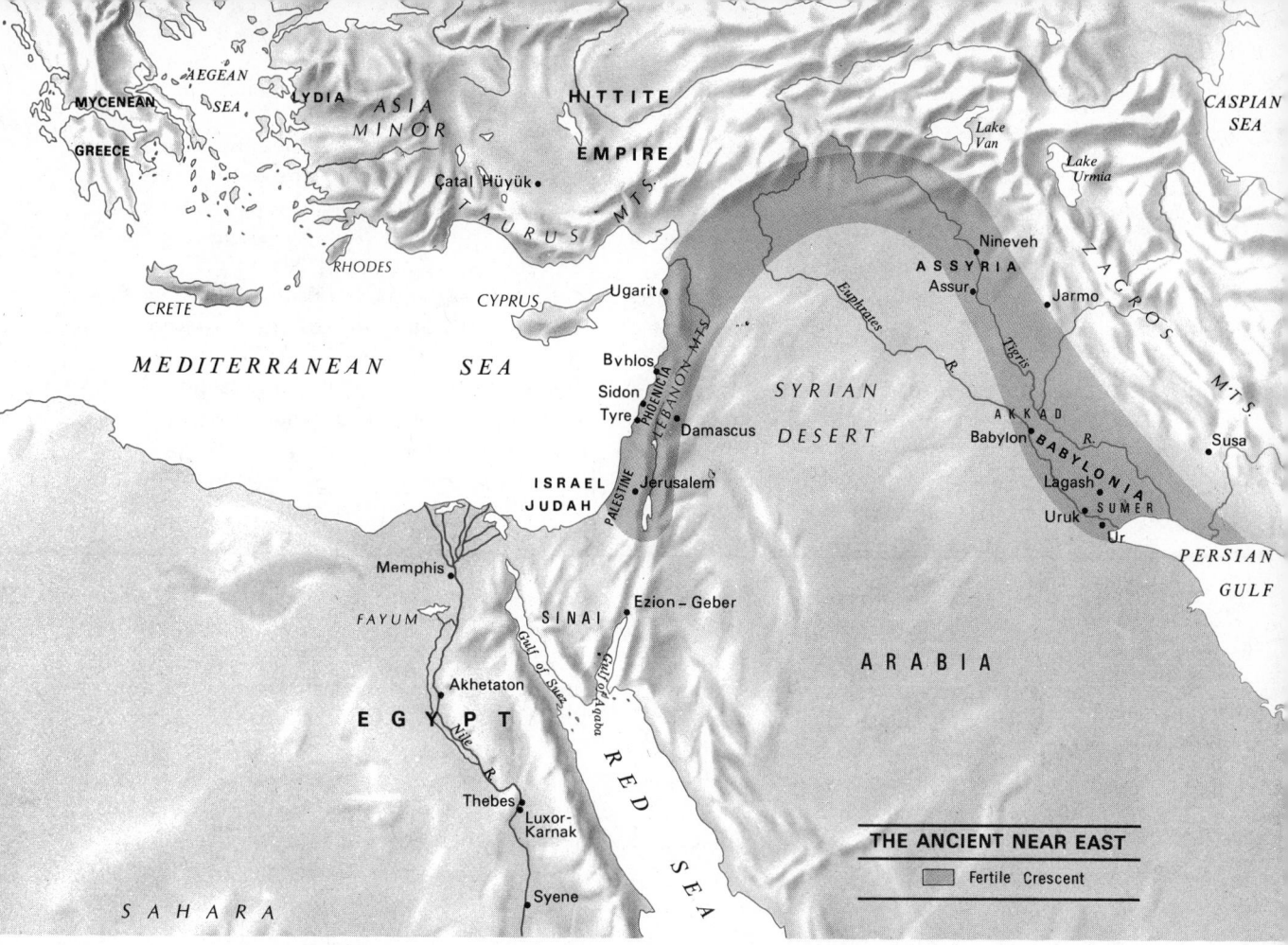

The map shows the following labels:

MYCENEAN GREECE · AEGEAN SEA · LYDIA · ASIA MINOR · HITTITE EMPIRE · CASPIAN SEA · Lake Van · Lake Urmia · Çatal Hüyük · TAURUS MTS. · Nineveh · ASSYRIA · Assur · Jarmo · ZAGROS MTS. · RHODES · CRETE · CYPRUS · Ugarit · Euphrates R. · MEDITERRANEAN SEA · Byblos · LEBANON MTS. · SYRIAN DESERT · Tigris R. · Sidon · PHOENICIA · AKKAD · Tyre · Damascus · Babylon · BABYLONIA · Susa · ISRAEL JUDAH · PALESTINE · Jerusalem · Lagash · SUMER · Uruk · Ur · PERSIAN GULF · Memphis · SINAI · Ezion-Geber · ARABIA · FAYUM · Akhetaton · Gulf of Suez · Gulf of Aqaba · Nile R. · EGYPT · RED SEA · Thebes · Luxor-Karnak · Syene · SAHARA

THE ANCIENT NEAR EAST
▢ Fertile Crescent

architectural forms are also thought to be of Sumerian origin. And it is probable that the example of Sumerian writing stimulated the Egyptians to develop a script of their own. These are examples of how cultures during their most formative stages may influence one another yet continue to develop unique features which stamp them as distinctive civilizations.

Sumerian writing. As we have noted, the symbols on the oldest Sumerian clay tablets were primarily pictures. However, many matters, including thought processes, cannot be depicted conveniently by pictures. Sumerian scribes overcame this problem by arbitrarily adding marks to the picture signs to denote new meanings. During the Proto-literate period some two thousand signs were in use. This cumbersome system could have been still further enlarged and complicated by the creation of more pictures and modifying marks. Fortunately, the Sumerians adopted an alternative solution whereby the signs represented sounds rather than ob-

jects or ideas. By giving the signs a phonetic value, the Sumerians could spell out names and compound words instead of inventing new signs. The use of syllabic signs reduced the number of signs to some six hundred by 2800 B.C.

In writing, a scribe used a reed stylus to make impressions in soft clay tablets. The impressions took on a wedge shape, hence the term *cuneiform* (Latin *cuneus*, "wedge"). The cuneiform system of writing was adopted by many other peoples of the Near East, including the Babylonians, Assyrians, Hittites, and Persians.

The Old Sumerian period. By 2800 B.C. the Sumerian city-states had emerged into the light of history. This first historical age, called the Old Sumerian (or Early Dynastic) period, was characterized by incessant warfare as each city sought to protect or enlarge its land and water rights. Each city-state was a theocracy, for the local god was believed to be the real sovereign. His earthly representative was the *ensi*, the high priest and city governor, who acted as the god's steward in both religious and secular functions. Though endowed with divine right by virtue of being the human agent of the god, the *ensi* was not considered divine.

Like life on a medieval manor, early Sumerian society was highly collectivized, with the temples of the city god and subordinate deities assuming the central role. "Each temple owned lands which formed the estate of its divine owners. Each citizen belonged to one of the temples, and the whole of a temple community—the officials and priests, herdsmen and fishermen, gardeners, craftsmen, stonecutters, merchants, and even slaves—was referred to as 'the people of the god X.'"[8] That part of the temple land called "common" was worked by all members of the community, while the remaining land was divided among the citizens for their support at a rental of from one third to one sixth of the crop. Priests and temple administrators, however, held rent-free lands.

In time, priests, temple administrators, and *ensis* became venal, usurping temple

These Old Sumerian period statues from the Abu Temple, Tell Asmar, are fashioned of limestone with inlaid shell and lapis lazuli eyes. These statues sometimes represented family groups and found their way into the temples often as a "substitute" for the actual persons. They possess some individuality between them as noted between the bearded man, shaven priest, and tunic-clad woman, but all hold the same rigidly frontal pose of religious concentration and have similar expressions.

property and oppressing the common people. This frequently led to the rise of despots called *lugals* (literally "great man" but usually translated "king") who rode to power on a wave of popular discontent. These secular rulers made the general welfare their major domestic concern. Best known is Urukagina, who usurped power at Lagash at the end of the Old Sumerian period. His reform inscriptions state that when he "had received the lugalship . . . he removed from the inhabitants of Lagash usury, forestalling, famine, robbery, attacks; he established their freedom . . . [and] protected the widow and the orphan from the powerful man."[9]

Akkadian dominance. Immediately north of Sumer lay the narrow region of Akkad, inhabited by Semites who had absorbed Sumerian culture. Appearing late in the fourth millennium B.C., the Akkadians were the earliest of the Semitic peoples who filtered into Mesopotamia from Arabia. A generation after Urukagina, Sargon I (2370-2315 B.C.), an energetic Akkadian ruler, conquered Sumer and went on to establish the world's first empire which, he claimed, extended "from the lower sea to the upper sea" (the Persian Gulf to the Mediterranean Sea).

Very proud of his lower-class origins, Sargon boasted that his humble, unwed mother had been forced to abandon him: "She set me in a basket of rushes . . . [and] cast me into the river."[10] Rescued and brought up by a gardener, Sargon rose to power through the army. As *lugal*, Sargon looked after the welfare of the lower classes and aided the rising class of private merchants. At the latter's request he once sent his army to far-off Asia Minor to protect a colony of merchants from interference by a local ruler. We are told that Sargon "did not sleep" in his efforts to promote prosperity; trade moved as freely "as the Tigris where it flows into the sea, . . . all lands lie in peace, their inhabitants prosperous and contented."[11]

Sargon's successors, however, were unable either to withstand the attacks of semibarbaric highlanders or to overcome the desire for independence of the priest-dominated Sumerian cities. As a result, the house of Sargon collapsed about 2230 B.C.

The Neo-Sumerian period. Order and prosperity were restored a century later by the *lugals* of the Third Dynasty of Ur (c. 2113-2006 B.C.). By creating a highly centralized administration in Sumer and Akkad, these rulers solved the problem of internal rebellion that had plagued Sargon and his successors. The formerly temple-dominated cities became provinces administered by governors who were watched closely by a corps of "messengers." The "church" became an arm of the state; the high priests were state appointees, and the temple economic organization was used as the state's agent in rigidly controlling the economy.

At the head of this bureaucratic state stood the now-deified ruler, celebrated in hymns as a heaven-sent messiah who "brings splendor to the land, . . . savior of orphans whose misery he relieves, . . . the vigilant shepherd who conducts the people unto cooling shade."[12] Much of what we now call social legislation was passed by these "vigilant shepherds." Such laws were called "rightings" (Sumerian *nig-si-sa*, usually translated "equity"), since their object was the righting of wrongs that were not covered by the old customary law (*nig-ge-na*, "truth"). The prologue to the law code of Ur-Nammu, founder of the dynasty, declared that it was the king's purpose to see that "the orphan did not fall a prey to the wealthy" and that "the man of one shekel did not fall a prey to the man of one mina (sixty shekels)."[13]

Disaster struck Ur about 2006 B.C., when Elamites from the highlands to the east destroyed the city. The Sumerians were never again a dominant element politically, but their culture persisted as the foundation for all subsequent civilizations in the Tigris-Euphrates valley.

For more than two centuries following the destruction of Ur, disunity and warfare again plagued Mesopotamia, along with depression, inflation, and acute hardship for the lower classes. Merchants, however, utilized the lack of state controls to become full-fledged capitalists who amassed fortunes which they invested in banking operations and in land. (These merchants used a form of double-entry bookkeeping which they called "balanced accounts." Their word for capi-

tal, *qaqqadum*, meaning "head," influenced later peoples; our word *capital* is derived from the Latin form, *caput*). The stronger local rulers of the period freed the poor from debt slavery and issued a variety of reform laws which are best illustrated by the legislation of Hammurabi.

Hammurabi and the Babylonian empire. Semitic Amorites (from *Amurru*, the "West"), under the rule of their capable king, Hammurabi of Babylon (c. 1792-1750 B.C.), again brought most of Mesopotamia under one rule by 1760 B.C.

Hammurabi is best known for his code of nearly three hundred laws whose stated objective was "to cause justice to prevail in the land, to destroy the wicked and the evil, to prevent the strong from oppressing the weak . . . and to further the welfare of the people."[14] Hammurabi's legislation reestablished a state-controlled economy in which merchants were required to obtain a "royal permit," interest was limited to 20 percent, and prices were set for basic commodities and for fees charged by physicians, veterinarians, and builders. Minimum wages were established, and debt slavery was limited to three years. Other laws protected wives and children, although a wife who had "set her face to go out and play the part of a fool, neglect her house, belittle her husband"[15] could be divorced without alimony, or the husband could take another wife and compel the first to remain as a servant. Punishments were graded in their severity; the higher the culprit in the social scale, the more severe the penalty.

In the epilogue to the code, Hammurabi eloquently summed up his efforts to provide social justice for his people.

Let any oppressed man, who has a cause, come before my image as king of righteousness! Let him read the inscription on my monument! Let him give heed to my weighty words! And may my monument enlighten him as to his cause and may he understand his case! May he set his heart at ease! (and he will exclaim): "Hammurabi indeed is a ruler who is like a real father to his people. . . ."[16]

Mathematics and science. Carrying on the work of the Sumerians, the Babylonians made advances in arithmetic, geometry, and algebra. For ease of computation with both whole numbers and fractions, they compiled tables for multiplication and division and for square and cube roots. They knew how to solve linear and quadratic equations, and their knowledge of geometry included the theorem later made famous by the Greek philosopher Pythagoras: the square of the hypotenuse of a right-angled triangle is equal to the sum of the squares of the other two sides. Perhaps their greatest achievement was the principle of place-value notation which gave numbers a value according to their position in a series.

The Babylonians achieved little that today deserves to be called science. They did observe nature and collect data, which is the first requirement of science; but in seeking intelligible explanations of natural phenomena, they did not go beyond the formulation of myths which explained things in terms of the unpredictable whims of the gods. The sun, the moon, and the five visible planets were thought to be gods who were able to influence men's lives; accordingly, their movements were watched, recorded, and interpreted.

Literature and religion. The Babylonians took over from the Sumerians a body of literature ranging from heroic epics that compare favorably with the *Iliad* and the *Odyssey* to wisdom writings that have their counterparts in the Old Testament books of Job, Proverbs, and Ecclesiastes. Longest and most famous is the *Epic of Gilgamesh*, which recounts the exploits of a heroic ruler of Uruk who lived about 2700 B.C. The central theme of the epic is Gilgamesh's hope of immortality. This leads him to seek out and question Ut-napishtim, the Babylonian Noah who was granted eternal life because he saved all living creatures from the flood. Ut-napishtim's story has many remarkable similarities with the Hebrew account of the flood. But Gilgamesh's quest is hopeless, and he is so informed on several occasions:

Gilgamesh, whither rovest thou?
The life thou pursuest thou shalt not find.
When the gods created mankind,
Death for mankind they set aside,

Life in their own hands retaining.
Thou, Gilgamesh, let full be thy belly,
Make thou merry by day and by night.
Of each day make thou a feast of rejoicing,
Day and night dance thou and play! . . .
Pay heed to the little one that holds on to thy hand,
Let thy spouse delight in thy bosom!
For this is the task of mankind![17]

The ancient Mesopotamians never went beyond this early view that immortality was reserved for the gods. Unlike the Egyptians (see p. 25), the Babylonians did not go on to develop a belief in an attractive life after death as a reward for good behavior on earth. They did come to believe in divine rewards for moral conduct, but these were rewards to be enjoyed in this life—increased worldly goods, numerous offspring, and many years of life. Thus, the sun-god Shamash was celebrated in hymns which proclaimed that "the honest merchant . . . is pleasing to Shamash, and he will prolong his life. He will enlarge his family, gain wealth . . . and his descendants will never fail."[18]

Fall of the Babylonian empire. The pattern of disunity and warfare, all too familiar in Mesopotamia, reasserted itself following Hammurabi's death. In 1595 B.C. the Hittites, an Indo-European people who had established themselves in Asia Minor (see p. 28), mounted a daring raid down the Euphrates, capturing and plundering Babylon. The next five centuries is a dark age about which little is known; yet it did preserve the cultural heritage left by the Sumerians and Babylonians. Meanwhile, in a neighboring river valley, another civilization had emerged.

EGYPT: GIFT OF THE NILE

Predynastic Egypt. Egypt is literally "the gift of the Nile," as the ancient Greek historian Herodotus observed. The Nile valley, extending 750 miles from the first cataract to the Mediterranean, is a fertile oasis cut out of a limestone plateau. Its soil is renewed annually by the rich silt deposited by the flood water of the river, which rises and falls with unusual precision. The rise begins early in July and continues until the banks are overrun, reaching its crest in September. By the end of October the river is once more contained within its banks.

By 4000 B.C. Neolithic villagers had begun to build dikes to catch and hold the Nile flood and to construct ditches and wells for irrigation. Population grew and social organization advanced, leading to the formation of two distinct kingdoms late in the fourth millennium: Lower Egypt comprised the broad Nile delta north of Memphis, while Upper Egypt extended southward along the narrow ten- to twenty-mile-wide valley as far as the first cataract at Syene (Aswan). Each kingdom contained about a score of districts, or *nomes,* which had formerly been ruled by independent chieftains.

The Predynastic period ended about 3100 B.C. when Menes (also known as Narmer), ruler of Upper Egypt, united the two kingdoms and founded the First Dynasty with its capital at Memphis. Because little is known of these first two dynasties, the period is called Egypt's archaic age.

The Old Kingdom (c. 2700-2200 B.C.). The pharaohs of the Third through the Sixth Dynasties—the period called the Old Kingdom or Pyramid Age—firmly established order and stability and the essential elements of Egyptian civilization. The nobility lost its independence, and all power was centered in the pharaoh (*Per-ao,* "Great House"). The pharaoh was considered a god rather than the human agent of a god, as was the rule in Mesopotamia. As the god of Egypt, the pharaoh owned all the land (although frequent grants were made to temples and private persons), controlled the irrigation system, decided when the fields should be sown, and received the surplus from the crops produced on the huge royal estates. This surplus supported a large corps of specialists—administrators, priests, scribes, artists, artisans, and merchants—who labored in the service of the pharaoh. The people's welfare was thought to rest on absolute fidelity to the god-king. "If you want to know what to do in life," advised one Egyptian writer, "cling to the pharaoh and be loyal. . . ."[19] As a consequence, the Egyptian felt a sense of security that was rare in Mesopotamia.

The belief that the pharaoh was a god led to the practice of mummification and the construction of colossal tombs—the pyramids—to preserve the pharaoh's mummy for eternity. The pyramid tombs, in particular those of the Fourth Dynasty at Gizeh near Memphis which are the most celebrated of all ancient monuments, reflect the great power and wealth of the Old Kingdom pharaohs. Their construction provided employment during the months when the land was inundated by the Nile.

Toward the end of the Sixth Dynasty the centralized authority of the pharaohs was undermined when the nobles assumed the prerogatives of the pharaohs, including the claim to immortality, and the *nomes* again became independent. For about a century and a half, known as the First Intermediate Period (c. 2200-2050 B.C.), civil war raged, and outsiders raided and infiltrated the land. The lot of the common people became unbearable as they faced famine, robbery, and oppression by petty tyrants. "The land trembled," wrote a contemporary, "all the people were in terror, the villages were in panic, fear entered into their limbs."[20]

The Middle Kingdom (c. 2050-1800 B.C.). Egypt was rescued from anarchy by the pharaohs of the Eleventh and Twelfth Dynasties, who reunited the country and ruled from Thebes. Stressing their role as watchful shepherds of the people, the Middle Kingdom pharaohs promoted the welfare of the downtrodden. One of them claimed: "I gave to the destitute and brought up the orphan. I caused him who was nothing to reach [his goal], like him who was [somebody]."[21] No longer was the nation's wealth expended on huge pyramids, but on public works. The largest of these, a drainage and irrigation project in the marshy Fayum district south of Memphis, resulted in the reclamation of 27,000 acres of arable land. Moreover, a concession that has been called "the democratization of the hereafter" gave the lower classes the right to have their bodies mummified and thereby to enjoy immortality.

Following the Twelfth Dynasty, Egypt again was racked by civil war as provincial governors fought for the pharaoh's throne. During this Second Intermediate Period (c.

1800-1570 B.C.), the Hyksos, a mixed but preponderantly Semitic people, invaded Egypt from Palestine about 1720 B.C. They easily conquered the delta and made the rest of Egypt tributary. It was probably at this time that some Hebrews entered Egypt, accepting the invitation of Joseph, who rose to high position under a friendly Hyksos king.

The New Kingdom or Empire (c. 1570-1090 B.C.). The Egyptians viewed the Hyksos conquest as a great humiliation imposed on them by detestable barbarians. An aggressive nationalism emerged, promoted by the native prince of Thebes who proclaimed: "No man can settle down, when despoiled by the taxes of the Asiatics. I will grapple with him, that I may rip open his belly! My wish is to save Egypt and to smite the Asiatics!"[22] Adopting the new weapons introduced by their conquerors—the composite bow, constructed of wood and horn, and the horse-drawn chariot—the Egyptians expelled the Hyksos and pursued them into Palestine. The pharaohs of the Eighteenth Dynasty, who reunited Egypt and founded the New Kingdom, made Palestine the nucleus of an Egyptian empire in western Asia (see Reference Map 1).

The outstanding representative of the aggressive state that Egypt now became was Thutmose III (c. 1490-1436 B.C.). This "Napoleon of Egypt" led his professional standing army on seventeen campaigns into Syria, where he set up his boundary markers on the banks of the Euphrates. Nubia and northern Sudan were also brought under his sway. The native princes of Palestine, Phoenicia, and Syria were left on their thrones, but their sons were taken to Egypt as hostages. Here they were brought up and, thoroughly Egyptianized, eventually sent home to rule as loyal vassals. Thutmose III erected obelisks—tall, pointed shafts of stone—to commemorate his reign and to record his wish that "his name might endure throughout the future forever and ever." Four of his obelisks now adorn the cities of Istanbul, Rome, London, and New York.

Under Amenhotep III (c. 1398-1361 B.C.) the empire reached its peak. Tribute flowed in from conquered lands; and Thebes, with its temples built for the sun-god Amon east of the Nile at Luxor and Karnak, became the most magnificent city in the world. The Hittites and the rulers of Babylonia and Crete, among others, sent gifts, including princesses for the pharaoh's harem. In return, they asked the pharaoh for gold, "For gold is as common as dust in your land."

During the reign of the succeeding pharaoh, Amenhotep IV (c. 1369-1353 B.C.), however, the Empire went into sharp decline as the result of an internal struggle between the pharaoh and the powerful and wealthy

The step-pyramid of Zoser at Sakkara was erected during the Third Dynasty (c. 2600 B.C.), and is a magnificent early example of Egyptian pyramid building.

priests of Amon. The pharaoh undertook to revolutionize Egypt's religion by proclaiming the worship of the sun's disk, Aton, in place of Amon and all the other deities. Often called the first monotheist (although, as Aton's son, the pharaoh was also a god), Amenhotep changed his name to Akhenaton ("Devoted to Aton"), left Amon's city to found a new capital (Akhetaton), and concentrated upon religious reform. Most of Egypt's vassal princes in Asia defected when their appeals for aid against invaders went unheeded. Prominent among these invaders were groups of people called the Habiru, whose possible identification with the Hebrews of the Old Testament has interested modern scholars. At home the army leaders joined with the Amon priesthood to encourage dissension. When Akhenaton died, his weak successor, Tutankhamen (c. 1352-1344 B.C.)—famed for his small but richly furnished tomb discovered in 1922—returned to Thebes and the worship of Amon.

One of the army leaders who succeeded Tutankhamen founded the Nineteenth Dynasty (c. 1305-1200 B.C.), which sought to reestablish Egyptian control over Palestine and Syria. The result was a long struggle with the Hittites, who in the meantime had pushed south from Asia Minor into Syria. This struggle reached a climax in the reign of Ramses II (c. 1290-1224 B.C.), the pharaoh of the Hebrew Exodus from Egypt. Ramses II regained Palestine, but when he failed to dislodge the Hittites from Syria, he agreed to a treaty. Its strikingly modern character is revealed in clauses providing for non-aggression, mutual assistance, and extradition of fugitives.

The long reign of Ramses II was Egypt's last period of national grandeur. The number and size of Ramses' monuments (see illustration, p. 22) rival those of the Pyramid Age. Outstanding among them are the great Hypostyle Hall, built for Amon at Karnak, and the temple at Abu Simbel, with its four colossal statues of Ramses, which has recently been raised to save it from inundation by the waters of the new High Dam at Aswan. (Syene). After Ramses II, royal authority gradually declined as the power of the priests of Amon rose.

Period of Decadence (1090-332 B.C.). During the early part of the Period of Decadence the Amon priesthood at Thebes became so strong that the high priest was able to found his own dynasty and to rule over Upper Egypt. Civil war grew increasingly common, and Egypt became, in the words of the Old Testament, a "broken reed," with the result that in 671 B.C. the Assyrians made Egypt a province of their empire.

Egypt enjoyed a brief Indian summer of revived glory during the Twenty-Sixth Dynasty (663-525 B.C.), which expelled the Assyrians with the aid of Greek mercenaries. The revival of ancient artistic and literary forms proved sterile, and after attempts to regain Palestine failed, "the king of Egypt came not again any more out of his land" (II Kings 24:7). Only the commercial policies of these rulers were successful. In about 600 B.C., to facilitate trade, Pharaoh Necho ordered a canal dug between the Nile mouth and the Red Sea (it was later completed by the Persians), and he commissioned a Phoenician expedition which circumnavigated Africa in three years—a feat not to be duplicated until 1497 A.D.

Egypt passed under Persian rule in 525 B.C., and two hundred years later this ancient land came within the domain of Alexander the Great. Persian rule marked the end of thirty Egyptian dynasties which had existed for nearly three thousand years.

Egyptian society and economy. Although most Egyptians were serfs and subject to forced labor, class stratification was not rigid, and people of merit could rise to a higher rank in the service of the pharaoh. The best avenue of advancement was education. The pharaoh's administration needed many scribes, and young men were urged to attend a scribal school: "Be a scribe, who is freed from forced labor, and protected from all work. . . . he directeth every work that is in this land." Yet then as now the education of a young man was beset with pitfalls: "I am told thou forsakest writing, that thou givest thyself up to pleasures; thou goest from street to street, where it smelleth of beer, to destruction. Beer, it scareth men from thee, it sendeth thy soul to perdition."[23]

Largely because all landed property de-

An Egyptian lord and his party are bird hunting, in this detail from a New Kingdom wall-painting found on a tomb at Thebes (c. 1400 B.C.). In addition to the visual background of hieroglyphics, the artist has painted the abundant vegetation and wildlife of the Nile Valley in realistic and loving detail.

scended from mother to daughter, the status of Egyptian women was exceptionally favorable. Upon the death of his wife a husband lost the use of the property, which was then inherited by the daughter and her husband. Brother and sister marriages often took place within the Egyptian ruling family to ensure the right of succession to the throne, which was always through the female line.

The economy of Egypt has been called "theocratic socialism" because the state, in the person of the divine pharaoh, owned the land and monopolized commerce and industry. Because of the Nile and the proximity to the Mediterranean and Red seas, most of Egypt's trade was carried on by ships. During the Old Kingdom boats plied regularly up and down the Nile, which, unlike the Tigris and the Euphrates, is easily navigable in both directions up to the first cataract at Aswan (Syene). The current carries ships downstream and the prevailing north wind enables them to sail upstream easily. Trade reached its height during the Empire, when commerce traveled along four main routes: the Nile River; the Red Sea, which was connected by caravan to the Nile bend near Thebes; a caravan route to Mesopotamia and southern Syria; and the Mediterranean Sea, connecting northern Syria, Cyprus, Crete, and Greece with the delta of the Nile. Egypt's

indispensable imports were lumber, copper, tin, and olive oil, paid for with gold from its rich mines, linens, wheat, and papyrus rolls — the preferred writing material of the ancient world.

Mathematics and science. The Egyptians were much less skilled in mathematics than were the Mesopotamians. Their arithmetic was limited to addition and subtraction, which also served them when they needed to multiply and divide. They could cope with only simple algebra, but they did have considerable knowledge of practical geometry. The obliteration of field boundaries by the annual flooding of the Nile made land measurement a necessity. Similarly, a knowledge of geometry was essential in computing the dimensions of ramps for raising stones during the construction of pyramids. In these and other engineering projects the Egyptians were superior to their Mesopotamian contemporaries. Like the Mesopotamians, the Egyptians had acquired a "necessary" technology without effecting a conceptual breakthrough to a truly scientific method.

Yet, what has been called the oldest known scientific treatise was composed during the Old Kingdom. Its author described forty-eight cases requiring surgery, drawing conclusions solely from observation and re-

2. Painted bichrome cow, Lascaux (c. 15000–14,500 B.C.). Dating back to the Upper Paleolithic period, this painting is found high on the wall in the interior of the Lascaux cave in central France. Discovered in 1940, Lascaux contains some of the finest examples of animal cave painting in existence. Paleolithic artists used paints prepared from natural deposits found in the soil, ground to a fine powder, and mixed with water. Pigment was applied with fingers, pointed tools, or pads of moss and fur. The lifelike images have been taken as evidence that Paleolithic art may express, in abstract form, a complex system of fecundity myths.

3. Egypt: Back of the throne of Tutankhamen (New Kingdom, c. 1350 B.C.). Fashioned of gold, and inlaid with enamel and semi-precious stones, this throne is an outstanding example of the treasures discovered in 1922 in the only intact tomb remaining in the Valley of the Kings. The scene portrayed is that of Tutankhamen and his young queen, Ankhesenamen, who appears to be anointing him with oil from a vessel she holds in her hand. In his brief nine-year reign, Tutankhamen restored Egypt back to its ancient belief in a multitude of gods. It was probably for this reason that he was buried along with many objects of incredible wealth and splendor.

4. Greece: Temple of Apollo at Delphi (c. fourth century B.C.). Delphi was famous throughout ancient Greece as the site of the temple and oracle of Apollo. It was considered by the Greeks to be the center of the earth and the place where the god Apollo communicated to man through oracles his knowledge of the future. As part of a religious ritual, a prophetess would deliver Apollo's message while in a trance-like state. Though now in ruins, the site was built in a sacred area and contained several temples, treasuries, and monuments. There were also stadiums, gymnasiums, theatres, and even a hotel to house visitors.

5. Room in a villa at Boscoreale, near Pompeii (first century B.C.). Rome's singular accomplishment in architecture included an attention to domestic buildings that reflected a traditional concern for home and family. Since the Roman country house had few doors and windows, a large amount of wall space was available for the lavish decoration that is a mark of so much Roman art. Wall paintings were often intended to create the illusion of space beyond the room and, as is evident here, the realistic Roman style convincingly achieved the illusion.

jecting supernatural causes and treatments. In advising the physician to "measure for the heart" which "speaks" in various parts of the body, he recognized the importance of the pulse and approached the concept of the circulation of the blood. This text remained unique, however, for in Egypt as elsewhere in the ancient Near East, thought failed to free itself permanently from domination by priests and bondage to religion.

The Old Kingdom also produced the world's first known solar calendar, the direct ancestor of our own. In order to plan their farming operations in accordance with the annual flooding of the Nile, the Egyptians kept records and discovered that the average period between inundations was 365 days. They also noted that the Nile flood coincided with the annual appearance of the Dog Star (Sirius) on the eastern horizon at dawn, and they soon associated the two phenomena. (Since the Egyptian year was six hours short of the true year, Julius Caesar in Roman times corrected the error by adding an extra day every four years.)

Egyptian religion. Early Egyptian religion had no strong ethical character. Relations between men and gods were based largely on material considerations, and the gods were thought to reward those who brought them gifts of sacrifice. But widespread suffering during the First Intermediate Period led to a revolution in religious thought. It was now believed that instead of propitiatory offerings the gods were interested in good character and love for one's fellow man: "More acceptable [to the gods] is the character of one upright of heart than the ox of the evildoer. . . . Give the love of thyself to the whole world; a good character is a remembrance."[24]

The cult of Osiris became very popular when it combined the new emphasis on moral character with the supreme reward of an attractive afterlife. "Do justice whilst thou endurest upon earth," men were told. "A man remains over after death, and his deeds are placed beside him in heaps. However, existence yonder is for eternity. . . . He who reaches it without wrongdoing shall exist yonder like a god."[25] Osiris, according to an ancient myth, was the god of

the Nile, and the rise and fall of the river symbolized his death and resurrection. The myth recounted that Osiris had been murdered by Seth, his evil brother, who cut the victim's body into many pieces. When Isis, the bereaved widow, collected all the pieces and put them together, Osiris was resurrected and became immortal. Osiris was thus the first mummy, and every mummified Egyptian was another Osiris.

But only a soul free of sin would be permitted to live forever in what was described as the "Field of the Blessed, an ideal land where there is no wailing and nothing evil; where barley grows four cubits high, and emmer wheat seven ells high; where, even better, one has to do no work in the field oneself, but can let others take care of it."[26] At the time of soul testing, Osiris weighed the candidate's heart against the Feather of Truth. If the ordeal was not passed, a horrible creature devoured the rejected heart. During the Empire the priesthood of Osiris became corrupt and claimed that it knew clever methods of surviving the soul testing, even though a man's heart were heavy with sin. Charms and magical prayers and formulas were sold to the living as insurance policies guaranteeing them a happy outcome in the judgment before Osiris. They constitute much of what is known as the Book of the Dead, which was placed in the tomb.

Akhenaton's religious reformation was directed against the venal priests of Osiris as well as those of the supreme god Amon. As we have seen, Akhenaton failed to uproot Amon and the multiplicity of lesser gods; his monotheism was too cold and intellectual to attract the masses who yearned for a blessed hereafter.

Monumentalism in architecture. Because of their impressive and enduring tombs and temples, the Egyptians have been called the greatest builders in history. The earliest tomb was the mud-brick mastaba, so called because of its resemblance to a low bench. By the beginning of the Third Dynasty stone began to replace brick, and an architectural genius named Imhotep constructed the first pyramid by piling six huge stone mastabas one on top of the other. Adjoining this Step Pyramid was a temple complex whose stone columns were not freestanding but attached to a wall, as though the architect was still feeling his way in the use of the new medium.

The most celebrated of the true pyramids were built for the Fourth Dynasty pharaohs Khufu, Khafre, and Menkaure. Khufu's pyramid, the largest of the three, covers thirteen acres and originally rose 481 feet. It is composed of 2,300,000 limestone blocks, some weighing fifteen tons, and all pushed and pulled into place by human muscle. This stupendous monument was built without mortar, yet some of the stones were so perfectly fitted that a knife cannot be inserted in the joint. The Old Kingdom's eighty pyramids are a striking expression of Egyptian civilization. In their dignity, massiveness, and repose, they reflect the religion-motivated character of Egyptian society.

As the glory and serenity of the Old Kingdom can be seen in its pyramids, constructed as an act of faith by its subjects, so the power and wealth of the Empire survives in the temples at Thebes, made possible by the booty and tribute of conquest. On the east side of the Nile stand the ruins of the magnificent temples of Karnak and Luxor. The Hypostyle Hall of the temple of Karnak, built by Ramses II, is larger than the cathedral of Notre Dame. Its forest of 134 columns is arranged in sixteen rows, with the roof over the two broader central aisles (the nave) raised to allow the entry of light. This technique of providing a clerestory over a central nave was later used in Roman basilicas and Christian churches.

Sculpture and painting. Egyptian art was essentially religious. Tomb paintings and relief sculpture depict the everyday activities that the deceased wished to continue enjoying in the afterlife, and statues glorify the god-kings in all their serenity and eternity. Since religious art is inherently conservative, Egyptian art seldom departed from the traditions established during the vigorous and self-assured Old Kingdom. Sculptors idealized and standardized their subjects, and the human figure is shown either looking directly ahead or in profile (see illustration, p. 24), with a rigidity very much in keeping with the austere architectural settings of the statues.

Yet on two occasions an unprecedented naturalism appeared in Egyptian sculpture. The faces of some of the Middle Kingdom rulers appear drawn and weary, as though they were weighed down by the burden of reconstructing Egypt after the collapse of the Old Kingdom. An even greater naturalism is seen in the portraits of Akhenaton and his beautiful queen, Nefertete. The pharaoh's brooding countenance is realistically portrayed, as is his ungainly paunch and his happy but far from god-like family life as he holds one of his young daughters on his knee or munches on a bone. The "heretic" pharaoh, who insisted on what he called "truth" in religion, seems also to have insisted on truth in art.

Painting in Egypt shows the same precision and mastery of technique that are evident in sculpture. However, no attempt was made to show objects in perspective, and the scenes give an appearance of flatness. The effect of distance was conveyed by making objects in a series or by putting one object above another. Another convention employed was to depict everything from its most characteristic angle. Often the head,

In contrast to conventional Egyptian art, this representation of Akhenaton is so naturalistic that it borders on caricature.

arms, and legs were shown in side view and the eye, shoulders, and chest were shown in front view.

Writing and literature. In Egypt, as in Sumer, writing began with pictures. But unlike the Mesopotamian signs, Egyptian hieroglyphs ("sacred signs") remained primarily pictorial. At first the hieroglyphs represented only objects, but later they came to stand for ideas and syllables. Early in the Old Kingdom the Egyptians began to use alphabetic characters for twenty-four consonant sounds. Although they also continued to use the old pictographic and syllabic signs, this discovery was of far-reaching consequence. It led to the development of the Semitic alphabet, from which our present alphabet is derived.

Egypt's oldest literature is the Pyramid Texts, a body of religious writing found inscribed on the walls of the burial chambers of Old Kingdom pharaohs. Their recurrent theme is a monotonous insistence that the dead pharaoh is really a god.

The troubled life that followed the collapse of the Old Kingdom produced the highly personal literature of the First Intermediate Period and Middle Kingdom. It contains protests against the ills of the day, demands for social justice, and praise for the romantic excitements of wine, women, and song. The universal appeal of this literature is illustrated by the following lines from a love poem, in which the beloved is called "sister":

I behold how my sister cometh, and my heart is
  in gladness.
Mine arms open wide to embrace her; my heart
  exulteth within me: for my lady has come to
  me. . . .
She kisseth me, she openeth her lips to me: then
  am I joyful even without beer.[27]

A classic of Egyptian literature is Akhenaton's *Hymn to the Sun*, which is similar in spirit to Psalm 104. A few lines will indicate its lyric beauty and its conception of one omnipotent and beneficent Creator.

How manifold are thy works!
They are hidden before men,
O sole god, beside whom there is no other.
Thou didst create the earth according to thy heart
While thou wast alone.[28]

The Rosetta Stone, discovered in Egypt in 1799 by an officer in Napoleon's army, supplied the means by which Jean Champollion was able in 1822 to decipher Egyptian writing. On the stone a decree, dated 196 B.C., is inscribed in three different scripts, as is shown by the section reproduced here. The bottom layer of writing is Greek, which Champollion could read. Working from the Greek he was able to decipher the hieroglyphic writing in the top layer. The middle layer is a simplified form of hieroglyphic writing, called demotic.

By the fifth century A.D. the ability to read ancient Egyptian writing had been lost. Not until fourteen hundred years later, when the Rosetta Stone was deciphered by Jean François Champollion (1790-1832), could modern man appreciate this ancient literature.

THE HITTITES

The Hittite empire. Except for brief mention in the Bible, very little was known about the Hittites until archaeologists began to unearth the remains of their civilization in Asia Minor in 1906. By 1920 their writing had been deciphered, and it proved to be the earliest example of a written Indo-European language. The Hittites are thought to have entered Asia Minor from the north about 2000 B.C., and their superior military means—particularly the horse-drawn chariot—enabled them to conquer the native people of central Asia Minor.

After 1450 B.C. a series of energetic Hittite kings created a more centralized government and an empire that included Syria, lost by the Egyptian pharaoh Akhenaton. Pharaoh Ramses II moved north from Palestine in a vain attempt to reconquer Syria. Ambushed and forced back to Palestine after a bloody battle, Ramses agreed to a treaty of "good peace and good brotherhood" in 1269 B.C. (see p. 23). The Hittites may have been eager for peace with Egypt because of the threat posed by a new movement of Indo-European peoples. Shortly after 1200 B.C. these barbarians, chief among whom were the Phrygians, destroyed the Hittite empire. Darkness settled over Asia Minor until after 800 B.C.

Hittite civilization. The Hittite state under the empire was modeled after the older oriental monarchies of the Near East. The king claimed to represent the sun god and was deified after death. The nobles held large estates from the king and in return provided warriors armed increasingly with iron weapons. The Hittites are credited with being the first people to work iron from local deposits, which afforded them a jealously guarded monopoly. Not until after 1200 B.C. did iron metallurgy become widespread.

The Hittites adopted the Mesopotamian cuneiform script together with some works of Babylonian literature. While their law code shows some similarity to the code of Hammurabi, it differed in prescribing more humane punishments. Instead of retaliation ("an eye for an eye"), the Hittite code made greater use of restitution and compensation.

The chief importance of Hittite culture lies in the legacy it left to the Phrygians and Lydians and, through them, to the Greeks who settled along the Aegean coast of Asia Minor. The Hittite goddess Kubaba, for example, became the great Phrygian goddess Cybele, the "Great Mother" whose worship became widespread in Roman times.

After 1200 B.C., with the Hittite empire destroyed and Egypt in decline, the Semitic peoples of Syria and Palestine ceased being pawns in a struggle between rival imperialisms. For nearly five hundred years, until they were conquered by the Assyrians, these peoples were able to play an independent and significant role in history.

THE ERA OF SMALL STATES

The Phoenicians. *Phoenician* is the name the Greeks gave to those Canaanites who dwelt along the Mediterranean coast of Syria, an area that is today the state of Lebanon. Hemmed in by the Lebanon Mountains to the east, the Phoenicians turned to the sea and by the eleventh century B.C. had become the greatest traders, shipbuilders, navigators, and colonizers before the Greeks. To obtain silver and copper from Spain and tin from Britain, Gades (Cadiz) was founded on the Atlantic coast of Spain. Carthage, one of a number of Phoenician trading posts around the shores of the Mediterranean, was destined to become Rome's chief rival in the third century B.C.

Although the Phoenicians were essentially traders, their home cities—notably Tyre, Sidon, and Byblos—also produced manufactured goods. Their most famous export was woolen cloth dyed with the purple dye obtained from shellfish found along their coast. They were also skilled makers of furniture (made from the famous cedars of Lebanon), metalware, glassware, and jewelry.

Culturally the Phoenicians were not creative. They left behind no literature and little art. Yet they made one of the greatest contributions to human progress, the perfection of the alphabet, which, along with the Babylonian sexagesimal system of notation, they carried westward. The origin of the alphabet is still a moot question. Between 1800 and 1600 B.C. various Canaanite peoples, influenced by Egypt's semialphabetical writing, started to evolve a simplified method of writing. The Phoenician alphabet of twenty-two consonant symbols (the Greeks later added the vowel signs) is related to the thirty-character alphabet of Ugarit, a Canaanite city (see map, p. 17) which, like the Hittite empire, was destroyed about 1200 B.C.

The half-dozen Phoenician cities never united to form a strong state, and in the last half of the eighth century B.C. all but Tyre were conquered by the Assyrians. When Tyre finally fell to the Chaldeans in 571 B.C., the Hebrew prophet Ezekiel spoke what reads like an epitaph to the once great role played by the Phoenicians:

When your wares came from the seas, you satisfied many peoples; with your abundant wealth and merchandise you enriched the kings of the earth. Now you are wrecked by the seas, in the depths of the waters; your merchandise and all your crew have sunk with you. [29]

The Arameans. Closely related to the Hebrews were the Arameans, who occupied Syria east of the Lebanon Mountains. The most important of their little kingdoms was centered on Damascus, one of the oldest continuously inhabited cities of the world. The Arameans dominated the camel caravan trade connecting Mesopotamia, Phoenicia, and Egypt and continued to do so after Damascus fell to the Assyrians in 732 B.C. The Aramaic language, which used an alphabet similar to the Phoenician, became the international language of the Near East. In Judea it displaced Hebrew as the spoken language and was used by Jesus and his disciples.

The Hebrew kingdoms. In war, diplomacy, inventions, and art, the Hebrews made little splash in the stream of history. In religion and ethics, however, their contribution to world civilization was tremendous. Out of their experience grew three great religions: Judaism, Christianity, and Islam.

Hebrew experience is recorded in the Holy Writ of Israel, the Old Testament of the Christian Bible, whose present content was approved about 90 A.D. by a council of rabbis. All of us are familiar with the power and beauty of some of its many great passages. As a work of literature it remains unsurpassed; but it is more than that. "It is Israel's life story—a story that cannot be told adequately apart from the conviction that God had called this people in his grace, separated them from the nations for a special responsibility, and commissioned them with the task of being his servant in the accomplishment of his purpose." [30]

The Biblical account of the history of the Hebrews (later called Israelites and then Jews) begins with the patriarchal clan leader Abraham. About 1800 B.C. Abraham led his people out of Ur in Sumer, where they had settled for a time in their wanderings, and eventually they arrived in the land of Canaan, later called Palestine.

About 1700 B.C., driven by famine, some Hebrews followed Abraham's great-grandson Joseph, the son of Israel (also called Jacob), into Egypt. Joseph's rise to power in Egypt, and the hospitable reception of his people there, is attributed to the presence of the largely Semitic Hyksos, who had conquered Egypt about 1720 B.C. (see p. 22). Following the expulsion of the Hyksos by the pharaohs of the Eighteenth Dynasty, the Hebrews were enslaved by the Egyptians. Shortly after 1300 B.C. Moses led them out of bondage and into the wilderness of Sinai, where they entered into a pact or covenant with their God, Yahweh. The Sinai Covenant bound the people as a whole—the nation of Israel, as they now called themselves—to worship Yahweh before all other gods and to obey his Law. In return, Yahweh made the Israelites his chosen people whom he would protect and to whom he granted Canaan, "a land flowing with milk and honey." The history of Israel from this time on is the story of the working out of this covenant.

The Israelites had to contend for Palestine against the Canaanites, whose Semitic ancestors had migrated from Arabia early in the third millennium B.C. Joined by other Hebrew tribes already in Palestine, the Israelites formed a confederacy of twelve tribes (clans of the twelve sons of Israel) and, led by war leaders called judges, in time succeeded in subjugating the Canaanites. In the meantime, however, a far more formidable foe had appeared. The Philistines, from whom we get the word *Palestine*, settled along the coast about 1175 B.C., having been uprooted from Asia Minor by the invasions that destroyed the Hittite empire (see p. 28).

Aided by the use of iron weapons, which were new to Palestine, the Philistines were well on their way to dominating the entire land by the middle of the eleventh century.

It became apparent that the loose twelve-tribe confederacy could not cope with the Philistine danger. "Give us a king to govern us," the people demanded, "that we also may be like all the nations, and that our king may govern us and go before us and fight our battles."[31] Saul, the first king of Israel (1020-1000 B.C.), died while fighting the Philistines, but his successor David (1000-961 B.C.) not only restricted the Philistines to a narrow coastal strip but became the ruler of the largest state in the ancient history of the area, stretching from the Euphrates to the Gulf of Aqaba.

The work of David was completed by his son Solomon, in whose long reign (961-922 B.C.) Israel reached a pinnacle of wordly power and splendor as an oriental-style monarchy. In the words of the Bible:

Solomon ruled over all the kingdoms from the Euphrates to the land of the Philistines and to the border of Egypt; they brought tribute and served Solomon all the days of his life. . . . And Judah and Israel dwelt in safety, from Dan even to Beersheba, every man under his vine and under his fig tree, all the days of Solomon. . . . And God gave Solomon wisdom and understanding beyond measure, and largeness of mind. . . . Now the weight of gold that came to Solomon in one year was six hundred and sixty-six talents of gold, besides that which came from the traders and from the traffic of the merchants, and from all the kings of Arabia and from the governors of the land. . . . The king also made a great ivory throne, and overlaid it with the finest gold. . . .[32]

But the price of Solomon's vast bureaucracy, building projects (especially the palace complex and the Temple at Jerusalem), standing army (1400 chariots and 12,000 horses), and harem (700 wives and 300 concubines) was great. High taxes, forced labor, and the loss of tribal independence led to dissension, and on the death of Solomon in 922 B.C. the realm was split into two kingdoms—Israel in the north and Judah in the south. These two weak kingdoms were in no position to defend themselves when new, powerful empires rose again in Mesopotamia. In 721 B.C. the Assyrians captured Samaria, the capital of the northern kingdom, taking 27,900 Israelites into captivity and settling foreign peoples in their place. The resulting mixed population, called Samaritans, made no further contribution to Hebrew history or religion.

The southern kingdom of Judah held out until 586 B.C. when Nebuchadnezzar, the Chaldean ruler of Babylonia, destroyed Jerusalem and carried away ten thousand captives; "none remained, except the poorest people of the land."[33] Thus began the famous Babylonian Exile of the Jews (Judeans), which lasted until 538 B.C. when Cyrus the Persian, having conquered Babylon, allowed them to return to Jerusalem where they rebuilt the Temple destroyed by Nebuchadnezzar.

Persian rule was followed by that of the Hellenistic Greeks and Romans. In 66-70 A.D. the Jews rebelled against Rome, and Jerusalem was totally destroyed in the savage

ANCIENT ISRAEL
8TH CENTURY B.C.

Damascus

Tyre
Kadesh

PHOENICIA

KINGDOM
OF
ARAM

MEDITERRANEAN
SEA

Sea of
Galilee

Megiddo

KINGDOM
OF
ISRAEL

Samaria

Jordan R.

Joppa
Shiloh
Bethel
Jericho
Jerusalem
Bethlehem

AMMON

PHILISTIA

KINGDOM
OF
JUDAH

Gaza
Hebron

DEAD
SEA

MOAB

Beersheba

NEGEV
(DESERT)

EDOM

Uncertain   Boundary

fighting that ensued. The Jews were again driven into exile, and the Diaspora—the "scattering"—was at its height.

Hebrew religion. From the time of Abraham the Hebrews worshiped one god, a stern, warlike tribal deity whose name Yahweh (Jehovah) was first revealed to Moses. Yahweh differed from the many Near Eastern nature gods in being completely separate from the physical universe which He had created. This view of Yahweh as the Creator of all things everywhere was inevitably to lead to the monotheistic belief that He was the sole God in the universe.

After their entrance into Palestine, many Hebrews adopted the fertility deities of the Canaanites as well as the luxurious Canaanite manner of living. As a result prophets arose who "spoke for" (from the Greek word *prophetes*) Yahweh in insisting on strict adherence to the Sinai Covenant and in condemning the "whoring" after other gods, the selfish pursuit of wealth, and the growth of social injustice.

Between roughly 750 and 550 B.C. appeared a series of great prophets who wrote down their messages. They sought to purge the religion of Israel of all corrupting influences and to elevate and dignify the concept of Yahweh. As summed up by Micah in a statement often cited as the essence of all higher religion, "He has shown you, O man, what is good; and what does the Lord require of you but to do justice, and to love kindness, and to walk humbly with your God?"[34] The prophets viewed the course of Hebrew history as being governed by the sovereign will of Yahweh, seeing the Assyrians and the Chaldeans as "the rod of Yahweh's anger" to chastise His stubborn, wayward people. They also developed the idea of a coming Messiah, the "anointed one" from the family of King David, who would inaugurate a reign of peace and justice.

Considered the greatest of the prophets are Jeremiah and the anonymous Second Isaiah, so-called because his message was incorporated in the Book of Isaiah (chapters 40-55). Jeremiah witnessed the events that led to Nebuchadnezzar's destruction of Jerusalem and the Temple and to the Babylonian Captivity of the Jews. He prepared the people for these calamities by affirming that Yahweh would forgive their sins and restore "a remnant" of his people and by proclaiming a "new covenant." The old covenant had been between Yahweh and the nation, which no longer existed, and it had become overlaid with ritual and ceremony and centered in the Temple, which had been destroyed. The new covenant was between Yahweh and each individual; religion was now a matter of a man's own heart and conscience, and both the nation and the Temple were considered superfluous. Second Isaiah, who lived at the end of the Babylonian Captivity, capped the work of his predecessors by proclaiming Israel to be Yahweh's "righteous servant," purified and enlightened by suffering and ready to guide the world to the worship of the one, eternal, supreme God. Thus were the Jews who returned from the Exile provided with a renewed faith in their destiny and a new comprehension of their religion which would sustain them through the centuries to come.

LATER EMPIRES OF WESTERN ASIA

Assyrian expansion. By 700 B.C. the era of small states was at an end. For two hundred years the Assyrians had been bidding to translate the growing economic unity of the Near East—evidenced by Solomon's trading operations and even more by the activities of Aramean merchants—into political unity. The Assyrian push toward the Mediterranean began in the ninth century and, after a lapse, was resumed in the eighth century, during which Babylon was also subdued. By 721 B.C. the Assyrians were the masters of the Fertile Crescent.

A Semitic people long established in the hilly region of the upper Tigris, the Assyrians had been schooled for a thousand years by constant warfare. But their matchless army was only one of several factors that explain the success of Assyrian imperialism: a

The militaristic nature of the Assyrians is reflected in this relief sculpture of sling-carrying warriors.

policy of calculated terrorization, an efficient system of political administration, and the support of the commercial classes that wanted political stability and unrestricted trade over large areas.

The Assyrian army, with its chariots, mounted cavalry, and sophisticated siege engines, was the most powerful yet seen in the ancient world. Neither troops or walls could long resist the Assyrians who, in Byron's well-known phrase, "came down like a wolf on the fold." Conquered peoples were held firmly in control by systematic terrorization. "From some I cut off their noses, their ears and their fingers, of many I put out the eyes. . . . I bound their heads to tree trunks round about the city"[35] is a characteristic statement from the Assyrian royal inscriptions. In addition, mass deportations were employed as an effective means of destroying national feeling.

The well-coordinated Assyrian system of political administration was another factor in the success of the empire. Conquered lands became provinces ruled by governors who exercised extensive military, judicial, and financial powers. Their chief tasks were to ensure the regular collection of tribute and the raising of troops for the permanent army that eventually replaced the native militia of sturdy Assyrian peasants. An efficient system of communications carried the "king's word" to the governors as well as the latter's reports to the royal court—including one prophetic dispatch reading: "The king knows that all lands hate us. . . ."[36] Nevertheless, the Assyrians must be credited with laying the foundations for the later more humane administrative systems of the Persians and Alexander the Great and his successors.

Assyrian culture. Culturally the Assyrians were not creative; their role was rather one of borrowing from the superior cultures of other peoples and unifying the best elements into a new product. This is evident in Assyrian architecture and sculpture, the work of subject artisans and artists. Both arts glorified the power of the Assyrian king. The palace, serving both as residence and administrative center, replaced the temple as the characteristic architectural form. A feature of Assyrian palace architecture was the structural use of the arch and the column, both borrowed from Babylonia. The palaces were decorated with splendid relief sculptures that glorified the king as warrior and hunter. Assyrian sculptors were especially skilled in portraying realistically the ferocity and agony of charging and dying animals.

Assyrian kings were interested in preserving written as well as pictorial records of their reigns. King Ashurbanipal (d. 631 B.C.) left a record of his great efforts in collecting the literary heritage of Sumer and Babylon, and the 22,000 clay tablets found in the ruins of his palace at Nineveh provided modern scholars with their first direct knowledge of this literature.

Downfall of the Assyrian empire. Revolt against Assyrian terror and tribute was inevitable when Assyria's strength waned and effective opposition arose. By the middle of the seventh century B.C. the sturdy Assyrian stock had been decimated by wars, and the Assyrian kings had to rely on unreliable mercenary troops and subject levies. Egypt regained its independence under the Twenty-

Sixth Dynasty, and the Medes refused further tribute. Then the Chaldeans, a new group of Semites who had filtered into Babylonia, revolted in 626 B.C. In 612 they joined the Medes in destroying Nineveh, the Assyrian capital. From one end of the Fertile Crescent to the other people rejoiced: "Nineveh is laid waste: who will bemoan her?"[37]

The Lydians and the Medes. The fall of Assyria left four states to struggle over the crumbs of empire: Chaldea and Egypt vied over Syria-Palestine, while Media and Lydia clashed over eastern Asia Minor.

After the collapse of the Hittite empire about 1200 B.C., the Lydians had followed the Phrygians, whose last king was the semilegendary Midas (d. c. 680 B.C.), in establishing a kingdom in western Asia Minor. When Assyria fell, the Lydians expanded eastward until stopped by the Medes at the Halys River. Lydia profited from being astride the commercial land route between Mesopotamia and the Aegean and from the possession of valuable gold-bearing streams. As a result, the Lydians invented coinage (about 675 B.C.), which replaced the silver bars hitherto in general use. Lydia's most famous king was Croesus, and the phrase "rich as Croesus" is a reminder of Lydian opulence. With his defeat by the Persians (see p. 34), Lydia ceased to exist.

The Medes were an Indo-European people who by 1000 B.C. had established themselves on the Iranian plateau east of Assyria. In the seventh century B.C. they had created a strong kingdom with Ecbatana as capital and with the Persians, their kinsmen to the south, as vassals. Following the collapse of Assyria, the Medes expanded into Armenia and eastern Asia Minor, but their short-lived empire ended in 550 B.C. when they, too, were absorbed by the Persians.

The Chaldean empire. While the Median kingdom controlled the highland region, the Chaldeans, with their capital at Babylon, were masters of the Fertile Crescent. Nebuchadnezzar, becoming king of the Chaldeans in 604 B.C., raised Babylonia to another epoch of brilliance after more than a thousand years of eclipse. By defeating the Egyptians in Syria, Nebuchadnezzar ended their hopes of re-creating their empire. As we have seen

earlier (p. 30), he destroyed Jerusalem in 586 B.C. and carried several thousand Jews captive to Babylonia.

Nebuchadnezzar built Babylon into the largest and most impressive city of its day. The tremendous city walls were wide enough at the top to have rows of small houses on either side; between the rows of houses was a space wide enough for the passage of a chariot. In the center of Babylon ran the famous Procession Street, which passed through the Ishtar Gate. This arch, which was adorned with brilliant tile animals, is the best remaining example of Babylonian architecture. The immense palace of Nebuchadnezzar towered terrace upon terrace, each resplendent with masses of ferns, flowers, and trees. These roof gardens, the famous Hanging Gardens of Babylon, were so beautiful that they were regarded by the Greeks as one of the seven wonders of the ancient world.

Nebuchadnezzar also rebuilt the great

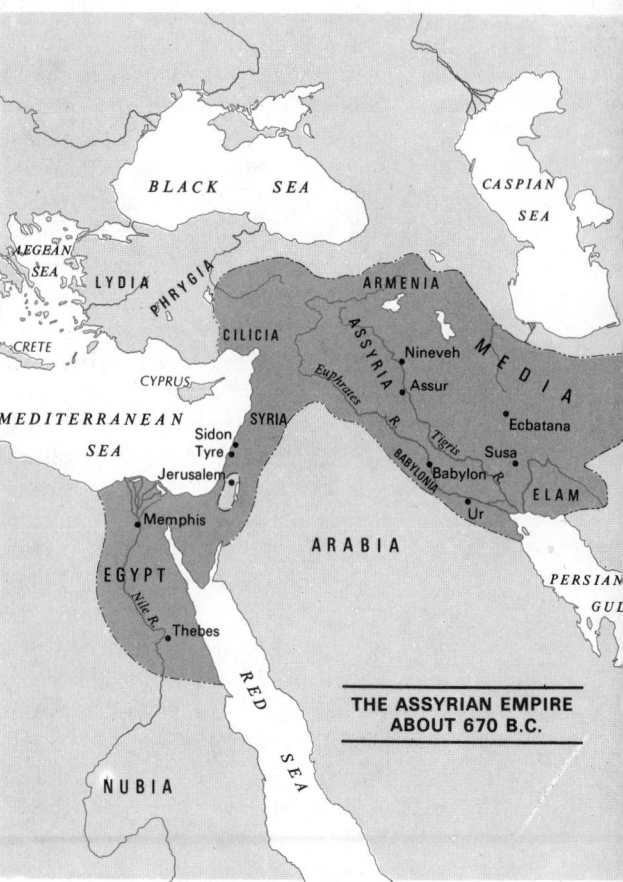

THE ASSYRIAN EMPIRE ABOUT 670 B.C.

temple-tower or ziggurat, the Biblical "Tower of Babel," which the Greek historian Herodotus viewed a century later and described as

a tower of solid masonry, a furlong in length and breadth, upon which was raised a second tower, and on that a third, and so on up to eight. The ascent to the top is on the outside, by a path which winds round all the towers.[38]

Nebuchadnezzar was the last great Mesopotamian ruler, and Chaldean power quickly crumbled after his death in 562 B.C. The Chaldean priests—whose interest in astrology greatly added to the fund of Babylonian astronomical knowledge—continually undermined the monarchy. Finally, in 539 B.C., they opened the gates of Babylon to Cyrus the Persian, thus fulfilling Daniel's message of doom upon the notorious Belshazzar, the last Chaldean ruler: "You have been weighed in the balances and found wanting."[39]

The Persian empire. Cyrus the Persian was the greatest conqueror in the history of the ancient Near East. In 550 B.C. he had ended Persian vassalage to the Medes by capturing Ecbatana and ousting the Median dynasty. The Medes readily accepted their vigorous new ruler, who soon demonstrated that he deserved to be called "the Great." When King Croesus of Lydia moved across the Halys River in 547 B.C. to pick up some of the pieces of the Median empire, Cyrus defeated him and annexed Lydia, including those Greek cities on the coast of Asia Minor which were under the nominal control of Lydia. Then he turned east, establishing his power as far as the frontier of India. Babylon and its empire, as we have seen, was next on his list. Following the death of Cyrus, his son Cambyses conquered Egypt. The next ruler, Darius I (522-486 B.C.), began a conflict with the Greeks that continued intermittently for more than 150 years until the Persians were conquered by Alexander the Great. Long before this event the Persian nobility had forgotten Cyrus the Great's answer to their suggestion that they "leave this small and barren country of ours" and move to fertile Babylonia:

Do so if you wish, but if you do, be ready to find yourselves no longer governors but governed; for soft lands breed soft men; it does not happen that the same land brings forth wonderful crops and good fighting men.[40]

Persian government. Although built upon the Assyrian model, the Persian administrative system was far more efficient and humane. The empire was divided into twenty provinces, or satrapies, each ruled by a governor called a satrap. To check the satraps, a secretary and a military official representing the "Great King, King of Kings" were installed in every province. Also, special inspectors, "the Eyes and Ears of the King," traveled throughout the realm.

Imperial post roads connected the important cities of the empire. Along the Royal Road between Sardis and Susa there was a post station every fourteen miles, where the king's couriers could obtain fresh horses, enabling them to cover the 1600-mile route in a week. "Nothing mortal travels so fast as these Persian messengers," wrote Herodotus. "These men will not be hindered . . . , either by snow, or rain, or heat, or by the darkness of night."[41]

The Persian empire was the first to attempt governing many different racial groups on the principle of equal responsibilities and rights for all peoples. So long as his subjects paid their taxes and kept the peace, the king did not interfere with local religion, customs, or trade. Indeed, Darius was called the "shopkeeper" because he stimulated trade by introducing a uniform system of gold and silver coinage on the Lydian model.

Persian religion and art. The humaneness of the Persian rulers may have stemmed from the ethical religion founded by the prophet Zoroaster, who lived in the early sixth century B.C. Zoroaster sought to replace what he called "the lie"—ritualistic, idol-worshiping cults and their Magi priests—with a religion centered on the sole god Ahura-Mazda ("Wise Lord"), who demanded "good thoughts of the mind, good deeds of the hand, and good words of the tongue" from those who would attain paradise (a Persian word). The new religion made little progress

THE CHALDEAN AND
PERSIAN EMPIRES

Chaldean Empire
About 586 B.C.

Persian Empire
About 500 B.C.

0 100 200 300 400 500

1" = 430 MILES

until first Darius and then the Magi adopted it. The Magi revived many old gods as lesser deities, added much ritual, and replaced monotheism with dualism by transforming what Zoroaster had called the principle or spirit of evil into the powerful god Ahriman, rival of Ahura-Mazda. The complicated evolution of Zoroastrianism is revealed in its holy writ, the *Avesta* ("The Law"), assembled in its present form between the fourth and the sixth centuries A.D. Zoroastrian eschatology—"the doctrine of final things" such as the resurrection of the dead and a last judgment—influenced Judaism. Following the Muslim conquest of Persia in the seventh century A.D., Zoroastrianism gradually died out in its homeland. It exists today among the Parsees in India.

In art the Persians borrowed largely from their predecessors in the Fertile Crescent, especially the Assyrians. Their most important work was in palace architecture, the best remains of which are at Persepolis. Built on a high terrace, the royal residences were reached by a grand stairway faced with beautiful reliefs. Instead of the warfare and violence that characterized Assyrian sculpture, these reliefs depict hundreds of soldiers, courtiers, and representatives of twenty-three nations of the empire bringing gifts to the king for the festival of the new year.

SUMMARY

This chapter has recounted the evolution of human affairs from primitive culture to civilization. The first great period in man's prehistory, during which man was a hunter and food-gatherer whose chief all-purpose tool was the hand-ax, is called the Paleolithic or Old Stone Age. Evidence indicates that the Paleolithic cultural stage may have begun in Africa over two million years ago. Some nine thousand years ago the Neolithic stage was initiated with the appearance of food-producing villages in western Asia. This revolutionary change from a food-gathering to a food-producing economy, quite probably the most momentous development in human history, made possible the rise of civilization.

Civilization rose in Mesopotamia and Egypt during the second half of the fourth millennium B.C. Both these civilizations were river-made, one by the Tigris and Euphrates and the other by the Nile. In each case the complex society we call a civilization was the result of human cooperation in taming the rivers to make them work for man.

The words *monumental* and *timeless* best describe Egyptian culture. The Egyptians built colossal statues and huge tombs; their burial customs were designed to outwit time itself. The state centered upon the absolute rule of the pharaohs—god-kings who eventually extended their rule from Nubia to the Euphrates River.

The story of ancient Mesopotamia is primarily concerned with the achievements of the Sumerians and the later adoption of their civilization by various invaders. The most important of these new states was the Babylonian empire created by Hammurabi. Babylon was sacked by the Indo-European Hittites of Asia Minor, who went on to duel with Egypt over Syria and Palestine.

By 1200 B.C. the first great Near Eastern empires—Babylonian, Egyptian, and Hittite—had collapsed, allowing the small Semitic peoples of Syria and Palestine freedom to make their own contributions—the greatest being the ethical monotheism of the Hebrews. Political diversity was ended by the rise of the Assyrian empire, which unified all of the ancient Near East for the first time. After the fall of Assyria, the Chaldean Nebuchadnezzar erected a new Babylonian empire, but it was soon terminated by the expansion of Persia. Stretching from India to Europe, the Persian empire gave the Near East its greatest extension and power—which produced an inevitable conflict with the Greeks. The next major phase in the history of civilization was to be centered on Greece.

SUGGESTIONS FOR READING

The Cambridge Ancient History, Vols. I-II, 3rd ed. (Cambridge Univ., 1975) incorporates the latest research on prehistory and the ancient Near East. R. Braidwood, **Prehistoric Men,*** 8th ed. (Scott, Foresman, 1975) is the best short survey. Also recommended: Grahame Clark, **World Prehistory: An Outline,*** 2nd ed. (Cambridge Univ.); D. Roe, **Prehistory: An Introduction** (Univ. of California); L. S. B. Leakey, **Adam's Ancestors: The Evolution of Man and His Culture*** (Torchbooks); and J. H. Coles and E. S. Higgs, **The Archaeology of Early Man*** (Penguin, 1976).

C. W. Ceram, **Gods, Graves, and Scholars*** (Bantam, 1972) and L. Cottrell, **The Anvil of Civilization*** (Mentor) are popular archaeological surveys. J. Deetz, **Invitation to Archaeology*** (Anchor) describes the techniques of the archaeologist. See also Evan Hadingham, **Circles and Standing Stones** (Walker, 1975) which accounts riddles of archaeology in Britain.

W. Hallow and W. Simpson, **The Ancient Near East*** (Harcourt Brace Jovanovich, 1971) is comprehensive. Other short surveys are M. Covensky, **The Ancient Near Eastern Tradition*** (Harper & Row); G. Childe, **What Happened in History*** (Penguin); H. Frankfort, **The Birth of Civilization in the Near East*** (Anchor); and S. Moscati, **The Face of the Ancient Orient*** (Anchor).

H. Saggs, **The Greatness That Was Babylon*** (Mentor) is a brief general history of Ancient Mesopotamia. See also S. N. Kramer, **The Sumerians** (Univ. of Chicago, 1971) and the same author's popular **History Begins at Sumer*** (Anchor).

Jon M. White, **Everyday Life in Ancient Egypt*** (Capricorn) and L. Casson, **Ancient Egypt** (Time-Life) are brief surveys. A. Gardiner, **Egypt of the Pharaohs*** (Galaxy) is a detailed political history. On the Empire period see G. Steindorff and K. Steele,

When Egypt Ruled the East* (Phoenix); C. Aldred, **Akhenaton and Nefertiti** (Viking, 1973); and C. Desroaches-Noblecourt, **Tutankhamen*** (New York Graphic Society, 1976).

H. Frankfort *et al.,* **Before Philosophy*** (Penguin) is a notable interpretation of Mesopotamian and Egyptian thought. John A. Wilson, **The Culture of Ancient Egypt*** (Phoenix) is recommended. O. Neugebauer, **The Exact Sciences in Antiquity*** (Torchbooks) is an authoritative work.

O. R. Gurney, **The Hittites*** (Penguin) and D. Harden, **The Phoenicians*** (Praeger) are authoritative surveys. See also Gerhard Herm, **The Phoenicians: The Purple Empire of the Ancient World** (Morrow, 1975) about the great mariners and traders.

J. A. Hexter, **The Judaeo-Christian Tradition*** (Harper & Row, 1966) is a succinct overview of Hebrew history and religion. Excellent longer surveys are H. M. Orlinsky, **Ancient Israel*** (Cornell); E. Ehrlich, **A Concise History of Israel*** (Torchbooks); B. W. Anderson, **Understanding the Old Testament,** 3rd ed. (Prentice-Hall, 1975); and O. Eissfeldt, **The Old Testament: An Introduction** (Harper & Row, 1965).

A. Olmstead, **History of Assyria** (Univ. of Chicago) and **History of the Persian Empire*** (Phoenix) are the standard accounts. See also R. Zaehner, **The Dawn and Twilight of Zoroastrianism** (Putnam).

H. Frankfort, **The Art and Architecture of the Ancient Orient*** (Penguin, 1971) and I. E. S. Edwards, **The Pyramids of Egypt*** (Penguin, 1975) give methods and reasons for the construction of the pyramids.

*Indicates a less expensive paperbound edition.

CHAPTER 2

Aegean, Hellenic, and Hellenistic Civilizations

The Glory That Was Greece

INTRODUCTION. Scarred by time and weather, the ruins of the Athenian Acropolis stand against a vivid blue sky and overlook the trees and buildings of a modern city sprawled beneath. These ruins are striking symbols of a departed civilization—the democracy of Athens at its height.

In the fifth century B.C. the temples and statuary of the Acropolis were gleaming and new, fresh from the hands of builders and sculptors. Five hundred years later Plutarch wrote:

The works are . . . wonderful: because they were perfectly made in so short a time, and have continued so long a season. . . . [The Acropolis looks] at this day as if it were but newly done and finished, there is such a certain kind of flourishing freshness in it . . . that the injury of time cannot impair the sight thereof. As if every one of those . . . works had some living spirit in it, to make it seem young and fresh: and a soul that lived ever, which kept them in their good continuing state.[1]

Today the Acropolis bears the heavy "injury of time"; yet for us no less than for Plutarch, ancient Athens has retained a "flourishing freshness." This quality, together with a refined sense of symmetry and proportion, is characteristic of the Greek spirit and the dazzling achievements of Greek civilization. The ancient Greeks repeatedly demonstrated an ability to regard the world about them from a "young and fresh" perspective and to inject a love of proportion not only into their architecture but into almost everything they attempted. Yet in the crucial sphere of politics, their sense of proportion failed them. Instead of compromising their differences, the city-states quarreled continually, and that fervid individualism which moved them to brilliant creative efforts blinded them to the necessity of cooperation. Thus the political life of the Greeks was marked by conflicts between the city-states until they were at last subjugated by King Philip of Macedonia and his son, Alexander the Great.

Yet Alexander, out of genuine admiration of the Greek cultural achievement, strove to perpetuate the learning of the city-states as he set forth to forge a world-state. Greece's accomplishment was to prove so enduring that its magnificent legacy of knowledge and art would provide much of the cultural heritage of the West and, to a lesser extent, of the East. Thus the English poet Shelley could say with justification, "We are all Greeks." Probably no other people has made so lasting an impression on man's intellectual history.

BACKGROUND FOR GREEK CULTURE

Aegean civilization. Greek civilization was unique in so many ways that a student of history might infer that Greek culture developed in a vacuum or, free from outside influences, sprang full-blown from the rocky hills of this small land. The Greek achievement, however, was preceded by an advanced civilization located on the lands surrounding the Aegean Sea. This Aegean civilization, which came into full flower about 2000 B.C. and collapsed suddenly following 1200 B.C., developed through two major periods. The first and longer period, which ended about 1450 B.C., is called "Minoan" after the legendary Cretan King Minos. Crete was the center of Minoan civilization, which spread to the Aegean Islands, the coast of Asia Minor, and mainland Greece. The last period of Aegean civilization, the two and one half centuries following 1450 B.C. when the center of Aegean political power and culture lay on the Greek mainland, is called "Mycenaean" after its most important site at Mycenae.

The Minoans. The narrow, 160-mile-long island of Crete was a stepping stone between Europe, Asia, and Africa. Stimulated by contacts with Mesopotamia and Egypt, a brilliant civilization emerged here.

Minoan prosperity was based on large-scale trade that ranged from Troy to Egypt and from Sicily to Syria and employed the first ships capable of long voyages over the open sea. Chief exports were olive oil, wine, metalware, and magnificent pottery. This trade was the monopoly of an efficient bureaucratic government under a powerful ruler whose administrative records were written on clay tablets, first in a form of picture writing and later in a syllabic script known as Linear A. Neither script can be read, but Linear A appears to contain some borrowed Semitic words, the result of Cretan trade with the coastal cities of Syria. Our knowledge of Minoan civilization is therefore scanty and imprecise; most of it is derived from the material remains uncovered by archaeologists.

It was the epoch-making discoveries of the English archaeologist Sir Arthur Evans that first brought to light this civilization, whose existence had previously only been hinted at in Greek legends and the epics of Homer. Between 1900 and 1905 Evans unearthed the ruins of a great palace at Knossos, the dominant city in Crete after 1700 B.C. Rising at least three stories high and sprawl-

THE AEGEAN WORLD

The Lion Gate at Mycenae was built about 1250 B.C. Mycenaean palaces served as hilltop fortresses and were enclosed by defensive walls of mammoth stone blocks. The Lion Gate is the most impressive remnant of these massive fortifications.

ing over nearly six acres, this "Palace of Minos," built of brick and limestone and employing unusual downward-tapering columns of wood, was a maze of royal apartments, storerooms, corridors, open courtyards, and broad stairways. Walls were painted with elaborate frescoes in which the Minoans appear as a gay, peaceful people with a pronounced liking for dancing, festivals, and athletic contests. Women are shown enjoying a freedom and dignity unknown elsewhere in the ancient Near East or classical Greece. Furnished with running water, the palace had a sanitation system surpassing anything constructed in Europe until Roman times and, after that, until the nineteenth

century. The palace was linked to other parts of Crete by well-paved roads lined with the luxurious dwellings of the nobility.

The glory of Minoan culture was its art—gay, spontaneous, and full of rhythmic motion. Art was an essential part of everyday life and not, as in the ancient Orient, an adjunct to religion and the state. What little is known of Minoan religion also contrasts sharply with conditions in the Near East: there were no great temples, powerful priesthoods, or large cult statues of the gods. The principal deity seems to have been the Mother Goddess, and a number of recovered statuettes show her dressed like a fashionable Cretan lady with flounced skirts, a tightly laced, low-cut bodice, and an elaborate coiffure. It is also noteworthy that the later classical Greeks believed that Zeus and other deities came from Crete.

The Mycenaeans. About 2000 B.C., or shortly thereafter, the first Indo-European Greek tribes, collectively called Achaeans, entered Greece, where they absorbed the earlier settlers and ruled from strongly fortified citadels at Mycenae, Pylos, Thebes, and other sites. By 1600 B.C. the Achaeans—or Mycenaeans, as they are usually called—had evolved their own civilization, based largely on borrowings from the Minoans, and were plying the seas both as pirates and as traders.

Some of the wealth accumulated by the kings of Mycenae—the greatest single hoard of gold, silver, and ivory objects found anywhere before the discovery of Tutankhamen's tomb—was unearthed in 1876 by Heinrich Schliemann, fresh from his even more sensational discoveries at Troy (see p. 41). The royal palace on the acropolis, or citadel, of Mycenae had well-proportioned audience rooms and apartments, fresco-lined walls, floors of painted stucco, and large storerooms. Noteworthy also were the royal "beehive" tombs, constructed of cut stone and covered with earth.

The expansive force of this hitherto unimagined Mycenaean civilization led to the planting of colonies in the eastern Mediterranean (Hittite sources refer to Achaeans in Asia Minor) and to the conquest of Knossos about 1450 B.C. The latter event was made possible by the destruction of the labyrinthian palace at Knossos by fire—the after-effect, it is now conjectured, of a great tidal wave caused by the eruption of the small volcanic island of Thera (Santorini) eighty miles north of Crete. The palace at Knossos was rebuilt by the Mycenaeans (to be finally destroyed about 1380 B.C. by earthquake and fire), and the center of Aegean civilization shifted to the Greek mainland.

This story of Achaean-Cretan relations was unclear until after 1952 when a young English architect, Michael Ventris, startled the scholarly world by deciphering a type of Cretan script known as Linear B, many examples of which had been found by Evans at Knossos and by later archaeologists at Pylos, Mycenae, and Thebes. When Linear B turned out to be an early form of Greek written in syllabic characters, it followed that the rulers of Knossos after 1450 B.C. must have been Achaean Greeks who had adopted the Cretan script to write their own language.

The Linear B texts, which are administrative documents and inventories, greatly add to our knowledge of Mycenaean life. The Mycenaean centers were fortified palaces and administrative centers and not, as in Crete, true cities. The bulk of the population lived in scattered villages where they worked either communal land or land held by nobles or kings. The nobles were under the close control of the kings, whose administrative records were kept daily by a large number of scribes. Prominent in these records are details of the disbursement of grain and wine as wages and the collection of taxes in kind. The most important item of income was olive oil, the major article in the wide-ranging Mycenaean trade which was operated as a royal monopoly. Perhaps it was their role as merchant-monopolists that led the Achaean kings late in the thirteenth century B.C. to launch the famous expedition against Troy in order to eliminate a powerful commercial rival.

Troy, site of the Homeric epics. The city of Troy occupied a strategic position on the Hellespont (the strait from the Aegean to the Black seas now known as the Dardanelles). Thus Troy could command both sea traffic through the straits and land caravans going between Asia and Europe. For many years scholars thought this city existed only in the epic poems of Homer. Heinrich Schliemann (1822-1890), a German romantic dreamer and amateur archaeologist, believed otherwise. As a boy, he had read Homer's *Iliad*, and thereafter he remained firmly convinced that Troy had actually existed. At the age of forty-eight, having amassed a fortune in the California gold rush and in world-wide trade, Schliemann retired from business to put his persistent dream of ancient Troy to the test.

In 1870 Schliemann began excavations at the legendary site of Troy, where he unearthed several cities, built one on top of the other. He discovered a treasure of golden earrings, hairpins, and bracelets in the second city, which led him to believe that this was the city of Homer's epics. Excavations in the 1930's, however, showed that the seventh city, over a thousand years more recent than the second, was the one made famous by Homer.

Neither the view that Troy was the victim of commercial rivalry nor the other widely held theory that it was destroyed by Achaean pirates seeking booty corresponds to Homer's view that the Trojan War was caused by the abduction of the beauteous Helen, queen of Sparta, by the Trojan prince Paris. Led by Agamemnon, king of Mycenae, the

This vase from Mycenae, with its six helmeted soldiers carrying lances and round shields, shows both the adventurous and martial nature of the Mycenaeans.

wrathful Achaeans besieged Troy for ten long years. Homer's *Iliad* deals only with a few weeks during the tenth year of the siege.

The fall of Mycenaean civilization. About 1200 B.C., not long after the fall of Troy, a new wave of Indo-Europeans, the Dorian Greeks, materially aided by weapons made of iron instead of bronze, burst upon Greece. First of the Mycenaean strongholds to fall was Pylos, whose Linear B archives contain numerous references to hastily undertaken preparations to repel the invaders. We find orders directing women and children to places of safety; instructions to armorers, "rowers," and food-suppliers; and a report entitled "how the watchers are guarding the coastal regions."[2] The preparations were in vain, however. Pylos was sacked and burned, and the destruction of the other major Mycenaean citadels soon followed. Mycenaean refugees found a haven at Athens and in Ionia on the western coast of Asia Minor.

The next four centuries, the Greek Dark Ages, were marked by the disappearance of the major characteristics of the relatively advanced Mycenaean civilization—political centralization, wide-ranging commerce, sophisticated art forms (including monumental architecture), and writing. Yet while the Dorian invasion was an undoubted catastrophe, it was also vital to the ultimate rise of a unique Hellenic (from *Hellas*, the Greek name for Greece) civilization that was not largely an offshoot of the Near East, as was Aegean civilization.

THE RISE OF HELLENIC CIVILIZATION

The influence of geography. Geographical factors played an important part in shaping the events of Greek history. The numerous mountain ranges which crisscross the peninsula severely hampered internal communications and led to the development of fiercely independent, autonomous political units—the city-states. Furthermore, the Greeks had every incentive to go down to the sea in ships. The numerous islands and indented coastlines of the Greek peninsula and of Asia Minor stimulated seagoing trade, and the rocky soil (less than a fifth of Greece is arable) and limited natural resources encouraged the Greeks to establish colonies abroad.

The Homeric Age. Most of our information about the Greek Dark Ages (c. 1150-750 B.C.) which followed the Dorian invasion is derived from the epics composed during the last century of this period and attributed to the blind Ionian poet Homer. Controversy surrounds the problem of Homer's existence and whether he or several poets composed the *Iliad* and the *Odyssey*. The Homeric epics retain something of the material side of the bygone Mycenaean period; yet in filling in the details of political, economic, and social life, the religious beliefs and practices, and the ideals that gave meaning to life, the poet could only describe what was familiar to him in his own age.

The values that gave meaning to life in the Homeric Age were predominantly heroic values—the strength, skill, and valor of the preeminent warrior. Such was the earliest meaning of *aretē*, "excellence" or "virtue," a key term throughout the course of Greek culture. To obtain *aretē*—defined by one Homeric hero as "to fight ever in the forefront and outvie my peers"—and the imperishable fame that was its reward, men welcomed hardship, struggle, and even death. Honor, like fame, was a measure of *aretē*, and the greatest of human tragedies was the denial of honor due to a great warrior. Homer makes such a denial the theme of the *Iliad*: "The ruinous wrath of Achilles that brought countless ills upon the Achaeans" when Achilles, insulted by Agamemnon, withdraws from battle.

To the Homeric Greeks, the gods were plainly human: Zeus, the king of the gods, was often the undignified victim of the plots of his wife Hera and other deities, and he asserted his authority through threats of violence. Hades, the abode of the dead, was a subterranean land of dust and darkness, and Achilles, as Homer tells us in the *Odyssey*, would have preferred to be a slave on earth than a king in Hades.

Society was clearly aristocratic—only the *aristoi* ("aristocrats") possessed *aretē*—and the common man was reviled and beaten when he dared to question his betters. Yet the common man had certain political rights as a member of the assembly that was summoned whenever a crisis, such as war, required his participation. Two other instruments of government described by Homer were the tribal king and his council. The king was hardly more than a chief among his peers, his fellow nobles, who sat in his council to advise him and to check any attempt he might make to exercise arbitrary power. Economic conditions were those of a simple, self-sufficient agricultural system much like that of the early Middle Ages in western Europe.

The city-state: origin and political evolution. The *polis*, or city-state, the famed Greek political unit consisting of a city and its surrounding plains and valleys, did not exist in the Greek Dark Ages. The nucleus of the *polis* was the elevated, fortified site—the *acropolis* —where people could take refuge from attack. With the revival of commerce in the eighth and seventh centuries B.C., a trading center developed below the acropolis. The two parts combined, forming the *polis*, from which our word *politics* is derived.

The political development of the *polis* was so rich and varied that it is difficult to think of a form of government not experienced— and given a lasting name—by the Greeks. Four major types of government evolved: (1) monarchy limited by an aristocratic council and a popular assembly, as described in the Homeric epics; (2) oligarchy ("rule of the few"), arising when the aristocratic council ousted the king and abolished or restricted the popular assembly; (3) tyranny, imposed by one man who rode to power on the discontent of the lower classes; (4) democracy ("rule of the people"), the outstanding political achievement of the Greeks, which emerged after the tyrant was deposed and the popular assembly revived and made the chief organ of government. After dissatisfaction with democratic government became widespread in the fourth century B.C., many of the city-states returned either to oligarchy or to one-man rule.

The Age of Oligarchy. By the middle of the eighth century B.C., the nobles, who resented the power wielded by the tribal kings, had taken over the government, ushering in the Age of Oligarchy. Ruthlessly exercising their superior power, the nobles acquired a monopoly of the best land, reducing many commoners to virtual serfdom and forcing others to seek a living on rocky, barren soil.

The hard lot of the common man under oligarchy produced the anguished protest of Hesiod's *Works and Days* (c. 700 B.C.). A commoner who had been cheated out of his parcel of land by his evil brother in league with "bribe-swallowing" aristocratic judges, Hesiod was the prophet of a more exalted conception of the gods and a new age of social justice. To establish a just society, Hesiod argued, men must learn to pursue moderation (*sophrosyne*) in all things—apparently the first expression of this famous Greek ideal—and realize that "far-seeing" Zeus and the other gods punish evildoers and reward the righteous. He redefined human excellence, or *arete*, in a way to make it attainable for the common man. Its essential ingredients were righteousness and work— honest work in competition with one's fellows being a form of strife in moderation. "Gods and men hate him who lives without work," Hesiod insisted. "His nature is like the drones who sit idle and eat the labor of the bees." Furthermore, "work is no shame, but idleness is a shame," and "esteem," "glory," and "riches" follow work.[3]

Hesiod's new ideals of moderation and justice took root slowly, and the poor found relief only by emigrating to new lands overseas. As Plato later noted, the wealthy promoted colonization as a safety valve to ward off a threatened political and economic explosion:

When men who have nothing, and are in want of food, show a disposition to follow their leaders in an attack on the property of the rich—these, who are the natural plague of the state, are sent away by the legislator in a friendly spirit as far as he is able; and this dismissal of them is euphemistically termed a colony.[4]

From 750 to 550 B.C. the Greeks planted colonies throughout much of the Mediterranean world, a development often compared with the expansion of Europe in modern

Examples of Greek painting have totally disappeared except for what has survived through vase-painting. This has become an invaluable source of what everyday life was like in ancient Greece. An affectionate domestic scene is depicted on this water-jug from the fifth century B.C.

times. Settlements sprang up along the northern coast of the Aegean and around the Black Sea. So many Greeks migrated to southern Italy and eastern Sicily that the region became known as *Magna Graecia*, or Great Greece. Colonies were also founded as far west as present-day France—at Massilia, modern Marseilles—and Spain and on parts of the African coast. Unique was Naucratis in Egypt, not a true colony but a trading post whose residents gained extraterritorial rights (their own magistrates and law courts) from the Egyptians.

In time colonization ameliorated Greece's economic and social problems. By 600 B.C. the use of coined money, learned from the Lydians, had created the beginnings of a middle class. The Greek home states gradually became "industrialized" as a result of concentrating upon the production of specialized wares—vases, metal goods, textiles, olive oil, and wine—for export in exchange for foodstuffs and raw materials. But before this economic revolution was completed, the continuing land hunger of the peasants con-

tributed to a political revolution. After 650 B.C. tyrants arose in many Greek states and, supported by the aggrieved peasantry and the rising merchant class, seized the reins of government from the nobility. These tyrants (the word meant simply "master" and did not at first have the unfavorable meaning it now possesses) not only distributed land to the peasants but, by promoting further colonization, trade, and industry, accelerated the rise of a mercantile class and the completion of the Greek economic revolution.

Athens to 500 B.C. Athens and Sparta, the city-states destined to dominate the history of Greece during the classical period (the fifth century and most of the fourth), underwent markedly different developments during the period prior to 500 B.C. While Athens' political, economic, and social evolution was typical of most other Greek states, Sparta's development produced a unique way of life that elicited the wonder and often the admiration of other Greeks.

During the course of the seventh century B.C. at Athens, the council of nobles became supreme. The popular assembly no longer met, and the king was replaced by nine aristocratic magistrates, called archons, chosen annually by the council to exercise the king's civil, military, and religious powers. The nobility acquired the good land on the plain; the peasants either stayed on as sharecroppers, who were often reduced to debt slavery, or took to the hills.

When the Athenian nobles finally realized that their failure to heed the cry for reform would result in the rise of a tyrant, they agreed to the policy of compromise advocated by the liberal aristocrat Solon. In 594 B.C. Solon was made sole archon with broad authority to reconcile the lower classes. Inspired by the new ideals of moderation and justice, Solon instituted middle-of-the-road reforms that have made his name a byword for wise statesmanship.

Solon provided a new start for the lower classes by canceling all debts and forbidding future debt bondage, but he rejected as too radical their demand for the redivision of the land. His long-range solution to the economic problem was to seek full employment by stimulating trade and industry. To achieve this goal, Solon required fathers to teach their sons a trade, granted citizenship to foreign artisans who settled in Athens, and encouraged the intensive production of olive oil for export.

Moderation also characterized Solon's political reforms—the common people were granted important political rights, but not equality. While laws continued to originate in the new aristocratic Council of Four Hundred, they now had to be ratified by the popular assembly, which Solon revived. And since wealth, not birth, became the qualification for membership in the Council and for the archonships, wealthy commoners acquired full political equality. Furthermore, the assembly could now act as a court to hear appeals from the decisions of the archons and to try them for misdeeds in office.

Unfortunately, Solon's moderate reforms satisfied neither party. The poor had received neither land nor political equality, while the nobles thought Solon a radical who had betrayed his class. Deeply discouraged, Solon described what is too often the lot of moderate reformers: "Formerly they boasted of me vainly; with averted eyes, now they look askance upon me; friends no more, but enemies."[5]

Solon had warned the Athenians to accept his reforms lest "the people in its ignorance comes into the power of a tyrant." He lived to see his prediction fulfilled. In 560 B.C., after a period of civil strife, Pisistratus, a military hero and champion of the commoners, usurped power as tyrant. He solved the economic problem by banishing many nobles, whose lands he distributed among the poor, and by promoting commerce and industry. Together with extensive public works and the patronage of culture—thus starting Athens on the road to cultural leadership in Greece—these reforms gave rise to a popular saying that "Life under Pisistratus was paradise on earth."

Pisistratus was succeeded by his two sons, one of whom was assassinated and the other exiled. When the nobles, aided by a Spartan army, took this opportunity to restore oligarchy, Cleisthenes temporarily seized power in 508 B.C. and put through constitutional reforms that destroyed the remaining power of the nobility. He disregarded the old noble-dominated tribes and created ten new ones, each embracing citizens of all classes from widely scattered districts. The popular assembly acquired the right to initiate legislation, while the new and democratic Council of Five Hundred, selected by lot from the ten tribes, advised the assembly and supervised the administrative actions of the archons. A final reform of Cleisthenes was the peculiar institution of *ostracism*, an annual referendum in which a quorum of six thousand citizens could vote to exile for ten years any individual thought to be a threat to the new Athenian democracy.

Sparta to 500 B.C. In sharp contrast to Athens was the rival city-state Sparta. Sparta had not joined the other Greek cities in trade and colonization but had expanded instead by conquering and enslaving its neighbors. To guard against revolts by the state slaves (helots), who worked the land for their conquerors, Sparta was forced to deviate from the normal course of Greek political development and transform itself into a militaristic totalitarian state. Aristotle called the government of Sparta a "mixed constitution"; for the small minority of ruling Spartans, it was a democracy, but for the great mass of subjected people it was an oligarchy. The government included two kings, a small Council of Elders, and an assembly of all Spartan citizens. True power resided in five overseers, the ephors, who were elected by the assembly and wielded more influence than the dual monarchs.

The state enforced absolute subordination of the individual to its will. Throughout his life every Spartan was first of all a soldier. Sickly infants were left to die on lonely mountaintops; boys were taken from their families when they were seven years old to live under rigorous military discipline for the rest of their lives; girls were trained to become healthy mothers of warrior sons. As their men marched off to war, Spartan women bid them a laconic farewell: "Come back with your shield or on it."

While Sparta developed the finest military machine in Greece, it remained backward culturally and economically. Trade and travel were prohibited because the city fathers feared that alien ideas might disturb the status quo. A self-imposed isolation forbade those cultural contacts without which no balanced civilization can develop. Sparta is a classic example of how intellectual stagnation accompanies rigid social conformity and military regimentation.

To provide additional assurance that its helots remain uncontaminated by democratic ideas, Sparta allied itself with oligarchic parties in other Peloponnesian states and aided them in suppressing their democratic opponents. The resulting Spartan League of oligarchic states, in operation by the end of the sixth century B.C., was shortly to be faced by an Athenian-led union of democratic states (see map, p. 48).

UNITY AND STRIFE IN THE HELLENIC WORLD

The Persian Wars. The leaders of the Greek economic and cultural revival after 750 B.C. were the Ionian Greeks, descendants of the Mycenaeans who had fled to the Aegean coast of Asia Minor and its offshore islands. Influenced by contacts with Phoenician traders (from whom they borrowed the alphabet in the eighth century), neighboring Lydia, and Egypt, the Ionians "first kindled the torch of Hellenism."

We have seen in Chapter 1 that when the Persians conquered Lydia in 547 B.C. they also annexed Ionia, which had been under nominal Lydian rule. Chafing under Persian-appointed tyrants, the Ionian cities revolted in 499 B.C., established democratic regimes, and appealed to the Athenians, who were also Ionians, for aid. Athens sent twenty ships, but to no avail. By 494 B.C. Darius I had crushed the revolt, burning Miletus in revenge.

The battle of Marathon. Darius knew that Ionia was insecure as long as Athens remained free to incite her kinsmen to revolt, and thus in 490 B.C. a Persian force of about twenty thousand men sailed across the Aegean and debarked on the plain of Marathon near Athens. Darius' aim of forcing the

Athenians to accept the exiled son of Pisistratus as a pro-Persian tyrant was frustrated when the Athenian army, half the size of the Persian, won an overwhelming victory, killing 6400 of the foe while losing only 192.

The battle of Marathon was one of the most decisive in history. It destroyed the belief in Persian invincibility and demonstrated, in the words of the Greek historian Herodotus, that "free men fight better than slaves." The victory also gave the Athenians the self-confidence that would soon make their city the leading Greek state.

End of the Persian Wars. Ten years later the Greeks were well prepared for a new Persian invasion under Xerxes, Darius' successor, whose objective was the subjection of all of Greece. Athens now had two hundred ships, the largest fleet in Greece, and Sparta had agreed to head a defensive alliance of thirty-one states.

The Persian army—reckoned by Herodotus at 1,700,000 but more likely 150,000 or so—was too huge to be transported by ship. Crossing the swift-flowing, mile-wide Hellespont on two pontoon bridges—a notable feat of engineering—the army marched along the Aegean coast accompanied by a great fleet carrying provisions. The Spartans wanted to abandon all of Greece except the Peloponnesus to the invaders but finally agreed to a holding action at the narrow pass of Thermopylae. Here three hundred Spartans and a few thousand other Greeks held back the Persians for three days, until a Greek traitor led them over a mountain path to the rear of the Greek position. The Spartans fought magnificently until all were slain, together with seven hundred other Greeks. The Spartan dead were immortalized on a monument erected at the pass: "Go tell the Spartans, thou that passeth by, / That here, obedient to their laws, we lie."

The Persians then burned Athens, whose inhabitants had fled, for they placed their faith in "wooden walls"—their fleet. Their faith was not misplaced; in the Bay of Salamis the Greek fleet, largely Athenian, turned the tide of victory with the shout: "On, sons of the Greeks! Set free your country, set your children free, your wives, the temples of your country's gods, your fathers' tombs;

now they are all at stake."[6] With 200 of his 350 ships destroyed and his lines of communication cut, Xerxes had no alternative but to retreat to Asia, although he left a strong force in Greece. The following summer (479 B.C.) the Greek army, with the Spartan contingent in the van, routed the Persian force at Plataea, and Greece was for the time being safe from invasion.

Culmination of Athenian democracy. Following the expulsion of the Persians, the Athenians "felt themselves suddenly to be 'on top of the world,' and from this in a large measure sprang the reckless confidence and boundless energy which now carried them forward to the greatest phase of their history. Athens' heyday lasted less than eighty years, and the number of her adult male citizens scarcely exceeded fifty thousand. Yet this handful of men attempted more and achieved more in a wider variety of fields than any nation great or small has ever attempted or achieved in a similar space of time."[7]

For more than thirty years (461-429 B.C.) during this Golden Age of Greece, the great statesman Pericles guided Athenian policy. In Pericles' time the actual executive power no longer resided in the archonship, which was filled by lot, but in a board of ten elected generals. This board operated much like a modern-day governmental cabinet. The generals urged the popular assembly to adopt specific measures, and the success or failure of their policies determined whether or not they would be reelected at the end of their annual term. Pericles failed of reelection only once, and so great was his influence on the Athenians that, in the words of the contemporary historian Thucydides, "what was in name a democracy was virtually a government by its greatest citizen."[8]

To enable even the poorest citizen to participate in government, Pericles extended payment to jurors (a panel of six thousand citizens chosen annually by lot) and to members of the Council. While his conservative opponents called this political bribery, Pericles insisted that it was essential to the success of democracy:

Our constitution is named a democracy, because it is in the hands not of the few but of the many.

But our laws secure equal justice for all in their private disputes, and our public opinion welcomes and honours talent in every branch of achievement, not as a matter of privilege but on grounds of excellence alone. . . . [Athenians] do not allow absorption in their own various affairs to interfere with their knowledge of the city's. We differ from other states in regarding the man who holds aloof from public life not as "quiet" but as useless; we decide or debate, carefully and in person, all matters of policy, holding, not that words and deeds go ill together, but that acts are foredoomed to failure when undertaken undiscussed.[9]

The majority of the inhabitants of Athens, however, were not recognized as citizens. Women, slaves, and resident aliens were denied citizenship and had no voice in the government. Nor did they have any standing in the law courts. If a woman desired the protection of the law, she had to seek out a citizen to plead for her in court.

Athenian imperialism. The victory over Persia had been made possible by a partial unity of Hellenic arms; but that unity quickly dissolved when Sparta, fearful of helot rebellion at home, recalled its troops and resumed its policy of isolation. Because the Persians still ruled the Ionian cities and another invasion of Greece seemed probable, Athens in 478 B.C. invited the city-states bordering on the Aegean to form a defensive alliance called the Delian League. To maintain a two-hundred-ship navy that would police the seas, each state was assessed ships or money in proportion to its wealth. From the beginning, Athens dominated the League. Since almost all of the 173 member states paid their assessments in money, which Athens was empowered to collect, the Athenians furnished the necessary ships.

By 468 B.C., after the Ionian cities had been liberated and the Persian fleet destroyed, various League members thought it unnecessary to continue the confederacy. In suppressing all attempts to secede, the Athenians were motivated by the fear that the Persian danger still existed and by the need to maintain and protect the large free-trade area so necessary for Greek—and especially Athenian—commerce and industry. The Athenians created an empire because they dared not unmake a confederation. By aiding in

GREEK POLITICAL ALLIANCES
ABOUT 431 B.C.

- Athens and Allies
- Sparta and Allies
- Neutral Greek States

the suppression of local aristocratic factions within its subject states, Athens both eased the task of controlling its empire and emerged as the leader of a union of democratic states.

To many Greeks—above all to the members of the oligarchic Spartan League and the suppressed aristocratic factions within the Athenian empire—Athens was a "tyrant city" and an "enslaver of Greek liberties." Pericles, on the other hand, justified Athenian imperialism on the ground that it brought "freedom" from fear and want to the Greek world:

We secure our friends not by accepting favours but by doing them. . . . We are alone among mankind in doing men benefits, not on calculations of self-interest, but in the fearless confidence of freedom. In a word I claim that our city as a whole is an education to Hellas. . . .[10]

The Peloponnesian War. In 431 B.C. the Peloponnesian War broke out between the Spartan League and the Athenian empire. While commercial rivalry between Athens and Sparta's ally Corinth was an important factor, the conflict is a classic example of how fear can generate a war unwanted by either side. According to Thucydides:

The real but unavowed cause I consider to have been the growth of the power of Athens, and the alarm which it inspired in Lacedaemon [Sparta]; this made war inevitable.[11]

Several incidents served to ignite the underlying tension, and Sparta declared war on the "aggressors."

Sparta's hope for victory lay in its army's ability to besiege Athens and lay waste its fields. Pericles, on the other hand, relied on Athen's unrivaled navy to import foodstuffs and to harass its enemies' coasts. Fate took a hand in this game, however. In the second year of the war a plague carried off a third of the Athenian population, including Pericles. His death was a great blow to Athens, for leadership of the government passed to demagogues. In the words of Thucydides:

Pericles, by his rank, ability, and known integrity, was able to exercise an independent control over the masses—to lead them instead of being led by them. . . . With his successors it was different. More on a level with one another, and each grasping at supremacy, they ended by committing even the conduct of state affairs to the whims of the multitude. This, as might have been expected in a great imperial state, produced a host of blunders. . . .[12]

Eight more years of indecisive warfare ended in 421 B.C. with a compromise peace. During the succeeding period Athenian imperialism manifested itself in its worst form through the actions of Pericles' unworthy successors. In 416 B.C. an expedition embarked for Melos, a neutral Aegean island, to force it to join the Athenian empire. Thucydides reported the specious logic the Athenians employed to justify their naked imperialism on this occasion:

We believe that Heaven, and we know that men, by a natural law, always rule where they are stronger. We did not make that law nor were we the first to act on it; we found it existing, and it will exist forever, after we are gone; and we know that you and anyone else as strong as we are would do as we do.[13]

The Athenians put all Melians of military age to death and sold the women and children into slavery.

The war was resumed in 415 B.C. with an Athenian expedition against Syracuse that was destined to end in disaster. Acting on the invitation of states that feared Syracusan expansion, the Athenians hoped to add Sicily to their empire and so become powerful enough "to rule the whole of the Greek world."[14] But ill luck and incompetent leadership resulted in two Athenian fleets and a large army being destroyed by the Syracusans, supported by Sparta. The war dragged on until 404 B.C., when Athens capitulated after its last fleet was destroyed by a Spartan fleet built with money received from Persia in exchange for possession of the Greek cities in Ionia. At home, Athens had been weakened by the plots of oligarchic elements to whom Sparta now turned over the government. The once great city was also stripped of its possessions and demilitarized.

Aftermath of the war. Anarchy and depression were the political and economic legacies of the Peloponnesian War. Having ended the "tyranny" of Athens over Greece, the Spartans substituted their own form of rule which made the Athenian empire seem mild in comparison. Everywhere democracies were replaced by oligarchies supported by Spartan troops. The bloody excesses of these oligarchs soon led to revolutions which Sparta could not suppress. As one of their generals admitted, the Spartans did not know how to govern free men. Incessant warfare filled the early fourth century as a bewildering series of shifting alliances, usually financed by Persia which wanted to keep Greece disunited and weak, sought to keep any state from predominating.

Political disintegration in turn contributed to the economic and social ills that plagued Greece during the fourth century B.C. Commerce and industry languished, and the unemployed who did not go abroad as soldiers of fortune supported demagogues and their radical schemes for the redivision of wealth. The wealthy, for their part, became increasingly reactionary and uncompromising. Even most intellectuals—including Plato and Aristotle—lost faith in democracy and joined with the wealthy in looking for "a champion powerful in action" who would bring order and security to Greece. They found him, finally, in the person of the king of Macedonia.

The Macedonian unification of Greece. To the north of Greece lay Macedonia, inhabited by hardy peasants and nobles who were related to the Greeks but were culturally inferior to them. Macedonia became a centralized, powerful state under the able and crafty Philip II (359-336 B.C.), who created the most formidable army yet known by joining the crack Macedonian cavalry of nobles with the infantry phalanx used by the Greeks. In his youth, Philip had been a hostage at Thebes, where he acquired an appreciation of Greek culture, an understanding of Greek political weakness, and a desire to win for Macedonia a place in the Hellenic world.

After unifying Macedonia—including a string of Greek colonies that had been established along its coast during the earlier centuries of Macedonia's weakness—Philip turned to the Greek city-states, whose wars afforded him the opportunity first to intervene, then to dominate. In vain did Demosthenes, the great Athenian orator and democratic leader, warn that "democracies and dictators cannot exist together" and urge the Athenians and other Greeks to stop Philip before it was too late. Belatedly, Athens and Thebes acted, but their combined forces were shattered at Chaeronea in 338 B.C. Philip then forced the Greeks into a federal league in which each state, while retaining self-government, swore to "make war upon him who violates the general peace" and to furnish Philip with men and supplies for a campaign against Persia. On the eve of setting out for Asia Minor, Philip was assassinated by a noble with a personal grudge, leaving the war against Persia as a legacy for his brilliant son Alexander.

Incapable of finding a solution to the anarchy that tore their world to shreds, the Greeks ended as political failures and at the mercy of a great outside power, first Macedonia and then Rome. They retained their cultural leadership, however, and the culture of the new Hellenistic Age and its successor, the world of Rome, was to be largely Greek.

THE GREEK GENIUS

The Greek character. The Greeks were the first to formulate many of the western world's fundamental concepts in philosophy, science, and art. How was it that a relative handful of people could bequeath such a legacy to civilization? The definitive answer may always elude the historian, but a good part of the explanation lies in environmental and social factors.

Unlike the Near Eastern monarchies, the *polis* was not governed by a "divine" ruler, nor were the thoughts and activities of its citizens limited by powerful priesthoods. Many Greeks, and most notably the Athenians, were fond of good talk and relished debate

and argument. The nature of the universe and of man, a person's duty to the state and to his fellow citizens, law and freedom, the purpose of art and poetry, the standards of a good life—these were a few of the numerous problems they discussed brilliantly and with pertinence for our times as much as theirs.

The Greeks felt a deep-seated need to discover an order in the flux of human life and in nature. This quest for order produced exceptional results in science, art, and philosophy. Beginning with Hesiod (see p. 43), the Greeks stressed the virtue of *sophrosynē* (moderation, self-control) as the key to happiness and right living. Its opposite was *hubris*, meaning pride, arrogance, and unbridled ambition. The result of human excesses and lying at the root of personal misfortune and social injustice, *hubris* invariably provoked *nemesis*, or retribution. According to the Greeks, an inexorable law would cause the downfall or disgrace of anyone guilty of *hubris*. The Athenian dramatists often employed this theme in their tragedies, and Herodotus attributed the Persian defeat by the Greeks to Xerxes' overweening pride, for "Zeus tolerates pride in none but himself." [15]

The Greeks exhibited human frailties and failings—at times they were irrational, vindictive, and cruel. But at their best they were guided by the ideals that permeate their intellectual and artistic legacy. The philosopher Protagoras is credited with the statement, "Man is the measure of all things"—a saying which sums up the outstanding feature of Greek thought and art. In short, the Greeks were humanists.

Greek religion. Early Greek religion abounded in gods and goddesses who personified physical elements. Thus Demeter was the earth and giver of grain, Apollo, the sun and giver of light, and Poseidon, who dwelled in the sea, was the ruler of the waters. Other deities had special functions, such as Aphrodite, the goddess of love, Dionysus, the god of fertility and wine, and Athena, the goddess of wisdom and the guardian of Athens. The Greeks of Homeric times believed in manlike deities, capable of malice, favoritism, and jealousy, and differing from ordinary men only in their immortality and their possession of supernatural powers. Zeus, the king of sky, earth, and men, supposedly ruled the world from Mount Olympus with the aid of lesser deities.

By the time of Hesiod, as we have seen (p. 43), a religious reformation had begun which changed the vengeful and capricious gods of Homer into austere arbiters of justice who rewarded the good and punished the wicked. Demeter and Dionysus gained prominence as the central figures of "mystery" cults whose initiates (*mystae*) were promised an afterlife of bliss in Elysium—formerly the abode of heroes only. And from the famous oracle at Delphi the voice of Zeus' son Apollo urged all Greeks to follow the ideal of moderation: "Nothing in excess" and "Know thyself" (meaning "Know your limitations").

Early Greek philosophy and science. Philosophy arose from the insatiable Greek curiosity about nature. As we noted in Chapter 1, the Mesopotamians were skilled observers of astronomical phenomena such as eclipses, which they attributed to magical and supernatural causes. The early Greek philosophers, beginning with Thales of Miletus (c. 636-546 B.C.), changed the course of human knowledge by insisting that the phenomena of the universe can be explained by natural causes. This rejection of the supernatural and the application of reason to discern universal principles in nature has been called the "Greek miracle." It led men to the threshold of today's world of science and technology.

Called "the father of philosophy," Thales speculated on the nature of the basic substance from which all else in the universe is composed. He concluded that it was water, which exists in different states or forms and is indispensable to the maintenance and growth of organisms. Thales' successors in Ionia proposed elements other than water as the primal substance in the universe. One called it the "boundless," apparently a general concept for "matter"; another proposed "air," out of which all things come by a process of "rarefying and condensing"; a third asserted that fire was the "most mobile, most transformable, most active, most life-giving" element. This search for a material substance as the first principle or cause of

all things culminated two centuries after Thales in the atomic theory of Democritus (c. 460-370 B.C.). To Democritus, reality was the mechanical motion of indivisible atoms, which differed in shape, size, position, and arrangement but not in quality. Moving about continuously, atoms combined to create objects. Scientists have used this theory to the present day, although we are now aware that the atom is neither indivisible nor indestructible.

While these and other early Greek philosophers were proposing some form of matter as the basic element in nature, Pythagoras of Samos (c. 582-500 B.C.) countered with the profoundly significant notion that the "nature of things" was something nonmaterial—numbers. By experimenting with a vibrating cord, Pythagoras discovered that musical harmony is based on arithmetical proportions, and he intuitively concluded that the universe was constructed of numbers and their relationships. His mathematical interpretation of nature greatly influenced Plato, and modern mathematical physicists have continued along the path he was the first to trod.

An important consequence of early Greek philosophical speculation was the undermining of conventional beliefs and traditions. In religion, for example, Xenophanes ridiculed the traditional view of the gods: "If oxen and lions had hands, . . . they would make portraits and statues of their gods in their own image." The eroding of traditional views caused Greek inquiry to turn away from nature to man—to a consideration of human values and institutions. During the last half of the fifth century B.C., the Sophists —"men of wisdom" who taught public speaking and prepared men for public life— submitted all conventional beliefs to the test of rational criticism. Concluding that truth was relative, they denied the existence of universal standards to guide human actions.

Socrates, a martyr to truth. The outstanding opponent of the Sophists was the Athenian Socrates (c. 470-399 B.C.), a snub-nosed, plain man but a fascinating conversationalist. Like the Sophists, Socrates turned from cosmic to human affairs; in the words of the Roman statesman Cicero, Socrates was "the first to call philosophy down from the heavens and to set her in the cities of men, bringing her into their homes and compelling her to ask questions about life and morality and things good and evil."[16] But unlike the Sophists, Socrates believed that by asking salient questions and by subjecting the answers to logical analysis, agreement could be reached about ethical standards and rules of conduct. And so he would question passers-by in his function of midwife assisting in the birth of correct ideas (to use his own figure of speech). Taking as his motto the famous inscription on the temple of Apollo at Delphi, "Know thyself," he insisted that "the unexamined life is not worth living." To Socrates, human excellence or virtue (*aretē*) is knowledge, and evil and error are the result of ignorance.

In time Socrates' quest for truth led to his undoing, for the Athenians, unnerved by the Peloponnesian War, arrested him on the charge of impiety and corrupting youth. By a slim majority a jury of citizens condemned Socrates to die, a fate he accepted without rancor and with a last request:

When my sons are grown up, I would ask you, my friends, to punish them, and I would have you trouble them, as I have troubled you, if they seem to care about riches, or anything, more than about virtue; or if they pretend to be something when they are really nothing, then reprove them, as I have reproved you, for not caring about that for which they ought to care, and thinking that they are something when they are really nothing. And if you do this, both I and my sons will have received justice at your hands.

The hour of departure has arrived, and we go our ways—I to die, and you to live. Which is better God only knows.[17]

Plato and his Theory of Ideas. After Socrates' death, philosophical leadership passed to his most famous disciple, Plato (427-347 B.C.). Like Socrates, Plato believed that truth exists, but only in the realm of thought, the spiritual world of Ideas or Forms. Such universals as Beauty, Good, and Justice exist apart from the material world, and the beauty, good, and justice that we encounter in the world of the senses are only imperfect re-

flections of eternal and changeless Ideas. Man's task is to come to know the True Reality—the eternal Ideas—behind these imperfect reflections. Only the soul, and the "soul's pilot," reason, can accomplish this, for the human soul is spiritual and immortal, and in its prenatal state it existed "beyond the heavens" where "true Being dwells."[18]

Disillusioned with democracy, Plato expounded his concept of an ideal state in the *Republic*, the first systematic treatise on political science. The state's basic function, founded on the Idea of Justice, was the satisfaction of the common good. Plato described a kind of "spiritualized Sparta" in which the state regulated every aspect of life, including thought. The family and private property, for example, were abolished on the grounds that both bred selfishness, and marriage was controlled in order to produce strong, healthy children. Individuals belonged to one of three classes and found happiness only through their contribution to the community: workers by producing the necessities of life, warriors by guarding the state, and philosophers by ruling in the best interests of all the people.

Plato founded the Academy in Athens, the famous school which existed from about 388 B.C. until 529 A.D. Here he taught and encouraged his students, whom he expected to become the intellectual elite who would go forth and reform society.

Aristotle, the encyclopedic philosopher. Plato's greatest pupil was Aristotle (384-322 B.C.), who set up his own school, the Lyceum, at Athens. Reacting against the other-worldly tendencies of Plato's thought, Aristotle insisted that Ideas have no separate existence apart from the material world; knowledge of universal Ideas is the result of the painstaking collection and organization of particular facts. Aristotle's Lyceum, accordingly, became a center for the analysis of data from many branches of learning.

To us today, Aristotle's most significant treatises are the *Ethics* and the *Politics*. They deal with what he called the "philosophy of human affairs," whose object is the acquisition and maintenance of human happiness. Two kinds of virtue (*aretē*), intellectual and moral, which produce two types of happiness, are described in the *Ethics.* Intellectual virtue is the product of reason, and only such men as philosophers and scientists ever attain it. Much more important for the good of society is moral virtue—for example, liberality and temperance—which is the product less of reason than of habit and thus can be acquired by all. In this connection Aristotle introduced his Doctrine of the Mean as a guide for good conduct. He considered all virtues to be means between extremes; thus courage, for example, is the mean between cowardice and rashness.

In the *Politics* Aristotle viewed the state as necessary "for the sake of the good life," because its laws and educational system provide the most effective training needed for the attainment of moral virtue and hence happiness. Thus to Aristotle the viewpoint that the state stands in opposition to the individual would be unthinkable.

Aristotle's writings on formal logic, collectively known as the *Organon* ("Instrument"), describe two ways in which new truths can be acquired. The first, induction, moves from particular facts to general truths. Deductive logic, on the other hand, moves from the general to the particular. To facilitate deductive reasoning from general truths, Aristotle devised the syllogism, a logical structure requiring a trio of propositions. The first two propositions (the major and minor premises) must be plainly valid and logically related so that the third proposition, the conclusion, inevitably follows. For example, (1) all Greeks are human; (2) Socrates is a Greek; (3) therefore Socrates is human.

There has probably never been another man whose interests were so widespread or whose knowledge was so encyclopedic as Aristotle's. He investigated such diverse fields as biology, mathematics, astronomy, physics, psychology, rhetoric, logic, politics, ethics, and metaphysics. His accomplishments won him renown, and he was ultimately requested to tutor the young prince of Macedonia, who became his most famous pupil—Alexander the Great.

Medicine. Preconceived and false ideas about the human body blocked the development of medical science until 420 B.C., when Hippocrates, the "father of medicine," founded a school in which he emphasized the value of observation and the careful interpretation of symptoms. The members of this school were firmly convinced that disease resulted from natural, not supernatural, causes. Writing of epilepsy, considered at the time a "sacred" or supernaturally inspired malady, one Hippocratic writer observed:

It seems to me that this disease is no more divine than any other. It has a natural cause just as other diseases have. Men think it supernatural because they do not understand it. But if they called everything supernatural which they do not understand, why, there would be no end of such things![19]

Despite their empirical approach, the Hippocratic school adopted the theory that the body contained four liquids or humors—blood, phlegm, black bile, and yellow bile—whose proper balance was the basis of health. This doctrine was to impede medical progress until modern times.

The writing of history. History for the Hellenic Greeks was not an account of legendary events and mythical figures, nor were the forces of history attributable simply to the whims of the gods. The Greeks viewed history as a humanistic study by which historians sought to learn about the actions and characters of men. As such, history could be subjected to rational standards and critical judgment.

If history be defined as an "honest attempt first to find out what happened, then to explain why it happened," Herodotus of Halicarnassus (484?–425? B.C.) deserves to be called the "father of history." In his highly entertaining history of the Persian Wars he discerned the clash of two distinct civilizations, the Hellenic and the Near Eastern. His portrayal of both the Greeks and the Persians was eminently impartial, but his fondness for a good story often led him to include tall tales in his work.

The first truly scientific historian was Thucydides (460–400? B.C.), who wrote a notably objective chronicle of the Peloponnesian War. Although he was a contemporary of the events and a loyal Athenian, a reader can scarcely detect whether he favored

Athens or Sparta. In describing the character and purpose of his work, Thucydides probably had Herodotus in mind:

With reference to the narrative of events, far from permitting myself to derive it from the first source that came to hand, I did not even trust my own impressions, but it rests partly on what I saw myself, partly on what others saw for me, the accuracy of the report being always tried by the most severe and detailed tests possible. My conclusions have cost me some labour from the want of coincidence between accounts of the same occurrences by different eyewitnesses, arising sometimes from imperfect memory, sometimes from undue partiality for one side or the other. The absence of romance in my history will, I fear, detract somewhat from its interest; but I shall be content if it is judged useful by those inquirers who desire an exact knowledge of the past as an aid to the interpretation of the future, which in the course of human things must resemble if it does not reflect it. My history has been composed to be an everlasting possession, not the show-piece of an hour.[20]

Hellenic poetry and drama. Greek literary periods can be classified according to dominant poetic forms which reflected particular stages of cultural evolution in Greece. First came the time of great epics, followed by periods in which lyric poetry and drama flourished.

Sometime during the eighth century B.C. in Ionia, the *Iliad* and the *Odyssey*, the two great epics attributed to Homer, were set down in their present form. The *Iliad*, describing the clash of arms between the Greeks and the Trojans "on the ringing plains of windy Troy," glorifies heroic valor and physical prowess against a background of divine intervention in human affairs. The *Odyssey*, relating the adventure-filled wanderings of Odysseus on his return to Greece after Troy's fall, places less stress on divine intervention and more on the cool resourcefulness of the hero in escaping from danger and in regaining his kingdom. These stirring epics have provided inspiration and source material for generations of poets in the western world.

As Greek society became more sophisticated, a new type of poetry, written to be sung to the accompaniment of the lyre, arose among the Ionian Greeks. Its authors sang not of legendary events but of present delights and sorrows. This new note, personal and passionate, can be seen in the following examples, in which the contrast between the new values of what is called the Greek Renaissance and those of Homer's heroic age is sharply clear. Unlike Homer's heroes, Archilochus of Paros (seventh century B.C.) unashamedly throws away his shield and runs from the battlefield:

My trusty shield adorns some Thracian foe;
I left it in a bush—not as I would!
But I have saved my life; so let it go.
Soon I will get another just as good.[21]

And in contrast to the older view of an unromantic, purely physical attraction between Paris and Helen, Sappho of Lesbos (sixth century B.C.), the first and one of the greatest of all woman poets, saw Helen as the helpless victim of romantic love:

She, who the beauty of mankind
Excelled, fair Helen, all for love
The noblest husband left behind;
Afar, to Troy she sailed away,
Her child, her parents, clean forgot;
The Cyprian [Aphrodite] led her far astray
Out of the way, resisting not.[22]

Drama, which developed from the religious rites of the Dionysian mystery cult, filled a civic-religious function in Greek society. In Athens, by the fifth century B.C., two distinct forms—tragedy and comedy—had evolved. Borrowing the old familiar legends of gods and heroes for their plots, the tragedians reinterpreted them in the light of the changing spirit of the times.

By depicting man in conflict with destiny, Aeschylus (525-456 B.C.) expressed the new concern for achieving harmony and avoiding the excesses which led to suffering. In his trilogy, the *Oresteia*, for example, he concerned himself with *hubris*, as applied to the murder of the hero Agamemnon by his false queen, and then proceeded to work out its ramifications—murder piled on murder until men through suffering learn to substitute the moral law of Zeus for the primitive law of the blood feud. Like the prophets of Israel, Aeschylus taught that while "sin brings misery," misery in turn leads to wisdom:

The Persian invasion made Athens a heap of ruins, but the withdrawal of the invaders left the Athenians free to reconstruct the Acropolis into a treasury of temples and statues. In the Parthenon, which housed Phidias' huge gold and ivory statue of Athena, great care was taken to design a structurally and visually perfect building. The tops of the Doric columns lean toward the center of each colonnade, the steps curve upward at the center, and the columns are more widely spaced in the middle of each row than at the ends—all these refinements create an illusion of perfect regularity which would be lacking if the parts were actually perfectly proportioned. The Parthenon was originally brightly painted, and painted sculpture adorned the gables and parts of the frieze, while another sculptured and painted frieze ran around the walls inside the colonnade. A reconstruction of the entire Acropolis appears at the right.

Zeus the Guide, who made man turn
Thought-ward, Zeus, who did ordain
Man by Suffering shall Learn.
So the heart of him, again
Aching with remembered pain,
Bleeds and sleepeth not, until
Wisdom comes against his will.[23]

A generation later, Sophocles (c. 496-406 B.C.) largely abandoned the problem of how to justify the ways of god to man and concentrated upon character. To Sophocles, a certain amount of suffering was inevitable in life. No man was perfect; there was a tragic flaw in the character of the best of men which caused them to make mistakes. Sophocles dwelled mainly on the way in which men react to suffering. Like his contemporary, the sculptor Phidias, Sophocles viewed man as an ideal creature—"Many are the wonders of the world, and none so wonderful as Man"—and he displayed man's greatness by depicting him experiencing great tragedy without whimpering.

Euripides (c. 480-406 B.C.), the last of the great Athenian tragedians, reflects the rationalism and critical spirit of the late fifth century. To him, the life of man was pathetic, the ways of the gods ridiculous. His recurrent theme was "Since life began, hath there in God's eye stood one happy man?" and for this he has been called "the poet of the world's grief." Euripides has also been called the first psychologist, for he looked deep into the human soul and described what he saw with intense realism. Far more than Aeschylus or even Sophocles, Euripides strikes home to modern man.

Comedies were bawdy and spirited. There were no libel laws in Athens, and Aristophanes (c. 445-385 B.C.), the famous comic-dramatist and a conservative in outlook, brilliantly satirized Athenian democracy as a mob led by demagogues, the Sophists (among whom he included Socrates) as subversive, and Euripides as an underminer of civic spirit and traditional faith.

The Greeks as builders. In the sixth century B.C. architecture flourished in Ionia and Greece with the construction of large temples of stone, the form having developed from earlier wooden structures which had been influenced by the surviving remains of Mycenaean palaces. Architecture reached its zenith in fifth-century Athens, then at the height of its power and wealth.

The Parthenon, the Erechtheum, and the other temples on the Athenian Acropolis exhibit the highly developed features that make Greek structure so pleasing to the eye. All relationships, such as column spacing and height and the curvature of floor and roof lines, were calculated and executed with remarkable precision to achieve a perfect balance, both structurally and visually. The three orders, or styles, usually identified by the characteristics of the columns, were the Doric, which was used in the Parthenon; the Ionic, seen in the Erechtheum; and the later and more ornate Corinthian.

Located where all men could see and enjoy them, the Greek temples afford an interesting comparison with those of Egypt. Whereas the Egyptian temple was enclosed and mysterious, the Greek temple was open, with a colonnade porch and single inside room containing a statue of the god. Sacrifice and ritual took place outside the temple, where the altar was placed.

Other types of buildings, notably the theaters, stadiums, and gymnasiums, also express the Greek spirit and way of life. In the open-air theaters the circular shape of the spectators' sections and the plan of the orchestra section set a style which has survived in principle to the present day.

Sculpture and pottery. Greek sculpture of the archaic period (c. 625-480 B.C.), although crude in its representation of human anatomy, has the freshness and vigor of youth. Influenced partly by Egyptian models, the statues of nude youths and draped maidens usually stand stiffly with clenched fists and with one foot thrust awkwardly forward (see photo, p. 57). The fixed smile and formalized treatment of hair and drapery also reveal how the sculptor is struggling to master the technique of his art.

The achievement of mastery of technique by 480 B.C. ushered in the classical period of fifth-century Greek sculpture whose "classic" principles of harmony and proportion have shaped the course of western art. Sculpture from this period displays both the end of technical immaturity and the beginning of

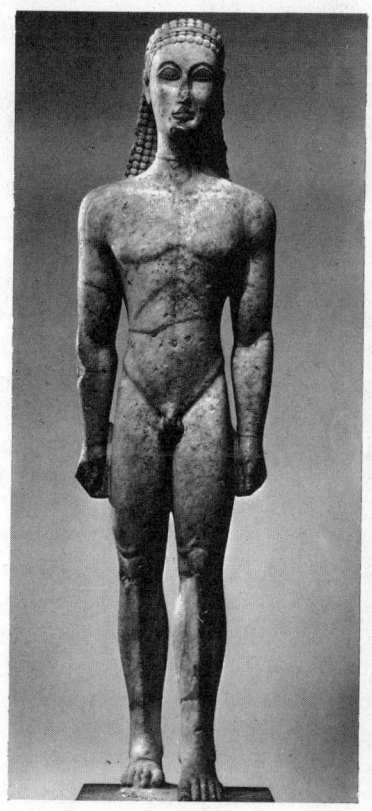

Between the sixth and fourth centuries B.C. Greek art developed from the rigid stylization, reminiscent of Egyptian art, of the *kouros* ("boy") figure (left) to the more complex, naturalistic, yet idealized Hermes by Praxiteles, shown holding the young Dionysus.

idealization of the human form which reached its culmination in the dignity and poise of Phidias' figures in the continuous frieze and pediments of the Parthenon. Carved with restraint and "calm exaltation," the frieze depicts the citizens of Athens participating in the Panathenaic procession in honor of Athena which took place every four years.

The more relaxed character of fourth-century B.C. Hellenic sculpture contrasts with the grandeur and dignity of fifth-century art. Charm, grace, and individuality characterize the work of Praxiteles, the most famous sculptor of the century. These qualities can be seen in his supple statues of the god Hermes holding the young Dionysus and of Aphrodite stepping into her bath.

The making of pottery was a highly developed art in Greece. The earliest vases were decorated with abstract geometric designs, then came paintings of scenes from mythology and daily life. From the surviving Greek pottery, we can get an inkling of what Greek painting, now lost, was like (see illustration, p. 44).

THE HELLENISTIC AGE

Alexander the Great. When Philip of Macedonia was assassinated in 336 B.C., his crown fell to his gifted twenty-year-old son, Alexander, who crushed rebellion in Greece and proved himself a resolute, ambitious king from the beginning of his reign.

Like his father, the youthful Alexander was alive to the glories of Hellenic culture, having as a youth been tutored by Aristotle. Reveling in the heroic deeds of the *Iliad*, Alexander may have seen himself as a second Achilles waging war against barbarians when he planned to revenge the Persian attacks on Greece. Two years after Philip's death, he set out with an army of 35,000 soldiers recruited from Macedonia and the Greek League that his father had organized (see p. 50). In quick succession he subdued Asia Minor, Syria, Palestine, and Egypt. Then the young leader marched into Mesopotamia and there, in 331 B.C., defeated the last powerful army of Darius III, the Persian monarch. Alexander was now master of Persia,

This mosaic from Pompeii is a copy of a fourth-century B.C. Greek painting depicting the defeat of Darius (at the right) by Alexander (at the left) at the Battle of Issus. While this mosaic can only be an imperfect realization of the original painting, the intricacy and vitality of the composition attest to the skill of the Greeks at painting, an art at which they themselves believed they excelled.

the proud empire that had controlled the Near East. He ventured as far east as the rich river valleys of India (see Chapter 4), where his weary soldiers forced him to turn back. In 323 B.C., while he was planning the circumnavigation of Arabia, Alexander died at the age of thirty-two, the victim of malaria. With the Greeks now masters of the ancient Near East, a new and distinctly cosmopolitan period in their history and culture began— the Hellenistic Age.

Alexander's legacy to political thought was the vision of a unified world and the brotherhood of mankind. Various of his military and administrative policies sought to unify the lands he conquered and to promote what he himself called "concord and partnership in the empire" between orientals and westerners. He blended Persians with Greeks and Macedonians in his army and administration; he founded numerous cities—seventy, according to tradition—in the East and settled many of his followers in them; and he married two oriental princesses and encouraged his officers and men to take foreign wives. Finally, for personal as well as political reasons, Alexander ordered the Greek city-states to accord him "divine honors."

The division of Alexander's empire. For several decades following Alexander's sudden death, his generals vied for the spoils of empire. Three major Hellenistic kingdoms emerged and maintained a precarious balance of power until the Roman conquests of the second and first centuries B.C.: Egypt, ruled by Ptolemy and his successors; Asia, comprising most of the remaining provinces of the Persian empire and held together with great difficulty by the dynasty founded by Seleucus; and Macedonia and Greece, ruled by the descendants of Antigonus the One-Eyed.

While the Antigonids in Macedonia followed the model of Alexander's father Philip in posing as national kings chosen by the army, the Ptolemies ruled Egypt as divine pharaohs, and some of the Seleucids became deified "saviors" and "benefactors." Ptolemaic and Seleucid administrations were centralized in bureaucracies staffed by Greeks, an arrangement which created a vast gulf between a ruler and his native subjects.

Plagued by native revolts, dynastic troubles, and civil war, the Hellenistic kingdoms soon began to crumble. Macedonia lost effective control of Greece when Athens asserted its independence and most of the other Greek states formed two federal leagues, the Aetolian in the north and the Achaean in the Peloponnesus, which successfully resisted Macedonian domination. The eastern reaches of Alexander's empire—India, Bactria, and Parthia—gradually drifted out of the Seleucid sphere of influence. Pergamum, in northwestern Asia Minor, renounced its allegiance to the Seleucids and became an independent kingdom famous for its artists and scholars. In the year 200 B.C. the new power of Rome entered upon the scene, and by 30 B.C. Rome had annexed the last remaining Hellenistic state, Egypt.

Hellenistic economy and society. The Hellenistic Age was a time of economic expansion and social change. In the wake of Alexander's conquests, thousands of Greeks flocked eastward to begin a new era of Greek colonization. An economic union between East and West permitted the free flow of trade, and prosperity was stimulated further when Alexander put into circulation huge hoards of Persian gold and silver and introduced a uniform coinage. The result was a much larger and more affluent middle class than had hitherto existed.

By the third century B.C. the center of trade had shifted from Greece to the Near East. Largest of the Hellenistic cities, and much larger than any cities in Greece itself, were Antioch in northern Syria and Alexandria in Egypt. The riches of India, Persia, Arabia, and the Fertile Crescent were brought by sea and land to these Mediterranean ports.

Alexandria outdistanced all other Hellenistic cities as a commercial center. Its merchants supplied the ancient world with wheat, linen, paper, glass, and jewelry. Boasting a population of about a million, the city had a double harbor in which a great lighthouse, judged one of the wonders of the ancient world, rose to a height estimated at 370 feet. Its busy streets were filled with a mixture of peoples—Greeks, Macedonians, Jews, and Egyptians. As in all other Hellenistic cities in the Near East, the privileged Greeks and Macedonians were at the top of the social scale and the mass of natives at the bottom. Harsh social and economic differences separated the rich from the poor, and the exploited workers frequently went on strike.

Hellenistic philosophy. Developments in philosophy reflected the changed environment of the Hellenistic Age. With the growing loss of political freedom and the prevalence of internal disorder, philosophers concerned themselves less with the reform of society and more with the attainment of happiness for the individual. This emphasis on peace of mind in an insecure world led to the rise of four principal schools of thought.

The Skeptics and Cynics reflected most clearly the doubts and misgivings of the times. The Skeptics achieved imperturbability by denying the possibility of finding

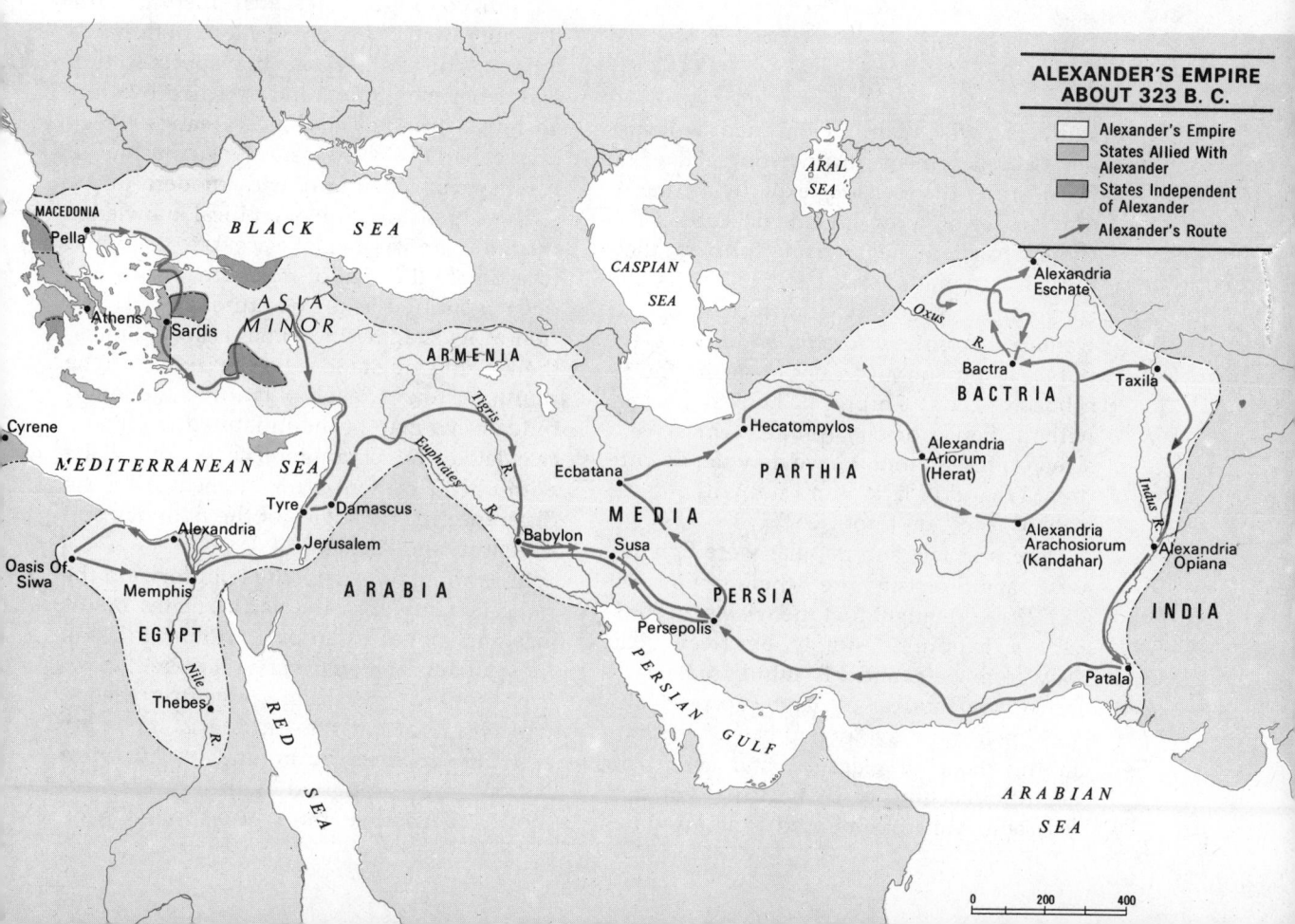

ALEXANDER'S EMPIRE
ABOUT 323 B. C.

Alexander's Empire
States Allied With Alexander
States Independent of Alexander
Alexander's Route

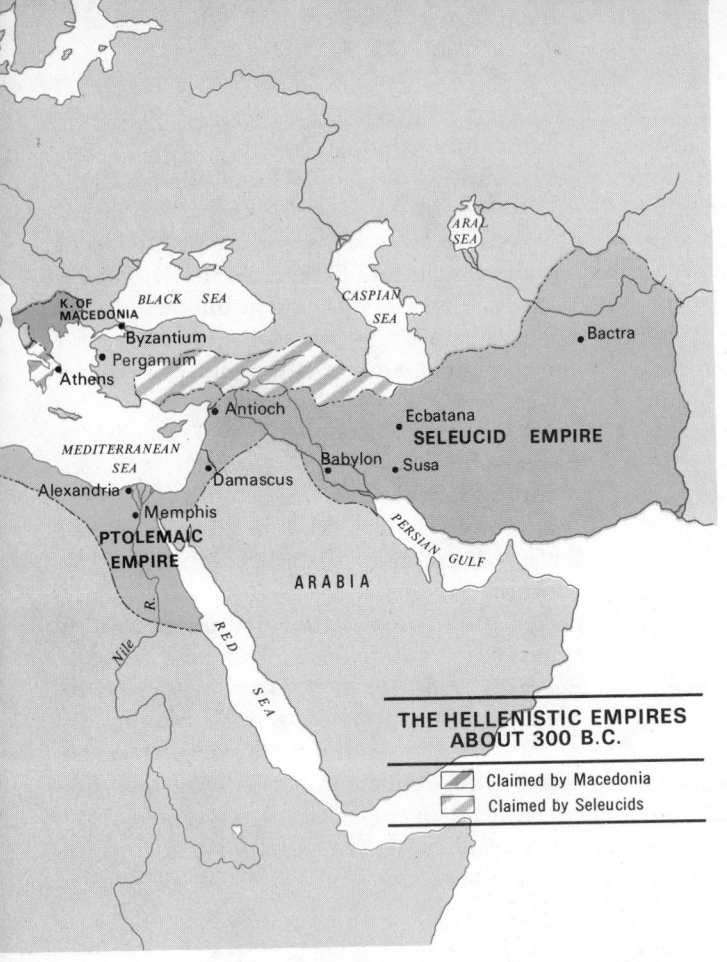

MEDITERRANEAN SEA

K. OF MACEDONIA
Byzantium
Pergamum
Athens

BLACK SEA

CASPIAN SEA

ARAL SEA

Bactra

Antioch

Ecbatana

SELEUCID EMPIRE

Babylon
Susa

Damascus

Alexandria
Memphis

PTOLEMAIC EMPIRE

PERSIAN GULF

ARABIA

Nile R.

RED SEA

THE HELLENISTIC EMPIRES ABOUT 300 B.C.

Claimed by Macedonia
Claimed by Seleucids

fall apart at death. Thus, beyond death there is no existence and nothing to fear. Epicurus maintained that the finest pleasures were intellectual, but many of his followers later distorted his teachings so that Epicureanism appeared to be concerned only with the gratification of sensual desires.

The Stoics, followers of Zeno (c. 336-c. 264 B.C.), a Semite from Cyprus, argued in contrast to Epicureanism that the universe is controlled by some power—variously called Reason, World Soul, Fortune, and God—which determines everything that happens. Fortified by this knowledge, the Stoic wise man conforms his will to the World Will and "stoically" accepts whatever part fortune allots him in the drama of life. With its insistence on duty and on the brotherhood of man in One Great City, Stoicism was particularly attractive to the Romans.

Science and mathematics. The Greek concern for rational, disinterested inquiry reached a zenith in the Hellenistic period, particularly at Alexandria where the Ptolemies subsidized a great research institute, the Museum, and a library of more than half a million books. Emphasizing specialization and experimentation, and enriched by Near Eastern astronomy and mathematics, Greek science in the third century B.C. achieved results unmatched until early modern times.

The expansion of geographical knowledge incited scientists to make accurate maps and to estimate the size of the earth, which had been identified as a globe through observation of its shadow in a lunar eclipse. Eratosthenes, the outstanding geographer of the century, drew parallels of latitude and longitude on his map of the inhabited world and calculated the circumference of the globe with only 1 percent error by measuring the difference in the angles of the noonday sun at Aswan and Alexandria.

In astronomy, Aristarchus put forward the radical theory that the earth rotates on its axis and moves in an orbit around the sun. Most of his contemporaries adhered, however, to the prevailing geocentric theory, which stated that the earth was stationary and the sun revolved around it. This view not only was supported by the powerful authority of Aristotle, but it also seemed to ex-

truth. The wise man, they argued, will suspend his judgment and not dogmatize; he has learned that sensory experience, man's only source of knowledge, is deceptive. The Cynics carried negativism further; their ideal was nonattachment to the values and conventions of society. Cynic philosophers wandered from city to city, haranguing the public to pursue a concept of virtue that is echoed by today's hippies: "Look at me, I am without house or city, property or slave. I sleep on the ground. I have no wife, no children. What do I lack? Am I not without distress or fear? Am I not free?"[24]

More practical and popular were Epicureanism and Stoicism. The Athenian Epicurus (342-270 B.C.) taught that the wise man could achieve happiness simply by freeing his body from pain and his mind from fear—particularly the fear of death. To reach this goal, men must avoid bodily excesses, including those of pleasure, and accept the scientific teaching of Democritus that both body and soul are composed of atoms which plain all the known facts of celestial motion. This was particularly true after Hipparchus in the next century added the new idea of epicycles—each planet revolves in its own small orbit while moving around the earth. Aristarchus' heliocentric theory was not revived until the sixteenth century A.D.

Mathematics also made great advances. Euclid systematized the theorems of plane and solid geometry, and Archimedes of Syracuse, who had studied at Alexandria, calculated the value of π, invented a terminology for expressing numbers up to any magnitude, and laid the foundations of calculus. Archimedes also discovered specific gravity by noticing the water he displaced in his bath. And despite his disdain for making practical use of his knowledge, he invented the compound pulley, the windlass, and the endless screw for raising water.

The Hellenistic Greeks extended the advances in medicine made earlier by Hippocrates and his school. By dissecting bodies of dead criminals, they were able to trace the outlines of the nervous system, to understand the principle of the circulation of the blood, and to ascertain that the brain, not the heart, was the true center of consciousness.

Architecture, sculpture, and literature. The host of new cities that sprang up in Hellenistic times served as a tremendous impetus to architecture. The new cities benefited from town planning: the streets were laid out according to a rectangular plan. The great public edifices were elaborate and highly ornamented; this was an age which preferred the more ornate Corinthian to the simple Doric and Ionic orders.

Hellenistic sculptors continued and intensified the realistic, dramatic, and emotional approach that began to appear in Hellenic sculpture during the fourth century B.C. Supported by rulers and other rich patrons in Alexandria, Antioch, Rhodes, and Pergamum, they displayed their technical virtuosity by depicting violent scenes, writhing forms, and dramatic poses—all with a realism which could make stone simulate flesh. Little evidence remained of the balance and restraint of classical Greek sculpture. The famous Laocoön group (see illustration) and the frieze from the altar of Zeus at

Pergamum, with their twisted poses, contorted faces, and swollen muscles, remind one of the Baroque sculpture of seventeenth-century Europe which replaced the classical art of the Italian Renaissance.

The quality of literature from the Hellenistic Age was generally inferior to that of the Hellenic Age, although the historian Polybius, who lived in the second century B.C. and described Rome's eastward expansion, ranks second only to Thucydides as an exponent of scientific history. Scholarship flourished, and we are indebted for the preservation of much of Greek classical literature to the subsidized scholars at the Alexandrine library—"fatted fowls in a coup," as a Skeptic philosopher called them. Yet, paradoxically, these sophisticated scholars produced superb pastoral poetry extolling the simple life of shepherds. The best was written by the scholar Theocritus at Alexandria in the third

The trend toward realism and increased complexity in sculpture begun in the fourth century B.C. culminated in the art of the Hellenistic period, which produced such intricate sculptures as the contorted Laocoön group.

century B.C. The following short example, written by a contemporary, well illustrates its character and appeal:

Would that my father had taught me the craft of a
  keeper of sheep,
For so in the shade of the elm-tree, or under the
  rocks on the steep,
Piping on reeds I had sat, and had lulled my
  sorrow to sleep.[25]

The Hellenistic contribution: the East. The greatest contribution of the Hellenistic Age was the diffusion of Greek culture throughout the ancient East and the newly rising Roman West. In the East, the cities that Alexander and his successors built were the agents for spreading Hellenistic culture from the Aegean Sea to India. Literate Asians learned Greek to facilitate trade, become members of the ruling circles of the Hellenistic states, and read Hellenic classics.

For a time the Seleucid empire provided the peace and economic stability necessary to ensure the partial Hellenization of a vast area. But with an insufficient number of Greeks to colonize so large an area as the Near East, the Greek city-states remained only islands in an Asian ocean. As time elapsed, this ocean encroached more and more upon the Hellenized areas.

The gradual weakening of the loosely knit Seleucid empire eventually resulted in the creation of independent kingdoms on the edge of the Hellenistic world. Bactria achieved independence in the middle of the third century B.C. Its Greek rulers, descendants of Alexander's veterans, were remarkably successful in enlisting native cooperation; and their prosperous state, which controlled the caravan route to India, lasted for over a century (see also p. 100).

Also in the middle of the third century, a nomad chieftain founded the kingdom of Parthia, situated between the Seleucid and Bactrian kingdoms. Claiming to be the heirs of the Persians, the Parthians expanded until by 130 B.C. they had wrested Babylonia from the Seleucids. Although Parthia was essentially a native Iranian state, its inhabitants absorbed some Hellenistic culture.

The Hellenistic contribution: the West. In the history of western civilization there is little of greater significance than Rome's absorption of Greek civilization and its transferance of that heritage to modern Europe. The stage on which this story began was the cosmopolitan Hellenistic Age, which "longed and strove for *Homonoia*, Concord, between man and man . . . [and] proclaimed a conception of the world as One Great City."[26] The process by which the Roman West was Hellenized will be described in the following chapter.

SUMMARY

The two most important centers of the Aegean maritime civilization were Knossos on the island of Crete and Mycenae on the Greek mainland. Aegean civilization reached its zenith first in Crete (2000-1450 B.C.), where the island dwellers fashioned a sophisticated urban culture, synthesizing cultural elements from the Near East. After 1450 B.C. the center of Aegean culture shifted to Mycenae on the Greek mainland. The Mycenaean phase lasted until the warlike Dorians invaded the Peloponnesus and forced the Mycenaeans to flee eastward to Ionia in Asia Minor. There, by the eighth century B.C., fiercely independent city-states evolved a distinctly Hellenic culture which was to come to fruition in the Hellenic Age (the eighth to fourth centuries B.C.).

Achilles, the hero of Homer's *Iliad*, would have lived forever had not a Trojan arrow pierced him fatally in the heel, the only vulnerable part of his body. Like Achilles, the Greek city-states of the Hellenic period had one fatal defect—in their case, an inability to submerge individual differences for the sake of common survival. The city-states failed to adapt themselves to the political realities of the fifth century B.C., which had resulted from the colonial expansion and economic revolution of previous centuries and which linked the destinies of Athens and other Greek cities with those of a larger Mediterranean community. Instead of developing the Delian League into a true Greek federation, Athens placed its own interests first and converted the League into an Athenian maritime empire, thus plunging the Greeks into the disastrous Peloponnesian War.

Fortunately for the Greeks, Philip II, the Macedonian ruler who conquered the city-states sixty years after the Peloponnesian War, sincerely admired Hellenic culture—an admiration which was shared by his son, Alexander the Great. It was the ambitious and gallant Alexander who conquered the Near East and laid the boundaries for three large empires carved from his conquered lands. The Hellenistic Age, which began after Alexander's death, was a period of economic expansion, cosmopolitanism, striking intellectual and artistic achievements, and the wide diffusion of Greek culture.

What is it about the Greeks that leads us to speak so admiringly? The secret lies in the originality with which they met every situation. Free of Near Eastern superstitions and traditions, they examined each problem in a spirit of critical inquiry and sought for an explanation that accorded with the natural world rather than supernatural law. Thus their view of life, something entirely new in the world's history, tended to be secular rather than religious, rational instead of credulous. This clear-cut, straightforward approach to life may have been the most lasting contribution of the Greeks to human history.

SUGGESTIONS FOR READING

P. MacKendrick, **The Greek Stones Speak*** (Mentor) is an account of the great archaeological discoveries in the Aegean area. See also R. W. Hutchinson, **Prehistoric Crete*** (Peter Smith); C. W. Blegen, **Troy and the Trojans** (Praeger); E. Vermeule, **Greece in the Bronze Age*** (Univ. of Chicago, 1972); and John Chadwick, **The Decipherment of Linear B*** (Vintage). M. Renault, **The King Must Die*** (Bantam, 1974) is an absorbing novel set in Mycenaean times.

A. R. Burn, **The Pelican History of Greece*** (Penguin); M. I. Finley, **The Ancient Greeks*** (Compass); and C. E. Robinson, **Hellas: A Short History of Ancient Greece*** (Beacon) are valuable analyses. Other good surveys include M. Bowra, **The Greek Experience*** (Mentor); H. Kitto, **The Greeks** (Peter Smith); and H. Lloyd-Jones, **The Greek World*** (Penguin). J. B. Bury, **A History of Greece to the Death of Alexander the Great,** 4th ed. (St. Martin's, 1975) is a standard detailed history. D. Kagan, ed., **Problems in Ancient History,** Vol. I, **Ancient Near East and Greece** (Macmillan, 1975) is a good survey of the formative centuries of Greek civilization. On Greek colonization see J. Boardman, **The Greeks Overseas*** (Peter Smith). On the transition from oligarchy to democracy see A. Andrewes, **The Greek Tyrants*** (Torchbooks); and W. G. Forrest, **The Emergence of Greek Democracy, 800–400 B.C.*** (McGraw-Hill).

Valuable special studies on politics, economics, and society include A. R. Burn, **Persia and the Greeks: The Defense of the West, 546–478 B.C.** (Funk & Wagnalls, 1968); H. Mitchell, **Sparta*** (Cambridge); A. E. Zimmern, **The Greek Commonwealth: Politics and Economics in Fifth-Century Athens*** (Galaxy); G. Glotz, **Ancient Greece at Work*** (Norton); V. Ehrenberg, **The Greek State*** (Norton); T. B. Webster, **Everyday Life in Classical Athens*** (Capricorn); Frank Frost, **Greek Society*** (Heath, 1971); and A. H. M. Jones, **Athenian Democracy** (Barnes & Noble). Plutarch, **The Rise and Fall of Athens*** (Penguin, 1975) contains nine biographies from the *Parallel Lives.*

Edith Hamilton, **The Greek Way*** (Avon) is a popular appreciation of the beauty and values of Hellenic literature. A. Lesky, **A History of Greek Literature*** (Crowell) is a detailed treatment, as is J. B. Bury, **Ancient Greek Historians*** (Dover).

C. Seltman, **The Twelve Olympians*** (Apollo) recounts myths about the Olympian gods and goddesses. See also M. Grant, **Myths of the Greeks and Romans*** (Mentor); W. K. Guthrie, **The Greeks and Their Gods*** (Beacon); and A. W. Adkins, **Moral Values and Political Behavior in Ancient Greece*** (Norton, 1973).

Good introductions to Greek philosophy and science include W. K. Guthrie, **Greek Philosophers from Thales to Aristotle*** (Torchbooks); F. M. Cornford, **Before and After Socrates*** (Cambridge); and G. E. R. Lloyd, **Early Greek Science: Thales to Aristotle*** (Norton, 1974) and **Greek Science After Aristotle*** (Norton, 1973). G. Majno, **The Healing Hand: Man and Wound in the Ancient World** (Harvard, 1974) is a major work describing ancient man's attempts to conquer pain and disease.

Recommended for fine arts students are J. Pollitt, **Art and Experience in Classical Greece*** (Cambridge, 1972); J. Boardman, **Greek Art*** (Praeger, 1973); Martin Robertson, **A History of Greek Art,** 2 vols. (Cambridge, 1976); and A. W. Lawrence, **Greek Architecture,*** rev. ed. (Penguin, 1975).

W. W. Tarn, **Hellenistic Civilization*** 3rd ed. (Meridian) is a detailed survey. Brief and well illustrated is J. Ferguson, **The Heritage of Hellenism: The Greek World From 323 to 31 B.C.*** (Harcourt Brace Jovanovich, 1973). On the career and motives of Alexander the Great see Robin Lane-Fox, **Alexander the Great** (Dial, 1974), a serious history and biography; W. W. Tarn, **Alexander the Great*** (Beacon); and A. R. Burn, **Alexander the Great and the Hellenistic World*** (Collier).

*Indicates a less expensive paperbound edition.

CHAPTER 3

The Roman World: 509 B.C. to 180 A.D.

The Grandeur That Was Rome

INTRODUCTION. As the Athenian saw the symbol of his city-state's democracy and culture in the rock-jutting Acropolis, so the Roman viewed the Forum as the symbol of imperial grandeur. Temples were to be found there, but in contrast to the Acropolis, the Forum was dominated by secular buildings —basilicas, the nearby Colosseum, and the great palaces of the emperors rising on the neighboring Palatine Hill. While the Acropolis was crowned with statues to Athena, the Forum gloried in triumphal arches and columns commemorating military conquests. Rome was the capital of a world-state, extending from the Rhine to the Euphrates, and its citizens were proud of their imperial mission.

Although the buildings in the Forum appear fundamentally Greek in style, they are more monumental and sumptuous. Here, then, are two clues to an understanding of the Romans: they borrowed profusely from the Greeks, and they modified what they took. *Adoption* and *adaptation* are key words in the study of Roman civilization.

Rome was the great intermediary—the bridge over which passed the rich contributions of the Fertile Crescent, Egypt, and especially Greece to form the basis of modern western civilization. The Romans replaced the anarchy of the Hellenistic Age with law and order and embraced the intellectual and artistic legacy of the conquered Greeks. As Rome's empire expanded, this legacy was spread westward throughout Europe.

Yet Rome was more than an intermediary, for it made many important and original contributions to our western culture. Throughout a history which led from a simple farming community in the plain of Latium to a strong state which became the master of the Mediterranean and finally of the entire known western world, the Romans met one challenge after another with practicality and efficiency. In the shadows of its marching legions went engineers and architects, so that today, scattered throughout the lands that once were part of the Roman world, the remains of roads, walls, baths, basilicas, amphitheaters, and aqueducts offer convincing evidence of the Romans' technical prowess. Most lasting and far-reaching of all were their administrative institutions—the legal codes and governmental systems they developed and modified to meet changing needs—which have served as the framework of western political life for many centuries.

ROME TO 509 B.C.

Early settlers of Italy. The Greeks and Romans were offshoots of a common Indo-European stock, and settlement of the Greek and Italian peninsulas followed broadly parallel stages. Between 2000 and 1000 B.C., when Indo-European peoples invaded the Aegean world, a western wing of this nomadic migration filtered into the Italian peninsula, then inhabited by indigenous Neolithic tribes. The first invaders, skilled in the use of copper and bronze, settled in the Po valley. Another wave of Indo-Europeans, equipped with iron weapons and tools, followed; and in time the newer and older settlers intermingled and spread throughout the peninsula. One group, the Latins, settled in the lower valley of the Tiber River, a region that became known as the plain of Latium.

For ages history had bypassed the western Mediterranean, but it was henceforth to become an increasingly significant area. During the ninth century B.C. the Etruscans, a non-Indo-European people who probably came from Asia Minor, brought the first city-state civilization to Italy. Expanding from the west coast north to the Po valley and south to the Bay of Naples, the Etruscans organized the backward Italic peoples into a loose confederation of Etruscan-dominated city-states. After 750 B.C. Greek colonists migrated to southern Italy and Sicily, where they served as a protective buffer against powerful and prosperous Carthage, a Phoenician colony established in North Africa about 800 B.C. Yet the future was not to belong to these various invaders, but to an insignificant village on the Tiber River, then in the shadow of Etruscan expansion. This was Rome, destined to be ruler of the ancient world.

Rome's origins. According to ancient legend, Rome was founded in 753 B.C. by the twin brothers Romulus and Remus, who were saved from death in their infancy by a she-wolf who sheltered and suckled them. Virgil's *Aeneid* preserves a different tradition that the founder of the Roman race was Aeneas, a Trojan who after the fall of Troy founded a settlement in Latium. Turning from fable to fact, modern scholars believe that in the eighth century B.C. the inhabitants of some small Latin settlements on hills in the Tiber valley united and established a common meeting place, the Forum, around which the city of Rome grew. Situated at a convenient place for fording the river and protected by the hills and marshes from invaders, Rome was strategically located. Nevertheless, the expanding Etruscans conquered Rome about 600 B.C., and under their tutelage Rome first became an important city-state.

Some aspects of Etruscan culture were borrowed from the Greek colonies in southern Italy, and much of this, including the alphabet, was passed on to the conquered

Romans. (Etruscan writing can be read phonetically but not understood.) From their Etruscan overlords, the Romans acquired some of their gods and goddesses and the practice of prophesying by examining animal entrails. From the conquerors, too, the conquered learned the art of building—especially the arch. Even the name *Roma* appears to be an Etruscan word.

The Roman monarchy. Rome's political growth followed a line of development similar to that of the Greek city-states: limited monarchy of the sort described by Homer, oligarchy, democracy, and, finally, the permanent dictatorship of the Roman emperors. We shall see that in moving from oligarchy to democracy, the Romans, unlike the Greeks, succeeded in avoiding the intermediate stage of tyranny.

According to tradition, early Rome was ruled by kings elected by the people. After the Etruscan conquest, this elective system continued, although the last three of Rome's seven kings were Etruscan. The king's executive power, both civil and military, was

called the *imperium*, which was symbolized by an eagle-headed scepter and an ax bound in a bundle of rods (*fasces*). The *fasces* symbol is found on the United States dime, and in the 1930's it provided both the symbol and the name for Mussolini's political creed of fascism.

Although the *imperium* was conferred by a popular assembly made up of all arms-bearing citizens, the king turned for advice to a council of nobles called the Senate. Each senator had lifelong tenure, and the members of this group and their families constituted the patrician class. The other class of Romans, the plebeians, or commoners, included small farmers, artisans, and many clients, or dependents, of patrician landowners. In return for a livelihood, the clients gave their patrician patrons political support in the assembly.

EARLY REPUBLIC, 509-133 B.C.: DOMESTIC AFFAIRS

Establishment of the Republic. In 509 B.C., according to tradition, the patricians expelled the last Etruscan king, claiming that he had acted despotically, and established what they called a republic (*res publica*, "commonwealth"), in which they held the reins of power. The *imperium* was transferred to two new magistrates, called consuls. Elected annually from the patrician class, the consuls invariably exercised their power in its interest. In the event of war or serious domestic emergency, a dictator could be substituted for the two consuls, but he was given absolute power for six months only.

Struggle for equal rights. For more than two centuries following the establishment of the Republic, the plebeians struggled for political and social equality. Outright civil war was averted by the willingness, however reluctant and delayed, of the patricians to compromise. This largely explains why it was unnecessary for the plebeians to resort to tyrants to help them gain their goals, as had happened in the Greek city-states. Much of the plebeians' success in this struggle was

Cheerful artwork frequently adorned Etruscan tombs. In this painting the youth at the right is playing a double flute, an instrument the music-loving Etruscans particularly enjoyed.

also due to their tactics of collective action and to their having organized a corporate group within the state. This unofficial body, a sort of state within a state, was known as the *Concilium Plebis* and was presided over by plebeian officials called tribunes, whose job was to safeguard the interests of the plebeians and to negotiate with the consuls and the Senate. Finally, Rome's constant wars gave the plebeians, indispensable in filling the ranks of the Roman conscript army, greater bargaining power.

The advancement of the plebeians during the early Republic took two main lines: the safeguarding of their fundamental rights and the progressive enlargement of their share of political power. Because the consuls often interpreted Rome's unwritten customary law to suit patrician interests, the plebeians demanded that it be written down and made available for all to see. As a result, about 450 B.C. the law was inscribed on twelve tablets of bronze and set up publicly in the Forum. The Law of the Twelve Tables was the first landmark in the long history of Roman law, and Cicero tells us that Roman schoolchildren were required to memorize it.

The plebeians in time acquired other fundamental rights and safeguards: they secured the right to appeal a death sentence imposed by a consul and to be retried before the popular assembly; the tribunes gained a veto power over any legislation or executive act that threatened the rights of the plebeians; and marriage between patricians and plebeians, prohibited by the Law of the Twelve Tables, was legalized. Important also was the abolition of the enslavement of citizens for debt.

Little by little the plebeian class acquired more power in the functioning of the government. In 367 B.C. one consulship was reserved for the plebeians, and before the end of the century plebeians were eligible to hold other important magistracies which the patricians had in the meantime created. Among these magistracies, whose powers originally had been held by the consuls, were the praetor (in charge of the law courts), quaestor (treasurer), and censor (supervisor of public morals and the letting of state contracts). The right to hold high political offices proved to be a stepping stone to the Senate, and some plebeians succeeded in gaining entry to that august body.

The long struggle for equality ended in 287 B.C. when the *Concilium Plebis* was recognized as a constitutional body, henceforth known as the Tribal Assembly, with the right to pass laws that were binding on all citizens, patricians as well as plebeians. The plebeians demanded this right because of the undemocratic organization and procedure of the older popular assemblies, which the patricians had been able to control. The Roman Republic was now technically a democracy, although in actual practice a senatorial aristocracy of patricians and rich plebeians continued to control the state. Having gained political and social equality, the plebeians were willing to allow the more experienced Senate to run the government during the remainder of this period of almost constant warfare down to 133 B.C.

After 287 B.C. conflict in Roman society gradually assumed a new form. Heretofore, the issue had been primarily social and political between hereditary classes. When equality was achieved, many plebeians were able to profit from new opportunities and amass prestige and wealth in the state's expanding economy. As a result, wealth instead of aristocratic descent was most important, and the old distinction between patrician and plebeian became much less fundamental than a new conflict between rich and poor which arose after 133 B.C.

The Roman citizen. The fundamental unit of early Roman society was the family. The father's power was absolute, and strict discipline was imposed to instill in children those virtues to which the Romans attached particular importance—loyalty, courage, self-control, and respect for laws and ancestral customs. The Romans of the early Republic were stern, hard-working, and practical. Man's relationship to the universe and the possibilities of immortal life did not concern them unduly, and religious practices were confined to placating the spirits (*numina*) of the family and the state. Under Etruscan influence the major spirits were personified. Thus the sky-spirit Jupiter became god of the universe; Mars, spirit of vegetation, became god of war; and Janus, whose temple doors remained open when the army was away at war, was originally the spirit of the city gate.

EARLY REPUBLIC, 509-133 B.C.: FOREIGN AFFAIRS

Roman conquest of Italy. The growth of Rome from a small city-state to the dominant power in the Mediterranean world in less than four hundred years (509-133 B.C.) is a remarkable success story. By 270 B.C. the first phase of Roman expansion was over. Ringed about by hostile peoples—Etruscans in the north, predatory hill tribes in central Italy, and Greeks in the south—Rome had subdued them all after long, agonizing effort and found itself master of all Italy south of the Po valley. Roman expansion was not deliberately planned; rather, it was the result of dealing with unsettled conditions, first in Italy and then abroad, which were thought to threaten Rome's security. Rome always claimed that its wars were defensive.

Rome's position was favored by geography. While the Italian peninsula has a great mountainous backbone, the Apennines, running down most of its length, the country is not so rugged as Greece. Consequently the mountains did not constitute a barrier to political unification. Also, the Alps in the north kept all but the most intrepid barbarian tribes from entering the Italian peninsula. In addition, the Latins occupied a central position on the peninsula, which made it difficult for their enemies to unite against them successfully.

Soon after ousting their Etruscan overlords in 509 B.C., Rome and the Latin League, composed of Latin peoples in the vicinity of Rome, entered into a defensive alliance against the Etruscans. This new combination was so successful that by the beginning of the fourth century B.C. it had become the chief power in central Italy. But the members of the Latin League grew alarmed at Rome's increasing strength, and war broke out between the former allies. With the victory of Rome in 338 B.C., the League was dissolved, and the Latin cities were forced to sign individual treaties with Rome. Thus the same year which saw the rise of Macedonia over Greece (see p. 50) also saw the rise of a new power in Italy.

Border clashes with aggressive highland Samnite tribes led to three fiercely fought Samnite wars and the extension of Rome's frontiers to the Greek colonies in southern Italy by 290 B.C. Fearing Roman conquest, the Greeks prepared for war and called in the Hellenistic Greek king, Pyrrhus of Epirus, who dreamed of becoming a second Alexander the Great. Pyrrhus' war elephants, unknown in Italy, twice routed the Romans, but at so heavy a cost that such a triumph is still called a "Pyrrhic victory." When a third battle failed to induce the Romans to make peace, Pyrrhus is reported to have remarked, "The discipline of these barbarians is not barbarous," and returned to his homeland. By 270 B.C. the Roman army had subdued the Greek city-states in southern Italy.

Treatment of conquered peoples. Instead of slaughtering or enslaving their defeated foes, the Romans treated them fairly, in time creating a strong loyalty to Rome throughout the peninsula. Roman citizenship was a prized possession and was not extended to all peoples on the peninsula until the first century B.C. Most defeated states were required to sign a treaty of alliance with Rome which bound them to adhere to Rome's foreign policy and to supply troops for the Roman army. No tribute was required, and each allied state retained local self-government. Rome did, however, annex about one fifth of the conquered lands, on which nearly thirty Roman colonies were established by 250 B.C.

The First Punic War. After 270 B.C. only Carthage remained as Rome's rival in the West. Much more wealthy and populous than Rome, with a magnificent navy that controlled the western Mediterranean and with a domain that included the northern coast of Africa, Sardinia, western Sicily, and parts of Spain and Corsica, Carthage seemed more than a match for Rome. But Carthage was governed by a commercial aristocracy which hired mercenaries to do the fighting. In the long run, the lack of a loyal body of free

Rhine R.

Danube

Rhone

Drava

A L P S

Sava

R.

R.

VENETIA

TRANSPADANE GAUL

Po R.

LIGURIA

Parma

CISPADANE GAUL

Genoa

A D R I A T I C   S E A

A P E N N I N E

Pisa

Arno R.

Florentia

UMBRIA MOUNTAINS

Rubicon R.

E T R U R I A

Spoletium

Tiber R.

CORSICA

S A M N I U M

A P U L I A

Rome

Ostia

LATIUM

Brundisium

MT. VESUVIUS

CAMPANIA

Tarentum

Pompeii

S A R D I N I A

LUCANIA

T Y R R H E N I A N   S E A

B R U T T I U M

M E D I T E R R A N E A N

Messina

S I C I L Y

MT. ETNA

S E A

Syracuse

Carthage

A F R I C A

ROMAN ITALY BEFORE AUGUSTUS

0   50   100

citizens and allies, such as Rome had, proved to be Carthage's fatal weakness.

The First Punic War (from *punicus*, Latin for "Phoenician") broke out in 264 B.C. when Rome sought to oust a Carthaginian force that had occupied Messina on the northeastern tip of Sicily just across from Roman Italy. According to Polybius, a Hellenistic Greek historian, the Romans "felt it was absolutely necessary not to let Messina fall, or allow the Carthaginians to secure what would be like a bridge to enable them to cross into Italy."[1] Rome lost 200,000 men in disastrous naval engagements before Carthage sued for peace in 241 B.C. Sicily, Sardinia, and Corsica were annexed as the first provinces of Rome's overseas empire, governed and taxed by Roman proconsuls.

The contest with Hannibal. Thwarted by this defeat, Carthage concentrated upon enlarging its empire in Spain. Rome's determination to restrict the Carthaginian sphere of influence led to the greatest and most difficult war in Roman history. While both powers jockeyed for position, a young Carthaginian general, Hannibal, precipitated the Second Punic War by attacking Saguntum, a Spanish town claimed by Rome as an ally. Rome declared war, and Hannibal, seizing the initiative, in 218 B.C. led an army of about 40,000 men, 9000 cavalry troops, and a detachment of African elephants across the Alps into Italy. Although the crossing had cost him nearly half of his men and almost all of his elephants, Hannibal defeated the Romans three times within three years.

Hannibal's forces never matched those of the Romans in numbers. At Cannae, for example, where Hannibal won his greatest victory, some 70,000 Romans were wiped out by barely 50,000 Carthaginians. On the whole Rome's allies remained loyal—a testimony to Rome's generous and statesmanlike treatment of its Italian subjects—and because the Romans controlled the seas, Hannibal received little aid from Carthage. Thus Hannibal was unable to inflict a mortal blow against the Romans.

The Romans finally found a general, Scipio, who was Hannibal's match in military strategy and who was bold enough to invade Africa. Forced to return home after fifteen years spent on Italian soil, Hannibal clashed with Scipio's legions at Zama, where the Carthaginians suffered a complete defeat (see map, p. 71). The power of Carthage was broken forever by a harsh treaty imposed in 201 B.C. Carthage was forced to pay a huge indemnity, disarm its forces, and turn Spain over to the Romans. Hannibal sought asylum in the kingdom of the Seleucids where he stirred up anti-Roman sentiment.

Roman intervention in the East. The defeat of Carthage left Rome free to turn eastward and settle a score with Philip V of Macedonia, who, fearing Roman expansion, had allied himself with Hannibal during the darkest days of the war. Now, in 200 B.C., Rome was ready to act, following an appeal from Pergamum and Rhodes for aid in protecting the smaller Hellenistic states from Philip, who was advancing in the Aegean, and the Seleucid emperor, who was moving into Asia Minor. The heavy Macedonian phalanxes were no match for the mobile Roman legions, and in 197 B.C. Philip was soundly defeated and his dreams of empire were ended when Rome deprived him of his warships and military bases in Greece. The Romans then proclaimed the independence of Greece and were eulogized by the grateful Greeks:

There was one people in the world which would fight for others' liberties at its own cost, to its own peril, and with its own toil, not limiting its guaranties of freedom to its neighbours, to men of the immediate vicinity, or to countries that lay close at hand, but ready to cross the sea that there might be no unjust empire anywhere and that everywhere justice, right, and law might prevail.[2]

A few years later Rome declared war on the Seleucid emperor who had moved into Greece, urged on by Hannibal and a few greedy Greek states that resented Rome's refusal to dismember Macedonia. The Romans forced him to vacate Greece and Asia Minor, pay a huge indemnity, and give up his warships and war elephants. The Seleucids were checked again in 168 B.C. when a Roman ultimatum halted their invasion of Egypt, which became a Roman protectorate, and a year later Rome supported the Jews in their successful revolt against the Seleucids (see p. 122).

Most of the East was now a Roman protectorate, the result of a policy in which Roman self-interest was mingled with idealism. But Roman idealism turned sour when anti-Romanism became widespread in Greece, particularly among the radical masses who resented Rome's support of conservative governments and the status quo in general. (The Romans, for example, helped crush a socialist revolution in Sparta.) The new policy was revealed in 146 B.C. when, after many Greeks had supported an attempted Macedonian revival, Rome destroyed Corinth as an object lesson, supported oligarchic factions in all Greek states, and placed Greece under the watchful eye of the governor of Macedonia, which was made a Roman province.

Destruction of Carthage. In the West, meanwhile, Rome's hardening policy led to suspicion of Carthage's reviving prosperity and to a demand by extremists for war—*Carthago delenda est* ("Carthage must be destroyed"). Treacherously provoking the Third Punic War, the Romans besieged Carthage, which resisted heroically for three years, destroyed the city in 146 B.C.—the same year of Corinth's destruction—and annexed the territory as a province.

Rome, supreme in the ancient world. In 133 B.C. the king of Pergamum, dying without heir, bequeathed his kingdom to Rome. Apparently he feared that the discontented masses would revolt after his death unless Rome, with its reputation for maintaining law and order in the interest of the propertied classes, took over. Rome accepted the bequest and then spent the next three years suppressing a proletarian revolution in its first Asian province.

With provinces on three continents—Europe, Africa, and Asia (see map above)—the once obscure Roman Republic was now supreme in the ancient world. But the next century, during which Rome's frontiers reached the Euphrates and the Rhine, would witness the failure of the Republic to solve the problems that were the by-products of the acquisition of an empire.

LATE REPUBLIC, 133-30 B.C.

Effects of Roman expansion. The political history of Rome thus far consists of two dominant themes: the gradual liberalization of the government and the expansion of Roman dominion over the Mediterranean world. Largely as a result of this expansion, important social and economic problems faced Rome by roughly the midpoint of the second century B.C.

One of the most pressing problems was the disappearance of the small landowner, whose energy and spirit had made Rome great. Burdened by frequent military service, his farm buildings destroyed by Hannibal, and unable to compete with the cheap grain imported from the new Roman province of Sicily, the small farmer sold out and moved to Rome. Here he joined the unemployed, discontented proletariat, so called because their only contribution was *proles,* "children."

On the other hand, improved farming methods learned from Greeks and Carthaginians encouraged rich aristocrats to buy more and more land and, abandoning the cultivation of grain, introduce large-scale scientific production of olive oil and wine, or of sheep and cattle. This trend was especially profitable because an abundance of cheap slaves from the conquered areas was available to work on the estates. These large slave plantations, called *latifundia,* were now common in Italy, while small farms were the exception.

The land problem was further complicated by the government's earlier practice of leasing part of the territory acquired in the conquest of the Italian peninsula to anyone willing to pay a percentage of the crop or animals raised on it. Only the patricians or wealthy plebeians could afford to lease large tracts of this public land, and in time they treated it as if it were their own property. As early as the fourth century B.C. plebeian protests had led to an attempt to limit the holdings of a single individual to 320 acres of public land, but the law devised for that purpose was never enforced.

Corruption in the government was another mark of the growing degeneracy of the Roman Republic. Provincial officials seized opportunities for lucrative graft, and a new class of Roman businessmen scrambled selfishly for the profitable state contracts to supply the armies, collect taxes in the provinces, and lease mines and forests. Although in theory the government was a democracy, in practice it remained a senatorial oligarchy, as we have seen (p. 67). The tribunes, guardians of the people's rights, had become mere yes-men of the Senate.

Thus by the middle of the second century B.C., the government was in the hands of the wealthy, self-seeking Senate, which was unable to cope with the problems of governing a world-state. Ordinary citizens were for the most part impoverished and landless; and Rome swarmed with fortune hunters, imported slaves, unemployed farmers, and discontented war veterans. The poverty of the many, coupled with the opulence of the few, hastened the decay of the old Roman traits of discipline, simplicity, and respect for authority.

The next century (133-30 B.C.) saw Rome convulsed by civil war, even while engaged in occasional foreign wars. The Senate was noticeably inefficient in carrying on foreign conflicts, but its most serious weakness was its inability to solve the economic and social problems following in the wake of Rome's conquests. This led to the establishment of a dictatorship and the end of the Republic.

Reform movement of the Gracchi. An awareness of Rome's profound social and economic problems led to the reform program of an idealistic young aristocrat named Tiberius Gracchus. Supported by a few liberal Senators, Tiberius was elected tribune for the year 133 B.C. at the age of twenty-nine. His reforming zeal was the product of the newly imported liberal learning of Greece and an awareness that the old Roman character and way of life was fast slipping away. He sought to arrest Roman decline by restoring the backbone of the old Roman society—the small landowner.

Tiberius proposed to the Tribal Assembly that the act limiting the holding of public land to 320 acres per person be reenacted.

Much of the public land would in the future be held by the present occupants and their descendants as private property, but the surplus was to be confiscated and allotted to landless Roman citizens. In his address to the assembly Tiberius noted that

it is with lying lips that their commanders exhort the soldiers in their battles to defend sepulchres and shrines from the enemy; . . . they fight and die to support others in wealth and luxury, and though they are styled masters of the world, they have not a single clod of earth that is their own.[3]

Although the Tribal Assembly adopted Tiberius' proposal by a wide majority, the Senate induced one of the other tribunes to veto the measure. On the ground that a tribune who opposed the will of the people thereby forfeited his office, Tiberius took a fateful—and, the Senate claimed, unconstitutional—step by having the assembly depose the tribune in question. The agrarian bill was then passed.

To ensure the implementation of his agrarian reform, Tiberius again violated custom by standing for reelection after completing his one-year term. On the pretext that he sought to make himself king, partisans of the Senate murdered Tiberius and three hundred of his followers. The Republic's failure at this point to solve its problems without bloodshed stands in striking contrast to its previous development by peaceful means.

Tiberius' work was taken up by his younger brother, Gaius Gracchus, who was elected tribune for 123 B.C. In addition to the reallocation of public land, Gaius proposed establishing Roman colonies in southern Italy and on the site of Carthage. To protect the poor against speculation in the grain market (especially in times of famine), Gaius committed the government to the purchase and storage of wheat and to its subsequent distribution to the urban masses at about half the former market price. Unfortunately, what Gaius intended as a relief measure later became a dole, whereby free food was distributed—all too often for the advancement of astute politicians—to the entire proletariat.

Another of Gaius' proposals would have granted citizenship to Rome's Italian allies, who were now being mistreated by Roman officials. This proposal cost Gaius the support of the Roman proletariat, which did not wish to share the privileges of citizenship or endanger its control of the Tribal Assembly. Consequently, in 121 B.C. Gaius failed to be reelected to a third term and the Senate was emboldened to resort to force again. Martial law was declared and three thousand of Gaius' followers were arrested and executed, a fate Gaius avoided by committing suicide.

The Senate had shown that it had no intention of initiating needed domestic reforms, or of allowing others to do so, and the Gracchi's deaths were ominous portents of the manner in which the Republic was henceforth to decide its internal disputes.

In foreign affairs, too, the Senate soon demonstrated its incapability. Rome was forced to grant citizenship to its Italian allies after the Senate's failure to deal with their grievances goaded them into revolt (99-88 B.C.). Other blunders led to the first of the civil wars that destroyed the Republic.

The first civil war: Marius vs. Sulla. Between 111 and 105 B.C. Roman armies, dispatched by the Senate and commanded by senators, failed to protect Roman capitalists in North Africa and to prevent Germanic tribes from overrunning southern Gaul, now a Roman province, and threatening Italy itself. Accusing the Senate of lethargy and incompetence in directing Rome's foreign affairs, the people elected Gaius Marius to the consulship in 107 B.C., and the Tribal Assembly commissioned him to raise an army and deal with the foreign danger. Marius first pacified North Africa and then crushed the first German threat to Rome. In the process he created a new-style Roman army that was destined to play a major role in the turbulent history of the late Republic.

In contrast to the old Roman army, which was composed of conscripts who owned their own land and who thought of themselves as loyal citizens of the Republic, the new army created by Marius was recruited from landless citizens for long terms of service. These professional soldiers identified their own interests with those of their commanders, to whom they looked for bonuses of land or money, and were ready to follow them in any undertaking. Thus the character of the army changed from a militia to a career service in which loyalty to the state was no longer paramount. Aspiring generals would soon use their military power to seize the government.

In 88 B.C. the ambitious king of Pontus in Asia Minor, encouraged by the growing anti-Roman sentiment in Asia Minor and Greece caused by corrupt governors and tax collectors, declared war on Rome. The Senate ordered Cornelius Sulla, an able general and a staunch supporter of the Senate's prerogatives, to go east. As a countermove, the Tribal Assembly chose Marius for the eastern command. In effect both the Senate and the Tribal Assembly, whose power the Gracchi had revived, claimed to be the ultimate authority in the state. The result was a series of civil wars between rival generals, each claiming to champion the cause of either the Senate or the Tribal Assembly. The first of the civil wars ended in a complete victory for Sulla, who in 82 B.C. had himself appointed dictator for an unlimited period with power to "issue edicts and reorganize the Republic."

Sulla set out to restore the preeminence of the Senate. He drastically curtailed the powers of the tribunes and the Tribal Assembly, giving the Senate the control of legislation which it had enjoyed two hundred years before. Convinced that his work would be permanent, Sulla voluntarily resigned his dictatorship in 79 B.C. His reactionary constitutional changes were not to last.

The second civil war: Pompey vs. Caesar. The first of the civil wars and its aftermath increased factionalism and discontent and nursed the ambitions of individuals eager for personal power. The first to come forward was Pompey, who had won fame as a military leader. In 70 B.C. he was elected consul, and, though he was a former partisan of Sulla, courted the populace by repealing Sulla's laws against the tribunes and the Tribal Assembly. Pompey then put an end to anarchy in the East caused by piracy, the protracted ambitions of the king of Pontus, and the death throes of the Seleucid empire. New Roman provinces and client states brought order eastward to the Euphrates and southward to Palestine (see map, p. 77).

Still another strong man made his appearance in 59 B.C., when Julius Caesar allied himself politically with Pompey and was elected consul. Following his consulship, Caesar spent nine years conquering Gaul, where he accumulated a fortune in plunder and trained a loyal army of peerless veterans. During his absence from Rome, he cannily kept his name before the citizens by publishing a lucidly written account of his military feats, *Commentaries on the Gallic War*.

Caesar's conquest of Gaul was to have tremendous consequences for the course of western civilization, for its inhabitants quickly assimilated Roman culture. Consequently, when the Roman Empire collapsed in the West in the fifth century A.D., Romanized Gaul—or France—emerged before long as the center of medieval civilization.

Jealous of Caesar's achievements in Gaul and fearful of his growing power, Pompey conspired with the Senate to ruin him. When the Senate demanded in 49 B.C. that Caesar disband his army, he crossed the Rubicon, the river in northern Italy which formed the boundary of Caesar's province. By crossing the Rubicon—a phrase employed today for any step that commits a person to a given course of action—Caesar in effect declared war on Pompey and the Senate. He marched on Rome while Pompey and most of the Senate fled eastward. Pompey was soon killed in Egypt where he sought refuge, but the last Pompeian army was not defeated until 45 B.C.

Caesar assumed the office of dictator for life, and during his brief period of autocratic rule he initiated far-reaching reforms. He granted citizenship liberally to non-Italians and packed the Senate with many new provincial members, thus making it a more truly representative body as well as a rubber stamp for his policies. In the interest of the poorer citizens, he reduced debts, inaugurated a public works program, established colonies outside Italy, and decreed that one third of the laborers on the slave-worked estates in Italy be persons of free birth. As a result, he was able to reduce from 320,000 to 150,000 the number of people receiving free grain. His most enduring act was the reform of the calendar in the light of Egyptian knowledge; with minor changes, this calendar of 365¼ days is still in use today.

Caesar realized that the Republic was, in fact, dead. In his own words, "The Republic is merely a name, without form or substance." He believed that benevolent despotism alone could save Rome from continued civil war and collapse. But Caesar incurred the enmity of many, particularly those who viewed him as a tyrant who had destroyed the Republic. On the Ides (the fifteenth) of March, 44 B.C., a group of conspirators, led by ex-Pompeians whom Caesar had pardoned, stabbed him to death in the Senate, and Rome was once more plunged into conflict.

Caesar's assassins had been offended by his trappings of monarchy—his purple robe, the statues erected in his honor, the coins bearing his portrait—and they assumed that with his death the Republic would be restored to its traditional status. But the people of Rome remained unmoved by the conspirators' cry of "Liberty! Freedom! Tyranny is dead!" The majority of them were prepared to accept a successor whose power and position stopped just short of a royal title. The real question was: Who was to be Caesar's successor?

The third civil war: Antony vs. Octavian. Following Caesar's death, his eighteen-year-old heir, Octavian, allied himself with Caesar's chief lieutenant, Mark Antony, against the conspirators and the Senate. Although he was not a conspirator, Cicero, the renowned orator and champion of the Senate, was put to death for his hostility to Antony, and the conspirators' armies were routed. Then for more than a decade Octavian and Antony exercised dictatorial power and divided the Roman world between them. But the ambitions of each man proved too great for the alliance to endure.

Antony, who took charge of the eastern half of the empire, became infatuated with Cleopatra, the last of the Egyptian Ptolemies. He even went so far as to transfer Roman territories to her dominions. Octavian took advantage of this high-handedness to arouse Rome and Italy against Antony. When Octavian's fleet met Antony's off Actium in Greece, first Cleopatra and then Antony deserted the battle and fled to Egypt. There

Antony committed suicide, as did Cleopatra soon afterwards when Alexandria was captured in 30 B.C. At the end of a century of civil violence Rome was at last united under one ruler, and the Republic gave way to the Empire. Two centuries of imperial greatness, known as the *Pax Romana* (the Roman peace), followed.

THE PAX ROMANA: 30 B.C. TO 180 A.D.

Reconstruction under Augustus. Following his triumphal return to Rome, Octavian in 27 B.C. announced that he would "restore the Republic." But he did so only outwardly by blending republican institutions with strong personal leadership. He provided the Senate with considerable authority, consulted it on important issues, allowed it to retain control over Italy and half of the provinces, and gave it the legislative functions of the nearly defunct Tribal Assembly. The Senate in return bestowed upon Octavian the title *Augustus* ("The Revered," a title previously used for gods), by which he was known thereafter.

Augustus never again held the dictatorship, and he seldom held the consulship. Where, then, did his strength lie? Throughout his career he kept the power of a tribune (which gave him the right to initiate and to veto legislation) and the governorship of the frontier provinces, where the armies were stationed. Augustus' control of the army meant that his power could not be successfully challenged. From his military title, *imperator* ("victorious general"), are derived our modern terms of *emperor* and *empire*.

Augustus thus effected a compromise "between the need for a monarchical head of the empire and the sentiment which enshrined Rome's republican constitution in the minds of his contemporaries."[4] He preferred the modest title of *princeps*, "first citizen" or "leader," which he felt best described his position, and his form of disguised monarchy is therefore known as the Principate. At the beginning of the Empire, then, political power was divided between the Senate and the *princeps*, and this *dyarchy* ("rule of two") lasted for more than two centuries, although the Senate slowly faded into the background.

Augustus faced the problems of curing a sick society and removing the scars resulting from a century of civil strife. The aristocracy was too decadent to be patriotic, and in the cities an unemployed mob favored with free bread and circuses had long since lost interest in hard work. Accordingly, Augustus concentrated on internal reform, although he did extend the Roman frontier to the Danube as a defense against barbarian invasions while failing in an attempt to conquer Germany up to the Elbe River (see map, p. 77). His thorough reconstruction of government and society laid the foundation for two centuries of order and prosperity. For example, he created a professional civil service, open to all classes—which greatly reduced the corruption and exploitation that had flourished in the late Republic—and a permanent professional army, stationed in the frontier provinces and kept out of politics. By means of legislation and propaganda, he also sought with some success to check moral and social decline and to revive the old Roman ideals and traditions. Augustus' reforms engendered a new optimism and patriotism which

The Gemma Augustea celebrates some of the great events of Augustus' reign. Holding the imperial staff, Augustus and the goddess Roma rest their feet on the weapons of conquered peoples. The emperor is receiving a laurel crown, the symbol of civilization. Tiberius, Augustus' successor, steps from a chariot at the left. Victorious Roman soldiers occupy the lower panel.

were reflected in the art and literature of the Augustan Age (discussed later in chapter).

The Julio-Claudian and the Flavian emperors. Augustus was followed by four descendants of his family, the line of the Julio-Claudians, who ruled from 14 to 68 A.D. Tiberius, Augustus' stepson whom the Senate accepted as his successor, and Claudius were fairly efficient and devoted rulers; in Claudius' reign the Roman occupation of Britain began in 43 A.D. The other two rulers of this imperial line were of a different stripe: Caligula was a madman, who demanded to be worshiped as a god and made his favorite horse a senator; Nero was infamous for his immorality, the murder of his wife and his mother, and his persecution of Christians in Rome.

During Nero's reign, in 64 A.D., a great fire raged for nine days, destroying more than half of the capital. The Roman historian Tacitus has left us a vivid account of how Nero made the unpopular Christians scapegoats for the fire:

. . . large numbers . . . were condemned—not so much for incendiarism as for their anti-social tendencies. Their deaths were made farcical. Dressed in wild animals' skins, they were torn to pieces by dogs, or crucified, or made into torches to be ignited after dark. . . . Nero provided his Gardens for the spectacle, and exhibited displays in the Circus . . . . Despite their guilt as Christians, and the ruthless punishment it deserved, the victims were pitied. For it was felt they were being sacrificed to one man's brutality rather than to the national interest.[5]

The Julio-Claudian line ended in 68 A.D. when Nero, faced by army revolts, committed suicide. In the following year four emperors were proclaimed by rival armies, with Vespasian the final victor. For nearly thirty years (69-96 A.D.) the Flavian dynasty (Vespasian followed by his two sons) provided the Empire with effective, if autocratic, rule. The fiction of republican institutions gave way to a scarcely veiled monarchy as the Flavians openly treated the office of emperor as theirs by right of conquest and inheritance.

The Antonines: "five good emperors." An end to autocracy and a return to the Augustan principle of an administration of equals—emperor and Senate—characterized the rule

of the Antonine emperors (96-180 A.D.), under whom the Empire reached the height of its prosperity and power. Selected on the basis of proven ability, these "good emperors" succeeded, according to Tacitus, in "reconciling things long incompatible, supreme power and liberty." Two of these emperors are especially worthy of notice.

Hadrian reigned from 117 to 138 A.D. His first important act was to stabilize the boundaries of the Empire. He gave up as indefensible recently conquered Armenia and Mesopotamia and erected protective walls in Germany and Britain, the latter an imposing structure of stone and turf twenty feet high. Hadrian traveled extensively, inspecting almost every province of the Empire. New towns were founded, old ones restored, and many public works were constructed, among them the famous Pantheon in Rome (see illustration, p. 83).

The last of the "five good emperors," Marcus Aurelius, who ruled from 161 to 180 A.D., approached Plato's ideal of the "philos-opher king" and preferred the quiet contemplation of his books to the blood and brutality of the battlefield. Yet, ironically, he was repeatedly troubled by the invasions of Germanic tribes across the Danube. While engaged in his Germanic campaigns, he wrote his *Meditations*, a philosophical work notable for its lofty Stoic idealism and love of humanity.

The "immense majesty of the Roman peace." In the finest period of the Empire, a vast area stretching from Britain to the Euphrates and from the North Sea to the Sahara and containing upwards of 100 million people was welded together into what Pliny the Elder, in the first century A.D., termed the "immense majesty of the Roman peace." Non-Romans were equally conscious of the rich benefits derived from Roman rule. To a Greek writer of the second century, it was

a world every day better known, better cultivated, and more civilized than before. Everywhere roads are traced, every district is known, every country opened to commerce. . . . There are now as many cities as there were once solitary cottages. . . . Wherever there is a trace of life there are houses and human habitations, well-ordered governments and civilized life.[6]

This quotation throws significant light upon the period known as the *Pax Romana*. While the economy remained predominantly agricultural, the Empire became progressively more urban in character as cities increased in number, particularly in the frontier provinces. The cities formed vital nerve centers linked together by a vast network of roads and waterways. The Empire lay secure behind natural frontiers guarded by well-trained armies, the roads were cleared of brigands and the seas of pirates. The *Pax Romana* also witnessed the creation of a cosmopolitan world-state where races and cultures intermingled freely.

The Graeco-Roman cultural synthesis. Writing during the rule of Augustus, the Roman poet Virgil was the spokesman for what enlightened Romans felt to be the mission of the Empire:

Others, doubtless, will mould lifelike bronze with greater delicacy, will win from marble the look of life, will plead cases better, chart the motions of the sky with the rod and foretell the risings of the stars. You, O Roman, remember to rule the nations with might. This will be your genius —to impose the way of peace, to spare the conquered and crush the proud.[7]

By "others," Virgil was referring to the Greeks, to whom the Romans willingly acknowledged a cultural debt. The Romans learned the Greek language, copied Greek architecture, employed Greek sculptors, and identified their gods with Greek deities. Although Greek ways of life introduced sophisticated habits which were often corrupting to the Roman virtues of self-reliance, personal integrity, family cohesion, and discipline, Greek influences made the Romans on the whole less harsh and insensitive. Largely because of their admiration for Greek culture, the Romans helped perpetuate the legacy of Greece. The *Pax Romana* was the acme of Graeco-Roman civilization.

Governing the diverse state. At the head of this huge world-state stood the emperor, its defender and symbol of unity as well as an object of veneration. The major theme of the many encomiums written to celebrate the enlightened, beneficent government of the Principate was that liberty had been exchanged for order and prosperity. The Empire was said to represent a new kind of democracy—"a democracy under the one man that can rule and govern best." "The whole world speaks in unison, more distinctly than a chorus; and so well does it harmonize under this director-in-chief that it joins in praying this Empire may last for all time."[8] Nevertheless, during the Principate the cities of the Empire continued to exercise a large measure of self-government, and although the central government increasingly intervened in their affairs, this was usually the result of the failure of city authorities to solve local problems.

Economic prosperity. Rome's unification of the ancient world had far-reaching economic consequences. The *Pax Romana* was responsible for the elimination of tolls and other artificial barriers, the suppression of piracy and brigandage, and the establishment of a reliable coinage. Such factors, in addition to the longest period of peace the West has ever enjoyed, explain in large measure the great expansion of commerce that occurred in the first and second centuries A.D. Industry also was stimulated, but its expansion was hindered since wealth remained concentrated and no mass market for industrial goods arose. Industry remained organized on a small-shop basis with producers widely scattered, resulting in local self-sufficiency.

Although the cities were the centers of political and cultural life, most of them, particularly in the West, were of secondary importance economically. They consumed much more than they produced and flourished only because the economy of the Empire remained prosperous enough to support them. Most were like Rome itself, into which so much revenue poured from the provinces that its citizens had the necessary purchasing power to buy immense quantities of goods from other parts of the Empire and even from regions far beyond the imperial frontiers.

The economy of the Empire remained basically agrarian, and the huge estates, or *lati-fundia*, prospered. On these tracts, usually belonging to absentee owners, large numbers of *coloni*, free tenants, tilled the soil as sharecroppers. The *coloni* were gradually replacing slave labor, which was becoming increasingly hard to secure with the disappearance of the flow of captives from major wars.

Despite the general prosperity, the Empire under the Antonines had already entered upon its "Indian summer." Once the Empire had ceased to expand geographically, its economy in turn became progressively more static. Late in the first century A.D. Italian agriculture began to suffer from the loss of its markets in the western provinces, which were becoming self-sufficient in the production of wine and olive oil. To aid the wine producers the Flavian emperor Domitian created an artificial scarcity by forbidding the planting of new vineyards in Italy and ordering the plowing under of half the existing vineyards in the provinces. This was followed by a program of state subsidies, inaugurated by the Antonine emperors. Loans at 5 percent interest were made to ailing landowners, with the interest to be paid into the treasuries of declining Italian municipalities and earmarked "for girls and boys of needy parents to be supported at public expense." This system of state subsidies to both producers and consumers was soon extended to the provinces. Also contributing to Roman economic stagnation was the continuing drain of money into the oriental luxury trade (see p. 117). This early evidence of declining prosperity foreshadowed the economic crisis of the third century A.D., when political anarchy and monetary inflation caused the economy of the Empire to decline rapidly (see Chapter 5).

Rome, imperial capital. At the hub of the sprawling Empire was Rome, with about a million inhabitants. Augustus boasted that he had found a city of brick and had left one of marble. Nonetheless, Rome presented a striking contrast of magnificence and tawdriness, of splendid public buildings and squalid tenements which often collapsed or caught fire. The crowded narrow streets, lined with apartment houses and swarming with all manner of people, are described by the satirist Juvenal early in the second century A.D.:

. . . Hurry as I may, I am blocked
By a surging crowd in front, while a vast mass
Of people crushes onto me from behind.
One with his elbow punches me, another
With a hard litter-pole; one bangs a beam
Against my head, a wine-cask someone else.
With mud my legs are plastered; from all sides
Huge feet trample upon me, and a soldier's
Hobnails are firmly planted on my toes.[9]

Social life. At the top of the social order were the old senatorial families who lived as absentee owners of huge estates and left commerce and finance to a large and wealthy middle class. In contrast to the tenements of the poor, the homes of the rich were palatial, as revealed by excavations at Pompeii, which was buried by the eruption of Vesuvius in 79 A.D. These elaborate villas contained courts and gardens with fountains, rooms furnished with marble walls, mosaics on the floors, and numerous frescoes and other works of art. An interesting feature of Roman furniture was the abundance of couches and the scarcity of chairs. People usually reclined, even at meals—a custom which may have had its value during the sumptuous dinners served by the wealthy gourmands, who were not above administering emetics to permit disgorging and starting afresh on more food and wine.

The lower classes in the cities found a refuge from the dullness of their existence in social clubs, or guilds, called *collegia*, each comprising the workers of one trade. The activity of the *collegia* did not center on economic aims, like modern trade unions, but on the worship of a god and on feasts, celebrations, and decent burials for members.

The living conditions of slaves varied greatly. Those in domestic service were often treated humanely, and their years of efficient service frequently rewarded by emancipation. Nor was it uncommon for freed slaves to rise to places of eminence in business, letters, and the imperial service. On the other hand, conditions among slaves on the large estates could be indescribably harsh. Beginning with Augustus, however, numer-

The Colosseum, built by the Flavian emperors, uses arch construction both to light the interior and to disperse weight. Largest of the Roman amphitheaters, it was used for gladiatorial combats, animal fights, and even for naval exhibitions—water pipes for flooding still exist in some arenas.

ous enactments protected slaves from mistreatment; Hadrian, for example, forbade private prisons and the killing of a slave without judicial approval.

Recreation played a key role in Roman social life. Both rich and poor were exceedingly fond of their public baths, which in the capital alone numbered eight hundred during the early days of the Empire. The baths served the same purpose as our modern-day athletic clubs. The larger baths contained enclosed gardens, promenades, gymnasiums, libraries, and famous works of art as well as a wide variety of types of baths. An old Roman inscription expresses an interesting philosophy: "The bath, wine, and love ruin one's health but make life worth living."

Foot races, boxing, and wrestling were minor sports; chariot racing and gladiatorial contests were the chief amusements. The cry for "bread and circuses" reached such proportions that by the first century A.D. the Roman calendar had 159 days set aside as holidays, 93 of which were given over to games furnished at public expense. The most spectacular sport was chariot racing. The largest of six race courses at Rome was the Circus Maximus, a huge marble-faced structure seating about 150,000 spectators. The games, which included upwards of twenty-four races each day, were presided over by the emperor or his representative. The crowds bet furiously on their favorite charioteers, whose fame equaled that of the all-American football heroes of our own day.

Scarcely less popular, but infinitely less civilized, the gladiatorial contests were also organized by the emperors as a regular feature on the amusement calendar. These cruel spectacles, which have no exact counterpart in any other civilization, were held in arenas, the largest and most famous of which was the Colosseum. The contests took various forms. Ferocious animals were pitted against armed combatants or occasionally even against unarmed men and women who had been condemned to death. Another type of contest was the fight to the death between gladiators, generally equipped with different types of weapons but matched on equal terms. It was not uncommon for the life of a defeated gladiator who had fought courageously to be spared at the request of the spectators. Although many Romans decried these blood-letting contests, there persisted a streak of cruelty in Roman public amusements which can scarcely be comprehended, far less condoned, today.

THE ROMAN CONTRIBUTION

The Roman spirit. The Roman spirit was compounded of many factors. Never completely lost was the tradition of plain living. Geography was another factor; for centuries the Romans were faced with the need to conquer or be conquered, and they had to stress discipline and duty to the state. But the Roman spirit also had another side. It could be arrogant and cruel, and its deep-rooted sense of justice was too often untempered with mercy.

By and large, the Romans lacked the creative fire of the Greeks, but they knew superbly well how to preserve, adapt, and disseminate civilization. Therefore we might characterize the Romans as synthesists rather than innovators—and at the same time pay respect to their recognition of cultural indebtedness. For all their limitations, the Romans had greatness as a people. The *Pax Romana* could have been fashioned and maintained only by a people grave in nature, mature in judgment, and conscious of their responsibilities to others.

Contributions in government. Roman political thinkers such as Cicero contributed the germinal ideas for many governmental theories destined to be influential in later centuries. Some of these deserve mention: the social-contract theory (that government originated as a voluntary agreement among citizens); the idea of popular sovereignty (that all power ultimately resides with the people); and the concept that law must be the paramount rule in government. Although the growing despotism of the Roman emperors corroded these concepts, they were never lost sight of and ultimately were transmitted to modern times. Important, too, was the Roman tradition of unity and order within a great imperial structure. As we will see in later chapters, this concept was to play an important role in the politics of medieval Europe.

The Romans laid the foundations for the political framework of modern Europe in still other ways. Many current administrative divisions, such as the county and province, are derived from Roman practice. In some instances European boundaries are little altered from those existing under the Caesars. The medieval Church also modeled its organization, administrative units, and much of its law after that of the Empire.

Evolution of Roman law. Of the contributions made by the Romans in government and politics, Roman law is preeminent. Two great legal systems, Roman law and English common law, are the foundation of jurisprudence in most modern western nations. Roman law is the basis for the law codes of Italy, France, Scotland, and the Latin American countries. Where English common law is used, as in the United States, there is also a basic heritage of great legal principles originated by ancient Roman jurists. In addition, Roman legal principles have strongly affected the development of the canon law of the Roman Catholic Church; and international law has borrowed principles inherent in the Roman system.

Roman law evolved slowly over a period of about a thousand years. At first, when Rome was a struggling city-state, the law was unwritten, mixed with religious custom, and harsh in its judgments. In the fifth century B.C., as we have seen (p. 67), the law was written down in the Law of the Twelve Tables. During the remainder of the Republic the body of Roman law (*jus civile*, "law of the citizen") was enlarged by legislation passed by the Senate and the assembly and, equally important, by judicial interpretation of existing law to meet new conditions. By the second century A.D. the emperor had become the sole source of law, a responsibility he entrusted to scholars "skilled in the law" (*jurisprudentes*). Holding to the idea of equity ("follow the beneficial interpretation"), and influenced by Stoic philosophy with its concept of a "law of nature" common to all men and ascertainable by means of human reason, these jurists humanized and rationalized Roman law to meet the needs of a world-state. Finally, in the sixth century A.D., the enormous bulk of Roman law from all sources was codified (see p. 151) and thus easily preserved for posterity.

Roman engineering and architecture. The Empire's needs required a communication system of paved roads and bridges as well as huge public buildings and aqueducts for the cities. Pride in the Empire led also to the erection of ostentatious monuments symbolizing Rome's dignity and might.

As road builders, the Romans surpassed all previous peoples. Constructed of layers of stone according to sound engineering principles, their roads were planned for the use of armies and messengers and were kept in constant repair. The earliest and best known main Roman highway was the Appian Way, running from Rome to the Bay of Naples, which was built about 300 B.C. to facilitate Rome's expansion southward. It has been said that the speed of travel possible on Roman highways was not surpassed until the early nineteenth century.

In designing their bridges and aqueducts, the Romans placed a series of stone arches next to one another to provide mutual support. At times several tiers of arches were used, one above the other. Fourteen aque-

ducts, stretching a total of 265 miles, supplied some fifty gallons of water daily for each inhabitant of Rome. The practical nature of the Romans and their skill and initiative in engineering were demonstrated also in the many dams, reservoirs, and harbors they constructed.

At first the Romans copied Etruscan architectural models, but later they combined basic Greek elements with distinctly Roman innovations. The structural simplicity of Hellenic buildings was too restrained for the Romans who, by utilizing brick and concrete as new building materials, developed new methods for enclosing space. The static post and lintel system of the Greeks was replaced with the more dynamic techniques of vaulting.

The barrel vault, basically a series of adjoining arches forming a structure resembling a tunnel, was a new method of enclosing space. In the barrel vault the piers, or supports, of the arches became heavy masonry walls to bear the weight of the vaulted roof. The Romans next developed the cross vault by intersecting two barrel vaults at right angles. Cross vaults were employed to great effect in public baths and basilicas.

Another important advance in architectural engineering was the Romans' success in constructing concrete domes on a magnificent scale. The weight of the dome was transferred directly to the walls, and since there was no sidewise thrust, no other support was necessary. The largest of the domed structures was the Pantheon (temple of "all

In the barrel vault, essentially a Roman contribution, the walls support the sideways and downward pressure of the material above. The walls of the cross vault, an advance in architectural engineering, did not need to be as thick as those of a barrel vault, because the weight of the material was spread over a larger area. Also, openings in the supporting walls furnished window space.

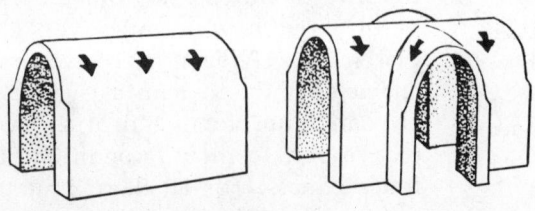

the gods"), which still stands (see illustration).

The standard type of Roman public building was the basilica, a colonnaded structure that became a model for early Christian churches (see illustration, p. 127). Rows of columns divided the interior into a central nave and side aisles, with the roof over the nave raised to admit light, creating a clerestory like those found in Egyptian temples. Perhaps the most famous Roman edifice is the Colosseum (see illustration, p. 80), a huge amphitheater about one quarter of a mile around on the outside and with a seating capacity of about 45,000. Its three stories of arches are decorated with Doric, Ionic, and Corinthian columns.

Roman buildings were built to last, and their size, grandeur, and decorative richness aptly symbolized the proud imperial spirit of Rome. Whereas the Greeks evolved the temple, theater, and stadium, the Romans contributed the triumphal arch, bath, basilica, amphitheater, and the multistoried apartment house. Many modern public buildings show the influence of Rome's bold new architecture.

Sculpture and painting. After the conquest of Greece thousands of statues and other art pieces were brought to Rome. Many Romans acquired a passion for art, and the homes of the wealthy were filled with all kinds of Greek art.

Although strongly influenced by Etruscan and Greek models, the Romans developed a distinctive sculpture of their own which was remarkably realistic, secular, and individualistic. Lifelike portraiture flourished particularly during the Republic, probably originating in the early practice of making and preserving wax images of the heads of important families. During the Principate, on the other hand, portraiture and relief sculpture tended to idealize the likenesses of the emperors (see illustrations, pp. 76, 84). Portraits on coins also served to glorify the Empire and particular emperors. Equestrian statues, sculptured coffins, or sarcophagi, and the reliefs found on imperial monuments were exceptionally fine works of art. The Romans developed a great fund of decorative motifs, such as cupids, garlands of flowers, and scrolls of various patterns, which are still used today.

What little Roman painting has been preserved clearly reflects the influence of Hellenistic Greek models. The Romans were particularly skilled in producing floor mosaics—often copies of some Hellenistic painting (see p. 58)—and in painting frescoes. The frescoes still to be seen in Pompeii and elsewhere show that the artist drew the human figure accurately and showed objects in clear though imperfect perspective.

Literary Rome. In literature as in art the Romans turned to the Greeks for their models. Roman epic, dramatic, and lyric poetry forms were usually written in conscious imi-

The Pantheon, built by the emperor Hadrian, is one of the best preserved buildings of Imperial Rome. It impressively harmonizes the Greek-style colonnaded porch with the Roman-style dome.

Sculpture, during the Augustan age, expressed itself best in portraiture—the finest examples combining expressive realism with the classical insistence on serenity. One of the most frequent subjects is the emperor Augustus Caesar, here presented in an idealized, militaristic pose.

ed from Hellenistic Greek originals but with many Roman allusions, colloquialisms, and customs added. Plautus' comedies are bawdy and vigorously humorous, and their rollicking plots of illicit love and stock characters of the shrewish wife, henpecked husband, lovelorn youth, clever slave, and swashbuckling soldier reveal the level of culture and taste in early Rome. The works of Plautus suggest many of the types that modern comedy has assumed—the farce, burlesque, and the comedy of manners. From him Shakespeare got ideas for his *Comedy of Errors* and *The Merry Wives of Windsor*.

The Golden Age of Latin literature. Latin literature entered its first great period of creative activity in the first century B.C., when an outpouring of intellectual effort coincided with the last years of the Republic. This period marks the first half of the Golden Age of Latin literature, known as the Ciceronian period because of the stature of Marcus Tullius Cicero (106-43 B.C.), the greatest master of Latin prose and perhaps the outstanding intellectual influence in Roman history.

Acclaimed as the greatest orator of his day, Cicero found time during his busy public life to write extensively on philosophy, political theory, and rhetoric. Some nine hundred of his letters still exist, and these, together with his speeches, give us insight into Cicero's personality, as well as into the problems and manners of republican Rome. Much of the value of Cicero's letters lies in the fact that most were not intended for publication and thus he spoke his mind freely. Cicero also made a rich contribution to knowledge by passing on to later ages much of Greek thought—especially that of Plato and the Stoics—and at the same time interpreting it from the standpoint of a Roman intellectual and practical man of affairs. He did more than any other Roman to make Latin a great literary language.

The Ciceronian period also produced the personal lyrical poetry of Catullus (c. 87-54 B.C.), a young man about town who wrote intensely of his loves and hates:

I hate and love—the why I cannot tell,
But by my tortures know the fact too well.[10]

tation of Greek masterpieces. Compared with Greek literature, however, Latin writing was more moralistic and less speculative and imaginative. But it remains one of the world's great literatures largely because of its influence upon medieval, Renaissance, and modern culture.

Formal Latin literature did not begin until late in the third century B.C. when a Greek slave named Livius Andronicus translated Homer's *Odyssey* and several Greek plays into Latin. By the end of the same century the first of a series of Latin epics dealing with Rome's past was composed.

The oldest examples of Latin literature to survive intact are the twenty-one comedies of Plautus (c. 254-184 B.C.), which were adapt-

Catullus' contemporary, Lucretius (99-55 B.C.), found in the philosophy of Epicurus an antidote to his profound disillusionment with his fellow citizens who, he wrote, "in their greed of gain . . . amass a fortune out of civil bloodshed: piling wealth on wealth, they heap carnage on carnage. With heartless glee they welcome a brother's tragic death."[11] His long philosophical poem, *On the Nature of Things*, will be discussed later in this chapter.

Augustus provided the Roman world with a stability that was conducive to a further outpouring of literary creativeness. The second phase of the Golden Age of Latin literature, the Augustan Age, was notable particularly for its excellent poetry. Virgil (70-19 B.C.) was probably the greatest of all Roman poets. His masterpiece, a great national epic called the *Aeneid*, glorifies the work of Augustus and eloquently asserts Rome's destiny to conquer and rule the world (see quotation, p. 78). Using Homer's *Iliad* and *Odyssey* as his models, Virgil recounted the fortunes of Aeneas, the legendary founder of the Latin people, who came from his home in Troy to Italy. The *Aeneid* breathes Virgil's deep and enthusiastic patriotism and is as much a piece of imperial symbolism as Rome's triumphal arches.

Horace (65-8 B.C.) was famous for both lyrical odes and satirical verse. Succeeding generations have turned to Horace because of his urbane viewpoint and polished style:

Happy the man, and happy he alone,
He, who can call to-day his own:
He who secure within, can say,
To-morrow do thy worst, for I have lived to-day.[12]

Quite a different sort was Ovid (43 B.C.-17 A.D.), a poet akin to Catullus in spirit and personal life, who combined a predilection for themes on sensual love with first-rate storytelling. In fact, it is largely through his *Metamorphoses,* a collection of Greek stories about the life of the gods, that classical mythology was transmitted to the modern world.

The Silver Age. The literature of the so-called "Silver Age," the period between the deaths of Augustus and Hadrian (14-138 A.D.), substitutes a more critical and negative spirit for the patriotism and optimism of the Augustan Age. Despite a great emphasis upon artificial stylistic devices, the Silver Age was memorable for its moral emphasis (seen in Tacitus, Plutarch, and Seneca) and its brilliant satirical poetry which reached its peak in Juvenal (55?-130 A.D.). This master of poetic invective flayed the shortcomings of contemporary Roman society (see also quotation, p. 79):

Whatever passions have the soul possessed,
Whatever wild desires inflamed the breast
(Joy, Sorrow, Fear, Love, Hatred, Transport, Rage),
Shall form the motley subject of my page.
For when could Satire boast so fair a field?[13]

The writing of history. Two Roman historians produced notable works during the Golden and Silver Ages. The first, Livy (59 B.C.-17 A.D.), was a contemporary of Virgil; his immense *History of Rome*, like the latter's *Aeneid*, is of epic proportions and glorifies Rome's conquests and ancestral ways. By assembling the legends and traditions of early Roman history and welding them into a continuous narrative, Livy, like Virgil, sought to advance Augustus' program of moral and social regeneration. He glorified the virtues of the ancient Romans—their heroism, patriotism, and piety—and sought to draw moral lessons from an idealized past.

Tacitus (55-117 A.D.), like his contemporary Juvenal, was concerned with improving society, but he used history rather than poetry to serve his ends. In his *Germania* Tacitus contrasted the life of the idealized, simple Germanic tribes with the corrupt and immoral existence of the Roman upper classes. In the *Annals* and *Histories* he used his vivid, epigrammatic prose to depict the shortcomings of the emperors and their courts from the death of Augustus to 96 A.D. Some of his brief, trenchant statements have been quoted for centuries; for example, "Tyrants merely procure infamy for themselves and glory for their victims"; "The more corrupt the state, the more numerous the laws"; and (in his description of Roman conquest) "They make a solitude and call it peace." Tacitus suffered from the bias of his own senatorial class; he looked upon the emperors as tyrants and thus could not do justice to the positive contributions of imperial government.

The most famous Greek author in the Empire was Plutarch (46?-120? A.D.). He lectured on philosophy at Rome before retiring to his small hometown to pursue research on the outstanding figures in Roman and Greek history in order to discover what qualities make men great or ignoble. His *Parallel Lives*, containing forty-six biographies of famous Greeks and Romans arranged in pairs for the purpose of comparison, is one of the eminently readable classics of Greek literature. Because many of the sources Plutarch used have been lost, his *Lives* is a mine of invaluable information for the historian.

Stoicism and Epicureanism. The Romans contributed no original philosophical theories, preferring to adapt existing Greek systems of thought to suit their needs. As men of action with grave governmental responsibilities, the Romans paid scant attention to such abstract problems as the nature of the universe and of human knowledge. But the corrupting effects of life in the late Republic on the old Roman virtues and traditions caused thoughtful Romans to be concerned over problems of behavior. As a consequence, they were attracted to the two chief Hellenistic ethical philosophies, Epicureanism and Stoicism.

Epicureanism made its greatest impact during the last days of the Republic, since men found its tenets comforting in a period of political upheaval when no one knew what the morrow would bring. As young men, Virgil and Horace embraced Epicureanism, but Lucretius was the most important Roman interpreter of this philosophy. In his *On the Nature of Things*, Lucretius followed Epicurus (see p. 60) in basing his explanation of the "nature of things" on materialism and atomism. He called on men to free themselves from the superstitious fears of the gods and of death, which were causing them to become converts to the emotional mystery religions of Greece and the East. Lucretius exhorted his readers to "make the most of today," but to seek pleasure in philosophical serenity, rather than in sensuous gratification, and to have no fear of death since souls, like bodies, are composed of atoms that fall apart when death comes:

What has this bugbear Death to frighten man,
If souls can die, as well as bodies can? . . .
So, when our mortal frame shall be disjoin'd,
The lifeless lump uncoupled from the mind,
From sense of grief and pain we shall be free;
We shall not feel, because we shall not be.[14]

More enduring, especially in the days of the Empire, was the appeal of Stoicism to the Roman ruling classes. It had a humanizing effect on Roman law by introducing such concepts as the law of nature (see p. 82), the brotherhood of men—including slaves—and the view that a man is innocent until proved guilty. The main emphasis of Roman Stoicism was on a just life, constancy to duty, courage in adversity, and service to humanity.

One of the outstanding Roman Stoics was Seneca (4 B.C.-65 A.D.), Nero's tutor and a writer of moral essays and of tragedies meant to be read rather than performed. He was regarded with high favor by the leaders of the early Christian Church, for his Stoicism, like that of the ex-slave Epictetus (d. 135 A.D.) and the emperor Marcus Aurelius, was a kind of religious creed. He stressed an all-wise Providence, or fatherly god, and the immortality of the soul. Seneca occupies an important place in the development of moral theory in Europe because his essays enjoyed a wide reputation among thinkers during the Middle Ages and the Renaissance.

Science in the Roman Empire. The Romans had little scientific curiosity, but by putting the findings of Hellenistic science to practical use, they became masters in engineering, applied medicine, and public health.

The Romans pioneered in public health service and developed the extensive practice of hydrotherapy—the use of mineral baths for healing. Beginning in the early Empire, doctors were employed in infirmaries where soldiers, officials, and the poor could obtain free medical care. Great aqueducts and admirable drainage systems also indicate Roman concern for public health.

Characteristic of their utilitarian approach to science was the Romans' predilection for amassing immense encyclopedias. The most important of these was the *Natural History* compiled by Pliny the Elder (23-79 A.D.), an enthusiastic collector of all kinds of scientific odds and ends. In writing his massive work, Pliny is reputed to have read more than two thousand books. The result is an intriguing mixture of fact and fable thrown together with scarcely any method of classification. Nevertheless, it was the most widely read work on science during the Empire and the early Middle Ages.

Pliny was well aware of the lack of creative scientific activity in his day. "In these glad times of peace," he wrote, "no addition whatever is being made to knowledge by means of original research, and in fact even the discoveries of our predecessors are not being thoroughly studied." To Pliny, the cause of this state of affairs was "blind engrossment with avarice," and he cited this example: ". . . now that every sea has been opened up . . . , an immense multitude goes on voyages—but their object is profit not knowledge."[15] Pliny himself was suffocated by a rain of hot ashes while he was studiously observing the eruption of Mount Vesuvius at Pompeii.

The last great scientific minds of the ancient world were two Greeks, Claudius Ptolemy and Galen, both of whom lived in the second century A.D. Ptolemy resided at Alexandria, where he became celebrated as geographer, astronomer, and mathematician. His maps show a comparatively accurate knowledge of a broad section of the Old World, and he used an excellent projection system (see illustration, p. 367). But he exaggerated the size of Asia, an error which influenced Columbus to underestimate the width of the Atlantic and to set sail from Spain in search of Asia. His work on astronomy, usually called the *Almagest* ("the great work") from the title of the Arabic translation, summed up the geocentric, or earth-centered, view of the universe that was to rule men's minds until the sixteenth century. In mathematics, Ptolemy's work in improving and developing trigonometry became the basis for modern knowledge of the subject.

Born in Pergamum in Asia Minor, Galen was a physician for a school of gladiators. His fame spread and he was called to Rome where he became physician to Marcus Aurelius. Galen was responsible for notable advances in physiology and anatomy; for example, he was the first to explain the mechanism of respiration. Forbidden by the Roman government to dissect human bodies, Galen experimented with animals and demonstrated that an excised heart can continue to beat outside the body and that injuries to one side of the brain produce disorders in the opposite side of the body. The most experimental-minded of ancient physicians, he once wrote: "I confess the disease from which I have suffered all my life—to trust . . . no statements until, so far as possible, I have tested them for myself."[16] His medical encyclopedia, in which he summarized the medical knowledge of antiquity, remained the standard authority until the sixteenth century.

SUMMARY

The story of how Rome rose from an insignificant muddy village along the banks of the Tiber to the mighty ruler of the Mediterranean world will always remain one of the most fascinating stories in world history. Emerging from obscurity about the middle of the eighth century before Christ, the Latin people who clustered about Rome and its seven hills succeeded in 509 B.C. in ousting their Etruscan overlords and establishing a republic. The history of the Roman Republic can be divided into two distinct periods. During the first, from 509 to 133 B.C., two themes are dominant: the gradual democratization of the government and the conquest of the Mediterranean.

By 287 B.C., thanks to the reluctant willingness of the patricians to compromise, the plebeians had succeeded in breaking down the privileged position of the patricians by obtaining recognition of their fundamental rights as citizens and by acquiring a progressively more important share of political power. Having achieved these gains, the rank and file of the citizens allowed the aristocratic Senate to continue exercising full control of the Republic.

The other theme in the early history of the Roman Republic was the conquest of the Mediterranean. Between the years 509 and 270 B.C. the Romans crushed all resistance to their rule in Italy. They then clashed with Carthage, and after a herculean struggle, Carthage surrendered in 201 B.C. Having conquered the West, the Romans found themselves drawn to the East, and by 133 B.C. Macedonia and Greece were ruled by Roman governors, the Seleucid emperor in Asia had been defeated and humbled, and Rome had acquired its first province on the Asian continent. But as the Mediterranean world succumbed to the Roman legions, the Republic itself faced civil war and degeneration.

The second and last period in the history of the Roman Republic, from 133 to 30 B.C., began with the attempts of the Gracchi brothers to persuade the senatorial oligarchy to allow the enactment of necessary reforms, but to no avail. Marius, Sulla, Pompey, and Julius Caesar mark the appearance of one-man rule and the end of the Republic. Augustus, the heir of Caesar, ruled Rome wisely and well. On the surface the old republican institutions, such as the Senate, were preserved, but Augustus wielded the real power in the new government, which is called the early Empire, or Principate. For two hundred years, during the *Pax Romana*, many millions of people in Italy and the Empire's provinces enjoyed peace and prosperity.

Through the Roman achievement of a single empire and a cosmopolitan culture, the Greek legacy was preserved, synthesized, and disseminated—and the Romans were able to make important contributions of their own. The Romans excelled in political theory, governmental administration, and jurisprudence. While the Greeks were individualistic, the Romans put a higher value on conformity, and their essentially conservative and judicious attitude of mind compensated for their lack of creativity. Primarily synthesists rather than innovators, the Romans willingly admitted their cultural indebtedness and by doing so exhibited a magnanimity characteristic of the Roman spirit at its best.

SUGGESTIONS FOR READING

D. R. Dudley, **The Civilization of Rome*** (Mentor); R. Barrow, **The Romans*** (Penguin); M. Grant, **The World of Rome*** (Mentor); and P. Arnott, **The Romans and Their World*** (St. Martin's, 1970) are brief excellent surveys of Roman history and culture. M. Cary and H. Scullard, **A History of Rome Down to the Reign of Constantine,** 3rd ed. (St. Martin's, 1975) is a standard detailed account, as is D. Kagan, ed., **Problems in Ancient History,** Vol. II, **The Roman World** (Macmillan, 1975).

M. Pallotino, **The Etruscans*** (Indiana Univ., 1975); and E. Richardson, **The Etruscans: Their Art and Civilization** (Univ. of Chicago) are detailed accounts. See also Raymond Bloch, **The Origins of Rome** (Praeger), an examination of the archaeological, historical, and legendary evidence. For an instructive survey of archaeological discovery in Italy, see P. MacKendrick, **The Mute Stones Speak*** (Mentor).

H. Scullard, **History of the Roman World from 753 to 146 B.C.** (St. Martin's, 1975) and F. B. Marsh, **History of the Roman World from 146 to 30 B.C.** (Methuen, 1971) are detailed accounts. H. Scullard, **From the Gracchi to Nero,** 3rd ed. (Barnes & Noble) covers the transition from the late Republic to the early Empire. E. Salmon, **History of the Roman World from 30 B.C. to A.D. 138,** 6th ed. (Methuen) details the history of the early Empire.

Recommended special studies: F. E. Adcock, **Roman Political Ideas and Practice*** (Univ. of Mich.); Richard E. Smith, **The Fail-** ure **of the Roman Republic** (Arno, 1975); R. Syme, **The Roman Revolution*** (Oxford); G. Ferrero, **The Life of Caesar*** (Norton); Lily R. Taylor, **Party Politics in the Age of Caesar*** (Univ. of Calif.); L. Cottrell, **Hannibal: Enemy of Rome** (Holt, Rinehart & Winston); J. Buchan, **Augustus** (Verry); and T. Africa, **Rome of the Caesars** (Wiley).

W. W. Fowler, **Social Life at Rome in the Age of Cicero*** (St. Martin's); S. Dill, **Roman Society from Nero to Marcus Aurelius*** (Meridian); M. Johnston, **Roman Life** (Scott, Foresman); J. Balsdon, **Roman Women** (Greenwood, 1975); and F. C. Grant, ed., **Ancient Roman Religion*** (Bobbs-Merrill) are all interesting. See also F. R. Cowell, **Life in Ancient Rome*** (Capricorn, 1975).

Other books of interest are Martin L. Clarke, **The Roman Mind: Studies in the History of Thought from Cicero to Marcus Aurelius*** (Norton, 1968); M. Grant, **Roman Literature*** (Penguin); Edith Hamilton, **The Roman Way*** (Avon); M. Wheeler, **Roman Art and Architecture*** (Praeger); and H. J. Rose, **Religion in Greece and Rome*** (Torchbooks).

Recommended historical novels: W. Bryher, **The Coin of Carthage*** (Harvest); T. Wilder, **The Ides of March*** (Avon, 1975); R. Graves, **I Claudius*** (Vintage); M. Yourcenar, **Memoirs of Hadrian*** (Noonday).

*Indicates a less expensive paperbound edition.

CHAPTER 4

Ancient India and China
to 220 A.D.

The Asian Way of Life

INTRODUCTION. Civilization had its genesis in four Afro-Asian regions: Egypt, Mesopotamia, and the valleys of the Indus and the Huang Ho. For some two thousand years these areas charted the path for the onward march of civilization. By 500 B.C. western peoples began to join this procession, making rapid progress in the civilized arts of life; and for a thousand years both great segments of the human race were roughly in equilibrium.

One of the basic themes of world history, therefore, may be called the Afro-Asian strand. The early chapters relating to this theme are largely concerned with the origins, growth, and flowering of the Afro-Asian cultures from the fifth century B.C. to the fifteenth A.D. During their classical period great civilizations emerged in Asia and northern Africa. Imbued with massive political power and economic opulence and graced with cultural magnificence, these civilizations of the East were not only comparable to those of the West, but from time to time, in important respects, superior. Although isolated sub-Saharan Africa suffered from inertia and a certain amount of cultural stagnation during this period, the accomplishments of its peoples were not trivial, and their worth has recently been rediscovered and truly appreciated.

An Indian scholar has written: "All that India can offer to the world proceeds from her philosophy."[1] Indian philosophers have consistently held a fundamental belief in the unity of life—a unity within which has been assimilated and synthesized a variety of beliefs and customs from both native and foreign cultures. Thus a basic concept dominates the life and thought of both ancient and modern India—unity in diversity. India's intricate religious philosophy developed in ancient times, along with a unique social pattern, the caste system.

Whereas religion has dominated the cus-

toms and attitudes of India's people, the Chinese have been more humanistic and worldly. Their attitude toward life has led to a concern for natural science, the art of government, the keeping of historical records, and the formulation of down-to-earth ethical standards. But despite the great differences in their cultures, these two Asian nations have much in common. Weighed down by poverty, both can look back to days of ancient glory; striving to direct their own affairs, both can remember foreign conquerors; hemmed in by age-old tradition and custom, both find themselves in a world of nuclear power and space science. The course that these countries follow in the future will inevitably be conditioned by all that they have experienced in the long centuries since their birth.

INDIA: UNITY IN DIVERSITY

Geography of India. We can think of India* as a gigantic triangle, bounded on two sides by ocean and on the third by the mountain wall of the Himalayas. Through the passes to the northwest came the armed conquerors, restless tribes, and merchants and travelers who did much to shape the turbulent history of this land.

For purposes of discussion, the land can be divided into four parts: Baluchistan, Hindustan, the Deccan, and Tamil Land (see map, p. 91). Our interest lies principally in Hindustan, for in the alluvial plain watered by the upper Indus and its tributaries (called the Punjab) and in the territory along the lower Indus (called Sind), India's earliest civilization developed.

In recent years scholars have come to the conclusion that the ancient Near East should not be considered as isolated from the Asian lands to the east. Rather, we should conceive of a "Greater Near East" which extended beyond the Fertile Crescent through Iran and Baluchistan to the Indus valley. By taking this larger western Asian setting as the subject for investigations, archaeologists are discovering significant trade and cultural relationships between Mesopotamia, Iran,

and prehistoric India. Scholars now emphasize that the transition from food gathering to food production, the all-important agricultural revolution, did not emerge independently in India. Food production began in Mesopotamia, then radiating in several directions, diffused eastward across the Iranian plateau into Baluchistan and hence into the Indus valley. In this northwestern area of India the new farming became the economic basis for India's first civilization.

The Indus civilization. How old is the Indus valley culture, the first Indian culture to reach a level of achievement that can be described as civilization? Unknown before 1920 when its remains were first uncovered, its pictographic script could not be read and its historical background was largely conjectured. In 1969, however, Finnish scientists claimed to have deciphered this ancient tongue and to have thereby discovered new insights into the origin of the Hindu caste system. Most scholars date the Indus civilization approximately 2300 to 1800 B.C.

The Indus civilization eventually extended

*Until the text deals with the creation of the separate states of India and Pakistan in 1947, the word *India* will refer to the *entire* subcontinent.

some 950 miles along the valley from the Himalayan foothills in the north to the coast, embracing an area estimated to have been twice the size of the Old Kingdom in Egypt and some four times the size of Sumer and Akkad. Harappa and Mohenjo-Daro, the two largest cities that have been excavated, were the political capitals and commercial centers of this region.

The Indus civilization comprised numerous cities and small towns, and although Harappa and Mohenjo-Daro were four hundred miles apart, the Indus River made possible the maintenance of a strictly organized, uniform administration and economy over the large area. In this stretch of territory, containing some three dozen settlement sites, houses were built of uniform-sized baked bricks. The people used stamp-seals, engraved with a uniform script, and a standard system of weights. They cultivated grains, domesticated cattle and sheep, worked metals, made textiles, and carried

on trade. There is evidence that considerable trade existed between the Indus cities and those of Sumer. While revealing characteristics typically Indian, the Indus valley civilization was based upon techniques and crafts similar to earlier Sumerian and Egyptian methods, indicating some possible borrowing of culture.

For centuries the people of the Indus valley pursued a meticulously regulated, efficient, but relatively static way of life. At Mohenjo-Daro, however, excavations show clearly the decline of the city in its latter days. Street frontages were no longer strictly observed, the brickwork was becoming shoddy, and residential areas were degenerating into slums. Finally, groups of skeletons huddled together in their dwellings suggest that this city and perhaps the civilization came to a sudden end. We can only speculate on what great disaster—a plague or a flood, perhaps—may have overtaken these people.

The Aryan invasions. About 1500 B.C. a group of Aryans migrating from the shores of the Black and Caspian seas began to invade India, coming into conflict with the native Dravidians, described as a short, dark people. In a few hundred years the Aryans conquered and settled the upper Indus valley and began penetrating the Ganges region. A tall people with fair skins and long heads, the Aryans fought readily and knew neither writing nor city life. The number of cattle a man owned was the measure of his wealth, and the word for war meant "a desire for more cows." Each tribe was headed by a rajah, women had a high social status, and marriage was monogamous and confined to the group.

Overcome by the storm of invasion from the north, the native Dravidians were enslaved or driven southward, much as the North American Indians were pushed back by the pioneers. As time passed, the Aryans contemptuously referred to the people they conquered as *Dasyu*, or slaves. The *Dasyu*, however, possessed a culture superior in some respects to that of the Aryans; and the invaders borrowed many customs and ideas from the conquered people, including their system of land tenure and taxation and their

ANCIENT INDIA

Indus Valley Civilization

village community. The native people of India also influenced the development of the Indo-Aryan tongue, Sanskrit.

Early Vedic Age (c. 1500-900 B.C.). Aside from the rajah, his tribal assembly, and the common tribesmen, there were few social gradations in the Aryan tribal structure prior to the invasion of India. In the process of subjugating and settling among the dark-skinned natives, the Aryans realized that they would be absorbed racially unless they took steps to prohibit intermarriage. Class division now took on a new purpose—that of preserving purity of race. This concept is intrinsic in the Vedic Sanskrit word for class, *varna*, which means "color." (It was translated later by Portuguese travelers as *casta*, from the Latin *castus*, meaning "pure"; hence, the term *caste*.)

The oldest examples of Sanskrit literature are the *Vedas*, collections of hymns, epic chants, and ritual formulas. The earliest— the *Rig-Veda*—reflects the events, religious beliefs, and heroic interests of the period of Aryan conquest. The *Vedas* also show that after the conquest the invaders in time settled down to village life and agricultural pursuits. In many ways village life was simi-lar to that of modern India, although complexities of later Indian life such as the restriction of women's rights and the prohibition against eating cattle did not exist at this time. The most important figure of the village was the headman, sometimes elected and at other times holding his position by hereditary right. The village was composed of a group of families, and the villagers worked as farmers or artisans or both.

Later Vedic Age (c. 900-500 B.C.). About the beginning of the ninth century B.C., the center of power and culture shifted eastward from the upper Indus valley to the upper Ganges valley. There the Aryans created small, isolated city-states, each sovereign unto itself. The epic poems describing these times tell of constant warfare and shifting military alliances among the city-states.

The cities of the Later Vedic Age were surrounded by moats and walls, and their streets were well planned. Usually occupying a palace located at the center of a city, the rajah possessed powers greater than those of the village headman of the Early Vedic Age. He had his own retinue of follow-ers and was advised by a royal council com-

Excavations at Mohenjo-Daro have unearthed mother-god-dess figurines and seals which may have had religious signif-icance. The seals bear Indus writing, essentially a picto-graphic script employing about 250 symbols and 400 charac-ters, which is still undeci-phered. Such seals have been found along the Iranian plateau trade routes and on an island in the Persian Gulf, indicating that trade existed between the Indus civilization and western civilizations. This seven-inch-high statue of a man also sug-gests contacts between the Mesopotamian and Indus valley civilizations because of its heavy beard, a common feature of contemporaneous Sumerian sculpture.

posed of his relatives and nobles. He received taxes and was probably, in theory at least, the owner of all land. In cities a tradesman class existed, and unskilled, menial tasks were performed by slaves. Trade contacts with Mesopotamia were renewed during this period, and merchants may have brought back from the West the use of coinage and the notion of an alphabetic system of writing that was eventually adapted to Sanskrit.

The village, caste, and family. In the Later Vedic period the three pillars of traditional Indian society—the autonomous village, caste, and the joint-family—were established. India has always been primarily agricultural, and its countryside is still a patchwork of thousands of villages. As we mentioned, the village in early times was made up of family groups who possessed certain rights and duties and were governed by the headman. An elected council of villagers, on which women were allowed to serve, distributed the land and collected taxes. Villages within a city-state enjoyed considerable autonomy, with the rajah's government hardly interfering at all as long as it received its quota of taxes. This system of self-governing villages continued until government became more centralized under British rule.

If the earliest caste division had been inaugurated to separate the Aryans from the *Dasyu*, by the Later Vedic period caste became more sharply defined and complex as the Aryans themselves split into castes. The four castes recognized at this time were ultimately ranked: (1) the Brahmins, or priests; (2) the Kshatriyas, or warriors; (3) the Vaisyas, or traders, merchants, and bankers; and (4) the Sudras, or farm workers and serfs. In addition there was a group of outcastes, or Pariahs, called "untouchables" because their touch was considered defiling to the upper castes. The non-Aryan population remained at the bottom of the social scale, as Sudras and outcastes.

At first the Kshatriyas had a higher social rank than the Brahmins; but as time went on, warfare declined while religion increased in importance. As educators, historians, and intermediaries between the gods and men, the priests assumed the dominant position which they have successfully maintained into the twentieth century. Eventually the four castes were subdivided into thousands of groups with special social, occupational, and religious significance. The definition and order of importance of the four castes have remained much the same, however, throughout India's history.

The third pillar of Indian society was the joint-family. "Joint in food, worship, and estate," the family was made up of descendants of a common ancestor. The joint-family was governed by the patriarch during his lifetime; after his death, authority was transferred to the eldest son. All males of the group had to be consulted on serious matters, since the property belonged to the family as a whole. Everything earned by individuals in the group went into a common fund, from which was drawn what was needed to supply each member. It was possible for a man to acquire property and to live in his own residence, but he had to show that his holdings had been obtained without use of the family patrimony.

The joint-family was not only a cooperative economic unit but also a powerful instrument for social cohesion. It encouraged a strong family life in which the individual was made to feel his subordination to the group. Marriage was all-important in protecting family ties, and the individual member's desires were considered less important than the family's interests. For thousands of years the joint-family concept dominated the socioeconomic life of the large majority of India's people.

The emphasis placed on the interests and security of the group rather than on the individual is a common denominator of the three pillars of Indian society—the autonomous village, the caste system, and the joint-family. Thus Indian society has always been concerned with stability rather than with progress in the western sense, and the individual Indian has tended to acquire a more passive outlook toward life than his western counterpart. This traditional emphasis upon the group also helps explain the socialistic approach of Nehru and his successors toward contemporary economic and social issues.

Language and literature. The Aryans were part of the huge Indo-European linguistic group and therefore bequeathed to India a language related to Persian, Greek, Latin, and most modern European languages, including English. The various dialects of the invading bands, mixed with the speech of the natives, developed into Sanskrit. By the fourth century B.C. Sanskrit had evolved in such a fashion that the vernacular differed from the traditional Sanskrit of the priests and bards. The chief modern Indian language, Hindi, is derived from the speech of this period.

After the composition of the *Vedas*, which passed orally from generation to generation, a series of prose commentaries on them were produced, including the famous *Upanishads* ("session," at which a teacher gave instruction). Written between 800 and 600 B.C., the *Upanishads* extend and replace the old Vedic concepts with profound speculations about the ultimate truths of life.

A different, and originally secular, Indian tradition produced two great epic poems. The *Mahabharata*, similar to the Greek *Iliad*, glorifies the Kshatriyan, or warrior, caste, as it recounts the struggle between two Aryan tribes. The most famous section of the *Mahabharata* is a philosophical poem called the *Bhagavad-Gita (The Lord's Song)*, which emphasizes that men must never shirk their duty or fear death. Some modern Indians have found in this ancient poem a justification for righteous warfare; others, notably Gandhi, have used it to support nonviolence and passive resistance.

The other magnificent epic, the *Ramayana*, has been likened to the Greek *Odyssey* because it tells of a hero's wanderings and his faithful wife's long vigil. Where the *Mahabharata* is a vigorous glorification of war and adventure, the *Ramayana* shows the growth of chivalric ideals among the Aryans. Both epics have provided all subsequent Indian literature with a vast supply of stories.

Religion in India. The power of religion in Indian life has always been extraordinarily strong. From this ancient land have come some of the most novel and complex religious ideas. These concepts constitute one of India's unique contributions to world civilization. Its religious values and philosophical tradition were not fully known to western scholars until the late eighteenth and mid-nineteenth century, when the *Rig-Veda* and the *Bhagavad-Gita* were translated into English by Max Muller and Sir Edwin Arnold. Throughout the nineteenth century Hindu philosophical and spiritual thought intrigued numerous western literary and intellectual figures, such as Thoreau, Emerson, Goethe, Wordsworth, and Tolstoi; and the founding of the famous Theosophical Society in the 1870's was a mark of the wide appreciation of the Hindu spiritual tradition.

What was to become one of the world's most complex religious and philosophical systems, touching upon all facets of life, had

The Kailasa Temple at Ellora, the largest and most elaborate of the Indian temples carved out of solid rock, contains intricate carvings of incidents and characters from the great epics, the *Mahabharata* and the *Ramayana*.

the most simple beginnings. The early Aryans had unsophisticated religious views; they worshiped various gods with sacrificial rites. The most popular deity was Indra, a boisterous god who wielded the thunderbolt, ate bulls by the score, and quaffed lakes of wine. The earliest Vedic philosophy was not complicated. After death the human soul experienced either eternal punishment or everlasting bliss. Gradually, however, there evolved the idea that Something existed beyond the everyday acts of both gods and men, Something which underlay all life, a Moral Law governing even the gods themselves. The *Vedas* show the evolution of Indian religion from a simple belief in many gods toward a complete pantheism, a conception of the universe and everything in it as God.

The Upanishads: core of Indian theology. The pantheistic conception was subsequently developed with great subtlety in the *Upanishads*, which form the core of all subsequent Indian religious thought and are the foundation on which Hinduism was built. The main teachings of the *Upanishads* may be summarized as follows:

1) Brahman is the Absolute, the eternal universal essence, the all-pervading force permeating the universe.

2) As part of this world force is its Atman, the Universal Soul, to which all individuals belong.

3) As individual souls living in a world of the senses, we think we exist apart from the One Soul—but this is *maya*, or illusion. As long as individuals exist in this world, they are kept from the desired goal of absorption into the Absolute, into Brahman.

4) While living in this state of illusion, of separateness from the One Soul, the individual places his faith in things that are meaningless, transitory, and unsatisfying. As long as such earthly goals as pride, power, and material success are sought, the result must be pain and sorrow. Deliverance and emancipation can only be attained by *moksha*, the ultimate absorption and loss of self into Brahman. The essence of *Upanishadic* thought is escape from illusion.

5) This release from the meaningless state of earthly existence and its attendant *maya*

is part of a cosmic and complicated process of reincarnation. The individual soul must go through a long series of wanderings—of earthly reincarnations from one body to another. A man's status at any particular point in time is not the result of fortuitous lot but depends on his soul's actions in previous existences.

6) Gradually Hinduism gave the caste system a religious significance by linking it to the process of reincarnation. In effect, caste became the essential machinery for the educative process of the soul as it went through the infinitely long succession of rebirths from the lowest categories in caste to that of the Brahmin, who presumably is near the end of the cycle.

7) *Karma* is the inexorable law of caste and salvation. A man must accept whatever caste he is born into. There is no favoritism in the universe, for a man brings his *karma* into the world and everything that happens to him springs from this fact. "Just as he acts, just as he behaves, so he becomes." If and as long as *karma* is defied, the soul is condemned to an infinite number of earthly existences and denied escape from the sufferings of *maya*. Central to *Upanishadic* teaching is the belief that death is only a single, essential incident in the foreordained cycle of rebirth. In the *Bhagavad-Gita* the Lord loftily proclaims:

Just as a man, having cast off old garments, puts on other, new ones, even so does the embodied one, having cast off old bodies, take on other, new ones.[2]

Hinduism: a religious synthesis. The philosophy of the *Upanishads* permeates Hinduism. Although the main tenets of Hinduism can be summarized, as in the preceding section, it has been said that Hinduism is less a religion than a way of life because it possesses no canon, such as the Bible or the Koran, no single personal founder, such as Christ or Muhammad, and no precise body of authoritative doctrine of belief.

In time literally thousands of deities, demigods, and lesser spirits came to be added to Indra and the early Aryan gods, forming the Hindu pantheon. Early Aryan and Dravidian gods merged, evolved, and acquired new characteristics and new names for many centuries. In this process of evolution any god accepted by Hinduism became identified with the central Reality. Hindus, therefore, do not think of their religion as polytheistic, for all gods and various spirits are manifestations of the Absolute Reality, Brahman, which pervades everything.

Gradually Hinduism acquired a trinity consisting of Brahma, the creator; Vishnu, the preserver; and Shiva, the destroyer. These names and others have often been used interchangeably for the Absolute Reality. In popular worship Vishnu and Shiva achieved special importance, a position they continue to maintain. Vishnu is a benevolent deity, working continually for the welfare of the world; his followers believe that he has appeared in some ten incarnations to save the world from disaster. The other great god, Shiva, personifies the Life Force and is worshiped as embodying power, in both its constructive and destructive aspects. Some representations portray Shiva in terrifying guise, garlanded with skulls; others show him as the Lord of Dancers, whose activities are the source of all movement within the cosmos. Although the basic teachings of the *Upanishads* remained constant, Hinduism from its earliest origins exhibited an unusual organic quality of growth and adaptation (see Chapter 7).

The simplicity of Gautama Buddha. During the time of the later *Vedas* and the *Upanishads* (900-500 B.C.), religious rites were supervised by the Brahmins. They kept strict control over the people and stressed religious ceremonies, costly sacrifices, and the passive acceptance of Brahmin dogmas. But many individuals criticized or even rejected Brahminic caste requirements and claims for special prerogative. Some would-be religious reformers sought to make the goals of *Upanishadic* thought available without priestly apparatus and sacrificial ritual. None did this more simply and effectively than Gautama, who became the Buddha ("The Enlightened One"). The Buddha (563?-483 B.C.) stands out as one of the most profound influences in the history of mankind because of two principal factors: the beauty and simplicity of his own life and the philo-

sophical depth and ethical purity of his teaching.

Gautama was the son of the ruler of a kingdom located at the foot of the Himalayas. As a privileged youth, he led a happy life and married his beautiful cousin, who bore him a son. One day, according to traditional Indian literature, Gautama was deeply shocked by the misery, disease, and sorrow that he saw as he walked through the streets of his native city. The happiness that his wife and son offered him only made the world's suffering appear more unbearable by contrast. He determined to abandon palace life and seek an answer to his questions about life and death in the outside world. For seven years he dwelt in a forest, practicing the self-mortification rites of the ascetics he found there. Gautama almost died from fasting and self-torture and at last concluded that these practices did not lead to wisdom.

One day, while sitting beneath a large tree meditating on the problem of human suffering, he received "enlightenment." From this insight, he constructed a religious philosophy that has affected the lives of millions of people for 2500 years. He soon attracted disciples, the most devoted being the faithful Ananda, who occupies the same position in Buddhist stories as the disciple John in the New Testament. Dressed always in a simple yellow robe, with begging bowl in hand, the Buddha wandered through the plains of the Ganges, preaching to the villagers who flocked to hear him. He spoke with everyone, regardless of caste, and, like Jesus, who congregated with sinners and publicans instead of the "respectable" Pharisees, the Buddha would decline the sumptuous banquets of nobles to partake of the simple hospitality of peasants and social outcasts.

At last, when eighty years old and enfeebled by his constant travels, the Buddha was invited by a poor blacksmith to a meal. According to legend, the food was tainted, but Gautama ate it rather than offend his host, although he forbade his disciples to follow his example. Later in the day the Buddha was taken with severe pains, and he knew death was near. Calling his disciples together, he bade them farewell. Ananda burst into tears, and the master gently reproved him, saying, "Enough, Ananda! Do not let yourself be troubled; do not weep!"

Buddhist teachings. The fundamental teachings of the Buddha, briefly stated, consist of the Four Noble Truths, which were revealed to the Buddha in the Great Enlightenment:

"1. 'the truth of pain,' as manifest in 'birth, old age, sickness, death, sorrow, lamentation, dejection, and despair';

"2. 'the truth of the cause of pain,' viz., craving for existence, passion, pleasure, leading to rebirth;

"3. 'the truth of cessation of pain,' by ceasing of craving, by renunciation; and

"4. 'the truth of the way that leads to the cessation of pain,' viz., the Middle Path, which is the Eight-fold Path consisting of 'right views, intention, speech, action, livelihood, effort, mindfulness, and concentration.'"[3]   ·

In addition to these teachings, the Buddha set forth certain moral injunctions: not to kill, not to steal, not to speak falsely, not to be unchaste, and not to drink intoxicating liquors. Nonviolence and respect for all life were strongly enjoined.

Buddhism should not be thought of as a completely new religion, for its founder's teachings were aimed at reforming an existing system, not at completely repudiating it. Buddhist and *Upanishadic* philosophies, though, differ in important aspects. Gautama taught that a man's caste, whether Brahmin or Sudra, had no bearing on his spiritual stature. Only by living the true philosophy could one win deliverance from illusion (*maya*). Nor was the Buddha interested in rituals or ceremonies or priestly mediation between gods and man. As a consequence, Buddhism (unlike Hinduism) has no trinity, nor does it even postulate the existence of a God or First Cause. When the whole cosmos attains its ideal state, all beings will be in perfect harmony.

According to the Buddha, the individual cannot hope to attain an ideal state so long as he remains attached by transitory desires to the wheel of birth and rebirth. Reincarnation is a necessary doctrine in Buddhism, for only by repeated lives can the individual come to realize that the world of the senses is but a spiritual illusion. Once this is learned, the path by which sorrow is removed opens to the seeker. The strict rules of the Eightfold Path will free him from the bondage of rebirth and make possible a reabsorption into the Universal Soul, the "slipping of the dewdrip into the Silent Sea"—the entry into *nirvana*. And unlike Hinduism, the process of rebirth could be long or short, depending upon the degree of morality of an individual's everyday life. Man, therefore, was essentially a free agent despite *karma*.

What is *nirvana?* Does it constitute the total annihilation of the individual or rather the end of the illusion of separateness from the One Soul? According to one Indian scholar, "*nirvana* is incommunicable, for the Infinite cannot be described by finite words. The utmost that we can do is to throw some light on it by recourse to negative terms. *Nirvana* is the final result of the extinction of the desire or thirst for rebirth . . . it is the incomparable and highest goal . . . [The] Buddha purposely discouraged questions about the reabsorption of the individual soul, as being of no practical value in the quest for salvation."[4]

A temple wall painting shows the many-armed Hindu god Shiva as the Lord of the Dancers. In his hands he holds symbols of the various aspects of his divine power.

The Buddha and later Buddhism. The Buddha reformed Indian religion. He censured the rites and dogmas of Brahmins, broke with the rules of caste, taught that all men are equal, and gave the world a code of morals whose purity is universally recognized. He founded orders of monks, and the monasteries gradually developed into important academic centers. During his lifetime his teachings were disseminated through central India. The beauty and nobility of his thought can be appreciated from the following excerpts from Buddhist literature:

Hatred does not cease by hatred at any time; hatred ceases by love.

All men trouble at punishment, all men love life. Remember that you are like unto them, and do not cause slaughter.

Not by birth does one become an outcaste, not by birth does one become a Brahmin. By deeds one becomes an outcaste, by deeds one becomes a Brahmin.[5]

Though the Buddha was a reformer, after his death many of the evils that he had attacked crept, ironically enough, into Buddhism itself. In spite of Buddha's denigration and rejection of deities, in time men prayed to him as a god who could assure their salvation. Subsequently his teachings were elaborated into metaphysical beliefs, and Buddhism in its new form spread throughout eastern Asia.

INDIA UNDER THE MAURYAS AND THE KUSHANS

Alexander the Great in India. By the sixth century B.C. nearly a score of royal states or tribal republics had been established in northern India. Of these the most important was Magadha (see map, p. 99), along the lower Ganges. In 326 B.C. Alexander of Macedon, continuing his conquest of the former Persian empire (see p. 57), brought his phalanxes into the easternmost Persian satrapy in the Indus valley, defeating local Punjab rulers. He turned back from a contemplated attack into the Ganges valley because of the near mutiny of his travel-weary troops. After Alexander died, the empire he had built in such meteoric fashion quickly disintegrated; by 321 B.C. his domain in the Punjab had completely disappeared. But from the towns he had founded in Bactria, beyond the northwest passes, were to come important Hellenistic influences on India in later times.

Chandragupta Maurya. By 322 B.C. a new era was at hand for India. In that year Chandragupta Maurya, who apparently had served as a Magadhan soldier, gathered an army and seized the Magadha state from an unpopular sovereign. In the next twenty-four years Chandragupta conquered much of north India and founded the Maurya dynasty, which endured until about 185 B.C.

The emergence of this Mauryan empire stemmed from three significant factors. First, by the sixth century B.C. important advances in agriculture, trade, and general prosperity in north India led to the emergence of a new merchant class whose interests were menaced by constant feuds and wars between numerous petty kingdoms. This middle class sought law and order and naturally favored the creation of large stable governments. Second, Alexander's invasion had broken the power of numerous small kingdoms, leaving behind a debris of weakness and confusion. Into this vacuum intruded the third factor: a new type of ruler who by force and craft created the "new kingship in India."

Chandragupta may be considered the first emperor of India, even though his power did not extend to the southern regions of the subcontinent. The Magadhan maintained contacts with the Greeks after he became emperor and fostered a friendly exchange of information between the Seleucid empire and his own. He lived in great splendor; his court included Greek courtiers and was run according to Persian ceremonial, factors which scarcely endeared him to his Indian subjects. So great was the danger of conspiracy that Chandragupta lived in strict seclusion, surrounded by a bodyguard of women who cooked his food, served his wine, and in the evening lulled him to sleep with music.

Life in the Mauryan empire. In its structure and the hierarchy of administrative divisions, the Mauryan empire was remarkably advanced. It was divided into a small number of provinces, each governed by a viceroy and a staff of officials. The emperor was not limited by any law, and the central government maintained a tight rein over the distant provinces. Over all, there were some thirty imperial departments overseeing such affairs as markets, canal irrigation, public works, and revenues. The municipal organization of the capital was amazingly comprehensive. Comprising six boards, it provided for the treatment of foreigners, birth and death statistics, retail trade, manufacturing, and the collection of a sales tax. Excellent roads connected the many villages and towns; and a postal service was maintained by royal couriers.

Practically the only work on statecraft in India that has survived from ancient times is the *Arthasastra*, written by Chandragupta's able chief minister, Kautilya. From this book we learn that justice was dispensed sternly but fairly in both civil and criminal cases. Under the supervision of a well-organized war office, the large army was fed, trained, and led. Apparently like the later Renaissance Italian author on statecraft, Machiavelli, Kautilya believed in deception or unscrupulous means to attain any desired end. The *Arthasastra* comments that "intrigue, spies, winning over the enemy's people, siege and assault" are the five means of capturing a fort. The main pillar of the government was the pervasive and dreaded secret service, which employed a large number of spies.

All land belonged to the state, and agriculture was the chief source of wealth. Irrigation and crop rotation were practiced, and famines were almost unknown. Trade was cosmopolitan; in the bazaars of Pataliputra, the splendid capital city known today as Patna, were displayed goods from southern India, China, Mesopotamia, and Asia Minor. Indian ships sailed the Indian Ocean to the head of the Persian Gulf and to Arabia, and from these points caravans carried Indian goods overland toward markets as distant as the cities of Greece. Manufactur-

ing was also important in the Mauryan empire. Greek accounts refer to the making of arms and agricultural implements and the building of ships; northwestern India was famous for cotton cloth and silk yarn.

About 297 B.C. Chandragupta was succeeded by his son Bindusara. A charming story about Bindusara indicates the close cultural relations which existed at this time between the Mauryan and Seleucid rulers. Writing to Antiochus, Bindusara asked for a sample of Greek wine, some raisins, and a Sophist. In his reply Antiochus stated that he was sending the wine with pleasure, but that "it isn't good form among the Greeks to trade in philosophers."[6]

Ashoka, propagator of Buddhism. Ashoka, a son of Bindusara, reigned from 273 B.C. to 232 B.C. He was one of the few early kings who pursued the arts of peace more diligently than the arts of war; his first military campaign was also his last.

In 262 B.C. Ashoka attacked the state of Ka-

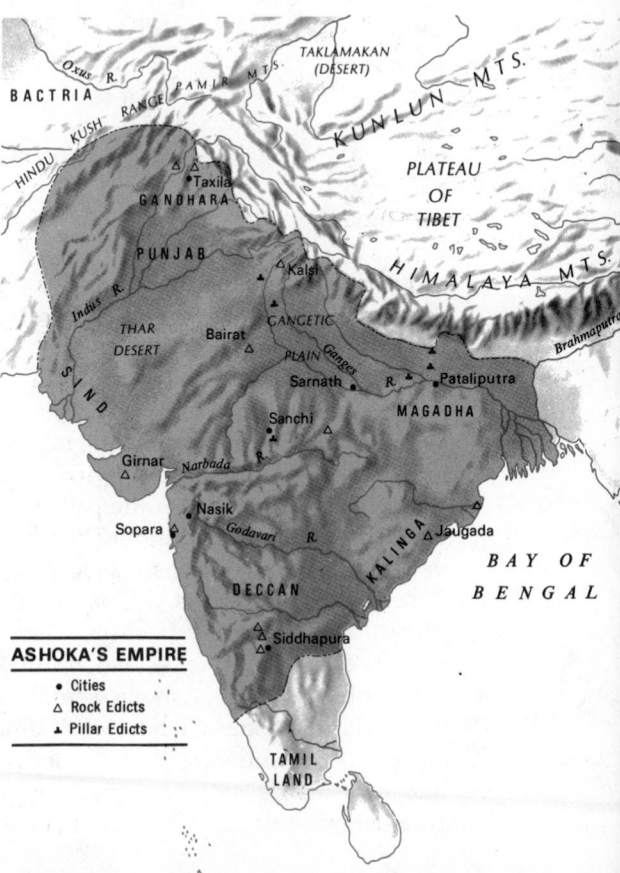

ASHOKA'S EMPIRE
- Cities
△ Rock Edicts
▲ Pillar Edicts

linga to the south, whose inhabitants stubbornly resisted his invasion. In the war of extermination that followed, victory fell to Ashoka, and at least 200,000 Kalingans were killed or captured. Thus Ashoka extended the Mauryan empire so that it included nearly all of India into the northern area of Tamil Land (see map, p. 99). But the cruelty of the campaign horrified him, and he resolved never again to permit such acts of butchery. Soon after this war, Ashoka was converted to Buddhism, whose gentle teachings increased his aversion to warfare.

As the years passed, Ashoka became even more deeply religious. Throughout his empire he had his imperial edicts carved on rocks and stone pillars. Some of the latter still stand today. These huge, polished sandstone pillars, thirty to forty feet high, together with a series of Rock Edicts, give little or no information concerning political events, but their inscriptions are invaluable for appreciating the spirit and purpose of Ashokan rule. Stressing compassion, kindness to all living things, truth, purity, and liberality, the edicts were a practical application of the teachings of Buddha. The inscriptions on Ashoka's pillars show not only that the art of calligraphy was highly developed but also that writing was commonly used for practical purposes throughout the empire.

Although a devout Buddhist, Ashoka believed in complete religious toleration; he did not persecute the Brahmins, who upheld Hindu tradition. A strong believer in the doctrine of *ahimsā*, or noninjury to men or animals, he forbade the sacrifice of animals in the capital, substituted royal pilgrimages to Buddhist shrines for hunting expeditions, and did away almost entirely with the slaughter of animals for meat at the palace. Ashoka ate no meat himself and probably encouraged vegetarianism among his subjects.

Termed "the first royal patron of Buddhism," Ashoka has been likened to St. Paul and Constantine—a successful propagator of his faith. Ashoka sent Buddhist missionaries to many lands—the Himalayan regions, the Tamil kingdoms, Ceylon, Burma, and even as far away as Syria, Egypt, and Macedonia—to teach the gospel of salvation

and equality. Thus transformed from a small Indian sect to a powerful religion, Buddhism began to make its influence felt beyond its homeland. Ashoka's missionary efforts had enduring success in neighboring Asian lands, particularly in Ceylon, where Buddhism is found today in nearly its original form.

Fall of the Mauryan empire. Almost immediately after Ashoka's death in 232 B.C., the Mauryan empire began to disintegrate. The last emperor was assassinated in 185 B.C., and the state was then invaded by a ruler from southern India and also by Demetrius, the fourth Bactrian king (see p. 62), who overran the Punjab in northwest India.

Although the Mauryan state had once been powerful, it crumbled almost overnight. So dramatic was the collapse and so grave the consequences that, like the decline and fall of the Roman empire, it has provoked much scholarly speculation. Whatever the reasons for the fall of the Mauryan empire, its contribution to world civilization survived, for "the moral ascendancy of Indian culture over a large part of the civilized world, which Ashoka was mainly instrumental in bringing about, remained for centuries as a monument to . . . [India's] glory. . . ."[7]

The Graeco-Bactrian kingdom. When Demetrius invaded India, he occupied Gandhara (see map, p. 99), whose inhabitants had been converted to Buddhism by Ashoka. The Bactrians organized the chief Gandharan town as a Hellenistic city and even fashioned an acropolis there. Demetrius also acquired Taxila (an administrative center of the Mauryan empire) and Pataliputra, the Mauryan capital. Thus he ruled an area stretching from the Persian desert to the middle of the Ganges valley.

Demetrius organized his domain much as a Seleucid kingdom. In keeping with Alexander's ideal of bringing East and West together on a basis of equality, Demetrius issued a bilingual coinage bearing Greek inscriptions on one side and Indian on the other. "His realm was to be a partnership of Greek and Indian. He was not to be a Greek king of Indian subjects, but an Indian king no less than a Greek one, head of both races."[8]

During the period of the Graeco-Bactrian kingdom, a prolific Graeco-Roman Buddhist school of art evolved from the fusion of Greek and Buddhist elements in Gandhara. Because of the Buddha's prohibitions against idolatry, artists had for centuries refrained from portraying the Buddha in human form, depicting instead only symbols of his life and teaching. In the capital from one of Ashoka's pillars, for example, the lion suggests Buddha's majesty and power while the wheel below is the Wheel of Law which was set in motion through his teachings. With the growth of the *Mahayana* school, however, artists began to create figures of the Buddha. Dating from the fifth century A.D., the head of Buddha from Gandhara shows Hellenistic influence in the modeling of the features and hair, while the elongated ear lobes, heavy-lidded eyes, mark on the forehead, knot of hair, and expression of deep repose are Indian. Eventually the *Mahayana* school of Buddhism and Graeco-Roman Buddhist art spread together throughout eastern Asia.

His general, Menander, who subsequently ascended the throne, continued the concept of partnership. Whereas in the West the Seleucid rulers had endeavored to create a basically Greek empire filled with Greek settlements, it was not possible to found Greek cities on any such scale in India. Thus Menander's kingdom was essentially Indian with a small Greek ruling class. The kingdom of Bactria attained a high state of culture before being crushed by the nomadic tribes that swept out of Central Asia about the close of the second century B.C.

The Kushan empire. A turbulent period followed the fall of the Bactrian kingdom. But by the first century A.D. the most important of the invading clans, the Kushans, had established themselves as masters of a large part of northwestern India and had founded another of the great empires in Indian history.

Kanishka, the most outstanding of the Kushan rulers, became king sometime between 78 and 128 A.D. (probably closer to the former date). All of northwest India, perhaps as far south as the Narbada River, and much of present Afghanistan to the north were under his sway. This enlightened monarch took over the civilization of the people he conquered. During his reign the arts and sciences flourished, imposing buildings were constructed, and advances were made in the field of medicine.

Mahayana and, Hinayana Buddhism. Whereas Gautama Buddha had concerned himself primarily with the removal of individual suffering through a life of purity and self-denial, later Buddhists added to this central doctrine more emotional and less purely philosophical concepts, together with myths and rituals. By the time of Kanishka this less austere approach with its great mass appeal had aroused the opposition of many Buddhists, who viewed it as a corruption of the original Buddhism.

In an effort to heal the growing split in Buddhism, Kanishka convened a great council of five hundred monks. But unity was not restored, and henceforth two major forms of Buddhism flourished: the more popular *Mahayana*, or "Great Vehicle," and the more orthodox *Hinayana*, or "Lesser Vehicle." The *Mahayanists* viewed the Buddha as a Bodhisattva, an exalted being who renounced *nirvana* in order to save mankind, and they claimed that their doctrine, less rigorous and more easily adapted to the needs of the common man, was the great vehicle by which enlightenment might be more easily achieved. With its message of hope and salvation for the masses, *Mahayana* Buddhism spread rapidly along the trade routes to Nepal, Tibet, China, Korea, and Japan. The *Hinayana*—which remained primarily an ethical philosophy, austere and rational—became the southern branch of Buddhism, spreading from India and Ceylon to Burma, Thailand, Cambodia, Vietnam, the Malay peninsula, and Indonesia.

Like Ashoka, Kanishka was a Buddhist convert who was instrumental in helping make Buddhism a world religion. Hinduism, however, still had a strong hold on the Indian people. While the Buddhists had disregarded caste and accepted both the Greeks and the Kushans, the Hindus rejected the foreign invaders as outcastes. Gradually, the Indians came to consider Hinduism a more characteristically Indian movement than Buddhism. Therefore, although Kanishka helped spread Buddhism to other countries, in the long run his support probably lessened its popularity within India.

Trade with the West. At the tip of the Indian peninsula lay the Tamil country, peopled by Dravidians who had long been absorbing elements of Hindu culture from the lands to the north. These states enjoyed commercial ties with the Hellenistic Greeks, particularly those in Egypt, and the vigor of the commercial contact is shown by some interesting examples of linguistic influences: the Hebrew term for peacock and the Greek words for ginger, cinnamon, and rice come from the Tamil language.

In Roman times trade with the Tamil kingdoms and that with the Kushans expanded. When Augustus became head of the Roman world, the Kushan and Tamil rulers sent him congratulatory embassies, an honor never before paid a western prince. The ambassadors took about four years en route and bore such gifts as "a gigantic python, huge tortoises, and an armless boy who could shoot arrows and throw darts with his feet!" In the period from Augustus' rule to the reign of the first Constantine, at least nine other embassies from India visited

the Roman emperors to arrange for the protection and well-being of Indian ships and traders at Roman ports.

Roman merchants dwelt in Tamil seaports, and through them precious metals, coins, wine, pottery, glassware, silverware, and even craftsmen and masons were brought to India. Tamil poets described Roman ships that carried a guard of archers to ward off pirates, while the Tamil kings themselves employed bodyguards of Roman soldiers, whose habit of wearing long coats aroused much comment in a land where comparative nudity was the rule. For its part, India was exporting drugs, pearls, silks, muslins, and spices. In view of the magnitude of the Roman-Indian trade, we can understand why Ptolemy showed considerable knowledge of the geography of India which is shown in his map (see p. 389).

Soon after 220 A.D. the Kushan empire collapsed, and northern and central India entered a chaotic period. In Chapter 7 we will continue the story of India. Now let us trace the development of civilization in the secluded land of China.

CHINA: THE FORMATIVE CENTURIES

The checkerboard land. Chinese civilization arose and developed in a vast land of over four million square miles which was for centuries almost completely isolated from the other centers of civilization by mountains, deserts, and ocean. This isolation helps explain the great originality of China's culture. For example, of all the world's writing systems today, only the Chinese and its derivatives are not based ultimately on the alphabet developed in West Asia.

Geographically, China looks like a vast checkerboard divided by mountain ranges and river systems. Two mountain chains cross the country from southwest to northeast, and three more extend from west to east, forming three great river valleys. The Yellow River (Huang Ho), traditionally known as China's Sorrow because of the misery caused by its periodic flooding, traverses the North China Plain; here was the original homeland of Chinese culture. This valley was eventually superseded by the Yangtze River valley in Central China as the most important economic and cultural region. The shorter rivers and valleys converging on present-day Canton form the third major river system.

These rivers were of crucial importance in the development of Chinese civilization. They provided water for irrigation and served as a cheap and efficient transportation system. As in Egypt, the beginning of political organization was linked with geography: governing bodies were needed to construct and control irrigation systems and to prevent ruinous flooding. The complex system of mountain ranges and river systems has, throughout China's history, created problems of political and military unity. At the same time, the great river valleys were suited to the growth of a homogeneous civilization extending over a greater land area than any other culture in the world.

The Shang dynasty: China enters history. The first Chinese state for which we possess written historical evidence, the Shang dynasty, flourished in the region of An-yang, a site in the Yellow River valley, from about 1500 to 1027 B.C. An-yang was a crossroads of influence from North and Southeast Asia as well as from West Asia and had long been a culture center. The remarkably advanced Shang civilization was distinguished from its predecessors by three important developments: bronze metallurgy, a writing system, and the emergence of a state organization in an urban environment.

Carrying bronze metallurgy, which probably originated in West Asia, to heights never surpassed in world history, the Shang people cast elaborate bronze ceremonial vessels and weapons, intricately decorated with both incised and high-relief designs. Different from anything found in prehistoric China or the West, Shang design may be the earliest example of a unique Pacific Basin style, characterized by frontal views of animal heads, in contrast to animal profiles which predominated in the West. The cere-

monial bronze vessels were required for religious rituals, which also fostered sacred dancing and music.

The Shang people invented or perfected a distinctive writing system, unquestionably Chinese in both language and form. They possessed sufficient written words, over two thousand, to express themselves with considerable facility. Some are still in use today. These characters, or graphs, representing individual words, rather than sounds, consisted of three types: pictographs, recognizable as pictures of observable objects; ideographs, representing ideas; and characters, formed in part on phonetic principles.

Shang society appears to have centered on a city-state and its surrounding settlements, ruled by hereditary kings. Shang kings and aristocrats lived in imposing buildings, went to battle in horse-drawn chariots, conducted human sacrifices, and buried live servants with their dead masters. In contrast, the common people lived in primitive pit dwellings and went to war on foot. Warfare was frequent, and the chariot, a new weapon, facilitated the spread of Shang power through large parts of the Yellow River valley. Both military and administrative inventions made

Shang artisans produced intricately detailed bronze vessels by a sophisticated casting process. This owl-like wine cup was used in religious ceremonies by the earliest emperors.

possible the emergence of a recognizable state by the late Shang period. Political and social authority rested on the aristocrats' monopoly of bronze metallurgy, their possession of expensive war chariots, and the king's religious functions.

Shang religion centered around the worship of deities, spirits, ancestors, natural phenomena such as the wind and the earth, and the cardinal points of the compass. Animal sacrifices were usual, and sometimes libations of a beerlike liquor were poured on the ground. One of the deities worshiped was Shang Ti (Supreme Ti). In Chinese mythology the Five Ti were early Chinese rulers, and Shang Ti was probably worshiped as a "supreme ancestor."

In the nascent urban centers people made a living in specialized occupations and trade. The majority of the population, however, consisted of peasants who grew wheat, millet, and rice and raised cattle, sheep, pigs, and horses. Farming methods were primitive; for a plow, farmers used a stick dragged through the soil.

Chou: the classical period. In 1027 B.C. (or 1122 B.C., according to some sources), the Chou people conquered the Shang. With their capital at Hao, near modern Sian, the Chou lived on the edge of Shang civilization and authority, sharing its culture and language. The Chou undoubtedly benefited from their proximity to nomadic tribes in the north and west, from whom they may have learned some of the martial skills that made their conquest of Shang possible.

The Chou kings conquered most of the North China Plain, but the lack of efficient communications made the development of a unified state impossible. Consequently, the kings delegated local authority, particularly in the east, to relatives or military chieftains and social magnates. These vassal lords, whose power was hereditary, recognized the suzerainty of the Chou kings and were responsible for supplying the kings with military aid. As the vassal states grew in size and developed their own bureaucratic and military organizations, they became virtually independent, and the Chou kings continued to reign only on the sufferance of the feudal lords.

The remnants of Chou royal power disappeared completely in 771 B.C., when an alliance of dissident vassal states and "barbarians" seized the capital and killed the king. Part of the royal family managed to escape eastward to Lo-yang, however, where the dynasty, now known as the Eastern Chou, survived for another five centuries. At Lo-yang, Chou royal functions were largely confined to performing state religious rituals and arbitrating differences among the feudal lords. As the stronger feudal states gradually absorbed their weaker neighbors, the domains of the Eastern Chou kings themselves diminished in size and strength in comparison with their vassals'. Warfare between the feudal states was incessant, particularly in the "Period of Warring States" (403-221 B.C.).

The interstate system. The disappearance of Chou influence over the vassal states during the Eastern Chou period led not only to rapidly increasing interstate warfare but to a decline in adherence to the traditional rules of the proper conduct of warfare and the establishment of legitimacy. Particularly in the fourth and third centuries B.C., many state rulers took the title *wang*, or king, formerly reserved for the Chou ruler alone. Enemy states sought to exterminate each other and to annex each other's territory. As the states grew in size, the scale of warfare grew too. In the latter years of the Chou some states could throw thousands of chariots and tens of thousands of peasant foot soldiers into battle. Interstate conferences were held to consider and conclude treaties and alliances and to develop disarmament proposals. Alliances were established and cemented through royal marriages, and hostages were exchanged to ensure loyalty.

The formation of leagues and alliances, the exchange of ambassadors, political marriages, and the holding of interstate conferences all resemble the interstate system that developed in Europe in late medieval and early modern times. By 221 B.C., however, the Period of Warring States ended when the state of Ch'in conquered all its rivals; and while Europe, after the fall of the Roman Empire, was never again to achieve political or administrative unity, China was never again permanently disunited.

Chou culture. The Chou destruction of Shang did not result in any sharp break in the development of Chinese culture. The writing system became more complex and sophisticated, and the Chou continued to produce bronze vessels, but with less elaborate designs than the Shang. During the sixth century iron was introduced and came into general use by the end of the Chou, when China had drawn abreast, if not ahead, of technological developments in the rest of the world. Iron weapons made warfare more efficient, and iron plows contributed to the expansion of agriculture.

The Eastern Chou is unrivaled by any later period in Chinese history for its energy and dynamic creativity. The ox-drawn iron-tipped plow, together with the growth of large-scale irrigation and water-control projects, led to population growth based on increased agricultural yields. Canals were constructed to facilitate the moving of commodities over long distances. Commerce and wealth grew rapidly, and a merchant and artisan class emerged. Cowrie shells, bolts of silk, and ingots of precious metals were the media of exchange, and by the end of the Chou period copper cash, small round coins with square holes, were being minted and starting to come into general circulation. In various weights and degrees of purity, and with various legends on the face, copper cash remained the basic coinage of China into the late nineteenth century. Chopsticks and lacquer were also in use at this time.

The art of horseback riding, which was developing among the nomads of Central and West Asia, deeply influenced Chou China. The horse contributed to the ease and growth of communications between east and west, and technological and intellectual developments in India and West Asia were gradually carried to China. In design, for instance, the typical western profile replaced the Shang highly stylized frontal view. Central Asian horsemen threatened China militarily, and in response the Chinese began constructing defensive walls, later joined together to become the Great Wall of China. Inside China itself, cavalry replaced the chariot in warfare, and the use of the horse improved internal communications, contrib-

uting to the process of political centralization. All these developments led to a growing self-consciousness on the part of the Chinese who, while divided into states fighting among themselves, began to distinguish between their own high civilization and the barbarian peasants and nomads. This sense of unique superiority of their own civilization became a lasting characteristic of Chinese culture.

The classes. Class divisions and consciousness were highly developed during the Chou and have remained so down to modern times. The king and the aristocracy were sharply separated from the mass of people on the basis of land ownership and family descent. The nobility were members of a territorially dispersed clan system, and the clans in turn were divided into families, each with a male head. Until the later stages of Chou, the nobility held the chief posts in the army and administration. The fact that the aristocrats' inherited privileges depended

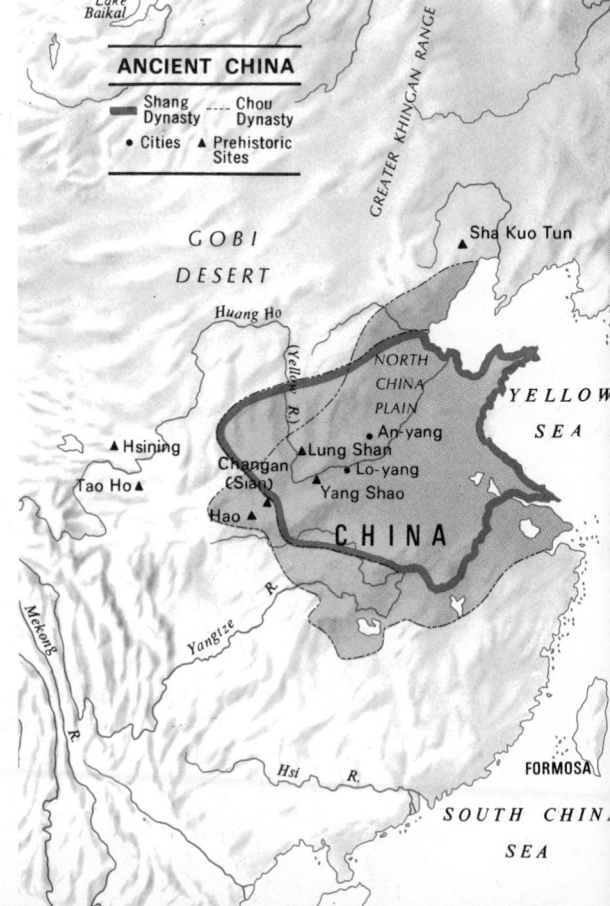

on proof of their noble ancestry was at least partly responsible for the great emphasis which the Chinese placed on ancestor worship.

The feudal nobles lived a far different life from that of farmers. Their customs can be compared in a general way to those of Europe's feudal nobility (see Chapter 8). Underlying the feudal structure was a code of chivalry, practiced in both war and peace. The intricate and complex code became so important to the nobility as a symbol of gentility that nobles devoted years to its mastery. Arrayed in breastplate and helmet, the Chinese noble waged war from his chariot and, to display his martial skill and social grace, "would come to the court of his seigneur to take part in tournaments of the noble sport of archery which was accompanied by musical airs and interspersed with elegant salutations, the whole regulated like a ballet."[9]

Village life. Agriculture, of course, was the occupation of the overwhelming proportion of the population. Large-scale irrigation, fertilizer, and the ox-drawn iron-tipped plow modified the traditional feudal land system, stimulating a gradual changeover to private land ownership based on increased productivity. But the masses generally had no political rights and, until the end of the Chou, little or no land. The peasants cultivated their fields as the tenants of nobles or landlords, paid taxes, and served as common soldiers. Families lived together in villages clustered about the residence of a noble or, after feudal times, a landlord. Eventually, the village community included members not related by blood to the original family group.

Despite increased agricultural productivity and changes in property structure, the farm population still had difficulty eking out an existence. A major problem in the Chinese economy has been that the majority of farmers worked fields so small that they could not produce a crop surplus to tide them over periods of scarcity. This problem, evident as early as 400 B.C., became especially acute from the eighteenth century on, when population pressures led to a marked decline in in the size of peasant holdings.

The rise of philosophical schools. By the fifth century B.C. rapid economic, social, political, and technological change, coupled with increasing warfare between the states, destroyed the apparent stability that had characterized Chinese society internally during the Shang, Western Chou, and early Eastern Chou dynasties. Educated Chinese became aware of the great disparity between the traditions inherited from their ancestors and the reality in which they themselves lived. Moreover, the nascent bureaucratic class had no place in the traditional scheme of Chinese society, with its two classes: the aristocracy and the peasants.

The tension between inherited tradition and existing reality led directly to the birth of social and personal consciousness in China on the eve of the Period of Warring States. Many scholars have noted with excitement the parallel between the flourishing intellectual life of fifth-century B.C. China and the Golden Ages of Greek philosophy and Indian religious thougnt at the same time. More than Indian and Mediterranean thinkers, Chinese philosophers concerned themselves primarily with man's control of himself and his society in an age when it appeared that he could no longer control either.

Although they often disagreed violently among themselves, most of the schools of Chinese philosophy in the Eastern Chou shared certain characteristics. Dismayed with the present state of man and society, they looked to the past for models on which to base the construction of a meaningful ethical system for man and the reconstruction of Chinese society. This led to a greater consciousness of history in China than in other world cultures. From this time on, the writing of history was a major literary activity, and down to the end of the nineteenth century all intellectual innovations sought their justification in the linear continuity of historical examples and classical writings. These influences are even present in Communist China today. All schools of Chinese thought also shared a common interest in the achievement of order in society and of a proper balance between man and man, and between man and nature.

Master K'ung, the sage. The first, most famous, and certainly most influential professional Chinese philosopher and teacher was K'ung-fu-tzu, Master K'ung, known in the West by the Latinized form of his name, Confucius (551-479 B.C.). His teachings had a greater and longer-lasting influence in China and the rest of East Asia than those of any other philosopher and became the official school of thought in Japan, Korea, the Ryukyu Islands, and Vietnam, as well as in China. He is still venerated as the official philosopher of the Nationalist Chinese government on Taiwan. The teachings of the sage and his most famous disciple, Mencius, were written down and form a crucial part of the Confucian canon, conventionally known in later dynasties as the Thirteen Classics. In the West what we largely know about Confucius is drawn from the *Analects*, a collection of Confucius' responses to his disciples' questions, each prefaced by the phrase, "The Master said."

Confucius was born in the small state of Lu, in modern Shantung province, into what was evidently a family of the lower aristocracy that had sunk into poverty. Orphaned as a child, he obtained an education and became a member of the new bureaucratic class. Tradition has it that he found employment for a while as an official in his native state, but he never achieved the prominent public position he sought. Dissatisfied with the conditions of Chinese social and moral life, he spent at least ten years wandering around the country advising princes and teaching young men, who, he hoped, might succeed where he had failed. Confucius was evidently a teacher of rare ability, and it is said that he had more than three thousand students. Confucius said of himself, "I am a transmitter and not a creator. I believe in and have a passion for the ancients." Living in an age of social, political, and moral turmoil, Confucius was probably the first Chinese to be conscious of tradition as tradition, and he sought to revive it by organizing it into a system of thought.

Confucianism is a social and moral philosophy, not a religion. While accepting the existence of Heaven (*T'ien*) and spirits, Confucius was fundamentally an agnostic who

Courtesy, Museum of Fine Arts, Boston, Bigelow Collection

Buddha, Lao-tzu, and Confucius were three of the great leaders of East Asian thought. In this Japanese painting from the Kano period (1336-1558) they are depicted conversing together. Although the three philosophers were not contemporaries, their discussion symbolically represents the interaction of the three philosophical schools.

believed that the basic concern of man is man. "We don't know yet how to serve men, how can we know about serving the spirits?" he said. And, "We don't know yet about life, how can we know about death?" "Devote yourself to the proper demands of the people, respect the ghosts and spirits but keep them at a distance—this may be called wisdom."

Confucius' home state of Lu was known for its conservatism, and the Master believed that the social and political problems of his day could be solved only if men would return to the traditions of the founders of the Chou dynasty. Society would be stable if only each man would play his assigned role: "Let the ruler be a ruler and the subject a subject; let the father be a father and the son a son." He advocated a paternalistic form of government in which the ruler made himself responsible for the welfare of his people and the family was the model for the state.

Government, according to Confucius, was primarily a problem of ethics. While he did not challenge the hereditary rights of the rulers, he insisted that their primary responsibility was to serve as an example of correct ethical conduct for the people. The cultivation of virtue depended on *li*, "propriety," which characterized proper conduct for those in a ruler's court; *li*, in turn, depended on education. Each man would play his proper role in society if he performed the rituals proper to his station. "By nature men are pretty much alike; it is learning and practice that set them apart."

The ideal man, according to Confucius, was the *chün-tzu*, the cultivated man. The primary virtues were integrity, righteousness, conscientiousness or loyalty toward others, altruism, and love for one's fellow man. Etiquette or decorum were essential expressions of virtue. Confucius said, "Courtesy without decorum becomes tiresome. Cautiousness without decorum becomes timidity, daring becomes insubordination, frankness becomes effrontery." The ruler who possessed the essential virtues and behaved with decorum, Confucius insisted, would be able to rule by example rather than force.

Mencius and the "Mandate of Heaven." The most significant transmitter of Confucian doctrine was Mencius (372-289 B.C.), who, like Confucius, failed to achieve a high position in government and became a wandering teacher. Mencius added important new dimensions to Confucian thought. He taught that man's nature was fundamentally good and could be developed by self-cultivation through education and a kind of spontaneous inner search resembling Taoist mystical experiences. Government should be guided not by opportunism but by ethical standards, he claimed. A moral ruler will behave benevolently toward his people, providing for their well-being. A true king must have the support of his people. Heaven manifests itself through the people, and if the people accept and support their ruler, he has the "Mandate of Heaven" to rule over them. If they overthrow their ruler, he has lost Heaven's mandate and his right to leadership. This rationalization of revolution had originally been used by the Chou to justify their revolt against the Shang. But Mencius now developed it into a full justification of revolution.

Modern commentators, both Chinese and western, have seen in Mencius' concept of the Mandate of Heaven a form of protodemocratic thought. Mencius evidently believed that all men were morally equal and that the good ruler needed the consent of his people. But it would perhaps be more accurate to define Mencius' political theories as advocating benevolent autocracy rather than popular democracy.

Taoism: intuitive mysticism. While Confucianism stressed reason and social cohesiveness, Taoism, the most important school of Chinese thought next to Confucianism, emphasized the individual man and insisted that man's greatest problem was to conform to nature, not to society. Taoism often represented the revolt of the man of sensibilities and the common man against the social and moral rigidity of orthodox Confucianism.

The *Tao te ching*, or the *Classic of the Way and Power*, is the most important Taoist work, and though attributed to Lao-tzu, apparently a mythical figure who tradition says was slightly older than Confucius, it probably dates only to the third century B.C. Because the *Tao te ching* is cryptic and overly concise, it has been subject to many different interpretations, and no two western translations agree on its precise meaning. Taoism's second most important book, the *Chuang-tzu*, was also written in the third century B.C., though it is attributed to a fourth-century philosopher of the same name. One of the most beautiful works of Chinese literature, it contains stories and passages of great poetic delight and philosophical insight.

Popular Taoism quickly degenerated into a religion of spirits and magic, but philosophical Taoism sought to define the "true nature" of man in abstract terms. The word *tao*, meaning "road" or "way," in Confucianism stood for the ideal society which that school advocated. The Taoists defined it to mean the scheme of nature to which man should conform. Man could live in harmony with nature only if he turned his attention inward and experienced oneness between himself and the universe. In the Tao there are no distinctions. Everything is relative. The Taoists' highest ideal was the state of original and complete simplicity, and they advocated a society in which individuals lived simply, without law or machinery, without striving to be more than a harmonious part of nature.

The Taoists believed that the only way to achieve union with nature was through inaction, doing nothing: "Do nothing and nothing will not be done." Spontaneity, not conscious planning, was the key to correct behavior. The ideal political system, according to Taoism, would be "a small country with a few inhabitants."[10] In the early history of Chinese thought Taoism represented a strain of romanticism in contrast to Confucian rationalism.

The school of law. Following the end of the Period of Warring States, a non-Confucian school of philosophy, the School of Law or Legalists, developed. The Legalists taught that man is by nature selfish and evil and that moralists like the Confucians contributed to evil by encouraging human desires. According to the Legalists, people primarily want security and social order, and this can be achieved only in a society where the uneducated citizen, living in a kind of Taoist primitive state, blindly follows an absolute ruler and is subordinate to the state. To achieve this kind of society, harsh punishments and the strictest laws would be necessary. People were to be mutually responsible for the enforcement of the law, and anyone who had knowledge of a crime but did not report it was considered as guilty as the criminal himself. The ruler, by nature, would seek to create a strong and secure state, and therefore only his desires would be right.

Chinese art and literature. In general the Chinese arts are marked by restraint, a quality probably derived from Chinese conservatism and serenity. For example, a poem seldom employs a great deal of highly ornate language, nor is it effusive in its effect.

During the Shang and Chou periods the Chinese were already skillful craftsmen and sensitive artists. Jade ornaments have been found in the earliest Chinese graves. From Shang times the Chinese cut jade into forms of fishes to use as "sound stones" which, when struck, emitted a clear tone for a considerable length of time. Strikingly beautiful ceremonial bronzes were produced during the Shang period and for the next 1500 years (see illustration, p. 103).

Taoism made a profound impression upon Chinese art. The Taoist and the Chinese artist alike are deeply introspective and intuitive in approach, seeking to understand the processes of nature that create the landscape. Painting to express his reaction to a scene is more important to the Chinese artist than depicting the landscape realistically. Unfortunately almost no examples survive of the earliest Chinese painting, but literary references indicate that it was an established art centuries before the birth of Christ.

During the Chou dynasty, the characters making up the Chinese written language assumed a form, which, with some modifications, has remained comparatively unchanged up to the present time. While the spoken language was broken up into dialects that were often mutually unintelligible, members of the educated classes shared a literary form of Chinese that differed, as far as we know, from colloquial speech but that was universal in meaning. Thus, scholars in all parts of China could communicate with each other in writing, although they read any given character in the pronunciations of their own dialects, just as the character meaning "white" [白] is today read *baak* in Canton and *bai* in Peking and Taipei. As a result, the written language served as a bond between scholars and has exerted a unifying effect on Chinese culture over the centuries.

Even today, a literate Chinese, with some special study, can read the original texts of the Chou period. Of the forty thousand characters that exist, a knowledge of four to five thousand is sufficient to achieve a good level of literacy. Because the characters are constructed of a limited number (214) of "radicals," or elements that give clues to general categories of meaning, and very often of simpler characters serving as phonetic elements, it is not difficult to enlarge one's knowledge of characters once a few hundred basic forms have been mastered. Further, words are built up of compounds consisting of two, three, or more characters. Therefore a knowledge of as little as 1000 characters provides a key to a large and often quite sophisticated vocabulary.

CHINA: THE FIRST EMPIRES

Rise of Legalist Ch'in. As we recall, China was experiencing significant growth despite, or perhaps because of, its division into many petty, warring states. No state strove more for internal centralization and wielded increasingly autocratic power than the state of Ch'in, which embraced the ruthless philosophy of Legalism (see p. 109). Bearing strong resemblances to modern totalitarian thought, Legalism contributed greatly to Ch'in's eventual success in conquering and unifying all China. Although it disappeared as a legitimate philosophical school with the fall of the Ch'in empire about 206 B.C., its advocacy of a strong ruler and a universal criminal code were important additions to Chinese statecraft and strongly influenced the orthodox philosophy, founded on the teachings of Confucius and Mencius, that was to dominate China for over two thousand years.

Ch'in, a frontier state located in the far northwestern part of China in what is now Kansu and Shensi provinces, was less bound by tradition and more innovative than states in the central region. The other Chinese states considered Ch'in a country of barbarians, uncivilized and ignorant. Gradually, however, Ch'in was more and more influenced by Chou culture, and in 352 B.C. Shang Yang, a scion of the ruling house of a small

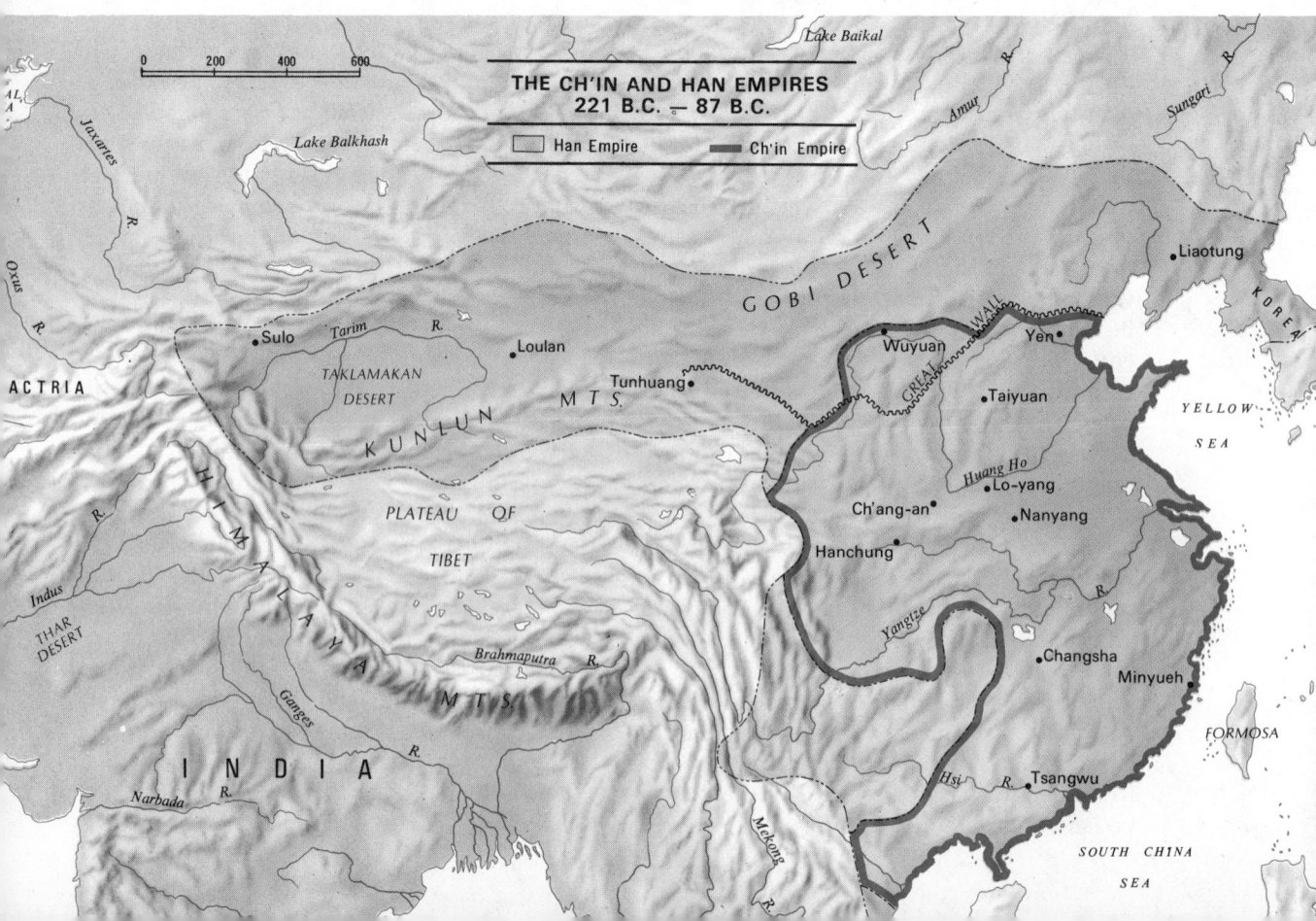

THE CH'IN AND HAN EMPIRES
221 B.C. — 87 B.C.

Han Empire　　Ch'in Empire

Chou state, became chancellor of Ch'in, ruling until 338 B.C.

Shang Yang instituted far-reaching changes in Ch'in government and society Recognizing that the growth of Ch'in's strength and power depended on a more efficient and centralized bureaucratic structure than could exist under feudalism, Shang Yang suppressed the old nobility and created a new aristocracy based on military merit. He divided the population into five- and ten-family units ruled directly by officials of the state and introduced a universal draft beginning at approximately age fifteen. Soldiers distinguishing themselves in battle were awarded with the services of five peasant families, and all noble ranks and access to a life of luxury were based on military accomplishment. Based on this new system, Ch'in eventually fielded and supported an army of one million men.

Economically, Shang Yang encouraged agricultural development and for the first time in the state's history levied direct state taxes on land in the place of the older system of communal work. Commerce, too, was encouraged, under a system of laws that protected merchants and their property.

These reforms made Ch'in the most powerful state of the time; and after Shang Yang's death Ch'in began to conquer the other states of Chou China, extending to the entire country the institutional innovations and social changes that had taken place in Ch'in as well as those that had occurred in the states it had conquered—for example, regulation of weights and measures, price control, state monopolies in the salt and iron mines.

Ch'in unites China. In the middle of the third century B.C. the Legalist Li Ssu, one of the most remarkable statesmen in Chinese history, helped the king of Ch'in conquer the other states of Chou China, establishing the first unified empire in Chinese history by 221 B.C. The king then assumed the title *Shih Huang-ti*, "First Emperor," taking for his title two terms that referred to the gods (Shang Ti) and the sage-emperors of the mythical age (the Three Huang and the Five Ti).[11] *Huang-ti* remained the title of Chinese emperors until the end of the imperial system in 1911.

Men of immense drive, skill, and imagination, Shih Huang-ti and Li Ssu carried out a revolution in Chinese society that went far beyond the unification of the country through centralization of bureaucratic administration. In effect, they created a precursor of the modern totalitarian state, particularly its fascist variety, in a premodern society. They gathered the complete aristocratic class—some 120,000 families, according to tradition—at the capital and replaced them with their own bureaucratic administrators in the provinces. With the exception of the imperial soldiers, the entire population had to surrender its weapons to the state. Shih Huang-ti standardized weights, measures, coinage, and axle lengths throughout the empire. The standardization of axle lengths was particularly important, for it permitted the creation of a unified road system radiating out from the capital, thus contributing to the ease of imperial control.

A single harsh legal code replaced all local laws and went far toward shattering long-standing traditions; the entire realm was divided into provinces, administrative units drawn to obliterate traditional feudal units and to facilitate direct rule by the emperor's own centrally controlled civil and military appointees. To destroy the source of the aristocracy's power and to permit the emperor's agents to tax every farmer's harvest, private ownership of land by peasants was allowed.

Vast public works of both a civilian and a military nature were undertaken for the greater security of the state and glory of the emperor. Shih Huang-ti's most spectacular public work was repairing the remnants of walls built in earlier times and joining them into the Great Wall, extending from the sea into Central Asia for a distance of over 1400 miles. The wall was both a line of defense against the barbarians who habitually raided China and a symbol of distinction between China's sedentary agricultural civilization and the nomadic animal-husbandry societies of Central Asia. It was meant to keep the nomads out and, at the same time, to keep the Chinese in.

One of the most important keystones of Ch'in imperial policy was intellectual control and enforced conformity. Li Ssu standardized the Chinese writing system, giving it essentially its modern form, thus facilitating written communication and inhibiting heterodox thought by destroying regional scripts. Furthermore, he tried to enforce intellectual conformity and make the Ch'in imperial system appear to be the only natural political order by attempting to destroy the historical memory of the intellectuals. In 213 B.C. he instituted the first literary inquisition in history, known as the "Burning of the Books." The Confucian classics, all works of history that did not support the Ch'in, and any other books that appeared to be of a subversive nature were destroyed; scholars who protested were banished from the empire or killed. The only exceptions were works of a utilitarian nature, according to Legalist philosophy: books on medicine, agriculture, divination, Ch'in history, and certain government libraries and documents. These measures, along with the centralized empire itself which had little room for cultural diversity, dealt a blow to Chinese thought from which it never fully recovered.

When Shih Huang-ti died in 210 B.C., his inept son was unable to control the rivalry among the First Emperor's chief aides. As the court sank into intrigue, anarchic popular rebellion swept the land; by 206 B.C. the Ch'in dynasty, which claimed that it would endure for "ten thousand generations," had completely disappeared. But the Chinese empire, which Ch'in created, lasted for more than two thousand years, evolving eventually into Communist China today. Although Ch'in itself disappeared, it created the longest-lived political institution in world history.

The Han dynasty: the Legalist state survives. In 202 B.C., the year in which the Romans defeated the Carthaginians at the battle of Zama, Liu Pang, better known under his posthumous title Kao Tsu (High Ancestor), won control of China and established the Han dynasty, with its capital at Ch'ang-an (see map, p. 110). The Han dynasty is traditionally divided into two parts: the Earlier Han, from 206 B.C. to 8 A.D., and the Later Han, from 23 A.D. to 220 A.D. It was interrupted by a short-lived dynasty under a usurper of the throne. The Han corresponded in the East to the Roman Empire in the West in time, significance, power, and prestige. Chinese today still call themselves "Men of Han," and the Japanese call the Chinese characters they use in writing their own language "Han characters," much as we speak of the "Latin alphabet."

Although the anti-Ch'in rebellions were characterized in part by a nostalgia for Chou society, the clock could not be turned back; the Legalist imperial state had become a permanent feature of the Chinese political landscape. Kao Tsu and his successors succeeded where the Ch'in had failed because they retained the Legalist state in all its essentials but tempered their approach to the intellectuals and the people with moderation. At first Kao Tsu and his immediate successors, faced with the problem of ruling a vast empire without efficient means of communications, reestablished some of the vassal kingdoms in distant regions, but they spent the first century and a half of their rule subjugating their own creations, returning to Legalist political institutions. Although the dynasty constantly faced internal threats and external danger, the population grew dramatically. A "census" of 2 A.D. listed the population of the empire as almost sixty million, a greater number of people than ever recognized Rome's rule.

In accord with Legalist principles, which were tempered by Confucian ideas, the Han emperors established complex administrative organs staffed by a salaried bureaucracy to rule their vast empire. Periodic searches were made for men of talent, chosen through a primitive examination and recommendation system and promoted by merit. By the first century B.C. the government employed more than 130,000 bureaucrats, or one for every 400 to 500 people in the empire. Relatively small by modern standards, the Han bureaucracy set the pattern for and influenced all subsequent periods of Chinese history down to the start of the current regime.

Although the examinations were theoretically open to all Chinese except merchants, the bureaucrats were drawn largely from the landlord class, because wealth was needed to obtain the education to pass the examinations. Consequently, the earlier division of Chinese society between aristocrats and peasants was now transformed into a division between landowner-bureaucrats and peasants.

Wu Ti, the "Martial Emperor." After sixty years of consolidation, the Han empire reached its greatest extent and development during the long reign of Wu Ti, from 141-87 B.C., who embarked on a policy of territorial expansion. He justified his conquests in terms of self-defense against the threat of attacks by nomads, but desire to control the trade routes of Central Asia may also have been a major factor. In the north, he drove the nomads into and beyond the Gobi Desert. In the west, he extended the Great Wall out into the desert of the Tarim Basin and settled some 700,000 Chinese on the borders of this barren region, bringing it under Chinese control. His armies conquered parts of what is now Russian Turkestan, and under one of his successors Han armies reached beyond this point, extending Chinese power farther from the capital than Roman power reached out from Rome at any time. In the east, Wu Ti conquered southern Manchuria and northern Korea, bringing these areas once and for all under the sway of Chinese culture. And to the south, he extended his empire along the coast well into North Vietnam.

Wu Ti's great conquests were based on far-reaching economic and financial reforms aimed at providing the government with revenue to administer the growing em-pire. The emperor increased taxes, made the laws more stringent, established state monopolies on such vital products as salt and iron, and used conscript and slave labor in constructing public works. As costs increased, taxes increased, until the government's fiscal situation grew precarious and the peasants' burdens led to revolt. This in turn increased the government's need for revenue to pay for the suppression of the rebellions its policies had caused. Moreover, as the government at the center grew weaker, it had to rely more and more on local military commanders and magnates for control of the population, giving them greater power and prestige at its own expense. This vicious circle of decline after an initial dynastic period of increasing prosperity and power has been the pattern of most Chinese dynasties since the Han; western historians of China call it "the dynastic cycle." In the Han this eventually led to the temporary usurpation of the throne that divided the Earlier from the Later Han.

The Later Han dynasty never reached the heights of its predecessor. Warlords in the provinces seized more and more power for themselves, and widespread peasant rebellions sapped the state's resources. Reduced to a political fiction for the last three decades of its reign, the dynasty finally collapsed completely in 220 A.D. when the throne was usurped by the son of a famous general. But China succeeded where Europe failed: after three and a half centuries of disunion, China

Built as a defense against invaders, and extending for 1500 miles, the Great Wall symbolizes China's self-enforced isolation. It remains today one of the greatest monuments of engineering skill in the preindustrial age.

once again was united and, with minor exceptions, has remained united to this day. In Europe, unification remains, even now, a dream.

Han intellectual developments. In his political style and policies, Wu Ti was almost as much a Legalist as the Ch'in First Emperor, and yet his court was strongly oriented toward Confucianism. While neither Wu Ti nor Kao Tsu, the founder of the dynasty, wasted affection on scholars, they recognized that a literate and educated bureaucracy was necessary for governing so vast an empire. Consequently the way was open for a revival of the intellectual life that had been suppressed under the Ch'in. In 191 B.C. the Han lifted the Ch'in ban on Chou literature, and some older men were apparently able to write down from memory texts they had memorized in their youth, before the Ch'in dynasty was established. Legend has it that other texts were found hidden in the walls of houses, where they had been put by scholars to escape the Ch'in book burning.

Han thought included ideas drawn from a variety of schools, which were woven into a new synthesis that was very different from Chou philosophy. The primary interest of scholars during the first century of Han was the recovery of Chou literature. Their understanding of the old texts was at times vague, however, and it was Confucius as the ideal image of the sage rather than Confucianism as a political and social philosophy that eventually triumphed during the Han. While Legalism as a philosophical school was anathema to the Han scholars, Legalist statecraft was redefined in Confucian terms (as understood by the Han scholars), and Chou ethical concepts tempered the harshness of Legalist practice. The result was a philosophy of benevolent imperial despotism, a far cry from Confucius' feudal concept of the *chün-tzu* and Mencius' doctrine of the Mandate of Heaven.

The Han dynasty witnessed many other important intellectual developments. The Five Classics were established as the primary Confucian canon and the basis of education. In 124 B.C. an imperial university was established, and by the latter half of the first century B.C. it was said to have had three thousand students. In the Later Han this increased tenfold. By 1 A.D. one hundred men a year entered government service through official examinations based on the Confucian classics, and Han Confucianism became the orthodox philosophy of the state in 58 A.D., when regular sacrifices to Confucius were ordered performed in all government schools.[12]

In Wu Ti's reign, Ssu-ma Ch'ien, a court astrologer, wrote the *Shih chi*, or *Historical Records*, a remarkable work which set the pattern for all subsequent Chinese historical writings but also determined their style and scholarly approach. Ssu-ma Ch'ien was an unusually sophisticated historian and his work, consisting of 130 chapters, is a kind of universal history. The first twelve chapters are the "Basic Annals" which record events from earliest times up to the reign of Wu Ti. This is followed by chronological tables, essays on such subjects as astrology, rituals, music, rivers and canals, and economics; the last seventy chapters are made up of biographies of important men and essays on other lands and their people. In the Later Han, Pan Ku compiled the *History of the [Earlier] Han*, which was limited to a single dynasty. This became the prototype for later dynastic histories and thereafter it was customary for each dynasty to write the official history of its predecessor.

Technological advancement. During the Han period China equaled and even surpassed the level of scientific and technological development in the rest of the world. Advances were particularly notable in the fields of mineralogy, alchemy and chemistry, pharmacology, zoology, and botany.[13] The Han Chinese invented a primitive seismograph, knew of sunspots, invented the water-powered mill, paper, and porcelain, and reckoned accurately the length of the year as early as 28 B.C. In textiles they were far ahead of the West. Although little remains of it, tradition indicates that the capital at Ch'ang-an must have rivaled Rome in wealth and splendor.

Buddhism and Buddhist art enter China. In Central Asia, where the Han had recently extended the *Pax Sinica*, the Chinese were in close contact with the Kushan empire in northwest India. This contact facilitated the spread of Buddhism from northwest India into China during the later Han dynasty, for Buddhist missionaries made their way through the heart of Asia along the same protected routes as the silk caravans. Transported to China along with the Buddhist faith were the Gandharan Graeco-Indian artistic techniques and the stupa architecture, from which the style of the Chinese pagoda is derived.

A first-century Han emperor gave Buddhism official recognition and so initiated its spread within China, although its impact was not felt strongly until after the Han period. At first progress was hindered by the suspicions of the Chinese that Buddhist monasticism did not fit into the country's family tradition. But much of Buddhist mysticism was like that of Taoism, and the resemblance facilitated its eventual approval by many of the Chinese. Both *Hinayana* and *Mahayana* Buddhism were imported into China, but the latter, with its acceptance of Bodhisattvas and even local Chinese gods, gained the ascendancy. As Buddhism rose in dominance over Taoism and Confucianism, much of the intellectual capacities of the Chinese was devoted to the translation and interpretation of its scriptures.

THE MEETING OF EAST AND WEST

Beyond the Roman frontiers. During its period of greatest prosperity, the Graeco-Roman world-state, centered in the Mediterranean basin, maintained trade contacts extending far beyond the imperial boundaries. In the market quarter of imperial Rome, Chinese silk was sold, and Indian merchants frequented the streets of Alexandria. During the four centuries after 334 B.C. (the year when Alexander the Great entered Asia), the frontiers of civilization were progressively enlarged until finally a great chain of intercommunicating states stretched across Eurasia from the Atlantic to the Pacific.

The eastward drive of Hellenism was ac-

Constructed with remarkable precision, this Chinese sundial from the Han period was superior to any devised in the West until the thirteenth century A.D. The base and vertical shaft have been reconstructed for this photograph.

companied by a marked increase in economic activity throughout western Asia and in the exchange of goods between East and West. The trade between India and the West took several routes (see map, p. 116). From northern India, caravans proceeded across Parthia, while ships from southern Indian ports sailed to meet overland routes across Mesopotamia, Arabia, and Egypt.

Monsoons encourage sea traffic. After Egypt and other Hellenistic areas had succumbed to Roman conquest, the Romans took over the rich trade with the East. From the Roman standpoint, the routes from India that centered on Syria had serious disadvantages: they led through Parthian territory, and the caravans were subject to heavy tolls by the Parthian government. The high profits that caravan merchants made as middlemen also boosted costs. Therefore Augustus and his successors encouraged the use of the southern sea route to India.

About 100 B.C. a most important discovery had been made when a Greek mariner found how to use the monsoon winds that blow from the southwest across the Arabian Sea from May to October. Eliminating the tedious journey along the coasts, sailors could now voyage from Aden to the west coast of India across the open sea. Furthermore, ships could return from India by using the countermonsoon blowing from the northeast between November and March. Thus round-trip voyages could be made in less than a year, and Strabo, the Greek geographer during the time of Augustus, stated that 120 ships sailed to India every year from Egyptian ports. This improvement in the sailing route encouraged western merchants to strike still farther east by ship, and they subsequently rounded the southern points of India and Ceylon.

The silk trade. The first move to pierce the land barrier separating China from the West was made by the Chinese rather than the Europeans. In 138 B.C. the Chinese emperor Wu Ti dispatched an ambassador into west Central Asia to seek allies against the Huns. Although the ambassador failed to secure

alliances, he aroused Wu Ti's curiosity by describing the lands beyond the Pamirs and by showing his ruler the alfalfa and grape seeds he had carried back with him to China. Wu Ti resolved to open up trade relations with the peoples to the west. Thus, as a result of Chinese initiative, the use of silk spread to the Mediterranean during the early part of the first century B.C.

The silk caravans from northwest China which passed through Turkestan and Parthia before reaching the Roman dominions were also subject to heavy tolls. By diverting the caravans around Parthia to Indian ports and by transporting goods in Roman ships from there to the Red Sea and Egypt, the price of silk was reduced. As a result of this seaborne competition, the silk trade became highly developed; the reduction of prices made this commodity available for more than just the wealthiest people in the West.

Severance of East-West contacts. Unfortunately for the cause of international relations,

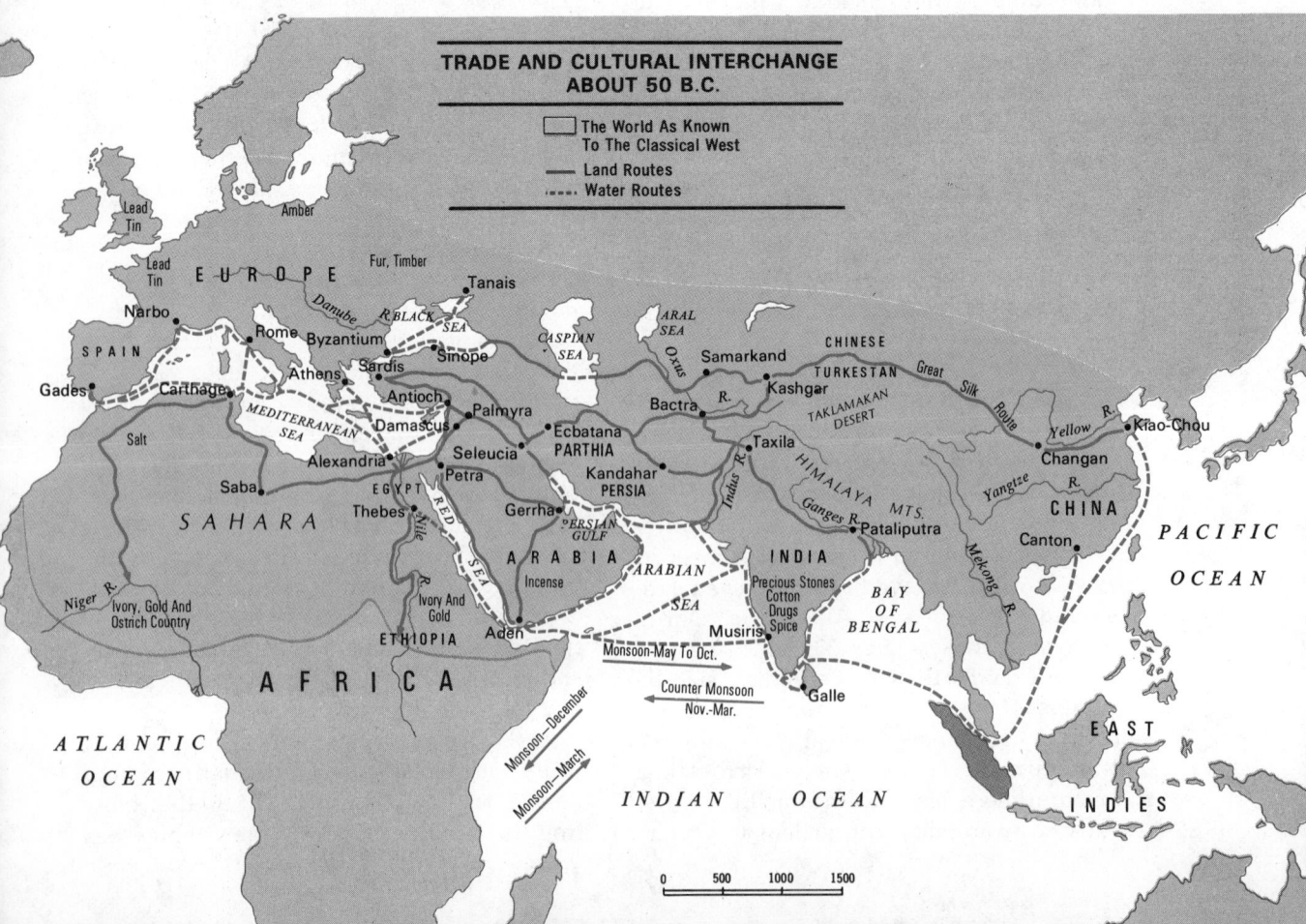

TRADE AND CULTURAL INTERCHANGE ABOUT 50 B.C.

commercial and cultural interchange among the three great civilizations of classical times was interrupted more and more frequently after the beginning of the third century A.D. With the overthrow of the Han dynasty in 220 A.D., China's power and prestige dwindled in Central Asia. By coincidence, at the same time the Kushan empire in northeast India succumbed, and Indian civilization also underwent a process of change and transition. About the same time, and probably most significant in the disruption of Eurasian relations, came the political and economic decline of the Graeco-Roman world (see Chapter 5).

An economic consequence of East-West trade. The volume of the Graeco-Roman world's oriental trade had been surprisingly large. Because Roman exports to the East did not match in quantity or value the empire's imports of silk, spices, perfumes, gems, and other luxuries, the West had suffered seriously from an adverse balance of trade. Thus precious metals were continually being exported to Asia. Pliny declared that India, China, and Arabia drained away annually at least 100,000,000 sesterces (about $5,000,000 at a time when dollars had more purchasing value than today)—"that is the sum which our luxuries and our women cost us."[14] The discovery of vast hoards of Roman coins in India supports Pliny's statement.

One scholar has estimated that between 31 B.C. and 192 A.D. alone, Rome's trade with the Orient cost Rome a net money loss of about $500,000,000. This serious drain, which took place at a time when the empire's known sources of gold and silver were being exhausted, was a prime cause of the deterioration of the imperial coinage and one of the factors in the general economic decline of the Roman world in the third century A.D.

The influence of West upon East. Roman contact with the East was made largely through trade with India and China and substantially increased the knowledge of both sections of the world about each other. But Greek influence was even more consequential.

There is little doubt that the strongest Greek influence on Indian civilization was in the field of sculpture, as demonstrated by the results of the Graeco-Buddhist school at Gandhara, which in turn affected art forms in China and even in Japan. For a time, Indian coinage also bore the strong imprint of Hellenistic influence. Indian astronomy, which made many significant advances in its own right, also benefited from Greek learning.

The influence of East upon West. The trade with both India and China made a powerful impact on the economy of the Graeco-Roman world, as we have pointed out, and those Romans and Greeks who could afford luxuries enjoyed a variety of spices, muslins, silks, and other goods.

Whatever the immediate impact upon the West may have been, the long-range consequences of its meeting with the East were quite significant. With the contact once established, cultural exchange was going to continue, even though sometimes at a slow pace and by indirect means. Medieval Europe was to benefit from the success of the classical civilizations in establishing contact with each other. For example, "Chinese technological inventions poured into Europe in a continuous stream during the first thirteen centuries of the Christian era, just as later on the technological current flowed the other way."[15] No longer can an educated westerner assume the attitude that the meeting of East and West has always demonstrated the superiority of the West.

SUMMARY

From about 2300 to 1800 B.C. the counterpart of the civilizations that developed along the Nile and the Tigris-Euphrates emerged along the Indus in India. Then about 1500 B.C. Aryan nomads invaded India, and as a result a new culture developed. During this Vedic Age the foundations of the unique socio-religious system of Hinduism were laid, and the three pillars of Indian society—the autonomous village, the caste system, and the joint-family—evolved. In the sixth century B.C. Gautama Buddha gave India a philosophy which has endured in Asia until the present.

During the fourth century B.C., shortly after the Hellenic Age in the West, the Mauryan emperors in India, especially the pious and gentle Ashoka, presided over a progressive and prosperous realm in India. This ruler sent missionaries throughout southern and eastern Asia, carrying the civilizing tenets of Buddhism. In turn the great Kushan monarch Kanishka further advanced Indian culture and encouraged the penetration of Buddhism into China.

The formative centuries of Chinese civilization began under the Shang dynasty about the end of Indus culture in India. Building on this advance, the Chou period (1027 or 1122-256 B.C.) was one of remarkable dynamism and creativity in technology and commerce. Its greatest achievement was the contribution to philosophy by Confucius, Mencius, and Lao-tzu. In the third century B.C. Ch'in, which embraced the philosophy of Legalism, established the first unified empire in Chinese history. While the Ch'in dynasty was short-lived, the imperial form of government it created was to endure for more than two thousand years. Its successor, the great Han dynasty (202 B.C. to 220 A.D.), gave China one of its most illustrious eras. Corresponding in time to the Roman Empire in the West, it carved out an extensive empire, especially in Central Asia.

During the centuries immediately preceding and following the birth of Christ, the great civilizations of the world—Graeco-Roman, Indian, and Chinese—were connected by tenuous routes of commercial and cultural exchange. Although this contact between East and West was eventually cut off, it continued long enough to establish a durable tradition in both the Orient and the Occident that beyond the mountains and the deserts to the east or to the west lay other great civilizations. This tradition incited adventurous spirits many centuries later to bring the "halves" of world civilization together once again.

SUGGESTIONS FOR READING

S. Piggott, **Prehistoric India*** (Penguin) describes the archaeological evidence for the Indus civilization. See also M. Wheeler, **Early India and Pakistan to Ashoka** (Westview, 1968); and Bridget and Raymond Allchin, **The Birth of Indian Civilization*** (Penguin). B. G. Gokhale, **Asoka Maurya** (Twayne, 1966); and R. Thapar, **Asoka and the Decline of the Mauryas** (Oxford) are two significant works on India's first empire. A. L. Basham, **The Wonder That Was India*** (Taplinger, 1968) is a comprehensive study of Indian culture prior to the coming of the Muslims in the elventh century.

S. Radhakrishnan, **The Hindu View of Life*** (Macmillan). Today's foremost Indian philosopher compares Hinduism with western philosophy. W. T. De Bary, *et al.* eds., **Sources of Indian Tradition,*** 2 vols. (Columbia) contains significant selections from Vedic and Upanishadic texts, with illuminating introductions. Excellent translations of Hindu religious texts are S. Prabhavananda and F. Manchester, trans., **The Upanishads: Breath of the Eternal*** (Mentor); and S. Prabhavananda and C. Isherwood, trans., **The Song of God—The Bhagavad-Gita*** (Vedanta).

C. Humphreys, **Buddhism*** (Penguin) describes the life of the Buddha and the rise of the major branches of Buddhism, as does Thomas Berry, **Buddhism*** (Apollo, 1975). E. A. Burtt, ed., **The Teachings of the Compassionate Buddha*** (Mentor) contains excerpts from Buddhist writings, including Chinese and Japanese.

John H. Marshall, **The Buddhist Art of Gandhara** (Cambridge); and H. Ingholt, **Gandharan Art in Pakistan** (Shoe String) are two books on the relationship of Indian and Graeco-Roman art. See also A. Coomaraswamy, **History of Indian and Indonesian Art*** (Verry), and **The Dance of Shiva*** (Noonday); and H. Zimmer,

Art of Indian Asia, 2 vols. (Princeton).

W. Watson, **China Before the Han Dynasty** (Praeger, 1966) is a good nontechnical survey. M. Granet, **Chinese Civilization*** (Meridian) covers the period down to Han times.

Fung Yu-lan, **A Short History of Chinese Philosophy*** (Free Press); and Liu Wu-chi, **A Short History of Confucian Philosophy*** (Penguin) are two excellent introductions. A. Waley, **Three Ways of Thought in Ancient China*** (Anchor) is a concise introduction to Confucianism, Taoism, and Legalism.

A major source of information and interpretation is J. Fairbank, E. Reischauer, and A. Craig, **East Asia: Tradition and Transformation** (Houghton Mifflin, 1973). W. T. De Bary, *et al.*, eds., **Sources of Chinese Tradition*** (Columbia, 1960) is an outstanding collection of translations with valuable commentaries.

I. Needham and Wang Ling, **Science and Civilization in China,** 7 vols. (Cambridge Univ.) is a major work. See also Chang Kuang-chih, **The Archaeology of Ancient China** (Yale, 1971).

On Chinese art see R. Grousset, **Chinese Art and Culture*** (Evergreen); and L. Sickman and L. Soper, **Art and Architecture of China*** (Penguin, 1971).

R. Wheeler, **Rome Beyond the Imperial Frontiers*** (Greenwood, 1972) is a well-illustrated study of Rome's trade with the East. See also E. C. Bagchi, **India and China: A Thousand Years of Cultural Relations,** 2nd ed. (Greenwood, 1971), a stimulating study.

*Indicates a less expensive paperbound edition.

The crowing of a cock awakened Marcus Ligustinus, who lived in the crowded, noisy, smelly working-class Subura district of Rome that stretched northward from the Forum. He knew that it was close to the first hour of the Roman twelve-hour day (and twelve-hour night), which began with sunrise. Since it was midwinter, the first hour began—in modern terms—at 7:30, and the twelfth hour would end with sunset at 4:30. (We follow the Romans in using the terms *ante meridiem*, "before midday," and *post meridiem*, "after midday," which we abbreviate as a.m. and p.m.) Marcus preferred the longer days and longer hours of midsummer, when the twelfth hour did not end until 7:30 and there was time for a siesta, even though sunrise came early. Most Roman commoners went to bed soon after sundown anyway, since both candles and the small olive oil lamps with their smoking wicks gave little light and were expensive.

The small bedroom was very stuffy and Marcus opened the tightly-closed window shutters and looked out on a large courtyard bounded by the wings of his four-story apartment building. Such apartment blocks were called *insulae* because they were "islands" surrounded on all four sides by streets. Flimsily built of wood by private capitalists in answer to the city's housing shortage, the *insulae* were one of Rome's gifts to civilization. They far outnumbered private homes and tenants could purchase their one- or two-room apartments (like modern condominiums), but renting was more common.

By our reckoning it was December 1, 107 B.C. To Marcus, too, it was December—the "tenth" month, so called because until 153 B.C., when it was changed to January 1, the Roman year had begun on March 1. The first day of the month was called the Kalends, from the verb *calo*, "to proclaim," since it was the day on which a priest announced which days had a religious significance. Marcus remembered it was also the day his rent was due and this made him angry, as it always did, at capitalist landlords.

Marcus awakened his two children, a boy of ten and a girl of eight. Back on their small five-acre farm his father had raised eight children, but in the city Marcus could not afford more than two. The number of Roman citizens was declining. Infant mortality had always been high—only one child in three reached the age of ten—and abortion had become common and would not be declared illegal until the end of the second century A.D. Marcus' wife, Turia, whom he had married when she was fourteen and he fifteen, had had two abortions (and several miscarriages) during

their ten-year marriage, but she was afraid to use the method of contraception favored by some of her friends—magical formulas and incantations. Some of Marcus' neighbors had also exercised their legal rights as heads of families to expose or abandon unwanted children.

The children rose from their cots and adjusted their woolen tunics, the basic garment worn day and night by all Romans. They followed their father to the adjoining room where Turia had just finished emptying the slop jar out of the one window onto the street three stories below. Before seating himself on one of the four stools beside the small table—the only furniture in the room— Marcus placed a bit of bread on a small boxlike shrine dedicated to the traditional spirits, the Lares and Penates, that guarded all Roman households. Then he addressed a prayer—taking great care not to stumble over the words lest the prayer lose its power—to Janus, the guardian spirit of the doorway for whom the month of January was named: "Father Janus, in offering to thee this sacrificial bread I make good prayers that thou be kind and favorable to me, my children, and my house and household."

A light breakfast was the first of the family's three daily meals, and Turia had taken from the cupboard a few olives, some wheat biscuits, and a round loaf of bread that Marcus had brought from the bakery where he worked as a miller. (Among lower-class Romans, men did all the shopping.) Marcus dipped his biscuit into a cup of warm wine to fortify himself against the long hours ahead before he returned for dinner at the ninth hour (1:30 in winter, 2:30 in summer). His dinner was always a thick porridge made from unground wheat, and supplemented by turnips, beans, olives, and figs. Sometimes honey, cheese, an egg, a bit of pork, or salted fish was added to the porridge. Marcus' third meal of the day, a light supper usually of bread and cheese, was eaten soon after sunset before retiring. Turia did all her cooking on a portable brazier filled with charcoal (coal was unknown), which also served as the sole source of heat in winter.

After breakfast Turia turned to her household chores, chiefly spinning woolen thread and weaving the rough cloth with which she made all the family's clothing. Marcus dropped his son off at the one-room school where he was learning reading, writing, and simple arithmetic with the aid of an abacus. Here a wealthy man had installed one of his Greek slaves as a teacher (*grammaticus*) of any boy whose father could afford the small fee. Marcus' son knew he was fortunate to be able to go to school, but he still looked forward to the long summer vacation from July 1 to October 15.

Like the school, the bakery where Marcus worked was located on the ground floor of his apartment building. Here the odor of freshly-baked bread mingled with that of a pig that served as a sort of vacuum cleaner to keep the floor clear of wheat husks. Marcus was in charge of the shop's stone flour mill which stood as high as a man and whose hollow top stone, into which the grain was poured, was rotated by a slave.

At midday all shops closed, and although they opened again after dinner, Marcus' working day was over. Throughout the year he usually worked six hours a day, and since the Roman work week consisted of seven days, he thus worked a 42-hour week. Marcus was a firm believer in the popular Roman slogan: "Six hours are enough for work: after that sample life."

Marcus "sampled life" in a variety of ways. Most exciting were the great state religious festivals called games (ludi). Each provided entertainment for a week or more for a total of 59 days during the year. On many days Greek and Roman tragedies and comedies were performed, but far more popular were coarse mimes which mimicked, usually without dialogue, the everyday life of the common people. Between acts jugglers, clowns, boxers, and wrestlers performed. A procession of nude girls served as a finale.

The most popular feature of the games was the chariot races held in the Circus Maximus. Marcus and his family, dressed in their formal togas, would leave home before dawn in order to find places on the wooden planks built up behind the stone seats that were reserved for senators and capitalists. Excitedly they would bet on a favorite charioteer and watch him risk life and limb as he whipped his horses around the oval course. Twelve races, each of seven laps (about five miles) were run each day. Sometimes the family would watch bloody fights to the death between gladiators (war prisoners and condemned criminals), animal fights (bulls against elephants, for example), and wild beast hunts, but these were privately promoted and not a part of the official games.

Other religious festivals that did not include games or other entertainment provided Marcus with another 45 public holidays during the year. Marcus' favorite was Anna Perenna on March 15, the festival of the first full moon during what had once been the first month of the Roman year. Held on the river bank north of the city, it was a veritable "pop festival" during which everyone drank much wine—a glass for every future year of one's life—and in the evening reeled homeward in a tipsy procession.

Rome had many wine shops catering to the lower classes, where heated wine and snacks were cheap and prostitutes charged six copper *asses* (the price of two loaves of bread), but Marcus seldom patronized such places. He was no puritan, but he could not be extravagant on his daily wage of 16 *asses*. He preferred the parties given by the miller's burial society (*collegium*), where he drank wine contributed by new members and munched on bread and sardines. The society's entrance fee was steep but it gave Marcus much satisfaction to know that when he died his body would not be thrown into a common pauper's grave outside the city walls. He would receive an honorable burial with his remains cremated and the ashes placed in an urn and set in one of the many niches of a wall-like tomb.

Marcus' favorite recreation was the public baths, where he spent most afternoons. The baths were privately owned, but the fee was nominal and often it was paid by some candidate for public office seeking votes. The baths provided Marcus many relaxing hours as he leisurely progressed through the sequence of rooms—the dry sweat room, the warm room where a slave scraped the sweat from his body (soap was unknown), the tepid room for cooling off, and the invigorating cold bath. Another popular room was the lavatory with its long row of marble toilets equipped with comfortable arm rests; here Marcus liked to sit for an hour or more chatting with other patrons.

When the baths closed at sundown, Marcus was usually in such a good mood that he would sometimes stop at a shop for some hot food to carry home for supper. And as he hurried homeward, he would break out in song: "Baths, sex, and wine our bodies undermine; Yet what is life but baths and sex and wine?"

6. (preceding page) **Hagia Sophia, Istanbul** (532-537 A.D.). By the sixth century the gradual decline of the Roman Empire had emptied the Graeco-Roman classical tradition of nearly all its strength. The imperial capital had been moved from Italy to Constantinople in 330. Christianity was now the state religion and already showing signs of becoming what it was destined to be: a primary force in shaping the world of the next 1000 years. Europe was on the brink of the Middle Ages. At this moment of climactic transition in western history, Hagia Sophia was erected, an immense stone symbol linking past and future. The grandeur of its construction — it is one of the greatest domed vaults of all time — recalls the glory of Rome, while its almost mystical il-

lumination and spiritualized atmosphere prefigure the coming dominance of the Christian faith. After Constantinople was captured by the Turks in 1453, Hagia Sophia became an Islamic mosque, serving in this capacity until recently, when it was converted into a museum. 7. (above) **Muhammad Ascending to Paradise** (sixteenth century). Islam's meteoric rise to power and subsequent hegemony in the whole Middle East were attended by notable, often superb, achievements in the arts. This manuscript page from Persia was executed at a time when influences from both Christianity and the Far East relaxed the abhorrence Muslims traditionally felt toward making images of Muhammad. Note, however, that the Prophet's face is blank.

8. Ireland: "Christ Enthroned" from **Book of Kells** (c. 800). With the final dissolution of the Roman Empire, the pendulum of European civilization swung to the north where the barbarian peoples were gradually converted to Christianity. The Irish assumed the spiritual and cultural leadership of western Europe during this period and their monasteries were centers of Christian culture. Their manuscripts were considered sacred objects that contained the Holy Writ and much effort was put into decorative embellishment largely detached from physical reality.

9. The French town of Conques, with the Church of Ste. Foy (eleventh century). By the eleventh century a wave of religious fervor swept across the Continent. Hosts of pilgrims traveled set routes to sacred sites, and along these routes towns sprang up. The towns erected churches, which were grander than ever before, and whose complex floor plans could more readily accommodate the traffic of the pilgrims. Christianity began to belong to the masses, and the flowering of the Middle Ages grew increasingly evident in the stately towers and arches of the monumental Romanesque style.

PART TWO
The Middle Ages

■ When we speak of the "fall" of Rome, perhaps we forget that the great classical tradition was carried on for another thousand years without interruption in Constantinople, or "New Rome." Until it fell in 1453 the Byzantine empire acted as a buffer for western Europe, staving off attack after attack from the east. The culminating series of attacks, resulting in the collapse of the empire, was launched by the adherents of Islam—a dynamic way of life developed by the followers of Muhammad, an eloquent prophet who instilled in his people a vital sense of their destiny to rule in the name of Allah. With unbelievable swiftness, the followers of the Prophet became rulers of the Near East, swept across North Africa and surged into Spain, and expanded eastward to the frontiers of China. The Muslims, the great middlemen of medieval times, shuttled back and forth across vast expanses, trading the wares of East and West and acting as the conveyors of culture. Throughout most of the Middle Ages, the East outshone the West even as Constantinople and Baghdad outdazzled in material magnificence and intellectual and artistic triumphs any capital in western Europe.

In Europe, after the inundation of the Roman Empire by Germanic tribes in the fifth century brought disorder and fragmentation, a painful search for stability began. Centuries of confusion followed until Charlemagne established a new "Roman" empire. This ambitious and laudable experiment was premature, however, and after its collapse a new system had to be created—one which would offer at least a minimum of security, political organization, and law enforcement. This was feudalism. Under this system, the landed nobility acted as police force, judiciary, and army. Accompanying feudalism was the manorial system—an economic order which provided food and life's necessities and divided men into two great classes: the fighters or nobles and the workers or serfs.

Crude as it was, feudalism served to mitigate the chaos which followed the fall of Charlemagne's empire. Yet feudalism and the manorial system were inherently rural and rigid, and by the eleventh century new forces were at work. Shadowy outlines of new kingdoms—Germany, England, France, and Spain—began to emerge under the direction of vigorous monarchs. Europe went on the offensive, ejecting the Muslims from the southern part of the Continent, breaking Muslim control of the Mediterranean, and launching crusades to capture Jerusalem from the infidel. The "closed" economy of the feudal countryside gave way before the revival of trade and communications, the growth of towns, the increased use of money as a medium of exchange, and the rise of a new class in society—the bourgeoisie.

The greatest stabilizing force in Europe during the medieval period was the Church. The Middle Ages has sometimes been characterized as the Age of Faith; to an extent greater than in classical or modern times, the attention of men living in those days was directed toward a religious goal —the salvation of the soul—and the Church was the great arbiter of human destiny. With the authority that stemmed from its vital spiritual service, the Church provided the nearest approach to effective and centralized supervision of European life. All men were born, lived, and died under its protection. In the thirteenth century, when popes such as Innocent III bent proud monarchs to their will, the Church reached the zenith of its influence as a kind of international government as well as the focus of medieval society, arts, and scholarship. The Church was the chief patron of poets and artists; its monasteries were repositories for precious manuscripts; and it fostered a new institution of learning— the university.

During the ten centuries commonly referred to as the medieval period in the West, great civilizations in India and China experienced their golden ages while Europe was struggling to build a new and viable civilization on the debris of the defunct Roman Empire. In Gupta India the government was stable, and science and the arts flourished. Under the rule of the T'ang and Sung dynasties, Chinese life was enriched by notable creativity. Later, Mongol conquerors, symbolized by Genghis Khan, put together the largest empire in the world, stretching west from China as far as Russia and Mesopotamia. And influenced greatly by China, the proud and independent Japanese developed a unique culture pattern characterized best by the *samurai*, the knight, and the *bushido*, the code of the warrior.

CHAPTER 5

The Rise of Christianity and the Fall of Rome

The City of God

INTRODUCTION. To the inhabitants of the Graeco-Roman world, Rome was the "Eternal City"—a proud designation which is still used today. When, therefore, in 410 A.D. the barbarian Visigoths responded to its magnetic lure by entering Italy and sacking the city, a cry of anguish reverberated throughout the crumbling Empire. In distant Bethlehem St. Jerome cried, "The lamp of the world is extinguished, and it is the whole world which has perished in the ruins of this one city."[1]

This chapter completes the history of Rome—it tells of the fall of the City of the Caesars and the emergence, like the phoenix arising from the ashes, of the "City of God." It was St. Augustine who, in the wake of the Visigoths' capture of Rome, devised that phrase to represent the rise of a new Christian society on the ruins of paganism and a once invincible Empire—and to assure Christians that the "community of the Most High" would endure, although the greatest city on earth had fallen.

This period in history has several facets.

One concerns the national history of the Jews, the coming of Jesus in the midst of their turbulent relations with the Romans, and the eventual triumph of his teachings. Another is the story of the progressive decline of the Roman Empire during the time of Christianity's triumph. A third element is the migration of the Germanic peoples and their settlement in Europe—a movement which completed the disintegration of the western half of the Roman Empire. A final aspect (to be discussed in the next chapter) is the shift in civilization's center of gravity —from the West, overrun by barbarians, to the eastern shores of the Mediterranean and even beyond.

THE RISE AND TRIUMPH OF CHRISTIANITY

Post-exilic Jewish nationalism. At the very time when the Principate of Augustus was laying the foundations of Rome's imperial greatness, events were taking place in the distant Roman province of Judea that would one day alter the course of western history. Following the conquests of Alexander the Great in the Near East, Palestine was ruled first by the Ptolemies and then by the Seleucids. Since their return from exile in Babylonia in 538 B.C. (see p. 30), the Jews in Palestine had created a theocratic community, based upon the Torah, God's Law, originally revealed to Moses and contained in the Pentateuch (the first five books of the Old Testament), and later supplemented by the teachings of the prophets and the writings of scholars. Religious life centered on the Temple at Jerusalem, which echoed with the cry "Hallelujah" ("Praise ye Yahweh") in thanksgiving for Yahweh's gracious dealing with his people. The most powerful figure was the high priest, assisted by the Sanhedrin, the high court for the enforcement of the Law. Since there was no distinction between civil and religious law, the jurisdiction of the Sanhedrin covered all aspects of Jewish life.

The Hebrews, the "People of God," were tightly knit; even the Jewish groups outside Palestine were linked by spiritual bonds to the Temple and to a law which they believed to be divinely inspired. But, being unable to participate in the services of the Temple at Jerusalem, the Jews of the Diaspora met in local synagogues (from the Greek word for "assembly") for informal worship and instruction in the Scriptures. In the long run, the synagogue, which probably first arose during the Babylonian Exile, outlived the Temple to become the heart of Judaism. It also influenced the forms of worship in the Christian church and the Muslim mosque.

During the Hellenistic Age, Greek influences were constantly at work among the Jews. Most Jews outside Palestine spoke Greek, and a Greek translation of the Hebrew Scriptures became a necessity. Called the Septuagint (Latin for "seventy") from the tradition that it was the work of seventy scholars whose independent translations were miraculously identical, it was produced at Alexandria in the third century B.C.

Greek influences contributed to factionalism among the Jews in Judea. Eventually, one extremely pious group came to blows with the aristocratic pro-Greek Sadducees, as they came to be called, who were favored by the Seleucid rulers of Palestine. The internal conflict gave the Seleucid king an opportunity to intervene, and in 168 B.C., seeking to completely Hellenize the Jews, he ordered the Temple dedicated to the worship of Zeus. Viewing this decree as a blasphemous defilement, the Jews rebelled. Under their leader, Judas Maccabaeus, they rededicated the Temple to Yahweh and in 142 B.C. won their independence from the Seleucids.

Although Judas and his immediate successors contented themselves with the title of high priest, later members of the family were known as kings. In time these rulers became worldly and corrupt, and factionalism again flared up, resulting in persecution and bloodshed. It was in the midst of a civil war that the Roman legions appeared on the scene.

Roman occupation of Palestine. Adopting the practice habitually followed by eastern Mediterranean states, one Jewish faction appealed to Rome for aid. Pompey, who was then completing his pacification of Asia Minor and Syria (see p. 74), ended the civil war in 63 B.C. by making Judea subject to the governor of Syria.

Eventually, Herod the Great, a half-Jewish, half-Arab leader from Edom just south of Judea, rose to power as a tool of the Romans. Appointed by Mark Antony, Herod served as king of Judea from 37 to 4 B.C. He erected a magnificent palace, a theater, a hippodrome, and rebuilt the Temple on a lavish scale. To the Jews, however, Herod remained a detested usurper who professed Judaism as a matter of expediency. Soon after his death, Judea was made into a minor Roman province ruled by governors called procurators, the best known of whom is Pontius Pilate (26-36 A.D.), under whom Jesus was crucified.

The Jews themselves remained unhappy and divided. During centuries of tribulation the prophets had taught that God would one day create a new Israel when righteousness prevailed under a God-anointed leader, the Messiah. In time, many Jews lost hope in a political Messiah and an earthly kingdom and instead conceived of a spiritual Messiah who would lead all the righteous, including the resurrected dead, to a spiritual kingdom. But a group of ardent Jewish nationalists, called Zealots, favoring the use of force to drive the hated foreigner out of God's land, precipitated a fatal clash with Rome.

Destruction of Jerusalem. In 66 A.D. violence erupted when the Roman garrison at Jerusalem was massacred. After a five-year siege, Titus, son of the emperor Vespasian, laid waste the city. What came to be called the "Wailing Wall," a small part of the Temple complex, remained standing. The story is that it was protected by angels whose tears cemented the stones in place forever. It was later prophesied that a third Temple would be erected on the site when the Messiah came. (The Dome of the Rock, a mosque built by the Muslims, has occupied the site since the eighth century A.D.) The wholesale destruction of Jerusalem in 70 A.D. spelled the end of the ancient Hebrew state. The Jewish dream of an independent homeland was to remain unrealized for almost nineteen centuries, until the republic of Israel was proclaimed in 1948.

Development of Jewish religious thought. The destruction of Jerusalem did not destroy the most important single aspect of Jewish culture—its religion. Through centuries of suffering, captivity, and subjugation, the Jews had been taught by a succession of prophets to cleave to their covenant with Yahweh and to safeguard their religious inheritance.

In the centuries just preceding and following the birth of Christ, Judaism exhibited vigor and strength. While the aristocratic Sadducees, who controlled the office of high priest, stood for strict adherence to the written Law or Torah, the more numerous Pharisees believed that, with divine guidance, men could modify and amend the Law. For example, they accepted the belief in personal immortality and the Kingdom of Heaven. From their ranks came the rabbis, scholars who expounded the Law and applied it to existing conditions. The "oral law" propagated by the Pharisees became the core of the later Talmud. Moreover, following the destruction of the Temple and the end of the high priesthood, the rabbinical schools of the Pharisees did much to ensure that Judaism would endure.

The Dead Sea Scrolls. In recent years the discovery of the Dead Sea Scrolls has added greatly to our knowledge of another Jewish sect, the Essenes. While exploring caves about the desolate western shore of the Dead Sea in 1947, two Bedouin boys came across several clay jars containing long manuscripts wrapped in linen. Later, many more scrolls were found in other caves. Nearby were the ruins of a monastery built by the Essenes "to separate themselves," as the scrolls state, "from the abode of perverse men." Occupied between the second century B.C. and 68 A.D., the monastery was destroyed by the Romans during the great Jewish revolt. Prior to its destruction the Essenes hid their manuscripts in the caves.

Some scrolls are portions of the Old Testament dating from the first century B.C. and

The partially unrolled Thanksgiving Scroll, one of the Dead Sea Scrolls preserved at the Hebrew University in Jerusalem, is composed of religious hymns which poetically develop the Essenes' theological doctrines.

thus are centuries older than the earliest text previously known. Jewish and Christian scholars alike have been thrilled to read the Book of Isaiah in such ancient manuscript and to discover that the version we have been using, although based on much later sources, has been accurate except in some details.

Those scrolls which describe the Essene sect in the first century B.C.—that is, just prior to the appearance of Christianity—have been said to constitute "a whole missing chapter of the history of the growth of religious ideas between Judaism and Christianity."[2] Some scholars have attached much significance to common elements in the beliefs and practices of the Essenes and early Christians. The Essenes' founder, a shadowy figure known as the Teacher of Righteousness, suffered persecution and perhaps martyrdom late in the second century B.C. The sect considered itself the true remnant of God's people, preached a "new covenant," and waited patiently for the time when God would destroy the powers of evil and inau-

gurate His Kingdom. Similar views concerning the transition from the "Old Age" to the "New Age" were held by many other Jews as well as by Christians. For the Christians, however, the gap had been bridged. The Messiah had come, and his resurrection was proof that the New Age had arrived. "The New Testament faith was not a new faith, but the fulfillment of an old faith. . . . Lines of continuity between Moses and Jesus, Isaiah and Jesus, the Righteous Teacher and Jesus, John the Baptist and Jesus should occasion no surprise. On the contrary, a biblical faith insists on such continuities. . . . [The Bible is] a history of God's acts of redemption."[3]

The life of Jesus. Whatever its parallels with the Essene sect—including baptism and a communal meal—Christianity bears the unmistakable imprint of the personality of its founder, Jesus of Nazareth. According to the Biblical account, he was born in Bethlehem during the reign of Herod; therefore he may have been born by the time of Herod's death (4 B.C.) rather than in the year which traditionally begins the Christian era. After spending the first years of his life as a carpenter in the village of Nazareth, Jesus began his brief mission, preaching a gospel of love for one's fellow man and urging people to "Repent, for the kingdom of heaven is at hand" (Matthew 4:17).

The fame of Jesus' teaching and holiness spread among the Jews as he and his twelve disciples traveled from village to village in Palestine. When he came to Jerusalem to observe the feast of the Passover, he was welcomed triumphantly by huge crowds as the promised Messiah. But Jesus was concerned with a spiritual, not an earthly, kingdom, and when the people saw that he had no intention of leading a nationalistic movement against the Romans, they turned against him. His enemies then came forward—the moneylenders whom he had denounced, the Pharisees who resented his repudiation of their minute regulations of daily behavior, the people who considered him a disturber of the status quo, and those who saw him as a blasphemer of Yahweh. Betrayed by Judas, one of his disciples, Jesus was condemned by the Sanhedrin for blasphemy "because he claimed to be the Son of God" (John 19:7). Before the procurator Pontius Pilate, however, Jesus was charged with treason for claiming to be the king of Jews.

"Are you the king of Jews?" he [Pilate] asked him. Jesus answered, . . . "My kingdom does not belong to this world; if my kingdom belonged to this world, my followers would fight to keep me from being handed over to the Jews. No, my kingdom does not belong here. . . . You say that I am a king. I was born and came into the world for this one purpose, to speak about the truth. Whoever belongs to the truth listens to me." "And what is truth?" Pilate asked.[4]

Jesus was condemned to the death that Rome inflicted on criminals—crucifixion.

With Jesus' death it seemed as though his cause had been exterminated. No written message had been left behind, and his few loyal followers were disheartened. Yet in the wake of his martyrdom the Christian cause took on new impetus. Reports soon spread that Jesus had been seen after his crucifixion and had spoken to his disciples, giving them solace and inspiration. At first there were few converts within Palestine itself, but the Hellenized Jews living in foreign lands, in contact with new ideas and modes of living, were less firmly committed to traditional Jewish doctrines. The new religion first made real headway among the Jewish communities in such cities as Damascus, Antioch, Corinth, and Rome.

Paul's missionary work. As long as the followers of Jesus regarded him exclusively as a Messiah in the traditional Jewish sense, requiring his followers to observe the Jewish Law, the new religion could have no universal appeal. Largely through the missionary efforts of Paul, this obstacle was removed.

Born Saul, of strict Jewish ancestry, and raised in a Hellenistic city in Asia Minor, this Christian saint possessed a wide knowledge of Greek culture. Saul was also a strict Pharisee who considered Christians to be blasphemers against the Law and took an active part in their persecution. One day, on the road to Damascus—in Saul's own words:

And as I was traveling and coming near Damascus, about midday a bright light suddenly flashed from the sky around me. I fell to the ground and heard a voice saying to me, "Saul, Saul! Why do you persecute me?" "Who are you, Lord?" I asked. "I am Jesus of Nazareth, whom you persecute," he said to me. The men with me saw the light but did not hear the voice of the one who was speaking to me. I asked, "What shall I do, Lord?" and the Lord said to me, "Get up and go into Damascus, and there you will be told everything that God has determined for you."[5]

Saul, henceforth known as Paul, turned from being a persecutor into the greatest of Christian missionaries.

Paul taught that Jesus was the Christ (from *Christos*, Greek for "Messiah"), the Son of God, and that He had died to atone for the sins of mankind. Acceptance of this belief guaranteed salvation to Jews and gentiles alike. The Law, with its strict dietary regulations and other requirements that discouraged the conversion of gentiles, was unnecessary:

A man is put right with God only through faith in Jesus Christ, never by doing what the Law requires. . . . So there is no difference between Jews and Gentiles, between slaves and free men, between men and women: you are all one in union with Christ Jesus.[6]

Tradition states that after covering eight thousand miles teaching and preaching, Paul was beheaded at Rome about 65 A.D. (as was also Peter, founder of the church at Rome) during the reign of Nero. By this time Christian communities had already been established in all important cities of the Roman Empire.

Persecution of Christians. The Roman government tolerated any religion that did not threaten the safety or tranquility of the Empire. Christianity, however, clearly appeared to be a subversive danger to society and the state. The Christians refused to participate in the worship of the emperor which, although not an official state religion, was considered an essential patriotic rite uniting all Roman subjects in common loyalty to the imperial government. To Christians there was only one God; no other could share their loyalty to Him. In the eyes of the Roman officials this attitude branded them as traitors. In addition, the Christians seemed a secret, unsociable group forming a state within a state—"walling themselves off from the rest of mankind," as a pagan writer observed. Many were pacifists who refused to serve in the army, and all were intolerant of other religious sects and refused to associate with pagans or take part in social functions that they considered sinful or degrading.

During the first two centuries A.D. persecution was only sporadic and local, like that at Rome under Nero (see p. 76). But during the late third and early fourth centuries, when, as we shall see, the Empire was in danger of collapse, three organized empire-wide efforts were made to suppress Christianity. By far the longest and most systematic campaign against the Christians, who now comprised perhaps one tenth of the population, was instigated by the emperor Diocletian from 303 to 311. But the inspired defiance of the Christian martyrs, who seemed to welcome death—"The blood of the martyrs is the seed of the Church" are the words of a third-century Christian[7]—could not be overcome.

Official recognition and acceptance. In 311 the emperor Galerius recognized that persecution had failed and issued an edict of toleration making Christianity a legal religion in the East. In the following year the emperor Constantine was swayed toward Christianity during a desperate battle with the army of a rival for the throne. At the height of the conflict, tradition has it that he saw emblazoned across the sky a cross with the words *In hoc signo vinces* ("By this sign thou shalt conquer"). Constantine won the battle, and in 313 he issued the Edict of Milan, which legalized Christianity throughout the Empire and put it on a par with all the pagan cults. Constantine favored Christianity by granting many privileges to the Church, but he waited until he was on his deathbed before receiving baptism. His successors, with one exception, were Christians.

In his brief reign (361-363) the scholarly emperor Julian, Constantine's nephew, who had been raised a Christian, renounced his faith and sought to revive paganism; as a result, he was branded the Apostate. Julian did not persecute the Christians ("Those who are in the wrong in matters of supreme importance," he wrote, "are objects of pity rather than of hate"[8]), and his efforts to revive paganism failed dismally. On his deathbed he is supposed to have said, "Thou hast conquered, O Galilean."

The Church of St. Apollinare in Classe, outside Ravenna, is an early basilica (from the Greek, *basilikos*, meaning "kingly") which Justinian erected on the site of a temple of Apollo. The Church itself dates from the sixth century; the round bell tower at the right is a tenth-century addition.

The final step in the triumph of Christianity was taken during the reign of Theodosius I (379-395), who made Christianity the official religion of the Empire. Henceforth paganism was persecuted, and even the Olympic games were suppressed.

Reasons for the spread of Christianity. In its rise to preeminence Christianity competed with the philosophies and religions of the day. The philosophies were becoming more religious and other-worldly, however, which made it easy for their adherents to accept a Christianity whose doctrines, as we shall see, were becoming more philosophical. During the early Empire most Roman intellectuals had embraced Stoicism which, unlike Epicureanism with its unyielding materialism, had room for God (see p. 86). The dominant philosophy of the third century, Neo-Platonism, rejected human reason and taught that the only reality is spirit and that the soul's principal objective is to escape from the material world and, by union with God, return to its spiritual home.

There were also the popular mystery religions such as the worship of the Phrygian Great Mother (Cybele), the Egyptian Isis, the Greek Dionysus, and the Persian Mithras, god of light who fought against darkness (Mithras was especially popular with soldiers). All of these cults presented the comforting idea of a divine savior and the promise of everlasting life. Their followers found Christian beliefs and practices sufficiently familiar so as to make conversion easy.

But Christianity had far more to offer than did the mystery religions. Its founder was not a creature of myth, like the gods and goddesses of the mystery cults, but a real historic personality whose lofty ethical teachings and whose death and resurrection as the divine incarnation of God were preserved in detail in a unique record—the New Testament. Also unique was the Christian God—the omnipotent, jealous yet loving God of the Hebrew Scriptures now universalized as the God of all mankind. Moreover, Christianity was a dynamic, aggressive faith. It upheld the equality of all men—Jesus' ministry was chiefly to the poor and downtrodden—taught that a loving Father had

A view of the interior of the Church of St. Apollinare looking toward the apse. The fine mosaic work throughout dates from the second half of the sixth century and reflects strong Byzantine influence. The richly ornamented interior of St. Apollinare is in sharp contrast to the austere brick exterior (see photo, p. 126). This is a characteristic of early Christian architecture and may have been intended to greatly emphasize the difference between the everyday world as contrasted with the spiritual magnificence of the Kingdom of God.

sent His only Son to atone for men's sins, and offered a vision of immortality and an opportunity to be "born again" cleansed of sin. Its converts displayed enthusiasm and zeal, and the courage with which they faced death and persecution impressed even their bitterest enemies. In time, also, a Church organization was created that was far more united and efficient than any possessed by its competitors.

Church organization. The years immediately following Christ's death had passed with little organization in the Christian movement. Viewing the present world as something that would end quickly with the imminent Second Coming of their Lord, the earliest converts saw no necessity for organization. But after it became clear that the Second Coming had been postponed, a definite Church organization began to emerge.

At first there was little or no distinction

between laity and clergy. Traveling teachers visited Christian communities, preaching and giving advice where needed. But the steady growth in the number of Christians made necessary special Church officials who could devote all their time to religious work, clarifying the body of Christian dogma, conducting services, and caring for the funds. The earliest officials were called presbyters (elders) or bishops (overseers). By the second century the offices of bishop and presbyter had become distinct. Churches in the villages adjacent to the mother Church, which was usually located in a city, were administered by priests (a corruption of *presbyter*) responsible to a bishop. Thus evolved the diocese, a territorial administrative division under the jurisdiction of a bishop. Furthermore, the bishops were recognized as the successors of the apostles and, like them, the guardians of Christian teaching and tradition.

A number of dioceses made up a province; the bishop of the most important city in each province enjoyed more prestige than his fellows and was known as an archbishop or metropolitan. The provinces were grouped into larger administrative divisions called patriarchates. The title of patriarch was applied to the bishop of such great cities as Rome, Constantinople, and Alexandria.

Primacy of the bishop of Rome. A development of outstanding importance was the rise of the bishop of Rome to a position of preeminence in the hierarchy of the Church. At first only one of several patriarchs, the Roman bishop gradually became recognized as the leader of the Church in the West with the title of pope—from the Greek word meaning "father."

Many factors explain the emergence of the papacy at Rome. As the largest city in the West and the capital of the Empire, Rome had an aura of prestige that was transferred to its bishop. When the Empire in the West collapsed in the fifth century, the bishop of Rome emerged as a stable and dominant figure looked up to by all. The primacy of Rome was fully evident during the pontificate of Leo i, called the Great (440-461), who provided both the leadership that saved Italy from invasion by the Huns (see p. 135) and

the major theoretical support for papal headship of the Church—the Petrine theory. This doctrine held that since Peter, whom Christ had made leader of the apostles, was the first bishop of Rome, his authority over all Christians was handed on to his successors at Rome. The Church in the East, insisting on the equality of all the apostles, has never accepted the Petrine theory.

Foundations of Christian doctrine and worship. While the administrative structure of the Church was being erected, Christian beliefs were being defined and systematized. This process of fixing the dogma began with Paul, who stressed the divinity of Jesus and interpreted his death as an atonement for man's sins.

In time differences of opinion over doctrinal matters caused clashes. One of the most important controversies was over Arianism. At issue was the relative position of the three persons of the Trinity—God the Father, God the Son, and God the Holy Spirit. The view that the Father and the Son were equal was vigorously denied by Arius (256-336), a priest of Alexandria, who believed that Christ was not fully God because he was not of a substance identical with God and, as a created being, was not coeternal with Him. The controversy became so serious that in 325 the emperor Constantine convened the first ecumenical Church council, the Council of Nicaea, to resolve the problem. With Constantine presiding, the council branded the Arian belief a heresy— an opinion or doctrine contrary to the official teachings of the Church—and Christ was declared to be of the same substance as God, uncreated, and coeternal with Him. This mystical concept of the Trinity, without which the central Christian doctrine of the incarnation would be undermined, received official formulation in the Nicene Creed. Despite persecution, Arianism continued to flourish throughout the fourth century, and we shall see that some of the German tribes had been converted to this Christian heresy before they invaded the Empire.

The liturgy in the early churches was plain and simple, consisting of prayer, Scripture reading, hymns, and preaching. The early Christian worshiped God and sought salvation largely through his own efforts. Following the growth of Church organization and dogma, however, the Church was believed to be the indispensable intermediary between God and man. Without the Church the individual could not hope to approach God.

The development of the Church's dogma owed much to the Church Fathers of the second through fifth centuries. Since most of them were intellectuals who came to Christianity by way of Neo-Platonism and Stoicism, they maintained that Greek philosophy and Christianity were compatible. Because reason (*logos* in Greek) and truth come from God, "philosophy was a preparation," wrote Clement of Alexandria (d. 215), "paving the way towards perfection in Christ,"[9] the latest and most perfect manifestation of God's reason. Thus Christianity was viewed as a superior philosophy which could supersede all pagan philosophies and religions.

In the West three Church Fathers stand out. The scholarship of St. Jerome (340-420) made possible the famous Vulgate translation of the Bible into Latin, which in a revised form is still the official translation of the Roman Catholic Church. St. Ambrose (340-397) resigned his government post to become bishop of Milan, where he employed his great administrative skills to establish a model bishopric. By reproving the actions of the strong emperor Theodosius I and forcing him to do public penance, St. Ambrose was the first to assert the Church's superiority over the state in spiritual matters. St. Augustine (354-430) was probably the most important of all the Church Fathers. At the age of thirty-two he found in Christianity the answer to his long search for meaning in life, as he relates in his *Confessions*, one of the world's great autobiographies. As bishop of Hippo in North Africa, he wrote more than a hundred religious works which became the foundation of much of the Church's theology.

The regular clergy. So far we have discussed the secular clergy, who moved through the world (*saeculum*) administering the Church's services and communicating its teachings to the laity. But another type of churchmen also arose—the regular clergy, so called because they lived by a rule (*regula*) within monasteries. These monks sought seclusion from the distractions of this world in order to prepare themselves for the next.

The monastic way of life was older than Christianity, having existed in Judaism, for example, among the Essenes (see pp. 123–124). Christian ascetics, who had abandoned the worldly life and become hermits, could be found in the East as early as the third century A.D. Some went so far as to denounce even beauty as evil and, in pursuit of spiritual perfection by subordinating their flesh, tortured themselves and fasted to excess. In Syria, for example, St. Simeon Stylites lived for thirty-seven years on top of a pillar sixty feet high.

As a more moderate expression of asceticism, Christians in Egypt developed the monastic life, wherein men seeking a common spiritual goal lived together under a common set of regulations. St. Basil (330-379), a Greek bishop in Asia Minor, drew up a rule based on work, charity, and a communal life in which, however, each monk retained most of his independence. The Rule of St. Basil became the standard system in the eastern Church.

In western monasticism the work of St. Benedict (c. 480-543) paralleled St. Basil's efforts in the East. About 529 St. Benedict led a band of followers to a hill between Rome and Naples, named Monte Cassino, where they erected a monastery on the site of an ancient pagan temple. There he composed a rule which gave order and discipline to western monasticism. Benedictine monks took the three basic vows of poverty, chastity, and obedience to the abbot, the head of the monastery. Unlike eastern monks, the daily activities of the Benedictine monks were closely regulated: they participated in eight divine services, labored in field or workshop for six or seven hours, and spent about two hours studying and preserving the writings of Latin antiquity at a time when chaos and illiteracy had overtaken the western half of the Roman Empire. Benedictine monasticism was to be the most dynamic civilizing force in western Europe between the sixth and the twelfth centuries.

DECLINE AND DIVISION IN THE ROMAN WORLD

The crisis of the third century. In the third century A.D., while Christianity was spreading throughout the Roman world, internal anarchy and foreign invasion drastically transformed the nature of the Empire. What can be called the constitutional monarchy of the first and second centuries (see p. 75) changed to a despotic absolute monarchy in which the emperors made no attempt to hide the fact that they were "army made." By the late third century the emperor was no longer addressed as *princeps*, meaning first among equals, but as *dominus et deus*, "lord and god." The Principate had been replaced by absolute rule known as the Dominate.

The transformation of the Roman Empire in the third century was foreshadowed by the reign of Commodus, who succeeded his father, Marcus Aurelius, in 180 A.D. Commodus was an incompetent voluptuary whose dissipations, cruelties, and neglect of affairs of state motivated a group of conspirators to have him strangled in 192 A.D. Civil war followed as rival armies fought for the imperial throne—on one occasion troops holding Rome sold the throne to the highest bidder—until Septimius Severus emerged on top and established a dynasty that provided some measure of order.

The Severan dynasty (193-235), like the reign of Commodus and its aftermath, marks the approaching end of the Principate. The Senate was ignored and the army pampered and enlarged. Septimius Severus' dying words to his sons, "Enrich the soldiers and scorn all others," reflect the trend of the times.

The dire effects of this toadying to the soldiery became apparent after 235, when the last member of the Severan dynasty was murdered by mutinous troops. During the next fifty years the Empire was rent from within by bloody civil wars and lashed from without by foreign invaders. The imperial scepter was dragged in the gutter by generals who murdered emperors with no compunction, intimidated all opposition, and put themselves or their puppets on the throne. Of the twenty-six who claimed the title of emperor during this long period of military anarchy, only one died a natural death.

Meanwhile, German tribes breached the imperial frontiers: the Franks devastated Gaul and Spain, the Saxons attacked Britain, and the Goths occupied Dacia (modern Rumania). For the first time since Hannibal's invasion five centuries earlier, it was felt necessary to protect Rome itself with a wall twenty feet high and twelve feet wide, which still stands. In Asia a powerful new menace appeared after 226—a reinvigorated Persia under the rule of the Sassanid dynasty, which proceeded to attack Syria.

Economic decline. As deadly to the well-being of the Empire as military anarchy and foreign invasions was prolonged economic decline. The Empire was no longer expanding; the economy had become static. In the past military expansion had paid off in rich booty, and the tapping of new sources of wealth had justified a large army. Now, however, wars were defensive, and the army had become a financial liability rather than an asset. Gold and silver were also being drained away because of the one-sided trade with India and China (see pp. 116-117).

The trend toward the concentration of land ownership in a few hands was greatly accelerated by the turbulent conditions of the third century. Small farmers abandoned their lands, which were then bought up cheaply by large landowners, and the emperors added to their vast estates through confiscation. The number of tenant farmers, or *coloni* (see p. 79), increased as small farming decreased and men fled the insecurity of city life to find jobs and protection on the large estates with their fortified villas. There they cultivated their patches of land, paying rent to the landowner and providing him with free labor at sowing and reaping time. The condition of the *coloni* worsened as they fell behind in their rents and taxes and, by imperial order, were bound to their tenancies until they had discharged their debts. This was a first step toward serfdom and the social and economic pattern of the Middle Ages.

Frequent civil wars disturbed trade and thus helped undermine the prosperity of the cities, whose populations decreased correspondingly. To make matters worse, inflation spiraled because the government spent more than it took in. In order to meet their military and administrative expenses, the emperors repeatedly devalued the coinage by reducing its silver content. Ultimately the amount of alloy reached 98 percent, and prices soared as people lost confidence in the debased currency. The government later refused to accept its own money for taxes and required payment in goods and services.

Diocletian. A much-needed reconstruction of the Empire was accomplished by Diocletian (285-305), a rough-hewn soldier and administrative genius whose work of stabilization is often compared to that of Augustus after a similar period of turmoil. But while Augustus had established a form of constitutional monarchy, Diocletian founded an undisguised oriental despotism.

To increase the strength of the government, Diocletian completed the trend toward autocracy. The Senate was relegated to the status of a mere city council, while the person of the emperor was exalted. Adorned in robes laden with jewels, the emperor surrounded himself with all the splendor of an oriental despot. An imperial etiquette was established which transformed the emperor into a veritable god; rigid ceremonial demanded that men bow low before him and address him as "the most sacred lord."

The imperial administration was greatly enlarged. Diocletian realized that the Empire's problems had become too great for one man. He divided the Empire, retaining the eastern half for his own administration. In the West he created a coemperor who, like himself, was designated an Augustus. Each Augustus in turn was to entrust the direct rule of half his realm to an assistant, termed Caesar. Since each Caesar would succeed his Augustus when the senior official died or retired, the problem of succession was supposedly solved.

Next, Diocletian greatly increased the number and variety of administrative units

Diocletian and his co-Augustus, each with his appointed Caesar, are shown in an embrace symbolic of the unity which Diocletian hoped to maintain despite administrative division of the empire. This sculpture now adorns St. Mark's Cathedral in Venice.

within the four divisions of the Empire. The provinces were reduced in size and more than doubled in number. (Italy lost its hitherto favored position and was divided into provinces.) The 120 provinces were grouped into thirteen dioceses, each under a vicar. The dioceses in turn were grouped into four prefectures, each under a prefect who served directly under one of the four emperors. Paralleling this civil administration was a separate hierarchy of military officials. Finally, a large secret service was created to keep close watch over this vast bureaucracy. Even the Christian Church did not escape the spreading tentacles of the new regimented state, as Diocletian's ruthless persecution of Christianity demonstrates.

Diocletian also made strenuous efforts to arrest economic decay in the Empire. He gradually restored confidence in the debased currency by issuing new standard silver and gold coins. In the meantime, in an effort to stem the runaway inflation, he issued an edict fixing maximum prices for all essential goods and services, which were set to cover a wide range from peas to beer, and from haircuts to freight rates.

Head of the emperor Constantine, which was once part of an enormous statue.

Constantine. After Diocletian and his fellow Augustus retired in 305, his scheme for the succession collapsed, and civil war broke out once again. Within a few years Constantine (306-337), the only one of five rival emperors who favored Christianity (see p. 126), forged to the front, and after sharing the Empire for a few years with an eastern rival, became sole emperor in 324.

Constantine carried on Diocletian's work of reconstructing and stabilizing the Empire. We have already noted his solution of the Christian problem. To stabilize the manpower situation, necessary for the production of essential goods and services as well as the collection of taxes, Constantine issued a series of decrees which froze people to their occupations and places of origin. Henceforth no *colonus* could leave the soil, and the children of a *colonus* had to accept the same status as that of their father. In the cities the same restrictions were applied to members of those guilds whose activities were essential to the state, such as baking and transportation. Born into and bound to their occupations, members had to marry within the guild and train their sons to carry on the same line of work. Thus, to serve the interests of the state and to arrest further economic decline, a veritable caste system was established.

Division of the Empire. The Roman world's center of gravity shifted eastward during the age of Diocletian and Constan-

tine. The administrative reforms swept away Italy's former primacy, and Rome even ceased to be a seat of imperial authority. Diocletian's coemperor in the West ruled from Milan, while Diocletian himself chose to govern the eastern half of the Empire and set up his court at Nicomedia in northwestern Asia Minor. His was a logical choice; the East had declined less than the West, and the greatest dangers to the Empire came from beyond the Danube River and from Persia. But even more strategic than Nicomedia was the old Greek colony of Byzantium, across the straits, selected by Constantine for a new capital. Reached only through a narrow, easily defended channel, Byzantium possessed a splendid harbor at the crossroads of Europe and Asia. Constantine dubbed his capital New Rome, but it soon became known as Constantinople.

The establishment of an eastern capital foreshadowed the impending division of the Empire into two completely separate states, the East and the West. For about fifty years following the death of Constantine in 337, the unity of the Empire was preserved, although there were often two joint emperors, one in the East and the other in the West. But after Theodosius I divided it between his two sons in 395, the Empire was never again governed as a single unit. Henceforth we can speak of a western Roman empire, which soon fell, and of an eastern Roman—or Byzantine—empire, which endured for another thousand years during which it adhered to the paternalistic and authoritarian pattern laid down by Diocletian and Constantine (see Chapter 6).

UPHEAVAL IN THE WEST

The Germanic tribes. Weakened by economic, social, and political decline, Rome had turned to the most extreme forms of absolutism in an effort to ride out the storm that threatened to engulf it. But its internal crisis was compounded by mounting external pressures that threatened to stave in its far-flung frontiers. The greatest danger lay to the north, the home of restless bands of fierce barbarians—the Germans. From the Franks on the Rhine to the Goths on the Black Sea, they were grouped into tribes (whose names will appear in the text as each makes its bid for the spoils of a tottering empire). Semi-nomads, the Germans were at a cultural stage midway between a pastoral and an agricultural economy. They engaged in so little commerce that cattle, rather than money, were sufficient as a measure of value.

According to the Roman historian Tacitus, the Germans were notorious as heavy drinkers and gamblers. On the other hand, Tacitus praised their courage, respect for women, and freedom from many Roman vices. A favorite amusement was listening to the tribal bards recite ancient tales of heroes and gods.

Each warrior leader had a retinue of followers, who were linked to him by personal loyalty. According to Tacitus:

On the field of battle it is a disgrace to the chief to be surpassed in valour by his companions, to the companions not to come up to the valour of their chief. As for leaving a battle alive after your chief has fallen, *that* means lifelong infamy and shame. To defend and protect him, to put down one's own acts of heroism to his credit—that is what they really mean by "allegiance". The chiefs fight for victory, the companions for their chief.[10]

This war band—called *comitatus* in Latin—had an important bearing on the origin of medieval feudalism, which was based on the personal bond between knights and their feudal lords. The heroic virtues associated with the *comitatus* also continued into the Middle Ages where they formed the basis of the value system of the feudal nobility.

In an effort to eliminate blood feuds, the Germanic system of justice was based on the principle of compensation. For the infliction of specific injuries a stipulated payment termed a *bot* was required. The amount of compensation varied according to the severity of the crime and the social position of the victim. For example, it cost forty times as much to kill a man of rank as a common man. Some crimes were botless—that is, so grave in character that compensation could not be paid. A person charged with such a crime had to stand trial and produce oath-helpers who would swear to his innocence. If unable to obtain oath-helpers, he was subjected to trial by ordeal, of which there were three kinds. In the first, the defendant had to lift a small stone out of a vessel of boiling water; unless his scalded arm had healed within a prescribed number of days, he was judged guilty. In the second, he had to walk blindfolded and barefooted across a floor on which lay pieces of red-hot metal; success in avoiding the metal was a sign of innocence. In the third, the bound defendant was thrown into a stream which had been blessed; only if the holy water accepted him and he sank was he believed innocent. Trial by ordeal, which was employed only where a strong presumption of guilt existed, lasted until the thirteenth century, when it was outlawed by Pope Innocent III and various secular rulers.

Roman-German contacts. During the many centuries that the Romans and Germans faced each other across the Rhine-Danube frontier, there was much contact—peaceful as well as belligerent—between the two peoples. Roman trade reached into Germany, and Germans entered the Empire as slaves. During the troubled third century many Germans were invited to settle on vacated lands within the Empire or to serve in the Roman legions. By the end of the fourth century the Roman army and its generals in the West had become almost completely German.

The Germans beyond the frontiers were kept in check by force of arms, by frontier walls, by diplomacy and gifts, and by employing the policy of playing off one tribe against another. In the last decades of the fourth century, however, these methods proved insufficient to prevent a series of great new invasions. A basic factor behind Germanic restlessness seems to have been land hunger. Their numbers were increasing, much of their land was forest and swamp, and their methods of tillage were inefficient.

Wholesale barbarian invasions. Meanwhile another restless people were on the move. The Huns, superb Mongolian horsemen and fighters, were nomads from Central Asia who had for centuries plundered and slain their Asian neighbors. In 372 they

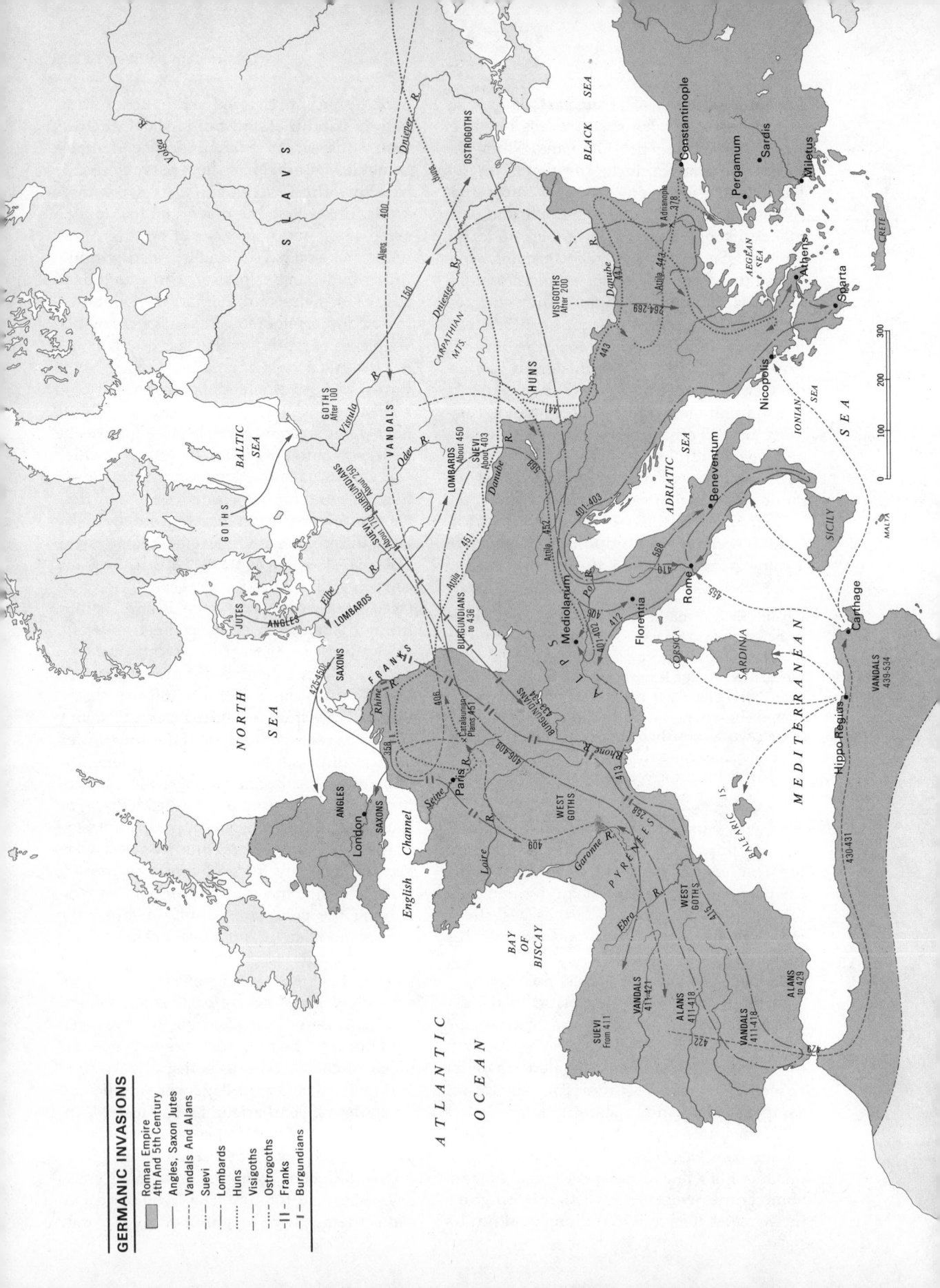

GERMANIC INVASIONS

	Roman Empire 4th And 5th Century
	Angles, Saxon Jutes
―――	Vandals And Alans
‒‒‒	Suevi
····	Lombards
·····	Huns
········	Visigoths
‒·‒·	Ostrogoths
‒ǁ‒	Franks
‒ǀ‒	Burgundians

ATLANTIC OCEAN

BAY OF BISCAY

NORTH SEA

BALTIC SEA

S L A V S

Volga

Dnieper R.

Alans 400

150

Dniester R.

CARPATHIAN MTS.

OSTROGOTHS

BLACK SEA

Constantinople

Adrianople 378

Attila 443

Atlila 441

Danube R.

264-269

VISIGOTHS After 200

Pergamum

Sardis

Miletus

AEGEAN SEA

Athens

Sparta

CRETE

443

Nicopolis

IONIAN SEA

300
200
100
0

GOTHS After 100

Vistula R.

VANDALS

Oder R.

Suevi Until 250

BURGUNDIANS About 250

LOMBARDS About 450

SUEVI About 403

451

Attila

588

Danube R.

HUNS

441

401-403

401-403

Attila 452

452

Po R.

406

401-402

412

Mediolanum

Florentia

Ben+eventum

588

476

Rome

455

ADRIATIC SEA

CORSICA

SARDINIA

SICILY

MALTA

MEDITERRANEAN SEA

Carthage

Hippo Regius

VANDALS 439-534

430-431

GOTHS

Elbe R.

JUTES

ANGLES

LOMBARDS

F R A N K S

SAXONS

425-450

358

Rhine R.

406

BURGUNDIANS to 436

Catalaunian Plains 451

BURGUNDIANS 443-534

406-408

406-408

409

413

413

258

258

Seine R.

Paris

Loire R.

WEST GOTHS

Garonne R.

P Y R E N E E S

Ebro R.

WEST GOTHS

WEST GOTHS

415

415

ANGLES

London

SAXONS

English Channel

VANDALS 411-421

ALANS 411-418

VANDALS 411-418

SUEVI From 411

422

ALANS to 429

429

429

BALEARIC IS.

I T A L Y

S E A

crossed the Volga and soon subjugated the easternmost Germanic tribe, the Ostrogoths. Terrified at the prospect of being conquered in turn by the advancing Huns, the Visigoths petitioned the Romans to allow them to settle as allies inside the Empire. Permission was granted, and in 376 the entire tribe crossed the Danube into Roman territory. But soon corrupt Roman officials cheated and mistreated the Visigoths, and the proud barbarians went on a rampage. The inept East Roman emperor sought to quell them, but he lost both his army and his life in the battle of Adrianople in 378.

Adrianople has been described as one of history's decisive battles: it destroyed the legend of the invincibility of the Roman legions and ushered in a century and a half of chaos. For a few years the capable emperor Theodosius I held back the Visigoths, but after his death in 395 they began to migrate and pillage under their leader, Alaric. He invaded Italy, and in 410 his followers sacked Rome. The weak West Roman emperor ceded southern Gaul to the Visigoths, who soon expanded into Spain. Their Spanish kingdom lasted until the Muslim conquest of the eighth century.

To counter Alaric's threat to Italy, the Romans had withdrawn most of their troops from the Rhine frontier in 406 and from Britain the following year. The momentous consequence of this action was a flood of Germanic tribes across the defenseless frontiers. The Vandals pushed their way through Gaul to Spain and, after pressure from the Visigoths, moved on to Africa, the granary of the Empire. In 455 a Vandal raiding force sailed over from Africa, and Rome was sacked a second time. Meanwhile the Burgundians settled in the Rhone valley, the Franks gradually spread across northern Gaul, and the Angles, Saxons, and Jutes invaded Britain. Although each of these several tribes set up a German-ruled kingdom within the confines of the Empire, only the Franks in Gaul and the Angles and Saxons in Britain managed to perpetuate their kingdoms longer than a few centuries.

While the Germans were taking over the western part of the Empire, the Huns pushed farther into Europe. Led by Attila, the "scourge of God," the mounted nomads crossed the Rhine in 451. The remaining Roman forces in Gaul, joined by the Visigoths, defeated the Huns near Troyes. Atilla then plundered northern Italy and planned to take Rome, but disease, lack of supplies, and the dramatic appeal of Pope Leo I—which was to give the papacy great prestige—caused him to return to the plains of Hungary. The Hunnic hordes disintegrated after 453, when Attila died on the night of his marriage to a Germanic princess whom legend immortalized as Krimhild of the *Nibelungenlied* (see p. 256).

The fall of Rome. What was happening to the imperial throne in the West during this turbulent period? As we have mentioned (p. 132), after the death of Theodosius I in 395, the Empire was divided between his two sons. Roman rule in the West grew increasingly impotent as a series of incompetent emperors sought safety behind marshes at Ravenna. The leaders of the mercenary soldiers, whose ranks were now mainly German, wielded the real power.

In 475 Orestes, the Germanic commander of the troops, forced the Senate to elect his young son Romulus Augustulus ("Little Augustus") as emperor in the West. In the following year another Germanic commander, Odovacar, slew Orestes and, seeing no reason for continuing the sham of an imperial line, deposed Romulus Augustulus and proclaimed himself head of the government. The deposition of the boy, who by a strange irony bore the names of the legendary founder of Rome and the founder of the Empire, marks the traditional "fall" of the Roman Empire.

Actually, no single date is accurate, for the fall of Rome was a long and complicated process. Yet 476 at least symbolizes the end of the Roman Empire in the West, for in this year the long line of emperors inaugurated by Augustus ended and the undisguised rule of Italy by Germanic leaders began.

Theodoric's kingdom in Italy. The disintegration of the Hunnic empire following the death of Attila freed the Ostrogoths to migrate as other tribes were doing. Under their energetic king, Theodoric (c. 454-526), who had spent some years as a hostage at Constantinople, the Ostrogoths were galvanized into action.

Theodoric accepted a commission from the emperor in the East to reimpose imperial authority over Italy, now in Odovacar's hands. In 488 he led his people into the Italian peninsula, where, after hard fighting, Odovacar sued for peace and was treacherously murdered. Theodoric then established a strong Ostrogothic kingdom in Italy with its capital at Ravenna. Because he appreciated the culture he had seen at Constantinople, Theodoric pursued a successful policy of maintaining classical culture on a high level. Following his death without a male heir in 526, civil war broke out in Italy, paving the way for a twenty-year war of reconquest (535-555) by the armies of the East Roman emperor Justinian. Italy was ravaged from end to end by the fighting, and the classical civilization that Theodoric had carefully preserved was in large part destroyed.

The Lombards. In 568, only three years after Justinian died, the last wave of Germanic invaders, the fierce Lombards, poured

Reminiscent of the classical architecture which the Ostrogothic king admired, Theodoric's tomb in Ravenna is remarkable for its dome, which is one enormous slab of stone, 35 feet in diameter and weighing 470 tons.

into Italy. The Eastern emperor held on to southern Italy, as well as Ravenna and Venice, and the pope now became the virtual ruler of Rome. Not until the late nineteenth century would Italy again be united under one government. The Lombard kingdom in Italy, weakened by the independent actions of many strong dukes, did not last long. In 774 it was conquered by the Franks, who, as we shall see in Chapter 8, had in the meantime established the most powerful and longest lasting of all the Germanic kingdoms that arose on the territory of the western empire.

The problem of the fall of Rome. The shock and dismay felt by contemporaries throughout the Roman world on learning of Alaric's sack of the Eternal City in 410 were to echo down the centuries, leaving the impression that the fall of Rome was a major calamity, one of the greatest in history.

Pagan writers attributed the sack of Rome to the abandonment of the ancient gods. In *The City of God* St. Augustine argued against this charge and put forth the theory that history unfolds according to God's design. Thus Rome's fall was part of the divine plan—"the necessary and fortunate preparation for the triumph of the heavenly city where man's destiny was to be attained."[11]

This view was challenged in the eighteenth century by Edward Gibbon, author of the famous *Decline and Fall of the Roman Empire*, who saw Rome's fall as the "triumph of barbarism and religion." Christianity, he argued, had played an important role in undermining the imperial structure: "The clergy successfully preached the doctrines of patience and pusillanimity; . . . the last remains of the military spirit were buried in the cloister."[12]

In our time some explanations of Rome's fall have been rooted in psychological theories. For example, the basic cause has been attributed to a weakening of morale in the face of difficulties, to a "loss of nerve." Or it has been argued that the ultimate failure of Rome came from its too complete success. The easy acquisition of power and wealth and the importing of ready-made cultures from conquered peoples led to "a changed attitude of men's minds" and indo-

lence and self-gratification among the ruling classes. Such subjective theories can scarcely be proven, however, or even fairly assessed.

Most historians account for Rome's decline in terms of a variety of interacting forces. On the political side, the failure of civil power to control the army following the death of Marcus Aurelius resulted in military anarchy, the disintegration of central authority, and the weakening of Rome's ability to withstand external pressures. Diocletian and his successors had to increase the military establishment despite a growing manpower shortage, caused in part by recurrent plagues from Asia (perhaps smallpox or measles). "Hence they found themselves on the horns of a dilemma. Either they could conscript Roman civilians for military service and so decrease still further production and the state revenues, or they could . . . make up the deficit with barbarians."[13] The decision they made led to Germanization of the army and to German colonization within the empire.

On the economic side, the small farmer class disappeared, and more and more land was consolidated into huge *latifundia*; civil war and barbarian attacks disturbed trade relations; a debased currency and a crushing tax burden undermined the confidence of the people. Eventually the rigid economic and social decrees of Diocletian and Constantine created a vast bureaucracy which only aggravated the existing ills in the western half of the Empire, already far gone along the road to decline.

Western Europe in the sixth century. In the West the Empire was no more than a memory by the sixth century. In its place were new states that foreshadowed the major political divisions of modern Europe: Visigothic Spain, Anglo-Saxon England, Frankish Gaul, and a divided Italy ruled by Lombard dukes, the Eastern emperor, and the pope.

Vast tracts of formerly cultivated land were left untilled, and the failure of communications and transportation, coupled with the flight of the labor force from the cities to the country, had brought on a progressive decentralization of the economy. With much industry transferred from cities to large country estates, scores of once flourishing towns near the frontiers ceased to exist, while those closer to the Mediterranean shrunk in size and importance. "Roman civilization had been essentially urban; medieval civilization was to be essentially rural. With the decline of the towns the general level of civilization was lowered and western Europe began to assume its medieval aspect."[14]

Yet the Germanic invasions were not as cataclysmic as was once thought. True, the invaders pillaged ruthlessly, and in certain sections of the empire, especially in Britain, Roman civilization was entirely wiped out. The Germans also seized a great deal of land, but most of this was either vacant or belonged to the emperors; few private landowners were displaced. In most areas the invaders still represented a minority of the population, and a gradual blending and fusing of the cultures and the blood of the two peoples began. Thus the barbarians in time lost their Germanic customs, religion, and speech; that is why hardly a trace of the Germanic languages remains in Italy, France, and Spain. The Church, under the dual leadership of Benedictine monasticism and the papacy, assisted the fusion between German and Roman.

By the sixth century the foundations for the spiritual and political power of the papacy, which would lead to the Church-state rivalry of the Middle Ages, had been laid. We have seen how Pope Leo the Great acquired the moral leadership of the West by successfully protecting Italy from the Huns, and how the Lombard conquests in Italy gave the papacy its opportunity to achieve independence. In addition, ready for future use was the doctrine of the supremacy of the Church over the state in spiritual matters, a doctrine implied by St. Augustine in his *City of God* and clearly expressed by St. Ambrose during his clash with the emperor Theodosius I.

By the sixth century, then, the three elements that were to create the pattern of western civilization in the Middle Ages were being interwoven: Graeco-Roman culture, the Christian Church, and the Germanic peoples and their institutions. Here, in a sense, were the mind, spirit, and muscle that were to work together in western man during the next thousand years.

Survival in the East. In our study of history thus far it is apparent that the most westerly focus of civilization was Rome, which was not only far removed from the "heartland" of civilization in the Fertile Crescent and Egypt but was also the cultural area most exposed at this time to counterforces. As a consequence, the western half of the Roman Empire was overwhelmed by those forces, while the eastern half, though seriously threatened, managed to ride out the storm.

Until 1453 the eastern—or Byzantine—empire maintained the Roman imperial tradition and administrative structure. Equally important was the preservation of Greek language and learning. The East also evolved its own Orthodox Church, which was to play a vital role in shaping the course of civilization in Russia and the Slavic world. For these reasons we must redirect our steps toward the East, where the Graeco-Roman legacy endured and from where it would one day be transmitted back to the West.

SUMMARY

Christianity's roots extend back into Jewish history long before the birth of Christ, and it is there that we find the concept of the Messiah, the divinely appointed leader who would create a new Israel. Under the rule of the Hellenistic Seleucid empire and later of Rome, many Jews hoped for such a Messiah to lead them to political independence; but when Jesus attacked the shortcomings of the established religion and refused to head a political revolt against the Romans, his enemies brought about his condemnation and execution. Yet his teachings did not die with his crucifixion. Interpreted through the efforts of St. Paul and the Church Fathers, they spread rapidly throughout the Roman Empire. Despite persecution, converts flocked to the new faith, and finally, with the Edict of Milan in 313, the emperor Constantine made Christianity a legal religion. Thereafter the Church grew and flourished, with an organization based on the imperial Roman pattern and a hierarchy of officials culminating in the pope at Rome.

From the death of Marcus Aurelius in 180 A.D., the Roman Empire declined as its rulers became pawns of the army. Only Diocletian and Constantine were able to check the downward trend, and in the long run their system of despotism failed to save the western half of the Empire from further deterioration. When the Visigoths, pushed by the Huns, defeated Roman forces at the battle of Adrianople in 378, the gates of the Empire burst open before the barbarian tribes. The date of the final collapse of Rome may be set at 476, when the last Roman emperor in the West was deposed.

The fall of Rome—one of the great dramatic developments in history—has been explained in a variety of ways by later historians. No single cause can be given; the collapse appears to have been the result of various interacting factors. Following the devastating invasions which overwhelmed the western half of the Empire, the gap left by the Caesars was filled by a powerful new agency, the Christian Church.

As the Roman Empire crumbled in the West, a new center of imperial strength arose in the East at Constantinople. To this city and its Byzantine civilization—a continuation of the Graeco-Roman but with original contributions of its own—we shall now turn.

SUGGESTIONS FOR READING

J. A. Hexter, **The Judaeo-Christian Tradition*** (Harper & Row) is a brief but highly valuable survey of the evolution of ancient Judaism and Christianity. On the late ancient history of the Jews see E. Bickermann, **From Ezra to the Last of the Maccabees: Foundations of Post-Biblical Judaism*** (Schocken); and D. S. Russell, **The Jews from Alexander to Herod** (Oxford).

Edmund Wilson, **The Dead Sea Scrolls, 1949-1969** (Oxford, 1969) is the most readable introduction to a fascinating subject. See also John Allegro, **The Dead Sea Scrolls: A Reappraisal*** (Penguin); G. Vermes, **The Dead Sea Scrolls in English*** (Penguin); and Frank M. Cross, **Qumram and the History of the Biblical Text*** (Harvard).

Albert Schweitzer, **The Quest of the Historical Jesus*** (Macmillan) surveys the attempts of scholars to discover the Jesus of history. See also E. J. Goodspeed, **A Life of Jesus*** (Torchbooks); M. Enslin, **Christian Beginnings*** (Torchbooks); R. Bultman, **Primitive Christianity*** (Collins-World) and H. Kee and F. Young, **Understanding the New Testament** (Prentice-Hall, 1973).

J. W. C. Ward, **A History of the Early Church to A.D. 500*** (Harper & Row, 1975); J. G. Davies, **The Early Christian Church*** (Anchor); and H. Chadwick, **The Early Church*** (Penguin) are excellent surveys of the first five centuries of Church history. See also Cyril Richardson, **Early Christian Fathers** (Macmillan, 1970); H. Mattingly, **Christianity in the Roman Empire*** (Norton); E. R. Dodds, **Pagan and Christian in an Age of Anxiety** (Cambridge, 1965); and C. N. Cochrane, **Christianity and Classical Culture: A Study of Thought and Action from Augustus to Augustine*** (Galaxy).

On early monasticism see H. Waddell, **The Desert Fathers*** (Barnes & Noble, 1974); and E. Duckett, **The Gateway to the Middle Ages: Monasticism*** (Univ. of Michigan).

S. Katz, **The Decline of Rome and the Rise of Medieval Europe*** (Cornell) is a concise, clear account. A. H. M. Jones, **The Decline of the Ancient World*** (Longman, 1975) is a recent detailed survey. See also F. Lot, **The End of the Ancient World and the Beginning of the Middle Ages*** (Torchbooks); R. MacMullen, **Constantine** (Dial, 1969); and H. Doerries, **Constantine the Great*** (Torchbooks, 1972).

Edward Gibbon, **The Decline and Fall of the Roman Empire*** (Dell), ed. by F. C. Bourne, is an abridgment of this eighteenth-century classic. For modern scholarly opinion on Rome's decline see Lynn White, Jr., ed., **The Transformation of the Roman World: Gibbon's Problem After Two Centuries** (Univ. of Calif., 1966); F. Walbank, **The Awful Revolution: The Decline of the Roman Empire in the West*** (Univ. of Toronto, 1969); R. M. Haywood, **The Myth of Rome's Fall*** (Apollo); and D. Kagan, ed., **Decline and Fall of the Roman Empire: Why Did It Collapse?*** (Heath).

J. B. Bury, **The Invasion of Europe by the Barbarians*** (Norton) is the best general work on the nature and effect of the Germanic invasions. See also H. Moss, **The Birth of the Middle Ages, 395-814*** (Galaxy); E. A. Thompson, **The Early Germans** (Oxford); and O. J. Maenchen-Helfen, **The World of the Huns** (Univ. of Calif., 1973).

*Indicates a less expensive paperbound edition.

CHAPTER 6

The Byzantine Empire, Early Russia, and Muslim Expansion

Citadel and Conqueror

INTRODUCTION. When we speak of the fall of the Roman Empire, we sometimes forget that in fact only the western portion of that empire succumbed to the German invaders and entered into what has been described as its "Dark Ages." In the East, despite many vicissitudes, the east Roman or Byzantine empire stood for a thousand years as a citadel protecting an unappreciative West slowly emerging from semibarbarism.

Furthermore, the Byzantine empire made great contributions to civilization: Greek language and learning were preserved for posterity; the Roman imperial system was continued and Roman law codified; the Greek Orthodox Church converted the Slavic peoples and fostered the development of a splendid new Graeco-oriental art that was dedicated to the glorification of the Christian religion. Situated at the crossroads of East and West, Constantinople acted as the disseminator of culture for all peoples who came in contact with the empire. Called with justification "The City," this rich and turbulent metropolis was to the early Middle

Ages what Athens and Rome had been to classical times. By the time the empire collapsed in 1453, its religious mission and political concepts had borne fruit among the Slavic peoples of eastern Europe and especially among the Russians. The latter were to lay claim to the Byzantine tradition and to dub Moscow the "Third Rome."

The only rival of Byzantine civilization close at hand was the culture developed by followers of the Prophet Muhammad, who united the Arabian peninsula under the banner of his new religion, Islam, with its fundamental teachings of monotheism. The dynamic faith of Muhammad spread so rapidly that within a hundred years after the Prophet's death his followers had established a vast empire stretching from the Pyrenees to the Indus. This breathtaking religious and political expansion was followed by a flowering of Islamic culture that rivaled the achievements of the Byzantine empire and far surpassed those of western Europe at this time. The Muslims share with the Byzantines chief credit for preserving and disseminating learning in the Middle Ages.

THE PRECARIOUS FORTUNES OF THE EASTERN EMPIRE

Constantine's city. At the southern extremity of the Bosporus stands a promontory that juts out from Europe toward Asia, with the Sea of Marmora to the south and a long harbor known as the Golden Horn to the north. On this peninsula stood the ancient Greek city of Byzantium, which Constantine enlarged considerably and formally christened "New Rome" in 330 A.D.

Constantine had chosen his site carefully. The city commanded the waterway connecting the Mediterranean and the Black seas and separating Europe and Asia. Moreover, the site favored defense; it enabled Constantinople not only to become the great warehouse for East-West commerce but above all to be a buffer protecting Europe from attack.

In Chapter 5 we saw how, during the fourth and fifth centuries, both the eastern and western provinces of the Roman Empire were beset by dangers from beyond the northern frontier. Storming into the Empire, Visigoths, Huns, and Ostrogoths pillaged the Balkans and threatened Constantinople. But the more populous eastern provinces, with their greater military and economic strength, were saved from the fate that befell Rome.

As the western half of the Roman Empire crumbled, Constantinople turned eastward for its livelihood and culture, becoming gradually less Roman and western and more Greek and oriental. A panorama of triumphs and defeats, Byzantine history for the next one thousand years can be divided into four main periods—expansion, peril, recovery, and disintegration.

Justinian's reconquests. The history of the empire in the sixth century focuses upon the reign of Justinian (527-565), whose ambition was to restore the Roman Empire to its ancient scope and grandeur. Much of his success he owed to his wife, Theodora, who had been a dancer and was said to be the daughter of a circus animal trainer. Theodora proved to be a brave empress and a wise counselor. In 532, early in Justinian's reign, occurred the Nike rebellion (named after the victory cry of the rioters), the most famous of many popular revolts that have led historians to characterize Byzantine history as a despotism tempered by revolution. Theodora's coolness and bravery inspired her hard-pressed husband to remain in the capital and crush the rebellion:

May I never be separated from this purple, and may I not live that day on which those who meet me shall not address me as mistress. If, now, it is your wish to save yourself, O Emperor, there is no difficulty. For we have much money, and there is the sea, here the boats. . . . as for myself, I approve a certain ancient saying that royalty is a good burial-shroud.[1]

To carry out his plan for recovering the lost half of the Roman Empire from the Germans, Justinian first bought off the Persian

Sassanid kings, who threatened Syria and Asia Minor (see p. 130). Then in 533 he seized North Africa and the islands of the western Mediterranean from the Vandals. But it took twenty years of exhausting warfare for his generals to regain Italy from the Ostrogoths. Rome and other great Italian cities lay in ruins, and the classical civilization that the Ostrogothic king Theodoric had taken care to preserve was virtually annihilated. Justinian also wrested the southeastern portion of Spain from the Visigoths. Yet his empire was still much smaller than the Roman Empire at its height. Only a small part of Spain was his; nor had he recovered Gaul, Britain, or southern Germany. Furthermore his reconquests had been accomplished at the price of exhausting the empire, both militarily and financially. Nor were Justinian's reconquests permanent; three years after his death most of devastated Italy fell to the Germanic Lombards, and the Persians made inroads into Syria.

In domestic affairs as in warfare, Justinian sought to restore the dignity and splendor of the Roman Empire. In this area are found his greatest accomplishments—the codification of Roman law and the erection of the great Church of Hagia Sophia, both described later in this chapter.

Three centuries of peril, 565-867. With Justinian's death, the first and perhaps the greatest period of Byzantine history ended.

The exhausted empire now entered an era of peril lasting from the middle of the sixth to the middle of the ninth century. By the time Heraclius (610-641) ascended the throne, the empire was in a desperate position. Slavic tribes had invaded the Balkans, a new wave of Asiatic nomads, the Avars, were being kept beyond the Danube only by the payment of tribute, and the Persians were in the process of conquering Syria, Palestine, and Egypt. Jerusalem fell in 614, and various sacred relics, including what was reputed to be the Holy Cross, were carried off to the Persian capital. While one Persian army conquered Egypt, another advanced to a point in Asia Minor opposite Constantinople. In three brilliant campaigns Heraclius virtually destroyed the Persian empire and regained Syria, Palestine, and Egypt, along with the Holy Cross.

Although the centuries-old menace of the Persians had now been removed, the Eastern empire was soon confronted with a new danger. The early part of the seventh century saw in Arabia the birth of a new faith—Islam. With fanatical zeal the Arabs attacked the weakened Persian and Byzantine empires, and by the middle of the century they had subjugated Palestine, Syria, Persia, Egypt, and much of North Africa (see map, p. 159). An Arab fleet even besieged Constantinople annually for several years, and the distracted empire was also threatened by a new Hunnish menace, the Bulgars, who in 680 settled

In this detail from a mosaic from the Church of San Vitale at Ravenna, the emperor Justinian prepares to present a gold plate to the archbishop of Ravenna. The mosaics of this period emphasize individuality in facial features along with magnificently patterned costumes.

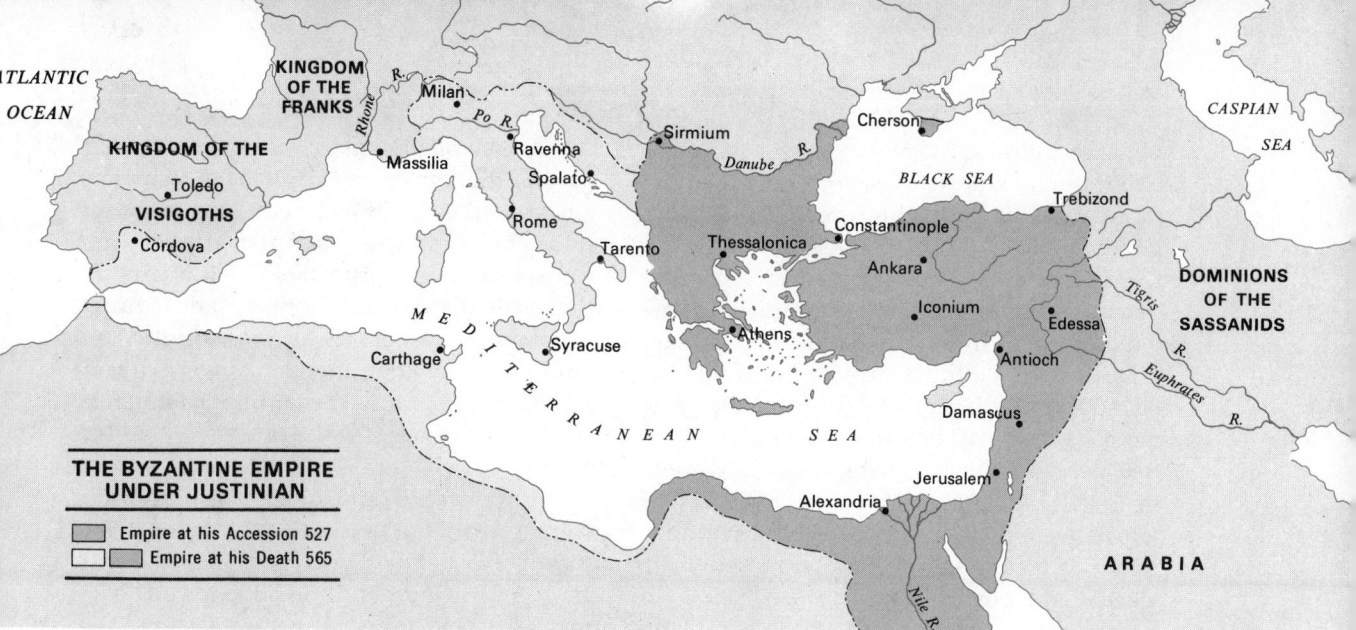

THE BYZANTINE EMPIRE UNDER JUSTINIAN

- Empire at his Accession 527
- Empire at his Death 565

in what is now Bulgaria. By 700 the Eastern empire stood on the brink of disintegration. In the Middle East it held only Asia Minor, while in the West it maintained a precarious hold on Sicily, southern Italy, Venice, and the exarchate of Ravenna, which extended from Ravenna southward through Rome.

The able Emperor Leo III (717-741) saved the hard-pressed empire. With the aid of a secret weapon, Greek fire (see p. 146), Leo repulsed the last great Arab assault on Constantinople in 718. He then turned to administrative and military reform. Civil and military authority in the provinces, separated by Diocletian (see p. 131), were reunited in the hands of provincial generals. Land was granted to the peasants in exchange for military service, and these free soldier-farmers, led by the powerful provincial generals, became the backbone of the Byzantine army. In contrast to the West, where the peasants were fast becoming serfs, a free peasantry continued to exist in the Eastern empire. Leo's religious policy, however, produced the iconoclastic controversy (see p. 147), which for over a hundred years caused widespread dissension.

Last days of grandeur, 867-1057. A little more than a century after Leo III's reforms had restored order to the hard-pressed empire, the strong Macedonian dynasty (867-1057) ushered in the third period of Byzantine history during which the empire went on the offensive. South Italy, which along with Sicily had recently been lost to the Muslims, was regained. The powerful Bulgarians, now Christianized and seeking to possess all the Balkans, were conquered, and the power of the Muslims in the East was shattered as the Byzantines regained the island of Cyprus and Antioch in Syria, both lost since the seventh century. It is also noteworthy that during this period of resurgence the emperors forged a new sphere of Byzantine influence in Russia.

The empire reached a high level of power under the energetic Basil II (976-1025). Byzantine military forces finally crushed their Bulgarian foes with great severity. On one occasion fifteen thousand Bulgars were blinded and only a handful, each with a single eye, were left to guide the rest home. The Bulgarian king is said to have died of shock when this sightless multitude returned. Basil the "Bulgar-slayer" incorporated the Bulgarian kingdom into the empire and the Byzantine frontier again reached the Danube.

Basil II was friendly with Vladimir, the prince of Kiev in southern Russia, and was instrumental in bringing about that ruler's conversion to Christianity. Other Russians also began to adopt Christian beliefs and various aspects of Byzantine culture. Trade augmented these relations.

Four centuries of decline: Part I, 1057-1204. At the end of the Macedonian dynasty in 1057, the Byzantine empire entered its last tempestuous period, one of decline, at times obvious and rapid, then again imperceptible and gradual. During these four centuries the foundations of Byzantine strength—a strong government, a prosperous economy, and a stable social order—suffered irreparable damage, and the weakened empire was shattered by both Christian and Muslim invaders.

During the tenth century a powerful landed nobility had begun to threaten the emperor's power. By absorbing the lands of the free peasants and reducing them to dependency, these landed magnates, whose interests were usually opposed to those of the central government, greatly increased their wealth and power. Since the free peasants had been the state's best taxpayers and the backbone of its armies, the empire's revenues and defenses became seriously undermined. At the end of the century Basil II twice had to repress the revolts of generals who represented the hostile aristocracy. Basil's successors held the great magnates in check until 1081, when one of them usurped the imperial throne.

In the meantime, within the orbit of Byzantine commerce a dangerous rival was emerging—the city of Venice, founded in the fifth and sixth centuries by refugees who fled the barbarian invasions of northern Italy and found safety on a cluster of small islands off the northern Adriatic coast. The island city of Venice was relatively safe from the barbarian hordes and thus remained under Byzantine sovereignty when most of the Italian peninsula was overrun. As subjects of the Byzantine empire, the Venetians enjoyed access to the eastern Mediterranean trade, but they were far enough away from Constantinople to run their own affairs. By the eleventh century Venice had acquired undisputed supremacy in the Adriatic, and ambitious Venetian merchants were dreaming of supplanting Byzantine commercial supremacy over all the eastern Mediterranean.

In the eleventh century also, the Byzantines were confronted with two new foes. The formidable Seljuk Turks (see p. 161) threatened Asia Minor; and the adventurous Normans, led by Robert Guiscard (see p. 207), began to carve out possessions for themselves in southern Italy. The Byzantine army was defeated by the Turks at the critical battle of Manzikert in 1071, and all of Asia Minor was soon lost. By an unfortunate coincidence, Bari, the empire's last stronghold in southern Italy, was captured by the Normans in the same year that the battle of Manzikert took place.

In 1081, when the empire stood deprived of rich possessions, sapped by growing commercial rivalry, and torn by the struggle with the landed aristocracy, a powerful landowner, Alexius Comnenus, became emperor by a coup d'état. Soon afterwards, in 1096, the first crusaders from the West appeared on the scene. Hoping to obtain some European mercenary forces to help defeat the

THE BYZANTINE EMPIRE ABOUT 814

Seljuk Turks, Alexius had appealed to Pope Urban II for assistance, but he was dismayed to find a host of crusaders, including the dreaded Normans, approaching the capital. The western response to Urban's appeal to save the Eastern empire and the Holy Land from the Seljuks was met with suspicion on the part of the Byzantines, who viewed the pope as heretical and the crusaders as potentially dangerous to the Eastern empire. Adroitly, Alexius encouraged the crusaders to forgo his hospitality as quickly as possible and attack his Seljuk enemies. The successful weakening of Muslim power by the First Crusade enabled Alexius to recover valuable portions of Asia Minor.

With the Fourth Crusade (1202-1204), the envy and enmity which had been building up for decades in the West against the Byzantine empire were converted into violence. Dependent upon the Venetians for ships and money, the crusaders were persuaded to attack first the Christian city of Zara in Dalmatia, a commercial rival of Venice, and then Constantinople. The Venetian goal was to obtain a monopoly on Byzantine trade.

Constantinople was so rent by factional strife that the crusaders had little trouble in capturing it. A French noble among the crusaders described the resulting sacking of the city:

[I saw] . . . the great churches and the rich palaces melting and falling in, and the great streets filled with merchandise burning in the flames. . . . The booty gained was so great that none could tell you the end of it: gold and silver, and vessels and precious stones, and samite, and cloth of silk, and robes vair [squirrel] and grey, and ermine, and every choicest thing found upon the earth . . . . never, since the world was created, had so much booty been won in any city.[2]

Priceless works of art were destroyed, yet many art treasures and sacred relics did find their way to the West.

The Fourth Crusade irreparably weakened the Byzantine empire. A tiny empire in exile held out around Nicaea in Asia Minor, while a Latin emperor ruled at Constantinople and Venice took over islands and coastal ports which enabled her to monopolize the eastern trade.

Four centuries of decline: Part II, 1204-1453. The Latin empire of Constantinople, hated by the native population upon whom it imposed the Roman Church, lasted only until 1261. In that year Michael Palaeologus of Nicaea, allying himself with Genoa, which was jealous of Venetian commercial supremacy in the eastern Mediterranean, reconquered Constantinople. Amid the rejoicing of the populace, a Greek patriarch was reinstated in Hagia Sophia.

The rule of the Palaeologi lasted until the demise of the Byzantine empire—a span of two centuries of decline. Internally, the empire lost strength and resiliency. A form of feudalism developed in which the great landed magnates resisted the authority of the emperor and the imperial bureaucracy. Taxes and customs duties diminished, coinage was debased, and the military and naval forces, composed increasingly of mercenaries, grew fatally weak. Bitter religious disputes arose between the clergy and the emperors who sought western aid in return for a promise to unite the Eastern and Roman churches.

Externally, the situation was critical. The empire held only a small portion of its former territory and was surrounded by ambitious rivals and foes. The Latins still retained southern Greece; the Venetians and Genoese each possessed coastal cities and island territories of the empire; and in the fourteenth century a powerful Serbian kingdom developed in the Balkans and menaced Constantinople.

In the meantime a new and ultimately fatal menace had arisen across the Straits in Asia Minor. In the late thirteenth century the Ottoman or Osmanli Turks, named after their early leader Osman, had received from the Seljuk sultan at Ankara a military fief along the Byzantine border south of Nicaea. The prospect of booty from raids across the border attracted swarms of recruits, with the result that Nicaea was taken in 1331. In 1356 the Ottomans crossed over to Europe and soon captured Adrianople, which became their capital. By 1390 they had overrun Bulgaria and Serbia and reached the Danube. The Ottoman Turks also expanded eastward in Asia Minor, until they were defeated in 1402 by the Mongol marauder Timur the Lame, or Tamerlane (see p. 173).

This defeat and the lack of a strong navy delayed the Turkish conquest of Constantinople. The end came in 1453. After a heroic defense of seven weeks, in which Constantine XI confronted the Turkish army of nearly 160,000 soldiers with only 9000 fighting men (half of whom were foreign mercenaries), the great eastern bulwark of Christian civilization collapsed before the might of Islam. As the Turks stormed the walls of the city, the emperor rushed to meet them, crying out as he was cut down: "God forbid that I should live an Emperor without an Empire! As my city falls, I will fall with it."[3]

The fall of Constantinople reverberated throughout the contemporary world. The last direct link with the classical era was shattered. First Rome had perished, now New Rome; an epoch that had seemed eternal had passed into history.

Reasons for endurance of the Byzantine empire. As the preceding résumé of Byzantine history attests, the empire's political life had always been stormy. During its thousand years of existence it experienced some sixty-five revolutions and the abdications or murders of more than sixty emperors. How did the empire manage to survive for such a long period?

One reason lay in its continuous use of a money economy, in contrast to the primitive barter economy then prevailing in the West. The use of money facilitated trade and the payment of taxes and enabled the empire to maintain standing military and naval forces. Until the latter days of the empire Byzantine military science was relatively advanced and the armed forces effective. Surviving military manuals indicate the efficiency of army organization, which included engineering and medical units. Also, the Byzantines had a secret weapon called "Greek fire," an inflammable chemical mixture whose main ingredient, saltpeter, made it a forerunner of gunpowder. As from a modern flamethrower,

As heirs of the Romans, the Byzantines were fierce and disciplined fighters. A detail from an illuminated manuscript shows their prowess in a naval battle.

Greek fire was catapulted out of tubes onto the decks of enemy ships.

Of great significance for the endurance, as well as the character, of the empire was the wholesale loss of African, Italian, and eastern territory by the year 700. The lands still under the emperor's control were now more homogeneous; most of the population was Greek. Thus historians speak of the seventh century as the period when the eastern Roman empire was transformed into the "Byzantine" empire—that is, transformed into a Hellenized civilization, taking its name appropriately from the original Greek settlement on which Constantinople had been built.

Another reason for the empire's endurance was its centralized system of administration. Where the West was broken up into numerous feudal principalities, the Byzantines were governed by a strong monarchy, aided by a well-trained bureaucracy. The emperor was the supreme military commander, the highest judge, the only legislator, and the protector of the Church. His authority rested on the claim that he was chosen by God to rule the Christian empire entrusted to him by God. So absolute was the emperor's control that his title *Autokrator* has been carried over into the English word *autocracy*, meaning "absolute supremacy." Only a successful revolution could depose him.

The Orthodox Church was another factor in the endurance of the empire. Linked closely to the state, the Church usually was the staunchest ally of the throne.

THE ORTHODOX CHURCH

Collaboration between Church and state. The Byzantine, or Orthodox, Church not only dominated religious and cultural life in the empire but was also interwoven with the political fabric. Whereas the Roman Church did not identify itself with the Roman Empire or any other state in the West but became an international body, the Orthodox Church was a state church ruled by God's vicar on earth—the king-priest who, surrounded by splendid pomp and ceremony, ruled the By-

zantine empire. In essence, the Church was a department of the state, and the emperor at times even intervened in spiritual matters. In many respects the patriarch of Constantinople had a position analogous to that of the pope in Rome, but with a significant difference—the patriarch, although elected by the bishops, was nominated by the emperor. Such blending of authority over Church and state in the office of emperor has been termed *Caesaropapism* (combining the functions of Caesar and pope).

The iconoclastic controversy. Relations between the eastern and western branches of the Church, continually undermined by what Constantinople viewed as Rome's excessive claims of primacy (see p. 128), deteriorated sharply in the eighth century as a result of the policies of the emperor Leo III. Although Leo had no use for Islam as a religion, he agreed with its contention that the employment of images and pictures in worship eventually led to idolatry. Therefore, in 726 Leo issued an edict forbidding the use of images (icons) of the sacred personages of Christianity, including Christ and all the saints. Statues were removed from churches, and church walls were whitewashed to cover all pictures.

In Constantinople rioting in protest against iconoclasm, or image breaking, broke out immediately. The demonstration was put down by troops, who killed some of the rioters. When the patriarch of Constantinople objected, he was replaced by another man more agreeable to the emperor's will. Riots continued to break out in Greece and Italy, and the pope at Rome, Gregory II, called a council of bishops who read out of the Church all those who had accepted iconoclasm. This caused an open breach between the papacy and the Eastern emperor.

Final separation of the churches. In 843 the iconoclastic controversy was finally settled by the restoration of images, but other sources of friction made permanent reunion of the Byzantine and Roman churches impossible. Exactly when the final breaking point was reached is difficult for scholars to determine. The traditional date is 1054, when doctrinal and liturgical disputes (the use of leavened vs. unleavened bread in the communion service, for example) caused the pope and the patriarch of Constantinople to excommunicate each other, thus creating a schism that was never to be healed. The important fact is that for centuries the papacy in the West and the Orthodox Church in the East steadily grew apart until they came to maintain distinctly separate existences, each viewing the other with suspicion and intolerance.

Missionary activity of the Church. The credit for converting many Slavic tribes to Christianity goes to the Orthodox Church. About 863 two monks who were also brothers, Cyril and Methodius, set out from Constantinople to bring the gospel to the pagan Moravians, a Slavic group living in what is now Czechoslovakia. They took with them translations of the Bible and the divine service written in an alphabet of modified Greek characters adapted to the Slavic languages. (The Cyrillic alphabet, used even now in Bulgaria, Serbia, and Russia, is named after Cyril, who invented it.) Although the Moravians and others of the westernmost Slavs eventually came under the sway of the Roman Church, the work begun by the two brothers triumphed among the Slavs to the east and south, so that ultimately the Orthodox Church extended throughout much of eastern Europe.

BYZANTINE ECONOMY, SOCIETY, AND CULTURE

Byzantine prosperity. During the early Middle Ages, Constantinople was called "The City"—with good reason. Visitors were fascinated by the pomp and pageantry of the court and Church, the scholarly and artistic endeavors, and the wealth, which far surpassed anything to be found in the West.

The complex urban civilization of the Byzantine world rested upon a foundation of strong and well-diversified economic activities. For centuries a stable agricultural system provided city and country folk with adequate food, and a varied industrial and commercial economy successfully supported large urban populations. The decline of population which had contributed to the collapse of the Roman Empire in the West did not occur in the East.

Geography was another major factor responsible for Byzantine prosperity. Constantinople stood at the crossroads of Europe and Asia, and its site ensured its being a port of transit for a great marine trading basin extending from the Adriatic to southern Russia. The merchants of Constantinople exported luxury goods, wines, spices, and silks to Russia and in turn imported furs, fish, caviar, beeswax, honey, and amber. Metalwork, leather goods, and other products manufactured in the empire went to India and China, while back to Constantinople came spices, precious stones, costly woods, and perfumes, some of which were transported on to the few western Europeans who could afford the luxuries of the Orient.

Trade supported, and was in turn stimulated by, the existence of a sound gold currency. In the West a decline in commerce had been attended by a shrinkage in the supply and use of money. The Byzantine empire, on the other hand, retained a currency of such excellence that its gold bezant was a medium of international exchange, remaining free of debasement until the eleventh century—far longer than any other coinage in history.

Besides being the greatest trading center of the early Middle Ages, Constantinople had industries that supplied Christendom with many products. The city specialized in luxury goods, and was famous for the manufacture of armor, weapons, hardware, and textiles. Until the time of Justinian, all raw silk for manufacturing fabrics had been imported from China, but after silkworms were smuggled out of China about 550 A.D., silk production began to flourish within the empire. Silken fabrics embroidered with gold and silver thread and fashioned into costly vestments for Church services or court attire were eagerly sought all over Europe. The silk industry was a profitable state monopoly.

The state controlled the economy through a system of guilds to which all tradesmen and members of the professions belonged. Wages, profits, hours of labor, and the price of foodstuffs—all were controlled "so that," as stated in a Byzantine handbook detailing such regulations, "men, being well directed thereby, should not shamelessly trample upon one another and the stronger should not do violence to the weaker."[4]

Constantinople, city of contrasts. The colorful social life of the empire was concentrated in Constantinople. The city itself had three centers: the imperial palace, the Church of Hagia Sophia, and the giant Hippodrome.

Court ceremonial was arranged to impress both foreigners and Byzantines with the emperor's exalted nature and his remoteness from mundane matters. An envoy to the palace was escorted through great lines of uniformed guards and dignitaries into a resplendent hall. At the appointed time a curtain was raised, disclosing the emperor clad in his imperial robes on his throne. Golden lions flanked the throne and golden birds perched in pomegranate trees. While the envoy prostrated himself, the throne would be raised aloft, symbolizing the unapproachability of the heir of the Caesars. During the audience the emperor remained motionless, silent, and aloof, while a court official spoke in his name.

Seating perhaps eighty thousand spectators, the Hippodrome was the scene of hotly disputed chariot races between the two major factions of the populace, the Blues and the Greens. Organized for political purposes as well as for sports, these factions used the Hippodrome as a forum to voice their opinions. The Blues tended to reflect the views of the great landowners, the Greens those of the merchants and the bureaucracy. In the Nike rebellion (see p. 141), Blues and Greens united in opposition to Justinian's costly policies.

Byzantine art: a unique synthesis. While Byzantine art was basically Roman in character during the reigns of the first Constantine and his immediate successors, the new capital's eastern location could not fail to bring additional artistic forces into play. Greek tradition had persisted in Alexandria and Antioch, and Constantinople was exposed also to influences from Persia. By the sixth century these elements were fused with the strong Christian spirit that had motivat-

This oldest known view of Constantinople, drawn in 1420, shows both its wealth of monumental architecture and its outstanding fortifications.

ed New Rome since its inception; the result was a new style of a uniquely Byzantine character.

Byzantine painting, for example, displays a synthesis of different—and even conflicting—cultural influences. The Greek tradition provided a graceful and idealistic approach; art historians point out, however, that while classical elements remained in Byzantine art, oriental influences—with their emphasis upon a more abstract and formalized style, vivid coloring, and ornamentation—eventually predominated.

Church architecture. The first great age of Byzantine art was associated with Justinian, who commissioned the magnificent Church of Hagia Sophia (Holy Wisdom), as well as many other churches and secular buildings. No other Byzantine church equaled Hagia Sophia in size or magnificence. According to Procopius, the historian of Justinian's reign, it was "a church, the like of which has never been seen since Adam, nor ever will be" (see Color Plate 6). The effect of light playing upon its multicolored marbles and bright mosaics moved Procopius to declare:

On entering the church to pray one feels at once that it is the work, not of man's effort or industry, but in truth the work of the Divine Power; and the spirit, mounting to heaven, realizes that here God is very near and that He delights in this dwelling that He has chosen for Himself.[5]

The dome is the crowning glory of Hagia Sophia both because of its beauty and because it represents a major advance in architecture. With forty windows piercing its base, Procopius described it as

marvellous in its grace, but by reason of the seeming insecurity of its composition altogether terrifying. For it seems somehow to float in the air on no firm basis, but to be poised aloft to the peril of those inside it.[6]

The Romans had been able to construct a huge dome on the Pantheon but had erected it upon massive circular walls which limited the shape of the building. The dome of Hagia

In this late tenth-century mosiac over the south door of Hagia Sophia, Constantine is offering his city and Justinian is presenting his church to the Virgin. The combination of oriental style and Christian subject matter is characteristic of Byzantine art.

Sophia was supported by pendentives, four triangular segments which received the weight of the dome and distributed it to four supporting piers. The use of pendentives made it possible to place a dome over a square area.

Over the centuries many other fine structures employed the pendentive principle. A favorite design, with symbolic appeal, was a church in the shape of a cross, surmounted by a dome. A still further development was the five-domed church, which was cross-shaped, with a central dome at the crossing and a smaller dome on each of the four arms. The most famous existing example of this design is St. Mark's in Venice, constructed in the eleventh century.

Vivid mosaics and decorative arts. The second outstanding period of Byzantine art began in the middle of the ninth century with the settling of the iconoclastic controversy and lasted until the sack of Constantinople in 1204. This age is notable for producing the finest examples of Byzantine decorative art.

In the decoration of churches, Byzantine artists made extensive use of mosaics—small pieces of multicolored glass or stone cemented into patterns to form brilliant decorations. Not only did the rich colors of the mosaics increase the splendor of the church interiors and heighten the emotional appeal of the rituals, but the representations also served as useful teaching devices by presenting the viewer with scenes from the Bible and with images of Christ, the Virgin, and the saints.

With their penchant for vivid colors and elaborate detail, Byzantine artists also excelled in such decorative arts as carving in ivory, the illumination of manuscripts, and the decoration of book covers, chests, thrones, and altars. Constantinople was renowned for its cloisonné technique, by which enamel was inlaid between thin gold bands to form the design.

Wall and panel painting. The third important period of Byzantine artistic activity took place during the fourteenth and fifteenth centuries when Byzantium was no longer wealthy. This revival expressed itself in brilliant paintings on walls and panels, a form of art necessitated in some measure by the need to find cheaper substitutes for expensive mosaics and enamels.

Like mosaics, Byzantine wall paintings were employed to decorate churches. In addition, icons—panel paintings of sacred personages—were used in daily worship. As in mosaics, the subject matter of Byzantine painting was treated symbolically rather than realistically: "like much of the art of today, which is not easy to understand at first glance, its significance lies below the surface; it is an art of the spirit rather than of the flesh, and must be approached from that point of view."[7]

The preservation of classical learning. The official adoption of the Greek language in the formative centuries of the Byzantine empire proved a stimulus to the preservation of classical works in philosophy, literature, and science. The scholars who perpetuated the Greek tradition were not clerics, as in the West, but members of the civil service; Byzantine monasteries produced many saints and mystics but showed little interest in learning or teaching. Byzantine scholars, concerned chiefly with recovering and classifying Hellenic and Hellenistic learning, were imitative rather than creative, and their own contributions tended to be a rehash of classical works. Yet when in the twelfth century the West began absorbing Greek science and Aristotelian philosophy from the Muslims in Spain, it was to Byzantine scholarship that the latter were indebted. Moreover, most of the West's knowledge of Greek literature and Platonic philosophy came from Constantinople in the fourteenth and fifteenth centuries.

One of the great achievements of Byzantine scholarship was the codification of Roman law. In 528 Justinian convoked a commission of scholars to gather and classify the vast, disorganized, and often contradictory mass of law that had accumulated during centuries of Roman government. The result was a great legal work popularly known as the Justinian Code and formally titled the *Corpus Juris Civilis*. It organized the imperial law of the last four centuries into the *Codex* and included as well the *Digest* of the writings of republican and imperial jurists, and the *Institutes*, a commentary on the principles

The Transfiguration of Christ is a twelfth-century example of Byzantine enamel work. The combination of oriental style and Christian subject matter is an important characteristic of Byzantine art.

underlying the laws. Appended to the main text were the *Novels*, the laws promulgated by Justinian and written in Greek, now the dominant language of the empire.

By this codification, Rome's priceless legal heritage was preserved and passed on to posterity. In holding that the will of the emperor is the source of law, that the judge is the emperor's representative in interpreting law, and that equity is the basic principle of law, Justinian's Code stands in sharp contrast to Germanic folk law (see p. 133). The Code was unknown in the West during the early Middle Ages, but in the twelfth century it slowly began to have a notable influence on the improvement of medieval justice and the emergence of strong monarchs, who borrowed for their own use the Roman doctrine of the emperor as a source of law.

EARLY RUSSIA

The Slavs. While the fortunes of the Byzantine empire had been ebbing and flowing, its culture had exercised continuous and substantial influence upon the development of Russia in its formative centuries.

The ancestors of the Russians were the Slavic tribes, whose original home is thought by some scholars to have been the wooded area of the Pripet Marshes (see map, p. 153). Moving into the lands vacated by the migrating Germans, in time three main groups developed. The Western Slavs—Poles and Bohemians—reached the Elbe and came under Latin Christian influences. Both the Southern Slavs, who moved into the Balkans, and the Eastern Slavs, the ancestors of the Russians who occupied the lands between the Carpathians and the Don, were subjected to Greek Christian influences.

Founding of a Russian state. About the time when their Viking brethren from Denmark and Norway were plundering and conquering throughout western Europe (see p. 194), Swedish Norsemen, called Varangians by the Byzantines, combined piracy with trade and began to venture along the waterways from the eastern Baltic to the Black and Caspian seas. The Slavic settlements along the rivers often hired the fierce Varangians as protectors. In 862 the people of Novgorod employed one such warrior, the half-legendary Rurik, who became prince of the city. His brothers and companions established themselves in other cities, one being Kiev.

By the late ninth century the Varangian ruler of Kiev had succeeded in establishing his supremacy over a large area which gradually became known as Russia, a name derived from *Rus* (meaning "seafarers"), by which the Slavs knew the Norse. The Kievan state operated as a loose confederation, with the prince of Kiev recognized as senior among his kinsmen who ruled the other Russian city-states. By the end of the tenth century the Norse minority had merged with the Slavic population.

Kievan Russia was less a political entity than a commercial entity, a coordinated group of princely states with a common interest in maintaining trade along the river routes. Kievan military expeditions against Constantinople itself began as early as 860, partly as typical Viking raids for plunder and partly to extort treaties which opened up a profitable Russian-Byzantine trade. Every spring after the ice had melted on the Dnieper, cargoes of furs, wax, honey, and slaves were floated down to Kiev. From there a great flotilla would descend the Dnieper and proceed along the Black Sea shore to Constantinople. Returning with silks, spices, jewelry, wines, and metalwares, the Kievans would pass these goods on to northeastern Europe via Novgorod and the Baltic.

Christianity in Kievan Russia. The official conversion of the Russians to Christianity took place about 989 under Prince Vladimir of Kiev. According to an early Russian chronicle, Vladimir shopped around before making his choice of religions. He rejected Islam because of its injunctions against the use of strong drink, Judaism because the God of the Jews could not be considered very powerful since He had allowed them to be ejected from their Holy Land, and Roman Christianity because the pope entertained dangerous ideas about his superiority to all secular rulers. There remained the Orthodox Church of the Byzantines, which was presented to Vladimir's subjects as his choice.

From the outset the Kievan princes followed the Byzantine example and kept the Church dependent on them, even for its revenues, so that the Russian Church and state were always closely linked. The Russians also copied the Byzantines in Church ritual, theology, and such practices as monasticism.

Apogee and decline of Kiev. Kiev reached its greatest splendor in the reign of Yaroslav the Wise (1019-1054 A.D.), who issued Russia's first law code (based on the customary law of the Eastern Slavs) and was a patron of art and learning. Byzantine architects and artists were brought to Kiev to build the cathedral of Hagia Sophia, named after its prototype in Constantinople. Yaroslav negotiated marriage alliances for his children with the royal families of Poland, Norway, Hungary, and France.

Following the death of Yaroslav, however, the princes of the various cities fought increasingly among themselves for possession of the Kievan state; and to these disruptions was added the devastation of the nomads who roamed uncomfortably close to the capital and cut the trade route to Constantinople. The trading and farming population around Kiev could not sustain such hardships, and they sought refuge in flight. Many fled northeastward to city-states in the neighborhood of present-day Moscow. When the Asiatic Mongols destroyed Kiev in 1240 (see p. 277), it had already lost much of its power, wealth, and population.

Byzantine aspects of Kievan culture. The commercial contacts between Constantinople and Kiev and the power of the Orthodox Church during the Kievan period were the chief factors responsible for the Byzantine influences in Russia. Architecture, for example, came within the province of the Church. The outstanding churches built at Kiev, Novgorod, and other cities show strong Byzantine influence. In time architects developed a distinctly Russian style, including the characteristic "onion dome," which is merely a fanciful "helmet" covering the dome. The decoration of churches also followed Byzantine models. In fact, the earliest mosaics, as well as mural and icon paintings, appear to have been the work of Byzantine artists who were brought to Russia. At Hagia Sophia in Kiev, some of these wall paintings still remain.

The adaptation of the Greek alphabet to the Slavic tongue and the translation of Church liturgy into Slavic stimulated the growth of Russian literature. Although at first Kievan literature consisted of translations of Byzantine works—chiefly sermons, saints' lives, and condemnations of Roman Catholicism—in time a literature of the Russian people emerged, as epics of their strug-

RUSSIA ABOUT 1000

‑‑‑‑ Varangian Trade Route

The Byzantine influence on Russian architecture is evident in Hagia Sophia in Kiev, originally built in the eleventh century by Yaroslav the Wise.

gles to resist the barbaric nomads from the steppes appeared. But the use of Slavic in the Church caused many churchmen to remain ignorant of Latin and to lack even a good knowledge of Greek; hence the majority of the learned had no direct contact with the literature in those two languages. Much of Russia's cultural isolationism in the past has been ascribed to this factor.

By the eleventh century, however, and particularly during the reign of Yaroslav the Wise, Kievan Russia could boast of a culture and an economy that were superior to what then existed in western Europe; for these achievements Kiev was primarily obligated to the Byzantine empire, which at the time enjoyed the highest cultural level in Christendom. In the wake of the fall of Constan-tinople in 1453, the Russians would appropriate even more of the Byzantine tradition, dubbing the new Russian center of Moscow the "Third Rome."

MUHAMMAD AND HIS FAITH

Pre-Islamic Arabia. In our examination of the Byzantine empire, we had occasion to mark the swift rise of a rival religious culture, Islam, imbued with expansionist aims. In 1453, adherents of that faith succeeded in conquering the eastern citadel of Christianity. We shall now trace the genesis and meteoric expansion of Islam, together with the splendid civilization it fostered.

The term *Islam*, meaning "submission to God," is derived from the Muslim holy book, the Koran. The followers of Muhammad, the founder of the faith, are known as Muslims. (This faith is often referred to as Muhammadanism, but Muslims frown on this term, which implies the worship and deification of Muhammad.)

The story begins in Arabia, a peninsula one third the size of the continental United States. Much of it is desert, and rainfall is scarce in the rest of the peninsula. Thus vegetation is scant and very little land is suitable for agriculture. Throughout much of Arabia, particularly in the interior, nomadism was the only way of life.

The nomads, or Bedouins, lived according to a tribal pattern; at the head of the tribe was the sheik, elected and advised by the heads of the related families comprising the tribe. Driven from place to place in their search for pastures to sustain their flocks, the Bedouins led a precarious existence. Aside from their flocks, they relied on booty from raids on settlements, on passing caravans, and on one another. The Bedouins worshiped a large number of gods and spirits, many of whom were believed to inhabit trees, wells, and stones. Each tribe had its own god, symbolized generally by a sacred stone which served as an altar where communal sacrifices were offered.

Although the Bedouins of the interior led a primitive and largely isolated existence, some parts of Arabia were influenced by neighboring—and more advanced—cultures. By the latter half of the sixth century Christian and Jewish groups were found throughout the Arabian peninsula. Their religious convictions and moral principles had a strong effect on the indigenous population, and their monotheistic beliefs were later incorporated into Islamic doctrine.

Mecca. Several of the more advanced cities were in Hejaz, among them Mecca, destined to be the key city in the Islamic religion. Fifty miles inland from the port of Jiddah, Mecca was favorably located for trade. Its merchants carried on business with southern Arabia, with Abyssinia across the Red Sea, and with the Byzantine and Persian empires. Mecca was controlled by the Quraysh, an Arab tribe whose members formed trading companies that cooperated in dispatching large caravans north and south.

The Quraysh merchants were also concerned with protecting a source of income derived from the annual pilgrimage of tribes to a famous religious sanctuary at Mecca. Known as the Kaaba (cube), this square temple contained the sacred Black Stone, by legend brought to Abraham and his son Ishmael by Gabriel. According to tradition, the stone was originally white but had been blackened by the sins of those touching it. The Kaaba supposedly housed the images of some 360 local deities and fetishes.

Muhammad, founder of Islam. Into this environment at Mecca was born a man destined to transform completely the religious, political, and social organization of his people. Muhammad (570-632) came from a family belonging to the Quraysh tribe. Left an orphan in early life, he was brought up by an uncle and later engaged in the caravan trade. Muhammad's formative years are known to us by legend only, but his first biographer relates that he was influenced by a monotheist named Zayd, who may have been either a Jewish or a Christian convert. When he was about twenty years old, Muhammad entered the service of a wealthy widow, Khadija, whose caravans traded with Syria. In his twenty-fifth year he married his employer, who was some fifteen years his senior. Despite the difference in their ages, the marriage was a happy one; and they had four daughters.

According to tradition, Muhammad frequently went into the foothills near Mecca to meditate. One night he dreamed that the archangel Gabriel appeared with the command, "Recite!" When Muhammad asked, "What shall I recite?" he was told:

Recite in the name of thy Lord who created
Man from blood coagulated.
Recite! Thy Lord is wondrous kind
Who by the pen has taught mankind
Things they knew not (being blind).[8]

This was the first of a series of visions and revelations.

Far from regarding himself as a prophet, Muhammad was at first afraid that he had been possessed by a spirit, and he even contemplated suicide. During his periods of doubt and anguish Muhammad was comforted by Khadija, and finally he became certain that he was a divinely appointed prophet of Allah, "*The* God." He became convinced that Allah was the one and only God—the same God worshiped by the Jews and Christians—who had chosen him to perfect the religion revealed earlier to Abraham, Moses, the prophets, and Jesus.

At first Muhammad had little success in attracting followers. His first converts were his wife, his cousin Ali, and Abu Bakr, a leading merchant of the Quraysh tribe who was highly respected for his integrity. Abu Bakr remained the constant companion of the Prophet during his persecution and exile and eventually became the first caliph of Islam. Most other early converts were slaves or oppressed persons. Opposition came from the leading citizens ("Shall we forsake our gods for a mad poet?"), who either ridiculed Muhammad's doctrine of resurrection (pre-Islamic Arabs had only vague notions concerning the afterlife) or feared that his monotheistic teaching might harm the city's lucrative pilgrimage trade to the Kaaba.

The Hijra and triumphal return to Mecca. The first encouraging development occurred when a group of pilgrims from Medina, a prosperous trading rival of Mecca with a large Jewish population, accepted the Prophet's teachings. Meanwhile, increased persecu-

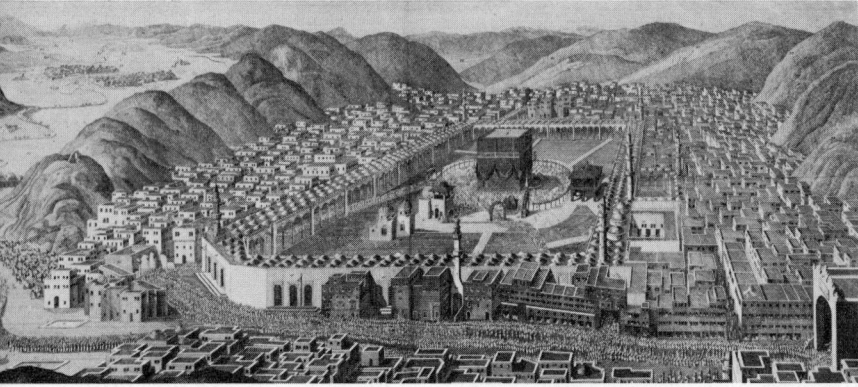

Mecca as it very likely looked in the Middle Ages. Each year thousands of Muslims make a pilgrimage to Mecca to worship at the Kaaba, a temple housing the sacred Black Stone that the angel Gabriel, according to legend, gave to Abraham and his son.

tion of the Muslims in Mecca encouraged the Prophet to migrate with his band to Medina.

Carried out in secrecy, this move took place in 622 and is known as the *Hijra*, which means "flight" or, in this context, "the breaking of old ties." The Hijra was such a turning point in Muhammad's career that the year in which it occurred is counted as the first in the Muslim calendar. In Mecca, Muhammad's own kinsmen had persecuted him, but in Medina he came to be acknowledged as a leader with divine authority in spiritual and temporal matters. He commanded the Muslims to turn toward Mecca when praying. This practice served to recognize the city as the spiritual capital of Islam and also emphasized the need for its conquest from the pagan trading oligarchy that governed it.

In the year 630 Muhammad marched on Mecca with an army. His old enemies were forced to surrender to the Prophet, who acted with magnanimity toward them. His first act was to cast out of the Kaaba its multitude of idols and fetishes; but the temple itself, together with the Black Stone, was preserved as the supreme center of Islam, the "Mecca" to which each devout Muslim should make a pilgrimage during his lifetime.

With Mecca and Medina both under his control, Muhammad became the undisputed master of Hejaz. In the two remaining years of his life tribe after tribe of Bedouins throughout Arabia offered him their loyalty. Upon his death in 632 the Prophet left behind a faith which had united Arabia and which was to astound the world with its militant expansion.

The Koran, the Muslim bible. Muslims believe that the Koran contains the actual word of God as revealed to Muhammad. The Prophet's revelations occurred over a period of more than twenty years, and before his death many of the messages had been written down. Abu Bakr, Muhammad's successor as head of the community, ordered the compilation of all these materials, including the passages that had only been committed to memory. Twenty years after the death of the Prophet, an authorized version was promulgated, which has remained the official text to the present day.

Because the Koran must never be used in translation for worship, the spread of Islam created a great deal of linguistic unity. Arabic supplanted many local languages as the language of daily use, and that part of the Muslim world which stretches from Morocco to Iraq is still Arabic-speaking. Furthermore, this seventh-century book remains the last word on Muslim theology, law, and social institutions and is therefore still the most important textbook being used in Muslim universities.

Theology of Islamic faith. Within the Koran one finds the central tenet of Islam—monotheism. There is only one God, Allah; this is proclaimed five times daily from the minaret of the mosque as the faithful are called to prayer:

God is most great. I testify that there is no God but Allah. I testify that Muhammad is God's Apostle. Come to prayer, come to security. God is most great."

While Allah is the only God, many other supernatural figures are acknowledged, as in Christianity. Islamic angels, for example, are similar to those described in the Bible. In addition, there exist *jinn*, who are spirits midway between angels and men. Some *jinn* are good, while others are evil. Islam recognizes the existence of prophets who preceded Muhammad. The Koran mentions twenty-eight, of whom four are Arabian, eighteen are found in the Old Testament, three in the New Testament (including Jesus), and one of the remainder has been identified as Alexander the Great. But to Muslims the greatest prophet is, of course, Muhammad. He is ascribed no superhuman status, although he was chosen to proclaim God's message of salvation. That message included the belief in the Last Judgment and the existence of paradise and hell.

Geography played an important role in the Prophet's concepts of heaven and hell: both are described in terms that incite an immediate reaction in people living in the desert. Those who have submitted to Allah's rule—the charitable, humble, and forgiving —and those who have fought for His faith, shall dwell in a Garden of Paradise, reposing in cool shades, eating delectable foods, attended by "fair ones with wide, lovely eyes like unto hidden pearls," and hearing no vain speech or recrimination but only "Peace! Peace!" This veritable oasis is far different from the agonies of the desert hell that awaits the unbelievers, the covetous, and the erring. Cast into hell with its "scorching wind and shadow of black smoke," they will drink of boiling water.

Islam imposes on all Muslims five obligations, known as the "Pillars of Faith"—belief in only one God and in Muhammad as His Prophet, prayer, almsgiving, fasting, and a pilgrimage to Mecca. Prayers are said five times a day, and each occasion calls for a sequence of recitations coordinated with a sequence of postures. They are to be repeated either alone or, preferably, in a mosque. The Muslim is required to give alms, a practice regarded as expressing piety and contributing to one's salvation. During the month of Ramadan, the ninth month of the lunar year, Muslims fast. Since food and drink are prohibited between sunrise and sunset, this is a very strenuous observance, although sick persons and travelers are exempted providing they fast for an equal length of time later. The second chapter of the Koran commands Muslims to make a pilgrimage to Mecca, where they go through traditional ceremonies, such as kissing the Black Stone in the Kaaba. Each Muslim should make the pilgrimage to Mecca at least once during his lifetime if he has the means.

The Koran also provides Muslims with a body of ethical teachings. Idolatry, infanticide, usury, gambling, the drinking of wine, and the eating of pork are all prohibited. Similarly, Islam encouraged the humane treatment of slaves and regulated such matters as the guardianship of orphans and divorce. Muslim men were allowed four wives (and an unspecified number of concubines), but if he could not treat them all with equal kindness and impartiality, a husband should retain but one.

Pervading Islam was the principle of religious equality. There was no priesthood—no intermediaries between man and God. There were leaders of worship in the mosques as well as the *ulema,* a class of learned experts in the interpretation of the Koran; but they were all laymen. In this way Islam was spared the priestly tyranny such as arose in India, where the Brahmins considered themselves superior to all other classes in the rigid caste system.

Islamic law. In addition to being a religion, Islam offered a system of government, law, and society. The Islamic community was an excellent example of a theocratic state, one in which all power resides in God in whose behalf political, religious, and other forms of authority are exercised.

Especially in the period of expansion after the Prophet's death, the Islamic state required detailed rules covering a variety of new situations. The code that was developed was based partly on pre-Islamic legal customs. Before Muhammad's time each tribe had its own *sunna*, or body of custom, which served as a law code. After the Prophet's death his followers prepared a Sunna based upon the "traditions" (*hadith*) of what he had said and done. Using the Koran and the Sunna as their sources, Islamic jurists developed a body of religious law which regulated all aspects of Muslim life. Its development and interpretation were in the hands of the *ulema*. Agreement among these scholars set the seal of orthodoxy on questions of text and doctrine, with the result that Islamic law became progressively authoritarian and static.

THE SPREAD OF ISLAM

Expansion under the first four caliphs. Upon the Prophet's death in 632 the question arose as to who should direct the fortunes of Islam. This was a dangerous moment. Muhammad left no son to succeed him; and, even if he had, neither his unique position as the Prophet nor Arab custom permitted any such automatic succession. Acting swiftly, Muhammad's associates selected the Prophet's most trusted friend and advisor, Abu Bakr, as his official successor, the caliph (from *khalifa*, meaning "deputy"). The second caliph was also one of Muhammad's companions, while the fourth was his cousin and son-in-law.

During the reigns of the first four caliphs (632-661) Islam spread rapidly. Their wars of conquest were aided by the Prophet's belief that any Muslim dying in battle for the faith was assured entrance into paradise. This concept of holy war (*jihad*) bred in the Arabs, already a fierce fighting people, fanatical courage. Moreover, the prospect of rich and fertile territory, as well as plunder, proved a strong incentive to a people who had been eking out a bare existence from the desert.

The Islamic cause was also aided by political upheavals occurring outside of Arabia. The Muslim triumphs in the Near East can be partly accounted for by the long series of wars between the Byzantine and Persian empires. Earlier Byzantine victories had left both sides exhausted and open to conquest. Moreover, the inhabitants of Syria and Egypt, alienated by religious dissent, were anxious to be free of Byzantine rule. In 636 Arab forces conquered Syria. The Muslims then wrested Iraq from the Persians and, within ten years after Muhammad's death, subdued Persia itself. The greater part of Egypt fell with little resistance in 640 and the rest shortly afterward. Thus, by the end of the reigns of the first four caliphs, Islam had vastly increased its territory (see map, p. 159).

The imposition of a head tax on all non-Muslims encouraged many to become converts to Islam. Contrary to exaggerated accounts in the West of the forceful infliction of Islam upon conquered peoples, the Jews and Christians outside of Arabia enjoyed toleration because they worshiped the same God as the Muslims.

Islam is one of the most effective religions in removing barriers of race and nationality. Apart from a certain privileged position allowed the Arabs, distinctions were mostly those of class. The new religion converted and embraced peoples of many colors and cultures. This egalitarian feature of Islam undoubtedly aided its expansion.

Arab domination under the Umayyads. The expansion of Islam under the first four caliphs produced a new type of claimant to the caliphate—powerful generals and governors of provinces. In 661 the governor of Syria proclaimed himself caliph, made Damascus his capital, and founded the Umayyad dynasty which lasted until 750. Thus the caliphate became in fact, although never in law, a hereditary office, not, as previously, a position filled by election.

The Umayyad navy held Cyprus, Rhodes, and a string of Aegean islands, which served as a base for annual sea-borne attacks on Constantinople from 674 to 678. With the aid of Greek fire, Constantinople was saved, and the Arab advance was checked for the first time. Westward across North Africa, however, the Umayyad armies had great success. The Berbers, a warlike Hamitic-speaking people inhabiting the land between the Mediterranean and the Sahara, resisted stubbornly until converted to Islam. The next logical jump was across the Strait of Gibraltar into the weak kingdom of the Visigoths in Spain. The governor of Muslim North Africa sent his general, Tarik, and an army across the Strait into Spain in 711. Seven years later the kingdom of the Visigoths had completely crumbled. The Muslims swept across the

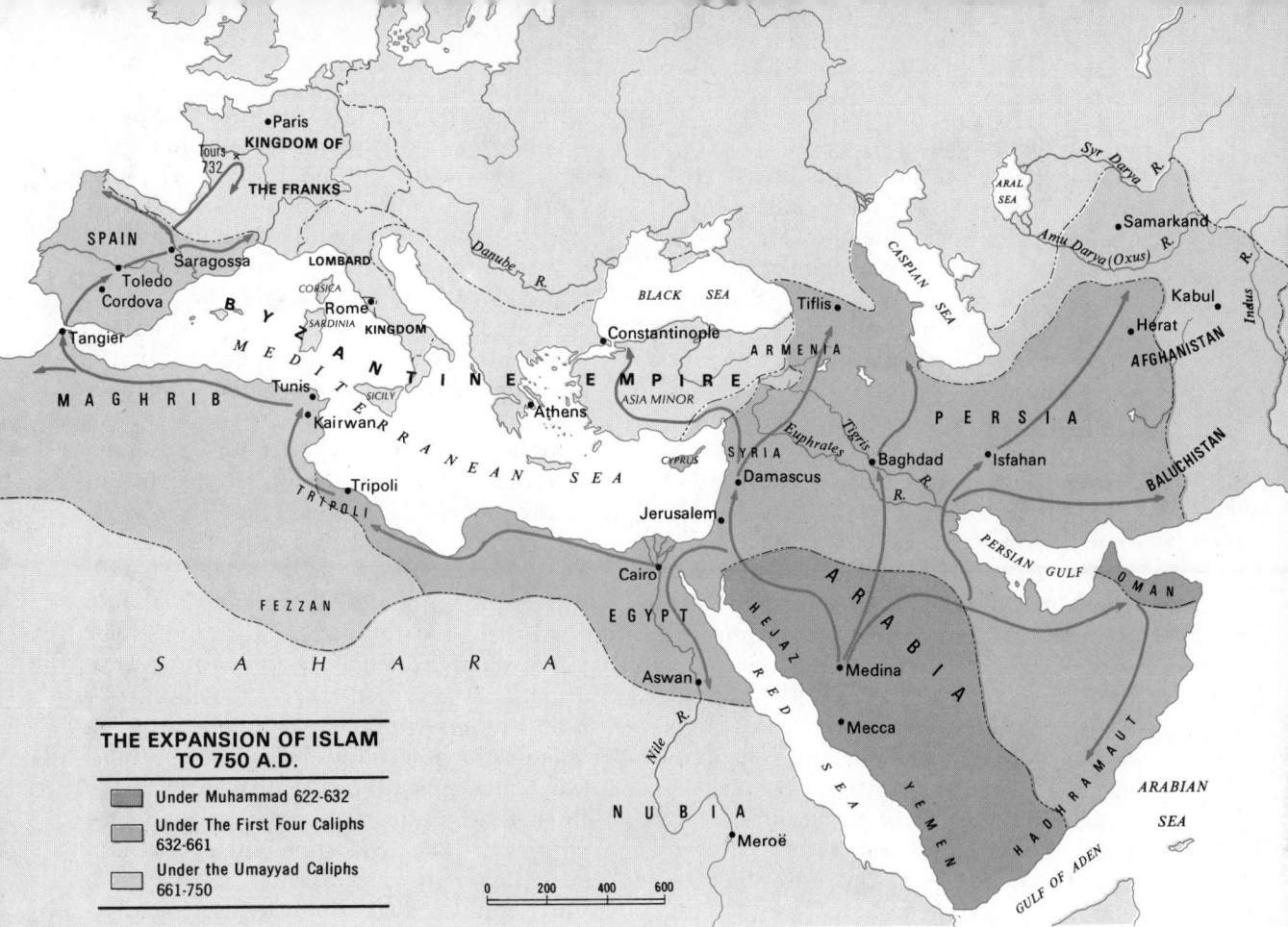

THE EXPANSION OF ISLAM TO 750 A.D.

Under Muhammad 622-632

Under The First Four Caliphs 632-661

Under the Umayyad Caliphs 661-750

0   200   400   600

Pyrenees and gained a foothold in southwest France, where they carried out a major raid to explore the possibility of a further northward advance. However, they were defeated by Charles Martel near Tours in 732 (see p. 190), in a battle which, together with their defeat by the Byzantine emperor Leo III in 718 (see p. 143), proved decisive in halting their westward expansion. Meanwhile the Muslims had been expanding eastward into Central Asia, and by the eighth century they could claim lands as far as Turkestan and the Indus valley.

The mainstay of Umayyad power was the ruling class of Arabs, who formed a privileged aristocracy greatly outnumbered by non-Arabic converts to Islam—Egyptians, Syrians, Persians, Berbers, and others. Many of these possessed cultures much more advanced than that of the Arabs, and the economic and cultural life of the Arab empire depended on these people. But because they were not Arab by birth, they were treated as second-class Muslims. They were not permitted to marry Arab women, and as soldiers they received less pay and booty than the Arabs. Resentment grew among the non-Arabic Muslims and eventually helped bring about the downfall of the Umayyads.

Shia movement against the ruling group. This resentment also found expression in the religious sphere, where large numbers of the non-Arabic Muslims joined the sect known as the Shia, formed when Ali, Muhammad's son-in-law and fourth caliph, was deposed by the Umayyads. The Shia continued to regard Ali and his descendants as the rightful rulers of the Islamic community. They believed that in every age a messiah-like leader would appear and that he must be obeyed. The Shia also rejected the Sunna, the body of later tradition concerning Muhammad that was not contained in the Koran; they insisted on the Koran as the sole authority on the life and teachings of the Prophet. Though originally an Arab party, the Shia in time became a general Islamic movement that stood for opposition to the ruling dynasty. The Shia evolved into one of the two major groups in Islam. The majority, named Sunnites because they were the "orthodox" perpetuators of Muhammad's Sunna, or tradition, upheld the principle that the caliph owed his position to the consent of the Islamic community. The numerical superiority of the Sunnites has continued to this day.

The Abbasids, high tide of Islamic civilization. In 750 the Umayyad dynasty was crushed by rebels, and a new dynasty, the Abbasid, ruled most of the Muslim world from 750 to 1258. The city of Baghdad was built in 762 as the capital of the new dynasty. The Abbasids owed their success to the discontent of the non-Arabic Muslims, who were the chief elements in the towns and in the Shia.

The fall of the Umayyad dynasty marked the end of Arab predominance; henceforth all Muslims were treated as equals. The Arab aristocracy had led the forces of conquest during the great period of Islamic expansion, but with the advent of more stable political conditions, the important status thus far held by the Arab soldier was given to non-Arab administrators and merchants. The traditional Arabic patterns of nomadism and tribal war were giving way before economic prosperity, the growth of town life, and the rise of a merchant class. The Abbasid caliph who built Baghdad forecast that it would become the "most flourishing city in the world"; and indeed it rivaled Constantinople for that honor, situated as it was on the trade routes linking West and East. Furthermore, Abbasid patronage of scholarship and the arts produced a rich and complex culture far surpassing that then existing in western Europe.

The location of a new capital at Baghdad resulted in a shift of Islam's center of gravity to the province of Iraq, whose soil, watered by the Tigris and Euphrates, had nurtured man's earliest civilization. Here the Abbasid caliphs set themselves up as potentates in the traditional style of the ancient East—and more particularly of Persia—so that they were surrounded by a lavish court that contrasted sharply with the simplicity of the Prophet.

The Abbasid dynasty marked the high tide of Islamic power and civilization. The empire ruled by these caliphs was greater in size than the domain of the Roman Caesars; it was the product of an expansion during which the Muslims had assimilated peoples, customs, cultures, and inventions on an unprecedented scale. This Islamic state, in fact, drew on the resources of the entire known world.

Trade, industry, and agriculture. From the eighth to the twelfth centuries the Muslim world enjoyed a prosperity such as post-Roman Europe did not experience until early modern times. In close contact with three continents, the Muslims could shuttle goods back and forth from China to western Europe and from Russia to central Africa. Trade was facilitated also by the absence of tariff barriers within the empire and by the tolerance of the caliphs, who allowed non-Muslim merchants and craftsmen to reside in their territories and carry on commerce with their home countries. The presence of such important urban centers as Baghdad, Cairo, and Cordova stimulated trade and industry throughout the Muslim world.

The cosmopolitan nature of Baghdad was evident in its bazaars, which contained goods from all over the known world. There were spices, minerals, and dyes from India; gems and fabrics from Central Asia; honey and wax from Scandinavia and Russia; and ivory and gold dust from Africa. One bazaar in the city specialized in goods from China, including silks, musk, and porcelain. In the slave marts the Muslim traders bought and sold Scandinavians, Mongolians from Central Asia, and Africans. Joint-stock companies flourished along with branch banking, and checks (an Arabic word) drawn on one bank could be cashed elsewhere in the empire.

Muslim textile industries turned out excellent cottons (muslins), silks, and linens. The steel of Damascus and Toledo, the leather of Cordova, and the glass of Syria became world famous. Notable also was the art of papermaking, learned from China. Under the Abbasids, vast irrigation projects in Iraq increased cultivable land which yielded large crops of fruits and cereals. Wheat came from the Nile valley, cotton from North Africa, olives and wine from Spain, wool from eastern Asia Minor, and horses from Persia.

The opulent reign of Harun al-Rashid. Just as the Abbasid was the most brilliant of Muslim dynasties, so the rule of Harun al-Rashid (786-809) was the most spectacular of the Abbasid reigns. He was the contemporary of Charlemagne, who had revived the Roman Empire in the West (see Chapter 8), and there can be no doubt that Harun was the most powerful ruler of the two and the symbol of the more highly advanced culture. The two monarchs were on friendly terms, based on self-interest. Charlemagne wanted to exert pressure on the Byzantine emperor to recognize his new imperial title. Harun, on the other hand, saw Charlemagne as an ally against the Umayyad rulers of Spain, who had broken away from Abbasid domination. The two emperors exchanged embassies and presents. The Muslim sent the Christian rich fabrics, aromatics, and even an elephant named Abu-Lababah, meaning "the father of intelligence." An intricate water clock from Baghdad seems to have been looked upon as a miracle in the West.

Relations between the Abbasid caliphate and the Byzantine empire were never very cordial, and conflicts often broke out along the constantly shifting border that separated Christian and Muslim territories. Harun al-Rashid once replied to a communique from the Byzantine emperor in the following terms:

In the name of God, the Merciful, the Compassionate. From Haroun, Commander of the Faithful, to Nicephorus, the dog of the Greeks. I have read your letter, you son of a she-infidel, and you shall see the answer before you hear it.[10]

Whereupon the irate caliph sent forth expeditions to ravage Asia Minor.

In the days of Harun al-Rashid, Baghdad's wealth and splendor equaled that of Constantinople, and its chief glory was the royal palace. With its annexes for eunuchs, officials, and a harem, the caliph's residence occupied a third of Baghdad. Resplendently furnished, the caliph's audience chamber was the setting for an elaborate ceremonial which continued that of the Byzantines and Persians.

Disintegration of the Abbasid empire. Despite the unprecedented prosperity of the far-flung Islamic world, the political unity of Islam began to disappear soon after the accession of the Abbasid dynasty. The first sign of political disintegration appeared in 756 when a member of the deposed Umayyad family founded his own dynasty at Cordova in Spain; in 929 his descendant assumed the title of caliph. Also in the tenth century the Fatimids—Shiites who claimed descent from Muhammad's daughter Fatima who had married Ali, the fourth caliph—proclaimed themselves the true caliphs of all Islam. From their capital at Cairo, which they founded, their rule eventually extended from Morocco to northern Mesopotamia.

Meanwhile, in the latter part of the tenth century Turkish nomads, called Seljuks, had migrated from Central Asia into the Abbasid lands, where they accepted Islam. After annexing most of Persia, the Seljuks gained control of Baghdad in 1055 and absorbed Iraq. Subsequently they conquered Syria and Palestine at the expense of the Fatimids and proceeded to annex most of Asia Minor from the Byzantines. It was the Seljuk's great advance that prompted the First Crusade in 1095. The Seljuks permitted the Abbasids to retain nominal rule, but a new and terrible enemy was now to appear and change everything.

Early in the thirteenth century Genghis Khan succeeded in uniting the nomads of Mongolia; he and his successors conquered eastern and central Asia (see Chapters 7 and 10) and swept into Persia and Iraq. In 1258 a grandson of Genghis Khan captured Baghdad and had the caliph put in a sack and trampled to death. Not only did the Abbasid dynasty come to an end, but so did most of the vast irrigation system that had supported the land since the beginning of civilization; Iraq was not to recover until modern times. The dynasty established by the Mongols survived for only a short time, and the Mongol ruling class was eventually absorbed into the native population of Persia and Iraq.

Muslim Egypt was saved from the Mongol advance by the Mamluks, captured slaves trained to become good Muslims and soldiers. They took over Palestine and Syria, ejecting the last of the crusaders in 1291. Ultimately they fell before the onslaught of another offshoot of the once great Seljuk empire, the Ottomans.

The Ottoman Turks. Having settled in northwestern Asia Minor in the thirteenth century as vassals of the Seljuks, the Ottoman Turks had organized their own aggressive state of Muslim frontier fighters by the end of the century (see p. 146). The Ottomans pitted their strength against the crumbling power of the Byzantines, and after capturing Constantinople in 1453 they pressed on into southeastern Europe. Driving as far as Vienna, they were turned back with difficulty in 1529 and again in 1683. Meanwhile, in 1517, the Ottomans had conquered the Mamluk territories, and within a few years they had added Iraq, much of Arabia, and all of the North African coastal belt to the borders of Morocco.

We have reviewed the expansion of Islam into western Asia and areas around the Mediterranean. In later chapters we shall trace its expansion as a missionary faith into India and Southeast Asia, and Chapter 17 will describe the medieval Afro-Muslim kingdoms of equatorial Africa. Although political solidarity was not maintained in the Islamic world, a form of unity was perpetuated by a common religion and culture. As a result, that world emerged in modern times as an almost solid ribbon of peoples stretching from Morocco in the west through Indonesia in the east. Today about one seventh of the world's population is composed of Muslim peoples, whose religious solidarity and cultural heritage provide the basis for a program of political resurgence.

ISLAMIC CULTURE

Borrowing the best from other cultures. The high attainment of the Muslims in the intellectual and artistic fields can be attributed not only to the Arabs, who as a group remained primarily concerned with religion, politics, and commerce, but also to those peoples who had embraced Islam in Persia, Mesopotamia, Syria, Egypt, North Africa, and Spain. Muslim learning benefited both from Islam's ability to absorb other cultures and from the native genius of the Islamic peoples. The cosmopolitan spirit permeating the Abbasid dynasty supplied the tolerance necessary for a diversity of ideas, so that the science and philosophy of ancient Greece and India found a welcome in Baghdad. Under Harun al-Rashid and his successors the writings of Aristotle, Euclid, Ptolemy, Archimedes, Galen, and other great Greek scientific writers were translated into Arabic. This knowledge formed the basis of Muslim learning, which in turn was later transmitted to scholars in western Europe (see p. 252). In addition to being invaluable transmitters of learning, the Muslims also made some original contributions of their own to science.

Advances in medicine. The two hundred years between 900 and 1100 can be called the golden age of Muslim learning. This period was particularly significant for advances made in medicine. In spite of a ban against the study of anatomy and a few other limitations imposed on Muslims by their religion, their medical men were in most ways far superior to their European contemporaries. Muslim cities had excellent pharmacies and hospitals, and both pharmacists and physicians had to pass state examinations to be licensed. Physicians received instruction in medical schools and hospitals.

Perhaps the greatest Muslim physician was the Persian al-Razi (d. 925), better known to the West as Rhazes. He wrote more than a hundred medical treatises in which he summarized Greek medical knowledge and added his own acute clinical observations. His most famous work, *On Smallpox and Measles*, is the first clear description of the symptoms and treatment of these diseases. The most influential Muslim medical treatise is the vast *Canon of Medicine* of the Persian scholar Avicenna (d. 1037), in which all Greek and Muslim medical learning is systematically organized. In the twelfth century the *Canon* was translated into Latin and was so much in demand in the West that it was issued sixteen times in the last half of the fifteenth century and more than twenty times in the sixteenth. It is still read and used in the Orient today.

Progress in other sciences. Muslim physicists were no mere copyists. Alhazen (d. 1039) of Cairo developed optics to a remarkable degree and challenged the view of Ptolemy and Euclid that the eye sends visual rays to its object. The chief source of all medieval western writers on optics, he interested himself in optic reflections and illusions and examined the refraction of light rays through air and water.

Although astronomy continued to be astrology's handmaiden, Muslim astronomers built observatories, recorded their observations over long periods, and achieved greater accuracy than the Greeks in measuring the length of the solar year and in calculating eclipses. Interest in alchemy—the attempt to transmute base metals into precious ones and to find the magic elixir for the preservation of human life—produced the first chemical laboratories in history and an emphasis on the value of experimentation. Muslim alchemists prepared many chemical substances (sulphuric acid, for example) and developed methods for evaporation, filtration, sublimation, crystallization, and distillation. The process of distillation, invented around 800, produced what was called *al-kuhl* (alcohol), a new liquor that has made Geber, its inventor, an honored name in some circles. Others claim that "Geber" became the etymological root of "gibberish."

In mathematics the Muslims were indebted to the Hindus as well as to the Greeks. From the Greeks came the geometry of Euclid and the fundamentals of trigonometry which Ptolemy had worked out. From the Hindus came arithmetic and algebra and the nine signs, known as Arabic numerals, whose value depends on their position in a series. The Muslims invented the all-important zero, although some scholars assign this honor to the Indians. Two Persians deserve mention: al-Khwarizmi (d. about 840), whose *Arithmetic* introduced Arabic numerals and whose *Algebra* first employed that mathematical term; and Omar Khayyám (d. 1123?), whose work in algebra went beyond quadratics to cubic equations. Other scholars developed plane and spherical trigonometry.

Muslim scholars devoted themselves to the study of science and medicine. In an observatory in Constantinople some astronomers make mathematical computations with the assistance of a variety of instruments, while others gather around a globe showing Asia, Africa, and Europe.

In an empire that straddled continents, where trade and administration made an accurate knowledge of lands imperative, the science of geography flourished. The Muslims added to the geographical knowledge of the Greeks, whose treatises they translated, by producing detailed descriptions of the climate, manners, and customs of many parts of the known world.

Islamic literature and scholarship. To westerners, whose literary tastes have been largely formed by Graeco-Roman classics, Arab literature may seem strange and alien. Where we are used to restraint and simplicity, "the Muslim writer excels . . . in clothing the essential realism of his thought with the language of romance."[11] Consequently, Arabic poetry abounds in elegant expression, subtle combinations of words, fanciful and even extravagant imagery, and witty conceits.

Westerners' knowledge of Islamic literature tends to be limited to the *Arabian Nights* and to the hedonistic poetry of Omar Khayyám. The former is a collection of often erotic tales told with a wealth of local color; although it professedly covers different facets of life at the Abbasid capital, it is in fact often based on life in medieval Cairo. The fame of Omar Khayyám's *Rubáiyát* is partly due to the musical (though not overaccurate) translation of Edward Fitzgerald. The following stanzas indicate the poem's beautiful imagery and gentle pessimism:

A Book of Verses underneath the Bough,
A Jug of Wine, a Loaf of Bread—and Thou
　Beside me singing in the Wilderness—
Oh, Wilderness were Paradise enow!

Some for the Glories of This World; and some
Sigh for the Prophet's Paradise to come;
　Ah, take the Cash, and let the Credit go,
Nor heed the rumble of a distant Drum! . . .

The Moving Finger writes; and, having writ,
Moves on: nor all your Piety nor Wit
　Shall lure it back to cancel half a Line,
Nor all your Tears wash out a Word of it.

And that inverted Bowl they call the Sky,
Whereunder crawling coop'd we live and die,
　Lift not your hands to *It* for help—for It
As impotently moves as you or I.[12]

The same rich use of imagery is found in much Islamic prose. As the first important prose work in Arab literature, the Koran set the stylistic pattern for Arabic writers even down to modern times. The holy book was designed particularly to be recited aloud; anyone who has listened to the chanting of the Koran can testify to its cadence, melody, and power.

Muslim philosophy, essentially Greek in origin, was developed by laymen and not, as in the West, by churchmen. Like the medieval Christian philosophers (see Chapter 11), Muslim thinkers were largely concerned with reconciling Aristotelian rationalism and

This map, made for Roger II of Sicily (note the size of Sicily in comparison to the rest of Europe), represents a direct contact between medieval Arab and European cartography. Arabia was placed near the top of the world; thus for clarity the map should be viewed upside down. Based on classical Ptolemaic models, the map uses a grid system of horizontal and vertical lines to divide the world into seventy geographical areas, thus producing a forerunner of the modern rendering of longitude and latitude.

religion. The earlier Muslim thinkers, including Avicenna, the physician with many talents, sought to harmonize Platonism, Aristotelianism, and Islam. Avicenna's work was widely read in the West, where it was translated in the twelfth century. The last great Islamic philosopher, Averroës (d. 1198), lived in Cordova where he was the caliph's personal doctor. In his commentaries on Aristotle's works, which gave the Christian West its knowledge of Aristotle long before the original Greek texts were obtained from Constantinople, Averroës rejected the belief in the ultimate harmony between faith and reason along with all earlier attempts to reconcile Aristotle and Plato. Faith and reason, he argued, operate on different levels; a proposition can be true philosophically but false theologically. On the other hand, Moses Maimonides, Averroës' contemporary who was also born in Muslim Spain, sought, in his still influential *Guide to the Perplexed*, to harmonize Judaism and Aristotelian philosophy. When St. Thomas Aquinas in the next century undertook a similar project for Christianity, he was influenced by these earlier attempts to reconcile faith and reason.

Islamic historiography found its finest expression in the work of ibn-Khaldun of Tunis (d. 1406), who has also been called "a father of sociology." Despite his busy life in public affairs, he found time to write a large general history dealing particularly with man's social development, which he held to be the result of the interaction of society and the physical environment. Ibn-Khaldun defined history as follows:

It should be known that history, in matter of fact, is information about human social organization, which itself is identical with world civilization. It deals with such conditions affecting the nature of civilization as, for instance, savagery and sociability, group feelings, and the different ways by which one group of human beings achieves superiority over another. It deals with royal authority and . . . with the different kinds of gainful occupations and ways of making a living, with the sciences and crafts that human beings pursue as part of their activities and efforts, and with all the other institutions that originate in civilization through its very nature.[13]

Artistry and precise observation combine to make this illustration from a thirteenth-century Islamic natural history text both graceful and accurate. Persian painters and book illustrators often ignored the prohibition about representing people and animals.

Ibn-Khaldun conceived of history as an evolutionary process, in which societies and institutions change continually.

Art and architecture. Religious attitudes played an important part in Muslim art. Because the Prophet inveighed strongly against idols and their worship, there was a prejudice against pictorial representation of human and animal figures. The effect of this prejudice was to encourage the development of stylized and geometrical design. Muslim art, like Muslim learning, borrowed from many sources. Islamic artists and craftsmen followed chiefly Byzantine and Persian models and eventually integrated what they had learned into a distinctive and original style (see Color Plate 7).

The Muslims excelled in two fields—architecture and the decorative arts. That Islamic architecture can boast of many large and imposing structures is not surprising, because it drew much of its inspiration from the Byzantines and Persians, who were monumental builders. In time an original style of building evolved; the great mosques

Graceful columns and arches frame the Court of the Lions, in the center of the Alhambra palace in Granada, Spain. This is the ultimate stage of refinement of Moorish architecture which combines both Spanish and Islamic elements.

embody such typical features as domes, arcades, and minarets, the slender towers from which the faithful are summoned to prayer. The horseshoe arch is another graceful and familiar feature of Muslim architecture.

On the walls and ceilings of their buildings, the Muslims gave full rein to their love of ornamentation and beauty of detail. The Spanish interpretation of the Muslim tradition was particularly delicate and elegant (see p. 208). Other outstanding examples of Islamic architecture are to be found in India; the Taj Mahal, for example, is based largely on Persian motifs.

Being restricted in their subject matter, Muslim craftsmen conceived beautiful patterns from flowers and geometric figures. Even the Arabic script, the most beautiful ever devised, was used as a decorative motif. Muslim decorative skill also found expression in such fields as carpet and rug weaving, brass work, and the making of steel products inlaid with precious metals.

SUMMARY

We have examined two rival but equally fascinating civilizations: first, the Byzantine, a citadel of classical and Christian culture; second, a dynamic Islam, conqueror alike of kingdoms and of the spiritual allegiance of populations stretching from Gibraltar to Java. With the conquest of Constantinople in 1453, this second civilization overwhelmed its rival.

When Constantine chose the site for New Rome, he picked a location that was geographically excellent for defense and trade. Constantinople's tradition as the eastern capital of the Roman empire encouraged Justinian to attempt to recover the western territory that had been under Roman rule; but these efforts failed, and in the long run Byzantium had to fight continually against invasions that diminished its empire on all sides. In 1453 the Ottoman Turks conquered "The City," and the empire of a thousand years was destroyed.

For a millennium the empire had acted as a buffer state, repulsing attacks while the weak, divided West grew in strength. And while learning was all but lost in medieval western Europe, the Byzantine world remained the custodian of classical knowledge and ideals until a resurgent West was able to assimilate its classical heritage. But Constantinople did much more than all this. Roman, Greek, and oriental elements were fused into a distinct and original culture; Slavic peoples were converted to Christianity; and the benefits of civilization were brought to Russia and neighboring lands.

The Norsemen who founded Kievan Russia also set up trade with Constantinople which continued for centuries. Through this medium, culture and religion were imported into Russia from the Eastern empire. While Constantinople itself fell, its heritage was in many ways maintained in the new Slavic state that was spreading across the vast Russian plain.

Muhammad (570-632), the founder of the Islamic religion, was born into a desert area populated by nomadic Bedouins and a few scattered groups of townsmen. Soon after Muhammad's death, his monotheistic teachings were compiled in the Koran, the Muslim bible.

During the reigns of the first four caliphs and the century of the Umayyad dynasty (661-750), great strides were made in annexing new territories and peoples. But the Umayyad dynasty was based on a ruling hierarchy of Arabs, and the resentment of the non-Arabs produced a revolution which set the Abbasid dynasty (750-1258) on a new throne in Baghdad.

During the early Abbasid period Islam reached the high point of its geographical expansion and cultural achievements, and a ribbon of Muslim peoples extended from Spain across three continents to the Far East. Unparalleled prosperity evolved from a combination of successful trade, industry, and agriculture. But the Muslims were not able to maintain an integrated empire; despite a religious unity, which still exists (though without formal organization), politically the empire broke up into smaller Muslim states.

The Muslims were especially gifted in science, literature, and philosophy. Muslim intellectual life was in good part the product of a genius for synthesizing varying cultures, and their diffusion of this knowledge was a tremendous factor in the revival of classical learning and the coming of the Renaissance in Europe.

Ironically, while the arts and learning were beginning to thrive in the West, Islamic civilization itself entered a period of cultural decline. Various reasons have been advanced for this phenomenon, including the influx of semibarbarous peoples into Islamic lands, intellectual stagnation resulting from rigid adherence to the Koran's sacred law, and the despotic and eventually corrupt rule of such Muslim dynasties as the Ottomans in Turkey, who destroyed all progressive political and economic movements.

SUGGESTIONS FOR READING

Charles Diehl, **Byzantium: Greatness and Decline*** (Rutgers) is highly recommended as a brief introduction. Also brief is R. Guerdan, **Byzantium: Its Triumphs and Tragedy*** (Capricorn). For greater detail see G. Ostrogorsky, **History of the Byzantine State** (Rutgers, 1969); **The Cambridge Medieval History,** Vol. IV, rev. ed., **The Byzantine Empire,** Pt. I, **Byzantium and Its Neighbors;** Pt. II, **Government, Church and Civilization.**

D. A. Miller, **The Byzantine Tradition*** (Torchbooks, 1966) is a brief perceptive survey of Byzantine civilization. See also J. Hussey, **The Byzantine World*** (Torchbooks); and S. Runciman, **Byzantine Civilization*** (Meridian).

John W. Barker, **Justinian and the Later Roman Empire** (Univ. of Wisconsin, 1966) is clear and lively, as is R. Browning, **Justinian and Theodora** (Praeger). See also G. Downey, **Constantinople in the Age of Justinian** (Oklahoma, 1968); and Dean A. Miller, **Imperial Constantinople*** (Wiley, 1969).

C. M. Brand, **Byzantium Confronts the West, 1184-1204** (Harvard, 1968); and D. Queller, ed., **The Latin Conquest of Constantinople*** (Wiley, 1971) describe the events marking the beginning of the disintegration of the Byzantine empire. See also M. Donald Nicol, **The Last Centuries of Byzantium, 1261-1453** (St. Martin's).

H. Magoulias, **Byzantine Christianity: Emperor, Church, and the West** (Rand McNally, 1970); and T. Ware, **The Orthodox Church*** (Penguin) are two good surveys. S. Runciman, **The Eastern Schism*** (Oxford) disentangles fact from legend.

See D. Talbot Rice, **Art of the Byzantine Era*** (Oxford); and A. Grabar, **Art of the Byzantine Empire** (Crown, 1966). For superb color reproductions of Byzantine mosaics see H. Newmayer, **Byzantine Mosaics*** (Crown).

F. Dvornik, **The Slavs in European History and Civilization** (Rutgers, 1975) emphasizes Byzantine influences. G. Vernadsky, **Kievan Russia,** 2nd ed. (Yale, 1973) is detailed and authoritative. M. Florinsky, **Russia: A History and an Interpretation,** Vol. I (Macmillan) is excellent on early Russia. See also G. Fedotov, **The Russian Religious Mind: Kievan Christianity, the Tenth to the Thirteenth Centuries*** (Torchbooks).

P. K. Hitti, **The Arabs: A Short History*** (Gateway) is an abridgment of a scholarly general history. See also C. Brockelmann, **History of the Islamic Peoples*** (Capricorn); and A. G. Chejne, **Muslim Spain** (Minnesota, 1974).

W. M. Watt, **Muhammad: Prophet and Statesman*** (Galaxy) is short and excellent. See also T. Andrae, **Mohammed: The Man and His Faith*** (Torchbooks); and M. Rodinson, **Mohammed** (Vintage, 1974). For an interpretation and translation of the Koran, see M. Pickthall, **The Meaning of the Glorious Koran*** (Mentor); H. A. R. Gibb, **Mohammedism: An Historical Survey*** (Galaxy) is outstanding.

P. Coles, **The Ottoman Impact on Europe*** (Harcourt Brace Jovanovich) is a lucid survey. See also S. Runciman, **The Fall of Constantinople, 1453*** (Cambridge); and N. Itkowitz, **The Ottoman Empire and Islamic Tradition*** (Knopf, 1972).

R. A. Nicholson, **A Literary History of the Arabs*** (Cambridge, 1969) traces the growth of Arab thought and culture through its literature, as does H. A. R. Gibb, **Arabic Literature,** 2nd ed. (Oxford, 1974). See also P. Hitti, **Makers of Arab History*** (Torchbooks) and D. Talbot Rice, **Islamic Art*** (Praeger).

*Indicates a less expensive paperbound edition.

CHAPTER 7

India, China, and Japan:
200-1350

The Guptas and the T'ang: Two Golden Ages

INTRODUCTION. The span of little more than a thousand years from the fifth to the fifteenth century was characterized in most parts of the world by numerous ethnic migrations and significant intercultural impacts. Later chapters will describe the ebb and flow of peoples—Vikings, Mongols, Magyars, and Germanic tribes—in medieval Europe; this chapter discusses the movement of peoples and cultural diffusion in Asia. During this period Indian culture expanded throughout Southeast Asia, enriching indigenous societies in what are now Burma, Indochina, the Malay peninsula, and Indonesia, while Buddhism exerted a profound influence upon China and Japan. Similarly, there was a continuous flow of Chinese culture eastward to the Korean peninsula and Japan. In the later part of this period, Muslim conquest appreciably influenced Indian society, and the repeated invasions by the Mongols and other nomadic peoples wrought important political and social changes in China.

The events related in this chapter point up a significant theme in history—the important role played by restless, nomadic peoples in the rise and fall of civilizations. In the decline of the Roman Empire, as treated in Chapter 5, we witnessed a classic example of this recurring phenomenon—nomad tribes pressing and probing "softer," more civilized, less dynamic groups, discovering the weak spots in their defenses, and finally overwhelming them. Again, in Chapter 6, we saw Byzantium assailed continuously for a thousand years until it at last fell victim to inexorable outside pressures. Perhaps the most awesome of all the nomads were the Mongols ruled by Genghis Khan, who led his hordes into China in search of booty and went on to create the greatest empire the world had yet seen—a vast realm extending all the way from the China Sea to eastern Europe. But if the assault of nomads is an important concern of this chapter, a corollary is how, once victorious, the predatory invader usually becomes respectable and sedentary, ceasing to be a menace to neighboring peoples.

In spite of these seemingly confused migrations and confrontations between peoples—or perhaps in part because of them—Asian civilizations reached a high peak during this period. In India the Gupta rulers came to power, and the subcontinent benefited from their enlightened government. Hindu culture entered a period of flourishing growth marked by important advances in mathematics, medicine, chemistry, textile production, and imaginative literature. In fact, in the realm of culture diffusion and creative thought, India played the major role in Eurasia during the four centuries from 200 to 600 A.D. In the following period, from the seventh through the tenth centuries, the T'ang dynasty held sway in China, reviving the greatness of Chinese civilization after a period of disorder and division. For the most part, the Chinese enjoyed prosperity and good government, and there was a flowering of scholarship and the arts. It was during the T'ang and Sung dynasties that such revolutionary inventions as printing, explosive powder, and the compass were devised. The Japanese archipelago, after being occupied by ancestors of the present inhabitants, was never successfully invaded until the twentieth century. Influenced greatly by China, the proud and independent Japanese gradually developed a unique culture pattern best symbolized by the *samurai*, the knight, and *bushido*, the code of the warrior. Here, too, was a development which centuries later affected world history.

INDIA: THE IMPERIAL GUPTAS

The Gupta empire. As we recall from Chapter 4, the Kushan dynasty, which had witnessed one of the richest periods in Indian civilization, crumbled about 220 A.D. Subsequent events in northern India followed a pattern that has recurred time and again in the history of the subcontinent: an epoch of distinction followed by an era of political disintegration and comparative cultural darkness.

With the advent of the Gupta empire in the fourth century, northern India came out of its dark era and entered upon another epoch of greatness. In about 320 A.D., the first ruler of the Gupta dynasty, Chandragupta I (not related to Chandragupta Maurya, p. 98), established himself as monarch of the Ganges valley; and his successor extended the imperial boundaries in all directions. As a result, much of northern India from the Himalayas south to the Narbada River was included within the Gupta empire, thus making it the most extensive and powerful Indian state since the days of Ashoka six centuries earlier. Nor had its limits been reached. The grandson of the dynasty's founder, Chandragupta II, extended the empire still farther west until it stretched from sea to sea (see map, p. 171). During his reign (c. 380-c. 413), the Gupta empire reached its zenith. In all its long history before the British conquest India probably came closest to political unity during the reigns of Ashoka, Chandragupta II, and the Mughuls (see Chapter 16).

Under the Gupta dynasty, India exhibited

a state of cultural integration and social harmony such as it has never since achieved. By comparison with the Roman Empire, which was nearing its demise, and China, which was enduring a troubled interim period between the two great eras of the Han and the T'ang, India was probably the most civilized region of the world at this time.

Dominance of Hinduism. Although religious tolerance was characteristic of the Gupta period, the Gupta rulers preferred Hinduism to Buddhism, and the Brahmin caste enjoyed imperial patronage. While Buddhism as a distinct faith became practically extinct, certain of its teachings—for example, *ahimsā*, nonviolence and respect for life—were incorporated into Hinduism. From about 185 B.C. to about 800 A.D., Hinduism not only became dominant in India but also gradually crystallized into its present form.

By recognizing all varieties of religious experience, Hinduism is capable of absorbing different and often even contradictory points of view—a factor that helps account for its tremendous tenacity. Names mean very little; God may be worshiped in many forms and by many names. Hinduism stresses conduct and ceremony rather than rigid belief. To be a Hindu it is only necessary to accept the leadership of the Brahmins and one's status in caste, thereby implying acceptance of the belief of reincarnation.

Notwithstanding the many invasions into India, all of the intruders—excluding the Muslims and later the British—were absorbed and found a place in Hinduism.

The caste system. By the Gupta period the caste system was rapidly assuming its basic features. Each caste was usually related to a specific occupation, was endogamous (a man was expected to select his bride from within his own group), and had its own *dharma*—rules regulating the types of food eaten, the manner of consumption, and with what other castes there could be social contact. The untouchables, the lowest rung in the caste ladder, had a degraded status.

In the light of modern democratic ideology, caste is a reprehensible system and indeed is so regarded by many of India's present leaders. Defenders of the institution, however, point out that a caste forms a kind of brotherhood in which all members are equal. Furthermore, within his caste the Hindu enjoys a sense of security that makes him feel part of a cosmic process in which no mistakes are made.

Achievements in Sanskrit literature. The Gupta period has been called the golden age of Sanskrit, the classical language of India. Court poetry was zealously produced, and the kings were generous patrons of many writers. The most famous writer, Kalidasa (c. 400-455), excelled as both a lyric and an epic poet and has been termed the "Indian

The best examples of Gupta painting are found in the caves at Ajanta in the Deccan. Hollowed out of solid rock and adorned with sculpture and murals, these twenty-nine worship halls and dwelling places served as a hermitage for Buddhist monks. Some of the paintings, which depict scenes from the life of Buddha and from Buddhist stories, date from the second century B.C.; the finest, however, were painted during the Gupta period. Presenting a brilliant panorama of contemporary life, the murals portray beggars, princes, peasants, women, children, beasts, and birds. This painting depicts the temptation of Buddha.

Shakespeare" because of his superb dramas. Characterized by a lack of action unfamiliar to western audiences, his plays abound in splendid imagery.

India presented an unusually fertile soil for the creation of fables and folklore. Since its religions stressed the unity of all life and the cycle of transmigration, it was not difficult for storytellers to reverse the positions of the animal and human kingdoms and to conceive of beasts acting like men and vice versa. Many Indian stories were eventually carried to Europe by the Muslims. Perhaps the most famous is the story of Sindbad, which found its way into the *Arabian Nights*. Boccaccio, Chaucer, La Fontaine, the Grimm brothers, and Kipling have all been indebted to Indian folklore.

Gupta science and technology. Scholarship and science were of a very high caliber during Gupta times. Students from all over Asia came to India's foremost university, situated at Nalanda. The most famous scientist was the astronomer and mathematician Aryabhata, who lived in the fifth century. In verse he discussed quadratic equations, the value of π, solstices and equinoxes, the spherical shape of the earth, and the earth's rotation. Other Indian astronomers predicted eclipses accurately, calculated the moon's diameter, and expounded on gravitation.

In astronomy and mathematics (except for geometry) the Hindus surpassed the achievements of any ancient western people. The Arabic numerals and the decimal system we use today appear to have come originally from India. Even the zero may have come from Indian rather than Arabic sources.

The Hindus were also remarkably advanced in chemistry; they discovered how to make soap and cement and were the finest temperers of steel in the world. Indian industry was famous for its superior dyes and fine fabrics; the methods of production were taken over by the Arabs, and from them by Europeans. The Arabs named one Indian cloth *quittan*—hence the word *cotton. Calico, cashmere, chintz,* and *bandanna* are also of Indian origin.

The development of Indian medicine was due to various factors, including an interest in physiology which resulted from Yoga. Some Gupta physicians were surprisingly modern in their techniques; they prepared carefully for an operation and sterilized wounds by fumigation. Caesarean operations, bone setting, and plastic surgery were all attempted. The Indians also used many drugs then unknown in Europe.

A period of instability. By 413, when Chandragupta II died, the Gupta empire had reached the zenith of its power. In the last half of the fifth century, while their kinsmen were ravaging Europe under Attila, "The Scourge," Huns invaded the Punjab. They soon gained control of northwestern India but were prevented from advancing into eastern India by a confederacy of Hindu princes.

In the seventh century the various states in the Ganges valley fought constantly with one another until at last a strong man arose. In the short space of six years (606-612) Harsha, rajah of one of the northern kingdoms, mastered much of the territory formerly

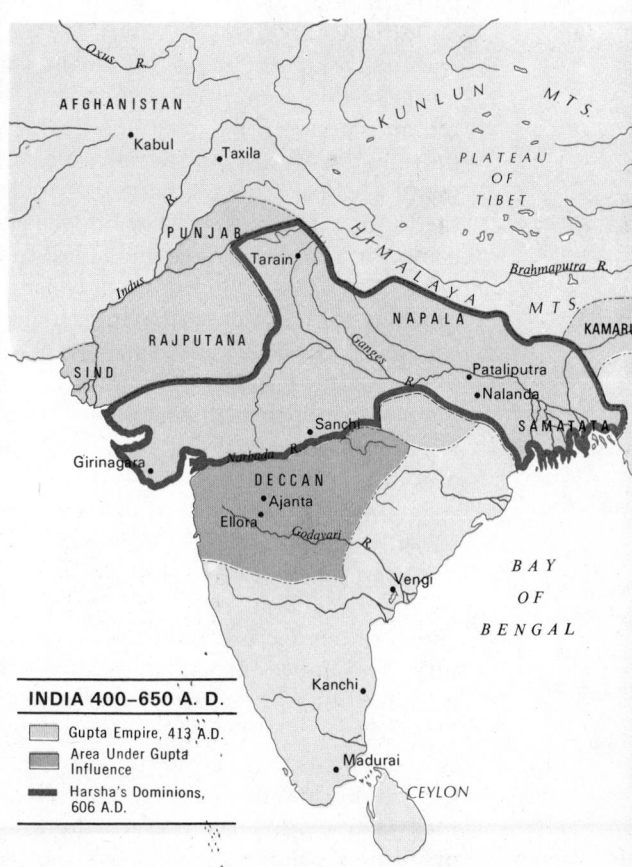

INDIA 400–650 A. D.

Gupta Empire, 413 A.D.

Area Under Gupta Influence

Harsha's Dominions, 606 A.D.

ruled by the Guptas. With his death in 647, northern India reverted to confusion and warfare which lasted for centuries.

Particularly warlike were the descendants of Central Asian peoples who had followed the Huns into northwest India in the fifth century and had intermarried with the local population. In time these people assumed the privileges of "blue-blooded" Hindus, haughtily called themselves Rajputs (Sons of Kings), and carved out kingdoms for themselves in parts of north India, especially in what became known as Rajputana, a strategic area between the Indus and Ganges valleys. The Rajputs possessed a code of chivalry not unlike that which existed in medieval Europe. Youths were brought up with the privileges and obligations of the warrior caste (the Kshatriya) and taught to respect women, spare the fallen, and demand fair play.

Expansion of Indian culture. For nearly one thousand years India sent her art, religious ideas, literature, and traders to many parts of Asia. The diffusion of *Mahayana* Buddhism into Central Asia, China, Korea, and finally Japan during this period was the most striking sign of the dynamic power of Indian culture. The relationship between India and China was especially strong, and many Chinese scholars made pilgrimages to the former. The most celebrated was Hsüan-tsang (or Yuan-chuang), who spent thirteen years (630-643) in Buddha's holy land. Returning to his native land, Hsüan-tsang brought back 657 manuscripts, together with many Buddhist relics, and devoted the remainder of his life to translating his treasures. His journal is one of the most valuable sources of information on medieval India.

Resulting mainly from peaceful trading activities, Indian cultural expansion in what has been called "Greater India" in Southeast Asia began about the second century A.D. and continued until the ninth or tenth century. The impact of Indian culture was not equally strong or enduring over all sections. One scholar has divided Greater India into two segments: the western zone (including Ceylon, Burma, the central part of Siam, and the Malay peninsula) received the full force of Indian colonizing activity and conse-

quently developed a culture that was largely a colonial imitation of the original; the eastern zone (comprising mainly Java, Cambodia, and Champa in Indochina) experienced Indianization that was very definite but not strong enough to prevent the indigenous peoples from developing their own distinctive cultures and ways of life.

From the second century A.D. on, the kingdoms established in Greater India were ruled by monarchs with Indian names. Some of these kingdoms endured more than a thousand years, persisting, in fact, after India itself had been overwhelmed by foreign invaders. Two monuments attest to the splendor of these states.

About 1100 one of the greatest architectural edifices in history was erected in Cambodia —Angkor Wat (see Color Plate 15). Long forgotten and swallowed up by the jungle, this vast complex was accidentally discovered by a French naturalist in 1861. It is surrounded by a stone enclosure measuring half a mile from north to south and two thirds of a mile from east to west. Nearby lay the Cambodian capital city, which may have had a population of close to one million.

In central Java one of the most imposing Buddhist shrines in the world is located: the immense monument of Borobudur. Erected on the top of a hill in nine successive terraces, Borobudur is covered with images of the Buddha, sculptures illustrating Buddhist texts, and carved scenes of everyday life. The art of Southeast Asia was unmistakably influenced by Indian styles and techniques, but in Angkor Wat and Borobudur the works created were larger than anything found in India itself.

THE MUSLIM CONQUEST OF INDIA

The Muslim invasions. In 711, the same year in which they invaded Spain, Arabs appeared in India. They made the southern valley of the Indus a province of the vast Umayyad empire, but the Rajput princes soon halted further Arab penetration of India.

At the end of the tenth century more Muslim invaders swept through the northwest passes. The newcomers were Turks and Afghans who, in 1022, annexed the Punjab. Despite destructive forays by various Muslim sultans, the Rajput and other Hindu kingdoms of the interior remained independent. Not until the closing years of the twelfth century did the Muslims establish a large Indian dominion.

The Delhi sultanate. The first important Muslim ruler was a former general who in 1206 established himself as sultan at Delhi, ruling a strong Muslim kingdom covering much of north India. The Delhi sultanate existed until the early years of the sixteenth century, and during the period of its greatest power (1206-1388), it gave northern India political unity. The early Delhi sultans also pushed Muslim authority and religion southward into the Deccan and in the first decades of the fourteenth century reached southernmost India. The Delhi sultanate, however, soon lost control in southern India to a rival sultanate in the Deccan and to other Muslim and Hindu states.

Tamerlane. In 1398 the Punjab was invaded by a Mongol who had already conquered Central Asia—Timur the Lame (Tamerlane). Defeating all armies sent against him, Timur looted wealthy Delhi, killing perhaps 100,000 prisoners. Afterwards, he departed westward for Samarkand, leaving Delhi's few surviving inhabitants to perish of famine and plague. After Timur's terrible visitation, nearly all semblance of political unity was destroyed in north India, and Muslim sultans maintained independent principalities in defiance of the ineffectual authority at Delhi.

Effects of Muslim rule. The Muslim conquest of India was unusually ruthless. To the Muslims, Hinduism with its many deities, elaborate ritual, powerful priestcraft, and fondness for images was the opposite of all that Islam held sacred. Hindu forces desperately resisted their Muslim conquerors and, after defeat, often suffered wholesale massacre. Many people clung tenaciously to their Hindu faith—the upper classes in particular—but a fairly large number of Hindus were converted to Islam. In some cases it was a choice between Allah or the sword; in others it was a voluntary matter: poor men sought to avoid the heavier taxes levied on infidels, low-caste Hindus became Muslims to escape their degraded status, and ambitious administrators accepted Islam in order to succeed in the official service of the Muslim rulers. One result of the Muslim intrusion was the emergence of a common spoken language—Urdu. This language was a combination of Persian, Turkish, and Arabic words which utilized the grammatical constructions of the Hindu languages. Urdu and the native Hindi became the languages most commonly used in northern India, and they are today the dominant languages of Muslim Pakistan and Hindu India.

The injection of the Islamic way of life into the pattern of Hindu society was to have profound effects upon the history of the Indian subcontinent. Fiercely proud of their own faith, and disdainful of Hinduism, the Muslims jealously retained their religion and ways of life. After the establishment of the powerful Delhi sultanate in 1206, therefore, the life of India was divided into two streams, the Hindu and the Muslim, which mingled only superficially and never really united. This division was to have momentous consequences in the twentieth century, when India, freed from British rule, split into two nations, India and Pakistan.

CHINA: THE MEN OF T'ANG

An age of political division. After the fall of the Han empire in 220 A.D., China was destined to suffer three and a half centuries of disorder and division before another great dynasty arose and reunited the country. The internal collapse of the Han empire —as with the breakdown of the Mauryan and Gupta regimes in India and of Rome in the West—allowed various nomadic peoples to penetrate the frontiers and raid and pillage. In North China these barbarians set up various petty states, especially after the opening of the fourth century.

Central and South China escaped these

barbarian intrusions and were now more intensively developed than before, especially by émigrés from the north. Hence the literate classical tradition was preserved in the south; and a sequence of regimes, with capitals at Nanking, kept alive the notion of a unified state under a "Son of Heaven."

Buddhism adapts itself. Although Buddhism had been introduced into China during Han times, this religion made its most important gains from the third century A.D. on. As the sober, balanced social order inculcated by Confucianism came to make less sense in a world run by warlords, all classes of Chinese were touched by Buddhism. Part of Buddhism's appeal resembled that of the mystery religions and of Christianity in the decaying Roman world: the assurance of inner consolation through faith and of salvation in a glorious afterlife even for humble folk. The monastic aspects of Buddhism appealed to many thousands of Chinese seeking seclusion and protection in the face of contemporary social chaos.

Political and economic conditions under the T'ang. After internal collapse and barbarian invasion, neither the Indian nor the Graeco-Roman world-state was ever able fully to regenerate itself politically. But in the late sixth and early seventh centuries the Chinese did just that, re-creating and improving on the Han model. After a short-lived reign of the Sui dynasty, the T'ang emperors (618-906) provided a long period of stable growth and cultural flowering, giving China renewed preeminence in all East Asia. As the Gupta empire represents tthe golden age of Hindu culture, the T'ang dynasty represents the golden era of China. Even today many Chinese like to consider themselves not only "Sons of Han" but also "Men of T'ang" in reference to these great ages.

The second emperor of the T'ang dynasty, T'ai Tsung ("Grand Ancestor"), reigned from 627 to 650 and is considered one of China's greatest emperors. After defeating the northern Turks decisively in 630, he took advantage of internal dissension in Turkestan to reestablish Chinese dominance over the Tarim Basin. Under his son, a successful war was undertaken against Korea, which was made a tributary vassal state. At this point China stood at the zenith of its power. The T'ang empire extended from Korea and Manchuria through Tibet and Central Asia to the borders of India and Persia (see map, p. 175).

A statesman as well as a great soldier, T'ai Tsung was energetic in instituting reforms. One of his major reforms was to strengthen the administrative system of the country. The emperor governed the center of his empire by means of a bureaucracy recruited through a civil service program rooted in Han precedent but now more elaborated. T'ang improvements also extended to land reform; laws were passed to curb the growth of large estates and to ensure equitable amounts of land for the peasants. Economic prosperity resulted from these reforms as well as from the more efficient transportation system which the T'ang developed by completing the Sui canal system. A thriving foreign commerce also contributed to the economic boom. Caravans arrived frequently from West and Central Asia; and great quantities of luxury goods were exported to such far-distant points as Jerusalem and Cairo.

T'ang scholarship. The T'ang period was outstanding in scholarly achievements. Two encyclopedias were compiled to assist bureaucrats in their work, and Buddhist scholars translated sacred texts into Chinese. T'ai Tsung ordered the publication of an elaborate edition of the Thirteen Classics of Confucianism and also stressed the value of historical writings:

. . . by using a mirror of brass you may see to adjust your cap; by using antiquity as a mirror, you may learn to foresee the rise and fall of empires.[1]

Li Po and Tu Fu, masters of T'ang poetry. An eighteenth-century anthology of T'ang poetry included hundreds of scrolls containing 48,900 poems by 2300 poets. The astonishing literary output of the T'ang era would almost appear to justify the remark: "[At this age,] whoever was a man was a poet."[2]

The two greatest poets of this era, Li Po (701?-762) and Tu Fu (712-770), were good friends who occasionally twitted each other in their works. Tu Fu summed up his fellow poet—a true Bohemian spirit who was notorious for his heavy drinking—in this fashion:

As for Li Po, give him a jugful of wine,
And he will write a hundred poems.[3]

And Li Po once addressed these witty lines to Tu Fu:

Here! is this you on the top of Fan-Ko
  Mountain,
Wearing a huge hat in the noon-day sun?
How thin, how wretchedly thin, you have
  grown!
You must have been suffering from poetry
  again.[4]

The poetry of Li Po exerted a great appeal for his countrymen. But the majority of Chinese scholars and poets today consider Tu Fu the greater poet, perhaps China's greatest.

T'ang artistic endeavors. The T'ang dynasty was the formative period of Chinese painting. The great Wu Tao-tzu furthered the development of a national school independent of foreign influences. The story is told that his last painting was a landscape to serve as a wall decoration for the emperor. As Wu and the emperor stood admiring the lifelike scene, the artist clapped his hands, a door in the painting opened, and Wu disappeared within, never to be seen again.

Sculptors used Buddhist subject matter, but their work bore the impress of indigenous artistic standards rather than those of India. *Mahayana* religious figures evinced a distinctively Chinese interpretation, with strong humanistic emphasis.

The invention of printing. In the first century A.D. the Chinese had discovered how to make paper, and in the fifth century they put ink stampings on documents by using seals fashioned from metal and stone. These

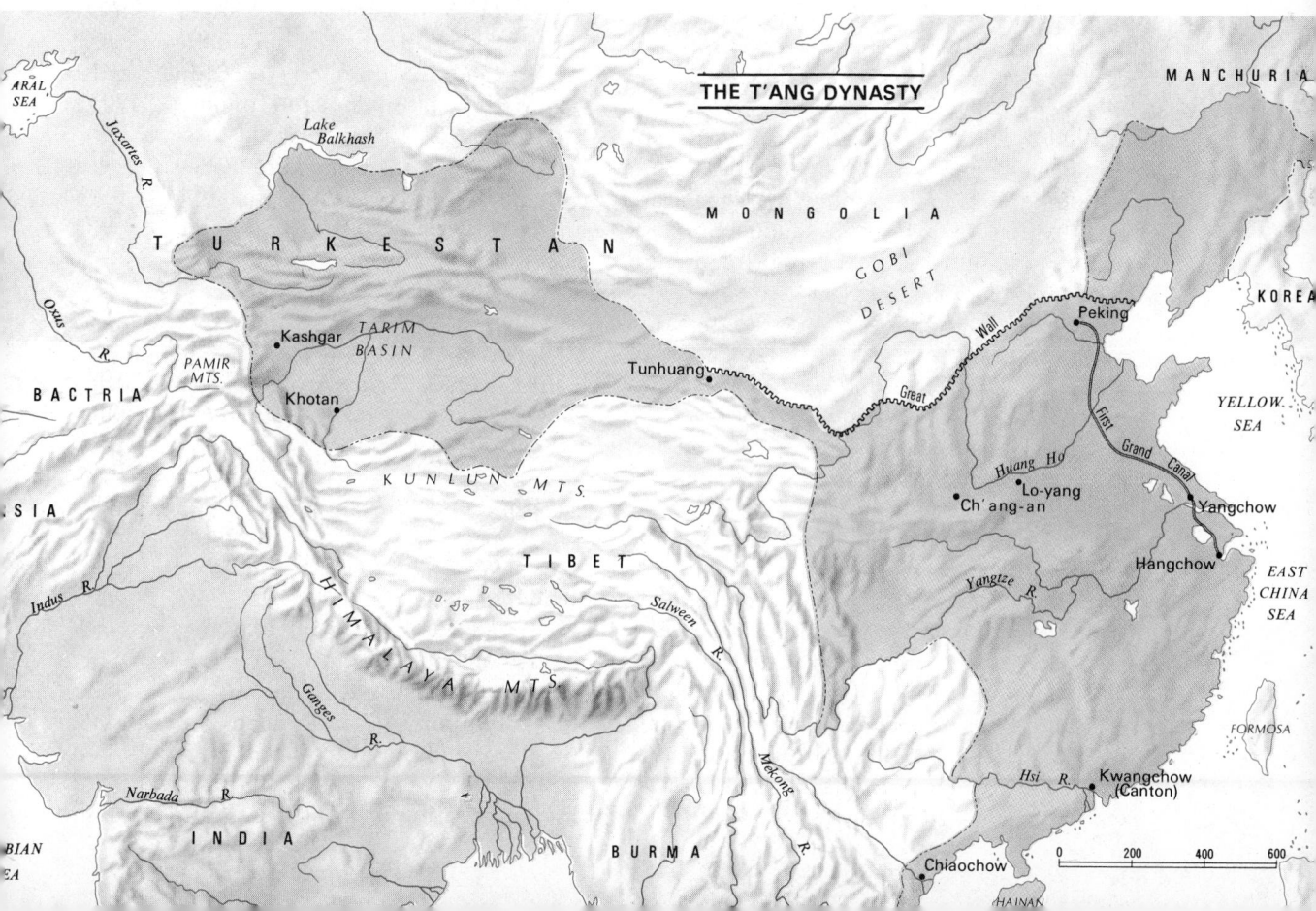

THE T'ANG DYNASTY

The Chinese invented block printing in about 600, and the earliest existing book printed by this method is the *Diamond Sutra*, dating from about 868.

technical discoveries paved the way for the culminating invention—printing.

Evidence would indicate that the process of block printing—printing from an image cut in a wooden block—was invented in China by about 600, although the earliest surviving examples come from Japan and date from 764 to 770. The first extant printed book is the *Diamond Sutra*, which was discovered in a cave in northwestern China. Printed in 868, the *Diamond Sutra* consists of six sheets of text pasted together to form a roll some sixteen feet long; the sheets are each two and a half feet by almost one foot in size and must have been printed from very large blocks.

Because the Chinese language is written not by means of an alphabet but by means of separate characters that represent entire words, the Chinese found block printing satisfactory. Nevertheless, they were the first to invent movable type, probably in the first half of the eleventh century.

T'ang decline: the end of an epoch. In the seventh century the T'ang dynasty still enjoyed a suzerainty that stretched from the Pamir Mountains in the west into Korea in the east, but during the next century divisive political forces arose. From mid-century on, the imperial boundaries contracted, and within the empire, decadence and disorder held sway. In 755 a revolt broke out, and the emperor was forced to flee, abdicating in

favor of his son. When the rebellion was finally put down, the weakened dynasty survived for a century and a half; in 906 the T'ang dynasty came to an end.

The Sung dynasty. The fall of the T'ang dynasty left China vulnerable to external attack and in another of its periods of internal disorder. This upheaval was followed by the founding of the Sung dynasty (960-1279). Early in the eleventh century the Sung emperors adopted the practice of "buying protection" by paying the Khitan Tatars in North China an annual tribute of 100,000 ounces of silver and 200,000 pieces of silk. In time the Sung were forced to increase these amounts and to begin paying tribute to other border kingdoms. Even though such payments did not represent a large percentage of the total state revenues, they were a drain on the imperial finances.

The unprecedented development of large estates whose owners managed to evade paying their share of taxes resulted in an increasingly heavy burden of taxation falling on the small farmers. The drop in the state revenues, a succession of budget deficits, and widespread inflation caused the emperor to seek advice from one of China's most fascinating statesmen and economists, Wang An-shih (1021-1086).

Wang An-shih believed that the ruler was responsible for providing his subjects with the necessities of life. He expressed his social philosophy thus:

The state should take the entire management of commerce, industry, and agriculture into its own hands, with a view to succoring the working classes and preventing them from being ground into the dust by the rich.[5]

To this end, he initiated an agricultural loans measure to relieve the farming peasants of the intolerable burden of interest which callous moneylenders exacted from them in difficult times and to ensure that lack of capital would not hinder the work of agriculture. To destroy speculation and break up the monopolies, he initiated a system of fixed commodity prices; and he appointed boards to regulate wages and plan pensions for the aged and unemployed. Wang An-shih also revamped the state examination system so that less emphasis was placed on literary style and memorization of the classics and more on practical knowledge.

In the next generation opposition from vested interests, difficulties in maintaining reforming zeal and efficiency among officials, the impracticality of some reform projects, and renewed foreign crises led to the victory of the conservative opposition and to the rescinding of most of Wang's "new laws." It is remarkable, nonetheless, to see how modern his theories were; the concepts of the welfare state and a planned economy are apparently not quite so new as we may have supposed.

The Neo-Confucian synthesis. Under the impact of Buddhist thought, many of Wang's opponents were interested in finding a better philosophic basis for the Confucian ethical system; consequently there developed, from elements of the old classic literature and Buddhist scriptures, a metaphysics that did not depend on the Buddhist church for ultimate explanations. This reinterpretation of tradition we call Neo-Confucianism.

The most important advocate of Neo-Confucianism was Chu Hsi (1130-1200), a brilliant scholar; the most influential commentator on the Chinese classics. Neo-Confucianism, while indebted both to Buddhism and Taoism, essentially represented a resurgence of Confucian thought. Its central and most pervasive influence was upon political and ethical institutions. Stressing the importance of good government in the hands of a benevolent ruler, it also advocated a bureaucratic state administered by intelligent and morally dedicated officials chosen by a rigorous examination system based on the classics.

Neo-Confucianism, as shaped particularly by Chu Hsi, became the dominant intellectual force down to the twentieth century with its revolutionary political and social changes.

Buddhism, institutionally under strict state control, lost its old prestige and intellectual respectability among the upper classes and survived principally as one of several popular cults among the masses.

The empirical sciences. Chu Hsi contended that self-cultivation required the extension of knowledge, best achieved by the "investi-

During the T'ang and Sung dynasties Chinese science and technology were far in advance of European science of the same era. One of the most complicated Chinese mechanical and scientific creations, this astronomical observatory, dating from about 1090, used a water-powered clock to rotate the instruments in time with the motion of the stars. It had previously been thought that the mechanical clock was a western achievement of the fourteenth century.

gation of things." As a consequence, Neo-Confucianism was accompanied by significant advances in experimental and applied sciences. The Sung period witnessed the production of large numbers of works concerning chemistry, zoology, and botany. Algebra was developed until it was the most advanced in the world. In medicine, inoculation against smallpox was introduced. Progress was also notable in astronomy, geography, and cartography; at this time, the earliest relief maps were constructed. By the end of the eleventh century the magnetic compass was employed as an aid to navigation. Another major development was the use of explosive powder—first in fireworks, then in warfare.

Excellence in Sung art. Many critics assert that "at its best Chinese painting is one of the outstanding expressions of man's ability to create beauty."[6] The Chinese painter believed that only days spent in meditation of a vista would reveal to him the scene's essential mood. When he had observed nature as long as he thought necessary, he would then paint the scene without looking at it. The awe and love felt for nature by Chinese painters was the force behind much of their work (see Color Plate 14).

Chinese paintings were not publicly displayed but were mounted on heavy scrolls and kept hidden away. Only on special occasions were they taken out for a short period of concentrated esthetic enjoyment. The painter was highly esteemed, for his techniques required years of intensive training. The use of ink on silk meant that he had to be sure of every line, for once the brush stroke had been made, no changes were possible. Calligraphy, or the use of the brush in writing the intricate Chinese word symbols, also provided excellent training.

Sung pottery—especially porcelain—was also of unsurpassed excellence. The Chinese loved the delicacy and beauty of the elegant porcelain pieces produced in this period.

Early modern China. During the eleventh century a group of people from Manchuria took northern China, ruling as the Chin dynasty (not related to the earlier Ch'in, p. 110). From 1127 on, the Sung had no control over northern China. They established a capital in the south of China, first at Nanking and then at Hangchow, and for the next one hundred years China was thus divided into two empires, the Sung and Chin.

Although militarily weak, the Southern Sung was economically and socially one of the greatest periods in Chinese history. Increased population, together with marked improvements in production, led to vastly increased internal and external trade. Commerce broke out of the controlled marketplaces, and shops began to line the streets of the towns and cities. More and more of the upper classes began to reside permanently in the urban centers rather than in the countryside. As Chinese foreign trade grew, large communities of foreign merchants settled inside China.

The growth of commerce required a more efficient monetary system. At first copper cash was used, but the advance of trade created such a money shortage that bank drafts and other forms of commercial paper were introduced in the ninth century. By 1024 the government began to issue paper money. This commercial revolution strongly resembled that which was to take place in Europe several centuries later. In the latter, however, feudalism was too rigid to develop within itself the new institutions required by commerce. In China very significant changes in society and culture did accompany the great economic growth and increased mercantile activity that took place from the eighth to the thirteenth centuries.

During the Southern Sung the bureaucracy, recruited more and more by examination and from the Yangtze valley area, began to replace the northern aristocracy as the main support of dynastic power. This professionalization of government service was an important factor in the early modernization of Chinese society. A change in the landholding and tax system, which occurred earlier in the eighth century, had weakened the power of the aristocracy and great landholders because it permitted the appearance of small- and medium-sized landholdings. The new "gentry" class which arose exerted its influence through the government bureaucracy, which drew most of its members from this class.

THE BARBARIAN CHALLENGE TO CIVILIZATION

China and the "barbarians." At the end of the twelfth century, with China split between the rule of the Chin and the Southern Sung, East Asian civilization faced a new threat from the north, greater than any in its previous history. By this time a recognizable pattern had emerged in China's relations with the nomadic peoples who surrounded her from the northeast to the southwest. Dynastic weakness encouraged "barbarian" invaders. The "barbarians" usually obtained the advice of Chinese administrators and military specialists, and they had superior military power based on the cavalry of the Central Asian steppe and use of the iron stirrup, which enabled an archer to shoot from the back of his horse without falling off. It was their excellent horsemanship that caused them to maintain military superiority over the peasant foot-soldiers.

As they acquired control over more and more settled Chinese territory, the "barbarians" usually adopted a policy of tolerance over the captured villages. They frequently employed the conquered Chinese in administration and tax collection, and also often employed other foreigners, feeling they could be trusted more than the Chinese.

All "barbarian" dynasties faced two great problems in their relationship with the Chinese. First, they sought to maintain their own identity by keeping their original homeland separate and by preserving their own language and customs. Always a small minority, they constantly faced the problem of losing their "barbarian" vigor by adopting the sedentary and "cultured" ways of the Chinese. Second, they had to control their new territories and alien population by military means. This meant stationing their forces at strategic locations throughout the country and defending major urban centers and economic regions from other "barbarians" and from internal revolt. Their resources were often not sufficient to accomplish this.

Rise of the Mongol onslaught. Up to the middle of the twelfth century the Mongol peoples had no national organization or identity but lived in scattered tribes spread over large areas. The majority lived as nomads, depending on animals for their needs; the protection of grazing routes through land as opposed to permanent domination of the land was a major nomadic concern. These nomads were never wholly independent from the sedentary civilizations like the Chinese, because they could not themselves produce the grains, metal goods, and other items they needed or desired.

This silk painting of barbarian royalty worshiping Buddha gives some indication of the extent of Chinese interaction with the outside world during the T'ang and Sung periods. Notice the many different kinds of dress and facial expression among the foreigners and the quality of caricature in their depiction, as compared with the portrayal of the serene and very Chinese Buddha with his disciples and guardians.

At the time of the birth of Genghis (also spelled Chinggis) Khan about 1162, no one leader had yet emerged to unite the Mongols as a whole. During Genghis' youth his father was killed. Brought up in a spirit of revenge, he slowly built up a personal following and overpowered his own overlord and other clans and tribes. At last, at a great meeting of the Mongol tribes in 1206, he was recognized as the ruler of all the Mongols and given the title by which he is known to history, Genghis Khan, which probably meant "ocean ruler" or "universal ruler."

Genghis was one of the greatest organizational geniuses of all time. Out of a population of a little over a million Mongols, he fashioned a war machine based on units of ten and trained in the most sophisticated cavalry techniques. With this machine he and his people conquered most of the known world from the Pacific to the Danube and the Mediterranean, terrorized the rest, and established a *Pax Tatarica* in eastern Europe, the Middle East, Central Asia, and the Far East that permitted the greatest development of travel and trade between the continents that the world was to witness before the seventeenth century.

Leading his magnificent army, Genghis campaigned against the Chin empire. In 1215 the Chin capital near Peking was sacked and its inhabitants massacred. Following this victory, the attack on the Chin slowed down because Genghis sent much of his army westward on a campaign through Central Asia and on into Russia. But the conquest of northern China was later renewed, and city after city was subdued. The Great Khan himself was killed, probably by assassination, in 1227. A Mongol legend claims that he will return one day to lead the Mongols to world conquest once more.

Genghis' death did not slow down the Mongol war machine. By 1234 the last remnants of the Chin empire were extinguished by his son, who then embarked on the slow process of conquering the Southern Sung. After years of heroic resistance the Chinese were vanquished by the new Mongol dynasty, the Yüan—the first "barbarian" dynasty in history to rule all China.

Although China was now incorporated into an empire that stretched across the world, it did not lose its separate identity. On the death of Genghis, portions of the empire had been administered by his sons and grandsons under the general leadership of one son elected as khan of all the Mongols. After 1260 the unity of an empire divided into a suzerain khanate and four vassal khanates was becoming a fiction, and Mongol China was a distinct state. The unity of the empire weakened after Kublai Khan, who from 1260 to 1294 held the suzerain khanate comprising China and Mongolia, moved his capital to Peking.

China under the Mongols. Instead of turning all of North China into one vast pasture land, the khans were taught the art of governing the sedentary Chinese and the advantages of maintaining a stable society in China from which the Mongols might obtain great benefits through taxation. While separating themselves from the Chinese by custom and law, the Mongols adopted most of the T'ang and Sung administrative institutions and even instituted an examination system to recruit bureaucrats. The Yüan also employed many foreigners in high positions, including Marco Polo. They set up a hierarchical system in which they were at the top and the Southern Chinese, the most numerous group, were at the very bottom.

The arts flourished during this "barbarian" dynasty. The drama, which was probably influenced by Central Asian dance performances, was popular, and what we now know as the "Chinese opera," a combination of singing, dancing, and acting accompanied by music, achieved its classical development during the Yüan. Growing out of the prompting books used by professional storytellers, the novel also developed rapidly.

The reign of Kublai Khan. For knowledge of Kublai Khan's reign, we are indebted to the famous Venetian traveler Marco Polo, author of probably the world's outstanding travelogue and what has been called the finest European account of Chinese civilization at this time. As a youth, Marco Polo accompanied his father and uncle, two Venetian merchants, eastward to Kublai Khan's court, arriving there about 1275. Received with honor and given posts in the imperial service, the Polos remained seventeen years in China. Marco Polo reported that the Great Khan maintained order throughout his dominions, improved the roads, constructed canals, revised the calendar, built granaries to store food surpluses, and aided the sick, orphans, and old scholars by means of state care.

After Marco Polo returned to Italy, he wrote of his travels. But his fellow Venetians were so incredulous of the figures he used in describing the wealth and power of China, whose civilization was superior to that of thirteenth-century Europe, that they dubbed him "Messer Millions." His account of black stones (coal) used for heating purposes and the people's habit of taking frequent baths seemed fabulous to them, since coal was unknown in medieval Europe and Europeans in the Middle Ages seldom, if ever, took baths.

Pax Tatarica: relinking of East and West. In the first centuries of the Christian era the West had been linked with India and China by the spice and silk trades. The subsequent centuries of mutual isolation were broken during the T'ang dynasty when its court attracted such diverse groups as Muslims, Christians, and Persians. With the advent of the nomadic Mongols, East and West were again linked together along the ancient silk routes. The resumption of this trade had permanent consequences. By making the trade routes across Asia safe and by tolerating diverse religions, the Mongol dynasty attracted European traders and missionaries to China.

With the unification, however temporary, of almost all Asia and the restoration of roads, communication was restored to the point where the Polos were far from being the only travelers to cross the great spaces separating East and West. One monk, from a Christian community in Peking, traveled in the thirteenth century as an envoy of Mongol Persia to the pope and also met the kings of England and France. The papacy sent various missions to the Far East in the same century, with the result that in the early fourteenth century a Roman Catholic community of several thousand persons existed in China.

Cultural interchange between China and the West was also considerable during medieval times. One authority believes that the Mongols and other Central Asian peoples conveyed gunpowder to Europe, and we know that the Muslims transmitted westward such invaluable Chinese inventions as the arts of papermaking and printing and the magnetic compass. China itself was enriched by its imports. One of the most important was a new food, sorghum, which was brought to China by way of India in the thirteenth century. By that time the abacus, a familiar sight in Far Eastern shops today, had also made its appearance. Ceramics and bronzes were affected by influences from civilizations to the west, especially Persia, while the cloisonné technique was undoubtedly borrowed from the Byzantines.

These are but random examples of a cultural interchange which certainly enriched East and West alike. Yet the profound psychological effect created in Europe by the accounts of Marco Polo and other travelers was perhaps even more far-reaching in the evolution of world history. Travelers' accounts had revealed that the Far East not only equaled but exceeded Europe in population, wealth, and luxury. Europeans now realized that the Mediterranean was neither the central nor the most important area of the world, and they began to develop new attitudes to fit this knowledge.

Decline of Mongol China. Actually, the prosperous appearances which Marco Polo described were largely deceptive. Kublai Khan's ambitious foreign wars and domestic works necessitated heavy government spending. Tax rates rose, and many peasants were dispossessed of their land and forced to work for greedy landowners of vast estates. Large issues of paper money depreciated in value, while hard currency diminished. Kublai Khan's projected invasion of Japan was a disastrous failure (see p. 184).

The seven other Yüan emperors who succeeded Kublai Khan all proved to be inadequate rulers. The Mongols allowed their armed strength to lapse; and the exclusion of Chinese from the imperial administration continued to fan the resentment of the people against the rule of foreigners. By 1368, less than a century after Kublai's final conquest of the Sung, rebellious forces from South China, led by an ex-Buddhist novice, took Peking and founded the Ming dynasty.

The nomad challenge of the Mongols was thus rebuffed in East Asia, but its scourge was longer felt elsewhere. Remnants of West Asian Mongols, converted to Islam, were part of continuing steppe-world invasions into India. Older Muslim centers in Mesopotamia never fully recovered. That segment of Mongols who had settled as overlords in southern Russia continued for more than two centuries to affect and condition Russian development.

THE EVOLUTION OF JAPAN

The geography of Japan. In the mountainous Japanese archipelago of over three thousand islands, only four are relatively large: Honshu, Hokkaido, Shikoku, and Kyushu (see map, p. 183). The oceanic sides of Kyushu and Honshu receive abundant rain and are warmed by the Japan Current (the Pacific's analog to the Gulf Stream); here have been the centers of Japanese life, past and present. Earthquakes, typhoons, and tidal waves are frequent catastrophes; yet the Japanese in all ages have expressed love for their native land and a sensitive appreciation of its scenic beauties.

Japan's distance from the major centers of older continental cultures has meant that while there have been crucial periods of close cultural borrowing (usually based on Japanese initiative), there have also been long periods of relatively isolated development. Japanese culture has been notably homogeneous, partly because in historic times there were no notable additions of new peoples—nothing equivalent to the British Isles' successive experience of Romans, Angles, Saxons, Danes, and Normans.

Origins of the Japanese people. In prehistoric times there must have been many strands of migration, particularly from Northeast Asia and the Asian mainland by way of Korea and from Southeast Asia and its adjacent islands by way of the island chain south of Japan. No precise theories concerning the origins of the Japanese people are possible, but the evidence points to a mixed origin. In time there developed a common ethnic community—predominantly Mongoloid though darker and hairier than Mongoloid types on the Asian mainland—with a single basic language belonging to the same Altaic family as Korean.

Early Japanese society. In ancient times the mountainous islands of Japan facilitated the growth of numerous small tribal states, each ruled by a hereditary chieftain who claimed descent from a tribal deity. According to Japanese folklore, the first emperor of Japan—Jimmu Tenno—descended from the Sun Goddess and became emperor in 660 B.C. Ever since, the same family has reigned in Japan, and thus the Japanese claim with justice to have the oldest unbroken dynastic line in the world. Historians believe that the ruling family of Japan originated with the most important tribal group —the Yamato clan—which occupied a fertile plain on Honshu.

The religion of the Japanese, known as *Shinto*, or "Way of the Gods," included the worship of forces and objects of nature and of ancestral spirits. With the growth of Yamato power, Shinto centered primarily on the Sun Goddess as the divine ancestress of the Yamato and, eventually, of all the Japanese people.

Agriculture was the foundation of the economy, with the clan rulers and nobles controlling the land. With the clans engaged in constant struggles for land, warfare was the order of the day. The rigid social structure was well suited for purposes of warfare; the subservient lower orders had to cater to the warrior nobles and their divinely descended chieftain. Thus the warrior in Japan has from earliest times tended to enjoy a social position and political power greater than that of his Chinese counterpart.

During the first few centuries A.D. the Yamato clan extended its power in central Japan. Its chieftain began to regard himself as a kind of emperor, while the chieftains of clans brought under the control of the Yamato attached themselves to the imperial court. Still, however, the Yamato had only nominal suzerainty over some of the more powerful clans.

Influence of China. While the Japanese archipelago is sufficiently removed from the Asian mainland to make invasion extremely difficult, it is close enough to allow commercial and cultural contacts. Thus much of Japan's history is the story of the influx of external ideas and institutions and adaption by the Japanese to form a unique culture pattern. During the Han dynasty (202 B.C.- 220 A.D.) Chinese rule was extended to part of Korea, and elements of Chinese culture were transmitted from there to Japan. In the succeeding centuries the influx of Chinese and Korean artisans, potters, weavers, painters, and farmers enriched Japanese culture. In addition, Chinese medicine and military science were introduced and the Chinese calendar adopted. Educated scribes brought to Japan the Chinese language with its character script and also the riches of Chinese literature. Transplanted from Korea in the

sixth century A.D., Buddhism was promoted by the rulers both as a means of weakening the clans with their allegiance to native Shinto and as a vehicle for the importation of Chinese ways and ideas.

The Taika reform: emulation of China. Faced by continued clan power and strife, the emperor and his advisers turned to T'ang China, probably the world's best-governed state in the seventh century, as a model for reforms that would change Japan from a clan and tribal society to a strongly centralized state. Inaugurated in 646, this "Great reform" (Taika) created a centralized bureaucracy and adopted the T'ang system of landholding and taxation. Law codes of the Chinese type were also drawn up. The Japanese state slowly began to take on the image of the T'ang government. Unlike the Chinese model, the emperor of Japan was claimed to be a divine personage and given the title of *Tenno* (heaven sovereign) so that rebellion against the throne constituted a religious crime. A court

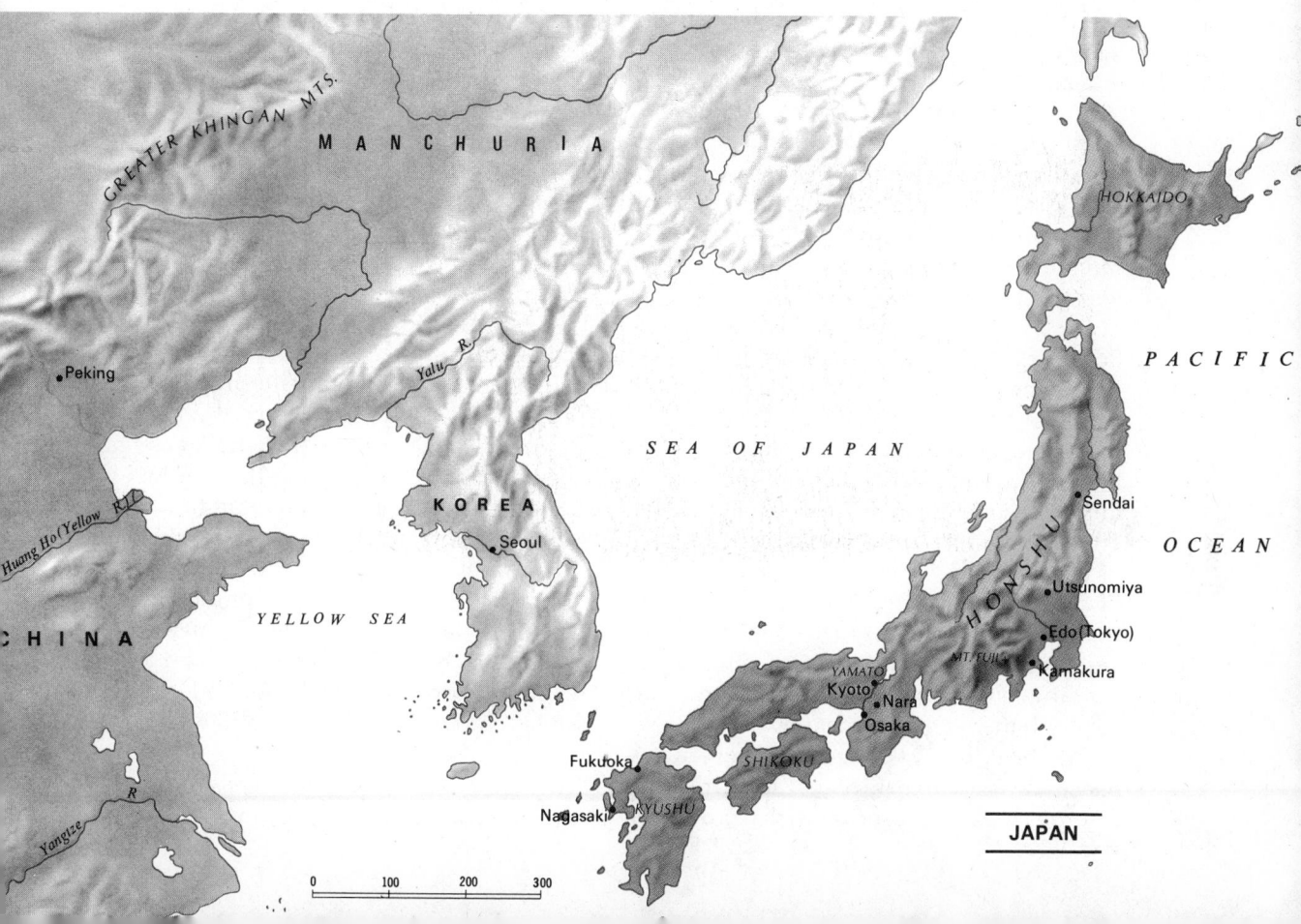

JAPAN

aristocracy was set up where officials owed their positions to imperial appointment which quickly became hereditary.

The Fujiwara regents (857-1160). In 784 the capital was removed from Nara, where a Chinese-type court had been established in 710, and ten years later settled upon Kyoto— then called Heian-kyo—where it remained until 1868. The early centuries at Kyoto are identified politically as the Fujiwara period.

The Fujiwara family had been prominent in the government at Nara and soon rose to dominate the imperial government at Kyoto. Holding vast provincial estates, this family acquired so much power that the emperors were reduced to the status of puppet rulers whose wives were chosen for them from Fujiwara women. Once a royal son had been born, the emperor would frequently be forced to abdicate and retire to a Buddhist monastery, leaving a Fujiwara grandfather or uncle to rule the country as regent for the new infant emperor. Between the ninth and twelfth centuries, the tradition was thus established that the emperor reigned but did not rule, for his powers were delegated to hereditary officials of an aristocratic civil bureaucracy.

At Kyoto, Japanese culture, hitherto an unashamed imitation of Chinese culture, began to develop its own distinctive character. A refined appreciation of beauty in all its forms emerged from the gay, sophisticated ceremonial of Fujiwara court life, in which women played a major role. This preoccupation with the esthetic inspired a sudden flowering of literature and art that established the classic canons of Japanese artistic tradition.

In time the hereditary bureaucracy of the Fujiwara grew inefficient and the government became impoverished. Taxable property steadily decreased, due to the exemption of temple lands and of estates that originally had been given to officials as payment for their services and which then remained hereditary. Eventually most of the land in the kingdom ceased to be a source of revenue for the imperial government.

The bankruptcy of the government finances was accompanied by an increase of disorder and lawlessness in the provinces.

To protect their estates, the provincial lords hired bands of professional soldiers, and a feudal society began to develop. By the twelfth century, power and authority had shifted from the civil aristocracy to a military nobility, who were destined to dominate Japanese history for the next seven centuries.

The Kamakura shogunate and the samurai. After the two leading military clans had battled from one end of the country to the other—a brutal struggle celebrated in present-day Japanese movies, television series, and historical fiction—one of Japan's outstanding soldier-statesmen, Yoritomo of the Minamoto clan, emerged victorious in 1185. He soon forced the emperor to grant him the office of *shogun* (generalissimo) and effectively ruled Japan through a feudal hierarchy of warrior nobility. From his residence at Kamakura, Yoritomo appointed constables and stewards in every province to prevent rebellion. Although he continued to pay the utmost respect to the emperor and governed at a discreet distance from the imperial court at Kyoto, the shogun, not the emperor, was the real ruler in Japan.

Following Yoritomo's death in 1199, control passed to the leaders of the Hojo clan who, copying the Fujiwara technique of rule, governed in the name of puppet shoguns. The outstanding event in the Hojo period was the repulse of invasions by Kublai Khan of Mongol China in 1274 and 1281, the only such external attacks the Japanese experienced until World War II. On both occasions nature in the form of a typhoon (thenceforth called *Kamikaze*, or "the Divine Wind") aided the Japanese by shattering the invading armadas.

The establishment of the shogunate gave prominence to the growing strength and importance of the *samurai* or *bushi*, the warrior nobility. Official recognition was now given to *Bushido* ("The way of the warrior"), the unwritten *samurai* code of conduct that resembled the western code of chivalry, but lacked its religious inspiration and idealization of women. This stern code was instilled in childhood with such injunctions as:

What a coward to cry for a little pain! What will you do when your arm is cut off in battle, or when, for the sake of honor, you must rip your stomach open with your sword?[7]

Stressing courage, fortitude, loyalty, and discipline, the code of *Bushido* approved the custom of ceremonial suicide—*seppuku*—which is generally known to westerners as *hara-kiri*. By means of *seppuku*, a warrior could atone for his crimes, escape disgrace if he had "lost face," or prove his loyalty to his lord.

The *samurai* spirit infused and strengthened the tightly knit system of noble privilege, military government, and national loyalty. It persisted long after the overthrow of the shogunate in 1868—until, in fact, the defeat of Japan in World War II.

Joined with the *samurai* spirit was Shinto's glorification of the nation and the emperor's sacred position, together with Zen Buddhism's stress on strict mental and physical discipline as the means of achieving enlightenment. Imported from China late in the twelfth century, the Zen sect discarded not only emphasis on ritual and learning but also the simple piety and devotionalism of the savioristic sects of Buddhism that were followed by the humbler folk.

The Ashikaga shogunate. In 1333 Kamakura, the seat of the shogunate since its establishment in 1192, was destroyed by the Ashikaga family, which succeeded in founding a new shogunate five years later with headquarters at the imperial city of Kyoto. The Ashikaga shoguns failed to establish effective control over the other great barons (*daimyos*) and the *samurai* retainers, and the whole country drifted into disorder. By 1500 Japanese society was completely feudalized in a fashion comparable to western Europe during the same period.

SUMMARY

At the very time when Europe was beset by the tribulations following the collapse of the Graeco-Roman world, Asia was being enriched by what were probably its most splendid centuries of cultural development. The first of these centuries saw the emer-

This Japanese Buddhist temple guardian figure illustrates both the unusual nature of Japanese Buddhism and the more salient aspects of Kamakura sculpture. Kamakura sculpture, influenced by contemporaneous Chinese Sung art, abounded in vivid realism.

gence of a golden age in India. With the Guptas, the zenith of Hindu culture was reached. Artists produced paintings of contemporary life and sculpture characterized by dignity and restraint; the Gupta poet Kalidasa wrote dramas which have been compared favorably with those of Shakespeare. In mathematics, the so-called Arabic numerals, the decimal system, and many of the basic elements of algebra came into use; and there were important discoveries in chemistry and medicine. So powerful was Gupta civilization that it diffused to many parts of Asia, thereby raising the cultural level of a large segment of mankind.

The Gupta age was followed in India by a period of internal dissolution and external invasion, culminating in the subjugation of the country by the forces of an uncompromisingly antagonistic religious culture, Islam. The consequences of that impact were in our own century to split the Indian subcontinent into two separate states: India and Pakistan.

China's outstanding achievement was the successful re-creation of a unitary centralized state on classical lines that had no analogy in India or the West. Barbarians were domesticated in the T'ang period, which also saw a rich flowering of poetry, painting, and sculpture, and the invention of printing.

The Sung period, despite its weakness in dealing with barbarian states, brought to perfection the bureaucratic civil service system, saw Buddhism lose ground to a secular Neo-Confucian philosophy among the upper classes, and refined many traditional arts and crafts, especially painting and ceramics. The invention of explosive powder for warfare, the magnetic compass, and paper money bear witness to the range of Chinese creative ability.

The short period of Mongol rule in China, through briefly uniting China with the West by trade routes, confirmed the growing Chinese tendency to be contemptuous of foreign ways and to accept despotic rule. Economic disorders and popular rebellion ended the Mongols' regime in China sooner than in other parts of their far-flung empire.

Japan was brought within the world of civilized communities by impulses radiating from the T'ang. The Japanese blended continental forms of government, social organization, religion, and the arts with their own native traits. They preferred patterns of hereditary aristocratic privilege to the social mobility found in China. Embracing Buddhism, they also retained their native Shinto in both public life and popular cult. While China was perfecting its centralized civilian administrative system, Japan was increasingly divided by the controls and ideals of a hereditary feudal military nobility.

SUGGESTIONS FOR READING

Sir Percival Spear, **India: A Modern History,** rev. ed., (Univ. of Michigan, 1972) contains one of the best introductory accounts of Gupta India and the coming of the Muslims. R. C. Majumdar and A. D. Pulsaker, eds., **The Classic Age** (Verry), Vol. III of **The History and Culture of the Indian Peoples** is the most comprehensive history of the Gupta period. See also B. G. Gokhale, **Samudra Gupta** (Asia, 1962).

For a well-illustrated account of the influence of India's art on neighboring countries, see B. Rowland, **The Art and Architecture of India*** (Penguin, 1971).

For the Islamic impact upon India the following are authoritative: K. S. Lal, **Twilight of the Sultanate** (Asia); and S. M. Ikram, **Muslim Civilization in India** (Columbia).

For the expansion of Hindu culture see D. G. Hall, **History of South-East Asia,*** 3rd ed. (St. Martin's, 1968); and G. Coedes, **The Indianized States of Southeast Asia** (East-West Center Press, 1975).

C. P. Fitzgerald, **China: A Short Cultural History,*** 3rd ed., (Praeger) contains an excellent account of the intellectual and artistic activities of the T'ang and Sung periods. See also John Meskill, **An Introduction to Chinese Civilization*** (Heath, 1973).

An excellent biographical study of a leading personality under the T'ang is C. P. Fitzgerald, **Son of Heaven: A Biography of Li Shih-min, Founder of the T'ang Dynasty** (AMS Pr.). The lives and works of the two greatest T'ang poets are treated authoritatively in A. Waley, **The Poetry and Career of Li Po: 701-762 A.D.** (Humanities); and W. Hung, **Tu Fu, China's Greatest Poet,** 2 vols. (Russell, 1969).

T. F. Carter and L. C. Goodrich, **The Invention of Printing in**

China and Its Spread Westward (Ronald) is the best detailed study. E. Kracke, **Civil Service in Early Sung China, 960-1067** (Harvard) is useful for an understanding of the Chinese political system.

John Meskill, **Wang An-Shih: Practical Reformer?*** (Heath) is an introduction, through readings and discussion, to the greatest premodern Chinese social theorist. See also H. R. Williamson, **Wang An-Shih: Chinese Statesman and Educationalist of the Sung Dynasty,** 2 vols. (Hyperion, 1973).

H. D. Martin, **The Rise of Genghis Khan and his Conquest of North China** (Octagon, 1970) relates the struggle of the Chinese with the neighboring Mongols.

Jacques Gernet, **Daily Life in China on the Eve of the Mongol Invasion*** (Stanford) has vivid descriptions of all facets of life, as does his **Daily Life in China in the Thirteenth Century** (Macmillan).

L. Olschki, **Marco Polo's Asia** (Univ. of Calif., 1960) is an exhaustive study of the life and times of Marco Polo. See also the same author's **Marco Polo's Precursors** (Octagon, 1971); and Henry Hart, **Marco Polo: Venetian Adventurer** (Univ. of Oklahoma).

G. B. Sansom, **A History of Japan,** 3 vols., (Stanford Univ., 1958-1963) is the best history in English. Also extremely valuable is E. O. Reischauer and J. K. Fairbank, **East Asia: Tradition and Transformation** (Houghton Mifflin, 1973). E. O. Reischauer, **The United States and Japan*** (Compass) is a synthesis of modern scholarship on Japanese history and culture. The relinking of East and West under the *Pax Tatarica* is treated in G. F. Hudson, **Europe and China** (Gordon Pr., 1976).

*Indicates a less expensive paperbound edition.

CHAPTER 8

The Rise and Fall of
the Carolingian Empire;
Feudalism
and the Manorial System:
500-1050

Europe's Search for Stability

INTRODUCTION. We last surveyed the fortunes of Europe at a crucial turning point in western civilization—the fifth century (see Chapter 5). The mighty Roman Empire in the West was breaking apart under the pressure of incoming Germanic tribes, and unity and stability gave way to fragmentation and disorder. What was the future of western Europe to be?

The first indication of the new forms that life and politics would take in the West came from the Germanic Franks in alliance with the Church. In the single century from 714 to 814, covering the reigns of the Frankish rulers from Charles Martel to Charlemagne, the Carolingian House of the Franks gave Europe an interim of stability and progress. A great empire was fashioned, Christianity was extended to barbarian tribes, and law and order were maintained.

This accomplishment of the Carolingians was premature, however. Charlemagne's empire could not endure, partly because it lacked the economic basis that had supported the Romans. By the ninth century

Muslim conquests had cut off what remained of European trade in the Mediterranean; inland trade shriveled up and urban life almost disappeared. In addition, the empire had no strong administrative machinery to compensate for the weak Carolingian rulers who followed the dominating figure of Charlemagne on the throne; the empire disintegrated amid civil wars and invasions.

Out of the ruins of the Carolingian empire emerged a new form of government known as feudalism. Based on local authority, feudalism was a poor and primitive substitute for a powerful, comprehensive central government; but it was better than no authority at all, and it survived for several hundred years. Also appropriate to the times was the rural, self-sufficient economy known as the manorial system. In sum, the poverty and localism of western Europe in the tenth century contrasts sharply with the contemporary societies of Byzantium and Islam.

NEW EMPIRE IN THE WEST

The kingdom of the Franks under Clovis. In the blending of the Roman and Germanic peoples and cultures, the Franks played an especially significant part. The kingdom of the Franks was not only the most enduring of all the Germanic states established in the West, but it became, with the active support of the Church, the center of the new Europe that arose upon the ruins of the western Roman empire.

Before the Germanic invasions the several tribes that made up the Franks lived along the east bank of the Rhine close to the North Sea. Late in the fourth century the Franks began a slow movement south and west across the Rhine into Gaul. By 481 they occupied the northern part of Gaul as far as the old Roman city of Paris, and in this year Clovis I of the Merovingian House became ruler of one of the petty Frankish kingdoms. By the time of his death in 511, Clovis had united the Franks into a single kingdom that stretched southward to the Pyrenees.

Clovis achieved his goal with the aid of an arsenal of weapons that included marriage alliances, treachery, assassination, and religion. As a first step, Clovis allied himself with other petty Frankish kings to dispose of Syagrius, the last Roman general in Gaul. The victor then turned against his Frankish allies and subdued them.

According to the sixth-century Gallo-Roman bishop and historian Gregory of Tours, whose *History of the Franks* is the fullest account of any Germanic people, Clovis became converted to Christianity in 496 as a result of a battle against the Alemanni, a pagan Germanic tribe whose name became the French word for Germany, *Allemagne*. On the verge of being defeated, Clovis called upon Christ for help:

"For I have called on my gods, but I find they are far from my aid. . . . Now I call on Thee. I long to believe in Thee. Only, please deliver me from my adversaries."[1]

Clovis won the battle and was baptized together with his whole army. He became the only orthodox Christian ruler in the West, for the other Germanic tribes were either pagan or embraced the heretical form of Christianity known as Arianism (see pp. 128, 242).

The conversion of the Franks must be considered a decisive event in European history. Ultimately it led to an alliance of the Franks and the papacy, and immediately it assured Clovis the loyalty of the Gallo-Roman bishops, the leaders of the native Christian population of Gaul. This was a political advantage not open to the heretical Arian Visigothic and Burgundian kings. Thus with the help of the native population of Gaul, Clovis was able to expand his realm in the name of Christian orthodoxy.

In 507 Clovis attacked the Visigoths, who ruled Gaul south of the Loire River and all of Spain (see map, p. 137). "Verily it grieves my soul," Clovis told his troops, "that these Arians should hold a part of Gaul."[2] The Visigothic king was killed, and his people abandoned most of their Gallic territory. Clovis died four years later at the age of forty-five—a ripe old age for a barbarian. Although never hardly more than a Germanic chieftain, he had created France.

Decline of the Merovingians. Clovis' sons and grandsons conquered the Burgundian kingdom and extended the Frankish domain to the Mediterranean and further into Germany. At the same time, however, the Merovingian House began to decay from inner weaknesses. The Germanic practice of treating the kingdom as personal property and dividing it among all the king's sons resulted in constant and bitter civil war. The royal heirs plotted murders and became adept at intrigue and treachery. The Merovingian princes also engaged in all manner of debaucheries, the least unpleasant of which was excessive drinking. Soon the Frankish state broke up into three separate kingdoms; in each, power was concentrated in the hands of the chief official of the royal household, the mayor of the palace, a powerful noble who desired to keep the king weak and ineffectual. The Merovingian rulers were mere puppets, the *rois fainéants* ("do-nothing kings").

A dark age. By the middle of the seventh century western Europe had lost most of the essential characteristics of Roman civilization. The Roman system of administration and taxation had completely collapsed, and the dukes and counts who represented the Merovingian king received no salary and usually acted on their own initiative in commanding the fighting men and presiding over the courts in their districts. International commerce had ceased except for a small-scale trade in luxury items carried on by adventurous Greek, Syrian, and Jewish traders, and the old Roman cities served mainly to house the local bishop and his retinue. The virtual absence of a middle class meant that society was composed of the nobility, a fusion through intermarriage of aristocratic Gallo-Roman and German families who owned and exercised authority over vast estates, and, at the other end of the social scale, the semi-servile *coloni*, who were bound to the land. These serfs included large numbers of formerly free German farmers.

The abstract transfigured Christ carved on a seventh-century Frankish tomb shows Jesus holding a spear. Even in a spiritual image, a militant rather than a meek Savior may have seemed most appropriate to the war-like Franks. (Courtesy of Rheinisches Landesmuseum, Bonn.)

Only about 10 percent of the peasant population of Gaul maintained a free status.

Coinciding with Merovingian decay, new waves of invaders threatened. A great movement of Slavic people from the area that is now Russia had begun about 500 A.D. (see p. 152). From this nucleus the Slavs fanned out, filling the vacuum left by the Germanic tribes when they pushed into the Roman Empire. By 650 the western Slavs had reached the Elbe River, across which they raided German territory. Another danger threatened western Europe from the south; in the late seventh century the Muslim Moors prepared to invade Spain from North Africa.

Charles Martel and the rise of the Carolingians. A new period dawned when Charles Martel became mayor of the palace in 714. His father, one of the greatest Frankish landowners, had eliminated all rival mayors, and Charles ruled a united Frankish kingdom in all but name. For the time being, however, the Merovingian kings were kept as harmless figureheads at the court.

Charles is best remembered for his victory over the Muslim invaders of Europe, which earned him the surname Martel, "The Hammer." In 711 an army of Moors from North Africa had invaded Spain, and by 718 the weak kingdom of the Visigoths had collapsed. With most of the peninsula under control, the Muslims began making raids across the Pyrenees. In 732 Charles Martel met them near Tours, deep within the Frankish kingdom. Muslim losses were heavy, and during the night they retreated toward Spain.

A major military reform coincided with the battle of Tours. For some time before this conflict, the effectiveness of mounted soldiers had been growing, aided by the introduction of the stirrup, which gave the mounted warrior a firm seat while wielding his weapons. To counteract the effectiveness of the quick-striking Muslim cavalry, Charles recruited a force of professional mounted soldiers whom he rewarded with sufficient land to enable each knight to maintain himself, his equipment, and a number of war horses. Such grants of land later became an important element in feudalism.

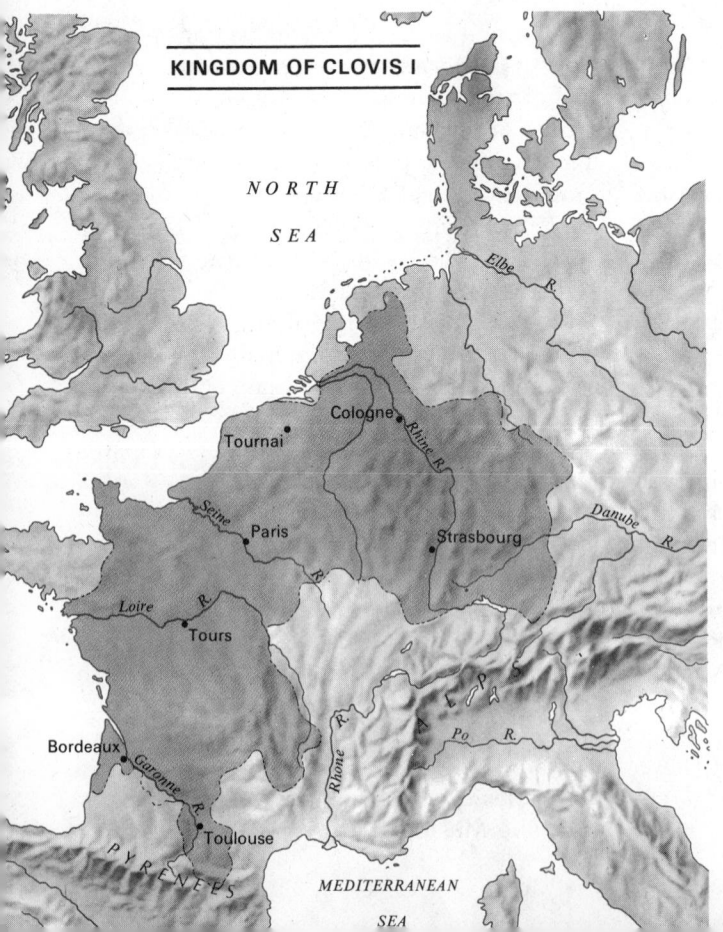

Pepin the Short. Charles Martel's son, Pepin the Short, who ruled from 741 to 768, was a worthy successor to his father. To legalize the regal power already being exercised by the mayors of the palace, he requested and received from the pope a ruling which stipulated that whoever had the actual power should be the legal ruler. In this maneuvering, St. Boniface (p. 242) was the intermediator, and in 751 Pepin was elected king by the Franks and crowned by St. Boniface. The last Merovingian was quietly shelved in a secluded monastery. In 754 the pope reaffirmed the usurpation by crossing the Alps and personally anointing Pepin, in the Old Testament manner, as the Chosen of the Lord.

Behind the pope's action lay his need for a powerful protector. In 751 the Lombards had conquered the exarchate of Ravenna, the seat of Byzantine government in Italy, and were demanding tribute from the pope and threatening to take Rome. Following the coronation, the pope secured Pepin's promise of armed intervention in Italy and his pledge to give the papacy the exarchate of Ravenna, once it was conquered. In 756 a Frankish army forced the Lombard king to relinquish his conquests, and Pepin officially conferred the exarchate of Ravenna upon the pope. Known as the "Donation of Pepin," the gift made the pope a temporal ruler over the Papal States, a strip of territory that extended diagonally from coast to coast (see map, p. 192).

The alliance between the Franks and the papacy affected the course of politics and of religion for centuries. It accelerated the separation of Latin from Greek Christendom by providing the papacy with a dependable western ally in place of the Byzantines, hitherto its only protector against the Lombards; it created the Papal States which played a major role in Italian politics until the late nineteenth century; and, by the ritual of anointment, it provided western kingship with a religious sanction that would in time contribute to the rise of monarchs strong enough to pose a threat to the papacy.

Charlemagne: the man and his conquests. Under Pepin's son, Charlemagne (Charles the Great), who ruled from 768 to 814, the

Frankish state and the Carolingian House reached the summit of their power. Einhard, in his famous biography of Charlemagne, pictured his king as a natural leader of men— tall, physically strong, and a great horseman who was always in the van of the hunt. Although he was preeminently a successful warrior-king, leading his armies on yearly campaigns, Charlemagne also sought to provide an effective administration for his realm. In addition, he had great respect for learning and was proud of the fact that he could read Latin.

Taking advantage of feuds among the Muslims in Spain, Charlemagne sought to extend Christendom southward into that land. In 778 he crossed the Pyrenees with indifferent success. As the Frankish army headed back north, it aroused the antagonism of the Christian Basques, who attacked its rear guard. In the melee the Frankish leader, a gallant count named Roland, was killed. The memory of his heroism was later enshrined in the great medieval epic, the *Chanson de Roland (Song of Roland)*. On later expeditions the Franks drove the Muslims back to the Ebro River and established a frontier area known as the Spanish March, or Mark, centered around Barcelona. French immigrants moved into the area, later called Catalonia, giving it a character distinguishable from the rest of Spain.

Charlemagne conquered the Bavarians and the Saxons, the last of the independent Germanic tribes. It took thirty-two campaigns to subdue the staunchly pagan Saxons, who lived between the Rhine and Elbe rivers. Charlemagne divided Saxony into bishoprics, built monasteries, and proclaimed harsh laws against paganism. Eating meat during Lent, cremating the dead (an old pagan practice), and pretending to be baptized were offenses punishable by death.

Like his father before him, Charlemagne intervened in Italian politics. Expansionist ambition drove the Lombard king to invade again the territories of the papacy. At the behest of the pope, Charlemagne defeated the Lombards in 774 and proclaimed himself their king. While in Italy, he cemented his father's alliance with the Church by confirming the Donation of Pepin.

The interior of the Chapel of Charlemagne in Aachen. Built as his tomb, it was modeled in an octagonal design after San Vitale in Ravenna and imported materials from Italy were used in the construction. The interior shows a conscious attempt to revert to arched Roman forms; it emphasized Charlemagne's desire to initiate an artistic renaissance.

The empire's eastern frontier was continually threatened by the Avars, Asiatic nomads related to the Huns, and the Slavs. In six campaigns Charlemagne decimated the Avars and then set up his own military province in the valley of the Danube to guard against any possible future plundering by eastern nomads. Called the East Mark, this territory later became Austria.

Charlemagne's coronation in Rome. One of the most important single events in Charlemagne's reign took place on Christmas Day in the year 800. The previous year the unruly Roman nobility had ousted the pope, charging him with moral laxity. Charlemagne came to Rome and restored the pope to his office. Then, at the Christmas service while Charlemagne knelt before the altar at St. Peter's, the pope placed a crown on his head amid the cries of the assembled congregation: "To Charles Augustus crowned of God, great and pacific Emperor of the Romans, long life and victory!"

This ceremony demonstrated that the memory of the Roman Empire still survived as a vital tradition in Europe and that there was a strong desire to reestablish political unity. In fact, Charlemagne previously named his capital at Aix-la-Chapelle (Aachen)

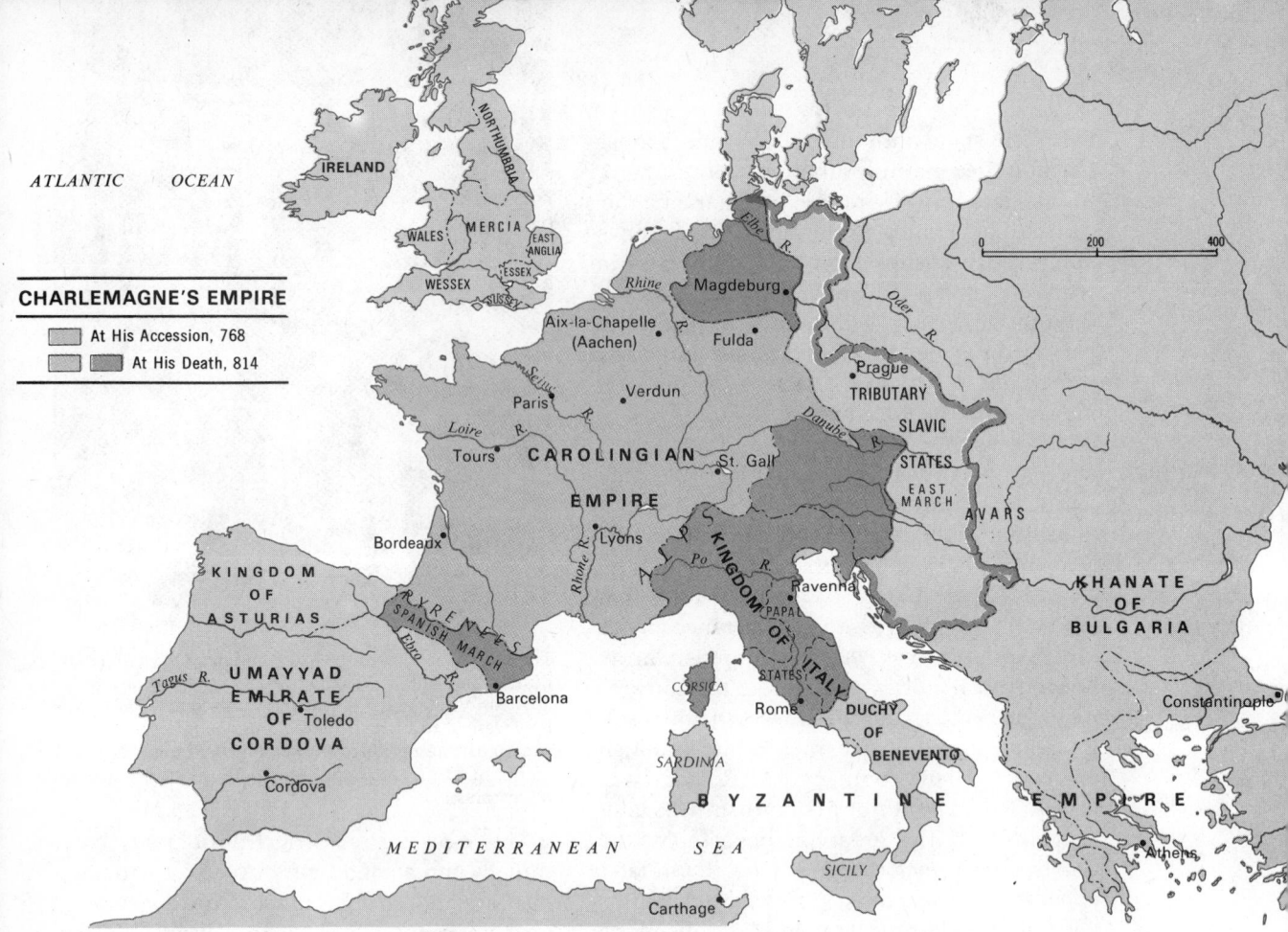

"New Rome" and was about to take the title of emperor and revive the Roman empire in the West. By seizing the initiative and crowning Charlemagne by the Grace of God, the pope assumed a position of superiority as the maker of emperors. A future clash between these two powers was inevitable, but it was postponed by the collapse of both the empire and the papacy in the ninth and tenth centuries, which came to be known as the age of feudalism.

Charlemagne's administration. The extent of Charlemagne's empire was impressive. His territories included all of the western area of the old Roman Empire except Africa, Britain, southern Italy, and most of Spain (see map). Seven defensive provinces, or marks, protected the empire against hostile neighbors.

The Carolingian territories were divided into some three hundred administrative divisions, each under a count (*graf*) or, in the marks along the border, a margrave (*mark graf*). In addition, there were local military officials, the dukes. In an effort to solve the problem of supervising the local officials, a problem that plagued all German rulers, Charlemagne issued an ordinance (capitulary) creating the *missi dominici*, the king's envoys. Pairs of these itinerant officials, usually a bishop and a lay noble, traveled throughout the realm to check on the local administration. To make the *missi* immune to bribes, they were chosen from men of high rank, were frequently transferred from one region to another, and no two of them were teamed for more than one year.

The Carolingian Renaissance. Charlemagne also fostered a revival of learning and the arts. His efforts in this area were destined to be far more lasting than his revival of the Roman Empire in the West, and they have prompted historians to speak of this period as one of cultural rebirth.

In 789 Charlemagne decreed that every monastery must have a school for the education of boys in "singing, arithmetic, and grammar." As he stated in a letter to the abbot of Fulda, Charlemagne was greatly concerned over the illiteracy of the clergy:

Since in these years there were often sent to us from divers monasteries letters in which . . . , owing to neglect of learning, the untutored tongue could not express [itself] without faultiness. Whence it came that we began to fear lest, as skill in writing was less, wisdom to understand the Sacred Scriptures might be far less than it ought rightly to be.[3]

At Aix-la-Chapelle, his capital, the emperor also sponsored a palace school for the education of the royal household and the stimulation of learning throughout the realm. Alcuin, an Anglo-Saxon scholar in charge of the school, began the arduous task of reviving learning by undertaking the first step of writing textbooks on grammar, spelling, rhetoric, and logic. "Ye lads," Alcuin exhorted his students, "whose age is fitted for reading, learn! The years go by like running water. Waste not the teachable days in idleness!"[4]

The reform of handwriting and the preservation of classical manuscripts were significant achievements of the Carolingian revival. Copyists labored in monasteries to preserve the classics of pagan and Christian thought with the result that the oldest manuscripts of most of the Latin classics that have come down to us date from the age of Charlemagne. The corrupt and almost illegible script of the Merovingian period was replaced by a more legible style of writing, known as Carolingian minuscule—"little letters," in contrast to the capitals used by the Romans—which became the foundation for the typeface still used in present-day printing.

At Aix-la-Chapelle Charlemagne also strove to recapture something of the grandeur of ancient Rome by building a stone palace church modeled after a sixth-century church in Ravenna. Its mosaics were probably the work of Byzantine artisans, and its marble columns were taken from ancient buildings in Rome and Ravenna.

Charlemagne's work on balance. Charlemagne must be considered one of the great constructive figures of world history. He extended Christian civilization in Europe, set up barriers against incursions of the Slav and Avar, and created a new Europe whose center was in the north rather than on the Mediterranean and in which a measure of law and order was again enforced after three centuries of disorder. Furthermore, his patronage of learning left a cultural heritage that later generations would build upon in producing a European civilization distinct from the Byzantine to the east and the Muslim to the south.

Charlemagne's empire afforded no more than a breathing space, however, for its territories were too vast and its nobility too powerful to be held together under existing conditions after the dominating personality of its creator had passed from the scene. Charlemagne had no standing army; his foot soldiers were essentially the old Germanic war band summoned to fight by its war leader, and his mounted warriors served him, as they had Charles Martel, in return for grants of land. Nor did Charlemagne have a bureaucratic administrative machine comparable to that of Roman times. The Frankish economy was agricultural and localized, and there was no system of taxation adequate to maintain an effective and permanent administration. Under Charlemagne's weak successors the empire disintegrated amid the confusion of civil wars and devastating new invasions. Progress toward an advanced civilization in the new Europe founded by Charlemagne was delayed for two centuries.

The division of the empire. Before his death in 814, Charlemagne himself, ignoring the pope, placed the imperial crown on the head of his only surviving son, Louis the Pious. Louis subsequently partitioned his realm among his sons, and bitter rivalry and warfare broke out among the brothers and their father. In 840 Louis the Pious died, a well-meaning man who was loved by the clergy, ignored by the nobility, and mistreated by his sons.

Strife continued among Louis' three surviving sons. Lothair, the elder, was opposed by the two younger—Louis the German and Charles the Bald. In 842 the younger brothers joined forces in the famous Strasbourg Oaths. The text of these oaths is significant in that one part was in an early form of French, the

NORTH SEA

THE DANELAW

ENGLISH KINGDOMS

ENGLISH CHANNEL

Aix-la-Chapelle (Aachen)

EAST KINGDOM OF LOUIS

FRANKS

TRIBUTARY

SLAVIC

Paris   Verdun

WEST   Strasbourg

Loire R.

FRANKS

KINGDOM OF CHARLES

KINGDOM OF LOTHAIR

Rhine R.   Elbe R.   Vistula R.

Danube R.

STATES

Rhone R.   Ebro R.

UMAYYAD EMIRATE OF CORDOVA

CORSICA

BYZANTINE EMPIRE

MEDITERRANEAN SEA

---

both Latin and Teutonic cultures, and although it was divided in 870 between Charles and Louis, the area was disputed for centuries. Lorraine remained one of the cockpits of Europe, a land drenched with the blood of countless French and German peoples.

The rival Carolingian houses produced no strong leaders worthy of being called "Hammer" (Martel) or "Great"; instead, we find kings with such revealing names as Charles the Fat, Charles the Simple, Louis the Child, and Louis the Sluggard. The last of the East Frankish Carolingians died in 911. In West Frankland the nobles, ignoring the eighteen-year-old Carolingian prince, chose Odo, the count of Paris, as king in 887.

The new invasions. During the ninth and tenth centuries the remnants of Charlemagne's empire were also battered by new waves of invaders. Scandinavians attacked from the north, Muslims from the south, and a new wave of Asiatic nomads, the Magyars, struck from the east. Christian Europe had to fight for its life against these plundering and murdering raiders, who did far more damage to life and property than the Germanic invaders of the fifth century.

From bases in North Africa, Muslim corsairs in full command of the sea plundered the coasts of Italy and France. In 827 they began the conquest of Byzantine Sicily and southern Italy. From forts erected in southern France they penetrated far inland to attack the caravans of merchants in the Alpine passes. What trade still existed between Byzantium and western Europe, except for that of Venice and one or two other Italian towns, was now almost totally cut off, and the great inland sea became a Muslim lake.

The most widespread and destructive raiders came from Scandinavia. During the ninth and tenth centuries Swedes, Danes, and Norwegians—collectively known as Vikings—stormed out of their remote forests and fiords. The reason for this expansion is not clear. Some historians stress overpopulation and a surplus of young men. Other scholars view these raiders as defeated war bands expelled from their homeland by the gradual emergence of strong royal power. Still others see a clue in the fact that the Vikings had developed seaworthy ships ca-

---

other in German. The first could be understood by Charles' followers, who lived mainly west of the Rhine; the other by Louis' followers, who lived east of the Rhine. These oaths are evidence that the Carolingian empire was splitting into two linguistic parts— East Frankland, the forerunner of modern Germany, and West Frankland, or France.

In 843 the brothers met at Verdun, where they agreed to split the Carolingian lands three ways. Charles the Bald obtained the western part and Louis the German the eastern; Lothair, who retained the title of emperor, obtained an elongated middle kingdom which stretched a thousand miles from the North Sea to central Italy (see map).

The importance of the Treaty of Verdun is that it began the shaping of modern France and Germany by giving political recognition to the cultural and linguistic division shown in the Strasbourg Oaths. Lothair's middle kingdom soon collapsed into three major parts, Lorraine in the north and Burgundy and Italy in the south. Lorraine encompassed pable of carrying a hundred men and powered by long oars or by sail when the wind was favorable. Viking sailors also had developed expert sailing techniques; without benefit of the compass, they were able to navigate by means of the stars at night and the sun during the day.

The range of Viking expansion was amazing. The Vikings went as far as North America to the west, the Caspian Sea to the east, and the Mediterranean to the south. Few areas seemed immune from their lightning raids, which filled civilized Europeans with a fear that is reflected in a new prayer in the litany of the Church: "From the fury of the Northmen, O Lord deliver us."

Three main routes of Viking expansion can be identified. The outer path, which was followed principally by the Norwegians, swung westward to Ireland and the coast of Scotland. Between 800 and 850 Ireland was ravaged severely. Monasteries, the centers of the flourishing culture attained by the Irish Celts, were destroyed. By 875 the Norwegians were beginning to occupy remote Iceland, and it was here rather than in their homeland that the magnificent Norse sagas were preserved, little affected by either classical or Christian influences. During the tenth century the Icelandic Norsemen ventured on to Greenland and, later, to North America (see Chapter 18).

Another route, the eastern line, was followed chiefly by the Swedes, who went down the rivers of Russia as merchants and soldiers of fortune and, as has been described in Chapter 6, forged the nucleus of a Russian state.

The Danes took the middle passage, raiding England and the shores of Germany, France, and Spain. By the 870's they had occupied most of England north of the Thames. Also in the middle of the ninth century their fury broke upon the Continent, where their long boats sailed up the Rhine, Scheldt, Seine, and Loire. In particular the Danes devastated northwest France, destroying dozens of abbeys and towns. Unable to fend off the Viking attacks, the weak Carolingian king Charles the Simple arranged an epoch-making treaty with a Norse chieftain named Rollo in 911. This agreement created

a Viking buffer state, later called Normandy, and recognized Rollo as duke and vassal of the French king. Like Viking settlers elsewhere, these Northmen, or Normans, soon adopted Christian civilization. By the eleventh century, as we shall see later, Normandy was a powerful duchy, and the Viking spirit of the Normans was producing the most vigorous crusaders, conquerors, and administrators in Europe.

Europe in 900. Europe's response to the invasions of the ninth and tenth centuries was not uniform. In England by 900 Viking occupation initiated a strong national reaction which soon led to the creation of a united English kingdom. Similarly, Germany in 919 reacted to the Magyar danger by installing the first of a new and able line of kings who went on to become the most powerful European monarchs since Charlemagne. The response to the invasions in France, however, is a different story.

The Viking attacks on France had the effect of accelerating the trend toward politi-

An example of the animal style common in the Celtic-Germanic art of the early Middle Ages, this wooden animal head of the early ninth century is the terminal of a post of a buried Viking ship found at Oseberg in southern Norway. It combines realistic details (nostrils, teeth, and gums) with the imaginative use of abstract geometric patterns derived from metalwork.

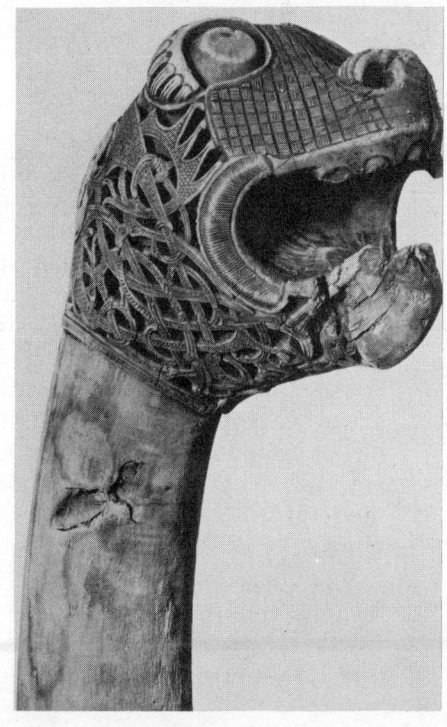

cal fragmentation that began under the Merovingians but was temporarily halted by the strong personal leadership provided by the Carolingians. When Charlemagne's weak successors were unable to cope with the incessant Viking assaults, people increasingly surrendered both their lands and their persons to the many counts, dukes, and other local lords in return for protection. The decline of trade further strengthened the aristocracy, whose large estates, or manors, became economically self-sufficient. In addition, the old Germanic levy of foot soldiers, who provided their own arms when called to battle, was dying out in favor of a professional force of heavily armed mounted knights, who received land grants from the king in return for military service.

Out of all these elements—the disintegration of central power, the need for protection, the decrease in the class of freemen, the rise of a largely independent landed aristocracy, and the creation of the mounted knight— new patterns of society, feudalism and the manorial system, took shape. Reaching their height in France during the tenth and eleventh centuries, feudalism and manorialism were the culmination of earlier trends that had been accelerated by the Viking attacks.

FEUDALISM

Nature and origins of feudalism. Feudalism can be defined as a type of government in which political power is exercised locally by private individuals rather than by the agents of a centralized state. It is often a transitional stage which follows the collapse of a unified political system; it serves as a stopgap until conditions permit the emergence of a centralized government. Feudalism has appeared in various areas and times in world history—in ancient Egypt and in modern Japan, for example—but the most famous of all feudal systems emerged in France following the collapse of Charlemagne's empire.

Fully developed feudalism was a fusion of three basic elements: (1) the personal element, called lordship or vassalage, by which one nobleman, the vassal, became the loyal follower of a stronger nobleman, the lord or suzerain; (2) the property element, called the fief (usually land), which the vassal received from his lord in order to enable him to fulfill the obligations of vassalage; and (3) the governmental element, meaning the private exercise of governmental functions over vassals and fiefs. The roots of these three elements run back to late Roman and early Germanic times.

By the fifth century the ability of the Roman emperor to protect his subjects had disappeared, and citizens had to depend on the patronage system, by which a Roman noble organized a group of less fortunate citizens as a personal bodyguard and in return looked after their wants and interests. A similar arrangement existed among the Germans—the war band or *comitatus*, described by Tacitus (see p. 133). Vassalage, the personal element in feudalism, arose from the combination of patronage and the *comitatus*.

The roots of the property element in feudalism, the fief, go back to Roman practices mainly. In the late Roman Empire the owners of great estates (*latifundia*) were steadily adding to their already extensive holdings. Unable to manage their tracts, the nobles granted the temporary use of portions to other people in exchange for dues and services. Such land was called a *beneficium*, or benefice (literally, a "benefit"). In late Merovingian times, when mounted warriors rather than old-style foot soldiers were needed to deal effectively with Muslim raiders from Spain, Charles Martel granted numerous benefices to compensate his mounted followers for this added expense. During the civil wars and foreign invasions of late Carolingian times, the competition among Charlemagne's successors for the available supply of mounted knights led not only to the wholesale granting of benefices but also to making the benefice hereditary. On the death of the vassal, the benefice now passed to his heir instead of reverting to the king. Hereditary benefices were commonly called fiefs.

The third basic element in feudalism, the exercise of governmental power by private individuals, also had antecedents in late Roman times. As the imperial government weakened, the powerful Roman landowners organized their own private armies to police their estates and fend off governmental agents, particularly tax collectors. The emperors also favored certain estates with grants of immunity from their authority, a practice which the Germanic kings often followed and which became the rule with Charlemagne's successors in their competitive efforts to fill their armies with mounted fief-holding vassals. And where immunity from the king's authority was not freely granted, it was often usurped.

With the coalescing of these three elements, feudalism can be said to have emerged as a definable—although highly complex and variable—governmental system in France by the end of the ninth century. To a greater or less degree the feudal system spread throughout most of western Europe, but our description of it applies particularly to the form it took in northern France.

The feudal hierarchy. In theory feudalism was a vast hierarchy. At the top stood the king, and theoretically all the land in his kingdom belonged to him. He kept large areas for his personal use (royal or crown lands) and, in return for the military service of a specified number of mounted knights, invested the highest nobles—such as dukes and counts (in England, earls)—with the remainder. Those nobles holding lands directly from the king were called tenants-in-chief. They in turn, in order to obtain the services of the required number of mounted warriors (including themselves) owed to the king, parceled out large portions of their fiefs to lesser nobles. This process, called *subinfeudation*, was continued until, finally, the lowest in the scale of vassals was reached—the single knight whose fief was just sufficient to support one mounted warrior.

Subinfeudation became a problem when a conflict of loyalties arose. Since the Count of Champagne, for example, was vassal to nine different lords, on whose side would he fight should two of his lords go to war against one another? This dilemma was partially solved by the custom of liege homage. When a vassal received his first fief, he pledged liege or prior homage to that lord. This obligation was to have top priority over services that he might later pledge to other lords.

Except for the knight with a single fief, a nobleman was usually both a vassal and a lord. Even a king might be a vassal; John of England was vassal to King Philip of France for certain French lands, yet he in no way thought himself inferior to Philip.

By maintaining a king at the head of the hierarchy, feudalism kept intact the vestiges of monarchy, which would in time reassert itself and restore centralized government. As one historian put it, feudalism "contained in its bosom the weapons with which it would be itself one day smitten."[5]

Relation of lord and vassal: the feudal contract. Basic to feudalism was the personal bond between lord and vassal. In the ceremony known as the act of *homage*, the vassal knelt before his lord, or *suzerain*, and promised to be his "man." In the oath of fealty which followed, the vassal swore on the Bible or some other sacred object that he would remain true to his lord. Next, in the ritual of *investiture*, a lance, glove, or even a bit of straw was handed the vassal to signify his jurisdiction (not ownership) over the fief.

The feudal contract thus entered into by

Warfare was a normal occupation for gentlemen during the feudal age, and even the more brutal aspects of combat were not considered ignoble subjects for art.

lord and vassal was considered sacred and binding upon both parties. Breaking this tie of mutual obligations was considered a felony, because it was the basic agreement of feudalism and hence of early medieval society. The lord for his part was obliged to give his vassal protection and justice. The vassal's primary duty was military service. He was expected to devote forty days' service each year to the lord without payment. In addition, the vassal was obliged to assist the lord in rendering justice in the lord's court. At certain times, such as when he was captured and had to be ransomed, the lord also had the right to demand money payments, called *aids*. Unusual aids, such as defraying the expense of going on a crusade, could not be levied without the vassal's consent.

The lord also had certain rights, called feudal *incidents*, regarding the administration of the fief. These included *wardship*— the right to administer the fief during the minority of a vassal's heir—and *forfeiture* of the fief if a vassal failed to honor his feudal obligations.

Feudal warfare. The final authority in the feudal age was force, and the general atmosphere of the era was one of violence. Recalcitrant vassals frequently made war upon their suzerains. But warfare was also considered the normal occupation of the nobility, for success offered glory and rich rewards. If successful, warfare enlarged a noble's territory; and, if they produced nothing else, forays and raids kept a man in good mettle. To die in battle was the only honorable end for a spirited gentleman; to die in bed was a "cow's death."

The Church and feudalism. Another unhappy result of feudalism was the inclusion of the Church in the system. The unsettled conditions caused by the Viking and Magyar invasions forced Church prelates to enter into close relations with the only power able to offer them protection—the feudal barons in France and the kings in Germany. Bishops and abbots thus became vassals, receiving fiefs for which they were obligated to provide the usual feudal services. The papacy fared even worse; during much of the tenth and early eleventh centuries the papacy fell into decay after becoming a prize sought after by local Roman nobles.

On the positive side, however, the Church in time sought to influence for the better the behavior of the feudal warrior nobility. In addition to attempting to add Christian virtues to the code of knightly conduct called chivalry, which will be described later in this chapter, the Church sought to impose limitations on feudal warfare. In the eleventh century bishops inaugurated the Peace of God and Truce of God movements. The Peace of God banned from the sacraments all persons who pillaged sacred places or refused to spare noncombatants. The Truce of God established "closed seasons" on fighting: from sunset on Wednesday to sunrise on Monday and certain longer periods, such as Lent. These peace movements were generally ineffective, however.

Class structure. Medieval society conventionally consisted of three classes: the nobles, the peasants, and the clergy. Each of these groups had its own task to perform. The nobles were primarily fighters, belonging to an honored society distinct from the peasant workers—freemen and serfs. In an age of physical violence, society obviously would accord first place to the man with the sword rather than to the man with the hoe. The Church drew on both the noble and the peasant classes for the clergy. Although most higher churchmen were sons of nobles and held land as vassals under the feudal system, the clergy formed a class that was considered separate from the nobility and peasantry.

THE MANORIAL SYSTEM

The manor in relation to feudalism. Having discussed feudalism, the characteristic political system of the ninth, tenth, and eleventh centuries, let us turn to the economic organization of the period, the manorial system. The feudal system was the means whereby protection was obtained for society; the manor was the agency that provided the necessary food for society's members. Feudalism and the manorial system evolved independently, but they were intimately connected.

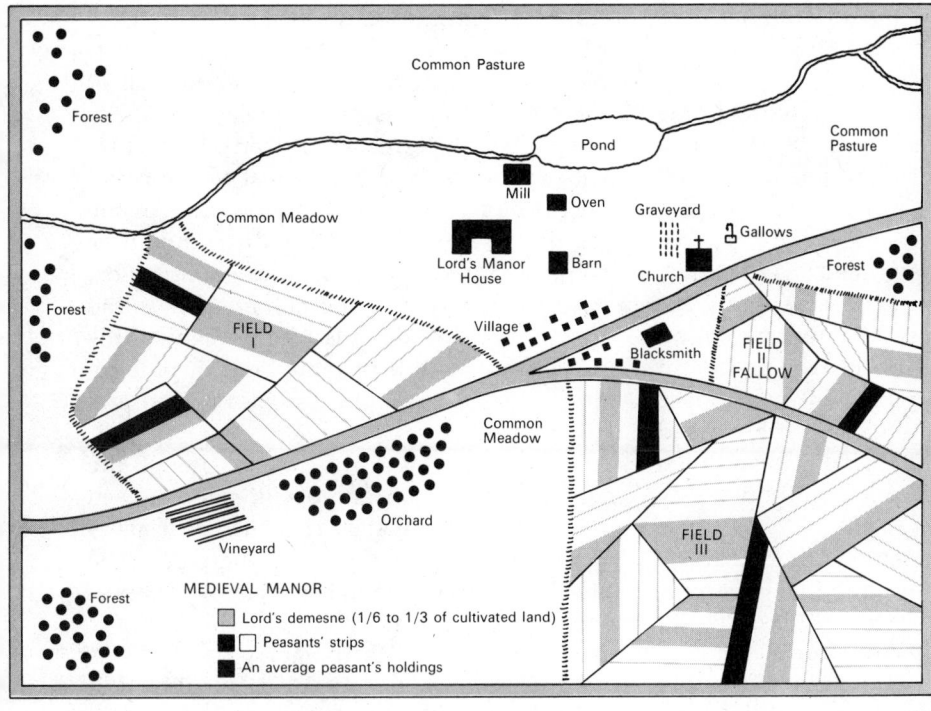

MEDIEVAL MANOR

- Lord's demesne (1/6 to 1/3 of cultivated land)
- Peasants' strips
- An average peasant's holdings

As the self-contained economic unit of early medieval life, the manor operated on a system of reciprocal rights and obligations based on custom. In return for protection, strips of arable land, and the right to use the nonarable common land, the peasant paid dues and worked on the lord's demesne. Under the three-field system, one third of the land lay fallow so that intensive cultivation did not exhaust the soil.

The term manorial system refers to the economic and social system that centered on the manors, the great estates whose origins go back to the Roman *latifundia* with their *coloni* workers (see p. 79). In Gaul, in particular, these estates survived the Germanic invasions. During the early Middle Ages they were held either by the descendants of their Roman owners or by Frankish kings, nobles, and the Church. The medieval serf was the direct descendant of the Roman *colonus* who worked the land, paid rent in kind, and could not leave the estate without the owner's permission.

Agriculture, the chief function of the manor. The manor varied in size from one locality to another. A small one might contain only about a dozen households. Since the allotment to each family averaged about thirty acres, the small manors probably included about 350 acres of tillable land, not counting the meadows, woods, wasteland, and the lord's demesne land. A large manor might contain fifty families and a total area of 5000 acres.

The center of the manor was the village, with the thatched cottages of the peasants grouped together along one street. Around each cottage was a space large enough for a vegetable patch, chicken yard, haystack, and stable. An important feature of the landscape was the village church, together with the priest's house and the burial ground. The lord's dwelling might be a castle or a more modest manor house.

Distribution of the land. Every manor contained two types of land, arable and nonarable. Part of the arable land, called the *demesne*, was reserved for the lord and was cultivated for him by his serfs. The remainder of the arable land was held by the villagers. The nonarable land, consisting of meadow, wood, and wasteland, was used in common by the villagers and the lord.

From one third to two fifths of the arable land was given over to the lord's demesne. The demesne might be either sharply set off from the tenures of the villagers or distributed among the lands of the tenants. The land not held in demesne was allotted among the villagers under the open-field system, whereby the fields were subdivided into strips. The strips, each containing about an acre, were separated by narrow paths of uncultivated turf. The serf's holding was not all in one plot, for all soil throughout the manor was not equally fertile, and a serious attempt was made to give each of the villagers land of the same quality.

Each tenant was really a shareholder in the village community, not only in the open fields but also in the meadow, pasture, wood, and wastelands. His rights in these common lands were determined by the number of acres he held in the open fields.

The wooded land was valuable as a place to graze pigs, the most common animal on the manor. Again the tenant was limited in the number of pigs that he might turn loose there. The tenant could also gather dead wood in the forest, but cutting down green wood was prohibited unless authorized by the lord.

Medieval farming methods. It is dangerous to generalize too sweepingly about agricultural methods, because differences in locality, fertility of soil, crop production, and other factors resulted in a variety of farming methods. But if we study farming as practiced in northwestern Europe, we can discover some common factors. The implements which the peasants used were extremely crude; the plow was a cumbersome instrument with heavy wheels, often requiring as many as eight oxen to pull it. (By the twelfth century plow horses were common.) There were also crude harrows, sickles, beetles for breaking up clods, and flails for threshing. Inadequate methods of farming soon exhausted the soil. It has been estimated that the average yield per acre was only six to eight bushels of wheat, a fourth of the modern yield.

In classical times farmers had learned that soil planted continually with one crop rapidly deteriorated. To counteract this, they employed a two-field system, whereby half of the arable land was planted while the other half lay fallow to recover its fertility. Medieval farmers learned that wheat or rye could be planted in the autumn as well as in the spring. As a result, by the ninth century they were dividing the land into three fields, with one planted in the fall, another in the spring, and the third left lying fallow. This system not only kept more land in production but also required less plowing in any given year.

Administration of the manor. Though the lord might live on one of his manors, each manor was administered by such officials as the steward, the bailiff, and the reeve. The steward was the general overseer who supervised the business of all his lord's manors and presided over the manorial court. It was the bailiff's duty to supervise the cultivation of the lord's demesne, collect rents, dues, and fines, and inspect the work done by the peasants. The reeve was the "foreman" of the villagers, chosen by them and representing their interests.

In status and function the various social classes that made up the manor community differed not only from locality to locality but from period to period. However, they can be roughly divided into three major categories: the lord and his officials, the free peasants, and the unfree peasants (serfs).

There often were freemen on the manor, however small a proportion of its population they may have represented. They possessed personal freedom and were not subject to the

In this fourteenth-century illumination peasants reap grain under the direction of the reeve.

same demands as the unfree peasants. The freeman did not have to work in the lord's fields himself but could send substitutes. He paid rent for his holding and, if he wanted to leave, could locate a new tenant for the land, provided the transfer took place in open court and the new man was acceptable to the lord. Aside from these privileges, however, the freeman was little different from the unfree man. His strips in the open field adjoined those of the servile worker, and he lived in a cottage in the same village.

The unfree peasants, the serfs, were bound to the manor and could not leave without the lord's consent. Serfdom was a hereditary status; the children of a serf were attached to the soil as their parents were. The lord of the manor was bound by the force of custom to respect certain rights of his serfs. So long as they paid their dues and services, serfs could not be evicted from their hereditary holdings. Although a serf could not appear in court against his lord or a freeman, he could appeal to the manor court against any of his fellows.

Whereas the peasants found their economic, political, legal, and social life in the manor, to the lord the manor was essentially a source of income from three obligations imposed on the peasantry: (1) services in the form of labor, (2) dues levied on the peasant, and (3) manorial monopolies.

The most important service was *week-work*. The peasant had to donate two or three days' work each week to the lord. The week-work included such jobs as repairing roads or bridges or carting manure to the fields. Because the lord's demesne "had always to be plowed first, sowed first, and reaped first," the peasant also had to perform extra *boon-work* at these times.

Various dues or payments—usually in produce, in money if it was available—were made to the lord. The *taille* (or tallage), a tax on whatever property a peasant managed to accumulate, was the most common. It was levied on all peasants one or more times a year. Another burdensome tax was imposed when a peasant died; before a son could inherit his father's cottage and strips, the lord claimed the best beast or movable possession as inheritance tax.

In addition to services and dues, the lord profited from certain monopolies. He operated the only grain mill, oven for baking bread, and wine and cider press on the manor, and he collected a toll each time these services were needed.

The weary round of peasant life. On the manors of the Middle Ages the margin between starvation and survival was narrow, and the life of the peasant was not easy. Famines were common; warfare and wolves were a constant threat; grasshoppers, locusts, caterpillars, and rats repeatedly destroyed the crops. Men and women alike had to toil long hours in the fields. A medieval poem vividly describes the life of a peasant family:

I saw a poor man o'er the plough bending. . . .
All befouled with mud, as he the plough followed. . . .
His wife walked by him with a long goad, . . .
Barefoot on the bare ice, so that the blood followed.
And at the field's end lay a little bowl,
And therein lay a little child wrapped in rags,
And twain of two years old upon another side;
And all of them sang a song that sorrow was to hear,
They cried all a cry, a sorrowful note,
And the poor man sighed sore, and said 'Children, be still.'[6]

The difficulties of the peasant's life were reflected in his home, a cottage with mud walls, clay floor, and thatched roof. The fire burned on a flat hearthstone in the middle of the floor; and unless the peasant was rich enough to afford a chimney, the smoke escaped through a hole in the roof. The windows had no glass and were stuffed with straw in the winter. Furnishings were meager, consisting usually of a table, a kneading trough for dough, a cupboard, and a bed, often either a heap of straw or a box filled with straw, which served the entire family. Pigs and chickens wandered about the cottage continually, while the stable was frequently under the same roof, next to the family quarters.

The peasant, despite his hard, monotonous life, was not without a few pleasures. Wrestling was exceedingly popular, as were cock-fighting, a crude type of football, and fighting with quarterstaves, in which both the con-

Into this medieval print the artist has crowded the whole life of the manorial village. A hunting party is shown in the foreground, the ladies riding behind the knights. The castle, with its moat and drawbridge, dominates the countryside. In the midst of the village houses, which are surrounded by a fence, stands the church. Note also the mill and the millrace at the left and what appears to be a wine or cider press to the right of the mill. In the upper right corner a serf is using the heavy plow common to northwestern Europe (the artist has shown only two draft animals). The nets were apparently set to catch hares, and below them stands a wayside shrine. Visible on the horizon is a gibbet with buzzards wheeling over it.

testants stood an excellent chance of getting their heads bashed in. Around the porch of the parish church the peasants often congregated to dance and sing on the numerous holy days. The Church preached in vain against "ballads and dancings and evil and wanton songs and such-like lures of the Devil." The peasants refused to give up these amusements, a small enough compensation for the constant exploitation they suffered. Yet medieval serfs also possessed a large degree of economic security, and in this respect they were perhaps better off than the factory workers of the early nineteenth century.

THE AGE OF CHIVALRY

Chivalry in feudal society. One of the most interesting and significant legacies of the Middle Ages is its concept of chivalry, a code which governed the behavior of all truly perfect and gentle knights. Such a paragon was Sir Galahad—"the gentlest man that ever ate in hall among the ladies." Early chivalry, however, which emerged during the heyday of feudalism in the eleventh century, was rough and masculine. It stressed the warrior virtues that were essential in a feudal society: prowess in combat, courage, and loyalty to one's lord and fellow warriors. The virtues of early chivalry are best expressed in early medieval epics, such as the eleventh-century *Song of Roland*, where they are summed up in the words of the hero who, surrounded by foes, cries: "Better be dead than a coward be called."

The later chivalry of the twelfth and thirteenth centuries contained new virtues which the Church and the ladies sought to impose upon the generally violent and uncouth behavior of feudal warriors. The chivalric romances that began to be written in the twelfth century mirror these new influences. In Chrétien de Troyes' *Perceval*, for example, the hero's mother sends him off to be dubbed a knight with these words of advice:

Serve ladies and maidens if you would be honored by all. If you capture a lady, do not annoy her. Do nothing to displease her. He has much from a maiden who kisses her if she agrees to give a kiss. You will avoid greater intimacy if you wish to be guided by me. . . . Above all I wish to beg you to go to churches and abbeys and pray to our Lord so that the world may do you honor and you may come to a good end.[7]

In sum, fully developed chivalry was a combination of three elements: warfare, religion, and reverence toward women. It required the knight to fight faithfully for his lord, champion the Church and aid the humble, and honor womankind. Unfortunately, practice often differed from theory. The average knight was more superstitious than religious, and he continued to fight, plunder, and abuse women, especially those of the lower class. The ideals of chivalry, however, have affected manners in later eras, and even today they color our concept of a gentleman.

Women in general shared the characteristics of the menfolk. They lived in a crude and often brutal age devoid of many of our modern refinements. Like their husbands, medieval women were heavy drinkers and eaters. It is said that a common compliment to a member of the fair sex was that she was "the fairest woman who ever drained a bottle."

Training for knighthood. From the time they were boys, men of the nobility underwent a rigid training for knighthood. At the age of seven, a boy was sent to the household of a relative, a friend, or the father's suzerain. There he became a page, learning the rudiments of religion, manners, hawking, and hunting. When about fifteen or sixteen, he became a squire and prepared himself seriously for the art of war. He learned to ride a war horse with dexterity and to handle the sword, the shield, and the lance correctly. The squire also waited on his lord and lady at the table and learned music, poetry, and games.

If not already knighted on the battlefield for valor, the squire was usually considered eligible for knighthood at twenty-one. By the twelfth century the Church claimed a role in the ceremony, investing it with impressive symbolism. The candidate took a bath to symbolize purity and watched his weapons before the altar in an all-night vigil, confessing and making resolutions to be a worthy knight. During the solemn Mass that followed, his sword was blessed on the altar by a priest. The climax of the ceremony came when the candidate, kneeling before his lord, received a light blow on the neck or shoulder (the *accolade*), as the lord pronounced these words: "In the name of God, Saint Michael, and Saint George, I dub thee knight. Be valiant." The ceremony was designed to impress upon the knight that he must be virtuous and valiant, loyal to his suzerain and to God.

Heraldry. With its unique decorative designs, worn proudly by each noble family on its armor, heraldry was one of the more colorful aspects of chivalry. The popularity of heraldry began to sweep through Europe in the twelfth century. The use of the closed helmet, which hid the face, required that some means of identification be developed. Ingenious feudal artists devised 285 variations of the cross and decorated the nobles' shields with such real and fictitious animals as the lion, leopard, griffin, dragon, unicorn, and a host of others in fanciful postures. A man's social position was evident in his coat of arms, for its quarterings, or divisions, showed to which noble families its owner was related.

Castles as fortresses and homes. The life of the nobles centered about the castle. The earliest of these structures, mere wooden blockhouses, were built in the ninth century. Not until the twelfth and thirteenth centuries were massive castles constructed entirely of stone.

The donjon, or central tower, was the focal point of the castle; it was surrounded by an open space that contained storerooms, workshops, and a chapel. The outside walls of the castle were surmounted by turrets from which arrows, boiling oil, and various missiles might be showered upon the attackers. Beyond the wall was the moat, a steep-sided ditch filled with water to deter the enemy. The only entrance to the castle lay across the drawbridge. The portcullis, a heavy iron grating which could be lowered rapidly to protect the gate, was a further barrier against unwanted intrusion.

A French manuscript illumination of a knight entering the lists to fight in a tournament gives some idea of the splendor with which such contests were frequently invested. These often brutal battles were considered suitable entertainment for noble ladies and gentlemen.

Life in the castle was anything but comfortable or romantic. The lord at first dwelt in the donjon, but by the thirteenth century he had built more spacious quarters. Because the castle was designed for defense, it possessed no large windows; and the rooms were dark and gloomy. The stone walls were bare except for occasional tapestries to allay the draft and dampness, and a huge fireplace provided the only warmth.

Amusements of the nobles. The average noble derived his pleasures primarily from outdoor sports, among which he included warfare. In peacetime the joust and tournament substituted for actual battle. The joust was a conflict between two armed knights, each equipped with a blunted lance with which he attempted to unseat the other. The tournament was a general melee in which groups of knights attacked each other. Often fierce fighting ensued, with frequent casualties.

The nobles were very fond of hunting, and the constant demand for fresh meat afforded a legitimate excuse for galloping over the countryside. Most hunting was done in the nearby forests, but at times an unlucky peasant's crops might be ruined during the chase.

A similar outdoor pastime, which lords, ladies, and even high church dignitaries delighted in, was falconry, a method of hunting with predatory birds. The hawks were reared with the utmost care, and large companies of lords and ladies spent many afternoons eagerly wagering with one another as to whose falcon would bring down the first victim. Nobles often attended Mass with hooded falcons on their wrists.

Indoor amusements included the universally popular diversions of backgammon, dice, and chess. The long, monotonous nights were sometimes enlivened by the quips of jesters. At other times a wandering minstrel entertained his noble hosts in exchange for a bed and a place at the table.

The decline of chivalry. The development of national governments under strong kings who enforced tranquility and order changed the whole basis of feudal society (see Chapter 10). Knights were no longer needed to fight for their lords, to rush to the succor of helpless maidens, or to take the law into their own hands in defense of personal honor. Yet chivalry continued on as an ideal, reaching its culmination in the fourteenth and fifteenth centuries. By the sixteenth century its code had become fantastic and even ridiculous, as is pointed out so cleverly in Cervantes' *Don Quixote*. Some knights continued to live in the past and obtained their excitement by becoming robbers, picking needless quarrels with their neighbors, or inventing imaginary females who had to be rescued from a fate worse than death.

SUMMARY

This chapter has surveyed the political, economic, and social history of the early Middle Ages (500-1050), during which the axis of European civilization was centered in France. The conversion of Clovis to Christianity and the subsequent Frankish alliance with the papacy meant that the most energetic of the Germanic tribes had united with the greatest existing force for civilization in western Europe—the Christian Church. The foundation of the new Europe whose center was no longer the Mediterranean was completed by Charlemagne, but his empire depended too heavily on the forceful personality of its founder and did not survive his inferior successors. After the Carolingian collapse, new political and economic patterns evolved to meet the turbulent conditions of the time.

Feudalism was a bridge between the centralized governments of the Romans and Carolingians and the national states of modern Europe. Like so many things in medieval civilization, feudalism was a blend of German and Roman customs, enriched and humanized by the ideals of Christianity. The people who held land under feudal tenure were a privileged caste of landed aristocrats whose main function was military service. Set apart from the feudal nobles but forming the backbone of economic life was the vast majority of the people—the peasants. On the manors, the economic units of early medieval life, the unfree peasants or serfs grew the food for all medieval people and performed the heavy labor needed. They were politically inarticulate, tied to the soil, and seldom masters of their own destinies.

One aspect of feudalism which has come down to the twentieth century as a highly romanticized tradition is chivalry. Although its practice in the Middle Ages fell far beneath its principles, its idealism became part of the medieval legacy to the twentieth century.

SUGGESTIONS FOR READING

M. Keen, **The Pelican History of Medieval Europe*** (Penguin); D. Hay, **The Medieval Centuries*** (Torchbooks); and H. Trevor-Roper, **The Rise of Christian Europe*** (Harcourt Brace Jovanovich) are valuable surveys of the Middle Ages. See also N. Zacour, **An Introduction to Medieval Institutions,** 2nd ed. (St. Martin's, 1976); and C. Erickson, **The Medieval Vision: Essays in History and Perception*** (Oxford, 1976).

J. Wallace-Hadrill, **The Barbarian West, 400-1000*** (Torchbooks); R. E. Sullivan, **Heirs of the Roman Empire*** (Cornell); and A. R. Lewis, **Emerging Medieval Europe, A.D. 400-1000*** (Knopf) are excellent brief surveys of the early Middle Ages. See John Morris, **The Age of Arthur** (Scribner's, 1973) for a history of the British Isles to 650 A.D. For greater detail see H. Moss, **The Birth of the Middle Ages, 395-814*** (Oxford); C. Dawson, **The Making of Europe*** (Meridian); M. Deanesley, **History of Early Medieval Europe, 476-911*** (Barnes and Noble); and G. Barraclough, **The Crucible of Europe: The Ninth and Tenth Centuries** (Univ. of California, 1976).

H. Fichtenau, **The Carolingian Empire: The Age of Charlemagne*** (Torchbooks) is the best work on the subject. See also R. Winston, **Charlemagne: From the Hammer to the Cross*** (Peter Smith); and P. Munz, **Life in the Age of Charlemagne*** (Capricorn). On the Carolingian Renaissance see F. Heer, **The World of Charlemagne** (Macmillan, 1975) which is scholarly and readable; E. Duckett, **Alcuin, Friend of Charlemagne: His World and His Work** (Shoe String); and M. Laistner, **Thought and Letters in Western Europe, A.D. 500 to 900*** (Cornell).

J. Brondsted, **The Vikings*** (Penguin); and Gwyn Jones, **A History of the Vikings** (Galaxy, 1973) are outstanding on Viking activities. G. Turville-Petre, **The Heroic Age of Scandinavia** (Greenwood, 1976) describes the Norse way of life as reflected in their heroic legends.

Carl Stephenson, **Mediaeval Feudalism*** (Cornell) is a clear introduction. See also F. Ganshof, **Feudalism*** (Torchbooks); and M. Bloch, **The Feudal Society,*** 2 vols., (Phoenix). S. Painter, **French Chivalry*** (Cornell) is a delightful essay on the feudal, religious, and courtly aspects of chivalry.

On rural life and the manorial system see **The Agrarian Life of the Middle Ages,** Vol. I in **The Cambridge Economic History of Europe,** 2nd ed. (Cambridge, 1967); and G. Duby, **Rural Economy and Country Life in the Medieval West** (So. Carolina, 1968). G. G. Coulton, **Medieval Village, Manor, and Monastery** (Peter Smith); H. S. Bennett, **Life on the Medieval Manor*** (Cambridge); and E. Power, **Medieval People*** (Barnes and Noble) are worthwhile accounts.

*Indicates a less expensive paperbound edition.

CHAPTER 9

The Crusades and the Rise of Trade, Towns, and a New Society: 1050-1450

The West Takes the Offensive

INTRODUCTION. Following the collapse of Charlemagne's empire, Europeans probably felt that the future held little promise. No longer was there an effective central government to maintain peace and enforce laws over large territories, and with political fragmentation had come economic localism in the form of the self-sufficient manorial system.

In this chapter we shall trace the rise of a new Europe—a Europe which in the eleventh century was to emerge from what is sometimes called the "dark ages." With the ejection of the Muslims from Sicily and the successful challenge to Muslim control of the Mediterranean, Christian Europe ceased to be on the defensive and took the offensive instead.

In northern Spain a few bands of Christians sparked a long struggle against the Muslims in a movement known as the *Reconquista*, meaning "reconquest"; but the most dramatic manifestation of Europe's new dynamism was the crusades. Spurred on by religious fervor, love of adventure, and hopes of personal gain, the crusaders set out to drive the Muslims from the Holy Land and free Jerusalem from the infidel. These expansive movements helped the recovery of international trade and the rise of flourishing towns. New markets stimulated the growth of industry and crafts; and the development of banking and the use of money, which superseded the old exchange by barter, made everyday business transactions more efficient. At the same time, men cleared and drained forests and swamps, and new lands went under the plow. All these factors—particularly the revival of urban life—sounded the death knell for the manorial system in western Europe.

Above all, the forces transforming the western world led to the growth of a new class in society—townsmen, the bourgeoisie or middle class. The status of a member of the middle class was based not on ancestry or ownership of large estates, as was the case with the feudal aristocrat, but on possession of goods and money. Gradually the bourgeoisie gained influence as well as wealth and began to exert a growing impact on history.

EUROPE AGAINST THE MUSLIMS

Norman conquests in Italy and Sicily. About the year 1000 southern Italy was a battleground for rival Lombard dukes, the Byzantine empire, and the Muslims. The Lombards ruled several duchies; the Eastern empire controlled the "heel and toe" of the peninsula, all that remained of Justinian's reconquest of Italy; and across the Strait of Messina Muslim princes ruled the island of Sicily.

In 1016 adventurers of Viking ancestry from Normandy plunged into this maelstrom of continual warfare. At first the Norman knights fought for hire, but soon they began to carve out large estates for themselves. The obscure house of Tancred of Hauteville was burdened with twelve husky sons, all of whom made their way to southern Italy. One blond giant of this family, Robert Guiscard, established his authority over his fellow Normans and by 1071 extinguished the last Byzantine foothold in southern Italy (see p. 144). Meanwhile Robert had allied himself with the pope, and in return the papacy recognized him as the ruler of southern Italy and of Sicily, still in Muslim hands. Under the leadership of Robert and his brother Roger, the Normans crossed the Strait of Messina and gained a footing in Sicily just a few years before another Norman, William the Conqueror, crossed the Channel to invade England. In 1072 these land-hungry Normans captured Palermo, and twenty years later the entire island of Sicily was theirs.

Venice, Genoa, and Pisa battle the Muslims. While the Normans had been ejecting the Muslims from Sicily, similar offensives had been going on elsewhere in the Mediterranean. Venice, still nominally a part of the Byzantine empire, had cleared the Adriatic Sea and in 1002 had won a great naval victory over a Muslim fleet. This enhanced Venetian trade with Byzantium. Genoa and Pisa also began to fight the Muslims, and by 1090 the western Mediterranean had been cleared of Muslim pirates and traders. The crusades to the Holy Land would shortly do the same for the eastern Mediterranean.

Muslim civilization in Spain. Although the offensive of the West had cleared the Muslims from the waters of the western Mediterranean, Muslim power remained in Spain. We will recall that with the fall of Rome in the fifth century, Visigothic tribes had settled in Spain; but they in turn had fallen to the Muslim invasion (see p. 190). Muslim Spain was ruled from Damascus until 756, when it became an independent Muslim state under the last remaining member of the Umayyad dynasty.

From their center at Cordova, the ancient capital of Roman Spain, the Umayyad rulers (756-1031) inaugurated a brilliant era. The Caliphate of Cordova, as Muslim Spain was called after 929, made many economic and cultural advances. Water power was harnessed to drive mills, new crops such as rice and sugar cane were introduced, and

The Great Mosque at Cordova is a fine example of the Islamic art that flourished in Spain during the Muslim rule of that country.

grain cultivation flourished. Other important products included wine, olive oil, leather goods, weapons, glass, and tapestries. Cordova's Great Mosque held 5500 worshipers, and its library held 400,000 volumes.

The Muslims of Spain were the most cultured people of the West. Literature and art became their glories, and learning flourished when the rulers, often men of letters themselves, invited some of the best scholars of the Muslim East to settle in Spain (see p. 165). By the twelfth century scholars from northern Europe were flocking to Spain to study, and through them much of the learning of the Arabs passed to Christian Europe.

The lot of the conquered Christians was not especially bad. Christian worship continued, and, generally speaking, tolerance was granted to all people—including Christians and Jews. The latter, who had been persecuted under the Visigoths, flourished in the professions and as officials of the state. Many Jews came from Christian Europe and the East, and the Talmudic school at Cordova became a leading center of Hebrew learning. Christians were converted to Islam, there was much intermarriage, and many of the later Muslim leaders were of Gothic or Hispano-Roman descent.

Politically, Muslim Spain was usually weak and disunited. Spain had been conquered by a medley of Arabs, Syrians, and Berbers who were often in discord and outnumbered by the native population. The Caliphate reached the height of its power in the tenth century but thereafter the caliphs were a mediocre lot, unable to withstand the pressures of factionalism. In 1031 the Umayyads were overthrown, and the Caliphate of Cordova was replaced by twenty-three small, warring states.

Early Christian victories in the Reconquista. During the period of Muslim dominance the following Christian states survived in the north of Spain (see map, p. 233): the county of Barcelona, nucleus of later Aragon, in the east; Leon in the west; and in between, Navarre, peopled by the fiercely independent Basques whom neither the Romans nor the Visigoths had wholly subdued.

Slowly gathering strength and resolution, these Christian states expanded south through the hills, with Leon leading the way. An offshoot of Leon was the county of Castile, named after the many castles built to defend it. In the mid-tenth century Castile became strong enough to throw off the rule of the king of Leon. The disintegration of the Caliphate of Cordova into small Muslim states after 1031 opened the way for further Christian advances: Castile captured a large part of what was to become Portugal, and the southern border of Castile was pushed from the Douro to the Tagus River. In 1063, a generation before the first crusade to the Holy Land, the pope proclaimed the *Reconquista* to be a holy crusade, and the first of many northern knights flocked to Spain to fight the Muslims. In 1085 the mighty bastion of Toledo fell to the king of Castile, and the end of the Muslim occupation seemed in sight. But Muslim resistance in southern Spain continued for another four centuries, and militant expansion in the name of Christianity would continue to color the formative years of Spain and Portugal.

THE CRUSADES: "GOD WILLS IT!"

The call to a crusade. The most dramatic expression of Europe on the offensive was the crusades. For hundreds of years peaceful pilgrims had been traveling from Europe to worship at the birthplace of Christ. By the tenth century bishops were organizing mass pilgrimages to the Holy Land; the largest of these, which set out from Germany in 1065, included about seven thousand pilgrims.

During the eleventh century, however, Christian pilgrims to the Holy Land became especially concerned and aggravated when the Seljuk Turks, who were new and fanatical converts to Islam, came sweeping and plundering into the Near East. The Seljuks seized Jerusalem from their fellow Muslims and then swept north into Asia Minor. Byzantine forces desperately tried to bar the invader, but at the battle of Manzikert (1071) the eastern emperor was captured and his army scattered. Within a few years Asia Minor, the chief source of Byzantine revenue and troops, was lost, and the emperor was writing to western princes and to the pope seeking mercenaries with which to regain lost territories. In addition, tales of alleged Turkish mistreatment of Christian pilgrims circulated throughout Europe, and though there is evidence that these stories were propaganda, men's minds became inflamed.

In 1095 Pope Urban II proclaimed the First Crusade to regain the Holy Land. Preaching at the Council of Clermont in that year, he exhorted Christians to take up the cross and strive for a cause that promised not merely spiritual rewards but material gain as well:

For this land which you inhabit . . . is too narrow for your large population; nor does it abound in wealth; and it furnishes scarcely food enough for its cultivators. Hence it is that you murder and devour one another. . . . Enter upon the road to the Holy Sepulchre; wrest that land from the wicked race, and subject it to yourselves.[1]

At the end of his impassioned oration the crowd shouted "God wills it"—the expression which the crusaders later used in battle.

Although the pope saw in the crusade an outlet for the restless energy of pugnacious nobles—their warring fervor would be channeled for the glory of God—the primary impetus behind the crusade was undoubtedly religious. It was viewed as a holy war, and following Pope Urban's appeal, there was a real and spontaneous outpouring of religious enthusiasm. The word *crusade* itself is derived from "taking the cross," after the example of Christ. (On the way to the Holy Land, the crusader wore the cross on his breast; on his journey home, he wore the cross on his back.) Pope Urban promised the crusaders that they would enjoy indulgence for their past sins. He also hoped that the religious enthusiasm following in the wake of the crusades would strengthen his claim to the moral leadership of Europe.

The First Crusade gains the Holy Land. From the end of the eleventh century to the end of the thirteenth, there were seven major crusades, as well as various small expeditions which from time to time tried their hands against the Saracen.

The First Crusade, composed of feudal nobles from France, parts of Germany, and Norman Italy, proceeded overland to Constantinople. Having expected the help of European mercenaries against the Seljuks, the emperor Alexius Comnenus was taken aback when confronted by an unruly horde of what Pope Urban himself had called "aforetime robbers." He hastily directed the crusaders out of Constantinople to fight the Turks. The First Crusade was the most successful of the seven; with not more than five thousand knights and infantry, it overcame the resistance of the Turks, who were no longer united. Above all, it captured the Holy City—Jerusalem. A contemporary account of the Christian entrance into Jerusalem reads:

But now that our men had possession of the walls and towers, wonderful sights were to be seen. Some of our men . . . cut off the heads of their enemies; others shot them with arrows, so that they fell from the towers; others tortured them longer by casting them into the flames. Piles of heads, hands, and feet were to be seen in the streets of the city. It was necessary to pick one's way over the bodies of men and horses. But these were small matters compared to what happened at the Temple of Solomon [where] . . . men rode in blood up to their knees and bridle reins. Indeed it was a just and splendid judgment of God that this place should be filled with the blood of the unbelievers, since it had suffered so long from their blasphemies.[2]

The First Crusade conquered a narrow strip of land stretching from Antioch to Jerusalem (see map, p. 143) and created the Latin kingdom of Jerusalem, which lasted until its last remnant fell to the Muslims in 1291.

When the kingdom of Jerusalem became endangered, the eloquent St. Bernard induced the kings of France and Germany to lead the Second Crusade in 1147. It never reached Jerusalem, having turned aside to attack Damascus where its forces were routed.

The "Crusade of Kings." The fall of Jerusalem in 1187 to the Muslims, reinvigorated under the leadership of Saladin, the Kurdish sultan of Egypt and Syria, served to provoke the Third Crusade (1189). Its leaders were three of the most famous medieval kings—Frederick Barbarossa of Germany, Richard the Lion-Hearted of England, and Philip Augustus of France. Frederick was drowned in Asia Minor; and, after many quarrels with Richard, Philip returned home. Saladin and Richard remained the chief protagonists.

To keep the Muslims united, Saladin proclaimed a *jihad*, or holy war, against the Christians, but he remained a patient statesman and chivalrous warrior. "Abstain from the shedding of blood," he once said, "for blood that is spilt never slumbers."[3] His commonsense approach to a settlement was evidenced when he proposed that Richard should marry his sister and be given Palestine as a wedding present, a proposal which shocked the Europeans.

Richard and Saladin finally agreed to a three-year truce and free access to Jerusalem for Christian pilgrims. Since Saladin would have granted this concession at any time, the truce scarcely compensated for the cost of such an expensive crusade.

The Fourth Crusade. The Fourth Crusade (1202-1204) reflects the decline of a religious ideal. No kings answered Pope Innocent III's call and the knights who did were unable to pay the Venetians the agreed-upon transport charges (see p. 145). The Venetians persuaded them to pay off the sum by capturing the Christian town of Zara on the Adriatic coast, which had long proved troublesome to Venetian trading interests. Then, in order to absorb all Byzantine commerce, the Venetians pressured the crusaders into attacking Constantinople. After conquering and sacking the greatest city in Europe, the crusaders set up the Latin empire of Constantinople (see map, p. 145) and forgot about recovering the Holy Land.

In this manuscript illumination Saladin wrests the cross, symbol of Christianity, from one of the leaders of the crusades.

Later crusades fail. The thirteenth century saw other crusades. The youngsters of the ill-fated Children's Crusade in 1212 fully expected the waters of the Mediterranean to part and make a path to the Holy Land, which they would take without fighting, but thousands of them were sold into slavery by Marseilles merchants. The Fifth Crusade in 1219 failed in its attack on Egypt, the center of Muslim power in the Near East. The unique Sixth Crusade in 1228 was organized and led by the excommunicated enemy of the pope, the emperor Frederick II, who by skillful diplomacy succeeded in acquiring Jerusalem, Bethlehem, and Nazareth from the sultan of Egypt without striking a blow. This arrangement ended in 1244 with the Muslim reconquest of the Holy City. The loss inspired the saintly Louis IX of France to organize the Seventh Crusade in 1248, but despite his zeal it ended in a fiasco when Louis was captured in Egypt and forced to pay an enormous ransom. This was the last major attempt to regain Jerusalem, and the era of the crusades ended in 1291 when Acre, the last stronghold of the Christians in the Holy Land, fell to the Muslims.

The crusader states. Altogether four crusader principalities, with the kingdom of Jerusalem dominant, had been established along the eastern Mediterranean coast. By the time Jerusalem fell to Saladin in 1187, however, only isolated pockets of Christians remained, surrounded by a vast hinterland of hostile Muslims. They were able to survive only by reason of frequent transfusions of strength from Europe in the form of supplies and manpower. It was natural for the European nobles who sought a permanent home in the Holy Land to adopt the customs of their Muslim neighbors and dress in light, flowing robes and turbans. Their houses were like Moorish villas, decorated and furnished with divans of brocade, Persian rugs, mosaic floors, and silk hangings. These transplanted Europeans became tolerant and easygoing, trading and even hunting with Muslims. Frequently there was bad blood between them and the newly arrived crusaders who had come for a short stay and a dash against the infidel.

The crusader states were defended by three semi-monastic military orders: the Templars, or Knights of the Temple, so called because their first headquarters was on the site of the old Temple of Jerusalem; the Hospitalers, or Knights of St. John of Jerusalem, who were founded originally to care for the sick and wounded; and the Teutonic Knights, exclusively a German order. Combining monasticism and militarism, these orders had as their aims the protection of all pilgrims and perpetual war against the Muslims. These men of the cross could put five hundred armed knights into the field, and their great castles guarded the roads and passes against Muslim attack. For two centuries the uniforms of these orders were a common sight in the crusader states; the Templars wore a white robe decorated with a red cross, the Hospitalers a black robe with a white cross, and the Teutonic Knights a white robe with a black cross.

The crusades evaluated. Even though the crusades failed to achieve their specific objective permanently, they cannot be written off as mere adventures. On the contrary, their influence extended over a much wider geographical field than just the Holy Land. Much of the crusading fervor carried over to the fight against the Muslims in Spain and the pagan Slavs in eastern Europe. Politically the crusades weakened the Byzantine empire and accelerated its fall (see Chapter 6). Although the early crusades strengthened the moral leadership of the papacy in Europe, the ill-success of the later crusades, together with the preaching of crusades against Christian heretics and political opponents lessened both the crusading ideal and respect for the papacy.

The contact with the East widened the scope of the Europeans, ended their isolation, and exposed them to a vastly superior civilization. Although it is easy to exaggerate the economic effects of the crusades, they did complete the reopening of the eastern Mediterranean to western commerce, which in turn stimulated the rise of cities and the emergence of a money economy in the West. The crusades as a movement were a manifestation of the dynamic vitality and expansive spirit of Europe, evident in many fields by the end of the eleventh century.

THE RISE OF TRADE
AND TOWNS

Revitalized trade routes. Although scholars have long debated the extent of trade and urban life that existed during the early Middle Ages, there is general agreement that fresh trade activity was evident even before the crusades. With the ending of Viking and Magyar attacks in the tenth century, a northern trading area developed which extended from the British Isles to the Baltic Sea. Closely related to this northern trade area was the route established by the Vikings as early as the ninth century, when they settled in Russia and created the lucrative Varangian route from the eastern Baltic down the rivers of Russia to the Black Sea and Constantinople (see p. 152).

The center of this northern trade system was the county of Flanders. By 1050 Flemish artisans were producing a surplus of woolen cloth of such fine quality that it was in great demand. Baltic furs, honey and forest products, and British tin and raw wool were exchanged for Flemish cloth. From the south by way of Italy came oriental luxury goods—silks, sugar, and spices.

Equally important as a catalyst of the medieval commercial revolution—whose impact on the Middle Ages deserves to be compared to that of the Industrial Revolution on the modern world—was the opening up of the Mediterranean trading area. In the eleventh century the Normans and Italians broke the Muslim hold on the eastern Mediterranean and the First Crusade inaugurated trade with the Near East. Arab vessels brought luxury goods from the East to ports on the Persian Gulf and Red Sea. From there they were shipped by caravan to Alexandria, Acre, and Joppa, and from those ports the merchants of Venice, Genoa, and Pisa transported the goods to Italy on their way to the markets of Europe. Other trade routes from Asia came overland, passing through Baghdad and Damascus and on to ports, such as Tyre and Sidon, in the crusader states. The easiest route north from the Mediterranean was via Marseilles, up the Rhone valley.

Early in the fourteenth century two more major trade lanes developed within Europe. An all-sea route connected the Mediterranean with northern Europe via the Strait of Gibraltar. The old overland route from northern Italy through the Alpine passes to central Europe was also developed. From Venice and other north Italian cities, trade flowed through such passes as the Brenner, sharply reducing the business of the Rhone valley route and the famous fairs of Champagne.

Fairs, centers of European trade. Along the main European trade routes, astute lords set up fairs, where merchants and goods from Italy and northern Europe met. During the twelfth and thirteenth centuries the fairs of Champagne in France (see Reference Map 4) functioned as the major clearing house for this international trade.

Fairs were important and elaborate events held either seasonally or annually in specified areas of each European country. The feudal law of the region was set aside during a fair, and in its place was substituted a new commercial code called the "law merchant." Special courts, with merchants acting as judges, settled all disputes which arose. In England such courts were called "pie-powder courts," from the French *pied-poudré*, meaning "dusty foot." Fairs also greatly stimulated the revival of a money economy and early forms of banking and credit.

Factors in the rise of towns. The resurgence of trade in Europe was the prime cause of the revival of towns. Trade and towns had an interacting effect on each other; the towns arose because of trade, but they also stimulated trade by providing greater markets and by producing goods for the merchants to sell.

In the revival of cities, geography played a significant role. Rivers, which were important in the evolution of ancient civilizations, were also important in the development of medieval towns. They were natural highways on which articles of commerce could be easily transported. Many communities developed at the confluence of two important streams; others arose where a river might be easily crossed by a ford or bridge, "Oxford" or "Cam-bridge," for example.

Often at a strategic geographic location a feudal noble had already erected a fortified castle, or *burg* (*bourg* in French, *borough* in English). Such a stronghold offered the merchants a good stopping place. The inhabitants of the burg were likely to buy some of the merchant's wares, and the castle offered him protection. In time a permanent merchant settlement, called a *faubourg*, grew up outside the walls of the burg. Frequently, too, merchants settled at an old Roman episcopal city like Cologne (Colonia Agrippina) or a fortified abbey or cathedral. Munich grew up around a monastery, and Durham was "half cathedral and half fortress against the Scot."

Another factor contributing to the rise of towns was the growth of population. In England, for example, the population more than tripled between 1066 and 1350. The reasons for this rapid increase in population are varied. The ending of bloody foreign invasions and, in some areas, the stabilization of feudal society were contributing factors. More important was an increase in food production brought about by the cultivation of wastelands, the clearing of forests, and the draining of marshes. Technological innovations such as the three-field system of crop rotation also increased production.

Interacting with the growth of towns was the decline of serfdom. Many serfs escaped from the manors and made their way to the towns. After living a year and a day in the town, a serf was considered a freeman.

The Hanseatic League. Sometimes a group of towns joined forces for mutual protection and to win special privileges. This was particularly true in Germany where by the thirteenth century a strong state capable of maintaining order did not exist. Most famous was the Hanseatic League, whose nucleus was Lübeck, Hamburg, and Danzig, but which by the fourteenth century comprised more than seventy cities. The League built up a lucrative monopoly on Baltic and North Sea trade. Its wealth came primarily from its control of the Baltic herring fisheries, its corner on Russian trade, and its rich business with England and Flanders. It established permanent trading stations in such leading European centers as London, Bruges, and Novgorod. Until the fifteenth century, when it began to lose its privileges and

A guild warden examines the work of an apprentice mason and carpenter before their admission as master craftsmen.

monopolies, the Hanseatic League remained the great distributor of goods to northern Europe. Its navy safeguarded its commerce from pirates and even waged a successful war with the king of Denmark when he threatened its Baltic monopoly.

Merchant and craft guilds. In each town the merchants and artisans organized themselves into guilds, which were useful not only for business but also for social and political purposes. There were two kinds of guilds: merchant and craft.

The merchant guild ensured a monopoly of trade within a given locality. All alien merchants were supervised closely and made to pay tolls. Disputes among merchants were settled at the guild court according to its own legal code. The guilds also tried to make sure that the customers were not cheated: they checked weights and measures and insisted upon a standard quality for goods. To allow only a legitimate profit, the guild fixed a "just price," which was fair to both producer and consumer.

When guilds first appeared, there was no adequate central government to protect merchants as they carried on their trading activities throughout the land. As a result the guilds assumed some functions which would otherwise have been governmental. If a merchant was imprisoned in another town, the guild tried to secure his release at its own expense. If a merchant of a London guild refused to pay a debt owed to a merchant of a guild in Bristol, the merchant guild in the latter town would seize the goods of any London merchant coming to Bristol.

The guild's functions stretched beyond business and politics into charitable and social activities. If a guildsman fell into poverty, he was aided. The guild also provided financial assistance for the burial expenses of its members and looked after their dependents. Members attended social meetings in the guildhall and periodically held processions in honor of their patron saints.

The increase of commerce brought a quickening of industrial life in the towns so that, as early as the eleventh century, the artisans began to organize. Craftsmen in each of the medieval trades—weaving, cobbling, tanning, and so on—joined forces. The result was the craft guild, which differed from the merchant guild in that membership was limited to artisans in one particular craft.

The general aims of the craft guilds were the same as those of the merchant guilds—the creation of a monopoly and the enforcement of a set of trade rules. Each guild had a monopoly of a certain article in a particular town, and every effort was made to prevent competition between members of the same guild. The guild restricted the number of its members, regulated the quantity and quality of the goods produced, and set prices. It also enforced regulations to protect the consumer from bad workmanship and inferior materials.

The craft guild also differed from the merchant guild in its recognition of three distinct classes of workers—apprentices, journeymen, and master craftsmen. The apprentice was a youth who lived at the master's house and was taught the trade thoroughly. Although he received no wages, all his physical needs were supplied. His apprenticeship commonly lasted seven years. When his schooling was finished, the youth became a journeyman (from the French *journée*, meaning "day's work"). He was then eligible to receive wages and to be hired by a master.

When about twenty-three, the journeyman sought admission into the guild as a master. To be accepted he had to prove his ability. Some crafts demanded the making of a "master piece"—for example, a pair of shoes that the master shoemakers would find acceptable in every way.

In the fourteenth century, when prosperity began to wane, the master craftsmen drastically restricted the number of journeymen who were allowed to become masters. The guilds either admitted only the relatives of masters or imposed excessively high entrance fees. When the journeymen then set up their own journeyman organizations, they were crushed by the wealthy guild masters, who usually controlled the town governments. By the fifteenth century most journeymen could not hope to become more than wage earners, and they bitterly resented the restrictions of the guild system.

Acquiring urban freedom. The guilds played an important role in local government. Both artisans and merchants, even though freemen, were subject to the feudal lord or bishop upon whose domain the city stood. The citizens of the towns resented the fact that their overlord collected tolls and dues as though they were serfs. The townsmen demanded the privileges of governing themselves—of making their own laws, administering their own justice, levying their own taxes, and issuing their own coinage. Naturally the overlord resented the impertinent upstarts who demanded self-government. But the towns won their independence in various ways.

One way was to become a commune, a self-governing town. The merchant guilds took the lead in acquiring charters of self-government for the towns. Often a charter had to be won by a revolt; in other circumstances it could be purchased, for a feudal lord was always in need of money. By 1200 the Lombard towns of northern Italy, as well as many French and Flemish towns, had become self-governing communes.

Where royal authority was strong, we find "privileged" towns. In a charter granted to the town by the monarch, the inhabitants won extensive financial and legal powers. The town was given management of its own

The horses pulling grain uphill in this illumination are wearing improved horseshoes which permit greater traction and collars which, by relieving pressure on their windpipes, greatly increase their pulling power.

finances and paid its taxes in a lump sum to the king. It was also generally given the right to elect its own officials. The king was glad to grant such a charter, for it weakened the power of his nobles and won him the support of the townsmen.

Founding new towns was still another way in which feudal restrictions were broken down. Shrewd lords and kings, who recognized the economic value of having towns in their territories, founded carefully planned centers with well-laid-out streets and open squares. As a means of obtaining inhabitants, they offered many inducements in the form of personal privileges and tax limitations. Among such new towns were Newcastle, Freiburg, and Berlin.

Technological advances. While in ancient societies men and animals were almost the only source of power, our medieval ancestors succeeded in greatly maximizing the muscle power of draft animals by three major developments. First, for the traditional horse collar which fastened around the animal's neck and choked him when pulling a heavy load, they substituted a harness fitted so that the shoulders bore the weight. Second, they developed a tandem harness in order to utilize the strength of several horses; and finally, they improved traction with a new type of horseshoe. These inventions are said to have done for the eleventh and twelfth centuries what the steam engine did for the nineteenth. In addition, our medieval forebears increased the number of

prime movers beyond sheer human and animal muscle power. They developed watermills (known but little used in the ancient world) and invented windmills for use in flat lands where waterfalls did not exist. Useful not only for grinding grains, these water- and windmills provided power for draining marshlands, for reclaiming areas from the sea (as in the Low Countries), and for fulling woolen cloth, which the West exported in quantity to the Byzantine and Muslim East.

The use of money, banking, and credit. All the aspects of Europe's expansion—the crusades, and the revival of trade, cities, and industry—had far-reaching effects on the financial structure. The first big change came with the reappearance of money as a medium of exchange. Coins were made from silver dug from old and new mines throughout Europe, but during the whole of the Middle Ages silver bullion was in short supply. In the thirteenth century silver coins were superseded in international trade by gold, especially the florin of Florence, which became a monetary standard for Europe.

When the English king Henry III invaded France in 1242, he carried with him thirty barrels of money, each containing 160,000 coins, to defray the expenses of the expedition. This incident graphically illustrates the need for instruments of credit and other forms of banking. All-important was the technique of "symbolic transfer." By this system a man deposited his money in a bank

In this representation of the Wat Tyler uprising, John Ball is shown at the head of a well-disciplined group of helmeted peasants bearing the banners of England and of St. George.

and received in return a letter of credit which, like a modern check, could later be cashed at any of the offices of the same bank. Letters of credit were common at fairs and very useful during the crusades, when the Templars arranged a system whereby crusaders could deposit money in the Paris office and withdraw it from the office in the Holy Land.

Banking also sprang from the activities of moneychangers at fairs and other trading centers. In addition to exchanging the coin of one region for another, these moneychangers would also accept money on deposit for safekeeping. The most important bankers, however, were Italian merchants from Florence and the Lombard cities, who by the middle of the thirteenth century were loaning their accumulated capital to kings and prelates. They found various ways of circumventing the Church's disapproval of all interest as usury. For example, if a sum was not repaid by a certain date, a penalty charge was levied.

THE EMERGENCE OF A NEW SOCIETY

The typical town. Medieval towns, which by the twelfth century were centers of an advanced culture as well as of trade and industry, were not large by modern standards. Before 1200 no town contained 100,000 inhabitants, and one of 20,000 was a metropolis.

Since the area within the walls was at a premium, medieval towns were more crowded than the average modern city. Shops were even built on bridges (as on the Ponte Vecchio, which still stands in Florence), and buildings were erected to a height of seven or more stories. The houses projected over the street with each additional story so that it was often possible for persons at the tops of houses opposite one another to touch hands.

The streets below were dark and narrow and almost invariably crooked, although they were often designed to be wide enough "to give passage to a horseman with his lance across his saddle-bows." The streets were full of discordant sounds—drivers yelled at pedestrians to get out of the way of the horses and oxen; dogs, pigs, and geese added their alarms; merchants bawled out their wares; people of every description jostled past one another, and unoiled signs above inns and shops creaked ominously in the wind, constantly threatening to crash down on some innocent passerby.

The bourgeoisie. The triumph of the townsmen in their struggle for greater self-government meant that a new class had evolved in Europe, a powerful, independent, and self-assured group, whose interest in trade was to revolutionize social, economic, and political history. The members of this class were called burghers or the bourgeoisie. Kings came to rely more and more on them in combating the power of the feudal lords, and their economic interests gave rise to a nascent capitalism. Also associated with the rise of towns and the bourgeoisie were the decline of serfdom and the manorial system and the advent of modern society.

A medieval townsman's rank was based on money and goods rather than birth and land. At the top of the social scale were the great merchant and banking families, the princes of trade, bearing such names as Medici, Fugger, and Coeur. Then came the moderately wealthy merchants and below them the artisans and small shopkeepers. In the lowest slot was the unskilled laborer, whose miserable lot and discontent were destined to continue through the rest of the Middle Ages and most of modern history.

The decay of serfdom. Attracted by the freedom of town life, many serfs ran away from their manors and established themselves in a town. As a result the remaining serfs became unreliable. Sometimes they secured enough money to buy their freedom by selling food surpluses in the towns, but often the lords freed their serfs and induced them to remain on the manor as tenants or hired laborers. As a first step in the emancipation of the serfs, the lords accepted a money payment from them as a substitute for their old obligations of labor and produce. The final step was for the lord to become a landlord in the modern sense, renting the arable land of the manor to free tenants. Thus former serfs became satisfied tenants or, on occasion, members of the yeoman class who owned their small farms. Serfdom had largely died out in England and France by 1500, although in the latter country many of the old and vexatious obligations, such as payment for the use of the lord's mill and oven, were retained. In eastern Europe serfdom persisted until the nineteenth century.

The depression of the late Middle Ages. While the twelfth and thirteenth centuries had been a boom period, during the late Middle Ages — the fourteenth and fifteenth centuries — the economy leveled off and then stagnated. By 1350 a great economic depression, which lasted approximately a century, was underway. Its causes are difficult to ascertain, but one of its symptoms, population decline, was probably also a major cause.

By 1300 the population of western Europe had ceased increasing, probably because it had expanded up to the limits of the available food supply. Famines had once again become common by the time of the Black Death, a bubonic plague from Asia carried by fleas on rats. The Black Death struck western Europe in 1347, decimating and demoralizing society. It is estimated that about one third of the population was wiped out. Hardest hit were the towns; the population of Florence, for example, fell from 114,000 to about 50,000 in five years. Coupled with this blow was the destruction and death caused by the Hundred Years' War between France and England (1337-1453).

Another symptom of economic stagnation was social unrest and tension. Individual folk heroes such as Robin Hood robbed the rich to benefit the poor, but more important was concerted group action. For the first time since the fall of Rome the common people organized themselves into pressure groups. Organized textile workers in the Flemish cities and in Florence, who resented the restrictions of the guild system (see p. 214), waged class war against guild masters and rich merchants, while peasant unrest flamed into revolt in France and England. A famous example of the latter was the Wat Tyler uprising in England in 1381. The decimation of the peasant population by the Black Death caused a rise in the wages of the day laborers and an increased demand for the abolition of serfdom. Parliament tried to legislate against the pay raise but succeeded only in incurring the anger of the peasants. This resentment was fanned by the sermons of a priest, John Ball, known as the first English socialist:

Ah, ye good people, the matter goeth not well to pass in England, nor shall not do so till everything be common, and that there be no villains or gentlemen, but that we may be all united together and that the lords be no greater masters than we be. What have we deserved or why should we be thus kept in serfdom; we be all come from one father and one mother, Adam and Eve.[4]

As in the case of other revolts, this uprising was crushed amid a welter of blood and broken promises.

Depression and economic stagnation began to be eased by 1450. A new period of economic expansion was at hand, promoted by a new breed of strong monarchs and stimulated by geographical discovery and expansion over the face of the globe (see Chapter 18).

SUMMARY

Constructive forces fashioning a new Europe became apparent in the period between 1050 and 1300. The great achievement of the eleventh century was expansion and offensive action by the forces of western Europe. The Muslims lost naval supremacy in the Mediterranean, and a Christian reconquest was initiated in Spain. Above all, a great movement, the crusades, was initiated in 1095. While the objective was to push the Muslims out of the Holy Land and particularly from Jerusalem, the crusades opened new doors for the narrow, ingrown Europeans.

During the eleventh century Europe was transformed by new forces: increased food production and population, revitalized trade, new towns, expansion of industry, and a money economy. A new society began to take shape; the bourgeoisie emerged and serfdom declined. (From 1350 to 1450, however, economic depression produced unrest among peasants and urban workers.) In the political realm, the tradition of kingship persisted in spite of feudalism with its many local sovereignties. Aided substantially by the new economic forces, the kings were to impose their will on the nobles and become masters of new nations. The beginnings of this movement, which were contemporary with the developments described in this chapter, will be set forth in Chapter 10.

SUGGESTIONS FOR READING

C. H. Haskins, **The Normans in European History*** (Norton); and D. C. Douglas, **The Norman Achievement, 1050-1100** (Univ. of Calif., 1969) are excellent studies of Norman power.

S. Runciman, **A History of the Crusades,*** 3 vols. (Cambridge) is highly recommended for both its literary and historical merit. R. A. Newhall, **The Crusades*** (Peter Smith) is a brief, lucid introduction to the subject. Also recommended are Hans E. Meyer, **The Crusades*** (Oxford, 1973); Zoé Oldenbourg, **The Crusades*** (Ballantine); G. Hundley, **Saladin** (Barnes and Noble, 1976); R. Dozy, **Spanish Islam: A History of the Muslims in Spain** (Barnes and Noble, 1969); and W. M. Watt, **A History of Islamic Spain** (Edinburgh).

R. M. Smail, **Crusading Warfare: 1097-1193** (Cambridge, 1967) describes the weapons, organization, and tactics of both the Latin and Muslim armies together with the nature and function of the Crusaders' castles. See also Smail's **The Crusaders in Syria and the Holy Land** (Praeger, 1974); and J. Beeler, **Warfare in Feudal Europe, 730-1200*** (Cornell, 1971). C. Oman, **The Art of War in the Middle Ages: A.D. 378-1515*** (Cornell) is the standard work.

R. Latouche, **The Birth of Western Economy: Economic Aspects of the Dark Ages*** (Torchbooks); and Robert Lopez, **The Commercial Revolution of the Middle Ages*** (Prentice-Hall, 1971)

throw new light on economic history. See also M. M. Postan, **The Medieval Economy and Society*** (Penguin); and G. Hodgett, **A Social and Economic History of Medieval Europe*** (Torchbooks, 1974). N. J. Pounds, **An Economic History of Medieval Europe** (Longman, 1974) is an excellent survey.

H. Pirenne, **Economic and Social History of Medieval Europe** (Harvest) and **Medieval Cities*** (Princeton) are two small classics on the revival of trade and growth of cities. F. Rörig, **The Medieval Town*** (Univ. of Calif.) treats urban life from the eleventh to the sixteenth centuries. See also A. R. Lewis, **Naval Power and Trade in the Mediterranean, A.D. 500-1100;** S. Baldwin, **Business in the Middle Ages** (Cooper Square, 1968); **Trade and Industry in the Middle Ages,** Vol. 2 of **The Cambridge Economic History of Europe** (Cambridge). More specialized accounts are A. Sapori, **The Italian Merchant in the Middle Ages*** (Norton) and S. Thrupp, **The Merchant Class of Medieval London*** (Univ. of Michigan).

D. M. Stenton, **English Society in the Early Middle Ages, 1066-1307*** (Penguin) is a brief, comprehensive, and readable account. See also A. Luchaire, **Social France at the Time of Philip Augustus** (Gannon); P. Ziegler, **The Black Death*** (Torchbooks); and Jeffrey B. Russell, **Witchcraft in the Middle Ages** (Cornell, 1972).

*Indicates a less expensive paperbound edition.

CHAPTER 10

Medieval Political History: 1050-1300

Nations in the Making

INTRODUCTION. Between 1050 and 1300, a period sometimes called the High Middle Ages, political as well as economic and social change was manifest in Europe. Not only did trade revive, cities grow, and a new bourgeois social class emerge, but kings developed their power at the expense of the feudal nobility. Inadequate to meet the demands of a new and progressive society in the making, feudalism was on the wane.

Perhaps the greatest weakness of feudalism was its inability to guarantee law and order. Too often feudalism meant anarchy in which robber barons, in the words of a twelfth-century observer, "levied taxes on the villages every so often, and called it 'protection money'" (see p. 224). Feudalism provided no consistently effective agency to deal with such ruffians. As a result, confusion, inefficiency, and injustice often prevailed.

The inefficiency inherent in the feudal system also hindered economic progress. Trade and commerce spread over ever larger areas, but the boundaries of many tiny feudal principalities acted as barriers to this expansion. Along the Seine River, for example, there were tolls every six or seven miles. Only by welding the confusing multiplicity of fiefs and principalities into a large territorial unit—the nation—could the irritating tolls and tariffs imposed by local barons be removed, trade advanced, the lack of a uniform currency be remedied, and justice established. In other words, the ills of feudalism could be cured only by the creation of unified and centralized national states. We shall see in this chapter how monarchs in England and France expanded their power and improved the machinery of government, thus laying the foundations for such states. In Germany and Italy, however, efforts to create a national state ended in failure, and in Spain unification was retarded by the formidable task of ousting the Muslims.

THE GENESIS OF MODERN ENGLAND

Britain after the Romans. When the Roman legions withdrew from Britain to Italy at the beginning of the fifth century, they left the Romanized Celtic natives at the mercy of the Anglo-Saxon invaders. These Germanic tribes devastated Britain so thoroughly that little remained of Roman civilization other than a splendid system of roads. Proof of the force with which the invaders struck is the fact that almost no traces of the Celtic language remain in modern English. Not only did the Anglo-Saxons push most of the Celts out of Britain, but they also fought among themselves. At one time there were more than a dozen little tribal kingdoms, all jealous and hostile, on the island.

The Anglo-Saxon monarchy. Gradually peace and a semblance of order came to the distracted island as rivalries among the kingdoms diminished and the overlordship of the island was held in turn by the different rulers. In the ninth century the kingdom of Wessex (see map, p. 192) held the dominant position. The famous Wessex king, Alfred the Great (871-899), was confronted with the task of turning back a new wave of invaders, the Danes, who overran all the other English kingdoms. After a series of disheartening reverses, Alfred defeated the Danes and forced them into a treaty whereby they settled in what came to be called the Danelaw (see map, p. 194) and accepted Christianity.

In addition to being a successful warrior, Alfred the Great made notable contributions in government in order, as he wrote, that he "might worthily and fittingly steer and rule the dominion that was entrusted to me."[1] He reorganized the militia of freemen (*fyrd*) so that part was always ready for battle while the rest tilled the soil, and the ships he built to repel future Viking attacks have won him the title of founder of the English navy. He also issued a set of laws, which reflect his desire to see the average man protected from wrongdoing and violence.

Following the example of Charlemagne, Alfred also advanced the intellectual life of his country. He invited learned men from abroad and founded a palace school. Since Latin was virtually unknown in England, Alfred urged the bishops to have translated into English the books "which are most necessary for all men to know." He also encouraged monks to keep an account of current affairs, the *Anglo-Saxon Chronicle*, which continued to be written for hundreds of years afterward.

Alfred's successors were able rulers who conquered the Danelaw and created a unified English monarchy. Danes and Saxons intermarried, and soon all differences between the two people disappeared. After 975, however, a decline set in. The power of the central government lagged and with it the ability to keep order at home and repel outside attacks. The impotence of the kingdom is well illustrated in the unhappy reign of Ethelred the Unready (978-1016), who was unable to keep a firm hand on the great nobles or to cope with a new attack by the Danes.

In its political structure, the major defect

of Anglo-Saxon England was the weakness of its central government: the inability of the king to control the great nobles, the earls, who were the king's deputies in their districts. But as a positive contribution to political history, the Anglo-Saxons developed local government to a strong degree. They left us a valuable legacy: the tradition of the people's participation in their government. In the local political divisions—the shires and their subdivisions, the hundreds—numerous assemblies or courts (moots) existed. Presided over by a royal official, the reeve, and composed of freemen of the area, the moots dispensed justice according to local custom and helped administer the realm. Here was one of the seeds of later democratic government. It is an interesting carry-over that American law students call their trial cases "moot court cases" and that our modern title of sheriff is derived from the shire's most important official, the shire reeve.

Following the reign of Ethelred, the Anglo-Saxons were again overrun by the Danes, and King Canute of Denmark ruled England as well as Norway. Canute proved to be a wise and civilized king and was well liked by his Anglo-Saxon subjects because he respected their rights and customs. Canute's empire fell apart after his death in 1035, and in 1042 the English crown was secured by Ethelred's son, Edward the Confessor. So pious that he remained a virgin all his life, Edward was a weak ruler who had little control over the powerful earls who had usurped most of the king's authority in their regions. This decline in government was reversed after the Normans conquered the island in 1066.

The Norman Conquest. The Norman Conquest of England really began in the reign of Edward the Confessor. Edward had spent most of his early life in Normandy, and as king of England he showed a strong pro-Norman bias. On his death without heir in 1066 the *Witan*—the council of the kingdom—selected Harold Godwinson, a powerful English earl, as the new ruler. Immediately William, duke of Normandy, claimed the English throne, basing his demand on a flimsy hereditary right and on the assertion that Edward had promised him the crown.

An outstanding statesman and soldier, William as duke of Normandy had subdued the rebellious nobles and established a new kind of centralized feudal state. William effectively controlled his vassals, and his feudal army of one thousand knights made him the most powerful ruler west of Germany. His centralized authority in Normandy contrasted sharply with the situation in England, where the powerful earls were continually embarrassing the king.

By promising to promote Church reform in England, William secured the sanction of the pope, which gave his invasion the flavor of a crusade. His well-equipped army of hard-fighting Norman knights and landless nobles from Brittany and Flanders looked upon the conquest of England as an investment that would pay them rich dividends in the form of lands and serfs.

The cross-Channel maneuver was hazardous; five thousand knights, bowmen, and supporting infantry, as well as many horses, had to be transported in open boats. On October 14, 1066, at Hastings, William's mounted knights broke the famed shield-wall of the English infantry, and resistance ceased when King Harold was slain. The defeat ended Anglo-Saxon rule and brought a new pattern of government that would make England the strongest state in Europe.

William the Conqueror's centralized feudal monarchy. As king of England, William directed all his policies at a single goal—the increase of his own power within the context of feudalism. And, sensibly, he utilized some of the institutions existing in England. He retained the Anglo-Saxon shires and hundreds as administrative divisions, along with the system of local courts and sheriffs. But the long arm of royal power also reached the local level through the king's commissioners, who occasionally toured the shires, and the sheriffs, who became the effective local agents of the king in collecting the feudal dues and in presiding over the shire courts.

Most important, William introduced the Norman system of centralized feudalism into England. As owner of all England by right of conquest, William retained some land as his royal domain and granted the remainder as fiefs to royal vassals called tenants-in-chief, among whom were bishops and abbots. In return for their fiefs, the tenants-in-chief provided William with a stipulated number of knights to serve in the royal army. To furnish the required knight service, the great vassals—most of whom were French-speaking Normans—subinfeudated parts of their fiefs among their own vassals. But from all the landholders in England, regardless of whether or not they were his immediate vassals, William exacted homage and an oath that they would "be faithful to him against all other men." Hence, both the tenants-in-chief holding fiefs directly from the king and the lesser tenants holding fiefs as vassals of the tenants-in-chief swore loyalty to the king, their feudal suzerain. This meant that a disgruntled noble could not call out his own vassals against the king, because every man owed his first allegiance to William.

William did not depend solely upon feudal levies, however; he retained the old Anglo-Saxon militia, in which every freeman was required to serve, and he hired mercenaries.

Thus the king had in readiness an independent fighting force to crush a rebellious baron. Furthermore, private feudal warfare was forbidden, and no castle could be built without royal permission.

The Domesday Survey is another example of the energetic and methodical manner in which William took over full control of England. Because William, like all medieval kings, constantly needed money, he ordered an accurate census of the property and property holders in his realm as a basis for collecting all the feudal "aids" and "incidents" (see p. 198) owed to him. Royal commissioners gathered testimony from local groups of older men who were put under oath and questioned. The complaints and even riots which the inventory caused are reflected in the *Anglo-Saxon Chronicle:*

So very narrowly did he cause the survey to be made that there was not a single hide nor a rood of land, nor—it is shameful to relate that which he thought no shame to do—was there an ox or a cow or a pig passed by that was not set down in the accounts. . . .[2]

The Bayeux tapestry, actually a woolen embroidery on linen, dates from the eleventh century. Over 230 feet long and 20 inches wide, it both depicts and narrates (in Latin) the events of the Norman Conquest of England in 1066. This section shows the English shield wall being attacked by the mounted French knights.

This seal was struck during the reign of William the Conqueror. The Latin inscription on the face reads "Know by this sign William, chief of the Normans"; the reverse reads "By this sign know the same William, king of the English."

In line with his policy of controlling all aspects of the government, William revamped the old Anglo-Saxon *Witan*, which had elected and advised the kings. The new Norman ruler changed its title to the Great Council—also called *curia regis*, the king's council or court—and converted it into a feudal body composed of his tenants-in-chief. The Great Council met at least three times a year as a court of justice for the great barons and as an advisory body in important matters. At other times a small permanent council of barons advised the king.

William also dominated the English Church. He appointed bishops and abbots and required them to provide military service for their lands. Although he permitted the Church to retain its courts, he denied them the right to appeal cases to the pope without his consent. Nor could the decrees of popes and Church councils circulate in England without royal approval.

Thus William formed the conquered island into one of Europe's most advanced states. In his determination to be master of his own house, he ruthlessly oppressed any opposition to his will. The nobility and the Church were burdened with feudal services, and the Anglo-Saxon freemen, oppressed by the exactions of their Norman lords, were in time reduced to serfdom. William advanced political feudalism and the manorial system and fused the two into a highly centralized feudal structure.

William's sons. William II, who succeeded his father in 1087, was a disappointing namesake. Utilizing his father's methods, but without his ability, William II stirred up several baronial revolts before being shot in the back—accidentally, it was said—while hunting. Succeeding him was his brother, Henry I (1100-1135), a more able and conciliatory monarch who met with only one baronial revolt.

While the Great Council, made up of the chief nobles, occasionally met to advise the king, the small permanent council of barons grew in importance. From it now appeared the first vague outlines of a few specialized organs of government. The exchequer, or treasury, supervised the collection of royal revenue, now greatly increased with the revival of a money economy. Notable was *scutage* or "shield money," a fee which the king encouraged his vassals to pay in lieu of personal military service. The well-trained "barons of the exchequer" also sat as a special court to try cases involving revenue. At times members of the small council were sent throughout the realm to judge serious crimes which endangered what was called the King's Peace.

Henry I's achievements in strengthening the monarchy were largely undone by the nineteen years of chaos that followed his death. Ignoring their promise to recognize Henry's only surviving child, Matilda, wife of Geoffrey Plantagenet, count of Anjou in France, many barons supported Henry's weak nephew Stephen. During the resulting civil war the nobility became practically independent of the crown and, secure in their strong castles, freely pillaged the land. According to the *Anglo-Saxon Chronicle:*

They levied taxes on the villages every so often, and called it "protection money." . . . If two or three men came riding to a village, all the villagers fled, because they expected they would be robbers. The bishops and learned men were always excommunicating them, but they thought nothing of it. . . .[3]

Henry II. Anarchy ceased with the accession of Matilda's son, Henry II (1154-1189), the founder of the Plantagenet, or Angevin, House in England. As a result of his inheritance (Normandy and Anjou) and his marriage to Eleanor of Aquitaine, the richest heiress in France, Henry's possessions stretched from Scotland to the Pyrenees. The English holdings in France far exceeded the land directly ruled by the French kings, who eyed their vassal rival with jealousy and

The White Tower, the oldest part of the Tower of London, was erected during the reign of William the Conqueror. This fortress was long used as a prison for those accused of crimes against the English throne.

fear. Henry's reign marks the outbreak of the strife between England and France, which runs like a red thread throughout the tapestry of medieval and modern history.

Stephen, Henry's weak predecessor, had left a sorry heritage. The judicial system was confused and corrupt. The royal courts administered by the king's justices faced strong competition from both the baronial courts, run independently by feudal lords, and the Church courts, which threatened to extend their supremacy over the whole realm.

Henry's chief contribution to the development of the English monarchy was to increase the jurisdiction of the royal courts at the expense of the feudal courts. This produced three major results: a permanent system of circuit courts presided over by itinerant justices, the jury system, and a body of law common to all England.

Itinerant justices on regular circuits were sent out once each year to try breaches of the King's Peace. To make this system of royal criminal justice more effective, Henry employed the method of inquest used by William the Conqueror in the Domesday Survey. In each shire a body of important men were sworn (*juré*) to report to the sheriff all crimes committed since the last session of the king's circuit court. Thus originated the modern-day grand jury which presents information for an indictment.

Henry's courts also used the jury system as a means of settling private lawsuits. Instead of deciding such civil cases by means of oath-helpers or trial by ordeal (see p. 133), the circuit judges handed down decisions based upon evidence sworn to by a jury of men selected because they were acquainted with the facts of the case. This more attractive and efficient system caused litigants to flock to the royal courts, a procedure facilitated by the sale of "writs," which ordered a sheriff to bring the case to a royal court. Not only was the king's income greatly increased by fees from the sale of writs, but the feudal courts of the nobility were greatly weakened.

This petit or trial jury eventually evolved into the modern trial jury whose members, no longer witnesses, determine guilt or innocence. Trial by jury became the most characteristic feature of the judicial system of all English-speaking nations and was carried to the far corners of the earth as a hallmark of justice.*

Henry's judicial reforms promoted the growth of the common law—one of the most important factors in welding the English people into a nation. The decisions of the royal justices became the basis for future decisions made in the king's courts, superseded the many diverse systems of local justice in the shires, and became the law common to all Englishmen.

Thomas à Becket, victim of Church-state rivalry. While Henry skillfully diminished the activities of the baronial courts by making the royal courts more powerful, he was not so successful against his other legal rival —the Church courts. When he appointed Thomas à Becket archbishop of Canterbury, the king assumed that his former boon companion and royal chancellor could easily be persuaded to cooperate, but Becket proved to be stubbornly independent, stoutly upholding the authority of the Church.

In 1164 Henry stipulated that clergymen found guilty by a Church court of committing heinous crimes, such as murder and grand larceny, were to be unfrocked and handed over to a royal court where punishments were more severe than in the Church courts. Henry's idea was to prevent the abuses resulting from "benefit of clergy"— the principle that the Church alone had legal jurisdiction over its clergy, among whom were included all who claimed to be students, crusaders, and even servants of clergymen. Becket refused to yield, claiming that clergymen would suffer unjust "double punishment" for a crime—unfrocked by the Church and punished by the state.

When Becket received no support from the English clergy, he fled to France and

THE DOMINIONS OF
HENRY II

- Inheritance
- Suzerainty
- Acquisitions by Marriage to Eleanor of Aquitaine
- French Royal Domain

Henry II was king, feudal suzerain, and vassal—all in one. He was king of England, feudal overlord of Scotland, Wales, Ireland, and Brittany, and vassal to the French king for the English holdings in France (although he held more territory there than the French monarch).

appealed to the pope for aid. After a few years the pope patched up the quarrel, and the archbishop returned to England. His first act, however, was to excommunicate the bishops who, in his absence, had crowned the eldest prince heir to the throne. When this news reached Henry, in a fit of passion he roared: "What a pack of fools and cowards I have nourished in my house, that not one of them will avenge me of this turbulent priest."[5] Responding to this tirade, four knights went to Canterbury and murdered Becket before the high altar of the cathedral. An eyewitness wrote that Becket "fell on his knees and elbows, offering himself a living victim, and saying in a low voice, 'For the name of Jesus and the protection of the church I am ready to embrace death.'"[6]

The resulting uproar destroyed all chance of reducing the power of the Church courts.

*The workings of Roman law offer an interesting contrast. "Under Roman law, and systems derived from it, a trial in those turbulent centuries, and in some countries even today, is often an inquisition. The judge makes his own investigation into the civil wrong or the public crime, and such investigation is largely uncontrolled. The suspect can be interrogated in private. He must answer all questions put to him. His right to be represented by a legal adviser is restricted. The witnesses against him can testify in secret and in his absence. And only when these processes have been accomplished is the accusation or charge against him formulated and published. Thus often arise secret intimidation, enforced confessions, torture, and blackmailed pleas of guilty."[4]

Becket became a martyr and, after miracles were reported to have occurred at his tomb, was canonized a saint. Although Becket was without much doubt a Norman, legend soon made him the symbol of English resistance to the yoke of Norman tyranny.

Richard the Lion-Hearted, knight-errant. As was the case after William the Conqueror's reign, the good beginning made by Henry II was marred by the mistakes of his successors. Having no taste for the prosaic tasks of government, Richard the Lion-Hearted wasted his country's wealth in winning a great reputation as a crusader (see p. 210) and in fighting the king of France. Richard spent only five months of his ten-year reign (1189-1199) in England, which he regarded as a source of money for his overseas adventures. The royal bureaucracy worked so well, however, that the king's absence made little difference.

John's powers limited by Magna Carta. Richard's successor, his brother John (reigned 1199-1216), was an able ruler who worked hard to promote his father's governmental system but who lacked his brother's chivalrous qualities. His cruelty and unscrupulous-

A detail from a medieval illuminated manuscript depicts the murder of Thomas à Becket.

ness cost him the support of his barons at the very time he needed them most in his struggles with the two ablest men of the age, Philip II of France and Pope Innocent III. As feudal overlord for John's possessions in France, Philip found the occasion to declare John an unfaithful vassal and his fiefs forfeit. John put up only feeble resistance, and after losing more than half his possessions in France he became involved in a struggle with Innocent III in which he was forced to make abject surrender (see pp. 245-246). In the meantime, John had completely alienated the English barons by attempting to collect illegal feudal dues and committing other infractions of feudal law. The exasperated barons rebelled and in 1215 forced John to affix his seal to Magna Carta, which bound the king to observe all feudal rights and privileges. People in later centuries, however, looked back upon Magna Carta as one of the most important documents in the story of human freedom.

To Englishmen of the time, this document did not appear to introduce any new constitutional principles. It was merely an agreement between the barons and the king, the aristocracy and the monarchy. But the seeds of political liberty were to be discovered in Magna Carta. Certain provisions were later used to support the movement toward constitutional monarchy and representative government:

Clause XII. [Taxation or feudal aids except those sanctioned by custom] . . . shall be levied in our kingdom only by the common consent of our kingdom [i.e., by the king's Great Council].

Clause XXXIX. No free man shall be taken or imprisoned or dispossessed, or outlawed, or banished, or in any way destroyed . . . except by the legal judgment of his peers or by the law of the land.

Clause XL. To no one will we sell, to no one will we deny, or delay right or justice.[7]

In 1215 these limitations upon the king's power applied only to freemen—that is, to the clergy, the barons, and a relatively small number of rural freeholders and burghers—not to the majority of the population, who were still serfs. As serfdom gradually disappeared, however, the term *freeman* came to include every Englishman.

The importance of Magna Carta does not lie in its original purpose but rather in the subsequent use made of it. Two great principles were potential in the charter: (1) the law is above the king; and (2) the king can be compelled by force to obey the law of the land. This concept of the rule of law and the limited power of the crown was to play an important role in the seventeenth-century struggle against the despotism of the Stuart kings; Clause XII was interpreted to guarantee the principle of no taxation without representation and Clause XXXIX to guarantee trial by jury.

The origins of Parliament. The French-speaking Normans commonly used the word *Parlement* (from *parler*, "to speak") for the Great Council, or *curia regis*, composed of the king's feudal tenants-in-chief. Anglicized as *Parliament*, the term was used interchangeably with Great Council and *curia regis*. Modern historians, however, generally apply the term to the Great Council only after 1265, when its membership was radically enlarged.

The first meeting of Parliament—the enlarged Great Council—took place in the midst of a baronial rebellion against Henry III, the son of King John. In an effort to gain the widest possible popular support, Simon de Montfort, the leader of the rebellion, summoned not only the barons but also two knights from every shire and two burghers from every borough to the Great Council in 1265.

Parliament gains stature. Parliament first became important during the reign of Henry III's son, Edward I (1272-1307), one of England's half-dozen outstanding monarchs. Beginning with the "Model Parliament" of 1295, Edward followed the pattern set by Simon de Montfort in summoning representatives of shires and towns to meetings of the Great Council. In calling Parliaments, Edward had no idea of making any concession to popular government. His aim was to enhance royal power by, in essence, packing his Great Council with representatives who would tend to support him rather than his opponents, the powerful barons. He could

Probably the earliest authentic view of Parliament in session, this picture shows a meeting called by Edward I. The dignitaries occupying the center benches are Church officials and secular lords. In the center are members of the judiciary seated on woolsacks to remind them that wool was vital to the English economy. Just below them are representatives from the towns and shires.

then expect to more easily obtain consent for new taxation, and he could use Parliament as an easy way of informing the country about royal policy. His utilization of the growing wealth and influence of the burghers to support royal power was soon copied by the king of France, Philip IV, who in 1302 began the practice of including representatives of the French bourgeoisie in his feudal council.

Early in the fourteenth century the representatives of the knights and the burghers, called the "Commons," adopted the practice of meeting separate from the lords spiritual and temporal. Thus arose the divisions of Parliament that came to be called the House of Commons and the House of Lords.

Parliament, particularly the Commons, soon discovered its power as a major source of money for the king. It gradually became the custom for Parliament to exercise this "power of the purse" by withholding its financial grants until the king had redressed grievances, made known by petitions. Parliament also presented petitions to the king with the request that they be promulgated as statutes, as the laws drawn up by the king and his council and confirmed in Parliament were called. Gradually the right to initiate legislation through petition was obtained. Again, Parliament's "power of the purse" turned the trick.

Edward I's statutes. Edward issued through Parliament a series of great statutes, many aimed at curtailing the power of the nobility that had greatly increased during the baronial revolts of his father's reign. The statute known as *Quo Warranto*, which demanded of a lord that he prove "by what warrant" he exercised certain rights and privileges, led to the recovery of lost royal rights. Another statute established the entail system which enabled a landowner to will his entire estate to his eldest son on condition that the property remain forever undivided. The younger brothers were thus forced to shift for themselves in governmental service, in the professions, or in commerce. By contrast, estates on the Continent were usually divided among all the sons in a family, a practice which encouraged the growth of a large and parasitic class of landowners. Edward also restricted the power of the Church, grown exceedingly rich through gifts of land. The Statute of Mortmain forbade the giving of more land to the Church without royal approval.

Widening the boundaries of the realm. Edward I was the first English king who was determined to be master of the whole island of Britain—Wales, Scotland, and England. In 1284, after a five-year struggle, English law and administration were imposed on Wales. As a concession to the Welsh, Edward gave his oldest son the title of Prince of Wales.

A dispute over the succession to the Scottish throne in the 1290's gave Edward his opportunity to intervene in the land to the north. After calling upon Edward to settle the dispute, the Scots accepted him as their overlord. Then Edward unwisely demanded that the Scots furnish him with troops to fight in England's wars. Under the courageous William Wallace, rebellion quickly flared up. After winning several victories against the English, Wallace was defeated and hanged as a traitor. But the fires of Scottish nationalism continued to burn despite numerous attempts to put out the flames. Edward II, the next English king, attempted to humble the Scots, but at the battle of Bannockburn (1314) the Scots, led by Robert Bruce, won their independence. The two peoples remained bitter enemies, with the Scots often joining the French in their wars against the English. Not until 1603 were the two kingdoms united under a common monarch.

THE BEGINNINGS OF THE FRENCH NATIONAL STATE

Political fragmentation. At the time William the Conqueror set sail, the monarchy in France barely existed. As we saw in Chapter 8, the later Carolingian rulers were generally weak and unable to defend the realm from Viking incursions. This task fell to the local counts and dukes, who built castles to protect the countryside and exercised the powers of the king in their territories. In France by the beginning of the tenth century there were more than thirty great feudal princes who were nominally vassals of the king but who gave him little or no support. Nevertheless, except for the short reign of Odo (see p. 194), the Carolingian kings maintained their precarious grasp on the throne. When the last Carolingian, Louis the Sluggard, died in 987, the nobles elected as his successor Hugh Capet, count of Paris and descendant of Odo.

The "kingdom" that Hugh Capet theoretically ruled was roughly comparable to, but smaller than, modern France. The territory Hugh actually controlled was a small feudal county extending from Paris to Orléans. It was almost encircled by rivers—hence, perhaps, its name: the Ile de France. The royal domain was surrounded by many independent duchies and counties, such as Flanders, Normandy, Anjou, and Champagne, which were a law unto themselves.

The early Capetians. Starting with little power and limited territory under their direct rule, the Capetian monarchs gradually extended their control over the great magnates. France was literally made by its kings, for ultimately the royal domain, in which the king's word was law, came to coincide with the boundaries of the realm.

In the late tenth and eleventh centuries, however, there was little tangible evidence that the Capetian kings would fulfill their destiny. They were weaker than many of their own vassals, and they had no hand in the stirring events of their time. While they remained historical nonentities, one of their vassals, the duke of Normandy, seized the throne of England; another, the count of Flanders, became a leader of the First Crusade and ruler of the kingdom of Jerusalem; and another vassal became the founder of the kingdom of Portugal.

The major accomplishment of the first four Capetian kings was their success in keeping the French crown within their own family. The nobles who elected Hugh Capet to the kingship had no thought of giving the Capetian family a monopoly on the royal office. But the Capetian kings, with the support of the Church, which nurtured the tradition of kingship as a sacred office, cleverly arranged for the election and coronation of their heirs. Before the king died, the young prince was crowned by the Church and became "associated" with his father in his rule. For three hundred years the House of Capet never lacked a male heir, and by the end of the twelfth century the hereditary principle had become so ingrained that French kings no longer took the precaution of crowning their sons during their own lifetime.

Louis the Fat pacifies the Ile de France. The advent of the fifth Capetian king, Louis VI (1108-1137), also known as Louis the Fat, heralded the end of Capetian weakness. Louis' pacification of the royal domain, the Ile de France, paralleled on a smaller scale the work of William the Conqueror in England.

With the support of the Church (which supplied him with able advisers), Louis determined to crush the lawless barons who were defying royal authority in the Ile de

France. According to Abbot Suger, his chief adviser and biographer:

A king, when he takes the royal power, vows to put down with his strong right arm insolent tyrants whensoever he sees them vex the state with endless wars, rejoice in rapine, oppress the poor, destroy the churches, give themselves over to lawlessness which, and it be not checked, would flame out into ever greater madness. . . .[8]

In the end the castles of the defiant vassals were captured and in many cases torn down. "And this," writes Abbot Suger, "they deserved who had not feared to raise their hand against the Lord's anointed."[9] Louis had made his word law in the Ile de France, established a solid base from which royal power could be extended, and so increased the prestige of the monarchy that the great duke of Aquitaine deigned to marry his daughter Eleanor to Louis' son. Unfortunately, Eleanor's behavior so scandalized Louis' pious son ("I thought I married a king," Eleanor

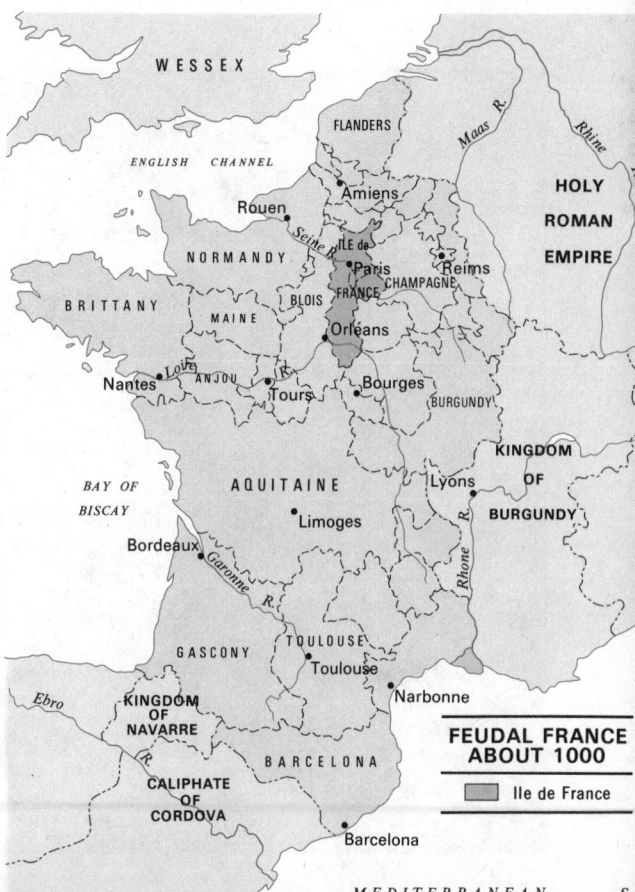

FEUDAL FRANCE ABOUT 1000

Ile de France

once exclaimed, "but instead I am the wife of a monk") that he had the marriage annulled, and Aquitaine passed to Eleanor's second husband, Henry II of England.

Philip Augustus extends royal rule. The first great expansion of the royal domain was the work of the next Capetian, Philip II Augustus (1180-1223), during whose reign the French king for the first time became more powerful than any of his vassals and France replaced Germany as the strongest monarchy in continental Europe.

Philip Augustus' great ambition was to wrest from the English Plantagenets the vast territory they held in France. Philip made little headway against Henry II, except to make Henry's life wretched by encouraging his faithless sons, Richard the Lion-Hearted and John, to revolt. As we have seen, Philip took Normandy, Maine, Anjou, and Touraine from John, thereby tripling the size of the royal domain.

Philip also greatly strengthened the royal administrative system by devising new agencies for centralized government and tapping new sources of revenue, including a money payment from his vassals in lieu of military service. New salaried officials, called bailiffs, performed duties similar to those carried out in England by itinerant justices and sheriffs. A corps of loyal officials, like the bailiffs recruited not from the feudal nobility but from the ranks of the bourgeoisie, was collected around the king. As in England, special administrative departments were created: the *parlement*, a supreme court of justice (not to be confused with the English Parliament, which became primarily a legislative body); the chamber of accounts, or royal treasury; and the royal or privy council, a group of advisers who assisted the king in the conduct of the daily business of the state.

In this early phase of consolidation of royal power, the papacy, which was struggling with the German emperors, usually allied itself with the French monarchy. As in England and Germany, however, the kings sometimes collided with the popes. Philip II defied Innocent III by having French bishops annul his marriage; but when the pope imposed an interdict on France, Philip backed down, and his wife again became his queen.

On the other hand, the Church inadvertently helped expand the royal domain. In southern France, particularly in Toulouse, the heretical Albigensian sect flourished. Determined to stamp out this sect, Innocent III in 1208 called the Albigensian Crusade, discussed in Chapter 11. Philip, faced with the enmity of King John and the German emperor, did not take part, but he allowed his vassals to do so. After Philip's death his son Louis VIII led a new crusade to exterminate the remnants of Albigensian resistance. Later in the century Toulouse escheated to the French crown when its count died without heir. The royal domain now stretched from the chilly coast of the

The *Très Riches Heures du Duc de Berry* is a devotional book containing prayers for each day of the year. The months are illustrated by full-page miniatures. This one, of October, depicts peasants sowing grain in fields on one bank of the Seine, while on the far bank is the Louvre as it appeared in the time of Philip II, who built the fortress as a storage place for his records and money.

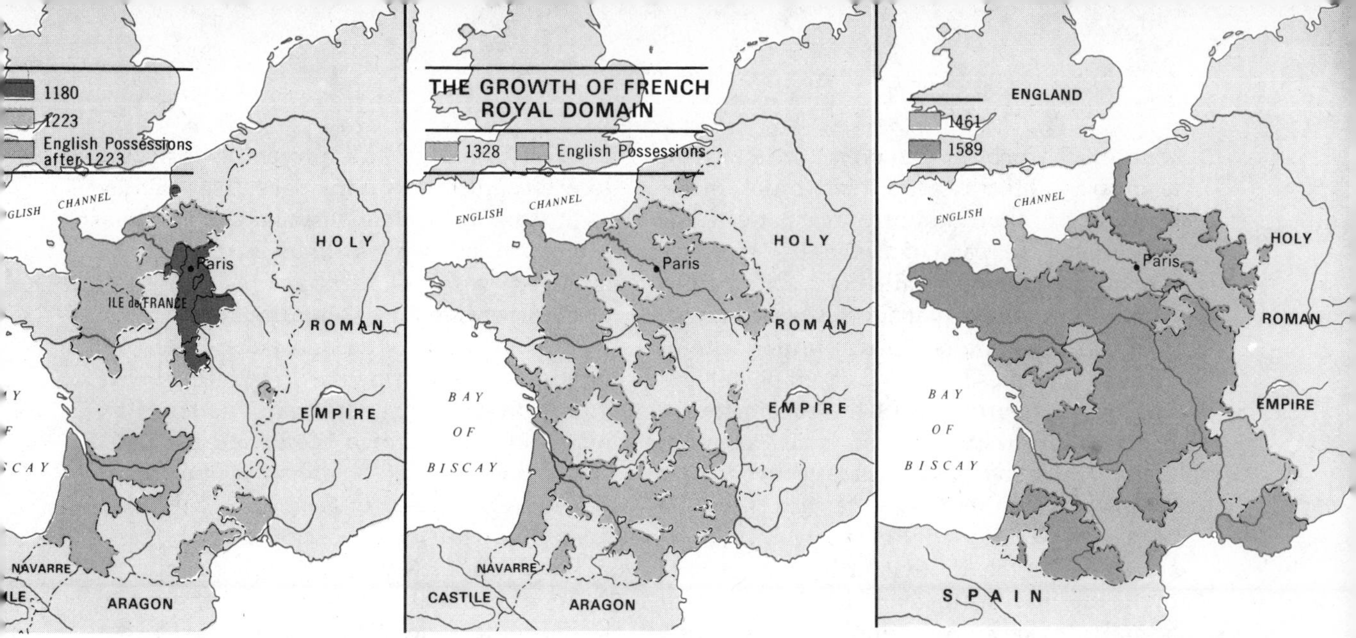
THE GROWTH OF FRENCH ROYAL DOMAIN
1180
1223
English Possessions after 1223
CHANNEL
HOLY
ROMAN
EMPIRE
Paris
ILE de FRANCE
NAVARRE
ARAGON
1328
English Possessions
ENGLISH CHANNEL
BAY OF BISCAY
CASTILE
ENGLAND
1461
1589
SPAIN

English Channel to the warm shores of the Mediterranean.

Louis IX dignifies the throne. After the brief reign of Louis VIII, France came under the rule of Louis IX (1226-1270), better known as St. Louis because of his piety and noble character. In contrast to the cunning opportunism of his grandfather, St. Louis' ideal was to rule justly, and he made some sacrifices to that end. For example, special officials were created to check on the bailiffs, who were forbidden to encroach on the feudal rights of the nobility. On the other hand, St. Louis believed himself responsible only to God, who had put him on the throne to lead his people out of a life of sin. Accordingly, St. Louis was the first French king to issue edicts for the whole kingdom without the prior consent of his council of great vassals. He also ordered an end to trial by battle and the time-honored feudal right of private warfare. Certain matters, such as treason and crimes on the highways, were declared to be the exclusive jurisdiction of the royal courts. Furthermore, St. Louis insisted on the right of appeal from the feudal courts of his vassals to the high royal court of *parlement* at Paris.

St. Louis' passion for justice impressed his contemporaries. He endeavored to hear personally his subjects' problems and complaints, and Joinville, his friend and biographer, whose *St. Louis, King of France* is a medieval masterpiece, has left us this sketch:

> Many a time it happened that in summer time he would go and sit down in the wood at Vincennes, with his back to an oak, and make us take our seats around him. And all those who had complaints to make came to him without hindrance from ushers or other folk. Then he asked them with his own lips: "Is there any one here who has a cause?" Those who had a cause stood up when he would say to them: "Silence all, and you shall be dispatched [judged] one after another."[10]

Just, sympathetic, and peace-loving, St. Louis convinced his subjects that the monarchy was the most important agency for assuring their happiness and well-being.

Climax of Capetian rule under Philip IV. The reign of Philip IV, the Fair (1285-1314), climaxed three centuries of Capetian rule. The antithesis of his saintly grandfather, Philip was a man of craft, violence, and deceit. He took advantage of the growing anti-Semitism that had appeared in Europe with the crusades to expel the Jews from France and confiscate their possessions. (Philip's English contemporary, Edward I, had done the same.) Again, heavily in debt to the Knights Templars, who had turned to banking after the crusades, Philip had the order suppressed on trumped-up charges of heresy.

Philip's need of money also caused him to clash with the last great medieval pope. As we shall see in Chapter 12, Pope Boniface VIII refused to allow Philip to tax the French clergy and made sweeping claims to supremacy over secular powers. But the national state had reached the point where such leaders as Philip IV would not brook interference with their authority no matter what the source. The result of this controversy was the humiliation of Boniface, a blow from which the medieval papacy never recovered.

In domestic affairs the real importance of Philip's reign lies in the increased power and improved organization of the royal government. Philip's astute civil servants, recruited mainly from the middle class, concentrated their efforts on exalting the power of the monarch. Trained in Roman law, and inspired by its maxim that "whatever pleases the prince has the force of law," they sought to make the power of the monarch absolute.

Like Edward I in England, Philip enlarged his feudal council to include representatives of the third "estate" or class—the townsmen. This Estates-General of nobles, clergy, and burghers was used as a means of obtaining popular support for Philip's policies, including the announcement of new taxes. Significantly, Philip did not need to ask the Estates-General's consent for his tax measures, and it did not acquire the "power of the purse" that characterized the English Parliament. Philip had sown the seeds of absolutism in France, but their growth was to be interrupted by the Hundred Years' War between France and England, which broke out twenty-three years after his death (see Chapter 12).

CHRISTIAN RECONQUESTS IN SPAIN

The Reconquista. The unification of Spain was a more complex process than that of either France or England. The customary rivalry between the feudal aristocracy and the royal authority was complicated by another significant element—a religious crusade. Unification required the ejection of the Muslims, with their alien religion and civilization. Unity also called for the integration of several distinct Christian states.

In Chapter 9 we noted the beginning of the *Reconquista*, or reconquest of Spain, up to the year 1085, when the Muslim stronghold of Toledo was captured. During this long struggle a mounting patriotism blended with a fanatical religious spirit. As early as the ninth century northern Spain became suffused with a religious zeal centering around Santiago de Compostela, reputed to be the burial site of the apostle St. James. His bones were enshrined in a great cathedral which thousands of pilgrims visited. Banners were consecrated there, and the battle cry of the Christian soldiers became "Santiago" (a contraction of *Sante Iago*, St. James' name in Spanish).

The Poem of My Cid. Another symbol of national awakening was an eleventh-century soldier of fortune, El Cid (Arabic for "lord"). His exploits against the Muslims thrilled Europe, and he became the hero of the great Spanish epic, *Poema de Mio Cid*. In the epic El Cid appears as a perfect Christian knight, although in reality he was an adventurer seemingly more interested in booty and power than in religion. The following characteristic lines begin with a reference to a victory over the Moors near Valencia:

His fame goes re-echoing even beyond the sea;
My Cid rejoiced, and all his company,
because God had given him aid and he had routed them there.
He sent out raiders, all night they rode; . . .
They destroyed the lands of the Moors as far as the seashore. . . .
Seizing and despoiling, riding at night,
sleeping in the daytime, taking those towns,
My Cid spent three years in the lands of the Moors. . . .
He sent forth a herald to Aragón and Navarre;
he sent his messages to the lands of Castile:
"Whoever would leave his toil and grow rich,
let him come to My Cid, whose taste is for battle.
He would now lay siege to Valencia to give it to the Christians."[11]

In 1212, at Las Navas de Tolosa, the Christians achieved one of the decisive victories of the Middle Ages. A few years later they captured first Cordova, whose great mosque was reconsecrated as a cathedral (see illustration, p. 208), and then Seville. By the end of the thirteenth century, when the reconquest halted until the latter part of the fifteenth century, Moorish political control was confined to Granada.

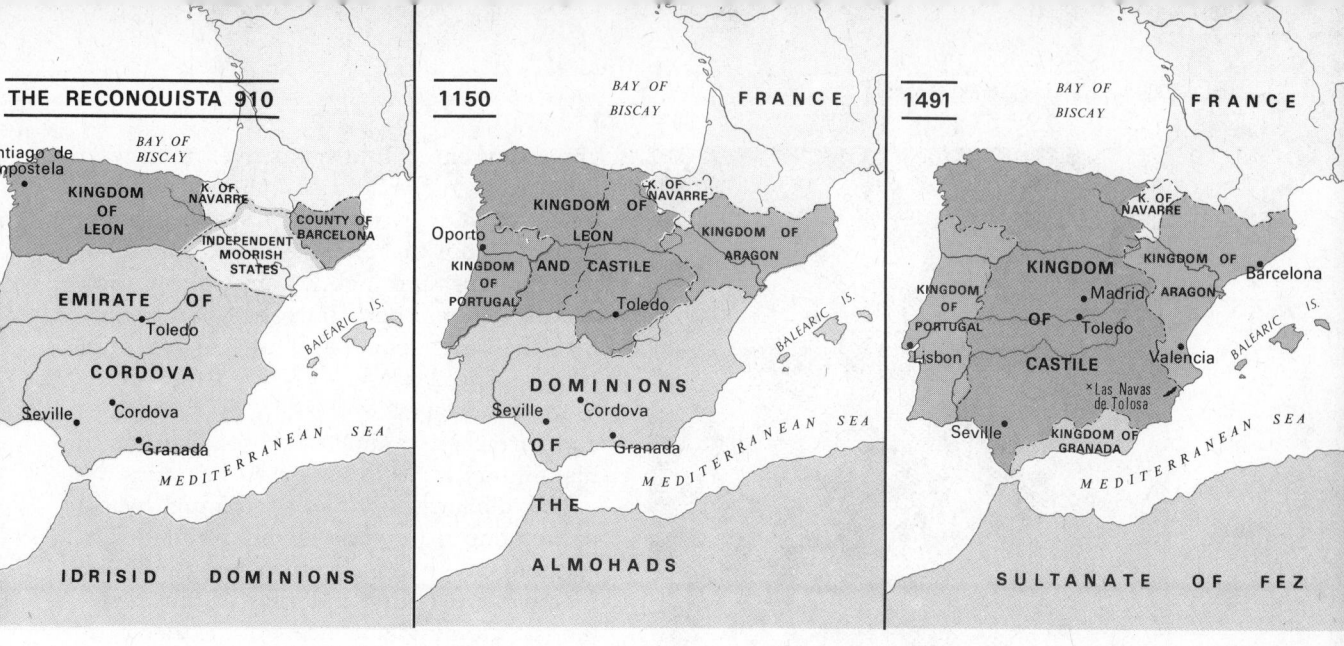

THE RECONQUISTA 910 | 1150 | 1491

It was usual for the Christian victors to allow their new Muslim subjects to enjoy their own religion and traditions. Muslim traders and artisans were protected because of their economic value, and Muslim culture—art in particular—was often adapted by the Christians.

FAILURES OF THE NATIONAL STATE: GERMANY AND ITALY

German tribal duchies. Following the collapse of the Carolingian empire, the tribal consciousness of its people kept Germany from falling into the extreme political fragmentation that characterized feudal France. When the successors of Louis the German, who received East Frankland in the Treaty of Verdun in 843 (see p. 194), proved incapable of coping with the attacks of savage Magyar horsemen in the late ninth and early tenth centuries, the task was taken over by the tribal leaders of the Saxons, Bavarians, Swabians, and Franconians who assumed the title of duke. The dukes of the five German duchies —including Lorraine, which Louis the German had acquired on the breakup of Lothair's middle kingdom—usurped the royal power and crown lands in their duchies and also took control over the Church.

When the last Carolingian, Louis the Child, died in 911, the dukes elected the weakest among them, Conrad of Franconia, to be their king. The new monarch ruled just eight years and proved himself incapable of meeting the menace of the Magyar raids. On his deathbed he recommended that the most powerful of the dukes, Henry the Fowler, duke of Saxony, be chosen as his successor. Henry founded the illustrious Saxon dynasty, which ruled until 1024 and made Germany the most powerful state in western Europe.

Henry the Fowler. After some initial opposition, Henry I (919-936) obtained recognition of his kingship from the other dukes. He exercised little authority outside of his own duchy, however, and his kingdom was hardly more than a confederation of independent duchies.

Against Germany's border enemies, Henry was more successful. He pushed back the Danes and established the Dane Mark as a protective buffer. Inroads were also made against the Slavs across the Elbe, where in 928 Brandenburg was set up as another defensive mark. Thus began the *Drang nach Osten* ("push to the East"), which became a permanent feature of German history. Further to the southeast, in Bohemia, Henry forced the Slavic Czechs to recognize his overlordship.

More spectacular was Henry's great victory over the Magyars in 933, following his refusal to pay the annual tribute demanded by these marauders. By this victory Henry

The crown of Otto I, which was probably made for his coronation, consists of eight gold plaques held together by hinges which open or close by means of pearl-headed pins. The crown was constructed in this portable fashion because Otto traveled a good deal and needed to have his crown with him for state occasions in various countries. Four of the plaques consist of pearls and gems held together by gold filigree. The other four plaques contain enamel panels showing God, David, Hezekiah with Isaiah, and (in the plaque visible here) Solomon. The upper part of the crown is an eleventh-century addition.

earned the gratitude of the German people, and when he died no one disputed the election of his son Otto to succeed him.

Otto the Great. Realizing that the great hindrance to German unity was the truculence of the dukes, Otto I, the Great (936-973), initiated a policy of gaining control of the unruly duchies by setting up his own relatives and favorites as their rulers. As an extra precaution he appointed, as supervising officials, counts who were directly responsible to the king. This policy was only temporarily successful, however, for both the counts and Otto's relatives and favorites proved unreliable. Even Otto's son, who was made duke of Swabia, rebelled against his father.

In the long run it was by means of an alliance with the Church that Otto constructed a strong German monarchy. The king protected the bishops and abbots and granted them a free hand over their vast estates; in return the church prelates furnished him with the officials, the income, and the troops that he lacked. Otto appointed the bishops and abbots, and since their offices were not hereditary, he could be sure that their first obedience was to his royal person. These prelates replaced the counts as the chief agents of the king in the duchies and furnished as much as three quarters of his military forces.

This alliance of crown and Church was a natural one at the time. At his coronation at Aachen, Otto had insisted on being anointed *rex et sacerdos* ("king and priest"), thus reviving the Carolingian concept of the theocratic ruler and the alliance between crown and Church. Furthermore, both partners feared the unruly and arrogant dukes whose usurpations included the right to appoint bishops and abbots in their duchies.

Otto also put an end to the Magyar menace, thereby enhancing his claim that the king, and not the dukes, was the true defender of the German people. In 955 Otto crushed the Magyars at Lechfeld, near Augsburg (see map, next page), another decisive battle of the Middle Ages. The people of the time compared Lechfeld to the battle of Tours more than two centuries earlier; and Otto the Great, like Charles Martel, was hailed as the savior of Europe. The remaining Magyars settled quietly in Hungary, and by the year 1000 they had accepted Christianity.

The eastward movement. Otto continued German expansion eastward against the Slavs, and the region between the Elbe and the Oder became more and more Germanized. Like Charlemagne earlier, Otto relied on the Church to Christianize the stubborn heathens, and Magdeburg and other bishoprics were established in the conquered lands.

This expansion has been called the greatest achievement of the medieval Germans. Had it not been for this move eastward, modern Germany would have been a narrow strip of land wedged in between the Rhine and the Elbe; it has been estimated that 60 percent of German territory before the First World War had been taken from the Slavs. On the other hand, because the borders between the German colonists and the Slav natives were never clearly defined, pockets of Slavs and Germans intermingled. This ethnic admixture has caused serious disputes and conflicts in modern times.

The German empire. Like so many men of the Middle Ages, Otto the Great tended to revere the past, and he regarded the Roman and Carolingian empires as golden ages. As one historian succinctly put it: "His objective was Empire, and his model was Charlemagne." This pursuit of an empire characterized the German monarchy until the middle of the thirteenth century and was a major factor in its collapse.

Italy in the tenth century, having split into warring fragments, was a tempting field for an invader. In the north the old Lombard realm, which had been a part of Lothair's middle kingdom, became the object of various rival contenders. In central Italy were the Papal States, ruled by the pope. During this century, however, the popes were ap-

pointed and controlled by the Roman nobility, and the power and prestige of the papacy was at its lowest ebb. Further south were two Lombard duchies; and, finally, at the extreme tip of the peninsula, the Byzantine empire retained a shaky foothold on the Italian mainland. Dotted here and there were cities, such as Venice, which had never become completely depopulated.

In deciding to invade Italy, Otto the Great was initially motived by defense. The dukes of the south German duchies of Swabia and Bavaria were hopeful of seizing Burgundy and Lombardy, and Otto believed that his position as German king would be endangered if those large remnants of Lothair's old middle kingdom fell into the hands of his German rivals. He first placed Burgundy and its weak ruler under his "'protection." Then he turned to Italy, where not only politics but, as chivalrous contemporary accounts explained it, romance also beckoned. Queen Adelaide, the widow of the former king of Lombardy, had been imprisoned by a usurper. Her plight suited Otto's political ambitions. In 951 he crossed the Alps, met Adelaide, who had escaped, and married her. He then dethroned her captor and proclaimed himself king of Italy.

On his second expedition to Italy in 962, Otto was crowned emperor by the pope, whose Papal States were threatened by an Italian duke. No doubt Otto thought of himself as the successor of the imperial Caesars and Charlemagne; and, in fact, his empire later became known as the Holy Roman Empire. But Otto also needed the imperial title to legitimatize his claim to Lombardy, Burgundy, and Lorraine, which had belonged to the middle kingdom of Lothair, the last man to hold the imperial title. Otto's coronation was a momentous event that brought Italy and Germany, pope and emperor, into a forced and unnatural union.

The distracting, even malevolent, effect of the German pursuit of empire in Italy is demonstrated by the reign of Otto III (983-1002), who eagerly promoted his grandiose scheme for "the renewal of the Roman Empire." Ignoring Germany, the real source of his power, he made Rome his capital, built a palace there, and styled himself "emperor of

NORTH SEA

FRIESLAND

la-Chapelle (Aachen)

LORRAINE

Mainz

Strasbourg

SWABIA

KINGDOM OF BURGUNDY

Milan

LOMBARDY

Genoa

CORSICA

SARDINIA

Brandenburg

SAXONY Magdeburg

Rhine

Frankfurt

FRANCONIA

Elbe R.

Saale

Danube R.

Lechfeld

Salzburg

BAVARIA

CARINTHIA

Po R. Venice

PAPAL

TUSCANY

STATES SPOLETO

Rome

Naples

TYRRHENIAN SEA

Prague

BOHEMIA

Vienna

Vistula R.

POLAND

Oder

HUNGARY

GERMANY ABOUT 1000

☐ Holy Roman Empire

Danube R.

CROATIA

SERBIA

ADRIATIC SEA

IONIAN SEA

the Romans." As the "servant of Jesus Christ," another of his titles, Otto installed non-Italian popes in Rome and conceived of the papacy as a partner in ruling an empire of Germans, Italians, and Slavs. But notwithstanding Otto's love for Italy, the fickle Roman populace revolted and forced him to flee the city. He died a year later while preparing to besiege Rome.

Despite the distractions in Italy, the Saxon rulers were the most powerful in Europe. They had permanently halted Magyar pillaging and, by utilizing the German Church as an ally, had curbed the divisive tendencies toward feudalism. Economically, too, there was progress. German eastward expansion had begun, and the Alpine passes had been freed of Muslim raiders and made safe for the Italian merchants who by the year 1000 were ready to act as middlemen linking western Europe with the eastern Mediterranean.

The Salian emperors vs. the papacy. Pioneers in nation-making, the Saxon kings were succeeded by a new royal line, the Salian House (1024-1125), whose members set about with increased vigor to establish a centralized monarchy. To the dismay of many nobles, a body of lowborn royal officials was recruited; and the power of the dukes was weakened further when the crown won the allegiance of the lesser nobles.

The reign of Henry IV (1056-1106) was a watershed in German history. The monarchy reached the height of its power, but it also experienced a major reversal. For a century the Ottonian system, by which the king had governed his kingdom through the clergy, whom he appointed, had functioned smoothly. Under Henry IV, however, the revival of a powerful papacy led to a bitter conflict, centering on the king's right to appoint Church officials who were at the same time his most loyal supporters. This conflict, known as the Investiture Struggle (see p. 244), resulted in the loss of the monarchy's major sources of strength: the loyalty of the German Church, now transferred to the papacy; and the chief material base of royal power, the king's lands, which were dissipated by grants to loyal nobles.

The real victors in the Investiture Struggle were the German nobles, many of whom allied themselves with the papacy and continued to wage war against the monarchy long after the reign of Henry IV. From the time of Henry's death in 1106 until the accession of Frederick Barbarossa in 1152, the Welfs of Bavaria and the Hohenstaufens of Swabia, along with other noble factions, fought over the throne, which they made elective rather than hereditary. The outcome was that the structure of a strong national state was wrecked and Germany became extensively feudalized. The great nobles usurped royal rights, built strong castles, and forced lesser nobles to become their vassals. On the other hand, the great nobles acknowledged no feudal relationship to the king. Many free peasants, in turn, lost their freedom and became serfs. The evil effects of this period were to hinder the development of a unified Germany until modern times.

Prosperity in divided Italy. Italy was even less unified than Germany. Jealous of one another and of their independence, the prosperous city-states in northern Italy joined the struggle between the German emperors and the papacy. The Welf-Hohenstaufen rivalry in Germany was reflected in Italy, where the rival factions were known as Guelphs and Ghibellines—the latter name derived from Waiblingen, the chief Hohenstaufen stronghold in Swabia. The former were usually pro-papal; the latter strongly favored the German monarchy's imperial claims in Italy. Yet, amidst the turmoil, the vitality, wealth, and culture of the northern Italian cities increased.

A brilliant civilization also flourished on the island of Sicily. By 1127 the Norman conquests (see p. 207) resulted in the establishment of the kingdom of Naples and Sicily which, under the able rule of Roger II (1130-1154), became one of the strongest and wealthiest states in Europe. Scholars from all over the East and Europe traveled to Roger's court, which ranked next to Spain's in the translation of Arabic documents. Life and culture in the Sicilian kingdom, which included Norman, Byzantine, Italian, and Arabic elements, was diverse and colorful. In the thirteenth century the history of Naples and Sicily became fatally entwined with the history of the German empire and hinged on the rise and fall of the powerful royal house of Hohenstaufen.

Frederick Barbarossa. The second Hohenstaufen emperor, Frederick I Barbarossa ("Red-beard"), who reigned from 1152 to 1190, realistically accepted the fact that during the preceding half century Germany had become thoroughly feudalized; his goal was to make himself the apex of the feudal pyramid by forcing the great nobles to acknowledge his overlordship. Using force when necessary, he was largely successful, and Germany became a centralized feudal monarchy not unlike England in the days of William the Conqueror.

To maintain his hold over his German tenants-in-chief, Frederick needed the resources of Italy—particularly the income from taxes levied on wealthy north Italian cities, which, encouraged by the papacy, joined together in the Lombard League to resist him. Frederick spent about twenty-five years fighting intermittently in Italy, but although some of the cities submitted to his authority, the final result was failure. The opposition from the popes and the Lombard League was too strong. Frederick did score a diplomatic triumph, however, by marrying his son to the heiress of the throne of Naples and Sicily. The threat of Hohenstaufen encirclement made it vital to the papacy that this royal house be destroyed.

Frederick Barbarossa died in Asia Minor while en route with the Third Crusade, and in time he became a folk hero in Germany. It was believed that he still lived, asleep in a cave in the mountains near Berchtesgaden in Bavaria. Some day, awakened by a flight of ravens, he would emerge and bring unity and strength back to Germany. "In the late nineteenth century, the artists of the Prussian court delighted to paint pictures of his last, and joyful, awakening in 1871, when the sky was full of ravens since a second German Empire had been called into existence. Statues of Frederick Barbarossa and Kaiser Wilhelm I were placed side by side to symbolize the 'fact' that where one had left off, the other had begun."[12]

Frederick II, a brilliant failure. It fell to the lot of Frederick Barbarossa's grandson,

Frederick Barbarossa is shown here with his two sons in a miniature dated around 1180. He is credited with originating the title "Holy Roman Empire" for the lands he claimed in Germany and Italy while seeking to centralize royal power in his empire.

Frederick II (1194-1250), to meet the pope's challenge to the threat of Hohenstaufen encirclement. Orphaned at an early age, Frederick was brought up as the ward of the most powerful medieval pope, Innocent III. During Frederick's minority the empire fell on evil days; the Welf and Hohenstaufen factions resumed their struggle over the throne, and the strong feudal monarchy created by Frederick Barbarossa collapsed. In 1215, one year before Innocent died and with his support, Frederick was elected emperor. Faced by a resurgent nobility in Germany, he soon turned his attention to wealthy Italy.

The papacy and the north Italian cities successfully defied Frederick throughout his reign, and in the end he experienced the same failure as had Frederick Barbarossa. Frederick also clashed with the papacy in another sphere. Embarking on a crusade at the pope's insistence, he turned back because of illness and was promptly excommunicated. A few months later Frederick resumed his crusade and was again excommunicated, this time for crusading while excommunicated. When Frederick acquired Jerusalem by negotiation (see p. 211) and agreed to allow Muslims to worship freely in the city, the pope called him "this scorpion spewing poison from the sting of its tail" and excommunicated him a third time.

Frederick sacrificed Germany in his efforts to unite all Italy under his rule. He transferred crown lands and royal rights to the German princes in order to keep them quiet and to win their support for his inconclusive Italian wars. Born in Sicily, he remained at heart a Mediterranean monarch. He shaped his kingdom of Sicily into a modern state. Administered by paid officials who were trained at the University of Naples, which he founded for that purpose, his kingdom was the most centralized and bureaucratic in Europe. Economically, too, it was far in advance of other states; Frederick minted a uniform currency and abolished interior tolls and tariffs, and his powerful fleet promoted and protected commerce.

As long as he lived, this brilliant Hohenstaufen held his empire together, but it quickly collapsed after his death in 1250. In Germany his son ruled ineffectively for four years before dying, and soon afterward Frederick's descendants in Sicily were killed when the count of Anjou, brother of St. Louis of France, was invited by the pope to annihilate what remained of what he called the "viper breed of the Hohenstaufen."

Significance of the fall of the Hohenstaufens. The victory of the papacy was more apparent than real, for its struggle against the emperors lost it much of its prestige. Men had seen popes using spiritual means to achieve earthly ambitions — preaching a crusade against Frederick II and his descendants, for example. More and more, popes acted like Italian princes, playing the game of diplomacy amid shifting rivalries. This involvement in worldly concerns and the accompanying decay in religious ideals help explain the increasing attacks on the papacy that would culminate in the Protestant revolt.

The Hohenstaufen kingdom of Naples and Sicily might have become the nucleus of a unified Italy. Unfortunately, the count of Anjou's seizure of the kingdom initiated a long period of bitter rivalry between Spaniards of the House of Aragon, who had married into the Hohenstaufen family, and Frenchmen representing Anjou. Beset by this interference, southern Italy and Sicily precipi-

tously declined amid alien rule, corruption, and, at times, horrible cruelty.

The Holy Roman Empire never again achieved the brilliance it last enjoyed during the reign of Frederick Barbarossa. The emperors usually did not try to interfere in Italian affairs, and they ceased going to Rome to receive the imperial crown from the pope. In German affairs the emperors no longer even attempted to assert their authority over the increasingly powerful nobles. After the fall of the Hohenstaufens, Germany lapsed more and more into the political disunity and ineffectual elective monarchy that remained characteristic of its history until the late nineteenth century.

SUMMARY

During the period from 1050 to 1300, England and France arose as pioneers in national unification and centralization. The essential pattern of historical development was similar in both nations, although each had its distinctive problems. (1) At first the kings were faced with serious competitors to their royal authority, the feudal nobility and the Church; (2) the kings became more powerful than their competitors, first by strengthening their power within the context of the feudal system, then by gradually establishing some of the military, judicial, and administrative agencies of a modern state; (3) the kings in effect made alliances with the rising middle class in the cities against their common enemy, the nobility. From the middle class came most of the money that the king needed to maintain a professional civil service, including a standing army that gradually replaced the often unreliable feudal levies.

In England William the Conqueror secured a unified kingdom in 1066 as a result of the Conquest, and successive English kings managed to keep their competitors under control and build up the machinery of royal administration. English development is also noteworthy for its legal and constitutional achievements: the common law, the jury system, circuit judges, and the first steps in the creation of representative government through Parliament.

In France the movement toward the consolidation of royal power started from a small area—the minuscule Ile de France. Each of the many counties and duchies that constituted feudal France had to be subordinated and brought within the framework of royal authority. It took the French kings three centuries to accomplish what William the Conqueror had done in one generation.

Nation-making in Spain was unique, since it was suffused with the religious fervor of a crusade. In the mid-eleventh century the Christian Spanish states began the *Recon-*

quista in earnest, but not until the end of the fifteenth century would the task be completed.

Although they had initial success in building a strong state at home, the German kings dissipated their energies by seeking the prize of empire over the Alps. For hundreds of years German rulers pursued this imperial phantom in Italy. In the face of resistance from the Italian cities, the treachery of the German nobles, and the opposition of the papacy, the German kings failed to achieve their goal. In both Germany and Italy after 1250, disunity and weakness prevailed; national unification was delayed until the nineteenth century.

SUGGESTIONS FOR READING

F. Heer, **The Medieval World: Europe, 1100-1350*** (Mentor); and S. Painter, **The Rise of the Feudal Monarchies*** (Cornell) are excellent syntheses. See also C. Brooke, **Europe in the Central Middle Ages, 962-1154,*** 2nd ed. (Longman, 1975).

H. Cam, **England Before Elizabeth*** (Torchbooks); G. Sayles, **The Medieval Foundations of England*** (A. S. Barnes); and C. Brooke, **From Alfred to Henry III, 871-1272*** (Norton) are valuable surveys of English history during the period covered in this chapter. See also F. Stenton, **Anglo-Saxon England,** 3rd ed. (Oxford, 1971), the standard account; and D. Kirby, **The Making of Early England** (Schocken, 1968).

R. Allen Brown, **The Normans and the Norman Conquest** (Crowell, 1970); H. Lyon, **The Norman Conquest*** (Torchbooks); and J. A. Matthew, **The Norman Conquest** (Schocken) are all outstanding treatments. H. Muntz, **The Golden Warrior** (Scribner's) is a first-rate novel dealing with the Norman conquest.

Works on English monarchs of the period include E. Duckett, **Alfred the Great: The King and his England*** (Phoenix); Amy Kelly, **Eleanor of Aquitaine and the Four Kings*** (Vintage); S. Painter, **The Reign of King John*** (Johns Hopkins); James A. Brundage, **Richard Lion Heart** (Scribner's, 1974); and W. L. Warren, **Henry II** (Univ. of Calif., 1973). See also R. Winston, **Thomas Becket** (Knopf, 1967); and T. M. Jones, ed., **The Becket Controversy*** (Wiley, 1970).

On English constitutional history see J. C. Holt, **Magna Carta: The Idea of Liberty*** (Wiley, 1972); G. L. Haskins, **The Growth of English Representative Government*** (A. S. Barnes); B. Lyon, **A Constitutional and Legal History of Medieval England** (Harper

& Row); and A. Pollard, **The Evolution of Parliament,** 2nd ed. (Russell).

For French history see R. Fawtier, **The Capetian Kings of France, 987-1328*** (St. Martin's), the best account. See also C. Petit-Dutaillis, **The Feudal Monarchy in France and England: From the Tenth to the Thirteenth Centuries*** (Torchbooks).

R. Merriman, **The Rise of the Spanish Empire in the Old World and in the New,** Vol. I, (Cooper Square) is the standard work on medieval Spain. Gabriel Jackson, **The Making of Medieval Spain*** (Harcourt Brace Jovanovich) is brief and highly readable with many illustrations. See also R. Menendez Pidal, **The Cid and his Spain** (Frank Cass, 1971).

J. Bryce, **The Holy Roman Empire*** (AMS Pr.) is an old masterpiece and should be supplemented by G. Barraclough, **The Origins of Modern Germany*** (Capricorn). See also the diverse scholarly opinions presented in R. Herzstein, ed., **The Holy Roman Empire in the Middle Ages: Universal State or German Catastrophe?*** (Heath). P. Munz, **Frederick Barbarossa: A Study in Medieval Politics** (Cornell, 1969); E. Kantorowicz, **Frederick the Second, 1194-1250** (Ungar); and T. van Cleve, **The Emperor Frederick II of Hohenstaufen** (Oxford, 1972) are instructive biographies.

William F. Butler, **The Lombard Communes: A History of the Republics of North Italy** (Haskell, 1969) is a reprint of a standard work. L. Salvatore, **A Concise History of Italy** (AMS Pr., 1976) is a good general survey.

*Indicates a less expensive paperbound edition.

CHAPTER 11

Medieval Religion, Thought, and Art: 600-1300

To the Glory of God

INTRODUCTION. In Paris, on a small island in the Seine, stands an edifice of weather-beaten stone, the Cathedral of Notre Dame. Dedicated to the glory of God and the veneration of Our Lady, this cathedral offers a fascinating glimpse into the life and spirit of medieval Europe. Notre Dame de Paris was built by cooperative community action between 1163 and 1235, during some of the most epoch-making years of the Middle Ages. While workmen were supporting the cathedral's vault with flying buttresses and carefully fitting the multicolored windows into place, churchmen and students lolled on the Petit Pont, a bridge that led to the Left Bank. The students wrangled over theology, accused one another of heresy, and occasionally composed blasphemous poems that parodied the sacred liturgy. Some of these students were one day to occupy episcopal thrones as princes of the Church; one of the mightiest occupants of the papal throne, Innocent III, once studied in Paris.

The underlying difference between our medieval ancestors and ourselves would appear to be one of perspective. To them theology was the "science of sciences," whereas today there are those who say that we have made science our theology. Yet this difference is not due exclusively to the extension of knowledge during the intervening centuries. It also lies in the fundamental premise governing the lives of our medieval forefathers. They believed in a world order, divinely created and maintained. For them, the universe possessed an inner coherence and harmony, which it was the function of the theologian and the scientist alike to discover. Revelation and knowledge, faith and reason, Church and state, spirit and matter—these dualities could be reconciled in a great spiritual and social synthesis.

In this chapter we will examine the methods by which medieval men sought to realize this synthesis and the measure of their success. As a first step, we shall trace the institutional growth of the one universal organization of medieval Europe, the Church. Next we shall watch its progressive assumption of secular powers, culminating in the triumphs of Innocent III. Finally, we shall see how, under the sponsorship of the Church, scholars and philosophers, scientists and inventors, and artists and artisans labored for the glory of God and the salvation of man.

THE CHURCH IN THE EARLY MIDDLE AGES

Gregory the Great and the early medieval papacy (600-1050). While Europe gradually recovered from the shock of the Roman Empire's demise, the Church—the papacy and Benedictine monasticism in particular—became the mainstay of European civilization. During the pontificate of Gregory I, the Great (590-604), the medieval papacy began to take form. Gregory's achievement was to go beyond the claim of papal primacy in the Church (see p. 128) to establish the actual machinery of papal rule, temporal as well as spiritual.

A Roman aristocrat by birth, Gregory witnessed and commented on the devastation of Rome as the city changed hands three times during Justinian's long struggle to retake Italy from the Ostrogoths:

Ruins on ruins. . . . Where is the senate? Where the people? All the pomp of secular dignities has been destroyed. . . . And we, the few that we are who remain, every day we are menaced by scourges and innumerable trials.[1]

Concluding that the world was coming to an end, Gregory withdrew from it to become a Benedictine monk. In 579 the pope drafted him to undertake a fruitless mission seeking Byzantine aid against the Lombards, who had invaded Italy a few years before. After the people of Rome elected Gregory pope in 590, he assumed the task of protecting Rome and its surrounding territory from the Lombard threat. Thus Gregory was the first pope to act as temporal ruler of a part of what later became the Papal States.

Gregory the Great also laid the foundations for the later elaborate papal machinery of Church government. He took the first step toward papal control of the Church outside of Italy by sending a mission of Benedictine monks to convert the heathen Anglo-Saxons. The pattern of Church government Gregory established in England—bishops supervised by archbishops, and archbishops by the pope—became standard in the Church.

The task of establishing papal control of the Church and extending the pope's temporal authority was continued by Gregory the Great's successors. In the eighth century English missionaries transferred to Germany and France the pattern of papal government they had known in England; and the Donation of Pepin (see p. 190), by creating the Papal States, greatly increased the pope's temporal power. The papacy's spiritual and temporal power suffered a severe setback, however, with the onset of feudalism. Beginning in the late ninth century, the Church, including the papacy, fell more and more under the control of feudal lords and kings.

Missionary activity of the Church. The early Middle Ages was also a vital period of missionary activity. By disseminating Christianity, the missionaries aided in the fusion of Germanic and classical cultures. Monasteries served as havens for those seeking a contemplative life, as repositories of learning for scholars, and often as progressive farming centers.

One of the earliest Christian missionaries to the Germans was Ulfilas (c. 311-383), who spent forty years among the Visigoths and translated most of the Bible into Gothic. Ulfilas and other early missionaries were followers of Arius, and thus the heretical creed of Arianism (see p. 128) came to be adopted by all the Germanic tribes in the empire except the Franks and Anglo-Saxons. As we saw in Chapter 8, the Franks' adoption of Roman Catholicism produced an alliance between Frankish rulers and the papacy that was important for European history.

Another great missionary, St. Patrick, was born in Britain about 389 and later fled to Ireland to escape the Anglo-Saxon invaders. As a result of his Irish missionary activities, monasteries were founded and Christianity became dominant. From these monasteries in the late sixth and seventh centuries a stream of monks went to Scotland, northern England, the kingdom of the Franks, and even to Italy. The Irish monks eagerly pursued scholarship, and their monasteries were repositories for priceless manuscripts.

Beginning with the pontificate of Gregory the Great, the papacy joined forces with Benedictine monasticism to become very active in the missionary movement. Gregory, as we saw, sent a Benedictine mission to England in 596. Starting in Kent, where an archbishopric was founded at Canterbury ("Kent town"), Roman Christianity spread through England, and finally even the Irish Church founded by St. Patrick acknowledged the primacy of Rome.

The English Church in turn played an important part in the expansion of Roman-controlled Christianity on the Continent. St. Boniface, the greatest missionary from England in the eighth century, spent thirty-five years among the Germanic tribes. Known as the "Apostle to the Germans," he established several important monasteries, bishoprics, and an archbishopric at Mainz before he turned to the task of reforming the Church in France. There he revitalized the monasteries, organized a system of local parishes to bring Christianity to the countryside, and probably was instrumental in forming the alliance between the papacy and the Carolingian house. Roman Catholic missionaries also worked among the Scandinavians and the Western Slavs.

The monks as custodians of knowledge. One of the great contributions of the monasteries was the preservation of learning. Writing in the sixth century, Bishop Gregory of Tours lamented:

A monk copies a manuscript in the *scriptorium*, surrounded by other manuscripts and such tools of his trade as inkpots, pens, and brushes.

In these times . . . there has been found no scholar trained in the art of ordered composition to present in prose or verse a picture of the things that have befallen.[2]

Learning did not entirely die out in western Europe, of course. Seeing that the ability to read Greek was fast disappearing, the sixth-century Roman scholar Boethius, an administrator under the Ostrogothic king Theodoric, determined to preserve Greek learning by translating all of Plato and Aristotle into Latin. Only Aristotle's treatises on logic were translated, and these remained the sole works of that philosopher available in the West until the twelfth century. Unjustly accused of treachery by Theodoric, Boethius was thrown into prison, where he wrote *The Consolation of Philosophy* while awaiting execution. This little classic later became a medieval textbook on philosophy.

Cassiodorus, a contemporary of Boethius who had also served Theodoric, devoted most of his life to the collection and preservation of classical knowledge. By encouraging the monks to copy valuable manuscripts, he was instrumental in making the monasteries centers of learning. Following his example, many monasteries established scriptoria, departments concerned exclusively with copying manuscripts.

During the early Middle Ages most education took place in the monasteries. In the late sixth and seventh centuries, when the effects of the barbarian invasions were still being felt on the Continent, Irish monasteries provided a safe haven for learning. There men studied Greek and Latin, copied and preserved manuscripts, and in illuminating them produced masterpieces of art. *The Book of Kells* is a surviving example of their skill.

The outstanding scholar of the early Middle Ages, the Venerable Bede (d. 735), followed the Irish tradition of learning in a northern England monastery. Bede described himself as "ever taking delight in learning, teaching, and writing." His many writings, which included textbooks and commentaries on the Scriptures, summed up most knowledge available in his age. Through Alcuin later in the century, Bede's learning influenced the Carolingian Renaissance (see p. 192). Bede's best known work, the *Ecclesiastical History of the English People*, with its many original documents and vivid character sketches, is our chief source for early English history.

THE CHURCH MILITANT

The Church-state rivalry. In the last quarter of the eleventh century a resurgent and militant papacy entered into a bitter and prolonged struggle with what was then Europe's strongest state, the German or Holy Roman Empire. By 1200 the papacy had emerged triumphant; under Pope Innocent III, the most powerful man ever to sit on St. Peter's chair, the theory and the practice of papal power coincided.

Medieval political theory begins with the concept of a universal community divided into two spheres, the spiritual and the temporal—a view based upon Christ's injunction to "Render therefore to Caesar the things that are Caesar's, and to God the things that are God's" (Matthew 22:21). As Pope Gelasius I declared in the fifth century, God had entrusted spiritual and temporal powers to two authorities—the Church and the state—each supreme in its own sphere. At first the question of ultimate superority between these authorities did not arise, although Gelasius had implied that the Church was superior to the state in the same way that the soul was superior to the body. The issue could not be permanently shelved, however; a fight for supremacy was in the long run inevitable.

When the German king Otto the Great revived the Roman empire in the West in 962 (see p. 235), his act reemphasized the concept of the dual leadership of pope and emperor. Otto claimed to be the successor of Augustus, Constantine, and Charlemagne, although his actual power was confined to Germany and Italy. At first the papacy looked to the German king for protection against the unruly Italian nobles who for a century had been making a prize of the papacy. From the Church's viewpoint, however, this ar-

During the fourteenth century the Church-state struggle produced a great amount of rival political theory, with the Church making much use of symbolism and allegory. In this illumination Christ hands the sword of temporal power to a worldly king, while St. Peter, as pope, receives the key to heaven, symbol of spiritual power. Christ's gaze is fixed on St. Peter, thus indicating that the Church was more important than the state.

rangement had its drawbacks, for the German kings continued to interfere in ecclesiastical affairs—even in the election of popes.

During the eleventh century controversy arose between Church and state over the problem of lay investiture. Theoretically, on assuming office a bishop or abbot was subject to two investitures; his spiritual authority was bestowed by a Church official and his feudal or civil authority by a layman—a feudal lord or a king. In actual fact, however, feudal lords and kings came to control both the appointment and the installation of church prelates. As noted earlier (p. 234), this practice was most pronounced in Germany, where control of the Church was the foundation of the king's power. The German Church was in essence a state Church.

The Cluniac reform. A religious revival—often called the medieval reformation—began in the tenth century and reached full force in the twelfth and thirteenth. The first far-reaching force of the revival was the reformed Benedictine order of Cluny, founded

in 910. From the original monastery in Burgundy, there radiated a powerful impulse for the reform of the feudalized Church. The Cluniac program began as a movement for monastic reform, but in time it called for the enforcement of clerical celibacy and the abolition of simony, the purchase or sale of a Church office. (The term *simony* comes from Simon the magician, who tried to buy the gift of the Holy Spirit from the apostles.) The ultimate goal of the Cluniac reformers was to free the entire Church from secular control and subject it to papal authority. Some three hundred Cluniac houses were freed from lay control, and in 1059 the papacy itself was removed from secular interference by the creation of the College of Cardinals, which henceforth elected the popes.

Gregory VII. The most ambitious proponent of Church reform was Pope Gregory VII (1073-1085), who claimed unprecedented power for the papacy. Gregory held as his ideal the creation of a Christian commonwealth under papal control. Instead of conceding equality between the Church and the state, he drew from the Gelasian theory the conclusion that the spiritual power was supreme over the temporal. In the *Dictatus Papae* ("Dictate of the Pope") Gregory claimed:

That the Roman pontiff alone can with right be called universal.

That he alone may use the imperial insignia.

That of the pope alone all princes shall kiss the feet.

That it may be permitted to him to depose emperors.

That he himself may be judged by no one.

That he who is not at peace with the Roman Church shall not be considered catholic.

That he may absolve subjects from their fealty to wicked men.[3]

The Investiture Struggle. In 1075 Gregory VII formally prohibited lay investiture and threatened to excommunicate any layman who performed it and any ecclesiastic who submitted to it. This drastic act virtually declared war against Europe's rulers, since most of them practiced lay investiture. The climax to the struggle occurred in Gregory's clash with the emperor Henry IV. The latter was accused of simony and lay investiture in appointing his own choice to the archbishopric of Milan and was summoned to Rome to explain his conduct. Henry's answer was to convene in 1076 a synod of German bishops which declared Gregory a usurper and unfit to occupy the Roman See:

Wherefore henceforth we renounce, now and for the future, all obedience unto thee—which indeed we never promised to thee. And since, as thou didst publicly proclaim, none of us has been to thee a bishop, so thou henceforth wilt be Pope to none of us.[4]

In retaliation Gregory excommunicated Henry and deposed him, absolving his subjects from their oaths of allegiance.

At last, driven to make peace with the pontiff by a revolt among the German nobles, Henry appeared before Gregory in January 1077 at Canossa, a castle in the Apennines. Garbed as a penitent, the emperor is said to have stood barefoot in the snow for three days and begged forgiveness until, in Gregory's words: "We loosed the chain of the anathema and at length received him into the favor of communion and into the lap of the Holy Mother Church."[5]

This dramatic humiliation of the emperor did not resolve the quarrel, nor do contemporary accounts attach much significance to the incident—public penance was not uncommon in those days even for kings. Yet the pope had made progress toward freeing the Church from interference by laymen and toward increasing the power and prestige of the papacy. The problem of lay investiture was settled in 1122 by the compromise known as the Concordat of Worms. The Church maintained the right to elect the holder of an ecclesiastical office, but only in the presence of the king or his representative. The candidate, such as a bishop, was invested by the king with the scepter, the symbol of his administrative jurisdiction, after which he performed the act of homage and swore allegiance as the king's vassal. Only after this ceremony had taken place was the candidate consecrated by the archbishop, who invested him with his spiritual functions, as symbolized by the ring and pastoral staff. Since the kings of England and France had earlier accepted this compromise, the problem of lay investiture waned.

The struggle between Church and empire continued for more than a century, sparked by the papacy's resentment at the emperors' continued interference in Italian affairs. We have already seen how the prosperous cities of northern Italy formed the Lombard League, defeated Frederick Barbarossa and Frederick II, and achieved the pope's aim of keeping the emperors out of Italy.

THE CHURCH TRIUMPHANT

The papacy's zenith: Innocent III. As demonstrated by Urban II's leadership of the First Crusade in 1095, the papacy emerged from the Investiture Struggle as the most powerful office in Europe. A century later the zenith of papal power was reached under Innocent III (1198-1216), a new type of administrator-pope. Unlike Gregory VII and other earlier reform popes, who were monks, Innocent and other great popes of the late twelfth and thirteenth centuries were lawyers, trained in the newly revived and enlarged Church, or canon, law. Innocent was like Gregory VII, however, in holding an exalted view of his office:

The successor of Peter is the Vicar of Christ: he has been established as a mediator between God and man, below God but beyond man; less than God but more than man; who shall judge all and be judged by no one.[6]

Innocent III told the princes of Europe that the papacy was as the sun, whereas the kings were as the moon. As the moon derives its light from the sun, so the kings derived their powers from the pope. So successful was the pontiff in asserting his temporal as well as spiritual supremacy that many states, both large and small, formally acknowledged vassalage to the pope. In the case of King John of England, a struggle developed over the election of the archbishop of Canterbury, and Innocent placed England under interdict and excommunicated John. Under attack from his barons, John capitulated to Innocent by becoming his vassal, receiving England back as a fief, and paying him an annual monetary tribute. Innocent forced Philip Augustus of France to comply with the Church's moral code by taking back as his queen the woman he had divorced with the consent of the French bishops. As for the Holy Roman Empire, Innocent intervened in a civil war between rival candidates for the throne, supporting first one, then the other. In the end Innocent secured the election of his ward, the young Hohenstaufen heir Frederick II, who promised to respect papal rights and to go on a crusade.

Within the Church itself, nothing better illustrates the power of the papal monarchy under Innocent III than the Fourth Lateran Council, which he called in 1215 to confirm his acts and policies. More than four hundred bishops, some eight hundred abbots and priors, and representatives of all leading secular rulers answered Innocent's call. The Council dealt with a wide range of subjects; for example, it outlawed trial by ordeal, required Jews to wear distinctive yellow badges, declared clergymen exempt from state taxation, and formally defined the Christian sacraments, setting their number at seven.

The sacramental system. Christian theology held that salvation was won only with the grace of God, and that God bestowed His grace on man by means of sacraments through the Church and its officials. Thus the Church was the necessary intermediary between God and man, a position strengthened when the Fourth Lateran Council decreed that every adult Christian must confess his sins and attend communion at least once a year.

The sacraments have been defined as outward or visible signs instituted by Christ to signify and to give grace. Until fixed at seven by the Fourth Lateran Council, as many as eleven sacraments had been accepted.

In the first of the seven sacraments, Baptism, the taint of original sin was washed away, and the person was given a Christian name, hence "christening." Confirmation strengthened the character of the recipient and confirmed his membership in the Church. The sacrament of Matrimony was instituted to give the married couple spiritual help—although celibacy was prescribed for those who entered the Church as a career. Holy Orders, or ordination into the priesthood, was administered by a bishop. This sacrament conferred the power and grace to perform the sacred duties of the clergy; the ordained priest was capable of administering all sacraments except Confirmation and Holy Orders. Penance enabled sins committed after Baptism to be forgiven through the absolution of the priest. Extreme Unction was administered when death appeared imminent; it forgave remaining sins and bestowed grace and spiritual strength on the dying Christian.

The most important and impressive sacrament was the Holy Eucharist, defined as "both a sacrament and a sacrifice; in it Our Savior, Jesus Christ, body and blood, soul and divinity, under the appearance of bread and wine, is contained, offered, and received." The significance of this sacrament as the core of Christian worship can be fully appreciated only when the doctrine of transubstantiation is understood. According to this doctrine—a subject of dispute until formally defined by the Fourth Lateran Council—when the priest performing the mass pronounces over the bread and wine the words Christ used at the Last Supper, "This is My Body . . . . This is the chalice of My Blood . . . ," a miracle takes place. To all outward appearances, the bread and wine remain unchanged, but in "substance" they have been transformed into the very body and blood of the Savior.

Church administration. The universality and power of the Church rested not only upon a systematized, uniform creed but also upon the most highly organized administrative system in the West. At the head was the pope, or bishop of Rome (see Chapter 5). He was assisted by the Curia, the papal council or court, which in the twelfth and thirteenth centuries developed an intricate administrative system. Judicial and secretarial problems were handled by the papal Chancery, financial matters by the Camera, and disciplinary questions by the Penitentiary.

Special emissaries called legates, whose powers were superior to those of local prelates, carried the pope's orders throughout Europe.

The Church was ahead of secular states in developing a system of courts and a body of law. Church or canon law was based on the Scriptures, the writings of the Church Fathers, and the decrees of Church councils and popes. In the twelfth century the Church issued its official body of canon law, which guided the Church courts in judging perjury, blasphemy, sorcery, usury (the medieval Church denounced the taking of interest), and heresy. Heresy was the most horrible of all crimes in medieval eyes. A murder was a crime against society, but the heretic's disbelief in the teachings of Christ or His Church was considered a crime against God Himself.

The papacy's chief weapons in support of its authority were spiritual penalties. The most powerful of these was excommunication, by which people became anathema, "set apart" from the Church and all the faithful. "They could not act as judge, juror, notary, witness, or attorney. They could not be guardians, executors, or parties to contracts. After death, they received no Christian burial, and if, by chance, they were buried in consecrated ground, their bodies were to be disinterred and cast away. If they entered a church during Mass, they were to be expelled, or the Mass discontinued. After the reading of a sentence of excommunication, a bell was rung as for a funeral, a book closed, and a candle extinguished, to symbolize the cutting off of the guilty man."[7]

Interdict, which has been termed "an ecclesiastical lockout," was likewise a powerful instrument. Whereas excommunication was directed against individuals, interdict suspended all public worship and withheld all sacraments other than Baptism and Extreme Unction in the realm of a disobedient ruler. Pope Innocent III successfully applied or threatened the interdict eighty-five times against refractory princes.

In the last analysis the Church's effectiveness depended upon the parish priest, whose importance was enhanced by the required confession and communion decreed by the Fourth Lateran Council. Although the priest

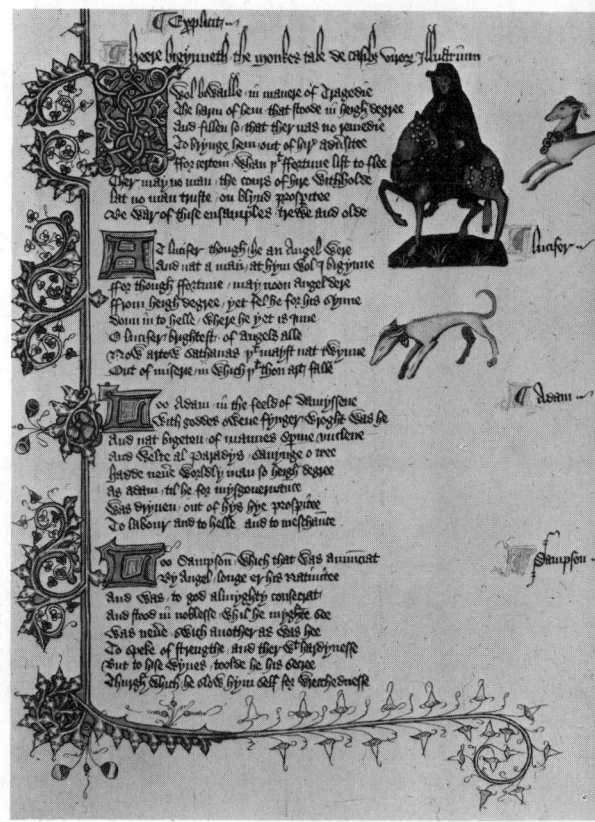

This detail from a fifteenth-century manuscript of Chaucer's *Canterbury Tales* shows the good parson.

was very likely of humble birth and little education, he was father confessor, social worker, policeman, and recreation director, all rolled into one. In most cases he was a credit to his Church. The "poor town Parson" in Chaucer's *Canterbury Tales* is a sympathetic portrayal.

> He was a kind man, full of industry,
> Many times tested by adversity
> And always patient. . . .
> Wide was his parish, with houses far asunder,
> But he would not be kept by rain or thunder,
> If any had suffered a sickness or a blow,
> From visiting the farthest, high or low,
> Plodding his way on foot, his staff in hand.
> He was a model his flock could understand.
> For first he did and afterward he taught.[8]

From the reign of Innocent III until the end of the thirteenth century, the Church radiated power and splendor. It possessed perhaps one third of the land of Europe, and all secular rulers and Church prelates acknowledged the power of Christ's vicar. Innocent III and his successors could and did "judge all and be judged by no one."

Yet while the Church's wealth enabled it to perform educational and charitable functions that the states were too poor and weak to provide, this wealth also encouraged abuses and worldliness among the clergy. Cracks were appearing in the foundation even while the medieval religious structure received its final embellishments. Weaknesses were evident in the lessening of religious zeal in the later crusades, in the need for renewed internal reform, and in the growth of heresy.

New monastic reforms. The medieval reformation gained momentum late in the eleventh century with a second movement of monastic reform brought on by the failure of the Cluniac reform to end laxity in monastic life. Among the new orders were the severely ascetic and hermit-like Carthusians and the very popular Cistercians.

The Cistercian movement received its greatest impetus from the zealous efforts of St. Bernard of Clairvaux in the twelfth century. The abbeys were situated in solitary places, and their strict discipline emphasized fasts and vigils, manual labor, and a vegetarian diet. Their churches contained neither stained glass nor statues, and the puritanical Bernard denounced the beautification of churches in general:

Oh! vanity of vanities! but not more vain than foolish. . . . What has all this imagery to do with monks, with professors of poverty, with men of spiritual minds? . . . In fact, such an endless variety of forms appears everywhere that it is more pleasant to read in the stonework than in books, and to spend the day in admiring these oddities than in meditating on the Law of God.[9]

Spurred on by this militant denouncer of wealth and luxury in any form, the Cistercian order had founded 343 abbeys in western Europe by the time of Bernard's death in 1153 and more than double that number by the end of the century. Yet in one important sense these austere new monastic orders were failures. Being exclusively agricultural and dwelling apart from society, these orders were unfitted to cope with religious discontent in the towns and the consequent rise of heresy.

Heresies. Heresy, defined as "the formal denial or doubt by a baptized person of any revealed truth of the Catholic faith,"[10] flourished particularly in the towns, where an increasing consciousness of sin and a demand for greater piety went largely unheeded by old-style churchmen. This fertile ground produced many heresies, among which the Albigensian and Waldensian were major ones.

Harking back to an early Christian heresy, the Cathari ("Pure") or Albigensians—so called because Albi in southern France was an important center—went to extremes in thinking of the world as the battleground of the opposing forces of good and evil. The Albigensians condemned many activities of the state and the individual, even condemning marriage for perpetuating the human species in this sinful world.

The Waldensians derived their name from Peter Waldo, a merchant of Lyons who gave his wealth to charity and founded a lay order, the Poor Men of Lyons, to serve the needs of the people. He had parts of the New Testament translated into French, held that laymen could preach the Gospel, and denied the efficacy of the sacraments unless administered by worthy priests. Because the Waldensian church still exists today in northern Italy, it has been called the oldest Protestant sect.

For ten years Innocent III tried to reconvert these heretical groups. Failing, in 1208 he instigated a crusade against the prosperous and cultured French region of Toulouse, where the Albigensian heresy was widespread. The crusade began with horrible slaughter to the cry of "Kill them all, God will know His own." Soon the original religious motive was lost in a selfish rush to seize the wealth of the accused. In time the Albigensian heresy was destroyed, along with the flourishing culture of southern France, and the Waldensians were scattered. Until the rise of Protestantism, the Church was generally successful in its efforts to crush heresy.

The Inquisition. In 1233 a special papal court called the Inquisition was established to cope with the rising tide of heresy and to bring about religious conformity. The accused was tried in secret without the aid of legal counsel. If he confessed and renounced his heresy, he was "reconciled" with the Church on performance of penance. If he did not voluntarily confess, he could be tortured. If this failed, the prisoner could be declared a heretic and turned over to the secular authorities, usually to be burned at the stake.

In any evaluation of the Inquisition, it should be remembered that the soul was considered incomparably more important than the body—therefore torturing a suspected heretic was justifiable if confession could save his soul from the greater torments of hell. Furthermore, the use of torture, secret testimony, and the denial of legal counsel prevailed in all courts that followed Roman law procedure.

The Franciscans and Dominicans. As a more positive response to the spread of heresy and the conditions which spawned it, Innocent III approved the founding of the Franciscan and Dominican orders of friars ("brothers"). Instead of living a sequestered existence in a remote monastery, the friars moved among their brother men, ministering to their needs and preaching the Gospel.

The Franciscans were founded by St. Francis of Assisi (1182?-1226), who, like Peter Waldo, rejected riches and spread the gospel of poverty and Christian simplicity. Love of one's fellow men and all God's creatures, even "brother worm," were basic in the Rule of St. Francis, which was inspired by Jesus' example:

Jesus called the twelve disciples together and gave them power and authority to drive out all demons and to cure diseases. Then he sent them out to preach the Kingdom of God and to heal the sick. He said to them: "Take nothing with you for your trip: no walking stick, no beggar's bag, no food, no money, not even an extra shirt. . . ." The disciples left and traveled through all the villages, preaching the Good News and healing people everywhere.[11]

The second order of friars was founded by St. Dominic (1170-1221), a well-educated Spaniard whose early career had been spent fighting the Albigensian heresy in southern France. There he decided that to combat the strength and zeal of its opponents, the Church should have champions who could preach the Gospel with apostolic fervor. Dominic's order of friar-preachers dedicated themselves to preaching as a means of maintaining the doctrines of the Church and of converting heretics.

The enthusiasm and sincerity of the friars in their early years made a profound impact upon an age which had grown increasingly critical of ecclesiastical worldliness. But after they took charge of the Inquisition, became professors in the universities, and served the papacy in other ways, the friars lost much of their original simplicity and freshness. Yet their message and zeal had done much to

The simple piety preached by St. Francis is reflected in this altarpiece, painted only nine years after his death, which shows the characteristically austere saint surrounded by six scenes from his life. The marks on St. Francis' hands and feet are stigmata—symbolic wounds representing his identification with Christ—which he received after a period of prayer and meditation.

provide the Church with moral and intellectual leadership at a time when such leadership was badly needed.

Veneration of saints and relics. Neither the Church's concern for theology nor its claims to universal authority appealed to ordinary men; they wanted solace on this earth and assurance of salvation in the next life. Such concerns enhanced the veneration of the Virgin Mary, one of the most potent forces in the medieval reformation. In an age when even the most educated persons believed that thunderstorms, plagues, and famines were the devil's work and that hell loomed perilously close, it seemed natural to pray to the Mother of Christ for protection and comfort. As an earthly mother supplicates for mercy on behalf of her erring child, so the Virgin Mary would supplicate her Son in heaven for her children on earth. Many magnificent Gothic cathedrals, such as Notre Dame (Our Lady) in Paris, were dedicated to Mary as symbols of the people's devotion.

Medieval people believed that relics of saints had miraculous powers. The bone of a saint, for example, supposedly would halt disease or create abundant harvests. The manner in which unscrupulous venders of fake relics sometimes duped Christians has been vividly recounted by Chaucer in his description of the Pardoner:

No pardoner could beat him in the race,
For in his wallet he had a pillow case
Which he represented as Our Lady's veil;
He said he had a piece of the very sail
St. Peter, when he fished in Galilee
Before Christ caught him, used upon the sea.
He had a latten cross embossed with stones
And in a glass he carried some pig's bones,
And with these holy relics, when he found
Some village parson grubbing his poor ground,
He would get more money in a single day
Than in two months would come the parson's way.
Thus with his flattery and his trumped-up stock
He made dupes of the parson and his flock.[12]

The crusades, and especially the sack of Constantinople in 1204, so flooded the West with relics that the Fourth Lateran Council prohibited, with little effect, the sale of relics and required papal approval of all new relics.

THE INTELLECTUAL SYNTHESIS

The medieval renaissance. "The meeting of Roman decrepitude and German immaturity was not felicitous."[13] This concise commentary on the character of early medieval civilization is especially relevant to the intellectual side of the period, and it remains a moot question among modern scholars whether the seventh century or the tenth was "the darkest of the Dark Ages." By the close of the sixth century even the most influential of early medieval popes, Gregory the Great, was contributing to the growing intellectual murkiness by voicing strong disapproval of secular literature, insisting that "the same mouth cannot sing the praises of Jupiter and praises of Christ." So feeble had the light of learning become by the end of the eighth century that Charlemagne found it necessary to order the monasteries to revive their schools and resume instruction in the rudiments of "singing, arithmetic, and grammar" (see p. 192).

In sharp contrast to the fate of his political achievements, Charlemagne's modest educational revival survived his death. At least partly as a result of this stimulus, western Europe by the late eleventh century was on the threshold of one of the most productive and energetic periods in the history of western thought—the medieval renaissance.

What was revived first of all during the medieval renaissance was intellectual curiosity, plainly evident from contemporary accounts, such as the following concerning an eleventh-century scholar from Liège:

Olbert was not able to satiate his thirst for study. When he would hear of some one distinguished in the arts he flew there at once, and the more he thirsted the more he absorbed something delightful from each master. At Paris he worked at Saint-Germain and studied the Holy Faith which glowed there. In Troyes he studied for three years, learning gratefully many things. . . . He felt obliged to listen to Fulbert of Chartres who was proclaimed in the liberal arts throughout France. Afterwards just like the bees among flowers, gorged with the nectar of learning, he returned to the hive and lived there studiously in a religious way, and religiously in a studious manner.[14]

Scholasticism. Living "religiously in a studious manner" aptly characterizes the scholars of the medieval renaissance and points up an essential difference between medieval thought on the one hand and early Greek philosophy and modern scientific thought on the other. With but few exceptions, medieval man did not think of truth as something to be discovered by himself; rather, he saw it as already existing in the authoritative Christian and pagan writings handed down from antiquity. Spurred on by a new zest for employing reason (called logic or dialectic), medieval scholars of the twelfth and thirteenth centuries succeeded in understanding and reexpressing those elements in the Christian and pagan heritage that seemed significant to them. Since this task was carried out largely in the schools, these scholars are known as schoolmen—or scholastics—and the intellectual synthesis they produced is called scholasticism.

Each scholar formed his own judgments and earnestly sought to convince others. This led to much debate, often uncritical but always exuberant, on a wide range of subjects. Most famous was the argument over universals known as the nominalist-realist controversy.

Nominalists and realists battled over the problem of universal Ideas, basing their arguments on indirect evidence, transmitted by Boethius and others, that Plato and Aristotle did not agree on the subject. Plato had argued that Ideas had reality apart from their existence in men's minds. A specific object was *real* only insofar as it represented the nature of its Idea (see p. 52). Thus Plato himself, for example, was real inasmuch as he partook of the Idea of Man. Aristotle, taking an opposite view, maintained that individuals existed as individuals—a human being was a real entity, not just a reflection of the universal Idea of Man. To the realists in the Middle Ages, only universal Ideas could be real and exist independently. To the nominalists, abstract concepts such as universal Ideas were only names (*nomina*) and had no real existence.

Both realism and nominalism—if carried to their logical extremes—resulted in conclusions equally abhorrent to the Church.

Realism became pantheism (the universe as a whole is God), and nominalism became materialism (the universe is composed solely of matter).

The contribution of Abélard. The extreme views of nominalists and realists, along with other examples of the sterile use of logic ("whether the pig is led to the market by the rope or by the driver"), outraged a brilliant young student named Pierre Abélard (1079-1142), later a popular teacher at the cathedral school of Notre Dame in Paris. Like many bright students in all ages, Abélard succeeded in antagonizing his teachers, both realist and nominalist. "I brought him great grief," he wrote of one, "because I undertook to refute certain of his opinions." Another teacher was mercilessly ridiculed:

He had a miraculous flow of words, but they were contemptible in meaning and quite void of reason. When he kindled a fire, he filled his house with smoke and illumined it not at all. He was a tree which seemed noble to those who gazed upon its leaves from afar, but to those who came nearer and examined it more closely was revealed its barrenness.[15]

Abélard's great contribution to medieval thought was freeing logic from barrenness and rerouting it to become again a means to an end rather than an end in itself. Conceptualism, his common-sense solution to the nominalist-realist controversy, held that universals, while existing only in the mind as thoughts or concepts, are nevertheless valid (real) since they are the product of observing the similar qualities that exist in a particular class of things. Thus, by observing many chairs and sitting in them, we arrive at the universal concept "chair."

In addition to redefining the purpose of scholastic thought, Abélard perfected the scholastic method. Like others before him, Abélard emphasized the importance of understanding, but whereas the former had begun with faith, Abélard started with doubt. We must learn to doubt, he insisted, for doubting leads us to inquire, and inquiry leads us to the truth. Abélard's intellectual skepticism was not that of modern experimental science, however; he never transcended superimposed authority. He aimed to arouse intellectual curiosity in his students and turn it into useful channels, bringing reason to bear on inherited truths in order to achieve understanding.

In an epoch-making work, *Sic et Non* (*Yes and No*), Abélard demonstrated his method. Listing 158 propositions on theology and ethics, he appended to each a number of statements pro and con taken from the authoritative writings of the Church. Abélard did not go on to reconcile these apparent contradictions, but he urged his students to do so by rational interpretation. Abélard's methodology was used by his successors to assimilate and reexpress the pagan as well as the Christian heritage of the past. The resulting scholarly compilations, which bear such apt titles as *concordantia* (concordance), *speculum* (mirror), and *summa* (sum total), constitute the crowning achievement of the medieval intellectual synthesis.

Abélard is remembered as a great lover as well as a great scholar—a rather uncommon combination. His ill-starred romance with his pupil, the learned and beautiful Héloïse, niece of the canon of Notre Dame, cut short his promising career as a teacher. The two lovers were married in secret, but Héloïse's uncle, falsely believing that Abélard planned to abandon Héloïse, hired thugs who attacked and emasculated the scholar. Both Abélard and Héloïse then sought refuge in the Church—Pierre as a monk and Héloïse as the abbess of a nunnery.

The new material and the task of reconciliation. In the twelfth century the study of Greek learning with its Muslim additions was undertaken by western scholars who flocked to Spain and Sicily and there translated Muslim editions of ancient writings. As a result of these translations a host of new ideas, particularly in science and philosophy, were introduced to western scholars. Western knowledge was expanded to include not only Arabic learning but also such important classical works as Euclid's *Geometry*, Ptolemy's *Almagest*, Hippocrates' and Galen's treatises in medicine, and all of Aristotle's extant writing except the *Poetics* and the *Rhetoric*.

As his works became known, Aristotle became, in Dante's words, "the master of those who know," and his authority was generally accepted as second only to that of the Scriptures. But because the Church's teachings were considered infallible, Aristotle's ideas, as well as those of other great thinkers of antiquity, had to be reconciled with religious dogma. Using Abélard's methodology, the scholastic thinkers of the thirteenth century succeeded in this task of reconciliation.

Scholasticism reached its zenith with St. Thomas Aquinas (1225?-1274). In his *Summa Theologica* this brilliant Italian Dominican dealt exhaustively with the great problems of theology, philosophy, politics, and economics. After collecting the arguments pro and con on a given problem—for example, "Whether it is lawful to sell a thing for more than its worth?"—he went on to draw conclusions. (His answer to the problem cited reflects the great influence of Christian ethics upon medieval economic thought: "I answer that, it is altogether sinful to have recourse to deceit in order to sell a thing for more than its just price, because this is to deceive one's neighbour so as to injure him." [16])

St. Thomas' major concern was to reconcile Aristotle and Church dogma—in other words, the truths of natural reason and the truths of faith. There can be no real contradiction, he argued, since all truth comes from God. In case of an unresolved contradiction, however, faith won out, because of the possibility of human error in reasoning. St. Thomas was so convincing in settling this conflict—the first clash between science and religion in the history of our western civilization—that his philosophy still has its followers today.

The decline of scholasticism. Having reached its zenith, scholasticism declined rapidly. The assumption that faith and reason were compatible was vigorously denied by two Franciscan thinkers, Duns Scotus (d. 1308) and William of Occam (d. c. 1349), who elaborated on Aquinas' belief that certain religious doctrines are beyond discovery by the use of reason. They argued that if the human intellect could not understand divinely revealed truth, it could hope to comprehend only the natural world and should not intrude upon the sphere of divine truth. Such a position tended to undermine the Thomistic synthesis of faith and reason. Realism and nominalism revived, the one promoting an increase in mystical, nonrational religion, the other contributing to the growing scientific spirit and to individualism and worldly concerns in general. For better or for worse, this trend toward the emancipation of human knowledge and action from the unifying authority of religion and the Church became a characteristic feature of western civilization.

After the thirteenth century scholasticism increasingly became a term of reproach, for its adherents were obsessed with theological subtleties, discouraged independent thought, and in general lost touch with reality. But it should be remembered that the scholastics sought to appropriate and make subjectively their own the store of Christian and pagan knowledge left to them by a more advanced civilization. In terms of their needs and objectives—an intelligible and all-embracing synthesis of faith, logic, and science—the scholastics were eminently successful, and people of our own age should not look askance at their accomplishments. Ironically, we today increasingly recognize the importance of reconciling science and faith in an age which has so much of the former and so little of the latter.

Medieval science. Because of the emphasis upon authority and the all-pervasive influence of the Church, the medieval atmosphere was not conducive to free scientific investigation. Those who studied science were churchmen, and their findings were supposed to illuminate rather than contradict the dogmas of the theologians. During the early Middle Ages scientific knowledge was limited to such compilations as the *Etymologies* of Isidore, bishop of Seville. Written in the seventh century, this naive and uncritical scrapbook of information remained a standard reference work in the West for three centuries. Isidore believed that the real nature of a thing was to be found in its name, and so he usually introduced each item with an often fanciful etymological explanation:

The liver [*iecur* in Latin] has its name because there is resident the fire [*ignis*] which flies up into the brain. . . . and by its heat it changes into blood the liquid that it has drawn from food, and this blood it supplies to the several members to feed and nourish them.[17]

The *Etymologies* has been called "the fruit of the much decayed tree of ancient learning."

When Greek and Arabic works were translated in the twelfth century, the West inherited a magnificent legacy of mathematical and scientific knowledge. Algebra, trigonometry, and Euclid's *Geometry* became available, and Arabic numerals and the symbol *zero* made possible the decimal system of computation. Leonard of Pisa (d. 1245), the greatest mathematician of the Middle Ages, made a great original contribution to mathematics when he worked out a method to extract square roots and to solve quadratic and cubic equations. On the other hand, Ptolemy's belief that the earth was the center of the universe—a fallacious theory destined to handicap astronomy for centuries—was commonly accepted.

Physics was based on Aristotle's theory of four elements (water, earth, air, and fire) and on his theories of dynamics—doctrines which took centuries to disprove. Some fourteenth-century nominalists were the first to challenge Aristotle's theory that a heavy object falls faster than a light one. Chemistry was based on Aristotelian concepts, mixed with magic and alchemy. Like the Muslim alchemist, his European counterpart tried in vain to transmute base metals into gold and silver and to obtain a magic elixir that would prolong life; in both cases the attempts did much to advance chemistry.

Frederick II and Roger Bacon. Two notable exceptions to the medieval rule of subservience to authority were the emperor Frederick II (see also p. 237) and the English Franciscan Roger Bacon. Frederick had a genuine scientific interest in animals and was famed for his large traveling menagerie, which included elephants, camels, panthers, lions, leopards, and a giraffe. He wrote a remarkable treatise, *The Art of Falconry*, which is still considered largely accurate in its observations of the life and habits of various kinds of hunting birds. "We discovered by hard-won experience," he wrote, "that the

In this picture from a fifteenth-century manuscript the university students oppose one another in "disputation," the class debates which went on for hours.

deductions of Aristotle, whom we followed when they appealed to our reason, were not entirely to be relied upon."[18] At his Sicilian court Frederick gathered about him many distinguished Greek, Muslim, and Latin scholars (including Leonard of Pisa), and he wrote to others in distant lands seeking their views on such problems as why objects appear bent when partly covered by water. He indulged in many experiments; one was a test to determine what language children would speak if raised in absolute silence. The experiment was a failure because all the children died.

Roger Bacon (1214-1292) also employed the inductive scientific method—he coined the term "experimental science"—and boldly criticized the deductive syllogistic reasoning used by scholastic thinkers. His *Opus Maius* contains this attack on scholasticism:

There are four principal stumbling blocks to comprehending truth, which hinder well-nigh every scholar: the example of frail and unworthy authority, long-established custom, the sense of the ignorant crowd, and the hiding of one's ignorance under the show of wisdom.[19]

Bacon never doubted the authority of the Bible or the Church—his interest lay only in natural science—yet his superiors considered him a dangerous thinker because of his criticism of scholastic thought.

Medieval medicine. By the thirteenth century learned Muslim commentaries on Galen and Hippocrates and on Aristotle's biology were available in the West. This knowledge, coupled with their own discoveries and improved techniques, made medieval doctors more than just barbers who engaged in bloodletting. Yet the overall state of medical knowledge and practice was, by our standards at least, still primitive. This can be seen in the prevalence of superstitious beliefs and the resort to magical practices, the general lack of concern for public sanitation, the periodic decimation of entire populations by epidemics such as the Black Death, and that significant indicator of the state of public health—the infant mortality rate, which was staggeringly high.

Origin of universities. Roman schools had a curriculum of seven liberal arts, separated into two divisions: a *trivium* consisting of grammar, rhetoric, and dialectic; and a *quadrivium* of arithmetic, music, geometry, and astronomy. When the Roman empire in the West fell, the task of education went to the Church; and the liberal arts were adapted to prepare youths for the ministry. Through the work of Cassiodorus in the sixth century (see p. 243), monasteries became important centers of learning. By 1100, however, monastic schools were overshadowed by the more dynamic cathedral schools established by bishops in such important centers as Paris, Chartres, Canterbury, and Toledo.

The renaissance of the twelfth century, with its revival of classical learning, its unprecedented number of students flocking to the schools, and its development of professional studies in law, medicine, and theology, led to the rise of organized centers of learning—the universities, which soon eclipsed the monastic and cathedral schools. Originally the word *university* meant a group of persons possessing a common purpose. In this case it referred to a guild of learners, both teachers and students, analogous to the craft guilds with their masters and apprentices. In the thirteenth century the universities had no campuses and little property or money, and the masters taught in hired rooms or religious houses. If the university was dissatisfied with its treatment by the townspeople, it could migrate elsewhere. The earliest universities—Bologna, Paris, and Oxford—were not officially founded or created, but in time the popes and kings granted them and other universities charters of self-government. The charters gave legal status to the universities and rights to the students, such as freedom from the jurisdiction of town officials.

Two systems: Bologna and Paris. Two of the most famous medieval universities were at Bologna in northern Italy and at Paris. The former owed its growth to the fame of Irnerius (d. 1130), who taught civil law. Because of his influence, Bologna acquired a reputation as the leading center for the study of law. The students soon organized a guild for protection against the rapacious townspeople, who were demanding exorbitant sums for food and lodging. Because the guild went on to control the professors, Bologna became a student paradise. In the earliest statutes we read that a professor requiring leave of absence even for one day first had to obtain permission from his own students. He had to begin his lecture with the bell and end within one minute of the next bell. The material in the text had to be covered systematically, with all difficult passages fully explained. The powerful position of the students at Bologna developed as a result of the predominance of older students studying for the doctorate in law.

At the university in Paris conditions developed differently. This university, which had grown out of the cathedral school of Notre Dame, specialized in liberal arts and theology and became the most influential intellectual center in medieval Europe. Its administration was far different from Bologna's. The chancellor of Notre Dame, the bishop's officer who exercised authority over the cathedral school, refused to allow the students or the masters to obtain control of the burgeoning university. Charters issued by the French king in 1200 and by the pope in 1231 freed the university from the bishop's authority by making it an autonomous body controlled by the masters.

The collegiate system. Universities owned no dormitories, and students lived in rented rooms or pooled their resources to obtain housing on a cooperative basis. With masters' fees and living expenses to pay, the impoverished student labored under decided handicaps. A philanthropic patron, however, sometimes provided quarters where poor scholars could board free of charge. One such patron was Robert de Sorbon, the royal chaplain to the saintly Louis IX. About 1257 Robert endowed a hall for sixteen needy students working for their doctorates in theology, thus founding the College de Sorbonne; the University of Paris is still popularly known by the name of its great benefactor.

As more colleges were established, the large universities became collections of colleges in which the students lived and studied. Although organization by colleges finally disappeared in the University of Paris where the system originated, at both Oxford and Cambridge the collegiate system has remained an integral part of the university to this day.

Curriculum and degrees. The degrees available at medieval universities were similar to those offered today. The bachelor's degree, which could be obtained after studying from three to five years, was not considered very important. For a master of arts degree, which admitted the holder into the guild of masters and was a license to teach, particular emphasis was placed on the works of Aristotle. In theology, law, and medicine the master's degree was commonly called a doctorate. It was no easy matter to get a master's degree (or doctorate) from a medieval university; many years of preparation were required, and at the final examination the candidate had to defend his thesis publicly for hours against the learned attacks of the masters. If successful in his defense, the candidate then stood the cost of a banquet for his examiners.

Latin literature. During the entire Middle Ages Latin served as an international means of communication. This common tongue provided much of the cohesion of the Middle Ages, for virtually all the crucial communications of the Church, governments, and schools were in Latin. Undoubtedly the most splendid medieval Latin is found in the Church liturgy, which was chanted by the priest.

Any misconception that the Middle Ages were simply "other-worldly" and long-faced will be rudely shattered by glancing at the Latin poetry written during the twelfth and thirteenth centuries by students. Known as Goliardic verse because its authors claimed to be disciples of Goliath, their synonym for the devil, it unhesitatingly proclaimed the pleasures of wine, women, and song:

'Tis most arduous to make
    Nature's self-surrender;
Seeing girls, to blush and be
    Purity's defender!
We young men our longings ne'er
    Shall to stern law render,
Or preserve our fancies from
    Bodies smooth and tender. . . .

In the public house to die
    Is my resolution;
Let wine to my lips be nigh
    At life's dissolution:
That will make the angels cry,
    With glad elocution,
"Grant this toper, God on high,
    Grace and absolution!"[20]

The Goliardic poets were brilliant at parodying and satirizing the ideals of their elders. They substituted Venus for the Virgin, wrote masses for drunkards, and were guilty of other blasphemies. Yet many of these poets later became respected officials in the Church.

In contrast, the great Latin hymns such as the *Dies Irae* and the *Stabat Mater Dolorosa* show the genuineness of the religious spirit of the twelfth and thirteenth centuries. The latter hymn movingly describes the Virgin Mary standing beside the cross:

By the cross, sad vigil keeping,
Stood the mournful mother weeping,
While on it the saviour hung;
In that hour of deep distress
Pierced the sword of bitterness
Through her heart with sorrow wrung.[21]

Vernacular literature. A rising tide of literature in the vernacular tongues began to appear by the twelfth century, with the epic as the earliest form. The greatest of the French epics, or *chansons de geste* ("songs of great deeds"), is the late eleventh-century *Song of Roland*, which recounts the heroic deeds and death of Count Roland in the Pyrenees while defending the rear of Charlemagne's army (see p. 191). The great Spanish epic, the *Poema del Mio Cid* (see quoted selection, p. 232), is a product of the twelfth century. These stirring epic poems, with their accounts of prowess in battle, mirror the masculine warrior virtues of early chivalry (see p. 202).

By the twelfth century in the feudal courts of southern France, poets called troubadours were composing short, personal lyrics dealing mainly with romantic love. "The delicacy and romanticism of the troubadour lyrics betoken a more genteel and sophisticated nobility than that of the feudal north—a nobility that preferred songs of love to songs of war. Indeed, medieval southern France was the source of the entire romantic-love tradition of Western Civilization, with its idealization of women, its emphasis on male gallantry and courtesy, and its insistence on embroidering the sex drive with an elaborate ritual of palpitating hearts, moonlight, and sentimental ties."[22] Typical are these lines written in adoration of the lovely Eleanor of Aquitaine:

When the sweet breeze
Blows hither from your dwelling
Methinks I feel
A breath of paradise.[23]

Nothing comparable to these lines exists in the *chansons de geste*, but during the last half of the twelfth century this new interest in love fused with the purely heroic material of the early epics. The result was the medieval romance, an account of love and adventure, to which was often added a strong coloring of religious feeling. Examples are Chrétien de Troyes' *Perceval* (see p. 202) and the tales concerning King Arthur and his Round Table of chivalrous knights who variously pursue adventure, charming ladies, and the Holy Grail. In Germany about the beginning of the thirteenth century, the old saga material dealing with Siegfried, Brunhild, and the wars against the Huns was recast into the *Nibelungenlied* (*Song of the Nibelungs*).

All the foregoing literary types were written for the aristocracy. The self-made burgher preferred more practical and shrewd tales. His taste was gratified by the bawdy *fabliaux*, brief, humorous tales written in rhymed verse; and the animal stories about Reynard the Fox, the symbol of the sly bourgeois lawyer who easily outwits King Lion and his noble vassals. In England during the fourteenth century the Robin Hood ballads celebrated robbing the rich to give to the poor and *Piers the Plowman* condemned the injustices of a social system that had brought on the peasant revolt in England (see p. 217 and quoted selection, p. 201).

Dante Alighieri. The vernacular was also used by two of the greatest writers of the period—Dante and Chaucer. Combining a profound religious sense with a knowledge of scholastic thought and the Latin classics, the Italian Dante (1265-1321) produced one of the world's greatest narrative poems. The *Divine Comedy*, which Dante said described his "full experience," is an allegory of medieval man (Dante) moving from bestial earthiness (hell) through conversion (purgatory) to the sublime spirituality of union with God (paradise). Dante describes how

Midway this way of life we're bound upon,
  I woke to find myself in a dark wood,
  Where the right road was wholly lost and gone.[24]

Dante then accepts the offer of Virgil, symbol of pagan learning, to be his "master, leader, and lord" to guide him through hell and purgatory. But it is Beatrice, the lady whom he had once loved from afar and who is now the symbol of divine love, who guides him through paradise. At last Dante stands before God, and words fail him as he finds peace in the presence of the highest form of love:

Oh, how fall short the words! . . .
The Love that moves the sun and every star.[25]

The wit of Chaucer. In the *Canterbury Tales*, Geoffrey Chaucer (1340?-1400), one of the greatest figures in medieval literature, reveals a cross section of contemporary English life, customs, and thought (see quoted selections, pp. 247, 250). The twenty-nine pilgrims who assembled in April 1387 at an inn before journeying to the shrine of St. Thomas à Becket at Canterbury were a motley group. The "truly perfect, gentle knight," just returned from warring against the "heathen in Turkey," was accompanied by his son, a young squire who loved so much by night that "he slept no more than does a nightingale." The clergy was represented by the coy prioress who "would weep if she but saw a mouse caught in a trap,"[26] the rotund

This fresco by Domenico di Michelino, an Italian painter of the Florentine school, has as its subject the early Renaissance poet and humanist, Dante Alighieri. The fresco is a method of painting which uses pigments mixed in water and applied to freshly laid wet plaster so that the colors become incorporated. Here Domenico has depicted the Cathedral of Florence, in which the fresco is located. Also shown are scenes from Dante's *Divine Comedy*, the allegory in which medieval man moves from hell (left detail), through purgatory, to heaven and union with God (center detail).

monk who loved to eat fat swan and ride good horses, the friar who knew the best taverns and all the barmaids in town, and the poor parish priest who was a credit to his faith. Also included in the group were the merchant who could talk only of business, the threadbare Oxford student, the miller with a wart on his nose, and the worthy wife of Bath, who had married five times and was now visiting Christian shrines in search of a sixth husband.

Chaucer's fame rests securely upon his keen interest in human nature and his skill as a storyteller. The Midland dialect he used was the linguistic base for the language of future English literature, just as Dante's use of the Tuscan dialect fixed the Italian tongue.

Rebirth of drama. Like Greek drama, medieval drama developed out of religious ceremonies; it was used by churchmen to instruct the faithful. The earliest forms were the mystery plays, which naively but forcefully dramatized Biblical stories, and the miracle plays, which described the miraculous intervention of saints in human affairs. At first the plays supplemented the regular service and were performed inside the church proper. As their popularity grew, they were presented either on the church steps or on a separate stage. By the fourteenth century another type, the morality play, had become popular. The actors personified virtues and vices, and the plot of the drama usually centered on a conflict between them. *Everyman*, an excellent example of a morality play, is still occasionally produced.

THE ESTHETIC SYNTHESIS

Artistic correlation. The *Summa Theologica* of St. Thomas Aquinas and the *Divine Comedy* of Dante represent the best intellectual expressions of the medieval spirit. Similarly, the Gothic cathedral is the ultimate artistic expression of the age. Each of these masterpieces represents a different aspect of the attempt to organize everything into an overall pattern that would glorify God.

The order and form of scholastic thought find their counterparts in the structure and style of the Gothic edifices. A scholastic treatise was systematically arranged in logical parts; the cathedral was similarly articulated in space. The main sections, the nave, transept, and apse, were individually distinctive yet integrated into a coherent structure.

Early Christian churches. Early Christian churches imitated the plan of the Roman basilicas. In this design a rectangle is divided into three aisles: a central aisle, or nave, ending in a semicircular apse, and a lower-ceilinged aisle on each side. Parallel rows of columns separated the nave from the side aisles. The roof over the nave was raised to provide a clerestory—a section pierced by windows to illuminate the interior (see illustration, p. 127). In the fourth century the basilica plan was modified by the addition of a transept across the aisles between the apse and the nave. This essentially "T" shape added Christian symbolism to the basic plan of the pagan-style building. Graceful belltowers were erected separate from the church building; the "leaning tower" of Pisa is a famous later example.

Romanesque architecture. In the eleventh century occurred a tremendous architectural revival, marked by the recovery of the art of building in stone rather than in wood, as was common during the early Middle Ages. At a much later date the name *Romanesque* came to be applied to this new style, because, like early Christian architecture, it was based largely on Roman models. Although details of structure and ornamentation differed with locality, the round arch was a standard Romanesque feature (see Color Plate 9). Both barrel and cross vaults were used, particularly in northern Europe, where the need to build fireproof churches made it impractical to follow the common Italian practice of using flat wooden roofs. While there was often one long barrel vault over the nave, the aisles were divided into square areas or bays with a cross vault over each bay. Thick outside walls and huge interior piers were necessary to support the heavy stone barrel and cross vaults. (In time diagonal ribs were built along the groins of the cross vault, transforming it into the ribbed-groin vault; see diagram.) Because the walls would be weakened by large window apertures, the clerestory windows were small or nonexistent. Thus the northern Romanesque interior was dark and gloomy, the exterior massive and monumental.

Gothic architecture. Actually, no clear-cut cleavage exists between Romanesque and Gothic. There was a gradual evolutionary process, which reached its culmination in the thirteenth and fourteenth centuries. The architects of the Gothic-style cathedral developed ribbed-groin vaults with pointed rather than round arches. This enabled them to solve the technical problem of cross-vaulting the nave, which, being wider than the aisles, could not easily be divided into square bays covered by Romanesque cross vaults (see diagram of floor plan, p. 261). Thus light ribbed-groin vaults, whose sides were of different length to fit the rectangular bays of the nave, replaced the heavy barrel vault, and the roof of the nave could be raised to permit the use of large clerestory windows. The thrust of the vaults over both the nave and the aisles was concentrated on a few strong structural supports. Part of the weight was carried down to the ground by columns within the building, and part by flying buttresses at points along the walls. With such vaulting and buttresses, the weight of the roof was largely shifted off the walls (see diagram of cross section, p. 261). Large stained-glass windows were set into the walls between the buttresses. The dark, somber interior of the Romanesque churches gave way to the jeweled light of the Gothic interiors.

Sculpture and stained glass. Most Romanesque and Gothic sculpture served an archi-

At the bottom of this detail of the "Last Judgment" scene at Autun Cathedral the dead rise from their graves in fear; at the top their souls are weighed in the balance. While the saved cling to the angels, the damned are seized by grinning devils and thrown into hell.

The ribbed-groin vault developed by Romanesque architects derived from the Roman intersecting vaults. The ribbed vault is made up of arches which span the sides of a square bay, with groin arches crossing diagonally from corner to corner.

tectural function by being carved to fit into the total composition of a church. To use sculpture to the best architectural advantage, the subject was often distorted to achieve a particular effect. Yet many thirteenth-century Gothic statues are masterpieces both in their fully developed craftsmanship and the grace and nobility of their content (see photos, pp. 261, 224). The relationship of the earlier Romanesque sculpture (see photo above) to the later Gothic reduplicates in large part that of archaic and classical sculpture in ancient Greece (see pp. 56-57).

Like sculpture, medieval painting in the form of stained-glass windows was an integral part of architecture. Composed of small pieces of colored glass held together in a

The Gothic age was the culmination of the Middle Ages, and the cathedral was the concrete synthesis of Gothic ideals. With his knowledge of weights and thrusts, the Gothic architect was able to raise his building to unprecedented heights and open it dramatically to light. The result, as evident in the cathedral at Cologne, is one of the most compelling unities of form and feeling in all of architecture.

pattern by metal strips which both braced the glass and emphasized the design, stained glass was an art whose excellence has not been duplicated in modern times. By adding various minerals to molten glass, thirteenth-century craftsmen achieved brilliant hues. Details such as hair were painted on the glass. The object, however, was not realism but the evoking of a mood—to shine with the radiance of heaven itself.

Secular architecture. What the cathedral was to religious life, the castle was to every-day living. Both were havens, and both were built to endure. The new weapons and techniques of siege warfare, which the crusaders brought back with them, necessitated more

massive castles. By the thirteenth century castle building in Europe reached a high point of development. The towers were rounded, and bastions stood at strategic points along the walls. The castle as a whole was planned in such a skillful manner that if one section was taken by attackers, it could be sealed off from the remaining fortifications. Whole towns were fortified in the same way, with walls, watchtowers, moats, and drawbridges.

Toward the end of the Middle Ages there was less need for fortified towns and castles. At the same time the wealth accruing from the revived trade and increased industry encouraged the development of secular Gothic architecture. Town and guild halls, the residences of the rich, and the chateaux of the nobles all borrowed the delicate Gothic style from the cathedrals.

SUMMARY

The traditional division of history into "ancient," "medieval," and "modern" is fundamentally arbitrary and artificial in that history is a continuous process. Applying the same common denominator—"medieval" —to the thousand turbulent years between the fifth and fifteenth centuries obscures the wide variations that existed during the period. For five centuries after the fall of Rome, Europe experienced a long period of decline sometimes called the "dark ages." But between 1050 and 1300 the West began a rapid recovery. In the words of a contemporary poet, "This long dead land now flames with life again." This renewed life in religion and culture has been the subject of this chapter. (Economic, social, and political recovery were described in earlier chapters.)

Emerging out of feudal decentralization ahead of the state, the Church developed the first unified system of law and administration in medieval Europe and intimately affected the life of every person. It gave man a sense of security against the dangers on earth and those beyond. To perform its historical mission, the Church required a hierarchy of clergy and an elaborate doctrine,

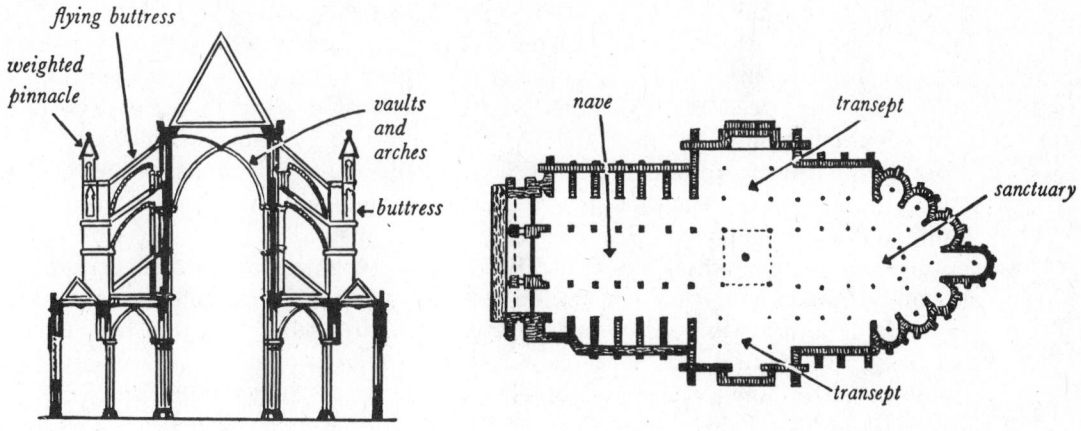

The fusing of sculpture and architecture is apparent in this detail of one of the doorways of Amiens Cathedral. Medieval cathedrals were rich in sculptures of saints and great men of antiquity, episodes from history and the Old and New Testaments, and allegorical representations of science, philosophy, and theology. The unified effect of the fully developed Gothic style is one of awesome, but ordered, intricacy, as the photograph of the entire front of Amiens Cathedral demonstrates. Above is a drawing of the cross section and floor plan of the same cathedral. Vaults, arches, buttresses, and weighted pinnacles were important structural elements in the Gothic style of architecture.

accompanied by methods for enforcing its will. We have followed the areas of reform, watched the Church's power reach its apex in the age of Innocent III, and noted signs of its eventual decline.

Within the Church, thinkers wrestled with philosophical issues, such as the realist-nominalist controversy. In the thirteenth century such famous scholastics as St. Thomas Aquinas made herculean attempts to reconcile faith and reason, Church authority and classical thought.

Stimulated by the acquisition of Greek and Arabic knowledge, education established new frontiers. The earliest universities grew from unorganized groups of scholars and students to important centers of learning. Bologna and Paris, in particular, directly affected other universities. In literature, Latin, the international language of the educated, slowly gave way to the vernacular tongues. Chaucer and Dante, giants in the literary field, both wrote in their native languages and did much to develop modern English and Italian respectively.

Evolving from Romanesque patterns, the splendid Gothic cathedrals were the greatest artistic achievement of the medieval period. The rounded arches and massive walls of Romanesque architecture were replaced by pointed arches, ribbed-groin vaults, and the flying buttresses of the soaring Gothic cathedrals. This style carried over from churches to castles, town halls, and urban dwellings.

SUGGESTIONS FOR READING

R. W. Southern, **The Making of the Middle Ages*** (Yale) is a brilliant topical treatment of the eleventh and twelfth centuries. F. Heer, **The Medieval World*** (Mentor) vividly pictures the society of the twelfth and thirteenth centuries.

M. W. Baldwin, **The Mediaeval Church*** (Cornell) is a perceptive essay on Church development. See also Jeffrey Russell, **A History of Medieval Christianity: Prophecy and Order*** (AHM); and M. Deanesly, **A History of the Medieval Church, 590-1500,*** 9th ed. (Barnes and Noble, 1969).

G. Barraclough, **The Medieval Papacy*** (Harcourt Brace Jovanovich) is brief and lavishly illustrated. S. R. Packard, **Europe and the Church Under Innocent III** (Russell, 1968) is short and admirable. For greater detail see W. Ullmann, **A Short History of the Papacy in the Middle Ages*** (Harper & Row, 1974); and R. W. Southern, **Western Society and the Church in the Middle Ages*** (Penguin). On Church-state political theory see K. Morrison, **Tradition and Authority in the Western Church, 300-1140** (Princeton, 1969).

D. Knowles, **The Monastic Order in England,** 2nd ed. (Cambridge) is considered to be the best introduction to medieval monasticism. See also H. Workman, **The Evolution of the Monastic Ideal*** (Beacon); and E. Duckett, **The Wandering Saints of the Early Middle Ages*** (Norton).

A. Turberville, **Medieval Heresy and the Inquisition** (Shoe String) is a standard account. Religious radicalism, particularly that inspired by the love ethic, is treated in N. Cohn, **The Pursuit of the Millennium*** (Galaxy).

C. H. Haskins, **The Renaissance of the Twelfth Century*** (Harvard) is the basic study of the medieval intellectual revival. C. Brooke, **The Twelfth Century Renaissance*** (Harcourt Brace Jovanovich) surveys all aspects of culture and is well illustrated. See also P. Wolff, **The Pelican History of European Thought,** Vol. I, **The Awakening of Europe*** (Penguin); and Colin Morris, **The Discovery of the Individual, 1050-1200*** (Torchbooks). D. Knowles, **The Evolution of Medieval Thought*** (Vintage) is an excellent introduction. Recommended for greater detail are W. Ullmann, **Medieval Political Thought*** (Penguin, 1976); and C. McIlwain, **The Growth of Political Thought in the West** (Cooper Square). See also J. Sikes, **Peter Abailard** (Russell, 1965); F. Copleston, **Aquinas*** (Penguin); and John H. Smith, **St. Francis of Assisi*** (Scribner's, 1974), a perceptive essay.

C. H. Haskins, **The Rise of Universities** (Gordon) is a brief survey. See also G. Leff, **Paris and Oxford Universities in the Thirteenth and Fourteenth Centuries** (Krieger, 1975).

William T. Jackson, **The Literature of the Middle Ages** (Columbia Univ.) and **Medieval Literature: A History and a Guide** (Collier) are recommended surveys. Outstanding also are Brian Stock, ed., **Mediaeval Latin Lyrics*** (Godine); C. S. Lewis, **The Allegory of Love*** (Galaxy); and E. Curtius, **European Literature and the Latin Middle Ages*** (Princeton).

Excellent on Romanesque and Gothic art are C. Morey, **Christian Art*** (Norton); O. von Simson, **The Gothic Cathedral*** ((Princeton); and A. Temko, **Notre-Dame of Paris*** (Viking). Stimulating interpretations of the interrelationship of medieval art, thought, and spirit are Henry Adams, **Mont-Saint-Michel and Chartres*** (Anchor); E. Mâle, **The Gothic Image*** (Torchbooks); and E. Panofsky, **Gothic Architecture and Scholasticism*** (Meridian).

*Indicates a less expensive paperbound edition.

This is the profile of members of a scholar-official's extended family. They live in Hsing-tsai (Quinsai in Marco Polo's account), the capital of the Southern Sung dynasty, which the Venetian traveler described as "the most noble city and the best that is in the world." The time is 1271, five years before its capture by the Mongols.

Hill beyond green hill, pavilion behind pavilion—at the
West Lake, will the singing and the dancing never cease?
It's the warm wind that lulls them and beguiles them
   into thinking
That *this* place is the other one we knew in times of peace.

Perhaps the sunset on the lake on this festival day has caused Wang Ch'eng-ta to recite Lin Sheng's lines from the previous century—or is it the presence on the barge of his cousin the general, who has come south from the frontier that separates civilization from the barbarians' occupation of the Wangs' traditional homeland? The general is always worried—that's his job—nevertheless Wang Ch'eng-ta has sufficiently overcome the long-held antipathy of scholars towards the military to convey to fellow administrators his cousin's concerns about the mounting Mongol buildup. However, they reply that enough money has been spent on coastal forces, the defense of the Yangtze towns, and equipping both the navy and army with new catapults for hurling molten metal and explosive bombs. Meanwhile, the general is being good-naturedly accused of undue pessimism by his other cousin, the merchant, who feels that today's festival calls for celebration. Certainly his own business affairs have never gone so well. He had originally made his fortune in the river trade, and had his home at the mouth of the Yangtze; then had expanded into overseas commerce. Now he has a fleet of compass-equipped junks—two of which can carry 500 people and several dozen tons of goods—which sail regularly to Japan and make occasional voyages as far south as Malaya and Java. Silks, brocades, and porcelain fetch a good price in Japan, while spices, rare woods, and ivory are much sought-after imports from the lower latitudes. Now, at his wife's insistence, he has moved to the capital and built a handsome house on Phoenix Hill, to the west of the Imperial Palace.

Wang Ch'eng-ta agrees: it has been a splendid day, one that fully justifies his renting of the *Seven Jewels*, built to hold 20 persons below a flat roof on which the crew stand and pole the boat slowly along the Western Lake. For much of the day, however, the *Seven Jewels* has been anchored near Thunder Point, a small promontory at the southern end of the lake from which rises an octagonal pagoda, about 170 feet high, built of blue brick in

975. At the stern of the boat, the three youngest males are being given a fishing lesson by their maternal grandfather, while at the prow are Wang Ch'eng-ta's son and daughter together with the merchant's son, waving at friends in neighboring craft—and with the young men also making indecorous calls to the pretty singing-girls being ferried in small boats to other barges. Meanwhile, at one of the cabin tables, WangTse-t'ien, his wife, is serving tea to her husband's mother and the wife of the merchant, with a servant bringing in a fresh supply of hot water and dishes with sweet cakes. They have serious matters to discuss: the forthcoming marriage that will further cement the ties between the official and merchant sides of the family.

Today, the Wangs have been celebrating the Festival of the Dead. Officials, merchants, and the general populace have gathered round Western Lake and on the surrounding hills. The Wangs arrived early at the family graves to sweep them, burn sticks of incense, and place offerings of food, for it is proper to honor one's ancestors who have provided the family and each of its members with both an identity and destiny. Moreover, the Wangs are proud that their illustrious forebears include the famous statesman, Wang An-shih (see p. 176), and Wang Ch'eng-ta has sought to instill in his son, Wang Kuo-chung, the ambition to serve his emperor as still another memorable scholar-official.

But Wang Ch'eng-ta has all but given up that hope. With the growth of population in the Sung dominions, now over sixty million, and of public education, the competition for higher office has become fierce. Of course the Wangs enjoy important advantages. Since Wang An-shih's service two centuries ago, there has always been a member of the family in the upper rungs of the imperial administration stationed in the capital. Gazing at the Thunder Point pagoda, Wang Ch'eng-ta realizes that his own upbringing had seldom been out of sight of that landmark. As a child, he had been particularly close to all his grandparents and happy with his tutor. Then, he had attended at Phoenix Hill the special school for the children of the upper classes where he had learned his twenty characters a day—which never gave him the trouble that his son, with his lack of concentration, always had. At college, instruction had been aimed at forming candidates suitable for the official examinations. Wang Ch'eng-ta remembers the trial of stamina involved in sitting for each successively harder examination, and his family's pride when he passed near the top in the final doctorate of letters examination held at the Imperial Palace. Promotion had been rapid—instead of being sent as a subprefect to some distant province, he was assigned a comparatively high administrative post in the imperial secretariat. He had once seen his own dossier; his superiors had commented favorably on his capacity for work, judgment, and conduct; he had given proof of filial piety and integrity. Wang Ch'eng-ta has a secure career; he has every chance for further promotion, though it is too much to expect an appointment to the emperor's council during the next decade before he retires around age 66. Still . . .

No such chain of thought enters his son's mind as he watches the conclusion of the jousts among the dragon-boats. Wang Kuo-chung envies the strength and agility of the athletes, but of course it is a sport for the common people. He has been missing classes and frequenting one of the capital's pleasure grounds. These are places "where no one stands on ceremony," acrobats and jugglers perform, singing, dancing, and the dramatic arts are taught, and they are staffed with women musicians and singing-girls. (Little wonder that a contemporary author writes that these establishments "have become places of debauch and perdition for society people and young men of good social standing.") Wang Kuo-chung has been making contingency plans against his expected failure in the examinations. It is not unusual for well-to-do families to buy a business in one of the luxury trades for sons who have failed as scholars. Wang Kuo-chung hasn't dared raise the matter with his father, but has already discussed it with his mother.

For her part, Wang Tse-t'ien has been busy these past few days. As the daughter of a scholar-official, and the wife of another, she shares her class's disdain for people born in trade—including her husband's merchant cousin and his wife. But they are useful. She wants the merchant to suggest the best type of business for her son, to use his influence in obtaining it, and to provide much of the capital for its purchase. In return Wang Tse-t'ien will use her husband's influence to buy a petty title of nobility that should gratify the merchant and his greedy wife—and which would pass in time to the merchant's son and her own daughter, soon to be married.

Some years earlier, at the time of the Festival of the Dead, Wang Ch'ing-chao's coming of age at fifteen had been celebrated by the placing of hairpins in her hair. This was an important milestone in her early life which had been spent in the family household where she had learned to spin and embroider. She had also been taught to read and write—and had even written some inconsequential poetry—but the attainment of literary skills served no practical purpose in her case. Wang Ch'ing-chao has always known that her primary function is to marry and have children, and thus perpetuate the family—and that marriages serve as alliances between families. Actually, she quite likes her fiancé, while he is captivated by the extent to which she exemplifies the Sung ideal of feminine beauty: she is slender, petite, and dainty. In addition to the political advantages which the marriage will bring, her future parents-in-law feel that she has her fair share of the feminine virtues most admired: modesty, chastity, conjugal fidelity, and filial piety towards themselves as her husband's parents. After marriage, Wang Ch'ing-chao will continue to lead a life of luxury and leisure. She will seldom appear in public, and will usually stay confined to her own apartment. But she will exert authority in a large household—and her mother has already discerned in her daughter elements of her own shrewdness, business acumen, and ambition.

The sun has long set, so that the clouds are no longer reflected on the lake. The *Seven Jewels* lies moored near Thunder Point and the Wangs are ashore among the jostling crowd. The young men have set out for the pleasure ground near one of the bridges over which the Imperial Way runs; the boys and their grandfather are going home on foot; the ladies are returning in curtained carry-chairs; and the senior Wangs are on horseback astride their splendid saddles. The general and the merchant have gone ahead, while Wang Ch'eng-ta stops by the pagoda, outlined against the new moon. All this beauty . . . this harmony of water and human skills . . . this legacy of centuries of cultivated living . . . He wonders if the general is right—will the barbarians pierce the northern defenses? And if so, will all be over? Or will the dragon in some cunning way devour its captor? Surely whatever fortune has in store, other springs will appear . . . the great cycle will never cease to turn, maintaining order and balance between Heaven and Earth, between *yang* and *yin*, between the Universe and the Sons of Han.

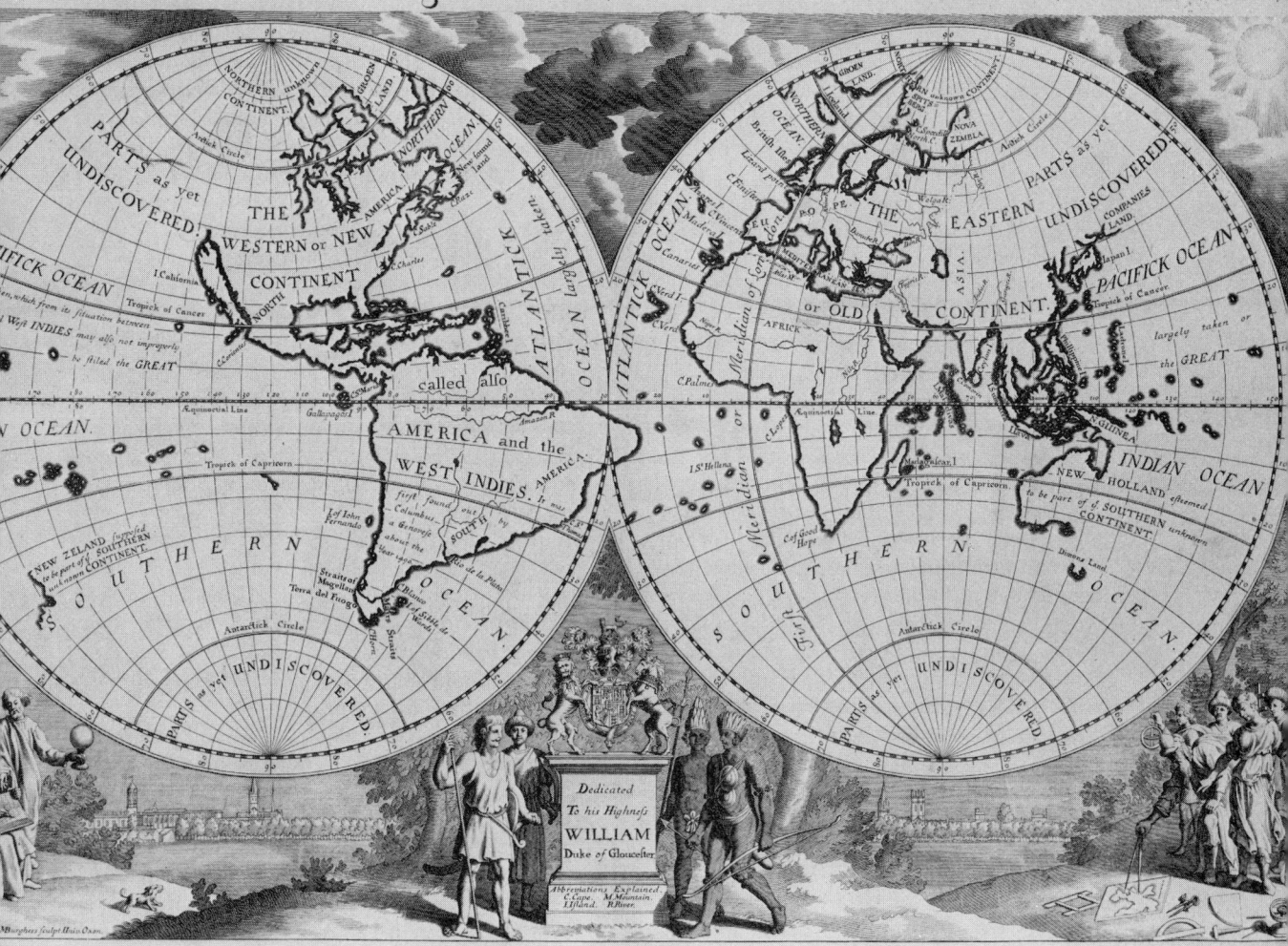

PART THREE
The Transition to Modern Times

■ So far in our study of history, we have encountered a number of societies which emphasized the group at the expense of the individual—societies such as that of ancient Egypt, for example, or of medieval Europe. In other societies, such as that of classical Greece, individualism counted for more than collectivism. During the period which historians speak of as early modern times, the interests and rights of the individual were again in the ascendant. In the political sphere, this emphasis upon individualism was manifested by the creation of nation-states; in the realm of thought and art, it produced the Renaissance; in the area of religion, it split Christendom through the Reformation; and in the field of exploration, it resulted in the discovery and colonization of the Americas and the reopening of the East to western trade.

By the end of the fifteenth century the medieval ideal of universal political unity had been shattered as national monarchies gained supremacy in England, France, and Spain. Despite opposition from popes and nobles alike, vigorous monarchs in these countries succeeded in their attempts at nation-making—a process that fostered and was in turn supported by a growing national consciousness among the common people. In Germany and Italy, however, unification was hampered by many obstacles, and in eastern Europe nation-making proceeded slowly, though Russia emerged as a powerful state after throwing off the Mongol yoke.

In the realm of thought, Italian scholars known as humanists discovered in the manuscripts of ancient Greece and Rome the same emphasis on individual freedom which was rapidly gaining momentum in their own day, and with this spirit of individualism sprang up an unashamed delight in the beauties and joys of life. Heeding Protagoras' ancient maxim that "Man is the measure of all things" and revolting against medieval authority and asceticism, Renaissance man was impelled by a new spirit of independence, a new hunger for experience. The creative vigor of the Italian Renaissance in literature, thought, and the fine arts surged throughout Europe, resulting in one of the most fruitful epochs in the cultural history of mankind.

Carried into the religious sphere, the resurgence of individualism shattered the universal supremacy of the Church and gave rise to the religious diversity of the modern western world. The followers of Luther, Calvin, and Zwingli substituted the authority of the Scriptures for that of the Roman Church and interposed no priestly mediator between the individual and his God. The Roman Church, which launched a vigorous reform movement of its own, nevertheless continued to be a potent force.

Finally, the economic structure of western Europe was transformed radically in early modern times. The quickening of town life abetted the rise of a new and forceful middle class, whose members were the chief supporters and benefactors of the system of economic individualism known as capitalism. Furthermore, overseas expansion stimulated trade, increased wealth, and introduced to European markets an abundance of products previously scarce or unknown. So important was the new trade and its many influences on European life and manners that it is referred to as the Commercial Revolution. The barter economy of the Middle Ages was superseded by one of money, banks, and stock exchanges; and Europe rapidly became the economic center of the world.

Up to the fifteenth century, Asia had been equal or superior to Europe in military power and cultural attainments. But as the West advanced, China and India declined in power and creativity. The European scramble for empire had serious consequences. In Asia, important trading concessions were wrung from the natives; in the New World, indigenous peoples were decimated and their cultures all but erased; in tropical Africa, the Europeans established a lucrative slave trade and reaped rich profits from this callous exploitation of human lives. From the mid-point of the seventeenth century to our own day, European civilization—the most creative, expansive, and aggressive on earth—was to be the dominant and pervasive influence in world history.

CHAPTER 12

Religion and Politics: 1300-1500

Europe in Transition

INTRODUCTION. In Europe the fourteenth and fifteenth centuries were marked by a decline of those institutions and ideas which we think of as typically "medieval" and which had reached their high point during the preceding two centuries. In thought and art an empty formalism replaced the creative forces which had given the Middle Ages such unique methods of expression as scholasticism and the Gothic style. Economic and social progress gave way to depression and social strife, with peasant revolts a characteristic symptom of instability.

The universal Church experienced a disintegration similar to that which had already fatally weakened its great medieval rival, the Holy Roman Empire. The Church's prestige was gravely weakened from within by the reformers and heretics, while external factors, chiefly political and economic, undermined its power and authority. By the sixteenth century these forces would be strong enough to bring about the Protestant and Catholic reformations.

Despite crises and setbacks—the Hundred Years' War came close to wiping out the gains made earlier by French and English monarchs—the process of nation-making continued during the fourteenth and fifteenth centuries. In western Europe the contrasting political trends clearly evident at the end of the thirteenth century—unification in England, France, and Spain, and fragmentation in Germany and Italy—reached their culmination. And in Slavic eastern Europe significant progress in nation-making was made in Russia. In much of Europe by the end of the fifteenth century, the conflicting aims of what are sometimes called the "new monarchies" were superseding the quarrels of feudal barons.

THE DECLINE OF THE MEDIEVAL CHURCH

Dangers facing the papacy. The history of the medieval Church divides roughly into three periods—dissemination, domination, and disintegration. In the initial period, which lasted from about the fifth through the eleventh centuries, Roman Christianity spread throughout the West. The advent of feudalism in the tenth century destroyed the Church's administrative apparatus centered on the papacy, but late in the eleventh century the Church revived under strong popes and became the most powerful institution in the West. The period of domination—the twelfth and thirteenth centuries—reached its zenith in the pontificate of Innocent III, who made and deposed temporal princes at will. The Church then seemed unassailable in its prestige, dignity, and power. Yet that strength soon came under new attack, and during the next two centuries the processes of disintegration were to run their course.

Papal power was threatened by the growth of nation-states, which challenged the Church's temporal pretensions. Joined by some of the local clergy, rulers opposed papal interference in state matters and favored the establishment of general Church councils to curb papal power. In addition, the papacy was criticized by reformers, who had seen the medieval reformation and the crusades transformed from their original high-minded purposes to suit the ambitions of the pontiffs, and by the bourgeoisie, whose realistic outlook was fostering growing skepticism, national patriotism, and religious self-reliance. During the fourteenth and fifteenth centuries these factors took their toll, and papal influence rapidly declined.

Boniface VIII. A century after the papacy's zenith under Innocent III, Pope Boniface VIII (1294-1303) was forced to withdraw his fierce opposition to taxes levied on the great wealth of the Church by Edward I in England and Philip IV in France. Emulating Innocent, Boniface threatened to depose the "impious king," as he termed Philip, but he gave way when Philip with the support of the Estates-General prohibited the export of money to Rome.

A final and more humiliating clash with the French king had long-range implications for the papacy. When Boniface boldly declared, in the most famous of all papal bulls, *Unam Sanctam* (1302), that "subjection to the Roman pontiff is absolutely necessary to salvation for every human creature," Philip demanded that the pope be tried for his "sins" by a general Church council. In 1303 Philip's henchmen broke into Boniface's summer home at Anagni to arrest him and take him to France to stand trial. Their kidnaping plot was foiled when the pope was rescued by his friends. Shocked and humiliated, Boniface died a month later.

The Avignon papacy. The success of the French monarchy was as complete as if Boniface had been dragged before Philip. Two years after Boniface's death, a French archbishop was chosen pope. Taking the title of Clement V, he not only exonerated Philip but praised his Christian zeal in bringing charges against Boniface. Clement never went to Rome, where feuding noble families made life turbulent, but moved the papal headquarters to Avignon in France, where the papacy remained under French influence from 1305 to 1377. During this period, the so-called "Babylonian Captivity" of the Church, papal prestige suffered enormously. All Christendom believed that Rome was the only rightful capital for the Church. Moreover, the English, Germans, and Italians accused the popes and the cardinals, who were also French, of being instruments of the French king.

The Avignon papacy added fuel to the fires of those critics who were attacking Church corruption, papal temporal claims, and the apparent lack of spiritual enthusiasm. Deprived of much of their former income from England, Germany, and Italy, and living in splendor in a newly built fortress-palace, the Avignon popes expanded the papal bureaucracy, added new Church taxes, and collected the old taxes more efficiently. This produced denouncements of the wealth of the Church and a demand for its reformation.

The Great Schism. When the papacy took heed of popular opinion and returned to Rome in 1377, it seemed for a time that the fortunes of the Roman Church would improve. But the reverse proved true. A papal election was held the following year, and the College of Cardinals, perhaps influenced by a shouting mob milling around the Vatican, elected an Italian pope. A few months later the French cardinals declared the election invalid and elected a French pope, who returned to Avignon.

The Church was now in an even worse state than it had been during the Babylonian Captivity. During the Great Schism, as the split of the Church into two allegiances was called, there were two popes, each with his college of cardinals and capital city, each claiming universal sovereignty, each sending forth papal administrators and taxing Christendom, and each excommunicating the other. The nations of Europe gave allegiance as their individual political interests prompted them. In order to keep that allegiance, the rival popes had to make concessions to their political supporters and largely abandoned the practice of interfering in national politics.

The Great Schism seemed to be permanent after the original rival popes died and each camp elected a replacement instead of working to heal the breach in the Church. Reli-

gious life suffered, for "Christendom looked upon the scandal helpless and depressed, and yet impotent to remove it. With two sections of Christendom each declaring the other lost, each cursing and denouncing the other, men soberly asked who was saved."[1] Heresy flourished as doubt and confusion caused many to break away from the Church.

The Conciliar Movement. Positive action came in the form of the Conciliar Movement, a return to the early Christian practice of solving Church problems by means of a general council of prelates (see p. 128). In 1395 the professors at the University of Paris proposed that a general council, representing the Universal Church, should meet to heal the Schism. A majority of the cardinals of both camps accepted this solution, and in 1409 they met at the Council of Pisa, deposed both pontiffs, and elected a third man. But neither of the two deposed popes would give up his office, and the papal throne now had three claimants.

Such an intolerable situation necessitated another Church council. In 1414 the Holy Roman emperor assembled at Constance the most impressive Church gathering of the period. For the first time voting took place on a purely national basis. Instead of the traditional assembly of bishops, the Council included lay representatives and was organized as a convention of "nations" (German, Italian, French, and English, the Spanish entering later). Each nation had one vote. The nationalistic structure of the Council was highly significant as an indication that the new tendency toward such alignments was being recognized by the Church's hierarchy. Finally, through the deposition of the various papal claimants and the election of Martin v in 1417, the Great Schism was ended, and a single papacy was restored at Rome.

Failure of internal reform. The Conciliar Movement represented a reforming and democratizing influence in the Church, aimed at transforming the papacy into something like a limited monarchy. But the movement was not to endure, even though the Council of Constance had solemnly decreed that general councils were superior to popes and that they should meet at regular intervals in the future. Taking steps to preserve his posi-

In this contemporary sketch of John Huss being led to execution, the reformer wears the headgear which branded him as a heretic condemned by the Council of Constance in 1415.

tion, the pope announced that to appeal to a Church council without having first obtained papal consent was heretical. The restoration of a single head of the Church, together with the inability of later councils to bring about much-needed reform, enabled the popes to discredit the Conciliar Movement by 1450. Not until almost a century later, in 1545, did the great Council of Trent meet to reform a Church which had already irreparably lost many countries to Protestantism.

Unfortunately, while the popes hesitated to call councils to effect reform, they failed to bring about reform themselves. The popes busied themselves not with internal problems but with Italian politics and patronage of the arts. Thus, "the papacy emerged as something between an Italian city-state and a European power, without forgetting at the same time the claim to be the vice-regent of Christ. The pope often could not make up his own mind whether he was the successor of Peter or of Caesar. Such vacillation had much to do with the rise and success . . . of the Reformation."[2]

Heresy: Wycliffe and Huss. Throughout the fourteenth century the cries against Church corruption became louder at the same time that heretical thoughts were being voiced. In England *Piers the Plowman* (see p. 257) mercilessly upbraided the corruption, ignorance, and worldliness of the clergy, and a professor at Oxford named John Wycliffe (1320?-1384) assailed not only Church abuses but Church doctrines. Because of his beliefs that the Church should be subordinate to the state, that salvation was primarily an individual matter between man and God, that transubstantiation as taught by the Church was false, and that outward rituals and veneration of relics were idolatrous, Wycliffe has been called the dawn-star of the Protestant Revolt. He formed bands of "poor priests," called Lollards, who taught his views; and he provided the people with an English translation of the Bible, which he considered the final authority in matters of religion. Although Wycliffe's demands for reform did not succeed, the Lollards, including the famous John Ball (see p. 217), spread a more radical version of Wycliffe's ideas until the movement was driven underground early in the next century.

In Bohemia—where a strong reform movement, linked with the resentment of the Czechs towards their German overlords, was under way—Wycliffe's doctrines were propagated by Czech students who had heard him at Oxford. In particular, his beliefs influenced John Huss (1369?-1415), an impassioned preacher in Prague and later rector of the university there. Huss' attacks on the abuses of clerical power led him, like Wycliffe, to conclude that the true Church was composed of a universal priesthood of believers and that Christ alone was its head. But Huss, who was more preacher and reformer than theologian, did not accept Wycliffe's denial of the validity of transubstantiation.

Huss' influence became so great that he was excommunicated. Later the emperor gave him a safe-conduct to stand trial for heresy at the Council of Constance. Huss refused to recant his views, and the Council ordered him burned at the stake in spite of his safe-conduct. This action made Huss a martyr to the Czechs, who rebelled against both the German emperor, who was also king of Bohemia, and the Catholic Church. The Czechs maintained their political and religious independence for more than a generation before they were crushed. In the sixteenth century the remaining Hussites merged with the Lutherans.

Reasons for Church decline. The reasons for the Church's decline during the fourteenth and fifteenth centuries can be divided into those that existed within the Church itself and those that were weakening it from the outside. By the early sixteenth century these forces were strong enough to bring about the Reformation.

As we have seen, trenchant criticisms of the clergy had come from a variety of sources, and the Conciliar Movement had gone so far as to challenge the supreme power of the pope himself. And while criticisms increased, the Church continued to decline in spiritual leadership. The worldly concerns of the fourteenth- and fifteenth-century popes—including their deep involvement in Italian politics—pushed the Church further in the direction of secularization.

Among the outside pressures that led to the Church's decline, the new spirit of inquiry encouraged by the Renaissance (see Chapter 13) resulted in a new critical attitude toward religious institutions. And the newly invented printing press provided the means for the rapid dissemination of ideas. In the socioeconomic field, the medieval Church was slow in adapting itself to the new environment of the towns. The problems arising from town life too often went unanswered by the Church, which failed to provide enough parish priests to keep pace with the growth of urban population. It is no accident that the towns became centers of heresy. Finally, the development of nationalism and the growing reluctance of kings to obey any opposing institution, including the Church, were evident in the encounters between Boniface VIII and the French ruler Philip IV.

CRISIS IN ENGLAND AND FRANCE

The Hundred Years' War. Nation-making in both France and England was greatly affected by the long conflict that colored much of their history during the fourteenth and fifteenth centuries. In both lands the crisis of war led to a resurgence of feudalism. Another deterrent to the rise of royal power was the increase in the power of the representative assemblies, Parliament and the Estates-General. Nevertheless, in the long run the increasing anarchy and misery of the times stimulated nationalistic feelings and a demand for strong rulers who could guarantee law and order. Thus by the late fifteenth century the French and English kings were able to resume the task of establishing the institutions of the modern nation-state.

The Hundred Years' War sprang from a fundamental conflict between the aims of the English and the French monarchies. The English kings wanted to regain the large holdings in France that had been theirs in the days of Henry II. The French kings, on the other hand, were determined not only to keep what had been taken from John of England but to expand further. Their ultimate goal was a centralized France under the direct rule of the monarchy at Paris.

Another factor was the clash of French and English economic interests in Flanders. This region was coming more and more under French control, to the chagrin of the English wool growers who supplied the great Flemish woolen industry, and of the English king whose income came in great part from duties on wool (see Reference Map 4).

The immediate excuse for the Anglo-French conflict was a dispute over the succession to the French throne. In 1328, after the direct line of the Capetians became extinct, Philip VI of the House of Valois assumed the throne. The English king, Edward III, maintained that he was the legitimate heir to the French throne because his mother was a sister of the late French king. The

French nobility disputed this claim, which became a pretext for war. Interrupted by several peace treaties and a number of truces, the conflict stretched from 1337 to 1453. At the naval battle of Sluys (1340) the English gained command of the Channel and thus were able to send their armies to France at will. Thereafter England won a series of great victories—at Crécy (1346), Poitiers (1356), and Agincourt (1415), where the French lost some 7000 knights, including many great nobles, and the English only 500.

The English armies were much more effective than those of the French. With no thought of strategy, the French knights charged the enemy at a mad gallop and then engaged in hand-to-hand fighting. The English learned other methods. Their secret weapon was the longbow, apparently taken over from the Welsh. Six feet long and made of special wood, the longbow shot steel-tipped arrows which were dangerous at four hundred yards and deadly at one hundred. The usual English plan of battle called for the knights to fight dismounted. Protecting them was a forward wall of bowmen just behind a barricade of iron stakes planted in the ground to slow down the enemy's charge. By the time the enemy cavalry reached the dismounted knights, only a few remained to be taken care of; the "feathered death" had done its work.

English military triumphs stirred English pride and what we now think of as nationalism—love of country, identification with it, and a sense of difference from, and usually superiority to, other peoples. However, patriotism was stirring in France also. The revival of French spirit is associated with Joan of Arc, who initiated a series of French victories.

Impelled by inward voices which she believed divine, Joan persuaded the timid French ruler to allow her to lead an army to relieve the besieged city of Orléans. Clad in white armor and riding a white horse, she inspired confidence and a feeling of invincibility in her followers, and in 1429 Orléans was rescued from what had seemed certain conquest. But Joan met a tragic end. Captured by the enemy, she was found guilty of bewitching the English soldiers and was burned at the stake, while the French king remained indifferent to her fate.

The martyrdom of the Maid of Orléans was a turning point in the long struggle. The nucleus of a permanent standing army was developed and the use of gunpowder to propel missiles began to transform the art of war. English resistance crumbled as military superiority now turned full circle; the English longbow was outmatched by French artillery. Of the vast territories they had once controlled in France, the English retained only Calais when the war ended in 1453.

Aftermath of war in England. The Hundred Years' War exhausted England, and discontent was rife in Parliament and among the peasants. (On the peasants' revolt of 1381, see p. 217.) Richard II (1377-1399), the last Plantagenet king, was unstable, cruel, and power hungry, and he foreshadowed modern absolute monarchs in believing that the king should control the lives and property

This illumination depicts a scene of late medieval warfare typical of the Hundred Years' War. Note the suits of armor, crossbows, longbows, and the early form of cannon.

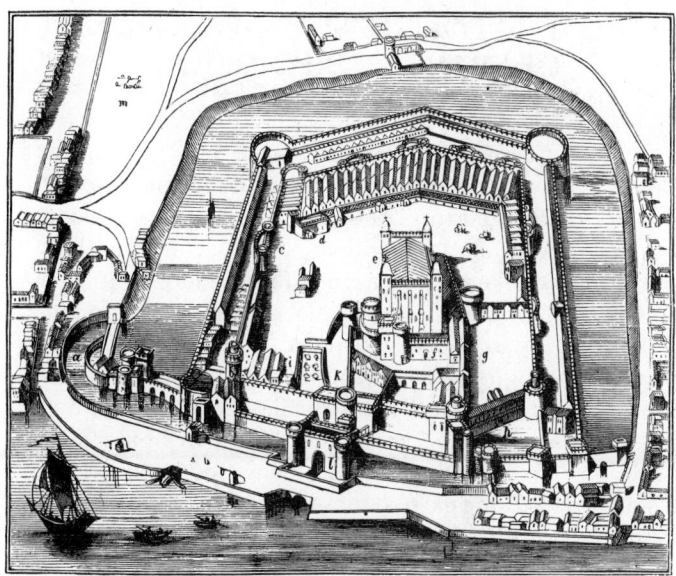

A sixteenth-century engraving of the Tower of London, long used as a prison for those accused of crimes against English monarchs, shows the complex network of walls, towers, living quarters, and fortress which was continually added to and modified from the time of William the Conqueror until well into modern times.

of his subjects. His seizure of the properties of Henry, the duke of Lancaster, led to a revolt in which Henry was victorious.

Henry IV established the House of Lancaster, which ruled England from 1399 to 1461. He was given the support of Parliament, which had deeply resented Richard's autocratic reign and was determined that its authority should not again be slighted. Hard-pressed for money to suppress revolts at home and carry on the war in France, the Lancastrian kings became more and more financially dependent upon Parliament. In return for money grants, Parliament acquired such gains as the guarantee of freedom of debate, the right to approve the appointment of the king's chief officials and members of his council, the stipulation that money bills must originate in the House of Commons, and the rule that the king's statutes should duplicate exactly petitions presented by the Commons. Not until 1689, when England became a constitutional monarchy, would Parliament again exercise such powers.

Baronial rivalry to control both Parliament and the crown flared up during the reign of the third Lancastrian king, and when he went completely insane in 1453, the duke of York, the strongest man in the kingdom, became regent. Two years later full-scale civil war broke out between the House of York and the partisans of the Lancaster family. The struggle became known as the Wars of the Roses; the white rose was the badge of the House of York, and the red rose that of the House of Lancaster. In 1461 the Yorkists managed to have their leader, Edward IV, crowned king. Ten years later Edward had succeeded in cowing the nobles and in winning the support of the middle class, who saw a strong monarchy as the only alternative to anarchy. Edward's power became practically absolute, foreshadowing the strong rule of the Tudors that soon followed.

The promise of the House of York ended in 1483 when Edward IV died, leaving two young sons as his heirs. Their uncle, Richard, bribed and intimidated Parliament to declare his nephews illegitimate and took the throne. The two boys were imprisoned in the Tower of London, where they were secretly murdered. The double murder was too much for the nation, and support was thrown to the cause of Henry Tudor, who, in his lineage and later marriage to Edward IV's daughter, united the Houses of Lancaster and York. At Bosworth Field in 1485 Richard died fighting as his army deserted him. According to tradition, his crown was found in a bush on the battlefield and placed on the head of Henry VII, the first of the Tudor line, which ruled England from 1485 to 1603.

Beginning of Tudor rule. Under Tudor rule England achieved the full status of a national state. During the reigns of the shrewd Henry VII (1485-1509) and his successor, Henry VIII (1509-1547), strong, almost absolute government was reintroduced into England, with the people supporting the monarchy because it held the nobility in check. The Court of Star Chamber, established by Edward IV, was the most effective royal instrument in suppressing the unruly barons; it bypassed the established common law courts, whose judges and juries were too often intimidated and bribed by powerful nobles, and operated secretly and swiftly without benefit of juries. Because the Tudor rulers restored order and promoted trade at home and abroad, they won the support of the people of middle rank—the burghers and landed gentry—and upon this support their power was primarily built. Though often high-handed, Tudor kings always worked through Parliament.

France after the Hundred Years' War: Louis XI. The Hundred Years' War left France with a new national consciousness and a royal power that was stronger than ever before. In 1438 the king had become the virtual head of the church in France by decreeing that it be run by a council of French bishops whose appointment was to be controlled by the monarch. Furthermore, the *taille*, a land tax voted during the war to support a standing army, became permanent, making the king financially independent of the Estates-General. Thus the purse strings, which the English Parliament used to gain concessions from the king, were kept firmly under royal control in France.

After the war the process of consolidating royal power was continued by Louis XI (1461-1483), son of the king aided by Joan of Arc. Physically unattractive and completely lacking in scruples, Louis earned himself the epithet, the "universal spider." In his pursuit of power he used any weapon—violence, bribery, and treachery—to obtain his ends. When the French nobles rose in revolt, dignifying themselves as the League for the Public Welfare, Louis outfoxed them by agreeing to their Magna Carta-like demands and then ignoring his pledged word.

Louis XI's most powerful antagonist was the duke of Burgundy, Charles the Bold, whose possession of Flanders and the other Low Countries or Netherlands (modern Holland, Belgium, and Luxemburg) made him one of Europe's richest rulers. After Charles' death in 1477, Louis seized most of Burgundy, while the remainder of the duke's possessions passed to his daughter Mary. When she married the German emperor Maximilian I, the Netherlands came into the hands of the House of Hapsburg (see map, p. 327). Like Henry VII of England, Louis XI was one of the "new monarchs" who created the absolute states which were to dominate Europe in the early modern period.

THE POLITICAL UNIFICATION OF SPAIN AND PORTUGAL

Ferdinand and Isabella: "One king, one law, one faith." Another "new monarchy" emerged in 1479 when Isabella of Castile and Ferdinand of Aragon, who had married ten years earlier, began a joint rule that united the Iberian peninsula except for Granada, Navarre, and Portugal. The "Catholic Sovereigns," to use the title the pope conferred on Ferdinand and Isabella, set out to establish an effective royal despotism in Spain. The Holy Brotherhood, a league of cities which had long existed for mutual protection against unruly nobles, was taken over by the crown, and its militia was used as a standing army and police force. The powerful and virtually independent military orders of knights, which had emerged during the *Reconquista*, were also brought under royal control.

Ferdinand and Isabella believed that the Church should be subordinate to royal government—a belief they shared with the other "new monarchs" of Europe. By tactful negotiations, the Spanish sovereigns induced the pope to give them the right to make Church appointments in Spain and to establish a Spanish Court of Inquisition, largely free of papal control. The Inquisition confiscated the property of most Jews and Muslims and terrified the Christian clergy and laymen into accepting royal absolutism as well as religious orthodoxy. Although the Inquisition greatly enhanced the power of the Spanish crown, it also caused many talented people to flee the land of persecution. About 150,000 Spanish Jews, mainly merchants and professional people, fled to Holland, England, North Africa, and the Ottoman empire. Calling themselves Sephardim, these exiles retained their Spanish language and customs into the twentieth century.

A final manifestation of Spanish absolutism, defined by Isabella herself as "one king, one law, one faith," was the virtual ignoring of the Cortes of Castile and Aragon. These representative assemblies had emerged in the twelfth century and were thus older than the English Parliament.

The most dramatic act of the Catholic Sovereigns was the conquest of Granada in 1492, the same year that Columbus claimed the New World for Spain. Before Ferdinand died in 1516, twelve years after Isabella, he seized that part of Navarre which lay south of the Pyrenees Mountains. This acquisition, together with the conquest of Granada, completed the national unification of Spain.

Results of Spanish unification. Royal absolutism and unification, coupled with the acquisition of territory in the New and Old Worlds, made Spain the strongest power in sixteenth-century Europe. But the process of unifying Spain had some unfortunate results: (1) Centuries of fighting against the Muslims left a legacy of warlike spirit and inordinate national pride. (2) Religious enthusiasm was whipped up as a means to an end, and the sequel was a heritage of religious bigotry and the death of that tolerance, intellectual curiosity, and sense of balance which had been characteristic of Muslim culture in Spain. (3) Spanish contempt for the Muslims created a scorn for those activities in which the unbelievers had engaged—trade, crafts, manual labor, and agriculture. This attitude hampered Spanish economic development in subsequent centuries.

Portugal. The nucleus of the area which eventually became Portugal was a part of Castile until 1095. In that year the king of Castile gave his daughter to Count Henry of Burgundy, one of many French knights who had helped take Toledo (see p. 208). Her dowry was the county of Portugal, named after its chief town Oporto ("The Port") at the mouth of the Duero River. The son of this marriage organized a revolt against his overlord, the king of Castile, and in 1139 proclaimed himself king of Portugal.

Attempts by Castile to regain Portugal ended in 1385 when John I, aided by English archers, decisively defeated the invader. The following year John signed an alliance with England which has been reaffirmed down the centuries and remains the oldest alliance in existence. In 1415 John took Ceuta in North Africa (see Reference Map 7), thus initiating Portuguese overseas expansion. Carried on by his son, Henry the Navigator, this policy eventually led to the creation of a great overseas empire (see Chapter 18).

DISUNITY IN GERMANY

The early Hapsburgs and the Golden Bull. Between 1254 and 1273 the German monarchy was made virtually nonexistent by the election of two rival foreign princes, neither of whom received wide recognition. Then in 1273 the imperial crown was bestowed upon the obscure Count Rudolf (1273-1291) of the House of Hapsburg—from Habichtsburg (Castle of the Hawk), their home in northern Switzerland. During the remainder of the Middle Ages and in modern times, the Hapsburgs had amazing success in adding to their ancestral lands. Rudolf himself acquired Austria through marriage, and thereafter the Hapsburgs ruled their holdings from Vienna. In the sixteenth century they obtained Bohemia and part of Hungary (see p. 276).

For the time being, however, the Hapsburg hold on the imperial crown proved to be brief. After Rudolf's reign it was passed from one family to another. Then in 1356 the nobility won another significant victory. The Golden Bull, a document which served as the political constitution of Germany until early in the nineteenth century, laid down the procedure for election of the emperor by seven German dignitaries—three archbishops and four lay princes. The electors and other important princes were given rights that made them virtually independent rulers, and the emperor could take no important action without the consent of the imperial feudal assembly, the Diet, which met infrequently. It has been said that the Golden Bull "legalized anarchy and called it a constitution"; in reality it stabilized the political situation in Germany by recognizing the independence of the princes, thereby encouraging them to emulate the new national monarchs and create stable governments in their principalities. It also ended disputed elections and civil wars over the succession. But with the emperor virtually powerless, people thereafter commonly referred to the welter of duchies, counties, bishoprics, and free cities as the Germanies, not Germany.

The imperial crown of Germany was returned to the Hapsburg family in 1438. From this time until 1806, when the Holy Roman Empire disappeared, the Hapsburgs held the imperial crown almost without a break. Maximilian I (1493-1519) helped make the Hapsburgs the most potent force in sixteenth-century Europe by taking as his wife Mary of Burgundy (see p. 272), heiress of the rich Low Countries, and by marrying his son to the heiress of Spain.

Inspired by the rise of the "new monarchies," Maximilian attempted to strengthen his power. His program for a national court system, army, and taxation was frustrated by the German princes who insisted on jealously guarding what they called "German freedom." The emperor continued to be limited in power; nor did the empire have an imperial treasury, an efficient central administration, or a standing army. And so the phantom Holy Roman Empire lived on as Voltaire later characterized it: "Neither Holy, nor Roman, nor an Empire."

ITALY: WEALTHY BUT DIVIDED

The northern city-states. The virtual ending of German imperial influence after 1250 left the three major divisions of Italy—the city-states of northern Italy, the Papal States, and the Kingdom of Naples (see map, p. 283)—free to follow their own devices. Such city-states as Venice, Florence, Milan, Genoa, and Pisa had grown wealthy from their thriving industries, lucrative trade, and banking houses that handled papal revenues and made loans to European monarchs.

Within each city there were intense rivalries and feuds. Unlike the situation in northern Europe, where the bourgeoisie inhabited the towns and the nobles lived on country manors, the Italian nobility had city houses as well as country villas. In some Italian cities arcaded streets enabled the townsmen to go about their business safe from the arrows which from time to time flew between the towered houses of feuding nobles.

In both the intracity rivalries and the struggles between city-states, mercenary soldiers under the command of leaders called *condottieri* were employed. Coming from all over Europe, these adventurers sold their swords to the highest bidder, but, in order to live and fight another day, they carried on their fighting with a minimum of bloodshed. Far different from the twentieth-century wars of annihilation, these petty conflicts did not hinder the spectacular progress in art and learning called the Italian Renaissance (see Chapter 13).

Civic patriotism advanced rapidly under the influence of the prosperous burghers, who finally succeeded in ousting the restless feudal aristocrats from positions of power. Ingenious city charters and civic constitutions were drafted, and there was much trial

A view of the Italian city of Siena looking toward several medieval towers built in the thirteenth and fourteenth centuries. In the center is the Mangia Tower of the Palazzo Pubblico, over three hundred feet high, and an excellent example of pointed Gothic architecture. Towers such as these were built to convey civic pride; often one community or noble family tried to outdo another in the grandness of the tower's construction.

and error in the art of government. Until the end of the thirteenth century the prevailing political trend in the cities was toward republicanism and representative government.

Two city-state republics were of unusual interest. Venice, the "Pearl of the Adriatic," was one of the richest cities of its time, controlling an empire of ports and islands in the eastern Mediterranean and carrying much of Europe's maritime trade in its great fleets. The government of this rich republic had been in the hands of a doge (duke), together with a popular assembly, but beginning in the thirteenth century the rich merchants gradually took over the reins of power. They alone sat in the Great Council, which replaced the popular assembly. This oligarchic council appointed the doge and the members of smaller councils which administered the government. Most famous among the smaller councils was the secret Council of Ten, which dealt swiftly with suspected enemies of the government. The merchant oligarchy of Venice provided good government and, unlike other Italian city-states, resolutely squashed internal strife.

Florence—the center of flourishing wool, leather, and silk industries—boasted merchants and bankers who were among the most prosperous in Europe, and its gold florin circulated in many lands as a standard coin. With its many checks and counterchecks of power, the Florentine constitution was bewilderingly complex. For example, the head of the state held office for two months only, and all measures needed a two-thirds majority in five different committees or assemblies to become laws. In theory Florence was a democracy but, as in Venice, real political power was wielded by wealthy businessmen.

During the fourteenth century republicanism declined and most Italian city-states came under the rule of despots. Conspiracy, confusion, and incompetence caused many citizens to welcome a strong leader as political boss or despot. Although Venice maintained the benevolent oligarchy of its merchants with the doge as a figurehead, Florence went under the thumb of the Medici family, and its republican institutions became largely empty forms. The Medici had

no aristocratic antecedents; their status was based on commerce and finance. The significance of the family emblem—six red balls on a field of gold—is unknown, but we are all familiar with the later modification of this insigne—the three balls of the pawnbroker.

The Papal States and the Kingdom of Naples. The Papal States, extending from fifty miles south of the mouth of the Tiber to the northeast across Italy as far as the mouth of the Po River, were poorly organized. The popes found it difficult to force their will upon various petty despots who defied their political authority. Although they headed the great international Church, in Italy the popes acted little differently from the rulers of the other states in the matter of hiring troops, waging wars, and making treaties.

The Kingdom of Naples covered the southern half of the Italian peninsula as well as Sicily. After 1250 the houses of Aragon and Anjou disputed over the kingdom (see p. 238) until Aragon won out early in the fifteenth century. Impoverished by the warfare of foreign armies, with its powerful nobles rebellious, and with brigandage rampant, southern Italy and Sicily sank into a backwardness that was to continue into the twentieth century.

EASTERN EUROPE

German eastward expansion. Since the early tenth century German barons and churchmen had been founding bishoprics and colonizing the land east of the Elbe. The German settlements, however, remained precariously isolated in the midst of large Slavic populations. Then, shortly after 1200, a new development occurred. The Teutonic Knights, a military-religious order founded at the time of the Third Crusade, transferred their operations to eastern Europe. Within fifty years the Knights had conquered the pagan Slavs in Prussia, and by 1350 they ruled the Baltic coastlands as far north as the Gulf of Finland. Assuming the role of a colonial aristocracy, the Knights built castles and towns, and a steady stream of German settlers moved into the conquered lands.

Poland and Lithuania. To the south of Prussia lived the Slavic Poles. They were first united into a state late in the tenth century, but the Polish nobility seldom allowed their monarch to exercise much power. Also in the late tenth century the Poles were converted to Roman Christianity, thus linking Poland to western European culture.

The continued threat of the aggressive Teutonic Knights caused the Polish nobles in 1386 to offer the Polish crown to the king of the neighboring Lithuanians, a pagan people who had expanded into a Russia weakened and fragmented by the Mongol conquest (see p. 277). Converted to Latin Christianity, the Lithuanians joined with the Poles in defeating the Teutonic Knights in the great battle of Tannenberg in 1410. The Knights never regained their former power, and in 1466 they turned West Prussia over to the Poles, retaining East Prussia as a fief of the Polish crown. This settlement was a great blow to German expansion, for the Poles obtained control of the Vistula River and a corridor north to the Baltic Sea, including the important port of Danzig. East Prussia was now cut off from the rest of Germany. In the history of modern Europe, the Polish corridor and Danzig have played an important role.

The Polish state, united with Lithuania in 1386 under a common sovereign, was the largest in Europe, but its promise was never realized. The nobility succeeded in keeping the monarchy elective and weak, and the middle class, composed largely of German settlers and Jewish refugees from persecution in western Europe, remained small and powerless. Above all, Poland faced the hostility of the ambitious tsars of Moscow who sought to rule over all Russians, including those in the huge Polish-Lithuanian state.

Bohemians and Magyars. Two other peoples appeared in the east European family in the Middle Ages. During the ninth and tenth centuries the Slavic Czechs established a kingdom on the Bohemian plain. German influence became strong in Bohemia, which was a part of the Holy Roman Empire, and the Golden Bull of 1356 made the Bohemian king one of the seven imperial electors. Living southeast of Bohemia in the wide and fertile plain known as Hungary were the Magyars, an Asiatic people. Originally the terror of eastern Europe because of their brutal raids (see p. 233), they became civilized, adopted Christianity, and in the eleventh century expanded their state.

The promise of both these rising nations—Bohemia and Hungary—was blighted by a common disaster. The king of Hungary, who was also king of Bohemia, met his death fighting against the Turks in 1526. Terrified at the prospects of Muslim rule, both the Czechs and Hungarians elected the same man to their vacant thrones—Ferdinand, the Hapsburg archduke of neighboring Austria. The Turks, however, occupied most of Hungary (which they would hold until the end of the seventeenth century), leaving Ferdinand only a narrow strip along the western border (see map at left). This intertwining of national fortunes explains how the Haps-

CENTRAL AND EASTERN EUROPE 1526
━━━ Hungary

burgs at Vienna came to rule a polyglot empire of Bohemians, Hungarians, and German Austrians.

South Slavs and Turks in the Balkans. The outstanding political development in southeastern Europe at the close of the Middle Ages was the disappearance of the Byzantine empire and the emergence of the Ottoman Turks as a threat to Europe. Before the end of the fifteenth century the Turks had extended their control over the Balkans and were pushing on toward Vienna. This huge new empire, with its center at Constantinople, was in no sense a national state but rather a bewildering mixture of Turks, Serbs, Hungarians, Bulgarians, Rumanians, Armenians, Greeks, and Jews.

Turkish rule delayed the rise of national states in southeastern Europe until the nineteenth century. The multiplicity of small countries in the Balkans in modern times and the resultant tensions and conflicts have made the peninsula a European danger zone, a source of constant worry to diplomats, and, as in 1914, the direct or indirect cause of wars.

The Mongol conquest of Russia. In Chapter 7 we followed the amazing career of Genghis Khan, who united the unruly tribesmen of Mongolia and then launched them like a thunderbolt on a campaign of world conquest. By 1240 the Mongols had conquered Kiev and other Russian principalities, and in 1242 they penetrated to the outskirts of Vienna. Western Europe seemed theirs for the taking, but the death of the great Khan in far-off Mongolia caused the Tatar, or Mongol, armies to return to the lower Volga pending the election of a new khan.

Central Europe was not molested again, but the Mongols continued to dominate Russia from their capital at Sarai on the Volga not far from the modern city of Volgograd. The various Russian principalities were allowed to govern themselves as long as they paid tribute to the Golden Horde, as the Tatars in Russia were called. The khanate of the Golden Horde was only one of the Mongol states, however; the successors of Genghis Khan ruled an empire stretching from Korea on the east to Poland on the west. On the south their holdings included

Persia and Afghanistan, as well as the area north of what is now India and Burma. Only since the Second World War has an empire arisen—that of Soviet Russia and its satellites—which could rival the vast expanse of contiguous territory controlled by the Mongols. In fact, the Russian empire together with Communist China not only rivals but nearly duplicates that of the Mongol khanates.

Mongol domination changed the whole course of Russian history; it completed the break between Russia and western European civilization initiated by the decline of Kiev. Asian cultural influences were strong—the status of women was lowered as they accepted the veil and oriental seclusion. Mongols and Russians intermarried freely; hence the saying, "Scratch a Russian and you will find a Tatar." Many authorities believe that the Mongol conquest was a wholesale calamity. Russia was cut off from Europe, and a new Russia north and east of Kiev began to develop. Its nucleus was the grand duchy of Moscow.

Alexander Nevski: pioneer of Russian greatness. Following the Mongol conquest, the most important Russian leader was the prince of Novgorod, Alexander Nevski, who also became the ruler of Vladimir. In 1238 and 1240, during the Mongol advance, this staunch warrior had won great victories over the Swedes and the Teutonic Knights. To the Orthodox Church and most princes, the westerners seemed a greater threat to the Russian way of life than the Mongols. Indeed, Nevski accepted Mongol domination and assistance in fighting invaders from the west, who, hoping to profit from the Russian collapse under the Mongol impact, tried to annex territory. Meanwhile, Nevski may have looked forward to the day when his successors would be strong enough to challenge Tatar rule.

Moscow, challenge to Tatar rule. Daniel, the youngest son of Nevski, founded the grand duchy of Moscow, which eventually expelled the Tatars from Russia. Well situated in the central river system of Russia and surrounded by protective forests and marshes, Moscow was at first only a vassal of Vladimir, but it soon absorbed its parent

GROWTH OF THE DUCHY OF MOSCOW

- Moscow c.1300
- Acquisitions: c.1300-1462
- Acquisitions Through Reign Of Ivan III, 1505
- Acquisitions Through Reign Of Ivan IV, 1584

SWEDEN

WHITE SEA

Arkhangelsk

N. Dvina R.

Golden Horde – Farthest Advance

Ob R.

Tobolsk

BALTIC SEA

Novgorod

Pskov

Yaroslavl

Kazan

Kama R.

Vladimir

Moscow

Smolensk

Ryazan

Volga R.

Kulikovo 1380

Warsaw

POLAND

Kiev

Dnieper

Don R.

Sarai

Budapest

HUNGARY

Danube R.

BLACK SEA

Astrakhan

Aral Sea

CASPIAN SEA

OTTOMAN EMPIRE

Constantinople

Tiflis

Ivan the Great. The Muscovite prince who laid the foundations for a Russian national state was Ivan III, the Great (1462-1505), a contemporary of the Tudors and other "new monarchs" in western Europe. Ivan more than doubled his territories by placing most of north Russia under the rule of Moscow, and he proclaimed his absolute sovereignty over all Russian princes and nobles by taking the title of "Great Prince and Autocrat of All Russia." Refusing further tribute to the Tatars, Ivan initiated a series of attacks that opened the way for the complete defeat of the declining Golden Horde, now divided into several khanates.

Ivan married Sophia Palaeologus, the niece of the last Byzantine emperor, and she brought with her to Moscow a number of gifted Italians. Among them were architects who designed an enormous walled palace called the Kremlin. Ivan not only adopted the double-headed eagle and court ceremonies of the Byzantine emperors but also claimed to be their legitimate successor. Thus Ivan sometimes used the title of *tsar*, derived from "Caesar," and he viewed Moscow as the Third Rome, the successor of New Rome (Constantinople).

"Two Romes have fallen, and the third stands." The doctrine that the Russian tsar was the successor of the Byzantine emperors was expressed by the monk Philotheos of Pskov late in the fifteenth century. "Two Romes have fallen," he wrote, "and the third stands, and a fourth one there shall not be." On the basis of the conviction that they were heirs of the Byzantine tradition, Russian rulers were later to press claims to the Dardanelles and parts of southeastern Europe. Moreover, as in the idea expressed by Philotheos when he said, "you are the only tsar for Christians in the whole world,"[3] the Russian tradition would henceforth encompass a great imperial mission.

Some historians see this Russian sense of destiny still operating in a new manifestation—communism—with the same fervor of the earlier Russian dedication to Orthodox Christianity. "Five centuries ago the words of Philotheos of Pskov may have sounded arrogant and foolhardy; but for us today, in the new constellation of world-

state. A major factor in the ascendency of Moscow was the cooperation of its rulers with their Mongol overlords, who granted them the title of Grand Prince of Russia and made them agents for collecting the Tatar tribute from the Russian principalities. Moscow's prestige was further enhanced when it became the center of the Russian Orthodox Church. Its head, the metropolitan, fled from Kiev to Vladimir in 1299 and a few years later established the permanent headquarters of the Church in Moscow.

By the middle of the fourteenth century the power of the Tatars was declining, and the Grand Princes felt capable of openly opposing the Mongol yoke. In 1380, at Kulikovo on the Don, the khan was defeated, and although this hard-fought victory did not end Tatar rule of Russia, it did bring great fame to the Grand Prince. Moscow's leadership in Russia was now firmly based, and by the middle of the fifteenth century its territory had greatly expanded through purchase, war, and marriage (see map).

forces after 1945, they echo through the centuries as the prophetic expression of the most momentous consequence of the fall of Constantinople . . . . on the wider stage of world-history the effects of the events of 1453 are only now making themselves felt."[4]

Ivan the Terrible. The next great ruler of Moscow was Ivan III's grandson, Ivan IV (1547-1584), called "the Terrible." Russia became more despotic as Ivan ruthlessly subordinated the great nobles to his will, exiling or executing many on the slightest pretext. With no consideration for human life, Ivan ordered the destruction of Novgorod, Russia's second city, on suspicion of treason. Another time, in a rage, he struck and killed his gifted eldest son. Yet Ivan was also a far-seeing statesman who promulgated a new code of laws, reformed the morals of the clergy, and built the fabulous St. Basil's Cathedral that still stands in Moscow's Red Square.

During Ivan's reign eastern Russia was conquered from the Tatars, and Cossack pioneers then crossed the Ural Mountains in their push to the Pacific—a movement which can be compared with the simultaneous expansion of western Europe across the Atlantic. Ivan's efforts to reach the Baltic and establish trade relations with western Europe were forcibly stopped by Sweden and Poland. Later, however, he was able to inaugurate direct trade with the West by granting English merchants trading privileges at the White Sea port of Archangel (Arkhangelsk) in the far north.

Ivan's death in 1584 was followed by the Time of Trouble, a period of civil wars over the succession and resurgence of the power of the nobility. Both Poland and Sweden intervened in Russian affairs, and their invasions across an indistinct frontier which contains no major natural barriers demonstrated again the danger from the West and contributed to Russia's growing tendency to withdraw into her own distinctive heritage. Order was restored in 1613 when Michael Romanov, the grandnephew of Ivan the Terrible, was elected to the throne by a national assembly that included representatives from fifty cities. The Romanov dynasty ruled Russia until 1917.

SUMMARY

The medieval ideal was unity—a Europe united as a Christian commonwealth and ruled by dual powers, the universal Church and an all-embracing Holy Roman Empire. In theory the emperor would rule in the temporal or earthly realm, and the pope in the affairs of the spirit. Because papal authority was not constricted to national boundaries, the Church was nearly all-encompassing. By contrast, the emperor's authority was limited for the most part to Germany and Italy, and even there imperial power was intermittent.

During the fourteenth and fifteenth centuries, forces were at work which threatened and ultimately undermined the medieval

St. Basil's Cathedral in Moscow, begun in 1554 by Ivan the Terrible, was consecrated in 1557 but not completed until 1679. It is polygonal in plan with richly ornamented onion-shaped domes. The building is a fine example of Byzantine architecture adapted to the Russian tradition.

ideal and the edifices stemming from it. The Church was badly weakened from within as a result of the Babylonian Captivity, the Great Schism, and the demands of reformers. And despite continuous opposition from both the Church and the feudal nobles, the national state had become a reality in Europe by the end of the period discussed in this chapter.

Influencing nation-making in both France and England was the Hundred Years' War, which stimulated nationalism in the hearts of Englishmen and Frenchmen alike. Other significant changes resulted from that conflict: in England, the power of Parliament was increased, and the upsurge in the power of the nobility led to the Wars of the Roses, which ended finally with the accession of the Tudors; in France, royal power was consolidated under Louis xi, and further progress in national unification was made. Ferdinand and Isabella completed the creation of a national state in Spain and laid the foundations for its future greatness. On the other hand, Germany and Italy continued divided and weak; their day of national unification would not arrive until the nineteenth century.

Eastern and southern Europe were on the periphery of most of the dynamic currents of change that were transforming western Europe. There was much movement of peoples, and the rise and fall of states culminated in the emergence of Poland, Lithuania, Bohemia, and Hungary. Russia, effectively isolated on its frozen plains, languished for years under the rule of the Mongols. But when the dukes of Moscow assumed leadership of the Russians, a long campaign was initiated against the alien Mongols—a historical movement somewhat similar to the *Reconquista* in Spain.

Truly, the late Middle Ages was an era of nation-making. The nation-states this period produced—in particular England, France, and Spain—would assume new roles in the stirring international drama that is the story of Europe from about 1500 to 1650, a story which will be taken up in Chapter 15.

SUGGESTIONS FOR READING

W. K. Ferguson, **Europe in Transition, 1300 to 1520** (Houghton Mifflin, 1963) is a comprehensive work. See also D. Hay, **Europe in the Fourteenth and Fifteenth Centuries** (Harcourt Brace Jovanovich); and E. Cheyney, **The Dawn of a New Era, 1250-1453*** (Torchbooks). R. E. Lerner, **The Age of Adversity: The Fourteenth Century*** (Cornell); and Jerah Johnson and W. Percy, **The Age of Recovery: The Fifteenth Century*** (Cornell) are lively, interpretative essays. M. Aston, **The Fifteenth Century: The Prospect of Europe*** (Harcourt Brace Jovanovich) is a well-illustrated, popular introduction.

A good account of Church history during this period is L. Elliott-Binns, **History of the Decline and Fall of the Medieval Papacy** (Shoe String, 1967). See also G. Leff, **Heresy in the Later Middle Ages**, 2 vols., (Barnes and Noble, 1967); K. McFarlane, **John Wycliffe and the Beginnings of English Nonconformity** (Verry); and M. Spinka, **John Hus: A Biography** (Princeton, 1968).

E. Perroy, **The Hundred Years' War*** (Capricorn) is the standard account.

A. R. Myers, **England in the Late Middle Ages*** (Penguin); and George Holmes, **The Later Middle Ages, 1272-1485*** (Norton) are excellent surveys of English history during the period. See also Faith Thompson, **A Short History of Parliament, 1295-1642** (Minnesota).

P. S. Lewis, **Later Medieval France** (St. Martin's, 1968) covers government and society in the late Middle Ages. Also recommended are two biographies: J. Michelet, **Joan of Arc*** (Michigan); and John H. Smith, **Joan of Arc** (Scribner's, 1973).

Gabriel Jackson, **The Making of Medieval Spain** (Harcourt Brace Jovanovich) is brief and highly readable with many illustrations. Other excellent surveys are F. Fernandez-Arnesto, **Ferdinand and Isabella** (Taplinger, 1975); J. H. Elliott, **Imperial Spain, 1469-1716*** (Penguin); and C. Roth, **The Spanish Inquisition*** (Norton).

G. Barraclough, **The Origins of Modern Germany*** (Capricorn) is the best account of this period of German history. J. A. Symonds, **The Renaissance in Italy,** Vol. I, **The Age of the Despots** (Peter Smith) is a celebrated account of Italian politics in the fourteenth and fifteenth centuries. D. Waley, **The Italian City Republics*** (McGraw-Hill); and D. S. Chambers, **The Imperial Age of Venice, 1380-1580*** (Harcourt Brace Jovanovich) are brief and well-illustrated.

Good introductions to Slavic eastern Europe are O. Halecki, **Borderlands of Western Civilization: A History of East Central Europe** (Ronald); and F. Dvornik, **The Slavs in European History and Civilization** (Rutgers, 1975).

N. Riasanovsky, **History of Russia,** 2nd ed. (Oxford, 1969); and G. Vernadsky, **History of Russia,*** rev. ed. (Yale) are excellent surveys. See also I. Grey, **Ivan III and the Unification of Russia*** (Collier); and S. Graham, **Ivan the Terrible** (Shoe String, 1968).

*Indicates a less expensive paperbound edition.

CHAPTER 13

The Renaissance: 1300 - 1600

Man Is the Measure

INTRODUCTION. In Italy during the fourteenth and fifteenth centuries men began to view the thousand years that had elapsed since the fall of Rome as the "dark ages"—a time of stagnation and ignorance—in contrast to their own age which appeared to them resplendent in wisdom and beauty. They exuberantly proclaimed that they were participating in an intellectual and esthetic revolution sparked by the "rebirth" *(renaissance)* of the values and forms of classical antiquity. Modern historians have accepted the term *Renaissance* as a convenient label for this exciting age of intellectual and artistic revival. But since the Middle Ages also made rich contributions to civilization, in what ways can the Renaissance be said to signify a "rebirth"?

First of all, there was an intense renewal of interest in the literature of classical Greece and Rome—a development known as the Revival of Learning. No longer were scholars confined to medieval translations of the famous writers of ancient Greece; many began to read the works of Plato, Aristotle, and others in the original Greek. In addition, they searched the monasteries for old Latin manuscripts and translated hitherto unknown works from Greek antiquity into Latin. Thus, the humanists, as these scholars were called, reintroduced classical learning into the mainstream of western thought. Second, while the scholars rediscovered classical thought, artists in Italy were stimulated and inspired by their study and imitation of classical architecture and sculpture.

But the spirit of the Renaissance was not characterized by a mere cult of antiquity, a looking backward into the past. The men of the Renaissance were the harbingers of the modern world, energetically and enthusiastically engaged in reshaping their political, economic, and religious environment, in pushing back geographical boundaries and extending the limits of human knowledge. Renaissance culture strikingly exhibits belief in the worth of man and his desire to think and act as a free agent and a well-rounded individual. The Renaissance spirit was admirably summed up by a versatile genius of the fifteenth century, Leon Battista Alberti, when he declared, "Men can do all things if they will."[1]

In some respects every age is an age of transition, but it may be fair to state that the Renaissance marks one of the turning points in western civilization. The dominant insti-tutions and thought systems of the Middle Ages were becoming devitalized; scholasticism, Church authority, and conformity were on the wane, and a more modern culture which depended on individualism, skepticism, and ultimately on science was taking its place.

We must be cautious in our analysis, however. The Renaissance did not burst forth simultaneously in all parts of Europe, and some medieval habits and institutions persisted for a long time; throughout the Renaissance the vast majority of illiterate common people clung to the ways of their forefathers.

The Renaissance originated with a relatively small, educated group dwelling in the cities of central and northern Italy. We shall begin with the Revival of Learning and the flowering of art in this locality and conclude with a discussion of other facets of the Renaissance as its ideas crossed the Alps to France, Germany, and England. It was in England that the underlying optimism and dynamism of the entire Renaissance period was epitomized by Shakespeare when he said:

> O, wonder!
> How many goodly creatures are there here!
> How beauteous mankind is! O brave new world,
> That has such people in't![2]

THE ITALIAN RENAISSANCE: THE BACKGROUND

The waning of the Middle Ages. By the fourteenth century there was a marked decline in medieval institutions and ideas. The feudal social structure was weakening before the growing power of the middle class, which sided with the new monarchs and thrived on the revival of trade and the growth of towns. The threat of armies using gunpowder was revolutionizing warfare at the expense of armor-clad knights. Heresy and schism racked the Church, and its temporal power was increasingly being challenged by aggressive national monarchs.

An empty formalism replaced the creativeness that had given the twelfth and thirteenth centuries their unique forms of ex-pression. Although asceticism remained a pious ideal, it gained few adherents among the acquisitive townspeople and was openly flouted by many of the clergy. Scholars still held learned disputations at the universities, but scholasticism was unable to satisfy the growing interest in man and society. In art the Gothic style of the twelfth and thirteenth centuries, superb in its balance and restraint, had given place to exaggeration and flamboyance. Decoration and ornamentation became ends in themselves.

Meanwhile, sophisticated Italian urban society no longer found medieval ideals of other-worldliness and asceticism satisfactory. Pious religious themes were not so engaging as satires directed against a sometimes corrupt clergy and the outworn conventions of chivalry. Searching for new modes of expression, thinkers and artists found what they wanted in the classical legacy of Greece and Rome.

Individualism and tradition in the Renaissance. In a sense, the Renaissance is the history of individual men expressing themselves brilliantly, and often tempestuously, in art, poetry, science, religion, and exploration. While the medieval way taught the unimportance of this life, stressed its snares and evils, and smothered the individual with a host of confining rules and prohibitions, the Renaissance beckoned man to enjoy beauty, to savor the opportunities of this world, and to be himself, regardless of restraints. Above all, the new spirit called upon its followers to adopt the concept of *l'uomo universale* ("the universal man" or "the complete man"). Life was best lived when the human personality showed its versatility by expression in many forms: ad-

vancement of the mind, perfection of the body, cultivation of the social graces, and appreciation and creativity in the arts.

Like any other movement, however, individualism had its negative aspects and its excesses. The lawlessness and political confusion of the Italian Renaissance and the strongly amoral character of its society were due in no small measure to the tendency of men to regard themselves as above the law.

Despite the prevalence of individualism, however, most men continued to share in the corporate life of the Church and the guilds, and many medieval customs and habits of thought persisted for centuries. In their love for Greek and Roman authors, Renaissance thinkers appear as subservient to the ancients as their medieval scholastic predecessors. Similarly, the artists of the Renaissance, who found inspiration in antiquity and whose works reflected a renewed interest in classical mythology and in the beauties of the human body, did not break completely with the subject matter and

artistic techniques of their medieval predecessors. Although their interest in rendering secular subjects increased, Renaissance artists still looked to the Church as their greatest single patron. Building churches, sculpturing saints and Madonnas, and painting religious murals continued to occupy the genius of hundreds of artists during this period.

Renaissance patrons. In the Italian cities the newly wealthy class of traders, bankers, and manufacturers conspicuously displayed their wealth and bolstered their social importance by patronizing artists and scholars. While leading commissions for artists in the fifteenth century were still obtained from such communal bodies as guilds and churches, individual patronage began to play a more important role.

Among the most famous patrons were members of the Medici family who, by acting as champions of the lower classes, ruled Florence for sixty years (1434-1494) behind a facade of republican forms. Lorenzo de' Medici, who was first citizen of Florence from 1469 until his death in 1492, carried on

Among the Renaissance concepts which superseded the hierarchic medieval view of the world was the notion of man as a free individual, capable of fashioning his own destiny. A prime incarnation of this idea was the vibrant Florentine nobleman, statesman, and patron of the arts, Lorenzo de' Medici, portrayed here by the sculptor Verrocchio.

his family's proud traditions and added so much luster to Florence that he became known as Lorenzo the Magnificent. His career signifies the zenith of Florentine leadership in the arts.

Other princes and despots of Italian city-states patronized the arts, and the popes were eager to sponsor artists. In the sixteenth century the popes outdid secular rulers in the splendor of their court. Pope Alexander VI (1492-1503), the father of the unscrupulous poisoners Cesare and Lucrezia Borgia, was a target for criticism because he devoted more time and thought to furthering the fortunes of his family than he did to religious matters. Wealthy families actively sought to control the papacy, and the Medici succeeded in placing two of their members, Leo X (1513-1521), son of Lorenzo, and Clement VII (1523-1534), nephew of Leo, in this office. Leo's pontificate, in particular, was one of great activity in the arts and learning in Rome.

A Renaissance artist had the benefit of the security and protection offered by his patron and enjoyed a definite advantage from working exclusively on commission. The artist knew where his finished work would repose, in cathedral, villa, or city square; this situation contrasts with some later periods, when artists painted when and as they wished and then attempted to sell the work to anyone who would buy it.

Manners and morals. During the Renaissance the newly wealthy citizens of the Italian cities sought refinement in every aspect of their culture. Believing that the mark of nobility was an elegance of manner as well as a cultivated mind, they eagerly read etiquette books to learn the rules of correct social behavior.

The most famous book on Renaissance manners, published in 1528, was *The Courtier* by Baldassare Castiglione (1478-1529), which established a model for the Renaissance gentleman. To Castiglione, good manners and deportment were essential to the ideal courtier, but his central idea was that a courtier's true worth was more commensurate with his strength of character and excellence of intellect than with his hereditary social position. The courtier should be a well-

Leonardo da Vinci, who had a wide knowledge of many fields besides painting, typifies the Renaissance ideal of the "universal man." Throughout his life Leonardo carried a sketchbook which he would fill with drawings and notes in his unusual handwriting, written inverted from right to left and best deciphered with a mirror. Although approximately two thirds of his original writings have been lost, nearly 5000 pages of his notes and drawings were compiled after his death. Leonardo would often follow grotesque-looking people, making numerous caricatures and studies like those in the sketch at the right. His interest in anatomy led to amazingly accurate subjects like the drawing of an embryo (far right). His detailed plans for tools of war (below) such as an armored tank which would not be built until centuries later, exemplify his seemingly limitless engineering skills.

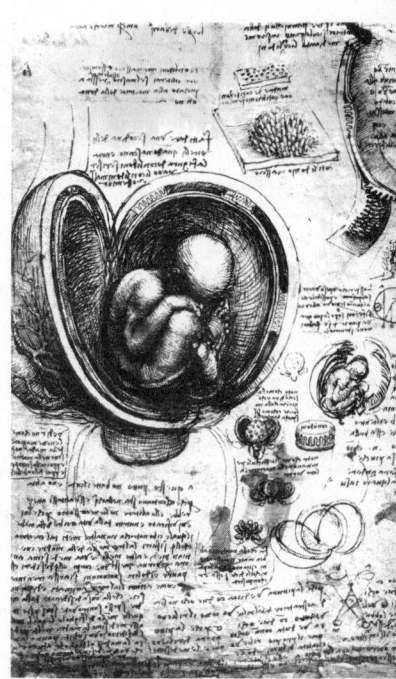

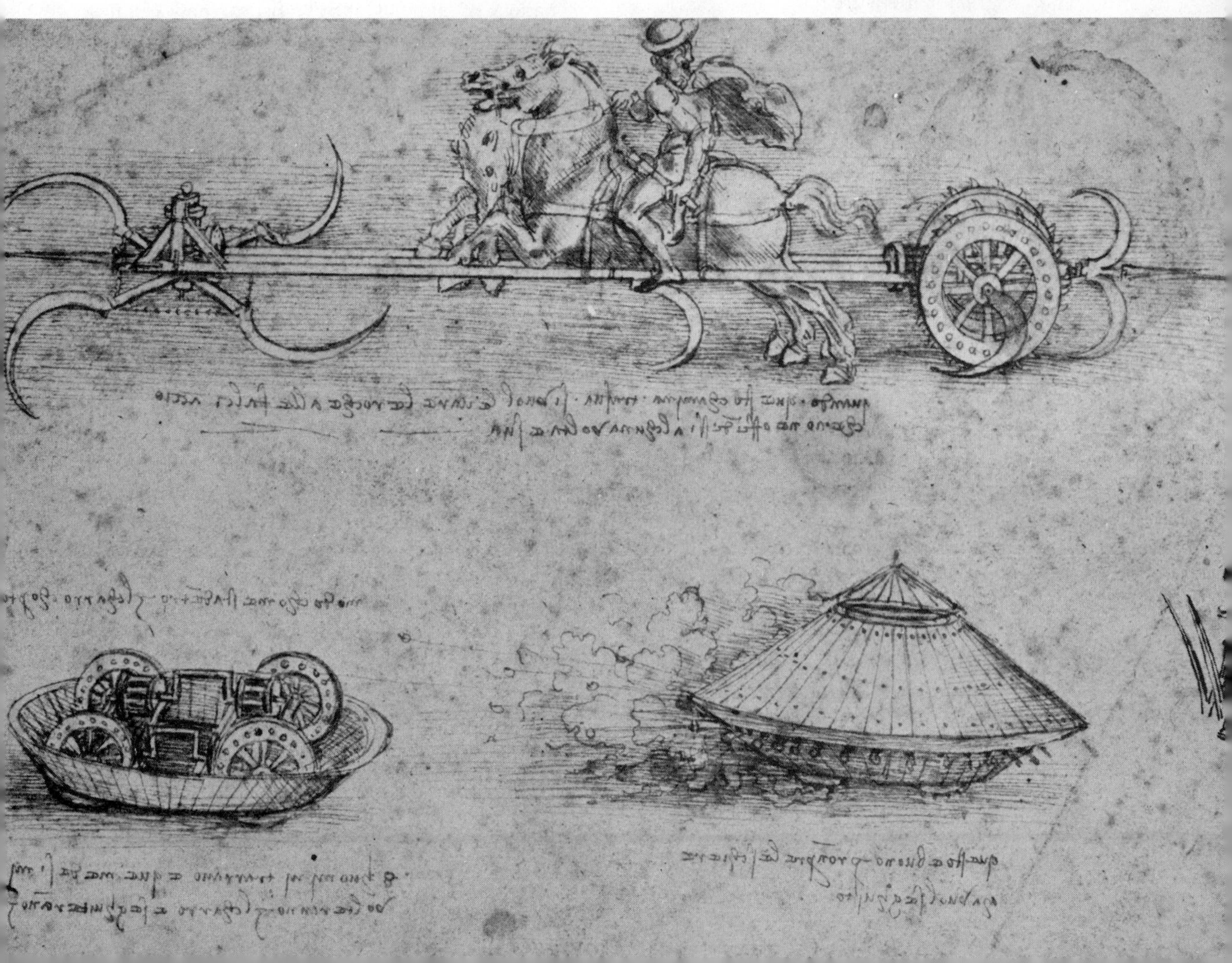

rounded individual, capable in the arts both of war and of peace.

The *Autobiography* of Benvenuto Cellini (1500-1571) gives us a vivid insight into Renaissance manners and morals, but it is no book of etiquette. Cellini was a bold and worldly adventurer, constantly embroiled in excitement and adventure—duels, love affairs, and prison terms. But he was also a fine sculptor (see Chapter 19). Vigorous and energetic, Cellini possessed *virtù,* a term used in the Renaissance to characterize a man of natural ability and abounding vitality. *Virtù* should not be confused with virtue; in fact, a man possessing *virtù* often appeared to be singularly deficient in virtue, as Cellini's life story reveals. Possession of *virtù* enabled a man to be considered *l'uomo universale*, the Renaissance ideal of greatness. While Cellini approximated this ideal, geniuses like Leonardo da Vinci and Michelangelo attained it in a greater measure.

THE REVIVAL OF LEARNING

Humanism and the classical revival. During the Middle Ages, Virgil, Cicero, and Caesar were popular authors; Aristotle was venerated much as though he were a Church Father; and Roman law greatly influenced Church, or canon, law. But in medieval times the writers of antiquity had been interpreted within the framework of the Christian religion and often cited as authorities to bolster Church dogma. Although many aspects of antiquity were avoided because of their disturbingly pagan quality, churchmen did make use of pagan literature for allegorical narratives which were Christian in character. Consequently, the true nature of the classical world was often distorted or obscured.

In fourteenth-century Italy, however, a new perspective was attained and a fresh appreciation of classical culture emerged. Successors to a small group of medieval teachers of grammar and rhetoric, the representatives of this new movement called themselves humanists, a name derived from the *studia humanitatis*, or "humanities," which Roman authors had used in the sense of a liberal or literary education.

Medieval scholastic education had emphasized the sciences and professional training in law, medicine, and theology at the expense of the "arts," or literary side of the curriculum. Hence the scholastics had centered their attention on Aristotle's scientific writings and other ancient works on astronomy, medicine, and mathematics. Stimulated by a rebirth of men's interest in the problems and values of human living, the humanists reversed this medieval emphasis and called attention to the importance of an education in the humanities—history, grammar, rhetoric, poetry, and moral philosophy. The humanists disdained the sciences because, as Petrarch—the first of the Italian humanists—wrote:

. . . they help in no way toward a happy life, for what does it advantage us to be familiar with the nature of animals, birds, fishes, and reptiles, while we are ignorant of the nature of the race of man to which we belong, and do not know or care whence we come or whither we go?[3]

Thus, despite the fact that both the humanist and the scholastic looked to the past and venerated its heritage, they differed widely in their choice of the ancient material to be revered.

Humanists and scholastics also differed in the manner in which they saw themselves in relation to the writers of ancient times. While the scholastic always felt himself inferior to the ancients and looked up to them as son to father or pupil to teacher, the typical humanist in his exultant individualism saw himself equal to the ancients and boldly hailed them as man to man and friend to friend. At the beginning of his *Divine Comedy* Dante described medieval man's reliance upon the authority of the ancients in allegorical terms. Dante (medieval man) is lost in the "dark wood" which is this life until he is rescued by Virgil (a favorite medieval symbol of ancient wisdom), who thereafter guides him along the right path. "Losing me," Virgil is made to say to Dante, "ye would remain astray."

The noticeably different attitude of the humanists was well expressed by one of their few medieval forerunners, John of Salisbury (d. 1180): "Most delightful in many ways is the fruit of letters that, banishing the irksomeness of intervals of place and time, bring friends into each other's presence. . . ."[4] It was in this spirit that Petrarch wrote his *Letters to Ancient Authors*, addressing Homer, Plato, Cicero, and others in familiar terms and sharing with them his own thoughts and experiences. This feeling of equality with ancient authors was also behind the humanists' practice of stuffing their own writings with apt quotations from the classics. The humanists' purpose, however, differed from that of the scholastics, who also quoted extensively from the ancients; as the humanist Montaigne explained in his essays (see p. 300), he quoted the ancients not because he agreed with them but because they agreed with him!

Petrarch, the "father of humanism." The "father of humanism" is a title that has been given to Francesco Petrarca, better known to us as Petrarch (1304-1374). Resentful as a youth of his father's desire to have him become a lawyer, he turned to reading Virgil and Cicero for consolation; and though he studied law at Bologna, he dreamed constantly of the glories of the classical age.

In 1327 he met the lady Laura and fell in love with her. Little is known of Laura or of the true nature of her relationship to Petrarch. But inspired by his love of her, Petrarch wrote sonnets which made him one of the greatest lyric poets of all time. In the love poetry of the age, his portrayal of Laura represents a fresh approach. Earlier poets had woven about their heroines an air of courtly love and religious idealization which made the characters quite unreal. Petrarch's Laura was a flesh-and-blood creature whom all readers could recognize as human.

The ancients wrote of the joys of this world, and their attitude toward life struck a sympathetic chord in Petrarch. In his *Secret* Petrarch has an imaginary conversation with St. Augustine which forcibly brings out the conflict between new ideas and those of medieval times. Petrarch concluded that, despite the importance of the world to come, the world of here and now held many delights which should not be shunned.

This inner conflict between his love of earthly things and his loyalty to the traditional medieval ideal of self-denial and other-worldliness exemplifies the transitional position Petrarch occupied in western culture. A product of medieval beliefs and attitudes, he nevertheless could not accept a depreciation of man's importance in the scheme of things or a constriction of his mental horizons. And thus he condemned the rigidity and arid logic of scholasticism and the extent to which medieval education was governed by dead tradition. He himself was not a careful scholar and never learned Greek, yet this versatile rebel had profound influence and gave humanism its first great impetus.

Boccaccio and the Decameron. Another early humanist was Giovanni Boccaccio (1313-1375), who began his career as a writer of poetry and romances. In 1348 the calamitous Black Death struck—a disaster which wiped out nearly two thirds of Florence's population. Boccaccio used this event to establish the setting of his masterpiece, the *Decameron*. To escape the pestilence, his characters—three young men and seven young women—sought seclusion in a country villa, where they whiled away the time by telling each other stories. Boccaccio suffused the hundred tales of the *Decameron*, based on the old *fabliaux* (see p. 257) and on chivalric accounts, with a new and different spirit. Recounted by sophisticated city dwellers, the tales satirize the follies of knights and other medieval types and express clearly the contempt which had developed for the old, and by then threadbare, ideals of feudalism. Many tales are bawdy and even scandalous—a charge which Boccaccio undertook to refute:

Some of you may say that in writing these tales I have taken too much license, by making ladies sometimes say and often listen to matters which are not proper to be said or heard by virtuous ladies. This I deny, for there is nothing so unchaste but may be said chastely if modest words are used; and this I think I have done.[5]

Nevertheless, the *Decameron* offers a wealth of anecdotes, portraits of flesh-and-blood characters, and a vivid (although one-sided) picture of Renaissance life.

The *Decameron* closed Boccaccio's career as a creative artist. Largely through the influence of Petrarch, whom he met in 1350, Boccaccio gave up writing in the Italian vernacular and turned to the study of antiquity. He attempted to learn Greek, wrote an encyclopedia of classical mythology, and went off to monasteries in search of manuscripts. By the time Petrarch and Boccaccio died, the study of the literature and learning of antiquity was growing throughout Italy.

The search for manuscripts. The search for manuscripts became a mania, and before the middle of the fifteenth century works by most of the important Latin authors had been found. The degree of difference between humanist and scholastic is indicated by the ease with which the early humanists recovered the "lost" Latin literary masterpieces: they were found close at hand in monastic libraries, covered by the undisturbed dust of centuries. The books had always been there; what had been largely lacking was a mature and appreciative audience of readers. In addition to these Latin works, precious Greek manuscripts were brought to Italy from Constantinople during the fifteenth century.

Individual scholars had their favorite classical authors, both Greek and Roman, but the highest universal praise was reserved for Cicero. Compounded of moral philosophy and rhetoric, his work displayed a wide-ranging intellect which appealed to many humanists. The revival of the art of writing classical Latin prose was due largely to the study and imitation of Cicero's graceful, eloquent, and polished literary style.

Revival of Platonism. As a result both of their rebellion against the Aristotelian emphasis upon natural science and of their search for a classical philosophy that stressed moral purpose and religious and mystical values, many humanists gravitated to Platonism during the fifteenth century. A factor in this revival was the study of Plato in the original Greek, particularly at Florence where Cosimo de' Medici, one of the great patrons of the Renaissance, founded the informal club that came to be known as the Platonic

Academy. Its leader, Marsilio Ficino (1433-1499), who always kept a candle burning before a bust of Plato, made the first complete Latin translation of Plato's works.

Ficino also sought to synthesize Christianity and Plato, much as St. Thomas Aquinas had done with Aristotle. In his principal work, *Theologia Platonica*, Ficino viewed Plato as essentially Christian and Plato's "religious philosophy" as a God-sent means of converting intellectuals. He coined the expression "Platonic love" to describe an ideal, pure love, and this concept found its way into much of Renaissance literature.

Aristotelianism. Despite its great attraction for many humanists, Platonism still had a formidable rival in Aristotelianism. Concerned chiefly with natural philosophy, logic, and metaphysics, Aristotelian commentators still dominated teaching in the Italian universities.

The most influential Aristotelians were the Latin Averroists, followers of the Muslim philosopher Averroës (see p. 165). The Averroists followed Aristotle in teaching that matter is eternal and in denying the immortality of the soul. Since such views were contrary to the Biblical story of creation and the belief in personal immortality, the Averroists advocated the doctrine of "double truth"—a truth in philosophy need not be valid in religion.

By the fifteenth century Padua had become the center of Aristotelianism, which reached its peak in the next century. By championing a secular rationalism that kept philosophy separate from theology, its adherents helped create an environment necessary for the triumph of scientific thought in the seventeenth century. As we shall see in Chapter 19, the new developments that Aristotelianism encouraged were to overthrow Aristotle's own brilliant but outmoded theories in physics and other fields of science.

Evaluation of humanism. We owe the humanists a debt of gratitude for reintroducing the whole of Latin and Greek literature into the mainstream of western thought. From their reading of the classics, humanists came to understand the classical world in a true historical perspective and corrected many misconceptions about ancient times which had existed in the Middle Ages. Medieval scholars, for example, had pictured Alexander the Great's soldiers as knights, but Renaissance historians no longer made such naive mistakes.

On the other hand, although the humanists condemned medieval restrictions, they themselves were often subservient to the authorities of antiquity. Indeed, theirs was a closed culture whose boundaries had been set by ancient Greece and Rome, so that the only course open to them was to retravel the ground, not to explore uncharted territory. Intent on returning to antiquity, so to speak, the humanists resented the centuries separating them from the golden days of Greece and Rome. Unfortunately, this viewpoint resulted in their disparagement of the best works produced in the Middle Ages.

The cult of classical letters gave rise to other defects. Humanist scholars were so dominated by Roman and Greek forms that they tended to imitate rather than to create for themselves. Their passion for Ciceronian Latin became pernicious; too often their writings were rich in form but barren in content. Worse still, their preoccupation with classical authors retarded the growth of a much more vital vernacular literature—as in the case of Boccaccio, who gave up writing prose and poetry in Italian to devote himself to Latin studies.

The humanists' contributions to philosophy were not extensive; they did little original thinking. Nevertheless the spread of humanistic influence resulted in a renewed and valuable emphasis upon the freedom and dignity of man as an individual and the importance of his place in the cosmos. This interest was manifested not only in literature but also in the fine arts.

ITALIAN RENAISSANCE ART

Transitional period in sculpture and painting. North of the Alps during the fourteenth and fifteenth centuries there was a continuation of "Gothic" art—in painting and sculpture, the same emphasis on realistic detail (see illustrations, pp. 230, 261); in architecture, an elaboration of the Gothic style. Fourteenth-century Italy, however, produced innovations in painting and sculpture that mark the beginnings of Renaissance art. Influenced by the humanistic spirit in thought and religion, a new society centered in rich cities, and a revived interest in antique art, Italian Renaissance art reached its zenith early in the sixteenth century.

The greatest figure in the transitional art of the fourteenth century was the Florentine painter Giotto (1266-1336), who, it was said,

Renaissance artists presented traditional subject matter in novel ways. Giotto's "Lamentation over the Dead Christ," one of thirty-eight frescoes painted for the Arena Chapel in Padua, lends a new drama and a new credibility to a familiar Biblical story.

"achieved little less than the resurrection of painting from the dead." While earlier Italian painters had copied the unreal, flat, and rigidly formalized images of Byzantine paintings and mosaics, Giotto observed from life and painted a three-dimensional world peopled with believable human beings dramatically moved by deep emotion (see illustration, p. 289). He humanized painting as St. Francis humanized religion.

Quattrocento painting. The lull in painting that followed Giotto, during which his technical innovations were retained but the spirit and compassion that make him one of the world's great painters were lost, lasted until the beginning of the *quattrocento* (Italian for "four hundred," an abbreviation for the 1400's). In his brief lifetime the Florentine Masaccio (1401-1428) completed the revolution in technique begun by Giotto. As can be seen in his various works, Masaccio largely mastered the problems of perspective, anatomical naturalism of flesh and bone, and the modeling of figures in light and shade *(chiaroscuro)* rather than by sharp line. Masaccio was also the first to paint nude figures whose counterparts can be found in classical, but not in medieval, art.

Inspired by Masaccio's achievement, most *quattrocento* painters constantly sought to improve technique. This search for greater realism culminated in such painters as Andrea Mantegna (1431-1506), whose "St. James on the Way to His Execution" well shows the results of his lifelong study of perspective.

While Masaccio and his successors were intent upon giving their figures a new solidity and resolving the problem of three-dimensional presentation, a later Florentine painter, Sandro Botticelli (1447-1510), proceeded in a different direction, abandoning the techniques of straightforward representation of people and objects. Botticelli used a highly sensitive, even quivering, line to stir the viewer's imagination and emotion and to create a mood in keeping with his subject matter, frankly pagan at first but later deeply religious. Movement and the patterning of hair and drapery in such allegorical and mythological works as the "Birth of Venus" are particularly sensitive (see illustration, p. 291).

Quattrocento sculpture. In the meantime progress was being made in sculpture, and it, like painting, reached stylistic maturity at the beginning of the *quattrocento*. In his two sets of bronze doors for the baptistery in Florence, on which he labored for forty-four years, Lorenzo Ghiberti (1378-1455) achieved the goal he had set for himself: "I strove to imitate nature as closely as I could, and with all the perspective I could produce." These marvels of relief sculpture (p. 292), which drew from Michelangelo the declaration that they were worthy to be the gates of

"St. James on the Way to His Execution," a fresco by Andrea Mantegna, is innovative in its perspective and use of classical models. St. James, at the left, is shown blessing a Roman soldier and healing a paralytic. Mantegna's interest in historical detail is obvious in both the classical buildings and the costumes of the soldiers.

The Renaissance emulation of the ideals of classical Greece and Rome extended to large-scale treatments of mythological subjects in painting and sculpture. The "Birth of Venus" by Sandro Botticelli contains the first important image since Roman times of the nude goddess in a pose similar to classical statues of Venus. This painting, done by Botticelli for the Medici family, was opposed to the Florentine artistic tradition of the period.

paradise, depict skillfully modeled human figures—including some classically inspired nudes—which stand out spatially against architectural and landscape backgrounds.

Although Ghiberti was a superb craftsman, he was less of an innovator than his younger contemporary in Florence, Donatello (1386-1466), who visited Rome to study the remains of antique statuary. Divorcing sculpture from its architectural background, Donatello produced truly freestanding statues based on the realization of the human body as a functional, coordinated mechanism of bones, muscles, and sinews, maintaining itself against the pull of gravity. His "David" is the first bronze nude made since antiquity, and his equestrian statue of Gattamelata the *condottiere* is the first of its type done in the Renaissance. The latter clearly reveals the influence of classical models and was probably inspired by the equestrian statue of Marcus Aurelius in Rome.

More dramatic than either of these equestrian statues is that of the Venetian *condottiere* Bartolomeo Colleoni (see p. 293), the creation of Andrea del Verrocchio (1435-1488). A versatile Florentine artist noteworthy as a sculptor, painter, and the teacher of Leonardo da Vinci, Verrocchio designed the statue of Colleoni to permit one of the horse's forelegs to be unsupported—a considerable achievement. The posture and features of the *condottiere* convey dramatically a sense of the supreme self-confidence and arrogance usually associated with Renaissance public figures.

Quattrocento architecture. Renaissance architecture, which far more than sculpture reflects the influence of ancient Roman models, began with the work of Filippo Brunelleschi (1377-1446). As a youth Brunelleschi

In 1403 the sculptor Lorenzo Ghiberti won a competition to design the bronze doors for the baptistry of the Florence Cathedral. His subject was scenes from the Old Testament; the panel shown is from the story of Esau and Jacob. The magnificently decorated doors well deserve the title given them by Michelangelo—the "Gates of Paradise."

accompanied Donatello to Rome where he employed measuring stick and sketchbook to master the principles of classical architecture. Returning to Florence, Brunelleschi constructed the lofty dome of the cathedral, the first to be built since Roman times. Although strongly influenced by classical architecture, Brunelleschi's buildings in Florence, which include churches and palaces, were not just copies of Roman models. Employing arcades of Roman arches, Roman pediments above the windows, and engaged Roman columns and other decorative motifs, Brunelleschi re-created the Roman style in a fresh and original manner.

The High Renaissance, 1500-1530. During the High Renaissance the center of artistic activity shifted from Florence to Rome and Venice, where wealthier patrons lived and where consequently greater opportunities were available to artists. The popes were lavish patrons, and the greatest artists of the period worked in the Vatican at one time or another. It did not seem inconsistent to popes and artists to include representations of pagan mythological figures in the decorations of the papal palace, and thus the Vatican was filled with secular as well as religious art.

The great architect of the High Renaissance was Donato Bramante (1444-1514) from Milan. Bramante's most important commission came in 1506 when Pope Julius II requested him to replace the old basilica of St. Peter, built by the emperor Constantine, with a monumental Renaissance structure. Bramante's plan called for a centralized church in the form of a Greek cross surmounted by an immense dome. The exterior of St. Peter's exemplifies the spirit of High Renaissance architecture—to approach nearer to the monumentality and grandeur of Roman architecture. In Bramante's own words, he would place "the Pantheon on top of the Basilica of Maxentius.'' Bramante died when the cathedral was barely begun, and it was left to Michelangelo and others to complete the work (see illustrations, p. 294).

High Renaissance architects also produced magnificent palaces and other secular buildings. Their decorative features show how classical details blended in a new fashion resulted in an impressive and refined structure. From the sixteenth century on, all Europe began to take to the new architecture.

The painters of the High Renaissance inherited the solutions to such technical problems as perspective space from the *quattrocento* artists. But whereas the artists of the earlier period had been concerned with movement, color, and narrative detail, painters in the High Renaissance strove to eliminate nonessentials and concentrated on the central theme of a picture and its basic human implications. By this process of elimination, many High Renaissance painters achieved a "classic" effect of seriousness and serenity and endowed their works with idealistic values.

Leonardo da Vinci. The great triad of High Renaissance painters consists of Leonardo da Vinci, Raphael, and Michelangelo. An extraordinary man, Leonardo da Vinci (1452-1519) was proficient in a variety of fields: engineering, mathematics, architecture, geology, botany, physiology, anatomy, sculpture, painting, music, and poetry. He was always experimenting, with the result that few of the projects he started were ever finished.

A superb draftsman, Leonardo was also a master of soft modeling in full light and shade and of creating groups of figures perfectly balanced in a given space. One of his most famous paintings is the "Mona Lisa," a portrait of a woman whose enigmatic smile has intrigued art lovers for centuries. Another is "The Last Supper," a study of the moment when Christ tells his twelve disciples that one will betray him. When he painted this picture on the walls of the refectory of Santa Maria delle Grazie in Milan, Leonardo was experimenting with the use of an oil medium combined with plaster, and, unfortunately, the experiment was unsuccessful. The painting quickly began to disintegrate and has had to be repainted several times. Last of the great Florentine painters, Leonardo combined an advanced knowledge of technique with deep psychological insight into many facets of human nature (see p. 285).

Raphael. The second of the great triad of High Renaissance painters was Raphael (1483-1520). By the time he was summoned to Rome to aid in the decoration of the Vatican, Raphael had absorbed something of Leonardo's intellectuality and Michelangelo's "body dynamics" and grandeur. His Stanze frescoes in the Vatican display a magnificent blending of classical and Christian subject matter and are imbued with a clarity and breadth of vision expressive of the High Renaissance at its best. Considered by some critics as unrivaled in the mastery of space composition, Raphael was equally at home in handling a single figure or in grouping masses (see illustration, p. 296).

Michelangelo. The individualism and idealism of the High Renaissance have no greater representative than Michelangelo

In Verrocchio's "Monument to Colleoni" the spirit of the great military leader is captured in the face, which is individual and very human rather than classical.

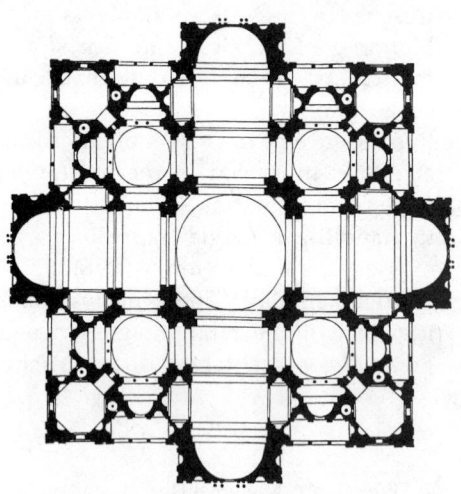

Bramante designed St. Peter's in the shape of a Greek cross with a dome similar to that of the Pantheon (see his architectural drawing). After his death, however, his plan was modified. Michelangelo redesigned the dome—which has been called the greatest achievement of Renaissance architecture—and later a long nave was added to the front of the church, giving it the form of a Latin cross rather than of a Greek cross. The courtyard view of the Palazzo Farnese in Rome shows the classical simplicity and symmetry which marked late Italian Renaissance palaces. The even spacing of the windows, the equal height of the three stories, and the repetition of decorative motifs all contribute to a feeling of unity in design.

Buonarroti (1475-1564). Stories of this stormy and temperamental personality have helped shape our ideas of what a genius is like. Indeed, there is something almost superhuman about both Michelangelo and his art. His great energy enabled him to complete in four years the entire work of painting the ceiling of the Vatican's Sistine Chapel, an area of several thousand square yards, and his art embodies a superhuman ideal of man. With his unrivaled genius for rendering the human form, he devised a wealth of expressive positions and attitudes for his figures in scenes from Genesis. Their physical splendor is pagan, but their spirit is Christian (see p. 296).

Michelangelo considered himself first and foremost a sculptor, and this *uomo universale*, who also excelled as poet, engineer, and architect, was undoubtedly the greatest sculptor of the Renaissance. The glorification of the human body, particularly the male nude, was Michelangelo's great achievement. Fired by the grandeur of such newly discovered pieces of Hellenistic sculpture as the Laocoön group and strongly influenced by Platonism, he expressed in art his idealized view of man's dignity and majesty (see Color Plate 11). Succeeding Bramante as chief architect of St. Peter's, Michelangelo designed the great dome (see p. 294), and was in the midst of creative activities when he died, almost in his ninetieth year, in 1564. He had long outlived the High Renaissance.

The Venetian school. Venice offered a congenial environment to artists. A prosperous merchant-prince could well afford to play the role of patron of the arts; trade with the East provided Venetians with luxuries and comforts which added splendor and color to daily life; and the beauty of the city itself would attract the eye of any artist.

This wealthy, sophisticated milieu produced a secular rather than a devotional school of painting. Most Venetian artists were satisfied with the here and now; they were not overly concerned with antiquity or classical canons. While they sometimes painted exquisite Madonnas, they more often painted wealthy merchants and proud doges, attired in rich brocades, jewels, and precious metals and grouped with beautiful young women who scarcely looked like Madonnas. There is a sensuousness in the Venetian painting of this period which is evident in the artists' love of decoration, rich costumes, radiant light and color, and striking nude figures.

Giorgione (1478-1511), like Botticelli, used classical themes and idyllic landscapes in his paintings. But unlike the Florentine master, who made his mythological figures imaginative and idealized, Giorgione's muses and Venuses were lovely Venetian models.

The pictures of Titian (1485?-1576) contain sensuous beauties of color and atmosphere. During his long working life he proved himself a master of a wide variety of subjects ranging from religion to pagan mythology. His portraits, which earned him the greatest fame among his contemporaries, show the Venetian love of color and texture of rich fabrics (see p. 296).

High Renaissance music. In contrast to the single-voiced or homophonic music—called plain song or Gregorian chant—of the early Middle Ages, the late medieval composers wrote many-voiced, many-melodied, or polyphonic music. Polyphony often involved a shuttling back and forth from one melody to another—musical counterpoint. By the fifteenth century as many as twenty-four voice parts were combined into one intricately woven musical pattern. The composers of the High Renaissance continued to produce complicated polyphonic music, but in a calmer and grander manner. Compared with the style of his predecessors, that of Josquin des Près (d. 1521), the founder of High Renaissance music, "is both grander and more simple. All stark intervals of early polyphony are ruled out; few dissonances are used, and the rhythms and forms used are based on strict symmetry and mathematically regular proportions. Josquin handled all technical problems of complicated constructions with the same ease and sureness one finds in the drawings of Leonardo and Raphael."[6] During the sixteenth century, also, instruments such as the violin, spinet, and harpsichord developed from more rudimentary types.

The Renaissance in Italy stimulated many

Michelangelo's "Creation of Adam" (top), one of the major scenes on the ceiling of the Sistine Chapel, depicts God, with Eve protected under His left arm, instilling life in Adam by merely pointing His finger. The frescoed figures have a sculptural quality that creates an illusion of roundness and depth. While Michelangelo used the human figure as an expression of spirituality and sublime beauty, Raphael's works stressed the earthly qualities of natural human beauty. Although the subject matter is religious, his "Madonna of the Chair" (bottom left) is endowed with a warm, human quality. This painting also demonstrates Raphael's concern for form and equilibrium within a composition. Titian's paintings are marked by their sensuousness and intense, jewel-like colors. His "Young Woman at Her Toilet" (bottom right) typifies his favorite theme of warm feminine beauty.

new forms of secular music, especially the madrigal, a love lyric set to music. The madrigal found favor in England, while French *chansons* and German *lieder* added to the growing volume of secular music.

THE NORTHERN RENAISSANCE

The northward spread of the Renaissance. The Italian Renaissance had projected man once more into the center of life's stage and permeated the intellectual and artistic environment with humanistic values. In time the stimulating ideas current in Italy spread to other areas and combined with indigenous developments to produce a French Renaissance, an English Renaissance, and so on.

While the wealthy burghers of the northern cities patronized the work of artists and scholars, the prime sponsors of the Renaissance north of the Alps were often the kings of the new national states. By importing artists and learned men from Italy or supporting native geniuses, the rulers added brilliance to their courts.

The influence of printing. Perhaps even more important in the diffusion of the Renaissance and later in the success of the Reformation was the invention of printing in Europe. The essential elements—paper and block printing—had been known in China since the eighth century. During the twelfth century the Spanish Muslims introduced papermaking to Europe; in the thirteenth century Europeans were in close contact with China (see Chapter 7) and block printing became known in the West. The crucial step was taken in the 1440's at Mainz, in Germany, where Johann Gutenberg and other printers invented movable type by cutting up old printing blocks to form individual letters. Gutenberg used movable type to print papal documents and the first published version of the Bible (1454).

Within fifty years after Gutenberg's Bible had been published, all the major countries of Europe possessed the means for printing books. It is said that the prices of books soon sank to one eighth of their former cost, thus placing books within the reach of a multitude of people who formerly had been unable to buy them. In addition, pamphlets and controversial tracts soon were widely circulated, and new ideas reached a thousand times more people in a relatively short span of time. In the quickening of Europe's intellectual life, it is difficult to overestimate the effects of the printing press.

Erasmus and northern Humanism. The intellectual life of the first half of the sixteenth century was dominated by Desiderius Erasmus (1466?-1536). Born in Rotterdam, he passed most of his long life elsewhere—in Germany, France, England, Italy, and especially Switzerland. The most influential and cosmopolitan of the northern humanists, he corresponded with nearly every prominent writer and thinker in Europe and knew

Although printing was a far superior system of reproducing books than hand copying, it still was a slow, tedious, and expensive process. A copy of the Gutenberg Bible cost forty-two gulden, a price equivalent to that of fourteen oxen. Although large books were beyond the means of most common people, the presses turned out small books, pamphlets, and circulars in large quantities for common consumption.

The high level of European portraiture in the sixteenth century reflected the man-centered outlook of the time. The traditional meticulous realism of the north was employed by Hans Holbein the Younger, who recorded the likeness of the humanist Erasmus—as well as other famous contemporaries—with jewel-like accuracy and brilliance.

personally popes, emperors, and kings. He was *the* scholar of Europe, and his writings were read eagerly everywhere.

Perhaps the most famous and influential work by Erasmus was *In Praise of Folly*, a satire written in 1511. Folly, the term used in the Middle Ages as a synonym for human nature, is described by Erasmus as the source not only of much harmless enjoyment in life but also of many things that are wrong and need correcting. A historian has described the work in these words: "At first the book makes kindly and approving fun of the ways of action and the foibles and weaknesses of mankind. It is not mordant, only amused. But gradually from fools innocent and natural and undebased, it passes to those whose il-

lusions are vicious in their setting and results."[7] Among such are merchants ("they lie, swear, cheat, and practice all the intrigues of dishonesty"), lawyers ("they of all men have the greatest conceit of their own abilities"), scholastic philosophers ("that talk as much by rote as a parrot"), and scientists ("who esteem themselves the only favourites of wisdom, and look upon the rest of mankind as the dirt and rubbish of the creation"). Most roughly handled are churchmen, in particular monks, who are "impudent pretenders to the profession of piety," and popes, cardinals, and bishops, "who in pomp and splendour have almost equalled if not outdone secular princes." While his satire is indeed harsh, Erasmus was himself balanced, moderate, and intolerant only of bigotry, ignorance, greed, and violence.

In Praise of Folly points up a significant difference between the northern humanists and their Italian predecessors. While both were repelled by much that seemed to them wrong in the life of their day, their reactions took different forms. The typical Italian humanists followed the course set by Petrarch: "In order to forget my own time I have constantly striven to place myself in spirit in other ages. . . ."[8] Disdaining such escapism, the great majority of northern humanists faced up to reality and became reformers of their society's ills. They also went further in broadening their interest in ancient literature to include early Christian writings—the Scriptures and the works of the Church Fathers. This led them to prepare new and more accurate editions of the Scriptures (Erasmus' Greek edition of the New Testament became famous and was used by Luther) and to compare unfavorably the complexities of the Church in their own day with the simplicity of primitive Christianity. Since the northern humanists held that the essence of religion was morality and rational piety—what Erasmus called the "philosophy of Christ"—rather than ceremony and dogma, it is not surprising that the Church became a major target of their reforming zeal.

Sir Thomas More's Utopia. The most significant figure in English humanism was Sir Thomas More (1478-1535), the friend of Erasmus. More is best known for his *Utopia*, the first important description of the ideal state since Plato's *Republic*. In his epoch-making work More criticized his age by using as his spokesman a fictitious sailor who contrasts the ideal life he has seen in Utopia (The Land of Nowhere) with the harsh conditions of life in England. More's denunciations centered on the new acquisitive capitalism, which he blamed for the widespread insecurity and misery of the lower classes. More felt that governments

are a conspiracy of the rich, who, in pretence of managing the public, only pursue their private ends, . . . first, that they may, without danger, preserve all that they have so ill acquired, and then, that they may engage the poor to toil and labor for them at as low rates as possible, and oppress them as much as they please.[9]

In Utopia, by contrast, no man is in want because the economy is planned and cooperative and because property is held in common. Utopia is the only true commonwealth, concludes More's imaginary sailor:

In all other places, it is visible that while people talk of a commonwealth, every man only seeks his own wealth: but there, where no man has any property, all men zealously pursue the good of the public. . . . in Utopia, where every man has a right to every thing, they all know that if care is taken to keep the public stores full, no private man can want any thing; for among them there is no unequal distribution, so that no man is poor, none in necessity; and though no man has anything, yet they are all rich; for what can make a man so rich as to lead a serene and cheerful life, free from anxieties; neither apprehending want himself, nor vexed with the endless complaints of his wife?[10]

More was the first of the modern English socialists, but his philosophy should not be considered a forerunner of the socialism of our day. His economic outlook was a legacy from the Middle Ages, and his preference for medieval collectivism over modern individualism was of a piece with his preference for a Church headed—medieval style—by popes rather than by kings, a view that prompted Henry VIII to execute him for treason (see p. 315).

Rabelais. One of the best known of the French humanists was François Rabelais (1494-1553). A brilliant, if coarse, lover of all life from the sewers to the heavens, Rabelais is best remembered for his work *Gargantua and Pantagruel* (published 1533-1552). Centering on figures from French folklore, this work relates the adventures of Gargantua and his son Pantagruel, genial giants of tremendous stature and appetite, to whom were ascribed many marvelous feats.

In the course of his pungent narrative, Rabelais inserted his views on educational reform and his humanistic belief in man's inherent goodness and ability to solve his problems by reason. He made vitriolic attacks on the abuses of the Church and the shortcomings of scholastics and monks, but he had little patience with overzealous Protestants either. What Rabelais could not stomach was hypocrisy and repression; and for those guilty of these tendencies, he reserved his choicest invective. In the following excerpt he bids his readers to flee from that

rabble of squint-minded fellows, dissembling and counterfeit saints, demure lookers, hypocrites, pretended zealots, tough friars, buskin-monks, and other such sects of men, who disguise themselves like masquers to deceive the world. . . . Fly from these men, abhor and hate them as much as I do, and upon my faith you will find yourself the better for it. And if you desire . . . *to live in peace, joy, health, making yourselves always merry*, never trust those men that always peep out through a little hole.[11]

Von Hutten: German humanist and patriot. One of the outstanding German humanists was Ulrich von Hutten (1488-1523). In him was blended a hatred of ecclesiastical abuses with romantic nationalist feelings. This scion of an aristocratic family, who wanted to unite Germany under the emperor, led a tumultuous life as a wandering Greek scholar and satirist. He supported Luther as a rallying point for German unity against the papacy, to which Von Hutten attributed most of his compatriots' ills. Although he neither reconciled his humanistic philosophy with Luther's theology nor formulated a practical political program, Von Hutten reflected the tensions and aspirations of the German people in the early years of the sixteenth century.

This portrait of Michel de Montaigne, the originator of the modern essay, is ascribed to the French School of Corneille de Lyon.

Montaigne. The last notable northern humanist was the French skeptic Michel de Montaigne (1533-1592). At the age of thirty-eight he gave up the practice of law and retired to his country estate and well-stocked library, where he studied and wrote. Montaigne developed a new literary form and gave it its name—the essay. In ninety-four essays he set forth his personal views on many subjects: leisure, friendship, education, philosophy, religion, old age, death, and so forth. He did not pretend to have the final answer to the subjects he discussed. Instead, he advocated open-mindedness and toleration—rare qualities in the sixteenth century, when France was racked by religious and civil strife.

Montaigne condemned the pedantry into which humanism and humanistic education had largely degenerated by the end of the sixteenth century, arguing that "To know by heart is not to know; it is to retain what we have given our memory to keep."[12] Even today's student may have cause to listen sympathetically to the following words:

Our tutors never stop bawling into our ears, as though they were pouring water into a funnel; and our task is only to repeat what has been told us. I should like the tutor to correct this practice . . . I want him to listen to his pupil speaking in his turn.[13]

Montaigne's final essay, entitled "Of Experience," which developed the thought that "when reason fails us we resort to experience," is an acknowledgment of the bankruptcy of humanism and a foreshadowing of the coming triumph of science.

Cervantes, creator of Don Quixote. The transition from feudal knight to Renaissance courtier finds its greatest literary expression in a masterpiece of Spanish satire, *Don Quixote de la Mancha*, the work of Miguel de Cervantes (1547-1616). By Cervantes' day knighthood had become an anachronism, though its accompanying code of chivalry still retained its appeal. It remained for a rationalist like Cervantes to show up the inadequacies of chivalric idealism in a world that had acquired new, and intensely practical, aims. He did so by creating a pathetic but infinitely appealing character to serve as the personification of an outmoded way of life.

Don Quixote, the "knight of the woeful countenance," mounted on his "lean, lank, meagre, drooping, sharp-backed, and rawboned" steed Rozinante, sets out in the Spanish countryside to right wrongs and uphold his lady's and his own honor. In his misadventures he is accompanied by his squire, the much less gallant but infinitely more realistic Sancho Panza, whose peasant adages and hard-grained common sense serve as a contrast to the unpractical nature of his master's chivalric code. Tilting at windmills, mistaking serving wenches for highborn ladies and inns for castles, and lamenting the invention of gunpowder as depriving ardent knights of a chance to win immortality, Don Quixote is, on the surface at least, a ridiculous old man whose nostalgia for the "good old days" is a constant source of grief to him. Thus the story represents a superb satire directed against the outworn ideology of the Middle Ages; in particular, it laughed the ideal of chivalric romance into the world of make-believe.

And yet *Don Quixote* is still more. Cervantes instilled in his main character a pathos born in large measure of the author's own career of frustrated hopes and ambitions. As a result, Don Quixote becomes more than a romantic lunatic; he serves to embody that set of ideals which each of us would like to see realized but which we must compromise in a world that has other interests to serve.

Secular drama appears. Like Greek drama, medieval drama developed out of religious ceremonies (see p. 258). A complete divorce of the Church and stage did not occur until the middle of the fifteenth century when the Renaissance era of drama began in Italian cities with the performance of ancient Roman comedies. In the following century appeared the *commedia dell'arte*, reflections of everyday life in vulgar and slapstick fashion usually improvised by the players from a plot outline.

As secular dramas grew in popularity, theaters were built as permanent settings for their presentations. Great ingenuity was shown in the design of elaborate, realistic stage scenery as well as in lighting and sound effects. Theaters embodying these innovations only gradually appeared outside Italy. Not until 1576 was the first public theater erected in London; three years later, a similar theater was constructed in Madrid.

Imitating the ancient models they admired, French and Italian writers followed what they believed were the rigid conventions of the classical drama and, to a large extent, catered to the aristocracy. By contrast, Spanish and English playwrights created a theatrical environment that was at once more socially democratic, more hospitable to national themes, and less concerned with classical models.

William Shakespeare. The spring of lyric song that bubbled up in the England of Henry VIII formed a veritable stream of verse that sparkled through his daughter Elizabeth's countryside. Her reign (1558-1603) climaxed the English Renaissance and produced such a galaxy of talented writers that some scholars have felt it necessary to go back as far as Athens in the fifth century B.C. to find an age as prodigal of literary genius. Strongly influenced by the royal court, which served as the busy center of intellectual and artistic as well as of economic and political life, their writings were highly colored, richly romantic, and often wildly extravagant

in spite of all their poetic allusions to classical times.

The supreme figure in Elizabethan literature and perhaps in all literature is William Shakespeare (1564-1616). We can only touch briefly upon a few facets of this versatile genius. His rich vocabulary and poetic imagery were matched only by his turbulent imagination. He was a superb lyric poet, and numerous critics have judged him the foremost sonnet writer in the English language.

Shakespeare wrote thirty-eight plays—histories, comedies, and tragedies. His historical plays reflected the patriotic upsurge experienced by Englishmen as their country grew stronger and more prosperous. For his comedies and tragedies, Shakespeare was content in a great majority of cases to borrow plots from earlier works. His forte lay in his creation of characters—perhaps the richest and most diversified collection conceived by the mind of one man—and in his ability to translate his knowledge of human nature

An early 1600's illustration based on Claes de Visscher's *View of London* shows the Globe Theatre on the south bank of the Thames, a short distance west of London Bridge.

Northern Renaissance painting, with its original Gothic realism, began to be affected by the Italian tendency toward naturalism and secularism at the end of the fifteenth century. One of the first German painters influenced by the Italian style was Albrecht Dürer. His copper engraving "Knight, Death, and the Devil" (lower left) is typical of his combination of the new style with medieval subject matter. In "The Harvesters" (above), the Flemish artist Pieter Brueghel the Elder has presented both a sweeping country landscape along with a memorable scene of peasant life.

into dramatic speech and action. Today his comedies are played to enthusiastic audiences: *The Taming of the Shrew, As You Like It, The Merchant of Venice, Merry Wives of Windsor,* to mention but a few. But it is in his tragedies that the poet-dramatist runs the gamut of human emotions and experience. Shakespeare possessed in abundance the Renaissance concern for man and the world about him. Hence his plays deal first and foremost with man's personality, passions, and problems. In such works as *Romeo and Juliet, Measure for Measure,* and *Troilus and Cressida,* the problems of love and sex are studied from many angles. Jealousy is analyzed in *Othello,* ambition in *Macbeth* and *Julius Caesar,* family relationships in *King Lear,* and man's struggle with his own soul in *Hamlet.* Shakespeare's extraordinary ability to build every concrete fact and action upon a universal truth makes his observations as applicable today as they were when first presented in the Globe Theater. Small wonder that next to the Bible, Shakespeare is the most quoted of all literary sources in the language.

Developments in painting. Before the Italian Renaissance permeated the artistic circles of northern Europe, the painters of the Low Countries had been making significant advances on their own. Outstanding was Jan van Eyck (1385?-1440), whose work has been called "the full flowering of the spirit of the late Middle Ages,"[14] for he continued to paint in the realistic manner developed by medieval miniaturists (see manuscript illuminations, pp. 215, 230). Van Eyck also perfected the technique of oil painting, which enabled him to paint with greater realism and also to devote more attention to detail.

The first talented German painter to be influenced deeply by Italian art was Albrecht Dürer (1471-1528) of Nuremberg. Dürer made more than one journey to Italy, where he was impressed both with the painting of the Renaissance Italians and with the artists' high social status—a contrast with northern Europe, where artists were still treated as craftsmen. Because he did not entirely lose many of the medieval qualities of the milieu in which he worked, his own work is a blend of the old and the new; but among German artists he went farthest in adopting the rational standards of Italian art. His "Knight, Death, and Devil" fuses the realism and symbolism of the Gothic with the nobility of Verrochio's statue of Colleoni (compare p. 293). In the long run Dürer became better known for his numerous engravings and woodcuts than for his paintings.

Another German painter, Hans Holbein the Younger (1497-1543), was less imaginative than Dürer; but whereas the latter lived principally in Germany and interpreted its spirit, the younger artist worked abroad, especially in England, and as a result his painting acquired a more cosmopolitan character. In his portraits of Erasmus and Henry VIII (pp. 298, 328), northern realism and concern for detail continues evident.

While many Flemish painters lost their northern individuality in the rush to adopt Italian techniques, Pieter Brueghel the Elder (1525?-1569) retained a strong Flemish flavor in his portrayal of the faces and scenes of his native land. He painted village squares, landscapes, skating scenes, peasant weddings and dances just as he saw them, with a reporter's eye for detail. He also took Biblical or mythological themes and depicted them as if the events were taking place in the Flanders of his own day. The depiction of everyday scenes in realistic fashion is known as *genre* painting; and in this medium, Pieter Brueghel and the Flemish school as a whole remained unexcelled.

SUMMARY

In the Middle Ages man had thought and acted primarily as a member of a community —a manor, a guild, or, above all, the universal Christian community represented by the Church and the Holy Roman Empire. But gradually, for a variety of reasons, he began to attach importance to himself as an individual and to develop an interest in worldly things for their own sake without relation to the divine. This new individualistic and secular spirit, the period in which it became prominent, and the ways in which it manifested itself in art, literature, and learning we call the Renaissance.

The change took place earliest in Italy and first expressed itself in the great intellectual movement known as humanism. In its early stages humanism was a revival of classical learning. Scholars eagerly searched for ancient manuscripts and introduced the literature of Greece and Rome into schools and universities. This reverence for antiquity led to the copying of classical literary and artistic forms, and many humanists wasted on such imitation talents which might better have been employed in creating original literature in their native language.

But humanism was much more than sterile imitation. It provided the West not only with a comprehensive knowledge of classical literature and thought but also with a more accurate historical perspective. The humanists absorbed classical ways of thinking, as well as classical modes of expression, and fostered an appreciation of the studies we know today as the "humanities." Above all, humanism reintroduced into western culture a much-needed emphasis on the dignity of man as an individual and on his place in the cosmos.

In its broader ramifications humanism stimulated a vital concern for the problems and challenges of the contemporary world. As we saw in this chapter and the one preceding, there was a progressive quickening of social life, resulting in sweeping changes in politics and economics and in men's minds. The common denominator of these changes was individualism.

Individualism manifested itself no less in the way in which the artist related his esthetic canons to the new man-centered view of the world. The extent to which the Renaissance sculptor, architect, and painter succeeded remains one of the glories of western civilization.

SUGGESTIONS FOR READING

J. Russell Major, **The Age of the Renaissance and Reformation*** (Lippincott, 1970) is a brief interpretive synthesis. W. K. Ferguson, **Facets of the Renaissance*** (Torchbooks) is an excellent survey of the Italian and Northern Renaissances. J. Huizenga, **The Waning of the Middle Ages*** (Anchor) is an influential study of "fading and decay" in the culture of northern Europe. J. Burckhardt, **The Civilization of the Renaissance in Italy*** (Mentor) is a classic study; it should be read in conjunction with W. K. Ferguson, **The Renaissance in Historical Thought: Five Centuries of Interpretation** (Houghton Mifflin); and T. Helton, ed., **The Renaissance: A Reconstruction of the Theories and Interpretations of the Age*** (Peter Smith).

F. B. Artz, **Renaissance Humanism, 1300-1550*** (Kent State) is a very brief introduction to humanism. P. O. Kristeller, **Renaissance Thought: The Classic, Scholastic, and Humanist Strains*** (Peter Smith) is an excellent analysis of Italian humanism. See also J. H. Whitfield, **Petrarch and the Renascence** (Haskell, 1969).

G. Brucker, **Renaissance Florence** (Wiley, 1969) contains much information as does F. C. Lane, **Venice: A Maritime Republic** (Johns Hopkins, 1973). See also C. Hibbert, **The House of Medici: Its Rise and Fall** (Morrow, 1975), from the emergence of this noted family to the end of the dynasty in 1743. Clemente Fusero, **The Borgias** (Praeger, 1973) is the role of another famous family in Renaissance Europe. See also E. R. Chamberlain, **Everyday Life in Renaissance Times*** (Capricorn); and F. W. Kent, **Everyday Life in Renaissance Florence** (Princeton, 1977).

Margaret M. Phillips, **Erasmus and the Northern Renaissance*** (Collier) is a valuable introduction. Outstanding studies of other Northern Renaissance figures include R. W. Chambers, **Thomas More*** (Univ. of Michigan); J. H. Hexter, **More's Utopia: The Biography of an Idea*** (Torchbooks); D. B. Lewis, **Doctor Rabelais** (Greenwood, 1969); and M. Chute, **Shakespeare of London.** Two solid studies of England's Renaissance man are S. J. Greenblatt, **Sir Walter Raleigh: The Renaissance Man and his Roles** (Yale, 1973); and Robert Lacey, **Sir Walter Raleigh** (Atheneum, 1974).

On printing and its effect on culture see P. Butler, **The Origin of Printing in Europe** (Univ. of Chicago); and Marshall McLuhan, **The Gutenberg Galaxy*** (Mentor).

F. B. Artz, **From the Renaissance to Romanticism: Trends in Style in Art, Literature, and Music, 1300-1830*** (Phoenix) is a fine overall view of the arts through six centuries. E. Newton, **European Painting and Sculpture*** (Penguin) is brief and valuable. Also recommended are Creighton Gilbert, ed., **Renaissance Art*** (Torchbooks, 1970); and A. Hauser, **A Social History of Art,** Vol. II, **Renaissance to Baroque*** (Vintage). B. Berenson, **Italian Painters of the Renaissance*** (Meridian); and H. Wolfflin, **The Art of the Italian Renaissance*** (Schocken) are two classics of art history. On northern painting see O. Benesch, **The Art of the Renaissance in Northern Europe** (Phaidon). See also B. Lowry, **Renaissance Architecture*** (Braziller).

Two excellent biographies of Renaissance artists are D. Merejkowski, **The Romance of Leonardo da Vinci*** (Hart, 1976) and H. Hibbard, **Michelangelo** (Harper & Row, 1975).

On music see Alfred Einstein, **A Short History of Music*** (Vintage); and G. Reese, **Music in the Renaissance** (Norton).

*Indicates a less expensive paperbound edition.

CHAPTER 14

The Protestant and Catholic Reformations

Here I Take My Stand

INTRODUCTION. On October 31, 1517, a professor of theology named Martin Luther nailed some papers on the door of the castle church in Wittenberg, Germany. It was the custom of the day for a man who wanted to engage in a scholastic debate with another to post his propositions publicly. In this respect Luther's action was not unusual, yet the forces he set in operation altered the entire religious pattern of the western world. A religious movement was to be launched that would split Christendom into numerous factions and sects.

Until his death in 1546, Luther believed that it might be possible to reform Catholicism to the conditions existing in early Christian times. From this standpoint the religious upheaval which he did so much to set in motion can be logically designated as the Reformation. On the other hand, because the struggle shattered western Christendom permanently, it might be described from a broader historical viewpoint as a revolution or, alternatively, as the Protestant Revolt. The sixteenth century also witnessed a significant revival of Catholicism itself. This renewal of the traditional faith was not solely a Counter Reformation in the sense that it represented a belated response to the challenge of Protestantism. As modern scholars have demonstrated, a strong Catholic Reformation had been gathering momentum even before Luther posted his theses.

The Reformation had both its negative and its positive aspects. In the name of God, men persecuted and killed their fellow men. Rulers anxious for absolute power used the conflicts engendered by the religious upheaval to serve their own political ends. Yet, much as in the early centuries of Christianity, when the blood of the martyrs became the seed of the Church, so the struggles of the sixteenth century, led by men afire with conviction and ready to sacrifice their lives for what they believed, renewed and stimulated the religious consciousness of western Europe. Luther declared: "Here I take my stand"; and in a broad sense this affirmation was echoed by Zwingli in the Swiss cantons, by Calvin at Geneva, and by the Catholic Church at the Council of Trent. Such staunch and uncompromising assertions of honest differences of doctrine gave institutionalized Christianity the new religious vitality and intellectual diversity that were to leave their mark on almost every phase of life in the West and bequeath us a rich legacy of values.

THE PROTESTANT REFORMATION

Passing of the medieval order. The Church's dominant position in European society depended on the continuance of the medieval world order; during the late Middle Ages, however, forces were slowly modifying every aspect of that order. The spirit of the Middle Ages was fundamentally one of faith, devotion to established institutions—the feudal order, the guild, and the Church—and the subordination of the individual's interests to those of the group. It was this spirit which fed the power of the Church. When the Renaissance changed this spirit, the universalities of the Middle Ages were shattered. Man became assertive. He began to rebel against all institutions which prevented him from acting as he wished.

Broadly speaking, the ideal of the Middle Ages was other-worldliness; the ideal of the Renaissance was present-worldliness. The Church represented the older ideal. Thus it was not simply that the Church's financial and moral abuses stood in need of correction, but that the Church's ideals no longer commanded the same respect and allegiance among all the population. The European townsman, for example, found himself increasingly out of sympathy with the Church's economic concepts of the "just price" and anti-usury statutes, for they conflicted with the new capitalism.

The Church itself embodied a dangerous contradiction at this time. In dogma it was medieval, yet its highest officials, including the popes, were patrons of a Renaissance culture deriving its inspiration from pagan Greece and Rome. The Church might denounce usury, but at the same time it utilized the services of powerful moneylending families.

As we have seen in Chapter 13, the northern humanists directed searching criticisms against the Church, though for the most part they wished to remain within it. But because it was primarily an intellectual movement, humanism could not create the dynamic drive necessary to inspire widespread reform. Having laid the intellectual groundwork for the pending religious revolt, the humanists left to other men—the militant and the martyrs alike—the task of arousing action. The time was ripe for the rise of a religious leader who would employ as his weapon not the conflict of Renaissance ideology with that of the Church, for that was a philosophical problem of which few were conscious, but rather the financial and moral abuses of the Church, which were common knowledge.

Religious ferment in Germany. The religious issue first came to a head in Germany. Aided by the invention of printing, devout

Germans had been studying the Scriptures carefully and censuring the behavior of many of the German clergy. Whereas in Italy familiarity bred a tolerance and rationalization of papal corruption, the Germans fiercely resented papal abuses and expected practice and theory to coincide.

The political situation also had a bearing on the religious question. Divided into hundreds of states, Germany lacked unity except for the nominal rule of the elected emperor of the Holy Roman Empire. The failure of imperial administrative reform (see p. 274) encouraged the many German states to imitate the new nationalism of countries to the west. With the religious affairs of each principality increasingly under the control of its ruler, a greater diversity of religious opinion could exist in fragmented Germany than in a state ruled by a centralized authority.

Nor must economic factors be overlooked. Trade and banking flourished, and the German burgher found no conflict between piety and profits. On the other hand, his piety and profits were both affected by the draining of German revenues by the Roman Church, especially when unscrupulous means were used to gather them. In short, Germany was ripe for religious revolt.

Martin Luther. The son of a German peasant who by virtue of thrift and hard work had become a petty capitalist, Martin Luther was born on November 10, 1483. Young Martin received a sound education which included university studies, but he accepted as a matter of course the prevalent beliefs in witchcraft and other superstitions. To the end of his life Luther believed vividly in the existence of devils and witches. The story goes that he once threw an inkpot at a devil whom he thought he saw leering at him. In 1505 he became a member of the mendicant order of Augustinian monks, a move which met with scant favor from his practical father, who wanted his son to study law. In 1508 Luther received a temporary appointment as a lecturer at the new University of Wittenberg, and a few years later he became professor of theology.

In the meantime Luther had struggled with

The deterioration of monasticism was responsible for much disenchantment with the Church. Monks were accused of every possible vice, from drunkenness and adultery to the frequenting of brothels. Such charges fostered the contempt vividly illustrated in this early sixteenth-century woodcut.

and solved for himself the spiritual problem that confronted many people in his time: In view of God's absolute power and man's powerlessness, how can man be certain of salvation for his soul? For many years Luther probed deeply this problem of eternal salvation. Finally, in 1515, while contemplating St. Paul's Epistle to the Romans (1:17), he came upon these words: "For therein is the righteousness of God revealed from faith to faith: as it is written, The just shall live by faith." Luther believed that his quest for spiritual certainty had been solved:

Night and day I pondered until I saw the connection between the justice of God and the statement that "the just shall live by his faith." Then I grasped that the justice of God is that righteousness by which through grace and sheer mercy God justifies us through faith. Thereupon I felt myself to be reborn and to have gone through open doors into paradise.[1]

Man was saved only by his faith in the "sheer mercy" of God, which alone could wash away sin and save him from the grasp of the devil. Luther had come to his famous doctrine of justification by faith, as opposed to the Roman Church's doctrine of justification by faith and good works—the demonstration of faith through virtuous acts, acceptance of Church dogma, and participation in Church ritual. Later, in a hymn that reflects his vigorous style of expression, Luther described his spiritual journey from anxiety to conviction:

In devil's dungeon chained I lay
　The pangs of death swept o'er me.
My sin devoured me night and day
　In which my mother bore me.
My anguish ever grew more rife,
I took no pleasure in my life
　And sin had made me crazy.
　　. . .
Thus spoke the Son, "Hold thou to me,
　From now on thou wilt make it.
I gave my very life for thee
　And for thee I will stake it.
For I am thine and thou art mine,
And where I am our lives entwine,
　The Old Fiend cannot shake it."[2]

The implications of Luther's doctrine were enormous. If salvation could come only through a personal faith in God's mercy, then an interceding priesthood became superfluous, for each man would then be his own priest. But Luther himself had no idea as yet where his views would eventually lead him and half of Christendom. It required a financial abuse by the Church to bring on the religious revolt.

Tetzel and the indulgences. Leo x, a cultured scion of the Medici family, "who would have made an excellent Pope if he had only been a little religious,"[3] wanted to complete the magnificent new St. Peter's in Rome, but he lacked money for the costly enterprise. Several papal agents were sent out to sell indulgences as a means of raising money. One of these agents, named Tetzel, discharged his mission "in the German archbishopric of Mainz in a manner which would be recognized in America to-day as high-pressure salesmanship."[4]

The Church's position in regard to indulgences has often been misunderstood. Although the sacrament of Penance absolved the sinner from guilt and eternal punishment, some temporal punishment remained. An indulgence was a type of good work, to be compared with praying, visiting shrines, and contributing to worthy causes, and like all good works it was a means of remitting or pardoning the temporal penalty for sins. Theologically, the concept of indulgences rested on the theory of a "treasury of merits," which held that Christ and the saints had won merit far in excess of their own needs and had thereby created a vast storehouse of good works. By means of indulgences the Church was able to draw upon and distribute this surplus to help those who felt they had not rendered sufficient penance to extinguish the punishment which they deserved.

It was the abuse attending the sale of indulgences to raise money that was chiefly responsible for provoking Luther's resentment. The common folk did not understand theology and thought that a payment of money would buy God's grace and insure their salvation. Tetzel did nothing to enlighten the populace as to the true nature of indulgences but rather exhorted them to give liberally for themselves and for their dead relatives in purgatory who were "crying to them for help." Thus Luther's case against indulgences rested on moral as well as theological grounds.

Development of Luther's ideas. On October 31, 1517, Luther, following a university custom, posted ninety-five propositions (theses) on the subject of indulgences on the church door at Wittenberg, at the same time challenging anyone to debate them with him. The following are typical:

6. The pope has no power to remit guilt, save by declaring and confirming that it has been remitted by God; . . .

21. Therefore those preachers of indulgences are in error who allege that through the indulgences of the pope a man is freed from every penalty.

36. Every Christian who is truly contrite has plenary remission both of penance and of guilt as his due, even without a letter of pardon.[5]

Luther wrote the ninety-five theses in Latin for the edification of his fellow theologians, but they were soon translated into the common tongue and six months later were well known throughout Germany. At first the Church at Rome did not seriously trouble itself. Heresy was anything but new, as the history of the Waldensians, Albigensians, and the followers of Wycliffe and Huss showed. But this particular "squabble among monks," as Leo X dismissed the matter, did not subside.

In 1519 Luther debated with the eminent Catholic theologian John Eck at Leipzig. Luther maintained that the pope ruled by virtue of human rather than divine authority and was not infallible; that Church councils did not exist by divine right either and could also err; and that Scripture constituted the sole authority in matters of faith and doctrine. When Eck pointed out that such views were similar to those of Wycliffe and Huss, Luther boldly declared that "among the opinions of John Huss and the Bohemians many are certainly most Christian and evangelic, and cannot be condemned by the universal church."[6] Yet in spite of these wide theological divergences, Luther continued to speak with affection of his "mother Church," which he hoped could be reformed

An anonymous caricature of Johann Tetzel, the German hawker of indulgences, entitled "Johann Tetzel and His Indulgence-Junk." The last two lines of the notorious jingle here ascribed to Tetzel read: "As soon as coin in the coffer rings, Right then the soul to Heaven springs."

and remain unified. By basing his position squarely on the doctrine of justification by faith alone, however, Luther found himself propelled by its implications to a position far removed from that of the Church.

Following the Leipzig debate, Eck initiated proceedings at Rome to have Luther declared a heretic. Luther in turn decided to put his case before the German people by publishing a series of pamphlets. In his *Address to the Nobility of the German Nation*, Luther called on the princes to reform ecclesiastical abuses, to strip the Church of its wealth and worldly power, and to create, in effect, a national German Church. Among numerous other proposals contained in this influential treatise, Luther urged a union with the Hussites, claiming that Huss had been unjustly burned at the stake.

The Babylonian Captivity of the Church summarized Luther's theological views. He attacked the papacy for having deprived the individual Christian of his freedom to approach God directly by faith and without the intermediation of the priesthood, and he set forth his views on the sacramental system. To be valid, a sacrament must have been instituted by Christ and be exclusively Christian. On this basis Luther could find no justification for making a sacrament of matrimony, which was also observed by non-Christians, or for any of the other sacraments except Baptism and the Lord's Supper (his term for the sacrament known to Roman Catholics as the Holy Eucharist). Luther rejected the doctrine of transubstantiation on the grounds that a priest could not perform the miracle of transforming bread and wine into the Body and Blood of the Lord. Nevertheless, he believed in the real presence of Christ in the bread and wine of the sacrament. In Luther's view, the bread and wine coexist with the Body and Blood without a change of substance.

Luther's third pamphlet, *The Freedom of a Christian Man*, which was dedicated to the pope in the slight hope that reconciliation was still possible, set forth in conciliatory but firm tones Luther's views on Christian behavior and salvation. He did not discourage good works but argued that the inner spiritual freedom which comes from the certainty found in faith leads to the performance of good works. "Good works do not make a man good, but a good man does good works."[7]

The breach made complete. In June 1520 Pope Leo x issued the bull *Exsurge Domine* ("Arise, O Lord, . . . Arise all ye saints, and the whole universal Church, whose interpretation of Scripture has been assailed"[8]), which gave Luther sixty days to turn from his heretical course. When Luther publicly burned the bull amid the applause of students and townsmen, he propelled himself into the center of German politics and brought about a showdown with Rome. In January 1521 Leo x excommunicated Luther.

Meanwhile, Charles v, who had recently been crowned emperor, found himself in a difficult situation. He was aware of popular German feelings and was not anxious to see papal power reconsolidated in his domains, yet he was bound by his oath to defend the Church and extirpate heresy. Moreover, Charles was orthodox in his own religious beliefs. It was decided that Luther should be heard at the emperor's first Diet, which was held at Worms. Summoned under an imperial safe-conduct, Luther was asked whether he intended to stand by everything he had written. He stood before the assembly and replied firmly:

In this workroom in Wartburg castle Luther completed his translation of the New Testament into German.

Your Imperial Majesty and Your Lordships demand a simple answer. Here it is, plain and unvarnished. Unless I am convicted of error by the testimony of Scripture or (since I put no trust in the unsupported authority of Pope or of councils, since it is plain that they have often erred and often contradicted themselves) by manifest reasoning I stand convicted by the Scriptures to which I have appealed, . . . I cannot and will not recant anything, for to act against our conscience is neither safe for us, nor open to us.

On this I take my stand [*Hier stehe Ich*]. I can do no other. God help me. Amen."

In May 1521 the Diet declared Luther a heretic and outlaw. He was, however, given protection by the elector of Saxony, in whose strongest castle he lived for almost a year under the guise of "Knight George."

During this period Luther began the construction of an evangelical church distinct from Rome. He wrote incessantly, setting forth his theological views in a collection of forceful sermons for use by preachers, in correspondence with friends and public figures, and in a treatise condemning monasticism. (In 1525 Luther married an ex-nun who had left the cloister after reading this treatise.) Luther also translated the New Testament into German, a monumental job accomplished in only eleven weeks. Later he translated the Old Testament. Luther's Bible was largely responsible for creating a standard literary language for all Germany.

Luther and the Peasants' War. Luther's teachings spread quickly through central and northern Germany. Pious persons who wanted the Church reformed embraced the new cause. Worldly individuals who believed that it would afford an opportunity to appropriate Church property also aided the movement, as did ardent nationalists like Von Hutten (see p. 299), who saw in it a means of uniting Germany. The emperor, meanwhile, was too deeply involved in a struggle with the French and the Turks to stamp out the new heresy (see p. 329).

Encouraged by Luther's concept of the freedom of a Christian man, which they applied to economic and social matters, the German peasants revolted in 1524. Long ground down by the nobles, the peasants included in their twelve demands the abolition of serfdom "unless it should be shown us from the Gospel that we are serfs"; a reduction of "the excessive services demanded of us, which are increased from day to day"; the fixing of rents "in accordance with justice"; and an end to "the appropriation by individuals of meadows and fields which at one time belonged to a community." [10] Luther recognized the justice of these demands, but when the peasants began to employ violence against established authority he turned against them. In a virulent pamphlet, *Against the Thievish and Murderous Hordes of Peasants*, Luther called on the princes to "knock down, strangle, and stab . . . and think nothing so venomous, pernicious, or Satanic as an insurgent." [11]

The revolt was stamped out in 1525 at a cost of an estimated 100,000 peasant dead, and the lot of the German peasant for the next two centuries was probably the worst in Europe. Luther had become a false prophet to the peasants, who either returned to Catholicism or turned to more radical forms of Protestantism. Politically and economically conservative, Luther believed that the equality of all men before God applied in spiritual but not in secular matters. This philosophy alienated the peasants but made allies of the princes, many of whom became Lutheran in part because it placed them in control of the church in their territories, thereby enhancing their power and wealth.

Local religious autonomy in Germany. At a meeting of the Diet of the Empire in 1529, the Catholic princes, with the emperor's support, pushed through a decree that the Mass must not be interfered with anywhere. This meant that while Lutheran activities were restricted in Catholic regions, those of the Catholics could be carried on even in Lutheran areas. In answer, the Lutheran leaders drew up a protest, and from this incident the word *Protestant* derives. The next Diet, meeting at Augsburg in 1530, was presented with a statement of Christian doctrine from the Lutheran viewpoint designed to conciliate the two parties. The Catholics refused to accept this statement, known as the Augsburg Confession, which became the official creed of Lutheranism.

The emperor now made public his intention to crush the growing heresy. In defense, the Lutheran princes banded together in 1531 in the Schmalkaldic League, and between 1546 and 1555 a sporadic civil war was fought. A compromise was finally reached in the Peace of Augsburg (1555), which allowed each prince to decide the religion of his subjects, gave Protestants the right to keep all Church property confiscated prior to 1552, forbade all sects of Protestantism other than Lutheranism, and ordered all Catholic bishops to give up their property if they turned Lutheran.

The effects of these provisions on Germany were profound. The Peace of Augsburg confirmed Lutheranism as a state religion in large portions of the Empire. Religious opinions became the private property of the princes, and the individual had to believe what his prince wanted him to believe, be it Lutheranism or Catholicism. Furthermore, by formally sanctioning state religion and thus enhancing a prince's power, the Peace of Augsburg added to Germany's political disintegration.

The death of Luther. In 1546, during the Schmalkaldic War, the founder of the new faith died. Martin Luther had been a born leader, genius, and zealot. His life had been molded by an absolute conviction of the rightness of his beliefs, which goes far to ex-

plain both his driving power and his limitations. "His weaknesses were manifest: intransigency in theological views, proneness to vehemence, narrowness of social concepts. . . . But Luther also had qualities to offset these: sincere desire for the truth, courage, determination, power of organization, an outstanding gift for identifying himself with the language and thought of the simple man. These were the qualities that permitted him to carry through what he had begun."[12]

In closing this account of Luther and the momentous movement which he set rolling, we might append an ironic footnote. The same sale of indulgences which furnished the money to build a fitting capital for a universal Church (St. Peter's in Rome) at the same time provided the occasion for destroying the unity of western Christendom.

Lutheranism in Scandinavia. In 1525 the Grand Master of the Teutonic Knights who ruled Prussia (see p. 275) turned Lutheran, dissolved the order, secularized its lands, and declared himself duke of Prussia. With this exception, outside Germany Lutheranism permanently established itself as a state religion only in the Scandinavian countries. Here emerging modern monarchs welcomed the opportunity to obtain needed wealth by confiscating church property and needed power by filling church offices with Lutherans who preached obedience to constituted authority. This was particularly the case in Sweden where Gustavus Vasa led a successful struggle for Swedish independence from Denmark. In 1523 he was elected king, and soon thereafter he declared himself a Lutheran and filled his empty treasury from the sale of confiscated Church lands. A century later his descendant, Gustavus Adolphus, would intervene in the religious wars in Germany and be instrumental in saving German Protestantism from extinction. In Denmark, which also ruled Norway, the spread of Lutheranism was encouraged by the king. In 1537 an ordinance, approved by Luther, established a national Lutheran church with its bishops as salaried officials of the Danish state.

Zwingli in Switzerland. Meanwhile, Protestantism had taken firm root in Switzerland.

Some of the giants of the Protestant Reformation are shown in this picture painted about 1530 by Lucas Cranach the Elder. At the far left is Luther, and at the far right his associate Melanchthon, who wrote the Augsburg Confession. Next to Melanchthon is Zwingli. In the center of the picture is John Frederick the Magnanimous, elector of Saxony, whose family supported Luther. John Frederick's uncle, Frederick III, once sheltered Luther in his Wartburg castle.

In the German-speaking area of that country —particularly in Zurich—the Reformation was led by Ulrich Zwingli (1484-1531). Like Luther, who was the same age, Zwingli repudiated papal in favor of scriptural authority, preached justification by faith, attacked monasticism and clerical celibacy, and drastically revised the sacramental system. But the differences between the two leaders proved irreconcilable when they met in 1529 at the University of Marburg, founded two years earlier as the first Protestant university in Europe. Whereas Luther looked on baptism as a means of helping to regenerate the individual, Zwingli considered it only a means of initiating a child into society. Nor did he believe with Luther that the real presence of Christ was found in the Lord's Supper. To Zwingli, who had been trained as a humanist and was therefore more of a rationalist than Luther, the bread and wine symbolized Christ's body and blood and the service was a commemoration of the Last Supper.

Zwingli was an ardent Swiss patriot who had once served as chaplain with Swiss mercenaries in Italy. The Swiss Confederation, comprising thirteen cantons, was a byproduct of the weakness and disunity of the Holy Roman Empire. Originating in 1291 as a defensive union of three cantons, the confederation expanded and repulsed all attempts of the emperors to exercise jurisdiction over it. Switzerland's independence was won by the valor of its hardy peasant pikemen, whose prowess became so famed that foreign rulers and popes eagerly sought their services. Garbed in colorful Renaissance costumes, Swiss mercenaries still guard the Vatican.

In 1531 war broke out between Protestant and Catholic cantons, and Zwingli was slain in battle. The war ended in the same year with an agreement that anticipated by a quarter of a century the Peace of Augsburg in Germany—each canton was allowed to choose its own religion. This settlement was largely responsible for keeping Switzerland from taking sides in the great religious wars that subsequently engulfed Europe. Furthermore, it helped set the policy of neutrality which the Swiss have followed to our own day.

These pen and ink sketches of John Calvin in his later years were drawn by one of his students.

John Calvin. The most famous sixteenth-century Protestant leader after Luther was John Calvin (1509-1564). A Frenchman of the middle class, Calvin studied theology and law at Paris, where he became interested in Luther's teachings. About 1533 he had what he called a "conversion," whereby he abandoned Catholicism and fled to the Protestant city of Basel in Switzerland. Here in 1536 he published the first edition of his great work, the *Institutes of the Christian Religion*, unquestionably one of the most influential books of systematic theology ever written. His capacity for creative thinking was overshadowed by his ability as an organizer and synthesist. Influenced by his legal training as well as by humanistic scholarship and the doctrines of Luther, Calvin set forth a system that was a masterpiece of logical reasoning.

Whereas Luther's central doctrine was justification by faith, Calvin's was the sovereignty of God. "Both Calvin and Luther had an overwhelming sense of the majesty of God, but whereas for Luther this served to point up the miracle of forgiveness, for Calvin it gave rather the assurance of the impregnability of God's purpose."[13] God was omnipotent and for His own purposes had created the world and also man in His image. Since Adam and Eve had fallen from a state of sinlessness, man was utterly depraved and lost.

Carrying these doctrines to their logical conclusions, Calvin defined man's relation to God in his famous doctrine of predestination. Since God is omniscient, He knows the past, present, and future. Consequently, He must always know which men are to be saved and which men are to be damned eternally. Man's purpose in life, then, is not to try to work out his salvation—for this has already been determined—but to honor God. While Calvin did not profess to know absolutely who were to be God's chosen—the elect—he believed that the following three tests constituted a good yardstick by which to judge who might be saved: participation in the two sacraments, Baptism and the Lord's Supper; an upright moral life; and a public profession of the faith.

Calvin's emphasis upon the sovereignty of God led him to differ with Luther on the relationship of church and state. To Luther the state was supreme, but to Calvin the church and its ministers, as representatives of the sovereignty of God, must dominate. Calvinist church government in turn was democratically oriented in that it was based on the authority not of bishops but of synods or presbyteries, elected bodies composed of ministers and elders. Although Calvin upheld lawful political authority, he also approved of rebellion against a tyranny "which overrides private conscience." Thus, wherever Calvinism spread it carried with it the seeds of representative government and of defiance against despotism.

Calvinist Geneva. In 1536 the Protestants of Geneva invited Calvin to become their leader, and there he put his ideas on government into effect. Calvin believed it was the duty of the elect to glorify God by establishing a theocracy that would be governed according to scriptural precept. Although the Bible was the supreme authority, the chief instrument of government was the Consistory, or Presbytery, a council of ministers and elders which made and enforced the laws. Calvin in turn dominated the Consis-

tory, which showed great zeal in disciplining the community and punishing or removing any person found guilty of unseemly behavior. Although the regime was high-minded, it carried its zeal to ridiculous lengths. Penalties were inflicted for being absent from sermons or laughing during the church service, for wearing bright colors, for swearing or dancing, for playing cards, or for having one's fortune told by gypsies.

In regard to more serious offenses, especially in the religious sphere, Calvin and his associates acted with a severity common to the Reformation age. They used torture to obtain confessions and banished citizens for heresy, blasphemy, witchcraft, and adultery. When the Spanish physician Servetus sought refuge in Geneva, having fled from Catholic persecution because he was a Unitarian who denied the doctrine of the Trinity, Calvin had him burned for heresy. "Because the Papists persecute the truth," Calvin explained, "should we on that account refrain from repressing error?"

The spread of Calvinism. From Geneva, Calvinism spread far and wide, imbued with its founder's spirit of austerity and a self-righteousness born of confidence in being among the elect of God. Many of its leaders studied at the Academy (today the University of Geneva), which trained students from other countries in Calvin's theology. In France, Calvinism made influential converts among both the bourgeoisie and the nobility. Known as Huguenots, the French Calvinists remained a minority but, as we shall see in the next chapter, their importance far outweighed their numbers. In Scotland the fiery Calvinist John Knox successfully challenged the authority of the Roman Church (see p. 316), and in Germany and the Netherlands Calvin's teachings formed the basis for the German and Dutch Reformed churches.

Henry VIII's quarrel with Rome. In Germany the revolt against the Church was primarily religious in nature, although it possessed political implications; in England the situation was reversed. There the leader was a monarch, Henry VIII (1509-1547), not a priest. Henry broke with Rome not for theological reasons but because the pope would not annul his marriage to Catherine of Aragon, daughter of Ferdinand and Isabella of Spain, whom he had married for dynastic reasons.

Catherine had given Henry a daughter, Mary, but no son, and Henry was convinced that a male heir was necessary if the newly established Tudors were to endure as a dynasty and England kept from reverting to anarchy. Catherine was the widow of his brother, and Church law forbade a man to marry his brother's widow. A special papal dispensation had been granted for the marriage, but Henry claimed the dispensation was not valid and in 1527 asked Pope Clement VII to revoke it.

Normally the pope might have acquiesced to Henry's wishes, for other popes had granted similar favors to monarchs and Henry had been loyal to the Church. In answer to Luther he had written a *Defense of the Seven Sacraments* (1521), in which he castigated Luther as a "poisonous serpent," the "wolf of hell," and the "limb of Satan." The pope gratefully bestowed on Henry the title "Defender of the Faith"—a title which English monarchs still possess. But much as he might have wished, the pope could not support Henry in his desires. There were two good reasons. First, the pope felt it would be dangerous for one pontiff to reverse the judgments of a predecessor. Second, the emperor Charles V, the most powerful monarch in Europe, was a nephew of Catherine and threatened the pope if he declared the marriage null and void. Clement decided to wait before giving his answer, hoping that in the meantime events would resolve themselves.

But Henry would not wait. He obtained from Parliament the power to appoint bishops in England without papal permission, designating Thomas Cranmer as archbishop of Canterbury—a willing tool who was sure to do his master's bidding. In 1533 Cranmer pronounced the king's marriage to Catherine invalid and legalized Henry's marriage to coquettish Anne Boleyn, whom he had secretly married three months earlier. At last goaded into action, Clement VII excommunicated Henry and maintained that Catherine alone was the king's true wife.

Establishment of the Anglican Church.
In 1534 Henry severed all connections with Rome. A sympathetic Parliament passed the famous Act of Supremacy, which stated that the king "justly and rightfully is and ought to be supreme head of the Church of England." It also enacted the Treason Act, which declared liable to the death penalty anyone who called the king a "heretic, schismatic, tyrant, infidel, or usurper." Turning on his old friend, Henry had Sir Thomas More beheaded because he would not acknowledge the sovereign as head of the English Church. In recent years More has been canonized by the Catholic Church not only for his saintly life but also for his martyrdom in opposing Henry VIII's divorce and break with the Church.

To replenish the royal coffers and to gain popular support, Henry, working through Parliament, dissolved the monasteries and sold their lands to the nobles and gentry. Thus Henry acquired accomplices, in a sense, in his conflict with Rome. It must be remembered that Henry and Parliament could not perhaps have effected such sweeping changes if many Englishmen had not been anticlerical.

In the same year (1539) in which Parliament acted to dissolve the monasteries, it also passed the Six Articles, which reaffirmed the main points of Catholic theology. By this act, both the Catholic who denied the supremacy of the king and the Protestant who denied the validity of transubstantiation were to be punished severely. Thus England threw off the supremacy of the pope without at that time adopting the Protestant faith; the elements of Protestantism in the English Church crept in after Henry's reign.

After Henry's death in 1547, his frail ten-year-old son mounted the throne as Edward VI. During his reign the growing Protestant party in England became ascendant. The Six Articles were repealed; priests were no longer held to their vows of celibacy; and the old Latin service was replaced by Cranmer's Book of Common Prayer, written in English, which brought the service much closer to the people and exerted a powerful influence on the development of the language. In 1553 the Forty-Two Articles defined the faith of the Church of England along Protestant lines.

Under the devoutly Catholic Mary (1553-

The lives of Europe's monarchs were often interwoven through ties of marriage and kinship; those bonds were emphasized or ignored according to the monarchs' nationalistic aims. Until she was widowed at eighteen, Mary Stuart had ruled France for two years as the queen of the youthful Francis II.

1558), the unfortunate daughter of the still less fortunate Catherine of Aragon, Catholicism was reinstated, and three hundred Protestants, including Archbishop Cranmer, were burned at the stake. But with the accession to the throne of Anne Boleyn's red-headed and fiery-tempered daughter, Elizabeth I (1558-1603), the Anglican Church took on a strong Protestant character. Realizing the political necessity for religious peace, Elizabeth worked hard to achieve a compromise settlement. Although the Church of England remained a state church under the control of the monarch, Elizabeth astutely changed her title from "Supreme Head" to the more modest "Supreme Governor." In accepting the Bible as the final authority, and in recognizing only Baptism and Holy Eucharist as Christ-instituted sacraments, Elizabeth's Thirty-Nine Articles (1563) were essentially Protestant, although many articles were ambiguously phrased in an effort to satisfy both parties. Much Catholic ritual was preserved, along with the ecclesiastical government of bishops in apostolic succession.

Presbyterianism in Scotland. The religious revolt in Scotland was largely the work of the zealous reformer John Knox (1505?-1572), who had become a disciple of Calvin in Geneva, which he called "the most perfect school of Christ that ever was on earth since the days of the Apostles." After returning to his native Scotland in about 1559, Knox became the leader of a group of Protestant nobles who wished to overthrow both the jurisdiction of the Roman Catholic Church and the monarch—Queen Mary Stuart, whose husband was king of France (see p. 333). In 1560 the Scottish Parliament severed all ties with Rome and accepted Knox's Articles of the Presbyterian Church, modeled after Calvin's views on theology and church government. When the beautiful but ill-fated queen returned from France one year later she found her bleak kingdom alienated from her own Catholic views. Her scandalous behavior (see p. 333) and her steadfast Catholicism led the Scots to depose her in 1567 in favor of her Protestant son James.

The Anabaptists. The most radical among those who rejected the religious establishment of the time were the Anabaptists ("rebaptizers"), so called because they denied the efficacy of infant baptism. They formed many sects led by self-styled "prophets" who carried to extreme Luther's doctrines of Christian liberty, priesthood of all believers, and return to primitive Christianity. Centered in Germany and the Netherlands, Anabaptism was predominantly a lower-class movement; many of the peasants whose hopes for economic and social reform had been crushed by the Peasants' War turned from Luther to the Anabaptists. In communities of their own, they shared their worldly goods with one another and lived as they thought the primitive Christians had lived, working and praying together. On occasion they employed force to purify society and establish a New Jerusalem. Mainly, however, they believed in the separation of church and state and advocated pacifism and the love-ethic. Today some portion of their spirit lives on among such groups as the Mennonites, the Amish, and the Quakers.

THE CATHOLIC REFORMATION

The background. The Catholic Reformation should not be viewed as only a retaliatory movement or a series of measures taken to stem the rising tide of Protestantism. The Roman Church had always retained latent forces of recuperation and strength which it could draw upon in challenging times. Before Luther had posted his ninety-five theses, evidence of renewed vitality and internal reform was visible in the Roman Church.

One of the prime examples of this resurgence occurred in Spain under Ferdinand and Isabella, ardent Catholics as well as autocrats. To deal with Moors, Jews, and heretics, the "Catholic Sovereigns" requested and got papal permission for a separate Spanish Inquisition under their control (see p. 272). The Inquisition soon came to dominate the Spanish Church, making it virtually a state church, and moved on to the problem of religious reform. Under the able Grand Inquisitor, Cardinal Ximenes (d. 1517), both the secular clergy and the monastic orders were invigorated by a renewal of spirit, discipline, and education—the latter including the scholarly study of the Bible at the University of Alcala, founded by Ximenes as a means of training able bishops. Thus Spain became a model Catholic state, where Protestantism would make few converts.

In a category of his own was the Dominican friar Savonarola (1452-1498), an ardent puritan, mystic, and reformer of Church and society. In 1494, when the Medici were expelled from Florence, Savonarola emerged as master of the city. For four years he ruled the Kingdom of God, as he called Florence, invoking the wrath of God upon worldly living and sinful luxuries. Bands of teenagers were organized to go about the city collecting and burning "vanities"—fashionable clothes, wigs, ornaments, and secular books and paintings. Savonarola also bitterly denounced the iniquities of the Borgia pope, Alexander vi, and called for a general council to reform the Church. But he lacked the power to reform the papacy and the Church, or even to maintain his hold on the fickle Florentines. Publicly humiliated by having his Dominican garb torn from him in the great square of Florence, Savonarola was hanged and burned, a victim of political intrigue. He was later hailed by Luther and the Protestants as a forerunner of their movement.

By the 1530's the inroads of Protestantism were apparent, and in retaliation the Church rallied its forces and prepared a powerful offensive. This renewal of strength, known as the Catholic Reformation—or, as some prefer, Counter Reformation—penetrated all areas of the Church. New monastic orders adapted monastic life to the needs of the time, the papacy headed a program of vigorous reform, and the Church regained much ground lost to the Protestants. Climaxing the whole movement was the Council of Trent, where the Church boldly reaffirmed its traditional doctrines and flatly refused to compromise in any way with the Protestants.

Reformist monasticism. In response to the same forces that had produced monastic reform during the earlier medieval reformation (see Chapter 11), a number of new monastic orders sprang up in the first half of the sixteenth century. Prominent among them were the Theatines, a body of devoted priests who undertook to check the spread of heresy by concentrating upon the regeneration of the clergy; the Capuchins, an offshoot of the Franciscan order inspired by the original spirit of St. Francis, who became notable for their preaching and for the care of the poor and the sick; and the Ursulines, whose special task was the education of girls. Reflecting both the reforming zeal of the new orders and the mystical reaffirmation of faith that characterized most reformers, Protestant as well as Catholic, was the order of barefoot Carmelites and their founder, the Spanish nun St. Theresa. These devout sisters slept on straw, ate no meat, and lived on alms. Quietistic mysticism, which teaches that spiritual peace can be attained by losing the sense of self in passive contemplation of God and His works, is well reflected in St. Theresa's written accounts of her ecstasies and visions.

Loyola and the Jesuits. The Society of Jesus, better known as the Jesuits, founded

Ignatius Loyola, flanked by members of the Society of Jesus, is pictured in this intricate seventeenth-century Spanish woodcarving. The Jesuits, as they were called, were founded primarily to convert the Moslem world and carried out successful missionary activities. In Europe their intellectual and political skill often raised them to places of great influence.

by the Spanish nobleman and ex-soldier Ignatius Loyola (1491-1556), played a vital role in the Catholic Reformation. While recovering from a severe battle wound, Loyola experienced a mystical religious conversion and vowed to become a soldier of Christ and "serve only God and the Roman pontiff, His vicar on earth." His "Company [*Societas*] of Jesus," founded in 1534 and given papal authorization in 1540, was organized along military lines with Loyola as "general." Members were carefully selected, rigorously

trained, and subjected to an iron discipline. One of the classics in the field of religious literature, Loyola's *Spiritual Exercises*, a work of great psychological penetration based on his own mystical religious experience, was used to inculcate disciplined asceticism and absolute obedience to superior authority. In addition to the usual monastic vows of chastity, obedience, and poverty, the Jesuits took a special vow of allegiance to the pope. As preachers, confessors to monarchs and princes, and educators, the Jesuits had remarkable success in stemming and even reversing the tide of Protestantism, particularly in Poland, Bohemia, Hungary, Germany, France, and the Spanish Netherlands (modern Belgium). In addition, the Jesuits performed excellent missionary work in America and Asia.

Papal reform: Paul III. A new era was at hand for the Church when Paul III, who reigned from 1534 to 1549, ascended the papal throne. He chose outstanding men as cardinals and appointed a commission to look into the need for reform. Their report listed the evils requiring correction, including the appointment of worldly bishops and priests, the traffic in benefices and indulgences and other financial abuses, the venality of some cardinals, and the absence of others from the papal court. Ignoring the opposition of some high churchmen, Paul made plans to call a general council to carry out needed reforms.

The Council of Trent. The Catholic Reformation came to a climax in the Council of Trent, which met in three sessions between 1545 and 1563. Rejecting all compromise with Protestantism, the Council restated the basic tenets of Catholic doctrine. It declared salvation to be a matter of both faith and good works, and it affirmed the source of doctrine to be not only the Bible, as interpreted by the Church, but also the "unwritten traditions, which were received by the Apostles from the lips of Christ himself, or, by the same Apostles, at the dictation of the Holy Spirit, and were handed on and have come down to us. . . ."[14] The Council also reaffirmed the seven sacraments, with special emphasis on transubstantiation, decreed that only Latin be used in the Mass, and approved the spiritual usefulness of indulgences, pilgrimages, veneration of saints and relics, and the cult of the Virgin.

At the same time, the Council sought to eliminate abuses by ordering reforms in Church discipline and administration. Such evils as simony, absenteeism, the abuse of indulgences, and secular pursuits on the part of the clergy were strictly forbidden. Bishops were ordered to supervise closely both the regular and the secular clergy, appoint reputable and competent men to ecclesiastical positions, and establish seminaries to provide a well-educated clergy. The clergy, in turn, were requested to preach frequently to the people.

In addition to freeing the Church of its worst abuses and formulating its doctrines clearly and rigidly, the Council of Trent strengthened the authority of the papacy. The pope's party in the Council, ably led by Jesuit theologians, defeated all attempts to revive the theory that a general council was supreme in the Church. And when the final session of the Council voted that none of its decrees were valid without the consent of the Holy See, the Church became more than ever an absolute monarchy ruled by the pope.

EFFECTS OF THE RELIGIOUS UPHEAVAL

Religious division but renewed faith. By 1550 Christendom was composed of three divisions—Greek Orthodox, Roman Catholic, and Protestant. With Protestantism predominant in northern Europe, the unity of western Christendom was split irreparably. The Catholics placed their faith in the authority of the pope and the need for a mediatory priesthood. The Protestants placed their faith in the authority of the Bible and held that every Christian could win salvation without priestly mediation. But since they differed among themselves in their interpretation of the Bible and the methods of church organization, in time hundreds of separate Protestant sects arose.

Although the religious upheaval fostered the religious diversity of modern times, it also represented in some aspects a return to medievalism. It was a great religious revival, a renewal of faith. Renaissance emphasis on free and secular thought gave way again to authority—for Protestants it was the Bible; for Catholics, the Church. The Renaissance movement, having fostered doubt and criticism of medieval values, was now engulfed in a return to some of those values. Thus, temporarily at least, the Renaissance spirit was stifled. But it was to prove stronger than this intense religious revival and in time was to profit from the passing of the single religious authority of the universal Church.

Another by-product of the religious upheaval was a new interest in education, already broadened by the intellectual and moral concerns of the humanists. Each faith wanted its youth to be properly trained in its teachings. As part of its campaign to win Protestants back to the fold, the Jesuits in particular developed a school system so superior and so attractive that many Protestant as well as Catholic youths attended. One feature of Protestantism eventually stimulated education a great deal. Its emphasis upon the importance of Bible reading encouraged the promotion of universal education; Luther, for example, insisted not only that the state should establish schools but that "the civil authorities are under obligation to compel the people to send their children to school."[15]

On the debit side the Reformation era witnessed an intensification of religious intolerance. There seems little choice between Catholics and Protestants in the degree of their detestation for one another and for religious liberty in general. Each religious sect assumed that salvation came through it alone, and all were equally intolerant when they had the power to be so. In the words of Sebastian Castellio (d. 1563), a one-time follower of Calvin who wrote a protest against the execution of Servetus:

Although opinions are almost as numerous as men, nevertheless there is hardly any sect which does not condemn all others and desire to reign alone. Hence arise banishments, chains, imprisonments, stakes, and gallows and this miserable rage to visit daily penalties upon those who differ from the mighty about matters hitherto unknown, for so many centuries disputed, and not yet cleared up.[16]

How can we call ourselves Christians, Castellio asked in effect, if we do not imitate Christ's clemency and mercy?

O Creator and King of the world, dost Thou see these things? Art Thou become so changed, so cruel, so contrary to Thyself? When Thou wast on earth none was more mild, more clement, more patient of injury. . . . O blasphemies and shameful audacity of men, who dare to attribute to Christ that which they do by the command and at the instigation of Satan![17]

Unfortunate, too, was the break between the humanists and the Protestants, which began when Luther broke with the Church.

Although both groups wanted to reform the Church by removing its abuses and returning to the practices and faith of early Christianity, Erasmus could say of Luther's revolt: "I laid a hen's egg: Luther hatched a bird of quite different breed."[18] The humanists, in other words, desired reform, not revolution. Furthermore, because they exalted the rationality and innate goodness of man, the humanists disagreed with the strong Protestant emphasis on man's depravity and the necessity of salvation by superhuman means. As Luther saw it, "The human avails more with Erasmus than the divine."[19]

Protestantism and capitalism. The Renaissance had encouraged a new individualism in economic matters, which contributed to a breakdown of the guild system and to the rise of the individual entrepreneur. While

Both Catholics and Protestants were guilty of incredible atrocities in their respective attempts to achieve religious conformity. Processions such as this became common in French cities as members of a "holy league" paraded through the streets seeking out Huguenots to execute for heresy.

Luther continued to accept the medieval concept of the "just price" and the ban against usury (receiving interest on money loaned), with the Calvinists investment of capital and loaning of money became respectable. Calvin encouraged individual enterprise by teaching that a man's career was a "calling" assigned to him by God and success in his calling was a sign of election to salvation. Indeed, it has been asserted that:

Calvin did for the bourgeoisie of the sixteenth century what Marx did for the proletariat of the nineteenth, . . . the doctrine of predestination satisfied the same hunger for an assurance that the forces of the universe are on the side of the elect as was to be assuaged in a different age by the theory of historical materialism. He set their virtues at their best in sharp antithesis with the vices of the established order at its worst, taught them to feel that they were a chosen people, made them conscious of their great destiny in the Providential plan and resolute to realize it.[20]

The business classes were among those that encouraged the revolt from Rome; we can now see that they were also among those that gained most by it.

Union of religion and politics. In many cases the religious division of Europe followed political lines. In Germany the Peace of Augsburg gave the ruler of each state the right to decide the faith of his subjects, thus controlling the church in his realm. Similarly, rulers of other countries, both Catholic and Protestant, developed national churches, so that Europe was divided religiously into an Anglican Church, a Dutch Church, a Swedish Church, and so on.

In many countries one effect of such division was to strengthen the hand of the king in building a unified state. The authority and prestige of the Protestant monarch was increased as he became the spiritual as well as the political ruler of his subjects. Even in Catholic countries, though the pope remained the spiritual ruler, the Church became national in sentiment, and it was the king rather than the pope who enforced religious conformity among his subjects. Conversely, where the split between Protestants and Catholics was deep, as in the Holy Roman Empire, the power of the central ruler was limited and national unity impeded.

Freedom of religion, as we have noted, was still far from a reality. Persecution flourished, partly because the clash between faiths engendered intolerance but even more because religious uniformity was the ideal of the rulers of the rising national states. Just as he sought to create a uniform system of law and justice throughout his realm, so the strong monarch endeavored to establish a single faith to which his subjects owed complete obedience. An incidental result of this policy was the emigration of religious minorities to areas where they could worship freely, as in the New World.

Political and religious developments continued to be closely related throughout the sixteenth and early seventeenth centuries. In the Religious Wars to be described in the next chapter political duels were superimposed on religious quarrels, resulting in some of the bloodiest and most prolonged warfare in human history. The founder of the Christian religion had given as a primary command, "Thou shalt love thy neighbor as thyself." But there was no brotherhood between Catholic and Protestant nor between political rivals who played on religious antagonisms to serve their own ends.

SUMMARY

The Renaissance represented a new emphasis on man's individuality, an outlook which could not fail eventually to have its impact on religion. An appeal for religious reform came from the northern humanists who criticized ecclesiastical abuses and called for a Christianity based closely upon the New Testament. By means of the printing press, which vastly increased the number of books available, the new ideas spread rapidly throughout Europe. Already beginning to revolt against all institutions which hampered them in their new economic freedom, many men of the middle class were sympathetic to the cry for Church reform. The new spirit also found an ally in the new nationalism and in the growing power of the kings, who were reluctant to be thwarted by any force, even the Church. When a leader appeared with a religious message in keeping with the spirit of the age, the long bottled-up forces of reform exploded.

Luther's open breach with the Church encouraged such Protestant leaders as Zwingli, Calvin, and other reformers to form their own churches. The essence of the new movements was an emphasis on Biblical authority, a denial of the need for priestly mediation for salvation, and a repudiation of the pope as head of organized religion. After the Protestant Revolt, churches were firmly tied to the political administration of the states. Thus Calvin and Zwingli established theocracies in Geneva and Zurich in Switzerland. In Germany each prince chose between Lutheranism and Catholicism for the religion of his subjects. In the Scandinavian countries the national churches were Lutheran. Without repudiating the basic elements of Catholicism, the English king broke with Rome and assumed the headship of the Anglican Church.

The challenge flung at the Church did not remain unanswered. As the medieval Church had arrested decline by new zealous orders of monks, so once again the Church was invigorated by various new religious brotherhoods and a resurgence of mysticism and morality. Pope Paul III and his successors carried out an energetic program to excise the abuses which had plagued the Church for centuries. Without any compromise with the Protestants, the Council of Trent reaffirmed the fundamental doctrines of the Church. But there was no possibility of the Church reuniting Europe.

Europe was plunged into an epoch of intolerance and bigotry from which it slowly emerged when, after the prolonged and bloody struggles to be described in the next chapter, it became apparent that no one faith could exterminate the others. But if the clock was set back in some ways, in other ways the religious upheaval furthered the transition from a medieval to a modern pattern of life. The revolt from the universal Church shattered the medieval ideal of unity and gave us the religious diversity of the modern world.

SUGGESTIONS FOR READING

H. J. Hillerbrand, **The World of the Reformation*** (Scribner's, 1973) is a fresh interpretation. G. L. Mosse, **The Reformation,*** 3rd ed. (Peter Smith); E. H. Harbison, **The Age of Reformation*** (Cornell); R. H. Bainton, **The Reformation of the Sixteenth Century*** (Beacon); and A. G. Dickens, **Reformation and Society in Sixteenth-Century Europe*** (Harcourt Brace Jovanovich) are all good brief surveys. J. Hurstfield, ed., **The Reformation Crisis*** (Torchbooks) contains brief, perceptive essays by noted scholars on major aspects of the Reformation era. See also J. Russell Major, **The Age of the Renaissance and Reformation*** (Lippincott, 1970); and R. L. DeMolen, ed., **The Meaning of the Renaissance and Reformation*** (Houghton Mifflin, 1974). J. Huizenga, **Erasmus and the Age of the Reformation*** (Torchbooks); and E. H. Harbison, **The Christian Scholar in the Age of the Reformation*** (Scribner's) are excellent on the northern humanists' criticism of the Church.

R. H. Bainton, **Here I Stand: A Life of Martin Luther*** (Mentor) is the most readable account. See also E. Erikson, **Young Man Luther*** (Norton); R. Marius, **Luther** (Lippincott, 1974); and E. Schwiebert, **Luther and his Times** (Concordia).

Williston Walker, **John Calvin: The Organiser of Reformed Protestantism*** (Schocken) is probably the best introduction. J. T. McNeill, **The History and Character of Calvinism*** (Galaxy) is a standard work. See also E. W. Monter, **Calvin's Geneva*** (Krie-

ger, 1975); and J. Ridley, **John Knox** (Oxford, 1968).

A. G. Dickens, **The English Reformation*** (Schocken); and T. M. Parker, **The English Reformation to 1558*** (Oxford) are excellent surveys.

On the "left wing" of Protestantism, see George H. Williams, **The Radical Reformation** (Westminster, 1962); and N. Cohn, **The Pursuit of the Millennium,*** rev. ed. (Galaxy).

A. G. Dickens, **The Counter Reformation*** (Harcourt Brace Jovanovich, 1969) is brief and richly illustrated. A sympathetic Catholic account is P. Janelle, **The Catholic Reformation** (Christian Classics). See also R. Ridolfi, **The Life of Girolamo Savonarola** (Greenwood); and J. Brodrick, **The Origin of the Jesuits** (Greenwood, 1976).

On the effects of the religious upheaval see R. H. Tawney, **Religion and the Rise of Capitalism*** (Mentor); R. Kingdon and R. Linder, eds., **Calvin and Calvinism: Sources of Democracy?*** (Heath, 1970); H. Kamen, **The Rise of Toleration*** (McGraw-Hill, 1967); E. Troeltsch, **Protestantism and Progress: A Historical Study of the Relation of Protestantism to the Modern World*** (Beacon); and E. W. Monter, **European Witchcraft*** (Wiley, 1969).

*Indicates a less expensive paperbound edition.

CHAPTER 15

Power Politics
and the New Diplomacy:
1500-1650

The Strife
of States
and Kings

INTRODUCTION. By acquiring a historical perspective we can do much to illuminate today's events and problems and bring them into focus. The period from 1500 to 1650 is particularly significant; it can serve as a laboratory in which we can watch the genesis and development of the statecraft of modern times.

The central factor in this troubled period was the rise of the competitive state system, involving the actions of independent and sovereign nations. These budding nations exhibited three fundamental features that contrasted sharply with the characteristics the same territories had possessed in earlier, feudal times: they had strong and effective central governments, their citizens displayed increased national consciousness, and their rulers claimed sovereignty—that is, supreme power within the boundaries of their own states. As we shall see in this chapter, these states were expansionist and aggressive, taking every opportunity to grow more powerful at the expense of weaker nations.

The decline of the medieval papacy and the religious revolt in the sixteenth century ended the Church's role as the arbiter of right and justice in disputes between secular rulers. The rulers of the sovereign states were thus completely free and untrammeled in the arena of international politics. Would one state be able to dominate all the rest? Would there be varying degrees of power among states without any one becoming supreme? Would these independent and sovereign nations be able to establish a pattern of cooperation, ensuring thereby a measure of peace and political amity in the western world? These fundamental questions were answered in Europe between 1500 and 1650. And the way in which they were answered set the pattern of international relations from that day to this.

The one hundred fifty years following 1500 are among the bloodiest and most complex in European history. The story of these years is chiefly one of battles, alliances, and treaties —in a word, drum-and-trumpet history. Yet running through the wars and complexities of this period two major threads can be discerned: the emergence of the modern diplomatic technique of the "balance of power" as a means of providing some degree of equilibrium to the new European state system, and the rise and fall of Spain as the dominant power in Europe.

THE COMPETITIVE STATE SYSTEM EMERGES

Sovereignty replaces suzerainty. Both the medieval ideal of universal empire and Church and the medieval actuality of decentralized feudalism were undermined by the rise of strong monarchs who defied popes and put down rebellious nobles. The century before 1500 had witnessed much disorder, civil conflict, and war; more and more, people looked to their kings to provide the state with a measure of stability and security. Rulers also took an active part in stimulating the economy of their nations, and in return they obtained from the bourgeoisie larger revenues which they used to expand administrative bureaus and government services. Of great importance was the fact that kings could now afford to hire soldiers for standing armies—monarchs were no longer feudal suzerains dependent upon the irregularly available feudal forces. Moreover, the king's army could easily squelch the retainers of a rebellious noble. Thus the power once distributed throughout the feudal pyramid was concentrated in the hands of the ruler.

The theory of centralized, unchallenged authority—that is, sovereignty—was given its first comprehensive expression by a French lawyer and university professor, Jean Bodin (1530-1596). Dismayed by the disorders of the religious wars in France (see p. 335), Bodin attacked both the feudal idea of contract and the universalism of empire and Church in his work *Concerning Public Affairs*. He supported the power of the monarch and his right of sovereignty, which he defined as "unlimited power over citizens and subjects, unrestrained by law."[1] According to Bodin, the king was free of all restraint save some rather shadowy limitation exercised by God and divine law.

The advent of power politics. Equipped with a standing army, royal courts, and new sources of revenue and backed by the growing support of the bourgeoisie, a European monarch was to a great extent master of his own state by the sixteenth century. And, equally significant, he was his own master in foreign affairs. The Church was no longer an international arbiter, and the factionalism of the Protestant Reformation was soon to reduce appreciably the Church's claim to universal influence. The international arena now consisted of a number of free agents who could keep what they could defend and take what they wanted if they had sufficient force. A nation-state depended for survival on the exercise of its power, and war was the chief instrument at hand. Thus statecraft became the politics of power, and the competitive state system emerged.

The rise of modern diplomacy. The development of the competitive state system gave rise to the practice of modern diplomacy. Rulers needed to be informed about the plans and policies of their rivals; states fearful of attack from stronger foes had to seek out allies; and, after wars had been fought, agreements between victor and vanquished required negotiations.

Medieval popes customarily sent envoys to reside at royal courts, but modern diplomatic practice had its real birth among the fiercely independent city-states of northern Italy. The republic of Venice—"the school and touchstone of ambassadors"—was particularly active; its authorities maintained diplomatic archives and sent their representatives throughout Europe with elaborate instructions. To act as a safeguard against poisoning, trusted cooks were part of a diplomat's retinue, but ambassadors' wives were forbidden to accompany their husbands on diplomatic missions for fear they might divulge state secrets. About 1455 the first permanent embassy in history was sent to Genoa by the duke of Milan. Within a short time most of the important nations of the day followed suit and posted representatives in European capitals.

On many occasions the new diplomacy encouraged negotiation and prevented war. Diplomatic methods so often involved deceit and treachery, however, that negotiations often fanned rather than diminished the fires of international hostility. A seventeenth-century Englishman defined an ambassador as "an honest man sent to lie abroad for the commonwealth."[2] Diplomacy during the past three hundred years often has done little to refute this definition.

Balance-of-power politics. One of the most important achievements of the new diplomacy was the technique known as the "balance of power," whereby a coalition of states could checkmate the swollen power of one or more rival states and thereby restore equilibrium. Balance-of-power politics then and later aimed not so much at preventing war as at preserving the sovereignty and independence of individual states from threatened or actual aggression. Yet as international relations more and more took the form of alignments aimed at preserving the balance of power, a sense of the interdependence of the European state system developed. The strong movement toward European unity in our day is the latest manifestation of this sense of interdependence.

The sixteenth century was the formative period for the behavior pattern of modern nations in international affairs. Unrestrained by religious or ethical scruples, the sovereign governments were about to begin an era of international strife with the quest for power as their only guide to success. With disunited Italy as a pawn in the game, the counters on the chessboard began to move.

ITALY: CASE STUDY IN POWER POLITICS

Charles VIII and the Italian Wars. Because of Louis XI's success as a statemaker (see p. 272), his son Charles VIII (1483-1498) entertained grandiose notions of imitating the exploits of Hannibal and Charlemagne by invading Italy, conquering Naples, and eventually wresting Constantinople from the Turks. In 1494 Charles crossed the Alps at the head of thirty thousand well-trained troops and initiated the Italian Wars that were to last intermittently until 1559. At first the expedition was little more than a holiday for the French. Charles' cavalry, pikemen, and light, quick-firing cannon won easy victories, and he soon took possession of Naples.

This quick conquest alarmed the rulers who had previously acquiesced to Charles' plan. Ferdinand of Spain suspected that Charles might next try to conquer the Spanish possession of Sicily, and the Holy Roman emperor became uneasy at the prospect of French dominance in Italy. In addition, Venice feared for its independence and took the lead in forming a league which also included the Papal States, the Holy Roman Empire, and Spain. Called the Holy League, it was the first important example of a coalition of states formed to preserve the balance of power in Europe. Its armies drove Charles out of Italy in 1495, thus halting French designs on the peninsula for the moment.

Machiavelli's works, which were translated into several different languages, had tremendous impact all over Europe.

End of the first phase of the Italian Wars. Following the death of Charles VIII in 1498, his successor, Louis XII, invaded Italy. The counters again moved on the chessboard: alliances were made and then broken, pledges went unhonored, and allies were deserted. Ferdinand of Spain offers a particularly good example of duplicity and treachery. Louis XII accused Ferdinand of cheating him on at least two occasions. Hearing this, Ferdinand scoffed: "He lies, the drunkard; I have deceived him more than ten times."[3]

In the first phase of the Italian Wars—which ended in 1513 with the French again ejected from Italy—one can see the new power politics at work, without benefit of rules and indeed without benefit of any moral or religious scruples. The only important objectives were glory, power, and wealth. In attaining these objectives "necessity knows no law," as Renaissance lawyers liked to observe. The conflict over Italy clearly prophesied the mode of future relations among modern sovereign states.

Machiavelli and Machiavellian politics. The primer for diplomacy and power politics was written by Niccolò Machiavelli (1469-1527), historian, playwright, and official in the Florentine republic. Outraged at the cavalier manner in which invaders had smashed their way into his beloved Italy, Machiavelli mourned his native land as being

more a slave than the Hebrews, more a servant than the Persians, more scattered than the Athenians; without head, without government; defeated, plundered, torn asunder, overrun; subject to every sort of disaster.[4]

Machiavelli's wide acquaintance with the unprincipled politics of the early Italian Wars produced his cynical and ruthless attitude toward men and politics. *The Prince*—one of a half-dozen volumes that have helped form western political thought—was written as a guide for an audacious leader who would use any means to win and hold power, free Italy from invaders, and end Italian disunity. A realist who wanted his leader-statesman to understand the political facts of life as they had been operating in Europe, Machiavelli wrote:

A prudent ruler . . . cannot and should not observe faith when such observance is to his disadvantage and the causes that made him give his promise have vanished. If men were all good, this advice would not be good, but since men are wicked and do not keep their promises to you, you likewise do not have to keep yours to them. Lawful reasons to excuse his failure to keep them will never be lacking to a prince.[5]

Machiavelli did not, of course, invent the precepts of ruthlessness in politics. Rulers had dishonored treaties and used force to attain their ends before *The Prince* was written. What Machiavelli did was to accept the politics of his day without any false illusions. He gave his prince many suggestions for survival and conquest in the brutal world of unrestrained power.

In the actions of all men, and especially those of princes, where there is no court to which to appeal, people think of the outcome. A prince needs only to conquer and to maintain his position. The means he has used will always be judged honorable and will be praised by everybody, because the crowd is always caught by appearance and by the outcome of events, and the crowd is all there is in the world. . . .[6]

Although "Machiavellian politics" is generally a term of condemnation, it should be noted that Machiavelli had an idealistic end in view: to "bring good to the mass of the people of the land" of Italy.[7]

EUROPEAN EMPIRE OR SOVEREIGN STATES?

Charles V. The manner in which the rulers of Europe practiced power politics is shown clearly by the events in Europe during the first half of the sixteenth century, a period often referred to as the Age of Charles V.

Charles' grandfather, Maximilian I, Archduke of Austria and Holy Roman emperor, had added the Netherlands and Franche-Comté to his realm by marrying Mary of Burgundy. (Franche-Comté was that part of Burgundy not seized by Louis XI; see p. 272). Maximilian's son (Charles' father) had married a daughter of Ferdinand and Isabella of

Spain. This calculated policy of dynastic marriages was to elevate the Austrian Hapsburgs to a position no ruler since Charlemagne had held. Following his father's death in 1506, Charles became ruler of the Netherlands; in 1516 his maternal grandfather, Ferdinand, bequeathed him Spain and its overseas empire and Naples and Sicily. The death of his other grandfather, Maximilian, gave him Austria and left vacant the throne of the Holy Roman Empire, to which Charles was elected in 1519 as Emperor Charles V.

Charles' efforts in protecting his dispersed territories, together with his dream of restoring royal authority and religious unity in Germany, led many of his contemporaries to believe that he sought to dominate all of Europe. Although he was essentially conservative and moderate, Charles found himself with too many irons in the fire; he was constantly frustrating plots, crushing rebellions, and repelling invasions in his many dominions.

EUROPE IN THE EARLY 16TH CENTURY

- Holdings of Charles V, 1520
- Acquired by Ferdinand, Brother of Charles, 1526
- Holdings of Henry VIII of England
- Holdings of French Kings
- Suleiman's Empire
- Holy Roman Empire

Two prominent kings on the European chessboard were Francis I (left, portrait by Jean Clouet) of France and Henry VIII (right, portrait by Hans Holbein) of England.

Charles' problems were inextricably connected with the activities of Francis I of France, Henry VIII of England, and Suleiman, ruler of the Ottoman empire. Out of the interplay of their rivalries unfolded the bloody drama of the first half of the sixteenth century.

New moves on the chessboard. The basic cause of Franco-Hapsburg rivalry was the fact that Charles' possessions encircled the realm of Francis I (1515-1547). In 1515, just before Charles V came into his inheritance, Francis invaded Italy, occupied Milan, and so set the stage for the renewal of the Italian Wars. Across the English Channel, Henry VIII followed the events closely, aiming to use his state, with its small population of 2,500,000, as a counterweight in the Franco-Hapsburg rivalry. Believing Francis to be militarily stronger than Charles, Henry allied himself with the Hapsburg emperor in order to check French power.

The test of strength began as Charles' forces drove the French from Milan. Francis soon recaptured it, but at the battle of Pavia (1525) the French were defeated and Francis was taken prisoner. Realizing that he had miscalculated, Henry VIII executed a sudden about-face, deserting Charles and supporting France and a coalition of lesser powers against the Hapsburgs. This use of England's power to equalize the strength of Continental rivals is a spectacular example of what now became the cornerstone of English foreign policy. Time and again in modern history, England has employed balance-of-power diplomacy to maintain European equilibrium.

Suleiman, ruler of the Turks. The Ottoman empire, which reached the height of its power under Suleiman the Magnificent (1520-1566), was far stronger than any European state. The outstanding feature of its efficient administrative and military system was the dominant role played by slaves. Although Christians were granted a separate religious and civil status under the leadership of their bishops, every five years between 2,000 and 12,000 Christian boys from the ages of ten to fifteen were enslaved and brought to Constantinople. There they were converted to Islam and trained to enter the administration, where even the post of grand vizier was open to them, or the army. In the latter instance they served as Janissaries, the elite 12,000-man core of the Turkish standing army, who were fanatical in their devotion to Islam.

The powerful Ottoman empire was still expanding. Suleiman's predecessor had given Europe a respite by turning eastward to conquer Syria and Egypt, but Suleiman resumed the advance westward. With the European states politically and religiously at odds, Suleiman faced no concerted resistance. In 1521 he captured Belgrade, the key fortress of the Hungarian frontier, and in 1526 on the plain of Mohacs the Janissary infantry crushed the cavalry of the Hungarian magnates. The Hungarian king and many of his magnates were killed, and Suleiman moved on to plunder Buda without organized resistance.

The king who perished at Mohacs had ruled both Hungary and Bohemia. Terrified by the prospect of new Turkish attacks, both the Bohemians and the Hungarians offered their vacant thrones to Ferdinand, brother-in-law of the dead king and brother of Charles v. Since most of Hungary had been occupied by the Turks, Ferdinand's rule extended only over the northwest portion of that country. Thus a Turkish victory placed the destiny of both Hungary and Bohemia in the hands of the Hapsburgs and established the Turks as a threat on Charles' Austrian borders.

Religion and politics on the chessboard. Following his release from captivity in 1526, after making promises he had no intention of keeping, Francis I decided upon an alliance with Suleiman. The enemies of the French king protested loudly against this "unholy alliance," but power politics took precedence over religion in both Paris and Constantinople.

Indirectly, the Turks aided the Protestant cause in Germany. In 1529 Suleiman's armies besieged Vienna, but supply difficulties and Hapsburg resistance forced the attackers to retire. To deal with the Turkish threat, Charles, who had been planning measures against the Lutherans, was forced to arrange a truce with the Protestant princes to gain their support against the Turks.

Suleiman now turned to the Mediterranean where Tunisia and Algeria became Ottoman vassal states and bases for Turkish pirates, known as corsairs, who preyed on Christian shipping and raided the coasts of Spain and Italy. The strength that Charles might have amassed to crush the French monarchy was diverted to his besieged lands bordering on the Mediterranean. A truce in 1544 halted the French-Hapsburg struggle, and Charles could at last concentrate his efforts on the German states, where in 1546 the Lutheran struggle flared into civil war. With France aiding the Lutherans and the Catholic princes

King Sapor of Persia Humiliating Emperor Valerian, School of Antwerp, ca. 1515-1525, oil on panel, 14⁹/₁₆ × 11¼ inches, 1934.64 (formerly believed to be a portrait of Emperor Charles V and formerly attributed to Cornelisz).

giving only half-hearted support to Charles lest he become powerful enough to dominate them, the Schmalkaldic War ended in 1555 with the compromise Peace of Augsburg (see p. 311). The Lutheran faith received official sanction, and Charles was thwarted in his cherished aim of restoring religious unity to Germany.

In 1556, five months after the Peace of Augsburg, the weary and discouraged emperor retired to a monastery. He turned over the Hapsburg possessions in central Europe to his brother Ferdinand, who was elected emperor, and gave Spain, the Netherlands, and his Italian possessions to his son Philip. Thereafter two Hapsburg dynasties, one Spanish and the other Austrian, ruled in Europe. A legend has it that Charles spent the two remaining years of his life trying to make several clocks keep exactly the same time—apparently an allegory suggesting that he was faced with so many problems that he could never settle all of them.

Significance for modern times. The eventful Age of Charles v had laid down much of the political and religious foundation for modern Europe:

1) It had been decided by force of arms that no single state was to dominate all of Europe. The balance of power was maintained.

2) German and Italian national growth was further stunted. Italy had been a battleground since 1494, and when the Italian Wars finally ended in 1559, Milan and Naples were Spanish possessions and Spain was to dominate Italy for nearly two hundred years.

3) Charles' wars with France and the Turks prevented him from applying pressure on the Lutherans and so saved the Reformation in Germany.

4) The Peace of Augsburg confirmed France's hold on the bishoprics of Metz, Toul, and Verdun in Lorraine, which the French had occupied during the Schmalkaldic War. French expansion toward the Rhine had begun, with momentous consequences for the future.

5) The advance of Ottoman power in Europe meant that Turkish control over the Balkans was handed down to later European statesmen as an explosive legacy. The alliance of France with Turkey, which also gave the French trading rights and a protectorate over the Holy Places in the Near East, became an enduring though irregular factor in European diplomacy.

6) The history of the first half of the sixteenth century made it quite clear that diplomacy a la Machiavelli was to be the order of the day. Deceit, treachery, surprise attacks, and broken promises were written into the record.

FAITH AND NATIONALITY IN WESTERN EUROPE

Era of the Religious Wars. While the threat of Hapsburg domination of Europe had been lessened after Charles v divided his lands, the Continent was still to witness convulsive rivalries and a century more of warfare. The period from roughly the middle of the sixteenth century to the middle of the seventeenth century is often referred to as the Era of the Religious Wars, for the religious issues which flamed forth from the Protestant upheaval—particularly that most international form of Protestantism, Calvinism—colored every political conflict.

Zenith of the Spanish state. The Era of the Religious Wars began in 1556 when Philip II, the son of Charles v, became king of Spain. Several factors made it seem that Philip's future would be impressive and successful. First, when his uncle Ferdinand received the Hapsburg Austrian lands together with the imperial crown of the Holy Roman Empire, Philip was freed of the political and religious complexities in middle Europe; that is, he had no "German problem." Second, the end of the Franco-Hapsburg wars over Italy in 1559 was followed by religious wars in France (see p. 335), leaving Spain without a rival on the Continent. Third, Philip inherited a new empire overseas which was more lucrative and more easily administered than his father's empire in the Germanies had been. From the New World came untold treasure to enrich the Hapsburg coffers at Madrid (see Chapter 18).

In addition to the riches of the Americas

and the Spanish possessions in Europe—the Netherlands, Franche-Comté, Naples, Sicily, and Milan—Philip had the best army of the time. The mercenary armies employed by other states could not rival the training and discipline of the native Spanish infantry. The dread of Spanish power caused people to say, as they had under Charles v, that "When Spain moves, the whole world trembles."

During his long reign (1556-1598) Philip sought three basic goals: to make his royal power absolute in all his possessions, to combat heresy and strengthen Catholicism, and to extend Spain's influence. Under Charles v the traditional parliaments, or Cortes, of Castile and Aragon had been largely superseded by a number of royal councils staffed by a well-trained civil service. Building on this foundation, Philip erected a centralized system of government in which every decision rested with the king and in which all agencies of government were subordinate to his will.

Philip was extremely devout and saw no distinction between the good of the Church and the interest of the Spanish state. At home the Spanish Inquisition both ferreted out heretics and strengthened royal power. Abroad, by championing the Counter Reformation Philip also justified his interference in the political and religious conflicts of other European nations.

One of Philip's great achievements was the uniting of the Iberian peninsula under the Spanish crown. In 1580 the direct line of the Portuguese royal family died out, and Philip claimed the throne through his mother, a Portuguese princess. When the Portuguese refused to accept him as their ruler, Philip invaded the country and seized the throne. The annexation of Portugal and its vast colonial empire brought new riches to Madrid from Brazil, Africa, and the East Indies.

Crusade in the Mediterranean. After Suleiman's death in 1566 the Turkish advance in the Mediterranean continued, and in 1570 the Turks captured the Venetian island of Cyprus, the last Christian outpost in the area. At the pope's urging, Christian Europe turned to Philip, the champion of the Catholic faith, to block Turkish expansion.

A Holy League was formed to raise a great fleet and destroy Ottoman naval power in the Mediterranean. Spanish and Venetian warships, together with the smaller squadrons of Genoa and the Papal States, made up a fleet of over two hundred vessels which was joined by volunteers from all over Europe. In 1571 the League's fleet and the Turkish navy clashed at Lepanto, on the western side of Greece. The outcome was a decisive victory for Christian Europe; Ottoman sea power was crushed, never to be restored as a major threat to Christendom. Lepanto is often considered the last crusade.

Unrest and revolt in the Netherlands. The conquest of Portugal and the defeat of the Turks were signal victories for Philip, but the specter of failure stalked him in the Netherlands. The seventeen provinces of the Low Countries (which included today's Holland, Belgium, and Luxemburg) had been restive under Charles v, who had imposed heavy taxes to help finance his wars. Yet he had continued to enjoy the confidence of the Netherlanders, who regarded him as one of themselves because he had been born in the city of Ghent. But the Netherlanders did not feel the same about Philip, whom they distrusted as a foreigner. Seeking to make his rule absolute in the Netherlands, Philip excluded the local nobility from the administration, maintained an army of occupation, and introduced the Inquisition to stop the advance of Calvinism.

Calvinism continued to spread, however, and in 1566 a series of violent anti-Catholic and anti-Spanish riots broke out. "The Council of Troubles"—soon dubbed "The Council of Blood"—was set up to stamp out treason and heresy. During the ensuing reign of terror some 8,000 were slain, 30,000 were deprived of their property, and 100,000 fled the country. At the same time Philip proposed new and oppressive taxes, including a 10 percent sales tax, which antagonized most Netherlanders, Catholic as well as Protestant. Under the Dutch leader, William the Silent of the House of Orange, discontent flared into open revolt in 1568.

In the first years of the revolt the puny forces commanded by the tenacious William the Silent were dispersed again and again.

The Dutch turned to the sea to outfit privateers to prey on Spanish shipping. Then in 1576 the incident of the Spanish Fury electrified the entire Netherlands. Usually well-disciplined, the badly fed and unpaid Spanish soldiers mutinied and marched on Antwerp where they burned public buildings and murdered seven thousand citizens. The calamity settled the local differences between the seventeen provinces that had prevented them from making a concerted effort against Spanish tyranny. The Pacification of Ghent, which the provincial representatives signed in 1576, declared that all Spanish soldiers must be expelled from the land, after which the representative body, the Estates-General, would govern the country.

Unfortunately for the rebels' cause, the seventeen provinces did not long maintain the unity manifested in the Pacification of Ghent. The Spaniards were able to take advantage of the differences between the Protestant provinces in the north and the predominantly Catholic provinces in the south. Employing a combination of diplomacy and force, the Spanish succeeded in reuniting the ten southern provinces with Spain in 1579. The Dutch in the north, however, continued to fight on, and in 1581 the Estates-General of the Dutch United Provinces (also called Holland because of the preeminence of that province with its flourishing city of Amsterdam) issued a declaration of independence. One of its provisions stated:

The people were not created by God for the sake of the Prince . . . but, on the contrary, the Prince was made for the good of the people.[8]

The declaration of 1581 set the model for later declarations justifying revolution in England, France, and the English colonies in America. It also established another landmark in modern history by decreeing freedom of worship for the large Catholic minority in the new nation. The stability of the state had become a greater concern than religious conformity.

Three years later the cause of Dutch freedom was placed in serious jeopardy when William the Silent was assassinated by a young Catholic fanatic and the Spanish stepped up their efforts to destroy the new republic. At this critical moment Elizabeth I of England, fearing that Philip planned to use the Netherlands as a base for an invasion of England, rushed troops to the aid of the United Provinces. The destruction of Philip's Armada by England in 1588 (see p. 334) further weakened the ability of Spain to crush the Dutch.

In 1609 a twelve years' truce was signed, which recognized the partition of the Netherlands along the line where the fighting had stopped. Not until the end of the Thirty

The 1566 rioting in the Netherlands was instigated by mobs of Calvinists who invaded Catholic churches, toppling images, smashing windows, and looting valuable articles. The Spanish reacted to such riots with ferocity.

Year's War in 1648 did the Dutch Republic gain from the Spanish formal recognition of its independence. The ten southern provinces, however, remained in Hapsburg hands and were known first as the Spanish Netherlands and then after 1713 as the Austrian Netherlands. In 1830 they achieved independence as the state of Belgium.

The English throne: Protestant or Catholic? On more than one occasion during the reign of Philip II, it seemed that England would come under Spanish domination. In 1554, two years before he ascended the throne of Spain, Philip had married Mary Tudor, the older daughter of Henry VIII. Mary adored her husband, and as queen she was strongly influenced by him, although he had no official status in the governing of England. After a brief reign Mary died, and in 1558 her half-sister, Elizabeth I, assumed the throne.

Elizabeth's disputed succession provided the next occasion for possible Spanish domination of England. The daughter of Henry by his second wife, Anne Boleyn, Elizabeth was considered illegitimate by English Catholics, who recognized only Henry's first marriage as valid. Furthermore, in the eyes of Catholic Europe, the rightful heir to the throne was the great-granddaughter of Henry VII, Mary Stuart, Queen of Scotland.

Brought up in France as a Catholic, Mary had wed the heir to the French throne and reigned for two years as queen of France. After the death of her husband, she returned to her native Scotland, where her French mother had been ruling as regent with the aid of French troops. Mary found Scotland in the hands of rebellious nobles and vigorous Protestant preachers under the Calvinist reformer John Knox (see p. 316). A widow of eighteen, famous for her charm, beauty, and grace, Mary proceeded to alienate her subjects by a series of blunders: she was too frivolous for her straitlaced Calvinistic subjects, she was unsuccessful in concealing her pro-Catholic sympathies, and, finally, she was accused of being involved in the sordid murder of her weakling husband, Lord Darnley. The Scottish Presbyterians revolted, and in 1568 Mary was forced to seek refuge with her cousin Elizabeth in England. There,

During the brief marriage of Philip II of Spain and Queen Mary of England, it appeared that Spain might come to dominate the island kingdom.

her Catholicism and her good claim to Elizabeth's throne made her an unwelcome guest, potentially dangerous to the Tudor monarch and to English Protestantism.

For his part, Philip had no compunctions about plotting to place Mary on the throne of England. Philip's ambassador in London became the center of a web of intrigue.

The island fortress: obstacle to Spanish hegemony. As Philip became the chief enemy of Protestant England, Elizabeth gradually emerged as the foremost obstacle to Spanish power. Unlike the impetuous Mary Stuart, who was often the blind instrument of her emotions, Elizabeth was realistic, calculating, and thoroughly Machiavellian. As the Spanish ambassador wrote to Philip:

. . . what a pretty business it is to treat with this woman who I think must have a hundred thousand devils in her body, notwithstanding that she is forever telling me that she yearns to be a nun and to pass her life in prayer.[9]

Elizabeth resorted to every subterfuge and trick available to her in the duel with Philip of Spain. Using her sex as a diplomatic weap-

A sixteenth-century Dutch drawing shows the execution of Mary, Queen of Scots. The inscription in old Dutch on the drawing reads, "On the VIII of February, Mary Stuart, Queen of Scots, fervent Roman Catholic, was beheaded, having tried to cause much unrest (and) to make herself mistress of England, which was completely proved against her by the Council of the Parliament."

on, she carried on long flirtations with the brothers of the French king, thereby helping to prevent an alliance between France and Spain. In addition she sent covert assistance to the Dutch, aware that their rebellion was sapping Spanish strength.

Elizabeth also secretly encouraged her sea captains to prey upon Spanish shipping and to attack the rich Spanish settlements in the New World. The most famous of Elizabethan Sea Dogs, Sir Francis Drake, sailed into the Pacific, plundered the western coast of Spanish America, and, after circumnavigating the globe, arrived in England with a hold full of gold and silver.

Aware of Elizabeth's duplicity, Philip planned to gain control over England by placing Mary Stuart on the English throne. But a plot against Elizabeth's life, in which Mary was obliquely implicated, was discovered. Parliament was convinced that as long as Mary lived, Elizabeth's life would be endangered, and therefore, in 1587, Elizabeth signed Mary's death warrant. But in a sense Mary had not failed. She had left behind in Scotland a son, James, who was destined to become the common monarch of England and Scotland, not by conspiracy or force but by common consent.

Philip and Elizabeth at war. After the discovery of the plot against her life, Elizabeth sought to hinder Philip's plans by openly sending arms and soldiers to the Netherlands, by aiding the Protestant cause during the French religious wars, and by authorizing Drake to destroy Spanish shipping. Philip meanwhile was planning his "great enterprise"—an invasion of England, blessed by the pope, to gain the kingdom for himself and wean its people from heresy.

Philip's strategy was to have a fleet of 130 ships, called by contemporaries the "Invincible Armada," join a large Spanish army in the Netherlands and then land this force on the coast of England. The Dutch, however, prevented the rendezvous by blocking the main ports in the Low Countries, and Philip's designs were ruined completely when the Elizabethan Sea Dogs trounced the Armada in the English Channel. The small, swift English ships outmaneuvered the bulky Spanish galleons, and a severe storm, the famed "Protestant wind," completed the debacle. The Armada limped home after losing a third of its ships.

The defeat of the Armada meant that England would remain Protestant, that it would soon emerge as a dominant sea power, and that the Dutch rebellion against Spain would succeed. By building new ships, Spain quickly recovered from the material effects of the defeat of the Armada, but it never overcame the psychological effects of that disaster. The Spanish people had been told that the Armada was "the most important [enterprise] undertaken by God's Church for many hundreds of years. . . . we are defending the high reputation of our King and lord, and of our nation; . . . and simultaneously our peace, tranquility and repose."[10] The optimism engendered by Spain's great past achievements soon vanished; in the words of a modern scholar, "If any one year marks the division between the triumphant

In July 1588 the English completely routed Spain's "Invincible Armada."

Spain of the first two Hapsburgs and the defeatist, disillusioned Spain of their successors, that year is 1588."[11]

The Wars of Religion in France. Soon after France and Spain ended their long conflict over Italy in 1559, France underwent one of the most terrible civil conflicts in its history. Persecution of Protestants had been sporadic under Francis I (d. 1547) and his son Henry II (d. 1559), who were more fearful of the Hapsburgs than of heresy, but by 1560 the Calvinist Huguenots numbered about one million out of a population of sixteen million. Huguenots were numerous in the cities, except in Paris, but the most influential element was the 40 to 50 percent of the nobility that had been attracted to Calvinism. The French nobility had long been restless; its numbers were increasing and it was frustrated by the loss of its former military and political preeminence.

Because the three weakling sons of Henry II had no heirs, the Valois line that had ruled France since 1328 (see p. 269) was nearing its end. This situation led to ruthless factional rivalry between two noble houses in France, both of which aspired to the throne. The Bourbons, who espoused Protestantism, had the better claim because they traced their

descent from St. Louis, the revered Capetian king of the thirteenth century. Champions of Catholicism were the powerful Guises, who claimed descent from Charlemagne. This was the setting for the series of civil wars, partly religious and partly political, that broke out in 1562.

During this period and until her death in 1589, the most powerful individual in France was Catherine de' Medici, the queen mother. Like her contemporary in London, Queen Elizabeth, Catherine was completely cynical and ruthless in statecraft. Even her youngest son referred to her as "Madame la Serpente." No matter how cruel or base, no technique was beneath her use; one of Catherine's political weapons was "'a flying squadron' of twenty-four maids of honor of high rank and low principles to help her seduce the refractory nobles on both sides."[12]

Determined to maintain the power of her sons, Catherine attempted to steer a middle course and to play one party off against the other. But as the Huguenots grew stronger, she resolved to crush them. Thus Catherine is blamed for the terrible Massacre of St. Bartholomew's Day. At dawn on August 24, 1572, with a signal from the bell of the Palace of Justice in Paris, the Catholics fell upon their Protestant rivals, and ten thousand Huguenots were slain.

The massacre did not destroy Huguenot power, however, and civil conflict continued. A new phase began in 1585, when Philip II entered the war on the side of the Catholics. He hoped first to extirpate Protestantism in France and then to control French policy, thereby gaining valuable support in crushing the Dutch revolt and in conquering England. In 1589, after assassins had eliminated both the Guise pretender and the last weakling Valois ruler, the Protestant Bourbon prince Henry of Navarre became King Henry IV of France by right of succession. Philip determined to crush the new king before he could consolidate his power. At this critical moment Queen Elizabeth intervened by sending Henry five thousand troops which turned the tide in his favor. Realizing that most Frenchmen were Catholic and sensing

that all were weary of civil war, Spanish intervention, and anarchy, Henry decided to place the welfare of France ahead of his own conscience and accepted the faith of Rome. "Paris is well worth a mass," he is supposed to have said, and soon Paris and other cities opened their gates to him. By 1595 the civil war was over and Philip was forced to withdraw his troops.

The Edict of Nantes. Although Henry IV changed his own faith, he sought to protect the liberties of the Huguenot minority in the Edict of Nantes (1598). When both Catholic and Protestant extremists denounced the measure, Henry refused to be intimidated: "I insist upon being obeyed. It is time that we all, having had our fill of war, should learn wisdom by what we have suffered."

The Edict of Nantes followed the example first set by the Dutch Republic of recognizing that more than one religion could be maintained within a state. To guarantee their religious freedom, Henry allowed the Protestants to fortify about a hundred French towns and garrison them with their own troops. As a result, the Huguenots in France constituted virtually a state within a state.

The failure of Philip II. Philip's failure in France was the last of his many setbacks. His final opponent, Henry IV, provided some fitting last words on Philip's hopes for Spanish dominance in Europe: while witnessing the departure of Spanish troops from Paris, Henry called out, "Gentlemen, commend me to your master, but do not come back."

While in the eyes of his Spanish subjects Philip was a wise, moderate, pious, and hardworking monarch, his enemies singled him out as a detestable example of trickery, cruelty, and religious intolerance. Yet Philip was not equal to Elizabeth in duplicity and diplomatic cunning, and it must be remembered that nearly all sixteenth-century European monarchs believed that the relentless persecution of noncomformists was essential to the welfare of the state. Philip's failures cannot be attributed to defects ingrained in his nature but to the fact that, in general, he was less skillful than his opponents in the game of power politics.

Most important, perhaps, is that Philip unwittingly pitted himself against the grow-

A contemporary drawing shows German cannoneers preparing to arm and fire a large mortar during the Thirty Years' War. During this period Gustavus Adolphus developed the tactical use of light and medium-weight artillery to be used in conjunction with infantry in open-field battles against the Hapsburg forces.

ing feelings of nationalism. Patriotism thwarted Philip's ambitions in the Netherlands and in England, and it also contributed to the failure of his intervention in the French religious wars.

Despite Philip's failures, Spain still enjoyed the reputation of being the first power in Europe. Spanish soldiers were the best on the Continent, and Spain's wealth from its vast overseas possessions seemed inexhaustible. Moreover, Spanish writers, scholars, and painters were outstanding; in fact, the last half of the sixteenth century and the first half of the seventeenth are usually regarded as the zenith of Spanish culture.

In the seventeenth century, however, Spanish power rapidly declined. Bad economic policies (see Chapter 18) coupled with continued overexertion in the game of power politics proved too great a burden for a nation of only eight or nine million people. The last of the so-called religious conflicts, the Thirty Years' War (1618-1648), accelerated the decline of Spain and left France the dominant state in Europe.

The issues of the Thirty Years' War. The Peace of Augsburg (see p. 311) failed to bring about a satisfactory religious settlement in the Germanies, and friction continued after 1555. The higher clergy and the princes who thereafter turned Protestant continued to take over Church lands within their jurisdiction. Furthermore, religious toleration for rapidly spreading Calvinism was now a burning issue, since the Peace of Augsburg had recognized only Lutheranism and Catholicism. A final religious factor was the progress being made by the Catholic Counter Reformation in the empire under the leadership of the Jesuits and the Jesuit-educated emperor, the Hapsburg Ferdinand II.

In addition to his deep antipathy toward heretics, Ferdinand wanted a united and subservient empire to strengthen his position in Europe. His desire to reassert imperial authority was opposed by the princes whose own power would remain strong with Germany divided and weak. Even the Catholic princes, who willingly supported Ferdinand as a Catholic leader against the Protestants, were opposed to any strengthening of imperial power. The papacy, too, was often

lukewarm in its support, regarding a strong emperor as a threat to the freedom of the Church in Germany and fearing that a too close association with the Hapsburgs would alienate the rulers of other states. Ferdinand could hope for unquestioned support only from his cousin, the Hapsburg king of Spain, who was still considered the most powerful ruler in Europe.

The varied religious and political issues in the empire created an atmosphere of tension in which one slight incident might upset the precarious peace. A prelude to the contest of arms was the formation of a Protestant League of German princes in 1608 and a similar Catholic League in 1609.

Phases of the Thirty Years' War. The complexities of the Thirty Years' War, which soon became an international struggle, can be divided into four phases: (1) Bohemian, (2) Danish, (3) Swedish, and (4) French.

The first battleground was Bohemia, preponderantly Protestant and strongly nationalistic, which had enjoyed a large measure of toleration under its Catholic Hapsburg kings. When Ferdinand withdrew that tolerance on mounting the throne of Bohemia in 1617, he precipitated a rebellion in 1618 which became a general religious war when the Bohemians invited the Calvinist head of the Protestant League to rule them. By the end of the following year Ferdinand had crushed the Bohemians, and his kinsmen, the Spanish Hapsburgs, had defeated the German Protestants supporting the Bohemian insurrection. Protestantism was stamped out in Bohemia, and the Protestant League in Germany was dissolved.

The second phase of the conflict began in 1625 when the Lutheran king of Denmark, who as duke of Holstein (see Reference Map 5) was also a prince of the empire, invaded Germany. The Danes sought not only to champion hard-pressed Protestantism but also to gain additional German territory and to thwart Hapsburg ambitions. However, the Hapsburg armies soon crushed the Danes.

This second defeat of the Protestants threatened to undo the work of the Protestant Reformation and to create a unified Hapsburg-ruled Germany. This prospect drew the leading Lutheran power, Sweden, into the fight in 1630. King Gustavus Adolphus told his people that "the papal deluge is approaching our shores"; he also hoped to acquire territories along Germany's Baltic coast as "guarantees against the emperor." The Swedish king was the founder of a new technique of warfare which stressed discipline, mobility, and morale; in Germany his well-drilled, hymn-singing veterans and mobile cannon quickly scored a series of brilliant victories. But after Gustavus Adolphus was killed in battle, a compromise peace was arranged in 1635.

The peace never went into effect, however, for Cardinal Richelieu, the chief adviser of the French king and the actual head of the government, decided that France would be secure only when the Hapsburgs of Austria and Spain, whose lands ringed France on three sides, had been defeated. Richelieu earlier had given secret aid to the German Protestants, the Danes, and the Swedes; now, in 1635, he came out in the open and the struggle became primarily a dynastic contest between Bourbons and Hapsburgs. The Swedes and the German Protestants kept the Austrian Hapsburg armies busy in Germany while French arms were concentrated against the Spanish Hapsburgs. In 1643 at the battle of Rocroi in the Spanish Netherlands the legend of the invincibility of the Spanish infantry came to an end, and the French turned to the Germanies. Although Richelieu had died in 1642, his successor, Cardinal Mazarin, continued his designs for weakening the power of the Hapsburgs.

The Peace of Westphalia. Peace negotiations began in 1644 without a cease-fire agreement, but they proceeded slowly. The delegates wrangled endlessly over such questions of protocol as who was to enter the conference room first and where they were to sit, and the fortunes of war frequently altered the bargaining power of the rival diplomats. Finally, in 1648, the longest peace negotiation on record ended in a series of treaties collectively known as the Peace of Westphalia. (Spain, however, stubbornly refused to make peace with France until 1659.)

A recapitulation of the various provisions of the peace would be very complex; suffice it to say that France moved closer to the Rhine with the acquisition of much of Alsace; Sweden and the Protestant state of Brandenburg made important territorial gains along Germany's Baltic coast; and Holland and Switzerland—the latter having successfully resisted its Hapsburg overlords since 1291—were granted independence. The Calvinists were given recognition in Germany, and Protestants were allowed to retain the Church lands they had taken before 1624.

The Peace of Westphalia permanently ended Hapsburg dreams of reviving the authority of the emperor in Germany. The sovereignty of the more than three hundred German states was recognized, with each state having the right to coin money, make war, maintain armies, and send diplomatic representatives to foreign courts. Henceforth the Hapsburg emperors worked to form a strong Danubian monarchy out of their varied Austrian, Bohemian, and Hungarian possessions.

The great significance of the Peace of Westphalia was that it symbolized the emergence and victory of the sovereign state which acknowledged no authority higher than its own interests and was prone to assume what Thomas Hobbes three years later called "the position of gladiators." More specifically, the conference established the basic principle underlying the modern state system—the essential equality of all independent sovereign states. It also instituted the diplomatic procedure of convening international congresses in order to settle the problems of war and peace by negotiation.

Thus the struggle against the Hapsburg encirclement of France begun by Francis I against Charles V early in the sixteenth century ended more than a century later. Changes had been wrought in the relative powers of nations. Both England and Holland had become great sea powers, and their commercial prosperity was increasing rapidly. The golden age of Spain was over, and France emerged as the greatest power in Europe. Although reports of devastation, population decline, and cultural retrogression in the Germanies have perhaps been exaggerated, the Thirty Years' War left a grievous legacy and thwarted German progress for a century. But by demonstrating that Protestants and Catholics were unable to exterminate each other, the Thirty Years' War—indeed, the entire Era of the Religious Wars—greatly promoted the cause of religious toleration in Europe.

THE CONTINUING SENSE OF EUROPEAN INTERDEPENDENCE

Proposals for keeping the peace. The irresponsible use of power was the outstanding feature of international politics in the late sixteenth and early seventeenth centuries. But gradually powerful rulers and diplomats realized that frequent wars threatened the growth of European trade and commerce and menaced even the existence of civilized society in the West. We have seen some of the early steps taken to improve international relations—the establishment of consular and diplomatic services, the formation of alignments to preserve the balance of power, and the first use of a general European peace congress to adjust conflicting interests after a great war. In addition, trade agreements and treaties formed the crude beginnings of a system of international law. Although these varied measures all too often had a negligible effect on the continued use of war as the means of settling disputes among nations, they reflect a continuing sense of the interdependence of the European state system—the Concert of Europe, as it would later be called.

The increased destructiveness of modern warfare had aroused the protests of many sixteenth-century humanists—Erasmus, for example, asserted that "war is sweet only to the inexperienced." In the early seventeenth century students of international affairs made some specific recommendations that are of particular interest today.

In 1623, Emeric Crucé, an obscure French monk, published a plan to eliminate war by means of an international organization which, he claimed, would be "useful to all nations, and agreeable to those who have

some light of reason and the sentiment of humanity." The central idea in his work was that all wars were harmful and their abolition would allow governments to devote themselves to the arts of peace. To this end he proposed that a permanent corps of ambassadors from all over the world be maintained at Venice as an international assembly for the settlement of all disputes through negotiation and arbitration. Crucé acknowledged that his plan for a seventeenth-century "United Nations" was in advance of his time, but added:

I have wished, nevertheless, to leave this testimony to posterity. If it serves nothing, patience. It is a small matter to lose paper and words. I have said and done what was possible for the public good, and some few who read this little book will be grateful to me for it, and will honor me, as I hope, with their remembrance.[13]

Either the first Bourbon monarch, Henry IV, or his chief minister, the Duke of Sully, devised the plan known as the Grand Design, which called for the establishment of a European federal union headed by a council of representatives from all states. The council was to secure disarmament and to control an international police force which would back its decisions by force. Each state was to contribute troops and money according to its strength. Despite its theoretical and utopian character, the Grand Design "shows that at the very moment when the modern national state, centralized within and dividing Europe into mutually hostile camps, emerged from the ruins of medieval unity, the ablest minds realized that eventually a new unity would have to be built out of these distinct entities, a United States of Europe. . . ."[14]

Grotius and international law. A number of European scholars were also at work laying the foundation for a science of international law by developing the principle that the nations formed a community based upon natural law. The first to obtain a hearing outside scholarly circles was Hugo Grotius (1583-1645), a gifted Dutch historian, theologian, practicing lawyer, and diplomat. In 1625 appeared *On the Law of War and Peace*, the work which gained Grotius instant fame and lasting recognition as the founder of international law. "Such a work," he declared, "is all the more necessary because in our day, as in former times, there is no lack of men who view this branch of law with contempt as having no reality outside of an empty name." And he continued:

I have had many and weighty reasons for undertaking to write upon this subject. Throughout the Christian world I observed a lack of restraint in relation to war, such as even barbarous races should be ashamed of; I observed that men rush to arms for slight causes, or no cause at all, and that when arms have once been taken up there is no longer any respect for law, divine or human; it is as if, in accordance with a general decree, frenzy had openly been let loose for the committing of all crimes.[15]

War and Peace are reconciled in the allegorical title page from the 1689 edition of Grotius' *De Jure Belli ac Pacis.* Four years before he wrote this great work, Grotius had escaped from a Dutch prison, where he had been sentenced to life imprisonment as a result of his campaign against the harsh Calvinist doctrine of predestination and for a more liberal regime in his own country, Holland.

Grotius endeavored to set forth a new code of international conduct based not upon the authority of the Church but on what he termed the fundamental idea of the law of nature. The law of nature was in turn founded on the dictates of reason, morality, and justice. If civilization was to endure, Grotius argued, humane considerations should prevail in the councils of the mighty, and rules of conduct binding all men should be established.

More realistic than his contemporaries Crucé and Sully, Grotius did not propose to eliminate war entirely. He sought instead to outlaw "unjust" wars and limit the effects of "just" wars. Wars were justified only to repel invasion or to punish an insult to God. Grotius' appeal fell largely upon deaf ears. Machiavelli's *The Prince* enjoyed more popularity in European palaces than *On the Law of War and Peace.*

SUMMARY

By the middle of the seventeenth century the pattern of politics in western Europe had changed significantly. Gone was the ideal of unity, whether based on empire or on universal Church; and sovereignty had replaced suzerainty. The new monarchies were largely absolute in authority within their own frontiers and free agents in the domain of international affairs. Following the principles of political behavior systematized by Machiavelli, these sovereign states pursued power, prestige, wealth, and security. No moral or religious scruples were allowed to interfere with these objectives. It was considered axiomatic that a nation had no permanent enemies or friends—only permanent interests. This maxim was illustrated by the manner in which alliances based on the new diplomatic technique of balance of power were formed on the European chessboard. We shall see in our study of later eras how the great powers have continued to alter their alliances in deference to the exigencies of the balance of power. It is also noteworthy that since balance-of-power diplomacy was the product of a felt need to preserve the security and independence of the new sovereign states, it

10. Giotto: "The Raising of Lazarus" (c. 1305). In 1300 a wealthy merchant from Padua, Enrico Scrovegni, acquired the ruins of an ancient Roman arena as the site for his palace and chapel. He engaged the Florentine artist, Giotto, to decorate the interior. Giotto painted a series of murals using the fresco technique of applying water-colors to a freshly plastered wall. In this powerful scene, Christ stands silhouetted against the blue background, calling Lazarus from the dead by a simple gesture of His hand. The scene is composed simply and clearly, divided into blocks of figures by broad diagonals, verticals, and curves. The figures have a three-dimensional quality, and a good sense of balance and depth. The whole work becomes a powerful religious statement.

11. (left) **Michelangelo: "Moses"** (c. 1515). The High Renaissance, more than any other period, developed the idea of artistic genius—of greater creative, even "divine" talent—in a single individual, who, by its possession, stood above the rules governing ordinary men. No one represented this concept more convincingly than Michelangelo—sculptor, painter, architect, and poet, who dominated the period like a colossus. The eight-foot-high statue of Moses, part of a vast sculptural program for the tomb of Julius II, was meant to be viewed from below and to project an awesome force and energy. The idealization and exaggeration of the human form expresses divine presence and conveys the sculptor's own deep religious feelings. **12.** (above) **George Gower: "Armada Portrait of Elizabeth I"** (c. 1588). This painting which is attributed to George Gower, a fashionable portrait painter in London, is probably the most magnificent Elizabethan costume portrait in three-quarter length, a popular style promoted to glorify the aging queen. It is a full-blown costume piece, using brilliant mosaics of color, and emphasizing delicate lines and details. The result is a distinctive style more medieval than Renaissance in origin. The details of the Spanish Armada prior to and after its defeat commemorate the stunning English victory.

13. Caravaggio: "The Lute Player" (c. 1595). Michelangelo de Caravaggio, one of the masters of the Italian Baroque, was a revolutionary artist who directed much of his work against the serenity of the Renaissance and the studied artificiality of his Mannerist contemporaries. Although a large portion of his work was in a religious vein, he also painted many secular subjects. Caravaggio was stubborn and often egocentric; he managed to scandalize the artistic Italian world by claiming that classical art and the great masters were not suffcient examples for the artist and that the natural world was the best teacher. "The Lute Player" is among the works Caravaggio produced while in Rome whose subjects are young boys ornamented by flowers, fruit, and musical instruments. Every detail of its story reveals the strength of its composition, with its sensitivity to color, accentuated by the severity of the surrounding outlines, and the emphasis on the central figure in relation to a neutral background.

reflected an early recognition of the interdependence of the European state system. The present-day movement toward European unity can be viewed as the latest expression of this recognition.

Power politics between 1500 and 1650 developed amid complex happenings, especially the so-called Religious Wars. Just what was religion and what politics was often difficult to determine, especially since religion was often used as a cover for political intrigue. With Philip II of Spain, for example, Catholic conviction appropriately coincided with Spanish national interests; to champion the Catholic Church was, in Philip's mind, to build a strong Spain. In other instances expediency, not religious principles, governed international politics: witness Francis I's alliance with the Turks and Richelieu's support of the German Protestants.

The revolt of the Dutch from Spain was the first large-scale example before 1650 of a successful countertrend to the increasing centralization of the monarch's power. The establishment of the Dutch Republic in the name of people's rights foreshadows the later and more famous revolts against absolutism which would establish constitutional government in England during the last half of the seventeenth century and in North America and France by the end of the eighteenth.

In the survey of European affairs in this chapter, two opposing principles were discussed: one, the right of a state to conduct its foreign affairs—even to waging war—without hindrance; the other, the concept that nations should accept some limitation of their freedom of action in international affairs. Ever since the early seventeenth century, when scholars began to think of limiting wars and the need for international law, national sovereignty and internationalism have been in competition. Sovereignty has gotten the best of it by far. But we will see that since Grotius' time, much effort has been devoted to a study of averting conflicts and subordinating disputes to the rule of law.

SUGGESTIONS FOR READING

The following are crisp, purposeful, and readable political surveys of all or part of the century and a half following the beginning of the Protestant Reformation: M. L. Bush, **Renaissance, Reformation, and the Outer World, 1450-1660*** (Torchbooks); H. Koenigsberger and G. Mosse, **Europe in the Sixteenth Century** (Longman, 1973); J. H. Elliott, **Europe Divided, 1559-1598*** (Torchbooks); T. Aston, ed., **Crisis in Europe: 1560-1660*** (Torchbooks); A. Moote, **The Seventeenth Century: Europe in Ferment*** (Heath, 1970); and J. R. Strayer, **On the Medieval Origins of the Modern State** (Princeton, 1970).

J. H. Whitfield, **Machiavelli** (Russell, 1965) is a sympathetic account. The older, unfavorable view is well presented in H. Butterfield, **The Statecraft of Machiavelli*** (Collier). S. Anglo, **Machiavelli: A Dissection** (Harcourt Brace Jovanovich, 1970) is a perceptive study with new insights. See also the brilliant study by G. Mattingly, **Renaissance Diplomacy*** (Sentry).

J. Lynch, **Spain Under the Hapsburgs**, Vol. I, **Empire and Absolutism, 1516-1598*** (Rowman, 1973) is an authoritative treatment. Also recommended are A. D. Ortiz, **The Golden Age of Spain, 1516-1659** (Basic Books, 1971); and R. Trevor-Davies, **The Golden Century of Spain, 1501-1621*** (Torchbooks). Fernand Braudel, **The Mediterranean and the Mediterranean World in the Age of Philip II,** 2 vols. (Harper & Row, 1975) is a masterful survey. See also K. Brandi, **Emperor Charles V: The Growth and Destiny of a Man and a World Empire*** (Humanities, 1968); and R. B. Merriman, **Suleiman the Magnificent** (Cooper Square, 1966).

G. Mattingly, **The Armada*** (Sentry) is the classic account. Popular and profusely illustrated is Jay Williams, **The Spanish Armada** (Harper & Row, 1966).

K. H. Haley, **The Dutch in the Seventeenth Century** (Harcourt Brace Jovanovich, 1972) is an excellent account. C. Wedgwood, **William the Silent*** (Norton) is a beautifully written biography.

Elizabeth Jenkins, **Elizabeth the Great*** (Capricorn) is short and lively. J. Neale, **Queen Elizabeth I*** (Anchor) is the most authoritative biography. Antonia Fraser, **Mary, Queen of Scots** (Delacorte, 1969) is a best-seller. See also J. Hurtsfield, **Elizabeth I and the Unity of England*** (Torchbooks); W. C. Richardson, **Mary Tudor, the White Queen** (Univ. of Washington); A. L. Rowse, **The England of Elizabeth*** (Macmillan); S. Bindoff, **Tudor England*** (Penguin); and R. Wernham, **Before the Armada: The Emergence of the English Nation, 1485-1588** (Norton, 1972).

J. Neale, **The Age of Catharine de' Medici*** (Torchbooks) describes the religious and political troubles of sixteenth-century France. For a briefer account see F. Palm, **Calvinism and the Religious Wars** (Fertig, 1972).

C. V. Wedgwood, **The Thirty Years' War*** (Anchor) is a vigorous account as is G. Pages, **The Thirty Years' War*** (Torchbooks). See also H. Holborn, **A History of Modern Germany,** Vol. I, **The Reformation** (Knopf) and Victor L. Tapié, **The Rise and Fall of the Hapsburg Monarchy** (Praeger, 1971) about the royal family that dominated central Europe and the Balkans.

*Indicates a less expensive paperbound edition.

CHAPTER 16

India, China, and Japan:
1300-1650;
Southeast Asia:
100-1650

Old Worlds Beyond the Horizon

INTRODUCTION. In this chapter, we once more pick up the narrative of the "old worlds" of the East begun in Chapter 4 and continued in Chapter 7. We now view the civilizations of India, China, Japan, and Southeast Asia during the period when they were at their peak of cultural accomplishment. Outside influences, such as the intrusion of the Europeans, were yet to come. At the same time when Europe was just beginning its rebirth of art, thought, and cultural values, these societies were continuing to build and develop their own rich heritage that had started some two thousand years before.

India expanded upon its period of flourishing growth that had developed in the age of the Guptas (see Chapter 7), an age which had played a major role in diffusion of culture and creative thought throughout the East. Under the influence of the Mughuls, who established a powerful dynasty which would reach its zenith in the sixteenth century, accomplishments in government, learning, and the arts continued their advance under the leadership of the great statesman,

Akbar. The Mughul empire came to compare favorably in its wealth and power with any of its contemporaries in the West.

In Southeast Asia and the Pacific, notable kingdoms influenced by contact with India and China over a long period had risen and fallen. This area in general presented a complex picture of ethnic and political flux resulting from diverse migrations of peoples and unstable governments.

In the period up to the seventeenth century, China and Japan continued to develop their indigenous cultures by following traditional patterns; these patterns were barely touched by European culture and grew in almost complete ignorance of the West. Indeed, repelled by what little they had seen of Europeans, both China and Japan sought to cut themselves off entirely from western influence. The great civilizations of the East were therefore left to pursue their own courses, unaware of the impending collision of cultures that would soon take place under the impetus of the Industrial Revolution, a collision that was to set the breakdown of China's culture into motion and from which Japan was to save itself by its swifter and more integrated response.

THE GLORY OF THE MUGHULS IN INDIA

Babur, founder of the Mughul empire. At the end of the twelfth century Hindu power in India was eclipsed by invading Muslims who established a powerful dynasty in Delhi. By 1500, however, a new Muslim force from the north was preparing to invade India. Two years after Columbus sailed westward toward what he hoped would be India, a descendant of Genghis Khan and Tamerlane mounted the throne of a little principality in Turkestan (see map, p. 175). The youthful ruler was Babur (the Tiger), an able general with the strength of a giant, who was to be the founder of the Mughul empire in India. In his memoirs Babur says that he used to think ceaselessly of the capture of Hindustan. At length he set out with an army of no more than twelve thousand men to achieve his goal. Defeating the large forces of the sultan of Delhi, who then ruled all Hindustan, Babur made himself sultan in 1526. A year later he subdued the Rajputs, who were trying to restore Hindu supremacy in northern India. The submission of the Rajputs placed the Mughul dynasty securely on the Delhi throne. (The name *Mughul* is a corruption of *Mongol*, a word much dreaded in India because of its association with Tamerlane, the ruthless destroyer of Delhi.) Babur himself did not live long to enjoy the fruits of his victory; worn out by his campaigns and adventures, he died in 1530.

Akbar, conqueror and administrator. Babur's grandson was Akbar, meaning "Very Great." In 1560 Akbar's empire consisted of a strip of territory some three hundred miles wide, extending from the northwest frontier eastward to Bengal. Sixteen years later Akbar had extended his rule over all of India north of the Vindhya Mountains, the natural boundary between Hindustan and the Deccan. Continuing southward, Akbar invaded part of the Deccan. When he died in 1605, his dominions ran from Kashmir in the far north well into the Deccan in the south, and his heirs were to extend them even farther.

Akbar's greatness should not be measured by his military conquests alone, however. He instituted innovations and reforms in the government and fostered cultural growth and religious toleration. As an administrator he had few equals. He divided his empire into twelve provinces (later increased to fifteen), ruled by governors whom he appointed and who were paid monthly salaries from the imperial treasury. Each province was divided into districts, and each district into smaller units.

Law was similarly well administered. In each village the headman was responsible for keeping law and order, while in the larger cities special officials were in charge of the administration of justice. Akbar himself often acted as a judge, for everyone in his do-

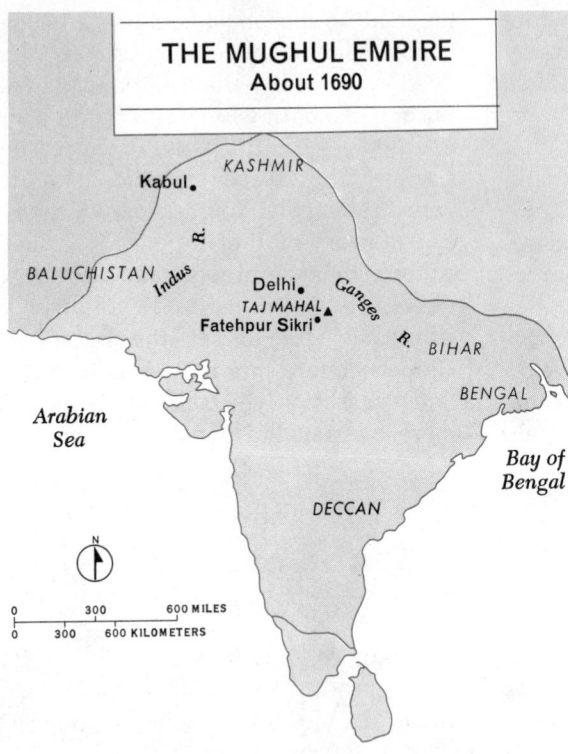

THE MUGHUL EMPIRE
About 1690

KASHMIR

Kabul.

BALUCHISTAN

Indus R.

Delhi.

Ganges R.

TAJ MAHAL
Fatehpur Sikri

BIHAR

BENGAL

Arabian
Sea

Bay of
Bengal

DECCAN

N

0   300   600 MILES
0   300   600 KILOMETERS

gious debates which often lasted far into the night. When the Jesuits arrived in India, Akbar had them stay at his court for periods of several years and treated them with every courtesy.

But the sultan never accepted any one religion completely; instead he created his own religion, called *Din Ilahi*, the "Divine Faith," which incorporated what he considered the best features of the other existing religions. By promulgating this new faith, he hoped to bring all India into common agreement on religious matters. But the older faiths were too strongly entrenched, and Akbar's religious theories died with him.

Monuments of Mughul architecture. At the crest of their power in the reigns of Akbar and his immediate successors, the Mughuls displayed one of the most magnificent civilizations of their time. In military strength, government efficiency, and patronage of the arts, they had few equals. Above all, they were great builders.

The Indo-Islamic style of architecture which the Mughuls developed for tombs, mosques, forts, and palaces was a blend of Indian and Persian elements characterized by a lavish use of mosaics, bulbous domes, cupolas, and lofty vaulted gateways. The Mughuls were also fond of formal gardens in which pools and fountains, architecture and greenery were carefully harmonized.

The Mughul style began with Akbar, an avid builder. Not far from the modern city of Agra, he erected a new capital, Fathpur Sikri, which he occupied for only fourteen years before abandoning it for Lahore. Fathpur Sikri is still preserved intact today, and a tourist strolling through its splendid buildings can feel the power of the great empire that made this city possible:

main had the right to appeal to him personally. The practice of *suttee* (burning a wife on her husband's funeral pyre), which had come into use during the Gupta age, was forbidden, and widows were permitted to remarry. Akbar prohibited child marriages and trial by ordeal, although he permitted such tortures as impalement, amputation, and death by elephant dragging. Nevertheless, in contrast to the barbaric punishments permitted in Europe at this time, the Mughul emperor probably had the most enlightened criminal code in the sixteenth century.

Despite the Mughul dynasty's allegiance to the Muslim faith, Akbar allowed complete freedom of religious belief in his empire, because he realized that religious strife made for political and social disintegration. Akbar's views were not based simply on political expediency, however; his own temperament was the chief reason for his enlightened policy. He felt that every faith had something of truth to offer but that all were untrue when they denied each other's sincerity of purpose. Every Thursday, Muslims, Brahmins, and members of smaller sects congregated in his Hall of Worship for reli-

Nothing sadder or more beautiful exists in India than this deserted city—the silent witness of a vanished dream. It still stands with its circuit of seven miles, its seven bastioned gates, its wonderful palaces, peerless in all India for noble design and delicate adornment; its splendid mosque and pure marble shrine . . . its carvings and paintings—stands as it stood in Akbar's time, but now a body without a soul.[1]

The Mughul rulers brought to India a rich Islamic style of art and architecture. Their court was magnificent with thousands employed to provide luxuries for them. In a contemporary painting (right) the great ruler Akbar is overseeing the construction of his new capital at Fathpur Sikri. A miniature painting (below) depicts an audience in the court of a Mughul ruler, while Hindu pilgrims (above) bathe at a shrine of the god Siva.

During the reign of Shah Jahan, Akbar's grandson, Mughul architecture reached its zenith. Shah Jahan had the red sandstone buildings of Akbar at Delhi demolished and erected a huge capital of marble containing fifty-two palaces. The famous Hall of Private Audience had ceilings of solid silver and gold and a Peacock Throne encrusted with costly gems. On the walls can still be seen the inscription by a Muslim poet: "If anywhere on earth there is a Paradise, it is here, it is here, it is here." Besides making Delhi a site of unrivaled splendor, Shah Jahan erected at Agra the famous Pearl Mosque and the Taj Mahal, the marble mausoleum built as a final resting place for himself and his favorite wife (see illustration below).

Signs of Mughul decline. The blend of Hindu-Islamic cultural elements under the Mughuls brought civilization in India to the highest point yet achieved there. It is unfortunate for world culture that the union of Muslim and Hindu genius could not continue to flower. But Akbar's tolerance and wisdom were lost in the fanaticism of his successors.

Shah Jahan, who came to the throne in 1628, held none of Akbar's views on religious

With its arches, decorations, domes, minarets, and formal gardens, the Taj Mahal, built about 1640 as a mausoleum, is a fine example of Islamic architecture influenced by the Indian imagination.

toleration. He officially promoted the Muslim faith, destroyed Hindu temples, and forcibly opposed the spread of Christianity. In 1630 Shah Jahan began the conquest of the Deccan; eventually it was subjugated and divided into four provinces. After Shah Jahan's health began to fail in 1657, a ruinous civil war broke out among his four sons, each of whom became an almost independent ruler. The last eight years of Shah Jahan's life (d. 1666) were spent as a prisoner of his son and successor, Aurangzeb. Despite his ignominious end, the reign of Shah Jahan marked the summit of the Mughul empire.

CHINA TURNS INWARD

Rise and fall of the Ming dynasty. The Ming (1368-1644) followed a pattern typical of Chinese dynasties, arising out of and ending in rebellion. With the weakening of Mongol power, the concentration of land in the hands of small numbers of wealthy landlords, and resentment against alien rule, the conditions were set by the middle of the fourteenth century for dynastic breakdown. Such a pattern, known as a dynastic cycle, was a feature of Chinese history common to most dynasties. Dynasties tended to rise while exercising a clean sweep of the political broom, beginning in strength and prosperity but succumbing to rebellions or invasions as the lands of the peasants fell into the hands of rich landowners. The final result was the overthrow of the dynasty. Rebellion broke out in southern China, Nanking falling in 1356 to forces led by a young monk, Chu Yuan-chang. It took Chu another twelve years before he at last drove the Mongol army out of Peking and established the dynasty in 1368, adopting the reign title, Hung-wu. (Chinese emperors were known by their reign titles rather than their personal names.)

The Hung-wu emperor, with Nanking as his capital, took a firm hand in reconstruction and in the restoration of traditional Chinese culture. A new code of law based on T'ang and Sung precedents was compiled, the examination system for selecting civil and military officials was reestablished, irrigation systems were repaired, and secret societies, so often breeding grounds for rebellion, were harshly suppressed. When Hung-wu died in 1398, he was succeeded by a grandson, who after a brief reign was overthrown in 1403 by his uncle Chu Ti, the Yung-lo emperor. It was under Yung-lo that the capital was transferred, in 1421, to Peking and the persistent attempts by the Mongols to retake China were at last stopped.

The Ming has been described as having been far more despotic than its predecessors. While harsh punishments for both the people and the members of the bureaucracy were characteristic of Ming rule, at the highest levels of government there was a progressive shift of power from the imperial house to the bureaucracy that ran parallel to the decline in Ming power. In 1380 Hung-wu took a major step in consolidating political power by abolishing the offices of chief councilor and the secretariat. By this move, he took full authority for decision-making into his own hands. Yung-lo, however, went back to relying on his grand secretaries (high court officials) for advice so that power began to shift toward the bureaucracy again. Under later emperors, the grand secretaries took over more and more of the initiative of government, with the emperors exerting a merely passive authority in accepting or rejecting their proposals. Other emperors relinquished their power to their eunuch attendants, whose growing influence contributed to the severe corruption that arose at the court and to the weakening of dynastic power.

Ming foreign policy followed a similar pattern of early strength and later decline. In 1403, Yung-lo sent missions of eunuchs to Tibet, Java, Siam, and Bengal. This venture was followed by a series of spectacular naval expeditions ranging from the South Seas to India and the Persian Gulf that began in 1405 and ended suddenly in 1431. Although historians are not sure why they were begun or why they were halted, at about this time an isolationist spirit took over the court and Chinese subjects were forbidden to leave the coastal waters of China. In the early Yung-lo period, the Chinese also exerted an aggressive military policy, bringing Annam (the

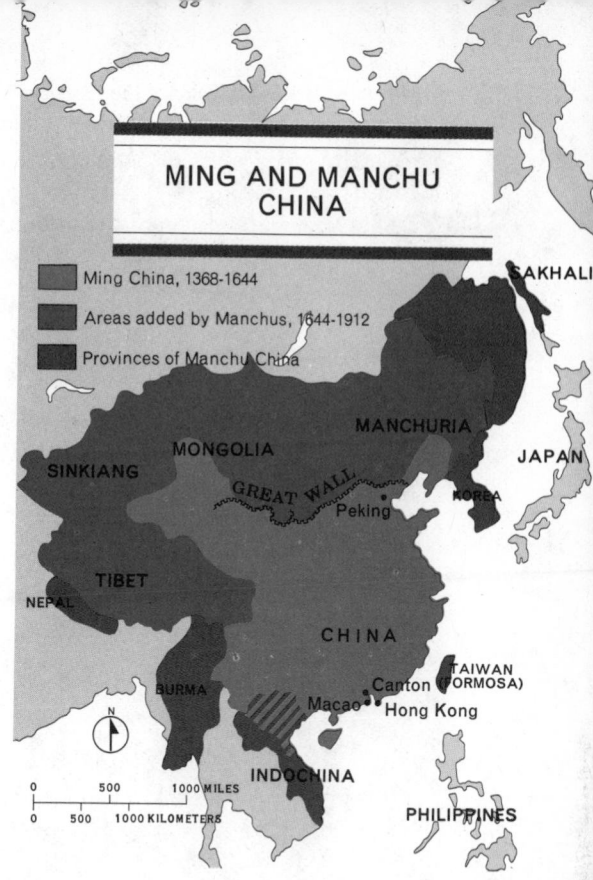

present Vietnam) back under Chinese domination in 1406. In 1421, Yung-lo led an expedition against the Mongols that culminated in successful drives across the Gobi desert. With their involvement in Annam, however, the Chinese armies became involved in long and bitter guerrilla warfare with which they could not cope, and, in 1427, the decision was made to withdraw. The breakdown of naval strength following the retreat to coastal waters opened the way for attacks by Japanese pirates, often aided by Chinese brigands, on the coastal provinces. In spite of this evident weakness, Chinese armies were able to stop the Japanese attempt to subdue Korea and then China by defeating the Japanese fleet in 1592.

The Ming dynasty was brought down by a combination of factors—military weakness, the corruption of the court under eunuch domination, and the exorbitant taxes and pitiable circumstances of the peasants typical of end-of-dynasty periods. Peasant uprisings broke out throughout China, and, had history followed its usual course, the dynasty would have fallen to the strongest of the rebel leaders. Instead, it fell, as had the Sung

The picture above demonstrates two methods of irrigation used in Ming China which were established earlier—a chain pump worked by treadmill operators contrasted with the more traditional style of a suspended rod with a bucket at one end and a weight at the other. Additional details of life in Ming China are shown in the sketch of a magistrate at work (left) and a spring river festival (below) in the midst of a busy commercial district.

before it, to an alien people, the Manchu from Manchuria in the north. Taking advantage of the disruption and weakness of the Chinese empire, they brought the dynasty to a close with the capture of Peking in 1644.

Foreign influences under the Ming. Although China turned inward under the Ming, influences from the outside world continued to filter in. Cotton culture, introduced earlier in the thirteenth century, was promoted by government edicts so that China had become, by the fifteenth century, a major cotton-producing nation. Western agricultural crops, corn, the sweet potato, and peanuts in particular were brought in. The Spanish peso and silver were also introduced, the latter replacing the copper currency to a great extent. Contact with the South Seas regions was maintained by an illegal trade that the government could not control.

Thus, China was not cut off from the material culture of the outside world. Nor was the governing class completely ignorant of western science and culture. The sixteenth century saw the arrival in China of the Jesuits, who through their writings and translations brought a knowledge of European sciences to the court and to China's intellectuals. In the end, however, these foreign intellectual influences were inconsequential. Rather, the Chinese remained turned inward to the traditional culture and ignored western thought until it was forcibly thrust upon them in the nineteenth century.

Ming society and culture. One reason for this inward turn of mind was the superiority of Chinese culture to other world cultures. At the beginning of the Ming dynasty, the Renaissance in Europe had not yet begun, while Confucianism provided a complete system of philosophy and ethics. Another key factor leading to the lack of Chinese receptivity to outside influences was the intellectual conformity fostered by Hung-wu's reinstitution of the examination system in a form that endured almost up to the fall of the Manchu in 1912. The examinations, which were given in a series beginning at the local level and continuing on to a final "palace" examination given under the supervision of the emperor himself, tested the candidates on their knowledge of the Confucian classics as interpreted by the Sung philosopher Chu Hsi. Success in the examinations, which was the primary means to upward mobility open to ambitious young men, not only made a man eligible for appointment as a government official but also brought him into a position of prestige and influence in his home locality. To this goal, the candidates devoted years of study. As a consequence, there was fostered among the intellectual and governing class a conformity of thought and an indoctrination into Confucianism, a philosophical orientation which supported this type of hierarchical social structure and was conducive to the maintenance of imperial power.

Although the humanistic course of Confucian thought tended to discourage development of the sciences, the Ming period was rich in the amateur writings of scholar-bureaucrats on topics ranging over the fields of zoology, botany, astronomy, mathematics, geography, agriculture, and medicine. A major work, the *Pen-ts'ao Kang-mu*, completed by the physician Li Shih-chen in 1578 after twenty-six years of research and field work, represented the most complete compilation of medical knowledge in China up to that time. However, in keeping with the spirit of Confucianism, the Chinese potential for scientific analysis was turned to the literary field in which impressive strides were made.

The bulk of intellectual activity under the Ming was directed toward traditional studies. Yung-lo commissioned extensive compilations of encyclopedias and dictionaries. Most notable was the *Yung-lo Ta-tien (Encyclopedia of the Yung-lo Period)*, a work of 11,095 volumes, now largely lost, that comprised all knowledge up to that time. Many Chinese scholars occupied themselves with philosophical writing, much of which was devoted to opposing or defending the views of a new school of Confucian thought developed by Wang Yang-ming. Wang, whose thought derived from one of the contending Neo-Confucian schools of the Sung period, held that knowledge was intuitive and should be sought through meditation. Aside from the writings of Wang, there was little that was new or creative in Chinese philoso-

The Temple of Heaven at Peking, built during the Ming dynasty, is a typical example of the pagoda form of Chinese architecture. Its cylindrical construction with three roofs is characteristic of the early pagoda style, introduced into China with the spread of Buddhism.

phy during the Ming. Government officials and local gentry took the responsibility for compiling gazetteers providing detailed accounts of local customs, history, geography, and political and social institutions.

In the arts, Ming painters produced many excellent works. Ming artisans tried to duplicate the standards of Sung pottery, but instead of emphasizing the beauty of form of the vessel, they concentrated on brilliant coloring and elegant decoration.

The Forbidden City, the imperial family's area of palaces and temples at Peking, was constructed in the early years (1403-1424) of the Ming dynasty. With its series of courtyards, brilliant lacquer work, and tile, marble, and alabaster decorations, it is typical of a period of richly ornamented architecture.

In literature, there was a significant new development. While the T'ang and Sung were the golden ages of poetry, popular fiction came to prominence during the Ming. Written in the colloquial speech of the time, which differed from the antiquated literary language of serious literature and philosoph-

ical discourse, it had its origins in the tales told by the oral storytellers who had been entertaining city dwellers since Sung times. Because of the complex twists of the plots, devised to string the audiences along, the storytellers often kept prompt books, some of which contain the earliest versions of such famous tales as the *Romance of the Three Kingdoms* and *All Men Are Brothers.* Although, from a moralistic Confucian standpoint, it was thought hardly proper for a serious scholar to demean himself with this form of writing, many did take up and elaborate on these stories, producing such popular tales as *Monkey* and the partially pornographic novel the *Chin P'ing Mei.* Later in the Ch'ing dynasty, this genre was to reach its culmination in the superb *Dream of the Red Chamber.* However, Ming fiction was not honored in its own time and serious works continued to be written in literary Chinese until the literary revolution of the 1920's, when use of the colloquial language in literature at last became accepted.

Thus, Chinese culture in the Ming period was integral and self-sufficient and it did not appear to the Chinese that the European "barbarians" had much to offer beyond more efficient means of warfare. Although the examination system was certainly responsi-

Glazed porcelain pieces, such as this ewer, were among the most highly prized trade items in the world.

ble for fostering a conservatism and intellectual sterility that were to serve China badly with the coming of the West in the nineteenth century, the self-sufficiency and superiority of Chinese culture itself perhaps played as great a part in hardening the Chinese mind against new ways of thought and new ideas. So it was that China's intellectuals came to look to their own past rather than to the future for their golden age.

JAPAN'S SELF-IMPOSED ISOLATION

Ashikaga state and culture. The decline of the Kamakura shogunate in Japan resembled the end of a dynasty in China. It was accompanied by economic difficulties, political and military strife, and the erosion of the bonds of feudal loyalty. Although the successors to the Kamakura shogunate, the Ashikaga, retained the shogunal office from 1338 to 1573, their government was so different from that of its predecessor that it represented a new stage in the history of Japanese feudalism.

Following the destruction of the Kamakura, Ashikaga Takauji set up a new emperor in Kyoto in 1336, a succession dispute arising when the former emperor escaped to the south and established a rival court. After Takauji became shogun in 1338, the Ashikaga family struggled for dominance over the contending feudal barons. In 1392, the succession dispute came to an end and the country settled into an unstable but relatively long period of peace. The Ashikaga, however, lacked the authority of the former Kamakura government and their effective control never extended far beyond Kyoto. Thus it was that the local lords, or *daimyo*, rather than the shoguns, were the key figures during this period. Furthermore, the warrior or samurai class had broken up into separate groups of lords and retainers, a relationship differing from past social arrangements in that it was based on vassalage.

Sporadic fighting among feudal lords persisted and spread until a civil war broke out between rival Ashikaga houses, lasting from

The Golden Pavilion, built at Kyoto in 1397, was the elegant home of the Ashikaga shoguns. The Japanese architectural style utilized here placed important emphasis on the setting and surrounding gardens of its buildings.

1467 to 1474. The civil war ended in a redistribution of feudal power but warfare continued in the provinces. The central government at last collapsed and by 1500 warfare had spread throughout the entire country.

Despite wars and political decentralization, the Ashikaga period was one of economic growth. The feudal lords encouraged trade and commerce in their own domains, and as the money economy grew, various merchants and even some Buddhist monasteries organized themselves into a kind of guild system to protect their interests and encourage trade across feudal boundaries. Towns began to develop at important geographical points and around castles and monasteries. Trade with China grew, inspired by the need for money to support the pretentious way of life of the Ashikaga shoguns, who, devoid of real power, still lived in elegance. The actual business of trade was undertaken by priests of the Zen sect, which was highly favored by the Ashikaga shoguns. This trade was extremely profitable and led to the development of seaports, one of the most important of which was Sakai, which was located just south of present-day Osaka and which became a strategic and financial center.

During the Ashikaga period the greatest art form of the Zen cultural influence was landscape painting. Here the artist portrays the spirit of nature by eliminating minor details and uses bold brush strokes to emphasize what he feels is essential. In these paintings, people and houses, bridges and boats, often appear as subordinate, blending into the great pattern of nature. This detail, from a screen by Sesshu done in ink on paper, is a fine example of painting in this tradition.

A major social development of the period resulting from the breakdown of the old feudal system was the emergence of the family as a social unit, with the interests of the family taking precedence over those of the individual. Women, who had enjoyed high political, social, and cultural status during earlier periods, gradually lost their rights and became both socially and legally inferior to men—a situation that was to continue well into Japan's modern period.

The roughly seventy-year period up to the beginning of the civil wars in 1447 was one of great artistic and cultural vitality. With ancient Kyoto as their capital and living in luxury and elegance in their Golden Pavilion, the shoguns promoted a distinctive new culture, fusing the once separate courtier and warrior cultures. It was to the Buddhist church and to Zen Buddhism in particular that the arts owed their survival in this age of turmoil, for the Zen monasteries were havens for artists. Perhaps for this reason, the Zen spirit exerted a strong influence on Japanese culture, which came to be pervaded by an urbane taste for things elegantly simple: the restrained and quiet contemplation of the tea ceremony, new architectural styles, monochrome painting, and landscape gardening. Among the masters of ink painting was Sesshu, whose works are felt to reflect Zen taste. In poetry, there was a passion for Chinese styles, and poets, writing in Chinese, strove to imitate and outdo their predecessors of the T'ang and Sung. The most enduring artistic development of the period was a form of lyric drama, the No, which combined stately mimetic dancing, music, and song.

Western influence first made itself felt with the arrival of the Portuguese in 1542. Francis Xavier, a Jesuit missionary, began to preach Christianity in western Japan and Kyoto in 1549. By the end of the century he may have converted as many as 300,000 persons to Christianity, including some of the feudal lords of Kyushu, who took up the new religion in order to gain commercial advantages and advanced military technology. Many feudal lords, for the same reasons, ordered the conversion of their vassals and just as promptly ordered them to give up Christianity when the expected advantages did not materialize. However, apart from Christianity and military technology, the Japanese took little interest in European culture and science and failed to adopt the new methods of scientific inquiry that were to shape the modern world.

Changes toward unification. Warfare among Japanese feudal lords sharpened following the civil war of 1467-1474, with the roughly 260 *daimyo* that existed before 1467 being reduced to about a dozen by 1600. During this long period of almost constant warfare, increasing economic burdens fell on the peasants and townfolk, so that riots and local uprisings became frequent. Between 1560 and 1600, however, a series of three able leaders, Oda Nobunaga, Toyotomi Hideyoshi, and Tokugawa Ieyasu, progressively established a single military power over all the *daimyo*. At first, this drive toward unification was conducted in the name of the last Ashikaga shogun, but Nobunaga, who had been his supporter, drove him out of Kyoto in 1573, bringing the line to an end. Nobuna-ga still had powerful enemies to contend with and next set himself to bringing the Buddhist church under submission. Once this was accomplished, he moved to subdue central and western Japan and by 1582 his armies under Hideyoshi had driven the powerful Mori family out of central Japan. Following the death of Nobunaga, Hideyoshi became regent in 1584. A series of battles against the remaining *daimyo* finally united Japan under a single government in 1590, creating a dictatorial power unique in Japanese history. Although theoretically the chief minister of the emperor, Hideyoshi ruled Japan through the feudal institution of vassalage. He disarmed the populace, and in attempting to create social change he tried to define more sharply than ever the various social classes and to prevent people from changing their class status. While Nobunaga had been personally attracted to the Jesuits and had allowed them to go about their religious activities unhampered, Hideyoshi in 1587 issued an edict banning the foreign missionaries. Nevertheless, perhaps out of a fear of alienating the Portuguese traders who were then the agents of the lucrative China trade, he did little to enforce the ban, although in 1597 there was a series of persecutions in which nine missionaries and seventeen Japanese converts were killed.

The arrival of Portuguese traders in Japan was initially greeted with interest by the Japanese who were intrigued by their odd style of dress. This screen painting portrays the strange foreigners who arrived from the south and became known in Japan as the "southern barbarians."

Scenes of life in Tokugawa Japan include a contemporary painting of people crossing a river by raft and on the backs of coolies (left), and a game being played in the teahouse (right). The sixteenth-century screen painting (below) depicts scenes from the *Tale of Genji*, a literary classic.

The Tokugawa shogunate. Hideyoshi, who died in 1598, was succeeded by Tokugawa Ieyasu. A brief period of dissension arose as a number of powerful families again vied for control of the nation. A decisive battle took place in 1600 at Sekigahara, out of which Ieyasu emerged victorious. He became shogun in 1603, but because of opposition to his plans to redistribute fiefs, he did not secure complete domination until his victory at the siege of Osaka in 1615. From his personal headquarters at Edo (Tokyo), he set up a rigid system of laws and institutions designed to perpetuate his family's position indefinitely. In this he was successful, for the Tokugawa family was supreme in Japan for the next two hundred and fifty years.

Like his predecessors, Ieyasu at first took a tolerant view of the Christian missionaries, and in his desire to maintain Japan's foreign trade, decided not to enforce the previous bans against Christianity. However, as he learned more about how missionary activities and the colonial aspirations of the European nations often went hand in hand, his suspicions grew. In 1612, 1613, and 1614, he issued edicts prohibiting Christianity and thousands of loyal Japanese Christians suffered martyrdom. Finally, the regime expelled European missionaries and traders and excluded all foreigners except the Dutch, who were not interested in missionary activity. They were allowed limited and rigidly controlled trade at Nagasaki. At the same time, all Japanese were forbidden to go abroad or even to build ships capable of navigating beyond coastal waters. Thus Japan, like China, chose to cut itself off from the West just as the fruits of the Renaissance were about to transform European culture and to lay the foundations for the dominance of the West.

This raises the intriguing question as to why in later years Japan responded so much more swiftly and effectively and with less internal dissension to the western challenge than did China. The contrast in the responses of the two countries is made even more striking by the fact that China by Ming times possessed a far more advanced technology in many fields than that of the West before the Renaissance.

One important factor was education. While education in China was very sophisticated, it was confined to a relatively small elite segment of society. The peasants, who made up the overwhelming majority of the population, were illiterate. In Japan, by contrast, there had grown up in Ashikaga times a type of school known as the *terakoya*, which became even more widespread during the Tokugawa period. Through the *terakoya* and similar schools, children from commoner families throughout all of Japan learned the basic skills of reading, writing, and computation. With a large literate population, Japan was in a better position for rapid modernization when confronted by the sudden western challenge.

But the Japanese had one other characteristic that was to serve them in good stead, a willingness to borrow and learn from foreign cultures. As inhabitants of a small island nation, the Japanese were conditioned to looking out and responding to the outside world. In earlier times, the Japanese had taken in the best of Chinese culture and had transformed it into uniquely Japanese forms. Japan's isolation during the Tokugawa period was, then, an aberration from the typical pattern of their culture. China, by contrast, was a vast, continental country with a rich indigenous culture. The Chinese saw China as the center of civilization and themselves as bearers of civilization to the inferior "barbarians" who came upon their shores or harassed their inner Asian frontiers. As a consequence, they had developed a spirit of self-sufficiency that has persisted even to the present day. No better examples can be found of how the prevailing attitudes among a people can affect the course of their history and civilization.

SOUTHEAST ASIA: BACKGROUND OF CONFLICT

The geographical foundations of disunity. At the southern tip of the Asian mainland, wedged between India and China and including a multitude of islands in both the Indian and Pacific oceans, lies Southeast Asia. Stretching over a combination of land and sea far greater in size than the United States, Southeast Asia is geographically, culturally, and politically one of the most complex regions in the world.

The Irrawaddy, Salween, and Mekong rivers, which flow south from the Tibet-Burma-China border region, provided avenues for the southward migration of distinctive ethnic groups from South China. North-south mountain chains, which divide Burma from Thailand and Thailand from Vietnam, provided barriers to communication that further emphasized the cultural and political differentiation between the peoples occupying the river valleys. Moreover, later migrants pushed earlier inhabitants out of the valleys and into the mountainous regions, making for further ethnic complexities. Unlike China, where some form of political unity and cultural homogeneity developed, Southeast Asia has always been characterized by political and cultural balkanization. The thousands of islands that make up the Philippine and Indonesian archipelagoes were also subject to natural division rather than unity. Pervasive influences exerted by the great civilizations of India and China added to the confusion.

Chinese, Islamic, and Christian influences in Southeast Asia. In addition to Hindu cultural penetration (discussed in Chapter 7), Chinese influence and on occasion political sovereignty has been a factor in Southeast Asia. During the past five hundred years especially, Chinese settlers migrated to urban centers in this region, where as merchants they came to dominate both local and foreign trade.

The spread of Islam to the Far East started only after the conquest of India by Turkish Muslims during the eleventh and twelfth centuries. As Muslim political and military power began to become dominant, many local rulers found it to their political and commercial advantage to become Muslims. During the fifteenth century, as Hindu rulers were driven from their thrones, Java was completely converted to Islam, which also spread to Sumatra, the Malay peninsula, and the other islands of the Indonesian archipelago. The one exception was the fabled island of Bali, which became the refuge of the former ruling family and has retained its basically Hindu culture into modern times.

In the fifteenth and sixteenth centuries Malayan and Indonesian merchants and settlers carried Islam into the Philippines particularly to the large southern island of Mindanao. But its influence was too late and too weak to spread further north, where Christianity was beginning to make significant inroads.

Spain began a concerted attempt to occupy the Philippines in the middle of the sixteenth century and established its colonial capital at Manila in 1571. By 1581, when Manila was made a bishopric, no fewer than four Catholic orders were active in the islands, and the Catholic university of Santo Tomàs was founded in 1611. By 1622 there were half a million Catholic converts in the Philippines, and this number increased to almost a million within a century. With the exception of Mindanao and some minor peripheral islands, the Philippines were destined to become the only Christian country in Southeast Asia.

The birth of nationhood. The heritage of geographical and ethnic complexity, of conflict between lowland immigrants and older settlers in the hills, and the waves of distinctive cultural influences from outside Southeast Asia, all made for uneven political development throughout the area in the centuries before the arrival of the West and it is almost impossible to make any generalizations that are valid for the entire region.

What is now Burma was occupied in successive waves and regions by various ethnic groups. Constantly at war with each other and with the neighboring Thais, and often in conflict with the Chinese to the north, the Burmese never succeeded in developing a unified kingdom with a centralized bureaucracy. There was often little continuity in succession from king to king, and though often successful in war, the Burmese kings were more given to raids and brief occupations than to the painstaking business of nation-building and statecraft.

The Thai, or Siamese, on the other hand,

A bas-relief from the temple of Angkor Wat in Cambodia details the *Davatas*, a minor type of genii. There are nearly 2000 of these figures reproduced throughout the structure, which is considered a superb example of Hindu architecture as combined with the influence of Southeast Asia (see Color Plate 15).

early developed a sense of nationhood and a durable administrative system. Furthermore, the Thais were culturally more homogeneous than the Burmese. By the early seventeenth century the Thai monarchs were already in active contact with the West, sending embassies to Holland and the court of Louis xiv. They were also in early contact with China, whose merchants purchased rice in Thailand. Chinese merchants and their families settled in Thailand early and in such numbers that they became a significant part of Thai society and were not even considered foreigners. Because the Chinese community was an important source of attractive women for the royal harem, many Thai monarchs were at least half Chinese, and the present dynasty and its capital, Bangkok, were founded by a half-Chinese general in the latter part of the eighteenth century.

Laos, lying in the northwestern part of the Indochinese peninsula, was a congeries of petty princedoms fought over by the Thais, Vietnamese, and Cambodians. The modern Cambodians are largely descended from the Khmer builders of the great empire which centered on Angkor Wat. Indonesia and Malaya remained the realm of petty Muslim princes and European colonies, which fought to control the rich resources of these lands

and the trade routes between eastern and southern Asia.

In the islands of the Indonesian archipelago, one kingdom and empire succeeded another on the great islands of Sumatra and Java. The sea was their thoroughfare, and the important Strait of Malacca, which controlled the trade routes between the Indian Ocean and the Far East, was a major prize of war. But the successive waves of cultural influence that traveled along the trade routes were not a sufficient basis for unification when faced with the geographical and ethnic divisions that plagued both continental and island Southeast Asia. The religious and political thought and institutions of *Hinayana* Buddhism, superimposed on early Brahminic Hindu influence, dominated, and continue to dominate today, Burma, Thailand, Laos, and Cambodia. Islam today pervades Indonesia, the southern Philippines, and the Malay peninsula.

The only region in Southeast Asia to come under Chinese cultural and political domination was what today constitutes North and South Vietnam. The Vietnamese people are the product of the integration of early migrants from South China with local populations, and their language, closely resembling Chinese, has marked Khmer and Thai elements. Spending over a thousand years of their history, beginning with the Han dynasty, under Chinese rule, and even longer under Chinese influence, Vietnam so closely resembled China culturally and politically that it has been called "The Lesser Dragon." Adopting *Mahayana* Buddhism, Confucian political thought, Chinese institutions, and the Chinese written language, the Vietnamese constructed a Confucian state on the Chinese model, complete with an emperor, a civil service bureaucracy recruited through the traditional Confucian examination system, a mandarin class, and court records and a literature in the Chinese style. Even the imperial palace at the capital at Hue in central Vietnam was built on the Chinese model. Sometimes more conservative than the Chinese themselves, the Vietnamese held onto tradition longer. For instance, Confucian examinations which were abolished in China in 1905, remained in force in Vietnam until the mid-1920's. But despite the amazingly strong Chinese influence on Vietnam and its culture, the Vietnamese throughout their history remained strongly conscious of themselves as Vietnamese. They constantly struggled for independence from China and, once independence was achieved, for the continuity and integrity of their own state.

SUMMARY

The great civilizations of the East—those of India, China, Japan, and Southeast Asia—seemed to reach their height in the period corresponding to Europe's Middle Ages and before the period of European domination. The alien Mughuls gave India its most brilliant period, surpassing the glories of the Guptas. The Mughul ruler Akbar is regarded as one of the greatest statesmen of all time. All facets of culture flourished under Mughul rule, but the noblest legacy was in architecture; the Taj Mahal and the buildings of Fathpur Sikri are ample evidence of the genius of Mughul builders.

As we have seen, China and Japan during this period were beset by internal changes that would in the end bear heavily on how these nations would respond to the coming challenge of the West. The overthrow of the yoke of Mongol oppression by the Ming led to a revival of traditional Chinese culture. Although touched by European influences, the Chinese tended to turn more and more inward, convinced of the superiority of their own culture. The result was a lack of preparedness for the challenge of the West and a set of attitudes that was to stand in the way of modernization in western terms.

In the fifteenth and sixteenth centuries, Japan underwent a long period of internal dissension and warfare that finally culminated in the formation of a closely knit state under the Tokugawa. Here too, a pattern of foreign exclusion was set that was to endure until the arrival of Admiral Perry's "black ships" in the nineteenth century. Nevertheless, the social and political stability and the great homogeneity of Japanese culture, with the widespread basic literacy of the time, as well as the Japanese willingness to learn from other countries, were to make Japan's response to the western impact more decisive than that of China. This allowed Japan to fend off the encroachments of the imperialist West that were to befall a China immersed in itself and lacking in homogeneity and political stability.

Although strongly influenced by Indian and Chinese cultures, the incredible political and ethnic complexities that characterized Southeast Asia inhibited the growth of the kind of cultural and national self-consciousness that marked China and Japan. Moreover, geographical considerations contributed to the inability of the peoples of this region to develop political unity and stability. These factors were to make Southeast Asia a relatively easy prey for Europe's expanding empires.

In following the detailed accounts of events in Europe and in the colonies that Europe would soon establish in Asia, we must not lose sight of the rich heritage of the peoples of the Asian continent. In the centuries to follow, they would move ever closer to the center of the stage of world history.

SUGGESTIONS FOR READING

W. T. de Bary, ed., **Introduction to Oriental Civilizations: Sources of Japanese Tradition,** 2 vols., **Sources of Chinese Tradition,** 2 vols., and **Sources of Indian Tradition,** 2 vols. (Columbia). These texts consist of brief introductory passages followed by translations of relevant documents. The best large-scale general survey of the Far East is E. O. Reischauer, J. K. Fairbank, and A. Craig, **History of East Asian Civilization,** Vol. I, **East Asia: The Great Tradition** (Houghton Mifflin, 1960). See also N. Peffer, **The Far East: A Modern History** (Univ. of Michigan, 1968), a good general text; and W. Bingham, *et al.,* **A History of Asia,** 2nd ed., 2 vols. (Allyn and Bacon, 1974).

M. Biardeau, **India** (Viking, 1960) is a well-illustrated introduction. See also Donald Lach, **India in the Eyes of Europe: The Sixteenth Century** (Univ. of Chicago); and S. M. Ikram, **Muslim Civilization in India** (Columbia, 1964). J. M. Shelat, **Akbar** (Verry) is an important biography.

Dun J. Li, **The Ageless Chinese: A History** (Scribner's) is a well-written full account. See also Donald Lach, **China in the Eyes of Europe: The Sixteenth Century** (Univ. of Chicago). On Sino-European contacts see G. F. Hudson, **Europe and China** (Gordon Pr., 1976).

Essays on Confucian thought include Arthur F. Wright, ed., **The Confucian Persuasion** (Stanford, 1960); D. S. Nivison and Arthur F. Wright, eds., **Confucianism in Action** (Stanford); and Arthur F. Wright and Denis Twitchett, eds., **Confucian Personalities** (Stanford, 1969). On Chinese literature see Chi-chen Wang, trans., **Dream of the Red Chamber** (Twayne); and Liu Tieh-yun, H. Shadick, trans., **The Travels of Lao Ts'an** (Cornell).

E. O. Reischauer, **Japan: The Story of a Nation,** rev. ed., (Knopf, 1974) is lucid and authoritative. A well-written account is D. Lach, **Japan in the Eyes of Europe: The Sixteenth Century** (Univ. of Chicago); and John W. Hall, **Japanese History,** (Greenwood). G. B. Sansom, **A History of Japan,** 3 vols., (Stanford, 1958-1963) is a detailed account. Other titles by the same author are **The Western World and Japan** (Knopf); and **Japan: A Short Cultural History** (ACC, 1962). More specialized books on Japan include T. C. Smith, **The Agrarian Origins of Modern Japan** (Stanford); R. P. Dore, **Education in Tokugawa Japan** (Univ. of Calif., 1965); and Robert Bellah, **Tokugawa Religion** (Free Press). On Japanese literature see Donald Keene, ed., **Japanese Literature: An Introduction for Western Readers** (Grove); and Donald Keene, ed., **Anthology of Japanese Literature: Earliest Era to the Mid-Nineteenth Century** (Grove).

Excellent general surveys on Southeast Asia are D. G. Hall, **A History of South-East Asia,** 3rd ed., (St. Martin's); Donald Lach, **Southeast Asia in the Eyes of Europe: The Sixteenth Century** (Univ. of Chicago, 1968); J. F. Cady, **Southeast Asia: Its Historical Development** (McGraw-Hill); and B. Harrison, **Southeast Asia: A Short History** (St. Martin's, 1966). See also R. C. Lester, **Theravada Buddhism in Southeast Asia** (Univ. of Michigan, 1973).

*Indicates a less expensive paperbound edition.

CHAPTER 17

Precolonial Africa:
3000 B.C.-1800 A.D.;
Native Cultures
in the Americas:
1000 B.C.-1500 A.D.

Before
the European
Impact

INTRODUCTION. Europe's isolation from Asia and its ignorance of sub-Saharan Africa and the Americas ended in the fifteenth century when a multitude of European explorers, traders, conquerors, and missionaries secured footholds in territories far from their homelands. Reaching out to trade, to conquer, and to spread the gospel of Christianity, they encountered civilizations and ways of life which dramatically revealed the limitations of their own knowledge and experience. The story of their explorations and discoveries will be taken up in Chapter 18; this chapter is concerned with the civilizations in Africa and the Americas prior to the arrival of the Europeans.

In describing the early history of sub-Saharan Africa and the Americas, we will introduce to the stage of world history peoples we have not previously encountered. In a number of instances we will take a giant step backward several thousand years, for both Africa and the Americas had inhabitants who, in the eighteenth century, were not so technologically advanced as some of their European and Asian counterparts had been two thousand years before. Yet both continents had fascinating cultures, some of which were to make important contributions to the civilization we know today. The variety of these contributions — from cotton, coffee, and Indian corn to the rhythms upon which jazz is based and sculpture which strongly influenced the development of modern art — reflects the remarkable diversity of the peoples of these lands, peoples who hunted, farmed, built cities, worshiped gods, and waged wars for centuries while Europeans remained totally ignorant of their existence.

Today a significant aspect of our world is the reawakening of old centers of civilization in the newer independent nations of Africa. Nationalistic fervor and brave hopes for the future have been built on pride in the past. For example, the former British colony known as the Gold Coast adopted the name of a long-dead African empire, Ghana, when it was granted independence in 1957. Rhodesia will once more be known as Zimbabwe when it is granted black majority rule. In the New World, Mexican artists take their themes and motifs not from their Spanish colonial heritage but from pre-*conquistadore* Indian cultures.

Thus, if we are to understand the new dynamic spirit that now moves many of these regions, we must know something of the sources of inspiration upon which their people draw. Some of these sources are outlined in the history of Africa and the Americas in the centuries covered by this chapter.

AFRICA: A CONTINENT OF MANY CULTURES

Records of Africa's past. Extending south from the southern fringes of the Sahara Desert to the Cape of Good Hope is sub-Saharan Africa. The terms "Africa" and "Africans" are often used to refer solely to this part of the African continent and its inhabitants who are mostly Negroid in physical characteristics. Africans are often thus distinguished from the Arab and Berber people of North Africa (north of the Sahara) who are mostly Semitic in physical characteristics and have been culturally involved in the Mediterranean world. Nevertheless, the Sahara has never been an impenetrable barrier, and the earliest written sources about sub-Saharan Africa come from North Africa: writings on Egyptian tombs, references in Greek and Roman histories, and trade manuals for North African merchants.

The Nile Valley was one of the original cradles of civilization and here, recorded on the tomb of a noble of the sixth dynasty of Egypt (c. 2340 B.C.), is the story of a trader named Harkhuf who made four long journeys south from Egypt along the Nile River, returning with African products. Conquest followed trade and soon the people of Nubia, as the lands south of ancient Egypt were called, were sending annual tributes of ivory, frankincense, gold, timber, hides, and black recruits for the Egyptian army. These tributes are recorded in pictures and written inscriptions in the temples and tombs of Egyptian royalty and constitute, with the story of Harkhuf, some of the earliest references available to historians about sub-Saharan Africa.

By the first millennium B.C. the thriving trade of the Mediterranean world led traders and travelers into better contact with Africa south of the Sahara, and surviving accounts provide more bits of information for historians. For example, a fifth century B.C. account by the Carthaginian admiral Hanno tells of a long journey taken by sea around the west coast of Africa. The Greek historian Herodotus, writing c. 430 B.C., described North Africans proceeding south into the Sahara with four-horse chariots. This account was thought to be false until the twentieth century, when ancient rock drawings of horse-drawn chariots were found in caves in the middle of the Sahara. The geographer Ptolemy (c. 150 B.C.) described the source of the Nile River as rising in the "Mountains of the Moon." This account was also thought to be imaginary until the nineteenth century when European explorers saw for themselves that the source of the Nile was the huge Lake Victoria fed by streams from the mist- and snow-covered mountains of East Africa.

By the end of the first century after Christ, a sailors' guide to the ports of the East African coast had been written. Ships from the Red Sea nosed their way along this coast exchanging iron tools and weapons for African ivory, tortoise shell, and some slaves. This was the period of the growth of Axum, a kingdom in what is now Ethiopia, whose busy ports along the Red Sea provided a crossroads for trade with India, Africa, and the Graeco-Roman world. Historians know much of Axum because the Axumites had their own written language which can be read easily today. That language, Ge'ez, is the parent of Amharic, the present-day Ethiopian language, and numbers of documents and inscriptions remain from the early Christian era.

Following the eleventh century A.D., documents concerning Africa became more numerous because much of West and East Africa had by then been drawn into the trading world of Islam. Arab travelers and scholars wrote a great deal about Africa. In West Africa the courts and traders of the great African kingdoms used Arabic for keeping some records. But the scholarship of Islam was not available to the Christians of Europe until after the Crusades and the Renaissance. Thus it was only after 1500 that Europeans became vitally concerned with Africa. Then for over three centuries that interest was primarily coastal and concerned the slave trade. Not until the nineteenth century did traders, missionaries, and explorers progressively penetrate what to Europe was a virtually unknown continent.

Europe's penetration of Africa came at a time when the West was experiencing remarkable advances in technology and the arts, stemming from the Renaissance and its subsequent scientific and industrial revolutions. To the intrusive Europeans, Africa south of the Sahara appeared static and many of its peoples backward. The absence of writing in many African societies and the fact that most Africans were not Christians molded western stereotypes of them. Preliterates and non-Christians were considered barbaric, a people without history and a people without civilized morals. In their rush for the ivory, gold, and slaves that Africans had to offer, the Europeans did not take time to study the epic poems and ancient rituals that many African societies had preserved for generations by memorization. They did not bother to examine the complex laws and morals that formed the "unwritten" constitutions of African political systems, and in most cases they would not and could not read the numerous Arabic manuscripts that could have informed them of much African history.

Rediscovery of Africa's past. Since 1945 however, great advances have been made in the approach to the study of Africa and in the recovery of the African past. The new view of Africa as an integral part of world history is one of the most exciting and rewarding events in contemporary historical studies.

This progressive rediscovery of Africa's past has been aided by the newly independent sub-Saharan states' interest in archaeological and historical research. In addition historians are now collecting and developing new criteria for interpreting oral tradition, i.e., the histories, poems, genealogies, and rituals which are memorized, often with great accuracy, by generation after generation of Africans. Oral traditions can sometimes relate accurate genealogies as far back as 700 years. Specialists from other fields such as geology, botany, biology, and linguistics are also working at revealing more and more the richness and importance of Africa's once unappreciated past.

Africans and geography. Africa has roughly four major ecological regions which run like bands across the continent. Beginning at the very north and south ends of the continent are two narrow strips of fertile coastline. Both these coastlines give way to deserts—the huge Sahara in the north (as large in area as the continental United States) and the smaller Kalahari in the south. The deserts merge into grassy plains called savanna which become more and more wooded as they near the equator. In the center and extending also along the West African coastline is the African forest of towering trees and abundant rainfall. As it approaches the East African coast, the forest gives way in places to wooded and grass savanna. East Africa is one of the continent's more interesting geological settings for in addition to broad sweeping plains there are also the highest mountains in Africa, and huge inland lakes.

The geography of Africa affects the way people live their lives and the progress of their history. The ecology of the northern coast is capable of supporting a large population and consequently it has been heavily settled for thousands of years. The Sahara is dry and forbidding, in parts even plants are unable to live in it. Only nomadic peoples can and do survive there. The camel has especially adapted to these dry conditions, while in the savanna donkeys, oxen, sheep, goats, and cattle are used both as beasts of burden and for meat. Many grain crops such as rice and millet can be raised as well; in this way large populations have been supported by the ecology of the savanna for the past two thousand years with farming villages scattered across the plains and large cities arising at key points of trade. Over one-half of the African continent is savanna and it is here where most Africans have lived and where many historical African states and governments have been located. It should be noted, however, that the lack of trees in the savanna has meant a shortage of wood for building, and this has prevented the adoption of many technological skills, particularly the construction of large storied buildings.

Many nutritious crops such as bananas, yams, and oranges which do not tolerate the drier conditions of the savanna thrive in the ecology of the African forest. All East Asian foods, they were introduced to Africa some time ago in the early centuries after Christ and created the potential for larger populations to live in the forest. However, an insect known as the tsetse fly lives in and near the forest, carrying a disease called trypanosomiasis, better known as sleeping sickness, which kills cattle, horses, and sometimes people. This precludes a plentiful supply of meat, and communication is often limited because of the absence of the horse and donkey and because of the difficulty of keeping

large roads cleared of dense undergrowth.

Peoples of Africa. A large variety of types of people inhabit Africa. Today there are over 850 ethnic (or tribal) groups and some 1000 different languages. The peoples can, however, be grouped into four major linguistic families.[1] The Afro-Asiatic speakers live between the Sahara and the Mediterranean in North Africa. This area has been peopled for at least five thousand years by the ethnic group known as Berbers. In addition there is in North Africa a prominent Semitic element, introduced through the immigration of both Jews and Arabs during the period of the Roman Empire and the era of Muslim expansion. Nilo-Saharan languages are spoken by black, Negroid type peoples in the central savanna south of the Sahara and by the tall, slender, lighter-skinned Nilote peoples in the lake region of East Africa. Niger-Kordofanian languages are spoken over most of Africa south of the Sahara and include the widely used Bantu languages. The Bushmen and Hottentots of southern Africa and a few hunting groups in East Africa, brown skinned but non-Negroid in physical characteristics, all speak the older Khoisan family of languages.

Language classification, however, while useful to scholars, can sometimes seem academic and not always practical. For example, the Masai of Kenya speak a Nilo-Saharan dialect but they still cannot be understood by their neighbors, the Luo, who speak a different Nilo-Saharan dialect. Perhaps more instructive is a classification of peoples according to their life-styles and their environment. The Pygmies and the Bushmen, though separated by many miles and speaking different languages, support themselves with primarily the same techniques: they use bows and arrows to hunt for meat and they collect wild roots and fruits. People living in this manner are called hunting and gathering societies, and their mode of existence traces far back into antiquity. Another type of society in Africa is the pastoral society in which the entire wealth and sustenance of the members comes from raising cattle. People living in these societies, such as the Fulani and Masai, organize their daily lives, work patterns, marriages, and politics around their herds of cattle. Farming societies represent another type of life-style followed by the majority of Africans, though this type can be broken down into two groups: those who must farm in the forest areas where they make clearings and those who farm the vast, more easily cultivated but less fertile areas of the savanna. Finally, there are urban societies in Africa and in these people live in large cities, producing and trading small products for their livelihood. Many large urban centers of Africa date back to 1000 A.D., and there is evidence that some such as Meroë and Nok existed in the first millennium B.C. Today many of these ancient cities have disappeared and large modern industrial cities have grown up on different sites. Yet archaeologists and historians know that urban life is nothing new to certain areas of Africa.

The formative period of Africa. It is now believed that during the Old Stone Age, Africa was among the most advanced areas in the world, a leader in the slow march toward civilization. In addition to developing the hand-ax, Africa produced the first true weapon of attack, the bolas, and its tool-making techniques may have been diffused to other continents by streams of migration.

The technique of plant domestication is thought by many scholars to be the next major step in people's effort to control their surroundings, after mastering weapon and toolmaking. According to present evidence, Africa was not the site of the earliest plant domestication. It appears that this first occurred in western Asia and then spread to the Middle East. Under the pharaohs, farming was flourishing in the lower Nile valley at least by the fifth century B.C. and possibly spread from there to sub-Saharan Africa. Some scholars believe, however, that Africans living in the upper Niger River valley independently developed domestic agriculture about 2000 B.C. Regardless of which theory is correct, crops of grains, mostly African rice and millet, were grown in the savanna by 2000 B.C. One of the earliest Neolithic farm cultures in Africa that has been excavated by archaeologists in detail is that of Nok, in central Nigeria, dating from 800 B.C. to 200 A.D. Its people were not only skilled farmers, but artisans who produced iron and tin tools and

This stylized terra-cotta head, dating from about 500 B.C., is an outstanding example of the highly developed level of sculpture reached by the Nok culture. The head represents a human face and was probably used for religious purposes.

decorations. The vitality of African neolithic culture can be sensed by examining Nok's most distinctive accomplishment, the production of strikingly beautiful terra-cotta (baked clay) sculpture.

During the first millennium B.C. the tempo of Africa began to quicken. Iron was introduced, and its use spread over much of the continent between 300 B.C. and 900 A.D. In West Africa, in the northwestern area of present-day Cameroun, Bantu-speaking peoples who farmed and worked iron began to increase in numbers. This "population explosion" led to historic expansion southward into the forest and eastern savanna regions. Bantu expansion in central and eastern Africa was supported by new types of crops, particularly a more nutritious type of banana called plantain, brought in the early centuries A.D. by Indian sailors who followed the wind currents from Asia to East Africa in search of trade. In addition, peoples moving south from the Nile Valley were bringing cattle and the techniques for raising them into East Africa and so provided increased protein supplies for the growing population. The Bantu increased rapidly and, as they pushed southward and eastward, they absorbed or displaced most of the hunting and gathering peoples they encountered, the latter being no match for the Bantu iron hoes and spears. By the eighth century A.D. the Bantu had reached the area of present-day Rhodesia, and by the sixteenth century they were nearing the tip of South Africa.

Africa's earliest civilizations. The first contacts with sub-Saharan Africa made by outsiders were probably by the ancient Egyptians. They sailed far up the Nile River and down the east coast of Africa in search of new markets and new conquests. The most famous expedition was sent by Queen Hatshepsut in c. 1470 B.C. to the land of "Punt" which probably was located in what is now Somaliland. Illustrations on Egyptian tombs show her sailors returning with live baboons, ivory, leopard skins, exotic trees, and bags of incense. Phoenicians also made contact with sub-Saharan Africa. The most famous of their several voyages was that of a fleet of sixty ships which in 520 B.C. was sent by the Phoenician colony at Carthage to explore northwestern Africa and to establish trading posts. There is evidence that the expedition sailed as far south as the modern nation of Sierra Leone, but today there is no indication of any trade post they may have established.

Along the valley of the Nile the pharaohs had extended their control well into Upper Egypt by 2000 B.C., and five hundred years later they gained mastery of the area known as Kush in the northern part of the modern state of the Sudan. In 750 B.C. this former colony of Egypt became so strong that it invaded and conquered Egypt. The Kushite kings, probably very dark-skinned peoples, made themselves the twenty-fifth dynasty of the pharaohs of Egypt, dominating their former masters until 600 B.C. when they were pushed back to their own land by the dissatisfied Egyptians. However, the Kushite kings continued to rule independently at their capital of Meroë, located not far from the modern city of Khartoum.

Meroë carried on lively trade with Egypt, Arabia, India, Ethiopia, and portions of Afri-ca to its south. Its trade goods of hides, ivory, and ebony indicate that the trade to sub-Saharan Africa was as substantial as that to Egypt and the Middle East. Most important for trade were Meroë's valuable iron ore deposits which the Kushites learned to smelt. Kush thus supplied Egypt and other African lands with tools and weapons. Today Meroë is uninhabited, but the extensive heaps of iron refuse and ruins of brick palaces, pyramids, temples, and homes can still be seen. Although Kush was influenced by Egyptian culture, as the Meroë pyramids show, it assuredly developed its own distinct culture influenced by sub-Saharan Africa. Its own system of writing has not yet been translated and this makes it difficult to know exactly what occurred in Kush during its centuries of power and what caused its gradual decline. Although not so famous as a result, Meroë can be considered along with Carthage and Egypt as one of the great civilizations of ancient Africa.

Kush was gradually superseded by a rival trading state to its east, Axum, in modern-day Ethiopia. Eventually the peoples of Kush became weaker, yet they began to raid the borders of Axum. King Ezana of Axum in 350 A.D. decided to crush his weak and worri-

Near the junction of the White and Blue Nile in the Sudan, the Kushites founded their fabulous capital, Meroë, building massive monuments, palaces, and sculptured gods. Their remains give a vivid impression of the city's former grandeur.

some rival and a lively description of his expedition remains today engraved on a monument in Axum. It reads:

And as I had warned them, and they would not listen but refused to cease from their evil deeds and betook themselves to flight, I made war on them . . . They fled without making a stand and I pursued them for 23 days, killing some and capturing others . . . I burnt their towns, both those built of bricks and those built of reeds, and my army carried off their food and copper and iron . . . and destroyed the statues in their temples, their granaries, and cotton trees and cast them into the river [Nile].[2]

Axum supplanted Meroë's importance and came to control a large share of the trade between Africa and the Mediterranean world, the Arabian peninsula, the Persian Gulf, and the Indian Ocean. Greek and Roman merchants lived at Axum, with Greek being the language of official records for some time, though this later was replaced by Ge'ez.

By the sixth century A.D., the documents indicate a high standard of living. Most people lived in stone houses and the king resided in a huge palace. He had chariots pulled by elephants and wore luxurious robes and splendid jewels; he was followed by a group of flute players. Axum's wealth was such that in the fields around Axum today one can still find its distinctive gold coins.

Axum's role in trade brought it into contact with Christianity at an early date. In 330 A.D. two young Byzantine Christian scholars were brought to the court of King Ezana where they converted the king to Christianity and persuaded him to make it the state religion. A large number of churches were then built throughout the countryside, and an archbishop was sent from Alexandria. At this time the Bible was translated into Ge'ez.

When the Arab empire began to expand in the seventh century A.D., its Muslim warriors were unable to conquer Axum and convert its Christians to Islam. Nevertheless Axum was surrounded by the Islamic world and cut off from ties with the outside for several centuries thus causing its decline. In the fourteenth century the descendants of the people of Axum reorganized and began to build the state that has grown to be Ethiopia today.

They trace the ancestry of their royal family back to ancient Axum, a historical tradition of unusual length.

The trans-Saharan trade. The kingdom of Axum had become prominent at the time of the Roman Empire, but the Romans were also interested in expanding trade all along the North African coast. Their chief competitors for a while were the people of Carthage who, as already mentioned, had explored the coast of Africa in search of new markets. Carthage was apparently aware of the rich gold deposits located in West Africa near the source of the Niger River. Although they probably did not reach this gold area, called Wangara, they did have trade contacts with it through local peoples across the Sahara. The Sahara is not the great barrier that first glance may make it seem. It is much more like an ocean which, though one cannot live there, one can cross rather quickly with the proper means, in ancient Roman times the horse, later the camel. Thus contact between the peoples on either side of this great desert has never ceased. This contact has been maintained partly because of the nature of the items that are traded across the Sahara, gold and salt. The gold of West Africa has always been valued and in exchange for it the people of North Africa have traded salt, an item essential for human health, particularly in warm climates, and painfully lacking as a natural resource in West Africa. Large supplies of salt are found in the ground in the northwestern part of the Sahara.

When Carthage was destroyed by the Romans in 146 B.C. the Romans fell heir to the trade routes across the Sahara, as their imports of gold, ivory, hides, and black slaves testify. Roman North Africa reached its peak in the third century A.D. and it was at this time that the camel was permanently introduced to the area from the Middle East. Thereafter, although Roman North Africa's prosperity declined along with the Roman Empire, the trans-Saharan routes became much more practical and permanent (see map, p. 367). After the amazingly rapid spread of the Islamic Arabs across North Africa in the seventh and eighth centuries, the trans-Saharan trade routes became more important. From this period on, written ac-

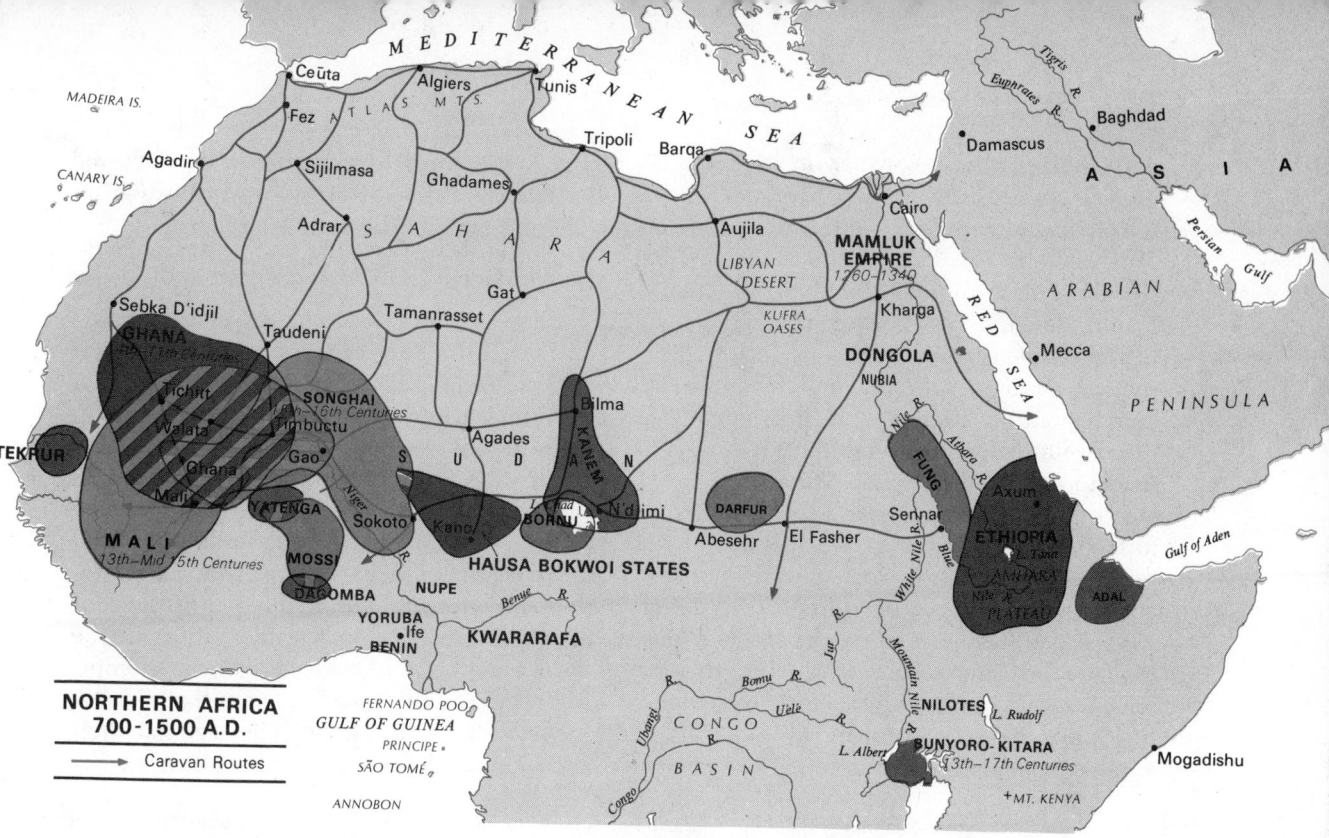

NORTHERN AFRICA
700–1500 A.D.

→ Caravan Routes

counts by Arab geographers and traveling traders make historical reconstruction easier.

Empires of the western savanna. The dangers of the desert—bandits, risks of being lost and dying of thirst—meant that preparations for a trading expedition across the Sahara were made with great care. Traders traveled in large groups of up to 10,000 camels, and the journey could take from eight to twelve weeks to complete with as much as three weeks between oases. The first site of ample water and rest, the Niger River, was a convenient stopping place. Here were located peoples who knew the African savanna better than the desert travelers and who could penetrate more easily the still distant gold-producing areas. Thus the Africans living near the bend of the Niger River became important middlemen in the trade of gold for salt across the Sahara. It was just west of the Niger that Ghana, the first of the great western Sudanic kingdoms developed. (The Sudan is a geographical term for the savanna lands of western Africa and should be distinguished from the modern nation of Sudan, south of Egypt.)

According to tradition, about 400 A.D. the kingdom of Ghana (not to be confused with

the modern state of that name) began to develop. Little is known about the early centuries of Ghana's growth, but by the eighth century, when Arab geographers began to write about it, Ghana had become a large empire based on lively trade and savanna-type agriculture. The government was strongly centralized, with the king being able to appoint and demote the main officers and advisers of the empire. Considered to be partly divine and able to intercede with the gods for the good of the empire, the king was also the ultimate judge of all court cases. When appearing in public he was surrounded by retainers holding gold swords, horses with gold-cloth blankets, and dogs with gold and silver collars. All the princes and advisers of the empire sat around him splendidly dressed as well.

The Arab writer al-Bakri was so impressed with Ghana that he wrote in 1067 that its army comprised 200,000 warriors with which to control the large variety of peoples in its territory. Although the primary occupation of most people in Ghana was agriculture, trade brought the kingdom its great wealth. The king claimed the right to every gold nugget coming from the mines of Wangara, though citizens could own as much gold dust as they could afford to buy. Taxes were levied on all goods entering and leaving Ghana. The wealth of this kingdom is evidenced by al-Bakri's description of the capital of Ghana, Kumbi-Saleh. It was really comprised of two towns about six miles apart, one occupied by the king and his officers and the other by merchants and strangers. In between were the dwellings of the inhabitants who grew food to supply the capital. The king's town was built like a fortress and the merchants' town, wrote al-Bakri, was even larger, with twelve mosques, two-storied stone houses, and public squares. The ruins of this latter town have been uncovered in modern-day Mauritania. Many *imama* (Muslim theologians), legal experts, and scholars lived there. Regarding the religion of the king of Ghana and his people, al-Bakri wrote:

The king's town is surrounded by huts and clumps of trees and copses, in which dwell the magicians of the nation, entrusted with the religious cult; it is there that they have placed the idols and tombs of their sovereigns.[3]

Although the king of Ghana was tolerant of the religion of Islam, he and the majority of his subjects never converted. In the eleventh century one section of the Almoravids, a group of zealous Muslim reformers living in the desert northwest of Ghana attacked Kumbi-Saleh. Ostensibly crusaders pledged to rid Ghana of its pagan practices, the Almoravids overran Ghana in 1076 and ruled for about ten years, enjoying the profits of the trans-Saharan gold trade as well as attempting religious reform. The people of Ghana, however, soon began to rebel against their conquerors and this in turn disrupted the

In this 1375 map from the Catalan Atlas, Mansa Musa, the wealthy king of Mali, awaits the arrival of a Musilim trader. The king—sometimes called Musa Mali, as in the following inscription—is holding a nugget of gold. The legend beside him reads: "This Negro lord is called Musa Mali, lord of the Negroes of Guinea. So abundant is the gold which is found in his country that he is the richest and most noble king in all the land."

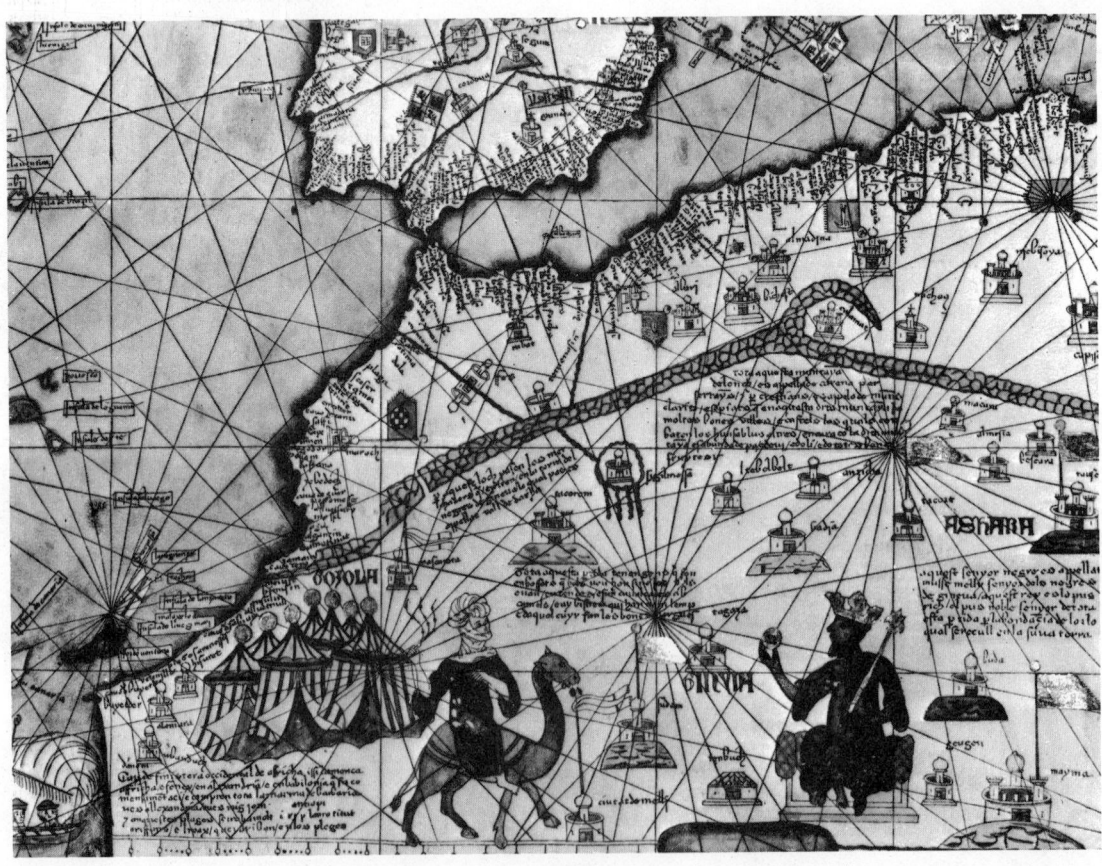

security of the long trade routes. Many traders moved away to other parts of West Africa, and many small states which had owed their allegiance to Ghana became independent.

One of the provinces which declared itself independent at this time was the kingdom of Mali. In 1235 its greatest leader, Sundiata, even succeeded in conquering its former suzerain, Ghana. Sundiata's eleven brothers had been murdered by the king of Ghana, according to the oral traditions concerning this period, but Sundiata miraculously survived this purge and his praises are sung by Malian historians today as the glorious founder of the Mali empire. Sundiata and his successors conquered vast territories, with the result that Mali became larger than Ghana had ever been. Although Sundiata was not himself Muslim, his descendants were. One of the most famous kings of Mali, Mansa Musa, is well known to historians for his pilgrimage to Mecca in 1324. The splendor of his caravan with thousands of retainers, gifts of gold and ivory, horses, camels, and slaves certainly deserves its fame.

Mali's, and Mansa Musa's, wealth was based on the gold mines of Wangara and the trans-Saharan trade, just as Ghana's had been. Its major commercial city, Timbuktu, succeeded Ghana as the main point of convergence for the caravan routes and became a great metropolis and center of Muslim learning. Muslim scholars from all over the world came to Timbuktu to study and to use its huge library. The famous Muslim traveler Ibn Batuta visited Mali in 1352 and wrote a detailed description of the country. He was most impressed by its security:

Among the admirable qualities of these people, the following are to be noted: 1) The small number of acts of injustice that one finds there; for the Negroes are of all peoples those who most abhor injustice. The sultan pardons no one who is guilty of it. 2) The complete and general safety one enjoys throughout the land. The traveler has no more reason than the man who stays at home to fear brigands, thieves, or ravishers.[4]

Ibn Batuta was surprised to find that the women of Mali were often educated and had more privileges and freedom of movement

No European ever saw Timbuktu until 1828, when René Caillé, disguised as a Muslim pilgrim, made the journey. The mixture of Muslim and native architecture is apparent in his drawing of the city. Caillé was most impressed by the difficulties the builders must have encountered in setting up a great city "in the midst of the sands."

than those he had observed in all his other travels. He admitted that he did not like the food very much during his stay, but was impressed with the wealth, comfortable living, and great amount of trade that was evident there. His only disappointment was to find that many Malians were not Muslim.

Mali at its height, c. 1350, controlled an area as large as western Europe, but the descendants of Mansa Musa were less and less able to control the huge empire. Many of the segments of the empire rebelled. One of these provinces, Songhai, with its capital of Gao further down the Niger River had reestablished its independence in the fourteenth century. One of the greatest of the Songhai rulers, Sonni Ali, captured Timbuktu in 1468 and proceeded to conquer much of Mali.

To some extent Sonni Ali merely conquered the empire of Mali and substituted himself as its ruler, though Songhai eventually was larger than Mali. After thirty years of ruthless military dictatorship and cruel warfare, this great conqueror died and was replaced by one of his generals, Askia Muhammad, who chose to institute major organizational changes. He set about reorganizing the entire empire so that it might be administered peacefully and not kept under control by force. He bureaucratized the government by appointing ministers and regional administrators who were directly responsible to him and no local intermediaries. He established a professional army and expanded the naval fleet of canoes which constantly patrolled the Niger River, supplying, policing, and keeping communications open with the different parts of the empire. Taxation was regularized and attempts were made to impose more consistent judicial standards, especially Islamic ones. Askia Muhammad also encouraged Islamic scholars and revitalized Timbuktu, which had been harassed for lack of cooperation by the militaristic Sonni Ali. A traveler writing after 1520 noted:

In Timbuktu there are numerous judges, professors, and holy men, all being handsomely maintained by the king who holds scholars in much honor. Here too they sell many handwritten books from North Africa. More profit is made from selling books in Timbuktu than from any other branch of trade.[5]

At the height of his power Askia Muhammad's influence reached from the Atlantic Ocean throughout much of the northern and western sections of the continent.

Songhai was supplying great quantities of gold across the Sahara in order to satisfy the demands of wealthy Italian city-states who were financing and inspiring the Renaissance. Once again Africa's neighbors to the north coveted the wealth of the rich middleman role of the West African empires and saw no reason to continue to pay the taxes of Songhai for its services. Hence, in 1590, the king of Morocco equipped an army of 5000 men to cross the Sahara and attack Songhai. Only about 1000 Moroccan soldiers were alive at the end of the desert crossing but they had brought guns with them. The superiority of these weapons over the swords and spears of Songhai was such that the Moroccans, although greatly outnumbered, were victorious in battle. Yet they were not powerful enough to take over the complex government of Songhai and during the following years large numbers of provinces, cities, and small kingdoms broke away, and the conquerors could do little about it. The historian Abderrahman es-Sadi was born in Timbuktu at this time and as he grew up he observed the progressive decay of the Songhai empire. His experiences later motivated him to write the *Tarikh es-Sudan (History of the Sudan)*, which is the source of much information about Songhai and which he introduced with the following comment:

When the Moroccan army arrived in the Sudan they found one of God's most favored countries in richness and fertility. Peace and security reigned throughout all its provinces . . . [but] . . . now all that has changed: Danger has replaced security; misery has replaced opulence; tranquility has been succeeded by trouble, calamities, and violence.[6]

Smaller states such as Kanem-Bornu, the Hausa city-states, and the Mossi kingdoms survived independently in the century after the Moroccan invasion.

The Sudanic empires of Ghana, Mali, and Songhai had a number of common features that incline historians to group them together. Their boundaries were ill-defined and embraced a variety of ethnically and culturally diverse peoples. Often established by conquest, these empires depended in many cases on military force and personal leadership for their perpetuation. But even the most stable systems of succession cannot guarantee that strong leadership will always be available for the throne, and thus incompetent rulers usually meant a rapid weakening of the empires. Ghana, Mali, and Songhai each endured for over two centuries, but they succeeded each other as empires rather than existing alongside each other in competition. For this reason historians consider them weak and illusive.

In addition, there was in all three empires an overlay of Islamic culture represented by the scholars, merchants, urban dwellers, clerics, and administrators of the government. This culture often clashed with the non-Muslim masses who were the labor force and suppliers of food to the wealthy and professional classes. Thus, despite its hold on West Africans, Islam never took deep root in the countryside. Customs, laws, and life-styles in rural areas for the mass of the people remained radically different from those of the towns, and this was an inherent weakness in the Sudanic empires.

However, the vast empires of the Sudan existed in order to manage the long-distance trade routes, to make them secure for travelers, to maintain order and consistency in the marketplaces—in short, to ensure that the lucrative gold and salt trade went as smoothly as possible and was not interrupted by quarrels and capricious laws in every little chiefdom en route. If this was accomplished and if peace was maintained, taxes paid, and sufficient foodstuffs and troop requisitions provided, then the provinces, chiefdoms, and kingdoms that made up the empires were left alone by the central government to follow their own customs, religion, and local rulers. Therefore a period of relative peace and gradual centralization endured in the Sudan from the tenth to the seventeenth centuries. But the overall lack of cultural unity had the potential of causing the whole system to dissipate into its separate parts when exposed to a major disruption, specifically, the Moroccan invasion of 1590.

The collapse of the system was hastened not only by Moroccan inability to govern, but by the simultaneous reorientation of the trade routes. The latter was the result of the appearance in the sixteenth century of Europeans for the first time on the southern West African coast trading for gold and slaves. These first Europeans were seeking, just like the Moroccan invaders, to avoid the Sudanic middlemen in obtaining gold. But the Europeans came around by sea and so began to draw the Wangara gold trade to the south and west rather than across the desert, thus sapping the prosperity of the Sudan. After the sixteenth century there was never again to be an empire in West Africa as territorially large as Songhai had been, though eventually others just as wealthy and efficiently governed were to arise.

The impact of trade in East Africa. From the beginning of the Christian era traders from India and Arabia followed coastlines and favorable winds to the coast of East Africa in search of ivory and tortoise shell. The trade continued and grew, as Greek and Roman coins found along the coast testify. Population also grew, for the plantain was introduced to Africa from Asia about this time and made possible its support.

As Roman trade waned in the fifth century, Arab and Indian trade expanded. By the time of Muhammad the trade routes and coastal towns were very familiar to the Arabs.

By the fourteenth century the trade of the East African coast had expanded tremendously, for the 1331 travelogue of the widely traveled Muslim, Ibn Batuta (who also visited West Africa) describes numerous trade cities and bustling ports all along the coast. One in particular, Kilwa, struck Ibn Batuta as the most beautiful and well-constructed town he had seen in the world. Archaeological excavations today, which bear out some of Ibn Batuta's description, reveal the stone ruins of enormous palaces, complex mansions and peaceful mosques, arched walkways, town squares, and public fountains. Coral and wood were used to make carved arches, doors, and windows. The main palace of Kilwa was built on the very edge of a cliff overlooking the ocean and contained over 100 rooms, as well as an eight-sided bathing pool in one of its many courtyards. The remains of at least thirty-seven cities along the East African coast have been uncovered today.

Through some written records from China we know, for example, that there were extensive trade contacts between China and East Africa. The city of Malindi even sent a giraffe as a gift to the emperor of China in 1415, and the emperor responded with a fleet of Chinese sailors and numerous gifts which accompanied the Malindi traders back to Africa. Chinese desire for large quantities of ivory coupled with East African demand for Chinese porcelain found in many of the ruined cities today accounts for much of this contact.

The trading cities of East Africa spread their influence and control along the coast, but there is as yet no evidence that their influence spread very far into the interior of the continent. Each city was a unit unto itself, usually in fierce competition with the other city-states. Each had its own government, laws, taxes, police force or army, and rulers. They rarely united for defense even in the face of severe outside threat, as the arrival of Europeans would subsequently be.

The ruins in the valley of Zimbabwe, meaning "the sacred graves of the chiefs," are dominated by the massive stone wall of the temple.

The peoples and rulers of the city-states were predominantly Bantu, with a minority being Arab, Persian, and Indian who soon intermarried with the local inhabitants. The Portuguese, arriving in 1500, described the coastal people as either black, tawny, or light—in all various stages of intermarriage. The language of the coast was Swahili, a Bantu language with some Arabic, Persian, and Indian word-borrowing. It was written in Arabic script, and by the seventeenth century poems, ballads, and letters, as well as trade and government documents, were commonly composed in Swahili. The architecture of the city-states was greatly influenced by Arab architecture of the Middle East but, although some Bantu converted to Islam, indigenous religious customs were common and Islam never spread far beyond the coast. The term "Swahili" can refer to the peoples of the coast and their cosmopolitan culture as well as to their language.

Zimbabwe. Partly in response to the active coastal trade, the prosperous Bantu state of Zimbabwe emerged in what is now Rhodesia. The rulers of this kingdom built the stone city of Great Zimbabwe over a long

period of time, from as early as the eighth century until the early eighteenth. Constructed of granite blocks without mortar or cement, and often in elaborate patterns, the massive walls of its temple ruins measure from ten to fifteen feet thick and from twenty to thirty feet high. The remains of the acropolis—built to be an impregnable fortress—can be seen on a nearby hill. Close by is the Valley of Ruins, the former site of a flourishing religious and administrative center.

Zimbabwe grew with the expanding coastal trade, even though it was 300 miles from the ocean, because it was the site of important gold mines. The trade of its gold with the coast was important, and many of the common people of Zimbabwe were involved in gold mining. Remains of over 7000 gold-working sites have been found, and much more gold was collected from streams. The mines were simple pits dug into the earth but some were as deep as fifty feet, and both men and women participated in the actual labor.

The Monomotapa, or king of Zimbabwe at this time, was thought by his subjects to be semidivine. He had the authority to judge the cases of the land, yet only his closest advisers were allowed to see him. He was expected to commit suicide if he became ill in order to maintain the health of the country. The main building in the Valley of Ruins was the palace of the king. Archaeologists estimate that about 1000 people occupied the site at one time; cooks, servants, farmers, and soldiers were housed with their families in smaller stone buildings that surrounded the main palace structure. Ruined stone buildings of the type found at Zimbabwe are much in evidence throughout the region. Some of the larger sites are thought to have been the sites of provincial administrative headquarters.

Early European contact. For some eight hundred years, beginning about 700 A.D., Islam was the most important outside influence in Africa and an important stimulant of trade between Africa, the Middle East, and India. Throughout this same period Islam was a dominant source of worry in Europe, as Christian enthusiasm for the Crusades against Islam demonstrates. In the fifteenth

14. Ch'iu Ying: "Peach Blossom Spring" (1530). The entire length of this hand scroll painting (detail shown) is over thirteen feet. It is done in ink and colors on silk in a precise, brilliantly refined style by one of the Ming dynasty's finest artists. It contains a careful blend of delicate and subtle colors with major attention devoted to detail. Landscape paintings such as this one are China's leading contribution to world art. Although limited in subject matter to mountains, forests, lakes, and sometimes agricultural scenes, their variations in mood are magnificently carried out. Landscape paintings of the Ming dynasty use bolder strokes, yet maintain the gentle lyricism of their predecessors.

15. (above) Angkor Wat, Cambodia (early twelfth century). Indian art styles spread far beyond the borders of India and in many cases not only retained vitality but increased it. Angkor Wat, the immense temple city of the Khmers in Cambodia, is considered by many to be the most perfectly realized example of Indian architectural technique. The gigantic size of the complex (its moat is two and one half miles long and one of its courtyards contains a half mile of sculptured reliefs) is matched by the brilliant spatial ordering of its profusion of galleries, sanctuaries, pavilions, and towers.

16. (right) Aztec mural: "Rain God's Heaven" (fifteenth century). Aztec art, as exemplified by this mural, is marked by strength and brutality. The work is painted in vivid colors and has no sense of spatial relationships, yet its strong emotional message is unmistakable. Much of the subject matter of Aztec art concerns human sacrifice which in itself was an integral part of their religion. The Aztecs believed that all their gods sprang from two deities, one male and one female. These gods in turn created the sun, the earth, and all creatures on the earth. The sun was created by one of the gods immolating himself, and to give it the energy necessary to move through the heavens, the other gods sacrificed themselves. Humanity then assumed this obligation for the gods and sacrifice to the sun became a sacred duty and necessary in order for the world to go on. Every time a human being was sacrificed, the disaster that always threatened to engulf the earth was postponed for a while. The conviction that human sacrifice was the key to life as opposed to death was so strong that it was considered a great honor to be chosen as one to be sacrificed.

17. (left) **Oni (king) of Ife** (thirteenth century). Characterized by a high degree of technical skill and a restrained, but stately realism, this bronze head is one of the masterpieces of an impressive collection of bronzes and terra-cottas discovered at Ife, Nigeria. The casting technique, called the *cire perdue* (lost wax) process, was possibly imported from the Mediterranean region. The modeling was done in wax over an earthen core, with another layer of earth packed around the head. The head was then heated to melt out the wax, and molten bronze was poured into the hollow form. Another theory, however, is that ancient Egypt may have been the source of Ife art, for terra-cottas dating from before the birth of Christ have been found in North Nigeria. Still other archaeologists believe that Ife art has neither European nor Oriental precedents. Although harmonious and noble in expression like the classical art of Greece and Rome, this head is related to other primitive art by the tribal scars on the face, the holes for attaching hair for realism, and its use in ancestor worship.

century, therefore, the Portuguese, who were in close geographical proximity to Muslim Spain and North Africa, decided that it might be possible to avoid traveling through Muslim lands to reach the spices and gold of India by sailing around them. With this in mind, they set about systematically exploring the coast of Africa, establishing several trading stations along the west coast. In 1498 Vasco da Gama succeeded in sailing around the southern tip of Africa, passed through the harbors of the East African city-states, and finally reached India.

The Portuguese explorers, a rather rough lot of sailors, were overwhelmed with the wealth and luxurious living they discovered along the East African coast. On the other hand, the suave Swahili peoples scorned the Portuguese for their lack of manners, unclean habits, and tawdry trade goods. However, the Swahili coast had been prosperous and peaceful for so long that there were few actual military defenses, and the Portuguese, certain that they could capture vast gold reserves quickly, attacked the cities, taking them by surprise and often without opposition. In most cases the towns were looted and burned. Kilwa, for example, was burned in 1505 after the Portuguese had marched ashore, said a mass, and removed all the cotton and silk stored there for trade to Zimbabwe. In the same year at Mombassa, Portuguese sailors broke into houses with axes, looted and killed, and then set the town on fire. In a letter of warning to the sultan of Malindi up the coast, the sultan of Mombassa wrote about the Portuguese:

He raged in our town with such might and terror that no one, neither man nor woman, neither the old nor the young, nor even the children however small was spared to live. His wrath was to be escaped only by flight. Not only people, but even the birds in the heavens were killed and burnt. The stench from the corpses is so overpowering that I dare not enter the town, and I cannot begin to give you an idea of the immense amount of booty which they took from the town. Pray harken to the news of these sad events, that you may yourself be preserved.[7]

Although the Portuguese built their own trade fort at Mombassa in 1590, they were unable to replace the functioning governments and complex trade networks they destroyed with anything of their own. The insecurity and fear which they instigated among the people caused the centuries-old Indian Ocean trade to wither. Swahili language and culture survived, but the trade did not revive until the early nineteenth century.

Interior East Africa. Throughout this period (500 to 1500) there were societies of peoples forming in the interior of East Africa as well. People such as the Kikuyu were organized in clans based on kinship ties and these clans in turn determined the division of land and farms which were the basis of their livelihood. Numbers of clans speaking the same language and acknowledging the same distant ancestors united to form tribes, or ethnic groups, as they are now called. But the rise and fall of these ethnic groups are barely known to historians, for no written and little archaeological evidence has survived concerning them. Oral traditions record that around 1300 A.D., tall, handsome, godlike warriors known as the Chwezi arrived in the area of Lake Victoria. They brought with them sophisticated knowledge of cattle-raising and state organization which they shared with the already present Bantu and stimulated the beginnings of the kingdom of Bunyoro-Kitara and its successor Buganda. The Chwezi disappeared as suddenly and mysteriously as they came, according to the epic poems of East Africa which immortalize them. However, the Bantu kingdoms influenced by the Chwezi continued to develop, many still being in existence in the early twentieth century.

Europeans and the slave trade. The Portuguese also made contacts with people along the west coast of Africa. Here they encountered some African kingdoms already centuries old whose prime interests were in trading with the empires of the savanna. One of these kingdoms was Benin, located in the forest of what is now southern Nigeria. The kings of Benin, called obas, had begun to rule over the area as early as the eleventh century. By the time the Portuguese arrived in 1472, the oba was very powerful with central religious and political responsibilities, living in a huge palace protected by a surrounding maze of courtyards. Benin had a powerful army and prosperous trade with the Sudan, exchanging forest products for items of the trans-Saharan trade.

The Portuguese, and the French, Dutch, and English traders who followed on their heels after 1500, were favorably impressed with the city and life-style of the Benin people. Benin was powerful enough not to suffer the fate of the East African city-states. Europeans were not allowed to live in Benin, but had to remain with their ships on the coast. They had to pay taxes and import duties and could trade only with the chosen representatives of the oba. The obas were powerful enough to enforce these rules.

Another kingdom encountered by the Portuguese was that of Kongo located near the mouth of the Congo River. The people of the Kongo, the Bakongo, responded differently to the arrival of the Europeans than had either the Swahili or Benis. Portuguese advisers and Catholic priests were welcomed by the Bakongo and invited to stay at the court of the king where their technical expertise was used to the best advantage and where

This drawing from Thomas Astley's *A New and General Collection of Voyages and Travels* depicts an audience given to Dutch traders in 1642 by Don Alvaro, king of Kongo. By this time so many Kongolese were taken into slavery that the population had become dangerously small.

large numbers of people were soon converted to Christianity. Letters of friendship and alliance passed between the Manikongo (king) and King Manuel of Portugal. Portuguese became the language of the court and many Kongolese learned to read and write it as well as church Latin. A Catholic cathedral was built and the people were encouraged by their king to adopt European dress and manners. The capital was renamed São Salvador and the king, Nzinga Myemba, took the name Dom Afonso. Schools were opened and by 1516 there were said to be over a thousand students in them.

But by the mid-sixteenth century the Portuguese had an ever increasing need for cheap labor to work in the mines and on the sugar plantations in their New World colonies and on the island of São Thome. Interest in furthering friendly relations with Kongo soon waned, except to gain slaves. At first Dom Afonso delivered his prisoners of war and criminals to the Portuguese traders and received in payment European cloth and metal. This trade was the precursor of what was to become the Atlantic slave trade, which endured into the nineteenth century. Soon Portuguese and Kongolese traders began to ignore the laws of the Kongo and developed the business of selling any person, not just criminals or prisoners of war.

The slave trade increased in Kongo rapidly. Eventually Dom Afonso wrote the king of Portugal protesting what was happening:

There are many traders in all corners of the country. They bring ruin to the country. Every day people are enslaved and kidnapped, even nobles, even members of the King's own family.[8]

Dom Afonso gradually curbed the slave trade in his country and hence the Portuguese began to engage in slave trade in other parts of Africa. Finally in 1540 Dom Afonso was shot by some disgruntled Portuguese traders while he was attending mass. This ended the good relations between Kongo and Portugal and to what many historians see as the first unsuccessful attempt to westernize and modernize an African kingdom.

By the seventeenth century, the slave trade had become the dominant commerical enter-

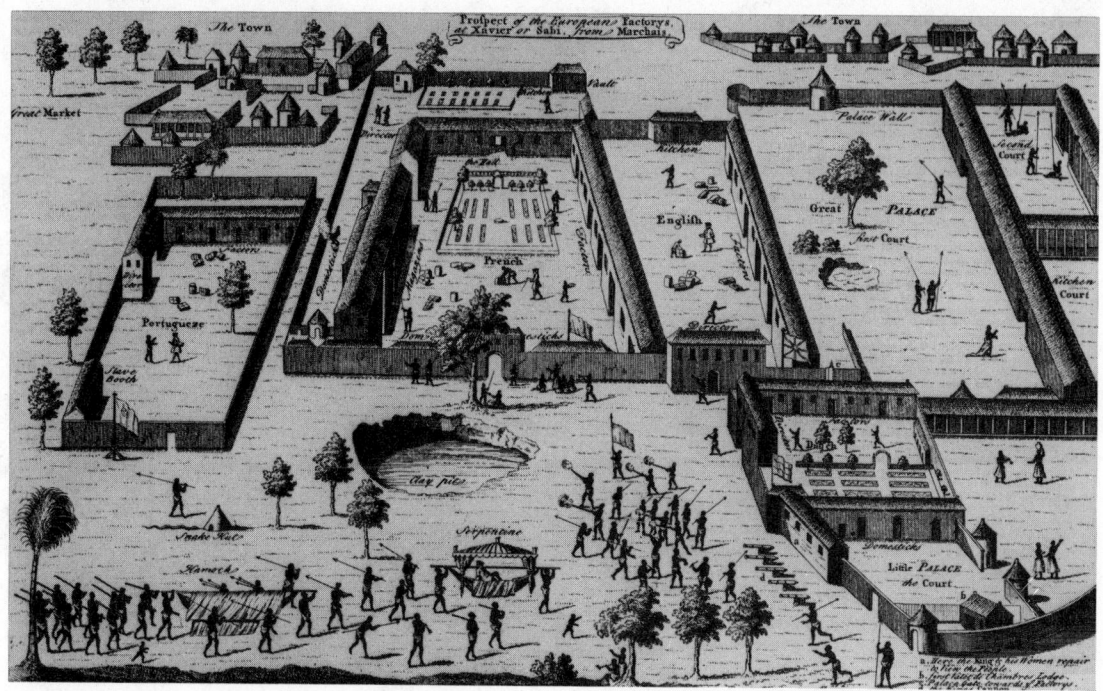

Slave compounds were often constructed on the West Coast of Africa where the captives were held before being shipped off to America or the West Indies. In this sixteenth-century map, a native king maintains "factorys" consisting of separate quarters for slave traders from Portugal, France, England, and the Netherlands.

prise along the West African coast. Domestic slavery had been practiced in Africa since ancient times, but the slave in African society was considered a part of the family, could marry, own property, own a slave of his own, and even inherit from his master. Slaves could achieve freedom, usually over several generations, by merging with the master family. Slaves might also be sold or beaten depending on the society and the individual. More harsh than this domestic slavery was the ancient slave trade which dates back at least to the time when the Egyptians sought African slaves for their armies. Over the centuries several hundred thousand slaves were exported from the coast of East Africa and across the Sahara to the Middle East. When European trade began, however, West African slaves were brought to the Americas in numbers approaching ten million from the period 1450–1850.[9] Furthermore, for every slave sold in the Americas, another is said to have lost his or her life in the cruel roundup in Africa or on the crowded slave ships.

The stimulant of the European-African slave trade was the plantation economy, es-

pecially sugar, of the West Indies and, much later, the cotton economy of the American South. Sugar was in great demand in sixteenth- to eighteenth-century Europe, and the West Indies was one of the few climates suitable for its growth. The sugar and cotton were exported to Europe where they were manufactured into goods such as rum, brandy, and cotton cloth. These, added to other manufactured items as guns and iron tools, were then shipped to the west coast of Africa. Here they were exchanged for the slaves who were packed in large numbers into the ships and taken to the West Indies where their cheap labor was essential for the production of the raw materials. This sequence is sometimes referred to as the triangular trade because all three points were needed to make it operate. The transport of the slaves across the Atlantic is called the "middle passage" and it was during that crossing that the most suffering and death occurred, for conditions on the ships were cramped and unsanitary.

Both Europeans and Africans accepted the trade and cooperated in it. It was a very lu-

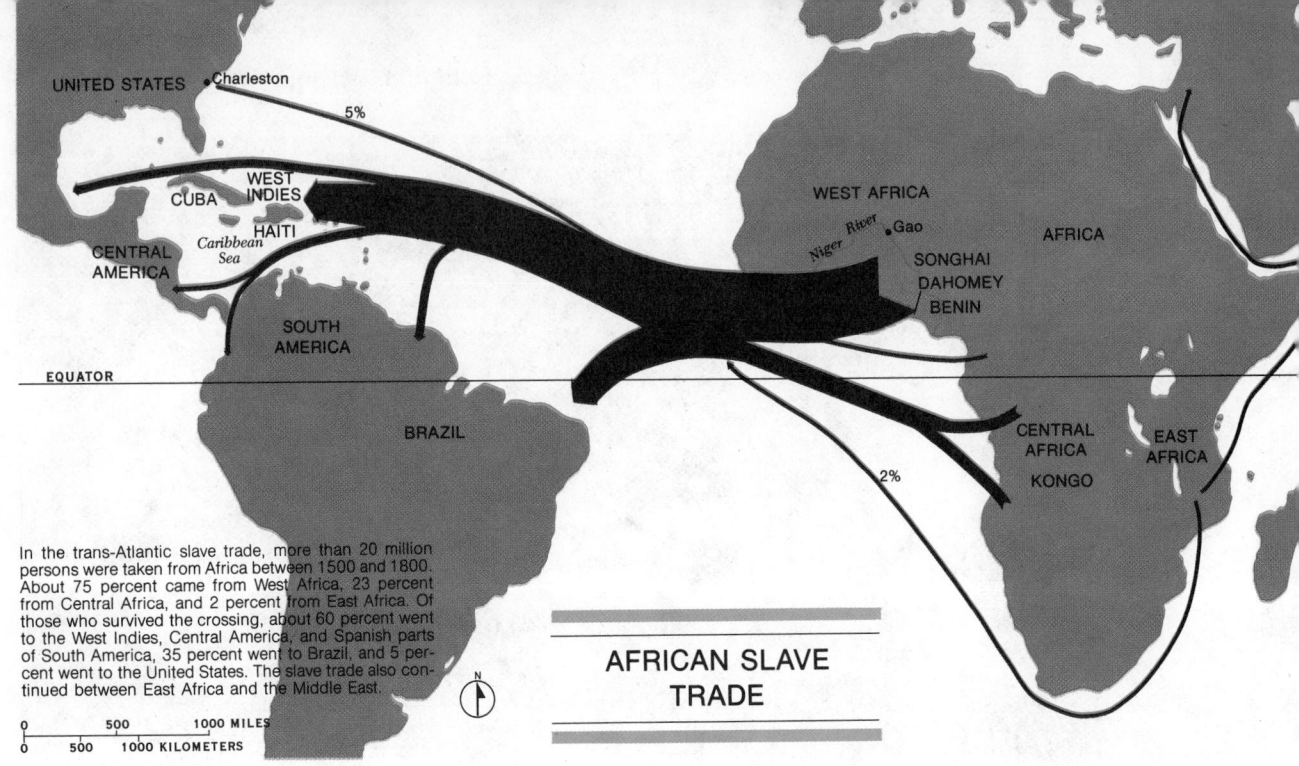

In the trans-Atlantic slave trade, more than 20 million persons were taken from Africa between 1500 and 1800. About 75 percent came from West Africa, 23 percent from Central Africa, and 2 percent from East Africa. Of those who survived the crossing, about 60 percent went to the West Indies, Central America, and Spanish parts of South America, 35 percent went to Brazil, and 5 percent went to the United States. The slave trade also continued between East Africa and the Middle East.

AFRICAN SLAVE TRADE

crative enterprise, bringing as much as 200 percent profit to some European and African traders. Slaves were obtained in the hinterland by Africans who then delivered the victims to the slave ships on the coast. African rulers and middlemen were very jealous of their trading rights and privileges. Hence Europeans were rarely permitted by Africans to penetrate into the interior of Africa. They were forced to live on ships anchored offshore, in special locales in the coastal towns, or in forts built on the shoreline.

The rise of West African forest states. Until the late fifteenth century all commercial contacts in West Africa had been north across the Sahara. With the arrival of Europeans the pattern of trade was revolutionized, routes shifting to the west and south by sea. As the trans-Saharan trade dwindled and the trans-Atlantic trade increased, the states along the savanna became less important, though they did not die out completely. Instead other kingdoms in the forest along the west coast of Africa developed. On the basis of the traffic in human beings, new West African states such as Dahomey, Oyo, and Asante rose to power and wealth. Dahomey, for example, was dependent and prospered on the slave trade until it decreased in the early

nineteenth century. Other states such as Oyo were adversely affected by the demoralizing experience of continuous slave raiding. Oyo's otherwise sound and fascinating system of complex government degenerated into a century of civil war which left it bitterly divided.

On the other hand, the state of Asante which developed in the late seventeenth century was able to diversify its economy such that it was not dependent on the slave trade alone. It had gold deposits for which Europeans and Arabs traded more eagerly than for slaves. It also had forest products which it deliberately cultivated, such as the kola nut, a type of chewy nut highly valued by Muslims. Thus Asante traded as much with the savanna-Muslim states to the north as with the European traders to the south. Asante was able to build up a highly centralized system of government, and even a certain sense of nationalism and patriotism emerged. Therefore it had a strength which, coupled with its economic advantage, helped it to resist the European imperialist attacks of the nineteenth century.

Historians continue to study and debate the long-term effects of the slave traffic, and researchers are reluctant to make sweeping generalizations about its effects in West Africa where it peaked in about 1790 and was outlawed by the British in 1807. Though its ultimate inhumanity and cruelty must not be ignored, the slave trade also resulted in a new type of contact with the outside world that was not completely evil. The slave trade helped introduce new medicines and tools, and it has led to the development of new, constructively organized state systems. The introduction of crops from the Americas such as maize, cassava, pineapples, and coffee was also a result. Depopulation caused by the slave trade was in many instances more than offset by an increase in population made possible by the more productive crops and by the stability and security of centralized states like Asante. It was in fact not until the end of the slave trade in the nineteenth century, and the subsequent recession in the African economy, that Europeans began to attempt serious geographic exploration and political domination of Africa's interior.

Some historians feel, however, that the origins of modern western racism lie in the years of participation in this dehumanizing activity—that Europeans developed theories of the blacks' inferiority in order to justify their participation in the slave trade. If this is so, it is indeed the most tragic legacy the slave trade has left.

The peopling of South Africa. One area of Africa which remained almost completely unaffected by the trans-Saharan trade, Islamic expansion, and even Portuguese greed, was the southern tip of the continent, from the Limpopo River to the Cape of Good Hope. Here the Khoisan people continued their hunting and pastoral existence, as yet unaffected by the Bantu expansion. In 1652, however, the Dutch chose the Cape of Good Hope as a site for a colony to serve as a supply station for their ships to India. As the colony of white settlers expanded, they slowly overwhelmed the native Khoisan, most of whom died off. The Bantu expansion of central and eastern Africa continued through the years and by the seventeenth century had reached the southeastern tip of the African continent. As the Bantu turned west, they and the expanding Dutch settlers, called Boers, encountered each other for the first

time in numbers at the Fish River in 1736. Then began a competition for land and livelihood between Boer and Bantu.

The Bantu response to the new competition for land was to become more militant. The Zulu people particularly, under their great leader Shaka (1787–1828), organized their various clans into a strict military society. Males and females served in the army from puberty until they were released for marriage. The military unit, not the village, came to be the focus of identity and organization. The Zulu made fierce warfare on their fellow Bantu starting in the eighteenth century, driving enemies back north and sending a wave of violence, insecurity, and population pressure through East Africa. Yet their greatest enemy was the ever expanding Boer coming from the west. Caught between the Boers and the sea, the Zulu and other Bantu groups were defeated again and again by the Boers as all parties struggled for the land—a struggle that continues in less overt forms to this day (see Chapter 36).

Indigenous culture of black Africa. What can be said of the collective achievement of the African before the European impact? The extent of control over nature and technological development certainly varied greatly from place to place in Africa. Hundred-ton barges moved goods up and down the Niger River, and Swahili *dhows* (large sailing vessels) plied the eastern coast while reed canoes alone were used by fishermen on some of Africa's interior rivers and lakes. Large stone houses in Zimbabwe, arched palaces in Kilwa, and multistoried houses in Asante and Timbuktu contrasted sharply with small mud and thatch huts scattered across the savanna where poor farmers labored for their meager crops. Shifting hoe cultivation, growing crops on a plot for only two or three years and then leaving it fallow for ten or twenty, was practiced by most African farmers. Yet Ethiopians plowed their fields with oxen, and the Kikuyu farmers terraced and irrigated their lands. In some parts of Africa the poor clothed themselves at best with the skins of animals. But in many areas, particularly in the savanna where cotton was grown, thread was spun and elaborate designs were woven into beautiful and colorful cloth on large looms. Some towns even had municipal dye vats for the use of the inhabitants. Although some very remote areas of Africa still used only stone tools, metalworking was highly developed throughout most of the continent, and weapons, shields, bridles, even chain mail, as well as utensils, containers, money, and exact weights and measures were produced. Later the blacksmiths were able to produce guns and ammunition modeled after European imports.

The skilled workers of African societies often organized themselves into tightly knit groups which tried to keep the secrets of their skill within their own families. Men were not permitted near where women fired the pots they sold, and blacksmiths were such a secretive group that people often attributed magical abilities to them. The miners, weavers, masons, shipwrights, and tanners all guarded the knowledge of their skills, demanding a fair value for their labor. Strikes were not unknown to historical Africa.

The type of manufacturing and technology that developed indigenously in Africa is called cottage industry, and as such it was not able to compete with the mass manufacturing and industrialized techniques of the Europeans in the eighteenth and nineteenth centuries. African-made guns and iron hoes for example could not be produced as quickly or consistently as those from English foundries. African-produced brass and leather jewelry could not compete with the flood of European glass beads. Thus African technology is often ignored or denigrated, even though Europe herself did not progress beyond cottage industry until the seventeenth and eighteenth centuries. Europe's amazing development of industrialization is indeed its major contribution to the centuries-old interaction of European and African culture, and industrialization will continue to be the one aspect of European culture that Africans feel they must acquire.

African cultures, however, have much to offer westerners who wish to study them. African societies in their laws, governments, education, and codes of social conduct were complex and efficiently regulated long before the European impact. Rules and conventions regarding the role of parents, worship of gods, education of children, and laws concerning land occupation and possession of property were carefully worked out. Effective social methods were at hand to compel the individual to conform without often resorting to use of a police force.

In political organization the basic unit for many Africans was the ethnic group, consisting of many clans who recognized a chief but often only as the first among equals. Hundreds of these ethnic units, microscopic or large, still exist in Africa today. Yet one of the most fascinating aspects of African society is the vast variety of forms of political organization it had. The people of Zimbabwe had a semidivine king while the Zulus organized themselves into a military state. The East African cities developed independently around trade and profit, the names of their leaders in many cases being unimportant and forgotten. The empires of Ghana, Mali, and Songhai became more and more bureaucratically organized, and yet more vast in size, incorporating a variety of peoples and life-styles. Other groups like the Asante achieved a centralized bureaucratic state, compact in area, and compelled by a sense of nationhood. Dahomeans had strict, statewide economic planning, with an annual census in order to determine what the taxes would be, how much food should be planted, and how many people could become traders or soldiers. Moreover, in almost all these cases, the African rulers, be they chiefs or kings or merchants, were rarely despots. They had to govern within the framework of accepted law and custom and seek and obey the advice of their council of elders, the representatives of the people.

Religion played an essential role in African life, touching every phase of it. While religious practices varied from tribe to tribe, they shared some aspects in common. Animism, as traditional religion is sometimes called, centered around the belief that the dead depart from this life but continue to observe and influence it. One had an obligation to honor and remember one's dead relations regularly, such as when eating, and to appease them if they became angry. Most African societies also believed in some sort of supreme being or highest power, but this power was far removed from this world.

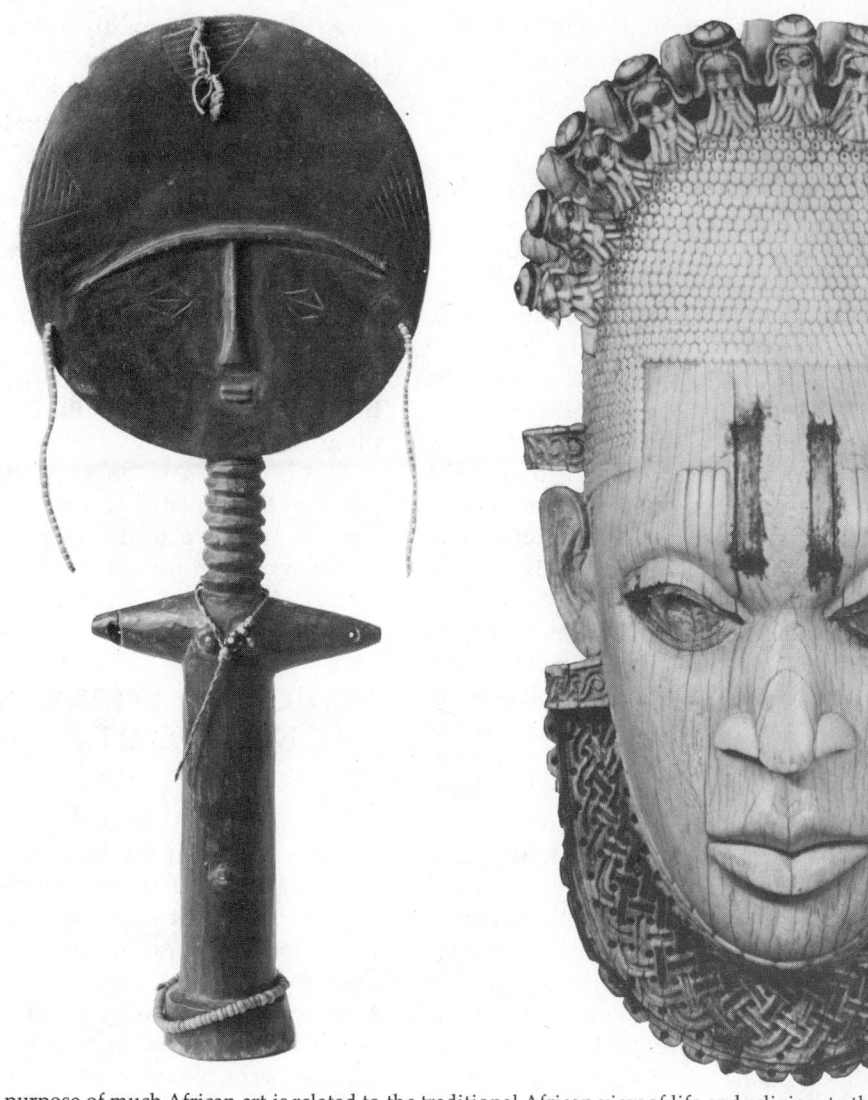

The purpose of much African art is related to the traditional African view of life and religion; to the powers and prejudices of the spirit world; and to symbolize the might and prestige of the kings and rulers. The doll from Asante (left) is carved of blackened wood; its round face is attached to a cylindrical body by a long neck. Fertility symbols such as these were carried by pregnant women and were considered to bring good luck and healthy children. The ivory mask of the king of Benin (right) was carved in the sixteenth century and features heads of Portuguese traders as its crown. It is thought to symbolize the divine kingship of its subject.

Rather, lesser spirits such as those of thunder or war or smallpox have the ability to affect directly such occurrences in life, and these gods must also be remembered and dealt with when necessary. The strict monotheism of Islam introduced another variation into the quite varied religious beliefs of Africans, at times conflicting with them, and at times converting them.

African arts are an integral part of African cultures and societies. They are not removed from life and hung in isolation in museums nor preserved under glass. African music, for example, is part of everyday life. African songs, much like western traditional folk songs, are about real-life situations: hunting, planting, cattle, love affairs, money, and famous heroes. Unlike the case of musical events in the western world where there are usually two parties—the artist and the audience, all Africans participate in the rendering of music. There are of course certain songs sung only on special occasions such as funerals, weddings, or coronations. Musicians were often kept at the courts of ancient kings such as in Mali and Axum to play whenever the king appeared. But on the whole African music is more communal than individual and audiences usually join in with clapping and dancing.

African visual art par excellence is sculpture. It is an ancient skill in Africa, with sculpted terra-cotta heads found in Nigeria dating to as early as 500 B.C. Sculpture is carved of wood, ivory, or soapstone, or cast in terra-cotta and bronze. Some of the bronze work has been compared to the best produced by Renaissance artists. A naturalistic bronze head found at the site of the ancient city of Ife in Nigeria, a forerunner of Benin, has been pronounced by art historians the finest surviving example of African art.

Sculpture often served a functional role too. For example, the kingdom of Benin not only created portraits of its kings and nobles but left a record of important events such as specific wars, alliances, good harvests, and the arrival of the Portuguese in plaques of bronze which were mounted on the walls of the oba's palace.

A rich body of folk tales and oral tradition attests to the artistry and imagination of Africans. Important literary and historical sources were produced written in Arabic, but not in the native languages. A perceptive reason for writing and studying history was given by the African historian es-Sadi of seventeenth-century Timbuktu in the preface to his Songhai *History of the Sudan:*

I saw the ruin of learning and its utter collapse and because learning is rich in beauty and fertile in its teaching, since it tells men of their fatherland, their ancestors, their annals, the names of their heroes and what lives these led, I asked divine help and decided to record all that I myself could gather on the subject of the Songhai princes of the Sudan, their adventures, their history, their achievements and their wars.[10]

African culture has indeed had a long tradition. While it would not compare materially with later European industrialization, and while it was uneven in development across the continent, it could boast outstanding sculpture, complicated and vital music, functional and well-organized political forms, prosperous commerce, crafts and cottage industry, and in some areas its own litera-

ture. Some tribes paid careful attention to family planning and population control. Capital punishment was rare, only the habitual murderer or thief being put to death. The rights of women—in relation to property, custody of children, and protection from abuse from the husband—were often more carefully spelled out than in western societies until very recent times. One of the most admirable traits of African society was the prevalence of the ideal of community. A built-in system of social security took care of the needy, the mentally ill, the old, the orphan, and the widow. Unlike the westerner with his emphasis on individual advance (often at the expense of the group), the African has always placed the group and family interests above his own.

OLD CIVILIZATIONS IN THE NEW WORLD

The earliest American immigrants. The question of when the Western Hemisphere was first settled remains uncertain. It is generally agreed that man did not originate in the Americas, for no bones of humans earlier than *Homo sapiens* have been found there. Man was already fully developed when he became the earliest immigrant to seek his fortune in the New World.

Making their way from Asia to Alaska via the Bering land bridge, nomadic groups spread out in various directions on the American continents. Until the 1920's it was thought that the Amerinds (American Indians) came to the Western Hemisphere as recently as three thousand years ago. The date of their arrival, however, has been progressively modified. Significant research in the 1960's has dated the Bering crossing as far back as 15,000 B.C. The most spectacular claim, not yet fully substantiated, is the discovery in central Mexico of crude tools dating back 40,000 years ago. It is apparent that the chronology of the Amerind migrations will be substantially rewritten in the near future.

The cultural levels achieved by different groups of Amerinds before the arrival of the

GULF OF MEXICO

PACIFIC

OCEAN

MEXICO

Tula
AZTEC
Teotihuacan
Tenochtitlán

Rio Las Balsas

Mayapán • Chichén Itzá
MAYA
Uxmal
YUCATAN
PENINSULA

BRITISH
HONDURAS
Tikal
MAYA
GUATEMALA HONDURAS
Copan

EL
SALVADOR NICARAGUA

COSTA RICA
PANAMA

**AZTEC AND MAYAN
CIVILIZATIONS**

Europeans varied. Most of the Indians of North America and of the Amazon region never progressed further than the Neolithic stage, with its dependence upon hunting, primitive agriculture, and village life. By contrast, the Mayas and the Aztecs in Mexico and Central America and the Incas in the Andes of Peru created advanced civilizations on a par with those which arose in Asia and the Near East. Perhaps the major reason for the more advanced cultures of the Mayas, Aztecs, and Incas was the efficient domestication of the all-important maize, or Indian corn, known as the "food of the gods." This former wild grass, skillfully bred into a basic crop, was capable of supporting large populations.

Unfortunately, we probably know less about these remarkable civilizations than about any great civilization of the Old World. In their fanatical zeal, many early Spanish *conquistadores* and missionaries destroyed libraries, dismantled cities, and suppressed as much of the native tradition as possible. The historical record of the Americas was damaged beyond repair.

The splendid culture of the Mayas. At its height, Mayan civilization was much more advanced than any other on the western continents. At least a thousand years before the birth of Christ, the Mayan Indians migrated into northern Central America. At the time that the Roman Empire and the classical civilization of the Mediterranean were collapsing, the Mayas had built wonderful cities in the southern part of their territory. Later, the

southern cities of what is called the Mayan classical period sank into decay, and the center of the Mayan civilization shifted northward to the Yucatán peninsula. From about 980 to 1200 a confederacy of independent city-states held sway; and during that period there occurred a splendid Mayan renaissance in architecture and art.

Within the city-states strict social stratification existed: the highest classes were the priests and nobles; below them were the farmers, craftsmen, and merchants; the last two levels included the lowest freemen and the slaves making up the bottom rank. The slaves performed the drudgery and heavy work; their lot was especially arduous, for until the arrival of the Spaniards there were no beasts of burden or wheeled vehicles in North and Central America.

Most of the populace labored in the fields surrounding the cities. The rich soil laid bare when the jungle was cleared away was made more productive by irrigation. The Mayas raised squash, pumpkins, chili peppers, and many grains and vegetables. But maize—the mainstay of their civilization—was the chief crop, supplying 80 percent of their food.

Religion permeated all phases of Mayan life. Dominated by a powerful priesthood, the government was a form of theocracy. Education was concerned primarily with religion, and reading and writing were the private domain of the clergy. The numerous gods of the Mayas were divided into three general groups: the deities of the sky, the earth, and the underworld. To maintain an accurate schedule of religious observances, which were intimately linked to their agricultural way of life, the Mayas constructed a calendar which approaches our own in accuracy. They also built several observatories, which were run by the priests; exactness in astronomical calculations was possible because of the excellent numerical system the Mayas devised.

Of all the Amerinds, the Mayas came the closest to developing an efficient system of writing. They used an advanced system of pictographs rather than alphabetic letters or

Tikal, located in what is now northern Guatemala, is the oldest and one of the largest of the Mayan temple centers. The Mayas lived close to their fields and only came to their cities for religious ceremonies and to work on necessary construction.

a syllabic system, but no Rosetta Stone has yet been discovered to give us a key to the hieroglyphics which adorned their monuments, buildings, jewelry, pottery, and books.

In architecture and sculpture the Mayas produced work of the highest quality. In the plaza of a Mayan city was a terraced mound or pyramid, topped by a temple. The highly stylized sculpture which decorated the temple terraces is regarded by some art experts as among the world's best, despite the fact that Mayan sculptors did their intricate carving without the aid of anything better than stone tools. Almost completely religious in inspiration, Mayan art depicted the deities and the animals connected with them—snakes, frogs, jaguars, and hummingbirds. Minor arts such as weaving, jade sculpture, ceramics, and gold and silver work were also highly developed and showed an extremely sophisticated sense of design which compares favorably with the best of Egyptian art.

Eventually the Mayan cities fell victim to internal strife, in which petty chieftains fought for supremacy. In addition to civil war, inroads were made by Toltec and Aztec invaders, who eventually conquered the Mayas. After the conquest, the Mayan population and culture declined. When the *conquistadores* came upon the scene, the country was in chaos; and the Spaniards found it a simple matter to subdue the Mayan peoples.

The warlike Aztecs. In the early centuries A.D. the peoples of the Mexican plateau were also advancing in civilization. They built cities, pyramids, and temples, which can be seen at Teotihuacán, near Mexico City. As warlike peoples came in from the north, empires arose, for example, the Toltec empire. The last and best known migrants, the Aztecs, entered central Mexico and, about 1325, founded a lake settlement called Tenochtitlán on the site of the present Mexico City. Then, allying themselves with other Mexican Indian tribes, they created a confederacy which in the fifteenth century ruled an area extending across Mexico from the Gulf of Mexico to the Pacific Ocean. Like the ancient Assyrians, the Aztecs glorified war, maintained a superb fighting force, and plundered the lands of their neighbors.

Dominating the one-quarter-square-mile Great Temple precinct in the Aztecs' capital city of Tenochtitlán was the huge double pyramid sacred to Uitzilopochtli, sun god and god of war, and Tlaloc, the rain god. The precinct was separated by a "serpent wall" and a moat from the rest of the city.

However, Aztec power lasted less than a century, for the arrival of Cortés in 1519 brought about its collapse.

Scholars have held different opinions concerning the Aztec form of government. Earlier writers looked upon it as an empire, ruled by an absolute king. Many historians today feel that the Aztec government was essentially a democracy. In Aztec society the main controller of rank was ability. As in our own society, a man could rise to any position if he had the requisite ability. Thus, through personal talent and initiative, a craftsman or farmer might become a priest or a member of the tribal council. Among the soldiers, rank was determined mainly by success in war. Chiefs were elected from powerful families and could be removed; sons or brothers of chieftains succeeded them only if they were capable.

While the Aztecs worshiped a pantheon of gods, their devotion to the sun was particularly important and unusually barbaric. In every city of their domain, great pyramids were built, topped by temples to the sun and rain. There, stone altars were set up, on which thousands of people were sacrificed to Uitzilopochtli, the god of war and the sun. Victims included men, women, and children, who were stretched out on a sacrificial stone where the priests tore out their hearts as offerings to the god. Aztec military superiority assured a large number of captives for these sacrifices.

Like the Romans, the Aztecs borrowed many aspects of their culture from their predecessors or captives. In fact, a fair analogy may be drawn between the Mayas and Aztecs in the New World and the ancient Greeks and Romans. Generally speaking, the Mayas were more artistic and intellectual than the Aztecs and remind us somewhat of the Greeks. The brusque and brutal characteristics of the Aztecs can be likened to the

A natural fortress, Machu Picchu was built by the Incas probably after 1440 on a narrow ridge between two mountain peaks. It appears to have been the residence and stronghold of the last Incan ruler after the Spanish conquest had begun. When the ruler died, the city was abandoned and lost until it was rediscovered in 1911.

tendencies which the Romans sometimes displayed.

The Incas. About the eleventh century some people known as Incas (children of the sun) settled in the heartland of the Andes. Some archaeologists believe that they wandered northward from the Lake Titicaca region until they came to the valley of Cuzco. From there they began to extend their dominion over the mountain peoples and the coastal dwellers. From 1438 until the arrival of the *conquistador* Pizarro in 1532, a vast Inca empire flourished, extending for about 2700 miles along the western coast of the continent and including an estimated population of ten million at the time of the Spanish conquest. Even today the bulk of the peoples on the Peruvian coast and in the highlands are descended from Inca stock.

The Inca form of government was a hereditary absolute monarchy, ruled by a king called the Inca, who exercised the power of life and death over his subjects. Actually, it was a true theocracy, for the people were sun worshipers who believed that the Inca was an offspring of the sun.

The power of the ruler depended largely on an excellent military organization based on compulsory and universal military training. Another source of power was control by the Inca of all the food throughout the empire. If any district produced more than it needed, he had the surplus stored for future use or transferred to a district which through drought or other misfortunes had failed to produce enough food.

The absolute control which the Inca exercised over his subjects made possible the magnificent construction projects in the empire. Immense slabs carved out of the mountain sides were trimmed at the quarry to fit exactly into a specific niche in a temple or fortress wall; no mortar was used by the Incas. Despite their lack of wheeled vehicles, the Incas transported the giant blocks for miles through the mountains. A splendid system of roads and trails radiated from Cuzco to every part of the Inca realm.

Why did the wealthy, powerful Inca and Aztec empires fall so easily before a handful of European conquerors during the sixteenth century? A primary reason is that both the great Indian empires of the Western Hemispheres were weakened by internal strife; the tribes ruled by the Incas and the Aztecs were restive under the control of their conquerors. Thus the Spanish with their firearms—weapons completely unknown to the Indians—were able to hasten a process of political dissolution perhaps already under way.

SUMMARY

Most of the Indians of North America never achieved what is usually called "civilization," but in Mexico and Central and South America a number of brilliant civilizations emerged—those of the Aztecs, Mayas, and Incas. The Aztecs have been compared to the Romans; they were practical, martial people, skillful at conquest and at governing subject peoples. By contrast, the Mayas have been likened to the Greeks; they were great builders and artists, and they were also scholars and scientists who invented a remarkable calendar, studied astronomy, and pursued mathematics. Of all the Indian nations of the Americas, the Incas should be remembered for developing one of the first totalitarian states in history.

During the many centuries covered by this volume, little has been seen of Africa south of the Sahara. This vast region lay on the periphery of great world movements; therefore much of African history was unknown and the achievements of its people usually dismissed as inconsequential. A more accurate evaluation, however, has developed in recent times. The continent of Africa has several different ecological regions. In the north and south are narrow regions of fertile coast. Farther inland are deserts—the Sahara and the

Kalahari. The deserts of Africa merge into large regions of savanna where populations have prospered because of the farming and pastoralism that are possible there. In the west-central section of the continent is the rain forest. The rivers of Africa connect the villages and cities and are a means for transporting goods for trade.

Throughout the centuries many great empires have risen and fallen. One of the earliest ironworking centers in Africa gave rise to the ancient kingdom of Kush. Axum was another rich empire that existed at this time and even supplanted Kush in its wealth and greatness. Ancient Ghana, Mali, and Songhai were three wealthy empires in the western savanna that existed from the ninth to the sixteenth centuries. They were based on the gold and salt trade across the Sahara, and their armies and governments controlled large areas. Their cities, such as Timbuktu, became centers of scholarship. From the seventh through the fourteenth centuries, trading ships from Arabia, India, and China carried on much trade with the East African coast. Thriving city-states grew there until the Portuguese destroyed much of the East African trade after 1500. Another great state that developed in the East African interior was Zimbabwe. The extensive ruins of large stone buildings are evidence of the power and wealth of this kingdom. Forest states, such as Benin, Dahomey, and Asante developed in conjunction with the arrival of the Europeans in search of trade and slaves. However, the slave trade did much damage to many African communities until it ended in the nineteenth century.

Throughout its long history, Africa has always maintained its own unique culture. Its sculpture, for instance, follows complex traditions and is comparable to the best work produced by European artists (see Color Plate 17). In recent decades, scholars, recognizing that Africans may not have attained the technological and industrial achievements of Europeans and Asians, have nevertheless pointed out the Africans' significant advances in social and political organization and in the arts.

SUGGESTIONS FOR READING

Basil Davidson, **Africa: History of a Continent** (Macmillan, 1972) is a superbly illustrated survey. E. J. Murphy, **History of African Civilization*** (Dell, 1974) is a good introductory general history of precolonial Africa. See also Harry A. Gailey, **History of Africa: From Earliest Times to 1800*** (Holt, Rinehart and Winston, 1970); and Robert July, **A History of the African People,** rev. ed. (Scribner's, 1974), two widely used surveys.

Margaret Shinnie, **Ancient African Kingdoms*** (St. Martin's, 1965) covers the early period of African history, discussing and illustrating archaeological findings. Easily read histories by regions are: Basil Davidson, **History of West Africa*** (Doubleday, 1966); and **History of East and Central Africa*** (Doubleday, 1969). See also Derek Wilson, **A History of South and Central Africa*** (Cambridge, 1975).

For additional facets of African history see J. D. Fage and R. A. Oliver, eds., **Papers in African Prehistory*** (Cambridge, 1970); Philip Curtin, ed., **Africa Remembered: Narratives by West Africans from the Era of the Slave Trade*** (Wisconsin, 1968). Other topics of interest are R. Oliver and C. Oliver, **Africa in the Days of Exploration*** (Prentice-Hall); F. Willett, **African Art: An Introduction*** (Praeger, 1971); and J. Maquet, **Civilizations of Black Africa*** (Oxford, 1972).

J. D. Fage, ed., **Africa Discovers Her Past*** (Oxford, 1970) contains essays evaluating new approaches to African history. Basil Davidson, **The African Genius: An Introduction to Social and Cultural History** (Little, Brown, 1970) is a sympathetic and scholarly analysis of indigenous cultures.

S. G. Morley, **The Ancient Maya** (Stanford) is the best general survey. V. W. von Hagen, **The World of the Maya*** (Mentor) is a brief survey.

F. Peterson, **Ancient Mexico*** (Capricorn) is a valuable account. Brief, lucid surveys of Aztec civilization are V. W. von Hagen, **Aztec: Man and Tribe*** (Mentor); and G. C. Vaillant, **The Aztecs of Mexico*** (Penguin). See also A. Caso, **Aztecs, People of the Sun** (Oklahoma Pr., 1970), a lavishly illustrated work; R. McC. Adams, **The Evolution of Urban Society: Early Mesopotamia and Prehispanic Mexico** (Aldine, 1966); and J. Soustelle, **Daily Life of the Aztecs on the Eve of the Spanish Conquest*** (Stanford).

J. A. Mason, **Ancient Civilization of Peru*** (Peter Smith) is an anthropological history of the culture and peoples of pre-Columbian Peru. See also V. W. von Hagen, **Realm of the Incas*** (Mentor); and B. Flornoy, **The World of the Inca*** (Anchor), a scholarly account of the Inca empire at its height.

*Indicates a less expensive paperbound edition.

This is the profile of a representative family of the influential *pochteca* class, merchants in charge of foreign trade who also played a strategic political role in Aztec society. The family lived at Tlaltelolco, the center of Mexico's commercial institutions. The time is 1519, immediately prior to the arrival of the Spaniards under Cortés.

Acamapichtli is restless and unable to sleep. Too much spiced iguana? Or is it tomorrow's festivities, in which the family will celebrate both Atototl's marriage and his own birthday? His daughter seems happy, and the young man's prospects are excellent. But the household won't be the same, and besides, birthdays make Acamapichtli pensive. He's getting old — 44 tomorrow — and still no grandchildren. What lies ahead for his family and himself?

From his second-story bedroom, he can see in the moonlight across much of Tlaltelolco to the twin city of Tenochtitlán. These two centers occupy a square of some 2500 acres on Lake Texcoco. Two centuries of labor have transformed the area into a network of raised earthworks and canals, and urban life is organized around the two principal centers, each possessing its pyramidal temple and square, together with palaces, residential districts, and government buildings. From the platform atop the 114-step pyramid at Tlaltelolco one can see the aqueduct bringing fresh water from Chapultepec as well as the causeways leading to the island capital. One axis runs from Tlaltelolco to the great temple at Tenochtitlán, and the capital's principal thoroughfares are wide and straight. Half of each street is surfaced with beaten earth, while the other half is occupied by a canal, along which ply boats and barges. Every day a thousand men clean the streets of the capital.

Acamapichtli belongs to an increasingly important class, the Pochteca, traveling merchants comprising a hereditary guild with its own gods, judges, and privileges. A level below the ruling class of chief priests, soldiers, and civil servants, the Pochteca were preoccupied not with prestige but with the power that wealth creates. Their essential role derived from the way that towns had developed — each specialized in certain goods, such as metalwork, woven cloth, and pottery; trade was regularly carried on between centers hundreds of miles apart. It was the Pochteca who organized and led the caravans of porters which journeyed from the central valley of Mexico to remote areas on the Pacific and Gulf coasts.

They bought and sold throughout the Aztec possessions and even beyond, exchanging the manufactured goods of the capital — embroidered clothes, golden jewels, and rabbit-hair blankets — for such luxury items as jade, amber, jaguar skins, and exotic plumes. Valuable as these exchanges were, however, they accounted only partly for the Pochteca's strategic role. Aztec rule had been created by conquest, and it existed by virtue of tribute levied on the conquered provinces. They had to provide annual taxes in the form of raw materials: gold discs and gold dust or vast amounts of cotton, corn, cacao, and rubber. This tribute was borne to the capital on the shoulders of porters led by the Pochteca.

These traders lived in their own urban districts — the most important was at Tlaltelolco, which had the largest marketplace in Mexico. There Acamapichtli felt secure in his wealth and status. He was a guild officer and no longer traveled himself, but supplied the younger traders with their material. He helped supervise the departure of the caravans and presided over the ceremonies on their return, represented the guild before the emperor, and served in the guild's own law courts.

Acamapichtli thought of his son who was already justifying his birth name, Quauhtlatoa (speaking eagle). As a young trading merchant, he had proved adept in learning the language of distant, and often hostile, tribes and had led caravans that were no less political than mercantile in their objectives. Quauhtlatoa and his young associates led a life of high adventure, spearheading alike the commercial and strategic campaigns of the state. Commerce preceded conquest, and the traveling Pochteca acted as spies, reporting on the strengths and weaknesses of still unconquered tribes, and even stirring up trouble so that the emperor could become "personally insulted" and undertake reprisals that culminated in territorial gains. Quauhtlatoa had quickly proved his ability as both merchant and warrior. On his second expedition to the north, he had personally captured three prisoners and had been present at the temple at Tlaltelolco when they were sacrificed to Yacatecutli, the god of commerce and merchants. He had thus proved his manhood and soon claimed his right of marriage which took place when he was twenty-two to the daughter of another merchant.

All Aztec children were entitled to an education, but the Pochteca were also allowed to send their male offspring to either the *calmecal* or *telpochcalli* type of school. One of Quauhtlatoa's cousins had shown a scholarly disposition and had gone to the *calmecal*. By its severe standards, requiring continuous fasts, penances, working on the temple's lands, and drawing blood from one's own ears and legs to sacrifice with incense to the gods, the *calmecal* prepared its students for the highest offices of state and the priesthood. Much less austere had been Quauhtlatoa's education at the *telpochcalli*, "the house of the young men." They had for their masters, not priests, but experienced warriors. Here they concentrated on learning the arts of warfare. As a student at the shool. Quauhtlatoa enjoyed a communal existence, enlivened by dancing and songs, and by the company of young women, the *auianime*, officially provided courtesans. Among his other amusements were *tlachtli*, the ancient Mexican ballgame played on courts marked by two carved stone rings on their side walls; *patolli*, a dice game where he could indulge the national passion for gambling; and hunting, for which his trading expeditions into the hinterland offered him scope. To other peoples, the Aztecs could give the impression of excessive zeal in warfare and atonement by human sacrifice, yet in personal behavior they instilled the virtues of restraint in manners, dress, and deportment and the sanctity of family life. So from childhood, Quauhtlatoa had been warned against alcoholic excesses and the stringent laws against public drunkenness. Similarly, he knew that not even the highest dignitaries would escape the punishment of death for both parties caught in adultery.

Acamapichtli's thoughts now returned to his daughter and tomorrow's wedding. He had always indulged her, and for good reason. As a little girl she had been bright and shown an aptitude for spinning, and subsequently had learned to spin cotton, grind corn efficiently, and use the loom to weave cloth of superior quality. Like other girls of her class, Atototl had been consecrated to the temple when young and for several years had stayed there for instruction from the elderly priestesses. She had become expert in making intricately embroidered materials and temple vestments, took part in the rituals, and offered incense to the gods several times a night. Prior to her marriage Atototl had little or no contact with the opposite sex. But now her girlhood was at an end—tomorrow a complicated marriage ceremony involving the two families and lasting some five days would begin. At its conclusion, she would enter into her full status in Aztec society: wife, mother, matron attending the many ceremonies open to her, matchmaker—and, when old, free to make speeches at the family feasts, as befits a society which honors longevity in both sexes.

The moonlit waters of the lake of Texcoco stretch eastward into darkness. Acamapichtli compares the gleaming temple to his left with its pyramidal twin in Tenochtitlán, their tops glowing from the ever-tended hearths. From them come the roll of drums and the piercing cries of the conches to mark yet another of the nine divisions of the day. While the priests are casting incense into the hearths and intoning their prayers, perhaps the emperor himself has risen in the palace to offer his own blood in the darkness. For the Aztecs are the "people of the sun"—and when the world was created, the sun itself was born from sacrifice and blood. In order to move, it required blood, and so some of the gods immolated themselves to provide the solar deity with the life to begin his course across the sky. Humanity had assumed the role of the gods. To keep the sun moving and prevent the darkness from overwhelming the world forever, they must provide their god every day with "the precious water" (*chalchiuatl*)—human blood. By means of this alchemy, the disaster that always threatened to engulf the cosmos could be averted for yet another day. Again the drums roll and the conches call from the temples. Humanity has come safely through the night and dawn is breaking. The state will endure. Acamapichtli can celebrate his birthday and Atototl's wedding.

CHAPTER 18

Exploration and
Colonization: 1450-1650;
The Commercial Revolution:
1450-1750

Seek Out, Discover, and Find

INTRODUCTION. One of the most potent forces molding modern world history was the thrust of European political power, commerce, and culture over the globe. Before 1500 the people of Europe existed largely on their own resources, supplemented by a slender trade with Africa and Asia. But within the next 150 years the picture was dramatically altered through the discoveries of new continents and trade routes. The riches of the entire world were funneled into Europe's economy, and the horizons of Europe's people were immensely widened—socially and intellectually as well as geographically. The discovery of hitherto unknown and unsuspected parts of the globe was probably more revolutionary than the space explorations of our own day.

Who wrought this miracle? First, there were the sea captains—da Gama, who made the first ocean voyage from Europe to India; Columbus, who introduced Europe to a New World; and Magellan, whose expedition ventured ever westward until its weary survivors had sailed completely around the world and dropped anchor once more in their home port. Close on the heels of such captains came the *conquistadores*—the "conquerors"—resourceful and ruthless soldiers like Cortés and Pizarro, who laid the foundations for a vast European empire by overwhelming flourishing native cultures in the New World.

Then came the task of exploiting what had been found and won. The European powers took advantage of the claims of their discoverers and explorers in one of two basic ways—through trade or by colonization. In Africa and Asia the emphasis was on trade; Europeans carried on their business from forts, acting as foreign merchants rather than as settlers. While in Africa their dealings were mostly with tribal peoples, in the Far East they faced venerable civilizations and urban cultures. There, they were the barbarians, and when their activities proved offensive by native standards, reprisals could be swift and severe.

The story of European expansion in the New World, on the other hand, is largely that of colonization, of the transplanting of European civilization to a new and exotic environment. Politically, the territories in the Americas were treated as extensions of the mother countries. The Spanish colonies, for example, were ruled directly by the king of Spain; the colonial economy was geared to

supplement that of the homeland; and the Spanish priests set out to bring the Indians into the spiritual fold with their Spanish masters. Similarly, the English and French who settled in North America brought with them the economic, political, and social institutions they had known at home.

For the native peoples of the New World, the arrival of the Europeans was cataclysmic. And the impact of the New World on the Old, while obviously quite different, was no less significant. As new stores of wealth were tapped by the immensely lucrative transatlantic trade, Europe's economic center of gravity shifted from the Mediterranean to the Atlantic seaboard; and the rapid influx of gold and silver made possible an unprecedented expansion of the economy. Nor was the revolution confined to economics: new medicines, foods, and beverages became available to Europeans, and even styles of dress were altered. Thus a handful of adventurers, ranging beyond the horizon in quest of El Dorado, the legendary city of gold which symbolized their hopes and dreams, set in motion a train of events which brought significant changes to European society and which ultimately influenced the very history of civilization.

CAPTAINS AND CONQUISTADORES

Medieval maps and adventurers. Early medieval maps were curiosities rather than documents of fact. They included lands which no man had ever seen; the oceans were shown abounding in sea dragons, while drawings of elephants and more fanciful animals were used to fill up empty land spaces, thereby adding to the picturesqueness of the map as well as conveniently concealing the ignorance of the map maker. Arabic works on astronomy and geography, acquired in the thirteenth century, proved that the earth was a sphere and greatly expanded geographical knowledge. Of greatest significance for the development of scientific geography, however, was the recovery in 1409 of Claudius Ptolemy's *Geography* (see

p. 87) with its elaborate map of the world. Although this second-century work added greatly to current knowledge, it contained a number of errors, two of which encouraged Columbus and other fifteenth-century explorers to sail boldly across the uncharted oceans. Ptolemy exaggerated the size of the known continents so that the distance between western Europe and eastern Asia appeared much smaller than it really is, and he underestimated the circumference of the world by five thousand miles.

Medieval adventurers also contributed to geographical knowledge, much of which influenced Columbus and his fellow explorers. The earliest prime examples were the Norsemen, who reached Iceland in the last half of

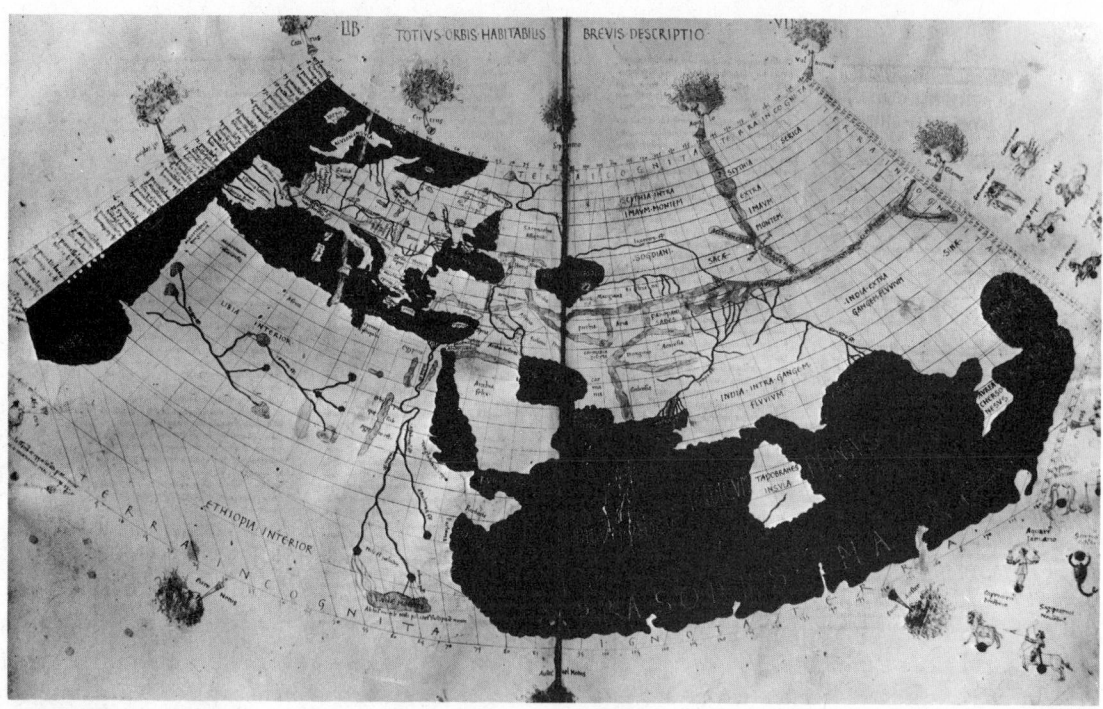

This map, published in the fifteenth century but based on one designed by Ptolemy in the second century, represents the first attempt to project the curved surface of the earth on a flat surface. The outline of the European continent (upper left) is fairly accurate.

the ninth century (see p. 195). In about 982 Eric the Red, son of a Norwegian noble, was banished from the Norse settlements in Iceland and sailed west to Greenland, which may have been discovered earlier in the century by Celtic refugees from Ireland, fleeing Viking raids on their homeland. Eric founded two settlements on the western coast of Greenland, which existed until about 1500 when they mysteriously vanished. It now appears that the first European to set foot on the North American coast was Bjarni Herjolfson. In 985 Bjarni was blown off course while sailing from Iceland to Greenland and made a landfall in Newfoundland. About fifteen years later Leif, son of Eric the Red, retraced Bjarni's route and named the country *Vinland* (Wineland) because of its wooded, vine-covered shore. A number of other voyages were made to Vinland, whose lumber was highly prized in treeless Greenland. Apparently no permanent settlement was made in Vinland, although archaeologists have recently discovered what appears to be the remains of a Viking camp in New-

foundland at L'Anse au Meadow.[1] But monumental as these voyages were, their implication were lost on contemporary Europeans, and they added little or nothing to European knowledge of geography.

In the thirteenth and fourteenth centuries a number of Europeans, many of them Christian missionaries, journeyed overland to the Far East. The most famous of these travelers was Marco Polo (see p. 180). But these exploits had little permanent effect because of political changes in Asia in the last decades of the fourteenth century. The Mongol dynasty in China, which had been friendly to European missionaries and merchants, was overthrown, and the succeeding Ming rulers proved anti-Christian. Meanwhile, the belligerent heathen Turks stood astride the eastern Mediterranean. These two developments put an end to further European penetration into the Orient, although trade continued at certain terminals controlled by the Muslims.

The search for new routes. The three major routes by which trade flowed from the

Far East to Europe had existed since Roman times (see map, p. 116). The northern one cut across Central Asia and the Caspian and Black seas to Constantinople (Byzantium); the middle route went by sea along the coasts of India and Persia through the Persian Gulf and the Euphrates valley to Antioch; and the southern route utilized the monsoon winds to strike across the Indian Ocean and up the Red Sea to Alexandria in Egypt. During the fifteenth century the commerce that flowed westward to Europe was rich indeed, even though the expansion of the Turks greatly reduced the importance of the northern route across Asia. The most important imports into Europe were spices—pepper, cinnamon, nutmeg, ginger, and cloves—highly valued as condiments and preservatives for food. Also in great demand were Chinese silk, Indian cotton cloth, and various precious stones.

The Mediterranean carrying trade in oriental goods was in the hands of Venice and other Italian city-states, which wielded an extensive and lucrative monopoly. Since the Arabs held a similar monopoly east of the Mediterranean, oriental goods were sold in the West at many times their price in India. As the demand for the products of the East increased during the latter half of the fifteenth century, the rulers of the new nations of western Europe became aware that an adverse balance of trade was draining their coined money away to Italy and the East. They determined to find new trade routes of their own, and, as rulers of powerful nation-states, they had the resources to support the stupendous feats of discovery and conquest that were needed.

Prince Henry the Navigator. It was the Portuguese who spearheaded the drive to find oceanic routes that would provide cheaper and easier access to oriental products. The man who set in motion the brilliant Portuguese achievements in exploration and discovery was Prince Henry the Navigator (1394-1460), whose original goal was to tap at its source the gold of Guinea and the African Gold Coast (see Reference Map 6), which came to Europe through Muslim middlemen (see illustration p. 368).

Henry employed skilled cartographers and navigators to construct accurate maps, and under his direction the caravel, the finest vessel afloat for long voyages, was developed. By utilizing the lateen rig, the triangular sail developed by the Arabs, the caravel revolutionized sailing by being able to tack into the wind. Augmenting Henry's innovations were other navigation aids. In the twelfth century the Europeans set their course with the aid of a magnetic needle floating on a straw in a bowl of water. By the time Henry's sailors were setting sail, the compass consisted of a needle which pivoted on a card showing the points of the compass. During the fifteenth century another great aid to navigation came into general use— the astrolabe, a graduated brass circle by which the altitude of stars could be estimated and latitudes more accurately measured.

The African voyages. Although Henry died before any of the numerous expeditions he sent forth had explored the entire length of Africa, his mariners did not fail him. In 1488 Bartholomew Diaz rounded the southern tip of Africa, from which point he noticed that the coast swung northeast. But his disgruntled crew forced him to turn back. Pleased with the prospect of soon finding a direct sea route to India, King John II of Portugal named the great cape rounded by Diaz "Cape of Good Hope."

Vasco da Gama commanded the first Portuguese fleet to reach India. Three ships left Lisbon in 1497 and, after rounding the Cape, crossed the Indian Ocean to Calicut in twenty-three days. The Arab merchants in Calicut sought to preserve their trading monopoly by delaying the return voyage, and it was not until 1499 that da Gama dropped anchor in Lisbon. He had lost two of his ships and one third of his men through scurvy and other misfortunes, but his one cargo of pepper and cinnamon was worth sixty times the cost of the expedition.

Lured by such fantastic profits another expedition set sail the following year and established a permanent base south of Calicut at Cochin. The Portuguese soon acquired a monopoly over trade in the Indian Ocean, and by 1516 their ships had reached Canton in China. The king of Portugal assumed the impressive title "Lord of the Conquest,

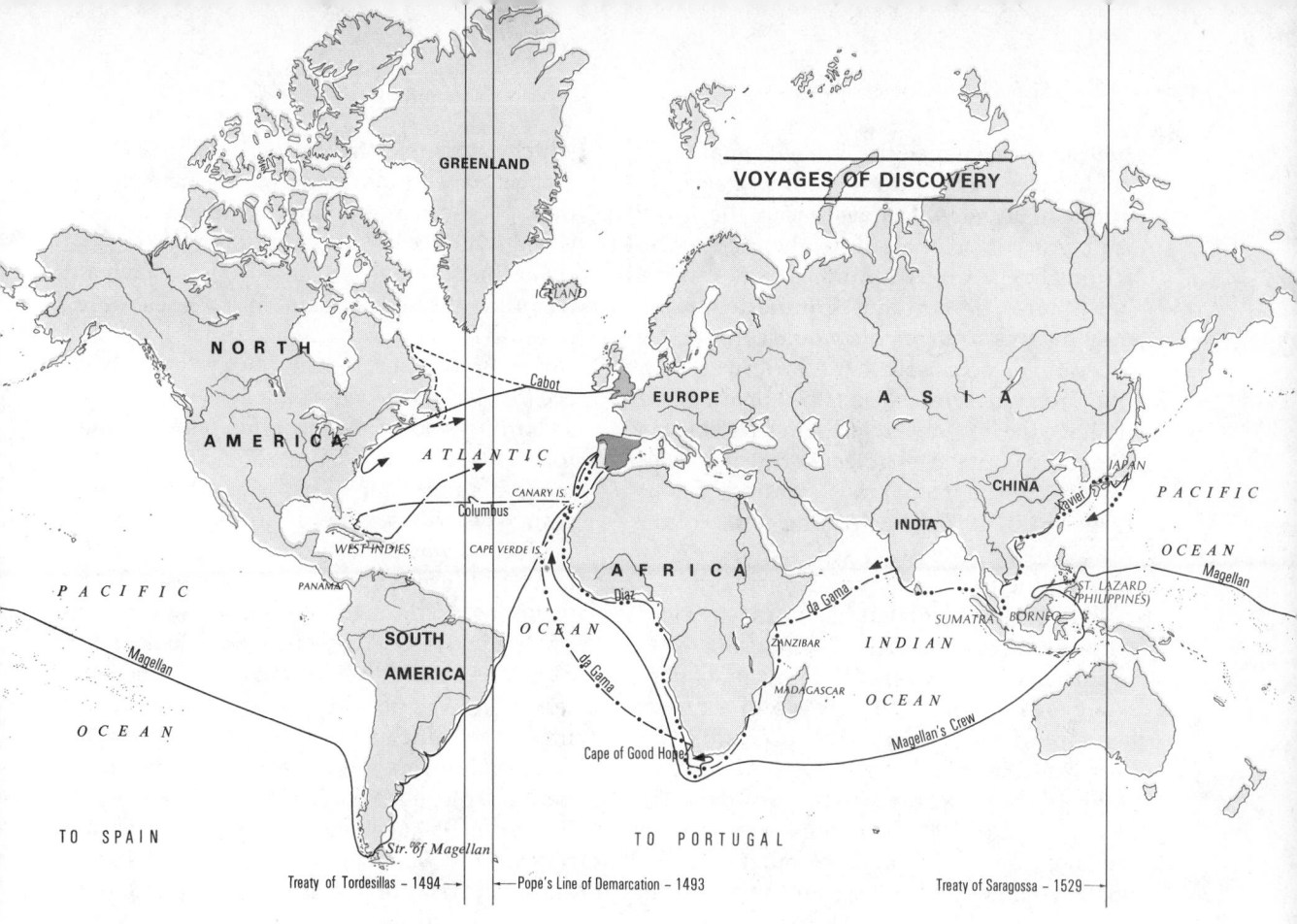

Navigation, and Commerce of Ethiopia, Arabia, Persia, and China."

Columbus discovers the New World. Meanwhile, Spanish ambitions for riches and prestige were realized through the exploits of a Genoese sailor named Christopher Columbus (1451?-1506). Influenced by Marco Polo's overestimate of the length of Asia and Ptolemy's underestimate of the size of the world, Columbus believed that Japan was less than 3000 miles from Europe (the actual distance is 10,600 nautical miles) and that it could be reached in one or two months by sailing westward. He tried unsuccessfully to interest the rulers of Portugal, England, and France in his enterprise before Queen Isabella of Castile agreed to sponsor his voyage. On August 3, 1492, Columbus set sail from Spain with three small ships and ninety men. On October 12 he landed on a small island in the West Indies. After he returned to Spain, Columbus announced that he had found the route to Asia, and the Spanish monarchs proclaimed him "Admiral of the

Ocean Sea, Viceroy and Governor of the Islands that he has discovered in the Indies."

Even after da Gama's voyage had opened up the eastward route to India, Columbus steadfastly refused to acknowledge that what he himself had discovered was in fact a massive obstacle on the route to the Far East. Although he made three more voyages to the New World in a vain attempt to find a direct opening to the Asian mainland, Columbus had already changed the course of history, though he did not know it. A New World had been revealed; old geographical views had been shattered; and the entire history of Europe was soon to be affected by the discovery of the new lands.

Spain and Portugal divide the new lands. An immediate repercussion of Columbus' first voyage was the destruction of Portugal's monopoly over discovery. Some sort of compromise had to be worked out between the two countries, and the Spanish monarchs invited the pope to define the pagan areas which Spain and Portugal might claim. In

1493 the pope issued the Bull of Demarcation, which drew a line from north to south running one hundred leagues west of the Azores and proclaimed that all heathen lands west of this line as far as the Indies were reserved for Spain. The Portuguese protested, claiming that this arrangement would confine their operations too closely to the African coast. By the Treaty of Tordesillas (1494) Spain agreed to have the line moved farther west. This new demarcation later enabled Portugal to claim Brazil after Pedro Cabral's sighting of South America in 1500 while sailing to the Indies. In 1529 another treaty fixed a similar demarcation line in the Eastern Hemisphere.

Balboa and Magellan. The search for riches drove the Spaniards to organize many expeditions to chart the coastlines and to penetrate the interior of the New World. One such enterprise was particularly successful. Having heard from Indians of a vast ocean only a short distance to the west, Vasco de Balboa led a band of 190 Spaniards across the Isthmus of Panama. On September 25, 1513, Balboa climbed to the summit of a hill from

The Spanish troops, aided by Indian allies, storm the main gate of Tenochtitlán in this illustration from a sixteenth-century Aztec manuscript.

which he beheld the Pacific Ocean—and in that act paved the way for European exploration of the largest single portion of the world's surface.

Ferdinand Magellan, a Portuguese navigator in the service of Spain, found a sea route into the Pacific. Encouraged by Balboa's discovery of the short distance between the two oceans, Magellan believed it was possible to sail around South America just as Diaz had rounded Africa. In August 1520 Magellan made his memorable discovery of the strait which bears his name. His five small ships made their way between huge ice-clad mountains and through tortuous passages. After a terrifying thirty-eight days they sailed out upon the western ocean, which looked so calm after the stormy straits that Magellan termed it "Pacific." Then followed a harrowing ninety-nine day voyage across the Pacific to Guam, during which rats had to be eaten for food. Magellan was slain by natives in the Philippine Islands, and only one of his ships returned to Spain in 1522 by way of India and the Cape of Good Hope. Its cargo of spices paid for the cost of the entire expedition. Magellan's tiny vessel had taken three years to circumnavigate the world, but henceforth no one could doubt that the earth was round and that the Americas constituted a New World.

Cortés conquers Mexico. While the Portuguese soon profited from their hold on the rich oriental trade, the Spaniards found that the islands and coasts of the New World did not immediately produce the harvest of riches which they had eagerly sought. Such wealth was not to be found along the seashore but in the unknown hinterland, where rich indigenous cultures flourished. Penetration of inland areas was the work of the *conquistadores*, the courageous but independent-minded and often brutal conquerors who looted whole native empires and planted the Spanish flag from California to the tip of South America.

In the same year that Magellan set forth (1519), the Spanish governor of Cuba dispatched Hernando Cortés on an expedition to Mexico, from which had come rumors of a great Aztec empire, flowing with gold. Montezuma, ruler of the Aztecs, had thousands of warriors, while Cortés had about six hundred men. But the Spaniards were equipped with horses, armor, and gunpowder, all unknown to the Aztecs. Two other factors aided the Europeans: the discontent of many subject tribes, which looked for a chance to break the Aztec rule; and an ancient Mexican legend which prophesied that the Aztecs would one day be conquered by the white-skinned descendants of an ancient god-king who had been repudiated by their ancestors.

Having made the fateful decision to march inland on the Aztec capital, Tenochtitlán, Cortés destroyed his ships to prevent his men from turning back. Crossing the coast lands and the mountains, the Spaniards entered the valley of Mexico. Cortés treacherously made a virtual prisoner of Montezuma and through his cooperation ruled peacefully until a popular uprising gave the Spaniards an excuse to plunder and destroy the capital. Yet Cortés was more than a plunderer; he built a new City of Mexico on the site of Montezuma's capital and demonstrated administrative skills in adapting the former Aztec confederacy to Spanish rule.

Pizarro in Peru. The conquest of the Incas in Peru was carried out with less skill and more enduring ill effects than Cortés' exploit in Mexico. Obsessed by tales of a rich and mighty empire in South America, a tough, illiterate peasant's son named Francisco Pizarro determined to explore and conquer it. In 1531 Pizarro sailed from Panama with 180 men and 27 horses. Landing on the Peruvian coast, the small band made its way across the barren mountains into the interior, where they seized the Incan monarch Atahualpa.

Attempting to buy his freedom by paying a huge ransom, Atahualpa offered to have a room measuring seventeen by twelve feet filled to a height of some seven feet with plates and vessels of gold and to have it filled twice over with silver. Despite this magnificent ransom, the Spaniards did not release the emperor but instead sentenced him on trumped-up charges to be burned to death. In the end, because Atahualpa accepted Christian baptism, he was merely strangled. The imprisonment and death of its ruler

rendered the highly centralized Incan government incapable of effective, organized resistance; and Pizarro soon captured the capital.

Within a decade civil war broke out among the conquerors, and Pizarro was murdered. When the Spanish royal government sought to protect the oppressed Indians from their colonial masters, Gonzalo Pizarro, a brother of Francisco, set up a government independent of Spain. But Madrid dispatched officials and soldiers to arrest the unruly *conquistadores* and to pacify the area so that silver could be mined for Spain and conversion of the natives to Christianity could proceed. Not until near the end of the sixteenth century was Spanish authority securely established over Peru. In time Spanish dominions in South America formed a huge, uninterrupted semicircle, while the Portuguese took possession of the vast hinterland of Brazil (see Reference Map 6).

Spanish penetration into North America. Using Mexico and the West Indies as bases, the Spanish explorers searched what is now the southern part of the United States for the treasures which rumors planted there. That the expeditions failed to find gold or other riches does not detract from the tremendous progress they made in opening up new and potentially wealthy areas. Not only mythical treasure but an equally mythical Fountain of Youth attracted Spanish *conquistadores*. In 1521 Juan Ponce de León lost his life trying to find the Fountain of Youth in Florida.

Eighteen years later Hernando de Soto, whose participation in the conquest of Peru had gained him a fortune, landed in Florida with a company of some six hundred adventurers. His search for treasure took him through the southern United States, and De Soto was possibly the first white man to sight the Mississippi River. He died without finding any treasure, and his followers buried him in the Mississippi.

Marvelous tales had persisted of a fabled land north of Mexico containing seven cities with golden towers, and in 1540 Francisco de Coronado set out from Mexico with a large band to find them. But the fabled cities turned out to be only adobe pueblos. In his vain search Coronado appears to have penetrated as far as Kansas, becoming the first European to behold the vast herds of buffalo roaming the American plains. The adventurer returned embittered by failure, and the Spanish authorities concluded that there was little to be gained in occupying the area north of the silver mines of Mexico.

English search for the Northwest Passage. The division of the overseas world between Spain and Portugal, as set forth by the Bull of Demarcation and the Treaty of Tordesillas, aroused little enthusiasm among other European powers, and it was not long before France, England, and Holland encroached on the private preserves of both Portugal and Spain.

In 1497—the same year in which da Gama embarked for India—John Cabot, an Italian mariner financed by the merchants of Bristol in England, sailed across the North Atlantic in a small ship manned by only eighteen men. After a turbulent six weeks' voyage, the expedition dropped anchor off the northern coast of the New World. When Cabot returned to England, Henry VII rewarded him with £10, the title of Grand Admiral, and the

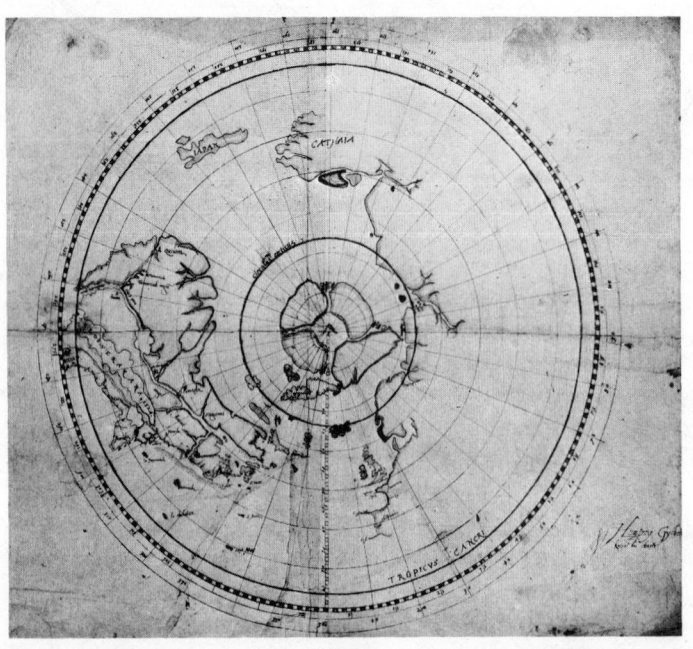

Drawn by Sir Humphrey Gilbert in 1582, this polar map shows a clear northwest route to the East. The belief in the existence of such a route helped stimulate the exploration of North America.

right to make another voyage. Cabot made his second voyage in 1498, coasting along the eastern shore of America in a vain attempt to find a passage to the Orient.

Cabot was the first European after the hardy Norse sailors to land on the mainland of North America; and, what was most important, his discovery laid the foundation for England's claim to the whole rich continent. Thus for £10 and a title England eventually acquired all of Canada and the territory along the Atlantic coast which constituted the thirteen American colonies— certainly an excellent business transaction.

For the next hundred years English seamen tried in vain to reach China through the illusive Northwest Passage, a sea route believed to exist north of Canada. Although similar expeditions trying to reach China by way of the Northeast Passage above Russia also failed, one of them reached Archangel and was granted trading privileges by Tsar Ivan the Terrible.

French explorations of inland America. France also joined in the search for the Northwest Passage. In 1523 Francis I commissioned the Florentine mariner Giovanni da Verrazzano to investigate the coast from North Carolina to Newfoundland. Eleven years later Jacques Cartier was sent on the first of three voyages that explored the St. Lawrence River as far as the present city of Montreal. These expeditions gave France its claim to sovereignty over eastern North America, a claim which duplicated England's.

Not until after its Wars of Religion did France resume its activities in the St. Lawrence region. Sponsored by the energetic first Bourbon ruler, Henry IV, Samuel de Champlain not only founded the first successful French overseas colony at Quebec (1608) but also journeyed over the lake which bears his name and westward to the Great Lakes. In 1673 Louis Joliet, a fur trader, and Father Marquette, a Jesuit missionary, reached the Mississippi River and followed it as far south as Arkansas in the hope of finding a short route to the Pacific. Nine years later René de La Salle explored the Mississippi to its mouth, taking possession of the entire territory and naming it *Louisiana* in honor of Louis XIV.

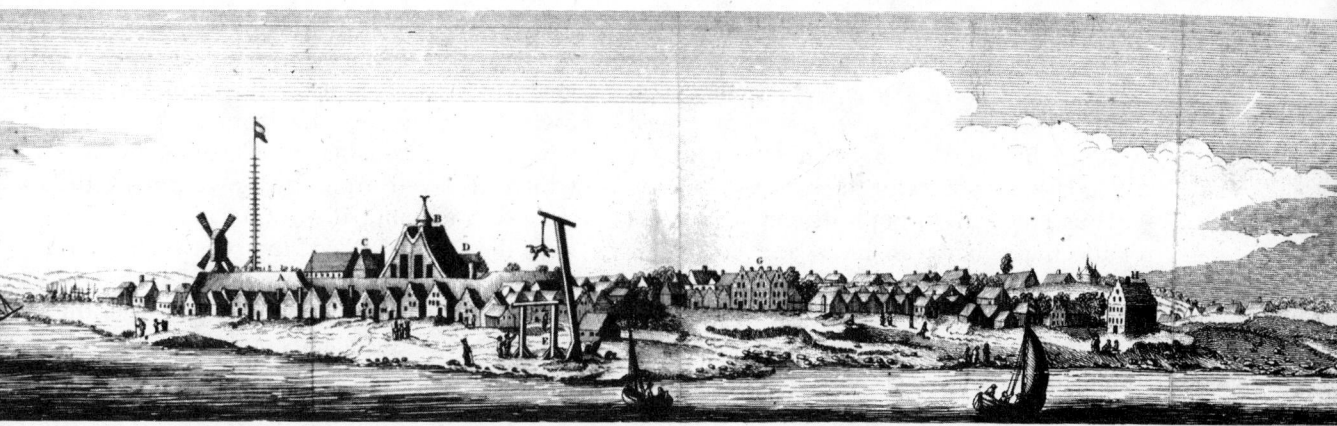

Pictured above is New Amsterdam (New York) as it appeared around 1640. In the center foreground are the gallows, to the right the West India Company stores (G), and to the left the governor's house (D), a church (B), the jail (C), and the fort (A).

The Dutch in America. Dutch interest in the New World coincided with the rise of the United Provinces (Holland) to a position of political independence and great economic strength during the first half of the seventeenth century. Dutch ambitions to find a shorter route to the Far East caused them to hire the English explorer Henry Hudson, who in 1609 sailed up the river that now bears his name. In 1621 the Dutch West India Company was founded for the purpose of trading in western Africa and the Americas. As part of its work, the company founded New Amsterdam on Manhattan Island in 1624 and permanently colonized Guiana, Curaçao, and Aruba in the Caribbean area.

EUROPE INVADES THE EAST

Portugal's eastern empire. Before the exciting era of exploration began to wane, the Europeans were faced with the problem of exploiting their newly found territories. In virtually every case, the natives suffered. Only in a few instances, notably in the Far East, were the indigenous people able to enforce their own policies. In most extreme contrast was Africa, where millions of natives were enslaved.

To ensure their toehold in Africa, the Por-

tuguese built fortified posts along the coast, began to develop a colony in Angola, and settled traders on the island of Zanzibar. Early in the sixteenth century Afonso de Albuquerque, the greatest of all Portuguese viceroys (1509-1515), resolved to consolidate his country's position in Africa and in the East. As a realist, he saw that Portugal could wrest commercial supremacy from the Arabs only by force, and he therefore devised a plan to establish forts at strategic sites which would dominate the trade routes and also protect Portuguese interests on land. The western end of the Arab trade routes was partially sealed off: Ormuz at the mouth of the Persian Gulf (see Reference Map 6) was captured, but the attempt to close the entrance to the Red Sea at Aden was only temporarily successful. To obtain a major base for a permanent fleet in the Indian Ocean, Albuquerque in 1510 seized Goa on the coast of India, which the Portuguese held until 1961. From Goa the Portuguese dominated the Indian ports that had supplied the Arab traders.

Albuquerque next set about securing control of the trade with the East Indies and China. His first objective was Malacca, which controlled the narrow strait through which most Far Eastern trade moved. Captured in 1511, Malacca became the springboard for further eastward penetration. The first Portuguese ship reached Canton on the south coast of China in 1516, but it was not until 1557 that the Portuguese gained a permanent base in China at Macao, which they still hold. About 1516, also, the first trading post was established in the rich Moluccas, or Spice Islands, source of the finest spices.

Thus Portugal, through its control of most of the traffic between India and Europe as well as the trade between India and the Far East, developed the first European commercial empire. Portugal's greatest poet, Luis de Camoëns, in 1572 celebrated his compatriots' overseas achievements in a memorable epic poem, *The Lusiads* ("The Portuguese"):

In golden treasures rich, distant Cathay,
And all the farthest Islands of the East,
And all the seas, to them shall homage pay.[2]

An already lucrative trade was vastly augmented when the Portuguese began to export slaves from Africa about 1500. Envying the rich profits, other nations—England, Holland, France, and Sweden—began to send in rival expeditions, and Portugal was forced on the defensive. In 1642 the Dutch drove the Portuguese out of the Gold Coast, and this rich trade and slaving area was left to other Europeans, especially the Dutch and English.

Dutch inroads in the East. Portugal's star was destined to set for many reasons, not the least of which was attacks on their commercial empire launched by the Dutch and the English—the beginning of a world-wide struggle over empire that lasted until 1763. Two events facilitated Dutch encroachment on the Portuguese monopoly of oriental trade. One was the Netherlands revolt against Spanish rule, and the other was the Spanish acquisition of Portugal. The Dutch looked on Spain's trade and colonies as fair game, and when the two crowns of the Iberian peninsula were joined in 1581, they felt free to attack Portuguese territory in eastern waters. Furthermore, the Dutch had previously enjoyed a rich trade carrying oriental goods from Lisbon to the ports of northern Europe; this traffic ceased when Spain took control of Portuguese ports. If Dutch trade was to survive, the Hollanders had to capture its source in the East.

In the 1590's a number of Dutch companies were formed to finance trading expeditions to the Far East. Because competition lowered their profits, in 1602 the companies amalgamated into the Dutch East India Company which received from the government the right to trade and rule in the area stretching from the Cape of Good Hope eastward to the Strait of Magellan. It was the Dutch East India Company that broke the power of the Portuguese in the islands of the Malay archipelago.

The governor-general of the East Indies who was appointed in 1618, Jan Pieterszoon Coen, laid the foundations for the Dutch empire in the East Indies. Whereas Albuquerque had felt that it was sufficient to occupy strategic points along the sea routes, Coen believed that the Dutch had to control the actual areas of production as well. He built a fortified trading station at Batavia on Java, a site which eventually became the capital of the Dutch East Indies, including Sumatra and the Moluccas. Dutch monopoly of the spice trade became complete after they drove the Portuguese from Malacca (1641) and Ceylon (1658), the latter the main source of cinnamon. In 1652 the Dutch established a colony at Cape Town on the southern tip of Africa as a port of call on the long journey to the Far East.

The English gain a foothold in India. The English meanwhile were staking out claims in India at the expense of the Portuguese. In 1600 Queen Elizabeth incorporated the English East India Company, granting it a monopoly of trade from the Cape of Good Hope eastward to the Strait of Magellan. By 1622 the company had put the Portuguese posts on the Persian Gulf out of business, and in 1639 it acquired Madras on the east coast of India. Through political stratagems, bribes, diplomacy, and exploitation of weak native rulers, the company prospered in India, where it became the most powerful political force in the subcontinent.

Europeans unwelcome in China. When the Portuguese first arrived in Canton in 1516, they were given the same privileges that Arab merchants had enjoyed for centuries. In response, the Portuguese behaved very badly, scorning the customs of the sophisticated inhabitants, and treating the "heathen" with arrogance and cruelty.

However, because trade was mutually profitable to both Chinese and foreign merchants, in 1557 the Portuguese were granted the right to trade at Macao. There, under close surveillance and subject to many strict regulations, the "ocean devils" conducted business. Stemming from this period is the mutual suspicion and hostility which characterized Sino-European relations in the nineteenth and early twentieth centuries.

A somewhat friendlier contact occurred when Jesuit missionaries arrived in China during the second half of the sixteenth century. They converted many important persons at the imperial court and in the provinces, thereby gaining protection for Christians generally.

Japan rejects European contacts. About 1542 three Portuguese ships from Macao were driven far off their course and landed at one of the southern Japanese islands. Before long, others visited the islands and began trading. Hearing about Japan after he had sailed from Lisbon for the Far East, St. Francis Xavier went there and started to convert the inhabitants. After Xavier's death in 1552, his work was carried on by other missionaries. By 1600 Japanese converts to Christianity numbered perhaps 300,000.

Suspicion on the part of the Japanese rulers that Christianity was endangering the status quo was reinforced by the bigotry of many Christians and by economic exploitation on the part of various unscrupulous Portuguese merchants. As we have seen in Chapter 16, the Japanese began persecution of the

Portuguese ships are shown anchored at the port of Macao on the Chinese coast in this sixteenth-century engraving.

AMACAO.

Jesuits and their converts, and in 1638 Japan cut itself off from the outside world:

For the future, let none, so long as the Sun illuminates the world, presume to sail to Japan, not even in the quality of ambassadors, and this declaration is never to be revoked on pain of death.[3]

Except for a small, closely watched Dutch post at Nagasaki, the islands were closed to western contact until 1853.

The Philippines. In the Far East, Spanish energies were concentrated primarily on the Philippine Islands. After 1565, cargoes of Chinese goods were transported from the Philippines to Mexico and from there to Spain. By this complicated route, Spain enjoyed some of the oriental commerce about which Columbus had dreamed. Spanish officials and missionaries brought Christianity and a degree of European civilization to the islands, which were henceforth a corner of the Far East fundamentally oriented toward the West, in contrast to Japan and China.

Renewal of the East-West contact. The remarkable series of geographical discoveries beginning in the fifteenth century which carried intrepid European explorers, soldiers, traders, and missionaries to the ends of the earth recalls a similar movement in the second and third centuries A.D. when rich contacts in commerce and culture existed among three intercommunicating empires— the Graeco-Roman, the Indian, and the Chinese. But the decline of Rome and other factors (discussed in Chapter 4) weakened and ultimately destroyed the lines of contact. For nearly a thousand years there was little exchange or communication between East and West.

Until the fifteenth century civilizations in the Near East, India, and China had been fully as advanced as those in Europe; and in some eras and in some aspects of culture they had surpassed the West. In the late Middle Ages, however, western Europe began to experience an astonishing resurgence —a "rebirth" which was reflected in the rise of powerful and well-administered nation-states, the increase of wealth and trade, the growing importance of the bourgeoisie, and the intellectual and artistic achievements of humanist scholars and artists. In contrast to the energetic West, the empires of India and China (as we saw in Chapter 16) were less dynamic both culturally and politically. And in Japan, isolation was the keynote of the Tokugawa shogunate—a regime no longer dynamic. Therefore, when the contact between East and West was renewed in the fifteenth century, it was not a meeting of equals. The discrepancies in effective political organizations, in disciplined armies, in energy and ambition prevented the resumption of East-West contacts on the same equal footing as had prevailed a thousand years earlier.

Europe's dominance begins. The same imbalance was readily apparent in both Africa and the Americas. In the Western Hemisphere promising civilizations among the Incas, the Aztecs, and the Mayas were no match for armed invaders. African potentialities had been restricted by isolation and harsh environmental forces, so that the natives fell an easy prey to the Europeans. Progress in sub-Saharan Africa was probably cut short by the effects of the slave trade.

The natural result of the impact of the strong upon the weak was that Europe took advantage of the other continents; the wider world became the servant of the West. The expansion of Europe and its mastery of much of the world is generally referred to as imperialism. Many of the conflicts and tensions in modern world politics find their source to a large degree in the imperial systems created by the West.

VICEROYS AND COLONISTS IN THE NEW WORLD

Spain consolidates its empire in the Americas. The *conquistadores* who carved out a mighty Spanish empire in the New World had been allowed to embark on their expeditions only after having secured royal permission. The crown's ultimate purpose was to replace these brilliant but erratic men of action with staid but reliable civil servants who would consolidate the territorial gains into a centralized colonial regime.

In theory, all overseas dominions were the personal property of the king, who made the major administrative decisions aided by one of his advisory councils, the Council of the Indies. Holding almost unrestricted power during the reigns of weak monarchs, the Council of the Indies formulated legislation, appointed colonial officials, and heard important colonial law cases. Before the end of the sixteenth century Spain possessed an American empire twenty times its own size, comprising in 1574 some 200 towns and about 160,000 Spanish settlers. For most of the colonial period the Spanish empire in the Americas was divided into two kingdoms: New Spain, which was made up of the West Indies, Venezuela, and the lands north of the Isthmus of Panama; and Peru, which consisted of all Spanish territory south of those lands.

Each kingdom had a viceroy who lived in splendor in Mexico City or Lima. Although the viceroys were the kings' representatives in America, they enjoyed only the appearance of great power. The Council of the Indies kept a tight rein on imperial affairs, judging the viceroys chiefly by their effectiveness in sending back treasure to Madrid. Under orders from the Spanish crown, the colonial regimes sharply restricted self-government. In the ten largest cities of the empire lawyers sent from Spain were in charge of courts called *audiencias*, which not only heard appeals against the decisions of viceroys and governors but also advised them in administrative matters. The crown levied head taxes, customs on imports, and excise charges on goods exchanged within the colonies, as well as demanding one fifth of all the gold and silver mined. The colonists were left no voice in the taxation. Membership in town councils was the only regular political outlet for the Spanish settlers, and there only the richest could participate. The Spaniards born in the Americas (Creoles) were regarded as potential rebels against the mother country, as indeed they proved to be in the nineteenth century.

For three centuries Spain was a potent agent in transmitting European culture and institutions to the New World. Its most important contributions were its language and literature. Also of lasting significance was the establishment of schools of higher learning. In 1551, eighty-five years before the founding of Harvard College, the first two universities in the New World—one at Lima, the other at Mexico City—were established. By the end of the seventeenth century no less than seven universities had been founded in Spanish America.

Mercantilism guides economic life. The economic theory current in the nation-states of Europe during this period was mercantilism, a doctrine which stressed the need of governmental intervention to increase the wealth and power of the state. Mercantilism had ramifications for the colonies as well as for the mother country. It postulated that a nation should be as economically self-sufficient as possible and that the colonies should be exploited for the gain of the ruling country. Each European nation wanted to export more than it imported, and the colonies provided ready-made markets for the finished products of the homeland. Thus Spain sent wines and finished goods to the New World but forbade the colonists to produce goods that would compete with those produced in Spain.

Under the mercantile system a nation's wealth was measured by the amount of precious metal it had accumulated, and the New World was a source of fantastic riches for Spain. Transporting the silver and gold to Spain was a perilous business. Each spring two well-guarded fleets left Seville or Cádiz, one heading for Mexico and the other for Panama. Laden with silver from the Andes and Mexico, the convoys returned to Spain in the autumn at great risk. After a rendezvous at Havana the combined fleets ran the gantlet back to Spain. Pirates and buccaneers were ever ready to swoop down on stragglers, as were warships of rival powers. Yet most of the treasure usually reached Spain, where the crown received its royal fifth.

In return for exploiting the virgin wealth of the New World, the Spanish introduced new products and methods which revolutionized agriculture, the mainstay of the American economy. To obtain farms, settlers often banded together to found a town in exchange for a royal grant of land, which was apportioned among the citizens. On the large estates of the aristocrats and the clergy, the forced labor of Indians and, later, African slaves was employed in the cultivation of cotton, vanilla, indigo, cacao, and other crops for export. The Spanish brought with them wheat, barley, rye, and rice, as well as coffee, sugar cane, and a variety of fruits. The importation of cattle and other livestock not only drastically modified the native diet but also stimulated such valuable new industries as breeding animals and exporting their hides. Originally the Indians had been their own pack animals, for the New World lacked beasts of burden except for the llamas domesticated by the Incas. The *conquistadores* introduced horses and mules and further revolutionized transportation by the introduction of the wheel. Through these imports and many more, the cultural state of certain areas in the Americas was abruptly jerked from a Neolithic level to a position approaching that of the Old World.

Indian plight eased by the Church. The desire to extend Christianity among the heathen had been one of the avowed objectives of every *conquistador*, but it was generally overlooked in the mad scramble to acquire gold and silver, jewels and slaves. In the islands of the Caribbean the forced labor and even enslavement of the Indians on the plantations proved so injurious that most of them died off. They were replaced by African slaves, who were imported to the islands about 1503 and to the American mainland a few years later. From the middle of the sixteenth century to the middle of the eighteenth century, some three thousand African slaves were imported annually, eventually transforming the racial composition of the Caribbean islands.

The work of the Church in establishing missions and persuading the crown to enact safeguards enabled the natives to survive in other areas of Spanish America. Early in the sixteenth century some clerics began to upbraid the Spaniards for their cruelties in exploiting the labor of the Indians. The most famous of these reformers was a Dominican friar, Bartolomé de Las Casas (1474-1566),

who insisted that the Indians, as subjects of the Spanish king, enjoyed the same rights as the Spaniards. He obtained royal permission to establish missions and settlements where the Indians and Spaniards could live on civilized terms. Las Casas' efforts also led to the promulgation of the New Laws of the Indies, directed at the greed of the plantation owners. But the attempt to improve the lot of the Indians was a losing battle, since the reforms ran counter to the economic interests of the settlers.

In order both to convert and to protect the Indians, a number of religious orders established mission towns. There, a few friars shielded the natives from white exploitation and taught them Christianity along with European habits and skills. The missionaries followed Las Casas in believing that the Indians should be converted not by force but by patient persuasion, "as rain and snow falls from heaven, not impetuously, not violently, not suddenly like a heavy shower, but gradually, with suavity and gentleness, saturating the earth as it falls."[4]

Portuguese activity in South America. Already burdened by its sprawling African and Asian interests, Portugal managed to establish a local administration in Brazil by the middle of the sixteenth century. In the 1570's Brazil's surge forward began as great numbers of African slaves were imported to cultivate sugar. This forced immigration continued for almost three centuries. During this period the crown imposed a highly centralized control on Brazil through its own officials, and a mercantilist policy was pursued in economic affairs.

After the Spanish king acquired control over Portugal, the Dutch and English regarded Portuguese possessions as lawful prizes to be won from their Spanish enemies. The Dutch took over land north of the mouth of the Amazon and founded Dutch Guiana. Subsequently, the English and French gained control over other parts of Guiana.

French colonization of North America. In 1608, as we noted earlier in this chapter, the city of Quebec was founded by Samuel de Champlain. To exploit the infant colony, a joint-stock company headed by Cardinal Richelieu was formed about twenty years

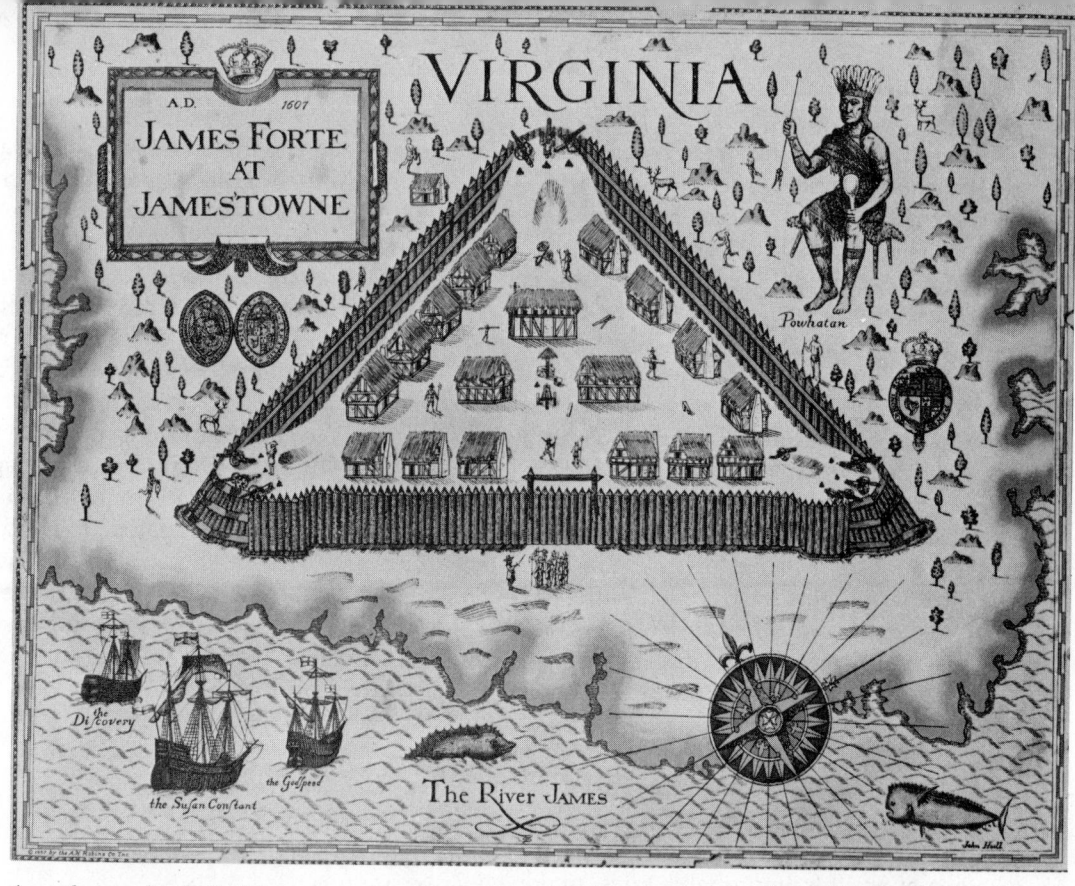

An early map details the Jamestown colony as it looked in 1607. Three ships, the *Discovery*, the *Sarah Constant*, and the *Godspeed* shown anchored in the James River were the ones that brought the original settlers from England. Also featured prominently is Powhatan, chief of an Indian confederation that was hostile to the early colonists.

later. In return for a perpetual monopoly on the fur trade and the title to certain lands, this company was supposed to bring several thousand settlers to Canada. But the company was unable to attract colonists. Stories of the severe Canadian winters frightened away most potential settlers; and the Huguenots, who would have been glad to escape religious restrictions, were not allowed to leave France.

By the middle of the seventeenth century New France had survived the initial, dangerous stages of an infancy marked by parental neglect. After La Salle in 1682 had explored the Mississippi River to its mouth, France also claimed the entire Mississippi valley. The French were at last firmly established in North America, ready to do battle with the English for the northern half of the continent and the Mississippi basin and prepared to resist any encroachment by the Spaniards from the Gulf of Mexico.

English colonies on the Atlantic seaboard. Like France, England was slow in following

up the valuable work of its explorers. Cabot had given it the means of claiming an entire continent, yet it was not until the days of Queen Elizabeth that Englishmen began to interest themselves in the potentialities of the New World. The defeat of the Spanish Armada in 1588 and the building of a strong English navy ensured safer passage from the Old World to the New. Reports of the wealth garnered by the Spaniards whetted the appetites of Englishmen to look for El Dorado. More important, the economic difficulties accompanying the spread of the enclosure movement—the diverting of land from food growing to sheep raising—brought unemployment and with it the desire by many to try their luck overseas. Added to these factors was the religious question. Although the Spanish and French governments forbade nonconforming religious elements to move to the New World, the English government saw emigration as an excellent means of getting rid of dissident sects. For their part, these strong-willed, God-fearing people were eager to migrate to a new land where they could worship freely.

Actually, the first successful English settlement was founded by a joint-stock company, called the London Company, whose shareholders hoped for substantial profit. (They were told that the lands to be developed were so rich that pots and pans were made of solid gold.) The company's charter, issued by James I, permitted it to act as a miniature government, even to the extent of coining money, levying taxes, and annexing territory.

In 1607 the London Company landed its first colonists at Jamestown in Virginia. For a number of years the colonists suffered from lack of food and other privations, but they were tided over this initial period by the dauntless Captain John Smith, whose motto was "It is less perilous to go forward than to go backward," and whose romantic rescue by the beautiful Pocahontas is one of the legends most cherished by Americans. Recent scholarship suggests that this story, like other of Smith's improbable tales, may have a basis in fact.

The first example of the transplantation to the New World of English common law and representative government is found in the royal charter to the London Company:

All and every the Persons, being our Subjects, which shall dwell and inhabit within every and any of the said several Colonies and Plantations, and every of their children . . . shall have and enjoy all Liberties, Franchises and Immunities within any of our Dominions . . . as if they had been abiding and born within this our Realm of England.[5]

In 1619 the governor of the Jamestown colony called a representative assembly to assist in the tasks of government. This body, which later became the legislature of the state of Virginia, is one of the oldest representative assemblies in existence.

Another great landmark in American history was the landing of the Pilgrims at Plymouth in 1620, after James I had granted them permission. This momentous royal decision in effect opened English North America to settlement by religious dissenters. Ten years later another Puritan group,

organized as the Massachusetts Bay Company, settled around Boston. Both groups had secured royal charters which allowed them to be virtually self-governing.

Between 1629 and 1642, as a result of increased hostility toward religious dissenters in England, some 25,000 Puritans migrated to New England. This movement, called the Great Migration, had important consequences for the future. It brought to the New World a number of educated and responsible people whose courage and intellectual attainments greatly stimulated the process of colonization. By the middle of the seventeenth century the English language and law and the religious and cultural institutions of England had become firmly rooted in North American soil.

THE COMMERCIAL REVOLUTION

The transformation of Europe's economic life. In the period between 1450 and 1750 Europe underwent a great economic transformation which is associated with the rise of capitalism and the shift from the town to the territorial state as the center of the economy. The period is often termed the Commercial Revolution because commerce and the activities of merchants were central to the great economic progress of the age.

The nature of capitalism. Capitalism is commonly defined by economists as an economic system in which capital, or wealth, is invested in order to produce more capital. Thus capitalism is an expanding economic system, ever producing more wealth. Other important characteristics are the private ownership of the means of producing wealth (such as land, raw materials, and factories) and the separation of capitalists and wage workers, which is not found in medieval guilds and manors or modern socialism. Also essential is the existence of the profit motive.

Four phases of capitalism. Much of the history of the five hundred years between the midpoint of the fifteenth century and the present day is concerned with the virtues and sins of capitalism, its defense and condemnation, and its development (as in the United States) or rejection (as in the Soviet Union). Its history can be traced in four distinct stages.

The first stage—commercial capitalism—is associated with geographical discoveries, colonization, and the astounding increase in overseas trade. These early capitalists, protected and encouraged by governmental controls, subsidies, and monopolies, made most of their profits from the buying and selling of goods.

Beginning about 1750, the second phase—industrial capitalism—was made possible by the accumulation of vast amounts of capital and its investment in machinery and the factory system of manufacturing. During the resulting Industrial Revolution the industrialist replaced the merchant as the dominant figure in the capitalistic system.

In the last decades of the nineteenth century, when the ultimate control and direction of large areas of industry came into the hands of financiers, industrial capitalism gave way to finance capitalism. The establishment of mammoth industrial empires and the ownership and management of their assets by men completely divorced from production were the dominant features of this third phase.

Since the great world depression of the 1930's, the state has played an increasingly dominant role in the capitalistic system, one well-known manifestation in the United States being the New Deal and its successor programs. This fourth phase is commonly known to economists as state capitalism and to its opponents by such terms as "creeping socialism."

Mercantilism. The body of economic theory and practice that accompanied commercial capitalism is called mercantilism. As previously noted (p. 399), mercantilism was a system of governmental regulation of economic matters in order to increase the wealth of the nation. In the words of Francis Bacon, its purpose was "the opening and well-balancing of trade; the cherishing of manufactures; the banishing of idleness; the repressing of waste and excess by sumptuary laws; the improvement and husbanding of the soil; the regulation of prices . . ."[6] A

similar program of stimulation and regimentation had characterized the economic life of medieval towns; now, under mercantilism, the new territorial state superseded the town and its guilds as the regulator of the economy.

Among the major tenets of mercantilism was bullionism, a doctrine which stressed the importance of accumulating precious metals. Mercantilists emphasized state power as the chief objective of economic policy, and "money," they liked to say, "is the sinews of war."

A second and corollary tenet of mercantilism was that a nation should maintain the most favorable balance of trade possible: it should export more than it imported so that foreign nations would have to pay the difference in precious metals. Only raw materials that could not be obtained at home were to be imported; after these materials had been manufactured into finished articles, they were then to be exported. Government subsidies, such as the granting of monopolies and the use of protective tariffs, encouraged the home production of manufactured goods.

Mercantilists believed that when raw materials were native, the profit to the home country was 100 percent. Therefore, if a country could not supply its own materials, it should acquire colonies from which they could be procured. Furthermore, colonies constituted not only sources of supply for raw materials but also markets for finished products. Because the mother country did not want competition for its infant industries, colonies were prevented from engaging in manufacturing. In addition, the colonies were prohibited from trading with foreign powers.

Mercantilism declined after 1750, when a new group of economic theorists challenged such basic mercantilist doctrines as the belief that the amount of the world's wealth remains constant and a nation can increase its wealth only at the expense of another. The more backward economic powers such as Russia and Prussia, however, still favored mercantilism long after other nations had turned to newer doctrines.

Decline of the early commercial centers. During the Middle Ages the central agency of European trade was the city-state. In northern Europe trade had been dominated by the confederacy of towns in the Baltic area known as the Hanseatic League. After the fifteenth century, however, the League rapidly declined, a victim of mercantile rivalry from the rising nation-states of Denmark, Sweden, and Russia. The absence of a strong central government in Germany left the League without adequate protection.

In southern Europe the merchants of the Italian city-states, with Venice in the lead, had for centuries acted as the great middlemen of Europe because they controlled the lucrative Asiatic trade. But the Portuguese smashed the Italian monopoly by discovering a new sea route to India and by obstructing the Red Sea and Persian Gulf routes that led to the Mediterranean ports. In addition, the Italian Wars of the sixteenth century had a disastrous effect upon the prosperity of the Italian city-states.

Portugal, temporarily paramount. With its limited population, Portugal could not permanently administer and protect an empire scattered over three continents. During the sixteenth century emigration, plague, and famine reduced the country's population from one and a half million to less than one, and the Portuguese were unable to man their ships and fortresses adequately. In 1580 Portugal came under the Spanish crown, and when it regained its independence in the following century, it retained only a few small possessions in the Far East, some islands in the mid-Atlantic, Brazil, and Mozambique and Angola in Africa. The economic power of Portugal ebbed away, not from lack of initiative so much as from lack of resources to support so great a task.

The economic decay of Spain. The decline of Spain's commercial might cannot be explained so simply. This nation apparently had everything—and failed. During the sixteenth century Spain had far more gold and silver than any of its rivals; and to this wealth was added that of Portugal and its possessions. Yet the wealth and power lavishly displayed during the reign of Philip II (1556-1598) were only surface deep. Farming was neglected, and industry was overburdened with governmental regulations. Religious

persecution and the expulsion of the Jews and Moors had deprived Spain of many of its skilled financiers and craftsmen. Since the Church and the upper classes were exempt from certain forms of taxation, the tax burden fell disproportionately on the classes engaged in trade, commerce, and industry.

An outward symbol of wealth, the rich flood of bullion from the Americas wreaked havoc in the Spanish economy by causing inflation. From 1500 to 1600 Spain experienced a fivefold rise of prices, a condition which attracted a stream of lower-priced products from Holland, France, and England, to the detriment of Spanish manufacturers. Spain's riches were drained off to purchase foreign manufactured goods—and even grain—and to pay the costs of Philip II's wars.

Antwerp's period of glory. As Spain and Portugal declined, the commercial center of Europe moved northward to Antwerp. To this great Flemish port came Europe's merchants and bankers. Antwerp was made a toll-free port, and the city fathers set up a merchants' exchange—the bourse—which, unlike the medieval fairs, operated continuously as an international commercial and financial center. It was said that Antwerp did as much business in one month as Venice in two years. Various institutions of modern capitalism evolved at Antwerp. Its bourse developed into the first stock exchange, trading in the shares of joint-stock companies. Life and property insurance came into use. But the spectacular prosperity of Antwerp was short-lived; in 1576, during the wars of the Netherlands against Spain, the city was sacked, and in 1585 the Dutch occupied the mouth of the Scheldt River and cut off the city's access to the sea. Henceforth Antwerp's trade and finances were largely appropriated by the Dutch city of Amsterdam.

Holland's golden age. During most of the seventeenth century Holland was the principal commercial, financial, and manufacturing country in Europe. Both the Dutch East India Company and the West India Company were markedly successful. The Dutch built better ships than their rivals and operated them more efficiently; their lower freight rates gained for them a monopoly on the carrying trade of Europe. The Dutch policy of religious toleration attracted artisans from abroad, and Holland became the leading industrial nation of Europe. Dutch exports included textiles, salted herring, glazed pottery, fine jewelry, and printed books. Trade, in turn, made Amsterdam the center of banking and credit.

Nevertheless, like Portugal, Holland was a comparatively small nation, and larger neighbors were presently to overtake it. Rivalry with England and France led to a series of wars during the latter half of the seventeenth century, and the Dutch lost much of their carrying trade to the English. Yet Dutch skill, together with the retention of the East Indies, enabled Holland to remain a significant factor in world commerce and finance.

France's rise and decline. With a population of about fifteen million in the seventeenth century, France was the premier nation of Europe. Its abundant economic resources were assiduously cultivated by Colbert (1619-1683), Louis XIV's astute minister of finance, who sponsored the colonization of Canada and chartered a number of trading companies which established slaving stations in Africa and trading posts in both India and the Caribbean sugar islands. Colbert also subsidized French industry by protecting it with high tariffs and granting monopolies, tax reductions, and loans without interest. In particular, Colbert subsidized the manufacture of those luxury items which the upper classes had habitually imported—tapestries, porcelains, laces, mirrors, glass, and fine woolens. There is no doubt that French commerce and industry gained much from Colbert's aggressive mercantilist policies.

After the death of Colbert in 1683, his mercantilistic system began to develop creaks and strains. Lacking Colbert's guiding genius, his followers added all kinds of minute and irksome regulations. The system's weaknesses also became apparent when, in retaliation for Colbert's restrictions against foreign imports, other nations refused to purchase French farm products and wines. Furthermore, the big governmental monopolies were increasingly unpopular with businessmen, who demanded the removal of governmental regulations and of controls by the old medieval guilds.

In addition, it has been estimated that between 1685 and 1715 France lost a million subjects through warfare, the surrender of colonies, and the drain of emigration. The revocation of the Edict of Nantes in 1685 resulted in the flight from France of a large group of industrious Huguenots, who took their capital and skills as artisans to neighboring countries. And the rivalry between France and England during the Seven Years' War (see Chapter 20) culminated in French disaster. Thus France lost to England the commercial supremacy which it might have had.

Rise of England's sun. Although England was inferior to France in area, fertility of soil, and population (between four and five million inhabitants), this island kingdom had many compensating factors in its favor. Geographical isolation discouraged military conquest from the Continent—the last successful invasion by a foreign power had taken place in 1066—and the English economy had not been burdened by the cost of maintaining large standing armies. After the union of England and Scotland in 1707, internal trade flourished in the largest customs-free area in western Europe. The aristocracy and middle class which controlled Parliament also controlled the principal trading and banking companies so that the growth of new enterprises was more peaceful and steady than anywhere else in Europe. The gradual control of the seas, the establishment of trading posts in exotic lands, and the shrewd policy of taking overseas territory as its booty from successful European wars enabled England to gain commercial benefits and to build the world's largest empire.

An important step in the rise of England's sun came in 1651 with the passage of the first Navigation Act forbidding the importation of goods into England or its dependencies except in English ships or in ships of the country producing the goods. The act was aimed at the Dutch carrying trade, and it provoked the first of three maritime wars with Holland noted previously. England soon outstripped Holland and by 1750 had laid the

On the Atlantic crossing, slaves were packed in so tightly that there was little room to stand, or even sit. When the weather permitted, they were allowed on the main deck for food and fresh air. An eyewitness drawing details slaves on the *Wildfire* on the way to Key West, Florida.

foundation for its economic domination of the world in the nineteenth century.

We shall see that England's textile industry was no small factor in accounting for its overall growth. Daniel Defoe, the author of *Robinson Crusoe*, maintained that the woolen industry in England was "the richest and most valuable manufacture in the world,"[7] of greater value to England than the rich mines of Peru and Mexico were to Spain.

More imports in Europe's markets. The discovery of sea routes to both Asia and the Americas provided an unparalleled impetus to the expansion of Europe and its commerce. The spice trade was especially profitable because there was no refrigeration for foods at this time, and slightly spoiled food could be made palatable by seasoning it with cloves, cinnamon, or pepper. Cloths from the East— calicoes, chintzes, and ginghams—became popular. The textile workers of England became so incensed at the foreign competition that they demanded a prohibition on the import of these inexpensive cotton fabrics, which they maintained were "made by a parcel of heathens and pagans that worship the Devil and work for 1/2*d.* a day."[8] Among other imports from Asia were silks, carpets, and rugs, precious stones, porcelain, brassware, and the all-important beverages tea and coffee.

From the New World came a variety of products which revolutionized the eating and drinking habits of the Europeans. The food supply of Europe was greatly improved by the addition of potatoes, maize (Indian corn), and tomatoes. From the Caribbean came sugar, which soon became so popular that it supplanted honey. An abundant supply of fish, primarily cod, came from Newfoundland's Grand Banks; and warm furs were obtained by trappers penetrating the interior of North America. The sacred beverage of the Aztecs, cocoa, found its way to Spain and thence throughout Europe.

The use of one commodity—tobacco— spread rapidly among rich and poor alike. It was used mainly in the form of snuff or for smoking in pipes. The medicinal qualities of tobacco were strongly recommended; even schoolchildren were forced to smoke during the Great Plague in London. Seventeenth-century claims for tobacco were as extravagant as some we hear today:

Divine Tobacco! which gives Ease
To all our Pains and Miseries;
Composes Thought, makes Minds sedate,
Adds Gravity to Church and State . . .[9]

Gold and ivory came to Europe from Africa, but the most important African export enriched the European powers indirectly. This export was that most misery-ridden produce —slaves. To obtain slaves to labor in the mines and on the plantations of the New World, slavers sailed to the Guinea coast, where they bought or stole their human freight. "A woman slave might change hands for a gallon of brandy, six bars of iron, two small guns, one keg of powder, and two strings of beads; a man slave might cost eight guns, one wicker-covered bottle, two cases of spirits, and twenty-eight sheets."[10] The voyage across the Atlantic to America cost the lives of from 10 to 25 percent of the Africans—inhumanly packed as they were in evil-smelling, suffocating quarters below deck—but the remainder were profitably disposed of at their destination. It is estimated that in three centuries some thirty million Africans were brought to the Americas.

The price revolution. The gold and silver brought to Europe from the New World in enormous quantities may have had a more direct effect on Europe's economy than any of the other products of Africa, Asia, or the Americas. By the middle of the fifteenth century Europe was confronted with a severe gold and silver shortage, caused both by the depletion of European mines and by increasing demands for currency to finance the new standing armies and navies and to pay for spices and other luxury commodities. The critical situation was partially relieved by the development of new European mines, by imports of gold from West Africa, and, above all, by the unprecedented quantities of precious metals from mines of Spanish America. The bonanza of bullion upset price levels throughout western Europe; between 1500 and 1650 commodity prices more than tripled.

This price revolution affected all classes. Merchants and manufacturers were benefited, but laborers were harmed because wages lagged behind prices. Except in parts of England, the landowners of western Europe, most of whom rented their land to peasants on long-term leases, suffered because their incomes were fixed. The peasants, on the other hand, benefited from rising prices for their farm products. In Europe east of the Elbe River, however, the situation was reversed. Here the landowners benefited from the rising price and growing market for grain in the West by the twofold process of increasing production and enserfing their peasants, who during the Middle Ages had been freer than those in western Europe. The subjection of the east European peasantry—as a means of obtaining a cheap labor force—contrasts sharply with the freedom of western Europe's peasant renters and farmers. Through the centuries the Elbe would continue to divide Europe economically and socially, and today it divides communist and capitalist Europe.

Banking becomes big business. One indicator of the resurgence of commerce was the growth of banking and related business practices. The word *bank* derives from the Italian *banca*, meaning "bench," on which medieval Italian moneylenders sat in the marketplace to carry on their business. When a man failed, the people broke his bench, and from this custom came the word *bankrupt*, or "broken bench." During the late Middle Ages moneylending became indispensable to the administration of both national monarchies and the Church so that traditional prohibition on usury was often ignored.

Large-scale banking was first developed in Italian cities, where merchant bankers arranged bills of exchange and negotiated loans. By 1350 some eighty banking houses were in business in Florence alone. In the fifteenth century the most illustrious of these families was the Medici, who established branch offices all over western Europe and acted as financial agents for the popes. Loans also were made to rulers who were continually in need of funds to carry on their wars.

The greatest of the sixteenth-century bankers were the Fuggers of Augsburg in Germany. They repeated the pattern set by the Medici, loaning money to the Church (half of the money collected by Tetzel from the sale of indulgences went to repay a Fugger loan), to Charles v to finance his election as emperor, and to the Spanish and Austrian Hapsburgs. The Hapsburg loans were secured by mining concessions, and the Fuggers gained a virtual monopoly on silver and copper mining in central Europe and silver and mercury mining in Spain. For decades the Fuggers realized an average yearly profit of over 30 percent, but they went bankrupt in 1607 when Spain for the third time defaulted on its loans.

By the seventeenth century the resources of banking families like the Fuggers were inadequate to meet the needs of the time, and private banks were superseded by public banks chartered by the government. The first of these great public institutions was the Bank of Amsterdam, chartered in 1609. Its main purpose was to facilitate trade by the conversion of various currencies into credits called bank money, which because of its standard value came to be preferred to coins. In 1694 the Bank of England was chartered as a means of financing England's wars. In return for a large loan to the government at 8 percent, the bank was granted a monopoly on such banking operations as issuing paper bank notes and marketing the government's securities. With banking there naturally evolved new financial techniques. Despite the increase in precious metals after 1500, the supply could not keep pace with the increase in trade, and the Bank of Amsterdam began the practice of issuing loans against its deposits. Because it could safely loan larger sums than had been deposited, the Bank of Amsterdam initiated a new, effective means of expanding credit. Bank notes also came to replace gold and silver currency.

Progress was also made in commercial arithmetic and in bookkeeping. Simple single-entry bookkeeping had been developed as early as the thirteenth century. Soon afterwards, double-entry bookkeeping came into use; it was well known in Italy by 1500 and in western Europe a century later. By listing a transaction either as a *debit* (meaning, "he owes") or a *credit* ("he believes" a promiser will carry out his promise), a businessman could readily determine his status in terms of profit and loss.

New methods of financing companies. Not only banks but also modern corporations were developed in response to needs arising from the expanded commerce of early modern times. Unprecedented difficulties resulted from trading at long distances overseas in strange lands. It was natural that those engaged in overseas trade should seek to combine their efforts both to provide mutual protection and to share losses as well as profits.

The companies were of two main types—regulated and joint-stock—and both were chartered, regulated, and granted monopolies by the state. In the regulated company individuals financed their own businesses and abided by the rules the group had accepted to protect the trade in which the members had a mutual interest. The earlier companies were of this nature.

The joint-stock companies involved an association of capital as well as of men. The members put their money into a common fund and gave over the management to a board of directors. Because of its advantages, the joint-stock company became almost universal. It had a permanent legal personality that did not expire, whereas the regulated company was not a legal entity, and in case of damages each member had to sue or be sued individually. As many people as wanted could contribute capital. Stock might be transferred as the owner saw fit, and at the same time, the company's policy underwent no serious change. The vast corporations of today grew out of this early type of business organization.

Stock exchanges and insurance. The creation of joint-stock companies gave impetus to the growth of stock exchanges, because the shares could be easily transferred from one person to another like any other commodity. A stock exchange made it easier to accumulate capital from many different sources, thereby enabling very large commercial companies to be formed. We have seen that the first stock exchange, the bourse at Antwerp, was primarily a commodity exchange. Later the two functions were separated.

Another method of sharing losses besides the joint-stock company was insurance. Since the loss of his vessel might well ruin an individual merchant, it came to be the practice to distribute losses among a group of traders by means of insurance. Interested merchants drew up an agreement by which each was responsible for a percentage of any possible loss. Because the merchants signed their names at the bottom of this document, the practice came to be known as underwriting.

The most famous of all marine insurance groups, Lloyd's of London, came into being about 1688. Lloyd's was not a stock company but an association of shipowners, merchants, and underwriters who first met together in a London coffee house owned by Edward Lloyd. Since its modest beginnings, Lloyd's has grown steadily and branched out into other forms of insurance. Today it is the world authority on matters of ship classification, and it publishes *Lloyd's List*, a daily paper which indicates the whereabouts of all registered vessels.

After the disastrous London fire of 1666,

fire insurance companies were started, and in the same period companies specializing in life insurance were also formed. In 1684 the Friendly Society was organized. This society was the first mutual company—an association in which policyholders received a share of the company profits.

Speculation and business bubbles. Toward the end of the seventeenth century, the accumulation of capital brought about a mania for speculation in the shares of joint-stock companies in England, France, and Holland. One authority comments on the fantastic nature of the wildcat schemes, "which promised to earn great dividends by trading in human hair, making square cannon balls, getting butter from beech trees, marketing an air pump for the brain, perfecting a wheel for perpetual motion, searching for rich wrecks off the Irish coast, or importing jackasses from Spain."[11] The two most notorious speculative companies were the South Sea Company in England and the Mississippi Company in France.

The financiers of the South Sea Company assumed the British national debt of about £9,000,000 in return for a 6 percent annual interest payment and a monopoly of British trade with South America and the islands in the South Seas. The price of company stock rose rapidly until it was far above the value of the company's earnings. In 1720, with a £100 share selling for £1,060, the huge speculative bubble burst when shareholders lost confidence and began to sell. Many lost not only their savings but also property they had mortgaged in the hope of getting rich quickly.

The Mississippi Company had a similar history. Formed to promote trade with France's Louisiana territory, where it founded New Orleans in 1718, the company soon acquired a monopoly on all French colonial trade. In addition, the company assumed the national debt and was granted the right to collect all indirect taxes in France and to establish a central bank with the privilege of issuing paper money. Speculative fever combined with currency inflation to bid up the company's stock to fantastic heights. Thousands suffered losses when shareholders began to unload and the company went bankrupt in 1720.

The demoralizing failure of these schemes left a legacy in both countries. In England Parliament passed the "Bubble Act," which drastically restricted the right of incorporation. In France distrust of paper money and the government's credit and solvency continued for generations.

The domestic system. In the Middle Ages manufacturing had been carried on under the guild system. The impetus of commercial expansion caused an important change in the organization of industry. The domestic, or putting-out, system evolved in the sixteenth century and reached its widest application in the textile industry of England. It operated in this fashion: a merchant capitalist would buy raw materials, assign them to artisans to be worked on in their own homes, take the finished product, and sell it to his customers. Thus, between producer and customer, a middleman intervened—an entrepreneur who accumulated capital by selling his goods at a profit. Because work was no longer planned and conducted by master and apprentice under one roof, this

The famous insurance association known as Lloyd's of London took its name from Lloyd's coffee house, where the insurance underwriters used to meet with merchants and shipowners. This satirical scene at Lloyd's dates from the late eighteenth century.

system widened the gulf between employer and employee, capitalist and worker.

The domestic system had many advantages. The accumulation of capital in the hands of the entrepreneur made possible the purchase of raw materials in greater bulk and allowed for marketing of finished products on a larger scale than had been possible under the guild system. The domestic system also contributed to an increased specialization of skills within an efficient system of overall production; an employer could have his raw wool sent to spinners, then to weavers, and finally to dyers. From the workers' point of view, it was now possible for agricultural tenants to augment the bare subsistence they eked from the soil by working at home. The capitalist employer, on the other hand, could operate without the restrictions imposed by the urban guilds.

The domestic system persisted for two hundred years in England, although in some trades workers were brought together in central shops long before the beginning of the machine age and the factory system proper. On the Continent, however, where the guilds were retained as agents of the mercantilist state in controlling industry, the guild system remained strong. Hence industrial production on the Continent lagged behind that in England, where industry was less restricted by guild practices.

Innovation in agriculture. The condition of agriculture was a basic socioeconomic factor in the life of the period, for agriculture provided the majority of Europeans with their livelihood. In England, especially, the advent of commercial capitalism wrought significant changes. The profit-making potentialities in farming attracted enterprising entrepreneurs, who bought up large tracts of land. Because the possession of land had always been the mark of nobility, the *nouveaux riches* consolidated their position in polite society by acquiring estates and marrying into the landed gentry. The alliance between land and trade created a powerful new group in Parliament—a class which promoted legislation favorable to its own needs and desires, often at the expense of the national good. But the satisfaction of the profit motive had a beneficial effect upon agriculture; the

new commercial landowners applied efficient business methods to the management of their estates. They encouraged the use of new tools and crops and were sympathetic to new ideas in stock breeding and soil development.

A pioneer agronomist was Jethro Tull (1674-1741), who advocated careful plowing of the land, planting seeds in neat rows by the use of a drill he invented, and keeping the plants well cultivated as they grew to maturity. By mixing clay and lime into the soil, Viscount Charles Townshend (1674-1738) restored the fertility of land that had once been worthless swamp and sand. He also suggested crop rotation as a method of soil restoration superior to the wasteful custom of allowing good farm land to lie fallow. He was so enthusiastic over turnips, his pet crop for livestock feed, that he was nicknamed "Turnip Townshend."

Robert Bakewell (1725-1795) was responsible for attacking the problem of livestock breeding. Haphazard breeding had resulted in sheep weighing only from twenty-five to forty pounds and cattle of about four hundred pounds. Through the select breeding of choice animals, Bakewell raised larger livestock, improved the quality of the meat, and increased the quantity of milk available from his dairy cattle. His methods attracted attention, especially from the wealthy farmers, but most of the rank and file were suspicious of his innovations and too poor to adopt them.

While the tempo of agricultural reform was much faster and more general in England than on the Continent, there was evidence of some progress in farming methods there also. In fact, the great advances in English agriculture owed much to Continental techniques and improved seeds, but these achievements were applied much more systematically in England.

The enclosure movement. The practice of enclosing open lands, a development which had begun in England even before Tudor times, was accelerated by the changes in farming methods. Aided by special acts of Parliament, members of the new commercial landowning class seized the opportunity to enclose the common lands, where for hundreds of years English villagers had grazed their cattle, and to purchase and fence in the small farms owned and operated by the sturdy, independent yeomen. These lands were consolidated into holdings which were, in effect, large-scale business enterprises requiring substantial capital for operation and upkeep. The demand for wool in the textile industry resulted also in the enclosure of large tracts of arable land for sheep raising.

The controversy over the enclosure movement reached its climax between 1750 and 1810. The advocates of enclosure justified amalgamation of small agricultural holdings by claiming that new methods of stock breeding and crop rotation could not be practiced on unfenced land. From an economic standpoint, enclosure was inevitable, and some historians believe that the enclosure movement resulted ultimately in a more careful use of a greater amount of land than had been available before. Better and more food was thus made available for a population on the verge of rapid increase. Like most drastic economic changes, however, the enclosure movement spelled misery and dislocation to a large number of countryfolk. The destruction of the yeoman class and the depopulation of many villages was ruefully pondered by Oliver Goldsmith in his poem, "The Deserted Village":

Ill fares the land, to hastening ills a prey,
Where wealth accumulates, and men decay.
Princes and lords may flourish, or may fade;
A breath can make them, as a breath has made;
But a bold peasantry, their country's pride,
When once destroyed can never be supplied. . . .
Ye friends to truth, ye statesmen, who survey
The rich man's joy increase, the poor's decay,
'Tis yours to judge how wide the limits stand
Between a splendid and a happy land.

The saga of the yeoman's misfortunes did not end with their departure from the villages; its finale took place in the cities. When the story of industrial capitalism is taken up in Chapter 22, we will view the bleak and harsh environment of displaced rural people as they labored long and hard in grimy factories and lived as best they could in ugly, disease-ridden slums.

SUMMARY

Braving the terrors of uncharted seas and the dreadful hardships of long voyages, a few daring sea captains opened up rich trade routes to the East and discovered new lands in the Western Hemisphere. In the New World the feats of the explorers were followed by the bold, and often cruel, exploits of the *conquistadores*, who carved out vast empires for their homelands.

Meanwhile, various European countries had erected forts on the African coast for the purpose of exploiting the slave trade. In the teeming lands of Asia, European penetration was secured only by the establishment of strongly fortified trading settlements at strategic sites. Using this system, the Portuguese controlled trade in the East during the 1500's but gradually lost out to the English and Dutch, who garnered most of the profits in the next century. While the Dutch concentrated more and more on the East Indies, the English East India Company built up a commercial stronghold in India. In China and Japan the behavior of the Portuguese caused native officials to restrict the westerners to a narrow theater of operations. In the East, European ways of life were successfully and permanently imposed only in the Philippines.

In sharp contrast to their failures in Japan and China, the western European powers were able to transplant not only their authority but also their institutions and culture to the sparsely populated lands of the Americas. The government and economics of the Spanish and Portuguese colonies were directly—and minutely—controlled by royal decrees and officials, whereas the development of the French, English, and Dutch colonies was left largely to private companies.

The impact of the New World upon the Old was so far-reaching as to intensify the Commercial Revolution, the name given to the first phase of our capitalistic economic system. The capitalism of this period, during which the economy in western Europe became nation-centered instead of town-centered, is called commercial capitalism because of the dominant part played by commerce as a producer of wealth. With the spectacular outburst of geographical discoveries and the creation of new trade routes, the areas which had thrived on the Mediterranean trade lost their leading roles to those along the Atlantic seaboard. The first great colonial empires were built up by Portugal and Spain, only to be superseded through the dynamism of Holland and later England and France. New products poured into Europe to augment diet, clothing, and the general standard of living, while the influx of gold and silver completed the change from a barter to a money economy and produced a price revolution.

This era also saw the development of large-scale banking and commercial practices. By the seventeenth century important banking institutions had been founded throughout western Europe. Because overseas trading ventures required large amounts of capital and entailed great risks, merchants pooled their resources by forming companies, the earlier ones of the regulated type, the later and more successful ones joint-stock companies—forerunners of present-day corporations. To serve as marketplaces for stock that could change hands readily, stock exchanges developed.

The geographical, political, and commercial expansion of Europe between the years 1450 and 1650 was so immense that it transformed the basic pattern of global existence. With it we enter the formative period of modern times. For the next three centuries the civilization of western Europe—carried to the four corners of the earth and stimulated by new and dynamic forces—was to dominate world culture.

SUGGESTIONS FOR READING

C. Nowell, **The Great Discoveries and the First Colonial Empires*** (Cornell); J. H. Parry, **The Establishment of the European Hegemony, 1415-1715*** (Torchbooks) and **The Age of Reconnaissance*** (Mentor) have excellent brief coverage. See also Robert L. Reynolds, **Europe Emerges: Transition Toward an Industrial World-Wide Society, 600-1750*** (Wisconsin, 1961); and D. Lach, **Asia in the Making of Europe,** Vol. 1, **The Century of Discovery** (Univ. of Chicago, 1965).

S. E. Morison, **The European Discovery of America: The Northern Voyages** (Oxford, 1971) and **The Southern Voyages** (Oxford, 1974) are engrossing surveys. The best book on Columbus is S. E. Morison, **Admiral of the Ocean Sea** (Little, Brown) condensed as **Christopher Columbus, Mariner*** (Mentor). On exploration in America before Columbus see H. Holand, **Norse Discoveries and Explorations in North America*** (Dover); and Carl Sauer, **Northern Mists*** (Univ. of California). On Portuguese explorations see S. E. Morison, **Portuguese Voyagers to America in the Fifteenth Century*** (Octagon); and E. Sanceau, **Henry the Navigator: The Story of a Great Prince and his Times** (Shoe String).

F. A. Kirkpatrick, **The Spanish Conquistadores*** (Meridian) is a colorful treatment. W. H. Prescott, **History of the Conquest of Mexico*** (Phoenix) and **The Conquest of Peru*** (Mentor), both abridged, are historical classics. On the same subject see Jorge E. Hardy, **Pre-Columbian Cities** (Walker, 1973); and J. E. Thompson, **The Rise and Fall of Maya Civilization,** 2nd ed. (Univ. of Oklahoma, 1973).

Good accounts of individual explorers are as follows: William W. Johnson, **Cortes** (Little, Brown, 1973); C. M. Parr, **Ferdinand Magellan, Circumnavigator** (Crowell); J. C. Beaglehole, **The Life of Captain James Cook** (Stanford, 1974); and G. M. Thomson, **Sir Francis Drake** (Morrow, 1972).

C. Boxer, **The Dutch Seaborne Empire, 1600-1800** (Knopf); and K. Haley, **The Dutch in the Seventeenth Century*** (Harcourt Brace Jovanovich, 1972) are lively portraits of Dutch society.

C. H. Haring, **The Spanish Empire in America*** (Harbinger) is the best introduction. See also J. H. Parry, **The Spanish Seaborne Empire** (Knopf, 1966); and L. Hanke, **The Spanish Struggle for Justice in the Conquest of America*** (Little, Brown).

A. L. Rowse, **Elizabethan Renaissance*** (Scribner's, 1974) is a highly readable account. C. Bridenbaugh, **Vexed and Troubled Englishmen, 1590-1642** (Oxford) describes the factors influencing English migration to America. Also recommended are Grace Woodward, **Pocahontas** (Oklahoma, 1970); and G. D. Langdon, Jr., **Pilgrim Colony: A History of New Plymouth, 1620-1691*** (Yale).

M. Dobb, **Studies in the Development of Capitalism,*** 2nd ed. (New World) is a useful introduction. The following are excellent special studies: R. De Roover, **The Rise and Decline of the Medici Bank, 1397-1494*** (Norton); R. Ehrenberg, **Capital and Finance in the Age of the Renaissance: A Study of the Fuggers and Their Connections** (Kelley); and V. Barbour, **Capitalism in Amsterdam in the Seventeenth Century*** (Harcourt Brace Jovanovich, 1972).

A. P. Thornton, **Doctrines of Imperialism*** (Wiley, 1965) contains good short accounts of early modern imperialism and mercantilism. On other aspects of the Commercial Revolution see E. J. Hamilton, **American Treasure and the Price Revolution in Spain, 1501-1650** (Octagon); R. H. Tawney, **The Agrarian Problem in the Sixteenth Century*** (Torchbooks); and B. H. van Bath, **Agrarian History of Western Europe, A.D. 500-1850** (St. Martin's).

On the African slave trade see D. Mannix and M. Cowley, **Black Cargoes*** (Compass); and J. Pope-Hennessy, **Sins of the Fathers: A Study of the Atlantic Slave Traders, 1441-1807** (Knopf). David B. Davis, **The Problem of Slavery in Western Culture*** (Cornell) is a historical review of ideas on slavery.

*Indicates a less expensive paperbound edition.

In the 1540's, as the reign of Henry VIII drew to a close, John Johnson and his family settled in at Glapthorn Manor in Northamptonshire. Compared to the noblemen's estates of the region, Glapthorn was small, with only a hundred acres of cultivated land and pasture and another hundred and fifty acres of meadowland and wooded hills. The manor was a few miles southeast of the old market town of Oundle, near the marshy Fen Country, in a belt of rich farmland and lush pasture encircled by deep forests of oak and beech. More than a thousand sheep grew fat in the enclosed grazing lands, whose wool John Johnson sent to his brother Otwell in London to be weighed and packed in the woolhouse and then sold to clothmakers in England and on the continent.

John and Otwell Johnson were partners in the firm of Johnson and Company, a loose association of woollen merchants who dealt in the fleeces and fells (skins) of English sheep. In the early 1540's their business was flourishing; the drapers of Calais and Bruges always wanted more wool than the English merchants had to sell, and as a result prices were rising higher and more rapidly than ever before. It was because his profits were so great that John Johnson had been able to rent Glapthorn Manor. Every merchant dreamed of living the life of a country gentleman on an estate far from the crowds of "the Street"—Lombard Street, where merchants met in the open air to transact business, find out international news and learn the latest rates of exchange on the currency of France, the Low Countries, Italy, and Spain.

The rent at Glapthorn was £8 a year, but with careful management and good luck in his business ventures John could afford it. As a merchant he had no fixed income; he was entirely dependent on the fortunes of the marketplace, the honesty of the traders he dealt with, and the soundness of the currencies that changed hands in the London counting houses. In a good year, John and his family lived well. His wife Sabine could spend £7 on cauldrons, pans, and kettles for the kitchen, and £11 on six silver goblets, and still have plenty of money to buy herself some of the sweet-smelling gloves that sold for six shillings the dozen. But in a bad year Sabine Johnson was hard pressed to keep the cellars stocked with the barrels of beer that cost four shillings tenpence, or to pay the hogsherd his five shillings a year in wages.

Sabine Johnson ran Glapthorn Manor whenever her husband was away, which was perhaps half the year. She was a lively, capable woman and the marriage was a happy one. Their letters—and they wrote often when John was abroad—were full of lighthearted endearments. John called Sabine his "loving heart"; "with all my heart, entirely beloved," she answered. "Would ye were in my bed to tarry me!" he wrote to her at the end of a long business day in Antwerp.

John had known Sabine since he was a young apprentice in his early twenties. She was the niece of his master, a wool merchant in London, and was then a child of nine or ten. While Sabine was still a girl, the young merchant had worked out the details of the marriage settlement with her father. She had a dowry of a hundred marks, and a good supply of sheets and blankets and furnishings. The dowry would help to set John up in business, the linens and furnishings would supply his first household, and the marriage would make the bond between John and his father-in-law more intricate and more enduring. Such were the practicalities of Tudor marriage; that John and Sabine loved one another was an unexpected dividend.

Sabine Johnson had been educated to serve as a dutiful helpmeet to her future husband. She had learned to read the Bible and devotional books, and to model herself on the perfect housewife— "of chaste thought, stout courage, patient, untired, watchful, diligent, witty, pleasant, constant in friendship, full of good neighborhood." She was taught to suppress her anger, to do as her husband told her, to endure his displeasure with a "mild sufferance," while remaining "ever unto him pleasant, amiable and delightful." Since her marriage at twenty, she had borne four children: three girls, Charity, Rachel, and Faith, and a boy, Evangelist. Another child, a boy, had lived only a few weeks and was buried in a tiny coffin in a nearby village churchyard.

The three Johnson daughters were sent at an early age to be educated in the home of their uncle Otwell Johnson. The son, however, was trained to carry on his father's profession. As soon as he was old enough Evangelist traveled with his father through the sheep farms of Northamptonshire and Buckinghamshire, watching John Johnson bargain with the wool growers and inspect the wool the shepherds showed him, learning to tell good fleeces from bad and to calculate in advance what price the wool might bring in the market at Calais. Several times he went up with his father to London, striding beside him through the confusion of bales and carts and coaches that choked the narrow streets and listening to the haggling of the merchants in Flemish, Italian, and French.

It was John Johnson's good fortune that, at a time when food prices were doubling, Glapthorn Manor was almost completely self-sufficient. Except for the delicacies sent up from London from time to time—hard white sugar, packed in chests, from the Canary Islands, boxed candies from the confectioners of Antwerp, ripe lemons and oranges bought at dockside from Spanish ships each autumn—all food eaten at Glapthorn was produced there. The bread was made from homegrown wheat and rye, stone-ground in the manor's own mill and risen with yeast from the ale vats in the brewhouse. The dairy yielded more than enough milk, butter, and cheese; the hens laid so abundantly that the surplus eggs had to be taken to Oundle market to be sold.

In more settled times the cook at Glapthorn would have sent four to six meat and fish dishes to the table at the noon dinner, but as things were, there were no more than two or three. (Noble households in the Tudor age were often served beef, mutton, veal, lamb, kid, pork, rabbit, capon, deer, and several varieties of ocean and freshwater fish at a single meal, with preliminary courses of poultry and game birds.) A salad began the Johnsons' meal, and fruit and sweets rounded it out, and with every course there was wine, preferably Bordeaux but sometimes lighter vintages from Orleans or Auxerre. At other times the family washed down a light meal of cheese and brawn (meat from baited bulls) with firkins of foaming beer—either the strong normal brew or the "double beer" that was twice as potent.

Meals were eaten in the great hall, a cavernous room with high ceilings filled with a long table for the family and guests and low benches for the servants. The manor house, a fifteenth-century stone and timber building set in a large garden, had three floors. On the ground floor the kitchen, pantry, and storage rooms led off the great hall. The bedrooms were on the second floor, and the third floor or attic contained the children's and servants' bedrooms. Every year at the hiring fair Sabine Johnson hired "mean drudges," servant girls who rose at dawn to light the fires, then spent their long days cleaning, washing, spinning, making candles, and beating the laundry clean with wooden bats. Sabine felt responsible for shaping her servants' characters as well as their work habits. She watched them carefully, and subtracted a few pence from their wages when they were late or slow in their work, or when they swore.

The Johnsons were a devoutly religious family. Along with his brother John Johnson held the Calvinist belief that only the elect of God would be saved, and was as eager to hear a good sermon as he was to condemn the pope as the "Antichrist of Rome." Both brothers took Bibles with them in their business travels, and would go miles out of their way to see a play on "the battle betwixt the Spirit, the Soul, and the Flesh." The religious enthusiasm of the family was evident at Glapthorn. The pictures on the walls (besides a portrait of the Supreme Head of the Church, Henry VIII) were of figures from the Bible. The books in the parlor were devotional books and stories from scripture, and the friends that came to visit there were almost exclusively Lutheran or Calvinist in their opinions.

But the family had other amusements as well. There was a chess set in the parlor, and an "old great Venice lute" that John played. In the summer there was hunting, hawking, and coursing hares. In spring came the festival of the sheep shearing, and village fairs with their entertainments of racing, wrestling, and morris dancing.

In 1551 a series of reverses struck the Johnson household. The sweating sickness, a virulent form of influenza with pulmonary complications, swept through southern England, reaching London and the merchant quarter in July. Otwell Johnson fell ill early one evening and was dead within eight hours. John Johnson barely had time to mourn his brother before he was caught up in the vast financial crisis brought on by the disastrous government policy of debasing the coinage. Johnson & Co. dealt daily with the merchants of Antwerp and Calais, and relied for its profits on a favorable rate of exchange between English pounds and foreign currencies. When the king and his council cut the value of English coins by half, continental creditors refused to accept payment in English money. Wool sales dropped drastically, and with no large reserves to fall back on, Johnson & Co. was forced to declare bankruptcy.

Immediately everything of value was seized by creditors—clothes, furniture, iron pots, and even the books off the shelves. Out of kindness the landlord allowed the family to stay on at Glapthorn rent free until such time as John could rebuild his fortunes, but his chances of recovery were slim, and he would in any case be encumbered with debt for the rest of his life. Two years later, with the accession of the Catholic Queen Mary Tudor, the Johnson family left England to join the colony of Protestant exiles in Geneva.

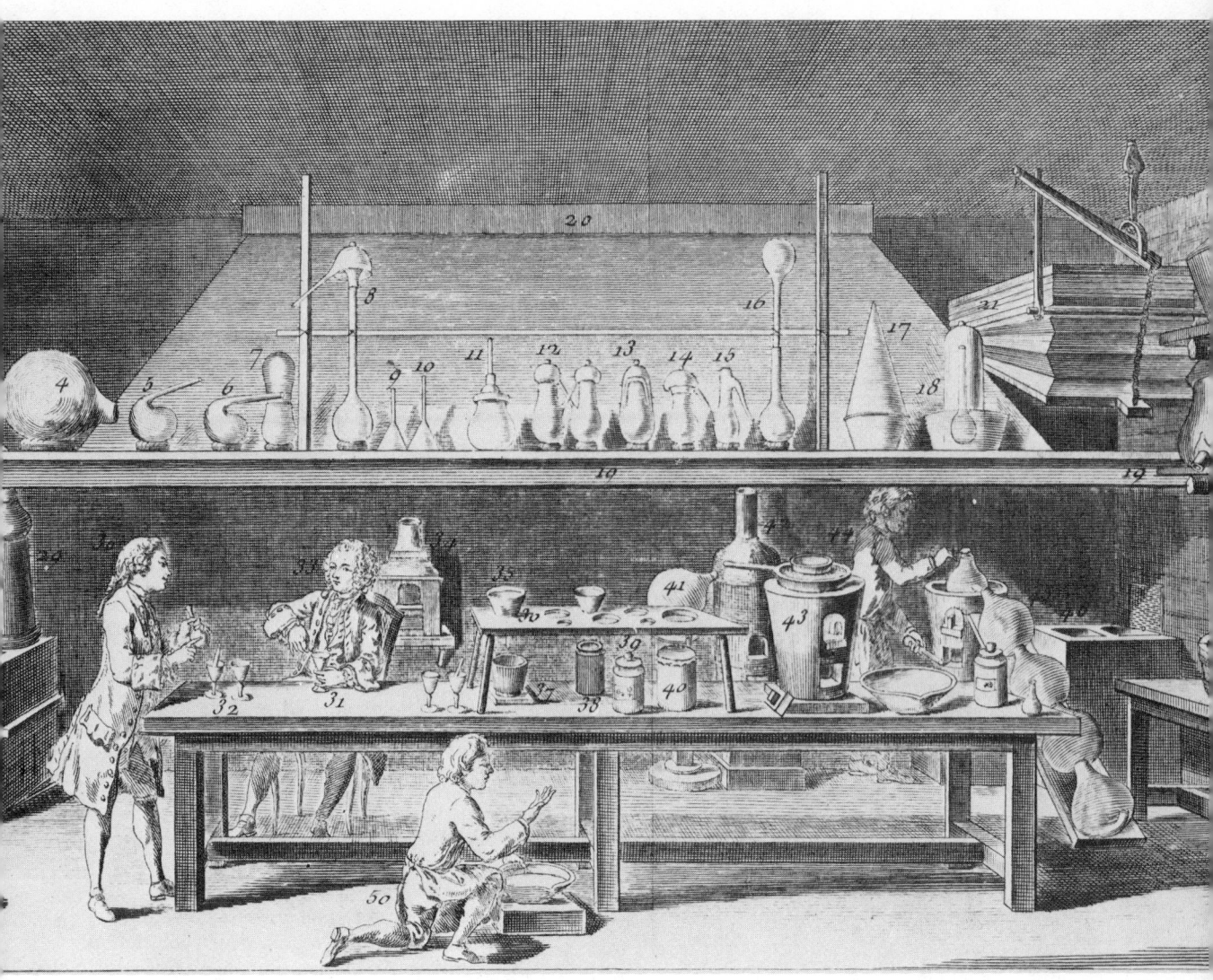

PART FOUR
Charting the Present

■ The story of Europe and the New World in the period from 1650 to 1815 forms one of the most complex chapters in world history. Following the challenge to the ideas and institutions of the Middle Ages posed by the Renaissance, the Reformation, and the great religious wars, the search for principles of order became a consistent theme in the writings of scientists as well as in literature and the fine arts. This search for order also played an important role in the ambitious domestic and foreign ventures of autocratic rulers.

A succession of fresh concepts about the universe (in the seventeenth century), about society (in the eighteenth century) and about man (in the nineteenth century) called into question and in some cases overthrew long-established beliefs and institutions. The first major advance was the development in the seventeenth century of the scientific method, which relied upon deductive reasoning. Other new ideas, many stemming from the spread of the scientific method, began to develop in the social and natural sciences.

In politics the late seventeenth century witnessed the high-water mark of absolutism under Louis XIV of France. But new political concepts rose rapidly to challenge royal prerogatives everywhere. The eighteenth century was the period of revolutions that established the precedents and voiced the ideology that were to become the inspiration for the whole liberal-democratic movement of modern times.

These political advances were accompanied, and indeed only made possible, by comparably important progress in thought. Outmoded ideas in economics and politics were attacked. So pervasive were the transformations in thought that they constituted an intellectual revolution known as the Enlightenment. Under the spell of the remarkable achievements of science—capped by the work of Newton—thinkers, writers, artists, and members of polite society sought to express a truly scientific, or at least rational, point of view. For many intellectuals, religion lost its emotional fervor and became a philosophical creed. Literature, in this Age of Reason, was guided by the mind rather than by the heart. Most painting and architecture was restrained and balanced in both form and spirit. In Paris, where the cult of reason reached its height, the salon was the temple of cultivated society. Here Europe's cosmopolitan intellectuals gathered to exchange views on all aspects of life; the result was witty, well-informed, and often brilliant conversation. The liberal tenets of the Enlightenment touched even the autocrats of the Continent; in Prussia, Austria, and Russia, benevolent despots made at least superficial attempts at reform.

The present owes much to the period from 1650 to 1815. That period provided us with the heart of our liberal political beliefs; it encouraged religious tolerance and freedom of inquiry; and, above all, it made man the focus of attention—his happiness, his freedom, his potentialities. All these developments made this period a time of hope for the future of mankind.

There was, however, a disquieting feature. The liberalism and rationalism we have discussed operated *within* but not *between* states. Humanitarianism did not touch international affairs. These were dominated by the competitive state system, in which each nation was a law unto itself and any weak neighbor was a potential victim. In this state of international anarchy the nations of Europe evolved the balance of power to check the grandiose ambitions of national rulers whose only law was force and to achieve some order in the relations between rival states. Thus a coalition of rival powers thwarted the plans of Louis XIV, of the French revolutionary leaders, and finally of the brilliant and unscrupulous Napoleon, who sought to control all of Europe under the pretex of spreading the ideals of equality and liberty. The discrepancy between benevolence and liberalism, on the one hand, and force and autocracy, on the other, was to become increasingly a paradox of modern civilization.

CHAPTER 19

Science, Thought, and
the Arts in the
Age of Reason: 1600-1800

New Dimensions of the Mind

INTRODUCTION. The first phase of the transition from medieval to modern times in the western world ended about 1600, to be followed by an even more epochal period of intellectual change. So important were the changes in this latter period that the intellectual movement they comprised is identified as the Enlightenment and the time span in which they occurred is known as the Age of Reason. In the broadest sense, the Age of Reason can be thought of as comprising the seventeenth and eighteenth centuries. The spirit and purpose of the Enlightenment were eloquently expressed by one of its spokesmen, the *philosophe* Baron d'Holbach, who wrote: "Let us then endeavor to disperse those clouds of ignorance, those mists of darkness, which impede Man on his journey, which block his progress, which prevent his marching through life with a firm and steady step. Let us try to inspire him . . . with respect for his own reason—with an inextinguishable love of truth . . . so that he may learn to know himself . . . and no longer be duped by an imagination that has been led astray by authority . . . so that he may learn to base his morals on his own nature, on his own wants, on the real advantage of society . . . so that he may learn to pursue his true happiness, by promoting that of others . . . in short, so that he may become a virtuous and rational being, who cannot fail to become happy."[1]

This message indicates how rapidly the heritage of the Middle Ages was being left behind. No longer was reason to serve faith, mind to obey authority, and man to spend his life in preparation for the next world. The thinkers of the Age of Reason believed in happiness and fulfillment in this world; they regarded mind rather than faith as the best source of guidance and were suspicious of emotion, myth, and supernaturalism. The chief support of the cult of reason was science, with its new laws and methods. The great age of science initiated by Copernicus in 1543 reached its climax in 1687 with Newton's explanation of the law of gravitation. The supreme achievement of the Enlightenment, however, was not in discovering additional scientific laws but rather in translating the advances of science into a new philosophy and world view.

Exaltation of science, faith in reason, and belief in humanitarianism led writers and thinkers of the Enlightenment to carry on a strenuous campaign of reevaluation of all aspects of society. They were positive that reason could solve all human problems. All thought was colored by a belief in progress and by a vigorous optimism regarding mankind's improvability. In religion a movement known as Deism, reflecting these views, sought to establish a "rational" faith; and in the study of mankind, the foundations were laid for the systematic disciplines of the social sciences.

Literature, music, and the fine arts were affected profoundly by the cult of reason. Everywhere there was supreme confidence in logic, a tendency to minimize spirit and emotion, and a close attention to the forms and rules which had characterized the classical era in Greece and Rome, when the splendor of human reason had first been extolled. In literature and music this emphasis on reason culminated in Neoclassicism, and in art it led from the grandiose Baroque and the more dainty Rococo styles to the pure Neoclassical style.

THE SCIENTIFIC REVOLUTION

From "authority" to "facts." The transition from the Middle Ages to early modern times represents a shift in emphasis from "authoritative" truth to "factual" truth. Medieval thought had enthroned theology as the "queen of the sciences" because the scholastics sought to relate human knowledge to ultimate divine purposes. Hence they made little distinction between a "fact" and a theological "truth." In their world view man was seen to be dependent upon a divine order in which God was responsible for mankind's origin and destiny alike. The medieval mind had also associated this earthly life with the loss of Eden and the physical world with the works of Satan. In order to justify modern man's extension of his environmental powers, it was first necessary to adopt a new attitude, namely, that God had revealed His

divine purpose both in scripture and in nature. As a consequence, interest shifted progressively to discovering the processes and laws governing the natural world. Instead of concentrating their attention on *why*, or final cause, men concerned themselves with *how*, or the manner of causation.

Important consequences derived from this conceptual shift. Men continued to regard scriptural revelation as providing certainty in the subjective world of faith and ethics. But increasingly they employed their reasoning powers to discover in the objective world of nature the principles of causation—and to do so in terms that were both mathematical and mechanical. Eventually this rationalistic emphasis upon the scientific method was to affect virtually every area of human activity, including the evolution of religious thought into Deism (see p. 423). Yet this view of a mathematical and mechanical nature was purchased at a high price: it threatened to drain the universe of all spiritual content and meaning and to reduce man himself to the status of an automaton. One day he would rebel against such a world view.

Progress of the scientific method. The birth of modern science is often regarded as marked by the publication in 1543 of Copernicus' heliocentric theory which denied that the earth was the center of the cosmos. This revolutionary theory challenged the teachings of religion and the traditional ideas concerning the nature of the universe and man's place in it. By the last half of the seventeenth century the Copernican system and the progress made in other branches of science besides astronomy had produced a change in man's outlook upon the world that is considered one of the greatest revolutions in the history of human thought. When Charles Darwin in the nineteenth century wrote that "science and her methods gave me a resting place independent of authority and tradition," he was describing what has been frequently called the fundamental faith of modern western man.

Basic to the growth of science was the development of the scientific method, a systematic and logical way of seeking truth. In the search for facts, this new servant relied on curiosity, healthy skepticism, and reason rather than faith. The foundations of the new method were laid in the first half of the seventeenth century by Francis Bacon in England and René Descartes in France.

Bacon's attack on unscientific thinking. Sir Francis Bacon (1561-1626) attacked humanism and scholasticism and derided Plato and Aristotle, maintaining that they had managed to survive for centuries only because of their shallowness, which had given them the necessary buoyancy to ride down the stream of time. In his *Novum Organum* (*The New Instrument*), published in 1620, Bacon described the course which science and a scientifically oriented philosophy should take. First, man must cope with four major prejudices (in Bacon's famous term, *Idols*) which had so far obstructed human progress. The Idols of the Tribe are the prej-

udices inherent in human nature itself; in particular, they represent the tendency to see only those facts which support an opinion one wishes to entertain. The Idols of the Cave are prejudices fostered in the individual by his particular environment—the circumstances of his birth, childhood, education, and so forth. The Idols of the Market Place are false opinions which spread when men consort together. Lastly, there are the Idols of the Theater, resulting from men's tendency to become attached to particular theories, schools of thought, and philosophies and to hold on to them long after the logical basis for their continuance has disappeared.

If better results were to be obtained, new ways of thinking and of approaching the world of nature had to be devised. Here we come to Bacon's famous method of induction, by which he advocated a systematic recording of facts derived from experiments. These facts would lead to tentative hypoth-

Sir Francis Bacon urged the need for experiment, because "men have been kept back . . . from progress in the sciences by reverence for antiquity, by the authority of men accounted great in philosophy, and then by general consent."

eses which could then be tested by fresh experiments under different conditions. Eventually it should prove possible for men to arrive at universal principles and scientific laws.

Bacon himself was an indifferent scientist. The significance of his work lies in the fact that he set forth a program to direct the course of scientific and philosophical inquiry at the time when the traditional modes of thought were crumbling. In his own words, "he rang the bell which called the wits together." Bacon also forecast the vast importance of the new science in enabling man to conquer his environment. In his *New Atlantis* (1627)—his description of a utopian society—emphasis is centered on a research institute called "Solomon's house," where experimentation and invention were subsidized and directed toward the goal of "the enlarging of the bounds of Human Empire, to the effecting of all things possible."[2]

Descartes, champion of the deductive method. As an advocate of the inductive method, Bacon undervalued the role of mathematics and deduction. Experimentation is not the only approach to scientific knowledge, as the mathematical approach attests. The mathematical approach is to begin with a self-evident axiom and then, by logical reasoning, to deduce various inferences. Applied to scientific investigations as a whole, this type of approach—known as the deductive method—advances by logical steps from simple self-evident truths to more complex truths. As we saw earlier, Aristotle had employed the syllogism to point out fallacies in human reasoning. It was the achievement of René Descartes (1596-1650) to make brilliant use of this method of reasoning in his attempt to extend the mathematical method to all fields of human knowledge.

Like Bacon, Descartes maintained that the first step in the search for truth was for men to rid themselves of preconceived notions and to take nothing for granted. Bacon had called for "minds washed clean of opinions," and Descartes began by being prepared to doubt everything except the fact of his own doubting. And if he doubted, he must in fact exist—hence his famous expression *Cogito, ergo sum* ("I think, therefore I am").

For Bacon, experiment was the next step in the quest for truth. Although Descartes by no means rejected the value of experimentation, he placed reliance above all on the attainment of knowledge through reason. By logical deduction, Descartes built up a concept of a unified, mathematically ordered universe which operated like a perfect mechanism; in this universe, supernatural phenomena were impossible and everything could be explained rationally, preferably in mathematical terms.

Some scientists criticized Descartes for not having made sufficient use of experiment, even as he had criticized Bacon for weakness in mathematics. As we well know, the experimental and mathematical methods are complementary. Before the mid-point of the seventeenth century, the two methods had been combined by Kepler and Galileo. ("Sense must be accompanied by reason"[3] was the way in which Galileo described the union of induction and deduction.) Thus a revolution in scientific thinking had been effected, and the foundation of modern science and modern philosophy had been firmly laid.

Science takes to the heavens. It was in astronomy that science made its first spectacular advance. For over a thousand years western Europe had accepted the view of Ptolemy, a Greek scholar of the second century A.D., that the earth was stationary. Rotating around it were concentric, impenetrable, crystalline spheres to which were attached the sun, planets, and fixed stars. The Ptolemaic system as expressed in the geocentric (earth-centered) theory was incorporated into the scholastic system of the Church. By the middle of the seventeenth century, however, a revolution in man's conceptions of the heavens had been attained through the labors of a Pole, Copernicus; a Dane, Tycho Brahe; a German, Kepler; and an Italian, Galileo.

Copernicus (1473-1543) was a contemporary of Martin Luther and Michelangelo. During visits to Italy for study, he read widely in the classical authors and was much impressed by the Platonist philosophy that beauty was supreme and that mathematics was the ideal science. As a mathematician, Copernicus found parts of the Ptolemaic

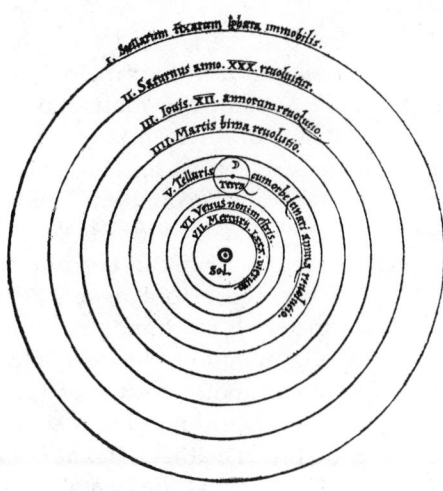

The 1559 engraving at right illustrates Ptolemy's system of the universe. Surrounding the earth are spheres containing the moon, sun, planets, and fixed stars. An additional sphere provides the system's motion. Beyond that is the Empyrean, where God dwells. The diagram above, illustrating the heliocentric theory of the universe, appeared in the first edition of Copernicus' *Concerning the Revolutions of the Heavenly Spheres* (1543). It places the sun in the center, surrounded by the first six planets in their correct order. The outer sphere was thought to be the home of all fixed stars.

theory "not sufficiently pleasing to the mind" and began to seek a more pleasing combination of circles to express the motions of the planets. He obtained such a model by assuming that the earth moves "like any other planet," while the sun stands still in the middle of the planetary orbits. Near the end of his life, he was persuaded to publish his views under the title *Concerning the Revolutions of Heavenly Spheres* (1543). In this work he refuted the theory that the earth remained stationary in the middle of the universe, contending instead that it rotated every twenty-four hours upon its axis from west to east and that it made an annual movement around the sun. As early as 1539 Luther attacked Copernicus' views as contrary to the truth of the Bible. Not until 1616, however, did the Catholic Church place Copernicus' book on the *Index of Prohibited Books* "until corrected," from which it was removed in 1620 after only minor revisions.

By brilliant mathematical and analytical reasoning, based on a slender body of facts, Copernicus had been able to bring one epoch in scientific thought to a close and to open

the door for another. However, the truth of his theory could be demonstrated beyond doubt only after a great number of accurate observations of the heavens had been charted. This need was in large part supplied by Tycho Brahe (1546-1601), although he himself never fully accepted the Copernican theory. For twenty-one years Brahe carried on accurate daily observations and carefully plotted the positions of hundreds of celestial bodies. He tracked the planets through the whole of their courses instead of contenting himself with picking them out at different points in their orbits. Thus in painstaking fashion he carried the science of observation as far as it could go prior to the invention of the telescope.

Brahe's data was used by his one-time assistant, Johann Kepler (1571-1630), a brilliant German mathematician. As a mathematician with a strong leaning toward Platonic idealism, Kepler quickly adopted the Copernican theory. While working with Brahe's data on the movements of Mars, Kepler had to account for the apparent irregularities in that planet's perplexing orbit.

After patiently applying one mathematical hypothesis after another, he was able to verify that the planet did not move in a circular orbit but described an ellipse. He then proceeded to assume that the other planets also traveled in elliptical orbits. Another planetary law discovered by Kepler was that the pace of a planet accelerated as it approached the sun. After reading Gilbert's book on magnetism (see p. 429), Kepler concluded that the sun emitted a magnetic force that moved the planets in their courses—an idea that formed a valuable basis for Newton's theory of gravitation.

A contemporary of Kepler, Galileo Galilei (1564-1642), discovered new facts to verify the Copernican theory but, as he wrote to Kepler:

. . . I have not dared to make [it] known, as I have been deterred by the fate of our teacher Copernicus. He, it is true, won undying fame amongst some few, but amongst the multitude (there are so many fools in the world) he was only an object of scorn and laughter.[4]

In 1609 Galileo made a telescope, and with it he discovered mountains on the moon, sunspots, the satellites of Jupiter, and the rings of Saturn. Thrilled with these discoveries, Galileo publicized his findings and beliefs. In 1616 he was constrained by the Church to promise that he would not "hold, teach, or defend" the heretical Copernican doctrines, and in 1633 he was forced to make a public recantation of his heretical doctrine. A legend has it that Galileo, upon rising from his knees after renouncing the idea that the earth moved, stamped on the ground and exclaimed, "Eppur si muove!" ("But it does move!")

Galileo was also the first to establish the law of falling bodies, proving that, irrespective of the weight or the size of the bodies, their acceleration is constant (the increase of velocity being thirty-two feet per second). Thus another entrenched belief inherited from the ancients was refuted: Aristotle's contention that bodies fall to earth at speeds proportional to their weight.

Newton and the law of gravitation. Great as the contributions of Brahe, Kepler, and Galileo had been to astronomy, their individual discoveries had yet to be united into one all-embracing principle or law which would explain the motion of all bodies in the planetary system and present the universe as one great unity operating according to unalterable principles. This goal was realized by Isaac Newton (1642-1727), the most illustrious scientist in the Age of Reason.

At the age of only twenty-four, Newton had made all his important discoveries: the law of gravitation, the principles of calculus, and the compound nature of light. At twenty-seven, the youthful genius was given a professorship in mathematics at Cambridge University. Although he had already discovered the principle of gravitation, he was not able to prove it mathematically until 1685. Two years later his momentous work was published in Latin under the title *Philosophiae Naturalis Principia Mathematica* (*Mathematical Principles of Natural Philosophy*). By this work all laws of motion, both celestial and terrestrial, were synthesized in a master principle for the universe, the law of gravitation, which was expressed in a concise, simple, mathematical formula:

Every particle in the universe attracts every other particle with a force varying inversely as the square of the distance between them and directly proportional to the product of their masses.[5]

The publication of the *Principia* climaxed the near century and a half in which scientists had struggled against static tradition and intolerant authority.

Advances in mathematics and scientific instruments. Meanwhile, mathematicians had been keeping abreast of the work of the astronomers and physicists and providing them with new tools. Indeed, as Galileo pointed out, mathematics was the language of science; of necessity these two fields had to progress hand in hand. Mathematical calculation was greatly simplified by the invention of time-saving devices and by the development of new forms of mathematical analysis. Decimals were introduced in 1585 and logarithms in 1614. Eight years later the slide rule was invented, followed in 1645 by the first adding machine. The degree to which these devices speeded up computation is indicated by the saying that John

Napier, the Scotsman who invented logarithms, doubled the lives of his fellow mathematicians by halving the time involved in solving intricate problems.

Two new branches of mathematical analysis helped make the seventeenth century the great age of science. Descartes "discovered the foundations of a wonderful science" (the words of his enthusiastic announcement) by uniting algebra and geometry into a unified discipline. The result, analytic geometry, permitted relationships in space to be translated into algebraic equations—a development of obvious value to astronomers, for example, since it helped them to represent astronomical phenomena in mathematical symbols and formulas.

Algebra was next applied to motion. The result was calculus, the greatest mathematical achievement of the seventeenth century, worked out independently by Newton and a German philosopher of remarkable versatility, Gottfried Leibnitz. This new calculus enabled scientists to consider quantitatively such problems as the movement of heat and the motion of stars, to compute quickly the content of circles, and to calculate stresses. Newton himself used it to arrive at and to prove his law of gravitation.

The work of science was no less dependent upon the development of new and more precise instruments. At the beginning of the seventeenth century the telescope and microscope appeared in Holland. We have already seen the invaluable use to which the first of these instruments was put by Galileo. After 1650, microscopic examinations of the lungs and other organs of the body were yielding vital information regarding their structure and functions. At this time also, Galileo and others were constructing crude thermometers; and a Dutchman, Christian Huygens, invented the pendulum clock and brought accuracy to the measurement of time. The micrometer, the barometer, and the air pump are other examples of seventeenth-century inventions that arose to serve science. The eighteenth century contributed the centigrade and the Fahrenheit thermometers, the chronometer, the sextant, and the anemometer, a device for measuring the force of wind.

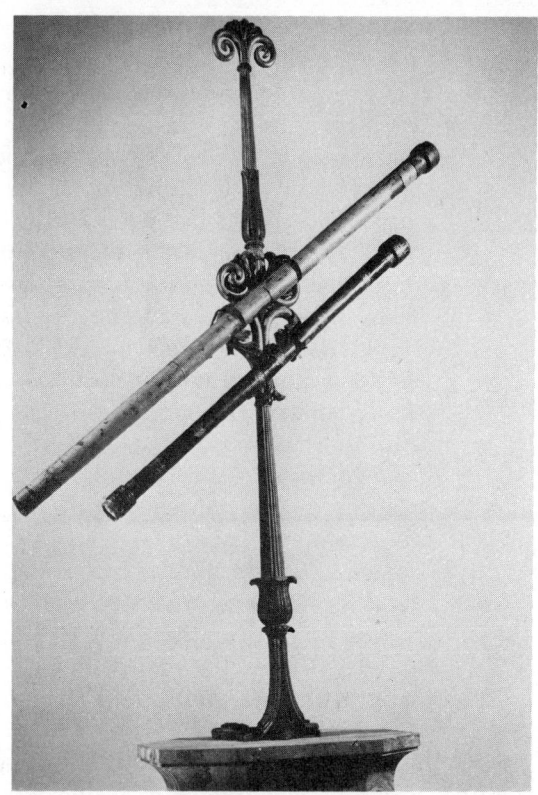

The instrument pictured above is Galileo's telescope; it was constructed in 1609 after a Dutch invention which arranged lenses in a tube to enable distant objects to be seen as if close by.

Another important factor in the progress of science was the establishment of scientific societies. The first, the Academy of Experiments, was founded at Florence in 1657. In 1662 the Royal Society of London received its charter from Charles II, and four years later the French Academy of Science was established in Paris. These societies concentrated upon the promotion of experimentation and the collection of scientific data.

THE CRISIS IN THE EUROPEAN CONSCIENCE

The spiritual crisis. In the latter half of the seventeenth century much of western Europe was undergoing a revolution—not in the realm of politics but in the minds of men. As a result of the impact of the scientific revolution, with Newton's discoveries as its crowning achievements, a new concept of a universe without supernatural or miraculous forces came into being. This universe could be understood; it was a smooth-running machine with all parts fitting into a harmonious whole. Scientists now were inclined to regard God not as a personal deity but as the embodiment of scientific natural law which operates the universe and holds the stars in their courses. "The ideal of a clockwork universe was the great contribution of seventeenth-century science to the eighteenth-century age of reason."[6]

By contrast to the harmony and reasonableness of the natural world revealed by the scientists, society and its institutions seemed more and more archaic and the world of man seemed one governed by intolerance, prejudice, strife, and unreasoning authority. But in the face of the teachings of science, many men were convinced that their world of religion, law, and government could also be brought under the control of reason.

The problem of how to reconcile old faiths with new truths had become, in the words of a noted French scholar, the "crisis in the European conscience."[7] Scholars and thinkers, therefore, set about seeing what could be reconciled between the old and new, what faiths if any might be left intact, and what should be completely discarded.

The dualism of Descartes. We must now return briefly to Descartes, for in addition to his many other endeavors this pioneer thinker sought to reconcile medieval religious faith with a mechanistic world in which supernatural phenomena were impossible and in which everything had to be explained rationally. According to Descartes, reason was the chief source of knowledge. By logical methods of thought, the nature of reality, the existence of God, and the existence of the human self could be demonstrated. Descartes' proof of the existence of God was based on his assertion that, since existence must be an attribute of perfection and since the Deity must by definition be the all-perfect Being, a God must perforce exist.

Descartes divided ultimate reality into two substances: mind and matter. He argued that there was no connection between the two realms except by God's intervention. The first was the realm of faith and theology, im-

penetrable and unknowable to science; the second was that of reason and the laws of nature, subject to the understandable processes of science. Thus Descartes, a loyal Catholic, sought to reconcile the old and the new by his system of philosophical dualism.

Spinoza and pantheism. Born in Holland to well-to-do Jewish refugees who had fled from the Inquisition in Portugal, Baruch Spinoza (1632-1677) was another thinker who sought to reconcile spirit and matter. Following the methods of Descartes, Spinoza strove to build a mathematical philosophy: his *Ethics* (1663) is filled with geometric axioms, postulates, and theories. But Descartes' dualistic system was rejected by Spinoza, to whom mind and matter were manifestations of one substance—nature, or God. In other words, the universe and God are one. While Spinoza was alive, both Jews and Christians persecuted him, but his true spirituality later was better understood. He has been called "the God-intoxicated man."

Locke and empiricism. In the main, the Continental philosophers were rationalists who believed that knowledge is gained through reasoning. By contrast, English thinkers tended to believe that knowledge came only from sensory experience, a school of thought known as empiricism. Its founder was John Locke (1632-1704), who felt that there was too much abstruse and flighty thought in Europe.

In 1690 Locke published *An Essay Concerning Human Understanding*, which sought to analyze the human mind. According to him, the mind at birth is like a blank tablet (*tabula rasa*), and the experience gained through the senses is recorded on this tablet. Unlike the rationalists on the Continent, Locke maintained that, of itself, the mind has no innate power to grasp reality. In acquiring knowledge, however, the mind is not completely passive. Locke believed that reflection also played a role: by the process of association, the mind combines new and old impressions to form a new idea.

Locke's empiricism was of fundamental importance in the cultural development of modern Europe. A true son of the Age of Reason, Locke believed that investigation of such basic philosophical questions as the existence of God and the fundamentals of morality would lead men to a state of universal reasonableness and thereby free them from the necessity of relying blindly on authority.

Deism: a solution to the spiritual crisis. By the end of the first quarter of the eighteenth century the crisis in the European conscience had eased. After this time most intellectuals pegged their faith to the new science and the new philosophy.

Upon this rationalistic, scientific basis they built their religion. Known as Deism, it stripped Christianity of most of its traditional dogmas. God—thought of as an impersonal force—became in their eyes the First Cause, the custodian of the world machine, the master "clockwinder" of the universe. God had been necessary to create the universe, but once the universe had been set in motion, its immutable laws could not be altered. It was regarded as useless to invoke the intercession of God to bring about a deviation from the laws of nature. Men must rely upon reason, not miracles, to solve the problems of society.

The Deistic concept of a "natural" religion included only a few basic beliefs: the existence of God as master of the universe, the necessity of worshiping God, the atonement by man for his sins, the doctrine of immortality, and the view that the aim of religion is virtue, or sensible living. All religions were to be based on these simple and rational essentials; anything additional was extraneous and not worth squabbling about. Deists maintained that if all creeds would give up or at least minimize their "extraneous" dogmas, religious intolerance and bigotry would cease. The God of Deism was universal and acceptable to all. It mattered little what He was called. In the words of Alexander Pope:

Father of all! in every age,
In every clime adored,
By saint, by savage, and by sage,
Jehovah, Jove, or Lord![8]

The philosophes, critics of society. By 1750 France was so decidedly the intellectual center of Europe that it has been said "an opinion launched in Paris was like a batter-

ing ram launched by thirty millions of men."[9] Here a group of thinkers and writers known as the *philosophes* brought the Age of Reason to its climax.

The term *philosophes* cannot be translated as "philosophers," because they were not philosophers in any strict sense but rather students of society who analyzed its evils and advocated reforms. Foremost among these *philosophes* were Voltaire and Diderot, whose influence will be noted in this chapter, and Rousseau and Montesquieu, whose importance in political reform will be discussed in Chapter 20.

Voltaire, prince of the philosophes. More than any other thinker, Voltaire (1694-1778) personified the skepticism of the eighteenth century toward traditional religion and the evils of the time. He enjoyed exercising a caustic pen, soon ran afoul of the law, twice was imprisoned in the Bastille, and finally was banished to England for three years. Upon his return to France, Voltaire again championed tolerance, popularized the science of Newton, fought for personal liberty and freedom of the press, and acted as an influential propagandist for Deism. He turned out a prodigious number of works: histories, plays, pamphlets, essays, and novels. In his correspondence—estimated at ten thousand letters—he wittily spread the gospel of rationalism and scathingly attacked the abuses of his day.

Voltaire achieved his greatest fame as the most relentless critic of the established churches, Protestant and Catholic alike. He was sickened by the intolerance of organized Christianity and disgusted by the petty squabbles which seemed to monopolize the time of many priests and clergymen. Yet, in spite of his vituperation against Christianity, Voltaire did not wish to wreck religion. He once said that if a God did not exist, it would be necessary to invent one.

Voltaire's short fictional satire *Candide* (1759) was a biting attack on the easy optimism of some *philosophes* and the view that this world is "the best of all possible worlds." As his hero, Voltaire used a naive young man, Candide, who learns after many hair-raising and comic adventures that the "best of all possible worlds" is rent by earthquakes, famines, plagues, greed, war, and injustice. The story ends with Candide advising his former tutor, Dr. Pangloss, that we must "cultivate our garden" (instead of concerning ourselves with unanswerable philosophical questions)—a succinct expression of Voltaire's common-sense approach to life.

Diderot and the Encyclopédie. Voltaire had many disciples and imitators, but his only rival in spreading the gospel of rationalism and Deism was a set of books—the famous French *Encyclopédie*, edited by Denis Diderot (1713-1784). The *Encyclopédie* constituted the chief monument of the *philosophes*, declaring the supremacy of the new science, championing tolerance, denouncing superstition, and expounding the merits of Deism. Its seventeen volumes contained articles whose authors—tradesmen as well as scientists and philosophers—criticized in a moderate tone unfair taxation, the slave trade, and the cruelty of the existing criminal code.

The Pietist reaction. In the middle of the eighteenth century there developed a reaction against both the rational approach of Deism and the cold formality of much organized religion. This new religious movement, known as Pietism, developed to restore faith, emotion, and the spirit as the mainsprings of worship.

Pietism was foreshadowed by the teachings of George Fox (1624-1691), the founder of the religious sect called the Quakers, or the Society of Friends. Fox believed that the external aspects of Christianity—dogma, organization, and ritual—were unimportant compared to the spiritual experience of the individual (the "inner light"). The Quakers criticized religious intolerance severely and condemned warfare.

The surge of Pietism got under way in England in 1738, when the brothers John and Charles Wesley began to preach to the people in a new way, discarding the formalism of the established church for a glowing

The French *philosophes* were not only acquainted with each other's ideas, but were also personal friends. In this eighteenth-century engraving some prominent *philosophes* are gathered for dinner and conversation—among them Voltaire, with his hand in the air, and Diderot, to the right of Voltaire.

emotionalism. Instead of stilted sermons, the Wesleys offered extemporaneous appeals charged with religious fervor. *Methodist*— at first a term of derision—came to be the respected and official name of the movement. After John Wesley's death in 1791, the Methodists officially broke away from the Anglican Church, and the new denomination became one of the most important religious forces in England's national life.

On the European continent, Pietists stressed "the religion of the heart" rather than that of unimportant externals. In some Catholic countries a religious movement similar to Pietism arose—Quietism—but it was quickly crushed by the alliance of Church and state.

Kant and the Critique of Pure Reason. The German philosopher Immanuel Kant (1724-1804) symbolized the revival of the heart and of faith. Thoroughly aroused by the exaggerated skepticism and materialism of the age, he determined to shift philosophy back to a more sensible position without giving up too much of its "rational" basis. Kant's answer, contained in the *Critique of Pure Reason* (1781), marked the end of eighteenth-century natural philosophy and ushered in philosophical idealism, so important in the first part of the nineteenth century.

To resolve the conflict between mind and matter, Kant resorted to dualism. Beyond the physical world, which is the legitimate realm of science or "pure reason," lies the world of "things-in-themselves," he believed, where science can never penetrate and which is the legitimate realm of faith or "practical reason." Kant agreed that the existence of God could not be demonstrated scientifically but declared that man's moral sense compels him to believe in the immortality of the soul and in the presence of God. Thus Kant put as the basis of religious faith not reason, which is subject to experience, but an absolute innate moral sense, a conscience which is independent of experience yet able to distinguish between right and wrong. On this basis, Kant believed that free will and the existence of God could be proven. Reason cannot prove that there is a just God behind the world as it is, but our moral sense demands such a belief. Thus there are truths of the heart above and beyond those of the head.

The new humanitarianism. Pervading the thought of the Enlightenment was a deep concern for the welfare of mankind. Belief in the helplessness of man and the depravity of human nature was superseded by recognition of man's mental and moral dignity. Intolerance and undue emphasis upon dogma and form were giving way to the practical application of Christ's teachings and to religious tolerance.

"It was the special function of the Eighteenth Century," wrote the English historian Trevelyan, "to diffuse common sense and reasonableness in life and thought, to civilize manners and to humanize conduct."[10] Notable among its humanizing functions was the emergence of the antislavery movement in England, spearheaded by the Quakers and the Methodists. A court case in 1772 in effect ended slavery in England itself, and the insistence that the black man anywhere should by law be considered as a human being rather than as property alone was prominent in litigation of the 1780's. The agitation against slavery found its foremost champion in William Wilberforce (1759-1833), who, beginning in 1789, introduced motions in the House of Commons to end trafficking in human misery, until in 1807 the slave trade in British territories was legally abolished. Not content with this victory, Wilberforce carried on his crusade to free all slaves in the British empire, a goal that was reached in 1833, the year in which he died.

One of the outstanding characteristics of the eighteenth century was its cosmopolitanism. This quality was so strong that even war did not necessarily breed extreme national hatreds. During the long period in which France was at war with most of Europe, English thinkers and their *philosophe* friends in Paris could fraternize with no difficulty. Proud of belonging to the European "republic of letters," the intellectuals of the time were gravely concerned with the problem of war. As we have seen, Voltaire made a scathing attack on war in *Candide*, and several works were written urging the creation of machinery to enforce peace.

TOWARD A NEW SCIENCE OF MAN

Birth of the social sciences. One of the great achievements of the eighteenth century was the application of the methods of science to the better understanding of man. The *philosophes* believed that by such application the laws governing society could be discovered. As one of them observed:

I believed that morals should be treated like all other sciences, and that one should arrive at a moral principle as one proceeds with an experiment in physics.[11]

This spirit of inquiry led to important innovations in the writing of history and the creation of those studies known today as the social sciences—political science, economics, anthropology, and psychology. In addition, important advances were made in criminology and education.

The ideas of progress and human perfectibility—concepts basic to the temper of the eighteenth century—were expressed most clearly by the Marquis de Condorcet, a member of the circle of *philosophes* around Voltaire. In his famous *Progress of the Human Mind* (1794) Condorcet asserts that there are no limits to human perfectibility and declares that progress will come by abolishing inequalities between nations, by securing equality for all men within nations, and by improving the human race in mind and body.

The writing of history. The greatest historian of this period was an Englishman, Edward Gibbon (1737-1794). The prose of this master craftsman was polished again and again until it emerged in glittering and sonorous sentences that carry the reader along with their majestic cadence. Gibbon shared the rational spirit of his day, and his *Decline and Fall of the Roman Empire* (1776-1787) was a vehicle for his ideas. He exposed the evils of tyrannical rulers and attacked the "barbarism and religion" that in his view had weakened the greatness of classical Roman culture.

Voltaire was also a historian of no mean merit, creating a new form, or school, of history, one that forsook the old reliance on wars and the foibles of rulers. He was interested in capturing "the spirit of the times" and in describing the progress and influence of ideas; in short, Voltaire approached history as an account of the evolution of civilization.

Men like the Italian Giovanni Battista Vico studied the "philosophy" of history—not the "what happened" so much as the "why." In his important *Principles of a New Science* (1725) Vico discussed the operation of laws in history, stressing the idea that every age is imbued with a certain "psychology," mood, or point of view and that each age is not only the product of the one preceding but also the creator of the next.

Other social sciences. The eighteenth century witnessed notable advances in political science, the study of government. In Chapter 20 we shall read of the writings of Hobbes, Bossuet, and Locke, and note the work of the *philosophes* Rousseau and Montesquieu as they analyzed the machinery and purposes of government.

Economics as a distinct subject for study emerged in the last half of the seventeenth century, much of it justifying the policy of mercantilism. Later, the Scotsman Adam Smith (see p. 467), and a number of the French *philosophes* known as the physiocrats made important contributions to economic theory by attacking the prevailing mercantilistic philosophy and initiating economic principles that were dominant down to the twentieth century.

As efforts were made to classify human races and to make comparative studies of various groups of people, the first halting steps were taken toward a science of anthropology. Much of the information used for these studies was provided by the writings of explorers, traders, and missionaries.

The science of criminology was established by the Italian Cesare Beccaria, whose *Essay on Crimes and Punishments* (1764) contained the plea that prison terms should be deterrents to crime rather than punishments for crime. Shortly thereafter, John Howard in England stressed the need for efficient prison administration and maintained that the chief aim of imprisonment should be reformation of the criminal.

New attitudes toward education. Until the eighteenth century education was almost unattainable for common people, the subjects taught often bore no relation to the needs of actual life, and the prevailing idea seemed to be that schoolchildren needed frequent beatings. In that century, however, educational thought began to reflect the humanitarianism of the age.

The scientific basis for the psychology of learning as well as for modern psychology in general was laid by the versatile British thinker John Locke at the end of the seventeenth century. His conception of the mind as a *tabula rasa* (blank tablet) at birth, and of the adult mind as one formed by experience through sensation and refined and tempered by reflection, memory, and judgment, was basic to the development of the discipline of psychology. One of the most important influences in education was that exerted by Jean Jacques Rousseau (1712-1778), whose novel *Émile* (1762) stated that the aim of education should be self-expression, not repression. Education must be many-sided to appeal to different children; and the pupil, not the subject matter, is most important.

Pietism, along with rationalism, entered into the motivation of education. In England the Sunday School movement, sponsored mainly by the Methodists, was a pioneer attempt to bring the rudiments of learning to the poor.

SCIENTIFIC PROGRESS CONTINUES

The dawn of modern medicine. We have seen the spectacular discoveries made in astronomy and mathematics and their profound impact on thought and religion. Meanwhile, scientific progress was being made in other branches of knowledge, with medicine being one of the first to be placed upon a scientific foundation.

Paracelsus (1493-1541), a contemporary of Copernicus, was an egotistical, opinionated German-Swiss physician who was so annoyed with the tyranny of tradition in his field that he advocated instead the value of experimental science. The gist of his teachings was that since the human body was basically chemical in its construction, the prescription of chemicals was in turn required to cure disease. He appears to have been the first to use such drugs as silver nitrate, copper vitriol, and arsenic and antimony compounds and to introduce the zinc oxide ointment commonly used today for treatment of skin diseases. One of his most original books dealt with the peculiar ailments of miners—the poisonous effects of metallic dusts that penetrated their skin, lungs, and mucous membranes.

Another scientist to find himself at odds with the followers of Galen and Hippocrates was Andreas Vesalius (1514-1564), a native of Brussels. Although he did not deny the merits of the Greek authorities, Vesalius contended that in medical schools, attention should first be given to the actual dissection of human bodies. At the age of twenty-three, Vesalius became a professor at the famous University of Padua. He was perhaps the first professor to perform dissection in the classroom. In 1543, within a few weeks of the appearance of Copernicus' masterpiece, Vesalius published his treatise *The Fabric of the Human Body*. This work exposed the errors made by classical scholars, showed the true structure of the human body, and by its revolutionary approach achieved for anatomy what Copernicus' book did for astronomy.

A commensurate advance in physiology (without which there could be no science of internal medicine) was made by the Englishman William Harvey (1578-1657), who had studied at Padua. Becoming interested in the problem of how the blood travels, Harvey plunged into painstaking research. Aristotle had declared that the blood was carried from the liver to the heart and thence sent by veins to the various parts of the body, and Galen believed that the arteries also contained blood. In Harvey's time doctors thought that the blood moved in the body, but they knew nothing of the functions of the heart nor did they know that the blood travels in a continuous stream, returning to its source. Harvey's description of the circulation of the blood,

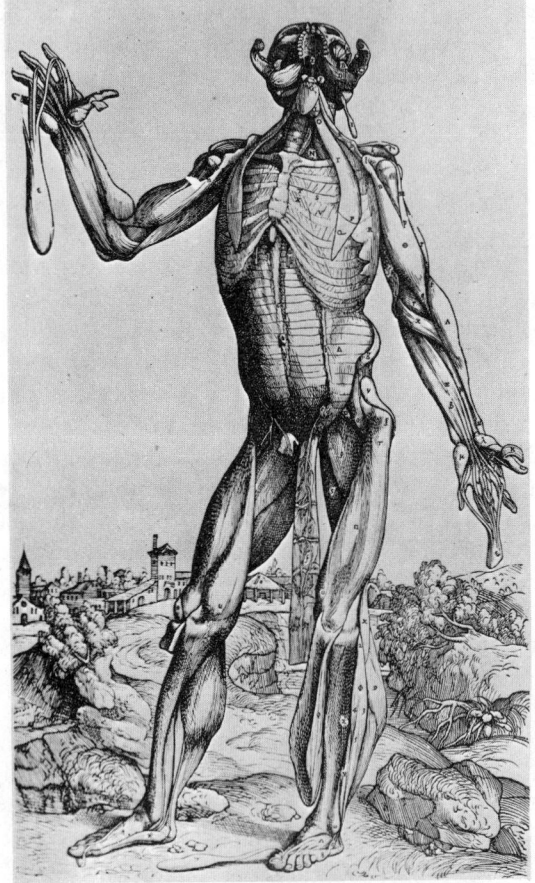

A detailed figure of a cadaver with its jawbone split and its muscles cut away appears in an illustration from *On the Fabric of the Human Body*, Vesalius' book on anatomy.

published in 1628 and entitled *Anatomical Exercise on the Motion of the Heart and Blood*, was a kind of master key to unlock the many doors leading to an understanding of how the human body functions.

In the eighteenth century, the most noteworthy advance in medicine was the introduction of inoculation against smallpox, then a fatal and widespread disease. About 1798 a perfected method, called vaccination, was introduced by the English physician Edward Jenner. A great step forward in the advance of medical diagnosis was the invention of the stethoscope, through which the sounds of the heart and respiratory organs could be heard. Still another advance was the study of blood pressure, one of the most important means of discovering disease. Although the method

employed was crude, it led to the making of modern-day apparatus.

Foundations of modern chemistry. The science of chemistry suffered from arrested development in the sixteenth and early seventeenth centuries as men followed the will-o'-the-wisps of alchemy and magic. Then appeared the son of an Irish nobleman, Robert Boyle, who is considered the father of modern chemistry. In 1660 he formulated the law that "at constant temperature, the volume of a gas varies inversely as the pressure upon it" (Boyle's law). And in his influential book *The Sceptical Chemist* (1661) he struck out against alchemy and urged the use of inductive inquiry in chemistry.

Joseph Priestley, an English chemist, isolated ammonia, the gas which in modern times plays an important role in the refrigeration process; and in 1774, he discovered the gas later named oxygen. His last important experiment in 1799 was the production of carbon monoxide gas. Much of the gas used in our homes for cooking and heating purposes is made by the method first devised by Priestley.

Through Boyle and Priestley, chemistry had come a long way from medieval alchemy, but it would not become an exact science until the phlogiston theory of combustion could be disproved. This theory contended that in all inflammable things there existed a combustible substance called phlogiston (from the Greek "to set on fire"), which was "a principle of fire, but not fire itself." Destruction of the phlogiston theory was the remarkable achievement of the eighteenth-century French scientist Antoine Lavoisier.

Supporters of the old theory maintained that phlogiston was removed during combustion. By using chemists' scales in his experiment, Lavoisier proved that nothing was given off, that, on the contrary, something was added. From this evidence Lavoisier reasoned that burning is a process in which the "dephlogisticated air" (oxygen) discovered by Priestley is taken from ordinary air and unites with the substance consumed. By decomposing the red powder he had obtained by burning mercury, Lavoisier conclusively proved his thesis; the loss of weight of the powder was exactly equivalent to the weight of the dephlogisticated air given off. To the element so essential in combustion Lavoisier gave a new name—*oxygen*.

In his experiments on combustion Lavoisier also discovered the law of the conservation of matter—that matter cannot be created or destroyed. With the knowledge that weight is a constant and that the scientist, aided by his balance, can accurately determine by weight the substances in any compound, measurements in chemistry could be made with the precision required of an exact science.

Beginnings of electricity. Only three hundred years ago practically nothing was known of electricity and its seemingly magical potentialities. The scientist William Gilbert was the first to use the term *electricity*, which he derived from the Greek word for amber (*elektron*). In his work *De Magnete* (1600) Gilbert described the attraction between magnets as well as the forces which are created when bodies such as amber are rubbed.

The next important step in the history of electricity was the creation of a crude machine to produce it. A device consisting of a globe of sulfur set in a glass sphere mounted on a revolving axis was invented in 1660. When rubbed by a cloth, it produced both sound and light. With this device an electric current could be sent from one end of a thread to the other—the first hint of possibilities for the transmission of electricity. The discovery in 1745 of the Leyden Jar at the University of Leyden in the Netherlands made possible the accumulation in a glass phial of the electricity which was produced by friction.

The next important advance is credited to Benjamin Franklin, who was America's first great name in science. Believing that lightning was identical with the static electricity in the Leyden Jar, Franklin in June 1752 carried out his famous kite experiment during a thunderstorm. Holding the kite string with a key tied to it, he soon felt the tingle of electricity in the key, through which electricity was freely conducted as the rain soaked the string. Franklin's experiment provided a rational explanation for what had been an awe-inspiring and terrifying phenomenon for thousands of years. The experiment led to the invention of the lightning rod, which soon became standard equipment on all important buildings.

Another great name in electricity is that of Alessandro Volta. In 1800 Volta, an Italian physicist, found a new way of generating electricity; he was able to make it flow continuously instead of discharging itself in one spark as was the case with the Leyden Jar. Volta's apparatus consisted of a set of glass tumblers containing water and a little sulfuric acid. In each solution two plates, one copper and one zinc, were immersed. The copper plate of one glass was wired to the zinc of the next. Electricity flowed through the connecting wires; the free copper plate carried a positive charge and the free zinc plate, a negative charge. Thus Volta's machine—the direct ancestor of modern electric cells and batteries—produced electricity simply but effectively. Volta's name has been immortalized in the term used for a unit of electrical measurement, the volt.

Advances in other sciences. Another science which made remarkable advances during the eighteenth century was geology. Here the most important figure was a Scottish gentleman farmer, James Hutton. His two-volume work, *Theory of the Earth* (1795), completely overthrew the catastrophic theory then current, which taught that the earth's surface was the result of sudden catastrophic action. In brief, Hutton maintained that behind all the various formations of the earth's surface two fundamental processes are at work in a constant and relatively imperceptible manner. The two processes are disintegration, or decay, and reconstruction, or repair. Through the action of water and wind and chemical decomposition, the former continually wears away the earth's surface. The process of reconstruction takes place as the material carried off and deposited on ocean, lake, and valley floors constantly forms new strata. By changing the concept of the earth as a static thing and stressing the immensity of geological time, Hutton gave the world an entirely new time perspective.

Exploration and scientific investigations in the seventeenth and eighteenth centuries brought to light a vast body of new information on plant and animal life which had to be classified. The old, unscientific method, which had designated all living things as fish, birds, beasts, trees, herbs, or shrubs, was inadequate to cope with the wealth of new data. The eighteenth-century Swedish naturalist Carolus Linnaeus worked out a logical system of plant classification, dividing the plant kingdom into classes, orders, genera, and species—still the basis of modern nomenclature. In the field of zoology the French scientist Georges Buffon performed the same function Linnaeus had performed in botany.

THE ARTS IN EARLY MODERN TIMES

The "anti-Renaissance" style: Mannerism. In Italy, where the Renaissance had initially burst forth, a countermovement in art appeared in the sixteenth century. There artists —who so often act as barometers to register sensitive changes in the cultural atmosphere

During the Renaissance renewed interest in classical antiquity resulted in the frequent use of subjects from Greek and Roman mythology. Benvenuto Cellini's salt-cellar represents Neptune, god of the sea, and Tellus, goddess of the earth. A virtuoso study in the technique of the goldsmith, it is less a utilitarian object than a piece of fine art. The boat in the foreground served as a salt receptacle, while an arch of triumph on the opposite side was designed to hold pepper.

—responded to the stresses of the Protestant and Catholic Reformations. The result was the development in Italian painting of a new, "anti-Renaissance" style called Mannerism. No longer was the artist working in that spirit of calm and balance, of harmony and proportion, which had prevailed in Renaissance art at its finest. The Mannerist artist lived instead in a state of doubt and indecision, and his work reflected those tensions. Technically speaking, Renaissance painters had mastered the problems of space and perspective, so that the artist placed his figures in balanced relationships enriched by vigorous and harmonious colors. By contrast, Mannerist painters such as Tintoretto (1518-1594) often defied the rules of perspective in order to obtain an oblique and even twisted point of view; their lines might be agitated, their designs asymmetric. They did not hesitate to distort the human figure in order to achieve emotional intensity and create new psychological effects.

Among the sculptors of the Mannerist period was the boastful Benvenuto Cellini (see p. 286), whose overelaborate compositions are typical of the extreme individualism and experimentation of the period. Some Mannerist architects sought to develop a more lavish classical style. The exaggerated magnificence of the Villa Rotunda near Venice, designed by Andrea Palladio (1518-1580), was achieved by grouping four identical temple facades on the sides of a square domed building. The Palladian style so impressed later generations that Thomas Jefferson used the Villa Rotunda as a prototype for his own Monticello.

Outside Italy the Mannerist style found its greatest achievements in the works of El Greco ("the Greek"). Born in Crete as Domenico Theotocopuli, El Greco (1547-1614) studied in Italy and later settled in Toledo in Spain. He was not concerned with depicting nature realistically but distorted space and perspective to create an often eerie world of the imagination. To achieve dramatic effects, he used *chiaroscuro* (strong contrasts of light and shade) and abrupt transitions in color. El Greco's paintings are easily recognizable for their elongated figures (see illustration, p. 432). To us he appears amazingly "modern,"

The Villa Rotunda, an aristocratic country house designed by Andrea Palladio in 1550, is one of his most famous buildings. It was to become the inspiration for later English and American architects.

and his works have had a decided influence upon twentieth-century painting.

Triumph of the Baroque style. Meanwhile, other developments had been pushing aside the doubts characteristic of Mannerism and were helping create a style expressing the varied facets of the seventeenth century: its intellectual zest, religious exaltation, sensuality, and violence. By announcing its regeneration with majestic voice, the Church of the Catholic Reformation indirectly exerted a powerful influence on the development of a new style of artistic expression—one that would proclaim the message of the revived Church with pomp and circumstance. This new style was the Baroque.

The Baroque style sought to synthesize two major traditions, one derived from the Middle Ages, the other from the Renaissance. The medieval esthetic tradition was transcendental in its purpose and marked by religious intensity, while the Renaissance was more natural in its conception and technically brilliant. In his synthesis the Baroque artist sought by the skill and grandeur of his treatment to arouse the strongest possible emotions in the beholder. As a result, by an emphatic use of color, gesture, ornamentation, and movement, he developed a style that tended to be grandiose and exaggerated. In keeping with the spirit of the times, moreover, the Baroque gave expression to two new forces in Europe; the Catholic Reformation and royal absolutism (see Chapter 20). "In its sacred branch it discharged the mighty task of realizing and consolidating a Catholic reform of art, of emphasizing the aesthetic and emotional side of religion. In the secular field it ministered to the pomp and pride of princes. To both church and throne it lent effulgence."[12]

The Baroque style merged painting, sculpture, and architecture in new, large-scale combinations marked by heroic proportions and dramatic arrangements of light and space. One of the creators of the Baroque in painting whose influence permeated western Europe was the Italian artist Caravaggio (1565-1609). He also painted religious themes but with a realism and solidity totally different from that of the Mannerists. By painting his models' faces in sharp light against a dark background, he substituted a down-to-earth naturalism for the artifices of Mannerism (see Color Plate 13).

The cool and objective point of view displayed by the canvases of the Spanish court painter Diego Velázquez (1599-1660) seem static alongside the sensuous exuberance of Rubens and the mannerisms of El Greco. Velázquez painted exactly what he saw in a style essentially his own, an unaffected and unadorned naturalism. He did not paint forms or surfaces so much as the movement of light over those surfaces, which produced an effect of the utmost reality. This preoccupation with light explains his "modernity" and especially his influence upon the French Impressionists of the nineteenth century.

The Dutch masters: Hals, Vermeer, Rembrandt. The first half of the seventeenth century was a golden age for Holland. Prosperous and comfortable, the burghers often acted as patrons of the arts. Their tastes in paintings differed greatly from those of kings, prelates, and aristocrats. These Dutch merchants and bankers favored familiar scenes of the flat lush countryside, seascapes in all seasons, and comfortable household interiors. A horde of competent Dutch painters arose in response to the demands of this republican art, and their overproduction soon depressed prices and created the image of the starving artist. Among the Dutch painters, the names of Hals, Vermeer, and Rembrandt stand out.

The robust Frans Hals (1580-1666) possessed a vigorous style that enabled him to catch with particular success the spontaneous, fleeting expressions of his portrait sub-

El Greco, the master of the Mannerist style, was deeply influenced by Tintoretto. Carrying the revolt against Renaissance style even further, El Greco distorted his figures to obtain the desired emotional intensity. In "St. Martin and the Beggar" the elongation gives the beggar's body a suggestion of weightlessness.

jects (see illustration, p. 433). His canvases provide us with a wonderful gallery of types—from cavaliers to fishwives and tavern denizens. As for Jan Vermeer (1632-1675), the subtle delicacy with which he handled the fall of subdued sunlight upon interior scenes has never been equaled (see illustration, p. 433). His few canvases raised *genre* painting to perfection, and today each commands a king's ransom.

The finest of Dutch painters—and one who ranks with the outstanding artists of all time—was Rembrandt van Rijn (1606-1669). His straightforward and realistic works gained him fame at an early age, but his later work declined in popularity as his style became more subtle. He concentrated progressively in his portraits on psychological and emotional qualities, and his work exhibits a strong element of the dramatic, which links Rembrandt to the mainstream of Baroque style (see illustration, p. 433).

Baroque architecture. The Baroque style endowed architecture with a new emotional significance, dynamism, and fluidity. Where the architecture of the Renaissance is severe and self-contained and emphasizes symmetry and "squareness," the Baroque sweeps us off our feet by subjecting us to an almost physical pull. It is a magnificent stage set, full of visual illusions intended to arouse an emotional response.

The capital of the new Baroque architecture was Rome, and the most renowned seventeenth-century architect of the Baroque school was Giovanni Lorenzo Bernini (1598-1680). He designed the colonnades outside the Basilica of St. Peter's, and his plan is typical of the Baroque use of vast spaces and curving lines. Besides being an accomplished architect and painter, Bernini was also a magnificent sculptor, as were many other artists of the Baroque. In fact the architect acted also as a sculptor, painter, and interior decorator, for the integration of Baroque art reached the point where it became difficult to see where one style of art left off and where another began (see illustration, p. 434).

After 1600 the Baroque style spread over much of Europe, being favored both by the Catholic Church and by rulers whose palaces

Seventeenth-century Dutch artists preferred portraits of the citizens themselves and scenes of daily life to religious subjects and grandiose display. Within these confines, however, they used various techniques and created different effects, as evident in these paintings of women in different walks of life. "The Bohemian Girl" by Franz Hals (left) shows the subject in a vigorous and joyful manner—the facial expression quickly conveys the mood. Hals' technique consisted of economical brushwork using a few vigorous strokes. The canvas may have the immediacy of a sketch but in reality it was done with careful precision. In "The Lacemaker" by Jan Vermeer (bottom left), the artist maintains complete equilibrium between visual perception and abstract organization. The fullness with which each is realized gives his paintings their great distinction. "Flora" by Rembrandt van Rijn (bottom right) is an example of the care and precision he used in describing his subject. An insight into the personality of the subjects sets the Rembrandt portrait apart from similar works of his contemporaries.

were designed to serve as symbols of power and magnificence. The Baroque features of the luxurious palace of Louis XIV at Versailles (see p. 445), an ideal which nearly every European prince hoped to attain, include the sweeping composition of its vast facade as well as its formal gardens with their imposing fountains, formal statuary, and elegant rows of hedges. In the interior, the silk and velvet draperies, rich marbles, and gilded carving created a background for profuse painted decoration. Although the Baroque won little favor in England or its colonies, Sir Christopher Wren's St. Paul's Cathedral, completed in 1710, blends the classical and the Baroque. Its Baroque features include the lantern atop its imposing dome and the two turrets flanking the facade.

The Rococo style. In France early in the eighteenth century a variation on the Baroque, called Rococo, appeared as a reaction to the Baroque's robustness and exuberance. Manifested chiefly in interior decoration and in painting, the Rococo is an intimate, gay, and dainty style. In the designing of interiors, the grandiose features of the Baroque are replaced by an almost effeminate delicacy (see below). The Rococo paintings of Jean Antoine Watteau (d. 1721) delicately blend fantasy with acute observation of nature and reflect the grace, ease, luxuriousness, and gentle artificiality of eighteenth-century French court life (see illustration p. 436).

Classicism and the arts. Even during the heyday of the Baroque in the seventeenth century, many of the arts continued to follow the tenets of classicism often reinforced by the cultivation of reason. This was generally true of all the arts in England and of some of the arts, particularly literature, in France.

By the eighteenth century a great classical revival, usually called Neoclassicism, was under way in all the fine arts as well as literature. Inspired in part by the order and symmetry of the world as revealed by science,

The influence of the Roman Baroque on aristocratic French interiors is evident in the Appartement du Roi in Cheverny, built before 1634 (right). Representative of the extravagant yet delicate Rococo style of interior decoration is the music room in the Potsdam palace of Frederick II (left).

and in part by a reaction against the Baroque and the Rococo, the creative artists of the Age of Reason were noteworthy for their rationalism, sophistication, balance, and self-control. Furthermore, the Enlightenment was a continuation of Renaissance humanism and its revival of antiquity, coupled with the new scientific outlook. In literature and the arts there was a respect for definite rules and conventions. The men of the time felt spiritually akin to Rome's Augustan Age and strove to exhibit the same stability, refined polish, and control over emotion. In consequence, every work of art tended to have a cold, rational aspect, whether it was a philosophical poem by Pope or a dainty symphony by Haydn. Inspiration sprang from the intellect, not the heart; from reason, not emotion. Generally speaking, classical forms were slavishly imitated; to writers the style of expression was considered so all-important that many of them were content to express old ideas so long as they were elegantly phrased.

French classical drama. The veneration for order and restraint was reflected in seventeenth-century French drama, with its emphasis on the rules of classical tragedy as first defined by Aristotle. His strictures had been expanded and redefined in the Renaissance as the three unities: unity of action (a single plot line shorn of irrelevant subplots), unity of time (confinement of a play's action to a single day), and unity of place (restriction of setting to one locale). It was believed that the illusion of reality, so essential to the success of the drama, would be destroyed if the unities were ignored. "Reason leads us to accept these rules," stated a French critic, truly a man of his times.

The works of the two greatest writers of tragedy in the seventeenth century—Pierre Corneille and Jean Racine—are important not so much for their scrupulous adherence to rigid conventions, however, as for their psychological insights and polished beauty of language. For plots, they relied on tales from Greek and Roman mythology or events of antiquity; for heroes and heroines, they drew idealized characterizations of the courtiers of their own day.

With its immensity, statuary, and ornate dome, the Sta. Maria della Salute in Venice, designed by Baldassare Longhena, is an outstanding example of the power and magnificence exuded by Baroque architecture.

The wittiest comedies of the period were those of Molière. As a true voice of the Age of Reason, he believed that moderation and good sense were the keynotes of life and that any deviation from reasonable behavior was fair game for comedy. With rapier-like wit, he spoofed the pretensions of learned females and the aspirations of the social-climbing bourgeoisie. But like all great writers, Molière created characters that were universal figures as well as individuals of his own time.

Alexander Pope. The foremost exponent of Neoclassicism in English literature was the poet Alexander Pope (1688-1744). An imitator of the classical satirists Horace and Juvenal, Pope ridiculed those who did not conform to the standards of the age:

Pains, reading, study are their just pretense,
And all they want is spirit, taste, and sense.[13]

Shying away from the robust heavy-handedness of the Baroque period, Watteau aspired to a more graceful, gentle art form. His "Réunion en Plein Air" displays the quick, supple line and light, sensitive brushwork characteristic of the Rococo style.

In his most famous poem, *An Essay on Man* (1733), Pope reduced to a series of epigrams the philosophy of his day. Reflecting the strong note of optimism so characteristic of the Enlightenment, Pope accepted the cosmos thus:

All are but parts of one stupendous whole,
Whose body nature is, and God the soul. . . .
All nature is but art, unknown to thee;
All chance, direction, which thou canst not see.
All discord, harmony not understood;
All partial evil, universal good;
And, spite of pride, in erring reason's spite,
One truth is clear: *Whatever is, is right.*[14]

The English novel. In conformity with the emphasis on clarity and simplicity in an age of science and reason, the eighteenth century was in general an age of prose. This contributed to the growth of a new literary form —the novel. Daniel Defoe's *Robinson Crusoe* (1719) is sometimes called the forerunner of the modern novel, but the title is probably better deserved by Samuel Richardson's *Pamela* (1740-1741), written in the form of letters. In line with the rationalistic temper of the age, Richardson's servant-girl heroine succeeds in holding her lecherous employer at bay with lectures on moral philosophy until virtue at length has its reward and the reformed rake proposes marriage.

With Henry Fielding the novel achieved full stature. Disgusted with Richardson's "goody-goodness," Fielding achieved fame by parodying the latter's smug sentimentality and, as the author of *Tom Jones* (1749), by composing one of the great novels in English literature. The hero Tom is a high-spirited, good-hearted young man who is continually being exploited by self-seeking worldlings and led astray by designing females. Finally, after many comic adventures, he learns eventually that he must check his natural impulsiveness with good sense and reasonable behavior.

In keeping with the Age of Reason's attack on irrational customs and outworn institutions, this period produced masterpieces of satire, such as Voltaire's *Candide*. One of England's outstanding satirists was Jonathan Swift, whose *Gulliver's Travels* (1726) ridicules the pettiness of man's quarrels, wars, and vices. For example, in the fictitious country of Lilliput, Captain Gulliver finds two opposing factions: the Big-endians, who passionately maintain that eggs must be opened at the big end, and the Little-endians, who are equally vehement that the small end should be used. This absurd quarrel satirizes a petty religious dispute then raging in England. It is ironic that a satire such as *Gulliver's Travels*, because of its absorbing adventures and strange characters, should have become (in adapted form) a favorite book for children.

The Neoclassical style in architecture. About midway in the eighteenth century, a reaction set in against both Baroque and Rococo, manifesting itself in a return to the intrinsic dignity and restraint of what a contemporary called "the noble simplicity and tranquil loftiness of the ancients." Too often, however, the Neoclassical imitations and adaptations of the antique were cold and pedantic. The Madeleine in Paris (see below) is a faithful copy of a still-standing Roman temple, and the Brandenburg Gate in Berlin is modeled after the monumental entrance to the Acropolis in Athens. In England, where the classical style had resisted Baroque influences, the great country houses of the nobility now exhibited a purity of design which often included a portico with Corinthian columns. Outstanding as examples of

Neoclassicism in colonial America are Mount Vernon and the stately mansion of Thomas Jefferson at Monticello. Interest in the classical style carried over through the nineteenth century, and today in the United States many libraries and government buildings are classical in derivation.

Painting and sculpture. The arts of painting and sculpture in the Age of Reason were dominated by the tastes of the aristocracy. Watteau's successors in France—Boucher and Fragonard—mirrored the artificiality and idleness in which the aristocrats at Versailles, sometimes thinly disguised as Greek gods and goddesses, spent their lives. In England the most famous beauties of the day and many prominent men sat for portraits painted in the "grand manner" by Sir Joshua Reynolds or Thomas Gainsborough.

Two great nonconformist painters, William Hogarth in England and Francisco de Goya in Spain, strove to reproduce realistically the

Modeled after a Roman Corinthian temple, the Church of the Madeleine in Paris has columns sixty-three feet tall, a height which surpasses that of the temple of antiquity. The church has no windows in the walls; light is furnished by rounded windows in the roof.

life around them in the gutter, the tavern, and the royal court, sometimes using their art to draw attention to the evils of the day. In his series of paintings called "The Harlot's Progress," "The Rake's Progress," and "Marriage à la Mode," Hogarth showed himself to be a pictorial pamphleteer, shrewdly exposing the vices of London life (see illustration p. 439). Goya's portraits of the Spanish royal family and the nobility display his keen insight into character. In the early years of the nineteenth century his art reached its peak in a series of etchings of the Napoleonic invasion and occupation of Spain. Called "The Disasters of War," they portrayed in powerful, shocking fashion the bestiality and misery wrought by war. A typical example of Goya's abhorrence of brutality is the stark depiction of an execution in his painting "Shooting of the Rebels of May 3, 1808."

In sculpture the works produced in the eighteenth century were mostly imitations of classical forms and personages. French portrait sculpture was more original. Houdon's "Portrait of Voltaire" is an example of Neoclassical sculpture at its best.

Developments in music. As we saw in Chapter 13, late medieval religious music was polyphonic, not homophonic, in form. By the sixteenth century many-voiced polyphonic music had become so excessively complicated that some Church reformers at the Council of Trent demanded an end to polyphonic music and a return to the homophonic Gregorian chant of the early Middle Ages. The results of the Council's compromise decision were best expressed in the sacred music of Giovanni Palestrina (d. 1594), who greatly simplified the prevailing style by uniting homophony with polyphony. The restrained yet powerful effect of Palestrina's music has earned him the honor of being called the "first Catholic Church musician."

In the seventeenth century the Baroque spirit was manifested in music by the development of new forms of expression and by experiments in harmony which moved away from the calm and exalted manner of Palestrina. For the first time instrumental music—in particular that of the organ and the violin family—became of equal importance with

vocal music. Outstanding among Baroque innovations was opera, which originated in Italy at the beginning of the seventeenth century and quickly conquered Europe. With its opulence, highly charged emotional content, and sweep of expression, opera was almost the perfect musical expression of the Baroque style. Here again we find an integration of the arts: dramatic literature, music, and acting, with the skills of the painter employed for elaborate stage settings.

The elaboration of polyphonic music during the Baroque era culminated in the sumptuous effects of the deeply religious music of Johann Sebastian Bach (d. 1750), the prolific German organ master and choir director. Bach's equally great contemporary, the German-born, naturalized Englishman George Frederick Handel (1685-1759), is known for his large, dramatic, and mostly homophonic operas, oratorios, and cantatas; he is best known today for his religious oratorio *Messiah* (1742).

To composers living in the latter half of the eighteenth century, the style of the Baroque masters Bach and Handel seemed too heavy and complex. Like the other arts of the Age of Reason, music now exhibited greater clarity and simplicity of structure and a strict adherence to formal rules and models. Emphasis was placed on a homophonic style and on simple, often folklike, melodies, and most compositions followed the sonata-form with its three clearly defined thematic sections—exposition, elaboration, and recapitulation.

New musical forms reflected new trends in instrumental music. As symphonies, sonatas, concertos, and chamber music appeared, music became more than the mere accompaniment to religious services and operatic performances. The chamber music played in courts and salons was written for wood winds and brasses as well as strings. Thus the modern orchestra developed along with the symphonic form.

The music of the latter half of the eighteenth century, with its emphasis on technical perfection of form, melody, and orchestration, was summed up in the work of the Viennese composers Franz Joseph Haydn and Wolfgang Mozart. The prolific Haydn

In "The Marriage Contract," a painting from Hogarth's series "Marriage à la Mode," a wealthy but low-born merchant is arranging the marriage of his daughter to the son of an impoverished but high-born noble. While the fathers talk business, the daughter listens to the blandishments of a young lawyer, and the son, a silly fop, takes snuff and stares into space. Typical of Hogarth's method of putting satirical meaning into every detail of his work are the two chained dogs (left corner) who represent the plight of the young couple.

wrote over one hundred symphonies in addition to numerous other works. For his part, Mozart, a child prodigy who at the age of six was composing minuets, wrote forty-one symphonies, climaxing his career with a trio of famous operas, *The Marriage of Figaro, Don Giovanni,* and *The Magic Flute.*

SUMMARY

The Age of Reason was a vigorous and productive period in the history of western culture. The promise of science initiated by Copernicus was fulfilled in Newton's brilliant postulation of the law of gravitation. New sciences, such as chemistry, electricity, and geology, were founded; and other sciences, such as astronomy, physics, and medicine, were put on a scientific foundation. Meanwhile, a system of scientific method, or investigation, was established. Two thinkers, especially, investigated the problem of developing new methods of inquiry.

Francis Bacon placed chief reliance upon the inductive method, in which facts drawn from experimentation are used to formulate hypotheses and eventually to reach universal principles and scientific laws. A younger contemporary in France, Descartes, was more interested in deduction and used the mathematical method to reason his way to the concept of a mechanically run universe. Actually, the mathematical and experimental methods were complementary and were soon combined to promote the further advancement of science.

By the mid-point of the seventeenth century it was apparent that respect for science and scientific attitudes was to be the keynote of the culture of the new era. To many of the intellectuals, little seemed left of faith and traditional Christianity; and as men ceased to believe in miracles and denominational theology, what has been termed the "crisis in the European conscience" arose. Some met the crisis by turning to a new form of rational, scientific religion in which faith became a matter of logic and intellect. And as science came to modify religion substantially, so it also came to be applied to the affairs of men in society, to what we now term the social sciences. A start was made in organizing systematic studies in history, government, economics, and criminology.

In the field of literature and the arts, no less than in religion and the social sciences, scientific law and the vogue of rule played their part. Writing had to be faultlessly phrased, witty, and elegant. This polished, sophisticated, classical style reached its acme in the verses of Pope. While poetry and drama, on the whole, were not of a high order, the eighteenth century was one of great prose. The novel (which largely escaped the bonds of Neoclassical restriction) came of age in this period.

Preceded by a style of painting known as Mannerism—the best example of this troubled, distorted style is the work of El Greco—Baroque art and music captured the imagination and allegiance of seventeenth-century Europe. This exuberant and grandiloquent style gave way, in the eighteenth century, to the lighter Rococo and Neoclassical styles.

The portraits of Reynolds, the landscapes of Watteau, and the elegant musical patterns of Haydn served to embellish the essentially aristocratic culture of the Age of Reason. There are some critics of twentieth-century culture who look back with nostalgia to the aristocratic culture of the age. These critics see contemporary culture, dominated by the machine and by the mass mind, as vulgarized. The essence of history, however, is change and not permanence. In the latter half of the eighteenth century there were important signs that the primacy of the aristocracy and the dominance of rationalism were coming to an end. New currents and forces were being released that would produce sweeping changes and mold the nineteenth century into another distinct age in the history of western civilization.

SUGGESTIONS FOR READING

Short but meaty treatments of European culture, with valuable bibliographies, are contained in the following volumes in **The Rise of Modern Europe Series*** (Torchbooks): C. J. Friedrich, **The Age of the Baroque, 1610-1660;** F. L. Nussbaum, **The Triumph of Science and Reason, 1660-1685;** J. B. Wolf, **The Emergence of the Great Powers, 1685-1715;** P. Roberts, **The Quest for Security, 1715-1740;** W. L. Dorn, **Competition for Empire, 1740-1763;** and L. Gershoy, **From Despotism to Revolution, 1763-1789.**

Intellectual developments are the focus of attention in P. Smith, **A History of Modern Culture, 1543-1776,*** 2 vols. (Collier); and J. Bronowski and B. Mazlish, **The Western Intellectual Tradition from Leonardo to Hegel*** (Torchbooks).

H. Butterfield, **The Origins of Modern Science, 1300-1800*** (Free Press); and A. R. Hall, **The Scientific Revolution, 1500-1800*** (Beacon) are two highly recommended books on the formation of a modern scientific attitude. Two well-written volumes in Harper & Row's **Rise of Modern Science** Series are Marie Boas, **The Scientific Renaissance, 1450-1630;** and A. R. Hall, **From Galileo to Newton, 1630-1720.** For a condensed account by these same authors see **A Brief History of Science*** (Signet). See also L. M. Marsak, ed., **The Rise of Science in Relation to Society*** (Macmillan); and Alan G. Smith, **Science and Society in the Sixteenth and Seventeenth Centuries*** (Harcourt Brace Jovanovich, 1973). On applied science see Thomas P. Hughes, ed., **The Development of Western Technology Since 1500*** (Macmillan). T. S. Kuhn, **The Structure of Scientific Revolutions*** (Phoenix) discusses the dynamic factors involved in major conceptual changes in science. See also W. C. Dampier, **A History of Science** (Cambridge).

A. Koestler, **The Sleepwalkers: A History of Man's Changing Vision of the Universe*** (Penguin) is a stimulating study of cosmological reconceptualization in early modern times—involving Copernicus, Brahe, Kepler, and Galileo. For discussion of the heliocentric theory see T. S. Kuhn, **The Copernican Revolution*** (Vintage). A. Armitage, **The World of Copernicus*** (Mentor) is a popular study. See also A. Koyré, **From the Closed World to the Infinite Universe*** (Torchbooks). G. de Santillana, **The Crime of Galileo*** (Phoenix) is an exciting account of the scientist's struggle against censorship.

H. Sigerist, **The Great Doctors*** (Peter Smith) is a notable biographical history of medicine. Also recommended are two books by C. Singer: **From Magic to Science*** (Peter Smith) and **A Short History of Anatomy and Physiology from the Greeks to Harvey*** (Dover).

F. B. Artz, **From the Renaissance to Romanticism*** (Phoenix) is a valuable view of the arts through six centuries. B. Willey, **The Seventeenth Century Background: Studies in the Thought of the Age in Relation to Poetry and Religion** (Columbia) is an excellent study. Arthur M. Wilson, **Diderot** (Oxford) is a definitive study of this individual. On art see W. Sypher, **Four Stages of Renaissance Style*** (Anchor); and V. Tapié, **The Age of Grandeur: Baroque Art and Architecture*** (Praeger). On music see M. Bukofzer, **Music in the Baroque Era** (Norton).

*Indicates a less expensive paperbound edition.

CHAPTER 20

Absolutism, Constitutionalism, and the Politics of Power: 1650-1775

L' État, C'est Moi

INTRODUCTION. The century following the Peace of Westphalia (1648) was a vitally important period in European politics. In the weighing scales of power and military might, the modern hierarchy of nations was being established. Some of the old political structures were decaying: the Holy Roman Empire, Poland, and the empire of the Ottoman Turks. Such powerful nations as Spain and Sweden were passing their golden ages and slipping into a tranquil state of ineffectuality in the realm of international affairs. In contrast, France and England were dynamic and aggressive; Prussia, Russia, and Austria had achieved stability and were advancing rapidly into the category of first-class powers.

What might be called the natural rise and fall of nations was accelerated by the deliberate policies of strong powers operating in the political climate termed the competitive state system. In the perpetual competition between nations, the decisive weapon was military force. No one nation, however, was allowed to become too strong; competitive states manipulated the balance of power to try to prevent the rise of a paramount nation

—France of Louis XIV in particular. Yet the prevalence of warfare during this age of absolutism should not blind us to the fact that the absolute monarchs provided the strong governments needed to achieve civil order after a long period of internal strife.

Offering a contrast to the pattern of growing absolutism on the Continent were the events taking place across the Channel. The Revolution of 1688 thwarted the growth of royal power in England and hastened its decline on the Continent. The system of government begun by that revolution—constitutional monarchy—was an important step toward ultimate democratic parliamentary government.

THE SYSTEM OF ROYAL ABSOLUTISM

Aspirations of absolutism. In the period from 1650 to 1775 the royal architects of the national state system reached the height of their power. During this age of absolutism the king was in theory an autocrat responsible to God alone. The outstanding example of the absolute monarch was Louis XIV of France, who is said to have once exclaimed to his fawning courtiers, "L'état, c'est moi" ("I am the state").

Under the system of absolutism the king aspired—although aspirations were often far different than realities—to exercise a tight control over his subjects. He was the supreme and only lawgiver. As head of the church he decided what religion his subjects were to follow and persecuted those who dissented. The worship of God was a matter of state, not of individual conscience. In accordance with mercantilist practice, the king sought to regulate every phase of economic life, from the establishment of new industries to working conditions and standards of quality. In addition, he was the arbiter of manners and fashion, the patron of arts and letters, and the personification of national glory. His will was enforced by an obedient and extensive bureaucracy—although far from the kind of administrative machinery that states today have at their disposal.

The aspirations of absolute monarchs were widely supported, for a powerful king stood for order, efficiency, security, and prosperity—values willingly exchanged for the uncertainties of upheaval and bloodshed such as had been experienced during the turmoil of the preceding era of religious wars.

Bossuet and Hobbes: defenders of absolutism. The new absolute state was explained and rationalized by a number of political theorists. Jacques Bossuet (1627-1704) was a prominent French churchman who had been entrusted with the education of Louis XIV's son and was finally elevated to the position of bishop. Utilizing the doctrine of the divine right of kings, Bossuet composed a brilliant justification of absolute monarchy:

It appears . . . that the person of the king is sacred, and that to attack him in any way is sacrilege . . . the royal throne is not the throne of a man, but the throne of God himself. . . . Kings should be guarded as holy things, and whosoever neglects to protect them is worthy of death. . . . the royal power is absolute . . . [and] the prince need render account of his acts to no one. . . . Where the word of a king is, there is power. . . . Without this absolute authority the king could neither do good nor repress evil.[1]

In the long run, it was Thomas Hobbes (1588-1679) who composed the most penetrating and influential justification of absolutism. To this English student of the new scientific thought, absolutism was not to be defended by resort to religion. In the *Leviathan* (1651) Hobbes drew upon science and its servant, psychology. From the excesses of the religious wars in France, the Thirty Years' War in Germany, and the Civil War that erupted in England, Hobbes discovered what he believed to be the essential nature of man when not restrained by law. A pessimistic, cynical observer of human conduct, Hobbes saw man "as a wolf to his fellow man" and mankind as essentially selfish and cruel. Before law and authority came into existence men lived under the adverse conditions of the state of nature, in which there is no place for industry . . . no culture of the earth . . . no arts; no letters; no society; and which is worst of all, continual fear, and danger of violent death; and the life of man, solitary, poor, nasty, brutish, and short.[2]

To create a workable society and escape from the intolerable evils of the state of nature, men had gladly surrendered all their rights and powers to a sovereign government, an action which bound them to an irrevocable contract. Hobbes did not actually believe that there had once existed a "state of nature" and that at some specific date in world history mankind had decided to create, by contract, a despotic, all-powerful government. But if not demonstrable by experience, his argument was natural in terms of rational thought as an explanation of the nature of government.

Hobbes' Leviathan, the sovereign state, could be any one of a number of forms of government. But, to Hobbes, monarchy was the most effective and desirable, for only thus could peace and security be maintained. There was no right of revolution, even against tyranny.

LOUIS XIV: THE EPITOME OF ABSOLUTISM

Inheritance of Louis XIV. The best example of political absolutism is offered by France in the days of Louis XIV, who reigned from 1643 to 1715. This proud Bourbon monarch inherited a realm which had been made powerful during the preceding fifty years. The previous century, the sixteenth, had been a sorry period in France's history. Wars with the Hapsburgs had been followed by religious civil wars that almost destroyed the nation. The reign of Henry IV (1589-1610), however, brought peace and laid the foundations of the great nation which was to enjoy economic, military, and intellectual leadership in the seventeenth century.

The death of Henry left Louis XIII, a boy of nine, on the throne, with the queen mother as regent. During the next fourteen years Henry IV's achievements were slowly undermined, until in 1624 Cardinal Richelieu, the clever protégé of the queen mother, became the real power behind the throne. For eighteen years the biography of Richelieu was truly the history of France. As chief advisor to Louis XIII, the "grim cardinal" set about restoring and furthering the accomplishments of Henry IV. He strove to exalt the power of France in Europe and of royal authority within the state. Richelieu himself loved power; while he made his royal master the first man in Europe, he made the king the second man in France.

Under Richelieu's direction the structure of absolutism quickly took shape. Castles of the nobility were torn down, officials of the central government called *intendants* replaced the nobility as the chief administrators in the provinces, and the Estates-General—a body that might have challenged the power of the king—was not summoned. In foreign affairs Richelieu was equally decisive and crafty. As we have already noted (p. 338), his intervention in the Thirty Years' War struck a staggering blow against the Hapsburgs and helped make France the greatest power in Europe.

After the deaths of Richelieu in 1642 and Louis XIII in 1643, the throne of France was again occupied by a child, Louis XIV, who was less than five years old. Richelieu had anticipated this emergency, however, by grooming a promising young Italian, Cardinal Mazarin, to be adviser to the regent. Mazarin governed France with a firm and efficient hand during the minority of the king, although the royal authority was seriously challenged by civil outbreak. For six years (1648-1653) France was convulsed by disorder. This civil war—a reaction against the excesses of the now powerful royal administration, known as the Fronde—had no effect in tempering absolutism. In fact, the violence of the struggle served to convince many Frenchmen that the only alternative to royal absolutism was anarchy.

Following the death of Mazarin in 1661, Louis XIV, then twenty-three years old, took over the personal management of state affairs. He found his people obedient and docile; Henry IV, Richelieu, and Mazarin had done their work efficiently.

France's rise to power in Europe was accompanied by the rise of French painting to a position of world leadership. The rulers of Bourbon France regarded art as a means of glorifying the monarchy, and they patronized the arts liberally. Philippe de Champaigne's "Triple Portrait of Richelieu," painted with keen precision and sophisticated use of colors, conveys the cool intellect, the poised manner, and the iron will of Richelieu. It is, moreover, a typical example of the classical realism of seventeenth-century French painting.

Louis XIV: the Sun King. Believing implicitly in the divine right of kings, Louis chose the sun as the symbol of his power. His courtiers dubbed him *Le Roi Soleil* (the Sun King), and he was also known throughout Europe as the Grand Monarch. Louis labored to enhance the power and prestige of the crown, which he frequently defended in haughty style:

All power, all authority, resides in the hands of the king, and there can be no other in his kingdom than that which he establishes. The nation does not form a body in France. It resides entire in the person of the king.[3]

The palace of the Louvre in Paris had been good enough for his predecessors, but Louis wanted a more magnificent symbol for his greatness—and a place where the nobility could be honored, watched, and held in check. On a barren marshland a few miles from Paris, Louis ordered the construction of the palace of Versailles. The marshland was transformed into a beautiful park surrounding the palace, whose facade was more than a quarter mile in length. The symmetry in the design of formal gardens and surroundings for the palace reflected the orderliness that Louis XIV, throughout his long reign, tried to impose on the society of his age.

Today the palace of Versailles is merely a historical monument, a symbol of royal elegance and glittering court life that has no place in our modern world. But two hundred years ago it was the most fashionable spot in Europe. During the day the French nobles promenaded with their king among the groves, terraces, and fountains of the park or hunted and hawked in the nearby woods and meadows. At night lords and ladies in powdered wigs, silks, and laces attended balls, masquerades, and concerts.

Just as science followed the rule of law, so life and manners conformed to the rules of etiquette. Studied elegance, formal manners, extravagant expressions of courtesy, and witty but superficial conversation all too often constituted the base of polite society, and manners were more important than morals. The aristocratic life of elegance, leisure, and polished deportment is well symbolized by the graceful minuet—a dance which "was a school for chivalry, courtesy and ceremony. . . ."[4]

Palace etiquette was carried to ridiculous extremes; the "cult of majesty" resulted in the king's being treated practically like a god. Louis was surrounded by fawning sycophants and servile courtiers, and his every action was made a regal ceremony based on the strictest precedent. For example, a nobleman of designated rank was required to dry the king after his bath, and only a very illustrious noble could hand the king the royal shirt or breeches during the public ceremony of dressing.

Louis' absolutism: the balance sheet. During the late seventeenth century France was the premier nation of Europe. In nearly every aspect—the splendor and formality of Versailles, the functioning of the central government, the organization of the military services—the absolute state of Louis XIV was the model.

Louis worked hard at what he called "the business of being king." He increased the powers of the *intendants* instituted by Richelieu; reorganized the army, making it the largest (nearly 400,000 men by 1703) and most modern in Europe; and instituted a wide variety of economic reforms to strengthen the French economy and increase revenue. Louis was fortunate in having as his finance minister the able Colbert, whose aggressive mercantilist practices (see Chapter 18) enabled a surplus to be accumulated in the royal treasury.

The positive side of Louis' reign—his own administrative zeal and the financial genius of Colbert—was counterbalanced by some unfortunate manifestations of Louis' lofty concept of the dignity of his office. The pomp and ceremony of Versailles is an example; Louis moved in a world of glitter and luxury, isolated from his people.

One extremely unwise act was the revocation of Henry IV's Edict of Nantes, which had guaranteed religious freedom for the Protestant Huguenots. To an absolute monarch like Louis, complete uniformity within his state was a cherished ideal, and legal toleration of religious nonconformity was a serious flaw in the system of absolutism. Therefore, in 1685, Louis revoked the Edict and caused thousands of industrious Huguenots to flee to other lands, taking with them

The epitome of the Baroque architectural style is the palace of Versailles as detailed in this view of the facade facing the garden. This magnificent building was designed by Louis Le Vau and Jules Hardouin Mansart, took fifty years to complete, and was in 1683 declared the official residence of Louis XIV and his court.

A detail from a portrait by Henri Testelin shows Louis XIV presiding over the opening of the Academy of Sciences and Foundation of the Observatory in 1667. French arts and sciences flourished during Louis' reign and other European monarchs sought to imitate French accomplishments.

skills and knowledge which were to enrich the enemies of France.

Finally, and most important of all, Louis squandered the resources of his realm in his passion for military conquest. War had become an all-important function of the state which required efficiency, organization, and discipline. Important changes were made in tactics and weapons: the improvement of firearms and the introduction of the bayonet eliminated the pike as the main infantry weapon; artillery and fortification methods were improved and so, in turn, were siege methods for the reduction of fortresses. Indeed, the tactics for siege warfare devised by Vauban, Louis' military engineer, established

the principles which governed that science until the twentieth century.

Possessing the strongest army and the most capable generals of the age, Louis embarked on a series of wars to attain for France her "natural boundaries" by extending French territory eastward to the Rhine at the expense of the Spanish and Holy Roman empires (see Reference Map 5). Louis' chief motive was not security for France but prestige for the monarchy.

France threatens the balance of power. Taking advantage of Spain's decline, Louis in 1667 marched in and laid claim to the rich Spanish Netherlands (modern Belgium). The Dutch, alarmed by the loss of a buffer state between themselves and France, formed an alliance with England and Sweden and forced Louis to renounce his claim and withdraw. To eliminate this obstacle to his plans, Louis bought off Holland's allies and in 1672 invaded the Dutch provinces. The Dutch were in desperate straits until the inspired leadership of William of Orange (great-grandson of William the Silent who had led the revolt against Spain) and the aid of their old enemies, the Spanish and Austrian Hapsburgs, enabled them to checkmate Louis. Weak Spain paid the price of the peace by ceding Franche-Comté to France (see Reference Map 5).

Louis precipitated a third war in 1688 by laying claim to various Rhineland districts, mainly in Alsace and Lorraine. William of Orange, who with his English wife Mary had replaced James II on the throne of England in 1689, became the vigorous leader of a new anti-French coalition consisting of England, Holland, Austria, Spain, Sweden, and a few German states. With England for the first time playing the part of a major power in European affairs, Louis again was held in check and in 1697 signed a compromise peace in which he gained little.

War of the Spanish Succession. The death of the childless king of Spain left the Spanish throne open to the conflicting claims of distantly related princes of both Hapsburg Austria and Bourbon France. In his will the dying king left this great prize to Louis XIV's grandson, Philip. All Europe realized that, with his grandson as king of Spain, Louis would have an empire rivaling in its extent and power the possessions of Charles V in the sixteenth century. Louis defied the Austrian claim and European sentiment by accepting the Spanish throne for Philip.

In answer to Louis' menacing move to dominate Europe, England organized another coalition against him. From 1702 to 1713 French armies fought the combined forces of this Grand Alliance in Spain, Italy, France, Germany, and the Low Countries. The allies were blessed with a remarkable English commander, John Churchill, the duke of Marlborough, an ancestor of Winston Churchill. Marlborough's most famous victory was the battle of Blenheim (1704); not until the French Revolution would French armies again terrorize Europe.

Treaty of Utrecht. In 1713 the War of the Spanish Succession ended with the forces of France considerably weakened and the Grand Alliance split by petty rivalries. Comparable in importance to the Peace of Westphalia, which had ended the Thirty Years' War, was the series of treaties signed at Utrecht between France and the members of the alliance. As a result of this peace settlement, a fairly satisfactory balance of power was maintained on the Continent for nearly thirty years without any major wars.

The most important terms of the Utrecht settlement were as follows: (1) Louis' grandson, Philip V, was permitted to remain king of Spain so long as the thrones of France and Spain were not united. (2) France was allowed to retain all of Alsace. (3) The Spanish empire was divided: Philip V retained Spain and Spanish America, while Austria obtained Naples, Milan, Sardinia, and the Spanish Netherlands (Belgium)—thereafter called the Austrian Netherlands. (4) England gained important colonies from France and Spain: Nova Scotia, Newfoundland, and the Hudson Bay territory, and valuable Mediterranean naval bases in the Balearic Islands and at Gibraltar. (5) As a reward for joining the Grand Alliance, the duke of Savoy was given Sicily and the title of king, and the Hohenzollern elector of Brandenburg was recognized as "king in Prussia." (In 1720 Savoy ceded Sicily to Austria in exchange for Sardinia.)

The significance of several provisions in this peace should be noted. The accession of the Bourbons to the throne of Spain after almost two centuries of Hapsburg rule marked the end of an era. The long-standing French-Spanish rivalry was now replaced by a strong French-Spanish family alliance since Bourbons occupied the two thrones. The English acquisition of important colonies and naval bases marked an important stage in the rise of Great Britain to world power. The treaty also gave recognition to two aggressive ruling families, the House of Savoy and the House of Hohenzollern. In the nineteenth century the House of Savoy would succeed in unifying Italy, and the Hohenzollerns Germany.

Consequences of Louis' wars. In 1715 Louis XIV died, leaving behind him a kingdom demoralized and debilitated by costly wars. France continued to be a first-class power and French culture was universally admired and imitated, but in retrospect we can see that Louis' reign did much to discredit the system of absolutism. He left behind a record of misery and discontent that paved the way for the French Revolution and the bloody downfall of his dynasty.

Louis' four wars strengthened the guiding principle of international diplomacy in modern times—the concept of the balance of power (see Chapter 15). To prevent France from dominating Europe, coalition after coalition had been formed. England was the balance wheel in the maintenance of this delicate equipoise, throwing support from one side to the other in order to maintain the balance of power on the Continent.

ENGLAND: CONSTITUTIONALISM VERSUS ABSOLUTISM

Background for the English Civil War. The victory of England over France involved more than just the matter of English superiority in arms or diplomacy. It was the victory of a constitutional monarchy, the product of a mold different from Louis XIV's absolutism. This new political form has been termed *aristocratic liberalism* and defined as "government in accordance with the agreed decisions of bodies which were drawn from a limited class but acted after free discussion and with some degree of tolerance and of consideration for the governed."[5]

The revolution in England that produced constitutional monarchy in the eighteenth century grew out of English experience with divine-right monarchy in the seventeenth century. The English Civil War (1642-1648) was a complex blend of religion and politics. (Recent attempts to uncover economic and social factors underlying the religious and political issues have not proved satisfactory.) Differences in religion were of central importance, and for this reason the English Civil War has been called the Puritan Revolution and the last episode in Europe's age of religious wars. But it was also a duel between those who upheld the power of the monarch and those who favored a government more representative of the people. The religious issue was important, but it has been overshadowed by the constitutional results stemming from the struggle. The outcome strongly influenced the development of constitutional government in modern times.

For hundreds of years English institutions had been developing slowly in the direction of constitutional, representative government. During the Wars of the Roses, which followed the Hundred Years' War, constitutional progress was almost submerged in feudal disorder. Then, largely with the cooperation of Parliament and the approval of the English people, Tudor monarchs had restored law and order to England, broken with the Church of Rome, and ruled with a strong hand. No consistent breach of opinion developed between the crown on the one hand and Parliament and the people on the other to raise constitutional issues or to challenge the royal power so skillfully wielded by the Tudors.

If the growth of constitutional government had been temporarily placed in cold storage, it had not been frozen. During most of Elizabeth I's reign the House of Commons was content to improve its procedures and gain parliamentary experience. Following the defeat of the Spanish Armada, however, Parliament began to reassert itself. On questions of taxation it became increasingly independent, and unpopular measures presented by the queen's advisors were occasionally rejected.

James I and Parliament. Elizabeth's successor was James Stuart, king of Scotland and the son of Mary Stuart. As James I of England, he reigned from 1603 to 1625. Scotland and England remained separate states, and not until 1707 did the Scots consent to the Act of Union which created the United Kingdom of Great Britain.

James had scholarly interests which led him to appoint a commission to make a new English translation of the Bible—the King James Version (1611), a masterpiece of English prose. But notwithstanding his erudition, the new king was totally unfitted for his position. He lacked common sense and tact; small wonder that the French dubbed him "the wisest fool in Christendom."

James' initial unpolitic move was to advocate the divine right of kings in his first address to Parliament:

The state of monarchy is the supremest thing upon earth, for kings are not only God's lieutenants upon earth and sit upon God's throne, but even by God himself they are called gods. . . . That as to dispute what God may do is blasphemy, . . . so is it sedition in subjects to dispute what a king may do in the height of his power . . . I will not be content that my power be disputed upon. . . .[6]

Disregarding the temper of his new English subjects and their institutions, James made it plain that he meant to be an absolute monarch. In 1611 he dissolved Parliament and ruled without it until 1621.

The religious issue. The constitutional issue of king against Parliament was complicated by religious issues. Some Englishmen were content with the Anglican Church as it then was. Others hoped to reintroduce more of the ritual and tenets of Roman Catholicism, although they had no desire to return to papal control. Still others took an extreme reformist position.

The most important members of the latter group were known as Puritans because they wished to "purify" the Anglican Church of its "papal rites" and ecclesiastical hierarchy. They were against any priest or ceremony standing between them and God. They also considered James overfriendly with Catholic sovereigns abroad and inclined to favor and protect Catholics at home.

Many Puritans belonged to the class of country gentlemen—the gentry—who were vigorously capitalistic. They and their allies, the city merchants, resented James' arbitrary taxation. Puritan lawyers revived the Magna Carta and the right of Parliament as ammunition against royal absolutism.

Charles I and Parliament. James' mistakes were repeated by his son Charles I (1625-1649)—and to an even greater degree. Like his father, the son espoused the divine right of kings, was contemptuous of the rights of Parliament, and supported the extreme anti-Puritan or High Church faction in the Anglican Church.

Insisting on absolute royal power, Charles opened his reign with stormy debates with Parliament; but in return for revenue grants he agreed in 1628 to the famous Petition of Right, which protected from arbitrary royal power two basic rights of every Englishman: his property and his person. The monarch was forbidden to tax without parliamentary consent or to imprison any person without due process of law.

Charles' capitulation was only temporary, and from 1629 to 1640 he ruled England without calling Parliament. During this period he resorted to methods of taxation which alarmed all property owners and which the supporters of Parliament considered illegal. In addition, Charles punished those who opposed his efforts to promote High Church Anglicanism.

Royalists vs. Parliamentarians. When Charles attempted to force his brand of High Church Anglican religion on the Presbyterian subjects of his Scottish kingdom, they promptly took up arms against their king. Faced by a hostile army and without sufficient funds to put a force of his own into the field, Charles was forced to convene Parliament.

When Parliament refused to vote any money until Charles had redressed certain grievances, Charles promptly dissolved it. But riots in London and a Scottish invasion compelled him to recall Parliament. Sensing the weakness in the king's position, Parliament immediately set to work to make its powers at least coequal with his. This session became known as the "Long Parliament" because it lasted nearly twenty years.

As the tension between the crown and Parliament increased, two bitterly antagonistic groups quickly developed: the Royalist "party" and the Parliamentary "party." While both groups included all classes, the Parliamentarians attracted most of the merchants and the Royalists most of the younger men—the latter apparently reacting to their elders' puritanism. The Parliamentarians were divided between Independents and Presbyterians, who differed over questions of church government but agreed in holding generally to a Calvinistic system of religion and in demanding further reductions in the political and religious prerogatives of the monarch.

The Royalists, whose leaders came mainly from the great landowners, opposed the extreme reforms urged by the Puritans. While agreeing with the Puritans in opposing royal despotism, they were unwilling to see the monarchy stripped of all its powers. This party also included a substantial number of clergy and laymen who, like their monarch, were believed by the Puritans to be pro-Catholic, ready to return the Anglican Church to the fold of Rome.

Civil war. Civil war erupted in 1642; within four years the Parliamentarians—by virtue of control of the sea, greater economic resources, superior generalship, and an alliance with the Scots—defeated the king's armies. A major factor in their triumph was Oliver Cromwell, a country gentleman and a military genius of the first order. Cromwell instilled in his troops a sense of discipline and religious mission and sent them into battle singing hymns. His God-fearing irresistible force became known as Cromwell's Ironsides.

By the end of 1646 the king had surrendered, and for the next two years he tried to play off his enemies—the Scots; the Presbyterians, who dominated Parliament; and the

Independents, who dominated the army—against each other. He actually succeeded in splitting Parliament and making a secret alliance with the Scots. The upshot was the rise of fierce resentment against the king in the ranks of the Independent army, and in 1648 the civil war resumed. The allies of the king were defeated, and in December 1648 all Presbyterian members of the House of Commons were purged from that body by the victorious Independent army. Following a brief trial, Charles I was executed in January 1649.

The Protectorate and Cromwell. Abolishing the House of Lords, the House of Commons proclaimed England a republic—the Commonwealth. But in 1653 the army, still distrusting Parliament, overthrew the Commonwealth and set up a new form of government, the Protectorate, in which Oliver Cromwell held the office of Lord Protector, assisted by a new Parliament. The structure and operation of the government was based on a constitution called The Instrument of Government, the first written constitution of modern times.

Now virtual dictator of England, Cromwell endeavored to achieve a religious settlement for the nation. Amid the rivalries between Independents, Presbyterians, Royalists, Scots, and others, he had been forced to assume the role of dictator, but at heart Cromwell was a moderate, believing in religious toleration for all Protestants and constitutional government. It was impossible, however, to reconcile the Independents, the Presbyterians, the High Church party, and other religious factions. The last three years of Cromwell's life were filled with disappointment and trouble. Although he did not favor it, his more extreme Puritan colleagues muzzled the press and foisted on a pleasure-loving folk hateful prohibitions which closed the theaters and stamped out wholesome as well as unwholesome popular amusements.

Cromwell died in 1658 amid rising discontent with his rule. One contemporary observer claimed: "it was the joyfulest funeral I ever saw for there were none that cried but dogs . . . ."[7] Seemingly, Cromwell's work had been a failure; yet his firm opposi-

tion to royal despotism and his advocacy of religious toleration were priceless legacies from the kingless decade. The Civil War and the Commonwealth had also generated a substantial body of liberal and democratic thought.

The magniloquent John Milton (1608-1674), author of the great Puritan epic, *Paradise Lost* (1667) and a member of Cromwell's administration, espoused political freedom in opposition to tyranny. Arguing that men are born free, that kings are elected deputies without power except that given by their subjects, Milton maintained that a republic is "held by wisest men of all ages the noblest, the manliest, the equallest, the justest government. . . ."[8] One of his best known tracts is *Areopagitica* (1644), an impassioned plea for freedom of the press:

Who kills a man kills a reasonable creature, God's image; but he who destroys a good book, kills reason itself, kills the image of God, as it were in the eye. Many a man lives a burden to the earth; but a good book is the precious life-blood of a master-spirit, embalmed and treasured up on purpose to a life beyond life. . . . We should be wary therefore . . . how we spill that seasoned life of man, preserved and stored up in books; since we see a kind of homicide may thus be committed . . . whereof the execution ends not in the slaying of an elemental life, but strikes at that ethereal and fifth essence, the breath of reason itself, [and] slays an immortality rather than a life. . . .[9]

A group known as the Levellers—made up of small merchants, farmers, and artisans, many of whom were in Cromwell's army—advocated democracy and a written constitution guaranteeing equal rights to all. Another group, known as the Diggers, deplored the existence of private property and unequal wealth. Such groups as the Levellers and Diggers eventually died out, but the slow ferment of their ideas influenced English political life.

Ironically enough, the Puritans—champions of liberty against the Stuarts—ruled England in more autocratic fashion than had Charles I. Oliver Cromwell was succeeded as Lord Protector by his son, who lost control of the army and resigned in less than a year. To most Englishmen the restoration of the monarchy seemed the only solution.

The serious and scholarly James I (left), with his close-cropped hair and relatively conservative clothing, contrasts sharply with the debonair elegance of his grandson, the Restoration king, Charles II (right).

Restoration of Charles II. When the exiled Charles Stuart, son of the late king, returned to England as Charles II in 1660, it was with the implicit understanding that the gains made by Parliament up to the outbreak of the Civil War in 1642 would be maintained. Constitutionally this meant that the struggle for power between the king and Parliament had not been settled. The king remained in full control of the administrative machinery of the state, but he was financially dependent on Parliament. Thus, should the king and Parliament fail to agree on policy, nothing could be done unless the king could find money outside the kingdom.

Behind the backs of his anti-French subjects, the king in 1670 negotiated a secret treaty with Louis XIV of France—the Treaty of Dover. In return for an annual subsidy from the French government, which made him more financially independent of Parlia-

ment, Charles agreed to become a Catholic; he agreed to make England a Catholic nation, and support Louis' war against Holland. After collecting a substantial sum from Louis, Charles had the effrontery to persuade Parliament to grant him money for waging war against the French king, his secret ally. No ruler has ever been able to give a better performance of running with the hare and hunting with the hounds.

In 1672 Charles suspended the operation of laws directed against English Catholics and Protestant Dissenters. Since the English had come to associate Catholicism with the menace of strong foreign foes and with despotic government, a political crisis resulted. One year later Parliament passed the Test Act, which excluded all Catholics and Dissenters from public office. Among its victims was the king's brother James, a staunch Catholic.

Monarch vs. Parliament. One notable consequence of the controversy between Charles and Parliament was the gradual rise of amorphous, but recognizable, political groupings that were forerunners of political parties as we define such groups today. To thwart Charles' pro-Catholic tendencies, some members of the House of Commons formed the Whig "party," which stood for the supremacy of Parliament, Protestantism, and the interests of the business classes. The Whig motto was "life, liberty, and property." Similarly, a group drawing heavily upon the landed gentry for support began to form, championing "the king, the church, and the land"—the Tory "party." Such vague associations to support particular Parliamentary interests did not function as a two-party system, however, before the end of the Stuart dynasty (1714).

A second important consequence of the conflict between king and Parliament was the passage of the Habeas Corpus Act in 1679. Anyone believing himself unjustly imprisoned could obtain a writ of *habeas corpus*, which compelled the government to explain why he had lost his liberty. Later this safeguard against arbitrary imprisonment became part of the Constitution of the United States.

James II and the Revolution of 1688. When Charles II died in 1685 and his brother James ascended the throne, the Whig opposition, and many Tories, soon came to believe that the cause of popular liberty and the Anglican Church were in serious danger. James adjourned Parliament after it refused to repeal the Test and Habeas Corpus acts and by royal order suspended all laws against Catholics and Dissenters. He also appointed many Catholics to important positions.

When James' second wife, a Catholic, unexpectedly gave birth to a son in 1688, the threat of a Catholic succession cost James his remaining Tory support. An invitation from both Whigs and Tories was extended to William of Orange, ruler of the Dutch, to assume the English crown. This choice was dictated by two factors: William was the husband of Mary, the older daughter of James II and the Protestant next in line to the throne; he was also considered the champion

In this anti-Catholic cartoon about the Glorious Revolution, fruit from the orange tree (representing the new ruler, William of Orange) knocks the crown from the head of James II and fells one of his officials. At the far right "the whole Heard of Papists and Jesuists" flee precipitately from the new Protestant king.

of Protestantism in Europe. In November 1688 William set sail for England and landed without opposition. The discouraged James, forsaken by his army, fled to France.

The Bill of Rights. Parliament offered the crown to William and Mary as joint sovereigns—an offer contingent on their acceptance of a declaration of rights, later enacted as the Bill of Rights. This declaration provided (1) the king could not suspend the operation of laws; (2) no taxes were to be levied or standing army maintained in peacetime without the consent of Parliament; (3) sessions of Parliament were to be held frequently; (4) freedom of speech in Parliament was to be assured; (5) subjects were to have the right of petition and were also to be free of excessive fines, bail, and cruel punishment; and (6) the king must be a Protestant. The Bill of Rights has exercised a tremendous influence on the development of constitutional government. The first ten amendments to the Constitution of the United States show their debt to the English declaration of 1688.

Results of the Glorious Revolution. The events which placed William and Mary on the English throne are referred to by Englishmen as the Glorious, or Bloodless, Revolution. Without bloodshed Parliament had deposed the old line of kings and laid down the conditions under which future English sovereigns were to rule. The theory of divine right was discredited, and Parliament was on the road to becoming the dominant element in government. In foreign affairs the events of 1688 resulted in a switch from the pro-French policy of Charles II and James II. Acting as the champion of Protestantism on the Continent, William used England's resources to check the territorial designs of Louis XIV.

The Revolution was consolidated by other actions supplementing the Bill of Rights. The Toleration Act of 1689 gave Protestant Dissenters the right of public worship, although they remained excluded from public office. In 1693 Parliament refused to pass the customary licensing act which former governments had used to muzzle the press. Given freedom of expression, the press thus became an increasingly important aid to representative government. Another act made judges irremovable and led to a more independent judiciary.

Significant as they were, the achievements of the Revolution were limited. The Bill of Rights and subsequent legislation guaranteed certain fundamental rights to the common people, but the nation was now governed by a small, wealthy minority of merchants, gentry, and landed nobility. However, the development of such concepts as popular sovereignty and the right of revolution which were established in England by the Revolution of 1688 were later to have a profound influence on the world's governments and peoples.

Locke's justification of the Revolution of 1688. John Locke, as we have already seen, was one of the most eminent thinkers of his day. In his "Of Civil Government," the second essay in *Two Treatises of Government*, published in 1690, Locke justified the overthrow of James II by expounding the following ideas:

Before government was established, all men, living in a state of nature, possessed certain natural rights. These rights consisted principally of the rights to life, liberty, and property. While life in a state of nature was not frighteningly ruthless, as Hobbes supposed, it was unsatisfactory because society was handicapped in many ways by the absence of government. There was no superior agency to enforce the law of nature, which is a body of rules ensuring the equality of all men and every man's enjoyment of his natural rights. Since men in a state of nature arrived at different interpretations of natural law, uncertainty and conflict often resulted.

Therefore, by common consent, an agreement, or contract, was entered into by which a sovereign was set up with power to govern and enforce the laws of nature. Through this contract the people give up some of their rights to the government, but their basic natural rights are in no way surrendered. Finally, the social contract is bilateral, or binding upon both parties. The government, for its part, can demand the obedience of the people, but the people may also expect that the government will keep its part of the contract by not in any way abridging the natural rights of the people. If these rights are violated, if the government rules unwisely and tyrannically, the people have a perfect right to overthrow their rulers. In short, the people are the real rulers, the custodians of popular sovereignty, which gives them the right of revolution. Thus, unlike Hobbes, Locke used the social contract theory to challenge rather than to support absolutism. His ideas were to find new expression in the American and French revolutions a century later.

Genesis of cabinet government. During the century following the Revolution of 1688 there slowly evolved what is known today as cabinet government—government by an executive committee, headed by a prime minister, which rules in the king's name but in reality is the instrument of the majority party in the House of Commons. A unique British contribution to the art of government, the cabinet system has spread to many parts of the world.

The evolution of cabinet government be-

Sir Robert Walpole, the first prime minister, dominated the British government from 1721 to 1742.

gan during the reign of William III and Mary (1689-1702). King William selected his own ministers and controlled their policies. Because Parliament and the king agreed on fundamentals, a clash did not arise. Politics in England were now controlled by an oligarchy of great landed nobles and country squires plus wealthy commercial and banking families often related to the nobility. The loyalties of these groups were divided between the Tories and the Whigs who, although they quarreled about particular issues, usually agreed on broad political principles.

William soon discovered that only when all his ministers were of the same party as the majority in Commons did the government function smoothly. Decisions were still frequently made by the monarch, sitting in conference with his ministers, but by 1714, at the end of the reign of William's successor, Queen Anne, the cabinet—as it was now known—was a distinct factor in policy-making.

The Hanoverians and the prime minister. By the Act of Settlement (1701), Parliament had provided for a Protestant succession through a granddaughter of James I (the Electress Sophia of Hanover), since neither William III nor Anne had surviving children to accede to the English throne. The accession in 1714 of the Hanoverian dynasty from the German state of Hanover stimulated the growth of cabinet government. The first Hanoverian, George I, was over fifty years old and thoroughly German in speech, habits, and interests. He so remained and could converse with his English chief minister only in French or in poor Latin. England interested him solely because its resources strengthened his hand in the game of petty politics in Germany.

Not much of an improvement as king was George II, also German-born, whose only claim to fame was that he was the last English monarch to lead his troops on the field of battle. Fortunately for English constitutional development, George's queen was a devoted friend of the chief minister, Robert Walpole, and through her influence the king was easily managed. Walpole served from 1721 to 1742 as leader of the Whig party and the House of Commons and real head of the government. In effect, he was the first prime minister.

Walpole established the principle that the entire cabinet had to act as the single administrative instrument of the House majority and that cabinet unanimity was a necessity. If any member refused to support the official policy, he had to resign. When Walpole eventually lost his majority in the Commons, he resigned. This act confirmed the principle that the executive branch of government—in theory the king but in practice the prime minister and cabinet—must resign when its policies are no longer supported in the Commons.

After the fall of Walpole, the next dominating figure in British politics was William Pitt the Elder (1708-1778), who was determined to cleanse British politics of corruption. Unfortunately, his health steadily declined, and his prestige and influence were cleverly reduced by a new power in politics. This was, surprisingly, the king.

Pretensions of George III. George III, who had come to the throne in 1760, was determined to "be a king," as his mother had long urged, and restore to the crown the power lost since the days of William III. In short, his object was to destroy the cabinet system by becoming his own chief minister. George III did not aspire to be a tyrant or to rule as a divine-right monarch; rather, he wished to rule as a "Patriot King," above political parties and in accordance with his own ideas.

It took George III only a few years to destroy the power of the Whigs and to secure control of Parliament. By 1770 all effective opposition to the king had been swept away, for George had filled the Commons with supporters known as the "King's Friends," bought by royal favors and pensions. For twelve fateful years George III was the effective head of the government. In this period Great Britain's thirteen North American colonies waged their successful war for independence.

Restoration of cabinet government. The disaster to British arms in America dealt the king's policies and methods a crushing blow. In a sense, by gaining their liberty, the Americans helped the Britons gain theirs. In 1780

the House of Commons resolved "that the influence of the crown has increased, is increasing, and ought to be diminished."[10] By 1782 George III had to dismiss Lord North, his subservient prime minister, and employ ministers who were willing to make concessions to public opinion.

In 1783 George III called the twenty-four-year-old son of the great war leader William Pitt (see p. 462) to be prime minister. Undoubtedly the king expected to control the youthful statesman, but he more than met his match. A new Tory party, reinvigorated by Pitt's leadership, took firm control of the affairs of state. The king was no longer consulted on the day-to-day details of government and only occasionally tried to intervene. When the king's mental instability and final insanity removed royal influence from governmental affairs, the prime minister and his cabinet colleagues assumed full control.

From the Glorious Revolution of 1688 until the passage of the Parliamentary Reform Bill of 1832, England was a perfect example of aristocratic liberalism—in essence, an oligarchy of landowners and merchants. A promising movement for parliamentary reform did begin in the 1760's, but it was cut short by fears of radicalism inspired by the excesses of the French Revolution. The British oligarchy was thus given a new lease on life.

THE RISE OF RUSSIA

Peter the Great and his objectives for Russia. In 1682 a new era in Russian history began with the accession of Peter I, who soon showed himself to be master of his unruly state, which was still a world apart from western Europe. The fourth member of the Romanov dynasty that had secured the throne in 1613 at the end of Russia's "Time of Trouble" (see p. 279), Peter grew up without benefit of discipline or formal education. But this six-foot-nine-inch giant possessed an excellent mind and such great stores of energy that his contemporaries contended that "he works harder than any *muzhik* [peasant]." Having a sound appreciation of what was essential for Russian progress, Peter

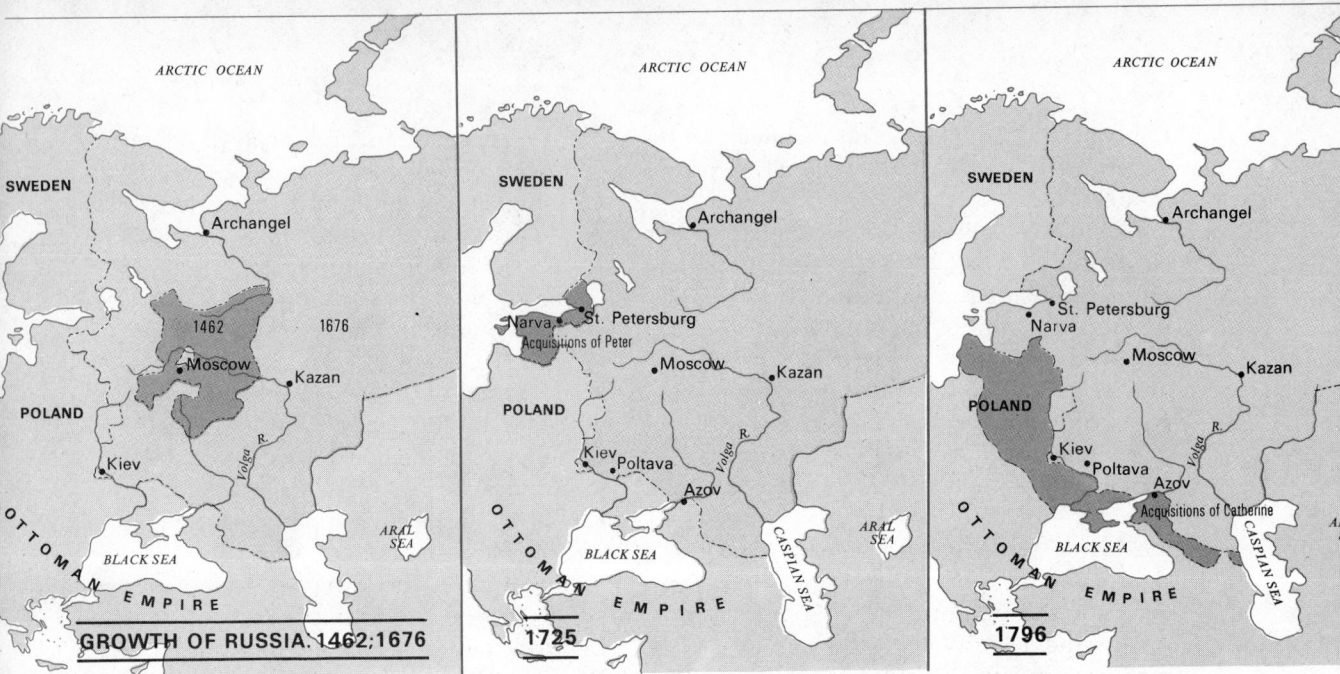

GROWTH OF RUSSIA: 1462;1676   1725   1796

pursued three basic policies during his long reign: (1) to Europeanize his people, (2) to obtain an outlet, "a window on the sea," and (3) to make his power absolute.

Peter's Grand Embassy. Peter first turned his attention to the Turks, who blocked Russia's way to the Black Sea. It took two expeditions to conquer Azov from the Turks, and Peter realized that he must learn from the West how to modernize his army and build a navy. He organized a Grand Embassy whose dual object was to secure allies against the Turks and to observe the most advanced European methods of warfare, government, industry, and education. Traveling as plain Peter Mikhailov, Peter visited Holland, England, and Germany. He astonished the rulers of western Europe by his curiosity as well as by his carousing and pranks. In Holland Peter worked as a common ship carpenter in order to learn Dutch methods of shipbuilding at first hand.

During his return trip to Russia Peter learned that his palace guard had revolted. He hurried back to Moscow and crushed the rebellion with savage cruelty, executing the leaders with his own hand. Peter then engaged European officers to build a western-type conscript army which in time numbered 100,000 men.

Peter obtained some seven hundred technicians from the West but no allies against the Turks. He therefore decided to direct his energies away from the Black Sea to the Baltic.

The Great Northern War. Peter's ambitions for a "window on the sea" led him in 1699 to make a secret alliance with Poland and Denmark against Sweden, which controlled most of the Baltic shores. Peter hoped to take advantage of the inexperience of Charles XII of Sweden, a youth of eighteen. Without waiting to be attacked, however, Charles launched the Great Northern War with an invasion of Denmark and quickly brought the Danes to their knees. The "Swedish Meteor" next landed at the other end of the Baltic, crushed Peter's army at Narva, and turned aside to deal with the Poles. Six years later, when Charles invaded Russia, the Swedish army was first weakened by Peter's "scorched earth" withdrawal into the heart of the Ukraine, then annihilated at Poltava (1709). The battle of Poltava amazed westerners and made them conscious for the first time of Russia's power.

Charles XII escaped to Sweden by way of Turkey—where he induced the sultan to attack Russia and regain Azov—only to be killed in 1718 in a skirmish with the Norwegians. The Great Northern War ended in 1721 when an exhausted Sweden sued for peace with the last of its foes, Russia. Sweden's days as a great power, inaugurated by Gustavus Adolphus, were over; except for Finland, almost nothing remained of its Baltic empire. Peter acquired four provinces situated south and east of the Gulf of Finland, thus securing his coveted access to the sea.

At tremendous cost in treasure and human life, western architects built the new capital of St. Petersburg as "a window opened upon Europe," replacing Moscow, the center of Russia's old way of life. Meanwhile Peter had bestowed on himself the titles "Father of the Country" and "the Great."

Attempts to westernize Russia. Peter resolved to change the age-old customs of his people in spite of their own opinions and desires. He instructed his male subjects to cut off their long beards, encouraged the adoption of European breeches instead of the flowing oriental robes which many men wore, and attempted to end the seclusion of women. Crude as he was, Peter endeavored to introduce the manners of polite European society into his country.

Responsible for the revision and simplification of the old Russian alphabet, Peter also established printing presses, promoted the study of foreign languages, sent many young men to western Europe to study, and started new schools for advanced training in engineering, navigation, and accounting. In the economic field he was a staunch mercantilist who sought to make his country as nearly self-sufficient as possible. Some of Peter's reforms, such as the establishment of new industries, failed shortly after his death. In addition, his aggressive program of westernization provoked much hostility, including that of the Church. Furthermore, Peter did nothing to alleviate the arduous lot of the Russian peasants, more than half of whom had been reduced to serfdom by their landlords with the consent of earlier Romanov tsars.

Absolutism of Peter the Great. Peter the Great accelerated the molding of Russia into an absolutist state. All vestiges of local self-government were removed, and Peter continued and intensified his predecessors' requirement of state service for all nobles. They were compelled to serve in the army, in the government, or in industry, and to send their sons abroad for study. In return, this "service nobility" was granted a free hand in dealing with their serfs.

The Church also became a tool of the state when Peter abolished the office of patriarch and appointed a Holy Synod of bishops to govern the Church. The new body was dominated by a layman called the procurator, who represented the tsar. For the next two hundred years the Church served as one of the most powerful agents and supporters of Russian absolutism.

Worn out from his exertions in politics and his excesses in drinking and brawling, Peter died in 1725 at the age of fifty-three. He had firmly established absolutism in Russia and ended its isolation from the West. Russia was now ready to play an important part in European history, but nearly forty years were to pass before an equally ambitious and ruthless monarch appeared on the Russian throne.

Catherine the Great. Catherine II was a German princess who married the Russian heir to the crown. Finding him half insane— "a moronic booby"—Catherine tacitly consented to his murder. It was announced that he died of "apoplexy," and in 1762 she became the ruler.

Catherine contributed to the resurgence of the Russian nobility that began after the death of Peter the Great. State service had been abolished, and Catherine delighted the

Catherine the Great was originally a German princess. Of Russia she said, "I came to Russia a poor girl. Russia has dowered me richly, but I have paid her back with Azov, the Crimea, and Poland."

nobles further by turning over most governmental functions in the provinces to them. The condition of the serfs, on the other hand, became so bad—for example, Catherine legalized the selling of serfs separate from the land—that in 1773 a terrifying peasant uprising occurred. Inspired by a Cossack named Pugachev ("Hang all the landlords!"), the rebels threatened to take Moscow before they were dispersed. Catherine had Pugachev drawn and quartered in Red Square, but his specter continued to haunt her and her successors.

Catherine served both her own interests and those of the Russian state with craft, shrewd diplomacy, and utter lack of conscience. She imitated the best features of the culture of Versailles and equaled its vices. In her own private life she was frankly immoral, and stories of her misconduct were common all over Europe. Just as the mistresses of Louis XIV graced the French court, so the male favorites of Catherine were openly paraded in her palaces.

This brilliant and unscrupulous monarch waged war successfully against the decaying Ottoman empire and advanced Russia's southern boundary to the shores of the Black Sea. Then, as we shall see later in this chapter, by plotting with the rulers of Prussia and Austria she annexed half of Poland and pushed the Russian frontier westward into central Europe. By the time of her death in 1796, Catherine's expansionist policy had made Russia a major European power.

THE EMERGENCE OF PRUSSIA

Rise of the House of Hohenzollern. If the rise of Russia was remarkable, the development of Prussia was even more amazing. History has scarcely a parallel example of the manner in which one royal house, the Hohenzollern, expanded its territory and exalted its power by fair means or foul.

The earliest Hohenzollerns were unimportant nobles occupying a castle on the heights of Zollern in south Germany. In 1417 a member of the family, who was one of the seven German electors (see p. 273), was made ruler of the unpromising Mark of Brandenburg, one of the border provinces carved out of Slavic lands east of the Elbe during the Middle Ages. By turning Lutheran during the Reformation, the Hohenzollerns gained wealth from seized Church properties, and the elector increased his authority as head of the new church in Brandenburg.

In the first decades of the seventeenth century the Hohenzollerns made further gains in territory, the most important being the acquisition of East Prussia. We saw earlier (pp. 276, 312) how the Teutonic Knights ruled East Prussia until the Protestant Reformation when the Grand Master, who was a member of the Hohenzollern family, turned Lutheran, dissolved the order, and ruled thereafter as hereditary duke of Prussia. In 1618, when the duke of Prussia died without immediate heirs, the duchy passed to the elector of Brandenburg.

Just four years before this windfall the elector had secured the lands of Cleves, Mark, and Ravensburg on the lower Rhine. (These territories were relatively unimportant until the Industrial Revolution of the early nineteenth century made the Ruhr valley a great industrial center.) Thus by the early seventeenth century the Hohenzollerns held territory as far east as the Niemen River and as far west as the Rhine, with Brandenburg and the small provincial town of Berlin located in the center. The policy of future electors was to bridge the gap between their detached lands and to forge a united state.

Creating the Prussian state. The Hohenzollerns were threatened with ruin during the Thirty Years' War, when Brandenburg was occupied by the Swedes from 1630 to 1643. The first of the four creators of the Prussian state was Frederick William (1640-1688), known as the Great Elector, who returned from exile in Holland determined to build a strong monarchy that would prevent such humiliations in the future. This meant the creation of a modern standing army and centralized bureaucracy, and the elimination of opposition from the nobility.

Frederick William's small but effective army cleared his lands of foreign troops and made good his claim to eastern Pomerania (along the Baltic coast) at the Peace of Westphalia. After the war he increased the army to 30,000 men and laid the foundations for a civil service which governed the scattered Hohenzollern possessions directly from Berlin. The bureaucracy and the army remained the two main pillars of the Prussian state down to modern times.

The Prussian nobility (Junkers) were encouraged to accept the new powerful state in return for important concessions—a monopoly of the key positions in the army and the bureaucracy, freedom from taxation, and a free hand in dealing with their peasants. As a result the rural masses of Prussia—as well as Russia and Austria, where a similar policy was followed—were forced deeper into serfdom at a time when the peasantry of western Europe had long been emancipated.

The Great Elector also promoted economic progress in his domains. Immigrants were brought in—diligent Dutch farmers, harassed Jews, and (after Louis XIV revoked the Edict of Nantes) thousands of skilled Huguenots.

The Great Elector's son, Frederick I (1688-1713), added lustre to the dynasty by obtaining the title "King in Prussia" as a reward for his support of the alliance against Louis XIV in the War of the Spanish Succession. He also took advantage of Sweden's defeat in the Great Northern War to annex western Pomerania. By the opening of the eighteenth century Prussia, as the combined lands of the Hohenzollerns now came to be called, had almost reached a position where it could embark on more ambitious and aggressive programs of expansion. The contribution of the next Hohenzollern was necessary, however, before this new phase in Prussian history could begin.

Like his grandfather, the Great Elector, Frederick William I (1713-1740) firmly believed that the destiny of Prussia, an artificial combination of lands without defensible frontiers, lay with its army. During his reign the army increased to 83,000 men—in size the fourth army in Europe and without a

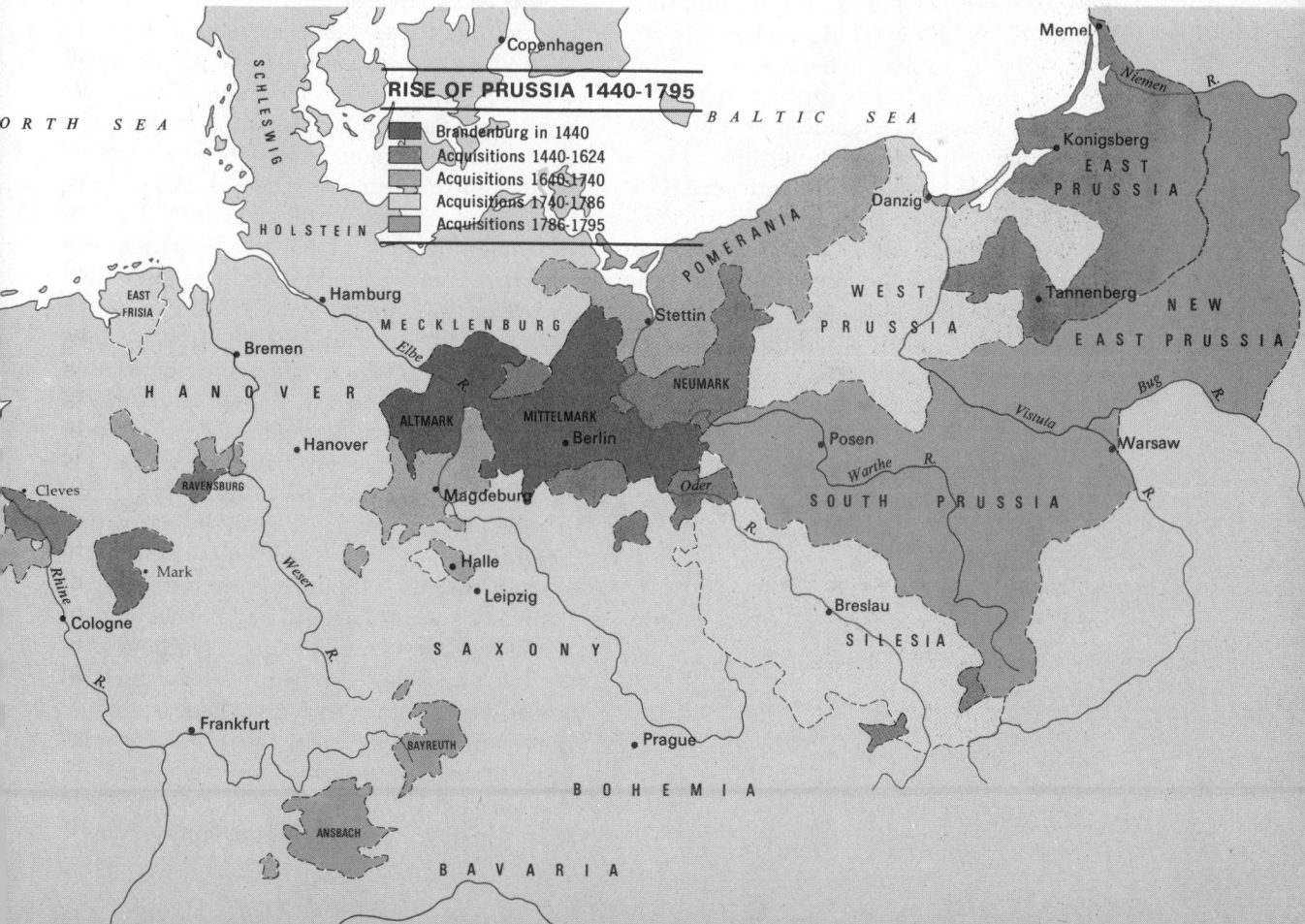

RISE OF PRUSSIA 1440-1795

Brandenburg in 1440
Acquisitions 1440-1624
Acquisitions 1640-1740
Acquisitions 1740-1786
Acquisitions 1786-1795

doubt the most efficient. As his contemporaries put it: "Prussia is not a State which possesses an army, but an army which possesses a State."[11]

King Frederick William also completed the task of creating a modern centralized government, run by a trained and efficient civil service and obeyed by a docile citizenry, who were told by their crusty king: "No reasoning, obey orders." He has well been dubbed "the Potsdam Führer," for it was through this ruler, with his maxims of "order, discipline, and work" and "Salvation belongs to the Lord, everything else is my business," that Germany developed its tradition of subordination to the state and blind confidence in the military point of view.

Frederick William I had high hopes for his son Frederick, who was subjected to a Spartan training. But Frederick loved music, art, and philosophy, and at eighteen he attempted to flee to France. Caught, he was forced to witness the beheading of his accomplice and best friend and was then subjected to more years of severe training and discipline. As the old king neared his last days he is supposed to have said: "O my God, I die content, since I have so worthy a son and successor." Frederick William was correct; his son was eventually to become the greatest soldier of his day and a master of Machiavellian diplomacy. Frederick II (1740-1786), known as Frederick the Great, brought Prussia fully into the arena of European politics. Moreover, he also continued his predecessors' work of building a powerful Prussian state at home. The remarkable rise of Prussia is illustrated by the chart below.

The Rise of Prussia

	1648	1740	1786
Population	750,000	2,500,000	5,000,000
Army	8,000	83,000	200,000
Annual revenue in thaler	?	7,000,000	19,000,000
Stored treasure in thaler	0	8,000,000	51,000,000

Adapted from S. B. Fay, *The Rise of Brandenburg-Prussia to 1786* (New York: Henry Holt and Co., Inc., 1937), p. 141.

POWER POLITICS AND THE DUEL FOR WORLD EMPIRE

Five great powers in conflict. In 1740 Europe had not seen a major war since the Peace of Utrecht in 1713 had brought the War of the Spanish Succession to a close. Political and economic forces were at work, however, which would in 1740 plunge the Continent into war, and the third quarter of the eighteenth century was to witness a series of destructive conflicts. France and Britain were becoming bitter rivals over commerce and colonies; Prussia under Frederick the Great was well armed and eager to secure additional territory; Russia under Catherine the Great was in a position to renew the expansionist policy of Peter the Great; and a fifth great power, Austria, had emerged along the middle Danube as the Hapsburgs, having failed as Holy Roman emperors, concentrated upon organizing their family lands into a monarchy that would be capable of holding its own in the competitive state system (see map, p. 484).

As the vigor and acquisitive appetites of the five major powers mounted, three once great states were lapsing into impotence. Spain was no longer a power to be reckoned with, and the Ottoman Turks no longer inspired fear. Following the death of Suleiman the Magnificent in 1566, the Ottoman empire had begun a gradual decline marked by the defeat at Lepanto in 1571 and the loss of Hungary to Austria in 1699. It was now caught in a net of intrigue woven by Russia and Austria. Poland still loomed large on the map of Europe (see Reference Map 5), but it lacked strong government and natural boundaries and was to become the most notable victim of aggression by powerful neighbors.

From 1688 to 1713, during the last three of Louis XIV's wars, England had not only been pitted against France on the Continent but the two states had also begun a long duel on a world-wide stage for colonial possessions in North America, the West Indies, and India. As the eighteenth century progressed, this colonial rivalry became increasingly intense. In line with the philosophy of mercantilism, one London merchant expressed the clash of economic interests in this fashion: "Our trade will improve by the total extinction of theirs."[12]

England came to realize that it could best checkmate French ambitions in Europe by destroying French commerce and sea power in North America and India. When war resumed on the Continent in 1740, the English had perfected the practice of obtaining and subsidizing allies to keep the French occupied in Europe while the bulk of British troops, especially naval forces, concentrated on the task of conquering the colonies and destroying the commerce of the French overseas, where distance served to neutralize France's advantages as a land power. The French, on the other hand, divided their energies by trying to play the game of power politics in Europe and at the same time endeavoring to compete with England over colonies. The result was to spell failure for France in both areas.

War of the Austrian Succession. It was the Austrian emperor who set the stage for a renewal of war on the Continent. Foreseeing the difficulties his young daughter, Maria Theresa, would have coping with greedy neighboring monarchs, he had drawn up in 1713 a document called the Pragmatic Sanction. The rulers who signed this document, including Frederick the Great's father, agreed to respect the territorial boundaries of Austria upon Maria Theresa's accession to the throne; but when the emperor died in October 1740, Frederick the Great, who had become king in Prussia in May of that year, had no intention of honoring the Pragmatic Sanction. He trumped up spurious claims to Maria Theresa's rich province of Silesia. On examining the document containing his demands, Frederick exclaimed to his advisers:

Bravo! This is the work of an excellent charlatan. If there is anything to be gained by honesty, then we shall be honest; if we must dupe, then let us be scoundrels.[13]

In December 1740 Frederick began the War of the Austrian Succession by occupying Silesia. France, Spain, Bavaria, and Saxony then threw in their lot with him to obtain a share of the loot. But having secured Silesia,

Frederick had no desire to continue fighting so that his allies also could filch territory from Austria. Thus in 1741 he withdrew from the conflict.

At first England was content to send subsidies to Maria Theresa, but in 1742 it entered the fray allied with Austria, Holland, and Hanover against the Franco-Spanish coalition. Meanwhile Frederick had reentered the war, and in 1745 his army roundly defeated the Austrians. Prussia and Austria then withdrew from the conflict, but fighting continued and the war broadened into a world-wide conflict involving the European colonial possessions. Thus it was, as the famous English historian Macaulay observed, "Because a monarch robbed a neighbor he had promised to defend, red men scalped each other by the Great Lakes of America, while black men fought on the [Indian] coast of Coromandel."[14]

The French triumphed in India, seizing the British outpost of Madras, but the British took the offensive in North America by capturing the French fortress of Louisburg, a stronghold guarding the entrance to the Gulf of St. Lawrence. On the seas, the British fleet successfully held off the French.

The war dragged on until 1748, when a general peace was signed at Aix-la-Chapelle. Louisburg was returned to the French and Madras to the English, and Frederick was confirmed in his possession of Silesia. The Peace of Aix-la-Chapelle—called "the peace without victory"—settled nothing. The rivalries that had ignited the conflagration continued to smolder, and in less than a decade they were to blaze forth in another major war.

The Diplomatic Revolution. The duel for world empire between England and France reached a decisive stage in the Seven Years' War (1756-1763), known in American history as the French and Indian War. The war was preceded in North America and India by preliminary skirmishes between English and French forces, and in Europe by a very significant regrouping of alliances in which two sets of traditional enemies became allies.

Placing the interest of her country above the age-old Hapsburg-Bourbon dynastic rivalry, Maria Theresa turned to Louis xv and suggested that an alliance be formed against

A major British victory in the Seven Years' War, the taking of Quebec in 1759, is depicted in an eighteenth-century engraving.

Frederick. The determining factor in Louis' decision to accept the Austrian offer was his realization that the English had replaced the Hapsburgs as France's most dangerous enemy. In the spring of 1756 Louis signed a pact whereby France joined Russia, Sweden, and various states in the Germanies as allies of Austria. (Five years later Spain was to join this coalition by declaring war on Great Britain.)

To check French ambitions on the Continent, England in the meantime had made an alliance with its recent foe, Prussia. So thoroughly had the traditional alignment of powers been reversed that this new grouping of nations—Austria and France vs. England and Prussia—is referred to as the Diplomatic Revolution of the eighteenth century.

Frederick opens the Seven Years' War. Frederick the Great applied the match to the international powder keg in 1756, making the droll observation: "If Austria is pregnant with war, I shall offer the service of the midwife."[15] Quickly attacking the coalition, he aimed heavy blows at Austria before France

and Russia could threaten him. But he soon was attacked on all sides. With brilliant strategy Frederick marched and wheeled his forces, winning battles but despairing of ever winning the war.

William Pitt's "system." In the colonial phase of the Seven Years' War, Great Britain at first suffered severe defeats. But the crisis ended when a remarkable statesman, William Pitt the Elder, came to power in 1757 (see p. 455) and, like Winston Churchill in 1940, gave England new heart and a new war strategy.

Pitt had supreme confidence in his own abilities, once saying: "I am confident that I can save the country and that no one else can." He developed a successful global strategy of war, known as his "system," which consisted of (1) providing large subsidies of money to Prussia, (2) destroying French sea power and thus preventing men and supplies from reaching the French possessions overseas, and (3) dispatching well-equipped English forces to the colonies to conquer the isolated French armies.

In 1759 one French fort after another fell in North America: Duquesne, Louisburg, Niagara, and Ticonderoga; and the defeat of France in North America was sealed when General Wolfe vanquished Montcalm's forces and captured Quebec. In India there was a similar chronicle of victories, the most decisive resulting from the infamous incident concerning the Black Hole of Calcutta. The ruler of Bengal, fearful of English influence, captured Calcutta and cruelly forced 146 English captives into a small dungeon, where during the night all but twenty-three died of suffocation and thirst. British forces commanded by Robert Clive avenged this act by defeating the ruler of Bengal in the decisive battle of Plassey (1757). Clive's victory laid the foundation for nearly two hundred years of British rule in India.

Survival of Prussia. The victories won by Great Britain contrasted markedly with the ordeals suffered by Prussia. In spite of Frederick's tactical victories, which made him a great hero and symbol for later Germans, Prussia lacked the necessary manpower to defeat the combined forces of Austria, France, and Russia. Attacked on all sides, Frederick compared himself to a man assaulted by flies:

When one flies off my cheek, another comes and sits on my nose, and scarcely has it been brushed off than another flies up and sits on my forehead, on my eyes and everywhere else.[16]

Frederick was saved by the narrowest of margins when a new tsar, the "moronic booby" whose wife Catherine was later called "the Great," recalled his armies from the gates of Berlin and withdrew from the war in 1762. Unable to continue without Russian support, Austria sued for peace in 1763. Prussia's hold on Silesia was confirmed, and the Continental phase of the war ended.

Treaty of Paris. In 1763 peace was also concluded between Great Britain and France and Spain. The Treaty of Paris provided for French cession to England of Canada and all the territory east of the Mississippi River. Spain ceded Florida to England and, as compensation, received from France the Louisiana territory including New Orleans. This marked the end of French rule in North America. France regained its trading posts in India as well as Martinique and other rich islands in the West Indies. The British also returned Havana and Manila to Spain.

By the Treaty of Paris, Great Britain became the greatest colonial, commercial, and naval power in the world. That a country of 6.5 million should triumph over a nation such as France, with a population of 23 million, was remarkable. As one Englishman wrote:

I shall burn my Greek and Latin books. They are the histories of little people. We subdue the globe in three campaigns, and a globe as big again as it was in their days.[17]

Partition of Poland. The eighteenth century offers many illustrations of the callous and cold-blooded manner in which wars were precipitated, promises broken, and allies deserted. Yet today, in an age accustomed to accepting the right of national self-determination, the most shocking example of completely unprincipled statecraft was the ruthless partition of Poland by Prussia, Russia, and Austria.

Without natural barriers to aid in its defense, Poland was a handicapped nation. In addition, it was dominated by a reactionary nobility whose insistence on retaining its feudal "liberties" rendered the central government virtually powerless. The monarchy was elective, and as the Poles usually could not agree on the choice of a king from among their own factions, only two native-born Poles had been elected to the throne in two hundred years. The Diet, composed solely of nobles, was completely impotent; by the *liberum veto* any single member could force the dissolution of this body. Such action was called "exploding the Diet," and during the century preceding 1764 forty-eight of fifty-five Diets were "exploded." This was not government but anarchy.

The first partition of Poland, in 1772, came about as a result of international tensions produced by the decline of the Ottoman empire. Austrian opposition to Russian designs on the Crimea and Moldavia (see Reference Map 7) brought the two states close to war. Frederick the Great, fearing that Prussia

THE PARTITION OF POLAND
1772-1795

☐ To Prussia
▨ To Russia
▨ To Austria

▬ Boundary of Poland after the
first partition 1772

▬ Boundary of Poland after the
second partition 1793

would be drawn into the conflict, then persuaded Catherine the Great to satisfy her territorial ambitions at the expense of helpless Poland. Frederick also aimed at annexing West Prussia (the Polish Corridor) in order to link East Prussia with the main body of Hohenzollern possessions. Maria Theresa of Austria reluctantly agreed to participate in the partitioning. In a wry comment on Maria Theresa's action, Frederick epitomized the ruthlessly competitive nature of international relations: "She wept, but she kept on taking."

In 1793, and again in 1795, while the rest of Europe was distracted by the French Revolution, Poland was again partitioned, Austria abstaining from the second operation. By the third partition Poland ceased to exist as an independent state. Under the alien rule of three different governments, the Poles continued to hope for the resurrection of their nation. Their faith was not rewarded until after the First World War.

SUMMARY

The concentration of power in the hands of absolutist kings resulted in a succession of wars that convulsed Europe between 1650 and 1775: the War of the Spanish Succession, the Great Northern War, the War of the Austrian Succession, and the Seven Years' War. Declining states, such as Turkey, and temporarily weakened states, such as Austria at the accession of Maria Theresa, were susceptible to the designs of their aggressive neighbors. In Poland's case, Prussia, Russia, and Austria joined in territorial banditry or, as it is more politely described, the "collective partition" of this helpless state.

By 1700 commercial and colonial rivalry added to the intense competitive spirit existing in Europe and culminated in the worldwide duel for empire between France and Great Britain. Great Britain, as the leader of various coalitions and the self-appointed caretaker of the Continental balance of power, emerged victorious over France and the monarchical despotism it symbolized. In England the successful Revolution of 1688 heralded the triumph of aristocratic liberalism—the rule of Parliament and of law. The most wealthy and influential elements in society controlled the government, and their support made for a stronger and more united government than that operating from Versailles. The English government thus proved fit to achieve victory in foreign diplomacy and warfare.

The interplay of international rivalries during the period had significant implications for modern times. In this period, which saw national interests supersede dynastic rivalry (the Diplomatic Revolution), it was determined that North America would be mainly Anglo-Saxon in culture; British rule was firmly established in India; and Britain's sea power gained the world-wide supremacy it was to hold well into the twentieth century. This period also saw the rise of the Prussian type of absolutism—the militaristic state—and the birth of the Russian policy of securing access to the Baltic and Mediterranean seas.

SUGGESTIONS FOR READING

Brief general introductions to the history of this period include J. M. Thompson, **European History, 1494-1789*** (Torchbooks); John B. Wolf, **Toward a European Balance of Power, 1620-1715*** (Rand, McNally, 1970); M. Beloff, **The Age of Absolutism, 1660-1815*** (Torchbooks); C. J. Friedrich and C. Blitzer, **The Age of Power*** (Cornell); F. Manuel, **The Age of Reason*** (Cornell); M. S. Anderson, **Eighteenth-Century Europe, 1713-1789*** (Galaxy); and O. and P. Ranum, eds., **The Century of Louis XIV*** (Torchbooks). A new interpretation is found in T. R. Rabb, **The Struggle for Stability in Early Modern Europe*** (Oxford, 1975).

The following are more detailed surveys: D. Maland, **Europe in the Seventeenth Century** (St. Martin's, 1966); A Moote, **The Seventeenth Century: Europe in Ferment** (Heath, 1970); David Ogg, **Europe in the Seventeenth Century*** (Collier); J. Stoye, **Europe Unfolding, 1648-1688*** (Torchbooks). See also Matthew S. Anderson, **Eighteenth-Century Europe, 1713-1789*** (Oxford); and David Ogg, **Europe of the Ancien Régime, 1715-1783*** (Torchbooks). Also valuable are the pertinent volumes in the **Rise of Modern Europe** series* (Torchbooks).

On the eighteenth-century power struggle see L. Dehio, **The Precarious Balance: Four Centuries of the European Power Struggle*** (Vintage); and A. Sorel, **Europe Under the Old Régime*** (Torchbooks).

An excellent survey is V. L. Tapié, **The France of Louis XIII and Richelieu** (Praeger). Others include L. B. Packard, **The Age of Louis XIV*** (Holt, Rinehart & Winston); M. Ashley, **Louis XIV and the Greatness of France*** (Free Press); David Ogg, **Louis XIV,** 2nd ed. (Oxford Univ.), a recent detailed study. See also William F. Church, ed., **The Impact of Absolutism in France: National Experience Under Richelieu, Mazarin, and Louis XIV*** (Wiley, 1969); and J. C. Rule, **Louis XIV and the Craft of Kingship** (Ohio State). W. H. Lewis, **The Splendid Century: Life in the France of Louis XIV*** (Anchor) is a popular account. Raymond F. Kerstead, ed., **State and Society in Seventeenth Century France*** (Watts, 1975) has interpretations of absolutist France. See also R. Hatton, **Europe in the Age of Louis XIV*** (Harcourt Brace Jovanovich, 1969) and O. Ranum, **Paris in the Age of Absolutism*** (Wiley, 1968).

R. Lockyer, **Tudor and Stuart Britain, 1471-1714** (St. Martin's, 1964); and Dorothy Marshall, **Eighteenth Century England** (McKay) are excellent general surveys. D. A. Baugh, ed., **Aristocratic Government and Society in Eighteenth-Century England** (Watts, 1975) is a new interpretation. M. Ashley, **England in the Seventeenth Century, 1603-1714*** (Penguin); and G. Aylmer, **A Short History of Seventeenth-Century England*** (Mentor) are brief and first-rate. The classic survey of the Stuart period is G. M. Trevelyan, **England Under the Stuarts*** (Barnes and Noble). On the English constitutional crises see Philip Taylor, ed., **The Origins of the English Civil War: Conspiracy, Crusade, or Class Conflict?*** (Heath); Christopher Hill, **The Century of Revolution, 1603-1714*** (Norton); and G. M. Trevelyan, **The English Revolution, 1688-1689*** (Galaxy). Books on Cromwell include Antonia Fraser, **Cromwell, the Lord Protector*** (Dell, 1975), an excellent character study; M. Ashley, **The Greatness of Oliver Cromwell*** (Collier); and C. V. Wedgwood, **Oliver Cromwell*** (Collier). On the Levellers and Diggers see M. Walzer, **The Revolution of the Saints: A Study of the Origins of Radical Politics*** (Atheneum).

B. Sumner, **Peter the Great and the Emergence of Russia*** (Collier); L. J. Oliva, **Russia in the Era of Peter the Great*** (Spectrum); and G. S. Thomson, **Catherine the Great and the Expansion of Russia*** (Collier) are good brief accounts. R. Coughlan, **Elizabeth and Catherine, Empresses of All the Russias** (Putnam, 1974) is an absorbing dual biography. Good reading also includes K. Waliszewski, **The Romance of an Empress: Catherine II of Russia** (Shoe String, 1968); I. Grey, **Catherine the Great** (Greenwood, 1975); and Otto Hoetzsch, **The Evolution of Russia*** (Harcourt Brace Jovanovich).

S. B. Fay, **The Rise of Brandenburg-Prussia to 1786,*** rev. ed. (Holt, Rinehart & Winston) is an admirable introduction. See also H. Holborn, **A History of Modern Germany, 1648-1840** (Knopf); H. Rosenburg, **Bureaucracy, Aristocracy, and Authority: The Prussian Experience, 1660-1815*** (Beacon); G. A. Craig, **The Politics of the Prussian Army: 1640-1945*** (Galaxy); and N. Mitford, **Frederick the Great*** (Torchbooks).

*Indicates a less expensive paperbound edition.

CHAPTER 21

Revolution in the Western World: 1776-1815

The Rights of Man

INTRODUCTION. The political changes that occurred during the last quarter of the eighteenth century and the first quarter of the nineteenth were world-shaking. John Locke's justification of the Glorious Revolution as a revolt against tyranny was a forerunner of the eighteenth-century attacks on the existing order. Physiocrats condemned the oppressive restraints of mercantilism, and *philosophes* attacked the irresponsible despotism of absolutism. Some monarchs heard the voice of reform and tried to uproot the evils of the Old Regime, but the momentous reforms that made the period from 1776 to 1815 a watershed in western political history were not imposed by authoritative decree from above but by revolutionary action from below.

In this chapter we shall follow the actions of the thirteen colonies as they successfully defy Britain and achieve their independence, we shall witness the overthrow of an ineffectual French king and watch a new republic rising from the bloodshed of revolution, and we shall observe the struggle of colonials in Latin America to throw off the shackles of repressive Old World regimes.

The rise of republican France was a challenge to despotic regimes throughout Europe, and the result was intermittent warfare on the Continent from 1792 to 1815. In the midst of this troubled era Napoleon came to power. Turning the new-born republic into a tool for conquest, this self-styled "man of destiny" threatened all Europe until defeat at Waterloo finally crushed his dreams of empire.

Before this period from 1776 to 1815, little is heard of the rights of the people; after it, representative government is in the ascendancy. Ever stronger voices speak forth for the rights of citizens, for bills of rights and constitutions—political concepts which have had an immeasurable influence on the course of western civilization.

THE INTELLECTUAL ASSAULT ON ABSOLUTISM

Criticism of existing governments. As we have seen in Chapter 19, eighteenth-century thought was characterized by a belief that all aspects of civilization should be based on reason, the ultimate touchstone of perfection. Faith in reason led the *philosophes* of the Enlightenment to reevaluate all aspects of society. These intellectuals were positive that reason could solve all human problems and that mankind's ability to improve itself was limitless.

The middle class, too, found much that was irrational and indefensible in the institutions of the day. Perhaps the most important factor in middle-class discontent was the government-controlled economy of mercantilism (see p. 403). Convinced that capitalism had outgrown the need for state assistance with its accompanying controls, the bourgeoisie were ready for a system of free enterprise. As early as the seventeenth century English merchants had denounced the hoarding of bullion, advocating instead that "the exportation of our moneys in trade of merchandise is a means to increase our treasure."[1] This growing concern for freedom of trade led the middle class to support the physiocrats, eighteenth-century economic thinkers who, as their name indicates, shared with *philosophes* the viewpoint that all human activity—economic, social, and political—was subject to natural laws similar to those governing the physical universe.

The physiocrats, laissez faire, and Adam Smith. The physiocrats believed that money should circulate naturally, much as the blood does in the human body, and that all eco-nomic activity should be freed from artificial restrictions. They believed in a "free market," the concept which implies that natural forces of supply and demand should be allowed to regulate the conduct of business. In sum, governments should adopt the policy of laissez faire (letting business alone).

The most influential advocate of laissez-faire economics was a Scottish professor of moral philosophy, Adam Smith (1723-1790). In 1776 his systematic formulation of the new science of economics, *An Inquiry into the Nature and Causes of the Wealth of Nations*, was published.

Smith was indebted to the physiocrats for his views of personal liberty, natural law, and the position of the state as a mere "passive policeman." He argued that increased production depends largely on division of labor, with each individual—and each nation—performing the work for which he is best fitted. By a wise division of labor, each member of society will perform quickly and efficiently the tasks for which he has an aptitude and will have a large field in which to exchange the results of his own labor for commodities produced by the labor of others. Smith maintained that every individual is and ought to be motivated by self-interest:

It is not from the benevolence of the butcher, the brewer, or the baker, that we expect our dinner, but from their regard to their own interest. We address ourselves, not to their humanity but to their self-love, and never talk to them of our own necessities but of their advantages. . . . Every individual is continually exerting himself to find out the most advantageous employment for whatever capital he can command. It is his own advantage, indeed, and not that of society, which he has in view.[2]

Smith looked on all fixing of wages, guilds and trade unions that limit apprenticeship, and tariffs and other governmental interference as injurious to trade, and he scoffed at the mercantilists' view that the wealth of a nation depends on achieving a surplus of exports, amassing bullion, and crippling neighboring countries. He insisted that trade works for the benefit of all nations the world over and that a country cannot thrive and its trade flourish if its neighbors are not prosperous.

Philosophes urge political reforms. Working with the physiocrats as they sought to remove outworn economic abuses, the *philosophes* carried on an offensive against tyranny, misgovernment, and unjust laws. The reform movements of the physiocrats and the *philosophes* were inseparably connected, for only by obtaining efficient and rational government could essential economic reforms be carried through.

The *philosophes* militantly advocated the end of arbitrary government and the adoption of such rights as civil liberty, trial by jury, and freedom of expression—freedoms which they construed as implicit in natural law. By expressing the belief that laws and institutions could be based on a natural law as immutable as Newton's laws of physics, they helped undermine the edifice of absolutism. Preeminent for their intellectual assault on absolutism were Baron de Montesquieu and Jean Jacques Rousseau, whose theories rank in importance with those of John Locke.

Montesquieu and The Spirit of Laws. Montesquieu (1689-1755), a French nobleman, was the most systematic and comprehensive student of government during the first half of the eighteenth century. His famous *Persian Letters* (1721), purporting to be the correspondence of two oriental gentlemen writing their friends in the East while traveling about France, was a devastating satire on French customs and institutions. The sophisticated French bourgeoisie were delighted as they read such comments as:

It is by sitting on chairs that nobility is acquired. A great noble is a man who sees the King, speaks to his ministers, and who possesses ancestors, debts, and pensions.[3]

Montesquieu's most important work was *The Spirit of Laws* (1748), a massive study of the salient features of numerous governments. Widely discussed in the French salons, it later became the political bible of important statesmen in England and colonial America. Unlike the English philosopher Locke and many of the *philosophes*, Montesquieu did not use the deductive method of analysis. He began not with the universal principles or natural laws but with facts. His method was to describe and analyze actual governments, both past and present, and then to show how they reflected the environment in which they functioned.

In *The Spirit of Laws* Montesquieu concluded that all governments conformed to certain specific factors of geography, economics, and race, which varied from country to country. Since the value of any governmental system depended on its relation to these specific factors, there could be no single "best" form of government.

Montesquieu was a relentless critic of tyranny and a champion of liberty. Although he did not endorse any one form of government, he admired the limited parliamentary monarchy of England. In the separation of executive, legislative, and judicial powers, he found the bulwark of liberty. Actually, Montesquieu misinterpreted the operation of the unwritten English constitution, for with its cabinet system of government England was moving toward unity of powers. However, this concept of separation of powers greatly influenced the planners of the American Constitution.

Rousseau and the Social Contract. Jean Jacques Rousseau (1712-1778) was one of the most enigmatic and significant persons of his time. Although believing in the general objectives of the *philosophes*, Rousseau distrusted reason and science. He gloried in impulses and intuitions, trusting emotions rather than thoughts, the heart rather than the mind. His early hand-to-mouth existence and the rebuffs and ridicule he suffered from polite society contributed to his hatred of the Old Regime and the status quo. He was also influenced by the ideal of the "noble savage" who lived "without faith . . . law . . . [with] neither king, nor judge, nor priest . . . nor taxes, nor prisons."[4] It was not surprising, then, that Rousseau excoriated the society that had refused to open its doors to him, urged the overthrow of artificial modes of life, and encouraged men to listen to their hearts and to the voice of nature rather than to their minds and the postulates of formal philosophy.

Rousseau's most important work and indeed one of the most influential books on political theory in modern times was his *Social Contract* (1762), which opens with the stirring statement: "Man is born free, but is everywhere in chains." In this work Rousseau endeavored to construct a theory of government based on the consent of the governed while reconciling the conflicting demands of individual liberty and social organization. In Rousseau's ideal society an individual surrenders all his natural rights— as envisaged by Locke—to the group and yet retains his freedom if the government follows what is called the "General Will." The General Will is defined as any action that is right and good for all; hence by obeying the General Will the individual is really obeying what is in his own best interest. Rousseau never made clear how the General Will was to be determined, except to imply that in an ideal society it would coincide with the will of the majority. In such a society the majority is always right, and the individual must obey its commands.

Rousseau defined the social contract in a way that emphasized the sovereignty of the people. By means of the social contract each individual surrenders his natural rights to the state, meaning the people as a whole. The people and the state are therefore identical, but the government is something quite different—it is merely the executive agent of the people's will:

. . . the depositories of the executive power are not the people's masters, but its officers; . . . it can appoint and dismiss them at pleasure; . . . for them there is no question of contract, but of obedience.[5]

Rousseau was hailed as the champion of democracy. But it is also true that his doctrine of the General Will later came to be used by ambitious despots. Claiming that he alone knew what constituted the General Will, a shrewd leader could justify his seizure of power. It is one of history's ironies that the *Social Contract*, written to justify democracy, was used later on to justify dictatorship.

Faith in enlightened despotism. The majority of the *philosophes* believed that the most logical way to attain desirable reforms was through the rule of an "enlightened despot": secure a well-meaning, intelligent monarch imbued with the philosophy of the Enlightenment and all would be well. In a sense, this theory of government was akin to the Platonic ideal of a society where philosophers would be kings.

Major rulers who were touched by the Enlightenment and became (or seemed to become) enlightened despots were Frederick the Great of Prussia, Catherine the Great of Russia, and the Austrian emperor Joseph II. Yet most of their reforms were continuations of well-established policies which owed nothing to the ideas of the Enlightenment.

Enlightened despotism in Prussia, Russia, and Austria. Dedicated to the improvement of the Prussian state, Frederick the Great expressed his concept of the enlightened monarch's role thus:

The monarch is only the first servant of the State, who is obliged to act with probity and prudence, and to remain as totally disinterested as if he were each moment liable to render an account of his administration to his fellow-citizens. . . . As the sovereign is properly the head of a family of citizens, the father of his people, he ought on all occasions to be the last refuge of the unfortunate.[6]

"Old Fritz," as his subjects affectionately called him, traveled about his kingdom a great deal, studying its problems and hearing complaints from his people. No aspect of government escaped his attention. His reforms included a law code and the most efficient courts in Europe, a system of primary education, and a policy of religious toleration. In economic matters, however, Frederick remained a mercantilist, seeking to

The ideas of Jean Jacques Rousseau found expression not only in his own writing but also in the writing and art of an era eager to accept his benevolent world view. This idealized scene of peasant life was influenced by Rousseau's advocacy of a return to the simple life.

make Prussia self-sufficient by subsidizing and controlling industry and commerce and by improving agricultural techniques. Although he admitted that serfdom was wrong he did nothing about it, not wishing to antagonize the Junker landowners. Until he died in 1786 at the age of seventy-four, Frederick worked diligently as the "first servant" of the state, aware that he had made Prussia a great European power.

In the early part of her reign Catherine II of Russia prided herself on being a patron of learning and the arts, a friend to the *philosophes*, and an exponent of the Enlightenment in government. The *philosophes* applauded her writings and her publicly announced policy of reform. They were the first to hail her as "the Great." But Catherine only posed at being a reformer, and little or nothing came of the changes she contemplated: the secularization of Church lands, the codification of the law, and the reform of local government.

The most sincere of the enlightened despots was Joseph II, the son of Maria Theresa. Joseph's reforms included the abolition of serfdom, toleration for Protestants and Jews, advancement of public education, equality of taxation, and centralization of the administrative and court systems.

Failure of enlightened despotism. Enlightened despotism was incapable of rooting out the deep-seated evils of the Old Regime. No matter how sincere and devoted to reform, an enlightened ruler such as Joseph of Austria could not achieve success against the entrenched power of the nobility and Church and the ignorance of the peasantry. Many of Joseph's reforms were hastily conceived and premature, and most of them died with him.

In most cases enlightened absolutism was nothing but a facade, a mere playing at reform because it was fashionable. "The Enlightenment was a fashion in Russia," it has been observed, "never a fact." Before her death in 1796, Catherine no longer quoted her "dear *philosophes*" or proclaimed their ideas. She had repressed a widespread peasants' rebellion with savage cruelty, and she had been frightened by the French Revolution, "the enemy of God and of the Thrones," as she called it.

As the last phase of authoritarian absolutism, enlightened despotism aimed more at strengthening the power of the state than at increasing the public welfare. As expressed by Frederick II, the monarch must concentrate on "the strengthening of his state and the growth of its power." The state was likened to a machine, and reforms were imposed from above on people who had not been educated to political realities. In the words of the British ambassador in Berlin:

The Prussian Monarchy reminds me of a vast prison in the centre of which appears the great keeper, occupied in the care of his captives.[7]

The successful reform movements were to come from below, from the revolutionary action of the people. It is noteworthy that in 1789, one year before Joseph II died a broken-hearted failure, a bourgeois revolution with a program in large part similar to Joseph's exploded in France. This French Revolution, inspired in part by the American Revolution, would end absolutism in France and sound its death knell throughout Europe.

THE AMERICAN REVOLUTION

Opposition to mercantilism. In 1776, with George III in full command of the British government (see p. 455), there began the stirring revolt that created in the western world a new nation, based on the political ideas espoused by Locke and Montesquieu. Many historians believe that the American Revolution was not so much a revolt against the tyranny of George III as a revolt of the American middle class against England's mercantilistic economic policy. In accord with the prevailing view that colonies existed for the benefit of the mother country, English navigation laws and other restrictive acts required the colonists to trade only with England and prohibited them from competing with English manufactured goods. For about a century these acts were not rigidly enforced, but finally the day of reckoning came.

After the Seven Years' War, England was saddled with a debt of nearly $700 million. The added expense of maintaining a strong force of British regulars in America, made necessary by a serious uprising of Indians in the Northwest in 1763, was therefore especially troublesome. The prime minister, George Grenville, having decided that the colonists should bear some of the expense of their own defense, induced Parliament to enact a series of acts designed for this purpose. A storm of protest arose in America, especially to the Stamp Act (1765), which levied duties on dice, playing cards, and—to the chagrin of newspaper publishers, lawyers, and merchants—on newspapers and legal and commercial documents. The Americans raised the constitutional principle of "no taxation without representation"; the British countered with the argument that Americans were indeed represented in Parliament because the members of that body represented not only the kingdom but the entire empire.

A revolution in minds and hearts. Although England's taxation measures precipitated the rebellion, it would be a mistake to interpret the American Revolution as resulting solely or even primarily from economic causes. Like all great historical movements, the American Revolution was a complex phenomenon. While admitting that the new taxes were ill timed, that they came too rapidly, and that the British government followed a confused policy of advance and then retreat under pressure, many historians deny that British mercantilism discriminated heavily against the colonists. The American colonies enjoyed a high degree of prosperity.

Agreement is growing among historians that the American Revolution was not so much brought about by a "cause" as by "conditions." As John Adams wrote in 1818:

But what do we mean by the American Revolution? Do we mean the American War? The Revolution was effected before the war commenced. The

King George III was the major target of American protest that resulted in a total break with England and led to the Revolutionary War. A painting by William Walcutt shows a crowd of New York colonists toppling a statue of George III in 1776.

Revolution was in the minds and hearts of the people. . . . This radical change in the principles, opinions, sentiments, and affections of the people, was the real American Revolution.[8]

It has been said that the separation movement really began when the first Englishman set foot on the soil of America. Many colonists had suffered religious persecution in the mother country and felt little love for their homeland. Many other colonists never had any connection with England. In 1775, out of a population of nearly three million, almost 40 percent were of non-English stock, mainly from Ireland and southern Germany. "To many Americans England had been an arbitrary and unkind mother; to a greater number she had never been a mother."[9] Of course, many other colonists considered themselves loyal Englishmen and opposed the break with the mother country.

The English colonial majority, however, prided themselves on their rights as Englishmen, rights stemming back to the Magna Carta. They had read the political writings of Montesquieu and Voltaire, and they accepted Locke's contract theory and the concept of the sovereignty of the people.

In summary, these were the conditions which predisposed the colonies to revolution: a fierce spirit of freedom, experience in self-rule in the colonial assemblies, the impact of liberal political ideas from the writings of the French *philosophes*, and the lessons of the Puritan Revolution and the Revolution of 1688 in England.

The war against England. Following the imposition of the stamp tax, events moved rapidly toward open hostilities. Colonial boycotts of British goods and English retaliatory measures, skirmishes at Lexington and Concord between British troops and colonial militia, and the well-organized movement for independence, led by such radicals as Samuel Adams and Patrick Henry, heightened sentiment against the mother country. On July 4, 1776, the revolt of the American colonies was formally proclaimed in the Declaration of Independence.

With the outbreak of war, Britain's state of unpreparedness was quickly exposed. After its victory in the Seven Years' War,

Britain had failed to build up any alliance system to offset the enmity of its vanquished enemies, Spain and France. The British armies and fleets were woefully neglected; commanders found it impossible to put fifteen thousand regulars in the field in America.

Even if Britain had been better prepared, the military situation was very difficult. Britain had to subdue a people now numbering almost one third of its own population on a battlefield three thousand miles distant. And unlike the situation today, when only highly industrialized powers are able to manufacture the complicated weapons of war, the colonists could make most of the gunpowder and muskets they needed as well as a substantial amount of artillery.

The struggle dragged on for seven years. Colonial forces were puny and colonial supplies inadequate, but the revolutionary cause was immensely strengthened by the courage, determination, and skill of its leaders—Washington, patient patriot and dedicated commander; Franklin, sage diplomat and famous scholar; Madison, skilled student of government; Jefferson, ardent and courageous champion of freedom; and Hamilton, adept politician and Washington's wartime aide. The defeat of the British general Burgoyne in October 1777 and the alliance with France in the following year turned the scales in favor of the colonies.

The participation of France, seconded by Spain and Holland, widened the conflict into another European colonial war. In essence, this conflict was a great world struggle, with England, devoid of allies, fighting in the West Indies, the North Atlantic, West Africa, and India as well as in North America. Faced with the active coalition of France, Spain, and Holland—plus a league of neutrality composed of Russia, Sweden, and Denmark—England granted independence to the thirteen colonies in 1783. They were now free to make their own destinies, unhampered by constraints from Europe.

In meeting the challenge of the great European alliance intent on destroying its empire, Britain was more successful than it had been in its attempt to crush the far weaker forces of the American colonists. Regaining mastery of the seas, Britain still maintained its world position.

Constitutional government. Just before the conflict with Great Britain ended, the American colonies ratified the Articles of Confederation (1781), setting up a loose league of independent states under a weak central government. This system produced civil strife and confusion, and tariff and boundary disputes raged between the states.

At this juncture a group of public-spirited men, including Hamilton, Madison, and Washington, urged the establishment of a strong central government. Their efforts led to the Constitutional Convention, which met at Independence Hall in Philadelphia from May to September 1787. After much debate between the advocates of a strong central government and those favoring sovereign states, a brilliant compromise was reached— the Constitution of the United States— which assured the supremacy of the federal government without making puppet governments of the states. In April 1789 George Washington took the oath of office as first president under the Constitution.

The American Constitution represented a clean break with the past and a promise of complete democracy in the near future. Manhood suffrage was not realized under the Constitution for several decades, but this delay does not detract from the importance of the advanced democratic philosophy which became the law of the land.

The American Constitution embodied certain fundamental principles. The first was the doctrine of popular sovereignty—all power ultimately resides in the people. Constitutional provisions required the participation of the people in amending the Constitution and denied this right to the national government acting alone. Another principle, revolutionary in its day, was that of limited government, which safeguards the rights of the people by setting up definite bounds and restraints on the actions of their public officials. A third important feature was the principle of federalism. In most countries all power resided in the central government, but in the United States power was divided between the state governments and the national government. The principle of strong federalism became one of America's greatest contributions to government.

Separation of powers was a fourth fundamental aspect of the new Constitution. The powers and duties of legislature, judiciary, and executive were carefully defined. Thus Congress makes the laws, the president applies and enforces them, and the courts interpret them. However, by a fifth feature— checks and balances—careful provision was made so that no one of the three governmental departments could become too independent or too powerful. The president, for example, can veto laws passed by Congress. But the legislature can by a two-thirds vote pass bills over the president's veto. In like manner, the Supreme Court stands as an ultimate safeguard because it can declare any law unconstitutional.

Finally, the Constitution contains a sixth basic principle, the protection of the rights of the individual, although in reality this principle appears in the first ten amendments to the Constitution—the Bill of Rights —instead of in the Constitution proper. No laws can be made encroaching upon freedom of religion, press, and speech, and all persons are safeguarded from arbitrary arrest and imprisonment.

THE FRENCH REVOLUTION

The Old Regime in France. In the eighteenth century France suffered greatly from the indifference and incompetence of its rulers. Unlike Louis XIV with his continued attention to the government, Louis XV, who reigned from 1715 to 1774, was preoccupied with personal pleasure and indifferent to matters of state. The next monarch, Louis XVI, was well meaning, but ill educated, indolent, and shy; he spent his happiest hours in a workshop tinkering with locks. Lack of uniformity in legal codes, tariff boundaries, weights and measures, and taxation added to the confusion and inefficiency of government.

Discrimination and injustice prevailed in the social structure; birth, not intelligence or achievement, assured success and social position. Of France's total population of 25,000,000 people, only 200,000 belonged to the privileged classes—the clergy and the nobility. These two groups controlled nearly half of the nation's land, monopolized the best positions in the Church, army, and government, and evaded much of the taxation. The peasants—80 percent of the population —were saddled with intolerable burdens. The *taille*, an income tax; the tithe, levied by the Church; the *gabelle*, a tax on salt; and various other taxes took nearly half of a peasant's income. In addition, while serfdom had nearly disappeared, peasants still paid their former lords fees for using the village mill, bakeoven, and wine press. Fishing, hunting, and keeping pigeons were reserved exclusively for the nobility, and peasants were forbidden to molest the deer and rabbits that destroyed their crops. Fields were often trampled underfoot by hunting parties of nobles, and swarms of pigeons gobbled up newly planted seed. Many nobles were absentee landlords who squandered their income from peasant tenant farmers and sharecroppers in ostentatious expenditures at Versailles.

The French middle class had wealth without responsibility, intelligence without authority, and ability without recognition. Practical and businesslike, they resented playing second fiddle to a parasitic nobility and were disgusted at the inefficiency of government. The extravagance of the royal court, the unfair methods of tax collection, the absence of a sound system of national bookkeeping, and the continuance of mercantilistic controls especially called forth censure. The middle class sought economic freedom and above all a constitutional monarchy in which they would be dominant.

Conditions in France were not the worst in Europe. France had the most prosperous middle class outside of England, and the peasants were better off than in any other Continental country. The revolution came to France because the middle class was keenly aware of the evils of the Old Regime.

As we shall see, the impending national bankruptcy, coupled with the selfishness of the nobles, finally brought on the crisis precipitating revolution. But in the background were the ideas of the *philosophes* and physiocrats. By criticizing the evils of the times, stimulating discontent—especially among the bourgeoisie—and offering a logical picture of what a well-ordered society might be, they created a widespread atmosphere of grievance and supplied political and economic philosophies for the future.

Effect of the American Revolution. In France the impact of the American Revolution was deep and widespread; the Americans showed the French how an antiquated government could be removed. War makes strange bedfellows. In France the government of a monarch who opposed freedom at home gave its support to American independence and painted an idyllic picture of the brave new republic. Many aristocrats who espoused the doctrines of the *philosophes* sympathized with the colonists. But, as one of them observed, "None of us stopped to think of the danger of the example which the New World set to the Old."

The financial crisis. Whatever its effect on the climate of opinion in France, the most immediate influence of the American Revolution upon France was acceleration toward bankruptcy. Participation in the American Revolution had cost France nearly $400 million. The credit of the government became so poor that it had to pay an interest rate of 20 percent on its loans, whereas England paid only 4 percent. By 1789 the government was faced with an annual deficit of $27 million, and interest payments on the national debt took half of the total national revenues.

When Louis xvi and his advisers proposed a program of tax equalization that would have put French finances in order, the nobility flatly turned it down. They insisted that the king convene the Estates-General, which they expected to dominate and thereby regain the power they had lost to the monarchy during past centuries. Thus by paralyzing the royal power and forcing the summoning of the Estates-General, the French nobility can be said to have initiated the Revolution. In the words of a nineteenth-century Frenchman, "The patricians began the Revolution; the plebeians finished it."

The Estates-General which was inactive since 1614 was composed of representatives of the First Estate (the clergy), the Second Estate (the nobility), and the Third Estate (the middle class and the peasants). As a gesture to the bourgeoisie, the Third Estate was granted twice the number of representatives allowed each of the other two estates.

The National Assembly. The calling of the Estates-General in 1789 precipitated a demand for reform all over France. For the guidance of the delegates to the assembly, the people prepared *cahiers* (lists) of grievances. The *cahiers* included demands for personal liberty, a national legislature to make the laws, a jury system, freedom of the press, and abolition of unfair taxation. Thus the *cahiers* presented a program of wide but moderate social and economic reform.

On May 5 the Estates-General was formally convened. The delegates of the Third Estate consisted of some six hundred deputies; half were lawyers, the remainder merchants, bankers, governmental officials, and farmers. According to custom the three estates were expected to vote by orders—that is, by estates rather than as individuals. This would mean that any scheme of reform formulated by the Third Estate could always be defeated by a two-to-one vote at the hands of the two privileged estates.

After five weeks of wrangling on the question of whether voting should be by order or by head, the members of the Third Estate proclaimed themselves the "National Assembly" of France, representing the whole "nation." A few days later they assembled at an indoor tennis court and solemnly took the Tennis Court Oath "never to separate but to meet in any place that circumstances may require, until the constitution of the kingdom is laid and established on firm foundations." Louis weakly yielded, and the Third Estate, augmented by most of the clergy and a few nobles, began its self-appointed task of framing a constitution for France.

Paris saves the Assembly. After giving in to the demands of the Third Estate, Louis XVI sought to shore up his authority by concentrating a large number of troops in and around Paris and Versailles. This gave substance to a rumor that the king was planning a military coup against the National Assembly. The rumor, coupled with rising living

Social stratification under the Old Regime in France is bitterly satirized in this cartoon which shows the First Estate and the Second Estate—the clergy and the nobility—riding on the back of the Third Estate, represented here by an aged, toilworn peasant.

costs—the price of bread had recently doubled—led to popular demonstrations in Paris. On July 14 the grim fortress known as the Bastille was stormed and destroyed by a mob seeking arms for themselves and freedom for political opponents of the Old Regime who were often imprisoned there.

Although the Bastille contained only seven prisoners, its fall influenced the king to dismiss his troops and grant full recognition to the National Constituent Assembly. The storming of the Bastille became the great symbolic act of the French Revolution, and July 14 was made the national holiday of France.

Renunciation of the Old Regime. The National Constituent Assembly was in session from June 1789 until October 1791. During this period the Assembly passed more than two thousand laws and effected a peaceful and moderate revolution. In the words of one historian, "No other body of legislators has ever demolished so much in the same brief period."[10]

One of the most important and dramatic

acts of the Assembly took place in the critical days of August 1789. The Bastille had just fallen, and peasants all over France, frightened by false rumors that brigands employed by nobles were burning peasant homes and fields and determined to destroy the records listing the surviving manorial obligations they owed to the lords, fell upon their hated oppressors. They killed some lords and destroyed the châteaux of others.

As the frightening news reached Paris, the deputies in the Assembly realized that immediate action had to be taken. During the night of August 4, noble after noble arose to renounce his feudal dues and privileges. By these proclamations, known as the August Decrees, serfdom was abolished (there were still some serfs in Alsace and Lorraine), old game laws were repealed, manorial courts were swept away, and tithes and all other fees of the Church were ended. It was declared that from that time on taxes were to be collected from all citizens irrespective of rank, the sale of judicial and municipal offices was to cease, justice was to be freely dispensed, and all citizens, regardless of birth, were eligible for any office.

The National Constituent Assembly passed other important reforms. It abolished the old provinces and replaced them with 83 equal administrative divisions called "departments." It also ended restrictions on the conduct of business and encouraged individual enterprise by abolishing guilds and prohibiting trade unions.

The Assembly also substantially changed the status of the Church. Monasteries were dissolved and all Church property confiscated. The former Church lands were used as collateral for paper money called *assignats*. By the Civil Constitution of the Clergy, the Church was secularized. Bishops and priests were now elected by the people, paid by the state, and required to swear allegiance to the new constitution of France.

The Declaration of the Rights of Man. Before drawing up the new constitution, the Assembly produced a document which summarized the principles upon which the new regime should be based—the Declaration of the Rights of Man. Its most important provisions were:

1. Men are born and will remain free and endowed with equal rights. . . .

2. The end and purpose of all political groups is the preservation of the natural and inalienable rights of Man. These rights are Liberty, the Possession of Property, Safety, and Resistance to Oppression. . . .

4. Liberty consists in being able to do anything which is not harmful to another. . . .

6. The Law is the expression of the will of the people. . . . the Law must be the same for all. . . .

9. Every individual . . . [is] presumed innocent until he has been proved guilty. . . .

10. None is to be persecuted for his opinions, even his religious beliefs, provided that his expression of them does not interfere with the order established by the Law.

11. Free communication of thought and opinion is one of the most precious rights of Man. . . .

17. The possession of property being an inviolable and sacred right, none can be deprived of it, unless public necessity, legally proved, clearly requires the deprivation, and then only on the necessary condition of a previously established just reparation.[11]

The Declaration of the Rights of Man embodied the ideals and rhetoric of the Enlightenment and the political liberalism underlying the Glorious Revolution in England and the revolt of the colonies in America. This French pronouncement appealed immediately to reform groups in all European nations, and during the nineteenth century it inspired many peoples to throw off the yoke of their own old regimes.

The Legislative Assembly. By September 1791 the National Constituent Assembly had formulated a new constitution which made France a limited monarchy. The chief organ of government was an elected single-chamber legislature called the Legislative Assembly. Louis XVI was given only a suspensive veto over legislation, a device which could retard action by the Assembly but could not block its will indefinitely. No longer could the king use the formula of Louis XIV, *L'état, c'est moi*; the monarch was now "Louis by the grace of God and the Constitution, King of the State."

Despite the rights guaranteed in the Declaration of the Rights of Man, the suffrage was given to only a minority of "active" citizens—those who paid a specified minimum amount of direct taxes. Thus one of the striking features of the French constitution of 1791 was its reflection of the interests of the influential bourgeosie.

This first phase of the French Revolution has been called the Bourgeois Revolution. After relatively little violence France had become a constitutional monarchy with the upper middle class in control. Their concern now was to "stabilize" the Revolution by blocking further change.

Opposition to the Legislative Assembly. The peasants were among the many elements in France that were discontented with the new government. Although the Constituent Assembly in the August Decrees had ruled that many privileges, such as possession of serfs, labor service, and hunting and fishing rights, were to be abolished without compensation, other old manorial dues and obligations were to be commuted into money payments. Most peasants, however, defied the government and refused to make the payments. Hatred against men of property and their agents in the Legislative Assembly grew.

Instead of accepting the moderate changes brought about between 1789 and 1791 and thus helping consolidate and strengthen the moderate revolution, Louis XVI remained opposed to constitutional monarchy. In June 1791, during the National Assembly, he and his family attempted to escape, which increased the suspicion that he was an enemy of the Revolution. Louis apparently did not understand that if constitutional monarchy failed, the Revolution would take a radical turn and the monarchy would be swept away.

The Civil Constitution of the Clergy had been condemned by Pope Pius VI, and consequently about half of the clergy refused to take the oath of fidelity to the constitution. These nonjuring priests told the people that sacraments administered by priests who had accepted the Civil Constitution of the Clergy were ineffectual. In the country districts the peasants supported their nonjuring priests, and serious disorders broke out. Thus, from the outset, the Legislative Assembly was faced with the enmity and opposition of a determined Catholic group.

The common people of the cities were especially disgruntled. The cost of living and

The idealization of the French Revolution is epitomized in Francois Rude's romantic "La Marseillaise" from the Arc de Triomphe in Paris. Classically garbed soldiers march forward dauntlessly under the guidance of the spirit of Liberty.

unemployment were increasing, and they saw no hope of relief in a government from which they were excluded. Largely illiterate and motivated by emotion, these urban workers could be aroused to wild passions of frenzy by eloquent leaders, and as time passed they became increasingly dangerous.

Factions in the Legislative Assembly. The division of opinion in the country at large was mirrored by factionalism in the Assembly itself. About one third of the deputies were conservatives; they made up the party of the Right, which supported the king and was satisfied with the achievements of the moderate revolution. Seated in the middle of the Assembly was the party of the Center, made up of representatives who had no particular program or principles. Next to the apathetic Center were the deputies of the Left, dynamic and aggressive young radicals who distrusted the king, were dissatisfied with the constitution of 1791, and wished the Revolution to continue. From the very start the enemies of the constitution assumed the leadership of the Legislative Assembly and worked for its downfall.

Leaders of the Jacobin movement. The enthusiastic radicals who were determined to advance the Revolution formed various clubs in Paris that were centers of agitation and revolutionary propaganda. The most important of these organizations met in an abandoned Jacobin (Dominican) monastery and took the name "Society of the Friends of the Constitution Meeting at the Jacobins in Paris." Their program was the overthrow of the monarchy and greater justice and opportunity for the masses. Soon, Jacobin Clubs sprang up all over France.

Most prominent in Jacobin circles were Jean Paul Marat, Georges Jacques Danton, and Maximilien Robespierre. As champion of the masses, Marat founded the newspaper *L'Ami du Peuple (Friend of the People)* and carried on a campaign for direct action by the people until 1793 when he was struck down by an assassin's dagger. Robespierre was deeply influenced by the works of Rousseau and became a fanatical reformer who quietly bided his time until he possessed the necessary power to establish an ideal republic based on virtue and justice. Danton, unlike the theorist Robespierre, was a practical republican who had little use for utopias.

Opposition to the Legislative Assembly outside France. Also plotting against the Assembly were many reactionary émigré nobles who had fled France when the Revolution wiped out their ancient privileges. Most of them had taken refuge in various states along the Rhine, where they found receptive ears for their conspiracies against the French government. Many German bishops and princes who possessed lands in French Alsace were indignant over the abolition of feudal dues and services. Furthermore, many German nobles feared that the abolition of the old manorial dues and obligations in France would lead to peasant insurrections on their own estates.

Although they were uneasy about the trend of events in France, the rulers of the large European states adopted a wait-and-see policy, hoping that factionalism in France would weaken the nation and perhaps reduce it to a state of impotency. However, Leopold II of Austria, brother of the French queen, became concerned over her safety and, with the king of Prussia, issued the Declaration of

The most dramatic of the events launching the French Revolution was the taking of the Bastille on July 14, 1789, as shown in this drawing. The day is celebrated by the French as their national holiday.

Pillnitz (August 1791), which declared that the restoration of absolutism in France was of "common interest to all sovereigns of Europe."

France vs. Austria and Prussia. Opposed from without and weakened from within, the moderate constitutional monarchy was doomed to failure. The shock of foreign war precipitated its downfall.

Nearly all the factions in France favored war—each for a different reason. The king and his supporters, as well as the émigré nobles, favored war because they believed the government would be defeated, discredited, and then overthrown. The radicals, especially a faction called the Girondists, who at first formed part of the Jacobin organization, were eager to involve France in a conflict because, in their opinion, war would discredit the monarchy and give them a chance to rise to power and establish a republic. Egged on by the Girondists, France declared war on Austria in April 1792. Prussia shortly afterward entered the conflict as an ally of Austria.

Yet, while eager for war, the French were utterly unprepared for it. During the summer of 1792, fortress after fortress fell to the invaders. On July 27 the Duke of Brunswick, commander of the allied forces invading France, issued a manifesto declaring that his object was "to restore to the king . . . the legitimate authority which belongs to him." He added that he would destroy Paris if the royal family was harmed. The actual result of the manifesto, however, was to bolster the position of the most radical groups, discredit the king completely, and end the monarchy in France.

Insurrection in Paris. The reply to the manifesto was the insurrection of the ninth and tenth of August instigated by radical Jacobin leaders. They set up a revolutionary "Commune" which controlled Paris and intimidated the Legislative Assembly into deposing Louis XVI and calling for the election, by universal male suffrage, of a National Convention to draw up a new constitution. As head of the Paris Commune, Danton became the virtual dictator of France.

The September Massacres. On September 2, news reached Paris that the fortress of

Stabbed by Charlotte Corday, a supporter of the Girondist faction, the Jacobin leader Marat lies dead in his bath in this famous Neoclassical painting by Jacques Louis David (1793).

Verdun had fallen to the invaders. As reinforcements were sent off to the front, the Paris Commune took care that no traitors were left behind at home. Many citizens believed that counterrevolutionists, in league with the enemy, would try to seize power. All suspected of sympathy for the monarchy were butchered. The prisons were emptied of nonjuring priests and nobles, who were then executed without trial. During the next five days nearly two thousand suspected royalists were killed.

Inauguration of the Republic. While the frenzy engendered by the September Massacres was spreading throughout France, the voters were electing representatives to the National Convention who were as a consequence overwhelmingly opposed to monarchy. Thus the first act of the newly assembled Convention on September 21, 1792, was to abolish monarchy in France. The Convention then proclaimed September 22, 1792, as beginning Year 1 of the Republic. France was now a republic, the former king Louis XVI a prisoner in fear for his life, and the first phase of the French Revolution—that of moderate reform—a failure.

Problems facing the National Convention. The National Convention remained in session three years. At the outset it was faced with serious problems: (1) foreign armies had to be driven out of France; (2) a vital decision had to be made as to what should be done with the king; (3) revolts throughout the country had to be suppressed; (4) a republican constitution had to be framed; and (5) the social and economic reforms initiated between 1789 and 1791 had to be completed and put into action.

Danton proceeded with alacrity to increase the armed forces and give them new spirit. During the autumn of 1792 the tide of foreign invasion receded as French armies took the offensive. They occupied the Austrian Netherlands (Belgium), the Rhineland, and Nice and Savoy.

Trial and execution of Louis XVI. The fate of Louis XVI was soon settled. The Girondists, now more moderate in their views and split from the Jacobins, wished to postpone the king's trial for treason until after the war, but the radical Jacobins demanded his death. A follower of Robespierre declared:

The death of the tyrant is necessary to reassure those who fear that one day they will be punished for their daring, and also to terrify those who have not yet renounced the monarchy. A people cannot found liberty when it respects the memory of its chains.[12]

The execution of Louis XVI was carried out on January 21, 1793. On the scaffold the king acted with quiet dignity and splendid fortitude. A French historian has declared: "he was greater on [the scaffold] . . . than ever he had been on his throne."[13]

European opinion turns against the Revolution. During the first years of the French Revolution a strong body of European opinion had acclaimed its reforms. Liberals cheered the news of the fall of the Bastille. The English romantic poet William Wordsworth described his feelings during those stirring days:

Bliss was it in that dawn to be alive,
But to be young was very Heaven! O times,

In which the meagre, stale, forbidding ways
Of custom, law, and statute, took at once
The attraction of a country in romance![14]

But there also had been voices raised in warning. In 1790 the influential English statesman Edmund Burke published his *Reflections on the Revolution in France.* A conservative, Burke feared the effect of the Revolution on English radicals and predicted that it would lead to mob violence and dictatorship in France. He likened the Revolution to "a strange chaos of levity and ferocity, and of all sorts of crimes jumbled together with all sorts of follies."[15] To Burke, the rule of the mob was as terrifying and as unjust as the rule of a capricious absolute monarch; stability, gradual change, and respect for the old as well as receptivity for the new were the basis of the good society.

Is it in destroying and pulling down that skill is displayed? . . . The shallowest understanding, the rudest hand, is more than equal to that task. Rage and frenzy will pull down more in half an hour than prudence, deliberation, and foresight can build up in a hundred years. . . . People will not look forward to posterity, who never look backward to their ancestors. . . . A disposition to preserve, and an ability to improve, taken together, would be my standard of a statesman.[16]

While the Legislative Assembly was in power and Louis XVI was on the throne, most observers thought Burke's arguments exaggerated; but they began to think differently after the September Massacres, the acquisition of territories outside of France, and the execution of Louis XVI.

In November 1792, after its armies had reached the Rhine, the National Convention declared that "France will grant fraternity and assistance to all peoples who shall desire to recover their liberty." This announcement in essence proclaimed an international revolution. In December the Convention stated that "it considered itself called to give liberty to the human race and to overthrow all thrones" and declared war on tyrants. It was also announced that in all countries conquered by the French, the inhabitants had to accept the principles of the Revolution; property belonging to counterrevolutionaries and to the Church was to be seized.

England as the leading anti-French power. In the face of French aggression—which, at the least, threatened the balance of power in Europe—England, Spain, Holland, and Sardinia joined Prussia and Austria in the First Coalition to wage war on the French Republic. Of all France's foes, England became the most implacable. From 1793 to 1815 England and France were at war almost continuously.

The prime minister in England at this time was William Pitt the Younger. Something of a liberal at the beginning of his career, Pitt wanted no war with France and considered Burke's dire warnings about the Revolution exaggerated. After the French occupied Belgium and threatened Holland, Pitt changed his opinions; he now believed that war with France was inevitable.

Pressures inside and outside France. In the spring of 1793 the armies of the First Coalition converged on France. The Revolution was again in peril. In addition to this foreign menace, France was rent by internal strife as moderate and radical factions fought for control of the National Convention. More representative of the bourgeois moderate revolution and of provincial support for federalism, the Girondists feared mob violence and radical reforms; to them the Revolution had gone far enough. By contrast, the Jacobins were tough realists who sided with the urban masses, welcomed more bloodletting, and were determined to advance the Revolution. The Jacobins finally ousted their rivals from the Convention and placed them under arrest. Some of the Girondists, however, escaped to the country, where they organized a rebellion against the tyranny of the radicals in Paris. Meanwhile, royalist Catholics rose again in rebellion. These disorders weakened the economy of the country, and bread riots broke out in Paris.

The Reign of Terror. To deal with the internal and external dangers, the National Convention entrusted its power to twelve men known as the Committee of Public Safety. It also passed a decree making liable to arrest every person of noble birth, anyone who had any contact with an émigré, and anyone who could not produce a certificate of citizenship.

The Committee of Public Safety inaugu-

The excesses of the French Revolution are typified by the guillotine, the instrument used during the Reign of Terror to behead thousands of Frenchmen, including Louis XVI, whose head is being displayed to the crowd. Ironically, the guillotine was first recommended by a Paris physician, Joseph Ignace Guillotin, who wanted a more humane method of punishment instead of the feudal tortures used to execute criminals. Before the Revolution only the nobility were allowed the relatively painless death of decapitation.

rated the Reign of Terror. Thousands of suspected royalists were arrested and thrown into prison. After a summary trial, many of them were thrown into carts—the tumbrels —and taken to the public square to be guillotined. During the fifteen months of the Terror, perhaps five thousand persons were executed in Paris; in the provinces the number was probably twenty thousand.

The "nation in arms." With subversive activity crushed on the home front, the leaders of the Republic turned their attention to the foreign danger. To meet its enemies, France forged a new weapon, the "nation in arms." Compulsory military service was introduced. In February 1793 the Convention passed a decree calling 300,000 men to the colors and making all men between eighteen and forty liable for military service. Military seniority was discarded, and brilliant young generals were given the highest commands. Results were demanded from these officers; it was victory or the guillotine.

In August 1793 the Convention decreed a general mobilization of the country. Scientists were enlisted to help the war effort, and workmen were conscripted and shifted from nonessential to war work. In Paris alone, 258 forges were set up out in the open to make 1000 gun barrels a day. Business was organized to produce vast quantities of medicines, shoes, and uniforms.

During 1794 and 1795 the new French armies carried out a series of great campaigns. The citizen armies of the Republic were motivated by a spirit not found in the professional and mercenary armies of their opponents. The French citizen-soldier believed he was fighting for his own liberty and for the right to enjoy the fruits of the Revolution.

By 1795, with Spain and Prussia no longer offering effective resistance to the French, the First Coalition had almost been dissolved. Holland was allied with France, Belgium was annexed outright, and French troops controlled all the territory up to the Rhine. In three years the Republic had gained the "natural frontiers" that Louis XIV had dreamed about. By 1795 only England, Austria, and Sardinia remained at war with France.

Social and economic changes. Among the significant reforms achieved during the period of the National Convention (also known as the Jacobin Republic) were the plan for a national system of education, abolition of slavery in French colonies, final eradication of manorial dues and obligations without compensation, and the establishment of a metric system of weights and measures. The welfare of the lower classes was promoted by placing ceilings on prices and by selling the confiscated estates of the émigrés. As a result of the latter measure, France became a land of small proprietors, and the once radical French peasant became a conservative.

The everyday life of the people was transformed in numerous ways. A strong anti-Christian movement was initiated; churches were closed and religious images destroyed. Everything that smacked of royalty and privilege was discarded. Knee breeches, a symbol of the aristocracy, were declared unpatriotic. In their place were substituted long trousers, the *sans cullotes* (literally, "without short breeches"), which "made all legs equal by concealment." Titles were discarded; the proper form of address became "citizen" and "citizeness." Both men and women gave up aristocratic wigs and powdered hair, and men adopted mustaches as a symbol of virility and patriotism. Streets formerly named for kings or nobles were renamed to commemorate revolutionary events or heroes. And men changed their names, especially if their Christian name was Louis. Even the name of the queen bee was changed to "laying bee."

The Terror continues. In the autumn of 1793 the Reign of Terror reached its height. The Girondists who had been expelled from the National Convention were executed, and the guillotine also claimed the queen, Marie Antoinette. By controlling the all-powerful Committee of Public Safety, Robespierre was now the dominant force in the government.

By the spring of 1794 there was no longer any justification for continuance of the Terror. But to the fanatical Robespierre, a "republic of virtue" had to be achieved, in which there would be no excesses of wealth, where every citizen would serve the public good, and where justice and love would prevail. To attain this utopian Jacobin commonwealth, Robespierre believed that "the people's prejudices must be destroyed . . . its habits altered, its vices eradicated, and its desires purified."[17] While a bewildered Paris looked on, many courageous leaders of the Revolution who dared to disagree with his fanatical views were executed. Among them was Danton, who wished to end the policy of terror. Disgusted at the bloodshed, the members of the Convention finally arrested Robespierre and sent him to the guillotine.

Reaction against the Terror. Frenchmen now hoped that the long period of excesses was over and that the nation could bind up its wounds and settle down to a period of tranquility and repose. Thousands of suspects were freed, the Paris Commune was dissolved, and the extraordinary powers of the Committee of Public Safety were swept away. In Paris gangs of young men attacked Jacobins, and in the provinces there was a veritable "White Terror" against the radicals. The Jacobin Clubs were closed and the Catholic churches were reopened. Conservatism was now the order of the day. It was not that the people wanted to go back to the old days. They wanted to see the gains of the Revolution safeguarded and perpetuated, but they were tired of extremists and fanatics.

THE NAPOLEONIC PERIOD

The Directory. The National Convention now drafted a new republican system of government, the Directory, which was composed of two legislative chambers and a weak executive body of five members called directors. The right to vote was restricted to some twenty thousand property owners.

Assuming power in 1795, the Directory faced opposition from extremists on the right and on the left. The royalists had boldly fomented an insurrection in Paris, which an obscure young general named Napoleon Bonaparte dispersed with a "whiff of grapeshot." In the spring of 1796 a radical working-class leader named "Gracchus" Babeuf plotted to seize the government and introduce a socialist economy. He ended as a guest of "Madame Guillotine"—and a martyr for modern Communists to honor—while the workers continued to suffer from inflation and unemployment.

Determined to smash the remnants of the First Coalition, the Directory commissioned three armies to invade Austrian territory. Two of these forces failed, but the one led by Napoleon Bonaparte crossed the Alps in 1796 and crushed the Sardinians and the Austrians. With a French army at the gates of Vienna, the Austrians were forced to accept the Treaty of Campo Formio (1797). Only Great Britain, protected by its fleet, remained at war with France.

Napoleon rises to power. Following his triumph over Austria, Napoleon obtained the consent of the Directory to invade Egypt in order to menace English interests in India. He is reputed to have said, "This little Europe does not supply enough glory for me." Evading the English fleet, Napoleon and his army landed in Egypt and were at first victorious. Efforts to crush Turkish forces were not successful, however, and in the meantime the English Admiral Nelson in 1798 destroyed Napoleon's Mediterranean fleet in the battle of the Nile. Aware that the Directory was becoming more and more incapable of coping with the problems of France, Napoleon in 1799 deserted his army and returned to France, where he was wildly acclaimed.

The France to which Napoleon returned was again in a state of crisis. A newly formed Second Coalition threatened to invade the country, inflation undermined the economy, and impressive gains made by monarchists and revived Jacobins threatened the regime. On the pretext of a Jacobin plot to set up a new Reign of Terror, Napoleon in 1799 swept the Directory from power and established a new government called the Consulate—ostensibly a republic but with nearly all power centralized in the thirty-year-old First Consul, Napoleon. The new constitution was approved by the people in a plebiscite; the vote was 3,011,007 to 1,526.

Napoleon's genius for leadership. What manner of man was this "savior" of France?

Born in Corsica in 1769, the young Napoleon was a member of the Corsican lower nobility of Italian origin. Educated in a French military school, he joined the French army at the beginning of the Revolution. His "whiff of grapeshot," which saved the Directory from a royalist coup, and his marriage to the morally lax Josephine de Beauharnais, who was influential with the directors, gained him his first big chance—command of the army of Italy.

Napoleon liked to describe himself as a "man of destiny." He also once remarked: "I am no ordinary man, and the laws of propriety and morals are not applicable to me." He had a great reservoir of energy which enabled him to be in the saddle all day and to pore over his maps most of the night. For fifteen years the Little Corporal amazed and confounded his opponents by his brilliant tactics and strategy and by the élan he inspired in his troops.

After becoming First Consul, Napoleon quickly scattered the forces of the Second Coalition. The Austrians were compelled to sign the Treaty of Lunéville (1801), and although Great Britain was not defeated, France and England arranged a truce in 1802.

Napoleon's domestic reforms. The First Consul then turned his attention to domestic reforms. The system of local government was reorganized to provide a completely centralized governmental structure. Prefects appointed by the central government were given almost complete charge of local affairs, an arrangement which made for efficiency at the expense of liberty. Next, Napoleon grappled with the financial problem. Graft and inequality in tax collection were ended, economies in public expenditures were effected, and most important, the Bank of France was established. It still exists today as a model of banking stability.

While irreligious himself, Napoleon shrewdly realized that the people demanded the reestablishment of the Church. In the

NAPOLEONIC EUROPE

- France in 1789
- Acquisitions of Napoleon to 1810
- Dependent States of Napoleon
- Allies of Napoleon
- → Napoleon's Campaigns

Concordat of 1801 with the Vatican, the pope was granted the right to approve of bishops appointed by Napoleon. In addition, seminaries were again permitted, and the state agreed to pay the salaries of the clergy. The Catholic Church was now restored in France, but without its former power and wealth.

Before 1800 scarcely 25,000 children in France were attending elementary school. To remedy this situation, Napoleon created a system of public education which provided an educational pyramid of public elementary schools, secondary institutions (*lycées*), special schools for technical training, and the University of France. The latter was not a teaching body but an administrative one; its function was to regulate and control the entire educational system.

Napoleon believed in rewarding ability and in opening the way for talent. In 1802 he created the order of the Legion of Honor to honor citizens who made outstanding contributions to society. Napoleon told his advisers that men "have one feeling—honour. We must nourish that feeling: they must have distinctions."[18]

Napoleon's most famous accomplishment was his codification of the numerous laws and decrees of the Revolution and some 360 local law codes. Completed in 1804, the great Civil Code was written with precision and clarity; it guaranteed many achievements of the French Revolution, such as religious toleration and the abolition of privilege. The Code Napoléon, as it was renamed in 1807, has exerted a marked influence upon the law of other countries, and Napoleon later claimed that he was prouder of it than of his forty battles.

When Napoleon declared himself emperor in 1804, a grateful and contented people overwhelmingly approved his action in another plebiscite. The First French Republic was now no more.

Napoleon at the height of his power. Just before Napoleon assumed the crown of emperor, war between Great Britain and France broke out once more. Napoleon welcomed war. His meteoric rise from a nonentity to the first citizen of France had not satisfied his lust for glory. During 1803 and 1804 he directed extensive preparations for an in-

vasion of England, but the inability of Napoleon's naval forces to gain control of the approaches to England and the formation of the Third Coalition (composed of Great Britain, Russia, Austria, and Sweden) compelled him to march eastward against his Continental enemies in 1805.

Meanwhile Napoleon's hopes of securing control of the seas and invading or at least starving out Britain were ended rudely in the smoke of Trafalgar (October 1805). In this decisive naval battle Lord Nelson defeated the combined French and Spanish fleets. Undaunted, Napoleon crushed the armies of Austria and Russia at Austerlitz, the most brilliant of his victories. In 1806 he occupied Berlin after the Prussians, still basking in the reflected glory of Frederick the Great, declared war. Napoleon organized the territory seized by Prussia in the partitions of Poland into a French dependency, the Grand Duchy of Warsaw. In 1807, at Tilsit, after suffering a third defeat, the Russian tsar agreed to assist France in disposing of the emperor's stubborn antagonist—England.

By 1808 Napoleon ruled over a France which extended from the North Sea to the Pyrenees and included much of Italy. He had placed several of his relatives on the thrones of nearby countries. Prussia and Austria were impotent before French power, and Russia appeared to be only a Napoleonic satellite.

Napoleon was now at the height of his great powers. Few men in history have possessed his gifts and achieved such amazing results. He was the dynamo and the brain of his "Grand Empire." But, as we shall shortly see, the load was too much for one man. The powers of Napoleon began to decline while his problems continued to increase.

Importance of British sea power. By 1808 it was apparent that British sea power was the all-important obstacle standing in the way of Napoleon's mastery of Europe. Safe behind warships, English factories turned out more and more war goods. British commerce and wealth increased, while French trade declined. Great Britain imposed a naval blockade against Napoleonic Europe. Seeking to crush England's economy by imposing a counterblockade, Napoleon prohibited the

In 1804 Napoleon declared himself emperor of France. In Jacques Louis David's painting of the coronation, Napoleon wears a laurel wreath in the manner of a Roman emperor as he prepares to crown himself. The pope and Josephine witness the ceremony. A romanticized painting by the Scottish artist Orchardson shows the defeated emperor brooding on the deck of the British ship, the H.M.S. *Bellerophon*, which carried him to his final exile.

entry of British vessels into countries under his control, a policy known as the Continental System. Fundamentally, the war was now a struggle between the sea power and industrial superiority of England and French military power on the Continent.

Reaction against French imperialism. Ostensibly "liberators" of subject people in Europe, Napoleon's armies disseminated the French revolutionary ideals of "liberty, equality, fraternity." But as Napoleon became more and more imperialistic, the people he had "emancipated" realized that they had merely exchanged one despotism for another. In posing as the champion of the Revolution, Napoleon had sown the seeds of nationalism and liberty which were to prove his undoing.

The occupation of Portugal (1807) and Spain (1808), in order to shore up in the Continental System, proved to be the first crack in the facade of Napoleon's Grand Empire. In both nations guerrilla warfare soon broke out, and a British expeditionary force joined the fighting against the French invaders.

All over Germany a wave of nationalism stirred the people to prepare for a war of liberation. Prussia in particular underwent a regeneration which caused German patriots to look to it for leadership. Liberal ministers began a program of social reform that included the abolition of serfdom, land for the peasants, and a degree of self-government in the cities. Although Napoleon had limited the Prussian army to 42,000 men, the Prussians undermined this provision by a subtle subterfuge: as soon as one army was trained, it was placed on reserve and a new army was called up for training. In this way Prussia managed to prepare a potential army of 270,000 men. Prussian intellectuals used education as a means of nationalistic propaganda. Founded in 1810, the University of Berlin became a center of strong nationalistic movements.

Invasion and retreat in Russia. Napoleon made a major misstep when, after Alexander I of Russia failed to enforce the Continental System in his own ports, he launched an invasion of Russia in 1812. Although Napoleon's Grand Army fought its way to Moscow, the enemy forces remained intact, and the Russians' scorched-earth strategy prevented the invaders from living off the country. While the French occupied Moscow, fires broke out, destroying three fourths of the city. After spending thirty-three days in the empty shell of Moscow vainly waiting for the tsar to agree to a peace, Napoleon gave the order to retreat.

As the Grand Army marched west along the frozen Russian roads, it rapidly disintegrated. Guerrilla forces hovered about the retreating columns, continually pouncing on stragglers. In the bitterly cold weather, campfires were inadequate, shoes soon wore out, and thousands died in the snow. Out of the 611,000 men who had crossed the Russian frontiers in June, a tattered fragment of about 100,000 was able to make a wintry escape from Russia to Germany.

Downfall of Napoleon. Prussia and Austria now joined Russia in the "War of Liberation." English troops commanded by the Duke of Wellington, "The Iron Duke," cleared French armies out of Spain, and in 1813 at Leipzig the allies inflicted a disastrous defeat upon Napoleon in the Battle of the Nations. Napoleon, however, spurned a peace offer:

What is it you wish of me? That I should dishonour myself? Never. I shall know how to die, but never to yield an inch of territory. Your sovereigns, who were born on the throne, may get beaten twenty times, and yet return to their capitals. I cannot. For I rose to power through the camp.[19]

After Leipzig the empire of Napoleon tumbled like a house of cards. In March 1814, allied forces entered Paris. Two weeks later the French emperor abdicated his throne, receiving in return sovereignty over Elba, a little island between Corsica and Italy. Nearly one year later, in February 1815, Napoleon eluded the British fleet, landed in France, and after a tumultuous welcome entered Paris and raised another army. In haste, the allies dispatched the British and Prussian armies toward France.

At the Battle of Waterloo in Belgium (June 18, 1815), Napoleon was outgeneraled and defeated by Wellington and soon thereafter sought asylum with the British. He hoped to live in exile either in England or the United States, but the British, taking no more chances, shipped him off to the bleak mid-Atlantic island of St. Helena, five thousand miles from Paris. Here, in 1821, he died of cancer at the age of fifty-one.

Why did the French empire, which appeared invincible under Napoleon, collapse? When Napoleon's physical vigor and mental brilliance began to flag after the destruction of the Third Coalition, his empire—the creation of one man's military and administrative genius—began to fall apart. A tired man, Napoleon fast became corpulent and lethargic. And if the emperor was tired, the French people were also suffering from war weariness. In addition, the resurgence of nationalism in Europe was bound to destroy any dictator who first stimulated it by prating about liberty, equality, and fraternity and then enslaved those he had "liberated."

Students of warfare point out that the defeat of Napoleon is explained chiefly by the relative importance in that day of sea power on the one hand and land power on the other. These military historians maintain that British command of the sea finally led to the Napoleonic collapse. Finally, some historians see Napoleon's greatest blunder in his invasion of Russia, which boomeranged and ended with the disastrous retreat from Moscow.

Accomplishments of Napoleon. Napoleon's rise to power is one of the most remarkable stories in all history, and his significance in history cannot be dismissed with only a negative verdict. It is true that his wars killed perhaps as many as six million people, but his interference throughout Europe spread French revolutionary ideals and kindled nationalism. In Germany, in addition, he contributed toward ultimate unification by allowing the larger principalities to annex their smaller neighbors, thus reducing the number of German states from more than three hundred to thirty-nine. He also did away with the hoary old Holy Roman Empire.

Napoleon is especially important because he preserved and disseminated many of the results of the French Revolution. In France he firmly established and safeguarded the social and economic gains of the Revolution, most of which benefited the middle class. The same can be said of French-occupied Europe: "the sale of sequestrated properties, the sweeping away of old feudal enclaves and immunities, the opening of careers to men of talent, . . . the liberation of the internal market from restrictive tolls and guilds . . . all helped to promote the growth and raise the social status of the bourgeoisie."[20] Outside of France after 1815 the Old Regime was restored, but the seeds planted by Napoleon in his self-styled role as "the son of the Revolution" could not be uprooted. During the nineteenth century they would come to flower as the middle-class movement called liberalism.

DISCONTENT AND REVOLUTION IN LATIN AMERICA

Climate for revolution. The wars for independence in Spanish America during the first quarter of the nineteenth century were another manifestation of the cycle of revolutions initiated by the Glorious Revolution in England in 1688 and followed by the American Revolution in 1776 and the French Revolution in 1789. All these movements sprang from the same body of political ideals.

During the eighteenth century the main intellectual and political currents in Europe penetrated to the colonies of the New World. One effect of the diffusion of liberal and reformist ideas was a partial rejuvenation of the Spanish and Portuguese empires in America. Colonial administration was made more efficient, the power of the Church in the colonies to suppress new ideas and censor educational activities was curbed, and greater prosperity was enjoyed.

Despite such progress, a good deal of discontent existed. The Creoles (Spaniards born in the colonies) resented the haughty *peninsulares* (the Spaniards sent from the homeland) who monopolized all the highest governmental positions. The rising young Creole generation feasted on the ideas of Montesquieu, Voltaire, and Rousseau. Although such works were banned after 1790, they were smuggled into the country in great numbers.

While government policy was reformist, it could not keep pace with the growth of liberal ideas, especially after the American and the French revolutions. The high degree of censorship and control infuriated the young intellectuals. There was, of course, no hint of the government giving people a greater voice in politics. While not so rigid, mercantilism was still in force, the courts were often corrupt, and the *peninsulares* dominated the Creoles and *mestizos* (those of mixed Spanish and Indian blood).

Thoughts of independence were in the air as the eighteenth century came to a close. Uprisings increased, and on occasion the English were asked for help. The most active of the so-called Precursors of Revolution was Francisco de Miranda (1750-1816), who spent thirty years traveling in the United States and Europe. His plans for emancipating the colonies from Spain received little support in England. In the United States he obtained a ship and some volunteers, but his incursion into Venezuela in 1806 ended in failure.

Toward independence. Only a spark set off by the Napoleonic wars was needed to ignite the revolutionary flame in Spanish America. When the news reached the colonies that Napoleon had unceremoniously removed the Bourbons and placed his brother Joseph on the throne, deep resentment stirred in Spanish America. The colonial authorities proclaimed their loyalty to Ferdinand VII, the former king, who was now interned in France. In a number of colonies liberal Creoles in 1810 ousted local officials and took charge, all the while proclaiming their loyalty to the absent Ferdinand. This "legal" phase of the revolution took place in Venezuela, the Argentine, New Granada (modern Colombia), and Chile.

The legal phase of the revolutionary movement was of short duration. Radical leaders demanded independence and an end to the fiction of loyalty to Ferdinand. Simón Bolívar (1783-1830), leader of the rebels in Caracas, went to England to obtain British aid and convinced Miranda that the time had come to strike for complete freedom. Miranda re-turned to Latin America in December 1810 and the following year proclaimed the independence of Venezuela.

Tragic reverses followed, and in 1812 Miranda felt compelled to make a humiliating surrender. Some of his fellow patriots, including Bolívar, were so furious with Miranda that they allowed him to be captured by the Spaniards. Thus repudiated, he was sent to a prison in Cádiz, where he died four years later. Successful royalist counterattacks in Venezuela ended the republican regime, and by 1815 Bolívar was in exile.

Other uprisings in Lima, La Paz, and Quito had been equally unsuccessful. The most tragic failure occurred in Mexico. In 1810 a premature effort for self-government led by a radical priest, Father Hidalgo (1753-1811), turned into a race war of Indian against white. Frightened by the specter of social revolution, wealthy Creoles and other conservatives supported the Spanish regime. Within a year Hidalgo was captured and executed, but his work for independence was carried on by another priest, Father José Morelos (1765-1815). In 1815 he suffered the same fate as Hidalgo.

The Liberators in action: Bolivar and San Martin. In 1814, following the defeat of Napoleon, Ferdinand VII was released by the French and was welcomed deliriously in Spain. Although the king might have rallied his subjects in the colonies by generous concessions, he ignored this opportunity and reimposed the Old Regime with all its hateful aspects. Soon embittered, the colonial independence forces rose from defeat to gain a complete triumph. This was the achievement of the Liberators, Simón Bolívar and José de San Martín (1778-1850), aided by a group of devoted and efficient lieutenants.

Bolívar, former leader of the abortive revolts in Caracas, was a wealthy Creole who gave his entire fortune to the revolutionary cause. A man of great personal charm, he was a born actor who liked to play the role of heroic leader and who sought the limelight and the plaudits of the crowd. Cultured, well traveled in Europe, and imbued with the liberal philosophy of the Enlightenment, he made the cause of independence both a crusade and an obsession.

LATIN AMERICA 1826

☐ European Colony

Map labels: UNITED STATES; MEXICO; Mexico City; CENTRAL AMERICA; HAITI; ATLANTIC OCEAN; Caracas; GREAT COLOMBIA; Bogotá; Quito; PERU; Amazon River; BRAZIL; Lima; La Paz; BOLIVIA; PARAGUAY; PACIFIC OCEAN; ARGENTINE PROVINCES; CHILE; Rio de Janeiro; Santiago; Buenos Aires; ATLANTIC OCEAN

naval supremacy in the waters off Peru, San Martín transported his troops to this viceroyalty in 1820. In 1821 he entered Lima, where he formally announced the independence of Peru.

The two Liberators met in 1822. At this meeting basic differences in policy and strategy developed. It is said also that Bolívar did not relish being outshone by any rival. Thereupon, without any recriminations, San Martín withdrew from the scene and spent the remainder of his life abroad. His greatness was only tardily realized; not until 1880 were his remains brought back to Buenos Aires and buried in the cathedral there. Today his life is studied in the Argentine schools just as Washington's is in the United States.

After San Martín's withdrawal, Bolívar was left to dominate the scene. In 1824 his army delivered the knockout blow to Spanish power by winning a decisive victory at Ayacucho, situated on a high Peruvian plateau nearly twelve thousand feet above the sea. Here the last Spanish viceroy in the New World surrendered. By 1825 the revolution had run its successful course.

Independence won in Mexico and Brazil. Royalist elements in Mexico were deeply offended by the revolution of 1820 in Spain and the brief triumph gained by the liberal party. For this reason, in 1821, the conservatives supported Agustín de Iturbide (1783–1824), a military man of dubious reputation. Joining the rebel forces holding out in the mountains, he proclaimed the independence of Mexico. After plans to establish a monarchy in Mexico under a Spanish prince fell through, Iturbide proclaimed himself emperor. Guatemala also announced its independence, though for a time it seemed that it would fall under Iturbide's rule.

Independence also came to Brazil, where the members of the royal house of Braganza had arrived in 1808, in flight from Napoleon's armies. Fond of their new abode, the Braganzas remained in Rio de Janeiro after Portugal was freed of the French armies of occupation. Under the paternalistic hand of King John, industries grew, commerce flourished, and European traders and bankers helped the cause of colonial development.

San Martín was the complete opposite; he had none of Bolívar's glowing enthusiasm. Reserved and uncommunicative, he was not moved by praise or blame if he believed his cause just. Doing his duty without any regard for his own interests, San Martín rightly called himself a stoic.

Bolívar began his comeback early in 1817. With a small force he defeated the Spanish armies in northern South America. The most dramatic incident of his victorious campaign was the successful crossing of the formidable Andes. The Republic of Gran Colombia (made up of modern Colombia, Venezuela, and Ecuador) was established, and Bolívar was named the first president of this huge new state.

Further south, in the Argentine, San Martín prepared for a spectacular offensive against the royalist forces. In 1817 he led his army over the Andes in a desperate three weeks' march, surprising and defeating the Spanish forces in Chile. Aided by a former British officer, Lord Cochrane, who won

In 1820 a liberal revolution aimed at establishing a constitutional monarchy occurred in Portugal. King John decided that he must return home in order to ensure his election as the new constitutional monarch. Before he left, he told his young son Pedro, who was acting as regent: "If Brazil demands independence, grant it, but put the crown upon your own head." Shortly after his father's departure, Pedro ripped the Portuguese colors off his uniform and shouted, "Independence or death!" The Brazilians defeated the Portuguese garrison troops with the help of a British naval force. In December 1822 Pedro was crowned emperor of Brazil, under a parliamentary system of government.

Both the North American and the Latin American revolutions enjoyed the leadership of remarkable men, and both were civil wars in which a part of the colonial population remained loyal to the mother country. But there were important differences. In Spain and Portugal only a small percentage of the people favored the colonies; in England a substantial portion of the population did.

And in Spanish America fighting ranged over larger areas and was more bloodthirsty and cruel. We shall also see in a later chapter (Chapter 27) that while freedom brought political unity to the United States, in Spanish America it was the harbinger of internal turbulence and political fragmentation.

SUMMARY

The *philosophes* created an enlightened climate of opinion and a widespread tendency toward reform which influenced a number of European monarchs. But these enlightened despots failed to ward off the ultimate downfall of the Old Regime because their reforms were not sufficiently comprehensive and thorough.

The ideas of the *philosophes* and John Locke found ready acceptance among the colonists in British America—particularly the middle class. The advanced political and economic state of the colonies was a more important

Although the Spanish were better trained and equipped, Simón Bolívar led his ragtag army with such personal valor that he managed to liberate four countries. Below Bolívar leads his men against the Spanish in the battle of Araure in Venezuela.

cause of the American Revolution than any specific act that precipitated the struggle.

Some historians have asserted that the upheaval in France could not have taken place without the successful revolution in the thirteen colonies. The American Revolution gave France the example of a functioning and stable system of free government. But the excesses of the Jacobin dictatorship led to a revulsion in public opinion and to the meteoric career of Napoleon Bonaparte. Motivated primarily by personal ambition, this dominating figure spread French revolutionary ideals throughout Europe. And, in a way, he was also responsible for the independence of Latin America. Revolution broke out in the Spanish colonies because the French emperor had invaded Spain and dethroned the royal family.

The French Revolution was more radical and influential than the English and American revolutions that preceded it. For the first time, the goal of universal manhood suffrage was envisaged, although the net result of the Revolution was the triumph of the bourgeois class and its enshrinement in the government. The French Revolution also constituted the first great stimulus to a new, fervid nationalism in Europe. Furthermore, the Revolution was social as well as political; intellectual, economic, and religious freedoms were all given strong emphasis. Much of the history of the nineteenth century is concerned with the struggle to extend the Revolution's heritage of patriotic nationalism, representative government, and intellectual, religious, and economic freedom. The use of violence to achieve these goals was an ominous part of the Revolution's legacy for the future.

SUGGESTIONS FOR READING

Peter Gay, **The Enlightenment: The Rise of Modern Paganism***(Vintage) is an eloquent treatment of the thinkers who greatly influenced the shape of modern society. R. Anchor, **The Enlightenment Tradition*** (Harper & Row) is a very brief overview. See also K. Martin, **The Rise of French Liberal Thought*** (Torchbooks); and W. H. Coates and H. V. White, **The Emergence of Liberal Humanism,** Vol. I of **An Intellectual History of Western Europe** (McGraw-Hill, 1966). J. Talmon, **The Origins of Totalitarian Democracy*** (Norton) stresses the influence of Rousseau. G. Bruun, **The Enlightened Despots,*** 2nd ed. (Holt, Rinehart & Winston) is good reading. See also J. Galiardo, **Enlightened Despotism*** (Crowell); and Henry F. May, **The Enlightenment in America** (Oxford, 1976).

C. Brinton, **The Anatomy of Revolution,*** rev. ed. (Vintage) is a comparative study of the English, American, French, and Russian revolutions. See also the detailed study by R. R. Palmer, **The Age of the Democratic Revolution: A Political History of Europe and America, 1760-1800,** 2 vols. (Princeton, 1969).

Edmund S. Morgan, **The Birth of the Republic, 1763-1789*** (Univ. of Chicago) is an excellent brief history of the American Revolution. See John Brooke, **King George III** (McGraw-Hill, 1972), a new evaluation. An excitingly narrated history of the American Revolution is Page Smith, **A New Age Now Begins: A People's History of the American Revolution** (McGraw-Hill, 1976). See also Gordon S. Wood, **The Creation of the American Republic, 1776-1787*** (Norton, 1972); Merrill Jensen, **The Founding of a Nation** (Oxford, 1968); and F. M. Brodie, **Thomas Jefferson: An Intimate History** (Norton, 1974).

Recommended books which examine Europe, the French Revolution, and its impact upon European society are: R. R. Palmer, **The World of the French Revolution** (Harper & Row, 1970); G. Rudé, **Revolutionary Europe, 1783-1815*** (Torchbooks); and N. Hampson, **The First European Revolution: 1776-1815*** (Harcourt Brace Jovanovich, 1969), which is profusely illustrated.

G. Lefebvre, **The Coming of the French Revolution*** (Princeton) stresses the role of the reactionary nobility in precipitating the Revolution. See Vincent Cronin, **Louis and Antoinette** (Morrow, 1975), for insights into two tragic figures. L. Gershoy, **The French Revolution, 1789-1799*** (Holt, Rinehart & Winston) is a brief survey. Longer perceptive surveys are C. Brinton, **A Decade of Revolution, 1789-1799*** (Torchbooks); Albert Soboul, **The French Revolution, 1787-1799*** (Vintage, 1975). F. Kafker and J. Laux, eds., **The French Revolution: Conflicting Interpretations*** (Random House, 1968) samples the opinions of leading historians. R. R. Palmer, **Twelve Who Ruled*** (Princeton) is good reading on the Reign of Terror. George Rudé, **Robespierre: A Portrait of a Revolutionary Democrat** (Viking, 1976); and J. M. Thompson, **Robespierre and the French Revolution*** (Collier) are brief biographies. See J. F. Bernard, **Talleyrand: A Biography*** (Putnam, 1974) for the biography of the French Revolution's supreme opportunist. The importance of the class struggle is stressed in G. Rudé, **The Crowd in the French Revolution*** (Galaxy).

F. Markham, **Napoleon and the Awakening of Europe*** (Collier) is a good popular introduction to the Napoleonic period. G. Bruun, **Europe and the French Imperium, 1799-1814*** (Torchbooks) is a notable survey. See also R. B. Holtman, **The Napoleonic Revolution*** (Lippincott, 1967). Vincent Cronin, **Napoleon Bonaparte*** (Dell, 1973) is a beautifully written biography, as is F. Markham, **Napoleon*** (Mentor). E. Longford, **Wellington: The Years of the Sword** (Harper & Row, 1970) spans his military career to Waterloo. P. Geyl, **Napoleon: For and Against** (Humanities, 1974) presents divergent evaluations by historians since 1815.

Irene Nicholson, **The Liberators: A Study of Independence Movements in Spanish America** (Praeger, 1969) is readable. Another lively account is John Lynch, **The Spanish American Revolutions, 1808-1862*** (Norton, 1973).

*Indicates a less expensive paperbound edition.

Stephen Upton first heard of the king's return to England in May of 1660 when the clerk of the kitchen summoned him to his office and told him there was to be a great banquet of celebration. Upton was the cook at Woburn Abbey, the great country house of the Earl of Bedford, and it would be up to him to plan and supervise the preparation of an elaborate dinner for fifty people. At about the same time Ann Upton, Stephen's wife, received her orders to start work embroidering the fine linen shirts that the earl and his son William would wear in the procession to welcome the new king to London. Ann Upton was housekeeper at Woburn, but in addition to overseeing the work of Abigail, Betty Buskin, Alice-about-the-house, and the other maids she spent hours doing fine needlework for the earl and his family. That night the Reverend John Thornton, tutor and household chaplain, informed the rest of the servants that God had been pleased to restore a king to reign over England (see p. 451), and the name of Charles II was heard for the first time at evening prayers.

The change in the government meant little to Stephen and Ann Upton and the others. The Uptons, who had been in service at Woburn for twenty-two years, could remember the days before the Civil War, when the new king's father Charles I had been king and when the earl their master had shouted oaths against him at the dinner table. When the war came the earl had taken the field for the Parliamentary side, but after a year he had gone over to fight for the monarchy. But the younger servants at Woburn knew nothing of this. They remembered only the rule of Master Oliver Cromwell and then of his son Richard, who was laughed at and called "Tumbledown Dick." And now Mister Thornton would teach them to honor Charles II along with all the others God had placed above them.

Woburn Abbey stood on the bank of the Thames near the village of Chiswick, and it was at Chiswick, in a fisherman's cottage, that Stephen Upton was born in the year King James died, 1625. By the age of six he had learned to make himself useful to the gardener on the nearby estate by scaring birds out of the kitchen garden for a penny a day. Later he hung about in the kitchen and did odd jobs in return for meat scraps and gravy, and at thirteen he was taken on as a turnspit for ten shillings a year plus board. Ann Upton had been born on the estate in 1627, and as soon as she was old enough her great-aunt, Old Susan, took her up to the manor house to help with the annual Great Washing. Unlike Stephen she attended the village school, so that when at twelve she went to live at Woburn as laundrymaid she knew how to read and to write a clear script. Both Ann and Stephen were clever and amiable; they rose in time to be housekeeper and cook.

Ann and Stephen Upton were married when she was eighteen and he twenty. They were given a wage of £20 a year and an apartment over the kitchen. The wages were paid out in monthly installments by the receiver general, and each servant signed his or her name in the wage book in token of receipt. Ann Upton wrote hers in large letters; Stephen Upton simply made a cross. Most of the servants were illiterate. Only three of the twelve footmen could write their names acknowledging receipt of their £2 or £6, and all of the maids signed with crosses for their pound a year. All wages were augmented by free room and board in the menservants' and womenservants' halls, and by gifts. The earl and countess customarily gave the Uptons ten shillings at birthdays and Christmas, and on special occasions such as the royal coronation. In addition to their liveries, menservants often had new boots every year, and the women new clothes. In 1660 Ann Upton noted with gratitude the receipt of a cloak and petticoat worth £6, "it being two years since I had any."

The forty-odd servants in the household occupied less than ten percent of the space in the sprawling ninety-room manor house. The large parlors, withdrawing rooms, and shell-lined grotto on the ground floor were reserved for the family, as were the great hall, salon, five living rooms and eleven dining rooms on the second floor. The entire west wing was reserved for state occasions. The earl and countess, their six living children, the earl's mother and unmarried sister lived in the north wing, where paintings of five generations of Bedfords looked down from the walls of the long portrait gallery.

Since the middle ages Woburn Abbey had stood grandly on the riverbank, ringed by the smaller households of the tenants who farmed the abbey lands. In the 1530's the ancestors of the present earl had acquired the abbey in the vast sale of monastic lands under Henry VIII. And in the early seventeenth century the earl's father ordered the abbey torn down and an imposing new house built on its ruins. Now all that was left of Woburn Abbey was the name and the ancient stones used in the foundation of the new house. But the time-honored pattern of dominance and subservience between master and servant, lord and tenant, familiar since medieval times still remained in force.

In the household at Woburn this pattern was repeated in miniature. The lives of the nobility and tenantry—for nearly all the servants were drawn from the tenant households of the neighborhood—intersected in the corridors and great rooms of the manor house. There was little friction between them; each knew and kept his or her place. In earliest childhood Ann and Stephen Upton had learned to recite, in the words of the catechism, how "the fifth commandment requireth the preserving the honor and performing the duties, belonging to every one in their several places and relations, as Superiors, Inferiors, or Equals." They were taught to abhor disobedience—the chief sin of Adam and Eve—as the root of all human vice, and to revere obedience as the prime virtue. It seemed natural to them that they should be called by their first names only, while they addressed the earl and countess as "my lord" and "my lady." And they took as a matter of course the occasional abuses, beating, and fines that fell to them when their work was not satisfactory or when the master or mistress was out of temper.

The Uptons' view of their place in the order of human society was strengthened by their understanding of the order and purpose of the world. The church taught that creation itself implied a ranking of life, with humans inferior to the angels and superior to the beasts. The social order seemed as logical—and as permanent—as the hierarchy of creation, ordained by God and therefore unsearchable by mankind. A servant ought always to have "a just fear and respect for his lord," a contemporary wrote, "because God hath placed him above him and he hath learnt that he ought to honor all his superiors."

It seemed entirely fitting, then, that Ann and Stephen Upton's lives should have no pace or direction of their own. The amount of work they had to do, the time in which they had to do it, all were set by the rhythm of the noble family's life. Not even the most serious crises in the Uptons' private lives were allowed to interfere with their dutiful service. The gravest of these crises occurred a few months after King Charles landed in England. Their sixteen-year-old son John ran off to sign on as a mercenary soldier, leaving a note saying he meant never to return. John Upton had grown up in the sewing room, pantry, and kitch-

en of the great house. At six he washed pots in the scullery; at nine he was a turnspit for his father; at sixteen he became a footman with full livery, but rebelled one day and struck the steward in the face. Rather than suffer the consequences—loss of a year's wages and a week on bread and water in the porter's lodge—he ran off.

John left in February of 1661. For a week Ann mourned for him as bitterly as if he had been killed, but she was forced to put aside her feelings as the month wore on, for the time of the annual move to London was approaching and her responsibilities crowded in.

Every year in March the earl and countess and their family took up residence in their London house for three or four months. Ann went on ahead to supervise preparation of the house, setting the maids to wash the windows and floors, clean and air the rooms, and scour the pewter with ashes and sand. Meanwhile at Woburn Stephen saw to it that all the great kettles and pans and cauldrons were packed into chests and loaded on wagons for the migration of the household. Finally when all was ready the caravan set off, first the master, mistress, and children in their painted coach, then the footmen and other menservants riding alongside them, and then the women sitting atop the heavily loaded wagons as they jolted along the muddy lanes of early spring.

If the servants formed a satellite community within the noble household, the earl and countess belonged to another satellite community—that of the court. The yearly stay in London was an obligation the earl owed to his superior the king. This year it had a special significance, for on St. George's Day, April 22, Charles II was to be crowned in Westminster Abbey. The menservants had new liveries for the occasion, though the earl himself wore his father's coronation robes, which Ann Upton sent out to be cleaned at a cost of £5.

On Coronation Day the servants went to Westminster to watch their master march in the royal procession carrying the king's scepter. Later, all work suspended, they joined the crowds that were celebrating in the streets in honor of the new king, and Ann almost forgot to think of her lost son as she danced with her husband around the bonfire.

PART FIVE
The European Primacy

■ **Europe's century.** Since continuity and change coexist in every age, historians are properly hesitant to characterize any period as being "revolutionary." But, during the four thousand years of recorded history, there have been epochs of drastic, far-reaching change. The nineteenth century, the century of European primacy, was one such revolutionary era.

Europeans went through what has come to be known as the Industrial Revolution during that time. They made the basic change from living in a world based on agriculture and the land, to participating in a society dominated by industries and cities. Not all countries made the transition at the same time: Britain headed the parade and the Balkan states marched at the rear. By 1914, however, Europe reacted to a set of economic, intellectual, cultural, and political conditions that were fundamentally different from those that prevailed in 1815.

In this Part we will discover why Europe possessed, by the end of the century, the material power, inventive intelligence, and governmental flexibility which enabled it to gain primacy over the planet. To do this we must first focus our attention on the factors leading to Europe's economic and material dominance. Then we will examine the brilliant cultural, intellectual, and scientific achievements of the European thinkers and artists. Only then, after we have studied the physical and mental strength of Europe, will we view the responses of political leaders to these developments. Through this examination, we can hope to learn the causes for both the achievement and subsequent loss of European primacy within the short space of a century.

The consequences of economic change. The explosive increase in productivity brought about by the Industrial Revolution—the change from animal power to machine power—had a widespread social and political impact. The middle classes and factory workers became major actors on the European stage, and the power structures of the old regimes could not deal effectively with these new elements. New political schemes and organizations were required to deal with the powerful forces at work in the industrializing countries and, simultaneously, with the rising tide of nationalistic sentiment throughout Europe.

When the established governmental and social patterns of former days were not changed quickly enough, revolutionary upheaval soon followed. In 1830 and 1848 turbulent currents battered the status quo. The Christian churches faced severe challenges in meeting the needs of the growing urban populations, as did the overburdened city governments. By the end of the century Europe's leaders were beginning to make calculated adjustments to the new order.

The wealth and power generated by the Industrial Revolution not only spread over all parts of European society, but, carried by the new means of transportation, soon affected the entire globe. The European primacy made itself felt directly in the far corners of the world through its economic and technological superiority and through the immigration of 40 million Europeans who created "new Europes overseas" in the Americas, Australia and New Zealand, and Africa.

Soon the Argentinean *gaucho,* the Australian sheepman, and the American cowboy—each a symbol of the "free individual" in his own country—were cogs in the global economic machine of constantly circulating raw materials and finished goods. Only the Japanese and the Americans were able to compete in some measure with the Europeans by the end of the century. Most of the rest of the world generally fell under the economic and political domination of industrialized Europe.

Artistic responses. The European artists were deeply affected by this turbulent era. Responding to the changing conditions in which they lived, they presented new esthetic ideas to the greatly enlarged middle-class audiences, often with far-reaching effect. The romantic movement that flourished at the beginning of the century expressed the opportunity and the peril of the times. Historians in every European country contributed to the redefinition of identity that became an essential part of modern nationalism. Novelists, especially in the last part of the century, found their audience expanded by the far greater number of literate people. In addition to providing a great deal of entertainment, novels helped make the newly expanded reading public conscious of the changing age through which it was passing.

Intellectual accomplishments. Europe's intellectuals were equal to the task of developing new ideologies to shape and reflect the changing European world. Nineteenth-century political thinkers and philosophers built on the strong bases of rational social inquiry provided by the Enlightenment. They also took inspiration from the ideals promised by the French Revolution—liberty, fraternity, and equality—to fuel the fires of liberal, socialist, and nationalist movements. The middle and lower classes had a rich menu from which to select their political programs.

Europe's scientists extended the advances of the scientific revolution to build such fundamental accomplishments as Darwin's theory of evolution, Einstein's theory of relativity, and Freud's and Pavlov's research into the workings of the human mind. The discoveries of the theoretical scientist were quickly felt by an increasingly literate and knowledgeable public.

During the first part of the century Europe's technologists, along with colleagues in the United States and Canada, developed inspired responses to old problems of production. Later, they led the way in converting scientific theory to practical applications in factories and homes.

Political responses to a changing age. The European states developed a broad variety of governmental structures in response to the material and intellectual developments. The revolutionary and evolutionary forces that altered Europe during the century produced unique political forms in each country. The great national, social, political, economic, and cultural diversity in Europe dictated that similar forces would produce different results in different countries.

The variety of political responses ranged from the gradually changing democracy of England to the reactionary Russian autocracy. Each nation in Europe experienced the growth of centralized state power and, ultimately, the voice of the common people in politics, either through revolutions in 1821, 1830, 1848, and 1905, through response to military events, or through rational reform.

This revolutionary century strongly tested the European state system. From time to time a major individual such as Talleyrand, Metternich, Bismarck, Cavour, or Disraeli would interpret events and opportunities in a sufficiently perceptive manner to take advantage of them. But by 1914, the outbreak of European war would prove that Europe's politicians had run a losing race in trying to keep up with the challenges and changes presented by the times. Nowhere did the leaders fall farther behind than in their failure after 1900 to defend their own best interests in the realm of foreign affairs. The forces of nationalism, militarism, and political and economic competition trapped the politicians in their outmoded alliance systems which eventually led the continent into a suicidal war.

The nineteenth century's legacy. This revolutionary century of European primacy bequeathed to the world most of the confusing, complex, and comfortable qualities it now has. The major problems facing the world today all find their roots in the previous century: overpopulation, environmental pollution, materialism on a large scale, racism, totalitarianism, political terrorism, fascism, communism, the alienation of the individual, and bureaucratic dominance. The resentment that many in the Third World now feel toward western Europe and the United States also stems from this period of European primacy. It is useless to try to comprehend Chinese, African, Latin American, and Indian attitudes toward the western world today without understanding the effects of European dominance on the developing world in the nineteenth century.

At the same time, most of the solutions we are now pursuing to the world's problems also have their roots in the last century. The Industrial Revolution, despite its initial abuse to the working class and environment alike, has also made possible the advanced standard of living, high productivity, better health standards, longer lifespans, and mobility that are present to a greater degree than ever before in the history of humanity.

CHAPTER 22

The Material Bases
of European Strength:
1815-1914

The Foundations for World Dominance

INTRODUCTION. Europeans in the nineteenth century established the economic and material foundations for their brief but thorough control of the world. They put together a number of essential factors to gain their global primacy. During that period the number of Europeans more than doubled, and the food supply grew at an even greater rate. Transportation and communications systems were vastly improved. The Industrial Revolution increased productive power and material strength beyond anything previously imagined; it built on the bases of more food and people and of improved transportation to transform age-old ways of life. Although the early stages of the industrialization process brought hardship and misery in the rapidly growing cities, most Europeans enjoyed more comfortable lifestyles by the end of the century than had their grandparents, and a look at the world map would assure them of their dominance of the planet.

Before we can examine nineteenth-century culture, thought, and politics, we must first focus on the role played by economic and material forces in human history. These forces serve much the same function in the life of a nation as gasoline does in the driving of a car. The fuel is important; it propels the car. It does not determine of and by itself the route chosen, the manner in which the car is driven, or whether or not the driver is skillful.

Europe's economic and material growth would fuel its rise to world primacy. But the skill that the European leaders would possess often would be inadequate to guide their nations safely along the winding and perilous roads of the nineteenth century.

The leaders had difficult tasks to perform because of the unprecedented changes through which their nations were passing. At the beginning of the period, Europeans depended on agriculture and the ways of life tied to it. By 1914 this picture had changed — most of Europe had gone through the Industrial Revolution and made the basic transition to a modern society. The change from human and animal power to machine power, from the limits of flesh and blood to the enormous capacities of coal, steam, and oil, and from local or regional markets and resources to a world economy brought about a transformation that drew a line between the old and the new Europe.

No aspect of European life was untouched by the events of that century. Society became wealthier, developed new sets of institutions, and produced a new way of life. The price paid to achieve the Industrial Revolution, however, was not cheap. In undergoing the change that permitted a much more efficient use of human labor and natural re-

sources, Europe's people suffered through difficult times, especially in the early years of industrialization. The rapid growth of cities overtaxed the available housing and increased the numbers of ugly, disease-ridden slums. As industry grew and became more complex, so too did the centralized bureaucratic states which developed new structures to collect the greater amounts of taxes needed to cope with the unprecedented challenges and demands on the political system. In pursuit of economic growth, businessmen and politicians — out of either ignorance or shortsightedness — inflicted major damage on the world's environment.

At the same time, the vast growth in material strength made it possible for most Europeans to live better. By the end of the century, especially in western Europe, major benefits could be seen. The industrialization process that initially made the cities such unpleasant places evolved to the point that there was a general increase in income and leisure time. Education became available for more people and with it came opportunities for greater social mobility.

The Industrial Revolution is still going on, in altered forms, in different parts of the world. Its social and environmental impacts remain powerful. Industrialization is clearly a determining factor in the ability of nations to survive, prosper, and influence other nations. As one scholar has noted, "Economic development is a great drama. It is the puberty of nations, the passage that separates the men from the boys."[1]

MORE FOOD FOR MORE PEOPLE

The agricultural revolution. The spectacular growth of the European industrial economy makes it easy to overlook the essential, great strides made in food production during the nineteenth century. Because of the improved global transportation network and better farming methods, the vastly increased number of city dwellers had more and better food to eat by 1914 than they had had in 1815.

At the beginning of the period, it is esti-

mated that approximately 60 percent of the capital and 85 percent of the population on the continent were devoted to farming. This large proportion of money and labor did not bring efficiency with it, because the major advances made in Britain during the eighteenth century had not spread in any large degree to the continent. During the century, however, progressive landowners gradually introduced improved farming methods.

They saw the financial opportunity that arose from the need to supply food to the growing city populations. The English advances in land use, planting practices, and cattle-breeding were first imitated, then improved on. In Russia and the German states farmers plowed new lands and tested higher yielding varieties of grain. In addition, commercial farmers—those engaged in supplying specialized items such as wine, cheese, and meat for the urban markets—improved both the quantity and quality of their products.

By 1914 the industrial nations—such as England, which had only ten percent of its population engaged in agriculture—imported more than one fourth of their food supply. The Americas, Australia, and New Zealand became important suppliers for the European table during the century. This foreign competition, which drove prices down, adversely affected those European countries in which a large proportion of the population continued to work on the land.

The advent of the Industrial Revolution and its increasing population demands put more pressure on farmers all over Europe to produce more and better food. For the peasants of the agricultural countries whose job it was to work the land, these increased pressures and demands only served to make their meager existence more miserable.

In 1914 for example, more than 70 percent of Russia's people still worked in agriculture. They became part of the international agricultural economy, and the pressures on them became severe. The tsarist minister of finance, who oversaw a program of grain export to attract foreign loans, stated that "we may go hungry, but we will export."[2] Export Russia did, but the famine of 1891 devastated the peasants in the European provinces of the country. Other farming classes also endured difficult times during the century, especially the Irish peasants, who in the 1840's suffered under the weight of the potato famine. The peasants generally maintained a tenuous existence during this century.

Population increases. The improvements in food supply occurred at the same time that Europe was undergoing a monumental population increase. In 1800, an estimated 175 million people lived in Europe. By 1910 there were around 435 million Europeans, an increase of 130 percent.[3]

At the end of the eighteenth century the views of the English clergyman, Thomas Robert Malthus (1766-1834), were being widely discussed. In his *Essay on Population*, Malthus had asserted that "the power of population is indefinitely greater than the power in the earth to produce subsistence for man."[4] In his own day Malthus could accurately point to a limited food supply and a population that was rapidly increasing. From this evidence he concluded that the inevitable fate of humanity was misery and ruin, since the number of people would increase geometrically and the amount of food would grow only arithmetically.

It was clear by 1900 that Malthus' gloomy assumptions had not come to pass in Europe. Without a continent-wide famine and war, a greater number of Europeans were enjoying a higher standard of living and eating more and better food. The Industrial Revolution, improvements in agriculture, and various methods of population control had—temporarily at least—disproven Malthus' theories.

The European population drastically increased because of the gradual decline in mortality rates, slightly better medical care, improved diet, earlier marriages, and better

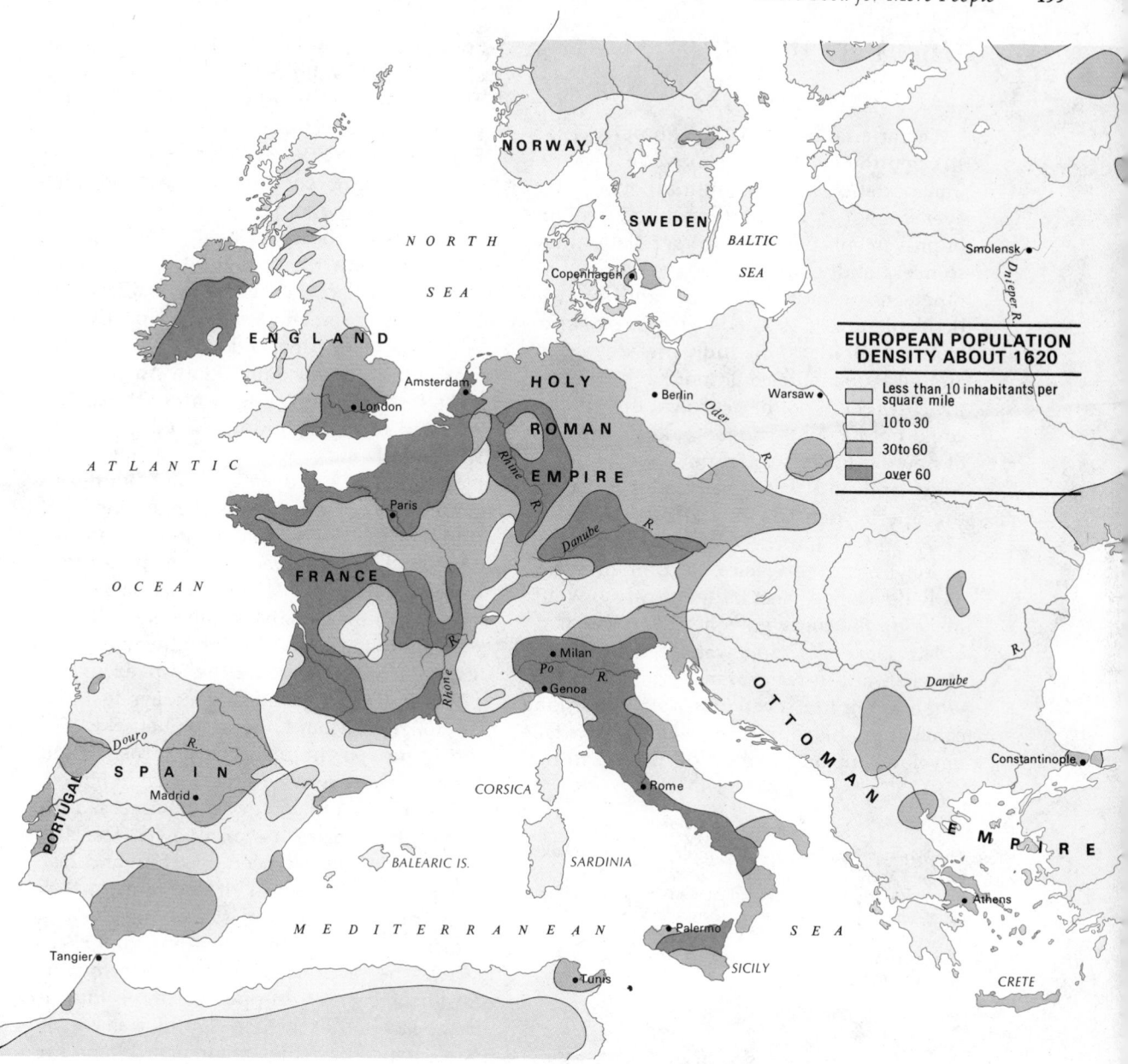

EUROPEAN POPULATION
DENSITY ABOUT 1620

Less than 10 inhabitants per square mile
10 to 30
30 to 60
over 60

hygienic conditions. The former balance of deaths per year versus births per year was lost—by the end of the century there were many more births than deaths annually.

This population growth was so great that 40 million Europeans could permanently leave their homes for other parts of the world and Europe would still show a population increase in one century that was greater than that of the previous two thousand years. In countries with efficient industrial economies (northern and western Europe), this growth in population could be absorbed. But in the poorer countries of southern and eastern Europe, the choice faced by the increasing multitudes was either overcrowding and starvation, or immigration.

The first two foundation stones for the European primacy in the nineteenth century, mutually supporting as they were, were the increasing food and population bases. Without them, it is very doubtful that Europe could have attained its global dominance (compare map above to map on p. 501).

THE TIES THAT BIND

The arterial network. The Europeans constructed the most complete and far-reaching transportation and communication network ever known to tie together the agricultural improvements, increased population, resources, and markets that evolved in the nineteenth century. Without rapid and dependable access to goods, customers, information, and ideas, the Industrial Revolution and all its benefits could not have occurred: the cities could not have grown, the factories could not have functioned, and the millions of new Europeans could not have been fed. New land and water passageways formed the arterial network of the new European body, and the improved means of communication, including electronic communication as it developed later in the century, would make up the continent's nervous system.

The Duke of Bridgewater made a major step forward in water transportation in 1759 when he built a seven and a half mile long canal from his mines in Manchester. This development cut the price of his coal in half

The Worsley-Manchester canal, built by James Brindley, enabled the Duke of Bridgewater to transport his coal and stone to Manchester and helped to start England's canal boom. This illustration shows the canal entering an underground tunnel that led to a coal mine. The crane was used to hoist blocks of quarried stone onto the canal boats.

and gave England a vivid lesson in the benefits of canal building. With strong governmental support nearly 4000 miles of improved rivers and canals were built in England by the 1830's. During the century canal building continued to spread, first through the industrialized world, and then to Egypt with the Suez Canal in 1869, and the Americas with the Panama Canal in 1914. The first project shortened the sailing time between London and Bombay by nearly half, while the latter canal did away with the necessity of sailing around South America.

At the beginning of the century streets and roads were often muddy, rutted paths that were impassable during the spring rains. Not until 1815 did a Scotsman, John Mc-Adam, change the nature of road construction by placing small stones in compact layers directly on the road bed. The pressure of traffic moving over the highway packed the stones together to give a fairly smooth, all-weather road. This type of highway enabled stagecoaches to increase their speed. In the 1750's it had taken over four days to travel the 160 miles from London to Sheffield; after the improvement in road construction the distance was covered in twenty-eight hours.

The nineteenth century also witnessed the transition from sail to steam power. The clipper ships may have been beautiful and fast, but in the last quarter of the century they were displaced by the sturdy steamships, which carried more cargo with greater regularity. The price of American wheat on the European market dropped by three fourths in the last part of the period; this was largely a result of the savings made possible by the steamships' larger cargo capacity and dependability. Further, trans-Atlantic passenger and mail service were improved by the use of steam to power sea-going vessels.

The most important element in the European arterial network was the railroad. Fifty years after the Englishman, George Stephenson, built a locomotive named the *Rocket* that attained the unheard-of speed of thirty-six miles per hour in 1830, rails linked every major market in Europe and in the United States. One student of French history maintains that the modern age did not begin in France in 1789, but with the transportation

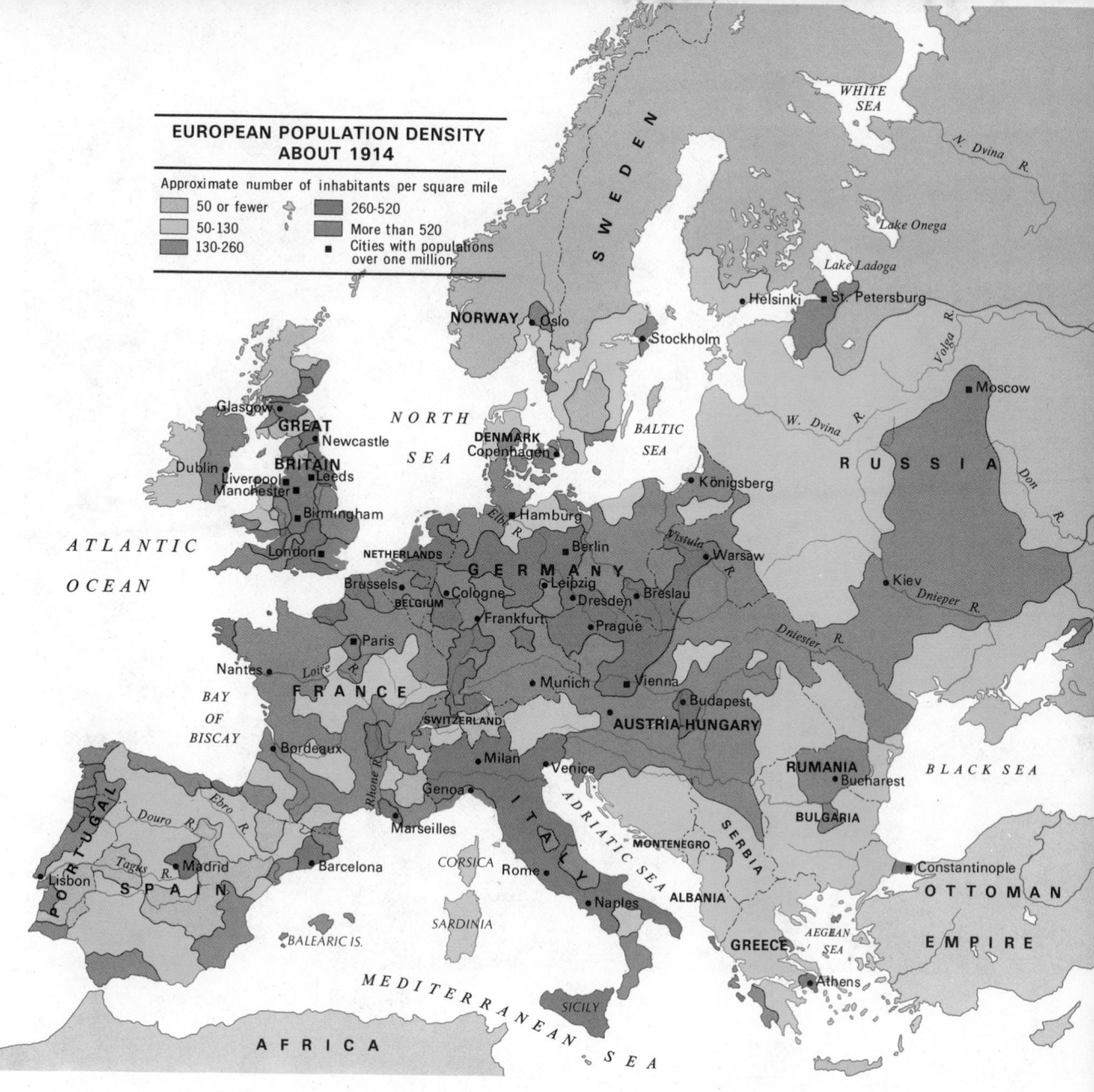

revolution and the railroad.[5] By 1903 the Russians had pushed the Trans-Siberian railroad to the Pacific Ocean. By carrying large amounts of material and people, the railroads knit the continents together and affected every aspect of life, from diet to vacations. The importance of the railroads at that time was symbolized in the massive and ornate stations that were built in the major European cities. Whether it was the Victoria Station, the Finland Station, the Südbahnhof, or the Gare de l'est, each station implied romance and dreams of faraway places. They came to be for the nineteenth-century cities what the

medieval cathedrals had been some 600 years earlier: a summation of the values and tastes of an era.

Transportation within cities also continued to improve, and by the end of the century urban rail lines and trolleys were introduced. The addition of electric power and improved motors made the train systems more dependable and less expensive. Later, suburban rail lines were introduced which made the daily "commute" a part of modern life. Subways were established first in Britain in the 1860's, Budapest in 1896, and Paris in 1900. By 1914 cheap and efficient urban transportation was

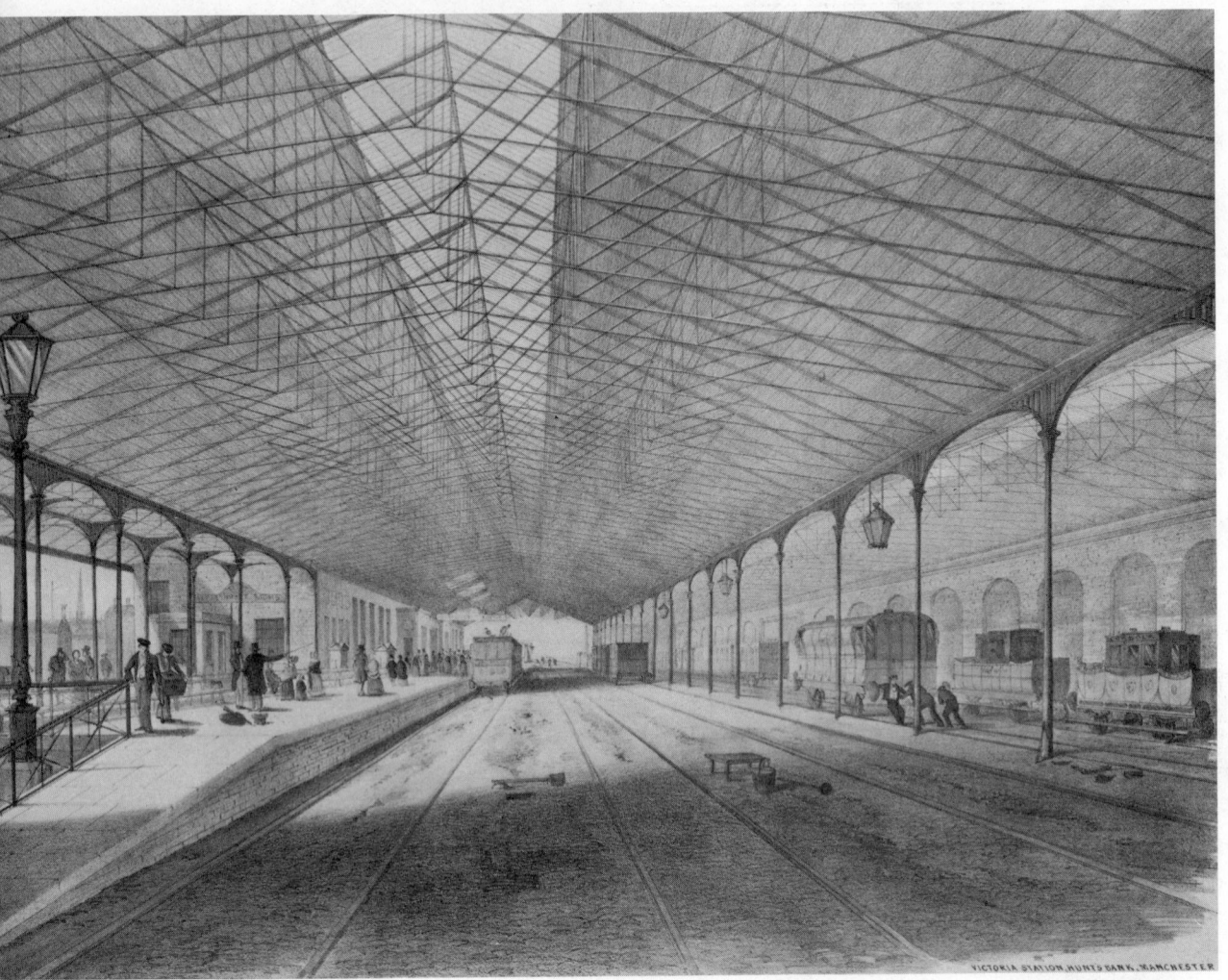

Victoria Station in Manchester, England, one of the typical ornate, nineteenth-century European railway stations.

widely available in all European cities. This greatly altered housing and business patterns by permitting a wider diffusion of workers over a greater area.

Communication changes. At the same time that the means to carry goods and passengers worldwide were changing, major improvements also came in the area of communications. Postal agreements among the various countries made cheap and dependable mail service possible. The modern postage stamp and the improved transportation system greatly increased the ability to deliver mail quickly and inexpensively. The Germans mailed 1.5 letters per inhabitant in 1840. By 1900 they were sending 60 per person per year. The United States Post Office sold 1.5 million stamps in 1850 and 4 billion stamps in 1900.[6]

Technological advances made during the century contributed to the general use of the electric telegraph, the undersea cable, the telephone, wireless telegraphy, and the typewriter. The telephone and typewriter, incidentally, contributed to the process of bringing women out of the home and into the office.

No longer would distance be a major obstacle after the communications and transportation revolutions. The world became a much smaller and more unified place to live by the end of the century.

THE FIRST PHASE OF THE INDUSTRIAL REVOLUTION: ENGLAND

England's advantages. The Industrial Revolution began in England in the middle of the eighteenth century and spread from there across the continent in the next century and a half. Devising new technologies and using new energy sources, the English gained a dominant position in the world economy, one which they kept without serious challenge until the last part of the nineteenth century.

England was neither the richest nor the most populous country in western Europe at the end of the eighteenth century, so England's advances cannot be explained as a consequence of her controlling wealth and labor supply. Instead, the English had the unique combination of elements that enabled them to industrialize first. As a result, sometime between the 1760's and 1780's they began to apply machine power as a substitute for animal and human power in the making of cotton cloth.

England possessed at virtually all levels of society a hard-working, inventive, risk-taking private sector which received strong support from the government. Capitalism in its modern form could not exist without the individual businessman who would take a chance on something new. England retained this close tie between private initiative and government support until the end of the century.

England had an expanding population that provided the supply of workers and the initial market for English products. This population had a larger per capita income than that of any other European state. The supply of factory workers did not come solely from peasants driven off the land by the Enclosure acts.[7] Rather, a gradual decline in the mortality rates and an increase in the birth rate led to increased population.

Thanks to early governmental support of road improvements and canal construction, England had a better transportation network than any other country in Europe. The English also possessed an undoubted mastery of the seas, a number of good ports, and a large merchant fleet. The English also profited by living securely on their island, away from any theater of war, even during the upheavals of the Napoleonic conflicts. The opportunity to industrialize in stable conditions gave the English the chance to profit from war contracts between 1792 and 1815. They could develop their industrial capacity without fear of battle damage or loss of life.

Probably the most important factor of all was the flexibility of the English social and political system. The British upper classes, unlike their continental colleagues, pursued their wealth in the new industrial framework with great enthusiasm. They worked more closely with the middle classes and artisans, and showed a belated sensitivity to the problems of the workers. Through their reform efforts later in the century they would blunt the possibility of revolution from below.

The revolution in textiles. The Industrial Revolution took place in England in the production of textiles. An idea of the massive increase made possible by the application of machines to cloth-making is evidenced by the amount of raw cotton England imported for use in its textile industry. In 1760 it imported a little over 1000 tons of raw cotton as compared to over 222,000 tons of cotton imported yearly by the middle of the nineteenth century.

This great change in productivity was not conceived in scientific laboratories by professional researchers. Practical men solving practical problems invented the machines. Each step forward in removing an obstacle to production posed new dilemmas which were, in their turn, resolved. In 1733 John Kay, a spinner and mechanic, patented the first of the great machines for the cloth industry—the flying shuttle. This device made it possible for one person to weave wide bolts of cloth by using a spring mechanism that sent the shuttle across the loom. Kay's innovation upset the balance between the weavers and spinners; one weaver required ten spinners to produce enough yarn to keep up with him. In 1764 James Hargreaves, a weaver and carpenter, devised the spinning jenny, essentially a mechanical spinning wheel, which allowed the production of the spinners to equal that of the weavers.

Five years later a barber named Richard Arkwright built the water frame, which made it possible to spin many threads into yarn at the same time. Ten years after that Samuel Crompton, a spinner, combined the spinning jenny and water frame into the spinning mule which, with variations, is still used today. The hand loom could no longer weave cloth as fast as the new machines could spin yarn, and a county vicar named Edmund Cartwright set about to solve this problem in 1785 by inventing the power loom, which mechanized the weaving process.

The capacity of the machines to make cotton far exceeded the ability of the cotton suppliers to provide their product. Since most cotton came from the United States, the demand outran the capability of the slave-based southern economy to maintain a sufficient supply. The best worker could not prepare more than five or six pounds of cotton a day. That problem was solved in 1793 when Eli Whitney invented the cotton gin, which enabled one worker to clean more than fifty times as much cotton a day.

These inventions were devised by men close to the work at hand who saw a particular problem to be solved. Tied together, they produced an expansion of productivity never before dreamed of. The essence of the Industrial Revolution is that it was a successful response to the age-old problems posed by limitations of human and animal power. The Industrial Revolution vastly increased the ability of human beings to make not only cloth, but many other essential goods as well. This liberation of humanity by machines from its own productive limitations is the great gift of the Industrial Revolution. The process described above would be repeated in countless other areas of work by the end of the nineteenth century.

New power sources. Before 1815 water power had been used to grind grain and make cloth. But this source of power was not sufficiently flexible. The application of steam power to machinery removed the geographical limitations on the use of machines and provided a virtually unlimited source of energy for the Industrial Revolution. Some authorities suggest that the introduction of steam power in the modern era was as important as the domestication of animals in prehistoric times.

In the first part of the eighteenth century an English mechanic, Thomas Newcomen, devised an "atmospheric engine" in which a piston was raised by injected steam. As the steam condensed, the piston returned to its original position. This device was used at first to pump water out of mines, but it proved to be unwieldy and inefficient.

James Watt, a builder of scientific instruments at the University of Glasgow, perfected the steam engine process and saved the tremendous amounts of energy lost by the Newcomen device. Watt's engine was first used to pump water out of mines too, but after 1785 it was also used to manufacture cloth and to propel ships and locomotives.

The application of this new power source to weaving made it possible to expand the mechanized cloth process to new areas of England. Until 1815, hand looms had continued to be widely used, but in the next three decades the undoubted superiority of the cloth-making machines made itself felt. By the end of the century hand weaving would be looked on as a craft, but not as a serious economic undertaking.

England's dominance. The increased use of machines, the growth of the factory system, and the urbanization that accompanied it made England the dominant European economic power until near the end of the century. After the conclusion of the Napoleonic wars, England flooded the continent with cheap goods. The continental nations were not able to compete effectively against English efficiency. When England started its march to industrialization before the upheaval of 1789 there were isolated areas on the continent, such as the French Le Creusot works, that might have been able to serve as the basis for a parallel advance, given the proper conditions. But twenty-six years of revolution and war made that widespread development impossible.

Cotton production continued its rapid increase, and at the turn of the nineteenth century was supplemented by the arrival of the Iron Age. In 1800 Russia and Sweden had contributed greatly to the English iron supply. By 1815, however, Britain exported more than five times as much iron as it imported. By 1848 the English iron works produced more of the metal than was turned out in the rest of the world.

A number of technological innovations enabled this development to occur. Refining of the brittle cast-iron was improved so that it became more malleable and tougher. At the same time more efficient mining processes for both coal and iron ore were implemented to insure a constant supply of these essential resources. By the middle of the century, England controlled the world market in both textiles and metal products.

The British extended their economic strength in other areas as well. By 1870 they had twice as much steam-generating capacity as the French. The combined capacity of English steam engines was about 4 million horsepower, roughly equal to the force produced by 6 million horses, or 40 million men. The engines were fed by the coal of England. The country could not have produced sufficient grain to feed the animal power required to perform the same tasks.[8]

In the 1850's Henry Bessemer devised a process by which steel, a harder and more malleable metal than cast iron, could be manufactured quickly and cheaply. Between 1856 and 1870 the price of British steel fell to one half the amount formerly charged for the best grade of iron. The drastic reduction in price had a positive impact on all areas of the economy.

England continued to produce more than two thirds of the world's coal, and more than one half of the world's iron and cloth. Industrial development had reached the extent that at mid-century more than one half of the population lived in cities and worked in industries. Germany would not match that particular distribution for fifty years. The British population continued to enjoy the highest per capita income in the world. In short, by any statistical measurement, Britain stood head and shoulders above the world in terms of economic and material strength.

Historians were not slow to catch the symbolic importance of the Great Exhibition in London in 1851. This fair was a forthright display of Britain's technological superiority to the world, and the building that portrayed England's advance, the Crystal Palace, was the wonder of the age.

The economic and technological dominance of England was undisputed throughout the world by the middle of the nineteenth century. To display this leadership, the Great Exhibition opened in London in 1851 at the famed Crystal Palace, not only to display past and present industrial achievements, but to also set the trends and directions for future growth and invention. The Crystal Palace, constructed of iron and glass, was a symbol both of the practical skill and the romance of industrialization.

THE SECOND PHASE OF THE INDUSTRIAL REVOLUTION: THE CONTINENT

Obstacles to industrialization. There were still many hurdles after 1815 in the paths of the continental powers as they pursued economic growth. The social structures of the various nations did not prove as favorable to economic change as did the British system. There was not as much mobility, communication, and cooperation among the classes as there was in England. The farther east and south the social system, the more repressive the structure; the farther east, the weaker and more isolated became the middle classes. In many parts of the continent the old noble classes had regained power, and they did not aid industrial development as much as did the English government.

Fragmented political boundaries, natural geographical obstacles, and a regressive system of toll-takers along major river and road systems hampered economic growth in Central Europe. These problems would not be solved until the mid-nineteenth century.

In 1815 the early stages of the Industrial Revolution were to be found in France, Belgium, and Germany and, to a lesser degree, in Sweden, Russia, and Switzerland. But the combined total of all these activities was miniscule when compared to England's economic development. Governmental commissions from across the continent traveled to London and to the northern industrial cities to search for the secrets of English success. English officials tried to maintain their lead by banning the export of machines and processes, but industrial espionage existed then as now. England's success could be studied, but it could not be easily transplanted. By the 1850's, only Belgium was able to industrialize to the point that it could compete with British products in its own markets. There, a combination of favorable governmental policies, good transportation, and a stable market helped this small country hold its own in dealing with British economic strength.

Improvements on the continent. After mid-century, France and the German states began to make major improvements in their economic conditions. During this period they were aided by the absence of major war, improved transportation networks in the forms of canal systems and railroads, more favorable governmental actions, and improved technical educational systems. Further, population increased some 25 percent in France and nearly 40 percent in Germany. Many of the English technological lessons were being applied, and improved upon, in continental factories. But the two most important developments came in banking and customs and in toll reforms.

After the Napoleonic wars, new banking houses appeared in major European cities to aid in supplying needed capital. The continental conflict had been a boon to bankers with international connections, and they were among the first to sense the great potential of the Industrial Revolution. Firms such as Hope and Baring in London, the Rothschilds in Frankfurt, Paris, Vienna, and London, and the numerous Swiss bankers were representative of the private bankers who had well-placed sources of information and intelligence. During the first part of the century these firms worked primarily with governments, but by mid-century they were investing in railroads and industry.[9]

Banking changed radically during this period as the demand for money greatly increased. Investment banks were formed to meet the needs of long-range capital, and new institutions were chartered to fill the need for short-term credit. The significance of these new banks was that the industrialists went to the middle classes—to the little people who put their money in banks—to raise capital. More could be gotten from the many small investors than from the few large bankers.

The other major development came in the German states. The *Zollverein* (customs union), which began to form under Prussian leadership in 1819, helped break down the trade barriers among the various German states which joined it. By 1842, the *Zollverein* attained its broadest influence, and one of the major obstacles to economic growth in central Europe was thus removed. In place of the more than 300 divisions fragmenting

With the spread of industrialization to the Continent, the iron and coal of the Saar region in Germany became increasingly important. Above is a metal foundry in the factory district of the Saar as it appeared about one hundred years ago.

Germany in 1800, by mid-century there was a veritable German free trade market, something Britain had enjoyed since the union of Scotland and England in 1707.

In the years after 1850, industrial development on the continent grew rapidly, aided by a high flow of credit. In addition, tariff walls throughout the area fell to a degree not to be matched until after World War II. Major industrial concerns, such as the German Krupp works and the major French silk factories, rose to claim portions of the European market, and the continent began to compete effectively with England in the economic arena.

Technological growth and advances. Although periodic business crises dealt setbacks to economic development, especially during the depressions of the 1870's and 1880's, substantial technological advances were made in the last third of the nineteenth century. New materials, new chemicals, and new means of transportation were introduced at a rapid rate. These new technologies helped solve many of the problems created in the earlier phases of the Industrial Revolution.

Perhaps the most fundamental change came in the introduction of electricity to everyday life and industry. The scientific principles behind electricity had been known for more than a century, but the problem that remained was to find a dependable way to generate it and transmit it across long distances. Research into the uses of this form of power went on in all major industrial countries. The first dependable dynamo, a device that changed energy from a mechanical into an electrical form, was perfected in 1876, and this enabled a plentiful supply of electricity to be generated almost anywhere. Inventors such as the American, Thomas A. Edison, began to apply the new resource quickly to industry, urban transport, lighting, entertainment devices, and conveniences for the home. Humanity had finally found a source of power that could be easily transportable and usable. England took the lead in applying electricity in home and industry, but by the end of the century the Germans were the most advanced in the use of electronic technology.

Another fundamental change, the use of oil and gas in the new internal combustion engines, came to be widespread in the last part of the century. The uses of steam had by then reached their limit; thus the newer forms of energy surpassed the century-old power source. The Germans in the 1870's and 1880's perfected the internal combustion engine as it is still known and used today.

Gottlieb Daimler's improvements in earlier designs permitted the use of gasoline in these extremely portable devices. In 1892 Rudolf Diesel invented the engine that bears his name, an engine which featured the burning of fuel instead of the explosion that drove the Daimler engine.

These new technological developments encouraged, in their turn, the search for petroleum and the beginning of the passenger car industry. By 1914 the automobile industry in Italy, Russia, Germany, England, France, and the United States came to be an important economic enterprise. At the same time pneumatic tire manufacturers, ball bearing makers, windshield suppliers—the list can go as far as the hundreds of elements that go into the making of an automobile—all

By the end of the nineteenth century the term *industrialization* had acquired worldwide significance. The technological revolution which originated in western Europe was now reaching every continent and affecting almost every aspect of life. In Germany Alfred Krupp discovered a new method for producing large quantities of steel and turned a small family company into the famous and self-sufficient Krupp munitions plant.

profited from the introduction of this new form of transport. Leaving aside the passenger car's economic impact, Europe's cities and people began to feel the impact of this new form of transportation, an impact that greatly extended the range of an individual's world and altered the noise level, quality of air, and character of the cities in which it came to be found.

Other new machines made their own impact in the markets, streets, and homes of Europe. Bicycles became commonplace in the 1890's, first as a form of entertainment and then as a means of daily transportation. The sewing machine found a place in an increasing number of houses as both a labor-saving device and as a money-saving investment. The Kodak camera, patented in 1888, made the snapshot a piece of preserved memory and a potential art form for the average person. These items illustrate the fact that never had humanity been so inventive; but more important, never had humanity had the technical ability to quickly transfer ideas into products accessible to the average person. This ability was another dividend of the Industrial Revolution.

The Germans compete. By the beginning of the twentieth century the Germans had become major competitors to the British economic system. Although the Germans did not outproduce the British in quantitative terms, the long-range projections indicated that England had leveled out in its economic growth and that Germany might surpass it within a few years.

The German unification in 1871 had completed a process of coordination begun with the *Zollverein* earlier in the century. The centralized German state ruled over a hardworking, well-educated nation that was more productive because of the newer and more efficient factories found there. Ironically, the British had taken some pleasure in the French misfortunes at the hands of the Germans in 1870-71, but by the end of the period they thought otherwise, since increased German competition threatened Britain's former economic superiority.

German exports were increasing rapidly, especially in the new chemical and electrical industries. Britain still dominated world shipping and banking and remained the world's richest nation, but it was no longer alone at the top. The Americans were making gains, but this was not as disturbing as the German competition.

The Germans were effectively organized. Their literacy rates were higher than the British and their workers were better trained. German businessmen were aggressively implementing new procedures and increasing their ability to sell their products on the world market. The German state worked actively to favor the industrial sector, while the British businessmen were confronted with a very politically potent and aggressive labor movement.

THE FACTORY SYSTEM AND ITS IMPACT

Considerations of cost. The Industrial Revolution brought about a major change in life for the individuals who were making the transition from the agricultural to the industrial economy. The old way of living in which the individual worked his fields during the summer and pursued his cottage industry during the winter slowly disappeared. With its disappearance went an era of individual enterprise—an era when a person set his own standards, worked at his own pace, and was master of his own fate, poor though it may have been. The transition from rural to urban life through which virtually all participants of the Industrial Revolution passed changed the ways of life, the value structures, living conditions, types and qualities of work, and social structures of those participants. It is not surprising that at the early stages of this process there was misery and hardship. Revolutions are rarely painless experiences. Whether or not the new industrial way of life was superior to the preindustrial style of life is a question that is still being debated.

Richard Arkwright may not have realized the implications of his invention that brought water-power to spinning, but he is known by some historians as the father of the factory system. The factory was a place where a number of people were brought together to process large amounts of material through specialized tasks with machines. This was a much more efficient system than individual enterprise, as it enabled workers to make more goods at a cheaper cost and, in some cases, with much higher quality. During the nineteenth century the factory developed from a rather primitive and often dangerous arrangement employing as few as five people, to a complex and sophisticated network of units using thousands of employees who worked in much-improved conditions. Greater productivity was achieved, but often at the price of major human problems.

Human problems. For all of its efficiency and improved output, the factory system raised substantial problems in its harmful effects on the human condition. Some of the dilemmas were solved by the technological improvements made during the course of the Industrial Revolution. However, some of the problems still remain.

In the factory system the workers labored and the employers owned. By the end of the century the gulf between owner and employee widened because the two sides had a conflict of interest. The owner wanted to gain the maximum return on his investment and get the most work from his employees. The employees, in turn, felt that they deserved

the profits because it was their labor that made production possible. The wage system that prevailed was dictated by the market conditions and modified by the profit claimed by the owner—not by the value of the product as the worker determined it.

The worker in the factory rarely got to do more than a single piece of work on a given product, usually a repetitive task done during a twelve-hour working day. The tyranny of the time-clock also made itself felt as the worker had to perform according to the demands of a mechanical device, and not according to his or her own standards.

The early factories were often miserable places to work. They featured bad lighting, lack of ventilation, dangerous machines, and the frustrations of frequent mechanical breakdowns. Workers in various industries would be exposed to dread diseases—those people working with lead paint risked lung problems, those who worked with pewter fell ill to palsy, and miners suffered from the black lung disease. Parliamentary commissions looked into these situations, but it was not until late in the century that health insurance and disability insurance came into effect. In some factories any accident that a worker suffered was held to be his own fault. Further, there was little job security since a worker could be fired for virtually no reason. Safety standards were lax and primitive

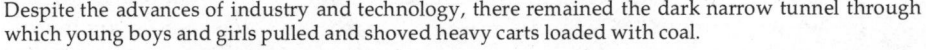

Despite the advances of industry and technology, there remained the dark narrow tunnel through which young boys and girls pulled and shoved heavy carts loaded with coal.

With the end of the Napoleonic Wars, England ceased its war spendings, which resulted in an industrial depression. Unable to make a living, hand-skilled workers responded with acts of protest and sabotage. Finally, in 1819, a large demonstration was staged in Manchester, where the discontented, waving "love" signs, demanded universal suffrage. What they got instead was a cavalry charge that took at least eleven lives and political repression in the name of "law and order."

machines posed a great danger to employees. Given the slightest miscalculation, an employee could easily lose a finger, hand, or his life in the maw of a machine.

The demand for plentiful and cheap labor resulted in the employment of women and children. A parliamentary report in England in the 1840's vividly proved that girls of six were used to haul carts of coal in the mines of Lancashire and that boys and girls of four and five years of age worked in textile mills. When they were not working, the women and children lived in horrid conditions in such wretched industrial cities as Lille, in France, where there were no sanitary, water, or medical services for the workers and working families were crammed twelve and fifteen people to a room in damp, dark cellars. In many areas improper diet and bad hygiene led to widespread outbreaks of cholera and typhus.

The generation of workers—men, women, and children—that endured the birth pangs of the Industrial Revolution inspired the best efforts of Charles Dickens, the English novelist, and Karl Marx. The former portrayed the tragic reality of that first generation of industrial urban life and the second sought solutions to the savage abuses he saw inflicted on the working class.

Often the workers in the first phase of industrialization were farmers attracted to the cities by the possibility of financial gain. Since most of them had never worked in an urban factory system before, the owners found it necessary to impose harsh discipline on them so that they would adapt their human spirit to the rhythm of the machines. At the end of the long, often dangerous days, the workers sought refuge in the local gin mill or tavern.

In Manchester, Lille, or Brussels the worker faced inadequate housing, nonexistent sewage and sanitation systems, impure water, and hostility from the more settled portions of the population. The Irish workers in England often faced the wrath of the English both from an economic point of view, in terms of competition for jobs, and religious terms, as the Irish Catholics encountered a Protestant population. The bitter price for the change in life-styles caused by industrialization was paid by that first generation of workers.

Later, by its very productivity and by the improvement it brought to the standard of life, the Industrial Revolution solved some of the problems faced in the early years of industrialization. As technological improvements increased, conditions in factories became better with improved lighting, ventilation, and safety standards. Further, factory owners came to recognize the fact that there was more profit to be made from an efficient factory with contented workers.

Workers and workers' movements. During the course of the century, improvements in the lives of the workers came from their organization into effective pressure groups. In England in the first decade after 1815 unemployment was high, especially among the handloom weavers and other high-skilled workers. In frustration, some of them struck out against the textile machines. The gangs of masked workers who took part in this violence were called "Luddites" after the legendary leader known as Ned Ludd. Incidents of Ludditism, worker strikes, and labor demonstrations such as that in 1819 in St. Peter's fields in Manchester occurred throughout the continent during the initial stages of industrialization.

Beginning in the 1820's in England, the movement toward organized labor unions received an important boost when the Combination Acts, legislation passed in 1799 against the formation of workingmen's associations, were repealed. Even though the early unions were weak, the bases were established for the powerful labor movement that gained its full strength by the end of the century.

On the continent workers turned to unions to gain better pay and working conditions. Their directions varied from the socialist and anarchist to the conservative workingmen's associations, but during the last quarter of the century unions made major advances. Their chief weapon was the strike, and their principal strength was their solidarity. As industry became more sophisticated and centralized, so too did the labor movement: the earlier artisans' associations and crafts unions were soon dominated by the trade unions. Across Europe the union movement took different forms. Some unions were established in a particular industry, while others were nationwide organizations. The English Trade Unions Congress was of the latter type, and came to have great power in affecting the major political parties.

By 1914 the workers could not negotiate on an equal basis with the owners, but they were in a far better situation than they were a century earlier when they had no organized strength. In England by 1914 there were almost 4 million union members. In Germany the unions engaged in a wide variety of activities ranging from handling life insurance to setting up vacations. Overall, the income gap between the rich and the poor began to close by 1914. Working hours were down, living conditions had improved, and the workers had found their voice.

Reform movements. During the century the working classes received some occasional aid from middle-class politicians and reformers. In England the reform movement was begun by intellectuals such as Thomas Carlyle and John Ruskin, and supported by the landowning aristocracy who did not like the often ostentatious and rude new-style businessmen. In the first half of the century a series of reforms passed through Parliament that limited the employment of young children, set maximum working hours for teenagers, established inspection procedures to ensure enforcement, and regulated working conditions for women. Some factory owners stated that these laws were bad for the country because they violated the freedom of contract between the worker and the employer, but the reformers were able to gain enough

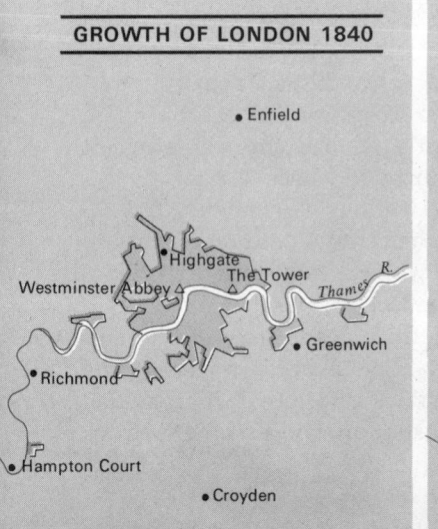

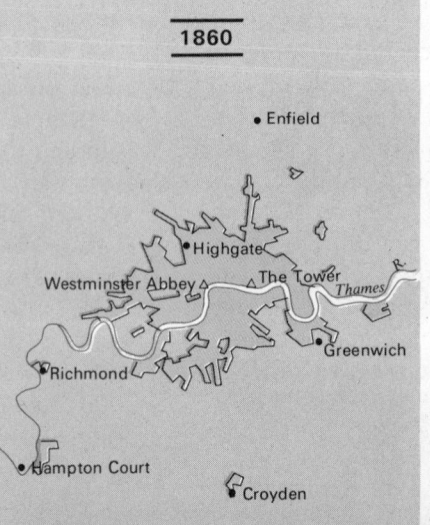

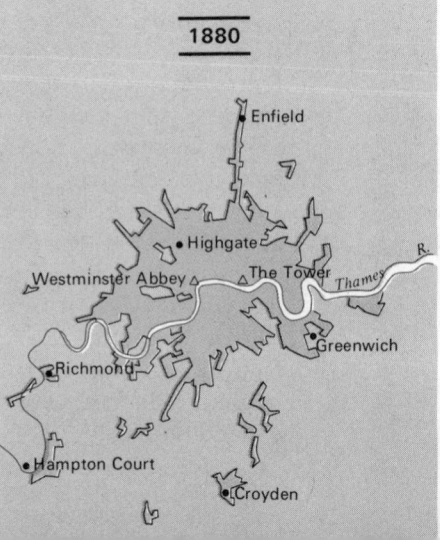

votes in Parliament to overcome this opposition.

Other nations followed England's lead in setting working standards. Massachusetts was the first state in the United States to limit child labor in 1836, while France and Germany followed suit with minor reforms in the 1840's. Finally, in an attempt to blunt the appeal of socialist politicians in Germany, Otto von Bismarck introduced a far-reaching series of reforms such as health insurance, accident insurance, and old-age insurance in the 1880's. He stated: "Give the workingman the right to work as long as he is healthy, assure him care when he is sick, and maintenance when he is old . . . ."[10] With these reforms, he set standards that would be copied by other European nations.

THE CRISIS OF THE CITIES

Rapid growth and its problems. During the nineteenth century European cities experienced massive growth in response to the population increases and new economic structures. Between 1800 and 1910 London grew from 831,000 to 4,521,000 people; Paris jumped from 547,000 to 2,888,000 inhabitants; Berlin expanded from 173,000 to 2,071,000 citizens; Vienna increased its count from 247,000 to 2,030,000; and St. Petersburg reached a total of 1,907,000 people as compared to the 220,000 dwellers found there at the first of the century.[11] New cities quickly grew in the northern parts of England, in northeastern France, and along the northern part of the Rhine. Even in European Russia, with more than 70 percent of the people working on the land, there were seventeen cities of more than 100,000 inhabitants by the end of the century.

As a substantial majority of the inhabitants of industrialized countries came to live in cities, urban leaders faced a serious crisis in maintaining the healthful environment, adequate social and sanitation systems, law enforcement, transportation, and housing needed for a decent quality of life. In almost every problem area mentioned above, let alone in the cultural and educational realms, European cities could not adapt quickly to the unfolding Industrial Revolution. Some of the urban problems experienced in the nineteenth century are still with us today.

Not until the end of the century were central heat, clean running water, adequate street lighting, access to primary education, and dependable sewage systems available in the major western European cities. Until mid-century waste disposal in some parts of Paris was taken care of either by dumping waste products in the streets or through manure collections. Thievery was common since police protection was inadequate. Not until a major urban renewal project was undertaken between 1853 and 1870 did the city gain a safe water supply, a sewage system,

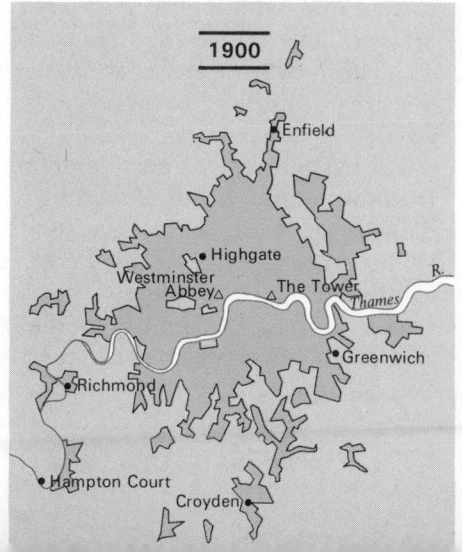
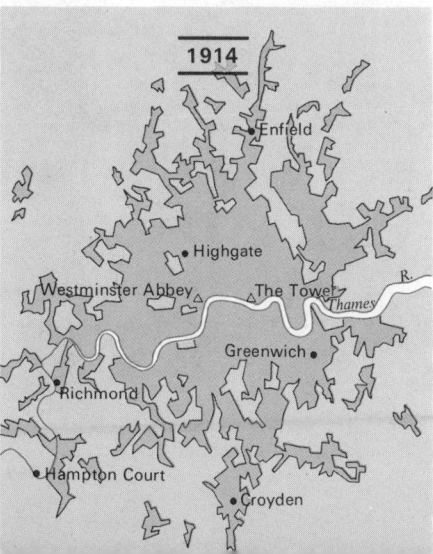

and the parks, squares, and boulevards tourists admire today. Other major cities shared the problems of Paris in greater or lesser degree. The East End slums of London remained a blight until they were firebombed by German planes in World War II. Every European city had, and still has, its quarter of filth and misery.

The new industrial towns were in even worse condition than the older centers during the middle part of the century. Charles Dickens described a typical English factory town at that time:

It was a town of red brick, or of brick that would have been red if the smoke and ashes had allowed it; but as matters stood it was a town of unnatural red and black, like the painted face of a savage. It was a town of machinery and tall chimneys, out of which interminable serpents of smoke trailed themselves for ever and ever, and never got uncoiled. It had a black canal in it, and a river that ran purple with ill-smelling dye, and vast piles of buildings full of windows where there was a rattling and a trembling all day long, and where the piston of the steam engine worked monotonously up and down, like the head of an elephant in a state of melancholy madness. It contained several large streets all very like one another, and many small streets still more like one another, inhabited by people equally like one another, who all went in and out at the same hours, with the same sound upon the same pavements, to do the same work, and to whom every day was the same as yesterday and tomorrow, and every year the counterpart of the last and the next.[12]

The middle classes. Dickens was not writing for those people he described so well. Instead, he was addressing himself to the new middle classes, those people who had the leisure, literacy, and security in their position to feel sympathy for those whose work made their better way of life possible. During the century the middle classes, the *bourgeoisie*, became the most important social, economic, and political group in Europe. This group had begun to rise in the twelfth century in concurrence with the development of the new cities. Their rapid ascension to dominance after 1815 was tied to the advances of the Industrial Revolution; this ascent was made possible by the social and legal changes of the French Revolution on the continent and by the flexibility of social institutions in the British Isles.

While it is difficult to formulate a strict definition of the *bourgeoisie*, it is easier to say who was *not* a member of this social class. Factory workers and peasants on the one hand, and aristocrats and nobles on the other were not part of the middle classes. Those closer to the working classes were called the lower-middle classes, or the *petite bourgeoisie*. Those who were near the elite were the upper-middle classes, or the *haute bourgeoisie*.

The first group was much more numerous than the second. Included in the lower-middle classes were such diverse people as skilled artisans, bureaucrats, clerks, teachers, shopkeepers, and the clergy. They were conscious of their proximity to the working classes and they desired to climb socially. Later in the century they profited the most from the compulsory education laws that were introduced in the major industrial

A lithograph by Daumier, made in 1848, contrasts the gluttonous bourgeois in his frock coat and top hat with the earnest working man in his shabby clothes. A merciless critic of the bourgeois society of his native France, Daumier was once sentenced to prison for a particularly vitriolic cartoon.

In 1837 an innocent seventeen-year-old girl—tenderly known as "Little Victory" by some—became queen of England. Until her death in 1901, the strong-willed Queen Victoria made domesticity and moral prudishness the ruling passions of her reign. Though her vision of progress was narrow, Victoria was in fact to reign over the most spectacular era of technological advancement in human history.

states. They served as some of the most avid consumers of the new wave of novelists, of the penny-press newspapers, and of state propaganda by 1914. A literate, numerous group, they came to play an important role in public affairs as the vote was extended to more people.

If their betters patronized the concert halls and art galleries, the lower-middle classes went to the music halls and the popular sporting events. By the end of the century the new transportation networks gave them the mobility to spend their vacations at resorts on the seashore or in the mountains. A whole new industry—mass tourism—was developing to meet their needs.

Bourgeois pretensions. The upper-middle class controlled a large portion of the wealth created by the Industrial Revolution. They came to gain access to many of the benefits of the aristocracy, such as the best schools, shops, restaurants, and cultural life. In fact, members of this group were often richer than some of the noble families. Factory owners, bankers, lawyers, architects, an occasional professor, doctors, and high gov-

ernmental officials entered the upper-middle class ranks. It was hard to gain admittance to this level of society, but money, taste, and aggressiveness could open the doors for those who so desired.

The *haute bourgeoisie* on the continent had made major social and legal advances, first in France and later in other countries after 1789. As the nineteenth century progressed they came to set the intellectual and political tone for the times. In England this class made itself felt even earlier. Because of the British commercial supremacy, England and things English came to be admired in European cities during the century.

This time has come to be labeled the Victorian period, in honor of the English queen, idealized as the ultimate "Mother, Wife, and Queen" by Tennyson. On the surface, the Victorians evidenced very little doubt regarding what was right and wrong, moral and immoral, and proper and improper during the latter part of the century. Underneath the surface, the middle classes may have felt insecure in their new-found dominance, and this may account for the emphasis on appearance and propriety that marked the age. The recent publication of some Victorian memoirs shows that a considerable undercurrent of sexuality and passion lay beneath the public display of sexual prudishness, staid conduct, and a too-earnest morality. Their straightlaced purity called for "cleaning up" Shakespeare or toning down some of the juicier parts of Gibbon's *Decline and Fall of the Roman Empire*.[13]

Their tastes ran to the heavy, the overstated, the sentimental in art, literature, and music, and to a touching love of devoted animals. Our century does not revere many of their cultural heroes. Appearance was very important to the *haute bourgeoisie*, especially in terms of home, furniture, dress, and servants. One estimate indicates that more than two and a half million English subjects worked as domestics at the century's end,

nearly a million more than farmed the land.

Yet for all of their pretentious posings, the upper-middle classes formed the vanguard for major drives against social evils such as slavery at the beginning of the century and the abuses of child labor at the end. From the ranks of the English middle classes the modern women's liberation movement got its most notable fighters. They also sent out warriors against the "evils" of alcoholism and pornography.

Against this positive record, however, must be set the smug assuredness of the upper-middle classes who constantly harped on the advantages of thrift, character, hard work, duty, and honesty. Abstract qualities such as those are hard to quarrel with, but they were prized more often than not after a person had arrived, not while he was fighting his way up.

A sketch from an early edition of *Bleak House* illustrates the way in which Charles Dickens satirized the aggressive, middle-class "do-gooders" whose willful and stern philanthropy was often worse than no philanthropy at all. When the particularly aggressive Mrs. Pardiggle visited, the poor bricklayer, lying on the floor, answered the prying questions he knew were forthcoming: "An't my place dirty? Yes, it is dirty—it's nat'rally dirty, and it's nat'rally onwholesome; and we've five dirty and onwholesome children, as is all dead infants, and so much the better for them, and for us besides. . . . How have I been conducting myself: Why, I've been drunk for three days; and I'd been drunk four, if I'd a had the money."

AN INTERNATIONAL ECONOMY

New business organizations. The increasingly complex technology of the Industrial Revolution required more money and improved business procedures. Businessmen came to live or die by their efficiency, and efficiency often meant consolidation. A large firm could amass the supply of money to buy the resources, install the technology, employ the work force, and market the finished product at the cheapest price more effectively than a smaller organization. Consolidation also helped in influencing politicians to make governmental policies favorable to the industry or economic sector. The gigantic firm came to be the dominant industrial force by the end of the century.

Business organizations took on a new look at this time. Some firms, such as that of Alfred Nobel, the Swedish industrialist who invented dynamite, established branches in many different nations. Others, such as John D. Rockefeller's Standard Oil, set out to control the market in one country for its product. With the need for more money, companies began to go to the public to sell stock. Joint stock companies were not new, but they had not been favored much in previous years since, if the company went broke, the investors were liable for the firm's debts. England led the way with laws designed to protect the small investor from business failure. Germany, France, and the United States followed with their own versions of limited-liability laws. More people began to "play the stock market." This came to be a substantial part of modern economic life and a useful device to raise capital.

Financial interests devised new strategies to control a certain segment of the market. One form was the trust, in which a body of trustees held a majority of stock in a given industry and thereby controlled the wage, price, and merchandizing policies of several companies. Another form of control was the holding company, in which a corporation was formed to accomplish the same functions as the more informal trust. In Europe these alliances took the form of huge industrial concerns known as cartels. These cartels, often secret, controlled such products as steel and rubber. Finally, there was the practice of monopoly, when one firm could gain control of the total economic cycle of a given product.

The new generation of industrialists developed more efficient management methods. The scientific management system of the American, F. W. Taylor, advocated breaking down every stage of the industrial process into its most minute piece, studying the efficiency of each stage of work, and finding the optimum speed of productivity that could be attained. The widespread use of interchangeable parts and, finally, introduction of the assembly line brought productivity to a high level by 1914.

Economic fluctuations. As a result of the Industrial Revolution the world came to be dominated by a European-based global economy. Non-Europeans came to play a role as suppliers of raw materials to the European industrial enterprises and as purchasers of the finished goods coming from Europe. The imperialistic economy increasingly tied the world to the rhythms of the economic booms and busts of the continent. Economic historians vary in their interpretations of the frequency and causes of the various stages of economic expansion and contraction in the business cycle. Whether one believes in a ten-year, twenty-year, or century-long cycle, the fact remains that the world became increasingly affected by European economic changes.[14] The depression that lasted from 1873 to 1896 is symbolic of the impact of economic events in Europe on the world. Overall, prices fell by roughly 30 percent in all products. Around the world human suffering was severe, especially in those areas that depended on shipping raw materials to cities or abroad and which had no control over the price their products could demand. But by 1896 a readjustment had been made, and the period up to the First World War was a generally prosperous one.

The industrialized world. By 1914 the world was divided into three stages of industrialization. Northern and western Europe, the northern United States, and Japan had passed through the Industrial Revolution. Russia, Italy, Spain, the Balkans, and Canada were going through the initial stages of the

Japan showed its ability to industrialize by taking its most profitable export item—raw silk—and employing a new silk-reeling method introduced from Europe in this factory at Tomioka.

process. The third area, much of which still has not industrialized—the Middle East, Africa, much of Asia, and Australia and New Zealand—had yet to engage in the machine age to any large extent.

Great Britain with its far-flung empire was still the richest nation. Even though it imported more goods than it exported, it earned nearly a billion dollars a year from overseas investments, shipping fees, and banking and insurance services. The United States increased its manufacturing output in the last half century from $2 billion in 1860 to $14 billion in 1900. America still depended on substantial foreign investment, but it was on the verge of establishing its financial superiority.

Germany had become the continent's economic giant. Its population had risen from 41 million in 1871 to 65 million in 1910. Close cooperation between the government and private industry paid off. Governmental tariff policies—protectionist after 1879—sup-

port for technical education, and encouragement of industrial cartels helped propel Germany to a position of competition with the British. France lagged behind Germany in both population and industrial output, but it made substantial progress in industrialization by 1914.

Japan's progress in the last half of the nineteenth century was miraculous. As the first Asiatic country to adopt western methods, Japan made good use of its large labor market and limited natural resources to increase exports from none in 1870 to $100 million in 1906.

European economic primacy. During the fifty years before 1914 international trade rose from $7 billion to $42 billion. European nations were, by and large, their own best customers, even with the tariff barriers erected on the continent after 1879. Europe became the chief supplier of world capital: Britain invested heavily in the Commonwealth and the United States, France made substantial loans to Russia, and Germany supplied major amounts of money to the Ottoman empire.

It was at the stage of large foreign investments that politics and finances began to work in common harness. The developing countries badly needed money to enable them to compete in the new world economic system. The industrialized countries naturally sought a healthy return on their spare capital. Financial interests could invest abroad in a number of different ways: they could purchase the bonds of strong nations—a safe investment, but with a relatively small return; they could make loans to underdeveloped countries—a riskier venture, but with a much higher rate of return; they could invest in countries that were stable but that needed capital in specialized areas—this insured a solid return on a safe investment. There were many other variations on the theme of foreign investment, all of which would pay off handsomely either directly in financial or indirectly in political terms.

But the results of these loans could be both helpful and devastating for the debtor countries. Needed capital could be gained and profitably used, as in the United States, with a minimum infringement on sovereignty. On the other hand, there was the example of the Ottoman empire, which received its first loan in 1854. Twenty-two years later the Turks were so deeply in debt that they had to place major portions of their tax base in foreign hands just to pay the interest. Of the more than 1 billion dollars the Turks borrowed, only 10 percent of the money was put to productive use. Russia found itself by 1914 with a funded debt of nearly 9 billion rubles, of which nearly half was owed to foreigners. Ten percent of Hungary's gross national product was paid to foreign investors to cover loans and interest in the immediate prewar years.[15]

Foreign investments of this magnitude could not help but have a profound political impact both on the creditor and debtor nations. But they also symbolized the undoubted economic control Europe exercised over the less developed world. In every economic and material sense, the Europeans had attained a mastery of the globe.

SUMMARY

Europeans by 1914 had extended their economic and material control throughout the globe. Building on the interrelated bases of increased food supply and a rapidly growing population, the European economic system supplied both the employees and the internal market needed for economic growth. Further, the extensive emigration by millions of Europeans helped to establish in the "new Europes overseas" the bridgeheads for European economic control. The rapid improvement in transportation and communication devices provided the ties that bound the formerly vast and disjointed world into an integrated economic system.

The main force behind the achievement of European primacy came from the Industrial Revolution, a series of technological and economic developments that increased human productivity to a formerly inconceivable degree. The first country to pass through the phase of industrialization was England, which was fortunate to possess the essential social, geographical, governmental, and technological advantages. The Revolution first took place in textiles, but the effect that the change from human and animal power to machine power had on the vastly improved ability to produce larger amounts of cloth was soon felt in metals and machines. New power sources and processes insured England's economic dominance to the end of the nineteenth century.

The continental nations lagged behind the British. Not until mid-century did they bring together the essential political, technological, economic, and social factors to enable them to compete. By the end of the century the Germans, specializing in the new chemical and electrical industries, came to pose a threat to British economic superiority.

As Europe passed through the Industrial Revolution, traditional society went through often painful changes. The factory system in its early stages posed serious human problems such as employee conflict with owners, bad working conditions, and the abuses of children's and women's labor in the mines and factories. A successful series of union movements developed through the century to the point that by 1914 labor leaders had a major voice in affecting both economic and political policies in the industrialized countries.

Economic change altered the traditional distribution of population. Europe passed from a predominantly rural-based continent to a place in which most of its people lived in cities. The substantial growth in city population, tied closely to the factory system and the Industrial Revolution, created wretched living conditions during the initial phases of the change. Some of the problems remain today. Yet the middle classes living in the cities came to dominate Europe both politically and economically, and they became the dominant class of the nineteenth century.

By the end of the century the combination of population increase, improved food production, better transportation, and the massive increase in human productivity brought about by the Industrial Revolution had transformed the basic conditions in Europe and enabled Europeans to reach out and directly control much of the world. The new, more efficient business organizations were able to survive the periodic booms and busts of the economic cycle and to reach to the far corners of the globe for resources and markets. The industrialized nations, especially Germany and England, gained substantial political influence along with their economic growth. They were not alone, however, as the United States, France, Belgium, and Japan were also involved to a lesser degree in the extension of their power. To those nations caught on the other side of industrialization, there could be no possibility of effective competition, at least in the near future.

SUGGESTIONS FOR READING

C. Singer *et al.*, eds., **The Late Nineteenth Century, 1850-1900**, Vol. V, **A History of Technology** (Oxford) is lavishly illustrated and clearly written, perhaps the best single work on technological accomplishments during this period. For a survey covering a longer time space, see D. S. Landes, **The Unbound Prometheus: Technological Change and Industrial Development in Western Europe from 1750 to the Present*** (Cambridge). On economic and industrial developments during the nineteenth century, see S. B. Clough, **Economic History of Europe**, rev. ed. (Walker, 1968). Also recommended are T. Ashton, **The Industrial Revolution: 1760-1830*** (Oxford); W. O. Henderson, **The Industrialization of Europe: 1780-1914*** (Harcourt Brace Jovanovich); and J. C. Chambers and G. E. Mingay, **The Agricultural Revolution** (Schocken, 1966).

The novels of Charles Dickens depict not only the more attractive aspects of traditional English country society but also the social injustices and urban degradation which often accompanied the advent of the Industrial Revolution. His novel **Hard Times** gives a very descriptive portrayal of "Coketown." Francis Sheppard, **London 1808-1870** (Univ. of Calif., 1971) is a first-rate account of a city going through the challenge of growth. Others that are helpful are Asa Briggs, **Victorian Cities** (Harper & Row, 1968); and E. J. Hobsbawn, **The Age of Revolution: Europe 1789-1848*** (Mentor).

A useful volume on the international aspects of European economic growth is Sidney Pollard, **European Economic Integration: 1815-1970*** (Harcourt Brace Jovanovich, 1974). See George Lichtheim, **Imperialism*** (Praeger, 1971) for the historical complexities of economic imperialism.

Vivid insights into the life and prevailing attitudes of the middle classes during the nineteenth century are provided by contemporary fiction and by biographical studies of leading personalities. Recommended, for example, are the novels of Stendahl, such as **The Charterhouse of Parma*** (Penguin) which portrays post-Napoleonic Italy and life at a reactionary court. The novels of Charles Dickens and of Honoré de Balzac, for England and France, also provide important insights.

*Indicates a less expensive paperbound edition.

CHAPTER 23

Art, Music, and Literature:
1815-1914

Cultural Responses to the Century of Change

INTRODUCTION. Artists, writers, and composers define and communicate the spirit, hopes, and values of their time. In so doing, they directly affect the mood, goals, and standards of the generations that come after them. Because their work seldom finds expression in governmental or economic policies, their importance might be overlooked by the student. To ignore, in this case, the nineteenth-century's artistic developments would be to lose a valuable window through which to view the essential contributions of creative individuals. In this chapter we will study the rich and varied influences of art, literature, and music on Europe during its century of change.

During this time cultural life went through stages dominated by romanticism, realism, and modernism. Artistic movements do not begin and end with the same precision as the reigns of monarchs or the terms of presidents. Within various art forms different artists may respond to unique conditions. Therefore it is difficult to establish precise chronological limits for movements of schools within the arts, and to determine the degree to which the individual artist is affected by a prevailing tendency. Generally speaking, until the middle of the century Europe's creative figures worked under the influences of the romantic movement, a cultural phenomenon that had a widespread artistic, intellectual, and political impact. For the next quarter-century artists and writers reacted to this romantic dominance, and responded to the currents produced by the age of science in the realism movement. From the end of the century, up to and beyond 1914, the artistic community experimented with a range of new forms and structures in the modernism movement.

During the century the artists, writers, and composers would provide the new "marching songs" in the forms of symphonies, poems, and paintings that would summarize and concentrate—in a melody, a line of verse, or an image—the feelings and thoughts of an entire nation. Often an artist's creation at one moment in history would transcend the limits of the period in which he lived—as well as his original audience—to become universal. An example of the lasting and varied impact of a work of art can be seen in Beethoven's Fifth Symphony, which has furnished different inspirations to succeeding generations. The work has remained a dependable item in symphony orchestra programs, in a way that Beethoven might have understood, but it has also been put to other uses. In the Second World War, the first four notes sounded for the Allies the strength of their destiny as democracies. Later the symphony served as the background for avant-garde motion pictures, and in the mid-1970's as the theme for a popular rock song.

Students debate the role of art in society—that it should be socially realistic, that it exists in pure isolation as the artist intended it, that it exists only in the eyes and ears of the beholder, and that it changes, reflects, or anticipates events. Yet there is no doubt that the art of the romantic and the post-romantic eras came to be a call from the soul of the artist to the world, a call that escapes the limits of the rational and mathematical and communicates itself to the soul and emotions of the beholder.

It does not really matter if the artistic pro-duction was written to pay the bills (in the cases of Dickens and Dostoevski), to show virtuosity (Paganini and Liszt), to make sweeping statements (Beethoven and Mahler), or merely to entertain. The creative artists of the last century, of all centuries, still speak to us today if we let them. We must cast off the stultifying layers of critics and authorities who have their own axes to grind in esthetic affairs, and meet the artists on a one-to-one basis. The interchange will teach us more about their times, and our own.

ROMANTICISM

Individuals and emotions. The romantic movement provided the basis of individuality and unleashed sensitivities that played a major role in forming the century's cultural and political changes. It is difficult to give a dictionarylike definition of romanticism that portrays its real power and force. The very fact that the movement emphasized the unique and the individual and laid out few rules, other than to identify its opposition to many of the classical esthetic standards, permitted many manifestations of romanticism.

In contrast to the rationalism of the eighteenth century, with its exaltation of self-restraint and self-discipline, the romanticism of the early nineteenth century was characterized by strong elements of individualism, idealism, and revolt against all rules and accepted authority. To the classicist, the human being is a rational, finite being—an integral member of society which is governed in accordance with law and with well-defined rules of conduct. Within this well-ordered social structure a person may find fulfillment, even as, in his intellectual and artistic expression, he emphasizes form and order and harmony. To the romanticist, on the other hand, the human being is a creature of feeling no less than of thought. He seeks after the infinite because he is not simply a cog in a finite human society but instead an irreplaceable part of nature and the whole creative process. The romanticist argues that society's laws and rules of conduct serve only to confine the natural soaring instincts of humanity. While the classicist insists upon the overruling claims of society, the romanticist supports the right of self-determination.

The classicist finds beauty in logic, elegance, symmetry, and order. The romanticist looks to the "natural," the wild, and the unruly. Because the movement emphasized the expressiveness of the individual creator and the escape from the constraints of classical forms, it provided the flexibility that the artists of the century needed to alter, mirror, and beautify every aspect of existence. Romanticism encouraged the genius of the individual and promoted the tremendous diversity of artistic productivity that would characterize the age. The romantics came to express their concepts of beauty in an often emotional and flamboyant way, in direct contrast to the elegant, measured, and balanced qualities of eighteenth-century art and music.

The fact that the individual was emphasized and treasured by the romantics over the socially accepted, structured facets of the previous century could be seen in the novels of authors such as Friedrich von Schiller (1759-1805) and Johann Wolfgang von Goethe (1749-1832). Their heroes and heroines were seldom cool, detached, and unfeeling. Goethe's *The Sorrow of Young Werther* (1774) tells the story of a sensitive, feeling, outcast young man who killed himself with the pistol of his rival after failing to gain his true love. Schiller's *Wilhelm Tell* (1804) describes the heroic struggle of the Swiss patriots in their drive for independence against tyranny. Unlike the brittle wit and irony of Enlightenment authors such as Voltaire, these stories were sentimental and emotional descriptions of people acting in response to what their hearts told them was right. It was better to experience a moving young death, or to rise up against impossible odds, than to look dispassionately and rationally at life.

By far the best known of Goethe's works was *Faust* (Part 1 came out in 1808, Part 2 in 1832). Based on German legend, it tells the story of Dr. Faust, the aging scholar who made a deal with the devil to give over his soul in return for twenty-four years of youth and pleasure. Faust eventually saved his soul by rejecting the devil's offer and serving mankind. Goethe effectively pointed out that human beings need a full realization of their own personalities in a number of intellectual, physical, and spiritual ways. At the same time the individual must ultimately integrate his personality with the collective good of society, to which he must dedicate himself.

A new life-style. The romantic movement's emphasis on the individual created, among some of its participants, a picturesque lifestyle. The classicists had seen man as a rational, finite being, an integral member of society who lives in accord with laws and rules of conduct. The romantics saw the individual as a creature of feeling no less than of thought. Rousseau had asserted that the human heart was the infallible source of wisdom, and that the individual should trust his instincts. He believed that human beings could find their truest happiness in nature, and he urged mankind to return to a more "natural" form of society by abandoning artificial conventions and institutions. To this end he popularized the cult of the "noble savage." This fit in nicely with the early romantic literature that sanctioned the valuing of the outsider or the rebel. The glory of Werther, for example, was that he did not sacrifice himself for social acceptance.

Not all of the romantics came to pursue the unconventional. Some, such as Victor Hugo (1802-1885) and Goethe, lived long, full, and respectable lives. But among European intellectual societies as far apart as England and Russia, young artists and writers were deeply affected by the romantic way of life. The list of creative artists living according to their own laws and dying at a young age is long. Whether they died in duels or wars, through suicide or by disease caused by their erratic life-styles, Byron, Pushkin, Lermontov, Galois, Shelley, Novalis, Petöfi, Chopin, Schubert, and Keats left the stage of life at the prime of their lives. Pushkin died at the comparatively advanced age of thirty-seven, but most of the artists on this list left life earlier. To some of the romantics, it was necessary to live intensely, according to the commandments of the heart and emotion, rather than to die fat, rich, bored, and bourgeois.

Romantic literature. Rousseau, Schiller, and Goethe helped set the stage for the literary advances in the nineteenth century. Schiller and Goethe, through their plays, novels, and poetry, aided the transition from classicism to romanticism by emphasizing the themes of independence, exalting the emotions, and delving into national legends. In other parts of Europe these trends were also being pursued. In the early nineteenth century the romantic novel took on many different aspects, all of them products of a state of mind in reaction to accepted values.

The novel, the dominant literary form of the nineteenth century, came into prominence in the eighteenth century. Buttressed by such romantic tendencies as interest in the folkways, ballads, and romances of the Middle Ages, the novel came to have ever larger audiences. Victor Hugo recreated the medieval past in romances such as *Notre Dame de Paris* (1831) with great popular success. In Britain, Sir Walter Scott (1771-1832) stirred the imagination of his countrymen by his collection of Scottish border ballads and poems. His most famous adventure story, *Ivanhoe* (1819), detailed medieval chivalry so effectively that it was imitated and followed with sequels still present in this century.

By mid-century, as if to mirror the drastic changes that Europe was undergoing, the novel began taking many different shapes. The historical novels of Scott were challenged by others with different themes that emphasized purpose, terror, manners, politics, social problems, love, psychological stress, adventure, and nature. By mid-century the noble works of Scott had been replaced in some homes by a preference for the works of the genial satirist and moralist William Makepeace Thackeray (1811-1863). In England, the snobbery and social climbing that went on in a society made highly fluid by the rise of the newly rich middle classes provided Thackeray with such rich characters as the unscrupulous but engaging figure of Becky Sharp, the heroine of *Vanity Fair* (1848).

European poets adapted quickly to the romantic current. Across the continent from Paris to Moscow, the classical traditions were overthrown. Romanticism's love of nature found strong expression in poetry. The intensity of the French poet Alphonse de Lamartine (1790-1869), who made the transition from classicism to the romantic style, was shared by poets in all major European languages.

In 1798 two young English poets, William Wordsworth (1770-1850) and Samuel Taylor Coleridge (1772-1834), published a volume of verse called *Lyrical Ballads*. In its preface Wordsworth defined poetry as "the spontaneous overflow of powerful feelings recollected in tranquillity." This was a concept that was at once romantic and very much at odds with the views of the previous century. In expressing "universal passions" and "the entire world of nature," he rejected the ornate and mythology-laden diction favored by the classicists. Instead, he used simple vocabulary to describe his deepest emotions. Wordsworth, especially in his earlier years, believed that by contemplating nature in all of its aspects, the soul of the observer would help grasp reality. Unlike the rationalists, he stressed the intuitive and the emotional in the intellectual process.

For his part, Coleridge pursued another facet of romanticism—interest in the supernatural and exotic. One need only read Coleridge's *Rime of the Ancient Mariner* and *Kubla Khan* to note his delight in the vivid descriptions his distant subjects gave him the chance to express. Coleridge's interest in the nonrational elements of human life would be shared later by other artists, as they pursued the areas of fantasy, symbolism, dream states, and the supernatural.

The romantic poets rebelled against the constraints of society, and often expressed their contempt for contemporary standards through their lives and works. In England, George Gordon (Lord) Byron (1788-1824) gloried in the cult of freedom, and when the Greeks rose against the Turks in 1821, he joined the cause of independence. Even though he died of fever rather soon after his arrival in Greece, his symbolic contributions became widely known. His friend, Percy Bysshe Shelley (1792-1822), believed passionately that human perfectibility was possible only through complete freedom of thought and action.

These romantic yearnings and dreams

were shared on the continent by the German poet Heinrich Heine (1797-1856). Like Byron, Heine was a cutting satirist of contemporary society and, like Shelley, a splendid lyricist. Heine is best remembered today for his *lieder*, or songs, many of which were set to music by Franz Schubert (1797-1828) and Felix Mendelssohn (1809-1847).

Another great romantic poet was John Keats (1795-1821), who was neither social critic nor charismatic rebel. Of prime importance to him was the pursuit and worship of beauty, which was the motive and message of his poetry. So it is that in the concluding lines of *Ode on a Grecian Urn* (1821) he tells us that "Beauty is truth, truth beauty—that is all Ye know on earth, and all ye need to know." Art for art's sake, beauty in itself, that is what Keats advocated, instead of the classical formulas of an earlier age or the socialist realism of the later part of the century.

Alexander Pushkin (1799-1837), Russia's greatest poet, liberated his nation's language from the foreign molds and traditions the eighteenth century had forced upon it. While serving as the transition between the classical and romantic ages, Pushkin came to occupy "the place of supremacy and centralness in Russian literature and civilization . . ."[1] His greatest contribution came in helping to create a truly Russian literature.

Art and architecture. The new century brought new tendencies to painting, as well as to other art forms. Some artists, such as the French master Eugène Delacroix (1798-1863), encountered major critical resistance. His flamboyant canvases were prime examples of the emotional approach used by the romantic artists. His "Massacre of Chios," painted in 1824 under the direct impact of the news of the Turks' slaying of Christians on the island of Chios, was dubbed the "Massacre of Painting" by conservative critics.

There is a great contrast between the precise draftsmanship and formal poses of the classical painters and the unrestrained use of color and new effects of the romantic artists. The new subject matter dealing with old legends, exotic scenes, and picturesque portrayals of industrial settings set the new school of painting off from the old.

Eugène Delacroix' "Massacre of Chios" established him as the foremost painter of the romantic era. Though inspired by a contemporary event, Delacroix aimed at expressing a "poetic truth" rather than at recapturing an actual occurrence. "Massacre" shows us an intoxicating mixture of sensuousness and cruelty.

The effects of the cult of nature were no less marked upon romantic painting than they were upon poetry. Artists were urged to look at nature with a fresh appreciation. The English painter John Constable (1776-1837) was in some respects the originator of the modern school of landscape painting. His choice of colors was revolutionary, as he used greens freely in his landscapes, an innovation considered radical by critics who had stressed the necessity of painting nature in browns.

Another English painter whose originality created a major stir was J. M. W. Turner (1775-1851). His vivid use of color and forceful imagination gave him the ability to create powerful atmospheric effects. He was clearly a forerunner of the French Impressionists in his use of perspective, color, and effects of climate.

Architecture was strongly affected by the romantic movement. Until about 1830 the architecture in Europe and America was based largely on classical models of Greece

Ludwig van Beethoven, the originator and spokesman for the music of the romantic era, once wrote: "Music is a higher revelation than any wisdom or philosophy. It is the wine that inspires new creations, and I am the Bacchus who presses out this wine for men and makes them spiritually drunk. . . ."

and Rome. But after that date, largely in response to the romantic movement, there occurred the great period of the Gothic revival, in which towers and pointed arches became the chief architectural characteristics.

The revival was stimulated in England by the romances of Sir Walter Scott, whose own residence at Abbotsford was designed along Scottish noble lines. In France the movement gained strength from the publication of Victor Hugo's *Notre Dame de Paris*, which discussed fifteenth-century life. For the next few decades architecture was dominated by backward-looking styles. Structures were designed in the Gothic and Rococo and other historic forms as well. Sometimes there would be an esthetically disastrous combination of forms, as the newly arrived middle classes decided that the best way to prove that they merited their new social status was to erect their houses and factories in styles formerly associated with the aristocracy.

In addition, in public buildings in the new towns major structures such as the train sta-

tions were designed in massive and ornamental style, calculated to reflect the civic grandeur and wealth of the community. From the standpoint of today's architects, there was a total lack of sensitivity in the way that buildings were related—or rather, unrelated—to their sites and functions.

Music. The impact of the nineteenth century on the development of musical composition can be seen today in the programs assembled by symphony orchestras throughout the world. The music of the romantics continues to enjoy enormous popularity both from audiences at symphony concerts and from the purchasers of phonograph records. Music was as much liberated by the romantic tide as was literature.

The nineteenth century brought radical changes in music. The regularity of the minuet, the precision of the sonata, and the elegant but limited small chamber orchestra were not sufficient to express the powerful forces of romanticism.

The genius who symbolized the transition from the classical to the romantic movement was the German composer Ludwig van Beethoven (1770-1827). One need only compare his relatively measured and restrained First Symphony with the compelling and intense Fifth or the lyrical, descriptive Sixth symphonies to hear the changes that he made. In a sense Beethoven was the ultimate romantic soul, a lover of nature and a passionate champion of the rights of man and of freedom. He spoke to the heart of humanity through the most emotional art form—music. While retaining the classicist's sense of proportion in the structure of his works, he added flexibility to music forms by developing new harmonies, and he enlarged the scope of the orchestra to handle them. He succeeded in freeing music from the somewhat arid formalism that had dominated up to the end of the eighteenth century.

The momentum of the forces which Beethoven set in motion carried through the entire century. Karl Maria von Weber (1786-1826), Louis Hector Berlioz (1803-1869), Felix Mendelssohn, Franz Schubert, and Robert Schumann (1810-1856) made major contributions in developing the musical repertoire of Europe by mid-century.

18. George Caleb Bingham: "The Trapper's Return" (c. 1844). Bingham was a nineteenth-century American *genre* painter who did much to give artistic form to the spirit of the western frontier. Bingham's ability to communicate the poetry of commonplace situations in a direct and effective manner is probably his greatest strength.

19. Edward Hicks: "Peaceable Kingdom" (c. 1848). This painting is a fine example of American Folk Art which is characterized by simple forms, neatly applied pigments, and a craftsmanlike precision. Hicks' favorite subject was based on a prophecy in the Book of Isaiah: "The wolf shall dwell with the lamb and the leopard shall lie down with the kid," and he painted many versions of this. "Peaceable Kingdom" details an assembly of different animals together with children in an idyllic setting. A secondary group of figures in the background reinforces the basic theme; in this case William Penn is signing a peace treaty with the Indians.

20. (above) **St. Pancras Station, London** (1868-1874). Much nineteenth-century architecture combined a revival of stylistic elements from past cultures with a growing nationalistic spirit. St. Pancras railroad station is an excellent example of the Gothic revival in architecture. The roof of its train shed spans 240 feet and is carried on Gothic arches springing from massive brick piers. The design makes use of other Gothic details such as the pointed arch and graceful stone tracery tying them in with classical elements in the columns and ironwork. The whole is a fine functional design, the elements of which are completely clear. This and other railway terminals which blended new building techniques with traditional methods were seen as the cathedrals of the nineteenth century. **21.** (right) **Claude Monet: "Gare St. Lazare"** (1877). Monet was prompted to settle in Paris by the fact that he was attracted to the St. Lazare station and he often set up his easel there. The vast enclosure with its glass roof, the incoming and outgoing trains, and the contrast between the sun and sky in the background and the steaming locomotives—all offered unusual and exciting subjects for Monet's impressionistic style.

22. (next page) **Paul Gauguin: "Contes Barbares"** (1902). In the late nineteenth century a growing disenchantment with the values and traditions of the West can be discerned among many European intellectuals. Paul Gauguin, for one, turned his back on the Paris society he had served as a stockbroker. His feeling for far-off exotic places ultimately became a conviction that his salvation and perhaps that of all contemporary artists lay in abandoning modern civilization and returning to some simpler and primitive life-style. Following his belief, Gauguin settled in Tahiti in 1895. This painting conveys the influence of Gauguin's attraction to Oriental, preclassical, and primitive art in which the origins of modern primitivism can be found. The bright colors and emphatic patterns affirm the beauty of the Tahitians with a robust simplicity that was in itself a departure from the affectations of most Parisian salon painters of the day.

THE REALISTIC RESPONSE

A "realistic" response. By the middle of the nineteenth century a new movement—realism—was having a profound effect on many of the European art forms. Realism concentrated in literature and painting on the concrete aspects of life, and found most of its early major proponents in France. Whereas romantic artists were to be true to their instincts and emotions, the realists were to observe and report all aspects of life in a dispassionate, precise manner. To the realists the function of art was not to find "truth in beauty," but to give all parts of the picture: the good, the bad, and the ugly. Instead of discussing a scholar's dialogue with the devil, the realist writer would concentrate on the commonplace and mundane. Most of all, the individual was seen to be strongly affected by the external conditions in which he was found. The details of the individual's surroundings were of as much interest to the realist as his soul. During the mid-century, the Industrial Revolution produced much for these writers and artists to portray.

The realistic novelists were reacting to the sentimental nature of many of the novels being written at that time, and also to the new ideological trends and the growing impact of science. A down-to-earth attitude became the order of the day. The result was a much more powerful form of the novel—the realistic novel—which did not hesitate to describe in graphic detail social and personal problems that others had ignored because they were not "nice."

The new trend had been foreshadowed in the work of Honoré de Balzac (1799-1850), the author of *La Comédie Humaine (The Human Comedy)*. This immense work was a panorama of ninety volumes concerning French life in the first half of the nineteenth century. He portrayed the life of Paris in such a detailed manner that his books serve twentieth-century students as a valuable reference for social history. In Balzac's novels, the crudities and greed of the French lower-middle classes were sketched in graphic detail and with devastating wit. The first thoroughgoing French realist was Gustave Flaubert (1821-1880). His masterpiece, *Madame Bovary* (1856), describes how the boredom of a romantic-minded young provincial wife led her into adultery, excess, and ultimately, suicide. By implication, Flaubert was pointing to the pitfalls of romanticism as a way of life.

A note of social protest pervades the works of Charles Dickens (1812-1870). He painted in vivid colors the everyday life of the middle classes and the poor, showing the struggle of the individual against the worst excesses of industrial expansion and social injustice. In *Oliver Twist* (1838), *Dombey and Son* (1847-48), *Hard Times* (1854), and other books, Dickens blended romantic and realistic elements by combining a fundamental optimism and belief in progress with merciless attacks upon existing slum conditions, the miseries of the poor, and the inhumane debtors' prisons. This note of reaction against mid-Victorian self-satisfaction was soon to swell into a chorus of attacks, both moderate and radical, upon the existing social order.

The realistic novel received its most developed presentation from the Russian novelists Leo Tolstoy (1828-1910) and Fëdor Dostoevski (1821-1881). Tolstoy's epic novel, *War and Peace* (1869), was a spectacular description of Russian life before and during the Napoleonic invasion of 1812. He stripped every shred of glory and glamour from that conflict, giving an exhaustive description of the various levels of society and of the intellectual trends of the time. He also provided a philosophy of history in the epilogue that has had significant influence. His *Anna Karenina* (1877) relentlessly detailed the story of two lovers who openly defied social conventions.

Dostoevski, perhaps the century's greatest novelist, traced the causes and effects of murder in two masterpieces of suspense and psychological analysis, *Crime and Punishment* (1866) and *The Brothers Karamazov* (1880). In the first he gave a chilling detailed view of life in St. Petersburg, and in the second a striking analysis of provincial life during a period of change.

A notable English realist was Thomas

Hardy (1840-1928), who dealt with the struggle of the individual — almost always a losing struggle — against the impersonal, pitiless forces of his natural and social environment. In America, Henry James (1843-1916) attempted, as he put it, to catch "the atmosphere of the mind," through an almost clinical examination of the most subtle details. Another well-known American writer of the period was Samuel Clemens (1835-1910), whose fame as Mark Twain should not blind us to the realistic character of his work. His writings show not only robust humor, but also accurate descriptions of the Middle and Far West. Like Dickens, he could use humorous satire to underscore social injustice. An American author whose work had a profound social and political impact was Harriet Beecher Stowe (1811-1896). Her novel *Uncle Tom's Cabin* (1852) captured the American public's attention and served to strongly influence the antislavery movement.

In the hands of some writers, realism developed into an extreme form of presentation known as naturalism. The naturalists declared that they wanted to apply scientific objectivity to their subject matter and to deal with their characters as with animals in a laboratory, whose every move was determined by environment or heredity. Émile Zola (1840-1902), the most outstanding follower of this literary doctrine, made a case study twenty volumes long of a middle-class family. In this series of works, which included *Nana* (1880) and *Germinal* (1885), Zola employed a clinical approach, amassing huge notebooks of information on such subjects as the stock market and the mining districts before describing those settings.

Comforting literature. If reading audiences at mid-century did not want to read works dealing with harsh reality, there was a wide range of reassuring and entertaining literature available. They could always turn to optimistic books such as Samuel Smiles' *Self Help* (1859), which sold 20,000 copies its first year and another 130,000 copies during the next thirty years. This work was rapidly succeeded by books with similarly pious titles, such as *Thrift, Character,* and *Duty,* which form a veritable catalogue of the Victorian "virtues." "This long series of smug lay sermons on the joys of industry and honesty [always connected] the practice of such virtues with the reward of material prosperity."[2] In the United States, Horatio Alger (1834-1899) wrote over a hundred novels following similar themes: virtue is rewarded, by struggling with temptation the good life will win out, and the heroes — usually poor but clean youths — will come to enjoy wealth and high honor.

English poetry also came to be expressed in a similarly smug and self-complacent way. The poets wrote in a moralistic and conventional manner for their middle-class audience, in stark contrast to the earlier romantic attitude of rebellion. Perhaps they preferred to come to terms with their world rather than fight against it. Their poetry, accordingly, lacks the high-flown nature of the earlier work.

The spokesman of Victorian England was Alfred Lord Tennyson (1809-1892). He was poet laureate from 1850 to the year of his death, and performed his duties with great distinction. Tennyson's popularity came from his sympathetic understanding of the ideas and goals of his countrymen. He shared their "high seriousness" and self-consciousness along with their love of sentiment. Yet the very qualities in his work that won his great acceptance in his own day have since worked against his popularity in this century. Today the beauty of much of his verse seems artificial, especially when measured against the romantics' poetry. His thought seems shallow and conformist. Perhaps his major error in twentieth-century eyes is that he was so much a man of the complacent times in which he lived. Another well-known English poet of the period was Robert Browning (1812-1889), whose sturdy optimism and faith in humanity won him many readers.

Drama. After mid-century, drama made major advances under the influence of the realistic movement. During the first part of the nineteenth century a great number of new plays had been brought to the European stage, to be performed along with the classics of Shakespeare and Molière. Some of the important authors such as Goethe in Germany, Hugo in France, and James S. Knowles (1784-1862) in the British Isles wrote the tragedies, love stories, and adventures that thrilled audiences.

Later in the century the plays of Ibsen, Shaw, and Chekhov brought new dimensions to stage productions. The exposure of social problems was an important aspect of these three writers. The problems facing the audiences and society toward the end of the century were more subtle in character than the obvious injustices of child labor and cholera-infested slums, which had monopolized the attention of social critics earlier in the century, and the works of these three writers focused on these newer problems of the day.

The dramas of the Norwegian, Henrik Ibsen (1828-1906), were the first of the problem plays. One of his best known works, *A Doll's House* (1879), assailed marriage without love as being immoral. In other works he attacked social greed masked by conventional respectability, and delineated with great skill the human dramas in the strains and stresses of ordinary life.

A disciple of Ibsen, and like the Norwegian an ardent assailant of bourgeois complacency, was the brilliant Irish playwright George Bernard Shaw (1856-1950). In a series of satirical and entertaining plays he bullied and shocked the English-speaking public into reassessing their conventional attitudes on a variety of social subjects ranging from private and public morality to militarism and religious beliefs.

In Russia, Anton Chekhov (1860-1904) gave penetrating presentations of his nation's society through his skillful portrayals of Russian life during a time of change. *The Cherry Orchard* (1904), his masterpiece, shows the impact of the emancipation of the serfs and its accompanying changes on the lives of a gentry family. His plays lack obvious plot and action, and depend on portrayal of detail to build a subtle tension.

Realism in painting. The major trends in literature after mid-century were paralleled by the equally major developments in painting. Already by the 1850's, various artists in France, led by Gustave Courbet (1819-1877), had been rebelling against traditional subject matter and techniques. Feeling that the canvases exhibited on academy walls were for the most part too "respectable" and hence artificial, they chose instead to paint life as they saw it.

Courbet, probably the most outstanding of the French realists, expressed his contempt for religious and neoclassical themes when he mocked: "Show me an angel and I will paint one." These prevailing themes were commercially profitable and their sentimentality made them comfortable items for the

George Bernard Shaw, one of the avant-garde playwrights of his day, brilliantly expressed through his plays his own optimistic faith regarding the possibility of man's perfecting himself through rational means. He expressed this belief with a wit and skill that is still popular today.

The revolutions in Europe in 1848 raised the issue of the dignity of labor as a major issue for the first time. Thus for the artists of the 1850's artistic subjects lay in turning to a more humane and authentic subject matter—portraying nature as it is and the dignity of men and women who labor in it, not the creation of allegories based upon ideals. Courbet provided the most direct and startlingly unvarnished image of contemporary work of the entire century in this painting "The Stonebreakers." Courbet was highly criticized for the lack of spiritual content in his works.

bourgeois market. When Courbet looked at life he consciously dropped the affectations of both the romanticists and neoclassicists and painted uncompromising, often brutal canvases. His view that "realism is an essentially democratic art" was shared by his compatriot, Honoré Daumier (1808-1879), who knew and portrayed Parisian life intimately. His lithographs were biting satires of life among the middle classes, in the law courts, and in political and financial circles.

Developments in music. Music was ill-suited to respond to the cultural demands made by realism. Nonetheless, in the period after 1850 the momentum of forces which Beethoven had set in motion created new advances in composition and presentation. Johannes Brahms (1833-1897), who carried on the traditions of romanticism, is generally regarded as the greatest symphonic composer in the second half of the century, and is also known as a master composer for string

quartets. Brahms did most of his best work in Vienna, which also served as the home for the century's two other great symphonic craftsmen, Anton Bruckner (1824-1896) and Gustav Mahler (1860-1911).

This was an age marked by an outpouring of post-romantic symphonies, overtures, concertos, and chorale works, all of which exploited the new and varied effects made possible by the expanded orchestra. At the same time, the increase in wealth led to a vastly larger audience that lavishly supported the major symphony orchestras. Major soloists were the idols of their day, as they showed their virtuosity in compositions which made use of romantic subject matter infused with sentiment, and not infrequently, showmanship.

In addition, many composers turned for inspiration to their native folk music and dances, especially in central and eastern Europe. Beethoven had used native themes, as had Schubert and Schumann in Austria and Germany. Frederic Chopin (1810-1849), even though doing most of his composing in France, drew heavily on Polish folk themes in his mazurkas and polonaises. Franz Liszt (1811-1886) in the middle of the nineteenth century, and Béla Bartók (1881-1945) and Zoltán Kodály (1882-1967) in the first decades of the twentieth century all drew inspiration from Hungarian folk themes. In Russia, Pëtr Ilich Tchaikovsky (1840-1893), Modest Moussorgsky (1835-1881), and Sergei Rachmaninoff (1873-1943) incorporated folk music in most of their major symphonies. In what would become Czechoslovakia, Bedřich Smetana (1824-1884) and Anton Dvorak (1841-1904) went to the people for many of their major themes, while Jean Sibelius (1865-1957) in Finland did the same. In music more than any other art form, the streams of individual genius, nationalism, and emotion blended to produce an art form that still strongly communicates its message after a century's time has passed.

Developments in opera were markedly influenced during the nineteenth century by the nationalism and romanticism that arose. In the fervid Germanic works of Richard Wagner (1813-1883) old Teutonic myths and German folklore were infused with typically romantic characteristics such as emphasis on the supernatural and the mystical. His *Ring* cycle was the culmination of a long and productive career. Wagner's descendants still manage the *Festspielhaus*, a theater in Bayreuth, Germany, he conceived of and his admirers financed.

Perhaps the greatest operatic composer of the century was Giuseppi Verdi (1813-1901), who composed such masterpieces as *Aida*, *Rigoletto*, *Il trovatore*, *La traviata*, *La forza del destino*, *Otello*, and many others. His operas, along with those of Wagner, form the core of most of the major opera house repertoires.

The music world rarely dealt with social problems or harsh realism. Its supporters were by and large the newly ascendant middle classes who had risen along with the veritable economic explosion produced by the Industrial Revolution. The middle class financed the building of new opera and symphony halls and maintained the composers and orchestras from the wealth produced by their commercial prosperity. Public concerts, symphony orchestras, quartet societies, piano and song recitals—all were attainments of the nineteenth century which had only faint beginnings in 1800.

MODERNISM

Beyond reality. As we have seen, the nineteenth century's cultural evolution began in the romantic response to the norms and accepted patterns of the classical age. The way was opened for an increasing diversity in forms, styles, and themes for the individual creative artist who was to be guided by his instincts and emotions. Romanticism thus encouraged the multifaceted pursuit of "truth in beauty." Partially in a response to the romantic emphasis on instinct and emotion, the realist movement, which did not affect all art forms in the same way, advocated a more objective rendering of the real world, in a dispassionate way that discouraged moralizing. Accuracy and precision in the analysis of detail made the realist movement especially effective in the novels of Tolstoy and Dostoevski.

By the end of the century a new movement—modernism—fragmented, disorganized, and united only in its reaction to the past, came to affect Europe's creative artists. The liberation of the individual artist in the new movement went far beyond the cultural strides made by the romantic movement in the face of classicism. It was as if the artist was freed from all rules of composition and form and obligations to communicate to a large audience. In music, old melodic structures and rhythms could be discarded. In poetry, former requirements of clarity and literalness could be ignored. In painting, the artists no longer felt the need to communicate the surface, photographic reality. Pure creativity to the ultimate degree possible for each individual artist, not easy communication with the audience in familiar language, form, and content, became the goal of the modernist movement.

Poetry was especially affected by this new tendency. Toward the end of the century, in reaction to the demands of realism, the Symbolism movement was begun in France by such poets as Stéphane Mallarmé (1842-1898) and Paul Verlaine (1844-1896). Poetry, rather than prose, best fit the Symbolists' goal of conveying ideas by suggestions rather than by precise, photographic word-pictures.

In a sense, all modern literature stems from the Symbolism movement. By vastly increasing the power of the poet to reach the readers' imaginations through expanded combinations of allusions, symbols, and double meanings, Symbolism gave new life to the written word. In a sense it was the final blow to classicism, the ultimate liberation of the individual writer. T. S. Eliot, Marcel Proust, William Butler Yeats, James Joyce, and Vladimir Mayakovsky could, in the twentieth century, trace their creative roots back to the Symbolists. But, in exploring new poetical realms and possibilities, they have left behind the majority of readers, who have been trained to see clarity, precision, simplicity, and definition as positive aspects of the written word.

Revolution in painting. Just as poetry was broken from its bond of literalness, painting at this time broke away from the necessity to be photographic. The French artists at the end of the century went beyond the mere technical problems involved in reproducing a scene literally. They became preoccupied with problems of color, light, and atmosphere, and they tried to catch the first impression made by a scene or object upon the eye in their paintings, undistorted by intellect or any subjective attitude. The result was that the Impressionists—as they were called—worked in terms of light and color rather than solidity of form. In so doing, they found that a more striking effect of light could be gained by placing one bright area of color next to another without any transitional tones. They also discovered that shadows could be shown not as gray but as colors complementary to those of the objects casting the shadows. At close range an Impressionist picture may seem little more than a splotch of unmixed colors, but at a proper

distance the eye mixes the colors, and a vibrating effect of light and motion emerges. Through their technique the Impressionists helped revolutionize modern painting.

Among the many outstanding French Impressionists, such as Claude Monet (1840-1926), Édouard Manet (1832-1883), Edgar Degas (1834-1917), and J. F. Millet (1814-1875), Pierre Auguste Renoir (1841-1919) stands out as the most representative. He painted all sorts of subjects, among them the Paris Opéra, landscapes, and houseboats on the Seine. His canvases all reveal a rich sense of color, as seen by his skillful use of it to capture flesh tones and texture, or by seeing how the sunlight plays across his paintings, giving the sense of a passing moment captured on canvas.

By conveying a sense of motion and of spontaneity, Impressionism had given painting a new vitality. But there was an esthetic price that had to be paid. For one thing its effects had been gained by sacrificing much of the clarity which continued to be a hallmark of the classical tradition. Again, while bringing the surface of things alive in an exciting fashion, the Impressionists seemed unable to give the objects the solidity and structure which were theirs by nature. How could the artists get the best of both worlds?

This was the difficult intellectual and artistic problem to which Paul Cézanne (1839-1906) addressed himself. For years this painter, a one-time realist and a friend of Zola, experimented with new techniques. He tried to simplify all natural objects by stressing their essential geometric structure. Cézanne believed that everything in nature corresponds to the shape of a cone, cylinder, or sphere. Proceeding on the basis of this theory, he was able to get below the surface and give his objects the solidity which had eluded the Impressionists. Yet, like the Impressionists, he made striking use of color in ways that helped to establish the relationships of his objects in space. The successful pioneering work of Cézanne was later to have important consequences.

One late nineteenth-century artist, Vincent van Gogh (1853-1890), had great success because of his individualism. The Dutch painter, whose short life of poverty and lone-

Auguste Renoir, the French Impressionist, used vibrant color and scintillating light to achieve delightful visual effects. Many of his paintings, such as "Canoeists' Luncheon" (top), portray the pastimes of the lower and middle classes in informal outdoor scenes. Influenced both by Impressionist works and by Persian art, Henri Matisse emphasized the arrangement of simple rhythmic forms, rich textures, and vivid areas of color in paintings like "Goldfish and Sculpture" (right).

Louis Sullivan and Walter Gropius produced revolutionary architectural designs born of the concept that external form should express the purpose of a building, its internal structure, and the materials used. Adhering to his maxim "form follows function," Sullivan expressed tremendous strength in the Carson, Pirie, Scott Store (left) with sharply cut horizontal windows which fulfilled their indispensable purpose—the admission of light. Similarly, Gropius achieved a very transparent effect in the Bauhaus (below) by means of a continuous glass curtain wall between two ribbons of white concrete.

liness was climaxed by insanity and suicide, used short strokes of heavy pigment which accentuated the underlying forms and rhythms of his subjects. He was not concerned with presenting simply a photographic representation of what lay before him, but wanted to convey the intense emotions he felt about the subjects of his work. As a consequence, he was ready to distort what he saw in order to communicate these sensations.

At the turn of the century artists became increasingly concerned with painting what they felt about an object, rather than just the object itself. This method of using an object as a means of expressing subjective feelings is known as Expressionism. This approach was quite close to that of the Symbolist school in literature.

Among the early Expressionists — or *les fauves* (the wild beasts), as they were derided by their critics — was Henri Matisse (1869-1954). He had learned to simplify form partly from African primitive art and had studied the color schemes of oriental carpets. His decorative style was to influence design strongly in our own day.

Experimentation took still other subjective forms. We have already noted that in order to achieve a sense of depth and solidity, Cézanne used geometric shapes and depth relationships on the two-dimensional painting surface. Further developments along these lines resulted in the emergence of a new school called Cubism. Cubists would choose an object, then construct an abstract pattern from it. In doing so, they went far beyond the traditional manner of reproducing the object from one vantage point; instead they viewed it from several points of view simultaneously. In a Cubist canvas one might see a given object — say, a violin — from above, below, inside and outside, with all the dissected elements interpenetrating. Such a pattern is evident in "Three Musicians" by the Spanish artist Pablo Picasso (1881-1974), probably the most influential single figure in twentieth-century painting.

Sculpture and architecture. Sculpture and architecture went through radical changes at the end of the nineteenth century. The premier sculptor of the time, Auguste Rodin (1840-1917), has been described as the father of modern sculpture. He gave his work a realistic honesty and vitality that made him the object of stormy controversy during much of his career. He shared with the Impressionist painters a dislike for finality in art, and preferred to let the viewer's imagination play on his sculpture. Rodin's technique of rough finish can best be seen in his bronze works. By this approach, he achieved two effects: a glittering surface of light and shadow, and a feeling of immediacy and incompleteness that emphasized the spontaneous character of the work.

While Rodin was making major contributions to the art of sculpture, architects in the United States and Europe were taking advantage of the new materials and technologies developed by the Industrial Revolution to make major strides in architecture. Helped by the new resources and methods, they were able to span greater distances and enclose greater areas than had hitherto been possible.

However much of a tragedy the Great Chicago Fire of 1871 may have been, it had the beneficial effect of levelling the city and permitting new building on a large scale. A new form of architecture emerged — the skyscraper. The steel-skeleton skyscraper enabled builders to reach far higher than they had ever been able to. Whereas high buildings had formerly required immensely thick masonry walls, a metal frame now allowed the weight of the structure to be distributed on an entirely different principle. Also, a far more extensive use of glass than ever before was made possible.

Outstanding among the pioneers in this new architecture was Chicago's Louis Sullivan (1856-1924). Like others, Sullivan saw the value of the skyscraper in providing a large amount of useful space on a small plot of expensive land. Unlike others, he rejected all attempts to disguise the skeleton of the skyscraper behind a false front and boldly proclaimed it by a clean sweep of line. Sullivan's emphasis upon the functional was to have a far-reaching influence.

One of Sullivan's pupils, Frank Lloyd Wright (1869-1959), originated revolutionary designs for houses. One feature of his houses was the interweaving of interiors and exteriors by the use of terraces and cantilevered roofs. He felt that the building should look appropriate on its site; it should "grow out of the land." His "prairie houses," with their long, low lines, were designed to blend in with the flat land of the Midwest. Much that is taken for granted in today's houses comes directly from Wright's experiments at the beginning of the century.

In Europe, the French engineer Alexandre Gustave Eiffel (1832-1923) planned and erected a 984-foot tower in Paris for the 1889 Exposition. Delicately formed from an iron framework, the tower rests on four masonry piers on a base 330 feet square. It stands today as a symbol of Paris, and of the innovations that made it possible.

In the decade prior to World War I there developed in Germany a widely accepted form of architecture that broke with tradition. The industrial age made itself felt in this new form that stressed the use of different techniques from the machine age. In 1914, one of the outstanding leaders of this movement, Walter Gropius (1883-1969), designed an exhibition hall in Cologne which, by emphasizing horizontal lines, using glass, exposing staircases, and not hiding its functionalism, would be accepted today as contemporary. The new movement in architecture resulted in the establishment of a school of functional art and architecture, the *Bauhaus*, in 1918.

Modern music. In the last third of the nineteenth century romanticism in music began to come under critical attack, as the composers who came after Brahms did not live up to the olympian standards of their predecessors. Although Tchaikovsky continued on in the tradition of writing symphonies in four movements, he spent an increasing amount of time writing music for ballets. Richard Strauss (1864-1949) kept some of the Wagnerian traditions alive into this century.

But there were striking departures occurring too. The French composer Claude Debussy (1862-1918) was strongly affected by developments in poetry and art, and began to delve into imitating the effects of the other two art forms in his composition. He engaged in "tone painting" to achieve a special mood or atmosphere. This device is immediately recognizable in Debussy's *"Prélude à l'après-midi d'un faune" (The Afternoon of a Faun)*, which astounded the musical world when it was first performed in 1892. The Impressionist painters had gained their effects by juxtaposing widely different colors. The composers in turn juxtaposed widely separated chords to create similarly brilliant, shimmering effects with sounds.

A number of other composers rebelled strongly against romanticism and engaged in striking experimentation. Breaking with the "major-minor" system of tonality, which had been the musical tradition since the Renaissance, some of them began to make use of several different keys simultaneously, a device known as polytonality. Outstanding among such composers, Igor Stravinsky (1882-1971) did for modern music what innovators such as Picasso accomplished for modern painting. Unlike the romanticists, Stravinsky was less concerned with melody than with achieving his effects by means of polytonality, dissonant harmonies, and percussive rhythms. Meanwhile, other composers were experimenting with atonality, the absence of any fixed key. In this regard, we should mention Arnold Schönberg (1874-1951), who developed the twelve-tone system. Compositions of this structure depart from all tonality and harmonic progressions, while at the same time stressing extreme dissonances.

With the work of composers like Schönberg, we arrive at Expressionism in music. Just as the Expressionist painters were trying to create a new inner reality, so composers sought to give shape to their innermost feelings by getting below the surface. Although harsh and unpleasant to many ears, these experiments with polytonality and atonality had validity for a century in which the old absolute values were being broken down—a century, as two world wars were to prove, of clashing dissonance.

POPULAR CULTURE

New pastimes for a new audience. As we noted in the last chapter, the urban working and lower-middle classes came to play an increasingly important role in the economic life of Europe. As literacy rates rapidly increased after 1870, and as social legislation increased the amount of leisure time, these groups also began to play an important role in the cultural life of their countries, as a mass audience able and willing to read or go to the music hall for entertainment. The consumers of the fine arts and music described above were rarely to be found among the lower-middle classes and working classes, except, perhaps, for their children who were pursuing an education. For most European city dwellers, the concert hall, the art gallery, and the thick, psychological novel were still distant objects.

At the turn of the century, the reading material for these people was generally to be found in the penny press and the "dime novel." The invention by Ottmar Mergenthaler (1854-1899) of the linotype machine had made printing a much speedier and less expensive proposition. Steam had been harnessed to the presses earlier in the century, so there were no technological obstacles to the mass-circulation press. The penny press served many functions: to inform, to entertain, to distract, to form opinion, and to sell goods through advertisements. Materials appeared for children as well as for adults, as the first comic strips made simultaneous appearances around the world at the turn of the century.

Pamphlets and books, materials of longer length, tended to deal with religious themes at the beginning of the nineteenth century. But in England it did not take long for sensationalism to be discovered, as first the confessions of criminals and fallen women were published for a scandalized, but fascinated public. Later, weekly newspapers much like those tabloids found at the check-out coun-

By the turn of the century the middle classes were heavily involved in all sorts of leisure-time activities—as spectators and participants—from reading to auto racing. Sunday afternoon sporting events like bicycle racing and football games became part of the popular culture.

ters of today's supermarkets appeared, some hitting a circulation of over a half million a week. By the turn of the century William Randolph Hearst (1863-1951) and Joseph Pulitzer (1847-1911) in the United States and Alfred Harmsworth (1865-1922) in England published newspapers which required minimal reading levels, but created much sensationalism (called "yellow journalism" in this country), and carried massive amounts of advertising that sold more than a million copies a day.

A new form of entertainment which diverted the mass audience resulted from developments in the Industrial Revolution. Coated celluloid film, improved shutter mechanisms, reliable projectors, and a safe source of illumination were discovered almost simultaneously in England, the United States, and France. Brought together, they helped revolutionize the whole concept of entertainment. The first public moving-picture performance took place in Paris in 1895, and soon after in London and the United States. Even though the new process would not be perfected until another twenty years had passed, the "movies" proved to be an instant success, reaching an infinitely larger audience than could ever be gained by live performers. The price of admission per member of the audience was much cheaper. In America admission came to be a nickel for the primitive films in the theaters, known as nickelodeons. In 1903 the first "plot" film was made, "The Great Train Robbery." Even though the early films were, by later standards, technically imperfect, they nonetheless had a shocking impact on the audiences. The unsophisticated viewers often reacted emotionally to such scenes as trains rushing toward them on the screen, villainous landlords evicting penniless widows from their lodgings, and the slapstick comedy that came to be popular. By 1914 movie theaters were open throughout Europe, catering to thousands of people nightly, people who would have never gone to an opera, a symphony, or an art gallery. Technology and democracy came together in the movie theater.

There were other pastimes that attracted popular attention. At the turn of the century, big-time sports made their appearance in Europe and the United States. Most of the sporting events enjoyed today have their roots far back in the Middle Ages. But until the end of the last century they were mainly the pursuits of the upper classes. With the advent of the six-day workweek, workers were provided with a day off to either participate in sports or to watch others play them.

In France, bicycle racing and boxing came to capture the public imagination. It was a Frenchman, Pierre de Coubertin, who reestablished the ancient Olympic games in 1896 in Athens, and who sensed that athletics might serve as a device to unite the world. Thirteen nations would take part in those first games.

Football became popular in its various forms—rugby and soccer in England and on the continent and its peculiarly American form in North America. The rules of all three varieties are almost a century old. In America, baseball and basketball became increasingly popular.[3] Throughout the British empire, the colonial officials took their games, especially cricket and soccer, and taught them to their subjects.

SUMMARY

At all levels of European society, life-styles, esthetic standards, and the means for self-expression were dramatically changed by the end of the nineteenth century. Cultural activities had passed from being the preserve of the elite and the elect, all sharing a common classical conception of what was "good" and "bad" in qualitative terms at the beginning of the century, to being as fragmented and diverse as the European world in 1900. The classicism of the eighteenth century at least had the advantage of unifying the participants, both creators and audience, in cultural activities. By 1900, in art, music, poetry, prose, and sculpture it would have been difficult to gain a consensus between the creative artist and his audience as to what was "good" and "bad."

Romanticism contributed the essential blow that freed the creative artist from the restrictions of accepted forms and contents. In music, literature, and art the romantic movement contributed figures of genius and works of excellence. At mid-century the realism movement brought a challenging response to the egocentric quality of much of the romantic artists and writers. It was at this time that the novel attained a level of perfection that has rarely been equalled. Realism's emphasis on detail and careful observation generated its own reaction in the modernism movement that arose in the 1890's. In painting, poetry, and music new revolutionary strides were taken to break any remaining limits and rules that might hamper the artist from gaining his creative potential. But in the process, the gulf between creator and audience widened, and has yet to be closed in some art forms.

A huge new group of consumers, the lower-middle classes and the working classes, were at the same time becoming participants in the new mass culture. They would have even less in common with the fine arts, and through their numbers and buying power they would come to have a greater effect on some parts of the creative community.

Never had the creators of poetry, art, prose, music, and sculpture had a greater opportunity to communicate to such a large audience. The new medium of cinema held out great promise as a powerful creative opportunity. And yet, the Symbolists, Cubists, polytonal composers, and avant-garde novelists were advancing to such a stage that they would seemingly be able to communicate to only a finely trained elite. In a sense, what was needed was a new series of classical definitions, forms, and functions upon which all could agree. But the romantic drive to individualism, which came to full flower through the century, has made that impossible. Even today, we still have the vast gulf between "mass culture" and the "fine arts."

SUGGESTIONS FOR READING

For English literature during this period see G. B. Woods, ed., **English Poetry and Prose of the Romantic Movement** (Scott, Foresman); and J. H. Buckley and G. B. Woods, eds., **Poetry of the Victorian Period,** 3rd ed. (Scott, Foresman). Outstanding studies of other notable literary figures are A. Maurois, **The Life of Balzac** (Harper & Row, 1966); H. Troyat, **Tolstoy** (Doubleday, 1967); and D. S. Mirsky, **A History of Russian Literature, from Its Beginnings to 1900*** (Vintage). For a discussion of romanticism on the continent see G. L. Mosse, **The Culture of Western Europe, the Nineteenth and Twentieth Centuries: An Introduction** (Rand McNally); L. A. Willoughby, **The Romantic Movement in Germany** (Russell, 1966); and B. Willey, **Nineteenth Century Studies*** (Torchbooks).

M. Raynal, **The Nineteenth Century: New Sources of Emotion from Goya to Gauguin** (Skira) is an excellent introduction to nineteenth-century painting. See also M. Brion, **The Art of the Romantic Era*** (Praeger), as well as relevant chapters in E. H. Gombrich, **The Story of Art*** (Phaidon, 1974); H. W. and D. J. Janson, **Picture History of Painting*** (Washington Square); and F. B. Artz, **From the Renaissance to Romanticism: Trends in Style in Art, Literature, and Music, 1330-1830*** (Phoenix).

For a better understanding of major developments in what has been described as music's "golden century," see M. Brion, **Schu-**

mann and the Romantic Age (Macmillan); A. Einstein, **Music in the Romantic Era** (Norton); P. A. Scholes, **Romantic and Nationalist Schools of the Nineteenth Century,** Vol. II of **The Listener's History of Music,** 5th ed. (Oxford); and H. C. Colles, **Ideals of the Nineteenth Century and the Twentieth Century,** Pt. III of **The Growth of Music** (Oxford). Well-written biographies of two titans in the world of music are M. M. Scott, **Beethoven** (Octagon); E. Valentin, **Beethoven, A Pictorial Biography** (Viking); and P. Latham, **Brahms** (Octagon).

For significant developments in esthetic theory and painting in the decades preceding World War I see C. Edward Gauss, **The Aesthetic Theories of French Artists: From Realism to Surrealism*** (Johns Hopkins); and E. F. Fry, **Cubism*** (McGraw-Hill World of Art Series). For an overall survey of developments during the past two centuries see H. L. C. Jaffe, **The Nineteenth and Twentieth Centuries,** Vol. 5 of **The Dolphin History of Painting*** (Thames and Hudson). A number of outstanding painters and their works are treated in individual publications; Fontana has issued a series of **Paintings*** in its **Art Books,** separately for Manet, Matisse, and Picasso. M. De Micheli has written **Cezanne*** and **Picasso*** (Grosset & Dunlap).

*Indicates a less expensive paperbound edition.

CHAPTER 24

Ideological and Intellectual Developments: 1815-1914

New Ideas in the Changing European World

INTRODUCTION. The major economic and material forces that changed Europe during the nineteenth century were complemented by the effects of a large number of new ideological and intellectual currents. The great importance of the era's doctrinal contributions can be gauged by searching for some of the roots of our political vocabulary in the *Oxford English Dictionary*. The terms that describe our ideological choices — socialism, liberalism, conservatism, capitalism, and communism — came to be commonly used in the first half of the nineteenth century.

In Chapter 24 we will examine the responses of the European thinkers and theorists to the complex times in which they lived. Romanticism's contributions in altering political thought will be discussed first. Then the origins and development of nationalism, conservatism, liberalism, and utopian and Marxian socialism will be investigated. Theoretical science made monumental advances and helped form the century's conceptual framework. However, when misapplied it also contributed to the sometimes arrogant assumptions that strengthened racism and imperialism. After assessing this incredibly productive period in political theory and science, it will be apparent that by 1914 the ideological and intellectual arena in Europe had changed as drastically as had the economic and material structure of the continent.

The nineteenth-century ideologists and intellectuals based their numerous and diverse contributions on the solid foundations of the western tradition. From Christianity they gained a strong element of morality and idealism concerning humanity's equality in the face of God. They were emboldened by the Renaissance's notion that man is the measure of all things. The Scientific Revolution had taught Europeans the value of rational observation and the experimental method to resolve problems. The thinkers were encouraged by the Enlightenment's exaltation of the powers of reason in the search for solutions to society's ills.

Europeans also had the instructive example of how ideas coming from John Locke and applied by the *philosophes* and the American colonists could either indirectly or directly lead to revolutions in America and France. The consequences of these two upheavals, especially the French, served to form the bases for some of the nineteenth century's most important movements. The ideals of liberty, fraternity, and equality would provide the foundations for liberalism, nationalism, and socialism. Reactions to the revolutions would give the fundamental impulse for the conservative movement.

As if the richness of the western tradition and the eighteenth century were not enough to spark Europe's intellectuals, the nineteenth century was ushered in by two forces that dealt devastating blows to the continent's political and economic framework— Napoleon and the Industrial Revolution. As he marched across Europe, the French emperor redrew the European map, destroying many institutions of the old regime in areas he conquered through his social and legal reforms. Even though there was an attempt to restore elements of the old structure in central and western Europe, the pre-1789 conditions could not take firm root again. As we have seen, the Industrial Revolution brought about wide-ranging changes in most of Europe by 1914, changes which invalidated any attempt to reintroduce the old order.

Political thought since 1789 has made the transition from the drawing rooms of the elite to the streets. Ideologies have, in the movement toward mass democracies in the twentieth century, gained more immediate impact. The conflicting ideologies that divide our world today came essentially in response to the same questions: What is humanity? What is humanity's potential? Is humanity perfectible or crippled by its own flaws? How best can humanity develop? Ideologies, once accepted, tend to shape the choices and policies of political leaders, and politics becomes the day-to-day application of those long-range principles to the changing environment. The questions that the nineteenth-century ideologists and intellectuals tried to answer, even with the aid of science, are still with us. Unless humanity becomes stagnant and ceases to change, they will always be with us.

ROMANTICISM'S IMPACT

A complex movement. Romanticism's liberating impact on art, literature, and music was equally felt in the political realm. As in the arts, the romantics' contributions in ideology were shaped by their responses to a number of different factors. At first they reacted to the classicism and rationalism of the eighteenth century. Later the romantics responded to French dominance between 1789 and 1815. Thereafter, the participants in the romantic tide were affected variously by post-1815 political repression on the continent, some aspects of industrialization, and middle-class propriety.

The first phase of this response set the tone for romanticism's contributions to European political thought. The romantics wanted to break out of the rational measured patterns of the classicists, who saw life as being made up of rules, structures, reasonableness, and defined behavior. The romantics viewed life as more than a matter of mastering the rules and living within the structure of accepted society. They pointed out that there were two levels of existence—the rational and the emotional. The two were not viewed as being mutually exclusive, but there was no doubt that the emotional level was the more important. A romantic would ask, "How does one rationally define beauty, love, friendship, anger—in short, all of the qualitative aspects of life?"

Rousseau believed that man must live more by his instincts and emotions than through the maze of intellect and rationalization erected by society (see p. 468-469). The "noble savage" exalted by Rousseau was to be admired because he was not contaminated; he was close to nature and therefore free. The romantic movement felt constrained by the structure of organized society. The romantics were not alone in voicing this view, as the Pietists in the Lutheran church were,

Jean Jacques Rousseau, one of the most enigmatic and significant persons of his time, gloried in impulses and intuitions, trusting emotion rather than thought, the heart rather than the mind. Though hailed as the champion of the masses, his writings have been used to justify such divergent political philosophies as democracy and totalitarianism.

J. J. ROUSSEAU

in a similar vein, trying to replace the rather austere and abstract religion of the intellectual theologians with warmth, fervor, and emotion. This emphasis on the individual, emotion, and criticism of the highly structured life would come to have an important influence on subsequent political movements.

The romantics looked to the past for their guide, but rarely with the detached, objective examination characteristic of twentieth-century historians. They had a great fascination with long-forgotten civilizations, symbolized by the fake ruins that came to be such an important part of European gardens. The medieval period also became the subject of much serious research. Romantic intellectuals paid a great deal of attention to myths and folklore as they tried to reclaim an "essential" part of their civilization. An example of this "looking backward" could be seen in Britain in the 1820's. There, the Philhellenism movement had created a wave of nostalgia for the Greece of Pericles. English intellectuals, led by the contentious and colorful Lord Byron, were caught up in an idealistic crusade which came to have important political implications during the 1821 Greek revolution.

By stressing the past, the unique, the emotional, and the individual aspects of life, the romantic movement paved the way for the rise of the fragmenting force of modern nationalism. By emphasizing the right of the individual to define his own standards instead of adhering to accepted eighteenth-century principles, the romantics contributed to the new political pressures that would be felt during the nineteenth century.

Romanticism in different areas. The romantic movement had its greatest impact in Germany. The cultural and national redefinition that occurred in the first part of the century led to the belief in the uniqueness of German civilization (see p. 487). Georg Wilhelm Friedrich Hegel (1770-1831), although not a romantic, was able to build on the movement's contributions in his lectures and writings at the University of Berlin. To Hegel, history was a process of evolution in which the supremacy of primitive instincts so dear to the romantics eventually gave way to the reign of clear reason and freedom—the "World Spirit"—that would be manifested in the state. Hegel believed that the Prussia of his day offered the best example of the state as a spiritual organism, because in Prussia the individual was given the greatest "freedom." Hegel saw this freedom not as the individual escaping from society, but as a situation in which there would be no conflict between the individual and society. The Prussian state, to him, blended the proper ingredients of national identity and structure to enable its individuals to attain their greatest growth. Hegel's high regard for the state was not shared by most of the romantic philosophers, but his exaltation of the Prussian state at the time when Germany was still fragmented had a powerful unifying influence.

The romantic movement took on a different form in England in the first part of the nineteenth century. The participants in the movement there reacted against the human costs of industrialization and against the pretensions of the new merchant classes. They were also deeply interested in the medieval pageantry of England, as well as in Philhellenism.

In France, Spain, Italy, Russia, and other parts of Europe the romantic movement made unique cultural contributions and aided in the sharpening of national identity. Giuseppe Mazzini (1805-1872) and Alessandro Manzoni (1785-1873), for example, contributed to the Italian unification movement as romantics, and in the other nations writers, philosophers, and statesmen participated in forming the new national movements.

Nationalism. By emphasizing research into the past and the picturesque to find their own roots, the romantics helped give birth to one of the nineteenth century's most potent movements—nationalism. They investigated their own history, folklore, linguistic backgrounds, and myths in the attempt to define their uniqueness. They saw the world not as a cosmopolitan and rational unit, but as a place of natural variety. In the first part of the century scholars across Europe investigated national myths and folklore, ranging from the Scandinavian sagas, to the French Chansons de Roland, to the Nibe-

George Gordon, Lord Byron, who died of fever while aiding the cause of Greek independence, was one of the romantic era's most colorful and impulsive figures. His masterpiece, *Don Juan*, gallantly expresses his rebellion against the constraints of society.

lungen stories in Germany. All were reprinted for an eager public. At the same time historical novels, such as those of Walter Scott, and various unauthoritative texts were published. During a century of uncertainty, stress, and change, this recovery of the national pasts was both comforting and uplifting.

The research and writings of the Germans, Johann Gottfried von Herder (1744-1803) and Jakob and Wilhelm Grimm (1785-1863 and 1786-1859), provided important historical support and the linguistic bases for the Slavic nationalistic movements. Herder conceived of a world spirit (*Weltgeist*) made up of component parts of the various national spirits (*Volkgeist*). Each of these national spirits was viewed as playing an essential role in world progress, and Herder believed the Slavs were soon to make an important contribution. The Grimm brothers' philological work aided the literary and linguistic revivals of many Slavic groups.

Composers, poets, and historians turned to national themes during the century. Beethoven in Germany, Dvorak and Smetana in Bohemia, Chopin in Poland, and Moussorgsky and Tchaikovsky in Russia all found inspiration in native songs. One need only read a portion of a sonnet Wordsworth wrote in 1802 upon his return from the continent to note this national pride:

. . . Oft have I looked round
With joy in Kent's green vales; but never found
Myself so satisfied in heart before.
Europe is yet in bonds; but let that pass
Thought for another moment. Thou art free,
My Country! and 'tis joy enough and pride
For one hour's perfect bliss, to tread the grass
Of England once again . . .[1]

Similar manifestations of national feeling could be found in the writings of Russia's great poet, Alexander Pushkin, and in the French novels of Victor Hugo. Romantic nationalism also made its impact felt in the writing of history by Leopold von Ranke in Germany, Jules Michelet in France, František Palacky in Bohemia-Moravia, and George Bancroft in the United States.

The increasing support of intellectuals buttressed the political strength of the European nationalities. The members of these groups knew their identity, as most of the European nations had been well defined for centuries. But the existence of nations and nationalities is not the same as nationalism. After 1789, this new ideological force emerged with its dominance over the cultural and political activities of the nation.

The spirit of fraternity projected by the French Revolution had a profound impact in uniting the French people. Napoleon's domination over the continent had a similarly strong effect of bringing people together in opposition to him, especially in Germany. The force of nationalism that surfaced in the course of the nineteenth century turned out to be the most enduring and least defined movement of the period.

Historians over the years have defined nationalism in conflicting ways. Unique conditions in various parts of the continent produced contrasting varieties of nationalism. Yet, even with this complexity there is no doubting the factor of sharing that is at the core of modern nationalism. Common land, language, folklore, history, enemies, and religion have drawn people together into the indivisible unit—the nation. The above elements can be combined in varying proportions under different external pressures, but the feeling of sharing, of being a part of a group, is the cornerstone of nationalism.

Nationalism can exist where there is no state structure, and can thrive in a country where the state does not respond to the needs of a minority nation. Nationalism, unlike patriotism, does not need flags and uniforms, although these devices can be used. All that is needed is a historical and emotional unity around which the members of a nation can gather, a unity that entails the cultural and political loyalty to the nation.

In the first part of the nineteenth century nationalism was seen from the Atlantic to the Urals. The fragmentation of Europe into a number of self-contained, egotistical units could be traced in the growing conflict between Sweden and Norway, the Denmark-Prussian strife, the rise of hostility between the Dutch and the Belgians, and the growth of nationalistic sentiment in Eastern Europe.

THREE NEW RESPONSES

Conservatism. The reaction to the events of the French Revolution, especially as expressed by Edmund Burke, provided the basis of nineteenth-century European conservatism. There were many serious intellectuals who did not believe in the liberty, equality, and fraternity slogans as defined by the revolutionaries. They did not believe that liberation could be attained by destroying the historically evolved traditions of the old regime. Freedom could be found only in order, and maintained solely by continual reference to precedents. A legitimate political and social life needed the framework of a historic tradition to survive.

The conservatives did not have faith in the individual as did the middle classes, nor did they share the love of pure emotion and spontaneity expressed by the romantics. Beginning with Burke, and going on through the first part of the century to the Frenchman Joseph de Maistre, the Russian Nicholas Karamzim, and the Spaniard Donoso-Cortes, there was a body of thinkers who found strength—not weakness—in the church and monarchy of the old regime; danger—not liberation—in the nationalistic movements; and degradation—not exaltation—in the new romantic art forms.

Conservatism took many forms during the nineteenth century, ranging from the romantic, to the patriotic, to the religious, to the secular. Yet whatever their approach in whatever country, conservatives stressed the need to maintain order through a constant reference to history. The welfare and happiness of mankind was seen to reside in the slowly evolving institutions of the past. Industrialism and the consequences of the French Revolution broke the organic continuity with the past, and were therefore dangerous. The conservatives were backward-looking, finding their standards and values in the proven events of the past, not in the untried reforms of the present.

Conservatives posed questions that would not go away: Was humanity better off as a result of the French Revolution? Is man truly equal? Can man engage in fraternity without the structure of the church and tradition? By advocating the old in a revolutionary century they formed the other part of the ideological dialogue.

Liberalism. At the same time that romanticism was making a major change in European intellectual circles, another major movement—liberalism—came to have a potent influence on thought and policy. Liberalism was associated almost exclusively with the ascendent middle class. Like romanticism, liberalism affirmed the dignity of the individual and the "pursuit of happiness" as an inherent right. Its roots were firmly set in the soil of the eighteenth-century trends of constitutionalism, laissez-faire economics, and parliamentarianism. Unlike romanticism, which accepted radical change as a justifiable means to give expression to the emotional needs of humanity, liberalism came to stand for gradual reform. Whereas the rationalists and some romanticists had tended to speak

of man in the abstract, conceiving him as a philosophical ideal, nineteenth-century liberals thought in terms of real individuals sharing basic rights in common, who worked together to gain parliamentary majorities and political power. Further, these individuals would use their power to make sure that each of them would be given a maximum of freedom from the state or any other external authority.

In economics, liberalism was best expressed in terms of fair competition among individuals responding to the laws of supply and demand, with a minimum of governmental regulation and interference. In his *Wealth of Nations* in 1776, Adam Smith stated that society benefited more from competition among individuals motivated by their self-interest than from governmental interference. The most intelligent and efficient individuals would gain the greatest rewards, society would prosper, and government could be kept in its proper place, that of protecting life and property.

The liberals faced severe challenges after 1815 as they tried to translate their ideology into public policy. Since most governments in Europe were controlled by the nobility and landed classes, the middle classes fought to gain political power that was equal to their economic strength. At the same time that they were trying to increase their amount of political influence, they also sought to limit the political base of the emerging working classes.

By the end of the century the bourgeoisie had largely achieved their goals and consolidated their control over the industrialized nations of the world. This was the major political transformation of the century. The class which was liberated from manual labor had sufficient income to spend its spare time in political pursuits. The middle-class liberals on the continent generally gained their success in the era of industrial capitalism after 1850. They were able to control the governments to the point that their economic interests would be protected and extended, while also granting sufficient social reforms to head off the possibilities of revolution. At the same time, they were able to gain substantial support for their points of view

At a time when the proponents of nineteenth-century liberalism were advocating the issue of civil liberties, John Stuart Mill helped define and place the problems in their proper perspectives. His essay *On Liberty* (1859) was an inquiry into "the nature and limits of the power which can be legitimately exercised by society over the individual."

through gaining control of the press and the universities.

Liberalism's major contributions came in the areas of support of civil rights, promotion of the rule of law through constitutional and governmental reform, and humanitarian enterprises. The twentieth-century student reading this description may be confused by the current use of the word liberal. The term still stands for reform, as it did in the nineteenth century. But in the realm of economics, liberalism has undergone a basic change. Unlike his nineteenth-century colleague, the twentieth-century liberal advocates an active governmental role in minimizing the extremes of wealth, in balancing the great power enjoyed by big business and labor, and in conserving natural resources. The twentieth-century liberal also advocates the state's intervention to aid the individual by providing social security and in opposing racial and sexual discrimination.

Some English variations. During the first half of the century, Jeremy Bentham and John Stuart Mill contributed some variations on the liberal theme. Bentham (1748-1832), a wealthy British lawyer, devised the doctrine of utilitarianism, or philosophical radicalism, based on the two concepts of utility and happiness. He connected these two terms by saying that each individual knows what is best for himself, and that all human institutions should be measured according to the amount of happiness they give. Bentham built on these two eighteenth-century concepts in forming the so-called "pain and pleasure principle."

He believed that the function of government should be to secure as great a degree of individual freedom as possible, for freedom was the essential precondition of happiness. Utilitarianism in government was thus the securing of the "greatest happiness for the greatest number." If society could produce as much happiness as possible and as little pain as possible, it would be working at maximum efficiency. Bentham recognized what later liberals would eventually enact — that the government would have to help out at all levels — but he gave no precise prescriptions.

This task was left to John Stuart Mill (1806-1873), who affirmed that the interests of the owners and the workers did not necessarily coincide. He proposed the theory that government should, if necessary, pass legislation to remedy injustices. Mill, much more firmly than Bentham, stated that when the actions of businessmen harmed the people, the state should intervene for the people's protection. The liberal theory of minimum governmental interference in the economic life of the nation was effectively challenged, and altered in the direction of the humanitarian tradition instead of the profit margin.

Mill admitted that maximum freedom should be permitted in the production process, and that natural law should dictate, in so far as possible, the relationship of citizens. But he also pointed out that the distribution of wealth depends on the laws and customs of society, and that these can be changed by the will of men. He upheld the rights of property and free competition, but only within reasonable limits. The liberty of the individual was not absolute — it had to be subordinated to the wider interests of society. Mill's ideas proved to be the germ of the welfare state, but he had little effect on legislation during his lifetime.

Above is a painting of Brook Farm, with its various buildings and expansive landscape, done by Josiah Wolcott in 1844. Among the illustrious names that graced Brook Farm in the mid-1800's were Ralph Waldo Emerson and Louisa May Alcott.

Socialism. The conservative and liberal ideologies did not respond to the needs felt by a growing and restless element of European society—the working classes. The early stages of the Industrial Revolution had caused great hardship for many people in the cities and farms, and the ultimate promise of the great economic change was not clearly seen. An ideology developed that attacked the capitalistic system as being both unplanned and unjust. Socialism condemned the increasing concentration of wealth and called for public or worker ownership of business. The nature of the industrial system also raised serious problems, dividing worker and owner, and the socialists insisted that harmony and cooperation among all humanity, and not ruthless competition, should control economic affairs.

The socialists were convinced that human beings were essentially good, and with the proper organization of society, they foresaw a happy future when "there will be no wars, no crimes, no administration of justice, as it is called, no government. Besides, there will be neither disease, anguish, melancholy, nor resentment. Every man will seek with ineffable ardor, the good of all."[2] This humanitarian and optimistic spirit also had its roots in the eighteenth century.

The early socialists of the nineteenth century are known as the Utopians, a name they received in a critical blast from Karl Marx. The first prominent Utopian was a French nobleman, Claude Henri de Rouvroy, Count de Saint-Simon (1760-1825). He defined a nation as "nothing but a great industrial society" and politics as "the science of production." He argued that humanity should voluntarily adopt the rule of paternalistic despotism of scientists, technicians, and captains of industry who would "undertake the most rapid amelioration possible of the lot of the poorest and most numerous class."[3]

François Marie Charles Fourier (1772-1837), another French reformer, also believed that future society must be cooperative. He spent much time in working out an ideal plan for a communal living unit, which he called a "phalanstery." Although his plan was endorsed by many prominent men of the day, attempts to found cooperative Fourieristic communities were unsuccessful. The famous Brook Farm colony in Massachusetts was one such short-lived experiment.

A more practical reformer and Utopian socialist was Robert Owen (1771-1858), a successful mill owner in Scotland, who made New Lanark, the site of his textile mills, into a model community. Here, between 1815 and 1825, thousands of visitors saw rows of neat, well-kept workers' homes, a garbage collection system, schools for workers' children, and clean factories where the laborers were treated kindly and where no children under eleven were employed. In 1825 Owen moved to the vicinity of Evansville, Indiana, where he established the short-lived colony at New Harmony.

The Utopian socialists were blinded by their own optimism in regard to the nature of humanity. Such colonies as Brook Farm and New Harmony were based on the nice, though naive, notion that humankind naturally loved one another, or could be educated to that blissful level. Because of their impracticality the experiments failed. The notion that capitalism corrupted humanity and that it was essential to remove this system became an article of faith for subsequent socialists. But the Utopians' attempts to change the order of things were too limited. Further, they brought no answer to the depressed nineteenth-century working classes as a whole. Eventually, the Utopians' views were overwhelmed by Marx's more complete and far-reaching plans.

In addition to the Utopians, another nineteenth-century school of socialism arose that drew its inspiration from the teachings of Christianity. This group, the Christian socialists, aimed at showing that the doctrines of the Sermon on the Mount were socialistic in character. Abhorring violence and drawing on traditional ideas of a universal Christian community, the Christian socialists preached good will among all classes and favored the socialist colonies' experiments. They worked for reforms in factories and tried to instill into organized Christianity a realization of the social aspects of the teachings of Christ.

Another approach to the problems of the times — anarchism — found its basis in the ideas of the French theorist Pierre Joseph Proudhon (1809-1865). This idealistic revolutionary advocated the organization of society on a purely voluntary basis. The anarchists opposed all state compulsion, proposing instead free cooperation among the members of society. The capitalistic society, and along with it the whole concept of property, had to be radically altered. The state had to disappear before the new order could emerge.

As a consequence of this view, anarchism split into two wings, becoming a violent movement dedicated to mayhem and overthrow on the one extreme, and pacifism and idealism on the other.

The 1840's witnessed a great transformation in the nature of European political thought. The ideologies and movements of the period all shared an essentially abstract point of view in answering the eternal questions. Their responses varied, but within their frameworks the romantics, the liberals, and the Utopian socialists were trying to do what was best for humanity in the most idealistic sense. The period after 1850 would make different demands on the intellectuals and ideologists, and a more concrete set of answers would come to the questions.

THE MARXIAN CONTRIBUTION

The mid-century crisis. By 1848 it became evident to many socialists that to liberate humanity, society would have to be totally and perhaps forcefully reorganized. The romantic and reformist responses to many of the social dilemmas of industrialism had been insufficient. As a testimony to its inadequacy, socialism remained a minor factor in European political thought. Consciousness of the problems of the working class was limited, and the sporadic reform efforts that resulted in France and England were sufficient to defuse revolution.

The mid-century did not in any way mark the arrival of the workers as a major political force in Europe. But at that time Karl Marx made his major contribution to the field of battle through his version of scientific socialism. It came to be a wide-ranging theory that justified violent revolution, preached the inevitable conflict of the classes, repudiated much of traditional religion and morality, and condemned contemporary politics. Marx established the enduring basis for the modern Communist movements and changed the history of the world. His organized body of doctrine would remain long after the emotions and sentiments of the romantics had faded.

Karl Marx (1818-1883) made the major transition from the philosophical and rather abstract approaches to social problems, to the direct application of theory to actual problems. Born in the ancient German Rhineland city of Trier, the son of Jewish parents who had converted to Protestantism, Marx went to the University of Berlin to work for his doctor's degree in philosophy. While at the university he joined a circle of intellectuals who considered themselves to be young Hegelians. After finishing his degree, Marx failed to receive an appointment to a university teaching position, so he returned to the Rhineland where he began writing for a local liberal newspaper.

It was at this time, in the mid-1840's, that the philosopher became the ideologist, moving from the goals of understanding the world to changing it. He was struck by the inequities he saw around him, and his readings of the French socialists such as Saint-Simon and Proudhon made him more aware of the economic factors in history. He went to Paris to continue his studies, and there met Friedrich Engels (1820-1895), the son of a manufacturer, with whom he would have a close, lifelong friendship. In 1845 Marx was expelled from France, at the request of the Prussian government, and went to Belgium where he continued his ideological work. He sharpened his distaste for capitalism, and learned of the human problems caused by industrialization in England from Engels. By the end of 1847 he and Engels had completed what still remains the best short introduction to Marxism, *The Communist Manifesto*. The book appeared in various European cities by January 1848, but it had little effect on the revolutions that broke out in that year. Nonetheless, it would have a substantial delayed contribution.

The *Manifesto* is both a masterful summation of communism and a tract calculated to stir the emotions. It opens with one of the most dramatic proclamations to be found in political literature: "A spectre is haunting Europe—the spectre of Communism." He warned the various reactionary forces of what was to come:

This photograph, taken in the 1860's, shows Karl Marx and his family with Friedrich Engels. From left to right: Laura, Friedrich Engels, Eleanor, Marx's wife Jenny, and Karl Marx.

"The Communists disdain to conceal their views and aims. They openly declare that their ends can be attained only by the forcible overthrow of all existing social conditions. Let the ruling classes tremble at a Communistic revolution. The proletarians have nothing to lose but their chains. They have a world to win. Working men of all countries, unite!"[4]

Marx had hoped that the 1848 revolutions would be the dawn of the new era, but he, like so many others, would be seriously disappointed. He was forced to flee the continent and seek refuge in England after the revolutionary movement collapsed.

From that time until the 1860's, he and his family lived a life of minimum comfort. Marx was supported largely by contributions from Engels and his friends as he single-mindedly constructed his doctrine. Virtually every day he would make his way to the British Museum where he collected material for his major works, especially *Das Kapital*. At night he would return home to his small apartment and write late into the evening. Times were especially difficult for him during the 1850's, when three of his children—two sons and a daughter—died, mainly because of the wretched conditions in which they lived. He could not afford a coffin for his dead daughter, and had to be helped out by friends. Although his standard of living improved, he never did recover from the bad effects of these years on his and his family's health.

Throughout his life, as Engels stated in his eulogy, "His mission . . . was to contribute in one way or another to the overthrow of capitalist society . . . to contribute to the liberation of the present-day proletariat. . . . Fighting was his element." His fight was best waged in the theories he constructed.

Marx's theories. Karl Marx worked from the 1840's until his death in 1883 to develop his ideology. At heart he was an optimist, believing that, given the proper conditions, the individual could be perfected. But the individual existed as a part of society, totally tied in a relationship to the means of production. Marx saw the capitalistic society in the mid-nineteenth century as destructive of human potential. His gigantic status in the western tradition stems from the fact that he developed a truly universal system of thought. As is the case with other ideologists, he built on the foundations erected by others, but he expressed his theories with a certainty and force that compelled attention.

Marx held a materialistic conception of history, stating that economic forces basically determine the course of human history. He did not deny the existence or importance of spiritual or philosophical forces in history, but he asserted that these were responses to the more fundamental and material facets of life. All nonmaterial factors, such as patriotism, religion, and esthetics, were seen to be "ideological veils" which obscured reality. He wrote that "it is not the consciousness of men which determines their existence, but, on the contrary, it is the existence which determines their consciousness."

Since material factors were fundamental, the way in which society organized its material and economic bases was the primary focus of history. For Marx, all history could be explained primarily in terms of the social organization best adapted to the means of economic production. When the economic organization of any era changed, it took the whole social and ideological structure with it to a new phase of history.

The process through which history progresses was viewed by Marx in dialectical terms. He owed a debt to Hegel, who believed that history is made up of a number of culture periods, each one the expression of a dominant spirit or idea. After fulfilling its purpose, a period is confronted by another contradictory idea or set of values. In Hegel's terms, the traditional "thesis" is challenged by the new "antithesis." Out of this struggle there comes a "synthesis" of old and new. Then the cycle starts all over again. Hegel saw history as a process of unfolding, determined by an absolute purpose or idea, which many Hegelians called God. The machinery of change was labeled the "historical dialectic."

The dialectic's great advantage was that it gave a rhyme and reason for change, and also a sense of progression. Marx adopted this concept of change, but modified Hegel's approach by predicting an exact end to the process—the victory of the proletariat and achievement of the classless society. To Marx, the combatants in world history were material forces, not ideas. As certain groups came to control the means of production—and thus the material forces—they formed a dominant, or exploiting group, which oppressed the lower, or exploited class. The history of the world was seen in terms of a history of class struggle, with the opposing classes forming the various theses and antitheses, be it slave against master in ancient Greece, plebeian against patrician in Rome, serf against lord in the Middle Ages, or proletariat against bourgeoisie in the nineteenth century.

The bourgeoisie, who had created the new capitalist society by gaining control of the means of production through organizing trade and industry, were now opposed by the proletariat. This latter class was politically active and conscious of its rights as a class. The bourgeoisie had themselves created the factory system, and with it the "seeds of their own destruction," the proletariat. Because of the inexorable logic of the dialectic, it was inevitable that when the proletariat realized its true power, it would overthrow its natural enemy, the bourgeoisie. Out of this conflict would appear the new and final synthesis — the classless society, the ultimate social organization of the modern industrialized era. It would be a place of harmony in which "each person works according to his ability, and receives according to his need."

The transition to that final phase might not be smooth, and Marx predicted that it would perhaps be necessary for an intermediate period, the dictatorship of the proletariat, to occur. Immediately after the revolution, there would still be many of the features of the old order around, and a dictatorship would be necessary to protect the proletariat from regressing. As the classless society achieved its existence, however, the state would wither away.

Marx identified a number of defects in the bourgeois phase of history that would supply the energy to fuel the inevitable revolution, among them the concepts of alienation and surplus value. Marx saw that in contemporary society the individual could not realize his potential because of the oppression of the capitalists, which made the world not a place of the individual's own making, but a hostile place in which he has no control. Since he is divorced from his own productive potential, he feels alienated from the world, and sees himself as no more than a cog in the machine. Under the capitalist system, Marx noted that the worker was not fully paid for all of the value that he created. A worker could produce in six hours the necessary economic value to supply his needs. However, the employer would keep the workers producing goods for twelve hours. The employer, thereby, was in possession of a "surplus value" of six working hours, which he has stolen from the worker. From this surplus value the employer makes his profit, thus robbing the workers of the fruits of their work.

Marx also stated that in the capitalist economy there would be a concentration of capital in fewer hands as the most ruthless of the bourgeoisie destroy more and more of their competitors, forcing them into the ranks of the proletariat. As the rich became richer and fewer, and the poor, in comparison, became poorer and more numerous, the possibility of revolution would increase. Further, because the masses cannot buy all of the goods they produce, economic crises with overproduction and unemployment will become the rule. In time the contradictions between the classes will become so acute that the proletariat will rise up and take over the means of production. In the words of the *Manifesto:* "The knell of capitalism is sounded. The expropriators are expropriated." In the new society there would be no private property, no state, no church, no exploitation of one class by the other, and a perfect harmony among individuals working according to their abilities and receiving according to their needs. Marx, too, had his Utopia.

Flaws and critics. Marx's combative personality attracted a large number of critics during his lifetime, and the universal pretensions of his theories have preoccupied a large body of commentators even to the present day. Further, enthusiastic disciples have turned his theories, some of them carefully defined and discussed by him and Engels, into a new "ism" — Marxism. He has, in the process, suffered the fate of all great thinkers who must see their work transmitted by lesser minds and opportunistic politicians.

Marx can be attacked at a number of different points. He never laid out a detailed battle plan for achieving the revolution. Beyond stating that it would inevitably occur, he did not leave a good road map detailing how to find Utopia. He never fully explained the degree of state ownership that would be necessary for a communist society to exist.

He also used rather outmoded assumptions and statistics in his "scientific work." Marx's scientific nature is often that of the ideologist with an axe to grind and a set of statistics — cunningly chosen — to put a fine finish on the blade. Writing in the 1870's, he relied on figures for an earlier time. He was incredibly nearsighted regarding the strengths and weaknesses of capitalism. He never fully understood the corporate ownership of capitalism and always saw it as a system owned by richer and richer individuals. This bias can still be seen in contemporary Soviet presentations of the American economy. Marx misunderstood the tremendous strength of nationalism, clinging to the concept of a world of workers, international workers. Having viewed the Industrial Revolution during its most wretched phase in England, he was unable to note that capitalism could be a flexible economic system, one that could spread wealth to a far greater degree than Marx had anticipated.

His optimism about the perfectibility of humanity is somewhat contradictory to the alleged "scientific" presentation of his doctrines. In his description of the proletarian phase of his schema, he is as much a dreamer and a Utopian as any thinker in the past thousand years. Ironically, it is this optimism, harnessed to a seemingly inevitable set of historical laws, that gave Marx's theories their great appeal. If one accepts his assumptions, and if one is oppressed by forces he perceives to be bourgeois or capitalist, then one has a recipe for hope and eventual victory. The "scientific" arguments for one's own eventual triumph are certainly appealing. It is from this context that Marx's popularity must be viewed, not from the picky arguments of intellectuals and middle-class scholars. Marx gave a program of hope to those who were suffering. That his disciples, self-proclaimed though they are, have distorted much of the optimistic nature of his thought, is not Marx's fault.

The First International. A brief mention must be made of Marx's lack of success in the world of politics. In 1864 in London, he helped to found an international organization of workers, the International Workingmen's Association. The group failed to make much progress because of the various squabbling factions. Marx and his forces commanded the majority, but the minority of Anarchists, led by Bakunin and non-Marxian socialists, would not cooperate. Marx had advocated using the state as the agency for initiating the classless society. The Anarchists, who believed that human nature is in-

herently good but is warped and depraved by authority, refused to go along with this extension of state activity. The First International limped along with minimal results.

Marx also aided the organization of various socialist parties in Europe and throughout the world as he continued his active correspondence to the end of his life. His impact as a political activist, however, was infinitesimal when compared to the effect of his doctrines on subsequent events.

THE TRIUMPH OF SCIENCE

New realities. In the second half of the nineteenth century, European scientists made major advances in the areas of biology, chemistry, and physics. The effects of these discoveries were soon felt outside the laboratories. The precision and far-reaching qualities of the discoveries supported nicely the widespread admiration of the practical, "realistic" men who came to dominate political thought. Science, in the service of *Realpolitik* (realism in politics) could, some thought, enable Europe to attain ever higher stages of progress.

The idealistic movements had set their goals too high to be attained by 1850. Liberty, fraternity, and equality were admirable principles, but not easily applicable in a rapidly changing, technological world. There was, accordingly, a decline in the level of abstract, idealistic, and political theorizing, as European thinkers sought more and more to tie their philosophical positions to science and realism. The result was a misuse of science, especially the theories of Charles Darwin, and a blithe arrogance in political affairs. The new politicians and their apologists began to plot their courses with little reference to the larger issues that should be the concern of ideologies and politics, and instead concentrated on dealing with immediate and real issues at hand. Political nearsightedness resulted, but there was also a sense of certainty.

In this age of scientism, many Europeans became buttressed in the assumption of their superiority, and believed that they had a monopoly on scientific knowledge and, by implication, on civilization. Even Fourier had not doubted that the word "civilization" could be applied only to Europe. Thinkers throughout the continent implicitly believed in the superiority of western culture, thereby confusing scientific and technological strength with esthetic and moral quality.

In the last half of the century Europeans would go out into the world in the certainty of their superiority—the French to bring civilization, the British to carry the White Man's burden, the Germans to bring order and efficiency, and, incidentally, the Americans to pursue their "manifest destiny." Never had Europe been more certain. The nagging accusations of Karl Marx and the conflicts between nations and classes were sublimated under the undoubted genius of European accomplishments, and scientists were often the unwilling witnesses for the European case to the world.

Darwin and biological advances. No scientific discovery fit in better with the new European certainty than that made by Charles Darwin (1809-1882) in his book *On the Origin of Species by Means of Natural Selection* (1859). Darwin's theory of evolution stated that all complex organisms have developed from simple forms through the operation of natural causes, and that no species is fixed and changeless. This view was first stated by some classical philosophers, and supported by investigations in the eighteenth century. In the first part of the nineteenth century Sir Charles Lyell's important study, *Principles of Geology* (3 volumes, 1830-1833), confirmed the views held by the Scottish geologist James Hutton (1726-1797) that the earth's development resulted from natural rather than supernatural causes. Lyell (1797-1875) helped to popularize the conception of geological time operating over a vast span of years, an understanding that was essential for the acceptance of any theory of biological evolution based on changes in species over many thousands of generations.

In the area of biology, Jean Baptiste Lamarck (1744-1829) argued that every organism tends to develop new organs to adapt itself to the changing conditions of its envi-

Skepticism was a typical reaction to Darwin's *The Origin of Species*. This *Punch* cartoon about the evolutionary process portrays man evolving from a worm through all of the intermediate stages, including a grotesque "missing link."

ronment. He theorized that these changes are transmitted by heredity to the descendants, which are thereby changed in structural form.

Darwin had these points of reference when he began his work on evolution. He had originally studied medicine and prepared for the ministry at Cambridge University, but in his twenties he became a naturalist. From 1831 to 1836 he studied the specimens he had collected while on a surveying expedition with the ship *Beagle*, which had sailed along the coast of South America and among the Galápagos Islands. The works of his predecessors, plus questions that were raised in his reading of Malthus' *Essay on Population*, served to help him define the problem that he pursued. Finally his book appeared, and in it was found the portentous statement that altered so many basic social and scientific conceptions:

. . . Species have been modified, during a long course of descent . . . chiefly through the natural selection of numerous successive, slight, favorable variations; aided in an important manner . . . by the direct action of external conditions, and by variations which seem to us in our ignorance to arise spontaneously.[5]

In this revolutionary work Darwin constructed an interpretation of how life evolves that upset the literal interpretation of the Bible found in many Christian churches. It radically affected the views of the scientific community about the origin and evolution of life on the planet. Further, through almost instantaneous popularization (it was originally printed in an edition of 1250 copies) the theory of evolution came to be widely read—and misapplied—in a broad variety of areas.

The dominant middle class responded enthusiastically to Darwin's points, finding a comfortable assurance of their own recently acquired position. The Darwinian hypothesis, when simplified, stated that all existing plant and animal species are descended from earlier, and generally speaking, more rudimentary forms. The direct effect of the environment causes species to evolve through the inheritance of minute differences in individual structures. In the struggle for survival, the fittest win out at the expense of their rivals. A species may also be changed by the cumulative workings of sexual selection, which Darwin declared to be the "most powerful means of changing the races of man." Some variations arise spontaneously, a view of Darwin's which pointed toward the doctrine of mutation.

The point that most appealed to the newly dominant middle classes was that regarding the survival of the fittest, and this aspect was emphasized in subsequent popularizations. The middle classes might employ the Darwinian theory to support their belief in the inevitable improvement of humanity; but while they shared this conviction with the romanticists, they had lost much of the latter's idealism and optimism.

After Darwin's evolutionary theories were announced, others working along similar lines helped to transform biology from a descriptive science into the search for genetic relationships between living organisms. In the 1870's the German biologist August Weismann (1834-1914), basing his research on an earlier theory that all living things originate and develop in very small structural units, or cells, distinguished two types of cells. One type—the somatic cell—dies with the individual, while the other—the germ cell—transmits through reproduction a continuous stream of protoplasm from one generation to the next. Later, Weismann produced experimental evidence that germ cells, which transmit hereditary characteristics, are not affected by changes in the somatic cells—in other words, that acquired characteristics cannot be inherited.

An Austrian monk, Gregor Mendel (1822-1884) formulated definite laws of heredity on the basis of experiments with the crossing of garden peas. Although he published his results in 1866, his work was not recognized until the end of the century. Mendel's laws not only proved a valuable help in the scientific breeding of plants and animals, but also demonstrated that the evolution of different species was more complex than had been deduced by Darwin.

From the works of Mendel and Weismann, biologists began to conclude that the nuclei of the germ cells possess chromosomes which carry the characteristics of an organism. Further research supported the mutation theory, which states that sudden and unpredictable changes within the chromosomes can be transmitted by heredity to produce new species. Scientists began to work with the very fundamental building blocks of life. The basis for the genetic engineering that is being experimented with in the last part of the twentieth century was established a hundred years ago.

Other scientific advances. In the last half of the nineteenth century, similar revolutions were underway in medicine, chemistry, and physics. In the first half of the century, medical practices were making the slow transition from the use of leeches and bleeding in 1800 to the fairly sophisticated surgical procedures available by the century's end. In the 1840's ether and chloroform began to be used to alleviate pain during operations. Major advances were later made in stopping the spread of infection into a wound by the Scottish surgeon Joseph Lister (1827-1912).

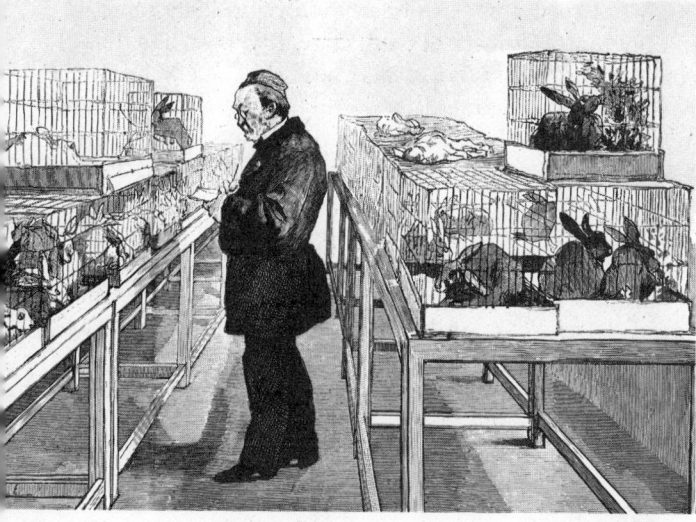

A nineteenth-century issue of the French magazine *L'Illustration* pictures Louis Pasteur in his laboratory.

Probably the most important single advance during the century was the substantiation of the germ theory of disease by Louis Pasteur (1822-1895) and Robert Koch (1843-1910). As a result of his search for a cure for anthrax, a fatal disease which in the late 1870's was destroying over 20 percent of the sheep in France, Pasteur established the principle that the injection of a mild form of disease bacteria will cause the formation of antibodies that will prevent the vaccinated person from getting the virulent form of a disease. Koch discovered the specific organisms that caused eleven diseases, including tuberculosis. As a result of the work of Pasteur and Koch, the twin sciences of bacteriology and immunology were placed on a firm footing, and the end of such deadly diseases as typhoid and smallpox was in sight.

Modern chemistry gained its foundations during this century, founded on the atomic theory advanced by an English Quaker schoolmaster, John Dalton (1766-1844). In 1869 the Russian chemist, Dmitri Mendeleev (1834-1907), drew up the period table in which all known elements were classified according to their weights and properties. From gaps in this table, chemists were able to deduce the existence of still other undiscovered elements. Advances were also made in the area of nutrition, in which the true significance of vitamins was discovered in 1912. Biochemical research threw light on the presence and function of the ductless glands. Chemotherapy made similarly large advances during the time with the discovery of a chemical that could destroy the syphilis bacteria, and of procedures that would lead to the discovery of sulfa drugs, penicillin, and other antibiotics.

Revolutionary developments occurred in physics during the century, in the areas of electricity and thermodynamics, in which the first law was formulated in 1847. Michael Faraday (1791-1867) prepared the way for the perfection of the dynamo, a device that would ultimately make possible changes in communication, including the transmission of current over long distances, and the development of the electric motor.

The Scottish scientist James Clerk-Maxwell (1831-1879) and the German Heinrich Hertz (1857-1894) conducted basic research into the nature of electromagnetic phenomena such as light, radiant heat, and ultraviolet radiation. By 1895 the X-ray and radioactivity were discovered. Pierre and Marie Curie (1859-1906 and 1867-1934) extracted radium from uranium ore in 1896, and the world began to become aware of the strength of radioactivity.

Perhaps the most important discovery was that made by the British physicist, Ernest Rutherford (1871-1937), who helped develop the electron theory. It was postulated that the atom contains negatively charged particles, known as electrons. Rutherford's contribution was his theory that each atom has a central particle, or nucleus, which is positively charged and separate from the electrons. These discoveries destroyed one of the foundation stones of traditional physics—that matter was indivisible and continuous.

NEW "CERTAINTIES"

Social Darwinism. The triumphs of science in the laboratory soon were to be applied to society, with varying degrees of success. The French philosopher Auguste Comte

(1798-1857) anticipated this tendency in a series of lectures and publications in the 1830's and 1840's. He stated that one could find the laws that controlled society in the same way that a scientist discovered physical laws. He saw humanity as part of a machine with neither free will nor the spark of God. Comte devised a new "science" to discover these laws—sociology—and stated that once humanity could rest its actions on science, and not on opinion, harmony would arise. He is also known as the father of positivism, a mechanistic way of thought that fit in nicely with the emphasis on "realism" in the last half of the nineteenth century.

The positivists, and people like them, took and abused Darwin's theories by applying them to areas Darwin had never dreamed of discussing. The dream of eternal progress, the dominance of science, the perfecting of humanity through obedience to the immutable laws of society, all found expression in the concept of Social Darwinism, the application of Darwin's biological concept of "the survival of the fittest" to human social, economic, and political activities. The simplistic approaches of the positivists and others of their kind are based on the theory that humanity is a cog in a machine. Their descendants live on to give easy answers to complex problems.

Intellectuals such as the English philosopher Herbert Spencer (1820-1903) sought to apply Darwin's theories dealing with organic matter to all aspects of human social and political life, and he had a profound influence in both Europe and the United States. Social Darwinism dominated western thought in the late nineteenth century since it was a convenient doctrine to justify the actions and philosophies of those atop the social structure.

Stressing the role of change and chance in nature, the Darwinian theory enforced the trend away from absolute standards and procedures. The American physicist Charles Sanders Peirce (1839-1914) broke new philosophic ground in this area. In the late 1890's, William James (1842-1910) popularized the approaches discussed by Peirce under the name of pragmatism. James stated, "An idea is true so long as to believe it is profitable to our lives." In effect, the pragmatists rejected any concept of truth or reality as an absolute.

New identities. The rapid social, political, economic, and intellectual changes that shook Europe led to new ways of defining individuals and groups. In the last half of the century European nationalism took on more blatant and bellicose qualities. The diversity that characterized the continent's people was sharpened by nationalistic strife. Aggressive nationalism became a new religion, and an effective way for politicians to mobilize their constituents. Nationalistic pressures became especially strong in Eastern Europe and the Balkans as political instability and economic underdevelopment created insecure conditions.

During the century several attempts were made to unite large ethnic groups into continent-wide movements. The Pan Slav movements which had begun before 1850 took on significant proportions in the last part of the century, as the Russian ideologists proclaimed Russia's destiny to create and rule a great Slavic empire. By the 1890's the Pan Germanic League had been organized to spread the belief in the superiority of the German race and culture.

On a global scale, spokesmen for the Anglo-Saxons and the Teutons espoused their superiority. In England and Germany it was believed that the world's leadership should naturally reside in London and Berlin, because the peoples there possessed the proper combination of religion, racial qualities, and culture to dictate the world's future.

During the last part of the century, modern "scientific" racism made its appearance. The application of biological theory to politics, whereby a nation is regarded as an organism, constituted perhaps the most perverted form of the use of science. One of the most influential advocates of this view was Joseph Arthur de Gobineau (1816-1882), who argued that different races are innately unequal in ability and worth, and that the genius of a race depended upon hereditary and not environmental factors. Gobineau stated a widely held belief among Europeans that the white peoples were alone capable of cultural creativity, and that intermixture with other races would destroy that creativity. Social

Darwinism fit naturally into such a schema to justify the European dominance on "scientific" grounds.

Latent anti-Semitism—hatred of the Jews—has been a part of European history since the widespread introduction of Christianity. But the movement attained a new strength and vigor in the last part of the century during the time of the new certainties. In Germany Heinrich von Treitschke (1834-1896) coined the phrase "The Jews are our calamity." In France anti-Semitism reached a climax in the scandal surrounding the expulsion of Alfred Dreyfus (1859-1935) from the French army. In Eastern Europe and Russia the Jewish minorities suffered many injustices.

As a response, the desire for a Jewish homeland grew among the Jews. In 1896 Theodor Herzl (1860-1904) came forward with the program of Zionism, which had as its purpose the creation of an independent state within Palestine. The first general congress of Zionists was held in Switzerland in 1897, and small-scale immigration to Palestine began. The tragic racial events of the twentieth century were presaged in its first decade when Karl Lueger successfully ran for mayor in Vienna, and stayed in power on an anti-Semitic platform. It was in this atmosphere that the young Adolf Hitler would spend some of his formative years.

The Christian response. The Christian churches faced severe challenges on all sides as they reacted to the forces released by the French Revolution, Napoleon, the scientific discoveries, and the new political and ideological forces. Darwin's discoveries and their subsequent widespread acceptance played havoc with the traditional Christian view of the origins of the world as contained in Genesis. A strong school of biblical criticism developed, mainly within the Protestant communities, to subject Holy Scriptures to rigid historical examination. It could be argued that the faith emerged stronger for the experience of the challenges, but it was not a pleasant episode for the major figures involved.

In 1864 Pope Pius IX (1846-1878) issued the *Syllabus of Errors*, which attacked the critical examination of faith and doctrine. In 1870 he called a general council of the Church, the first in centuries, to proclaim the doctrine of papal infallibility. By the end of the century, however, his successor, Leo XIII (1878-1903) reversed the Church's stand to a certain extent. In his pronouncement *Rerum novarum* ("concerning new things") in 1891, he inaugurated what became known as "Christian democracy." Leo condemned Marxism and upheld capitalism, but he also severely criticized the evils affecting the working classes. To improve their lives, he advocated social legislation and the formation of Catholic labor unions and political parties.

The emphasis of the romantic movement on the individual and emotionalism aided the evangelical Protestants. The Methodists continued their growth in England and the United States, while on the continent the evangelical manifestations of pietism reached to affect individuals as diverse as the Tsar of Russia, Alexander I, and German settlers in Bessarabia. Middle-class propriety was built around church attendance, and the churches were built and rebuilt, and generally filled on Sunday. The rapid changes through which Europe was passing brought pressure on the Protestants too, and severe doctrinal disagreements led to the creation of the large number of Protestant denominations that exist today.

SUMMARY

The century that had begun with the romantics reacting to the classicism of a more ordered age ended with evolution, atomic energy, and anti-Semitism. Perhaps most of the peasants of Europe were not directly touched by the ideological and intellectual ferment that stretched and tested the European mind. But the extent and nature of the range of knowledge was much more varied than it had been in 1800. This change did not imply a greater amount of wisdom, just a broader spectrum of choices. The fundamental questions that motivated the thinkers and theorists remained the same, however, except to a few dogmatic positivists who still saw humanity as part of a machine. In 1914 there was a choice of answers to those questions ranging from the anarchist, to the Marxist, to the liberal, to the racist.

Europe's material and economic strength had unquestionably expanded in the course of the century, and the intellectuals and theorists matched this growth with a proliferation of ideologies and scientific discoveries. Romanticism contributed to this expansion by emphasizing the individual response to the challenges and questions of life. This sanctioning of individual thought and the democratic assumptions implicit in the value placed on the individual's creations generated a wide variety of activity in various parts of Europe. Most importantly, romanticism acted as a catalyst for the formation of the modern nationalist movements which helped to define the goals, values, and identities of the continent's diverse peoples.

Other major ideological positions also took shape during the first part of the century in response to the changing conditions. Conservatism reacted to the reforms and forces emerging from the French Revolution and tried to reestablish a tie to the organic processes of the previous century. Liberalism sought to take advantage of the increased opportunities for the middle-class individual that were presented by the Revolution and the industrialization process. Working through parliaments, parties, and financial interest groups, the liberals gained great success in placing their goals before the public and in gaining power. The socialist schools that emerged during the first part of the century attempted to respond to the needs of the working classes and peasants. Stressing the goal of equality, the various socialist ideologists worked for a more equitable distribution of wealth. Hampered by the weakness of their constituency and their idealism, the early socialists were unable to make more than symbolic contributions. By mid-century the dreams of the French Revolution—liberty, fraternity, and equality—had not been attained in the forms as defined in 1789. New conditions and new forces called for new ideologies.

Karl Marx gave one ideological formula to the industrial world that has remained as a viable force, if in altered form, today. Marx declared the capitalist world in which he lived to be obsolete, and he devised a universal ideology that gave not only an explanation to world history and an analysis of the present, but also a definition of ideals and a formula for the future. His ideology would not gain major success in terms of power during the nineteenth century, but it did gain the roots needed to affect our days.

The major scientific advances made during the century revolutionized the understanding of many things that were previously mysteries, among them the understanding of human development, the nature of the atom, the geological history of the earth, and the nature of disease. Humanity gained the foundations for both self-destruction and an infinitely better life. The ways in which these discoveries would be used to achieve either result still hang in the balance.

The initial application of scientific discoveries, on the public stage, did not give immediate cause for optimism. The work of serious theoretical scientists came to be used by less admirable public figures and intellectuals to justify European dominance, racism, and an inequitable social and economic structure. Less profound thinkers misused the discoveries of Darwin and constructed new certainties about their superiority. Underneath the popularly accepted veneer of belief in inevitable progress, there appeared new doubts and fears. The eighteenth century had, in its classic forms, standards, values, and morals which were observed in theory, if not in practice. The nineteenth-century's thinkers had, in their incredibly active era, bequeathed a legacy of flux.

SUGGESTIONS FOR READING

H. D. Aiken, ed., **The Age of Ideology: The Nineteenth Century Philosophers***(Mentor) explores selections from the works of Hegel, Mill, and others. For a brief study of Marx and his ideas, see I. Berlin, **Karl Marx: His Life and Environment*** (Galaxy). R. Payne, **Marx** (Simon & Schuster, 1968) provides a portrait of the personal life of Marx. For a lively interpretation of the great economic philosophers see Robert L. Heilbroner, **The Worldly Philosophers,** 4th ed. (Touchstone). There are many paperback editions of the writings of Marx and Engels available, among them are K. Marx and F. Engels, L. S. Feuer, ed., **Basic Writings on Politics and Philosophy*** (Anchor). See also G. Hegel, J. Loewenberg, ed., **Selections*** (Scribner's); and K. Marx, S. Levitsky, ed., **Das Kapital*** (Gateway).

One of the nicest general surveys of nineteenth-century European thought is to be found in G. L. Mosse, **The Culture of Western Europe, The Nineteenth and Twentieth Centuries: An Introduction*** (Rand McNally). Edmund Wilson, **To the Finland Station*** (Anchor) remains one of the best, most literate surveys of the development of socialism. See also works by Adam Smith, Jeremy Bentham, and John Stuart Mill for a study of liberalism and its various interpretations. For a study of conservatism, see Hans Rogger and Eugen Weber, eds., **The European Right: A Historical Profile** (Univ. of Calif.).

C. Darwin, **Voyage of the Beagle*** (Anchor, 1962) is a journal of Darwin's experiences and observations about natural history and geology that led to his writing **On the Origin of Species*** (Collier). Making use of unpublished documents, G. Himmelfarb, **Darwin and the Darwinian Revolution** (Norton, 1968) sheds valuable light on both the character of Darwin and the age in which he lived. C. C. Gillispie, **Genesis and Geology: The Decades Before Darwin*** (Harper & Row) is a review of the controversy between religion and science which preceded the publication of **On the Origin of Species.** The involvement of Darwin and Thomas Huxley in the intellectual furor is dealt with in W. Irvine, **Ape, Angels, & Victorians: The Story of Darwin, Huxley & Evolution*** (McGraw-Hill). In R. Hofstadter, **Social Darwinism in American Thought*** (Beacon) the author details the cult of force, struggle, and militarism in the United States during the period of social Darwinism.

Excellent biographies of important scientific researchers include W. W. Cheyne, **Lister and His Achievements** (Longmans, 1925); E. Curie, **Madame Curie*** (Pocket Books); and R. Dubos, **Louis Pasteur: Free Lance of Science** (Little, Brown, 1950). See also B. Hoffman and H. Dukas, **Albert Einstein** (Viking, 1972). J. Bronowski, **The Ascent of Man*** (Little, Brown, 1976) is an invaluable and humane treatment of the development of science. O. Mannoni, **Freud*** (Vintage, 1974) is a good introduction to the life of the psychologist.

A valuable survey of the last years of the period is Heinz Gollwitzer, **Europe in the Age of Imperialism: 1880-1914*** (Harcourt Brace Jovanovich).

*Indicates a less expensive paperbound edition.

CHAPTER 25

From the Politics
of Reaction
to the Politics of Power:
1815-1871

Political Responses to Changing Conditions: The Half Century After Waterloo

INTRODUCTION. The upheaval created by the French Revolution and the Napoleonic wars left Europe in a disorganized state by 1815. The previous twenty-six years had witnessed the development of powerful economic changes, the emergence of radical new cultural and intellectual currents, and the redrawing of the political map. The leaders of Europe faced unsettled conditions as they tried to put their nations' affairs in order. Rarely in history had statesmen had to adjust to forces as earthshaking as the Industrial Revolution, the emergence of the middle classes, and the challenges of nationalism, liberalism, and socialism.

In this chapter we will discuss the variety of political responses to the changing conditions by those individuals both in and out of power during the half century after Waterloo. In 1815 most of the crowned heads of Europe and their representatives met in Vienna to build a political system that would apply conservative solutions to the aftermath of a revolutionary epoch. In the next decade the Concert of Europe tried to maintain the 1815 system by putting down any attempts to upset the status quo. This unsatisfactory response to changing conditions on the continent would lead to a rash of revolutionary outbreaks.

The political structure built at Vienna could not control the currents of individualism, freedom of thought, pride in nation, and equality under the law that had been unleashed after 1789 by the French attack on the Old Regime. Although the military battles were finished by 1815 and peace was at hand, the middle classes and underprivileged in many parts of Europe remained dedicated to these liberal concepts. As we have seen, liberalism emphasized individual freedom and rights in both politics and economics and the exercise of power through the voting box and representative government. The settlement at Vienna did not satisfy the middle classes, who came increasingly to advocate liberalism, and most of the governments on the continent tried to ignore their demands. In addition, the spirit of nationalism had taken hold, either as a direct response to French dominance as in Germany or indirectly through the effects of the romantic movement in Eastern Europe. The forces of liberalism and nationalism sparked a flurry of revolts that broke out in Spain, Italy, and Greece in 1820 and 1821 and in France, Belgium, and Poland in 1831. After these tests showed the weaknesses of the 1815 structure, the revolutions of 1848 across the continent completed the destruction of the reactionary position established at Vienna.

At the geographical extremes of the continent—England and Russia—the pattern of widespread outbreaks and unrest described above did not occur. England showed the capacity for political adaptability and institutional flexibility that enabled it to avoid serious popular strife. Russia, after the Decembrist revolt in 1825, endured a thirty-year period of reaction and repression that effectively snuffed out any possibility of serious political disturbances. By the end of the period, however, the strengths of the first and the weaknesses of the second would be easily apparent.

After the 1848 watershed France, the Germanies, the Hapsburg monarchy, and the Italian states experienced major political changes. France would turn to another member of the Bonaparte family to try an imperial path to achieve its destiny. In Prussia, after a period of constitutional crisis, Otto von Bismarck would make his appearance on the political stage and would help bring about the unification of Germany. The Hapsburg monarchy would struggle unsuccessfully with its nationalities problems before making a major compromise in 1867. The Italian peninsula, under the leadership of Sardinia, would achieve political unity.

Running through the century was the unanswered Eastern Question posed by the disintegrating Ottoman empire and its very strategic control of the Straits, and ultimately, the Eastern Mediterranean. The close attention of all of the great powers would be drawn to the area by the Crimean War and its aftermath, but the Eastern Question would remain unanswered.

STABILITY AND STRESS

The settlement at Vienna. During Napoleon's exile on Elba in September 1814, representatives from every European power except the Ottoman empire gathered at Vienna to build a new political and diplomatic structure for Europe. As is often the case, once the object of the wartime alliance—in this case the French emperor—had been successfully disposed of, the participants could return to the pursuit of their own interests. Their work went slowly during the ten-month-long Congress. Most of the major decisions about the future of the continent were made in small secret conferences of the leaders—Tsar Alexander I of Russia, Lord Castlereagh of Great Britain, Talleyrand of France, and Prince von Metternich of Austria. Metternich came to dominate the conference, as much by

This engraving of a painting by J. B. Isabey depicts Europe's statesmen gathered at the Congress of Vienna being introduced to the Duke of Wellington, seen in profile at the far left. Metternich is standing before an empty chair, and Talleyrand appears at the right with his arm resting on the table. Although there was a great deal of work to do at the Congress of Vienna, there was also opportunity for entertainment and relaxation. The illustration at right shows a horse show staged to amuse the distinguished guests.

his diplomatic skill as by his ability to impress on the participants the need for stability on the continent.

The Congress dealt with substantial issues, as it had to decide the status of post-Napoleonic France, define the new set of political boundaries, and gauge the proper response to the new democratic, liberal, and nationalistic sentiments that were sweeping the continent. In the first instance, the victorious allies chose not to be vengeful toward France and to allow her, at first, the same boundaries that she had possessed in 1792. After Napoleon's escape from Elba and his so-called "Hundred Days" of freedom, he was defeated at Waterloo. The enthusiastic response of much of the French population caused the Congress later to cut back the boundaries and impose a war indemnity. Nevertheless, the French boundaries were more extensive than they had been in 1789.

The revolutionary and Napoleonic wars had led to a drastic revision of the European map, including the disappearance of the Holy Roman Empire. To place Europe back on a pre-Napoleonic footing, four principles

were followed: legitimacy, encirclement of France, compensations, and balance of power. Under the first principle, the Congress determined that those royal houses which had been expelled from their thrones, such as the Bourbons in France, Spain, and Naples, the House of Savoy in Sardinia-Piedmont, and the House of Orange in Holland, would be returned. The new map of Europe would resemble the 1789 map, with the exception that the Holy Roman Empire would remain dissolved. In the place of the hundreds of independent governments formerly existing in Germany, the thirty-nine remaining German states were retained and organized into the German Confederation, to be dominated by Austria. In the process of redrawing the boundaries, the Congress constructed a protective belt to surround France and to make future French aggression more difficult.

The principle of compensation assured that no important power suffered a major territorial loss as a result of the post-Napoleonic readjustments. For example, Austria was compensated for the loss of the Austrian

Netherlands by gaining territory in Italy and along the Adriatic coast, and Sweden received Norway in return for permitting Russia to keep Finland.

The desire to reestablish the balance of power remained at the center of the Congress' attentions. As each of the large powers pursued its self-interest, conflicts became apparent over the exact definition of what constituted a proper European balance of power. Russia's ambitions in Poland endangered the negotiations, and Britain believed that an enlarged Russian state was a threat to peace. Prussia wanted all of Saxony, while Austria feared a growing Prussia. While the victors disputed, Talleyrand wormed his way into the good graces of Britain and Austria. A secret treaty was arranged, pledging the three countries to use force, if necessary, to restrain Russia and Prussia. The latter two powers eventually reduced their claims for more Polish and Saxon territory in the face of the French, British, and Austrian front, and a balance of power was achieved that endured until mid-century.

The Congress of Vienna has been criticized because it virtually ignored the democratic, liberal, and nationalistic forces that had gained strength since 1789. Yet in looking to gain a pre-Napoleonic settlement, the political leaders were not totally and blindly reactionary. Many of the changes that had occurred as a result of the French Revolution and the Napoleonic wars were retained. The forty years of general peace that followed is testimony to the success of Metternich and his colleagues in gaining stability. But by refusing to acknowledge the forces of change, the new political system that followed insured its own ultimate failure.

Order and revolution. To protect the structure of stability that had been erected at the Congress of Vienna, the great powers set out to coordinate their policies. Symbolically, in the autumn of 1815 Tsar Alexander had proposed the formation of a Holy Alliance to be based on "the precepts of justice, Christian charity, and peace." No one was quite sure what Alexander meant by this pact, but every ruler in Europe signed it except the king of England, the Turkish sultan, and the pope. The Holy Alliance may well have been, as Castlereagh stated, "a piece of sublime mysticism and nonsense," but it expressed the tsar's view that perhaps a new age had arrived, one of unity and cooperation.

In November 1815 Austria, Prussia, Russia, and England signed the Quadruple Alliance. Three years later it became the Quintuple Alliance when France joined the great powers. For a few years thereafter, the allies pursued their goals through what came to be known as the Congress System, a formidable European-wide network for maintaining order, tranquility, and stability which was a truly significant experiment in collective security.

After 1818, Metternich and his partners had to deal with the forces of nationalism and liberalism. In the Germanies, Greece, Spain, Italy, and Latin America national and liberal movements posed a severe challenge to the laboriously reconstructed status quo. The most violent revolutions broke out against the reactionary regimes in Italy and Spain. In 1820, in response to the misgovernment of the restored Spanish Bourbon King Ferdinand VII, there was a mutiny in the Spanish army. This touched off a general uprising that forced Ferdinand to give in to the rebels' demands for a representative government based on a liberal constitution. The news of the successful Spanish revolt spread rapidly to the Kingdom of Naples and Sicily, governed by a Neapolitan Bourbon king, Ferdinand I. Much the same results occurred there, as the king was forced to grant his people a constitution patterned after the Spanish model.

Metternich arranged for the Congress System allies to meet at Troppau and Laibach in 1820 and 1821 to deal with the revolution in Italy. Ferdinand I appeared at Laibach, supported intervention, reneged on his granting of the constitution, and welcomed the arrival of Austrian troops that eventually placed him back on his throne. In 1822 the Congress System participants convened at Verona to consider intervention in Spain. The French, themselves ruled by a restored branch of the Bourbon family, volunteered to put the affairs of Spain in order, and sent in their army to crush the Spanish liberals.

The Congress System's victories in Spain and Italy marked the high point of reactionary success. The System was weakened by England's withdrawal after 1820 into "splendid isolation" from permanent international commitments on the continent. The growing strength of English liberalism played an important role in forcing the government away from its ultraconservative allies. Then, the allies overreached themselves when they tried to restore the Spanish king's authority over his rebellious subjects in Latin America. Great Britain cared little for the renewal of Spanish control in the new world, and the threat of the British fleet exercised a sobering influence on the reactionaries. As if British opposition was not enough, President James Monroe in 1823 warned the European states that the United States would view the proposed intervention in Latin America as an unfriendly act. A combination of the strengths of the new revolutionary forces and the narrowly defined self-interest of the allies would be sufficient to put an end to the Congress System in the 1820's.

1830: RESTORATION AND REVOLUTION

The Bourbons restored. In 1814 and 1815 Louis XVIII, the new French king and brother of the slain Louis XVI, assumed the difficult task of leading France out of the previous quarter century of revolution and Napoleonic rule into a new state of reconciliation with the Bourbon family. He tried to blend elements of the revolutionary period with the remnants of the old regime. The mixture of the two provided a basis of instability that plagued the country throughout the century. He "granted" his subjects a charter that established a form of constitutional monarchy. The king kept all executive power, controlled legislation, and dictated the composition of the legislature. In terms of social, religious, and legal rights, there was little attempt made to return to the institutions of the old regime. Louis kept Napoleon's Civil Code, the Concordat with the papacy, and the bu-

reaucratic reforms of the Napoleonic period. In short, the restoration was moderate in nature, but it had the backing of only a minority of the French population. The ultraconservatives felt that the charter conceded too much to the bourgeoisie while the liberals and radicals asserted that Louis XVIII had not gone far enough in making reforms. The king tried to steer a middle course in his nine years on the throne, but his attempts were unacceptable to both sides.

Louis was succeeded on his death in 1824 by his brother, Charles X, who had no concern for maintaining the political balance. He did not accept any of the changes of the age, and in 1829 announced that he "would rather saw wood than be a king of the English type." So out of tune was he to the spirit of his age that in July 1830 he drove the usually submissive legislature to the point that it refused to support his ultraroyalist program. In response, Charles immediately dissolved the legislature and at the same time issued a series of ordinances gagging the press and limiting the right to vote even further. Galled by this violation of the constitution, liberal leaders, journalists, and radicals protested and rose in rebellion. At the end of July the then narrow streets of Paris were blocked with overturned carts, boxes, tables, and paving stones. Behind these barriers crouched the armed revolutionaries who ably held off the fire of the soldiers.

After three days a new liberal faction took over the government, and Charles fled to England and exile. A new government was put together under an agreement between the French republicans—led by the aging Marquis de Lafayette, hero of the American Revolution and the first years of the French Revolution—and the liberal monarchist supporters of the Orleans branch of the Bourbon family. The new king, Louis Philippe, who came to be known as the "citizen king," more accurately reflected the interests of the upper-middle classes.

1830 in Belgium and Poland. Tremors of the July Revolution in Paris were felt throughout the continent, but only in Belgium did the liberals achieve any lasting results. After the Congress of Vienna, the Belgians had been united with Holland under

The barricades, symbol of revolution in France, are immortalized in Eugène Delacroix' painting of the July Revolution of 1830, "Liberty Leading the People" (1831).

the Dutch crown. This union proved to be an unhappy one because of the wide cultural differences that separated the two peoples: The Dutch were mainly Protestant, the Belgians, Catholics; the Dutch were seafarers and traders, the Belgians, farmers and industrial workers; and in addition there were linguistic and economic conflicts between the two peoples.

In August, Belgian liberals requested that King William I of Orange grant them their own administration. When action was not forthcoming, rioting sprouted in Brussels and Dutch troops were sent in to put the revolution down. After repulsing the Dutch forces, the Belgians declared their independence and drew up a liberal constitution. In the meantime, William appealed to conserva-

tive forces for aid, but none was forthcoming as most of the major powers had all but given up the old principle of legitimacy as a pretext for intervention. In the summer of 1831 the Belgian national assembly met in Brussels, and chose Prince Leopold of Saxe-Coburg-Gotha as king. Finally, by a settlement in 1839 the international status of the new state was settled, and Belgium was recognized to be a "perpetually neutral state."

Not every country that rose up in the cause of liberal and nationalistic principles gained success in 1830. As a consequence of the Congress of Vienna, the Poles in and around Warsaw gained a special status within the Russian empire with their own constitution and substantial powers of local government, granted in 1818. After the death of Alexander ı in 1825, the Poles became more and more restless under the rule of the reactionary Tsar Nicholas ı. The Polish intellectuals were strongly affected by the influence of romanticism, and found a distinct contradiction as they compared the glories of their past with their status as a powerless, stateless nationality. The Poles had been strongly affected by the July Revolution in Paris, and in the winter of 1830-31 they rose in rebellion against the Russians. Internally divided and badly outmanned and outgunned, the rebels were crushed. Ironically, by drawing the attention of the Russian army to Warsaw for half a year, the Poles may well have kept Nicholas from answering the Dutch King William's call for help, and thereby helped save the Belgian revolution.

THE CALM BEFORE THE STORM: 1830-1848

The "citizen king." After the July Revolution Louis Philippe, the duke of Orleans, took the French throne. From the first he took great pains to exhibit a new, bourgeois point of view. Like William ııı of England after the Glorious Revolution of 1688, he received the crown from the people, and became known as the "citizen king." The rule of popular sovereignty replaced that of divine right, and as a token of this the revolutionary tricolor once more replaced the white flag of the Bourbons as the emblem of France.

Within a year the new king began to be criticized heavily by radicals who felt that their interests were being ignored. The government's policies supported the upper-middle classes, and virtually shut the workers and lower-middle classes out of the political arena. What had been assumed to be the first broad middle-class-dominated government on the continent turned out to be responsive only to a narrow part of the political spectrum. Yet, during Louis' reign France enjoyed prosperity and industrial growth, and the new government followed a moderate path in trying to maintain the status quo.

Had Louis ruled in more stable times his

In his early years on the throne the "king of the bourgeoisie," Louis Philippe, made a point of walking about the streets of Paris in a frock coat and top hat and carrying a walking stick like any solid middle-class citizen. For a time he allowed ordinary citizens to flock through his palace, much as their American contemporaries poured through the White House during the presidency of Andrew Jackson.

reign might have been more successful. The rapid changes introduced by the Industrial Revolution brought about workers' protests. The laboring classes accurately sensed that the government ignored their legitimate demands. Liberals' suggestions for reforms were shunted aside as the government followed the policy of divide and conquer in dealing with the opposition. The "September Laws" of 1835 were passed to bring the growing radical movement under control. But under the placid calm of the "citizen king's" reign, serious pressures of revolution were building. As the government disregarded the danger signs, Louis Philippe came to be seen as a dull and colorless individual who ruled through a corrupt and privileged regime. By 1848 France faced a serious crisis.

The challenges of nationalism. In the Germanies, the Italian peninsula, and the Hapsburg monarchy the post-1815 period witnessed the growing strength of the forces of nationalism. In the first two areas, nationalism would lead to movements toward unification. In the third region, nationalism would be a force for disintegration.

Napoleon had performed a great—if unwitting—service for Germany. By revising the European map he left a much more rational distribution of political units. The Vienna Congress had insured Austrian domination over the German Confederation, and Metternich knew full well the dangerous qualities of nationalism. Napoleon's domination of the Germanies had also helped to form the basis for a strong wave of patriotism, which remained even after 1815.

In the period immediately after the Congress of Vienna, the currents of romanticism found forceful expression in the works of German poets and philosophers and in the lectures of German professors. In the face of Metternich's opposition, nationalism and liberalism made major advances in central Europe. A great patriotic student festival took place in 1817 at Wartburg Castle, where Luther had taken refuge three centuries earlier. The high point of the October celebration came when some liberals burned reactionary books and pamphlets on the great bonfire. Student protests against the status quo continued both openly and secretly in the *Burschenschaften* (liberal societies). Metternich's response to these movements was immediate and harsh. He convinced the Diet of the German Confederation to issue the Carlsbad Decrees (1819), which dissolved the student associations, muzzled the press, and restricted academic freedom. Even in the face of this opposition, the forces of liberalism and nationalism would continue to build in the next twenty years, despite Metternich's policies.

Italy was seen by Metternich to be only a

Stupidity and indifference characterize the paunchy, middle-class members of the French legislature in Daumier's scathing portrayal of the lawmakers in session in 1831, entitled "Le Ventre Législatif."

Giuseppe Mazzini's lifework was revolution. Catalyst of the *Risorgimento* (Resurgence), Mazzini decried the doctrine of individual rights as a breeding ground for selfishness and competition and espoused a "universal" nationalism whereby all men would be brothers.

"geographical expression," and not a nation. In support of that belief, the Congress of Vienna had sanctioned its division into areas dominated by the Bourbons, the Papal States, and the Austrians. The settlement may have been consistent with the principles of legitimacy and compensation, but it ignored the fact that during the period after 1789 the Italians had known more liberty than ever before and had experienced more effective government. With the return of the old, inefficient ways high taxes, corruption, favoritism, and banditry resumed their traditional roles in the peninsula.

It was perhaps natural that this fragmented, individualistic land should produce the most notable romantic nationalist in Europe,

Giuseppe Mazzini (1805-1872). With the defeat of the revolutionary movements in 1820 and 1821 by Austrian troops, Mazzini began to work actively for independence. In 1830 he was implicated in an unsuccessful revolution against the Sardinian royal government and imprisoned for six months. After his release he started a new patriotic society, based in London, known as Young Italy, through which he launched his appeals to students and intellectuals for the Italian nationalist movement. The forces of reaction were able to weather the nationalist pressures until 1848.

The persistent forces of nationalism posed the greatest threat after 1815 to the continuation of the Hapsburg monarchy. It was the last of the major dynastic states, tied together by the oaths of loyalty to the Hapsburg family made by the many different nationalities controlled by Vienna. This multinational empire survived the initial wave of romantic nationalism during the revolutionary phases of 1820 and 1830. But Vienna had a great deal to fear if nationalism became strong among the Magyars to the east, the Czechs to the north, and the southern Slavs. The Germans comprised only about 20 percent of the total population, yet they controlled the levers of power. With an understanding of the fragmented basis of Austrian power, Metternich's fear of popular government and nationalism becomes much more understandable. In a very real sense, liberal and nationalistic philosophies would destroy the basis of his government's power, and with it the hoped-for stability that he desired.

Except for Bohemia and the areas immediately around Vienna, the middle class of the Hapsburg empire was quite small. A great majority of the inhabitants were peasants, either powerless serfs as in Hungary or impoverished tenant farmers who ended up owing one half of their time and two thirds of their crops to their landlords. Government was autocratic, and the regional assemblies possessed little power and represented mainly the nobility. The social, political, and economic structures were extremely vulnerable to the winds of change that arrived in 1848.

THE REVOLUTIONARY
YEAR: 1848

From idealism to reality. After 1830 the shell of the reactionary structure built at Vienna remained to cope with the varied forces of change. Revolutionary outbreaks in France, Germany, Austria, and Italy in 1848 and upheavals in other European countries gave vivid proof of the old order's inability to adapt to the new ideological and economic forces. Never had Europe seen such a variety of political and social pressures at work at the same time, and in such a fragmented way. The romantics, the socialists, the nationalists, the middle classes, the peasants, and the students could all agree that there had to be an overthrow of the reactionary structure of Europe, but each group had a different way to achieve that change, and a different view of what the world should be. As it spread

from Italy to Paris in February and to Vienna, Berlin, and Prague in March, the revolutionary discontent was strengthened by a series of bad harvests. Louis Philippe fell in Paris, Metternich was forced to flee Vienna, and the Prussian king was forced to acknowledge the revolutionary tide in Berlin.

But the movements fell apart as soon as they had destroyed the remnants of the 1815 structure. The revolutionaries' diversity, lack of experience, conflicting purposes, and their lack of armed strength doomed their efforts to failure. The revolutions of 1848 would see a bitter defeat for the idealistic themes of nationalism and liberalism, and a profound reevaluation of the nature of political power across the face of Europe.

France. All of the pressures that had been building in France since 1830 broke out in February 1848. The liberals resorted to a series of banquets at which they voiced their criticism of the government. In this seemingly harmless arena, they pushed for an end to corruption and reforms in the electoral system. The government saw a threat to its existence in these gatherings, and prohibited the holding of the Paris banquet planned for February 22. In response to this repressive action, mobs of excited citizens threw up more than 1500 barricades in the Parisian streets, and violence broke out. Republican leaders took the opportunity to establish a provisional revolutionary government, and proclaimed the introduction of universal manhood suffrage. The "citizen king" fled across the English Channel into exile.

The new regime, known as the Second Republic, had a brief and inglorious existence. The leaders had little preparation for running the government, and most of the new voters had no political experience. The reformers who united to overthrow the king

Discontent with the bourgeois, nonchalant reign of Louis Phillipe was the catalyst for the 1848 revolutions in France, which produced some of the most bitter fighting France had ever seen. In this painting government troops are shown storming the barricades in Paris during the bloody "June Days."

split immediately into moderate and socialist wings. The first group wanted middle-class control within the existing social order, while the latter pursued an economic and social revolution. By the summer the new government faced a major crisis over the issue of national workshops sponsored by the socialist, Louis Blanc (1811-1882). The workshops were to be the state's means to guarantee every laborers' "right to work." The moderate-dominated government voiced its belief in Blanc's principle of full employment, but it entrusted the plan's administration to men determined to discredit it. As a result, the workshops became a national joke as the laborers were assigned meaningless jobs such as carrying dirt from one end of a park to the other. When the workshops were disbanded, a violent insurrection known as the "June Days" broke out in Paris. The unemployed workers raised a red flag as a sign of revolution—the first time that the red flag had been used as a symbol of the proletariat. With the cry of "Bread or lead," the demonstrators reerected the barricades and tried to overthrow the government. The most bloody fighting Paris had seen since the Reign of Terror gave the insurgents far more lead than bread, and the movement was crushed. After that, the bourgeoisie and the workers would be on the opposite sides of political strife, and the moderates would look elsewhere for their political future.

Germany. The waves of the French February Revolution did not take long to cross the Rhine River and affect central Europe. At public assemblies convened throughout Germany patriotic liberals demanded, among other things, German unification. Rapid political changes occurred with a minimum of casualties. Barricades went up in Berlin on March 15, when the subjects of the Prussian King Frederick William IV finally gave vent to some of their long-repressed political dreams. The next day Prussian troops caused some bloodshed as they attempted to restore order. Seeing that the danger of widespread loss of life was becoming ever greater, the king decided to make concessions rather than kill his own subjects. He ordered the regular army troops out of Berlin and tried to make peace with his "dear

A session of the ill-fated Frankfurt Assembly, which frustrated the hopes of the German liberals, is shown in this woodcut.

Berliners'' by promising a parliament, a constitution, and a united Germany. Upon receiving news of this development the rulers of the other German states agreed to establish constitutional governments and guarantee basic civil rights.

The crowning symbol of 1848 in Germany was the Frankfurt Assembly, which opened its first session on May 18. Over 500 delegates attended, coming from the various German states, from Austria proper, and even from Bohemia. The heavy middle-class membership of the Assembly was made up of around 200 lawyers, 100 professors, plus many doctors and judges. Popular enthusiasm reached a peak when the Assembly's president announced that ''We are to create a constitution for Germany, for the whole Empire.'' The Assembly deliberated at length over the issues of just what was meant by Germany and what form of government would be best for the new empire. Some debaters affirmed that a united Germany

should include all Germans in central Europe, even Austria and Bohemia. Others did not want the Austrians included, for a variety of religious and political reasons. A major split developed over the question of whether the new imperial crown should be given to the Hapsburgs in Vienna or the Hohenzollerns in Berlin.

The course of German history was changed drastically by the Assembly's failure to apply a liberal solution to the political problems of Germany. The greatest tragedy of 1848 came to be found in the failed dreams of the Assembly and the loss of the liberal cause. From May to December the Assembly wasted time in splendid debates over often nonessential topics. Gradually, the German conservatives recovered from the shock of the spring revolts and began to rally around their rulers, urging them to undo the work of the reformers. In Prussia, Frederick William regained his confidence, as the army remained loyal and the peasants showed little interest in political affairs. The Berlin liberals were soon isolated, and the king was able to regain full control.

The Frankfurt Assembly continued its work, even though the antiliberal forces were running at full tide. It approved the Declaration of the Rights of the German People, an inspiring document that set forth the progressive political and social ideals of 1848. In April 1849, a constitution was approved for a united Germany, with an emperor advised by a ministry and a legislature elected by secret manhood suffrage. Austria was excluded for the simple reason that it refused to join the new union. When the leadership of the new German Reich was offered to King Frederick William, he refused to accept it, later declaring that he could not "pick up a crown from the gutter." After this contemptuous refusal most of the members of the Assembly sadly returned home. Outbreaks against the conservative domination continued to occur, but the Prussian army effectively put them down. Thousands of prominent, middle-class liberals fled, many migrating to the United States.

Italy. The news of the revolutions in Paris and Vienna triggered a rash of uprisings on the Italian peninsula. In Sicily, Venice, and Milan outbreaks demanding an end to foreign domination and despotic rule occurred. In response, King Charles Albert of Sardinia voluntarily issued a new liberal constitution. Other states such as Tuscany also granted their people liberal constitutions, and absolute government in Italy almost disappeared. In the Papal States a program of reform had begun as early as 1846.

But, as in the rest of Europe, the liberal and nationalist triumphs and reforms were quickly swept away by the reactionary tide. The Austrians were able to regain their mastery in the north of the peninsula in the face of the disunited Italians. In July 1848 they defeated Charles Albert at the decisive battle of Custozza. After another defeat a year later, he abdicated his throne in favor of his oldest son, Victor Emmanuel II. Austria helped restore the old rulers and systems of government in Italy to their pre-1848 conditions.

The final blow to the Italian revolutionary movements came in November 1848 when Pope Pius IX, who had begun a program of reform, refused to join in the struggle against Catholic Austria for a united Italy. He was forced by his subjects to flee from Rome, and the papal lands were declared a republic, with Mazzini as the head. The pope's flight prompted a uniform reaction from conservative Europe, and the French sent in an army to crush the republic in July 1849. The restored Pope Pius IX returned to Rome, and remained bitterly hostile to all liberal causes and ideas until his death in 1878.

The Hapsburg monarchy. The 1848 upheavals took a particularly large toll in the Hapsburg empire. When the news of the Parisian events was received in Vienna and Budapest at the beginning of March, reformers made immediate calls for change. In Budapest, the zealous liberal and fiery nationalist Louis Kossuth (1802-1894) gave a memorable speech as he castigated the "stagnant bureaucratic system" and spoke of the "pestilential air blowing from the Vienna charnel house and its deadening effect upon all phases of Hungarian life." He demanded parliamentary government for the whole of the empire.

This speech had a major impact in Vienna and inspired some Austrian students and workers to demonstrate in the streets. The movement soon gained the force of a revolt, and the frightened Austrian emperor forced Metternich, the symbol of European reaction, to resign. Meanwhile, the Hungarian Diet expressed the desire for liberal, parliamentary government under a limited Hapsburg monarchy. The Vienna-controlled Danubian region, that mosaic of nationalities, appeared to be on the verge of being transformed into a federation.

The diversity of the empire soon became a characteristic of the revolutionary movement, as the various nationalities divided among themselves. The Hungarians wrote a new constitution that was quite liberal, calling for a guarantee of civil rights, the ending of serfdom, and the destruction of special privileges. In theory, all political benefits to be found in the constitution were to be applied to all citizens of Hungary, including non-Magyars. The emperor accepted these reforms and promised, in addition, a constitution for Austria. At the same time he also promised the Czechs in Bohemia the same reforms granted the Hungarians.

By the summer the mood suddenly shifted, as the German and Czech nationalists began to quarrel and the Magyars began to oppress the Slavic nationalities after they demanded their own political independence. The divisions among the liberal and nationalistic forces gave the conservatives in Vienna time to regroup their forces, and also gave them the obvious tactic to follow to regain their former dominance: divide and conquer the subject nationalities. In June demonstrations broke out in the streets of Prague, barricades were thrown up, and fighting began. The Austrian forces lobbed in a few shells, Prague surrendered, and any hope for an autonomous kingdom of Bohemia was ended. In Hungary, Kossuth—as an advocate of Magyarization—announced that he would offer civil rights but not national independence for the minority nationalities found under his control. In protest, South Slavs under the Croatian leader Jellachich attacked the Magyars, and civil war soon followed. Taking advantage of the situation, the Austrians made him an imperial general. Following his attack against the Magyars, Jellachich was ordered to Vienna, where in October he forced the surrender of the liberals in control of the capital. By the end of the year the weak and incapable Emperor Ferdinand I abdicated in favor of his nephew, Francis Joseph. The Austrians began to repeal their concessions to Hungary, arguing that the new emperor was not bound by the acts of his predecessor. The Hungarians were infuriated by this cunning move, and declared complete independence for their country. Against the invading Austrian armies and the 100,000 Russian troops sent by Tsar Nicholas I, the Hungarians fought a bloody and hopeless struggle. By the summer of 1849 they were defeated, and Kossuth fled the country. The revolutionary movement in Hungary had reached its conclusion.

The 1848 outbreaks dealt a rude blow to the idealistic liberals, nationalists, and romantics who had failed in the pursuit of their various goals. In France some moderates learned that a revolution in the name of liberal principles could unleash forces that would, in their turn, threaten the middle classes. In the Hapsburg monarchy the various nationalities which had tried to free themselves from Vienna's control found that the nationalism that motivated each of them also doomed their struggle for freedom by making a unified attack impossible. By the end of 1848, the leaders of Germany and Italy were able to discard most of the liberal demands of the revolutionaries, but to retain the potent nationalistic forces that would eventually lead to unification.

THE NEW SEARCH FOR STABILITY: 1848-1871

France. The moderates in the cities and the conservatives in the countryside reacted to the events of the June Days by electing Louis Napoleon (1808-1873), nephew of the great emperor, to the presidency of the republic. After the troublesome days of 1848 and the mediocrity of Louis Philippe's reign, the very name of Napoleon seemed to promise great improvement. The new president had worked hard for almost twenty years to build that impression and to gain power. He had tried to overthrow the "citizen king" in 1836 and 1840, and had failed miserably both times. At one of his trials he showed his abilities as a demagogue by addressing the nation, saying "I represent . . . a principle, a cause, a defeat. The principle is the sovereignty of the people: the cause is that of the Empire: the defeat is Waterloo."[1] In prison and in exile he sought a cause he could ride to the power which, he was sure, destiny intended for him. He returned to France in 1848 where, spared of any involvement in the June Days, he was able to parlay his name into broad national support for the presidency. The constitution for the Second Republic gave strong powers to the president, and Louis Napoleon took advantage of his position and the overwhelming majority he received to entrench himself. During the next two years conservative forces dominated political affairs, and Louis Napoleon gained strength. The constitution under which he served, however, did not allow for a second term, and in December 1851 Louis' allies carried out a coup that dissolved the assembly and violated the constitution. After the mass arrests of his opponents and the brutal suppression of a workers' revolt, Louis set up a plebiscite which gave him a result that would have pleased his uncle—virtually unanimous support. In 1852 he proclaimed himself emperor, and the Second Republic was replaced by the Second Empire.

During its eighteen-year span the Second Empire experienced glory, prosperity, order, discipline—nearly everything a great nation could desire, in fact, except liberty. And even in this last area, Napoleon III was making some progress toward the end of his reign. Outwardly the government kept the form of a parliamentary regime, but the suffrage was juggled to give the emperor's supporters a safe majority in the legislature, which had little power anyway. The secret police kept track of potential political opponents, while the press was heavily censored and rarely reported any bad news.

The French seemed willing to pay for their newfound prosperity with the limitations on their liberty. The Industrial Revolution made its positive effects felt in this period as production doubled in two decades. The French supported the building of the Suez Canal, while railway mileage increased fivefold. The workers' conditions improved in a number of ways, including the partial legalization of labor unions and the right to strike. An ambitious program of public works under Baron Georges Haussmann (1809-1891) transformed Paris into a city of broad boulevards and harmonious architecture. The first improvement made it difficult to erect barricades, while the second enterprise made Paris Europe's most beautiful city.

Napoleon III claimed to be a man of peace, but his reign was marked by an interventionist foreign policy. He allied with England in the Crimean War, supported Cavour—momentarily—in Italy, and assured a foothold in Indochina. Napoleon also raised the French flag over Tahiti and penetrated the Senegal River in West Africa. In the 1860's he made a harebrained attempt to establish a foothold in the new world by placing Maximilian, a Hapsburg prince, on the Mexican throne. Forty thousand troops were involved in this adventure, which culminated in the retreat of the French forces and the capture and eventual execution of the Hapsburg prince by Mexican patriots. After 1866 he met his match in the Prussian chancellor Otto von Bismarck, as his blunders contributed to a quick Prussian victory over Austria. Finally in 1870 he gambled on a successful war with Prussia, a gamble which he lost, and the Second Empire died.

Italian unification. The 1848 romantic phase of the Italian unification movement was in ruins after the successful conservative response. One of the few centers of independence left was Sardinia, where the young King Victor Emmanuel II refused to withdraw the liberal constitution granted by his father. It was there that the Italian unification movement would find its base and its leader, Count Camillo Benso di Cavour (1810-1861).

THE UNIFICATION OF ITALY 1859-1870

- Kingdom of Sardinia to 1859
- To Kingdom of Sardinia 1860
- Annexed to Kingdom of Sardinia 1861; establishes Kingdom of Italy
- To Kingdom of Italy 1866
- To Kingdom of Italy 1870

Born of a noble family and trained for a military career, he became a liberal after traveling in Switzerland, France, and England. In 1852 he became the Sardinian prime minister, and concentrated his efforts on freeing Italy from Austrian domination. He knew that Sardinia could not take on Austria by itself; allies were needed, and to that end Sardinia joined Britain and France in their fight against Russia in 1855 in the Crimean War. Although this step appeared to be ludicrous, it enabled Cavour to speak at the peace conference after the war, where he stated Italy's desire for unification.

Cavour's statements won the support of Napoleon III. The two opportunists found that they could both make gains by drawing Austria into war, and they agreed that if Cavour could lure the Vienna government into a war, France would come to Sardinia's aid and help eject the Austrians from Lombardy and Venetia. In return France would receive Nice and Savoy from Sardinia. The scheme worked to perfection. In April 1859 Austria played into Cavour's hands by declaring war. The French and Sardinian armies defeated the Austrians at Magenta and Solferino and drove them out of Lombardy. At the same time revolts broke out in Tuscany, Modena, Parma, and Romagna. Napoleon III was proclaimed the savior and liberator of Italy.

But before the allies could invade Venetia, Napoleon reversed himself and made peace with Austria. He awoke to the fact that he was supporting a movement that would eventually unite the peninsula, a development that would not be in his interests. The Sardinians were furious with the French move, but they could do little but agree to a peace settlement in which Lombardy was added to Sardinia, the exiled rulers of Parma, Modena, Tuscany, and Romagna were restored, and an Italian confederation was created in which Austria was included.

A year later Cavour was able to make a major change in the peace settlement. Largely under the auspices of Great Britain, plebiscites were conducted in Italy, and Tuscany, Modena, and Parma voted to join Sardinia. Even with the cessions of Nice and Savoy to France, Cavour and Sardinia stood as the dominant forces on the peninsula. With northern Italy unified, the center of interest now shifted to the south and to a new leader, the flamboyant Giuseppe Garibaldi (1807-1882). In 1860 this former follower of Mazzini, secretly financed by Cavour, led his one thousand tough adventurers—The Red Shirts—to the conquests of Sicily and Naples, and prepared for a march on the Papal States. Cavour, however, feared that a march on the pope's holdings might provoke French intervention. Moreover, he wanted to assure that Sardinia would maintain its dominance over the unification movement. After reassuring Napoleon of the pope's safety, Cavour rushed troops to Naples and convinced Garibaldi to surrender his power to Victor Emmanuel II. By November 1860 Sardinia had annexed the former kingdom of Naples and Sicily and all the papal lands except Rome and its surrounding territory.

A parliamentary meeting at Turin in March 1861 formally proclaimed the Kingdom of Italy, a new nation of 22 million people. But there still remained the problems of Austrian-controlled Venetia and the papal control of Rome. Cavour, who died in 1861, did not live to see the full fruits of his life's work, but he knew that unity was not far off. In the decade following his death Italy gained Venetia in 1866 by acting as Prussia's ally in the Austro-Prussian War. When the Franco-Prussian War broke out in 1870, French troops were withdrawn from Rome, and Italian forces took possession of the Eternal City. In 1871 Rome became the capital of a unified Italy.

The methods used by the Sardinians have been criticized for their amorality. Cavour made no attempt to hide the true nature of his policies. He once said: "If we did for ourselves what we do for our country, what rascals we should be."[2] He fully realized the rules of the game in post-1848 state relations, and his skill in playing the game to the utmost effectiveness and in gaining Italian unification cannot be doubted.

Germanic competition. In the generation after 1848 the two major centers of German power, Vienna and Berlin, made their respective adjustments to the post-revolutionary situation. Austria's victory over the

Hungarians gave them only temporary comfort. The collapse of the liberal and nationalistic movements in the Hapsburg empire was followed by a stern repression which may have kept order, but did little to address the basic political problems facing the rulers in Vienna. The policy of centralizing all governmental activities in Vienna and the attempt to Germanize the subject nationalities served only to stimulate the feelings of nationalism in the empire. Ten years of this policy did little to improve the governing of the empire, and after their defeat by the French and Sardinians in 1859, Francis Joseph began to contemplate changes in Austria's political structure. In 1861 a new imperial constitution was framed in which representatives were to be elected from the various provincial parliaments to a central, imperial Diet. This might have pleased the other nationalities, but the Hungarians, by far the strongest and most stubborn of the subject peoples, demanded concessions that would make Hungary into a virtually independent state. These political problems greatly weakened the Austrians as they faced the challenge of Prussian power.

Prussia too had been shaken severely in the 1848 outbreaks, but in the post-revolutionary phase it did not have the nemesis of the nationalities problems that faced Austria. In 1850 the king issued his own constitution, a document that paid lip service to parliamentary government, but kept the real power in his hands and the hands of the upper class. At the same time, the Berlin court lacked the strength to achieve some of its diplomatic goals. Prussia sponsored a confederation of north German states, without Austria, and with Frederick William as head. This project alienated Austria and Russia, both of which feared the idea of a strong, Prussian-dominated Germany. A conference of the three powers followed at Olmütz in 1850, and the Prussian king was pressured to drop his plan. It was agreed to restore the German Confederation as set up at Vienna in 1815, with Austria as the major German power. Prussian ambitions were momentarily checkmated, but anti-Austrian Prussians never forgot or forgave the "Humiliation of Olmütz."

Prussia did gain success in other areas, however. The Berlin government kept Austria out of the *Zollverein* (customs union) and fought off Vienna's efforts to weaken the German tariff union. The conservative Prussian leaders strengthened their control over domestic policies by suppressing the liberals and instituting virtually total noble control over all state functions. The government and public administration were modern and efficient, especially when compared to the government in Vienna. Public education reached more citizens in Prussia than in any other European state.

By the end of the 1850's a new ruler, William I, came to power. He had a more moderate interpretation of the constitution granted in 1850, and the liberals and moderates again had the chance to make their views heard. But a serious constitutional crisis arose in 1862. The king wished to strengthen the army, but the Chamber of Deputies would not vote the necessary money. The liberals in parliament asserted the constitutional right to approve taxes and the king asserted his right to build up the army. To aid him during this crisis, William called Otto von Bismarck (1815-1898) home from his post as Prussian ambassador to France and made him prime minister. On Bismarck's advice, the king defied the legislature and continued to collect the needed taxes without legislative approval. Bismarck knew the necessity of armed strength for the achievement of Prussia's diplomatic goals. Ironically, his later military victories would gain him the support of many of the very liberals whom he had encouraged the king to defy.

Bismarck and German unification. The constitutional crisis of 1862 was undoubtedly an important issue in German history. But Bismarck's arrival in Berlin to dominate Prussian affairs at that time was even more significant. One of the main themes of 1848 in Germany had been the call for unity. This dream survived the debacle of the revolutionary year, in the form suggested by the German historian, Heinrich von Treitschke — "There is only one salvation! One state, one monarchic Germany under the Hohenzollern dynasty."[3]

The government at Berlin, through its

leadership in the *Zollverein*, sponsorship of the confederation of north German states, and efficient bureaucracy, offered impressive credentials for its claim to be the center of the unified German people. With the arrival of Bismarck the Prussians gained the necessary leadership for the difficult task of unification. He followed a political line subsequently characterized as *Realpolitik*—i.e., realism in politics which disdains high-flown theory or idealism and emphasizes the practical application of power to achieve state goals, no matter the damage done to ethics or morality. Bismarck's major gift was his ability to accurately assess the actual state of conditions; his major talent was his ability to move skillfully; and his major contribution was to be able to set a goal, and to achieve it.

Bismarck was a master image-maker, and so effective was he that historians have picked up his epithet "blood and iron" to describe his career. Yet few statesmen have ever accomplished so much change with such a comparatively small loss of life or controlled use of war. He was a master politician who knew that war was the final card to be played, to be used as the servant of diplomacy and not its master.[4]

The future German chancellor was a firm supporter of the Prussian aristocracy and an opponent of liberal ideals. As a student he showed more ability as a consumer of white wine than as a scholar, but he gained renown as a duelist. In 1847 he entered state service and soon joined the diplomatic corps, serving at such important posts as St. Petersburg and Paris.

After weathering the 1862 constitutional crisis, he turned his attention to the several steps that had to be taken before unification could occur. First, good relations with Russia had to be assured, and this was achieved in 1863 when Bismarck promised to aid Russia in all Polish-related problems after the abortive revolt by the Poles in that same year.

Prussian wars with Denmark and Austria. In 1864 Bismarck invited Austria to join Prussia in waging war on Denmark. The cause of conflict was the status of two duchies bordering on Prussia and Denmark— Schleswig and Holstein—both of which were claimed by the Germans and the Danes. The

Otto von Bismarck, the shrewd and consummate prime minister of Germany from 1862 to 1890, used his almost artistic ability to maneuver people and situations to bring about the unification of Germany in 1871. Though his epithet "blood and iron" characterized his devotion to the political philosophy of *Realpolitik*, his finesse in actually handling political affairs enabled him to achieve his goals with relatively little bloodshed.

Prussians—aided by Austrian forces—easily smashed the Danish defenses, and the administration of Holstein was awarded to Austria, while Schleswig came under Prussian rule.

With his eastern and northern flanks stabilized, Bismarck set out to isolate Austria and to force it out of its dominant position in German affairs. The new kingdom of Italy was promised Venetia if it would assist Prussia should war come, and the French emperor was induced to remain neutral by Prussian intimations of support should France seek to widen its frontiers. Austria was going through severe domestic crises, and found itself isolated on the continent. Bismarck provoked war with Vienna by expressing alarm at the way the Austrians were ruling Holstein, and sending troops into the province. Hostilities broke out in 1866 and lasted only seven weeks. At the battle of Sadowa the Austrians were defeated by the superior Prussian forces. The humiliation at Olmütz was avenged. To avoid, in turn, humiliating Austria, Prussia offered a moderate peace settlement, ending the old German Confederation. In its place the North German Confederation was formed under Prussian domination, with Austria and the south German states being excluded. As can be seen by the map on p. 594, Bismarck annexed several territories that allowed him to bring his lands together for the final push to unite Germany, such as Hanover, Mecklenburg, and other states north of the river Main.

In the Hapsburg lands, the impasse between Vienna and Budapest finally ended in 1866, after the Austrians' disastrous defeat by Prussia. Francis Joseph was forced to offer the Magyars an equal partnership with the Germans in ruling the empire. The offer was accepted, and in 1867 the constitution known as the *Ausgleich* (compromise) was promulgated. Under the document the Dual Monarchy came into existence, in which the Hapsburg ruler was both the king in Hungary and the emperor in Austria. Each country had its own constitution, language, flag, and parliament. Finance, defense, and foreign affairs were under ministers common to both countries. The common ministers were supervised by "Delegations" which consisted of sixty members from the Austrian parliament and an equal number from the Hungarian side. They did not meet together, except in extraordinary circumstances. The compromise was to be renegotiated every ten years. The problems of the multinational empire remained, except that now instead of one nation dominating, two directed the affairs of the chaotic state. Prussia's superiority in Central Europe was unquestioned.

The Franco-Prussian War. After 1867 Bismarck turned his attentions to the west, to France and Napoleon III. The French emperor had anticipated a long war between the Austrians and Prussians, one from which he could profit. He had foolishly allowed himself to be talked into neutrality during the war with Austria, in return for some ill-defined territorial concessions from Bismarck. In August 1866 he approached Bismarck for his share of the fruits of victory, but Bismarck stated that he had no recollections of promises made to France. Inexplicably, Napoleon III, through his ambassador, demanded Luxemburg and Prussian approval of the French takeover of Belgium. Bismarck had Napoleon's envoy put these requests in writing, and then avoided making a definite response. The chancellor made good use of this document four years later when he sent it along to the British in order to gain England's support for Prussia during the Franco-Prussian War. After the French participation in the Crimean War, there was no chance of the Russians coming to Napoleon's aid. Austria, which discovered Napoleon's cooperation with Bismarck, would not aid the French. France was deftly isolated by 1870 through Bismarck's diplomatic maneuvers.

It was a simple matter for Bismarck to maneuver the French into war. The immediate cause centered on the succession to the Spanish throne, left vacant after a revolution had exiled the reactionary Spanish Queen Isabella. Leopold, a Hohenzollern prince, was invited to become a constitutional king of Spain, something France would not allow because this would be an unwelcome extension of Prussian influence. Leopold withdrew his candidacy after France protested, but this was not enough for Paris. The French government sent its ambassador to Ems, where the Prussian king was vacationing, to demand that William I promise that no Hohenzollern would ever sit on the Spanish throne. This was an unreasonable request and the king refused to agree to it. He directed that a dispatch be sent to Bismarck (the famed "Ems dispatch") telling him the results of the interview. The chancellor altered the dispatch slightly to give the impression that the French ambassador had insulted the Prussian king, and that the king had returned the insult. When this version of the dispatch was published, both the French and the Prussian people were infuriated.

France declared war in July 1870, partially in response to the Ems dispatch and partially to reflect the view of the growing "war party." The French and Prussian forces were evenly matched, but the Germans had superior leadership. In two months the Prussians overwhelmed the French armies. The crowning disaster for Napoleon came at the battle of Sedan when he and his army were forced to surrender. The united strength of the north and south German states was put to good use, as they besieged Paris for four months before the final French capitulation.

By the Treaty of Frankfurt, France lost Alsace and a part of Lorraine to Germany, and was required to pay a large indemnity. For the next forty years the call for revenge became a staple of French politics, and World War I gave the French the chance to gain compensation for the humiliation suffered in 1870-1871.

THE EXTREMES OF EUROPE: ENGLAND AND RUSSIA

English flexibility. In the half century after Waterloo, England was able to avoid the revolutionary turmoil experienced by the western and central European states. England's politics did not develop within a vacuum. The English felt many of the same political pressures as, for example, the French during that time. Political life, especially in the first decade after 1815, was marked by occasional violence and disruption as some working class groups and radicals pushed for a program of rapid reform. But buttressed by its advanced industrial system and naval supremacy, the English became the world's most powerful and richest nation. The first quality assured a century of security while the second quality contributed to an increasing per capita income. The dominant political circles helped England to avoid revolutionary situations by slowly spreading democratic participation to the working classes by the end of the century. England, therefore, experienced political evolution, and not revolution.

The first decade after the Napoleonic wars was a difficult time for the island nation. Economic problems were felt throughout the country when the English shifted back to a peacetime economy. Unemployment increased, factories shut down, and prices and salaries dropped. The first major strains of industrialization began to be felt. Some handskilled workers were put out of work by the increasing use of machines. In response, "Luddism" occurred when workers wrecked some factories and destroyed the machines. In 1816 and in 1819 mob violence broke out. The worst case occurred in August 1819 in the Peterloo Massacre when a large meeting at St. Peter's fields in Manchester was dispersed by a charge of the army. In both cases the crowds had gathered to advocate parliamentary reforms and not to cause trouble, but the approach of the authorities sparked violence.

England's ruling classes, still recoiling from the excesses of the Jacobins during the French Revolution, at first refused to note the misfortunes of the poor or the large numbers of the unemployed. Instead they declared that the doctrine of "peace, law, order, and discipline" should be their guide. As a result, in a series of acts after 1815 the Habeas Corpus Act was suspended, public meetings were restricted, liberal newspapers were repressed, and heavy fines were imposed on literature considered to be dangerous.

But conditions began to change for the better after 1820. Tory cabinet ministers more favorable to the need for reform such as Robert Peel and George Canning began to act in a number of different areas. The reformers passed laws that abolished capital punishment for over one hundred offenses, created a modern police force for London, began the recognition of labor unions, and repealed old laws that kept non-Anglican Protestants from sitting in Parliament. In response to Irish pressure, they also passed the Catholic Emancipation Act that gave Roman Catholics voting rights and the right to serve in Parliament and most public offices. Further, substantial gains were made toward free trade. The July Revolution in Paris emphasized the conservatives' fear of popular uprisings, and aided the British reformist tendencies. The flexible nature of the English system allowed for the gradual changes that were needed to satisfy the business and professional peoples who were determined to break the aristocracy's governmental monopoly. In addition, the working classes' rising complaints gained an ever greater audience.

The need for reform was so generally felt that in 1830 the Duke of Wellington, as prime minister, was out of touch with the times when he made a fateful speech in which he declared that the country's constitution was quite satisfactory for all its needs. This so aroused public opinion that the "Iron Duke" was forced to resign, and Lord Grey, the Whig party's leader, became head of government, ending sixty years of almost continuous Tory rule. Grey recognized his mandate, and set out immediately to reform Parliament. The abuses were easily identifiable. Representation in the House had no relation to the population, as 3 percent of the population dictated the election of the members. The rapidly growing industrial towns such as Manchester and Birmingham—each with over 100,000 inhabitants—had no representatives, while other areas, virtually depopulated, had representation. Grey's program called for reform in the areas of parliamentary representation, an expanded franchise, and representation for the industrial cities. After being stymied by aristocratic interests first in the House of Commons and then in the House of Lords, the reform bills were finally passed when the king, William IV, threatened to create enough new peers who would vote for the bills in order to pass them through the Lords. Grey's reform bills did not bring absolute democracy to England, but they pointed the way toward the attainment of a more equitable political system.

Reform and stability. Other changes came in the 1830's and 1840's. In response to years of abolitionist crusades, slavery was abolished in the British empire in 1833. The Parliament passed laws initiating regulation of working conditions and hours. In 1835 the Municipal Corporations Bill introduced a uniform system of town government with popular elections. England learned that change was necessary. "Reform, that you may preserve," was the lesson learned from observing the events of the 1830 revolution in France.[5] The British profited from flexibility in their political structure, the accession of the popular young Queen Victoria in 1837, and a rising per capita income to ride out the stormy period with a relative degree of stability.

Despite these reforms, England had not yet attained a government which responded justly to all of the people. There was still major work to be accomplished. In the 1830's and 1840's a strong popular movement known as Chartism developed. Its leaders summarized England's political needs in six demands: universal manhood suffrage, secret voting, no property qualifications for members of Parliament, payment of Parliament members so that the poor could seek election, annual elections, and equal electoral districts. In 1839, 1842, and 1848 the Chartists presented their demands, backed by over a million signatures on their petitions, but each time they failed to gain their goals. The movement declined after 1848, but by the end of the century all of their demands, except that for annual parliamentary elections, had been enacted into law.

Another major trend in British politics by mid-century was toward economic liberalism, the political policy that would best help further England's world commercial dominance. A policy of free trade came to be favored. The Corn Laws, protective duties on imported grain which had favored the dominant farming gentry, no longer suited the industrialized English economy. These laws had been designed to encourage exports and to protect the English landowners from foreign competition. By the middle of the century the population had grown to such an extent that English farmers could no longer feed the country, and the price of bread rose alarmingly. The potato-crop famine in Ireland in 1845, which led to the death of perhaps as many as 500,000 people, dramatically spotlighted the situation and the need for low-priced wheat from abroad. The repeal of the Corn Laws made possible the importation of low-priced grain, cheaper food for the masses, and a more contented labor supply for the factory owner. This was also a victory for the free-trade forces over those who favored protective tariffs. Soon England abandoned customs duties of every kind, and Adam Smith's doctrines of 1776 finally won out. England had such a commercial and industrial supremacy that her economic structure needed no protection. The English economy boomed under the stimulus of cheap imports of raw materials and food.

By the end of the period, the enlightened self-interest of the political elite and the economic strength of the British Isles combined to insure controlled change, stability, and growth. Except for the Irish insurrection in Tipperary and some isolated Chartist threats, England was not affected by the continent-wide revolutionary upheavals of 1848. For the next twenty years an alliance of the landed gentry and the middle classes worked together to dominate the government and to keep the lower classes "in their stations." The newly ascendant middle classes believed that the political reforms, which had been in large measure advantageous to them alone, had gone far enough. The symbol of this conservatism was Lord Palmerston, who dominated the direction of foreign affairs from the 1830's until his death and ended his career by acting as prime minister during much of the period from 1855 to 1865. A viscount himself, he was quite satisfied with the rule of the aristocracy and the middle class. But underneath the calm surface, the demands for reforms such as those enunciated by the Chartists remained.

Russia—the inability to reform. In the half century after Waterloo, the autocratic Russian government also was able to avoid the revolutionary currents of 1830 and 1848. But unlike England, Russia possessed neither the economic strength nor the social and political flexibility to change with the times. Tsar Alexander I (1801-1825) sensed some of the political, economic, and social problems facing his empire. Educated in the traditions of the Enlightenment by his grandmother, Catherine II, Alexander understood the reformist trends of his time.

Russia was based on the social institution of serfdom and governed through the political structure of autocracy. Both its social institution and its political structure were in need of major reform. Serfdom was socially repressive and economically inefficient. The autocratic form of government no longer was adequate to administer the world's largest state. During his reign Alexander experimented with limited serf emancipation, constitutionalism, and federalism. His dilemma was that as an autocrat he was all powerful in

A contemporary cartoon shows a demonstration of the kind that helped bring about repeal of the Corn Laws in 1846.

theory, but in reality he was dependent on a social and political structure that could not easily adapt itself to modern conditions. He also had the misfortune to rule during the Napoleonic wars, and for the first fifteen years of his reign he had to devote substantial amounts of time and money to foreign affairs. His reform plans were never carried through to completion. Russia's tragedy was that not until the 1850's would there be another tsar with the willingness to make the fundamental social and political reforms needed for the vast empire to compete successfully in the industrializing world.

In the reactionary decade of the 1820's discussion of reform in Russia did not gain official favor, even if the reforms had been discussed by the tsar. Nonetheless, there were a number of well-educated, well-traveled Russian officers who met in a group of secret societies to discuss the need for change in Russia. When Alexander failed to follow through with his plans for reform, the intensity of their deliberations increased. When the tsar died at Taganrog on the Black Sea in December 1825, there was a time of confusion over who would succeed to the throne. The period between the death of Alexander and the confirmation of Nicholas I gave a small circle of liberal nobles and army officers the chance to advance their ill-defined demands for a constitution. On December 26 a small uprising in St. Petersburg—known as the Decembrist Revolt—broke out, but lasted less than a day. It could have been put down even earlier if Nicholas had been more decisive. An hour's dose of grapeshot fired at the two regiments in the Senate square was all that was needed to disperse what some later historians have called the first Russian Revolution. This abortive, ill-planned attempt doomed any chance of liberal or democratic reform in Russia for thirty years.

Nicholas I and reaction. Even though subsequent investigations revealed clearly how weak the Decembrist Revolt was, the new tsar was badly shaken. He remained ultrasensitive to revolutionary and liberal movements, no matter where they occurred. In response, he encouraged a movement toward what has been called official nationalism. The new ideology identified the foundations of Russia as "Autocracy, Orthodoxy, and Nationalism"—the Romanovs, the Russian Orthodox church, and Russian nationalism. To promote the three-pronged identity foreign visitors and publications were carefully screened and would not be permitted in the country if they contained the slightest hint of liberalism. Even musical compositions were checked to see if the notes were a secret code. The government closely monitored schools and universities and carefully regulated students' reading material. "Dangerous people," some 150,000 of them, were exiled to Siberia. The tsar feared the influences of free ideas and intellectuals in his reactionary state. The millions of non-Russians in the empire came to experience a limitation of their identity through the process of Russification. The tsar may well have strengthened his immediate control over his holdings, but he failed to address the major social and political reforms needed to convert his autocratic empire into a competitive, modern state.

For all of his efforts to control intellectual and political life, Nicholas failed. Russian intellectuals since the time of Peter I had been closely tied to foreign influences, and even with censorship, repression, and travel restrictions, Russian thinkers and writers were fully aware of the romantic movement, especially the works of the German philosophers and poets. In the 1840's and 1850's a new type of intellectual appeared, thinkers devoted to achieving political goals—the *intelligentsia*. Although they would not make their strength felt until after the 1860's, the *intelligentsia* established strong roots during Nicholas' reign. Alexander Herzen (1812-1870) and Michael Bakunin (1814-1876) were the pioneers of this peculiarly Russian movement. Herzen was a moderate socialist who advocated the freeing of the serfs, liberalization of the government, and freedom of the press. In 1847 he went into exile in London where he founded the famous paper, *Kolokol (The Bell)* ten years later. It was widely read in Russia, supposedly appearing mysteriously on the tsar's table. Bakunin was more radical, and is regarded as the father of Russian anarchism. Despairing of moderate reform in Russia, he advocated terrorism, calling it the "propaganda of the deed." He preached that anarchy—complete freedom—can be the only cure for society's ills. He too went to the west, and actively participated, with little result, in the 1848 revolution.

The European economic, intellectual, and political currents had a great impact on Russia during this time, but the greatest challenge posed by Europe's changes was that of the future path Russia should follow. The question of whether Russia should imitate Europe or pursue its own traditions had been posed since the time of Peter I. The westerners' response to the question was that if Russia were to survive it had to imitate the basic aspects of western life and thought and renounce much of its own past. The Slavophiles, the other side of the dialogue, renounced Europe.[6] As one of their number wrote: "In Europe the principle of

This drawing, done by a staff artist of the *Illustrated London News* in 1861, shows a group of Russian serfs in the peasant village of Goumnist. The general reaction of the serfs to the Emancipation Proclamation was disappointment, as they soon realized how unemancipated they remained in their new situation.

personality is supreme; with us it is the communal principle. Europe is pagan, Russia—holy Christian. In the west reigns an apparent liberty, a liberty like that of a wild animal in the desert. The true liberty is found among us, in the East."

By the 1850's Nicholas had been able to control his country to the extent that the impacts of the 1830 and 1848 revolutions were not felt to any large degree in Russia. But the basic doubt about Russia's future, the dissident intellectuals, the economic and social weaknesses of serfdom, and the political stagnation of autocracy did not bode well for Russia.

Alexander II and the Great Reforms. Russia's generally inept participation in the Crimean War (1854-1856) clearly spotlighted the country's inadequate social, economic, and political structure. When Alexander II (1855-1881) came to the throne, even the conservatives among his subjects acknowledged the need for reform across the entire

social and political structure. Alexander moved first to change the basis of the whole autocratic system—the institution of serfdom. After long deliberations, a committee appointed by the tsar to study the matter drew up the Emancipation Proclamation, which was duly issued as a *ukaz* (edict of the tsar) in March 1861. By this reform, 23 million people who had no civil rights, who could not own property, and who owed heavy dues and services were to begin the transition to land ownership and citizenship. The government paid the landlords a handsome price for the land which was to be turned over to the peasants. In return the peasants had to pay for the land over a period of forty-nine years by making payments to the government. The drawn-out nature of the land transfer was a disappointment to the former serfs, who had expected a portion of the lords' land to be turned over to them without charge. The peasants complained that they had been given the poorest land.

Further, all the land turned over to the peasants was to be owned collectively by the *mir*, the village community, which would divide the land among the peasants and be collectively responsible for the taxes. Even though they were granted ownership of their cottages, farm buildings, garden plots, domestic animals, and implements, the restrictions placed on the peasants by confining them to their villages constituted a serious problem. New generations of peasants would bring a large population increase, with no corresponding increase in their amount of land.

The emancipation of the serfs was the single most important event in the domestic history of nineteenth-century Russia. In its train it brought about reforms of the army, the judiciary, the municipal government, and the system of local self-government. One of the most important reforms came in 1864 when local government was transformed by the Zemstvo Law. In the country elective local boards *(zemstvos)* were established on

which the gentry, the middle class, and the peasants were represented. These boards gained the power to collect taxes for roads, asylums, hospitals, and schools. The *zemstvos* became one of the most successful governmental organizations in Russia.

THE EASTERN QUESTION TO 1870

The Balkans. The Balkans, the area of southeastern Europe below the line formed by the Sava and Danube rivers and the south flank of the Carpathian mountains, existed under the uncertain dominance of the decaying Ottoman empire in the half century after Waterloo. Of all the areas in Europe, the Balkans were the least advanced economically and politically, as they had fallen under Turkish control in the fourteenth and fifteenth centuries and had been cut off from western developments since that time.

By the end of the eighteenth century Ottoman power had substantially declined in the Balkans. This could be seen in 1799 when Sultan Selim III acknowledged the independence of the mountainous nation of Montenegro, after its long and heroic struggle against the Turks. Further proof of Ottoman weakness could be found in 1804 when some renegade Turkish troops in Belgrade went on a rampage, disobeyed the sultan's orders, and forced the Serbian people to defend themselves. This initial act of self-protection blossomed into a rebellion that culminated, after eleven difficult years, in the Serbs gaining an autonomous position under Turkish rule.

The chaotic nature of the Ottoman administration of Greece similarly contributed to the Greek revolution of 1821. Unlike the Serbian uprising, the Greek movement gained substantial outside support from Philhellenic societies in Great Britain. Even though Metternich through the Congress System hoped the revolt would burn itself out, the Greeks were able to take advantage of great power intervention to gain their independence. Tsar Nicholas I wanted to weaken Turkey in order to pave the way for

THE TREATY OF ADRIANOPLE 1829

Russian control of the Dardanelles; so much so that he overcame his hatred of revolutions and set aside his obligation to support the European balance of power. England became alarmed at this policy, and the upshot was an agreement in 1827 in which Britain, France, and Russia pledged themselves to secure Greek independence. The Turks were eventually defeated by the Russians, and in the 1829 Treaty of Adrianople the Greeks gained the basis for their independence while Serbia received autonomy. The Danubian Principalities of Moldavia and Wallachia became Russian protectorates.

The Greek revolution had brought the great powers forcefully into the Balkans and in the process had shown that the reactionary ideology of the Congress System would be forgotten when the self-interest of the various states was involved. It also brought the Eastern Question sharply into focus.

In its simplest expression the Eastern Question was the dilemma presented to the great powers by the disintegrating Ottoman empire. Because the Turks possessed responsibility for more territory than they could govern effectively, there were parts of the Ottoman empire that were under no consistent control. The power vacuums that were created presented tempting opportunities for the empire's neighbors. But because of the strategic nature of the empire's holdings — controlling the Straits, the eastern Mediterranean, the Balkans, and the Suez — the empire's fate was of interest to everyone. During the nineteenth century the indigenous peoples, infected by the spirit of nationalism, added yet another explosive element to the Eastern Question. By the 1830's it became apparent that the Turks were to be an object of rather than a subject in European diplomacy. The sultan's government had few admirers in Europe, but the European powers arrived at a consensus to prop up the decaying structure rather than to allow one nation to gain dominance over the strategic area.

The Crimean War. The conflict between Russian and British interests in the Near East, which culminated in the Crimean War, had ancient roots. Russia had made a substantial advance toward the Mediterranean during the reign of Catherine II. In her pursuit of the ancient Russian goal of controlling Constantinople and the Straits, she turned the Black Sea into a Russian lake. By the Treaty of Kuchuk Kainarji (1774) the Russians gained rights of navigation in Ottoman waters and the right to intervene in favor of Eastern Orthodox Christians in the Ottoman empire. The English were not happy with the Russian advance, and in 1791 the prime minister, William Pitt the Younger, denounced Russia's ambitions to dismember Turkey. Only the common threat of Napoleon from 1798 to 1815 diverted the two from their competition in the Eastern Mediterranean. During the Greek revolt the British feared that Russia would use the Greek independence movement as an excuse for further expansion at Turkish expense. The British intervened skillfully and the Greeks were able to gain their independence without a major Russian advance toward the Straits.

In 1832 the Ottoman empire seemed on the point of exhaustion when the able Mehemet Ali, the virtually independent governor of Egypt, attacked his overlord, the sultan. To prevent the establishment of a new and probably stronger government at the Straits, Nicholas I sent an army to protect the Ottoman capital, extracting in return the Treaty of Unikar Skelessi (1833) which made Turkey a virtual protectorate of Russia. The British resolved to deprive Russia of the advantage, and in less than a decade, after substantial diplomatic pressure from France, Great Britain, and Austria, the tsar agreed to renounce Unikar Skelessi and sign a general guarantee of Turkish independence. These agreements did little to improve the condition of the Ottoman empire, and in 1844 while visiting England, Nicholas referred to Turkey as a "dying man" and proposed that the British join in a dissection of the Ottoman carcass.

The Eastern Question flared up into an international crisis in 1851 in a quarrel over the management and protection of the holy places in Palestine. Napoleon III upheld the Roman Catholics' right to perform the housekeeping duties, in a move to gain support from Catholics and the military in France. Acting under the Kuchuk Kainarji treaty, Nicholas stated that the Orthodox faithful should look after the holy places. From this minor conflict the Crimean War eventually emerged, as the great powers all intervened in the discussions to protect their interests. The tsarist ambassador, Menshikov, tried to use the dispute to improve Russia's position in the Ottoman empire, while the British ambassador counseled the Turks to stand firm against the Russian moves. After the Russians occupied the Danubian Principalities in an attempt to show the sultan the seriousness of their demands, the Turks declared war on them in October 1853. By the next summer, the French, Sardinians, and British had joined the Turks. Napoleon saw the war as a chance to enhance his dynasty's reputation, the Sardinians found an opportunity to gain allies for their drive for Italian unification, and the British took steps, under the impact of anti-tsarist public opinion, to halt the Russian advance toward the Straits. The stated aim of all the allies was, of course, the defense of the Ottoman sultan.

A combination of the military strength of the combined allies and tsarist inefficiency led to a Russian defeat. Russia sued for peace, and in the resulting Treaty of Paris (1856) there was a redefinition of the Eastern Question. The integrity of the Ottoman empire was affirmed. The Black Sea was to be a neutral body of water, and the Straits were closed to foreign warships. It was declared that no power had the right to interfere on behalf of the sultan's Christian subjects. Russia's control over the Principalities was ended.

The Crimean War momentarily stopped the Russian advance into the Balkans, but it did little to cure any of the problems of the Ottoman empire, the "sick man of Europe." The legacy of unsolved problems bequeathed by the Treaty of Paris included the desire of the Balkan nationalities still under Turkish control to be free, the increasing financial indebtedness of the Ottoman empire to western financial interests, and the antagonism that emerged between Austria and Russia as the former "tilted" in favor of Britain and France. The Eastern Question, what to do with the Ottoman empire, was not answered in the nineteenth century. It was postponed again and again until 1914. Three Russo-Turkish wars, and two wars in which

The Russian fortress of Sevastopol was the major scene of battle for most of the Crimean War. Fortified by the famed military engineer E. I. Todleben, the town withstood the attack of the allied army for eleven months.

France, England, and Russia fought either with or against the Turks did little to bring a solution to the geo-political problem. Today the area is still a focus of world tensions as the Arab-Israeli conflict, tied in with the Russian-American rivalry, endangers world peace.

SUMMARY

In the half century after Waterloo, aside from the Crimean conflict, Europe avoided a major continental war. Part of this record of relative peace could be credited to the skill of the diplomats after 1815 who constructed the system to place Europe back on a basis of pre-Napoleonic stability. But perhaps the major cause for this period of general peace was the major challenge faced domestically by each country to adapt to the political, social, intellectual, and economic forces of the time.

The Vienna settlement had dealt with the challenges of liberalism and nationalism as much as it had confronted the classic problems of balance of power and compensation. The epidemic of revolutions in 1820-21 and again in 1830 definitely showed that the European pattern laid out in 1815 at Vienna could not be maintained. In 1848 the major movements emerging from the French Revolution combined to overpower the political structures in France, Italy, Germany, and the Hapsburg empire. A larger and more prosperous middle class had come into prominence, together with a numerous body of intellectuals who had been strongly moved by the gospels of freedom and nationalism. In the cities the Industrial Revolution was creating a growing mass of workers who resented their own poverty and who also had dreams of their own.

The revolutions in 1848 enjoyed spectacular successes as well as tragic failures. The diversity of the movements made any international cooperation impossible. The leaders of the revolutions had little or no experience, and often were infatuated with their ideals while bored with the reality in which they would have to work. The force of nationalism, so powerful an enemy of autocracy, soon showed itself to be a fragmenting force among the various liberated nationalities. The middle classes and the workers discovered that their interests could be quite contradictory. The combination of these factors doomed the idealistic revolutionaries, and introduced a new range of political alternatives to the continental stage after 1848.

The generation after 1848 in France turned to Louis Napoleon Bonaparte in a search for stability and prosperity. The French gained both, at the price of initially reduced liberty and also diplomatic and military defeat. The Italians achieved national unification under the leadership of Cavour in Sardinia. The Hapsburg empire, after nearly twenty years of trying to deal successfully with its fractious nationalities, redefined itself as the Dual Monarchy in 1867, as Germans and Magyars would try to govern the mosaic of peoples in the Danubian area. In Prussia, after a period of reaction to the uprisings in 1848, a constitutional crisis would lead to the rise to power of Otto von Bismarck and the march to German unification.

Two nations on the extremes of Europe, England and Russia, escaped the pattern of revolution and reaction after 1815. The first possessed the economic strength, social and political flexibility, and skilled leadership to make the needed changes to adapt to the powerful new ideological forces and the conditions created by the Industrial Revolution. A half century after Waterloo, England rested strong, rich, and secure. Russia began the period under consideration as the liberator of Europe from Napoleon, and her armies helped restore the Bourbons to the throne in Paris. At the end of this time, however, she lay weak, defeated, and in need of massive reforms. The Crimean War had indicated the degree to which Russia had failed to adapt to the new economic, social, and political pressures sweeping Europe. For much of the time, especially during the reign of Nicholas I, Russia had been seen as the Gendarme of Europe, a force against change. The defeat at Crimea had shown the failure of continued reaction.

SUGGESTIONS FOR READING

The following are excellent on the general background of the period: J. McManners, **European History, 1789-1914*** (Torchbooks); A. J. May, **The Age of Metternich, 1814-1848,*** rev. ed. (Holt, Rinehart & Winston), which is very brief; E. Hobsbawm, **The Age of Revolution: Europe, 1789-1848*** (Mentor); J. Droz, **Europe Between Revolutions, 1815-1848*** (Torchbooks); F. Artz, **Reaction and Revolution, 1814-1832*** (Torchbooks); W. L. Langer, **Political and Social Upheaval, 1832-1852*** (Torchbooks); J. Talmon, **Romanticism and Revolt: Europe, 1815-1848*** (Harcourt Brace Jovanovich); P. Stearns, **European Society in Upheaval: Social History Since 1750*** (Macmillan, 1975); and R. C. Binkley, **Realism and Nationalism: 1852-1871*** (Torchbooks).

H. Nicolson, **The Congress of Vienna: A Study in Allied Unity, 1812-1822*** (Compass) is good reading. L. Seaman, **From Vienna to Versailles*** (Colophon) is a short diplomatic history especially good on the Congress System. See also Henry A. Kissinger, **A World Restored: Metternich, Castlereagh, and the Problems of Peace, 1812-1822*** (Sentry); and Henry F. Schwartz, ed., **Metternich, the "Coachman of Europe": Statesman or Evil Genius?*** (Heath).

G. Fasel, **Europe in Upheaval: The Revolutions of 1848*** (Rand McNally, 1970) is a valuable short synthesis of recent scholarship. Priscilla Robertson, **The Revolutions of 1848: A Social History*** (Princeton) is colorful and entertaining. A scholarly reassessment is F. Fejto, ed., **The Opening of an Era, 1848: An Historical Symposium** (Fertig). G. Rudé, **The Crowd in History, 1730-1848*** (Wiley) describes how crowds were turned into bellicose mobs.

John B. Wolf, **France, 1814-1919: The Rise of a Liberal-Democratic Society*** (Torchbooks); and A. Cobban, **A History of Modern France,*** Vol. II (Penguin) are notable surveys. For greater detail see F. Artz, **France Under the Bourbon Restoration, 1814-1830** (Russell); T. Howarth, **Citizen King: The Life of Louis-Philippe, King of the French** (Verry); G. Duveau, **1848: The Making of a Revolution*** (Vintage); and F. A. Simpson, **Louis Napoleon and the Recovery of France** (Greenwood, 1975).

Two valuable surveys on England are Asa Briggs, **The Making of Modern England, 1783-1867: The Age of Improvement*** (Torchbooks); and E. L. Woodward, **The Age of Reform, 1815-1870,** 2nd ed. (Oxford). On social and economic change from 1815 to 1885 see S. Checkland, **The Rise of Industrial Society in England** (St. Martin's).

A. J. P. Taylor, **The Course of German History*** (Capricorn) is a short essay on German national history since the French Revolution. T. Hamerow, **Restoration, Revolution, Reaction: Economics and Politics in Germany, 1815-1871*** (Princeton) is highly praised. L. Namier, **1848: The Revolution of the Intellectuals*** (Anchor) is critical of the German liberals in the Frankfurt Assembly. W. Medlicott, **Bismarck and Modern Germany*** (Torchbooks) is an excellent introduction to the era. Also recommended are E. Eyck, **Bismarck and the German Empire*** (Norton); and A. J. P. Taylor, **Bismarck: The Man and the Statesman*** (Vintage), which is generally hostile. Notable scholarly surveys are O. Pflanze, **Bismarck and the Development of Germany: The Period of Unification, 1815-1871** (Princeton); and H. Holborn, **A History of Modern Germany, 1840-1945** (Knopf).

Barbara Jelavich, **The Hapsburg Empire in European Affairs, 1814-1918*** (Rand McNally) is an excellent brief history of the empire. A. J. P. Taylor, **The Hapsburg Monarchy, 1909-1918*** (Torchbooks) is chatty and spirited.

A. J. Whyte, **The Evolution of Modern Italy, 1715-1920*** (Norton) is a sound survey. G. Salvemini, **Mazzini*** (Collier) is an authoritative biography. See also C. Delzell, ed., **The Unification of Italy, 1859-1861: Cavour, Mazzini, or Garibaldi?*** (Holt, Rinehart & Winston, European Problem Studies).

M. Karpovich, **Imperial Russia, 1801-1917*** (Holt, Rinehart & Winston) is brief and valuable. H. Seton-Watson, **The Russian Empire, 1801-1917** (Oxford), and **The Decline of Imperial Russia, 1855-1914*** (Praeger) are excellent longer surveys. W. E. Mosse, **Alexander II and the Modernization of Russia,*** 2nd ed. (Collier) is a brief biography.

Matthew S. Anderson, **The Eastern Question, 1774-1923** (St. Martin's) is a new clarification of the Eastern Question. See also H. Kohn, **Pan-Slavism: Its History and Ideology*** (Vintage).

*Indicates a less expensive paperbound edition.

CHAPTER 26

Great Power Competition: 1871-1914

The Growth and Dominance of State Power

INTRODUCTION. Since 1500 the European political system had been going through a process of competition and concentration, as the more powerful states grew and the weaker units, with few exceptions, were swallowed up. In the four centuries to 1900 the number of independent countries declined from approximately 500 to roughly 25.[1] In the half century before World War I six major countries—England, Germany, France, Russia, Italy, and the Austro-Hungarian monarchy—remained as the leading competitors in the European arena. This chapter will discuss their attempts to adapt to the new economic, social, political, and intellectual conditions in Europe in the period before 1914.

The Industrial Revolution gave some of these states the immense material and economic power as well as the communications technology to affect the everyday lives of their citizens through the construction of huge conscript armies, universal educational systems, and communications networks. The states became more efficient in collecting taxes from their expanding populations; at the same time the citizens in western and central Europe came to have a larger voice in political decisions through the introduction of mass democratic parties. In line with these developments, England, Germany, and France led the way in building modern state systems, while the other major powers in Russia, Italy, and the Austro-Hungarian monarchy were trying to improve their governments in order to compete and survive.

As these states grew in strength they competed for areas to dominate outside of their national boundaries. The nagging Eastern Question seemed to defy solution and remained a dangerous point of contention. Further, the competition among these states took on global proportions during the last part of the century as all of the major powers except the Austro-Hungarian monarchy initiated an unprecedented wave of imperialism that carved up Africa and parcelled out portions of Asia for control. Because the European states had such great economic and military strength by the end of the century, these foreign involvements came to pose a threat to world peace, as the traditional European competition was projected to worldwide dimensions.

The major reason for the increase in European power was the improved ability of the states to mobilize their citizens and resources. Literacy became increasingly important in the modern industrial state, since the citizen had to be able to fulfill his governmental responsibilities and perform complex tasks in his work. Rulers from Napoleon I to Kaiser William II had noted the essential political importance of universal public education in order to build a dependable citizenry.[2] By the end of the century most of the states had declared war on illiteracy and had invested heavily in public education. The increase in literacy rates and the mass circulation press that developed during the latter part of the century brought politics to the common people, and changed the quality of political life. The schools thus became the training ground for citizenship as well as for vocation.

The states were active not only in the schools but also in the armed forces, the controlling of the food supply, the economy, the training of technical personnel, the police, and the important area of compiling and keeping the statistics and records of each citizen's life. As populations increased and as the number of state services grew, the number of bureaucrats increased correspondingly. In Germany, for example, the employees working in the postal services and railroads soared from 245,000 to nearly 700,000 between 1880 and 1910.[3] Military conscription, in all the states except England, directly touched the lives of many young men. By 1897 France and Germany each had nearly 3,500,000 men in the field or on reserve, and these soldiers were better and more expensively armed than ever before.

The increase in state functions had to be financed through more taxes and borrowing. Fiscal income in the German empire went from 263 million marks in 1873 to over 1200 million marks in 1909.[4] Other states registered a similar increase in income.

Thus in the political realm as in the areas of material and economic growth, cultural transformation, and intellectual and ideological development, Europe went through a revolutionary change by the end of the nineteenth century. An examination of the various states' responses to changing conditions in the last part of the century indicates the diversity of challenges facing Europe's statesmen. By the end of the period, those states that had shown the greatest flexibility in adapting to the new conditions — England, Germany, and France — would stand as Europe's most powerful countries.

THE ROAD TOWARD DEMOCRACY: ENGLAND 1865-1914

Gladstone and Disraeli. Profiting from its economic superiority and tradition of reform, England made considerable progress toward a truly democratic political structure in the half century before World War I. The state continued its support for industry and trade while at the same time becoming more closely involved with the welfare of its citizens. Two great statesmen, William Ewert Gladstone (1809-1898), a Liberal, and Benjamin Disraeli (1804-1881), a Conservative, dominated the first part of this period with their policies of gradual reform. These two alternated with one another as prime minister from 1867 to 1880. After Disraeli's death, Gladstone prevailed in British politics until he retired in 1894.

Gladstone and Disraeli came from sharply contrasting backgrounds. The son of a rich Liverpool merchant, Gladstone had every advantage that wealth and good social position could bestow. He entered Parliament in 1833 at the age of twenty-four, and quickly made a reputation for himself as one of the greatest orators of his day. He began as a Conservative in politics, following the path of the Tory reformer, Robert Peel. But gradually, he shifted his allegiance to the newly formed Liberal party that appeared in the 1830's. In the next thirty years he became a strong proponent of laissez-faire economics, and constantly worked to keep government from interfering in business. His record as a social and economic reformer was not imposing, but in the realm of political reform he made major advances.

Disraeli, on the other hand, had few of Gladstone's advantages. The son of a Jew who became a naturalized British subject in 1801, Disraeli was baptized an Anglican. He first made a name for himself as a novelist with *Vivian Grey* (1826). In contrast to Gladstone, Disraeli swung from liberalism to conservatism in his political philosophy. He stood for office as a Conservative throughout his career, and eventually became the leader of the Conservative (Tory) party.

Both Liberals and Conservatives had to face the fact that the complacent pace of government during the "Victorian Compromise" from 1850 to 1865 could not be maintained much longer. During that time an alliance of the landed gentry and the middle class worked together to keep the lower classes " in their stations." Serious problems remained to be dealt with. With only one adult male out of six having the right to vote, severe popular pressure for a more represen-

The English satirical magazine *Punch* portrayed Benjamin Disraeli and William Gladstone as rival stars in the theater. Much to the displeasure of Gladstone, Disraeli had just become prime minister.

tative government came to be felt by both parties. Both the Liberals, supported by the middle classes, and the Conservatives, drawing their strength from the landowning gentry, realized that reform must come, and each hoped to gain new political strength from the passage of a reform bill.

It was Gladstone's turn first. In 1866 he introduced a moderate reform bill giving the vote to city workers. When the proposal failed to pass, political agitation and riots rocked the country. The outbreaks evidently had an impact on the members of Parliament, because when the Conservatives came into power in 1867, Disraeli successfully sponsored a reform bill that added more than a million city workers to the voting rolls, thus increasing the electorate by 88 percent. Although women and farm laborers could still not vote, England advanced further down the road to political democracy. It must be mentioned that these reforms were not put into effect without considerable opposition from some conservatives who asserted that the day of revolution was brought nearer by increasing the franchise.[5]

Surprisingly, although the Conservatives had passed the reforms, the new voters brought the Liberals back into power in 1868. Gladstone began his so-called "Glorious Ministry," which lasted until 1874, and saw the introduction of a wide variety of reforms. With the granting of the vote to the urban masses, it became imperative to give their children an education. The Education Act of 1870 promoted the establishment of local school boards authorized to build and maintain government schools. Fees could be charged and attendance could be made compulsory between the ages of five and thirteen. Private schools received governmental subsidies if they could meet certain minimum standards. In ten years attendance in elementary schools jumped from 1 to 4 million.

Other reforms included a thorough overhaul of the civil service system. Previously, in both government and the military most appointments and promotions depended upon patronage and favoritism, but in 1870 employment in these areas was finally based on open examinations. In the army, enlistment terms were improved, flogging was

abolished, and the purchase of commissions was eliminated. The justice system was improved through measures which made it more efficient. The secret ballot was introduced, and some of the restrictions on the labor unions' activities were removed. By 1872 the "Glorious Ministry" had exhausted itself, and Disraeli wittily referred to Gladstone and his colleagues in the House of Commons as a "range of exhausted volcanoes."

Disraeli's government succeeded the "Glorious Ministry" in 1874, and in the next six years he set out to "give the country a rest." He was no standpat conservative, however. He advocated an approach known as Tory democracy that attempted to weld an alliance beween the landed gentry and the workers against the middle class. Even during this time of rest, Disraeli's government pushed through reforms in public health, housing, food and drug legislation, and union rights. Under the latter, the rights to strike and to peacefully picket were legalized.

Gladstone returned to power in 1880 and continued the stream of reforms with the Third Reform Bill that extended the vote to agricultural workers. This act brought Britain to the verge of universal manhood suffrage. He also gained the passage of the important Employers' Liability Act which gave workers rights of compensation in case of accidents on the job.

The Irish problem. One dilemma escaped, and continues to escape, the solutions of well-meaning reformers in England, and that was the problem of Ireland. The British handling of Ireland over the centuries stands exposed to serious criticism. In the seventeeth century the British placed large numbers of Scottish emigrants in the province of Ulster, in northern Ireland, where a strong colony of Protestants—the so-called Orangemen, or Scotch-Irish—developed. In the eighteenth century a number of oppressive laws were passed against Irish Catholics, restricting their political, economic, and religious freedom, and effectively dispossessing them of their lands.

With the passage of the Act of Union in 1801, the Irish were forced to send their representatives to the Parliament in London. A

This sketch of Irish tenants being forcibly evicted by British landlords bears sad witness to the realities of the Irish woes during the nineteenth century.

large part of the Irish farm land passed into the hands of parasitic landlords who leased their newly gained lands in increasingly smaller plots to more and more people. Many peasants could not pay their rent and were evicted from the land; thus in the first half of the nineteenth century the Irish lost both their representation and their livelihood. In 1845 the potato crop—the main staple of diet—failed, and a terrible famine ensued in which perhaps as many as 500,000 people died. A huge exodus to America began at that time, and the Irish population rapidly diminished. Between 1841 and 1891 the population fell from 8,770,000 to less than 5,-000,000.

The Irish gained a few concessions from the British during the century in the form of the Catholic Emancipation Act (1829) and protection from arbitrary eviction for tenants during the "Glorious Ministry." Further, the Irish Anglican Church lost its favored position in which Roman Catholics had to pay tax support to a church they did not attend. In 1881 Gladstone pushed through an act that allowed the Irish peasants the chance of gradually regaining the land that had once been theirs.

None of these concessions, however, made up for the lack of home rule, and in 1874 the Irish statesman Charles Stewart Parnell began to work actively to force the issue through Parliament. Gladstone introduced home rule bills in 1886 and 1896, but both were defeated. A home rule bill was finally passed in 1914, but by this time the Ulsterites strongly opposed the measure and prepared to resist by force incorporation into Catholic Ireland. The outbreak of war with Germany postponed civil strife, but this was only a two-year delay until the Easter Uprising of 1916. Not until 1921, however, did southern Ireland finally attain the status of a British dominion, as the home rule bill of 1914 was never put into effect.

Rule of the New Liberals: 1905-1914. Gladstone's fight for Irish home rule split his party and paved the way for a decade of Conservative rule in Britain (1895-1905). Partly because of foreign and imperial affairs, the Conservatives departed from the reformist traditions of Tory democracy. By 1905 the

A picture of the young Winston Churchill who, despite his support of many unpopular positions during his early political career, rose to become one of England's most magnanimous statesmen. A writer and painter as well as a politician, Churchill's countenance of vigor, forcefulness, and wit provided England with the necessary leadership to sustain itself through two world wars.

need for social and political reform again claimed the attention of the parties.

Over 30 percent of the adult male workers made the unacceptably low wage of less than seven dollars a week. It was impossible to save for the increasing periods of unemployment. Numerous strikes vividly reflected the workers' discontent. Partially in response to the laborers' needs the Labour Party was founded in 1900 under the leadership of J. Ramsay MacDonald (1866-1937), and the Liberals found themselves threatened on both their left and right flanks. They decided to abandon their old laissez-faire economic concepts and embrace a bold program of social legislation. In the words of the British politician David Lloyd George, "four spectres haunt the poor: Old Age, Accident, Sickness, and Unemployment. We are going to exorcise them."[6]

Led by prime minister Herbert Asquith, Lloyd George, and Winston Churchill, who at this time was just beginning his distinguished career, the Liberal party—with the aid of the Labour bloc—put through a thorough program that provided for old-age pensions, national employment bureaus, workmen's compensation protection, and sickness, accident, and unemployment insurance. In addition, labor unions were not to be held financially responsible for losses caused by a strike. Members of the House of Commons, up to then unpaid, were granted a moderate salary. This last act allowed an individual without private means to pursue a political career.

The House of Lords had tried to block the Liberal reform program. When they failed to pass the 1909-1910 budget which laid new tax burdens—including an income tax—on the richer classes in order to pay for the new programs, the Liberals and Labour directly attacked the rationale for the Lords' existence. They argued that a hereditary, irresponsible upper house was an anachronism in a democracy. The result was the Parliament Bill of 1911 that took away the Lords' power of absolute veto. Asquith announced

that the king had promised to create enough new peers to pass the bill if needed (a tactic used with the 1832 Reform Bill). The Lords had to approve, and thereafter could only slow up and force reconsideration of legislation.

By 1914 the evolutionary path to democracy and a modern democratic state structure had been largely completed. Britain stood as proof that revolution and bloodshed were not needed for the attainment of a more equitable society.

THE RISE OF GERMANY: 1871-1914

The Second Reich. The most important political event in Europe in the half century before World War I was the unification of Germany. Within the brief span of one lifetime the fragmented German areas of central

THE UNIFICATION OF GERMANY
1815–1871

- Prussia 1815-1866
- Annexed by Prussia 1866
- Joined Prussia in forming the North German Confederation 1867
- Joined with Prussia to form the German Empire 1871
- Alsace-Lorraine ceded to German Empire by France 1871
- German Confederation 1815-1866

With Paris about to fall to the Prussian armies, King William of Prussia is proclaimed German emperor by his princes in the Hall of Mirrors of the Palace of Versailles. Smiling with satisfaction, Bismarck stands foremost at the foot of the dais.

Europe united under Prussian leadership to challenge England for world economic and political dominance. Germany united around the Hohenzollern dynasty in Berlin. But the source of its strength was to be found in the rapid economic growth and population increase up to 1914, and the efficient German political structure. The unification movement had the support of major intellectuals and artists and the leadership of Otto von Bismarck. Bismarck had taken advantage of events to put together the Second (Hohenzollern) Reich, or empire, that was proclaimed in January 1871 in the Hall of Mirrors at the Palace of Versailles. King William I became the German emperor. The new Reich would be a federal union of twenty-six states with a population of 41 million. The new empire had a few parliamentary trappings, but behind this facade of the Bundesrat (representing the ruling houses of the various states) and the Reichstag (representing the people through its 397 members elected by manhood suffrage) stood the undoubted power of Prussia and the kaiser (emperor). William I controlled military and foreign affairs, and

enough votes (17) in the Bundesrat to veto any constitutional change. The chancellor, who was appointed by the kaiser and responsible to him alone, was the actual head of government. He could defy or ignore the legislature when it served his purpose, but he had to operate within the constraints of a federal state in which substantial powers of local government were reserved to member states.

Bismarck built the modern German state and distrusted those institutions that were not subordinate to it. The Catholic Church had sent a large bloc of representatives to the Reichstag in 1871, and these members supported the complete independence of the Church from state control. They denounced divorce, secular education, and freedom of conscience. Many of the Catholics were also strong supporters of the new dogma of papal infallibility.

Within Protestant Prussia anti-Catholic policies came to be enforced in a conflict that was known as the *Kulturkampf* (the civilization struggle). The so-called "May laws" made it a penal offense for the clergy to criticize the government, regulated the educational activities of religious orders, expelled the Jesuits from Germany, made civil marriages mandatory (this law was applied across the empire), and required all priests to study theology at state universities. Pope Pius IX declared these acts null and void and called on loyal Catholics to refuse to obey them. Also, many of the laws applied to Protestants, and they were actively disliked on that side of the religious spectrum. Bismarck struck back at the Catholics, imprisoning priests, confiscating church property, and closing pulpits. Yet the chancellor had met his match. He came to realize that he could not afford to create millions of martyrs, and showing his usual shrewd political sense he retreated and repealed most of the anti-Catholic laws.

Bismarck faced a more severe challenge to his position from the Social Democratic movement. The growth of the socialist movement coincided with the rapid growth of the industrial sector in Germany after 1860. Its founder, Ferdinand Lassalle, opposed violence as a method to gain power. After his death the party grew to the point that Bismarck saw it as a substantial threat even though it retained its essentially passive character. The Social Democratic party was established in Germany in 1875, and its leaders demanded not only a true parliamentary democracy, but also comprehensive social legislation. Their popular strength grew, and in 1878 the chancellor decided to act.

Two attempts were made on the emperor's life in that year, and although the Social Democrats had no connection with the acts, Bismarck launched an all-out campaign to weaken their political base. He was not one to let a good opportunity pass. He dissolved extra-legal socialist organizations, suppressed their publications, and imprisoned their leaders. Despite these measures, the supporters of the socialist movement increased. Bismarck changed tactics and began to undercut the socialist opposition by implementing important social legislation during the 1880's. He introduced sickness, accident, and old-age insurance bills that were passed and helped respond to many of the abuses of the Industrial Revolution. The Social Democrats did not wither away, and their party continued to grow in size and influence. Bismarck had, however, defused a potential social revolution by incorporating his opponents' goals into his own program.

Kaiser William II. In 1888 William II, the grandson of William I, became emperor of Germany. Just as Bismarck had been the dominant figure in central Europe since 1862, so too would William II dominate that part of the world until 1918. Here was a person who, without Bismarck's finesse, advocated the policies of "blood and iron." Where Bismarck might have known the limits and uses of force, William II lacked the diplomatic sensitivity of the old master. He was a militarist, a believer in the divine right of kings. He constantly reminded those around him that "he and God" worked together for the good of the state. The new kaiser saw not a guide but a threat in Bismarck and stated that "it was a question whether the Bismarck dynasty or the Hohenzollern dynasty should rule."[7] The young emperor and old chancellor conflicted on a number of points, and finally in March 1890 Bismarck resigned.

At the beginning of the twentieth century Germany presented a puzzling picture to the world. On one hand the blustering kaiser at the head of the powerful German state made fiery and bellicose statements. He encouraged the militaristic movement among all levels of society, from the aristocratic Prussian Junkers down to the large portions of the patriotic German masses at the bottom. Many Germans who shared in the increasing prosperity of the Second Reich would do their jobs in the knowledge that *"Alles kommt von oben"* ("Everything comes down from above").

On the other hand, Germany made substantial scientific, cultural, and industrial advances during the same period. A close observer of German society could note that not all Germans marched in four-four time at the kaiser's request. The Social Democratic party could claim the support of one third of the voters, an indication that a democratic system was in a full process of growth.

The outbreak of the war in 1914 was to nip

During the civil war of 1871 between the government and the Paris Commune, many atrocities were committed. Illustrating the violence which occurred on both sides, this photograph shows the Communards assassinating sixty-two hostages.

the possibility of a democratic movement in the bud. The only force that could bind all of Germany together—nationalism—was invoked by the kaiser in his war declaration speech. He stated, "I recognize no parties, but only Germans!"[8] Most of the political spectrum stepped forward in agreement.

THE THIRD REPUBLIC: 1871-1914

Precarious beginnings. Born in 1871 amidst the humiliation of military defeat, the French Third Republic went through many years of shaky existence before it gained a firm footing. It began with the bitter task of making a peace with Germany which would deprive it of part of Lorraine and all of Alsace and would impose a huge indemnity on the country. The Republic then had to undergo violent social conflict in Paris. The new national assembly, which was overwhelmingly royalist, set about drafting a new plan of government which had conservative overtones. The combination of the humiliating peace settlement and the right-wing assembly touched off a revolutionary outburst which culminated in the Paris Commune

(1871). The people of Paris had suffered greatly during the siege of the city, so much so that the food shortages had driven them to eat some of the animals in the municipal zoo. When it turned out that their sacrifices had brought them nothing but a tragic peace and a conservative government, the republican and radical portion of the city formed a Commune, in the tradition of the Paris Commune of 1792, to save the Republic. The Communards advocated governmental control of prices, wages, and working conditions (including the abolition of nightwork in the bakeries). After several weeks of civil strife, the Commune was savagely suppressed, leaving France with a deep-seated heritage of class hatred. The Commune's spirit would continue to live in the various revolutionary movements.

The national assembly finally approved a republican constitution for France four years later, in 1875. The delay occurred largely because the various monarchist factions were unable to reach an agreement, and a republic seemed to be the least disagreeable form of government. The improvised constitutional laws of 1875 were passed by a margin of one vote. Under the new statutes, there was election by direct manhood suffrage to the Chamber of Deputies, the influential lower house. There was also a Senate, elected indirectly by electoral colleges in the major administrative districts—the departments. The president was elected by the legislature, but his powers were so limited as to make him merely a figurehead. The ministry exercised the real power, and was appointed by whatever coalition of parties or factions held a majority in the legislature.

The Boulanger and Dreyfus affairs. The Third Republic faced a series of crises up to 1914, such as increased anarchist violence, culminating in a series of bombings in 1893, and financial scandals such as that surrounding the Panama Canal, which implicated a wide range of leading figures in business and politics. The most serious crises, however, were the Boulanger and Dreyfus affairs. The Republic was both threatened and embarrassed by the public cries for vengeance uttered in 1886 by General Boulanger, the minister of war. "Remember," he would say, "they are waiting for us in Alsace!" All of the anti-republican elements saw the general as a man on horseback who would sweep away the Republic by a coup d'état, as Louis Napoleon had done in 1851. When the government ordered his arrest on the charge of conspiracy, Boulanger fled the country and later committed suicide.

The Dreyfus case was a far more serious crisis for the Third Republic because it divided and embittered French opinion and challenged the fundamental ideals of French democracy. Captain Alfred Dreyfus, the first Jewish officer on the French general staff, was accused in 1894 of selling military secrets to Germany. He was tried by his fellow officers, found guilty, publicly stripped of his commission, and condemned to solitary confinement on Devil's Island, a notorious convict settlement near French Guiana. Even with the Dreyfus case settled, military secrets continued to leak to the Germans, and subsequently a royalist, spendthrift officer named Major Esterhazy was accused, tried, and acquitted. At that time the French writer Émile Zola entered the controversy, and in his famous letter "J'accuse" (1898) attacked the military judges for knowingly letting the guilty party—Esterhazy—go, while the innocent victim, Dreyfus, remained in prison. By

1899 Esterhazy had admitted his guilt, but the Dreyfus case had split France for the most part into two camps—the army, Church, and royalists, who were anti-Dreyfus, and the intellectuals, republicans, and socialists, who were pro-Dreyfus. When the case was placed under review, the court, ignoring Esterhazy's confession, continued to find Dreyfus guilty. However, the president of France pardoned him, and finally in 1906 the highest civil court in France found him completely innocent.

The case had a greater significance than just freeing a wrongly imprisoned man. The Church had actively campaigned against Dreyfus' release, and it would soon have to pay for its part in the Dreyfus affair. Many republicans believed that the Church was an enemy to democratic government, and they demanded an end to the clergy's connection with the state. The anticlerical movement gained successes in 1901 when all Church schools were closed and in 1905 when the ties between the Church and state were finally ended, thus putting an end to Napoleon's century-old Concordat with the papacy.

By 1914 the Third Republic had weathered the forty years of intermittent crises and had attained stability and prosperity. The workers' movement became a real power in the country as the various radical and socialist movements came together for mutual support in the National Labor group, the *Confédération Générale du Travail*. Monarchist and other right-wing parties still held considerable strength, even though they were weakened by the Dreyfus affair. But across the political spectrum French republicanism generally had wide support. Most Frenchmen enjoyed basic democratic rights, such as manhood suffrage, freedom of the press, and equality before the law. Under the basic statutes of the Third Republic, the multiparty political system reflected the extreme individualism of the French public. But the various cabinets that were constructed from the diverse parties were unstable, and were dissolved at the slightest pressure. French prime ministers came and went with bewildering rapidity. Yet, France was the most important democracy on the continent and one of the world's great powers.

RUSSIA: REVOLUTION AND REFORM

Revolutionary response. At the same time that the tsarist autocracy attempted to reform itself, the revolutionary movement became stronger. In the 1850's the remarkable movement known as Nihilism developed in Russia. The Nihilists questioned all old values, championed the independence of the individual, and delighted in shocking the older generation. At first they tried to convert the aristocracy to the cause of reform. Failing there they turned to the peasants, and a veritable missionary movement ensued. Some idealistic college students joined in the movement to become laborers and work in the fields with the peasants. Others went to the villages as doctors and teachers to preach reform to the people. This "go to the people" campaign was known as the Narodnik movement (*narod*, "people"). However, to a large degree the peasants ignored the outsiders' political message.

For the twenty years after his great reform in 1861, Alexander II suffered under increasing revolutionary attack. It was as if each reform was seen by the opposition not as an improvement but as a sign of weakness to be exploited. In Poland Alexander had tried to reverse the Russification program of his father, and in return he saw the Polish insurrection of 1863. He was also subjected to a number of assassination attempts. In the 1870's the revolutionary violence increased, as the collapse of the Narodnik movement drove the opposition more and more to the practice of terrorism. The radical branch of the Nihilists — under the influence of Bakunin's protégé, S. G. Nechaev — pursued a program of total destruction, to be achieved by a revolutionary elite. In his *Revolutionary Catechism* Nechaev stated that "everything that promotes the success of the revolution is moral and everything that hinders it is immoral." The soldiers in the battle — the revolutionaries — were "doomed men," having "no interests, no affairs, no feelings, no habits, no property, not even a name."[9] The revolution dominated all thoughts and actions for these individuals. Other groups carried out, perhaps unknowingly, Nechaev's theories. One after another, prominent officials were shot down or killed by bombs. Finally, Tsar Alexander II himself was assassinated in 1881, on the very day he had approved a proposal to call a representative assembly to consider new reforms.

Autocracy and reaction. The slain tsar's son Alexander III (1881-1894) could see only that his father's reforms had resulted in increased opposition and, eventually, assassination. During his thirteen-year reign he tried to return Russia's government to a policy of "Autocracy, Orthodoxy, and Nationalism." Under the guidance of Constantine Pobedonostsev, his chief advisor, the tsar pursued a repressive policy of censorship of "dangerous" publications, regulation of schools and universities, and increased secret police activities. Aside from renewing a rigorous policy of Russification among the nationalities, he also permitted the oppression of the Jews, who were bullied and sometimes massacred in terrible drives called pogroms. The revolutionaries may have been driven underground or executed (such as Vladimir Lenin's brother), and the nationalities may have been kept in their place. But under Alexander III Russia lost thirteen valuable years in its attempt to become competitive with western Europe.

Alexander was succeeded by his son, Nicholas II (1894-1917), an altogether decent but weak man. He inherited the reactionary policies of his father and tried to enforce them during his reign. But the forces of the Industrial Revolution and rural overpopulation spawned a wide range of political pressures that the autocratic structure could not adequately control. A wide range of political movements developed during the early years of Nicholas' reign, and most of them had to operate in secret. The Liberal party (Constitutional Democrats, or *Kadets*) wanted a constitutional monarchy and believed in peaceful reform on the English model. The Social Revolutionaries combined socialism with the Narodnik tradition and advocated "the whole land to the whole people." These agrarian socialists wanted the distribution of land among those who actually worked it — the peasants. The Social Democrats, exponents of Marxist principles in a Russian framework, attracted the radical intellectuals and the politically educated workingmen in the cities. They worked for complete social, economic, and political revolution. In 1903 they split into two wings—the Mensheviks and the Bolsheviks. The Mensheviks believed that Russian socialism should grow gradually and peacefully in accord with Marxist principles of development and historical evolution, and were prepared to work within a framework dominated by bourgeois political parties. They were sure that they would gradually and inevitably become the dominant political force and achieve the socialistic society. The Bolsheviks, led by Vladimir Lenin, advocated the formation of a small elite of professional revolutionaries who would be subject to strong party discipline and who would lead the proletariat. Lenin wanted to speed up the historical process as described by Marx.

The government worked energetically to put down the opposition by placing secret agents among the opposition parties to act as spies, launching outright attacks on the opponents, and carrying on diversionary anti-Semitic activities with bands of thugs called Black Hundreds. Yet by attacking the opposition, the government was concentrating on a symptom of Russia's problems and not the causes. Once again a failure in war—this time against Japan—exposed the weaknesses of the autocratic regime, and disorders spread throughout the land in the last days of 1904. On January 22, 1905, the Cossacks opened fire on a peaceful crowd of workers who had advanced on the Winter Palace in St. Petersburg carrying a petition asking for the tsar's help. A general strike broke out, with the strikers demanding a democratic republic, freedom for political prisoners, and the disarming of the police. Soviets—councils of workers—appeared in the cities to direct revolutionary activities. Most business and government offices closed and the whole machinery of Russian economic life creaked to a halt. The country was virtually paralyzed.

Pushed to the wall, Tsar Nicholas issued the October Manifesto of 1905 which prom-

ised "freedom of person, conscience, assembly, and union." A national Duma (legislature) was to be called without delay. The right to vote would be extended, and no law would go into force without the Duma's confirmation. The moderate groups were satisfied, but the socialist groups rejected the concessions as insufficient. They tried to organize new strikes, but the tsar's manifesto had created disunity among the ranks of the opposition.

When the first Duma met in the spring of 1906 it was boycotted by most of the radical forces. As a result the *Kadets* were the dominant force. After hearing the extensive criticism from the Duma of the government's policies in the Russo-Japanese war, treatment of minorities, and handling of political prisoners, the tsar dissolved the legislative body. Its members, he said, "would not cooperate." An appeal by the liberal leaders of the Duma for popular support met with apathy from the Russian people. Sensing the decline in political fervor, the tsar appointed a conservative prime minister, Peter Stolypin, who cracked down on some of the radical elements.

Unlike previous tsarist functionaries, Stolypin knew that changes had to be made, especially in the area of agriculture. Even without the tsar's full support he pushed through reforms that abolished all payments still owed by the peasants under the Emancipation law, and permitted peasants to withdraw from the village communes and become private owners of their lands, with substantial financial aid from the state. Stolypin was well on the way to finding a solution to that most enduring of Russian problems, the peasant problem. He was in the process of developing a class of small farmers when he was assassinated by a Social Revolutionary in 1911, who, in the strange mode of the day, was also an agent of the secret police. In spite of the reactionary tsar, Russia made major gains after 1905 toward becoming a constitutional monarchy. Stolypin's death, however, deprived the government of needed leadership, and the coming First World War gave the regime a test it could not pass.

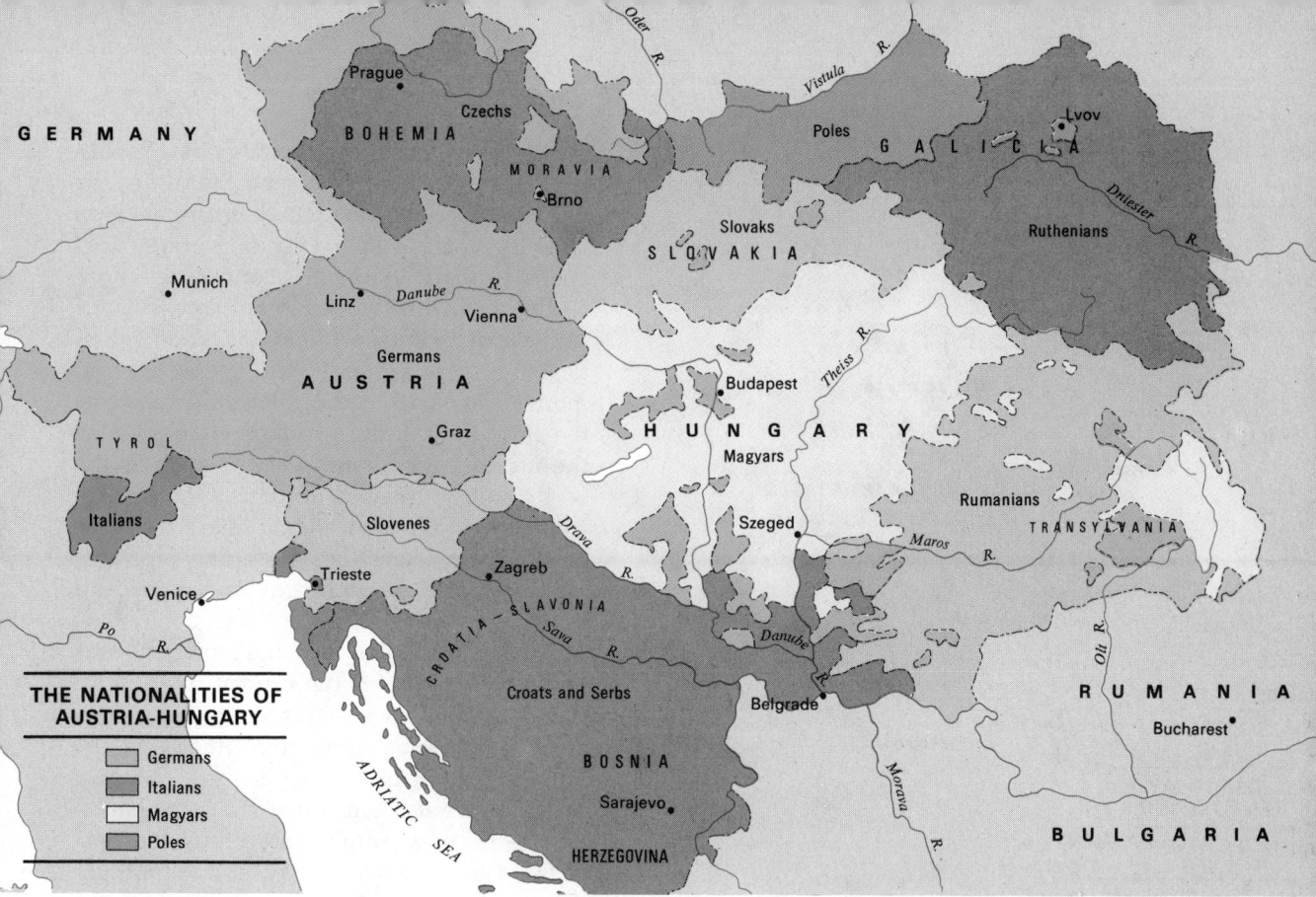

THE NATIONALITIES OF
AUSTRIA-HUNGARY

	Germans
	Italians
	Magyars
	Poles

THE LESSER GREAT POWERS

Italy. After the heady triumphs of unification in 1871, Italy had to face serious problems. The country had few natural resources, and the interests of the north and south rarely coincided. The religious issue seriously weakened the state, since the spiritual father of most of the Italians—the pope—did not reconcile himself to the new political situation. The taking of Rome, the last remnant of the Papal States, confirmed the pope's antipathy to the newly united state. Calling himself the "prisoner of the Vatican," the pope encouraged Italians to refrain from voting. In an attempt to come to terms with the pope, the Italian government passed the Law of Papal Guarantees by which the pontiff was to retain the Vatican as a sovereign state and to be given an annual sum of $600,000 (roughly the amount of money he had received from his previously held lands). Pius IX rejected the offer, but the state refused to repeal the law.

The Italian government carried on an impressive program of railroad building, naval construction, and attempts at social and welfare legislation. But major social problems remained, especially with the peasantry in the south of the country. Radical political parties made their presence felt, especially after the turn of the century, in the form of widespread strikes. In 1900 King Umberto, who had taken the throne in 1878, was the victim of an anarchist assassin. Change proceeded slowly after that, and not until 1912 did the country achieve universal manhood suffrage, a time when there was still widespread illiteracy. The political parties of the peninsula proved unable to coordinate effectively, and instability dominated governmental life. Another grievous burden for the country was its leaders' ambition to have Italy play a grand role in the world and thus fulfill the dreams of greatness built up during the drive for unification. Too much money was spent on the army, at the expense of needed investments in education and social services. National resources were squan-

RUSSIA

AUSTRIA - HUNGARY

Vienna

Budapest

Trieste

BOSNIA
HERZEGOVINA

Belgrade

SERBIA

RUMANIA

Bucharest

BLACK
SEA

MONTENEGRO

Sofia

BULGARIA

Constantinople

San Stefano

ADRIATIC

SEA

ITALY

Salonika

AEGEAN
SEA

OTTOMAN

IONIAN
SEA

GREECE

Smyrna

Athens

EMPIRE

CRETE

**THE TREATY OF
SAN STEFANO 1878**

Bulgaria as proposed by
the Treaty

dered in the unrewarding pursuit of building an empire in Africa.

Even though liberal and socialist politicians joined together to work for reforms such as compulsory education, freedom of the press, and better working conditions for the masses, Italy still faced severe crises by 1914. In June of that year a general strike spread through the central part of the peninsula. A major part in that movement was played by an editor of a socialist journal named Benito Mussolini. The conditions of economic hardship and high taxes that had driven thousands of Italians to emigrate to the United States remained, as the industrial gains in the north of the country were not shared by the south.

The Austro-Hungarian Monarchy to 1914.
After the 1867 *Ausgleich* (compromise) Francis Joseph still ruled over a multinational state in which there were 12 million Germans, 10 million Magyars, over 24 million Slavs, and some 4 million Rumanians. Although the Germans of Austria had recog-

nized the equality of the Magyars of Hungary in the 1867 arrangement, the rest of the nationalities continued to live under alien rule. But instead of having to work against one dominant national group, they now had to deal with two. In some cases, such as in the prospering, cosmopolitan, and sophisticated area of Bohemia, the people wanted more rights within the Hapsburg realm as the minimum and an independent state as the maximum demand. Others, such as the Serbs, sought the goal of joining their countrymen living in adjacent national states. The nationalities question was an explosive problem for the authorities in Vienna and Budapest.

The functioning of the Dual Monarchy was best symbolized by the official bank notes that were printed in eight languages on one side and in Magyar on the other. On the Hungarian side of the Monarchy the Magyar aristocracy governed under the constitution of 1848 that was reintroduced after the *Ausgleich.* The Hungarians refused to share political power with the Croats, Serbs, Slovaks, and Rumanians found under their rule. The small, powerful, landowning class dominated the mass of backward, landless peasants. Under conservative leadership, a virtual process of Magyarization was carried out among the various nationalities. Serious conflict broke out with the Austrians over the use of Hungarian in the Monarchy's common army and over the allocation of taxes.

In the Austrian half, political life was dominated by wealthy German businessmen and the landed aristocracy. But even with this concentration of power, the governmental patterns were more democratic, especially after 1907 when the bicameral legislature of Austria came to be elected by general manhood suffrage. Strong national hatreds impaired the functioning of what seemed to be, on paper at least, a liberal constitution. Political parties came to be based not on principle but on nationality. Each major group had to work with the German ruling elite, even though it might fear and detest it. The nationalities all too often disliked each other as well, and this stopped the possibility of a coalition of non-German elements against the Austrians. By 1914 the Austrians had given their subject nationalities substantial local self-government, but this concession did little to quiet the discontent.

Despite the governmental problems of the *Ausgleich* agreement, the defenders of the compromise on both sides could still tell themselves that they were, after all, citizens of a "great" empire. The Monarchy occupied a strategic geographical location and possessed enough military strength to be very influential in southern and eastern Europe. The Dual Monarchy also possessed considerable economic potential. Hungary had wheat while Croatia and Slovenia exported livestock. Prague and Vienna could boast industrial growth and prominent banking houses. But Francis Joseph ruled over a disjointed conglomeration of peoples whose economic and political strength could not compare with Germany or even France.

STATES IN CONFLICT ABROAD

The unanswered Eastern Question. In the generation after the Crimean War the problems posed by the disintegrating Ottoman empire became more severe. The Slavic nationalities still found under Turkish control began their drive for independence. To the north the Russians, who could do little militarily in the Balkans during their period of intensive internal reforms, broadcast the message of Slavic solidarity to their "little brothers" through the ideological weapon of Pan Slavism, which advocated the brotherhood of Slavs under Russian protection. The Austrians also kept a wary eye on developments in the Balkans.

The Bulgarians, who had been under the Turkish yoke since the fourteenth century, started their national revival in the late eighteenth century. By the 1860's an organized liberation movement was in existence, which was strengthened in 1870 by the founding of the Bulgarian Exarchate, a Bulgarian wing of the Greek Orthodox faith. They could gain strength from the example of the Rumanians, who after centuries under Turkish domi-

nance and a quarter century as a Russian protectorate had gained their independence in 1861, largely due to great power influence. During the 1860's the Serbian leader Michael Obrenovich had worked toward a Balkan union against the Turks. During all of this maneuvering and ferment, the Turks showed no ability to strengthen their rule over areas theoretically under their control.

Finally in 1875 peasants revolted in the district of Bosnia, a Turkish-governed province populated by a religiously diverse group of Slavs. Following this insurrection Serbia and Montenegro declared war on the Turks. In the summer of 1876 the Bulgarians broke into revolt, which the Ottoman forces were able to put down very forcefully. When highly emotional accounts of the Turkish massacres were published in the west, the incident became known as the "Bulgarian horrors," and drew British attention to the Balkans. The Pan Slav faithful in Moscow and St. Petersburg were naturally thrilled at the exploits of their "little brothers," and money and "volunteers" flowed southward.

The series of nationalistic uprisings in the improperly governed Ottoman holdings had captured the attention of the great powers, and by the end of 1875 the Eastern Question, with all of its myriad aspects, was once again the main focus of international diplomacy. The "sick man of Europe" was still strong enough to devastate the Serbs and Montenegrins in the field. They were forced to sue for peace, a possibility that drew Tsar Alexander II and the Russians into war with Turkey in 1877. After a hard-fought campaign the Russians broke through in early 1878 and were close to achieving their final goal of taking Constantinople when the sultan sued for peace.

The resulting treaty of San Stefano in March 1878 recognized the complete independence of Serbia and Rumania from the theoretical Ottoman sovereignty and reaffirmed Montenegro's independence. A large Bulgarian state was set up, nominally tributary to Turkey, but actually dominated by Russia. The Straits were effectively under Russian control, as the Bulgarian state would have a coast on the Aegean. The Eastern Question was almost solved. But Britain and

The new imperialism. It is ironic that the European states would have such great difficulty in dealing with the Eastern Question, and such comparative ease in amassing the power to extend their economic and political control to most of Asia and virtually all of Africa. Perhaps it was the fact that there was so much territory and wealth for the taking that kept the Europeans from engaging in too much conflict as they extended their influences throughout the world.

Whether the European states gained direct control over an area or merely skimmed the profits off the top of a given region, the movement went by the same name—imperialism. Imperialism is the ultimate expression of a state's ability to impose its will on another region, without the oppressed region having the chance to say yea or nay. In the period after 1870 imperialism was motivated by a broad array of forces, ranging from the economic needs of industrialized societies for resources and markets, to humanitarian impulses to "Take up the white man's burden," to missionaries wanting to save the heathen from eternal damnation.

From the end of the Middle Ages to the close of the eighteenth century a large part of Europe was expansionist, seeking colonies and monopolies in overseas trade. But a combination of political and economic factors helped dampen the imperialistic drive between 1815 and 1870. The loss of the thirteen American colonies in 1783 affected Britain's desire for empire, and France lost nearly all of its colonial possessions by 1815. Further, the laissez-faire school of economics argued against the possession of colonies.

When the tide turned, however, it came with a rush. In his six years as English prime minister, Disraeli annexed Fiji and Cyprus, fought a war against the Zulus in southeastern Africa, purchased a controlling interest in Suez Canal shares, and proclaimed Queen Victoria empress of India. The other major European powers, except the Austro-Hungarian Dual Monarchy, eagerly followed Britain's lead, and the colonial scramble began in earnest. The extension of European dominance around the world came about with amazing rapidity. It has been estimated that in 1800 fully one half of the world's surface

Austria correctly perceived a major shift of the balance of power in Russia's favor, and the two of them forced a reconsideration of the San Stefano treaty at the Congress of Berlin in June and July of 1878. Held under the supervision of Bismarck, the self-styled "honest broker," the Congress compelled Russia to agree to a revision of Bulgaria's status, and the large state created in March was broken into three parts—the northernmost would be independent, paying tribute to the Turks, while the other two parts would be Turkish controlled. Austria got the right to "occupy and administer" the provinces of Herzegovina and Bosnia.

The Congress turned back the Russian advance, stymied the national independence movements, and did little to impel Turkey to put its house in order. The Austrian gains caused great bitterness among the Serbs and the Russians, a mood which would add to tensions in the Balkans. The Balkans remained an arena of local nationalistic conflicts that would be projected eventually to affect the diplomacy of all the great powers.

was unknown to Europeans. A century later more land had been explored and acquired than in the entire period from the middle of the fifteenth century to the midpoint of the eighteenth. By 1914 European nations could claim control of about 60 percent of the earth's surface.

The modern nation-states had accumulated the material strength, ideological unity, and population surplus needed to overcome the only concrete limits they faced — those of territorial boundaries. Modern imperialism is as much a testimony to the undoubted strength of the advanced technological nation-state as it is to any laws of economic determination. The growth and the extension of state power can be as much a factor in imperialism as the strict profit motivation that Marxian socialists stress. In his famous and influential work, *Imperialism, the Highest Stage of Capitalism* (1916), Lenin argued that the wages of the workers did not represent enough purchasing power to absorb the output of the capitalist factories and that the vast amounts of capital that were accumulated could not be invested profitably in the home country. Therefore, to Lenin, imperialism was an inevitable phase in the development of capitalism. Lenin was correct in assessing that the profit motive is strong in modern imperialism, but it is not the only motive. False too is the notion that imperialism is a policy exclusive to capitalist powers, as can be proved by examples of communist imperialism in the twentieth century. The material power that the modern industrial state can generate is more than just a measure of surplus capital seeking a profitable home.

Other motives for imperialism can be found in a broad variety of areas, such as patriotism and the pride of seeing the state's flag in some far-off part of the world. The expanding nation-states most certainly could point to the need for colonies for defense purposes. As balance of power came to be measured in global rather than European terms, the states expanded to gain areas for use as naval bases and buffer states. Europe's sense of superiority also came into play, as many administrators in the colonies honestly felt that they were improving the natives' lives by bringing them "civilization." Many missionaries felt justified in altering the cultures of the peoples with whom they came into contact if that was the price that had to be paid for saving their souls from an eternity in hell.

We will assess the extent and influence of the imperialism of the later nineteenth century in the next part. But there can be no better way to conclude the chapter on state dominance than by noting that European states came to control the bulk of the world by 1914.

SUMMARY

By the beginning of the twentieth century England and Germany were the most powerful states in Europe. Statesmen in London and Berlin made the necessary adjustments to the new economic and social forces generated by industrialization to build state structures based on mass democratic participation. In return for the fiscal and political support of the common people, the states gave increased accident, health, and old-age protection. In the half century after 1865, England went from the complacency of the "Victorian Compromise" to the social concerns of the new Liberals and the Labour party. During the same time, under the leadership of Bismarck, the German states unified around the Hohenzollern throne and formed a potent economic and political force. Given the pattern of concentration and competition through which the European state system had passed in the previous four centuries, it is not surprising that the two major state powers would be found on opposite sides at the outbreak of World War I.

Russia and France emerged from defeats in wars in 1856 and 1871 to reform or rebuild their state structures. Under Tsar Alexander II the Russians carried on a thorough reform of their social and political systems. The emancipation of the 23 million serfs altered the entire foundation of Russian life, and the successful completion of the reforms would have been difficult in the best of times. Revolutionary opposition, culminating in the assassination of the tsar in 1881, led to a quarter century of reaction. During that time Russia underwent major economic and population changes, and a wide range of opposition parties developed. After the Russian failure in the war with Japan, the 1905 revolution forced the tsar, Nicholas II, to grant substantial reforms. In the nine years before World War I substantial reforms were made to respond to the changing conditions, but it would prove to be too little too late. In France, the Third Republic emerged from the ruins of the Franco-Prussian war and from the social conflicts of the Paris Commune. It weathered the Boulanger and Dreyfus crises successfully and withstood the pressures of financial scandal and conflicts over the Church's role. By 1914 the Third Republic, even with its multitude of parties, was relatively stable and prosperous as the French made a successful response to the pressures posed by industrialization.

Italy, united in 1861 and territorially filled out by 1870, and the Austro-Hungarian Monarchy, set in motion by the 1867 *Aus-*

gleich, faced overwhelming problems. The Italians had to deal with the conflicting differences between the north and the south of the peninsula, the dilemma of relations with the papacy, a lack of natural resources, and a politically inexperienced populace. The Dual Monarchy had to work through a cumbersome structure to govern a mosaic of nationalities. Neither state could compete as an equal in economic or military terms with England, Germany, France, or even Russia.

By 1900 the European power balance would be dominated by these six states. Their interests were in conflict on the Eastern Question, as seen by events of the 1870's. The tentative solutions emerging from the Congress of Berlin insured that the Balkans would remain a focus for state competition. But the entire globe also became a field of contest for the major states, and the complex strands of their competing interests would span the world and change what had formerly been disinterested spectators of Europe's struggles into active participants.

SUGGESTIONS FOR READING

C. J. H. Hayes, **A Generation of Materialism: 1871-1900*** (Torchbooks); and J. Munholland, **Origins of Contemporary Europe, 1890-1914*** (Harcourt Brace Jovanovich, 1970) are both outstanding syntheses. A. J. P. Taylor, **The Struggle for Mastery in Europe, 1848-1918** (Oxford); and L. Seaman, **From Vienna to Versailles*** (Colophon) are also well-written surveys of international relations.

K. Minogue, **Nationalism** (Basic); and E. H. Carr, **Nationalism and After** (St. Martin's) are brief and stimulating historical surveys. B. C. Shafer, **Nationalism: Myth and Reality*** (Harcourt Brace Jovanovich) is an outstanding fuller account. See also H. Kohn, **The Idea of Nationalism*** (Collier), and **Prophets and Peoples: Studies in Nineteenth Century Nationalism*** (Collier); and Peter F. Sugar and I. Lederer, eds., **Nationalism in Eastern Europe** (Univ. of Washington, 1969).

D. Thomson, **England in the Nineteenth Century, 1815-1914*** (Penguin); and J. Conacher, ed., **The Emergence of Parliamentary Democracy in Britain in the Nineteenth Century*** (Wiley) are both valuable brief accounts. See also the surveys cited in Chapter 25 and F. Ensor, **England, 1870-1914** (Oxford); G. Kitson Clark, **The Making of Victorian England*** (Atheneum); George M. Young, **Victorian England: Portrait of an Age*** (Galaxy); P. Magnus, **Gladstone*** (Dutton); and Robert Blake, **Disraeli*** (Anchor). G. Dangerfield, **The Strange Death of Liberal England, 1910-1914*** (Capricorn) describes the inability of the Liberals to deal with major problems.

Donald J. Harvey, **France Since the Revolution*** (Free Press, 1968); and D. W. Brogan, **The French Nation: From Napoleon to Pétain*** (Colophon) are two short, perceptive surveys. See also B.

Gooch, **The Reign of Napoleon III*** (Rand McNally, 1970); D. Thomson, **Democracy in France Since 1870,*** 5th ed. (Oxford); Roger L. Williams, ed., **The Commune of Paris, 1871*** (Wiley, 1970); and N. Halasz, **Captain Dreyfus: The Story of a Mass Hysteria*** (Simon & Schuster, 1968).

Michael Balfour, **The Kaiser and His Times** (Houghton Mifflin) describes the impact of William II on Germany and Europe. See also A. Rosenberg, **Imperial Germany: The Birth of the German Republic, 1871-1918** (Oxford, 1970). The rebellious spirit of German youth is described in W. Laqueur, **Young Germany: A History of the German Youth Movement** (Basic).

R. Charques, **The Twilight of Imperial Russia*** (Oxford) surveys the reign of the last tsar, Nicholas II. See also R. Massie, **Nicholas and Alexandra*** (Dell); G. Robinson, **Rural Russia Under the Old Regime*** (Univ. of California); A. Yarmolinsky, **The Road to Revolution: A Century of Russian Radicalism*** (Collier); and J. Joll, **The Anarchists*** (Universal).

P. T. Moon, **Imperialism and World Politics** (Macmillan) is a keen analysis of why Europe shouldered the "white man's burden." Other provocative studies on nineteenth-century imperialism are G. H. Nadel and P. Curtis, eds., **Imperialism and Colonialism*** (Macmillan); H. M. Wright, ed., **The "New Imperialism"*** (Heath); and A. P. Thornton, **Doctrines of Imperialism*** (Wiley).

*Indicates a less expensive paperbound edition.

In the autumn of 1815 the Bocage family of Paris endured the food shortages and high prices generated by the last years of the Napoleonic wars. They had suffered very little from the direct effects of the wars, and the father, a thirty-nine-year-old stonemason, had profited from the work needed to construct Napoleon's military installations on the outskirts of town. He was aided by his second wife, age twenty-three, who helped raise the children from their first marriage (the first wife had died of tuberculosis) and her own infant daughter. Living with the family was the sixty-year-old grandfather, a widower who had lost his wife to typhoid fever ten years earlier.

For the last decade the father had been working mostly on military buildings and facilities, and he feared that the arrival of peace might take what had been a dependable source of work from him. He had averaged thirteen hours of labor a day in the summer, with two one-hour periods out for meals. In the winter he worked as long as daylight allowed.

He employed the older of his two teenaged sons and sent the younger off to work with a friend. As most of the jobs the men worked on were within walking distance of their home, the family was able to share at least the evening meal together. But for the men of the family, life revolved around work and an occasional chance for a drink or a game of cards. The teenaged sons did not know the leisure that students in the twentieth century, even with the burden of their studies, enjoy. Adulthood arrived early, and so did all of the responsibilities that went with it.

The wife ran the home, cooked, sewed clothing, and supplemented what income the men were able to bring in by working eight to ten hours a day at home making lace. She was helped by the ten-year-old daughter from the husband's first marriage who looked after the baby and helped with the mending and cooking. None of the women in the family ever had the opportunity to go to school, and the day-to-day drudgery of work characterized their lives.

The grandfather was the patriarch of the family, and only he had the opportunity for leisure. His life of hard work, bad diet, and too much inferior wine, made him an economic drain on the family, a fact which the wife was not slow to grumble about.

Altogether the stonemason's family earned, in contemporary American terms, around three dollars a day. They had enough to eat. The father made half of the family income, the sons contributed perhaps a third, while the wife's lace making provided the rest of the money. Three fourths of their monthly income went for food, while the balance was spent on rent, candles, wood, and clothes, Without the wife's labor, the family's margin of security would have been disturbingly slim.

The Bocage family lived in the working-class Bondy district, on the third floor of a six-story building. They paid their rent to the agent who managed the building for a war contractor who had invested in real estate during the 1790's. Paris at that time was not a city of light, far from it. The streets were dark after sunset and became the haunts of petty thieves and prostitutes. The family had to walk everywhere as there was no public transportation in the narrow streets, which were rarely paved. Walking in the Bondy district required great diligence, as the Bocage family constantly had to avoid being splashed or muddied from the unpaved streets or else showered from above by the human waste emptied from chamber pots.

Their apartment contained two rooms, and was reached by walking up a narrow, cluttered staircase. They had no central heat, no running water, and no toilet facilities. In the bitter cold of the autumn mornings, the same fire had to serve as a source of heat and as an oven for cooking. The fire had to be kept going (matches would not be readily available for another thirty years), and the open fires posed a danger of setting off a major conflagration against which the inefficient Paris fire department could do little. Keeping the house clean was next to impossible for Madame Bocage. The overworked wife had little success in combatting lice, cockroaches, silverfish, fleas, and rats.

Shopping for food in the local markets was often a frustrating experience for the Bocage women. Maintaining an adequate diet was a serious challenge, especially during the economic problems of the post-Napoleonic period. The basic source of nourishment was bread, of which the family ate fifty pounds a week. Meat and dairy products, beans, potatoes, fruit in season, and an occasional fish completed the diet. Madame Bocage was limited in what she could buy at the local open air street market by the availability of local products. Often the meat and produce were spoiled and the fruits and grains not properly ripened. The family suffered gastric distress and bowel problems from eating bad food. They found sugar still to be a luxury and they drank coffee only on special days.

In their apartment, they owned a table and a few chairs, a complete set of cooking utensils, and spare sets of clothing. Undergarments were rarely changed and the bed linens were used till they fell apart. The problems of personal hygiene created by the lack of cleanliness in the apartment were increased by the fact that they rarely took baths or used soap. Personal dental health was virtually ignored, and the grandfather had not had a full set of teeth for twenty-five years.

Bad personal hygiene and primitive civic sanitation services contributed to the family's health problems. Those who could afford to, paid water carriers to bring water to their apartments. The water carriers claimed that the water was pure, but in fact they generally dipped their buckets from the river Seine, which served both as a place to dump sewage and gain drinking water. The Bocage family, and the others in their building, dumped their solid waste in a manure pile found in an alley by the side of the building. It was removed once a week to be sold in the country as fertilizer.

There was little time for leisure. For the father and the sons, drinking was a form of recreation, whether at home or at the neighborhood bar. There was more free time in the winter, when working hours were shortened by the lack of daylight. At that time they would play cards or visit the local brothel. At other times they would take advantage of the Sabbath or legal celebrations to go fishing, engage in lawn bowling, or walk outside the city limits where shops sold wine at cheaper rates, free from the city taxes. The ten-year-old daughter did not know the joys of playing with toys and games, although she on occasion accompanied her parents on walks or in other pastimes.

The Bocage family did not have access to public schools, and only the father, who had taught himself, could read. Their contact with political authority was limited to paying the indirect taxes, especially the one on wine which was highly resented. One of the teenaged sons had been called up for the draft, but he was found to be too short. The king, Louis XVIII, was only a figure of shadowy importance, far away. As the father never had to go to court, he was able to avoid the tangled judicial system.

The church was visited at those special moments of birth, marriage, and death, and the major religious days of All Saints Day, Christmas, and Easter. Other than that, the family was not notably pious. Death and disease surrounded the Bocage family. Measles, smallpox, tuberculosis, typhus, typhoid, and syphilis affected them and their neighbors at various times. They were made more susceptible to disease by undernourishment and bad hygiene.

In such difficult conditions, the Bocage's dreams and hopes revolved around the themes of having enough to eat, living a comfortable life, and accumulating a few possessions. Their horizons extended as far as they could walk and their economic and intellectual conditions limited their chances for a better life.

PART SIX
The Interdependent Planet

■ By 1914 Europe had brought together enough material strength, intellectual vitality, and governmental flexibility to dominate the planet. The explosive increase in productivity made possible by the Industrial Revolution and Europe's massive population growth contributed the power and personnel to extend economic and political control from the western tip of the Eurasian landmass to the entire world.

So dynamic was Europe's advance that it is tempting to portray a stagnant world awaiting the arrival of the Europeans. As we have seen in previous chapters, this was not the case. Until the fifteenth century the world's major centers of civilization developed separately and uniquely, each establishing its dominance over a defined part of the globe. In 1500 the Ottoman empire was perhaps the most vigorous military force in the world. The major civilizations of Central and South America developed complex socio-religious and cultural structures. China rested secure in its assumed superiority, while in Africa a rich variety of cultures evolved. Europe was fragmented and relatively weak.

Yet in the four centuries after 1500 the European state structure became concentrated in fewer, more efficient units. By 1900 the major powers of Europe could project their strength to infringe on the areas formerly dominated by the other major world cultures. The full force of the European advance came in the last thirty years of the nineteenth century, and in this chapter we will be dealing with the consequences of that advance for Europe and the affected countries.

As we will see in Part Six, the arrival of the Europeans — with their advanced technology, their developed political ideologies, their bureaucratic techniques, and their capitalist systems — posed severe challenges for the rest of the world. The indigenous peoples faced serious threats to their culture and their identity as the Europeans, with few exceptions, possessed sufficient economic and military strength to overwhelm them. There were two major types of European overseas involvement — the new Europes abroad and the colonies of exploitation.

The most direct method by which the Europeans extended their domination was the export of their own people. Millions of people from across the continent took part in the greatest transplantation of human beings in history. They went to the Americas, South Africa, Australia, and New Zealand, and carried their ways of life with them. In all of the new Europes there were common problems — the challenge of exploring and occupying hitherto unknown lands, dealing with the indigenous peoples, overcoming natural obstacles, and setting up governments. In this process, European culture was extended to the far corners of the world.

The other major type of European involvement abroad came in the colonies of exploitation. In the Middle East, Africa, and South and East Asia — with the notable exception of Japan — the European states established colonies for economic gain. These colonial areas, which were often seen by the Europeans as being unsuited for settlement, were usually governed by a minority of foreign officials and soldiers who controlled the majority of the native peoples. These indigenous peoples often strongly resisted the imperialistic takeover by the European states. By the end of the nineteenth century practically all of Africa had been partitioned and placed under European rule. Although China remained technically independent, it was controlled in many areas by the European powers. India fell directly under British control, as did many parts of the Ottoman empire. Japan was alone in successfully modernizing itself, and thus avoided to a certain extent being caught in the imperialist net.

The nineteenth century really ended not in 1899 but in 1914 with the outbreak of World War I. The century of European primacy came to a close with this suicidal struggle of the European nations, and the forces that were unleashed during that time of strife were communicated across the globe through the lines of communication spread by the imperialists themselves. The peoples in Asia and Africa would see that the Europeans — who had shown such abilities to scale the intellectual mountains and spread their power across the globe — had not found the answer to the basic problem of how to get along with each other.

Some historians suggest that implicit in the western tradition was an egotism that stopped the nation-states from effectively cooperating. This egotism led them to justify their actions solely in terms of self-interest, and represented the major cause for World War I. Indeed, that may be the underlying reason for the tragic conflict. But it is more revealing to note that the forces released more than a century earlier — of liberty, fraternity, and equality — had generated energies and movements so contradictory in nature that they could not be harmonized. When harnessed to the tensions released by competition among the major powers, these century-old forces led to war and, ultimately, the end of an era: the era of European primacy.

CHAPTER 27

The United States,
the British Dominions,
and Latin America:
1650-1914

New Europes Overseas

INTRODUCTION. In the four centuries before the twentieth, the greatest transplantation of peoples in human history took place as millions of Europeans left their homelands, crossed oceans, and made for themselves new homes in overseas lands. These immigrants brought with them what has been aptly called their "cultural baggage"—their language, religion, folk habits, and political institutions. At the same time, the slave trade brought vast numbers of Africans to the Americas.

In the new areas of settlement—the Americas, South Africa, Australia, and New Zealand—new Europes were founded and developed. In many ways these settlers perpetuated the culture of their homelands. Moreover, the most important developments in Europe after Waterloo—the ambitions of the middle class, the search of the masses for full political rights, the increased interest in a better standard of living, and the pervasive force of nationalism—all these became important factors in the overseas communities. Yet if the history of the new Europes is to be studied profitably in comparison with that of Europe itself, it should be re-

609

membered that certain common conditions and problems distinguished the history of these new nations: the challenge of geographical exploration, the problem of what to do with the indigenous peoples, and the search for a new national way of life. In the Americas there was also the problem of how best to treat the Negro, as a slave and then as a free man. Furthermore, some historians have stressed the deep influence in all the new Europes of frontier life with its fostering of democracy, individualism, resourcefulness, and optimism. As a complete explanation of the course of history in the new Europes, this thesis has been overdone. But some of its relevance remains.

In this chapter we shall see how the founding of colonies in Canada, Australia, New Zealand, and the Union of South Africa illustrates the transplanting of British culture to remote parts of the world. One interesting aspect of the story of the new Britains overseas during the nineteenth century is that they finally arrived at a status of full national independence or sovereignty without recourse to arms. At the same time they remained closely associated with the mother country as members of the British Commonwealth of Nations. Since the political development of Canada was a model for other English colonies, we shall emphasize Canadian history in our survey of the British dominions.

The United States stood apart from the other republics in the New World by reason of its spectacular economic advances, political stability, and successful democratic system. Its greatest failure was its inability to avoid the costly Civil War and delay in recognizing the legitimate aspirations of its black citizens.

Latin America faced certain unique problems in its struggle to win greatness. Here the Indian problem was far greater than it was in the United States, and relations between the two races were very different. From the time of the successful revolt against Spain and Portugal in the first quarter of the nineteenth century, the history of Latin America has been marked by civil wars and local struggles for political power. As this chapter discloses, threats from the outside and attempts by other powers to gain economic if not political control of Latin America did much to retard the growth of Latin America as a whole. Nevertheless, by the first quarter of the twentieth century a degree of stability and prosperity had been achieved in parts of Latin America, and the cultural patterns that developed there constitute a valuable component of world civilization.

THE MAKING OF A NEW NATION: THE UNITED STATES

Brave new world. The revolutionary movements in Europe during the nineteenth century had a two-pronged problem: they faced the vestiges of a feudal order of lord and peasant in which political, economic, and social privilege was concentrated in an aristocratic class; or they faced restless nationality groups that sought to unite under their own government by throwing off alien rule —or both. The nineteenth-century movements in the United States were not quite the same, since there was no significant heritage of feudal lord and peasant relationship in *English* North America and no counterpart to the conflicts with outside powers over national unification that troubled the Germans, Italians, Serbs, and other peoples of central and southeastern Europe. In place of these problems the United States had two major and interrelated problems of its own— the annexation, settlement, and development of a sparsely populated continent, and slavery. Free land and unfree men: these were the sources of the many political confrontations that culminated in the Civil War, the greatest revolutionary struggle in nineteenth-century America.

Democratic influences of the frontier. In 1783, the year the United States became a sovereign state, the young nation could not be called a democracy. Six years later only one male in seven possessed the franchise.

Religious requirements and property qualifications kept many of the common people
from participating in governmental affairs.
For the first forty years of its existence the
government of the United States was largely
in the hands of established families from the
South, such as those of Washington and
Jefferson, or of men of wealth and substance
from the middle class of the North, such as
Adams. It has been said that it took fifty
years after the Declaration of Independence
"to reach a vital belief that the people and
not gentlemen are to govern this country."[1]

The influence of the western frontier
helped move America closer to full democracy. Even before the Constitution was
ratified by the thirteen states, thousands of
pioneers crossed the Appalachian Mountains
into the new "western country." Here on
the frontier, land was to be had for the asking. Here social caste did not exist; one man
was as good as another. Vigor, courage, and
self-reliance counted, not birth or wealth.
Throughout most of the nineteenth century,
as pioneers moved westward, the West was
to be a source for new and liberal movements
which challenged the ideas prevalent in the
more conservative and settled areas of the
country.

Until the War of 1812 the growth of democracy was slow. In 1791 Vermont had been
admitted as a manhood-suffrage state, and
the following year Kentucky followed suit;
but Tennessee, Ohio, and Louisiana entered
the Union with property and tax qualifications for the suffrage. After 1817 no new state
entered the Union with restrictions on male
suffrage except for slaves. Most appointive
offices became elective, and requirements
for holding office were liberalized.

Jacksonian democracy. In 1828 Andrew
Jackson was elected to the presidency, following a campaign which featured the slogan
"Down with the aristocrats." Jackson was
the first president produced by the new
West; the first, excepting Washington, not
to have a college education; and the first
to have been born in poverty. He owed
his successful election to no congressional
clique but to the will of the people. The common people idolized "Old Hickory" as their
spokesman and a fearless leader of men.

The triumph of the democratic principle
in the 1830's set the direction for political
development down to this day. With the new
president came the idea that any man, by
virtue of being an American citizen, was
worthy of holding any office in the land.
Educational opportunities were widened
with the growth of the public school system,
class barriers became less important, and
government became more responsive and
responsible to the average or common man.
Indeed, it has been thoughtfully said that
"the 1830's saw the triumph in American
politics of that democracy which has remained pre-eminently the distinguishing
feature of our society."[2]

Acquisition of new lands. From 1800 to
1860 the westward movement proceeded at
an amazingly rapid pace. The Louisiana
territory, purchased from France for about
$15 million in 1803, doubled the size of the
United States. The annexation of Texas in
1845 was followed by war with Mexico in
1846. Two years later Mexico signed a peace
treaty whereby California, all title to Texas,
and the country between California and
Texas were ceded to the United States. The
same year that war broke out with Mexico,
the Oregon territory was occupied after the
settlement of a boundary dispute with Great
Britain (see p. 629). As a result of these acquisitions, by 1860 the area of the United
States had increased nearly two thirds over
what it had been in 1840.

The slavery issue. The acquisition of new
territory forced the issue of whether slavery
should be allowed in these areas. At the same
time, the whole issue of slavery was being
vigorously condemned by abolitionists in
the North, particularly in New England.
Henry Clay's Missouri Compromise of 1820,
by which slavery was permitted in Missouri
but forbidden in the remainder of the Louisiana Purchase, had satisfied both sides temporarily, but the antislavery forces grew
more insistent. In the senatorial campaigns
of 1858, Abraham Lincoln declared:

"A house divided against itself cannot stand."
I believe this government cannot endure permanently half slave and half free. I do not expect
the Union to be dissolved—I do not expect the

house to fall—but I do expect it will cease to be divided. It will become all one thing, or all the other.[3]

Slavery was a fundamental issue; from its existence stemmed many differences and tensions which separated the North from the South. In a sense the North and the South had become two different civilizations. The former was industrial, urban, and democratic; the latter was mainly agricultural, rural, and dominated by a planter aristocracy. The South strongly opposed the North's desire for higher tariffs, government aid for new railroads, and generous terms for land settlement in the West.

The Civil War. Soon after the inauguration of Lincoln as president, the southern states seceded from the Union and formed the Confederacy. The first shot of the Civil War was fired at Fort Sumter in 1861. Four agonizing years of conflict and the bloodiest war experienced by any western nation to that time followed. The Civil War ended

when General Lee surrendered to General Grant at Appomattox in April 1865; a few days later the joyful North was stunned by the assassination of President Lincoln. With the final collapse of the Confederacy before the overwhelming superiority of the Union in manpower, industrial resources, and wealth, the Civil War became the grand epic of American history in its heroism, romance, tragedy, and incalculable results.

In the largest sense the American Civil War can be explained in its relation to the great historical movements of the nineteenth century—liberalism, democracy, and nationalism—which were transforming Europe. It was the desire for freedom that sparked the revolutions in Europe in 1830 and 1848; and likewise in the United States many people had come to believe that slavery was an inhuman and immoral institution. The sentiment of nationalism was equally strong in Europe and in the United States. Just as wars were fought to attain German and Italian unity, a great struggle took place in

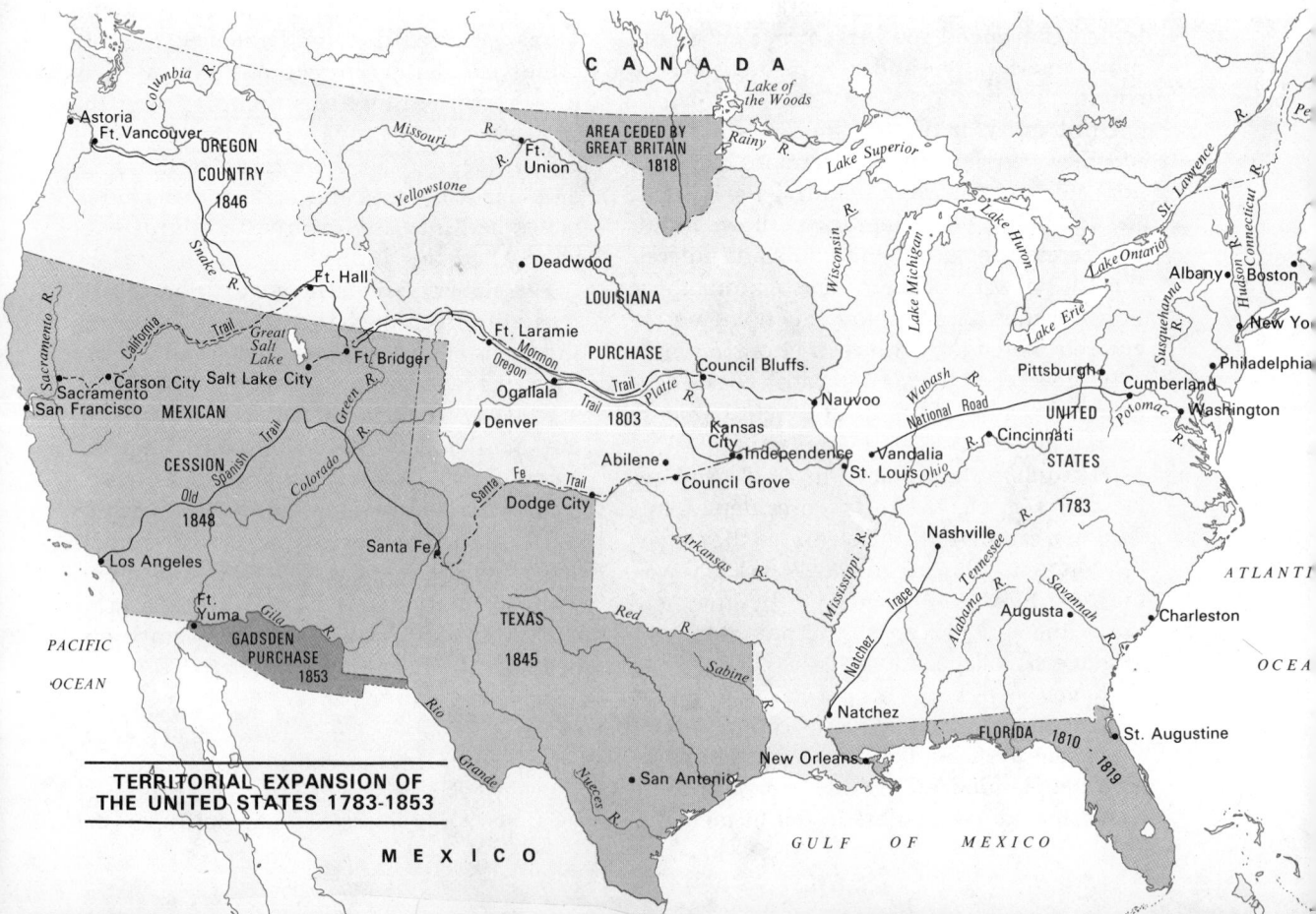

TERRITORIAL EXPANSION OF THE UNITED STATES 1783-1853

THE DIS-UNITED STATES—A BLACK BUSINESS.

The growing tensions between the North and South gained world-wide attention. *Punch*, the English humor magazine, viewed the situation like this in 1856.

America to maintain national unity. If the causes of the American Civil War are complex, the all-important result was simple. It settled the issue of whether the United States was an indivisible sovereign nation or a collection of sovereign states. The Federal Union was preserved, and nationalism triumphed over the sectionalism of the South.

Aftermath of the Civil War. Following the conflict, federal military occupation and force were used to try to convert the South to democratic voting and property rights for the Negro. Eventually this so-called Reconstruction period (1865-1877) was ended by a tacit political agreement between the industrial North and white southern leaders. The latter now proceeded to deprive Negroes of their voting rights. As second-class citizens, freed but landless, the ex-slaves became essentially a sharecropping class. More than one hundred years after the Civil War, black Americans had still not achieved the place in a politically and economically free society which radical reformers attempted to ensure at the beginning of the Reconstruction. In a sense, the civil rights movement of the twentieth century is the belated aftermath of uncompleted Reconstruction.

Industrial expansion. The victory of the North also foreshadowed an irresistible trend toward industrialism. In its lasting effects the economic revolution in the United States that followed the Civil War was more significant than the conflict itself. Railroads were built across broad prairies, and the first transcontinental railroad, the Union Pacific, was completed in 1869. Thousands of settlers swarmed westward.

Between 1850 and 1880 the number of cities with a population of 50,000 or more doubled. The number of men employed in industry increased 50 percent. In 1865 there were 35,000 miles of railroads in the country; eight years later this figure had been doubled. By 1900 the trackage was estimated to be about 200,000 miles, more than in all of Europe. In 1860 a little more than a billion dollars was invested in manufacturing; by 1900 this figure had risen to twelve billion. The value of manufactured products increased proportionately. In 1870 the total production of iron and steel in the United States was far below that of France and England. Twenty years later the United States had outstripped them and was producing about one third of the world's iron and steel.

In the age of rapid industrialism and materialistic expansion, many who pursued profits lost sight of ethical principles both in business and in government. In five years, between 1865 and 1870, the notorious Tweed Ring cost the city of New York at least $100 million. Ruthless financiers, such as Jay Gould and Jim Fisk, tampered with the financial stability of the nation. During General Grant's administration as president, the country was shocked by scandals and frauds. A new rich class, elevated to power and wealth overnight, failed to appreciate its responsibilities to society. Corruption in business was a blatant feature of the new economic order.

End of the era of expansion. For roughly a century the gospel of the new nation of America had been rugged individualism. As in Europe, government interference in business was unwelcome because it was felt that the individual should be free to follow his own inclinations, run his own business, and enjoy the profits of his labors. In an expanding nation where land, jobs, and opportunity beckoned, there was little to indicate that the system would not work indefinitely. By

1880, however, the end of the frontier was in sight. Free land of good quality was scarce, and the frontier could no longer act as a safety valve to release the economic and social pressures of an expanding population.

Between 1850 and 1900 the United States became the most powerful state in the Western Hemisphere, increased its national wealth from $7 billion to $88 billion, established an excellent system of public education, and fostered the enjoyment of civil liberties. But there were many disturbing factors in the picture. Unemployment, child labor, and industrial accidents became common in the rapidly growing industrial areas. In large cities, slums grew and served as breeding places for disease and crime. Strikes, often accompanied by violence, demonstrated the tension developing between labor and capital.

The progressive movement. The United States obtained its independence in 1783, became a political democracy early in the nineteenth century, and prevented the collapse of the Federal Union between 1861 and 1865. By 1890 a new challenge had arisen—the need for economic reform. At this point, as had happened in England and elsewhere at about the same time, a powerful movement whose object was the removal of economic inequalities began. The so-called progressive movement agitated for the elimination of sweatshops, of exploitation of foreign labor, and of waste of the nation's natural wealth. This era of the muckrakers lasted roughly from 1890 to 1914.

The success of the progressive movement was reflected in the constitutions of new states admitted to the Union and in their introduction of the direct primary, the initiative and referendum, and the direct election of senators. All these measures tended to give the common man more effective control of his government. After the enactment in 1887 of the Interstate Commerce Act, which had introduced federal regulation of the railroads, a steady expansion of governmental regulation of industry began. As president of the United States from 1901 to 1909, Theodore Roosevelt launched an aggressive campaign to break up the trusts, to conserve national resources, and to extend the regulation of the national government over the railroads, food, and drugs. In 1913 President Woodrow Wilson inaugurated a militant campaign of reform called the "New Freedom." The tariff was reduced because it was too much the instrument of special economic privilege; banking reform was effected by the Federal Reserve Act in 1913; and governmental regulation of business for the protection of public interests was further extended both by the passage of the Clayton Anti-Trust Act in 1914 and the establishment of the Federal Trade Commission in the same year.

The United States in 1914. In 1914 the United States was the most populous, rich, and influential of the new countries which had sprung from motherlands in Europe. In 1790 the population of the United States had been just under 4 million; the census of 1910 showed an increase to nearly 99 million. During the nineteenth century and the first decade of the twentieth century, more than 25 million immigrants had made America their new home. Since the days of George Washington, the national wealth had increased at least a hundredfold. Once the producer of raw materials only, the United States in 1914 was the greatest industrial power in the world. In 1900 it was producing more steel than Great Britain and Germany combined; and one of its concerns—United States Steel—was capitalized for $1,460 million, a sum greater than the total estimated wealth of the country in 1790. In 1914 many people in the United States and in the rest of the world failed to appreciate the significance of the amazing growth of the United States. Only World War I could give tangible proof that the New World nation had surpassed the power and economic importance of its mother country.

THE UNITED STATES AND WORLD AFFAIRS

Beginnings of isolationism. The tremendous development of the United States in wealth, population, and industrial power during the nineteenth century was reflected in its growing importance in world affairs. After the achievement of independence in 1783, three purposes may be identified as controlling American foreign policy: a basic concern for national security, the desire to protect and foster foreign trade, and, last, the feeling of a national mission in sympathizing with and encouraging the growth of freedom throughout the world.

During the first quarter century after gaining its independence, the new republic fought a brief naval war with France, became embroiled with Britain in the War of 1812, and sent two expeditions to the Mediterranean to teach the Barbary pirates a lesson. These complications notwithstanding, isolationism became the cardinal principle of American foreign policy. Thomas Jefferson's words on the subject have been quoted often:

Peace, commerce and honest friendship with all nations—entangling alliances with none.[4]

The Monroe Doctrine. Early in the 1820's the policy of noninvolvement was seriously challenged when the conservative Quadruple Alliance gave notice of helping the Spanish monarchy regain control over its rebellious colonies in Latin America. Both Britain and the United States regarded this possibility with alarm. George Canning, the British foreign secretary, suggested that his government and that of the United States make a joint declaration warning against European intervention in South America. This invitation was considered seriously by President James Monroe, but joint action was not deemed necessary. In his message to Congress in December 1823, Monroe warned the European powers against any attempt to extend their system to the Western Hemisphere and also made it clear that the United States had no intention of interfering in European affairs. In 1823 we could have our cake in foreign affairs and eat it too. The complications and dangers inherent in European intervention had been avoided—and without the necessity for any formal alliance. The shield of the British fleet stood behind the Monroe Doctrine with or without an alliance between Washington and London.

Challenges to American isolationism. On occasion, difficulties arose in reconciling isolationism with American interest in the cause of freedom throughout the world. Although much sympathy was expressed for the cause of the Greeks as they fought against Turkish tyranny in the 1820's, this sympathy did not lead to active support. In an Independence Day address, an elder statesman made it quite plain that while the United States was sympathetic to the cause of freedom

she goes not abroad in search of monsters to destroy. She is the well-wisher to the freedom and independence of all. She is the champion and vindicator only of her own.[5]

Some modifications of the American policy of isolationism became apparent in the two decades before 1860, however. The United States began to evince a growing interest in the Pacific and Asia (see Chapter 29). In 1844 the United States made its first treaty with China, opening certain Chinese ports to American trade and securing the right of our merchants and sailors to be tried in American tribunals in China. In 1853 Commodore Perry visited Japan, and by his show of force he persuaded the Japanese to open some of their harbors to American vessels. By 1854 the government of the United States was considering the annexation of the Hawaiian Islands. In 1867 the United States purchased Alaska from Russia for the amazingly small price of $7,200,000.

After the Civil War came to an end, the United States also moved to strengthen the Monroe Doctrine, which had been challenged by France's emperor, Napoleon III, while the United States was preoccupied with civil conflict. With French bayonets, Napoleon III had established a Mexican empire under Maximilian. Warnings by the United States secretary of state went unheeded until after the Civil War, when the protests to Napoleon were backed up by the force of 900,000 veterans. The French position in Mexico was now untenable, and Napoleon was forced to withdraw his military and financial support from Maximilian. In 1867 the emperor died before a Mexican firing squad.

After this post-Civil War flurry of activity in foreign affairs, isolationism again came to the fore as the United States set about domestic development. The building of railroads, the opening of western lands, the assimilation of millions of immigrants, the expansion of industry—all these activities monopolized attention. Foreign affairs were almost forgotten. A New York newspaper reflecting the prevailing mood went so far as to suggest the abolition of the diplomatic service!

By 1885, however, new forces began to emerge that were to carry the United States increasingly away from isolationism in the closing years of the nineteenth century. The United States began to seek an outlet for its vast national energy now that the frontier had disappeared and most of the fertile land was occupied. Foreign trade increased from a value of $393 million in 1870 to more than $1,333 million in 1900. Investments abroad in the same period increased from practically nothing to $500 million. At the same time, American missionary activity in Africa, in the Middle East, and in Asia greatly expanded. In common with the same intellectual trend in Europe, many American leaders were influenced by Darwinism, especially by its application to political affairs. The slogan "survival of the fittest" had its followers in Congress as well as in the British Parliament, the French Chamber of Deputies, and the German Reichstag. In order to be great, many argued, the United States must expand and must assume a vital role in world politics.

In Chapter 29 the growth of an American colonial empire will be described as the Stars and Stripes came to wave over Guam, the Philippines, Hawaii, and Puerto Rico. This urge to acquire dependencies did not long endure, however; by 1905 it was definitely waning. Nevertheless, the imperialistic urge was a manifestation, however fleeting, of deeper currents of history that were carrying the United States into the full stream of world affairs. The ambitions of expansionist powers such as Germany and Japan and the advance of technology that would soon destroy American geographical remoteness were rapidly eroding the time-honored belief that isolationism was the best buttress of national security.

New dynamism in foreign affairs. In 1883 the building of a modern navy was begun, and by 1890 the buildup had accelerated greatly. Care was taken not to alarm isolationist circles, however, for the new ships were officially known as "seagoing coastline battleships," a nice nautical contradiction. When this naval program was initiated, the United States Navy ranked twelfth among the powers; by 1900 it had advanced to third place.

The growing international stature of the United States was given startling confirmation in the border dispute between Britain and Venezuela in 1895. While Britain dallied before agreeing to submit the issue to arbitration, the State Department of the United States drafted a blunt note to the British Foreign Office. According to the United States, grave consequences would follow a refusal to accept arbitration, and it was added:

To-day the United States is practically sovereign on this continent, and its fiat is law upon the subjects to which it confines its interposition . . . its infinite resources combined with its isolated position render it master of the situation and practically invulnerable against any or all other powers.[6]

Fortunately for the cause of peace, Britain was too occupied with the Boers in South Africa, with tensions with Germany, and with rivalry with France in the Sudan to offer strenuous objections. Arbitration was accepted, and the greater part of the disputed area was awarded to British Guiana.

In Asia there was also evidence of the new dynamism in American foreign affairs. In 1899 the American secretary of state, John Hay, took the initiative in maintaining equal commercial rights in China for the traders of all nations, and the Open Door Policy in China became a reality. And in the melodrama of the Boxer Rebellion, the United States again was a leader rather than a follower (see Chapter 29).

Theodore Roosevelt. The quickened activity of the United States in international affairs is best symbolized by the ideas and actions of Theodore Roosevelt (1858-1919). In his terms as president he was one of the leading figures on the world stage. At the request of the Japanese, he assumed the role of peacemaker in the Russo-Japanese War. The peace conference, which met at Portsmouth, New Hampshire, 1905, successfully concluded a treaty, and in 1910 Roosevelt received the Nobel Peace Prize.

Roosevelt was not always a man of peace, however. Whenever he believed the legitimate interests of the United States to be threatened, he had no compunctions about threatening to use force or actually using it. The most significant illustration of Roosevelt's determination to protect vital national interests took place in the Panama incident. In 1901 the British conceded the exclusive right of the United States to control any Isthmian canal that might be dug. For $40 million the United States bought the rights of a private French company which had already begun work on a canal; and a lease was negotiated with Colombia, through whose territory the canal would be built. But the Colombian senate refused to ratify the treaty, claiming that the compensation was too small. Roosevelt is reputed to have explained, "I did not intend that any set of bandits should hold up Uncle Sam."[7] The upshot was a revolution, financed with money borrowed from J. P. Morgan; and Panama—the new republic which seceded from Colombia in 1903—concluded a satisfactory canal treaty with the United States. In 1914 the canal was opened.

By the first decade of the twentieth century, the United States had moved far from its traditional isolationism. But while active in international affairs, it was not yet willing to commit itself to definite foreign entanglements. A few observers warned of dangers soon to come. They stressed the importance of supporting nations whose interests coincided with those of the United States. Some publicists in America identified Russian imperialism as the great potential danger; others were more concerned over German ambitions. The history of the first half of the twentieth century was to prove both schools of observers correct.

LATIN AMERICA STRUGGLES TO WIN GREATNESS

Early disappointments in freed Latin America. Influenced by the liberal intellectual currents of the Age of Reason in Europe and irked by oppressive and corrupt controls from Madrid and Lisbon, the first decades of the nineteenth century witnessed an irresistible movement for independence in the Latin American colonies (see Chapter 21) By 1825 Spanish and Portuguese power was broken in the Western Hemisphere, and nine new political units emerged in Latin America. Mexico, Guatemala, Great Colombia, Peru, Bolivia, Paraguay, Argentina, and Chile were free of Spain, while Brazil, retaining a liberal monarchy, had gained its independence from Portugal. While the stirring military achievements of the rebel armies under Bolívar, San Martín, and others should not be underemphasized, it was British and American sympathy, as we have already seen, that helped the Latin American republics attain their independence.

For most of the new nations, unfortunately, the first half century of independence was a period of retrogression and disillusionment. The great Liberators were unable to maintain control of the nations they had freed, nor were the liberal, urban Creoles who had begun the independence movement able to agree with one another on elementary political matters. Impractical and inexperienced, they soon lost power to crude military leaders, or *caudillos*, whose armed gangs seized and lost the seats of power in a confusing series of tumults. A growing sectionalism appeared, and the mammoth states broke up into puny republics which in turn were threatened with localism.

The unpromising heritage. The Spanish colonial system had offered American-born whites little responsibility or opportunity in government, and the tradition of autocracy and paternalism was a poor precedent for would-be democratic republics. The emphasis on executive power inspired later presidents, generals, landowners, tribal leaders, and even clerical officials to wield authority with extreme arrogance. Independent legislative organs never flourished. Spain's economic system encouraged concentration of land and other forms of wealth in a few hands and an extractive economy. Finally, the Church, with its great properties and its hold on education and welfare agencies, was to complicate the politics of every new nation.

The effects of the wars of independence were also ruinous. Some of the most productive areas were devastated. Hatreds and divisions long persisted. Also, many men who had fought the royalists remained armed, fond of a life of violence and pillage, and likely to group themselves about the *caudillos* who promised them adventure or gain in revolutions.

Racial disunity. When independence was achieved in the first quarter of the nineteenth century, there were from fifteen to eighteen million people in the former Spanish empire. About three million of these were whites, among whom were included almost all the property-owning and educated groups. (Immigration from Europe did little to increase their numbers until the last third of the century, when a deluge began.) About the same number of people were *mestizos*, who scorned the Indians but were usually not accepted by the whites, though they were steadily increasing in number and ambition during the period when new nations were being formed. During the nineteenth century at least half of the population in some states was Indian. Deprived of the small protection once offered by the Spanish crown, they either sank into peonage or lived in semi-independence under their tribal rulers. Finally, in Brazil and most of the Caribbean islands, Negroes, most of them slaves, were in a large majority. Conflicts of interest quickly developed between these broad racial groups, particularly between the Creoles and the *mestizos*.

Mexico. The pernicious effects of these divisive factors in the newly independent Latin American world can be seen in the experiences of each nation. Mexico, which had seemed such a promising new country in 1821, had half a century of turmoil. The empire of Iturbide (see p. 490) lasted only a few months, and a federal republic was then established. In less than ten years, however, a preposterous military leader named Antonio López de Santa Anna (1795-1876) had become dictator. (It was Santa Anna who massacred the defenders of the Alamo in 1836). The debasement of Mexican public life and the humiliation of Mexico by the United States in the war of 1846-1848 must be charged to this strutting, corrupt *caudillo*. Upon his final overthrow in 1855, the injuries inflicted on Mexican pride during his regime brought more thoughtful and circumspect men into politics; and the liberals, whose eventual leader was the Indian Benito Juárez (1806-1872), set out to implement their program, the *Reforma*. They planned to establish a more democratic republic, to destroy the political and economic force of the Church, to hasten the inclusion of *mestizos* and Indians in political life. A terrible civil war followed their anticlerical measures; it ended in 1861 with the apparent victory of Juárez, but inability to meet payments on debts owed to foreigners brought an invasion of Mexico by European powers and the establishment of a French puppet regime (see p. 490).

When pressure from the United States had driven French troops from Mexican soil, Juárez again set about instituting the *Reforma*, but the poverty of the country hampered progress. Soon after Juárez died, power went to one of his adherents, Porfirio Diaz (1830-1915), who served as president from 1877 to 1880 and from 1884 to 1911. Under his administration Mexico became an orderly country. Foreign capital entered in large amounts. Factories, railroads, mines, trading houses, plantations, and enormous ranches flourished, and Mexico City became one of the most impressive capitals in Latin America. Yet Diaz' rule, though outwardly conforming to the constitution, was a dictatorship. If there was much encouragement of art and letters, there was no liberty. The Indians sank lower into peonage or even outright slavery, and the Indian heritage was disdained. In spite of the anticlerical laws of the Juárez period, the Church was quietly permitted to acquire great wealth; and foreign investors exploited Mexico, creating a long-lasting hatred of foreigners.

In 1910 the critics of Diaz found a spokesman in a frail, eccentric man named Francisco Madero (1873-1913), who undertook to lead a revolutionary movement and surprised the world by succeeding. The Diaz machine crumpled abruptly in 1911. Although Madero was murdered two years later and Mexico underwent another period of turmoil in which the country was controlled mainly by self-styled local rulers, a determined group was able to organize a revolutionary party and to bring about the only genuine social revolution that Latin America had experienced until the First World War. As we shall see in a later chapter, the Mexican constitution of 1917 has served as an inspiration to much of Latin America.

Argentina. Probably the most advanced Spanish-speaking country in the world, Argentina attained this position in a period of sudden growth that followed half a century of torpor. Its beginning as a free nation was promising. Soon, however, the bustling port city of Buenos Aires, whose energetic population sought to encourage European capital and commerce, found itself overawed by the great ranchers of the interior, *caudillos*, and their retainers, the primitive *gauchos*—colorful, nomadic cowboys and bandits, whose way of life is now regarded as romantic. The *caudillos* intimidated the adherents of constitutional government in

This mural by Diego Rivera depicts the historical and cultural forces behind the Mexican Revolution. Ostensibly only a group picture, it really shows a hierarchy of power. The foreign companies, wielding the most pervasive influence, are pictured at top. The degree of power then moves downward to the two opposing political leaders Madero and Diaz pictured with swords, the journalists and intellectuals, and, at bottom, the Indian, sunk pitifully into peonage. The Catholic Church, regarded as an enemy of the Revolution, is portrayed by the grim-faced padre near the top left.

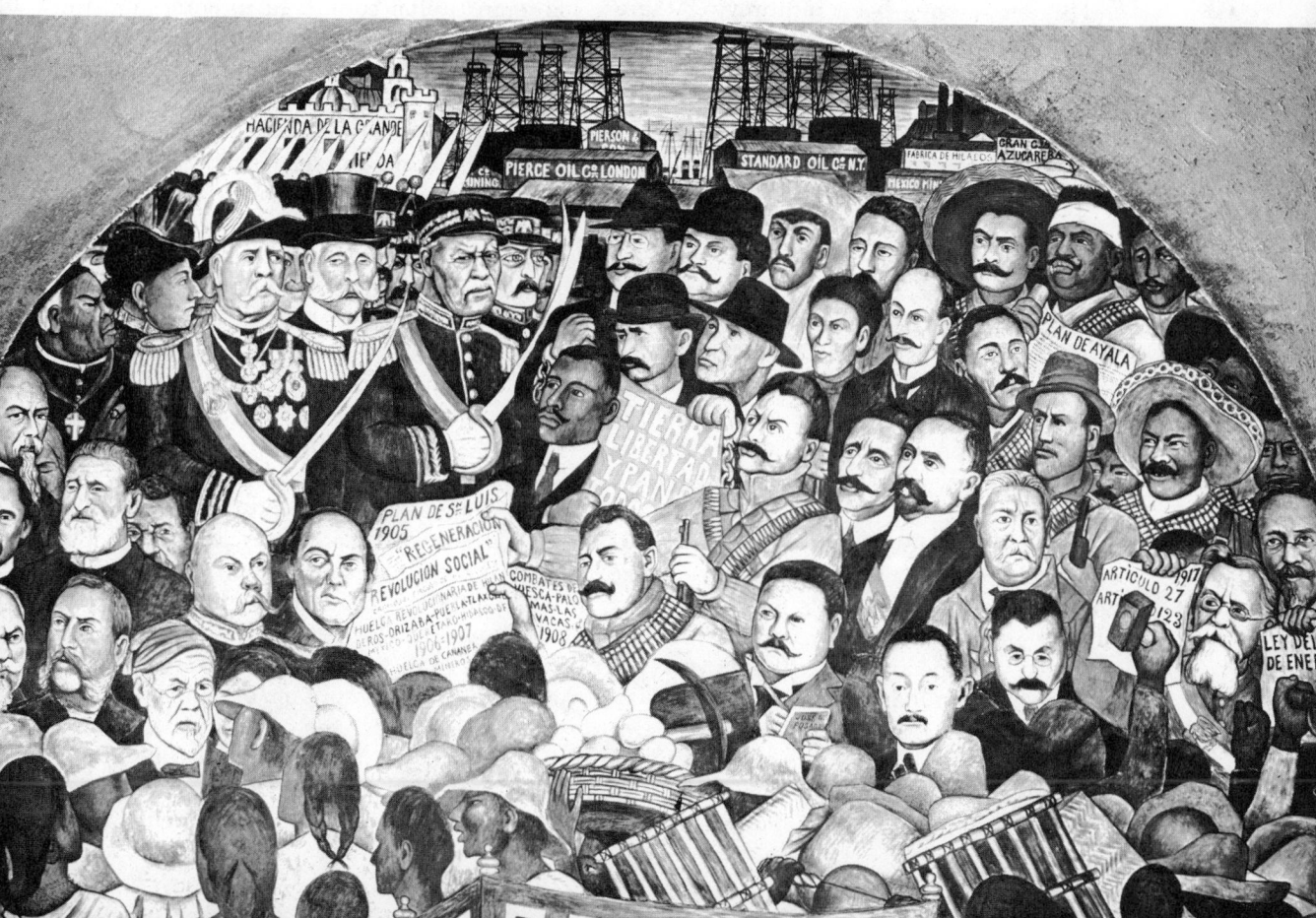

Buenos Aires, and until mid-century Argentina was not a republic but rather a *gaucho* paradise, isolated and ruled by men who wanted to keep European influences out.

In 1852 a combination of progressive elements overthrew the *gaucho* leader; commerce with Europe was revived, and by 1862 Argentina at last became a united republic and began a period of admirable stability. The constitution was usually observed, and individual rights were respected to a high degree. Immigrants poured in, and soon the population of Argentina became the most European of any major land of the New World, for it had few Indians or Negroes. Foreign capital, especially British, brought about amazing developments; port facilities, railroads, light industries, and urban conveniences were among the most advanced in the world. Buenos Aires became by far the largest and most beautiful city in Latin America, despite its location on a monotonous flat plain beside a muddy estuary.

This flat plain, or pampas, is perhaps the richest land in the world for grass and wheat; and livestock have been multiplying there for centuries. About 1880, refrigerated ships made it feasible to transport enormous quantities of fresh beef to Britain in exchange for capital and finished goods. About 1900 wheat joined beef as a major Argentine export. This intimate commercial relationship with Britain, which lasted until after World War II, affected nearly every aspect of Argentine life. Nevertheless, though top-drawer society was dominated by leaders who were pro-British in business and pro-French in culture, a true Argentine nationalism was developing. Along with the growth of this powerful sentiment came urgent demands for more democracy and wider distribution of wealth.

Brazil. For many years the former Portuguese colony of Brazil escaped the turbulence and disorders that befell its Spanish-speaking neighbors, probably because it had achieved independence without years of warfare and military dominance and because it enjoyed the continuity and legitimacy afforded by a respected monarchy. A constitution was granted by the first emperor, Pedro I, in 1824, and the secession to the throne of Pedro II in 1840 inaugurated a period of political liberty and economic and cultural progress that was to endure throughout his fifty-year reign.

Immigrants were attracted to this peaceful land in the New World, and foreign investments were heavy, though not with the arrant exploitation that Mexico experienced under Diaz. But economic growth tended to favor the southeastern part of the country at the expense of the great sugar plantations in the tropical north; and when the sugar lords were further injured in 1888 by the abolition of slavery, they ranged themselves in opposition to the emperor. Joining them were army officers, who resented the civilian nature of Pedro's regime, and a small number of ideological republicans. In 1889 the aging emperor was forced to abdicate.

For nearly ten years the new federal republic of Brazil underwent civil wars and military upheavals not unlike those in other Latin American countries. Finally, the republic was stabilized with the army in control, and Brazil resumed its progressive course. Foreign capital continued to enter, and immigration from Europe remained heavy. By World War I Brazil was generally stable and prosperous, with a growing tradition of responsible government.

Other Latin American nations. Political turmoil, geographical handicaps, and racial disunity all played a part in the development of the other new nations in Latin America. Bolivia, named so hopefully after the Liberator, underwent countless revolutions which to an outsider seem almost pointless. Peru's course was almost as futile. The state of Great Colombia dissolved by 1830, and its successors—Colombia, Venezuela, and Ecuador—were plagued by instability and civil wars. Paraguay endured a series of dictatorships; and Uruguay, created in 1828 as a buffer between Argentina and Brazil, long suffered from interventions by these two countries. An exception to the prevailing pattern of political chaos was the steady growth of the republic of Chile. In 1830 Chile came under the control of a conservative oligarchy. Although this regime proved to be generally enlightened, the country was kept under tight control for a century and was ruled for the benefit of the large landlords and the big businessmen.

Central America narrowly escaped becoming part of Mexico in 1822. After a fifteen-year effort to create a Central American confederation, Guatemala, San Salvador, Honduras, Nicaragua, and Costa Rica asserted their independence. Except for Costa Rica, where the whites comprised the bulk of the population, racial disunity delayed the creation of national feeling. In the Caribbean the Dominican Republic, after decades of submission to more populous but equally underdeveloped Haiti, maintained a precarious independence.

Foreign investments. The Industrial Revolution came into full stride just after the Latin American republics were born. The great industries of western Europe, and later those of the United States, demanded more and more raw materials and new markets in which to sell the finished products. Capital accumulated, and investors eagerly sought opportunities to place their money where high rates of interest could be obtained. This drive for markets, raw materials, and outlets for surplus capital led to the movement known as economic imperialism. As the following chapters show, imperialism was particularly active in Asia and Africa, and Latin America did not escape unscathed.

The continual disorder and the lack of strong governments in Latin America gave businessmen ample opportunity to obtain rich concessions and float huge loans. Many of the Latin American governments, created by revolution and interested only in filling their own pockets, often resorted to the vicious practice of selling concessions to foreign corporations for ready cash. Political bosses bartered away the economic heritage of their lands, for Latin America was rich in minerals, oil, and other important resources. Sometimes the foreign investor acted in good faith, providing capital at a reasonable rate of interest to Latin American regimes which, it developed, had no intention of fulfilling the contract. On other occasions unscrupulous capitalists took full advantage of officials in ignorant or helpless governments. In many cases defaults occurred and controversy ensued.

The injured foreign investor usually appealed to his government to intercede in his behalf, and an unending stream of diplomatic correspondence over debt claims was begun, for neither the United States, Great Britain, Germany, France, Italy, nor Spain— the chief investor states—would see its nationals mistreated in their ventures into foreign investments.

Roosevelt and the Monroe Doctrine. Another threat to Latin America developed in 1902 and 1903. A dispute between Venezuela and a coalition formed by Germany, Great Britain, and Italy provoked the three European powers into blockading Venezuela and even firing upon coastal fortifications to remind the Venezuelan dictator of his obligations to some of their nationals. At first inclined to stand by and let Venezuela take its punishment, the United States soon became suspicious of German intentions. President Theodore Roosevelt matched threat with threat; and the European nations retreated quickly into the safer field of international arbitration. The Venezuelan imbroglio was resolved, but it left the United States and President Roosevelt with an increasing determination never again to allow Europe so much rope in the Western Hemisphere, no matter how just the cause.

If the Monroe Doctrine was to prevent Europe from pursuing the legitimate task of protecting its nationals—even to the employment of force—then it was natural for Europe to charge the United States with the responsibility of protecting European creditors as well as its own. In 1904 the American president proclaimed the Roosevelt Corollary to the Monroe Doctrine. This doctrine was a frank statement that chronic wrong-doing on the part of Latin American governments might force the United States to exercise an international police power. Picturesquely described as the policy of speaking softly but carrying a big stick, the Roosevelt pronunciamento thus launched the era of the Big Stick. The United States not only established a customs receivership in the Dominican Republic but exercised similar control in Nicaragua and Haiti. In addition, the Monroe Doctrine was now used not only for its original purpose of keeping out European political interference in Latin America but also as an agency for expanding the commercial interests of the United States.

Cuba becomes a protectorate. In 1898 the United States went to war with Spain over the way the Spaniards were ruling Cuba. For decades the mistreatment of the Cubans had offended humanitarian sentiments of the Americans—an altruism strongly colored by the fact that the evils of Spanish rule also injured American commercial interests in the island. Victory in the brief, dramatic Spanish-American War brought the United States recognition as a world power and a conglomeration of islands in the Pacific Ocean as well as in the Caribbean. Puerto Rico was annexed; the Philippines were brought under American rule. Sensitive of accusations of outright imperialism in Cuba, the government offered Cuba an imperfect, closely tutored independence, and the Cubans were obliged to acknowledge by law the right of the United States to intervene for the "preservation of Cuban independence" and the "maintenance of a government adequate for the protection of life, property, and individual liberty." These and other restrictions on Cuban independence were embodied in the so-called Platt Amendment (1901) to the new Cuban constitution. Thus the United States established its first American protectorate. Panama soon became another protectorate of the United States. In all these areas American business interests throve, but so did the material welfare of the inhabitants.

Dollar diplomacy. The next manifestation of the imperialistic mood of the United States has been appropriately called dollar diplomacy, an American policy which prevailed from the Theodore Roosevelt through the Coolidge administrations. Dollar diplomacy referred to the coordinated activities of American foreign investors and their State Department, who worked in close cooperation to obtain and protect concessions for investors, especially in those sections of the Caribbean countries which produced sugar, bananas, and oil. From 1890 to 1914 this policy acutely affected nearly a dozen of the Latin American republics. The United States government could in the last

analysis—and at times did—control the policies of these states.

The "Colossus of the North." Although the growing assertiveness of the United States in the Western Hemisphere was accompanied by increasing alarm among the Latin American peoples, a movement which held hope for greater harmony between the United States and the Latin American states was developing. Some liberal thinkers in the United States had long envisioned a fraternity of the Americas indissolubly linked by common bonds of geography and democratic political ideals. Expressed by periodic conferences, the first of which was held in 1889, and the establishment of a permanent secretariat in Washington known as the Pan American Union, Pan-Americanism was carefully nursed by Washington officialdom.

Yet barely a decade after the first Pan-American Conference, United States imperialism shook the foundations of the new movement. If Latin American nations had ever felt a grateful appreciation for the protection afforded by the Monroe Doctrine, its benign aspect was forgotten in their concern over what they now chose to call the "Colossus of the North." Recognizing the familiar stamp of "made in the U.S.A.," the more suspicious of the Latin Americans began to see Pan-Americanism as a "skillful move in the expansionist policy of the North, and a suicidal tendency of the simple-minded South."[8] By 1913 the general resentment evoked such charges of hypocrisy that an important South American diplomat undiplomatically felt prompted to state in all sincerity: "There is no Pan-Americanism in South America; it exists only in Washington."[9] More sarcastic colleagues referred to the Pan American Union as the Colonial Division of the Department of State.

Latin America in 1914. Thus by 1914 Latin America's relations with the outside world were neither healthy nor comforting. Although a century of independence had elapsed, Latin America still lingered on the margin of international life. Left to shift for itself in the face of a future shaded by Yankee imperialism, Latin America saw only a hard road ahead in its relations with the outside world.

BLACK AFRICANS IN THE NEW EUROPES

Migration in history. Mankind has been a wanderer as much, or perhaps more so, than a home stayer. It has well been said that "Man's history is a story of movement, of the conquest of land from nature and from fellowman, of adaptation to new environment, of the blending of blood and the intermixture of cultures."[10] Intercontinental migration constituted one of the significant dynamics of modern world history from 1500 to 1900. During this period various major types of migration can be singled out, such as (1) from all of Europe to North America, (2) from Latin Europe to Central and South America, and (3) from Great Britain to South Africa, Australia, and New Zealand.

There was, however, another form of migration. Millions of Africans were seized and forcibly transplanted to the Americas. The slave trade in Latin America began shortly after 1502. As many native Indians died off and could not supply the mounting demand for the labor required by the plantations, the influx of black slaves increased rapidly. The first to be imported into Brazil came in 1538. By 1600 blacks formed the basis of the economy in Brazil, along the Peruvian coast, in the hot lands of Mexico, in Santo Domingo and Cuba, and in the mines of Colombia. By 1800 the population of Haiti was predominantly black or mulatto, and the African element was substantial in Brazil and Cuba and much less in the Dominican Republic, Panama, Venezuela, and Colombia.

Slavery in the English colonies. A century after the African was brought to Latin America, he appeared in the English colonies to the north. The first Negroes were landed in Jamestown in 1619, but their status was uncertain for some fifty years. Between 1640 and 1660 there is evidence of enslavement, and after the latter date the slave system was defined by law in several of the colonies. The labor of white immigrant indentured servants—initially an important factor in these colonies—provided unfree, cheap labor for only brief terms and declined as the use of black, lifetime slaves proved to be a less costly labor supply in the plantation system. In 1790 when the white population was just over three million, there were some 750,000 Negroes in the United States.

During the American Revolution there was a quickening of conscience about the rightness of slavery. For some people there was an embarrassing contradiction between the ideals of the Declaration of Independence and human bondage. The incipient antislavery sentiment waned, however, as concern mounted over a bloody slave insurrection in Santo Domingo, unrest among American slaves, and the unsettling economic and social consequences of liberal opinion. Slave rebellions in the early 1800's shocked many quarters. It was the Industrial Revolution in England, however, that did the most to fasten slavery on the economy of the southern states. An increased supply of cotton was needed for the new textile mills early in the nineteenth century. New technology and new lands made the plantation system more profitable, creating a rising demand for slaves even as the importation of slaves was ended in 1808. Eventually the belief in Negro inferiority was elevated into a pseudoscientific racist doctrine defending slavery.

Emancipation without equality. While human servitude was legally outlawed after the defeat of the Confederacy in the Civil War, the full "blessings of freedom" were denied to the "free" Negro during the remainder of the nineteeth century. In fact, while social Darwinists (see p. 556) upheld the rectitude of European imperialism's rule over the "lesser breeds" in Africa and Asia, an analogous American school of thought, based upon the spurious logic of biology, championed beliefs apportioning blacks a lowly and subordinate role in society. Following emancipation Negroes in the South were progressively disfranchised by state laws or by various devices such as poll tax requirements, literacy tests, property qualifications, and naked intimidation. A pattern of segregation in schools, restaurants, parks, and hotels was more thoroughly applied. Laws were passed prohibiting interracial marriage, and blacks were generally excluded from unions. Between 1885 and 1918 more

Editor of the *Crisis*, official publication of the NAACP and an important organ of Negro expression in the United States, W. E. B. DuBois directs the operations of the newspaper's editorial offices.

than 2500 Negroes were lynched in the United States. Blacks were generally poorly educated, socially denied, and economically depressed; it has been said that "the years from 1890 to 1920 were the darkest for the dark people of America."[11]

Notwithstanding numerous and often painful obstacles, however, black Americans in 1913, fifty years after the Emancipation Proclamation, could point to some solid advances: a professional class estimated at 47,000, at least 70 percent literacy, ownership of 550,000 homes, 40,000 businesses, and savings of some 700 million dollars. Their churches, banks, and insurance companies had become substantial institutions.

In addition to improving their own lot, blacks made rich and distinctive contributions to American culture. In music, folk spirituals are known all over the world, and modern rhythmic forms so dominant after World War I had their origin in black rhythm and blues. At the turn of the century Henry Ossawa Tanner was recognized as a distinguished painter specializing in biblical scenes. Receiving over fifty-seven patents for his various inventions, Elijah McCoy was a pioneer in perfecting automatic lubricating devices; appliances for lubricating railroad cars were not considered adequate without the "McCoy" trademark. The achievements of George Washington Carver in the field of agricultural chemistry illustrate the contributions of black Americans in science. W. E. B. DuBois, a social scientist of national stature, began the first effective black protest early in the century. In the 1920's New York experienced its Harlem Renaissance, as such notable black writers as Alain Locke, Claude McKay, and Langston Hughes produced outstanding literature. The first phase of this Renaissance ended in 1930, but its dynamism and strength carried on and still continues.

Africans in Latin America. The history of African peoples in the new Europes of Latin America has generally been different from that north of the Rio Grande. Long contact of the Spanish and Portuguese with the dark-skinned Moorish people in the Iberian peninsula and their early African explorations had helped prevent the development of the form racism took in North America. There was also an important difference in the status of the slave in North and South America. In the former, the slave was regarded as a mere chattel with no legal or moral rights. In the latter, partly explained by the tradition of the Roman law and some influence of the monarchs and the Catholic Church, slaves had a legal personality and moral status. Thus while the slave status was generally considered to be perpetual, manumission was not difficult in Latin America. By 1860 free blacks outnumbered slaves 2 to 1 in Brazil, while slaves outnumbered free blacks 8 to 1 in the United States. In 1888 slavery ended in Brazil without armed conflict.

There has been greater racial mixing in Latin America. The greatest meld of races—white, red, and black—in the history of the world has taken place. Perhaps more than half of the population has mixed blood. This intermingling may have eased racial tensions and made impossible North American practices such as segregation.

What did the African contribute to the new Europes of Latin America? Demographically, he helped fill the vast empty tropical spaces. Economically, he played a vital role in the production of colonial wealth as a herdsman, an artisan, and a farm worker. "During this era, the frontiers of European influence in the New World tropics were established on the base of African manpower."[12] Culturally, he contributed to the life style of the society in which he lived. Reflecting on this contribution and the racial blending that has taken place, a historian of South America has written: "The African peoples . . . have a rich cultural heritage and have transferred this heritage to the New World; the talents, the temperament, the beliefs, the physical traits of the Negro are ingredients in that new race of man—the American."[13]

SOUTH AFRICA, AUSTRALIA, AND NEW ZEALAND

Dutch settlement of South Africa. The area later known as the Union of South Africa, located at the tip of Africa, first came within the ken of Europe when Bartholomew Diaz reached the Cape of Good Hope in the year 1487. Ten years later Vasco da Gama

rounded the Cape on his way to the Indies. In the seventeenth century, when large fleets of merchantmen from Holland made their way around Africa to the Indies to trade for spices and oriental wares, the Cape became of great importance as a place to obtain fresh water and to replenish supplies.

In 1651 the Dutch established a settlement at the Cape of Good Hope named Cape Town, which grew slowly. As the Dutch settlers pushed into the interior, they came into conflict with the Kaffirs, or Bantu native people, who put up stout resistance against the expansion of the whites.

British rule. The Dutch period of South African history came to an end when Great Britain acquired the colony in 1806 during the Napoleonic Wars. From the beginning of English rule, there was bad blood between the two nationalities. The English did not cater to the sensitivities of the Boers, the Dutch burghers, who were a proud and independent people. The Dutch had many slaves, and the British emancipation of all slaves in the empire in 1833 caused much ill feeling. Moreover, the Boers disliked the attitude of the missionaries, who were continually accusing the Dutch of abusing the natives.

In 1836 the Boers began an epic journey in their great ox-drawn wagons to a new country where they could pursue their way of life without interference. This Great Trek was a folk movement similar in its importance to the covered-wagon epic of our own West. For several years the Boers were on the march. Finally, on the high veld, they established two little republics far away from the British—the Orange Free State and the Transvaal. The British, in the meantime, extended their settlement along the eastern coast north of the Cape and founded the colony of Natal.

The Great Trek did little to solve the difficulties of the Boers. In the mid-nineteenth century there was much fighting with the natives. The British government was forced to intervene because the native warriors, out to "blood their spears," made no distinction between Boer and Briton. In 1852 and 1854 the British government made treaties with the Boers, acknowledging their independence but retaining a shadowy right to have a voice in the foreign affairs of the two little republics.

The Boer War. The discovery of gold in the Transvaal in 1885 indirectly brought on the Boer War. Thousands of Englishmen and people of other nationalities thronged to the mines, and in a few years the boom town of Johannesburg numbered more than 100,000 inhabitants. Paul Kruger, president of Transvaal from 1883 to 1900, distrusted the British and was determined that the alien element should not gain control. Heavy taxes were imposed on the miners, or *Uitlanders* (foreigners), who complained that they paid taxes but that their children were denied adequate educational facilities and that it was almost impossible to become a naturalized Boer citizen. In their anger the *Uitlanders* appealed to the British authorities for assistance. Relations between Boer and Briton went from bad to worse, and in 1899 hostilities broke out between Great Britain and the two Dutch republics.

The world was amazed at the developments in the war which followed. The Boers were

During the Boer War farmers left their fields to take up arms against the British.

crack shots and splendid horsemen. Knowing every inch of the ground on which they fought, they frequently outmaneuvered the British troops. But the tide turned in 1900 when Lord Roberts and General Kitchener inflicted several disastrous defeats upon the Boers.

Formation of the Union. After the Boers surrendered in 1902, the British government treated them magnanimously. Loans were furnished to rebuild burned farmhouses and buy cattle. In 1906 the right of self-government was given to the Transvaal and, two years later, to the Orange Free State. The Liberal government in Great Britain then permitted the Boer and English states to unite and form the Union of South Africa in 1909. Only seven years after the war Boer and Briton joined hands in creating a new self-governing dominion in the tradition of Canada and Australia. The first prime minister of the Union was Louis Botha (1863-1919), who had been a Boer general in the late war. Botha's primary purpose was to create not an English or a Boer nationality but a blend of the two in a new South African patriotism.

Discovery and development of Australia. The discovery of Australia dates back to the seventeenth century, when Dutch explorers sighted its shores. It was the South Seas voyage in 1769 of the famous English explorer Captain Cook, however, that paved the way for English settlement. In 1788 a group of English convicts were transported to Australia and settled at Sydney. From the parent colony of Sydney, later called New South Wales, five other settlements were founded.

Although most of the first Europeans in Australia were convicts, in general they were not habitual criminals but political prisoners and debtors. After seven years of servitude many were liberated and as "emancipists" entered civil life and became valuable citizens. Quite early in the nineteenth century many free settlers also came to Australia. Soon they began to agitate against the transporting of convicts, and the first step in this direction was taken by Britain in 1840. By 1850 the Australian colonies were enjoying a liberal form of self-government.

During the first half of the nineteenth century the Australian colonies grew slowly. Sheep raising became the principal basis of economic prosperity. In 1850 the population of the country was about 400,000; a decade later it had nearly doubled. Although the discovery of gold in 1851 quickened the tempo of development, agriculture continued to be the mainstay of Australia's economy. Railway mileage was expanded, and large amounts of foreign capital flowed in to assist the young nation in developing its resources. In the decade preceding 1914 the population increased from just under four million to five million people.

The Commonwealth formed. In 1901 the six Australian colonies formed a federal union known as the Commonwealth of Australia, which bore many resemblances to the American system of government. The Commonwealth has a legislature composed of a House of Representatives and a Senate. The members of the latter house, six for each state, are elected without regard to changes in population, while the lower house is made up of members elected by each state in accordance with its population. As in Canada, however, the Commonwealth government makes the chief executive, the prime minister, responsible to the legislature and thus does not provide him with the fixed tenure guaranteed the American president.

New Zealand's development. About a thousand miles from the Australian mainland is a group of islands, two of which are of particular importance. These lonely projections of British influence in the South Pacific constitute the self-governing Dominion of New Zealand. The total population of this country, which has an area five sixths the size of Great Britain, is just over 3,148,000. The earliest settlers were desperate convicts who had escaped from the penal settlements in Australia. The activity of other colonizers forced the British government to assume protection of the islands in 1840, and a treaty was signed by British agents guaranteeing certain rights, especially land rights, to the indigenous Maoris.

New Zealand gradually became a rich pastoral, farming, and fruit-raising country. The chief export, then as now, was wool. Later the development of refrigeration enabled large quantities of meat and dairy products to be shipped to foreign markets, especially to Great Britain.

Social advances in the dominions. New Zealand and Australia have been termed sociological laboratories because of their pioneer activities in democratic government and social welfare legislation. As early as 1855 the state of Victoria in Australia introduced the secret ballot in its elections. The Australian ballot was later adopted in Great Britain, the United States, and the world over. Woman suffrage was introduced in New Zealand in 1893 and in Australia nine years later. In New Zealand a program of "land for the people" was carried out by imposing heavy taxes on large tracts of land held by absentee landlords. This dominion led the world in the adoption of noncontributory old-age pensions in 1878 and the establishment of a national infant welfare system in 1907. Before 1914 Australia had passed similar measures.

BICULTURISM IN CANADA

French Canada. From 1534—the year Jacques Cartier sailed up the St. Lawrence River and claimed the area for France—until 1763, Canada was part of the French empire. Unlike the English colonies in the New World, the French colony of Canada was rigidly supervised by the home government. All trade activities were carefully regulated; the Catholic Church monopolized education; and few Protestants were allowed to settle in New France. The French king granted huge tracts of land to nobles, who in turn parceled their estates out to peasant farmers. On the whole this introduction of an adaptation of European feudalism seriously restricted the development of the colony; it retarded expansion by denying free land to pioneers, and it subjected the "habitant" to unduly rigid control by priest, seigneur, and royal official.

The French-British quarrels. Early in the history of New France, English activities in North America plainly endangered the future of French Canada. In addition to England's interest in its Atlantic seaboard colonies, English fishermen frequently landed at Newfoundland, and in 1670 the Hudson's Bay Company was founded to carry on trading activities, especially in furs, with the Indians in the territory around Hudson Bay. When war broke out in Europe between England and France, their colonies in the New World went to war also (see Chapter 20). The ultimate English victory in the struggle for the New World was foreshadowed by the Treaty of Utrecht (1713) in which France ceded Acadia (later known as Nova Scotia), surrendered claims to Newfoundland, and recognized the Hudson Bay territory as British.

The British acquire Canada. Peace in New France was interrupted by renewals of the duel for world empire between Great Britain and France. The last of four colonial wars ended in a complete victory for Britain. In 1763, by the Treaty of Paris, Canada passed entirely into British hands. The victors took care to assure the loyalty of the French Canadians by means of a royal proclamation guaranteeing the political rights of the inhabitants and their freedom to worship as Roman Catholics. In 1774 the British government passed the famous Quebec Act, termed the "Magna Carta of the French Canadian race." This act reconfirmed the position of the Catholic Church and perpetuated French law and custom. No representative assembly, such as existed in the English-speaking colonies, was provided for, however, because the French lacked both interest and experience in self-government.

Canada's formative period. Great Britain's conquest of Canada ushered in Canada's formative period, which lasted from 1763 to 1867 and was characterized by the following important developments: the addition of an English-speaking population, the repulse of an attempt at conquest by the United States, the grant of local self-government, and, finally, the confederation of Canada into a dominion in 1867.

The addition of an English population to French Canada came as a result of the American Revolution. Although the rebellious colonists tried to conquer Canada, the French remained loyal to Britain, largely because

of the liberal concessions of the Quebec Act, and the invasion failed. Those inhabitants of the thirteen colonies not in favor of separation from Great Britain (Tories) suffered at the hands of the patriots, and a large number of them emigrated to Canada. The immigrants, known as United Empire Loyalists, settled in Nova Scotia, along the St. Lawrence River, and north of the Great Lakes.

The newcomers resented the absence of representative government in their new home and agitated for a measure of self-government. Numerous controversies also arose between the French Canadians and the newly arrived Loyalists. To meet this situation the British government in 1791 divided British North America into two separate provinces called Upper and Lower Canada and granted each a representative assembly. The quarrel between the French and English continued, causing discontent with the government in both provinces of Canada.

Open rebellion in 1837 was quelled only after serious fighting. From London, a special commissioner, Lord Durham (1792-1840), was sent to Canada to study the problem and make recommendations. A statesman with vision, Durham realized that a much larger degree of self-government must be granted if the home country was to hold the loyalty of its colonies. He recommended that certain matters of imperial concern, such as the control of foreign relations, should be left to the discretion of the mother country, but that Canada alone should control its own domestic affairs. By the mid-nineteenth century local self-government was granted to Canada. Unlike the thirteen colonies, who severed their connection with the mother country by revolution, Canada achieved virtual independence peacefully and remained loyal to Britain.

Confederation. Fear of the United States, the need for a common tariff policy, and a concerted effort to develop natural resources led Canadians into confederation. A plan of union—the British North America Act—was drawn up, approved by the British government, and in 1867 passed by the Parliament in London. This act united Canada (then divided into the provinces of Quebec and

THE GROWTH OF MODERN
CANADA

Canada in 1841
Canada Today

ALASKA
(U.S.) *Yukon R.*

BEAUFORT SEA

BANKS I.

VICTORIA I.

BAFFIN
BAY

GREENLAND
(Den.)

B A F F I N   I.

HUDSON
BAY

N O R T H W E S T

T E R R I T O R I E S

YUKON
1898

*Great
Bear L.*

MACKENZIE

*Great
Slave L.*

D I S T R I C T   O F   K E E W A T I N

(To Newfoundland 1809)

UNGAVA
(To Quebec 1912)

LABRADOR
(To Newfoundland 1927)

NEWFOUNDLAND
1949   St. Johns

*Prince
Rupert*

BRITISH

COLUMBIA
1871

A T H A B A S K A
(To Alberta 1905)   (To Saskatchewan
1905)

Edmonton

•Port Nelson

VANCOUVER

•Vancouver

ALBERTA
1905

SASKATCHEWAN
1905

Columbia R.

ASSINIBOIA
(To Saskatchewan 1905)

*Lake
Winnipeg*

(To Ontario 1912)

MANITOBA
1870

•Winnipeg

Missouri R.

Columbia

Lake Superior

ONTARIO
1867

*Lake
Huron*

Toronto

Lake Michigan

*Lake
Ontario*

Lake Erie

QUEBEC
1867

Montreal

St. Lawrence R.

PRINCE
EDWARD ISLAND
1873

NEW
BRUNSWICK
1867

NOVA
SCOTIA
1867

Halifax

ATLANTIC

OCEAN

U N I T E D   S T A T E S

Ontario), Nova Scotia, and New Brunswick. Canada was now a federal union of four provinces, somewhat similar in political organization to the United States. The government of Canada, however, adopted the English cabinet system with its principle of ministerial responsibility. As a symbol of Canada's connection with the mother country, provision was also made for a governor-general who was to act as the personal representative of the British king.

Obstacles to Canadian development. With the passage of the British North America Act in 1867, Canada's national existence began. But the new nation encountered many problems. Communications were poor. In 1869 the Dominion purchased the vast territories of the Hudson's Bay Company;* in 1871 a new colony, British Columbia, far off on the Pacific coast, joined the Dominion on the promise of early construction of a transcontinental railroad to link British Columbia with eastern Canada.

Another disturbing factor was the lack of cordial relations with the United States. After the Civil War anti-British sentiment was fanned by Irish patriots in the United States who, in the cause of freedom for Ireland, conducted armed forays over the Canadian border. But in 1871 the major differences between Canada and the United States were ironed out in the Treaty of Washington, a landmark in the use of arbitration.

*The Hudson's Bay Company had been incorporated in 1670 as the company of Gentlemen Adventurers of England Trading into Hudson's Bay. Early in the nineteenth century the company established posts throughout the Canadian west, and the vast territory extending from what is now the province of Ontario to British Columbia was administered by this great trading organization. In 1824 the company built Fort Vancouver on the Columbia River (in the present state of Washington), which was the trading center for the Oregon territory. Here the serious boundary dispute that developed between the company and American settlers caused Americans in 1844 to raise the cry "54-40 or fight" and "All of Oregon or none." Two years later the controversy was settled amicably when Great Britain and the United States accepted a boundary at the 49th parallel. The history of the Canadian west and even that of the United States was greatly influenced by this company. While the company no longer possesses its former administrative powers, it still continues to play an important part in the economic life of Canada.

The United Empire Loyalists, former colonists still loyal to England, fled north from the United States to escape persecution by those favoring independence and helped settle Canada above the Great Lakes. This addition of an English-speaking population marked the beginning of Canada's cultural pluralism. Above is a new Loyalist settlement at Johnston, Ontario.

One state: two nations. Canada has aptly been called "a classic instance of a two-fragment society," a pluralism that has seriously hindered its development. As we have seen, this dualism was not born with the British conquest in 1761. At this time the entire population was French, but an historic change began with the American Revolution, when English-speaking American Loyalists wishing to retain their British allegiance fled to Canada. In 1761 there were only 65,000 people in New France; by 1815 the population of all the British North American colonies had increased to 600,000, of whom only 250,000 were French. Between 1815 and 1850 a second wave of immigrants from Britain brought the entire population to 2,400,000, of whom less than one third were French. During the nineteenth century, and indeed down to the present, the population of French origin has remained between 28 and 31 percent of the total.

From the first arrival of significant numbers of British, the relations between the French and English have been strained. In his investigation of Canadian unrest in 1837, Lord Durham eloquently observed, "I found two nations warring in the bosom of a single state; I found a struggle not of principles but of races." In this reference to the ill will and on occasion downright hostility between English and French Canadians, Durham singled out the most persistent and disturbing problem in Canadian national life.

The reasons are complex and numerous. The memory of the British conquest has often rankled the French; the English, on the other hand, have felt pride in this victory and with their tie to "mother country." There was also a clash in the religious field. New France was highly conservative, ruled by an authoritarian regime. When this political authority was removed, the Catholic Church in Quebec became the main defender and citadel of French Catholic culture. The English-speaking Canadians, however, tended to be antagonistic to this Catholic role.

Complicating the situation was the fact that the French minority was largely agricultural with a high rate of illiteracy. The French lived an unhurried existence, dominantly rural, suspicious of the outside world. Their education, often centered in convents and seminaries, was classical and theological in emphasis. The more secular-minded English, on the other hand, eagerly sought training in economics and science. It was natural, therefore, that the English dominated business. And while the federal constitution sought to create a bilingual society and a dual school system, the French were bitter over the progressive erosion of this guaranteed equality in the western provinces, where no appreciable French population developed. Tension was also generated by the inclination of some English Canadians to assume a pose of superiority; they denigrated French-Canadian culture and made little effort to learn French.

At the end of the nineteenth century, while Canada was a united federation in political structure, a common Canadianism had not been achieved. The French had no intention of being absorbed by the culture of the majority. How to create a single nationality comprised of two separate but officially equal cultures was to emerge in the mid-twentieth century as Canada's cardinal problem.

Canada's national development. Under the leadership of the Dominion's first prime minister, Sir John A. Macdonald (1815-1891), Canadians resolutely set about the task of national development. Bounties were offered to new industries; a railroad was completed from the east to British Columbia in 1885; and an active program for attracting immigrants was pursued.

Macdonald's work was carried on by Sir Wilfrid Laurier (1841-1919), who as prime minister dominated Canadian politics from 1896 until 1911. Between 1897 and 1912 Canada received 2,250,000 new citizens, bringing the country's total population to over 7,000,000. New provinces were also carved out of land formerly controlled by the Hudson's Bay Company so that in 1914 the Dominion consisted of nine provinces.

After the turn of the century certain problems began to appear as the result of the country's rapid growth. The advance of industrialism produced labor problems and discontent among the common people. The influence of big business began to permeate the halls of the Canadian parliament. The competition of wheat from Russia, South America, and the United States and the vagaries of the climate had serious economic effects on the Canadian farmer. This period saw the rise of agrarian unrest resembling the Populist movement in the western United States about 1890. In 1904 the Canadian government created a body for regulating the railroads similar to the Interstate Commerce Commission of the United States. Canada was becoming a mature nation, with all the accompanying problems of depressions, the maldistribution of wealth, and the need of governmental restraint of business.

COMMON DENOMINATORS

Immigration. The vast, fertile lands of the new Europes provided an almost magnetic attraction for the poor and landless peoples of Europe. A tremendous tide of immigration entered the new lands; it is estimated that 40 million emigrants sailed from their European homes from 1815 to 1914. By the latter date the number of people of European stock living in the new Europes totaled 200 million—a figure which is almost equivalent to the total population of Europe at the time of Napoleon's defeat.

For some 350 years this mass movement from Europe was accompanied by an equally significant forced migration from West Africa to the Americas. The number transported in the slave trade ran into the millions, and since many died from ill treatment at the time of capture and at sea during the nefarious Middle Passage—the forty-day voyage across the Atlantic—this trade perhaps cost Africa 50 million of its people; this estimate does not include the Arab slave trade from the East African coast.

In various and different ways the new Europes reflected the nineteenth-century movements that had originated in western Europe —nationalism, democracy, industrialism, and even imperialism. In addition, they had problems and opportunities which sprang specifically from factors and conditions shared in their new environments. These common denominators, with some variants, will be considered here.

Exploration. In all the new Europes vast spaces had to be explored, paths to the interior mapped, and natural resources evaluated. In what is now Canada, Alexander Mackenzie in 1789 traveled to the Great Slave Lake, then down the river that now bears his name to the shores of the Arctic. Four years later he crossed the Rocky Mountains to the Pacific and thus became the first European to traverse North America at its greatest width. In the United States the famous expedition of Meriwether Lewis and William Clark started from St. Louis in the winter of 1803-1804, blazed a trail through the unknown Northwest, and reached the Pacific two years later. For half a century the process of exploration and mapping continued, reaching its climax in John Frémont's expeditions to Oregon and California during the 1840's.

The most famous figure in the exploration of South America was the German naturalist Alexander von Humboldt, who from 1799 to 1804 carried on explorations in Mexico, Cuba, and South America; he investigated the valley of the Orinoco, crossed the Andes, and studied the sources of the Amazon. Although others have carried on the work he began, the huge Amazon basin—a tropical wilderness covering an area as large as the United States—has not been completely explored to this day.

Not until after the midpoint of the nineteenth century was the continent of Australia crossed from north to south. Between 1860 and 1862 John McDouall Stuart made three attempts before he successfully completed the journey from Adelaide to Van Diemen's Gulf. The penetration of the interior of South Africa differed from explorations in the other new Europes. It was achieved by the gradual expansion of white settlement in such valiant movements as the Great Trek rather than by expeditions of exploration, although discovery further north was accomplished by such men as Livingstone and Stanley (see Chapter 28).

Race problems in the new Europes. Race relations have been an important component in the history of most of the new Europes and have remained so in some. Estimates of the number of Indians in North America at the time of the coming of the white man are conjectural. In Canada the estimate is about 200,000; in the United States, about 850,000. Since the coming of the white man, the number of Indians in North America has been reduced by approximately half. In Canada, where the Indian population was not so great as in the United States, the Canadians encountered less difficulty with the natives as they moved westward to the Pacific. In the United States, however, there were frequent Indian wars and, generally speaking, a much more severe impact of an advanced civilization upon the culture patterns of the Indians. While in modern times some attempts have been made to help the Indian make a place for himself in contemporary urban society, these efforts have generally been inadequate. The Indian remains the most neglected and isolated minority in the United States.

The aborigines of Australia and Tasmania—numbering possibly 300,000 at the time of the arrival of the Europeans—could not withstand the ravages of new diseases and of the intoxicating liquors brought by the white men. Nor could they adapt themselves to new ways of life made necessary by the disappearance of their hunting lands. At times they were treated brutally: in some localities they were shot in batches; sometimes the whites got the natives drunk and then gave them clubs to fight each other for the amusement of the "civilized" spectators. The natives of Tasmania are now extinct, and the aborigines in Australia are a declining race.

In New Zealand the native Maoris had a more advanced culture than the Australian aborigines and were better able to stand up to the whites. After serious wars in the 1860's peace was finally secured, and slowly the Maoris accommodated themselves to the new world created by the whites. Since 1900 the Maoris have shared the same political rights and privileges as the European settlers and have obtained the benefits of advanced education. In the 1920's the pure Maori community was estimated to be fifty thousand. They now constitute 5 percent of the population, and their numbers are increasing.

In two of the areas colonized by European stocks, Latin America and South Africa, the indigenous peoples greatly outnumbered the white pioneers. Some authorities, for example, estimate that the population of Latin America in pre-Columbian days was at least 25 million. While a large percentage of these people died out following the initial European impact, because of disease, war, and famine, in the long run native stocks did not dwindle away but substantially increased. There was much racial mixing between the Indians and Europeans, giving rise to the *mestizo*, and this mixed strain together with the Indian soon outnumbered the white population. In the early twentieth century population statistics were estimated to be: 20 million pure Indian, 30 million *mestizos*, 26 million black and mulatto, and 34 million white. Only in Argentina, Chile, and a few smaller states such as Costa Rica, Cuba, and Uruguay have European stocks overwhelmed the Indian.

Although the indigenous peoples in South Africa were not exterminated, neither were they given the opportunity to share in European civilization. The fierce fighting between the European frontiersmen (mainly the Dutch) and the Bantu caused constant misunderstanding and fear. Despite many political and economic disabilities, in the nineteenth century the South African natives showed a substantial increase in numbers. By 1904 the Europeans numbered about 1,150,000, as compared with about 7,000,000 others, mainly Bantu, "coloured,"* and a small community of Indians originally brought to the country as indentured workers from India. Unlike the situation in Latin America, the European minority—both English and Boer—have resolutely opposed any miscegenation with the indigenous Bantu peoples. Socially, politically, and economically there has been implacable segregation. This horizontally stratified society made up of endogamous classes, set apart by color, has been defined as "pigmentocracy."

Isolation. Another common denominator in the new Europes was that generally the new nations remained outside the main current of world affairs in the nineteenth century. The British overseas nations accepted British leadership in international affairs. They were also effectively sheltered by the British fleet, a dependence that largely explains their reluctance to assert their complete independence.

During most of the nineteenth century the United States lavished its main efforts upon the exploitation of its vast natural resources and on the Americanization of the millions of immigrants who flocked to its shores. Evidence of its future role in world affairs became increasingly apparent, however, as the century drew to a close. In fact, the en-

The indigenous Maoris and the white colonialists in New Zealand fought two series of bloody wars over land rights. The courage the Maoris displayed during these wars won them the colonists' respect, and they were given representation in the New Zealand parliament. Eventually they adapted to the dominant white culture.

trance of the United States onto the world stage was to be one of the cardinal factors in the drama of twentieth-century international affairs.

It would not be wholly correct to say that the nations of Latin America remained aloof from the flow of world politics. Politically unstable but rich in natural resources, these countries were tempting bait for great powers in Europe and also for the "Colossus of the North"—the United States. But the cruder imperialistic partitions and outright annexations so evident in Africa, China, and Southeast Asia were avoided. This lack of complete exploitation was due to luck rather than to the virtue of the outside powers. The national interests of the United States and to some extent of Britain coincided with the maintenance of the independence of various Latin American nations.

Progress of democracy. In general the liberal and equalitarian trends originating in western Europe found a fertile soil in the new Europes. Opposition to authority and

Coloured is a special South African term used to refer to the Cape Colored, a people of mixed racial ancestry.

to long-established traditions were at the heart of the revolutions that expelled the influence of Britain, Spain, and Portugal from the New World. Some historians have emphasized another factor in the progress of democracy—the influence of the frontier. Among the frontiersmen existed an absence of class distinctions, a refusal to truckle to authority, and a strong belief in the rights and capacities of the individual.

It is interesting that this frontier thesis worked in reverse in Australia. In this new Europe, land was not free or as productive as in the United States. As a result, in the remote "outback" vast sheep and cattle stations were established as rural capitalistic enterprises. On what has been called the "big man's frontier" there was little opportunity for the squatter and little man. This rural proletariat, therefore, escaped to the city. In this urban environment it supported radical and reformist causes that help explain the strong democratic trend in late nineteenth-century Australian politics. To a striking degree the same reverse frontier development occurred in Argentina.

In the United States the impediments to social democracy remaining after independence were largely removed by the 1820's; and during the remainder of the nineteenth century the country progressively perfected its democratic structure. In Canada the greatest stimulus to the growth of democracy was the achievement of responsible government. The trend toward social democracy evident in the United States was outstripped in Australia and New Zealand. In fact, New Zealand led the world in the direction of what is known as the welfare state.

With few exceptions, such as Mexico under the first Juárez administration, the Latin American republics in the nineteenth century paid mere lip service to the concept of social and political democracy. Society did not have the mobility existing in the United States and Canada. The new Latin American nations suffered from chronic political instability; changes in government came too frequently from bullets, not ballots.

Search for a nationality. Among all the new Europes, the United States has found the quest for nationality easiest. Its power,

size, available resources, and heritage of freedom and the rule of law from its mother country have all contributed to a distinctive and recognizable national ideal. The greatest threat to national sovereignty—the Civil War—ended with the triumph of the forces of national union. In the nineteenth century the United States was the melting pot for thousands and thousands of immigrants; it stood for nonmilitarism and for the hope of the common man. And this democratic ideology consisted not only of faith but also of works.

The search for a national identity has not been easy in Canada. The establishment of the Confederation in 1867 increased nationalistic sentiment. But the Canadian, then as now, continued to be drawn like a magnet to the colossus of the south. He prefers baseball to cricket; he even joins affiliates of American labor organizations. Another problem complicating the search for a national identity is the existence of a closely knit French Canadian minority that tenaciously clings to its own language and culture. To some, Canada is a country with two nationalities: Toronto the symbol of one and old Quebec that of the other.

Nationalism has burned as brightly in each of the Latin American nations as in the other new Europes. In fact, the sentiment of nationalism has seemed the stronger as if in compensation for the obvious failures in political stability. The eight major administrative divisions in the late colonial era have fragmented into nineteen states—a process accompanied by costly and bloody wars. The whole of Latin America, however, exhibits a cultural homogeneity which has perhaps been some compensation for political turmoil.

Australia and New Zealand have found the search for nationality difficult. Remote from Europe, these islanders have clung to the traditions and ways of life of their forebears. New Zealanders brag about being more English than the English. This sentiment notwithstanding, a recognizable national character has developed in both countries—strongly equalitarian and fiercely nationalistic in its pride of the immensity and beauty of its lands.

Unlike Canada, where the original European community became a national minority in a new country created by the victorious British, the Union of South Africa has a majority of Boers instead of British in its European community. Of all the people of the new Europes, the South African Boers, who now call themselves Afrikaners, have developed the strongest sense of national identity. Continuously challenged by the alien culture of their English neighbors and potentially endangered by the Bantu majority, these beleaguered people have developed a distinctive, unbending culture. Two of its main pillars are a rigid Calvinism brought from Europe in the seventeenth century and a new language, Afrikaans, developed from the Dutch tongue. As in the case of Canada, a unicultural and national South Africa (at least as far as Europeans are concerned) has been weakened by the antipathy between its English and Afrikaner segments. In recent years, however, this division has been lessened by a common fear of Bantu domination and also by resentment directed against the outside world for its criticisms of South African racial policies.

SUMMARY

In little more than two and one half centuries (1650-1914) the greatest human migration from the smallest of continents, Europe, had taken place. It surpassed in scope such momentous human wanderings of the past as those of the Indo-Europeans into India and southern Europe and the historical incursions of the Germanic tribes into the Roman Empire. Transoceanic in character, this mass movement originated in Europe which, during this period, forged ahead of the rest of the world in industry, technology and science, wealth, and military power.

These advances were reflected in the tremendous increase in Europe's population that reached full tide in the nineteenth century. From 1815 to 1914 that continent's numbers increased from 200 million to 460 million; yet, during this time span, more than 40 million immigrants sought homes in the new Europes overseas. In 1815 there were less than 20 million abroad. By 1914 the figure had grown to 200 million. As many people of European stock lived outside Europe by this latter date as had been in it when Napoleon was defeated at Waterloo in 1815. Concurrent with the European immigration to the Americas was the transfer of millions of Africans to the New World by the slave trade.

The transoceanic dispersal of Europeans has been treated mainly in the history of the United States, the British Dominions, and Latin America. The story of the United States, albeit familiar to most students, has been treated at some length because it is by far the most important of the new Europes in the nineteenth century and because of the profound differences in its development, despite a common European heritage. The frontier and slavery both influenced the formation of a distinctive society, and the latter bequeathed to the country the most intractable of its twentieth-century domestic problems. The Civil War had more "revolutionary" consequences, socially, economically, and politically, than any other event occurring in the new Europes.

African peoples were a potent economic factor in developing the vast natural resources of their new homes; and where they constituted a substantial ethnic element, they made significant contributions to the culture of their society. In Latin America there was considerable racial intermingling, abolition of slavery was progressive and peaceful, and discrimination by whites over blacks relatively mild. In the United States, a new Europe and to some extent a new Africa, the concept of Negro inferiority was more potent, and even after emancipation blacks continued to be treated as second-class citizens. Only in the last two decades, following the migration of hundreds of thousands of blacks to northern cities and the general ascendancy of the concept of human rights in the world, has the demand of black Americans for the full rights of citizenship initiated a critical phase in race relations in the United States.

The British Dominions became self-governing without breaking the political tie binding them to Britain. With the exception of South Africa, these communities were dominantly British in stock. Their language and culture were English; their governmental habits Anglo-Saxon. In the case of Canada, however, there was a strong French Canadian minority in Quebec inherited from the original French regime. In South Africa, following a confused history of rivalry and finally a war between the British and Dutch colonies, a rather shaky union was achieved in which the Dutch were the dominant element. There were no complications of rival nationalities in Australia and New Zealand. These colonies were settled by the British in the beginning and did not have to adjust themselves to an influx of other European peoples.

Both Australia and Canada, continental areas in their dimensions, took a leaf out of United States history. They attained their political unity by the merging of a number of colonies into a single government. Canada as a dominion became a confederation in 1867, and Australia attained the same status as a commonwealth in 1901.

Much the same problems of exploration, pushing back the frontier, and development of natural resources that were found in the American and British new Europes were also factors in the development and growth of Latin America. But instead of political unity, the sequel to the Spanish empire was fragmentation and a multiplicity of nationalities. There were also intermittent civil wars; revolutions and new regimes came and went with alarming and costly regularity. Dictators rather than democrats called the tune. In such an atmosphere economic development could not thrive; the bulk of the people lived in poverty. This internal disorder and weakness invited foreign intervention. The United States, in particular, extended its influence, political and economic, into Central America and the Caribbean region.

SUGGESTIONS FOR READING

O. Handlin *et al.*, eds., **The Harvard Guide to American History** (Harvard) is an indispensable bibliography. R. B. Morris, ed., **Encyclopedia of American History** (Harper & Row, 1976) is the most convenient reference work. Recommended general surveys are S. E. Morison, **The Oxford History of the American People** (Harper & Row), which is a graphic survey by a distinguished historian; and R. Hofstadter, **The American Political Tradition*** (Vintage) which is a brilliant and unorthodox interpretation of men and ideas from the Founding Fathers to F.D.R.

For a brief and stimulating survey of the first half of American history see M. Cunliffe, **The Nation Takes Shape: 1789-1837** (Univ. of Chicago). Also recommended is A. M. Schlesinger, Jr., **The Age of Jackson*** (Mentor), a Pulitzer Prize-winning study. A. Craven, **The Coming of the Civil War*** (Phoenix) is a challenging discussion of the various forces responsible for the conflict. One of the best treatments of the war is B. Catton, **This Hallowed Ground*** (Pocket Books). Also recommended is Carl Sandburg, **Abraham Lincoln: The Prairie Years and The War Years,*** 3 vols. (Dell).

R. W. Logan, **The Negro in the United States*** (Anvil) traces the progress of the American Negro. See also C. Vann Woodward, **The Strange Career of Jim Crow*** (Oxford, 1974); Lerone Bennett, Jr., **Before the Mayflower*** (Penguin); Winthrop D. Jordan, **White Over Black*** (Penguin); and L. H. Fishel and B. Quarles, **The Black American,*** 3rd ed. (Scott, Foresman, 1976), which is a comprehensive anthology. For two excellent historical surveys on the subject see Alex Haley, **Roots** (Doubleday, 1976); and E. D. Genovese, **Roll, Jordan, Roll: The World the Slaves Made** (Random House, 1976).

A critique of the American scene which has become a classic in the field of political analysis is Alexis de Tocqueville, R. D. Heffner, ed., **Democracy in America*** (Mentor). For an analysis of politics and military policy by a renowned military historian see W. Millis, **Arms and Men*** (Mentor). Brevity and scholarship mark the following two biographies: H. F. Pringle, **Theodore Roosevelt*** (Harvest); and E. M. Hugh-Jones, **Woodrow Wilson and American Liberalism*** (Collier). An excellent introduction to intellectual history since the 1880's is H. S. Commager, **The American Mind*** (Yale).

T. H. Raddall, **The Path of Destiny** (Doubleday) is a history of Canada from the British conquest to self-government in 1850. For two important aspects of Canadian history see Bruce Hutchison, **The Struggle for the Border** (Longmans, 1955), a lively account of Canadian-American relations; and J. B. Brebner, **Canada, A Modern History** (Univ. of Michigan).

John Harre and Keith Jackson, **New Zealand** (Walker) is a study of a multiracial society: Europeans and Maori. For provocative studies of history and society see O. H. K. Spate, **Australia** (Praeger, 1968); and Douglas Pike, **Australia** (Cambridge, 1969). On the rise of the gold and diamond industries and the background of the Boer War see C. W. De Kiewiet, **A History of South Africa, Social and Economic** (Oxford). Also recommended is L. M. Thompson, **The Unification of South Africa, 1902-1910** (Oxford). For a comparative cultural study of the new Europes see Louis Hartz, **The Founding of New Societies** (Harcourt Brace Jovanovich); and C. Hartley Grattan, **The Southwest Pacific Since 1900** (Univ. of Michigan).

*Indicates a less expensive paperbound edition.

CHAPTER 28

Africa and the
Middle East: 1800-1914

Cultural Clashes of Imperialism: The Islamic World and Africa

INTRODUCTION. In the eighteenth and nineteenth centuries the Middle East and Africa increasingly came to feel the pressures of the European advances. The civilizations in both areas faced serious challenges from the technologically and militarily superior Europeans. The diversified nature of the various cultures did not lend itself to a successful repulsion of the western invaders. By 1900 the Middle East would become caught up in the great powers' competition for dominance of the area, supremacy on the continent of Europe, and command of the Mediterranean Sea and Indian Ocean. During the same time the continent of Africa would experience a major change in its relations with Europe, as seven European powers would come to control all of its territory, with the exception of the countries of Liberia and Ethiopia.

In this chapter we will examine the impact of European imperialism on the Middle East and Africa, and the response of the two areas to the foreign forces. In the Middle East the religious unity produced by the prevalence of Islam was unquestioned. However, the political disunity of the region, especially the disintegration of the former dominance enjoyed by the Ottoman empire, made the introduction of European economic and political controls easier. In Central Asia the Persians and the Afghans were caught in the great power rivalry between the British and the Russians, and found their economic and political futures dictated by outside forces. But by 1914, potent nationalistic reform movements made their presence felt in many parts of the Middle East, as the indigenous peoples tried to regain control of their destinies.

In Africa the diversification of the socioreligious structures made a unified response to the Europeans impossible. From northern to southern Africa a rapid and massive influx of European states overwhelmed the indigenous cultures. The native cultures that had developed in response to separate and special environmental circumstances could not successfully hold off the technologically and bureaucratically efficient Europeans. By the end of the century the African peoples had begun the slow but steady process of adaptation to the industrialized world that is still not completed.

The European powers in both the Middle East and Africa gained considerable advantage from their incursions. In Central Asia, the Russians and British were able to dictate the terms on which they would come to control the area, both economically and politically. In the former Ottoman holdings along the Mediterranean, the English, French, and Italians would come to control the coast from the Straits of Gibraltar to Turkey. In Africa, Europeans would funnel off the continent's economic wealth and dictate the various nations' politics for over a half century after 1870. In return, the continent gained capital investment, development of natural resources, and certain educational and cultural benefits. But the damage caused by Europe's imposition of its political and economic structure had consequences which can still be felt today, shown in one way by the policies of many Asian and African leaders towards Europe in the United Nations and other international forums.

THE MIDDLE EAST

The Islamic world. By the nineteenth century the Islamic world extended from the Atlantic Ocean to the Pacific, in a broad band that reached across North Africa, the Middle East, Central Asia, and down to Indonesia. The faith retained much of its original vigor by 1900, and continues today to be one of the fastest growing religions in the world. Yet, not one area of the Islamic world was able to compete economically or politically with the advancing European community. The strength of the secular, industrial west was too much for the assorted nations of Moslems caught in the route of march.

The Islamic world presented a picture of great unity, and also one of great contrast. The unity resulted from the religious training and traditions which emphasized the basis of the *Koran*, the pilgrimages to Mecca, the daily prayers, and fasting. By the late nineteenth century more than 175 million Moslems performed their religious duties daily. Across the broad band of believers there was the same sacred language, law, morality, and institutions. Every year the number of believers traveling to Mecca grew. It is estimated that more than 50,000 Indians and 20,000 Malays made the trip each year by the end of the century. The contrast in the Islamic world came from the great diversity of peoples, environments, and external pressures affecting the faith from Ceuta in Morocco to Djakarta in Indonesia. Even among devout Moslems there existed some difference of opinion about the nature of the theological basis of the religion. Nonetheless, the Islamic world exhibited an impressive religious and cultural unity, especially given the large swath of the earth which it dominated.

In the nineteenth century the Middle Eastern portion of the Islamic world found itself caught up in the political and economic competition of the great European powers. That the Middle East is the site of such strategic locations as the Straits, the Suez, the overland routes to India, and Russia's access to the Indian Ocean and the Persian Gulf is a fact that condemned the nations located there to a tumultuous time. During the century the Ottoman empire, Persia, and Afghanistan had difficulty in constructing an adequate political structure or a sufficient economic base to defend themselves against such powers as Britain and Russia. The modern, secular state structure—with its professional bureaucrats, broadly based nationalism and patriotism, ideologies, mass literacy, and civil law structure—didn't exist for many of the Islamic rulers. To a large degree the major occupations of western Europe in the last part of the nineteenth century—research scientist, party politician, state functionary, technologist, and industrial worker—were not present in the Islamic world. The function of warrior remained prime, and the state structures fluctuated between the despotic and the nonchalant. Efficient government was hampered by corruption, social decay, lack of education and literacy, and a generally repressed population. In short, the Middle Eastern states were generally unable to mobilize their resources or to motivate their citizens. The Europeans were able to move in to take advantage of the political and economic vulnerability of the Islamic world.[1]

The Ottoman empire—the need to reform. The Ottoman empire went into a state of decline at the end of the seventeenth century, and the effects of this decline, as we have seen, presented European diplomats with the unsolvable Eastern Question. Yet in the nineteenth century it was still the biggest and most prestigious country in the Islamic world, theoretically controlling land stretching from north Africa to the Indian Ocean. By the end of the century there were an estimated 40 million inhabitants living under the sultan's authority.

But the control the sultan exercised was often weak and sporadic. The lines of power and communication to the empire's myriad of peoples were not dependable. The farther one went from Istanbul—to the end of the Arabian peninsula or to North Africa—the

less secure was Turkish control. The Ottoman administration, once a picture of effectiveness in the sixteenth century, declined in the next two-and-a-half centuries as the merit basis for administration came to be replaced by bribery and favoritism. The armed forces—once the most feared in all of Europe—also declined in power, and they came to be as much a threat to the sultan as to foreign enemies.

The empire had been founded on its ability to wage war, and to insure its stability the Turks needed the momentum of continuous victory. The very success that had pushed Ottoman control to its extreme limits of the Atlas and Caucasus mountains made short-range wars of conquest impossible. The European states became stronger and were able to inflict defeats on the Turkish forces. The empire was unable to adapt to the new western strength and to the absence of the reassuring victories it had enjoyed in previous centuries. As the European states became more dynamic, the Ottoman empire became stagnant, earning the epithet "the sick man of Europe," and stood in danger of losing its holdings.[2]

The decline of this once formidable state and the advance of the Europeans took place over a period of three centuries. During that time the European states went through the Renaissance, Reformation, Scientific Revolution, Enlightenment, Commercial Revolution, and Industrial Revolution. The Ottoman empire had profited from none of these seminal developments, which had given the western system its material, intellectual, and political dynamism, nor had it tried to. The forces of European nationalism and patriotism had no major effect in the Ottoman realm as devices to mobilize the population. Instead, the Turks dedicated themselves to the defense of their foundation of life and law—Islam.[3] In the nineteenth century, this was not a sufficiently flexible basis for competition in the international arena.

From the late eighteenth century on, there were some attempts made to reform the Turkish system. The Koran was the foundation for Islam, and although it was the most important basis for a Moslem's daily existence, it did not contain all of the answers to the questions of technological change. Firearms and artillery had been accepted from the infidel for centuries because they could be used in defense of the faith. The clock and the printing press, two symbols of the western advance, were not accepted. No printing was allowed in Istanbul in either Turkish or Arabic until 1729, and then the publication of books was sporadic until the end of the century. After the 1780's foreign influences were increasingly felt in the Ottoman empire; military advisers and diplomats entered at an increasing rate and the Ottomans began establishing permanent diplomatic posts in Europe. As is the case with developing states today, the military in the empire came to be the most advanced social element, since the training in modern technology brought with it the need to learn foreign languages and political theory. A whole new group emerged, trained to look outside the Koran for their information and even inspiration.[4]

The drive for reform was hesitant at best. Those who went too fast, such as Sultan Selim III (1789-1807), were overthrown. During the nineteenth century, sultans concerned with becoming more competitive with the Europeans were hampered in their reform attempts by the administrative chaos of the empire, which stopped the improvements from making much of an impact outside the walls of Istanbul. During the century the Turks went deeply in debt to the European powers. Their Balkan holdings erupted in nationalist movements in Serbia (1804), Greece (1821), and Rumania and Bulgaria later in the century. Russia continued to pressure the Turks while the other powers intruded more and more into the sultan's affairs. Vassals in Albania, Egypt, and Macedonia rose up in revolt. Particularly serious was the Egyptian challenge, as in 1824 Mehemet Ali conquered Crete and took Syria in 1832-1833. Three years later he pushed his gains to the Persian Gulf and the Indian Ocean. By 1840 a combination of the great powers eventually pushed him back to Egypt, which he would control henceforth as a viceroy.

The prelude to the Crimean War, in which Russia and France squabbled over the holy places and Istanbul became an arena in which Europe's diplomats debated the Turks' fate, showed the extent to which the once mighty empire had fallen. Even though the Turks emerged from the turmoil with their great power status guaranteed, it was apparent to all that the empire was kept alive only because the Europeans could think of no other alternative. In 1860 France gained the right to intervene in Syria. In 1874 the Ottoman financial structure collapsed, just at the time of renewed uprisings in the Balkans. The intermittent reform attempts had done little to stop the empire's decline.

Reaction and revolution to 1914. In 1876 Midhat Pasha, a proponent of reform, unveiled a plan for a new, western-style political structure in the Ottoman empire. Under the scheme the empire was declared to be a unitary state with the guarantees of free press, freedom of conscience, equality under the law, and equal taxation. Further, Midhat Pasha proposed the creation of an Ottoman citizenship. The new plan was proclaimed in Istanbul in December 1876. Unfortunately for the empire, Abdul Hamid II — the new sultan who came to the throne soon after — destroyed the reform plans, dismissed Midhat Pasha, and suspended the parliament. By the spring of 1877 Abdul Hamid was trying to rule as his predecessors four centuries earlier had ruled — absolutely. Spies spread throughout the country to track down liberals and other opponents. Censorship was applied, and those who had advocated reforms mysteriously disappeared or were forced into exile. At a time when he needed unity and change to preserve his crumbling holdings, Abdul Hamid chose to split up potential opponents and destroy them.

The sultan faced severe challenges on all fronts. Throughout his realm nationalist movements threatened his rule. The European powers continued their economic and political pressures on his holdings: France annexed Tunis in 1881; Britain occupied Egypt in 1882; and in 1900 Italy cast a covetous eye on Tripoli. Abdul Hamid's basic problem was not the constitutional movement at home, but the reactionary thrust of his policy prohibited him from seeing this.

Remaining under Turkish rule were the Arabs of the Middle Eastern area. They were primarily Moslem in their religion, with a significant Christian minority in certain areas, and some of them were beginning to be touched by the same nationalistic spirit which had affected nineteenth-century Europe. They too began to press upon the weak Ottoman structure. By the beginning of the twentieth century opposition to the sultan's tyranny and misrule was widespread among his subjects.

A nucleus of opposition formed among a group of exiled reformers who had been educated in western European universities. In 1902 these opponents—the Young Turks—and other national groups oppressed by the sultan met in Paris to form a united opposition to Abdul Hamid. At the same time a number of young army officers also became Young Turks, and gave the movement the needed military power and coordination for a successful rebellion. In 1908 the Young Turks told the sultan to put the 1876 constitution into effect or else face an armed uprising. Abdul Hamid saw the weakness of his position and agreed to the demands. But after gaining their initial goal, the revolutionaries split deeply over the question of the status of non-Turks in the new regime. Some of the Young Turks wanted to grant full political rights to the minorities, while others advocated severe restrictions. The new Turkish parliament that came into existence after the restoration immediately got bogged down over the issue of what rights should be extended to the subject nationalities. The sultan was encouraged by the division within the parliament and attempted a counter-revolution to regain power. When he turned against the Young Turks—who had gained substantial popular support by this time—he was overthrown.

Arabs in Syria, Lebanon, and the vast peninsula of Arabia were not happy with the new regime. They, along with the Albanians in the Balkans, were repelled by the Young Turks' program of Turkish supremacy and their policy of centralization which would obviously leave no hope for Arab home rule. When World War I broke out in 1914 the British—once an Allied victory was assured—had little difficulty in turning the Arab nations against their overlord, the Turkish

In 1909 the rebellious Young Turks forced Abdul-Hamid II from his throne. This photograph shows the victorious insurgent forces on the march.

sultan. Other parts of the empire fell away during the young Turk revolt and its aftermath. In 1908 Austria-Hungary annexed Bosnia and Herzegovina, Greece annexed Crete, and Italy—in the course of a short but difficult war—seized Tripoli and Cyrenaica. Finally, in 1912 and 1913, the Balkan nations fought two wars which resulted in the partitioning of Macedonia, thereby completing the destruction of the once mighty Ottoman empire.

Anglo-Russian rivalry. The area between the Caspian Sea and the Persian Gulf came to be a focus of Anglo-Russian conflict during the nineteenth century. The attentions of these two major powers could not have been welcomed by either Persia or Afghanistan. Persia, one of the more strategically located areas of the Islamic world, contained many different peoples (Turks, Arabs, Persians, Jews, Armenians) and religions (Islam, Zoroastrianism, Judaism, and Armenian Christianity). Ruling over this crossroads area was the Kajar dynasty, which would have to deal with the Russians to the north and the British to the south of the country.

Afghanistan, which lay to the east of Persia, controlled the Khyber pass, the most direct land route from Russia to British-controlled India. This mountainous country had been divided previously between the Mongols and Persians. By the nineteenth century the shah in Kabul, Afghanistan's capital city, ruled over the tribal confederations that roamed the country.

Russia had begun its advance toward the region in the middle of the sixteenth century. From that time to the present, the Russian state has had a deep and abiding interest in the fate of Persia and Afghanistan. The advance toward the Islamic world in general stemmed from a diverse set of motives. Russia needed a warm-water port, the military leaders desired a defensive buffer zone between European Russia and Asia, and a number of tsars wanted a direct trade route to India. Throughout the eighteenth and nineteenth centuries the Russians extended their control around the Black Sea, the Caucasus, and into Central Asia, to the frontiers of Persia, Afghanistan, and China.

As Russia advanced across the Asian continent, the British became more and more concerned about the tsarist threat to their interests in the subcontinent. They wanted to maintain control of the sea lanes of the Eastern Mediterranean and after 1869 also wanted sole access to the Suez Canal. European balance of power politics had aided the British in helping thwart the Russian drive to control the Straits, Constantinople, and the Eastern Mediterranean. But the Russian expansion across the Urals threatened English interests from another flank—through Central Asia. Defense of India's land frontiers to the north came to join the protection of the Suez Canal, the Red Sea, and the Persian Gulf to become twin elements in British foreign policy during the nineteenth century.

During the first half of the century Persia and Afghanistan were caught up in armed conflicts with the Russians and the British. The Persians, defeated in two wars by the Russians, lost large amounts of territory and had to pay substantial indemnities. In an attempt to secure control of the Khyber pass, the British fought the Afghans in 1839-1842. In the first part of the conflict a

3000-man British force was massacred. Later on English troops from India secured control of the region. As the two major European forces expanded their power from north and south, Persia and Afghanistan lost control over their own policies.

While the British consolidated their hold on India, Russian expansion reached the Pacific. Both nations began to advance toward each others' holdings. Many indigenous peoples, such as the Mongols, Afghans, Turkomans, and Tatars, entered Russia's political structure, and their cities, such as Samarkand, Tashkent, and Bokhara, became tsarist administrative centers. Britain's advances were controlled by a well-trained colonial government and a strong army. Russia's advance was won not only by the bravery and resolution of Russian troops, but also by the construction of the Trans-Caspian Railway, which at its completion in 1888 reached 1064 miles into the heart of Asia. The Orenburg-Tashkent Railway, completed in 1905, stretched 1185 miles farther. Both lines vastly increased Russia's ability to maintain military pressure on and

A contemporary Russian drawing shows a construction train on the Trans-Caspian Railway. The completion of this railroad allowed Russia to convey and supply troops in Central Asia and to greatly extend its economic influence there.

economic superiority over the area. The feats of Russian arms and engineers inspired some great Russian imperialists to dream of conquering Afghanistan, and even of penetrating India itself.

Although Britain did not rule out the latter possibility, it was thought probable that Russian pressure against India was designed primarily as a counter against Britain in other areas of the globe. As a Russian general admitted, "The stronger Russia is in Central Asia, the weaker England is in India and the more conciliatory she will be in Europe."[5]

By the end of the nineteenth century Afghanistan and Tibet continued to be serious areas of tension. Russian designs against the former were blocked by effective measures taken on the part of Britain, and the intrusion of Russian influence into Tibet was countered by a British military expedition to Lhasa in 1904. Persia, however, remained a problem more difficult to solve.

Britain made gainful economic inroads into Persia during the century, gaining substantial control over much of the area's mineral wealth and banking operations. A telegraph line to England was completed in 1870, symbolizing the ties of that country to the far-off province. During the last part of the century the Persians attempted a program of extensive westernization, complete with a new capital at Teheran. Major attempts were made to establish hospitals and a school system, as well as an army, but all of this would cost money. The British and the Russians made huge loans to the Persians, and in return gained control of substantial portions of the area's economy.

The British, by the end of the century, may have forestalled the Russian advance in other parts of Asia, but Persia remained an area of concern. The royal navy, based at Aden, was charged with keeping communications routes open from India to the Suez and with protecting the entry to the Red Sea. Along the Arabian coast the English gained control, through treaties with a number of friendly, miniscule sheikdoms such as Muscat, Oman, Bahrein, and Kuwait. The maintenance of this sphere of influence was effective in blocking German and French efforts to gain footholds along the Persian Gulf. The former had tried unsuccessfully to build a terminus on the gulf for its projected Berlin-to-Baghdad railroad. In 1903 the British foreign secretary issued what has been termed a British Monroe Doctrine over this area: "I say it without hesitation, we should regard the establishment of a naval base or a fortified port in the Persian Gulf by any other power as a very grave menace to British interests, and we should certainly resist it by all means at our disposal."[6]

Although Britain had discouraged German attempts to build a railroad in Persia, there was still the possibility that the Russian Trans-Caucasian Railway might be extended south through Persia to the warm waters of the Persian Gulf. In this event the tsar's government might not only profit commercially, but might also build a naval base that would be a potential threat to the British sea route to India.

Persia was in no position to resist Russian pressure. Its government was corrupt and inefficient, and Russia took advantage of its weakness. By the beginning of the twentieth century parts of northern Persia were in the control of the Russians. Tsarist forces trained the Persian army, put up telegraph lines, established a postal system, and pursued trade. Some Persian workers crossed into Russia to work in the Caucasus' oil fields. The Russian ministry of finance even set up a bank — "The Discount and Loan Bank of Persia" — with branches in many parts of the nation. This bank loaned the Persian government 60 million rubles, and provided 120 million rubles to Persian merchants to enable them to buy Russian goods.

The British government had no desire to see Russian power along the Persian Gulf. To counter this threat to the British-Indian lifeline, the English went into southeastern Persia and set up the Imperial Bank of Persia. At the same time they gained a profitable tobacco monopoly.

To complicate matters, the proponents of a reformist and patriotic persuasion in Persia initiated a successful revolution. In 1906 a parliament was established and the work of reform of Persia by Persians was carried on with the aid, at the same time, of American advisers. This development, plus the changing diplomatic situation in western Europe occasioned by the increase in tensions with the Germans, brought Russia and Britain together in 1907 to sign an agreement which, on the surface, ended their rivalry in Central Asia.

By the terms of the Anglo-Russian Entente, Russia agreed to deal with the sovereign of Afghanistan only through the British government. For its part, Great Britain agreed to refrain from occupying or annexing Afghanistan so long as it fulfilled its treaty obligations. Persia was split up into three zones: the northern was a Russian sphere of interest, the middle was a neutral zone, and the southern portion was under British control. Persia became an Anglo-Russian holding.

The partnership was, however, only a marriage of convenience brought on by larger pressures in Europe. Russia continued intervening in Persian domestic politics, throwing its support to the shah, who was willing to do its bidding. Though upset by the Russians' activities, the British chose not to alienate them because of more important national interests. Britain had fears closer to home; namely, the Germans and their ambitions. England needed Russia's help, and abided by the compromise arrangement in Persia.

The nineteenth century extension of European state power over the Middle East reflected each great power's views of its own trade and defense needs. But the colonial powers ignored the desires, goals, and legitimate demands of the indigenous population who had not, after all, mastered the techniques of the century of European primacy.

AFRICA TO 1914

Africa north of the Sahara. As we have seen, the Ottoman empire maintained a tenuous hold over the North African states during the nineteenth century. At the beginning of the period, the empire controlled all of the African coast along the Mediterranean, with the exception of Morocco. The disintegration of Turkish power during the century, how-

ever, made the areas either virtually self governing or subject to foreign pressures. By 1914 all of North Africa from Casablanca to Cairo had come under direct European control.

Europe had long been fascinated by Egypt, and Napoleon's invasion of that country had served to heighten interest in both its historic sites and economic potential. As the Ottoman control over Egypt weakened in the first years of the nineteenth century, the dynamic Mehemet Ali came to be the dominant figure in the country. He was able simultaneously to increase his authority in the theoretically Turkish-controlled land and carry out economic and agricultural changes. By the 1830's he had expanded his power, as has already been discussed, to the point where the great powers had to step in to protect the sultan from the Egyptians.

Yet with all of this activity, the life of the Egyptian *fellah* (peasant) remained one of poverty, disease, and ignorance up until the middle of this century. Most Egyptians continued to depend on the narrow green strip along the Nile River for survival, just as they had for thousands of years. Mehemet Ali's economic policies did not bring Egypt prosperity, and in the 1850's the government had to borrow a substantial amount of money from Great Britain. Dependence on foreign finance continued, as the Egyptians attempted to build the railroads, schools, and factories needed to improve their economy. One of the foremost projects undertaken was that of the Suez Canal, built in cooperation with the French from 1859 to 1869. The more the Egyptians built, the more their debts increased.

By 1875 Ismail, the ruler of Egypt, was forced by his financial difficulties to sell his block of 175,000 shares in the Suez Canal. The stock was snapped up by the astute prime minister of Great Britain, Disraeli, and gave the British virtual control of this essential water link between Europe and the East. When Ismail tried to repudiate his debts in 1879, Great Britain and France took over the financial control of Egypt and forced Ismail to abdicate in favor of his son. The Egyptian ruling classes and officer corps did not relish foreign control, and violence broke out in

1881 and 1882. The worst outbreak came at Alexandria where many Europeans lost their lives during rioting. The British moved in, put down the revolt, and took responsibility for the administration of the country.

To reorganize Egyptian finances, eliminate corruption from the administration, and improve the all-important (for the British) cotton industry, Sir Evelyn Baring, later Lord Cromer, was sent to Egypt to oversee the country's affairs from 1883 to 1907. He overhauled the system of government, curbed the use of forced labor, and carried on substantial public works projects. Some authorities have maintained that the best record of British imperialism is to be found in Egypt, as European technology, governmental expertise, and financial practices aided the country's development. Nevertheless, the twentieth century was barely underway before the Egyptians were voicing a growing demand for self-government.

To the west of Egypt, in Tripoli, Tunis, Algeria, and Morocco, the Europeans also made steady inroads during the nineteenth century. These four areas lacked a fertile green belt along a river such as Egypt possessed with the Nile; they also lacked both the economic basis and political leaders to attempt such grandiose projects as those pursued by the Egyptians. By the end of the century the rest of the north coast of Africa came under the control of the Italians and the French.

The political force centered at Tripoli had gained its independence from the Turks in the first part of the eighteenth century. For the next century the area served as a base for Mediterranean pirates, but in 1835 it once again went under Turkish control. In the last part of the nineteenth century the Italians focused their attention on Tripoli, and after gaining the consent of the great powers, they declared war on the Turks. After a more difficult campaign than they had expected, Italy finally forced the Turks to cede the area to them in 1912.

The Ottoman empire extended control over Tunis in 1575, and held it until the French established a protectorate in 1881. As in the case of Tripoli, the power of the indigenous central authority was quite weak, and the coastline harbored pirates and thieves. As in Egypt, the Tunisian government became indebted financially to European lenders even before the French takeover. After 1881 most of the country's wealth went abroad, and the majority of the population remained in a poverty-stricken state.

Algeria's coastline also served as a base for piracy from the sixteenth to the nineteenth century. In the 1820's the French complained forcefully of the piratical activities along the Algerian coast. When in 1827 the Algerian ruler insulted the French consul in public by hitting him on the head with a flyswatter, France was furnished with a pretext for intervention. The French sent a large army to occupy the country in 1830, but seventeen years passed before they succeeded in subduing the fierce Berber tribes. Algeria was then made an integral part of the French state.

From the 1840's to the end of the century, French interests also dominated in Morocco, the first country to experience overseas expansion by Europe. But the area remained contested over by European interests until 1914, and the Moroccan question increased tensions between Germany and France up to the beginning of World War I.

In general, the north African countries west of Egypt lacked the vigorous leadership, strong economies, and unified populations needed to withstand the European advances in the nineteenth century. The geographical obstacles also posed a severe challenge, as a nomadic population had to search continuously for the scarce means of existence.

Sub-Saharan Africa to 1870. As we have seen in Chapter 16, a great and diverse cultural growth took place in sub-Saharan Africa to 1650. The cities of Ghana and Timbuktu featured rich courts, extensive trade, stable governmental units, and, in the latter city, a center for Islamic studies. Major advances had taken place in the areas of law, government, and religion. The basic political unit, however, remained the tribe, of which there were hundreds. Mirroring the rich complexity of sub-Saharan Africa were the more than 400 different languages that developed.

Europe approached Africa slowly during

the first two centuries after 1500. The Portuguese had made the first stop in Africa in the fifteenth century, and they were soon followed by the Spanish, French, English, Danes, Swedes, and Dutch. As we saw in Chapter 27, the latter group established Capetown in 1652 as a supply station for the Dutch fleet. Until the end of the seventeenth century the Europeans kept their distance, staying on the coasts and trading with the major African groups as equals, but no more.

Human beings constituted the main item of exchange. In the mid-fifteenth century the Portuguese took the first group of twelve slaves out of Africa, and by 1501 the slave trade was underway. In the sixteenth century one estimate places the number of slaves landing in the new world at 125,000. The seventeenth century saw the arrival of 1,280,000 slaves, while the eighteenth century witnessed the importation of over 6 million Africans. Perhaps as many as 15 million Africans were forcibly uprooted from their homes.[7]

Throughout western Africa and the Congo, especially during the first phase of European-African relations, various African kings and nobles provided much of the human stock in trade that made slavery such a profitable business. They became increasingly dependent on European trade goods, and their participation in the slave trade is possibly explained by their desire for European luxuries and the fact that they did not understand the inhumane nature of slavery as practiced in the new world.

In political terms the Asante and Benin empires, among others on the west coast of Africa, grew rapidly, partially as a result of the slave trade. The trade increase indirectly led to a weakening of the major kingdoms that were present before the arrival of the Europeans in Angola and East Africa. In demographic terms the loss of slaves was a major tragedy. In economic terms speculators and investors would soon gain substantial control over the African resources. But for the African continent, even greater hardships were soon to come, as the Europeans finally "discovered" the interior of the continent.

Until the nineteenth century this great continent, many times the size of Europe, was virtually unknown to most Europeans. Still less was known about the 150 million people found in the area. But this state of affairs changed rapidly thanks to the intrepid investigations of some European explorers. The most successful representative of this group was David Livingstone, a Scottish missionary who crossed vast barren wastes and jungles from the Cape of Good Hope to Lake Tanganyika. He began his exploratory work in 1853 and "discovered" Victoria Falls and the Zambezi River for the Europeans. After his death in 1873, his work in the interior was carried on by Henry M. Stanley, the British explorer and journalist who had located Livingstone in 1871 and had casually greeted him, "Dr. Livingstone, I presume."

By the end of the century Africa was mapped and charted. The source of the Nile had been located, the flow of the Niger and Congo had been traced, and rich resources of the continent had been identified.

The arrival of the Europeans: 1870-1914. In 1870 only 10 percent of the African continent was directly under European control. The two most important foreign holdings were French-administered Algeria and the Cape Colony, governed by Great Britain. Most of the other European holdings were mere coastal ports. In the last thirty years of the century the European powers turned their full attention to carving up Africa. The diversity of the African peoples, their lack of mastery of the technological, political, and military arts, and their economic weakness condemned them to a state of helplessness in the face of the imperialists' advance.

The widely publicized results of Stanley's explorations galvanized the European nations into action. The first leader to take a firm stand to move into Africa was King Leopold II of Belgium. In 1876 he organized the International Africa Association and brought Stanley into his service. The association, composed of scientists and explorers from all nations, was ostensibly to serve humanitarian purposes, but the crafty king had other motives. As an agent of the association, Stanley went to the Congo where he made treaties with several African chiefs and, by 1882, obtained over 900,000 square miles of territory.

Slaves brought to the new world were obtained in four main ways: domestic slaves who were re-sold; criminals sold as punishment by their rulers; persons obtained from raids upon the various villages; and prisoners of full-scale wars. Studies show that the principal sources of the slave trade were raids and wars, no doubt similar to this raid of slave-traders on an African village.

England's occupation of Egypt and the Belgian acquisition of the Congo moved Bismarck in 1884 to call a conference of major European powers in Berlin to discuss potential problems of unregulated African colonization. This assembly of diplomats paid lip service to humanitarianism by condemning the slave trade, prohibiting the sale of liquor and firearms in certain areas, and expressing concern for proper religious instruction for the Africans. Then the participants turned to matters they considered much more important. They set down the rules of competition by which the great powers were to be guided in their search for colonies. They agreed that the area along the Congo River was to be administered by Leopold of Belgium, but that it was to be a neutral territory with free trade and navigation. No nation was to stake out claims in Africa without first notifying the other powers of its intention. No territory could be claimed unless it was effectively occupied, and all disputes were to be settled by arbitration.

In spite of these encouraging declarations, the competitors ignored the rules when state interests demanded they take such a course. On several occasions, as events transpired, war was barely avoided, and the humanitarian ground rules were rarely adhered to. The methods Europeans used to acquire lands continued in many cases to involve the deception of the Africans. The European colonialists obtained huge land grants by presenting uneducated chiefs with treaties which they could not read and whose contents they were not permitted to comprehend. In return, the natives were rewarded with bottles of gin, red handkerchiefs, and fancy dress costumes. The comparison between the European treaty methods and those of the Americans in the negotiations with the Indians is dishearteningly striking.

The ethical and cultural differences between the Africans and the Europeans were especially vast regarding the subject of land ownership. Since in many cases native custom reserved ownership of land to tribes, allowing individuals only the use of it, the chief granted land to European settlers with no idea that he was disposing of more than its temporary use. When later the settler claimed ownership, the natives were indignant, feeling that the tribe had been robbed of land, contrary to tribal law.

The division of Africa. In addition to the north African nations that were taken over by England, France, and Italy by 1914, the rest of the continent was also divided up by European imperialists. By the end of the period, only Liberia and Ethiopia would remain under self-rule.

Shortly after the Berlin conference, King Leopold organized his African territories into the African Free State, subject to his control alone. He began to exploit the colony's economic resources by granting concessions to private companies, reserving for his own administration an extensive rubber area ten times as large as Belgium. A system of forced labor was introduced, and soon stories of filthy work camps, horrible whippings, and other atrocities leaked out of the "Free State," now undergoing the process of "civilization," as the Belgians referred to it. In the face of a rising tide of international outrage, Leopold was forced to turn the "Free State" over to the Belgian government in 1908. The conditions of the colony, renamed the "Belgian Congo," improved under the direct administration of the government.

In the 1880's Germany acquired three colonies on the west coast of Africa: German Southwest Africa, Togoland, and Cameroons. They made their most important gains, however, on the east coast of the continent. German penetration there was largely the work of one man, Carl Peters, a student of British colonization methods. In 1884 he and three other colonial enthusiasts, disguised as English workingmen, set out on a secret mission to eastern Africa. Peters succeeded in obtaining treaties from local chiefs giving him control of sixty thousand square miles. The next year, Bismarck proclaimed the region to be German East Africa.

The British had been laying claims to the region directly north of Peters' concessions. Contradictory German and British claims were settled amicably in 1886 and 1890. After the agreements, which included the British concession of the strategic Helgoland Island in the North Sea, the British held Uganda, along the shores of Lake Victoria, British East Africa (later known as Kenya), the rich spice island of Zanzibar, and the area of Nyasaland. Germany's claim to its protectorate in East Africa (later called Tanganyika) was recognized by the British.

Meanwhile, by 1884 the British had gained control over a stretch of African coast fronting on the Gulf of Aden. This protectorate

Before the European scramble for Africa began, western nations controlled only 10 percent of the continent. By the early 1900's, however, Great Britain alone commanded over three million square miles of African territory, wielding power over such strategic areas as the Suez and the headwaters of the Nile. Made commander-in-chief of the Egyptian army in 1892, Lord Kitchener here reviews the troops.

(British Somaliland) was of great strategic value since it guarded the lower approach to the Suez Canal. Equally important were the headwaters of the Nile, situated in the area known later as the Anglo-Egyptian Sudan. In 1898 the British gained control of this area. Among the British acquisitions on the west coast of Africa, the most important were the territories around the mouth of the Niger, stretching back toward the Sudan. These British possessions included Gambia, Sierra Leone, the Gold Coast, and Nigeria.

During this same period Great Britain's influence in southern Africa had expanded northward from Cape Colony to German East Africa. The main force behind this drive came from the British capitalist Cecil Rhodes, who dreamed of an uninterrupted corridor of British territory from the Cape of Good Hope to Cairo. In the 1880's Rhodes became the leading figure in the fabulously wealthy De Beers diamond syndicate and the owner of many valuable goldmining properties in the Transvaal. By 1890 his annual income was estimated to be at least 5 million dollars. By unscrupulous methods the empire builder gained extensive settlement and mining rights to the high and fertile plateau through which flowed the great Zambezi River. In 1890 the capital, Salisbury, was founded and the region was named Rhodesia. After that date he had one remaining task—to unite the Boers and Britons in South Africa into a single nation. But, as we have seen in Chapter 27, his methods only widened the breach between the two peoples, and helped bring on the Boer War.

If overpopulation, lack of trade, and widespread poverty constitute the most compelling reasons for gaining colonies, Italy should have obtained the most extensive areas in Africa. But Italy came out of the scramble for colonies with very little territory. The Italians gained a piece of Red Sea coast and a slice of barren and desolate land on the Indian Ocean. But these areas were of little value without the rich plateau of Abyssinia (Ethiopia) in the hinterland. An attempt to take the ancient empire in 1896 ended in the humiliating destruction of a 20,000-man Italian army.

In 1884 France developed an ambitious

Cecil John Rhodes, the British statesman and business magnate for whom the country Rhodesia is named, spent most of his life mining, organizing, and exploiting South Africa. Rhodes left nearly all of his huge fortune to public service, one of the chief benefactions being the Rhodes Scholarship to Oxford University.

colonial program with its acquisition of a large section of equatorial Africa along the right bank of the Congo River. From trading posts along the west coast of the continent, France pushed into the interior and obtained most of the basins of the Senegal and Niger rivers. Expeditions from her north African holdings penetrated the Sahara. Although France did not succeed in getting to the Nile, by 1900 it controlled the largest empire in Africa, one which stretched eastward from the Atlantic to the western Sudan and southward to the Congo River. In addition, the French took the large island of Madagascar in the south Indian Ocean under their control. They completed their colonial gains in 1911—over German protest—by making Morocco a French protectorate.

Colonial profits and losses. The economic wealth of Africa surpassed the expectations of the most avid imperialist. By the first decade of the twentieth century it was the world's greatest producer of gold and diamonds. In addition, rich resources of tin, phosphates, and copper were discovered. Africa also served as a large supplier of rubber, coffee, and cotton. In addition the European imperialists gained the labor capacities of millions of Africans. The amounts of land and people coming under European domination are mind-boggling.

For the Africans coming under European domination, there were severe adjustments to make. The process of acculturation, that is, the social change caused by the interaction of significantly diverse cultures, was profound and widespread in Africa. For the first time many villagers were compelled to pay money taxes to a distant central authority. In most cases the Africans had lived within a small tribal area of law and political affiliation. With the advent of imperial rule, dozens of formerly distinct—and often antagonistic—tribes were gathered together, as in the case of Nigeria, into one colony. In other cases of imperialism, large tribes were split into two or three European colonial segments. Colonies were not, usually, homogeneous nations in the modern sense. This fact later proved to be a serious complication when these colonies became independent nation-states following World War II.

The process of colonization in Africa added up to the massive impact of a dynamic, self-confident, and technologically advanced civilization upon cultures that had been isolated from the mainstream of world affairs, politically and technologically arrested and overawed. Kinship and family ties were weakened when villagers sought wage employment in distant towns and mines. In some areas, as many as 50 percent of the young males sought employment in order to pay the new hut taxes, or else to buy the cheap, enticing European wares.

Undoubtedly, wage remittances from absent husbands did help raise standards of living, but the effect on family ties and tribal loyalties was destructive. The old ways of life were most disrupted in colonies that attracted European settlement, such as Kenya and Southern Rhodesia. In such areas Africans were limited to "native reserves" or to segregated areas in the towns. On occasion large tracts of land were allocated exclusively for European use. It was in these plural societies that racial tensions most rapidly developed.

For some fifty years after the scramble for colonies began, the incidence of social change was uneven. In some remote areas Africans may never have seen a white man, let alone worked for him. But tribal life was gradually transformed by the introduction of new forms of land tenure, enforcement of alien systems of law, and the growth of the money economy. In an attempt to imitate the technologically and militarily superior Europeans, many Africans tried to adopt the ways of their new rulers. As a result, some of them became "detribalized" and often bewildered, as they were alienated from much of their traditional culture but unable to understand fully and be part of the new.

Although the transformation of Africa was desirable—and probably inevitable—at some point, it was unfortunate that this revolutionary change occurred so quickly, and at the hands of intruders whose motives were so mixed. Much too frequently these imperialist intruders denigrated all African culture, dismissing the Africans as barbarous and uncivilized. Perhaps colonialism was a necessary—if abrupt and rude—awakening to the new day of the industrialized world, but there were several benefits. The arrival of the Europeans did introduce more peace between the tribes by imposing more efficient law enforcement methods, and the international slave trade was also stopped. Some of the material and technological advances of Europe were brought in, such as telegraph and telephone communications, railroads, improved harbors, and improved medical standards. The organizational and educational techniques of Europe were also introduced in the form of better administrative systems, widespread schools, and a money economy. All of these things may well have been necessary for Africa to have before the continent could enter the modern age, but the price paid by the Africans was extremely high.

SUMMARY

By 1914 the European states had established their primacy over the Middle East and Africa. There was no doubting the nature and extent of Europe's material and technological dominance over southwest

Asia and Africa. While thousands of Persians crossed into Russia to work in tsarist oil fields, thousands more black Africans worked in the bowels of European-owned mines. Both groups were grudgingly bearing witness to Europe's economic strength. While London-, Berlin-, and Paris-based financiers skimmed the profits off the top of their newly controlled areas, European officials and diplomats dictated policy for most of the region.

Yet even before 1914 the forces that would eventually remove European dominance in the next half century were at work. Those forces gained strength from European ideals. All of the apologists in Europe who spoke of carrying the "white man's burden" or of spreading "civilization" to the "lesser peoples" had a major blind spot in their world view. They confused technological and material strength with cultural strength. There could, of course, be no doubting the European material superiority over the Middle East and Africa. There was no military, economic, or technological arena in which the non-Europeans could claim superiority by 1914. Yet, the identities of the peoples caught under the European dominance did not disappear. Rather, under the influence of the European ideologies and political structures that accompanied the diplomats and industrialists, their identities became more sharply defined.

Nationalism—the very force that was driving Europe toward the brink of the First World War—was emerging in the Middle East and Africa. The Europeans may have had technological superiority, but the First World War would prove that they did not possess cultural superiority. The Turkish officers who had studied in the west to learn how to fight better had picked up the essential spirit of national revival, and they had portrayed it in their Young Turk movement. Their overemphasis on Turkish supremacy had, in turn, helped spark the growing Arabic movements in the Near East. During the twentieth century the various African cultural units would experience a similar reaction, ultimately using the Europeans' own weapons and ideas against them.

The rapid expansion of European primacy over the Middle East and Africa would, then, fail to establish firm roots. Europeanization would be a surface phenomenon, affecting mainly the material aspects of life. Islam would retain its strength and the African peoples would retain the essence of their identities. The contact of both areas with the dominant European state systems was immediately tragic for them, but not fatal. Armed with the technological, intellectual, and political lessons they would learn from the Europeans, the Middle East and Africa could hope, someday, to compete on an equal basis.

SUGGESTIONS FOR READING

R. H. Davison, **Turkey*** (Prentice-Hall) is a brief, well-written general history. See also Bernard Lewis, **The Emergence of Modern Turkey,*** 2nd ed. (Oxford); and F. Ahmad, **The Young Turks** (Oxford, 1970). William Miller, **The Ottoman Empire and Its Successors, 1801-1927** (Octagon) is a standard work. L. Stavrianos, **The Balkans, 1815-1914*** (Holt, Rinehart & Winston) is a brief examination. P. Coles, **The Ottoman Impact on Europe*** (Harcourt Brace Jovanovich, 1968) is a lucid survey.

G. S. Were and D. A. Wilson, **East Africa Through a Thousand Years*** (Africana, 1968) and J. D. Fage, **An Introduction to the History of West Africa*** (Cambridge) are brief, useful studies, as is J. B. Webster and A. A. Boahen, **History of West Africa** (Praeger, 1967). See also R. Hallett, **The Penetration of Africa** (Praeger); R. Slade, **Belgian Congo*** (Oxford), which is a detailed history from 1885 to 1908; Ronald Robinson and J. Gallagher, **Africa and the Victorians** (St. Martin's); and Peter Duignan and L. H.

Gann, eds., **Colonialism in Africa** (Cambridge), which contains perceptive essays on the motivation of imperialism. English historian Reginald Coupland gives a vivid picture of the horrors of the slave trade and of the long campaign against it in **The British Anti-Slavery Movement,** 2nd ed. (Barnes and Noble). The challenge of Britain's imperial mission in Africa is mirrored in the lives of three men: F. Gross, **Rhodes of Africa** (Praeger); Lord Elton, **Gordon of Khartoum** (Knopf); and M. Perham, **Lugard, The Years of Adventure** (Shoe String). See also A. Moorehead, **The White Nile*** (Torchbooks) and **The Blue Nile*** (Dell), fascinating accounts of exploration in central Africa; R. and C. Oliver, eds., **Africa in the Days of Exploration*** (Spectrum); Adu Boahen, **Topics in West African History*** (Humanities); and Basil Davidson, **African Slave Trade: Pre-Colonial History, 1450-1850*** (Little, Brown).

*Indicates a less expensive paperbound edition.

CHAPTER 29

South and East Asia: 1650-1914

European Advance and Asian Adaptation

INTRODUCTION. During the eighteenth and nineteenth centuries India, the nations of Southeast Asia, China, and Japan all reached a fateful turning point in their histories. The religious and cultural fragmentation in the subcontinent made the Mughul rule increasingly weak. The Indochina peninsula and the islands in the Indian and Pacific Oceans had long been subjected to European influences, but not to the extent that they would experience them in the next two centuries. China, with its unbending ethnocentrism and sense of cultural superiority, refused to recognize a changing world. Japan, with its tradition of borrowing from the outside, faced the necessity of making fundamental economic and political adjustments. At various times during the eighteenth and nineteenth centuries these areas would be forced to deal with the challenge of the Europeans' advance. Their condition at the time they faced this turning point in their history, and their various responses in the face of the European challenge, will be the subject of this chapter.

The nations of South and East Asia were

ill-equipped by their economies, social structures, political systems, and traditions to repel the oncoming Europeans and Americans. By the end of the nineteenth century only Japan made the necessary transition in its state structure, and it entered the twentieth century as a modern, industrial power. The question that naturally presents itself is, "why did the Japanese adapt to the western forces, and the Chinese, the Indians, and the other nations of Southeast Asia lag behind?"

All of South and East Asia shared similar problems and challenges. The area contained many regions of densely populated territory, which made large-scale agriculture impossible. The population of the area, on the whole, was concentrated in villages, with the exception of a few large cities. In nineteenth-century India, for example, roughly 80 percent of the people lived in communities of less than 2000 inhabitants. Most of the labor was based on human power. The area was and still is very susceptible to natural disas-ters such as tidal waves, earthquakes, and occasional droughts. In the eighteenth and nineteenth centuries the population generally suffered under bad living conditions, high infant mortality rates, endemic diseases, and lack of adequate nutrition—problems which are not yet completely solved.

In contrast to the individual-oriented western tradition, the force of religion and age-old habits in South and East Asia implicitly fostered feelings of acceptance and passivity in most of that area's population. The family—not the individual—was the most important element in society. This is just one example of a vivid difference in values that helped give rise to the mistrust and the hostility often shown toward the Europeans, who were seen in China and Japan as little more than smelly barbarians. Europe and Asia underwent several severe cultural conflicts—with often tragic results—by the end of the nineteenth century, as the Far East had to adjust to the radically new set of ground rules established by the Europeans.[1]

INDIA TO 1914

The subcontinent under the Mughul. The seventeenth century witnessed the extension of Mughul power to its greatest extent and the arrival of Europeans to establish trading posts. The reign of Shah Jahan (1628-1658) marked the height of the dynasty's power. The riches that were present in India during his tenure were reported back to Europe by missionaries, ambassadors, and businessmen. He passed on a powerful realm to his son Aurangzeb (1658-1707). This shah was a ruthless and fanatical man who intended to rid India not only of all vice, but also of all art and all views alien to the Islamic faith. He fought until his death at the age of 91 to impose order on his racially and religiously diverse subjects. He terrorized millions of Hindus with his fanaticism. In 1669 he prohibited the practice of the Hindu faith, an act that produced uprisings throughout the empire. But he also gained some successes, and by 1690 Mughul holdings took in the whole of the Indian peninsula.

This period of dominance, however, was followed by one of decline, as the empire began seething with corruption, oppression, and revolt. Fifty years after Aurangzeb's death the Mughul political power crumbled. The shahs who succeeded him were nicknamed the "Jolly" and the "Heedless," and the foreign invaders and merchants were not slow to take advantage of the region's political weaknesses. The prosperity that had been present during the earlier parts of the Mughul period had attracted European attention, and from 1650 on the traders seeking tea and spices came in ever greater numbers. The British prospered, as they became the favored merchants under the Mughuls. As political disorder increased, the trading centers were fortified so that the foreigners could protect themselves.

For the indigenous population, the conditions during this time may be summed up in one word—misery. Marauding armies, nobles bent on gaining power, and officials who oppressed the people brought anarchic conditions to India. The situation worsened in 1739 when Persian invaders sacked Delhi. Eighteen years later raiders from Afghanistan also attacked the capital. Even though the Mughuls would retain their imperial title until 1858, their dynasty would be a mere shadow of its former grandeur and strength.

After the first invasion of Delhi the British and French entered Indian politics more seriously. Disaster for the Mughuls became opportunity for the Europeans who, equipped with stronger weapons and better techniques, gained the ascendancy on the subcontinent.[2] For more than 100 years the two European powers had fought one another for supremacy through the agencies of their trading companies, and by the middle of the eighteenth century a great duel for empire took place. During the Seven Years' War (1756-1763) Robert Clive, the British leader in India, defeated the ruler of Bengal at the decisive battle of Plassey (1757). This victory ushered in the beginning of a new period in Indian history—that of British rule. The Brit-

After Robert Clive, as the servant of the British East India Company, had defeated the ruler of Bengal, thus becoming the real power in this province, he decided to continue the fiction of Indian authority. In this contemporary print Clive receives "Dewanee," the right to collect taxes, from the Mughul emperor.

ish defeated the French in 1760, a victory made possible by England's naval supremacy. The French could not adequately supply their forces in the field, and their influence in the subcontinent was virtually eliminated.

The traders soon became rulers. The most important problem facing the East India Company (see p. 396) was its relationship with the Indian people. As the Mughuls more and more became puppet rulers, anarchy spread. Finally in 1818 the company accepted the role of policeman on the subcontinent, and became India's master. Some local rulers were forced to accept the company's overlordship, while others were deprived of their territories. The area became divided into British India, administered directly by the English, and Indian India, where native dynasties ruled under British supervision. The British parliament, disturbed by the idea that a great business concern interested primarily in profits was controlling the destinies of millions of people, passed acts in 1773 and 1784 which gave it the power to control company policies and to appoint the highest company official to India, the governor-general. This system of dual control lasted until 1858.

The British introduced several important reforms in India. The practice of *suttee*, in which widows burned themselves on the funeral pyres of their deceased husbands, was prohibited. The custom in some areas of killing girl babies was opposed. The notorious system of banditry and murder called *thuggee* (hence our word *thug*) was broken up by the British secret police. In addition a comprehensive educational system was established.

Rebellion and reform. In the spring of 1857 a serious rebellion interrupted the progress of reform. This uprising was initiated by Indian troops, called *sepoys*, who formed the bulk of the company's armed forces. The sepoys complained that a new cartridge issued to them was smeared with the fat of cows and pigs. This infuriated the Hindus, who regarded the cow as sacred, and horrified the Moslems, who considered the pig unclean. Fortunately for the British, many areas in India remained loyal or at least calm. But the revolt in the affected areas was crushed only after fierce fighting and the loss of many lives.

One important consequence of the Indian mutiny was the final collapse of the Mughul dynasty. The mutineers proclaimed the last of the Mughul emperors permitted to maintain a court at Delhi as their leader. After order was restored, the British exiled him to Burma. The uprisings also ended the system of dual control under which the British government and the East India Company shared authority. The government relieved the company of its political responsibilities, and in 1858, after 258 years of existence, the East India Company ended its rule.

Under the new system the governor-general gained additional duties and a new title—viceroy. He was responsible to the cabinet officer of secretary of state for India. In the subcontinent the English maintained direct control of most of the high positions in the capital, while Indians were trained to carry out the governmental responsibilities in the provincial and subordinate systems. The

courts and law codes were reformed and the army and public services were reorganized. English became the administrative language of the country. On rare occasions, the native civil officials could rise to higher positions in the bureaucracy, but overall India was governed by and for the British. By 1900 there was still 90 percent illiteracy for the men and 99 percent for the women. Access to primary and secondary schools was simply not there for the vast majority of the people. The rural population carried most of the tax load through their payments on beverages and salt.

The subcontinent's infinite diversity of contrasting religions, languages, castes, and principalities (over 700 separate political units) made a policy of divide and rule both feasible and convenient. The contrasts between the European and the Asiatic ways of life in the cities of Bombay, Delhi, and Calcutta was as great as the difference between night and day.

India provided rich resources and vast markets for the British economy. In return the British introduced improved health standards, better water systems, and political stability to the area. The country was brought together by the English language and the English railroads more than it had ever been before. The British justified their economic dominance over the subcontinent by pointing out that they were helping to improve the lives of nearly one fifth of the human race.

But such self-serving rationales did not suffice to stop the rapidly growing Indian nationalist movement. In 1885, with the aid of several Englishmen who had interested themselves in Indian political ambitions, the Indian National Congress was formed. The British educational system, though it touched only a minority of the people, served as one of the most potent forces behind the new movement. As Indians became acquainted with the story of the rise of self-government in England, their desire for political freedom in their own land grew. Unable to rise past a certain level in the government, and disdainful of manual labor, thousands of newly educated but unemployed Indian youths turned in anger against

BRITISH INDIA 1914

British Territory
Dependent States

RUSSIA

CHINA

Kabul
AFGHANISTAN
KASHMIR
PUNJAB
BALUCHISTAN
Lahore
Indus
TIBET
Delhi
Lhasa
Ganges R.
RAJPUTANA
NEPAL
Lucknow
BHUTAN
Benares
ASSAM
Ahmadabad
BENGAL
Dacca
Calcutta
BURMA
Nagpur
ORISSA
Bombay
Cuttack
HYDERABAD
Rangoon
Hyderabad
ARABIAN
SEA
GOA (Port.)
MADRAS
BAY
MYSORE
OF
Bangalore
Madras
BENGAL
Pondichéry (Fr.)
CEYLON
Colombo

INDIAN OCEAN

the government. Confronted by the spread of violence, the British carried through a major shift in policy between the years 1907 and 1909. The various provincial legislatures in India were granted elected Indian majorities, and an Indian was seated in the executive council of the governor-general. The legislature of the central government, however, remained under British control. Moderate nationalists were satisfied for the time being, but their more radical comrades were not appeased. The twentieth century would see the spirit of nationalism become ever more insistent.

SOUTHEAST ASIA TO 1914

European imperialism. The peoples of Southeast Asia—that complex area at the southern tip of the Asian mainland, wedged between India and China and including the multitude of islands in the Indian and Pacific Oceans—had begun to come under European colonial rule in the sixteenth century. Throughout the area western rule made a substantial economic and political impact. A plantation economy was established by foreign investors to develop the coffee, tea, pepper, and other tropical products demanded by the world market. Important mineral deposits were discovered and exploited. The Europeans attempted to introduce law and order, for the purpose of limiting the chronic civil war and banditry that plagued the area. As was the case in India, the impact of European ways of life, especially western education, created a new generation of nationalists. In the Dutch East Indies, French Indochina, and the Philippines young intellectuals aspired to complete independence for themselves and their countries.

In the eighteenth and nineteenth centuries Great Britain came to control Ceylon, Malaya, and Burma. The first colony, taken from the Dutch in 1796, became one of the most valu-

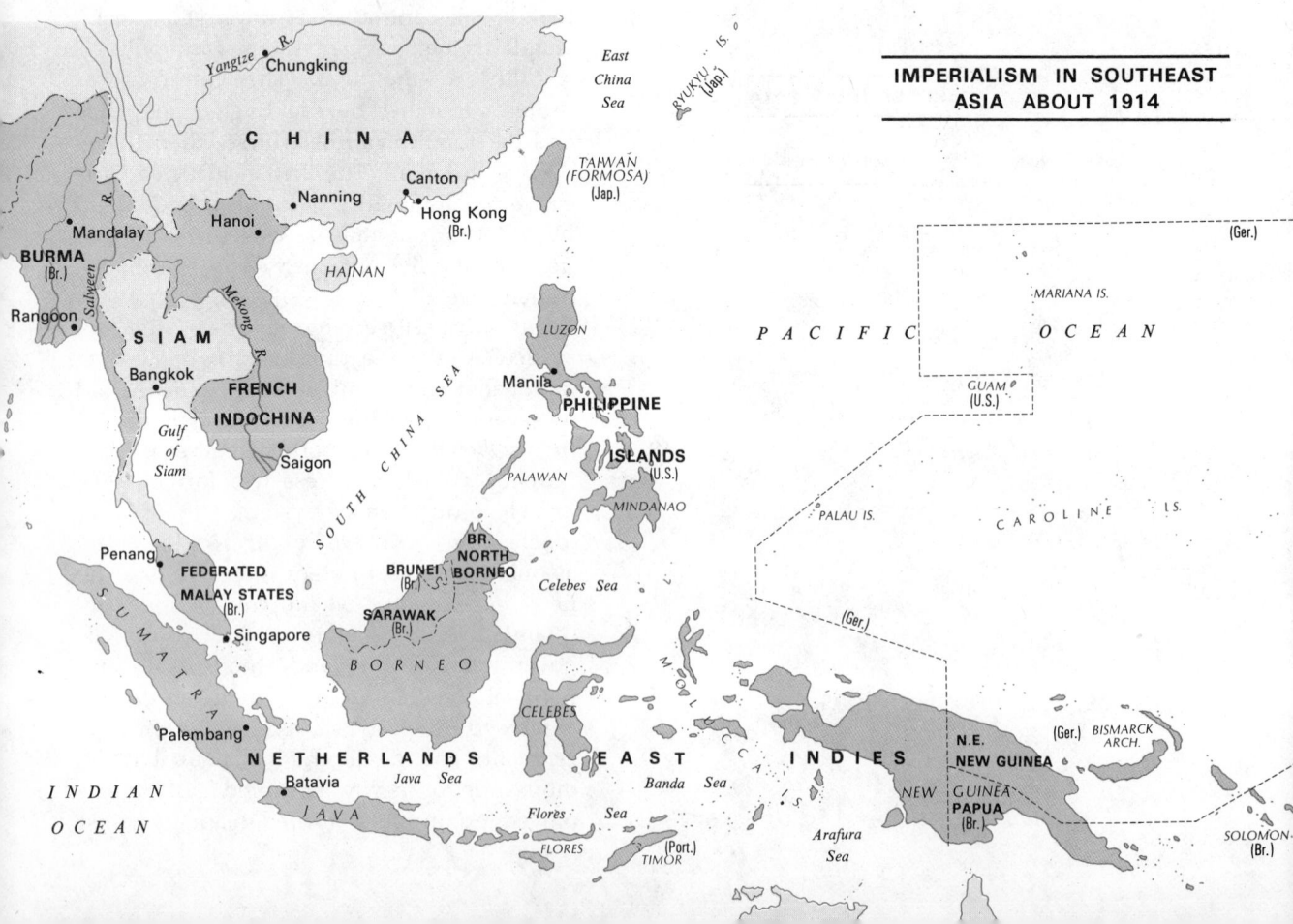

IMPERIALISM IN SOUTHEAST ASIA ABOUT 1914

able British holdings, producing such prized commodities as tea, rubber, lead, and sapphires. The Malayan peninsula, with the important island of Singapore, provided a vantage point from which Britain could dominate the seas surrounding southern Asia and export valuable supplies of tin and rubber. The British conquered Burma in three wars between 1823 and 1885 and annexed it to India.

France returned to the Southeast Asian area to pursue its interests in the nineteenth century. French commercial and religious interests were established in Indochina as early as the seventeenth century, but no concerted effort at stabilizing the French position was possible at that time in the face of British strength in the Indian Ocean. Not until the mid-nineteenth century did France increase its interest in Indochina. Anti-Christian persecutions in the area in 1856 and the fear that Catholicism would be eliminated if France did not go to its aid moved the French to join the British against China and Vietnam. By 1860 French forces occupied Saigon. From there, France's influence and power expanded through treaties, exploration, and outright annexation. They took Hanoi in 1882, governed Cochin China as a direct colony, and held Annam (central Vietnam), Tonkin, and Cambodia as protectorates in one degree or another. Laos too was soon brought under French "protection." By the beginning of the twentieth century France had created an empire in Indochina nearly 50 percent larger than the mother country. Only Siam (Thailand) managed to hold off the French advance and retain its independence.

Late in the sixteenth century the Dutch had taken most of the East Indies from the Portuguese, and in 1602 the Dutch East India Company was organized to exploit the resources of the Spice Islands. By 1798 the company's holdings were transferred to the Dutch crown. For some time the spice trade had been declining, and early in the nineteenth century the Dutch set about raising new products. In the 1830's the so-called "culture system" was introduced, under which one fifth of all native land was set aside to raise crops for the government. One fifth of all the natives' time was also required to till these lands, but the production of sugar, tobacco, coffee, tea, and other products increased tremendously. In the long run the culture system gave the islands a prosperous system of raising crops, but because it was based on forced labor it often prevented the natives from having enough land for their own use. Conditions for the natives improved in 1900 when the Dutch abandoned the system. Less favorable for the indigenous population was the Dutch neglect of higher education and their failure to prepare their wards for eventual self-government.

American imperialism. While the Europeans were pursuing their economic and political interests in the Far East, a new imperialist power was emerging in the Pacific—the United States. In 1867 the Americans occupied the Midway Islands and purchased Alaska from the Russians. The next step of the American advance was in the Hawaiian Islands. During the nineteenth century Americans and Europeans had developed large sugar plantations on these islands. By the end of the century the United States still continued to pour capital into them, and by 1881 the American secretary of state referred to the islands as being part of the "American system." To insure United States control, a revolt in 1893—engineered with the assistance of the U.S. Marines—deposed the Hawaiian queen and set up a republic. Five years later the islands were annexed by a joint declaration of both houses of Congress.

As we saw in Chapter 27, the United States' successful war against Spain in 1898 touched both Cuba and the Philippines. Admiral Dewey destroyed the Spanish fleet at Manila in May of that year and American soldiers set foot in the Philippines. Here, as in Cuba, resistance crumbled quickly, and in the treaty of December 1898 Spain ceded the Philippines, Guam, and Puerto Rico to the United States. One year later the Americans occupied the small Pacific outpost of Wake Island.

Some of the liberal Filipino patriots who had rebelled against the Spanish in 1896 had assisted the Americans against the Spanish, but they had no wish to exchange one master for another. When it became evident that

After "liberating" the Philippines from Spanish rule in 1898, a direct result of the Spanish-American War, the United States failed to grant the independence expected by the islanders. Hostilities broke out in 1899 between Filipino patriots and American occupation forces (captured insurrectionists above), an ironic replay of the fighting between native resisters and Spain three years earlier. Many Americans, disillusioned by imperialism, were ready to lay down the "white man's burden."

they would not quickly gain self-rule, fighting broke out. The hostilities, which began in 1899, lasted for three years. The ironic spectacle of American forces being used in a second conquest of the Philippines brought about a strong revulsion against imperialism in many quarters of the United States. A New York newspaper plaintively addressed Kipling, the spokesman of imperialism, in this way:

> We've taken up the white man's burden
> Of ebony and brown:
> Now will you kindly tell us, Rudyard,
> How we may put it down?[3]

American colonial administration in the Philippines proved to be liberal and well-intentioned for the most part. In 1913 the legislature became dominantly native, although final authority in the most important matters was still reserved for the United States Congress. The Philippine tariff was shaped to favor American trade, and large amounts of capital from the United States were invested in the islands. Increased educational facilities produced Filipinos among whom the

desire for independence grew increasingly strong. In their eyes, American government in the Philippines, no matter how efficient or humanitarian, was no substitute for self-government.

There could be no doubt that by 1900 the United States sat astride the Pacific basin as did no other power. The consequences of this Pacific imperial posture were to become a major and costly constituent of American life in the twentieth century. A massive conflict with Japan, another in Korea, and a tragic war in Vietnam lay in the future. Whether such involvement was essential for American basic interests was to become a crucial and painful question in the second half of the twentieth century.

CHINA TO 1914

China under the Manchus. In the middle of the eighteenth century China had a population of 300 million and comprised an area of more than 4 million square miles. The ruling dynasty was the Ch'ing, established by the Manchus from Manchuria, who in 1644 had superseded the Ming. These descendants of the Tatars appreciated Chinese civilization and adopted a conciliatory attitude toward their subjects. They refused, however, to allow intermarriage with the Chinese, for they realized that only their blood difference kept them from being assimilated and conquered. By and large, however, the Manchus gradually became Chinese in their attitudes and habits.

The Manchu emperors were remarkable conquerors. The reign of Ch'ien-lung (1736-1795) was a period of great expansion. At that time the Manchu government attained overlordship in eastern Turkestan, Burma, and Tibet. By the end of the eighteenth century Manchu power extended even into Nepal, and the territory under Ch'ing control was as extensive as under any previous dynasty.

Jesuit missionaries were active in China during the seventeenth century, occupying high positions in Ming and Ch'ing courts. They made important contributions to Chinese scientific information and technology and helped the government survey its territories. Until the last half of the eighteenth century the Jesuits were an important factor in Ch'ing dynamism. At the same time the Jesuits communicated back to Europe several important elements of Chinese culture. The concepts they introduced played an important role in the intellectual and artistic climate of the European Enlightenment, and the influence of the Chinese civil service system also affected western views of the way government should function.

In spite of these evidences of dynamism, however, uncritical acceptance of and reverence for traditional thought (particularly Confucianism) tended to make Chinese culture excessively backward-looking and conservative. The civil service received scholarly training not in administrative science but in the classics. Thus the amazing continuity which Chinese civilization has exhibited for

In 1689 China and Russia concluded a treaty—the first treaty between China and any western power—providing for frontier control and triennial visits of Russian trade caravans to Peking. In this contemporary print the Russian caravan passes through a gate in China's Great Wall. In the valley beyond the gate the caravan of horses and camels laden with trade items passes the walled city of Xogon Koton.

thousands of years was gained at the heavy price of falling seriously behind the technologically advanced Europeans in the nineteenth century. In addition, the prevailing attitude of superiority to the cultures of all other peoples was an unwholesome one for China, leading to what has been called "progressive sterility."[4] Evidence of the problems China faced could be found in the eighteenth century revolts in Formosa, Kansu, Hunan, Kueichou, and Shantung. All of them were suppressed, but clearly something was amiss.

To be sure, in her dealings with foreigners to the first part of the nineteenth century, China continued to act in the same imperious way. Merchants from western Europe came to China in increasing numbers, pursuing their trade in the face of great difficulties. Trade restrictions confined the foreign merchants to Canton and the Portuguese colony of Macao. In Canton the Chinese controlled both trade and taxes. In spite of their active dislike of these obstacles, the foreigners made enough money to compensate for their being treated as inferiors by the Chinese government.

China knew that the foreigners needed Asian products more than they themselves required European goods. In addition, the Manchus would neither recognize nor receive diplomatic representatives of foreign powers. In 1793 the imperial court responded to the British request for a permanent trade representative in Peking in this manner:

. . . to send one of your nationals to stay at the Celestial Court to take care of your country's trade with China, . . . is not in harmony with the state system of our dynasty and will definitely not be permitted . . . there is nothing we lack, as your principal envoy and others have themselves observed. We have never set much store on strange or ingenious objects, nor do we need any more of your country's manufactures.[5]

Europe's response. The foreigners were irritated by the high customs duties the Chinese forced them to pay and by the attempts of Chinese authorities to curb the growing import trade in opium. In 1800 its importation was forbidden by the imperial government. Despite this, the opium trade continued to flourish. Privately owned vessels of many countries, including the United States, made huge profits from the growing number of Chinese addicts. The government in Peking noted that the foreigners seemed intent on dragging the Chinese down through the encouragement of opium addiction.

Early in the nineteenth century serious internal weaknesses developed in the Manchu empire. The standing army became corrupt and tax farmers fleeced the people. The central bureaucracy declined in efficiency, and the generally weak emperors of the dynasty came to be unable to meet the challenges of the time. Further, the balance of trade turned against the Chinese in the 1830's to the point that the British decided to force the issue of increased trade rights. The point of conflict would be over the opium trade, which by the late 1830's had grown to the point that more than 30,000 chests were brought in annually by the various foreign powers. In the spring of 1839 Chinese authorities at Canton collected and burned the foreign opium in the port city. In response to this act the British occupied positions around the trading city.

In the war that followed, the Chinese could not match the technological and tactical superiority of the British forces. In 1842 China agreed to the provisions of the Treaty of Nanking. Hong Kong was ceded to Great Britain, and other ports, including Canton, were opened to British residence and trade. It would be a mistake to view the conflict between the two countries simply as a matter of drug control. As a Chinese historian has observed: "The war between China and England, caused superficially by the problem of opium prohibition, may actually be viewed as a conflict of Western and Eastern cultures."[6]

The French and the Americans approached the Chinese after the Nanking Treaty's provisions became known, and in 1844 gained the same rights as the British. The advantages granted the three nations by the Chinese set a precedent that would dominate China's relations with the world for the next century. The "most favored nation" treatment came to be extended to the point that China's right to rule in her own territory was limited. This began the period referred to by the Chinese as the time of unequal treaties—a time of unprecedented degradation for China. The humiliation the Central Kingdom suffered is still remembered and strongly affects important aspects of its foreign policy. Incidentally, the opium trade continued to flourish.

China was again defeated in a second "Opium War" in 1856 by England and France. By the terms of the Treaty of Tientsin (1858), the Chinese opened new ports to trading and allowed foreigners with passports to travel in the interior. Christians gained the right to spread the faith and to hold property, thus opening up another means of western penetration. The United States and Russia gained the same privileges in separate treaties.

The Manchu's empire appeared to be well on the way to ultimate physical dismemberment and economic control. Three provisions of these treaties caused long-lasting bitterness among the Chinese: extraterritoriality, customs regulation, and the right to station foreign warships in Chinese waters. Extraterritoriality meant that in a dispute with a Chinese, a westerner had the right to be tried in his own country's consular court. Europeans argued that Chinese concepts of justice were more rigid and harsh than those in the west. But the Chinese viewed extraterritoriality as being not only humiliating to China's sovereignty, but also discriminatory in favor of western nations. The other two provisions greatly weakened China's fiscal and military structure. After 1860, China was a helpless giant.

Chinese responses to the western advance. The Chinese competition with the Europeans had been carried on in military and economic terms. But the basic conflict was to be found in the realm of civilization and values. The Chinese could note the obvious, that the Europeans possessed technological and military superiority. The question they faced was how to adapt the strength of Europe to the core of Chinese civilization. In Chinese terms, this was the *t'i-yung* concept. *T'i* means "substance" and *yung* means "use." Under this concept, China should make use of the western advances so as to become able

to effectively compete with the West. The combination of the two elements presented severe problems of attaining a proper balance. By the twentieth century there was a debate between those who wanted to keep the old culture and those who wanted to westernize the country. In 1860 concerted attempts were made to strengthen the Manchus through an effort known as the *T'ung-chih* Restoration. In response to the western challenges, serious efforts were made to preserve Chinese culture while trying to make use of western technology.

If these attempts at adaptation could have been carried on in a time of peace, perhaps the Chinese could have adjusted. But they did not enjoy the luxury of tranquility. The concessions to the "foreign devils" resulted in a great loss of prestige for the Manchus. Serious internal difficulties further diminished their power, and the Taiping Rebellion of 1850 to 1864 almost overthrew the dynasty. The uprising was one of the most costly movements, in human terms, in modern history. It was felt in seventeen of China's eighteen provinces. Estimates of the number of deaths run from 20 million to 40 million people. The rebellion, even more than the foreign intervention, showed the extent to which China had sunk in its condition. It was based on the widespread discontent with the social and economic conditions of the Manchu rule, combined with the virtual lack of authority coming from Peking.[7]

That the Manchu dynasty managed to survive another half century was largely due to the abilities of a remarkable woman, Tzu Hsi, the dowager empress. From 1861 until her death in 1908 the "Old Buddha," as she was called, was the real power behind the throne. Shrewdly and unscrupulously, Tzu Hsi crushed internal revolts and restored a measure of prestige to China. She pursued reactionary policies, based on her conviction that China's security lay in holding to ancient traditions and customs. She encouraged antiforeign sentiment—an attitude her subjects shared.

A relatively weak central government and general lack of national unity, however, made it impossible for China to resist foreign encroachments. From 1870 to 1895 China

went through a brief period of tranquility, in which the Europeans introduced many aspects of their technological superiority in the forms of factories, railroads, and communications.

Carving up the Central Kingdom. During the first wars against the Europeans, the Chinese began the process of ceding territory and spheres of influence to foreigners. By 1860, as a result of the Treaty of Peking, Russia gained the entire area north of the Amur River, and the strategic city of Vladivostock was founded. In 1885 France had taken Indochina and Britain had seized Burma. In 1887 Macao was ceded to Portugal. China was too weak to resist these encroachments on its borders. But the crowning blow came not from the Western nations, but from Japan—a land which the Chinese had long regarded with amused contempt.

Trouble had brewed for some time between China and Japan, especially over the control of Formosa and Korea. In a dispute over China's claim to control over Korea, war broke out in 1894. The brief Sino-Japanese struggle resulted in a humiliating defeat for China. By the Treaty of Shimonoseki (1895), China was forced to recognize the independence of Korea and hand over the rich Liaotung peninsula and Formosa.

The Chinese defeat was the signal for the renewal of aggressive actions by western powers, who forced Japan to return the strategic Liaotung peninsula to China. Shortly thereafter, the European powers made their demands of the Manchu. Germany demanded a ninety-nine year lease to Kiaochow Bay and was also given exclusive mining and railroad rights throughout Shantung province. Russia obtained a twenty-five year lease to Dairen and Port Arthur and gained the right to build a railroad across Manchuria, thereby achieving complete domination of that vast territory. In 1898 Britain obtained the lease of Weihaiwei, a naval base, and France leased Kwangchowan in southern China.

A halt—or at least a hesitation—in the process of disintegration was brought about by the United States, not from high-minded desires but largely because Washington was alarmed at the prospect of American businessmen being excluded from China because the United States had no sphere of influence. In 1899 secretary of state John Hay asked the major powers to agree to a policy of equal trading privileges. In 1900 several powers did so, and the famous Open Door Policy was born.

The humiliation of the defeat by Japan had incensed the younger Chinese intellectuals who agitated for liberation from foreign dominance. Sympathetic to their cause, the young emperor in 1898 instituted what came to be known as the "hundred days of reform." Unhappily for China, however, the reactionaries at court viewed all innovation with disfavor and formed a powerful faction around the dowager empress. In September 1898 she imprisoned the emperor and took over the government.

After the suppression of the reform movement, a group of secret societies united in an organization known as the "Righteous Harmony Fists," whose members were called "Boxers" by the westerners. At first the Boxers were strongly anti-Manchu, but by 1899 the chief object of their hatred had become the foreign nations who were stripping China of land and power. The Boxers started a campaign to rid China of all "foreign devils." Many Europeans were killed, and the legations at Peking were besieged. In August 1900, an international army forced its way to Peking and released the prisoners. China was forced to apologize for the murder of foreign officials and to pay a large idemnity.

Only a decade after the conclusion of the Boxer rebellion, a revolution broke out all over China, and in 1912 the Republic of China was proclaimed with Sun-yat-sen as president. The revolutionary Chinese leaders knew that there had to be radically new approaches taken in the "Central Kingdom" in order to compete effectively with the West. As Hsüeh Fu-ch'eng wrote in the 1890's:

Western nations rely on intelligence and energy to compete with one another. To come abreast of them, China should plan to promote commerce and open mines; unless we change, the Westerners will be rich and we poor. We should excel in technology and the manufacture of machinery; unless we change, they will be skillful and we clumsy . . . . Unless we change, the Westerners will cooperate with each other and we shall stand isolated; they will be strong and we shall be weak.[8]

THE JAPANESE RESPONSE

Japan under the Tokugawa. India, Southeast Asia, and China were overwhelmed by the European powers by the end of the nineteenth century. Japan, however, responded in a united and alert way, successfully adapting elements of strength from the West to its own structures and ways of life.

At the beginning of the eighteenth century Japan was ruled from Edo (now Tokyo) by the head of the Tokugawa clan, who in 1603 had made himself *shogun.* As a military dictator with a retinue of feudal lords and warriors, the shogun kept the country united and at peace. The Tokugawa strengthened the feudalistic framework of unity and stability that would help give Japan the basis for a successful response to the European challenge. The Japanese structure was crowned by the emperor, in residence at Kyoto, who served as a figurehead with no real function other than as a symbol around which the nation could rally. The Tokugawa ruled the country from Edo, working through their feudal lords, the *daimyos.* These officials governed their regions with the aid of the *samurai,* the soldiers who also acted as administrators and governed and taxed the peasants. Below the peasants on the social scale were the artisans and merchants centered in the cities.

Strict rules and regulations controlled every aspect of social and political life. The government assured the citizens' obedience by enforcing a series of strong penalties on wrongdoers. The combination of force and obedience extended to the point that the daimyos had to spend a certain part of each year at the shogun's capital at Edo, to discourage any feelings of independence. Loyalty to the structure, be it the family or the state, was enforced through the feudal links in the chain of command and justified by neo-Confucian philosophic assumptions. The centrality of Edo was constantly reinforced by the travel between the city and the most distant holding. The stratified society may well have insured the power of the Tokugawa, but over a period of two centuries it was tested by peasant uprisings in the countryside and discontent in the cities. The peasant rebellions could be suppressed by force. But in the cities in the late eighteenth and early nineteenth centuries there was remarkable economic growth, accompanied by rapid urbanization. New social and political forces would pose difficulties for the Tokugawa structure. The spread of education and the increase in wealth helped spur the growth of new urban classes drawn from young, aggressive samurai, merchants, and intellectuals. These social forces could not be dealt with so easily by the Tokugawa governmental structure.

By the nineteenth century the shogunate lost much of its force and authority. Changing conditions in the cities and the flow of western information from the open port of Nagasaki worked to undermine the traditional system.

The western advance. By 1850 foreign traders and missionaries still found their ability to move throughout the country greatly limited. Both European and American merchants and diplomats tried to open relations with Japan during the first part of the nineteenth century. Within the country the question of how and when to open up to the West was finally discussed. Such European innovations as the daguerrotype, vaccinations, new crops, and manufacturing techniques had made their appearance, but the decision on Japanese policy toward the foreigners would not be defined until 1853. On July 7 of that year the United States fleet, under the command of Commodore Matthew Perry, sailed into Edo Bay. Perry, commanding a force of two steam frigates and two sloops of war, had been sent by the American government to convince the Japanese that a treaty opening trade relations between the two countries would be of mutual interest. He had been instructed to be tactful and to use force only if necessary. After delivering a letter from the American president, he remained in port ten days. When he departed, he told the authorities in Edo that he would return in a year for an answer. He actually came back eight months later, in February 1854. The Americans returned with more ships and before the deadline because they feared that the French or the Russians might gain concessions sooner from the Japanese.

The shogun, after a period of intense debate within his country, prudently decided to agree to Perry's requests. The Treaty of Kanagawa, the first formal agreement between Japan and a Western nation, was signed. By its terms shipwrecked sailors were to be well-treated, and two ports were opened for the provisioning of ships and a limited amount of trade. European traders soon obtained similar privileges, plus the right of extraterritoriality.

The entry of the West placed a severe strain on the 250-year-old political structure of the shoguns. On the one hand antiforeign sentiment grew while on the other hand many Japanese recognized that accommodation with the West was bound to come. The western representatives in Japan were caught in the middle, as there were a number of attacks against their presence. Finally, by 1867, after a time of strife and confusion, the country reached the point of revolution. In 1863 and 1864 European and American fleets illustrated their military superiority by bombarding Kagoshima and Shimonoseki, and thereby convinced some of the antiforeign elements of the folly of their position. In 1867 the system of dual government, with the emperor at Kyoto and the shogun at Edo, was given up. The capital was moved from Kyoto to Edo and renamed Tokyo (eastern capital), the largest city in the country.

The Meiji restoration. The new leaders of the country who oversaw the ending of the dual power system were remarkably young and largely of samurai origin. They understood the nature of western power and the threat it posed to their country. They proposed as Japan's best defense the forming of a "rich country and strong military," based on western technology and institutions adapted to their country's needs. The young emperor, whose reign was known as the *Meiji* (enlightened government), ruled from 1868 to 1912. During that time Japan became a dynamic, semimodernized power which the European nations had to recognize as an equal.

Centuries earlier the Japanese had gained a great deal from China. Now they set out to learn the lessons of how to construct an industrialized, bureaucratized state from the West. For the next generation the results of those lessons would be applied in a broad variety of areas. The restoration of the emperor's supreme authority was aided by the voluntary abolition of feudal rights. In 1871 the end of the feudal system was officially announced, although it was far from an actual fact. At the same time the government established a new territorial division and reformed the educational and mail systems. In 1882 a commission went out to study the world's various governmental systems in order to write a new constitution for Japan. The committee members were particularly impressed by Bismarck's German system,

The Japanese Response 665

and the new constitution promulgated in 1889 gave the premier in Japan a position analogous to that held by the chancellor in Germany. Under the new system the cabinet was responsible to the emperor alone. Only the army and the navy could appoint their respective ministers. Since no statesman could form a cabinet without a war minister and the army could overthrow any cabinet by simply withdrawing its minister, final control of policies rested in the hands of the military interests. The constitution provided for a Diet, which wielded influence in financial matters through its power to hold up an unpopular budget in peacetime by refusing to approve it. Under the new system the emperor was considered to be "sacred and inviolable" and possessed sovereign power.

The Japanese also showed skill in exploiting the lessons they learned from the West in other areas. In 1876 national conscription went into effect, and a modern military machine was created. The army officers were trained by the French and the Germans and the naval officers received their instruction from the British. The government initiated the founding of banks, factories, and business concerns. Later, when they became successful, these establishments were turned over to private ownership and management. Japan also changed to the modern calendar, in effect symbolizing her entry into the modern age.

Although the Japanese went to Europe and America to seek the best ways to modernize their country, the major changes they made were accomplished under Japanese leadership. The railways, telegraphs, lighthouses, and dockyards might have been constructed by foreigners and the warships might have been made in England, but the authorities in Tokyo retained their control.

The successful adaptation. The modernization of Japan was one of the amazing phenomena of modern world history. But there were some disturbing features from the western point of view in the way European technology and institutions were adapted by the Japanese for their own purposes. On the surface, the Japanese government was liberal and parliamentary. In reality, however, it was ultraconservative, giving the emperor

The influence of western technology and culture is evident in a Japanese woodcut of Yokohama harbor in the late nineteenth century. A steam locomotive carries passengers along the dock as Yokohama citizens dressed in western attire watch a ship set sail.

and his cabinet dominant power. Though Japan was the first Asian nation to achieve a high degree of literacy, education remained the tool of the government and one of its chief functions was to produce docile servants of the state. The press was subjected to wide control and censorship.

The army was used as a means of instilling conscripts with unquestioning loyalty and obedience to the emperor. In army barracks young soldiers learned that the noblest fate was death on the battlefield. Unlike the Chinese—who revered the scholar most of all—the Japanese admired the soldier; warfare was the supreme vocation. The Japanese were ready to seize the new methods and new ideas of the West to serve their own militant ends. It should not be forgotten, however, that ultimately this was how the West had forced home the notion of its own superiority on Asia.

In adopting many of the aspects of the western state system—with its universal military force, professional bureaucracy, mass literacy, and ideology—some Japanese institutions had to change. The samurai, who had formerly made their living as warriors or serving their feudal lords, had to change their life-styles. Many of them made the transition to the new system effortlessly. The conservative samurai were upset when the government passed a law forbidding the carrying of swords in public and lessening their financial advantages in 1876. Civil war broke out in some districts, and the government's forces put down the recalcitrant samurai and their armies.

The oligarchy that carried out the revolution through which Japan passed was able to keep a fair amount of control. They brought all of the people into the new system in one form or another. They could make such a major revolution with a minimum of strife because "so much that was new could be introduced in the name of so much that was old, in particular, the institution of the emperor." The emperor became the center of the revolution and the basis of the new ideology. "The emperor and the state were considered to be one and the same thing." Through the virtual state religion of Shintoism, the restoration leaders devised the ultimate political and religious ideology. In Shinto the emperor, directly descended from the Sun Goddess, can demand unlimited loyalty to himself. He expresses the gods' will. As a former president of the privy council, Baron Hozumi wrote:

The Emperor holds the sovereign power, not as his own inherent right, but as an inheritance from his Divine Ancestor. The government is, therefore, theocratical. The Emperor rules over his country as the supreme head of the vast family of the Japanese nation. The government is, therefore, patriarchal. The Emperor exercises the sovereign power according to the Constitution, which is based on the most advanced principles of modern constitutionalism. The government is, therefore, constitutional. In other words, the fundamental principle of the Japanese government is theocratic-patriarchal constitutionalism.[9]

At the same time that Japan underwent this fundamental social and political revolution, it also underwent the process of industrialization. In attaining a rapid growth in industrial power, the Japanese encountered the problems of rapid population growth and urbanization faced by the Europeans in their path through the Industrial Revolution. Social and cultural discontent naturally followed from such a rapid transformation. But the ideological and political structure constructed in the Meiji restoration was sufficient to hold the country together while at the same time repelling the Europeans and Americans.

Japan's victory in the war with Russia in 1904-1905 astounded the world. In the eyes of European diplomats, Japanese prestige began to increase soon after the conclusion of the Sino-Japanese War of 1894-1895. In 1902 Japan scored a diplomatic triumph by allying itself with Great Britain, in an alliance viewed by both nations as a deterrent to Russian expansion. When, a year later, the Russians rebuffed the Japanese attempts to negotiate a sphere-of-influence agreement over Korea and Manchuria, the Tokyo government attacked Port Arthur and bottled up Russia's fleet, without a declaration of war. The quick series of Japanese victories that followed forced the Russians to agree to the Treaty of Portsmouth in September 1905. Japan gained half of the island of Sakhalin, the leaseholds on the Liaotung peninsula and Port Arthur, and various Russian railway and mining rights in southern Manchuria. Japan's paramount position in Korea was also conceded, paving the way for its annexation of that nation in 1910. Japan had successfully met the challenge of European primacy, and was now accepted as a first-class power in its own right.

SUMMARY

In our examination of the Indian subcontinent, Southeast Asia, China, and Japan in the eighteenth and nineteenth centuries, we have seen a variety of reactions to the European advance. In India the Mughul dynasty became unable to control the myriad of peoples and religions over which it ruled, and the resulting instability furnished a convenient pretext for the ultimate imposition of British control. Only Siam maintained its independence, because the French and British wanted a buffer state in Southeast Asia. China suffered a distressing decline in the nineteenth century, from its position as the "Central Kingdom" to a helpless giant split into spheres of influence. Only Japan was able to adapt to the point that it could compete with the Europeans on a field of battle.

Japan possessed a number of advantages. Its position as an island protected it from the ravages of overland invaders. Its feudal structure gave it a tradition of unity and control. The Japanese leadership possessed a group of young officials in the 1860's with the ability to take advantage of the opportunities presented them, to move quickly, and to begin to make changes. They knew that to be successful the major reforms would have to be built on the substantial basis of Japanese society and culture. Those elements that would not fit in, such as the carrying of swords by the samurai class, would have to be sacrificed to the new order. The Meiji restoration leaders also commanded the expertise to go abroad and bring back the best possible elements from the industrialized world to apply them to the Japanese reforms. The speed with which they accomplished the transformation of their land, barely forty years after the fall of the shogun, is an impressive indication of the strength of Japanese society.

The other areas lacked the unity (India), geographical protection (China), and the feudal basis that Japan possessed. They also lacked the indefinable quality of luck, such as the politically fortunate deaths of the shogun at Edo and the emperor at Kyoto in 1867 which gave the leaders the opportunity to make their changes.

The Japanese defeat of the Russians in 1905 did not alter any basic power relationships. Yet it was the first step in a new direction. The nineteenth century, by and large, saw the Europeans expand their holdings over the various colonies of exploitation through their technological and economic superiority. The ancient cultures of South and East Asia could not withstand the sheer physical and technical superiority of the West. At the same time, Europe's successes often did not fundamentally change the cultural identities of the indigenous peoples. The Japanese indicated one example the underdeveloped world could follow in its response to western strength. In the twentieth century, the other areas under European domination would find their own paths to reassert their self-rule, after they too had mastered some of the European tools and techniques.

SUGGESTIONS FOR READING

For valuable insight into British rule and its consequences see M. Edwardes, **British India** (Taplinger, 1968); and S. Gopal, **British Policy in India** (Cambridge). See also P. Speare, **Twilight of the Mughuls** (Cambridge), a description of the once mighty Indian dynasty on the eve of its oblivion; S. N. Sen, **Eighteen Fifty-Seven** (India Ministry of Information, Delhi, 1957), is the official history of the Indian Mutiny of 1857; P. Woodruff, **The Men Who Ruled India,*** 2 vols. (Schocken); and Francis G. Hutchins, **The Illusion of Permanence** (Princeton), which deals with the problems of British imperial rule in India.

Li Chien-nung, **The Political History of China** (Van Nostrand) is the best history of Chinese domestic affairs in the nineteenth century. J. Meskill, ed., **The Pattern of Chinese History** (Heath) is a useful collection of articles from various interpretive schools. See also A. Feuerwerker, ed., **Modern China** (Prentice-Hall); and F. Wolfgang, R. A. Wilson, trans., **China and the West** (Harper & Row). P. S. Buck, **Imperial Woman*** (Pocket Books) is a lengthy, colorful, biographical novel of the last empress of China, who rose from concubinage to the throne of the Manchu. Other useful studies of China include Immanuel Hsu, **The Rise of Modern China** (Oxford, 1975); Wolfgang Franke, **China and the West*** (Torchbooks); D. J. Li, **The Ageless Chinese: A History*** (Scribner's, 1972), a survey of the western impact; Franz Michael, **The Taiping Rebellion** (Univ. of Washington, 1972); and P. W. Fay, **The Opium War, 1840-1842** (Univ. of North Carolina, 1975), the full story of the "opening of China." Key documents of the period are contained in Ssu-yu Teng and John K. Fairbank, **China's Response to the West: A Documentary Survey, 1839-1923** (Atheneum, 1966).

W. B. Beasley, **The Modern History of Japan*** (Praeger) is a useful study. O. Statler, **Japanese Inn*** (Pyramid, 1972) gives a dependable overview of Japanese history in the last three centuries. See also Mikiso Hane, **Japan: A Historical Survey*** (Scribner's, 1972), which has good sections on modernization. For an investigation into the early contacts between Europe and Asia see George B. Sansom, **The Western World and Japan** (Knopf). Other useful books are R. P. Dore, **Education in Tokugawa Japan** (Univ. of Cal.); G. B. Sansom, **Japan, A Short Cultural History** (Appleton-Century-Crofts); Robert Bellah, **Tokugawa Religion** (Free Press); T. C. Smith, **The Agrarian Origins of Modern Japan** (Stanford); and George Akika, **Foundations of Constitutional Government in Modern Japan: 1868-1900** (Harvard). G. M. Beckmann, **The Modernization of China and Japan** (Harper & Row) interrelates modernization of these two nations.

Recommended for the coverage of events in Southeast Asia are D. G. E. Hall, **A History of Southeast Asia** (St. Martin's, 1968); and H. J. Benda and J. A. Larkin, **The World of Southeast Asia** (Harper & Row). See also J. Cady, **Southeast Asia** (McGraw-Hill); and D. Dubois, **Social Forces in Southeast Asia** (Harvard).

*Indicates a less expensive paperbound edition.

CHAPTER 30

Hope and Holocaust:
1871-1918

The Waning of European Primacy: World War I

INTRODUCTION. The nineteenth century was Europe's century. Emerging from the drastic upheavals of the French Revolution and Napoleonic Wars, the continent's leaders constructed a political and diplomatic structure that, if it did not bring lasting peace, prevented the widespread conflicts that had given birth to the age. Given the revolutionary changes Europe underwent during this time, this was no small accomplishment.

The French Revolution's themes of liberty, fraternity, and equality bore potent and often conflicting fruit in the various countries of the European community. Each of the movements had universal appeal and particular application. During the first half century the old structure, symbolized by Metternich, maintained sufficient pressure to impose a certain fragile order on the growing tides of romanticism and liberalism. The Metternichean framework broke apart in 1848, as the idealists and the reactionaries clashed and both sides lost.

The new political order that came to dominate after 1850 imposed more effective control within the individual state structures.

Bismarck, for example, effectively took advantage of the resources and opportunities presented to him and engineered the unification of Germany. The British ruling circles throughout the century made timely and profitable concessions to the middle and working classes. France endured Bourbon restoration, revolutions, and another Napoleon before it finally attained the delicate balance of national drives and forces in the Third Republic. Russia and the Hapsburg monarchy made unsuccessful attempts at reforming outmoded political structures, while Italy gained unification and, with it, severe governmental problems.

The complexity and diversity of Europe's peoples and environments made for very individual applications of the themes of liberty, fraternity, and equality. That these principles came to be applied, or reacted against, during a period when the continent underwent unprecedented material and intellectual advances added to the revolutionary potential of the age. The Industrial Revolution coupled with the huge population increases gave the continent the material power and population to span the globe. At the same time the increased competition among the major states gave Europe's diplomats a substantial challenge. For most of the century they dealt very well with it by working out agreements for the carving up of Africa and the division of China into spheres of influence, and by avoiding major continental wars.

In 1900 there were many reasons why Europeans could be optimistic about their future, and, when looking over the previous three generations, maintain a sturdy belief in progress. Scientists were probing the innermost structures of the atom and the human mind. Living conditions had vastly improved. The massive social conflicts foreseen by some political theorists at mid-century were not coming to pass, as both labor and owners showed the ability to compromise. Concerted efforts toward international cooperation and peace seemed to indicate that, perhaps, a new age was at hand.

But to those who cared to see them, there were danger signs. Across the globe philosophers, revolutionaries, and nationalists questioned Europe's claims to world primacy. Within Europe the conflicting energies generated by the various state structures came to be harnessed into two competing alliance systems, with increasingly less ability to adapt to changing conditions or local crises. In the mass democratic politics of the time the forces of nationalism gloried in imperial expansion, took pride in massive armies, and complacently exalted in their own superiority. The unanswered question of the nineteenth century, the Eastern Question, finally found its own solution when in 1914 a nineteen-year-old revolutionary from Bosnia assassinated an Austrian archduke in a town few Europeans had heard of. With that, the camel's back was broken. The alliance systems went into operation, taking the continent into a suicidal conflict that came to be known as the First World War.

BASES FOR EUROPEAN OPTIMISM

Scientific superiority. During the nineteenth century scientists had made major contributions in the struggle against diseases, poverty, and malnutrition. Darwin's theories greatly challenged the accepted biblical view of humanity's origins. In the first part of the twentieth century Max Planck, Albert Einstein, Ivan Pavlov, and Sigmund Freud contributed greatly to our understanding of the universe and of ourselves. The physicists and psychologists pointed out better than most the fact that the old beliefs and foundations on which the European world rested had to be rethought. Science, as always, answered old questions with new questions, and the results were revolutionary and renewing to the old order.

As we saw in Chapter 24, the British physicist Ernest Rutherford advanced the theory in 1911 that each atom has a central particle, or nucleus, which is positively charged. This did away with the belief that the atom was indivisible and solid. On the continent, even greater discoveries were being made.

Max Planck (1858-1947) studied radiant heat, which comes from the sun and is identical in its nature with light. He found that energy emitted from a vibrating electron proceeds not in a steady wave—as traditionally believed—but discontinuously in the form of calculable "energy packages." To such a package, Planck gave the name *quantum*, hence the term *quantum theory*. This jolt to traditional physics was to prove invaluable in the rapidly growing study of atomic physics.

The scientific giant of the modern age, Albert Einstein (1879-1955), supported Planck's findings. In 1905 he contended that light is propagated through space in the form of particles, which he called photons. More-over, the energy contained in any particle of matter, such as the photon, is equal to the mass of that body multiplied by the square of the velocity of light (approximately 186,300 miles per second). The resulting equation— $E = mc^2$ —provided the answer to many mysteries of physics. For example, issues such as how radioactive substances like radium and uranium are able to eject particles at enormous velocities and to go on doing so for millions of years could be examined in a new light. The magnitude of the energy that slumbers in the nuclei of atoms could be revealed. Above all, $E = mc^2$ showed that mass and energy are convertible.

In 1905 Einstein revealed his Special Theory of Relativity, which called for a radically new approach to explain the concepts of time, space, and velocity. For example, he maintained that time and distance are interrelated and that the mass of a body increases with its velocity. Again, as mentioned above, he showed that mass and energy are convertible, i.e., $E = mc^2$.

In 1915 he produced his second installment, or the General Theory, in which he incorporated gravitation into relativity. He showed that gravitation was identical to acceleration, and that light rays would be deflected in passing through a gravitational field—a prediction confirmed by observation of an eclipse in 1919 and by various experiments carried out in the American space programs in the 1960's and 1970's.

The theory of relativity has been subsequently confirmed in other ways as well. The interconversion of mass and energy was dramatically demonstrated in the atomic bomb, which obtains its energy by the annihilation of part of the matter of which it is composed. In the process, the Newtonian views of the universe were upset. The universe, as conceived by Einstein, is not Newton's three-dimensional figure of length, breadth, and thickness, but a four dimensional space-time continuum in which time itself varies with velocity. Such a cosmic model calls for the use of non-Euclidean geometry. Einstein's theory has changed our attitude toward the structure and mechanics of the universe, and its relativistic implications have permeated not only this century's

Considered one of the greatest physicists the world has ever known, Albert Einstein is shown here outside of his laboratory in Berlin in 1920. Einstein wished his theories to have a simplicity and beauty which he thought fitting for an interpretation of the universe, but some of his work was so far advanced that it is either not widely understood or incapable of being tested with present knowledge.

scientific theories but our philosophical, moral, and even esthetic concepts as well.

Planck and Einstein investigated the infinite extent of the external universal, with massive impact on the state of knowledge. At the same time, the equally infinite extent of that universe known as the mind also began to be studied in greater depth than ever before.

The Russian scientist Ivan Pavlov (1849-1936) gave the study of psychology a marked impetus. In 1900 he carried out a series of experiments in which food was given to a dog at the same time that a bell was rung. After a time, the food and bell became inseparably identified by the dog. Henceforth when the bell was rung alone, the dog produced saliva, just as if food had been brought. Pavlov demonstrated the influence of physical stimuli on an involuntary process. The psychology of "conditioned reflexes" achieved a wide popularity, especially in the United States, where it was used to help prove the tenets of a school of behaviorism which considered man more or less a machine responding mechanically to stimuli. Behaviorism stressed experimentation and observational techniques, and did much to create relatively valid intelligence and aptitude tests. It also served to strengthen the materialistic philosophies of the period.

Probably the most famous name associated with psychology is that of the Austrian Sigmund Freud (1856-1939). Placing far greater stress than any predecessor on the element of the unconscious, Freud was the pioneer of psychoanalysis. This form of psychotherapy is based on the theory that mental symptoms express forbidden desires which are not consciously acknowledged. Freud treated emotional disturbances by bringing back deeply repressed "pathogenic" motives and memories to the surface with the help of dream interpretation and free association. He believed that the source of all adult male adjustments and maladjustments is the Oedipus complex, whereby the male child is sexually drawn to the mother, and jealous of the other parent. All in all, in revealing the heretofore unappreciated intricacies of the human mind, Freud had a far-reaching influence on the understanding of human behavior.

The field of psychoanalysis was pioneered and greatly influenced by the work of Sigmund Freud, whose theories have received mixed reactions from professionals and laymen alike, mostly because of his heavy emphasis concerning the supposed effects of repressed sexual energies on human thought and action.

International cooperation and peace. While Europe's scientists continued their profound investigations and maintained the continent's primacy in basic research, progress was being made in the area of international cooperation. As if to herald the coming of a new age, there was an unprecedented amount of international contact to organize the multinational lines of communication. Idealistic statesmen made substantial attempts to defuse wars, and Europeans viewed the efforts to bring order and peace to the world with some optimism. The wars of the nineteenth century were generally local and not too lengthy. The assumption spread that a general continental war would not last long, both because of the new spirit of cooperation and the terrible nature of the new weapons.

The spirit of internationalism and the yearning for peace grew rapidly among the peoples of the world. Indeed, some Social Darwinists believed that humanity might be evolving from the stage of fighting wars. The growth of world trade augmented by the new communication and transportation networks created for the first time a true world community.

Internationalism came to be expressed in a number of different ways. Large numbers of world conferences met to discuss international cooperation. In 1865 a meeting was held in Paris to discuss the coordination of telegraph lines and the problems of a unified rate structure. The International Telegraph Union, made up of twenty nations, was formed. To aid in the handling of mail the world over, the Universal Postal Union was set up in 1875. As a protection for authors' rights, an agreement was drawn up in 1886 by an international copyright union. As we have seen (Chapter 23), in 1896 the Baron de Coubertin, as a part of the growing internationalism, revived the ancient Greek Olympic games. Held every four years, the games attracted participants from nearly every nation.

In addition to the attempts at international cooperation, the organized world peace movement gained a foothold and increased influence during the nineteenth century. Motivated by Christian principles, the British Society for the Promotion of Permanent and Universal Peace was formed in 1816. Thirty years later workers for peace began the League for Universal Brotherhood in the United States. Although the first phase of the pacifist movement was, for the most part, religiously based, a new, more practical variety appeared in the late 1860's.

This improved approach to peace emphasized such practical matters as the improvements in international law, the rules of warfare, and the creation of agencies for arbitrating disputes. The first Pan-American Conference assembled in 1889 at Washington D. C. The eighteen countries present discussed the problems of peace as well as those of economy. Although accused by some as a tool of American interests, the conference nonetheless instituted a system of organized communications in the hemisphere.

Perhaps more significant was the opening of the Hague Conference in 1899. The Russian foreign minister invited the great powers to attend a conference at this Dutch city to discuss arms reductions. Although no progress was made on disarmament, the conference did adopt a number of points in international law on rules of war relating to the treatment of prisoners, outlawing the use of poisonous gas, and defining the conditions of a state of belligerency. An international court of arbitration, the Hague Tribunal, was established. A list of jurists from which nations could select judges was drawn up. Recourse to the court was voluntary, as was acceptance of its decisions. Yet arbitration between nations appeared to be on the increase. In the ten years after 1903 various powers signed 162 arbitration treaties, pledging the signatories to arbitrate international disagreements such as conflicts over fishing rights.

The contributions of notable individuals were also important in the world peace movement. Alfred Nobel, the Swedish manufacturer of dynamite, established the Nobel Peace Prize two weeks before his death in November 1896. The first prizes were awarded in 1901. Another philanthropist, Andrew Carnegie, founded the Carnegie Endowment for International Peace and built a peace pal-

Alfred Nobel contributed greatly to the age of cooperative internationalism with his philanthropy and pacifism. The Nobel Prizes remain a lasting memorial to his life and works.

ace at the Hague to be used for international conferences. Ironically, the building was finished just before the outbreak of the First World War.

Social compromises. While the advances in science and in international cooperation gave firm basis for optimism at the end of the nineteenth century, compromises between labor and owners also gave cause for hope. From the standpoint of conditions in 1848, it looked as though Marx's predictions in the *Communist Manifesto* — the inevitability of revolution and the destruction of capitalism and the bourgeoisie — would come true. In reality, the capitalist system proved to have much more strength and flexibility than had been anticipated, and the class revolution did not take place in the industrialized countries. So successful was the Industrial Revolution in improving conditions, contrary to Marx's perspective, that a Communist revolution has never occurred in an industrialized country.

Three basic improvements were made throughout Europe in the period before the First World War that led to this evolutionary change in conditions: the granting of such basic political rights as universal suffrage, civil liberties, and free expression of opinion; a more equal distribution of wealth; and the spread of education. The more effective state structures, thereby, found increased strength in the mass democracies by the end of the century.

The glaring contrast of complete opulence and utter poverty began to lessen, though by no means did the gulf disappear. The poor got less poor, while the rich got richer. In the advanced countries of western Europe there was a more equal sharing of the national wealth. The growth of labor unions gave workers more bargaining power with their employers, and they used this power to gain better wages. It has been estimated that the "real wages" of workers (the amount of goods that their wages could actually buy) increased 50 percent in industrial nations between 1870 and 1900.

Not only did real wages improve, but the states increasingly guaranteed the popular standard of living as western Europe moved toward the modern welfare-state concept.

Governments began to make it their business to provide such benefits as unemployment insurance, old-age pensions, and accident compensation. Because this social legislation was paid for out of tax revenues, England introduced a graduated income tax, by which every individual paid a sum relative to his earnings. In the United States, the government entered into the regulation of certain business activities and began the attack on trusts and monopolies.

Business management took on a broader social view, realizing that a contented and healthy work force would be more productive. Further, labor unions began to assert their right to have some say in the operation of industry. By the beginning of the twentieth century labor was more effectively organized than ever before, and in France, Italy, and England they were able to inflict paralyzing strikes on the nation in order to gain the goals of the workers. The increased power of the laboring masses, no doubt, also encouraged business to become more enlightened in its treatment of the workers.

Workers also tried to make business decision making more democratic and products less expensive by establishing cooperatives. Capital was secured by the sale of stock, goods were sold at prevailing prices, and profits were distributed annually to stockholders in proportion to the amount of goods each had purchased. By 1913 at least half of the British population was buying some of its goods from cooperatives.

The final aspect of the improvements leading to lessened social tensions in the second half of the nineteenth century was education. When the common people got the right to vote it was very apparent that they needed at least the rudiments of education to vote intelligently. As a result of the education bill passed in 1870, school attendance in England jumped from 1 to 4 million in ten years. Similar acts were passed in France, Germany, the Low Countries, and Scandinavia. Educational progress lagged in southern and eastern Europe, but in those regions substantial progress was being made by 1914.

Religious and ideological adjustments. The increased social concerns of the late nineteenth century received the official stamp of approval of the Roman Catholic Church. Reversing the position of Pope Pius ix, whose *Syllabus of Errors* (1864) had bluntly stated that it was wrong to believe that "the Roman Pontiff can and should reconcile and align himself with progress, liberalism, and modern civilization," Leo xiii (1878-1903) reconciled the Church with the modern age. He revived the progressive outlook of St. Thomas Aquinas, and in his pronouncement *Rerum novarum* ("Concerning new things") in 1891, began what became known as "Christian Democracy." The pope condemned Marxism and upheld capitalism, but he seriously criticized the evils afflicting the working class. To improve workers' lives, Leo advocated social legislation and the formation of Catholic labor unions and political parties. Soon Catholic parties, using the slogan and often the name of Christian Democracy, began to play a major role in European politics, and they continue to do so today.

The socialist movement also adapted to the changing times. In the early 1870's the growth of socialism was slow, but as the decade progressed the movement gained momentum. The Social Democratic party, organized in Germany, became the strongest of its kind in Europe and a model for similar parties in other nations. In the 1880's Marxist parties also developed in Italy, Austria, Scandinavia, and the Low Countries. In France the socialist movement, discredited by the Paris Commune of 1871, broke into a number of acrimonious factions. In England, the socialists were influenced to a greater degree by the maxims of Christianity than by the dogmas of Marx. British socialists placed their faith in parliamentary reform rather than in any uprising by the proletariat.

The most important British socialist group was the Fabian Society, organized in 1883 and including such brilliant intellectuals as George Bernard Shaw, Sidney and Beatrice Webb, and H. G. Wells. (The Fabian group gained its name from the cautious Roman general, Quintus Fabius Maximus, who wore down Hannibal by being content with small advances.) Chiefly through the efforts of the Fabian Society, the Labour party was formed in 1900 with the support of trade unions and various socialist groups.

A photograph of Beatrice and Sidney Webb, two of the intellectuals who were members of the Fabian Society.

Moderate socialists were not limited solely to England, for the approach of moderation — or revisionism as it came to be called — appeared in different forms on the continent. Encouraged by a general improvement in the life of the common man, the socialists became less revolutionary and more willing to cooperate with governments which were genuinely interested in raising the standards of living for the working people. In the 1890's the movement grew rapidly, and revisionist socialists gained power in a number of different governments. The German workers' representatives in the Reichstag numbered only 2 in 1871, but in the 1912 election the socialists won 110 seats in the lower house. Through a coalition of the various parties, the socialists in France had attained 102 seats in the Chamber of Deputies by 1914. Socialists from many countries joined the Second International after its founding in 1889; by 1914 it boasted a membership of 12 million.

By the turn of the century many of the potential social conflicts were on the way to being defused. The state and capital structures were sufficiently flexible to recognize that it was in their own best interests in a mass state to guarantee the citizens and workers a decent standard of living. This, along with the scientific advances, progress in international cooperation, and more democratic conditions, justified much of the optimism and belief in progress held by Europeans at the beginning of the twentieth century.

DANGER SIGNALS FOR EUROPE

Tremors. As substantial as the bases for European optimism may have been, there were danger signals to be seen by observant critics of the European primacy. In economic terms, the United States was beginning to outstrip the old continent. The blow struck by Japan at Russia in 1904-1905 was an indication that the tide of western domination might be turning, and that the non-Europeans could master the technological skills of the Europeans and apply them to their own culture for their own ends. In South Africa, Mohandas K. Gandhi (1869-1948) began to form his tools of passive resistance that would later in the twentieth century lead to successful political protests in India and the United States. The Chinese revolutionary movement was under way by 1914, laying the foundation for the return of the world's most populous nation to great power status by mid-century. In the streets of Vienna, Adolf Hitler developed his racial theories that would bear tragic results in the 1930's and 1940's. In Mexico, the forces that would carry out a pioneering social revolution gained strength. In Africa, the movements that would culminate in the expulsion of the Europeans gained their roots. In short, all the forces that would come to dominate our century were in their formative stages before 1914.

At the same time there were forces among the labor movement that were not content with the orderly rapprochement that was being worked out between the unions and the owners, and a new form of radicalism began to emerge. The progress of revisionist socialism seemed to be going against the dire prophecies of Marx, but there were radicals who refused to discard the doctrines of revolution, who viewed the growing moderation of the socialists with dismay, and who suspected that their old leaders were becoming the tools of the efficient capitalists. The new radical movement, known as syndicalism (from the French word *syndicat*, meaning "trade union"), appeared in the 1890's in France. Syndicalism's ultimate goal was imprecise, and the movement never possessed effective leadership. Apparently, the syndicalists believed that the bourgeois state could be overthrown by a general strike, and society thereafter would consist of "cells," each representing an industrial union. This underlying hostility was to be a continuous theme, although the syndicalists themselves didn't pose a major threat.

Lenin and the future. Western Europe may have remained relatively strong and secure, but Russia presented another picture entirely. Russia was just going through the throes of the Industrial Revolution at the beginning of the twentieth century, and on a different basis than the western European countries. Russia remained an overwhelmingly agricultural society in which industrialization was paid for by using grain produced by the peasants for export on the depressed world market. The regimes of Alexander III and Nicholas II had done little to aid the transition from an agricultural to an industrial society. The governmental reforms of the 1860's and 1870's were drowned out by the more recent memories of ruthless suppression of the opposition political movements. There were, then, no traditions of gradual reform or compromise such as existed in England. The use of force by the government generated terrorism from its opponents.

At first Marx's impact on Russia was slow in developing. Marx himself was not convinced that Russia would be a favorable laboratory for his theories, and he was surprised when *Das Kapital* was translated into Russian in 1872. He was quite pleased by the broad impact of his theories of class war and revolution in Russia. Not until 1898, however, would there be an attempt to establish a Russian Marxist party.

There was some dispute in Russia as to the way Marx's theories should be implemented in the peculiar environment of the Eurasian empire. The thinker and actor who would eventually devise the victorious method to apply (and often distort) Marx was Vladimir I. Lenin (1870-1924). Born in Ulyanovsk, formerly Simbirsk, a small city along the Volga River, Lenin grew up in the moderate and respectable circumstances provided by his father, a school administrator and teacher. In 1887 his elder brother, Alexander, was arrested in St. Petersburg for plotting against the life of the tsar, and was executed. Shortly thereafter, Lenin began to pursue the writings of Marx and to study the situation in which Russia found itself. He was a brilliant individual, overcoming major obstacles from tsarist officials to pass his law exams from St. Petersburg University without formally attending classes.

After 1893 he continually worked for the revolution and began to compile his body of tactics and strategy that still forms the bulk of twentieth-century revolutionary dogma. In 1895 he was sent to Siberia, exiled for his political activities. He spent the time in conditions that would seem luxurious when compared to the treatment his regime would

Vladimir Ilyich Ulyanov, better known by his pseudonym Nikolai Lenin, was the main force and organizer behind what is now known as the Soviet Union. His speeches and writings are regarded as gospel by his successors and followers, and his remains are still on view in a mausoleum on Red Square in Moscow.

offer its opponents after 1917. He had complete liberty of movement in the district, and was allowed to hunt, fish, swim, study and read, and keep up a large correspondence. His future wife, Nadezhda K. Krupskaya, joined him there, and the two of them were married. Together, they translated Sidney and Beatrice Webb's *The History of Trade Unionism.* What one of Lenin's biographers, Louis Fischer, called "the good life" of exile came to a close in 1900.[1] Lenin and Krupskaya made their way to Switzerland where they helped to found the socialist paper *Iskra* ("*Spark,*" whose motto was "From the spark—the conflagration").

In applying Marx to Russian conditions, Lenin found it necessary to sketch in several blank spots left by the father of modern communism. Lenin's methods would differ from those of other Social Democrats. In 1903 the split came within the Russian Social Democratic party between the Mensheviks, which means "the minority" in Russian, and Lenin's Bolsheviks, which means "the majority." The Mensheviks, who were actually the numerical majority as well as the more orthodox Marxists, believed that capitalism would inevitably break down of its own accord. The Bolsheviks, under Lenin, advocated the formation of a small elite of professional revolutionists, the vanguard of the proletariat. These professional revolutionists, subject to strong party discipline, would lead the proletariat, and in effect speed up the historical process described by Marx. The Bolsheviks, contrary to their name, constituted a rather small minority of the Social Democrats. The split between the two wings of the Marxist movement would be seen most forcefully in 1917 when Lenin would advocate the quick seizure of power, while the Mensheviks would counsel moderation.

For the next seventeen years Lenin developed his own approaches to bring about the revolution, a task in which he enjoyed little success. He advocated a socialism whose weapon was violence and whose tactics allowed little long-range compromise with the bourgeoisie. Lenin did, however, see the advantages of flexibility when a temporary deviation might serve the goals of the working class. He took little for granted, and reasoned that the development by the Russian proletariat of the necessary class unity to destroy the capitalists might have to be helped along. He devised a technique of revolution in which the elite leadership would enforce its dictates on the populace with iron discipline and which would sanction the infiltration of government, police, and army while also participating in peaceful and legal workers' movements. He agreed with Marx's philosophy and overall goals, but he devised his own tactics and politics.

In the process he distorted some of the fundamentals of the Marxist position. Engels and Marx did not want a police state, but rather a workers' republic. Engels wrote in 1891: "If anything stands, it is that our party and the working class can only come to power under the form of a democratic republic. This is the specific form of the dictatorship of the proletariat."[2] By emphasizing the gaining, and later, retention, of power by the elite party, Lenin destroyed much that was humane and optimistic in Marx, and prepared the basis for a modern totalitarian state.

He had relatively little firsthand impact on events in Russia until the late spring of 1917. His ideological and tactical work, however, was of major importance. He could do little until the First World War had forced all political institutions in Russia to grind to a halt. But when the opportunity came, he was ready.

Antagonisms. By the opening of the twentieth century, Europe's greatest dangers came not from the critics abroad or Lenin, but from major forces of antagonism focused and strengthened by the state system. These antagonistic forces served as the underlying, long-range causes of the First World War—militarism, rival alliances, secret diplomacy, economic imperialism, and nationalism.

On the eve of the war Europe consisted of some twenty-five independent political units. The major states recognized no higher authority, and each went its own way. International law was obeyed only if its dictates did not clash with the state's interests. The great powers were ready to take advantage of any neighbor's weakness, and to threaten war if the prize to be taken or the danger to

be avoided was substantial enough. War was an instrument of national policy, an extension of politics, to be used whenever peaceful methods did not work.

When force is the ultimate arbiter in international affairs, military strength becomes extremely important. By the end of the 1870's five of the six major European powers had introduced compulsory military training. Although Britain had not, they were in the process of stepping up their production of ships for their fleet, thus heating up the arms race. By the first decade of the twentieth century, the great powers had nearly 4.5 million men in the military and were spending annually more than $2 billion on arms. The arms race had begun, and the making of weapons became an important part of the various national economies.

Living in this state of international anarchy and distrust among neighbors, most states did not feel strong enough to rely solely on their own military resources for protection. Therefore, nations whose interests ran along parallel lines joined together to muster more fighting power. But this, in turn, provoked nations outside the alliance to form a union capable of matching strength with strength to maintain a balance of power. While the creation of two major rival alliances—the Triple Alliance of Germany, Austria, and Italy and the Triple Entente of England, France, and Russia—was a feature of European diplomacy in the years before 1914, it brought no security to the states involved. In fact, the possibilities of a major war were vastly increased because the alliances made it virtually impossible for a conflict to be localized.

Closely tied with the system of alliance was the practice of secret diplomacy. Some diplomats threatened, intimidated, jockeyed for power, and offered bribes. The activities of spies, the secret reports, and the unscrupulous methods of the European foreign offices poisoned the atmosphere of international politics and increased the tension still further, and also thwarted the attempts of decent and honorable statesmen to maintain tranquility.

Economic competition and tariff rivalries also became a source of tension, and the world's markets came to be viewed as a battlefield of sorts. A new kind of mercantilism in which the state structures acted as aggressive champions for their own businesses came into existence. One of the most significant features of this new system was the economic imperialism that was involved in the struggle to control the colonial world. In some cases, economic competition led to war: Japanese designs on the Asian mainland led to war with China in 1894; Great Britain fought the Boer War in South Africa in 1899-1902; Japan and Russia fought over Manchuria in 1904-1905; and Italy took Tripoli from Turkey in 1912.

Nationalism came to be the greatest force fueling the increase in antagonism on the continent. The spirit of unity and identity that had developed during the period was one of the most potent political tools for Europe's statesmen. By the end of the century nationalism came to take on narrow, blatant, and bellicose qualities as it was used to unite the populations of Europe behind various national leaders. It was one of the major contributing factors to the outbreak of the First World War. Among both subordinate and ruling groups, national loyalty was an intense, explosive emotion. Inflated nationalism became a new religion, an essential adjunct of power politics.

In great powers and small, nationalism was used to mobilize the various nations to action. As it turned out, the greatest danger to peace came in the nationalistic ambitions of the Balkan nations. Proud of their new freedom, they were determined to extend it to their brothers still under the Turks or Austrians. Serbia in particular was ready to liberate the other Slavic groups and unite itself with Slavs in Bosnia, Herzegovina, and Albania.

The Achilles tendon. If Europe could maintain stability and respond to the number of unifying elements that served its self-interest, the danger signals could be dealt with. The potential challenges—such as the non-European critics, revolutionaries such as Lenin, and the various national antagonisms—could be defused. Europe was Christian, in background if not totally in practice.

Europe was capitalist. Europe was white. Europe was generally industrialized. Europeans shared the same basic cultural inheritance. Europe's rulers were related to each other. But for all that, Europe was fragmented by its state system, a structure that emphasized the continent's diversity, and not its unity.

By 1914 the European structure had come to a point of no return. The individualism that had characterized western man for the preceding 500 years, with its ancient roots in Athens and the Judeo-Christian tradition, came to be expressed in the international anarchy of the state system. All of the intellectual challenges of the previous five centuries—the Renaissance that proclaimed that man was the measure of all things, the Reformation that stated the direct link between the believer and God, the Scientific Revolution that asserted man's ability to reason and question for himself, and the Enlightenment that spread the belief in the glories of the individual's reason—went to buttress the assumption of the superiority of the individual to the common will.

During the nineteenth century the European individual gained liberation from the constraints of animal power. As the individual became more powerful and productive, the state—the mediator between individuals in the liberal conception—also grew. More wealth produced per capita came to be fed to the state structure through increased taxes and customs duties. The primacy of the individual came to be translated into the primacy of the individual state, and the living out of values expressed through the state.

The international state system, equipped with all of the tools, communications devices, and economic strength of the Industrial Revolution, came to be a system of international anarchy in which each unit was answerable only unto itself. The individualism that had once formed the essence of western civilization came to be, in its inflated state system form, a grotesque parody, a selfish defense of national ego, and the triggering mechanism that tripped the sequence of events that led to Europe's suicidal plunge into the First World War.

DIPLOMATIC FAILURE

Bismarck's system. From 1870 to 1890 the German chancellor Otto von Bismarck dominated European diplomacy. He set out, after Prussia defeated the French, to build a foreign policy devoted to isolating France diplomatically by depriving it of potential allies. He reasoned that the French would try to take revenge on Germany and regain Alsace and Lorraine, but knew they could do little without aid from the Austrians or the Russians. In 1873 Bismarck made an alliance, known as the Three Emperors' League, with the tsarist empire and the Dual Monarchy.

The conflicts between the Austrians and the Russians in the Balkans soon put a strain on the Three Emperors' League, and at the Congress of Berlin (1878) Bismarck was forced to choose between the claims of Austria-Hungary and Russia in southeast Europe. He chose to support Austria for a number of diplomatic reasons, including fear of alienating Great Britain if he backed the Russians. Further, he felt that he could probably dominate Austria more easily than Russia. This momentous shift paved the way for a new arrangement. A year later Bismarck negotiated the Dual Alliance with the Austrian government, and in 1882 a new partner — Italy — was secured. This brought the Triple Alliance into existence.

The choice of Austria as a close ally in preference to Russia did not mean that Bismarck was reconciled to the loss of the latter's cooperation. In 1881 the Three Emperors' League was renewed, but when rivalries between Austria and Russia in the Balkans made it impossible for these two powers to be in the same group, the alliance once again collapsed in 1887. To fill the gap, Bismarck negotiated a separate alliance with Russia called the Reinsurance Treaty.

Under the shrewd hand of the chancellor, Germany kept diplomatic control over the continent for twenty years. Bismarck knew his goals and understood the states with which he worked. Every effort was made to avoid challenging Britain's interest and to encourage the English policy of "splendid isolation" from the continent's affairs. Bismarck effectively kept France in diplomatic quarantine, isolated from any allies of importance. Germany was not surrounded by enemies, because the chancellor was able to avoid alienating Russia while keeping an alliance with Austria.

In a single year, however, twenty years of work was effectively endangered. The preponderance of power built up by Bismarck and all of the advantages for Germany that went with it were lost by the new German kaiser, William II. In 1890 he dismissed the old chancellor and took German foreign policy into his own hands.

France had been attempting to escape from its impossible diplomatic position for some time. The kaiser gave the French the opportunity they needed by foolishly allowing the Reinsurance Treaty to lapse. He unwittingly encouraged Russia to seek new allies, and the French were not slow to respond. They poured millions of francs into Russian bonds for the capital-starved tsarist economy. In 1894 France received what it had sought for twenty years — a strong military ally. The Triple Alliance was now confronted by the Dual Alliance. Further, Germany now faced potential enemies on her eastern and western boundaries.

England ends its isolation. At the end of the nineteenth century Britain found itself involved in bitter rivalries with Russia — both in the Balkans and the Middle East — and with France in Africa. During the Boer War, all the great powers in Europe were anti-British. Only the dominance of England's fleet effectively discouraged the development of an interventionist movement. More and more, Great Britain became worried by its policy of diplomatic isolation. It was these circumstances which explained British overtures to Germany.

On the surface, nothing seemed more natural than that the two dominant European powers adjust their national interests so that they could avoid conflict. From the 1880's to 1901 several approaches were made from both sides to investigate an "understanding" between the major sea power, England, and the strongest land power, Germany. Tradition and dynastic relations spoke in favor of a closer tie between the two. By 1900, Berlin and London may have competed in economic and imperialistic terms, but they were far from any major strife in either area. Yet the two countries could not come together in an alliance. Even though there were important figures on both sides who could see the advantages of a German-English rapprochement, strong forces worked against this development. The two powerful nations' interests did not coincide to the point that each country could gain equal advantage from an alliance. The kaiser's truculence also offended many British leaders as he sought to expand his country's influence in the Middle East and the Balkans. But the major threat, as seen by England, was the German plan to build a fleet which would be a strong deterrent to Great Britain. Berlin initiated a huge naval program in 1900, providing for the construction of a fleet strong enough to challenge Britain's naval supremacy within twenty years.

The English were not slow to sense that the new German program was aimed directly at them. They were disturbed by the possibility of Germany becoming both a dominant land and sea power. For England, the supremacy of the Royal Navy was a life-or-death matter. Since food and raw materials had to come by sea, it was crucial that the navy be able to protect British shipping. The British became increasingly alarmed by the tremendous economic progress made by the Germans. The kaiser's threatening and irresponsible speeches and unpredictable behavior further increased their uneasiness.

Challenged by Germany, Britain looked elsewhere for allies. In 1904 Britain and France settled their outstanding differences and proclaimed the *Entente Cordiale,* a French term meaning "friendly understanding." The Entente Cordiale, together with England's alliance with Japan in 1902, ended Britain's policy of diplomatic isolation and brought it into the diplomatic combination pitted against Germany's Triple Alliance. In 1907 Britain settled its problems with Russia, thereby establishing the Triple Entente. Great Britain made no definite military commitments in the agreements with France

and Russia. Theoretically, it retained freedom of action, but for all this it was now part of the alliance system.

The Moroccan crises. For a decade before the First World War, Europe experienced a series of crises brought about as the two alliance systems flexed their muscles and probed each other's strength. As each diplomatic crisis arose, Europe came closer to war.

The first serious test occurred in 1905 over Morocco. France sought control of this territory in order to establish a continuous line of dependencies from the Atlantic across the North African coast to Tunisia. Carefully timing their moves, the Germans arranged for the kaiser to visit the Moroccan port of Tangier, where he declared that all powers must respect the independence of the country. The French were forced to give up their immediate plans for taking over Morocco and agree to Germany's suggestion that an international conference be called at Algeciras (1906) to discuss the matter.

At this meeting the Germans hoped for a split between the British and the French; however, this did not occur. On the contrary, all but one of the nations in attendance — even Italy — supported France rather than Germany. Only Austria remained at the kaiser's side. The conference agreed that Morocco should still enjoy its sovereignty, but that France and Spain should be given certain rights to police the area. The events at Algeciras, followed by the British agreement with Russia in 1907, caused great concern in the German government.

In 1911 a second Moroccan crisis heightened the tension. When France sent an army into the disputed territory "to maintain order," Germany countered by dispatching the gunboat *Panther* to the Moroccan port of Agadir. Great Britain came out with a blunt warning that all of its power was at the disposal of France in this affair. A diplomatic bargain was finally struck in which France got a free hand in Morocco and Germany gained a small area in Equatorial Africa.

The Balkan crises. The two rival alliance systems had managed to avoid war over Morocco. Feelings were soothed when the imperial powers compensated each other with pieces of African landscape. But the situation in the Balkans would produce a different result. In that complex peninsula, the forces of local nationalism sparked the military activities of the rival alliances, and these sparks resulted in war.

Austria and Russia had long kept a wary eye on each other's policies in southeastern Europe. During the nineteenth century each country had a very definite interest in the Balkan holdings of the "sick man of Europe." Neither side could afford for the other to gain too great an advantage in the area. Throughout the last part of the nineteenth century the two had occasionally disagreed over issues involving Macedonia, railroads, and boundary revisions. In 1908 a crisis erupted that threatened to draw Europe into war.

The issue that increased hostility was Austria's annexation of Bosnia and Herzegovina in that year. The Dual Monarchy had administered the two areas since 1878, and the annexation in actual terms of influence changed very little. But is was seen as a slap in the face

to the South Slavs, and to their "protector," Russia. The fact that the Russians had initiated the train of events that led to the Austrian annexation through an ill-considered plan made the whole affair doubly frustrating for the Slavs. A tsarist diplomat had initiated discussions whereby the Russians would give approval to the annexation in return for increased Black Sea rights for the Russians. The *quid pro quo* (something for something), questionable though it was, never came off.

Serbia was outraged by the incorporation of more South Slavs into the Hapsburg domain, and she expected her Slavic and Orthodox big brother, Russia, to do something about it. The Russians had come out of their war with Japan (1904-1905) badly bruised, and they were still dealing with the consequences of the 1905 revolution. Aside from making bellicose noises, they could do little of a concrete nature.

Austrian interests in the Balkans were concerned primarily with defense and with

DIPLOMATIC CRISES 1905-1914

keeping Serbia under control. The Dual Monarchy was going through serious domestic strains at home, as the polyglot empire limped along under the terms of the 1867 *Ausgleich.* The lofty Austro-Hungarian pretentions to being a great power badly outdistanced their ability to fulfill the role of greatness.

Germany's motives in the Balkans were largely economic in the long-range perspective, and diplomatic in the short term. The overall German plan envisioned a great continuous economy stretching from the Baltic Sea to the Persian Gulf. In addition, she could not afford to alienate her Austrian ally through lukewarm support.

That this transfer of two strips of territory from an administrative holding to a fully annexed possession could result in a diplomatic crisis is an indication of the lack of maneuverability produced by the alliance systems. Russia misplayed its diplomatic cards in setting off the train of events that produced the crisis, and became stuck in a prestige-damaging dilemma. Serbia perceived a direct threat, for which her protector could not offer any helpful assistance. Austria pursued an old goal and gained success and an inflated notion of her own power. Germany received the pleasant opportunity to exercise its diplomatic muscles by telling the Russians that forceful support of the Serbs would lead to a dangerous encounter between Berlin and St. Petersburg.

After 1908 tensions remained high in the Balkans. The Austrians sought to increase their advantage, knowing they had the support of their German ally. Serbia searched for revenge, while Russia found itself backed into a corner. The Russians would in the future be forced to act strongly and encourage aggressive policies on the part of their Balkan allies or lose forever their position of prestige in the Balkans. The 1908 crisis had changed relatively few of the major features of the competition for influence in the Balkans,

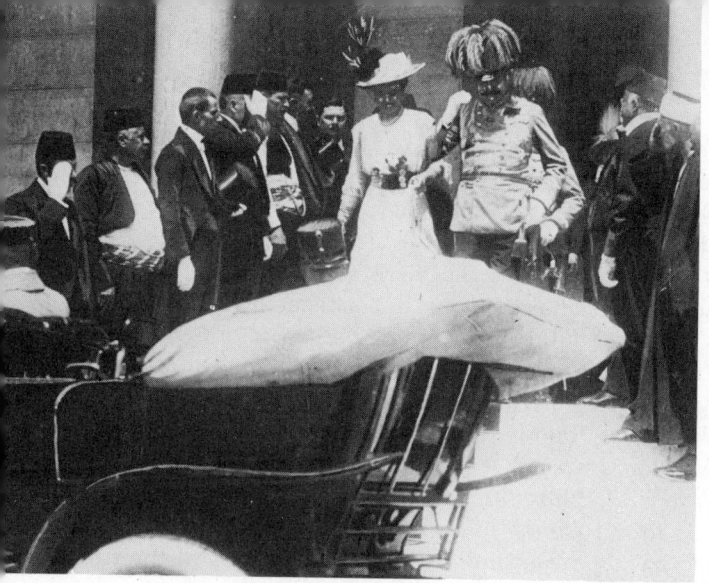

The photograph on the left, taken on June 28, 1914, shows Archduke Francis Ferdinand and his wife as they leave the Senate House in Sarajevo, Bosnia. Five minutes later they were both assassinated, allegedly by Gavrilo Princip, a Serbian terrorist, whose arrest is shown at right. A high-school student at the time of the assassination, Princip died in prison and remains a Serbian hero.

except to limit still further the major powers' options.

In 1912 Serbia and its neighbors, especially Greece and Bulgaria, formed an alliance with the objective of expelling Turkey from Europe. The First Balkan War began later in the year, and was quickly terminated as Turkish resistance crumbled. The victorious nations each had their own particular goals in mind in fighting the Turks. When the great powers stepped in to maintain a balance, and specifically to keep Serbia from gaining a seacoast, problems arose. Denied Albania by Austria and the Italians, the Serbs turned on their former Bulgarian ally—which had made major gains in the first war—and, supported by the Greeks, demanded territory promised to the Bulgarians. Bulgaria attacked its former allies, and Turkey and Rumania in turn entered the war against the Bulgarians, who were no match for their numerous opponents. A peace was signed by which Bulgaria gave its former allies most of the territory taken from Turkey. The Turks retained only a precarious toehold in Europe—the small pocket around Constantinople.

Had the great powers been able to place a fence around the Balkans and allow the squabbling nationalities to fight their mini-wars in isolation, then the Balkan conflicts of 1912 and 1913 would have had little significance. As it was, however, they added to the prevailing state of tension. The two competing alliance systems effectively tied the policies of the great powers to the narrow constraints of the Balkans. In effect, the tail wagged the dog, as the alliances reacted to every flareup in the turbulent peninsula.

By the end of 1913 no permanent solution had been found to the Balkan problem. Austria was more fearful than ever of Serbia's expansionist desires. Serbian ambitions had grown larger, since its territory had doubled as a result of the recent wars. The Serbian prime minister stated that "The first round is won; now we must prepare the second against Austria." As for Russia, its dreams of Balkan grandeur had not been blocked, but only interrupted. The rest of Europe lay divided between the two sides.

Assassination and war. The spark that set off the flames of war was struck on June 28, 1914 with the assassination of the heir to the Austrian throne, Archduke Francis Ferdinand. The archduke and his wife made a visit to the Bosnian town of Sarajevo, and while driving in their huge touring car through the narrow streets of the town, they were shot by a young, nineteen-year-old Bosnian student named Gavrilo Princip. The assassin had been inspired by propaganda advocating the creation of a Greater Serbia, and assisted by Serbian officers serving in a secret organization. The direct complicity of the Serbian government was not proved; even so, it seems likely that the Belgrade authorities were involved, at least indirectly.

A study of the events leading up to the assassination reveals a record of almost criminal neglect on the Austrian side and adolescent inefficiency on the revolutionists' part. Authorities in Vienna had knowledge of the dangers that the archduke might face on his visit to Sarajevo, but they failed to take appropriate actions to protect him. On the bright and warm Sunday of June 28, Francis Ferdinand and his wife were easy targets for the at least seven potential assassins that waited along the sunlit streets. Only two of the revolutionaries carried out their grim job. One of them threw a bomb at the archduke's car, but it rolled under the following vehicle where it exploded and wounded an officer. The procession then continued, but the drivers had been given incorrect information about the route to be followed. After a wrong turn was made, the drivers maneuvered their unwieldy cars to get back on the proper road. The other revolutionary, Gavrilo Princip, approached Francis Ferdinand's car, shot the archduke in the neck and with his second shot, by accident, killed Ferdinand's wife. Any one of a number of security measures would have most likely saved the archduke. But these measures were not taken, and Princip's bullets started the chain of events that plunged Europe into war.

The legal details of the case were lost in Austria's rush to put an end to the problem of Serbia. Count Leopold von Berchtold, the Austrian foreign minister, believed that the assassination in Bosnia justified crushing the anti-Austrian propaganda and terrorism coming from Serbia. The Austrians hesitated to act, however, without gaining assurances from the Germans. The kaiser felt that everything possible must be done to prevent Germany's only reliable ally from being weakened, and so he assured the Austrians of his full support. Berchtold received a blank check from Germany. Vienna wanted a quick, local Austro-Serbian war, and Germany favored quick action, to forestall Russian intervention.

On July 23 the Austro-Hungarian foreign ministry presented an ultimatum to the Serbs. Expecting the list of demands to be turned down, Berchtold demanded unconditional acceptance within forty-eight hours. On July 25 the Austrian government announced that Serbia's reply, which was conciliatory, was not satisfactory. The Vienna authorities immediately mobilized their armed forces. Meanwhile the Germans urged Austria to negotiate with Russia, which was following developments closely. Russia realized that if the Austrians succeeded in humbling the Serbs, Russian prestige in the area would suffer irreparably. The French in the meantime assured the Russians of their full cooperation and urged strong support for Serbia, while the British advised negotiations, but without success.

Europe had reached a point of no return in which the Austrians had committed themselves to the task of removing a serious opponent, and in which the Russians could not permit this to happen. Neither side would back down, and each had allies ready to come to its aid. Fearful that Serbia would escape from his clutches, Berchtold succeeded on July 27—thanks in part to a deception—in convincing the Hapsburg emperor that war was the only way out. On the following day, the Austrians declared war against Serbia.

As the possibilities of a general European war loomed, Berlin sent several frantic telegrams to Vienna. The German ambassador was instructed to tell Berchtold that "as an ally we must refuse to be drawn into a world conflagration because Austria does not respect our advice."[3] Had the Germans spoken to their ally in such tones a month earlier, war might have been avoided. But Austria's belligerency moved the Russians to act. The tsar ordered mobilization on July 30.

Germany was caught in a dilemma that Bismarck would never have allowed. Surrounded by potential enemies, the Germans had to move quickly and decisively or else face defeat. The Russian mobilization threatened them, because in the event of war on the eastern front, there would also be war on the western front. The best plan to Berlin, one that had been worked out much earlier, seemed to be to launch a lightning attack against France—which could mobilize faster than Russia—crush France, and then turn to meet Russia, which would gain military readiness more slowly. To allow Russian mobilization to proceed without action would jeopardize this strategy.

On July 31 the Berlin government sent out ultimatums to Russia and France, demanding from the former cessation of mobilization and from the latter a pledge of neutrality. Failing to receive satisfactory replies, Germany declared war on Russia August 1 and on France August 3. On August 2 the German ambassador in Brussels delivered an ultimatum to the Belgian government announcing his country's intention to send troops through Belgium. The Belgian cabinet refused to grant permission and appealed to Russia, France, and Great Britain for help in protecting its neutrality.

A majority of the British cabinet did not favor war, but with the news of the German ultimatum to Belgium, the tide turned. Sir Edward Grey, the British foreign secretary, sent an ultimatum to Germany demanding that Belgian neutrality be respected. This Germany refused to do, and on August 4, Great Britain declared war.

On the basis that Germany and Austria were not waging a defensive war, Italy refused to carry out its obligations under the Triple Alliance and for the time being remained neutral. In the latter part of August, Japan joined the Allies. Turkey, fearing the designs of Russia, threw in its lot with the Central Powers, Germany and Austria.

In the last few days of peace, diplomats tried desperately to avert general war. Through confusion, fear, and loss of sleep, the nervous strain among them was almost unbearable. Many broke down and wept when it became apparent that they had failed. This atmosphere of anguish and gloom is reflected in a passage from Sir Edward Grey's autobiography:

A friend came to see me on one of the evenings of the last week (before the war)—he thinks it was Monday, August 3. We were standing at the window of my room in the Foreign Office. It was getting dusk and the lamps were being lit in the space below on which we were looking. My friend recalls that I remarked on this with the words: "The lamps are going out all over Europe; we shall not see them lit again in our life-time."[4]

"The lamps are going out all over Europe . . ."—these words of Sir Edward Grey, the British foreign secretary, are illustrated in a *Chicago Daily News* cartoon of July 30, 1914, a few short days before World War I became a reality.

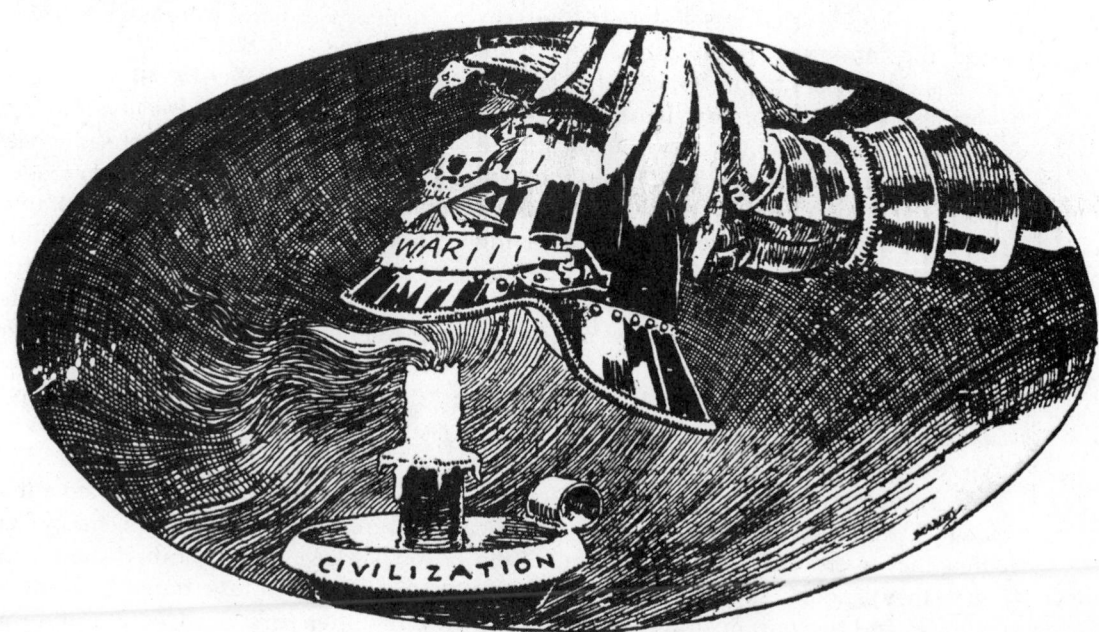

THE FIRST WORLD WAR

The scope of the conflict. Although the terrible struggle that racked mankind from 1914 to 1918 was fought chiefly on the European continent, it can justly be called the First World War. Altogether, twenty-seven powers became belligerents, ranging the globe from Tokyo to Ottawa and from Rio de Janeiro to Capetown. Tremendous fighting strength was mustered. The Central Powers —Germany, Austria, Bulgaria, and Turkey— mobilized 21 million men; their opponents, the Allies, called 40 million men to arms, of whom 12 million were Russians.

The sides were more competitive than the figures would indicate, however. Since the Russian divisions were often poorly equipped and ineffectively used, the apparent advantage of the Allies was not that great. Furthermore, in the German army, the Central Powers boasted superb generalship and discipline. Another advantage was that they fought from an inner or central position, and were therefore able to transfer troops quickly and efficiently to various fronts.

In their favor the Allies had greater resources of finance and raw materials. Britain, helped by its naval dominance and empire, could command vast material strength. In addition, because Germany was effectively shut off by British control of both the seas and the communications lines, the United States came, perhaps unconsciously, to be a major souce of support for the Allies.

The warring nations went into battle in a confident mood. Each side believed the conflict would soon be over, concluded by a few decisive battles. Each side, perhaps believing the messages from its own propaganda machine, assumed that it would win. It was generally believed that the war would be over by Christmas.

Campaigns of 1914 and 1915. The war plans had been on the books for years. The Germans knew that the Allied naval supremacy would cut them off from needed sources of raw material from abroad. They realized that they were potentially surrounded and that they should strike a quick knockout blow to end the war. Pushing the heroic Belgian resistance aside, German armies drove rapidly south into France. The strategy was to wheel west of Paris, outflanking the French forces, and then to drive them toward Alsace-Lorraine, where they would be met by another German army and destroyed by this hammer-anvil maneuver. Meanwhile, a small German force would be holding the presumably slow-moving Russians at bay in East Prussia.

But this strategy failed. After advancing so close to Paris that the top of the Eiffel Tower was within their sight, the Germans were hurled back by a bold counteroffensive, aided by a gap that opened between their armies. The French, aided in this attack— known as the battle of the Marne—by a small British expeditionary force, then marched rapidly north in a race with the Germans to reach and control the vital ports along the English channel. After much desperate fighting, battle positions were stabilized, and the "western front" was created in a solid line of opposing trenches, stretching from the Channel to the Swiss border. A new and grisly form of war of attrition resulted.

On the "eastern front" rapidly moving Russian armies penetrated East Prussia and overran the Austrian province of Galicia. However, the Russians—through confused leadership—suffered two catastrophic defeats in East Prussia, and the eastern frontiers of Germany were never again seriously menaced.

By the end of 1914, all of the combatants began to realize that they were in a new type of war, one of horrible consequences. Single battles devoured hundreds of thousands of lives, and the toll during the first few months of the conflict ran as high as a million and a half dead and wounded. Domestically, the new concept of total war, in which every element of society had to be mobilized, came to introduce radical changes. A new form of thought control came to be introduced in order to motivate the nations to fight and work harder.

In 1915 the British attempted a major campaign to force open the Dardanelles, closed by Turkey when it joined the Central Powers. This plan, attributed to Winston Churchill, then first lord of the admiralty, was

designed to open up a sea route to Russia, which was badly in need of war supplies. After heroic and costly attacks, Allied Australian and New Zealand troops—known as Anzacs—were compelled to withdraw from their landing positions on the Gallipoli peninsula in European Turkey.

Another major Allied setback in 1915 was the defeat of the Russian forces in Poland. More than 1,200,000 Russians were killed or wounded, and the Germans captured nearly 900,000 prisoners. Although Russia somehow remained in the war, fighting well against the Austrians, it ceased to be a major threat to the Germans. These defeats gener-

ated rising criticism against the tsar's government, and the Russians' morale began to break down.

Serbia was the next victim. Its conquest was made all the easier because in September, Bulgaria entered the war on the side of the Central Powers. Surrounded by enemies, Serbia was helpless and resistance was quickly crushed. The Austrians had finally gained their goal, but in the context of the continental conflagration, this development was hardly noticed.

The only bright spot for the Allies in 1915 was the Italian entry into their ranks. Italy had remained neutral in August 1914 by its defection from the Triple Alliance, of which it had been—at best—a symbolic member. Its entry into the war was gained in 1915 by promises the Allies made in a secret treaty in London. This agreement promised Italy lavish concessions of territory following a victory by the Allies.

1916: stalemate and total war. The Allied strategy was to restrict attacks in France to intermittent nibbling, thus saving manpower and at the same time concentrating on their naval blockade. Denied badly needed imports, the German war effort would be seriously weakened. Countering this tactic, the German high command launched a massive offensive against the important fortress of Verdun in the spring of 1916. This forced the Allies to throw hundreds of thousands of men into battle. The slaughter brought on by massed artillery and infantry charges between the trenches was horrible. The total loss of wounded and dead from this battle came to some 700,000 men.

To ease the pressure against Verdun, the British army began an offensive along the Somme on the western front. The attackers' losses were tragic: 60 percent of the officers and 40 percent of the men became casualties on the first day of the battle. Despite these awesome figures—which included the British firing 2 million shells at the first battle of the Somme—the attacks continued for several months without any substantial gains. The total German casualties at Verdun and on the Somme were slightly less than those of the allies. Europe was bleeding to death.

The battle of Jutland in 1916 (May 31-June 1), in the North Sea west of Denmark, was another crucial engagement since control of the seas was vital to Britain. At Jutland—the only major naval engagement of the war—the Germans maneuvered brilliantly and took risks. They could afford to gamble, for defeat could in no way worsen their existing strategic position. The British fleet, on the other hand, acted with great caution, since the British admiral was the one man who could "lose the war in an afternoon."[5] The British losses were heavier, but the German battleships retreated to their base to remain there for the duration of the war. British naval supremacy continued.

On the eastern front in 1916 the Russians continued their generally successful campaigns against the Austrian forces, but German armies saved the Austrians from destruction. Rumania, impressed by the Russian victory, threw in its lot with the Allies and launched an attack on Hungary. Despite initial success, Rumania was later invaded by German and Bulgarian forces and compelled to capitulate.

At the close of 1916, after more than two years of fighting, neither the Central Powers nor the Allies could envisage victory. The war had turned into a dreary contest of stamina, a far cry from the glories predicted by the militaristic propaganda.

Total war and the home front. War was no longer fought simply between armies. It was fought between states, and every component within the state participated. War had branched out into a whole new dimension—the struggle to sustain the will of the civilian population. As an English observer put it:

World War I produced the most fierce fighting and tragic loss of life the world had ever known to that point. Trench warfare became a way of life for the millions of soldiers who had to constantly keep an eye out for the enemy as well as try to advance their own strategic battlefield positions.

The war has passed out of the phase of mere battle. It is now a contest between the will and determination of whole nations to continue a life-and-death struggle in which "battle" takes a very small part.[6]

The citizens of the warring nations were urged to eat less food, buy more bonds, and make more weapons. Women were urged to take men's jobs—a notable social change—in order to release more men for military purposes. People were deluged by a barrage of propaganda inciting them to hate the enemy, to believe in the absolute righteousness of their cause, and to support the war effort without complaint or criticism.

Civil liberties suffered, and in some cases distinguished citizens were thrown into prison for opposing the war effort. In England, for example, the philosopher and mathematician Bertrand Russell was imprisoned for a short time. Governments took over the control of their national economies. Strikes were outlawed, and currencies and foreign trade were rigidly controlled.

On the home front all was flag waving and enthusiasm in the summer of 1914. The international socialist movement, whose policy it was to improve the international proletarian unity, fell victim to the patriotism that encouraged the workers of one country to go out and kill the workers of another in the name of the state. There was much idealism, sense of sacrifice, and patriotism, with little understanding at first of the horror, death, and degradation accompanying modern mechanized war. The spirit was expressed by the English poet Rupert Brooke when he wrote:

If I should die, think only this of me:
That there's some corner of a foreign field
That is forever England. There shall be
In that rich earth a richer dust concealed;
A dust whom England bore, shaped, made aware,
Gave, once, her flowers to love, her ways to roam,
A body of England's breathing English air,
Washed by the rivers, blest by suns of home.[7]

But this early idealism, this almost romantic conception of death in battle, gradually changed to one of war weariness and total futility. This growing mood is illustrated by

Total war required total cooperation—from every segment of the home front society. Posters exhorting conservation, preservation, and increased production at home, as well as a barrage of near-comic evangelism against the enemy, could be found in full view of the public eye. This poster, "Can the Kaiser," is a blend of domestic and militaristic propaganda messages.

the poetry of the young British officer and poet Wilfred Owen, himself a victim on the western front, who poignantly observed:

What passing-bells for those who die as cattle?
Only the monstrous anger of the guns. . . .

No mockeries for them; no prayers nor bells,
Nor any voice of mourning save the choirs,—
The shrill, demented choirs of wailing shells;
And bugles calling for them from sad shires.[8]

By the end of 1916 there was a deep yearning for peace. Sensing this mood, leaders on both sides put forth rather half-hearted peace feelers. But these achieved nothing. Continuance of the war was made possible largely through the use of propaganda. All the people in the warring nations were made to believe that they were part of a crusade for a better world. The Germans were named "Huns" by the Allies and the Russians were called "savages" by the Germans.

1917: Allied fatigue and American entry. In 1917 British and French military strength reached its highest point, only to fall to unprecedented depths. Allied commanders were hopeful that the long-planned breakthrough might be accomplished, but a large-scale attack by the French was beaten back with horrible losses. French regiments mutinied rather than return to the inferno of "no man's land" between the trenches. The Brit-

ish army meanwhile launched several massive offensives, only to lose hundreds of thousands of men without any decisive results. The Allies also launched unsuccessful offensives in Italy, where catastrophe threatened. Aided by the Germans, the Austrians smashed the Italian front at the battle of Caporetto (1917), an event vividly described by Ernest Hemingway in *A Farewell to Arms*. Italian resistance finally hardened, but collapse was barely averted.

The frustration of Allied hopes was deepened by the growing menace of the German submarine campaign. By 1917 shipping losses had assumed dangerous proportions.

Below is an aerial view of a typical "dogfight" scene between German and Allied planes during World War I. Although the aircraft of those days are now obsolete, their maneuverability has never been matched.

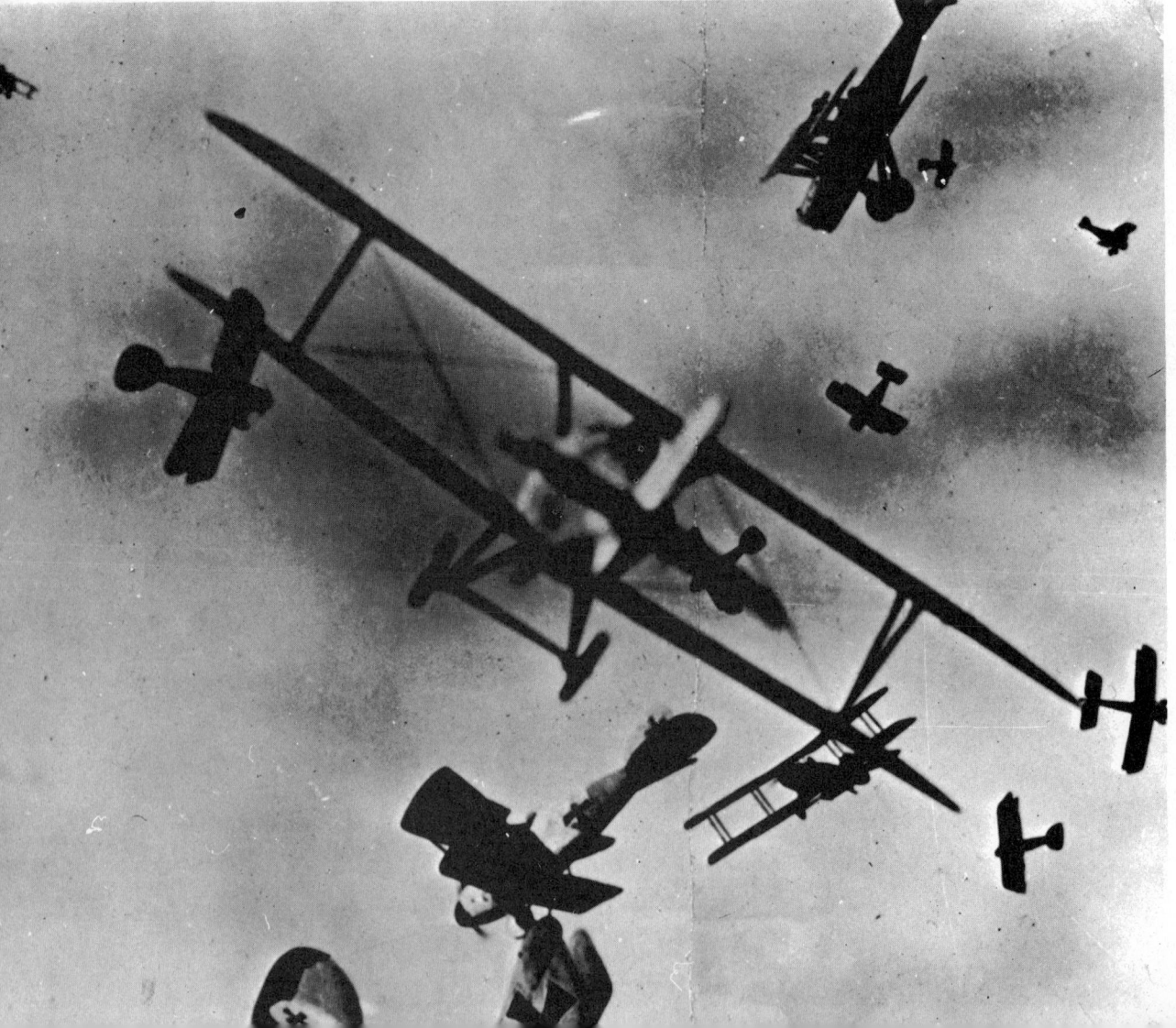

In three months 470 British ships alone fell victim to torpedoes. Britain had no more than six weeks' supply of food, and the situation became critical for the Allies. But the very weapon that seemed to doom their cause was to prove their salvation, for the submarine brought the United States into the war on the Allies' side.

The Americans had declared their neutrality in 1914 when President Wilson announced that the American people "must be impartial in thought as well as in action." The events of the following two years showed this to be no easy task. From the beginning of the conflict, American sentiment was predominantly with the Allies. There was a strong tradition of friendship with France because of that country's help to the American colonies during the Revolutionary War, and between England and America there were strong cultural ties of language, literature, and democratic institutions.

British propaganda, in addition, had the United States as its special target, and because of English control of the communications and transportation networks in the Atlantic, England effectively managed the news of the war. Another factor favoring the Allied cause was the American belief that Germany had grossly violated international law by invading Belgium. Partly because of the kaiser's saber-rattling speeches, the German government was regarded as undemocratic, unpredictable, and unstable. In some circles it was believed that a German victory would

The participants of World War I experienced a tragic consequence of industrialization as the tools of peacetime prosperity became the weapons of wartime destruction. Due to their effectiveness in surprise attack, submarines achieved widespread use as military weapons. Above a submarine takes on supplies while moored in a German harbor.

The British used deception—as did everyone else—to try to gain the advantage during the Great War. Under the pretext of building water tanks, the British secretly developed the military tank in 1916, and German soldiers were terrified when these strange steel monsters first appeared on the scene.

upset the world balance of power and that a victorious and expansionist Germany would imperil American security.

These attitudes were reinforced by substantial economic factors. As the war progressed, it became apparent that the British blockade would permit United States trade to be carried on with only the Allies, and before long American factories and farmers were producing munitions and food exclusively

Confident of victory and exhilarated at the prospect of gaining military glory for the Fatherland, German troops leave for the front at the outbreak of World War I (top). Well-trained, well-led, and well-equipped, the German soldier had every reason to expect an early victory. But after facing the terrible realities of battle and experiencing the numbing shock of defeat, his mood changed to one of exhaustion and despair (bottom).

for Great Britain and France. Industry expanded and began to enjoy a prosperity dependent upon the continuance of Allied purchases. Between 1914 and 1916 American exports to the Allies quadrupled. During 1915 and 1916 Allied bonds totaling about $1.5 billion were sold in the United States. It was quite apparent to the Germans that there was precious little neutrality on the economic front in the United States.

The immediate cause of the United States entry into the war on the Allied side was undoubtedly the German submarine campaign. Blockaded by the British, the Germans decided to retaliate by halting all shipping to the Allies. Its submarine campaign began in February 1915, and one of the first victims was the luxury liner *Lusitania*, torpedoed with the loss of more than a thousand lives, including one hundred Americans. This tragedy aroused public opinion in America.

In the fall of 1916 Wilson was reelected to the presidency. One of his election slogans was "He kept us out of war." But this boast was soon invalidated by the force of events. The discovery of German plots to involve Mexico in the war against the United States and more submarine sinkings drew violent American resentment. Finally, on April 6, 1917, the president asked Congress to declare war against Germany.

A wide range of causes brought Wilson to the point of involving the United States in the war. Once in the conflict, the president was intent on the struggle "to make the world safe for democracy." The spell of Wilson's lofty principles caused a great welling of idealism among Americans.

Germany's last drive. While the United States mobilized its tremendous resources of manpower and materials, the German government moved to try to win the war before American aid became effective. The British army had been bled white from the fruitless offensives of 1917, and the French divisions had barely recovered from the mutinies. Furthermore, the Russian war effort had collapsed after the February/March revolution. In November 1917 the Bolsheviks under Lenin took power and began to negotiate for peace. By the treaty of Brest Litovsk early in 1918, they made peace with Germany. The terms were harsh, as Russia lost 1,300,000 square miles of territory and 62 million people.[9]

Freed from the necessity of fighting on the Russian front, the Germans unleashed a series of major offensives against British and French positions in the spring of 1918. During one of these attacks, a brigade of American marines symbolized the difference the United States' entry into the war would make by stopping a German charge at Chateau-Thierry. A final effort was made to knock the French out in July 1918. It was described as the *Friedensturm,* the peace offensive. The Germans made substantial gains but did not score the essential breakthrough. By this time the momentum of the conflict was slowing down, and more than 1 million American "doughboys" had landed in France. The last German offensive was thrown back after a slight advance.

Hardly had the drive been stopped when the supreme Allied commander, Marshal Foch, counterattacked. Badly beaten and continually harassed, the German troops fell back in rapid retreat. By the end of October the German forces had been pushed out of most of France, and Allied armies were advancing into Belgium. The war of fixed positions separated by "no man's land" was over. The Allies had smashed the trench defenses and were now in open country.

On October 1, the German High Command urged the kaiser to sue for peace, and three days later the German chancellor sent a note to President Wilson requesting an end to hostilities. The president's reply notified the German government that peace was impossible so long as the autocratic regime in Germany existed. Although the German chancellor tried to keep the monarchy by introducing certain liberal reforms, it was too late. Revolution broke out in many parts of the country, the kaiser abdicated, and a republic was proclaimed.

While Germany was staggering under the continual pounding of Foch's armies, the German allies were suffering even greater misfortunes. Bulgaria surrendered on September 30, and Turkey capitulated a month later. Austria gave up the struggle against Italy on November 3. Nine days later the Hapsburg empire collapsed when Emperor Charles I fled Vienna for sanctuary in Switzerland.

At five o'clock on the morning of November 11, 1918, in a dining car in the Compiègne Forest, the German delegates signed the terms presented by Marshal Foch. At eleven o'clock the same day hostilities were halted. Everywhere the news was received with an outburst of joy. The world was once more at peace, confronted with the task of binding up its wounds and removing the scars of conflict. Delegates from the Allied nations were soon to converge on Paris, where the peace conference was to be held.

For the troops of the victorious Allies, November 11 meant returning home to a joyful conqueror's welcome; to those of the Central Powers, it meant a return saddened by the realization of failure. The exodus of German forces has been vividly described by the German novelist Erich Maria Remarque:

> Along the road, step upon step, in their faded, dirty uniforms tramp the grey columns. The unshaved faces beneath the steel helmets are haggard, wasted with hunger and long peril, pinched and dwindled to the lines drawn by terror and courage and death. They trudge along in silence . . . into peace.[10]

SUMMARY

The western tradition suffered a serious blow during World War I, as a half millennium of traditions and assumptions were endangered by this irrational conflict of Europeans against Europeans. The peace may have been restored in November 1918, but the world was a far different place than it had been four years earlier. Europe had sustained a damaging blow to its world dominance, as could be seen by the increase in the status of the United States in the councils of war and peace. The German empire, the Hapsburg monarchy, the Russian empire, and the Ottoman empire were either destroyed or in the process of disappearing. The fatigue brought on by the war would be felt in all of the colonial areas.

In Russia, the war gave Vladimir Lenin the opportunity to gain power and implement his particular variety of Marxian socialism. In Germany, the defeat laid the foundation for a decade of political instability which would ultimately lead to the Nazi party gaining power, taking advantage of all of the discontent and economic dislocation emerging from the war. England and France had both lost a generation of the best and bravest of their sons, in addition to incurring a drastic social and financial cost.

By the end of the nineteenth century Europe had undergone a veritable revolution in many basic aspects of its pattern of life that enabled it to gain world primacy. Europe's golden age was brought to an end by a combination of tragic forces: militarism, rival alliances, economic imperialism, secret diplomacy, and most important of all, narrow and bellicose nationalism. These forces operating within the state structure were sufficient to overwhelm the many qualities in Europe that would have served the continent's self-interest. Europe had great strength and a sound basis for being optimistic about the future. The few factors that might have impelled one to be pessimistic could have been dealt with.

But for more than four years the science, industry, wealth, and power of Europe were concentrated upon destruction. The same forces that had been applied positively for a century were used to destroy much of the progress that had been made. Germany would be made the recipient of guilt for this tragedy, but the European community as a whole equally shared in permitting the conditions to develop which made the suicidal strife possible. Germany made serious blunders by violating Belgian neutrality and declaring war on Russia and France, and thereby lost support and sympathy throughout the world. The structure of the Treaty of Versailles, as we shall see in the next chapter, rested in large part on the assumed "war guilt" of Germany, a guilt the Germans were forced to bitterly accept. Yet in the final analysis, it is futile to try to blame one country or another for the tragedy that came from the great flaw of European society—that of the state system's international anarchy.

SUGGESTIONS FOR READING

Two standard accounts of underlying causes of the First World War are W. L. Langer, **European Alliances and Alignments, 1871-1890*** (Vintage), and **The Diplomacy of Imperialism, 1890-1902** (Knopf). Bernadotte Schmitt, **Triple Alliance and Triple Entente** (Fertig) is a compact introduction. See also R. Albrect-Carrié, **A Diplomatic History of Europe Since the Congress of Vienna** (Harper & Row).

G. L. Sulzberger **The Fall of Eagles** (Crown, 1977) covers the grandeur and fall of three imperial dynasties. S. B. Fay, **The Origins of the World War,*** 2 vols., 2nd ed. (Free Press) is sympathetic to Germany and Austria and long considered the standard guide; but see now F. Fischer, **Germany's Aims in the First World War*** (Norton); and W. Laqueur and G. Mosse, eds., **1914: The Coming of the First World War*** (Torchbooks). See also L. Lafore, **The Long Fuse: An Interpretation of the Origins of World War I*** (Lippincott, 1965); Oron J. Hale, **The Great Illusion, 1900-1914*** (Torchbooks); D. Lee, ed., **The Outbreak of the First World War*** (Heath); and V. Dedijer, **The Road to Sarajevo** (Simon & Schuster, 1966). Colin Simpson, **The Lusitania** (Little, Brown, 1973) is a suspenseful account of this ship's sinking. See also Alexander Solzhenitsyn, **August 1914*** (Bantam).

A. J. P. Taylor, **The First World War: An Illustrated History*** (Capricorn); H. Baldwin, **World War I*** (Grove); and C. Falls, **The Great War*** (Capricorn) are good short accounts. Excellent special works include Barbara Tuchman, **The Guns of August*** (Dell); A. Moorehead, **Gallipoli: Account of the 1915 Campaign*** (Torchbooks); A. Horne, **The Price of Glory: Verdun, 1916*** (St. Martin's, 1975); and E. Coffman, **The War to End All Wars: The American Military Experience in World War I** (Oxford). See also J. Costello and T. Hughes, **Jutland, 1916** (Holt, Rinehart & Winston, 1976), which is a dramatic account of a famous naval battle.

*Indicates a less expensive paperbound edition.

August 1, 1914, promised to be a warm and bright day. The Bocage family looked forward to taking their yearly vacation by train up to the Normandy coast. They gave little thought to the rumors of a war with Germany as they boarded the subway to head for the railway station, the Gare Saint Lazare. Their trip would be abruptly halted by news at 3:55 p.m. that France had mobilized. The war that would plunge Europe into immense tragedy had not been totally unexpected, but the Bocage family had fervently wished that it might be avoided. Now that war seemed inevitable, none of them knew what to expect. They were worried, because they had much to lose if things went badly.

The father, forty-five-years-old, worked as a supervisor in the central post office. He had performed the functions assigned to him with diligence for nearly a quarter century, rising from a humble position to his present chair of power behind a large desk. His take-home pay, 5700 francs, was not very large, but it provided him and his family with a comfortable life. Even though he would never be rich, he still took great pride in the prestige of his office, and proudly placed on his lapel the row of ribbons that symbolized his good work and slow but steady rise through the ranks. As a careerist, he found great comfort in the pension that awaited him when he retired. He had no doubts about the importance of the work that he and his fellow half-million civil servants accomplished. He felt himself to be a part of the force of stability that kept France moving forward. He had little patience for the public, which did not respect his seniority and which launched attack after attack against the civil service. The public did not understand the narrow, though important, context in which he pursued his ambitions.

The thirty-seven-year-old wife remained at home, supervising the running of the home and bringing up the children. Her husband shared the view along with other Frenchmen that his wife should be cherished, maintained, and protected within the walls of the home. But both the husband and the wife were in general agreement that her role in the world at large was determined by her mate. Their two lives were tied together by law, but rarely did they come together sexually. This suited the wife as she had been trained to believe that this was the way life must be. She did not desire the vote, liberation, or divorce (the only major legal breakthrough for French women in the previous century). She was comfortable. Her apartment was her kingdom and her children were her subjects and sources of comfort. The church gave her consolation and a reason for her submissiveness. Eight years younger than her husband, she knew that she had, in all probability, a long period of widowhood ahead of her.

The sixteen-year-old son went to the *lycée*, a public secondary school, where he prepared himself to follow his father's example and enter the bureaucracy. He did not perform very well academically, and his teachers had discouraged him from planning to go to the university. His major preoccupations were playing soccer and learning the intricacies of the opposite sex. Soccer had taken hold of France some thirty years earlier, and the intensity with which the youth of the country played it was encouraged. Government officials believed that the game taught teamwork and discipline. As was the case with earlier generations, the son made his first visit to a brothel with some school chums the preceding summer, a fact that his father knew about and secretly approved of. In general, he was anxious to leave school and to serve his country, either in the civil service or else in the army fighting the Germans.

The fourteen-year-old daughter went to the local parochial school. She was being trained both at home and at school to follow the example of her mother, to marry, to have children, and to take care of the house. Society, church, and family all encouraged her to be complacent and obedient. Her life goal, though she only dimly realized it at that time, was to make a good marriage. She studied music, some literature, homemaking arts, and religion. Her major preoccupation, much to the mother's chagrin, was bicycle riding through neighboring streets. She was soon coming to the age where such unchaperoned activities would have to be stopped.

The family's modest seven-room apartment near the Porte Vincennes was purchased mostly through the wife's dowry of some 10,000 francs. The father's income, though modest, was sufficient to support his family's pretensions. After spending approximately half of the income on food and fuel, the family had enough money left over for such luxuries as their vacation to Normandy, clothing for special events, and an occasional trip to the theater or music hall.

Life was pleasant on the outskirts of Paris. The opening of the subway some twenty years earlier made it possible for the Bocage family to live in a more comfortable section of town and still make a living. The father was able to commute, leaving the apartment at 7:30 and taking the subway downtown. He returned home around six o'clock, early enough to relax in the comfort of his home. The apartment featured two comparatively luxurious public rooms, a living room and dining room, with paintings, good furniture, linens, and carpets. The mother read about the rich members of society in the newspapers and observed their behavior in her trips into the city. The father studied the habits and ways of life of his superiors, and they both modeled their goals and life-styles after the example of their "betters." Conspicuous consumption was easily evident, especially when one passed from the public to the private rooms and noticed the comparison between the richness of the former with the spartan qualities of the latter.

The apartment had electric lights and dependable and clean running water. A coal stove served heavy duty in the kitchen, while heat still came from open fires in the fireplaces. There were no indoor toilets—a trip to the backyard outhouse was still required. The standards of cleanliness inside the house were strictly observed by the cleaning woman who came three times a week.

Everything had to be proper if it was to be viewed by the public. The proper manners, the proper ways of speaking, the proper fashions, the proper posture, and the proper opinions to be held were all carefully sought after. A quarter-century's climb through the labyrinth of the post office bureaucracy may not have brought the father much financial wealth, but it certainly gave him a sense of position, of being beneath a certain number of superiors, and more importantly, of being above a certain number of humanity. In the bureaucratic, paper-shuffling life-style, appearance and position, not work accomplished or quality of finished product, came to be all important.

By 1914 the Bocage family had a great choice of leisure opportunities, and two days a week to pursue them. The father enjoyed following the new sports of bicycle and automobile racing while his son was a fan of the local soccer team. The ease of transportation made weekend trips and picnics easily available, and the family often took walks in the various parks and forests in and around Paris. Since the father's last promotion six years earlier, they had regularly gone to Honfleur in Normandy for their August vacation. During the winter the family read during the long evenings from the popular press, novels, and magazines that were available. The father and son both appreciated the pornographic sheets that came to be so popular at that time. The family attended the light musicals of the time, especially during the winter. Once a year, the mother treated herself and her daughter to a ballet performance at the Opera. Earlier in the year the father had gone to the cinema, but he found it to be so ludicrous and clumsy that he dismissed it as a serious art form. He preferred to spend his leisure time, especially on his way home, at the new American style bar where he stopped for a drink, usually of scotch whiskey.

The Bocage family had enough to eat and an adequate choice of clothing. Year around there was a selection of vegetables, meats, fish, and fruit brought in from the far corners of France and North Africa. The improvement in diet was matched by the widespread selection of ready-made clothes which made reasonably stylish dress available at a modest price.

The family could look forward to a longer, more healthy life span as a result of the great improvement in diet and sanitation that had taken place at the turn of the century. The major health hazards affecting their level of society were more apt to be those of dental problems and venereal disease than those of typhus, typhoid, and tuberculosis.

The father was caught up in the highly politicized atmosphere of the times. He was generally conservative, and followed the anticlerical attitudes that were strong among the governmental community. He feared the socialists and the syndicalists on the left and the royalists on the right. The more than one thousand strikes in 1909 also frightened him. The mother, however, took little interest in politics. Their hopes and dreams were closely tied to the milieu in which they found themselves—the bureaucratic middle class. The father dreamed of rising still higher within the ranks of the civil service. The son wanted to follow in his father's footsteps, enjoy his sports, and have a good time. The daughter was caught within the traditional framework that deprived her of the freedom of choice her brother enjoyed. The role of the church was most important in the lives of the mother and daughter, who attended mass faithfully. The son attended services less frequently, and the father went hardly at all.

But on that August day, one event overwhelmed the whole family, their lives, their goals, their standard of living, and their dreams, and that was the arrival of war. All aspects of the life that they enjoyed came to be wrapped up in love of *la patrie*. And when the mobilization posters went up at sunset, the Bocage family was about to enter a radically new way of life.

PART SEVEN
The World Adrift

■World War I had been described as a major watershed in modern history. It brought to a dramatic close a century of relative peace and ushered in what has been referred to as the Age of Violence. As we have seen, before 1914 Europe was the center of the world in political influence, cultural creativity, and military and financial power. This small continent ruled a vast colonial structure and with it hundreds of millions of dependent peoples. Ideologically, political liberalism and parliamentary institutions had flourished and multiplied. Democracy, it seemed, was destined to spread all over the globe. And capitalism was the prevailing economic creed, with the middle class its master and chief beneficiary.

First of the total technological conflicts, the 1914-1918 conflagration had far-reaching consequences, which include World War II in turn. Because of the fearful price paid by the men who endured World War I, they had to believe that a better world would emerge. They were soon disillusioned. Although the statesmen of the victorious Allies had championed the democratic and humanistic traditions of western civilization, their motives in making the peace were often as vindictive and nationalistic as any preparations for war. And though internationalism was activated in the form of the League of Nations, it was given neither the strength nor the support required to bring peace and security during the troubled 1920's and 1930's.

In these years democracy began its struggle with new totalitarianisms. In war-exhausted Russia, Marxist tenets were embraced by revolutionaries, and a Communist society took shape under Lenin. Another authoritarian system, Fascism, gripped Italy. And the most frightening ideology of all, Nazism, grew to terrifying fruition in Germany, where a people embittered by the humiliation of World War I and the Treaty of Versailles staked their future on a madman named Hitler.

By the 1920's and 1930's the non-European world had discovered the concept of nationalism. In the Middle East, Arab national ambitions had flared in 1916 into a revolt against Ottoman rule. The immigration of European Jews to Palestine led to conflict between Arabs and Jews, which was to increase as time passed. In North Africa, the Middle East, India, southeastern Asia, and Oceania, the indigenous peoples were gathering strength in their battle to oust the Europeans completely and govern themselves; and in the huge colonial area south of the Sahara, Africans were beginning to stir restlessly against European rule. Even China, tradition-bound for centuries, turned to revolution to regain the power and prestige it had lost during the era of imperialism. But though Chiang Kai-shek won an internal power struggle and organized the government, the country remained poor and weak. Meanwhile Japan continued its amazing technological, industrial, and military growth and became as a world power.

The world depression in the 1930's gave the totalitarian movements an opportunity to expand their despotism at home and to launch aggression abroad. From 1931 to 1939, starting with the Japanese invasion of Manchuria, their belligerence mounted. The new dictatorial regimes went from one success to another, glorifying militarism and the potency of the state, regimenting their citizens, and intimidating their neighbors. The older democratic nations, such as Britain and France, were paralyzed with indecision and fear and did little to halt the dictators. Appeasement was tried, but the aggression continued. Finally, in 1939, the British and French realized that their own nations were next in Hitler's march of conquest and took up arms. The Second World War began. In 1941 the Soviet Union, which had been allied earlier with the Nazis, and the United States, which for two decades had been attempting to ignore the mounting tensions abroad, were forced into the struggle. The horrors which this global conflict brought were the familiar ones of ruthless enemy occupation, the rigors of battle, and the loss of life and property, and the new ones created by dread new weapons and methods of warfare, the organized slaughter of certain nationality groups, and the repeated bombing of civilian centers.

Victory came to the Grand Alliance in 1945 and with it total defeat of Hilter's Third Reich and the fascist states established in Italy by Mussolini and in Japan by Tojo. As in 1919 the victors were confronted with the immense task of rebuilding and reestablishing a great part of the world. This task was made more difficult by the knowledge of the failures of the peace of 1919 and the dismaying realization that as the Second World War was more encompassing and vastly more destructive than the First, so a Third World War would be more shattering than the Second and, with the advent of nuclear weapons, might bring about the annihilation of man.

CHAPTER 31

The Course of Politics in the West: 1918 - 1930

New Vistas and Ominous Fears

INTRODUCTION. When World War I ended in 1918, a weary world began the herculean task of transforming its efforts from those of war to peace. Underlying this transition was the prevalent belief that somehow the sacrifices made during the war would lead to a better life for all mankind. Accordingly, there were roseate predictions of the ultimate triumph of democratic institutions everywhere. Had not four antidemocratic imperial governments—in Germany, Turkey, Austria-Hungary, and Russia—been overthrown? And millions of people, invoking nationalism's creed of self-determination, were escaping alien rule and establishing their own democratic governments. In addition to this faith in democracy and nationalism, there was an ambivalent adherence to the cause of internationalism so eloquently espoused by President Wilson. A new international order was to be achieved by the creation of a world organization designed to outlaw war and encourage amity between nations.

Europeans generally viewed their continent's prospects optimistically. They were prone to believe that Europe could regain its preeminence in the world—in finance, industry, and military power. It soon became evident, however, that such hopes were not justified. The war's economic consequences were both underestimated and only dimly understood. Nations such as Great Britain had lost export markets; disagreements over war debts and reparation claims against former enemies, as well as runaway inflation, plagued various nations after 1918. Economic recovery was also hindered, and the general morale tarnished, by the destruction of millions of Europe's young men on the battlefields of the Marne, Tannenberg, and Verdun.

The postwar decade soon exposed the lack of realism concerning nationalism and democracy. Newly created democracies in central and eastern Europe, whose people had little experience in representative government, were soon superseded by dictatorial regimes. Most challenging to the future of democracy was the establishment of two dictatorships—the Communist in Russia and the Fascist in Italy. Another menacing portent was the emergence of a racist and antidemocratic Nazi movement in republican Germany. Democratic institutions were destroyed in Russia and Italy, and even in the traditional bastions of democracy, in Great Britain, France, and the United States, there seemed to be a lack of purpose, of vitality, and of confidence. While France and Britain failed to come to grips with their basic problems, the United States, mainly aloof from world affairs, concentrated on what appeared to be dazzling prosperity. During the postwar decade all three nations exhibited various symptoms of moral fatigue and disillusionment.

Against this background, and confronted by the defeated nations' belief that the peace treaties were unjust, the newly created League of Nations began its task of safeguarding world peace and encouraging international conciliation. In retrospect, it is hardly surprising that its record was not impressive. Its usefulness was also compromised by the refusal of the United States to become a member of the League.

As the 1920's neared an end, the general course of international affairs seemed reasonably calm; former enemies such as France and Germany were apparently burying the hatchet, and economic recovery and prosperity was fairly widespread. Yet below the surface remained serious tensions and problems, both political and economic, bequeathed by the First World War. These, then, were the historical ingredients of the complex 1920's, which were ushered in following the end of hostilities by the immediate and crucial task of trying to fashion a "just peace" between the victors and vanquished.

THE PEACE SETTLEMENT

Wilson's blueprint for peace. Woodrow Wilson had declared that World War I was

a war for freedom and justice and self-government amongst all the nations of the world, a war to make the world safe for the peoples who live upon it and have made it their own, the German people themselves included.[1]

In January 1918, in an address before both houses of Congress, the president had enunciated his famous Fourteen Points as the basis for a lasting peace. With this speech, Wilson made himself a new kind of world leader, representing not wealth and power but morality and justice. Millions of men and women, at home and abroad, in the Allied nations, in the enemy countries, and in neutral states, flocked to his standard. The Fourteen Points seemed to open the way not only for a speedy cessation of hostilities but for a peace that could endure.

The first five points were general in nature and may be summarized as follows: "Open covenants openly arrived at"; freedom of the seas in peace and in war alike; the removal of all economic barriers and the establishment of an equality of trade conditions among all nations; reduction of national armaments; a readjustment of all colonial claims, giving

Thirty-two Allied nations sent representatives to Paris to put the stamp of finality and justice on the "war to end all wars." But the settlements which came out of the Peace Conference were marked by national rather than global interests, and by hostility rather than assistance for the defeated nations. Four influential men who clashed over their individual plans for a lasting peace were David Lloyd George, prime minister of Great Britain; Vittorio Orlando, prime minister of Italy; Georges Clemenceau, premier of France; and Woodrow Wilson, president of the United States.

the interests of the population concerned equal weight with the claims of the government whose title was to be determined. The next eight points dealt with specific issues involving the evacuation and restoration of Allied territory, self-determination for submerged nationalities, and the redrawing of European boundaries along national lines. The fourteenth point in Wilson's speech contained the germ of the League of Nations: the formation of a general association of nations under specific covenants for the purpose of affording mutual guarantees of political independence and territorial integrity to great and small states alike.

Cross-currents at the peace conference. All the Allied powers sent delegations to the peace conference at Paris, but the vanquished nations were not accorded representation. This exclusion was not in the spirit of Wilson's idealistic pronouncements before the armistice.

Three personalities dominated the Paris Conference: Wilson, Lloyd George, and Clemenceau. In the eyes of the war-weary and disillusioned peoples of Europe, Wilson was a veritable Messiah. But it soon became

apparent that he would be unable to prevent his ideals and promises from being sabotaged by the other Allied statesmen. Against the wily Lloyd George and the cynical Clemenceau, the idealistic American scholar had little chance of holding his own. In addition, certain factions in Congress were preparing to repudiate Wilson's program. Handicapped by a cold and imperious personality, Wilson (1856-1924) was so thoroughly convinced of the validity of his own ideas that he seldom recognized a need to "sell" them to others and often refused to consider the possibility of merit in the ideas of his opponents.

Lloyd George (1863-1945), the prime minister of Great Britain, was a consummately clever politician who could use the arts of diplomatic bargaining with a rare skill. He came to the conference just after a triumphant victory at the polls in which his party had promised the electorate the "hanging of the kaiser" and the "squeezing of the German lemon until the pips squeaked." He was determined to destroy the commercial and naval power of Germany, to acquire the German colonies, and to compel Germany to pay a large share of the cost of the war.

The strongest personality of the conference was the French premier—the seventy-seven-year-old Clemenceau (1841-1929), who for more than half a century had been a colorful part of French life and politics. A fierce individualist, Clemenceau had continuously opposed corruption, racism, and antidemocratic forces. His burning ambition was to ensure the security of France in the future; his formula was restitution, reparations, and guarantees. Clemenceau had little confidence in what, to him, were the unrealistic and utopian principles of Wilson, observing, "Even God was satisfied with Ten Commandments, but Wilson insists on fourteen."

Prearmistice peace principles and secret treaties. The Germans had surrendered with the understanding that the peace would in general follow the Fourteen Points and coincide with Wilson's speeches. In February 1918 the president had announced, "There shall be no annexations, no contributions, no punitive damages"; on July 4 he had said that every question must be settled "upon the basis of the free acceptance of that settlement by the people immediately concerned."

Complicating the promises of Wilson, especially the Fourteen Points, were the secret treaties the Allies had made during the war. In 1915 Italy had been induced to enter the conflict by promises of Austrian territory which would make the Adriatic an Italian sea. Italy was also promised an extension of its African colonies and a sphere of influence in Asiatic Turkey. Nearly all these proposed transfers violated the Wilsonian concept of national self-determination.

Other secret treaties gave Russia the right to take over the Dardanelles and Constantinople, Rumania the right to secure substantial territory at the expense of Austria-Hungary, and Japan the right to retain the German territory of Kiaochow in China. In return for Arab aid against the Turks, Britain had made vague promises of independence for the Arabs. In 1916, however, Britain and France had divided Turkish Iraq and Syria into their respective spheres of interest. Palestine, with its holy places, was to be placed under international administration; and in 1917 Great Britain pledged its support

of the "establishment in Palestine of a national home for the Jewish people."

President Wilson professed ignorance of the existence of the treaties, but their contents were common knowledge before the end of the war. In fact, in 1917 the Bolshevik government had released their texts, which were then published in American and English newspapers. Wilson may have believed that the secret agreements could be ignored, for he hoped to sway European statesmen to the necessity of founding the peace on his principles.

The League Covenant. When the statesmen assembled in their first plenary meeting on January 18, 1919, the first difficulty arose over the question of a league of nations. Wilson was insistent that the initial work of the conference must be to agree upon a covenant of a league of nations which was to be made part of the peace treaty. After much wrangling, the Covenant was approved by the full conference in April 1919. In order to gain support for the League, however, Wilson had to compromise on other matters. His Fourteen Points were thus partially repudiated, but he believed firmly that an imperfect treaty incorporating the League was better than a perfect one without it.

The Covenant of the League of Nations specified its aims: "to guarantee international cooperation and to achieve international peace and security." To implement this goal, Article x, the key article of the Covenant, stipulated that:

The Members of the League undertake to respect and preserve as against external aggression the territorial integrity and existing political independence of all Members of the League. In case of any such aggression or in case of any threat or danger of such aggression the Council shall advise upon the means by which this obligation shall be fulfilled.[2]

Redrawing German boundaries. The conference also faced the task of redrawing German boundaries. Alsace-Lorraine was turned over to France without question, in accordance with one of the Fourteen Points. Three districts formerly belonging to Germany were given to Belgium, after a dubious plebiscite conducted by Belgian officials. Another plebiscite gave half of Schleswig back to Denmark.

Clemenceau was determined that a buffer state consisting of the German territory west of the Rhine should be established under the domination of France. In the eyes of the American and British representatives, such a crass violation of the principle of self-determination would only breed future wars; and a compromise was therefore offered Clemenceau, which he accepted. The territory in question was to be occupied by Allied troops for a period of from five to fifteen years; and a zone extending fifty kilometers east of the Rhine was to be demilitarized. In addition, Wilson and Lloyd George agreed that the United States and Great Britain, by treaty, would guarantee France against aggression. The importance of this pledge cannot be overemphasized.

Along Germany's eastern frontier the creation of the Polish Corridor, which separated East Prussia from the rest of Germany, raised grave problems. Large sections of German territory in which there were Polish majorities but also a goodly number of Germans were turned over to Poland. (The land in question had been taken from Poland by Prussia in the eighteenth century.) A section of Silesia was likewise given to Poland, but only after a plebiscite. Danzig, a German city, was handed over to the League for administration. All in all, Germany lost 25,000 square miles inhabited by some six million people.

Although Clemenceau also claimed the Saar Basin, a rich coal area, this was not given outright to France but instead was placed under the administration of the League. The French were given ownership of the mines to compensate for the destruction of their own in northern France. It was agreed, however, that after fifteen years a plebiscite would be conducted to determine the future status of the Saar region.

The mandate system. A curious mixture of idealism and revenge determined the allocation of the German colonies and certain territories belonging to Turkey. Because outright annexation would look too much like unvarnished imperialism, it was suggested that the colonies be turned over to the League, which in turn would give them to certain of its members to administer. The colonies were to be known as mandates, and praiseworthy precautions were taken to ensure that the mandates would be administered for the well-being and development of the inhabitants. Once a year the mandatory powers were to present a detailed account of their administration of the territories to the League. The mandate system as such was a step forward in colonial administration, but Germany nevertheless was deprived of all colonies, with the excuse that it could not rule them justly or efficiently.

Reparations. Germany had accepted the armistice terms with the understanding that it was to pay for damage done to the Allied civilian population. At the conference the British and French delegates went much further by demanding that Germany pay the total cost of the war, including pensions. The American representatives maintained that such a claim was contrary to the prearmistice Allied terms and succeeded in achieving a compromise. It was agreed that, except in the case of Belgium, Germany was not to pay the entire cost of the war, but only war damages, which included those suffered by civilians and the cost of pensions. These payments, called reparations, were exacted on the ground that Germany was responsible for the war.

Although the Allies agreed that Germany should be made to pay, they were unable to decide on the sum. Some demands ran as high as $200 billion. Finally it was decided that a committee should fix the amount and report no later than May 1921. In the meantime Germany was to begin making payments which, by the time the reparations committee's report was ready, would total nearly $5 billion.

Other Allied demands. Germany was required to hand over most of its merchant fleet, construct one million tons of new shipping for the Allies, and deliver them vast amounts of coal, equipment, tools, and machinery. In military matters the demands were even more drastic. Germany was permitted a standing army of only 100,000 men, the size of the fleet was drastically reduced, possession of military airplanes was forbidden, and munitions plants were to be placed under close supervision. The treaty also provided that the kaiser be tried by a tribunal "for a supreme offense against international morality and the sanctity of treaties" and cited some eight hundred German officials for trial on charges of war atrocities. But the kaiser had fled to Holland after the German revolution; and when that country refused to surrender him, no further steps were taken by the Allied governments, which had inserted the clause providing for the punishment of the kaiser largely for home consumption.

The Treaty of Versailles signed. The Treaty of Versailles was built around the concept that Germany was responsible for the war. It stated explicitly that:

The Allied and Associated Governments affirm and Germany accepts the responsibility of Germany and her allies for causing all the loss and damage to which the Allied and Associated Governments and their nationals have been subjected as a consequence of the war imposed upon them by the aggression of Germany and her allies.[3]

Before coming to Paris in April 1919 to receive the Treaty of Versailles, the German delegation had been given no official information as to its terms. Upon obtaining the treaty on May 7, the German foreign minister stated:

It is demanded of us that we shall confess ourselves to be the only ones guilty of the war . . . . We are far from declining any responsiblilty . . . but we energetically deny that Germany and its people . . . were alone guilty. . . . In the last fifty years the Imperialism of all the European States has chronically poisoned the international situation . . . .[4]

The menace of Allied invasion gave the Germans no alternative but to sign, and the government therefore instructed its delegates to accept the treaty for Germany "without abandoning her view in regard to the unheard-of injustice of the conditions of the peace." On June 28, on the anniversary of the assassination of Archduke Francis Ferdinand and in the Hall of Mirrors at Versailles where the German empire had been proclaimed in 1871, the treaty was signed.

After witnessing this ceremony, an American delegate wrote in his diary:

I had a feeling of sympathy for the Germans who sat there quite stoically. It was not unlike what was done in ancient times, when the conqueror dragged the conquered at his chariot wheels. To my mind, it is out of keeping with the new era which we profess an ardent desire to promote. I wish it could have been more simple and that there might have been an element of chivalry, which was wholly lacking. The affair was elaborately staged and made as humiliating to the enemy as it well could be.[5]

Other World War treaties. The Allies also concluded treaties with the rest of the Central Powers. The treaty with Austria, the Treaty of St. Germain (1919), legalized the nationalist movements of Czechs, Poles, and South Slavs and converted the rest of the empire into the separate states of Austria and Hungary. By the treaty terms, the Austrian empire was reduced in area from 116,000 to 32,000 square miles and in population from 28,500,000 to 6,000,000. *Anschluss*—union of the Germans in Austria with their kinsmen in the new German republic—was forbidden. The treaty also awarded Italy sections of Austria—the territory south of the Brenner Pass, South Tyrol, Trentino with its 250,000 Austrian Germans, and the northeastern coast of the Adriatic with its large number of Slavs. To complete its acquisition of the Adriatic, Italy needed to obtain a slice of the Dalmation coast and the port of Fiume. The latter, however, was the natural port for the newly created state of Yugoslavia and had not been promised to Italy in 1915. Wilson declared that the Italian claim was in flat contradiction to the principle of self-determination; the ensuing controversy nearly wrecked the peace conference. The explosive issue of Italian claims in the Adriatic was not settled until 1920, when Italy renounced its claims to Dalmatia and when Fiume became an independent state. Four years later, however, Fiume was ceded to Italy.

By the Treaty of Sevres (1920) the Ottoman empire was placed on the operating table of power politics, dissected, and divided among Greece, Britain, and France. Greece was given nearly all of European Turkey and some islands of the Aegean Sea. The city of

Newly Created States
Ceded Territories

Smyrna was put under Greek administration, but Armenia achieved full independence. Syria was mandated to France, and Palestine and Iraq to England. To the Arabs, these transfers to Britain and France were a violation of wartime pledges. As for the Straits, this strategic waterway was to be under international control.

Two other treaties affected the Balkans. By the Treaty of Trianon (1920) Hungary lost territory to Czechoslovakia, Yugoslavia, and Rumania. The Treaty of Neuilly (1919) cut off Bulgaria from the Aegean Sea, imposed an indemnity, and provided for compulsory demilitarization. Bulgaria lost nearly one million subjects.

Evaluation of the peace settlement. During the first postwar decade tons of paper and barrels of ink were used in hot justification or acrid denunciation of the peace settlement. On the whole, the peace settlement was inadequate and unrealistic. In his indictment of the economic provisions of the peace, the world-famous economist John Maynard Keynes wrote in 1919:

The treaty includes no provisions for the economic rehabilitation of Europe,—nothing to make the defeated Central Empires into good neighbours, nothing to stabilise the new States of Europe, nothing to reclaim Russia; nor does it promote in any way a compact of economic solidarity amongst the Allies themselves; no arrangement was reached at Paris for restoring the disordered finances of France and Italy, or to adjust the systems of the Old World and the New.[6]

One of the weakest aspects of the peace settlement was the complete disregard of Russia. While the peace conference was in session, Russia was convulsed by civil war, complicated by the intervention of Japanese, American, French, and British troops. The Allied representatives at Paris disagreed on the policy to adopt toward the Communist government in Russia. The Soviets proposed to accept the huge prewar debts contracted by the tsar's government if the Allies would stop aiding the anti-Communist forces and restore normal commercial and diplomatic relations. The statesmen at Paris did not take this offer seriously, for they believed that the Communist government would soon collapse. Whether the new regime in Russia and the Allies could have reached some kind of an agreement leading to Russian participation in the peace settlement is uncertain, but the possibility was not seriously explored. George F. Kennan, an American authority on Soviet affairs, maintains that the sacrifice of this possiblilty had tremendous consequences for "the long-term future of both the Russian and American peoples and indeed of mankind generally."[7]

Some historians blame the errors of the treaties upon the defects of the personalities who made them. This view oversimplifies the problem and furthermore assumes that the statesmen at Paris were free agents. In truth, the delegates were the prisoners of their own people, who had been so influenced by propaganda, whose enmity was so bitter, and whose knowledge was so meager that any indication of reasonableness shown to the ex-enemies would have meant the repudiation of the harassed peacemakers. Perhaps no one possessed enough wisdom to cope with the many problems created and accentuated by four years of global war. Perhaps no other group of leaders could have made a better peace.

PROBLEMS OF STABILITY AND SECURITY

The "new world" and the powers. The prophecy that peace would usher in "a world fit for heroes" was quickly repudiated in the early troubled years of the postwar decade. The unity among the Allies wrought by the necessities of war did not long survive victory. During the Paris Conference and in the years following, serious differences emerged over such basic issues as reparations, war debts, disarmament, and the structure and functions of the League of Nations.

Italy was angry with its former allies for being so niggardly with the spoils of war. Great Britain was ready to let bygones be bygones; the "nation of shopkeepers" was anxious to see prosperity return to central Europe. On the other hand, France feared a resurgent Germany and was determined to enforce all the peace treaties.

And what of the vanquished? Germany was resentful of the peace settlement and determined to repudiate it. Hungary, Austria, and Bulgaria held similar views. Alone of the defeated powers, Turkey was fairly content, as it had been able to secure better treatment in a new treaty — the Treaty of Lausanne signed in 1923.

The United States refuses to join the League. In 1919, the year of its establishment, the League of Nations constituted a promising agency for improving the status of mankind everywhere. At the outset, however, it suffered a great blow to its prestige: the United States refused to become a member of the League. During the war Americans had been proud of Wilson's proposals for a new world order. After the war, however, their sense of a world mission and crusade for internationalism quickly ebbed away.

Disillusionment with the consequences of the peace settlements rekindled isolationism, and idealism born during the conflict was superseded by apathy and cynicism over world affairs. Unfortunately, President Wilson was both physically unable and politically maladroit in campaigning for Senate ratification of the League Covenant. In 1920 his program was repudiated at the polls, for the victory of Warren G. Harding, the Republican candidate for president, meant that the Covenant would never be ratified by the Senate.

The United States refusal to support the League was a fateful decision and, in retrospect, probably a serious blow to the cause of world peace. When the United States did join an international organization, the United Nations, in 1945, obstacles to world peace were much more complicated and obdurate than in 1919. But at the outset of the 1920's the chaos of the future and the coming of World War II were hidden in the yet unturned pages of history. The mass of Americans lapsed into complacent isolationism and normalcy with Harding.

France and the Little Entente. When both Britain and the United States repudiated the treaty guaranteeing France from aggression, the French, having little faith in the League as an instrument for their security, set about establishing their own military system. Allies were obtained through defensive treaties made, between 1920 and 1927, with Belgium, Poland, Czechoslovakia, Rumania, and Yugoslavia. The last three states constituted a diplomatic bloc, the Little Entente, whose power rested upon huge French loans and military assistance. For a brief ten years France with these allies dominated Europe; Germany was economically weak and militarily impotent.

The shift to a peace economy. One of the chief obstacles to postwar peace was the confused and desperate situation into which the European economy had been plunged. It has been estimated that the cost of the war was about $350 billion. It was the financial consequences of war that did the most to continue the enmity between victors and vanquished and also to alienate the nations, formerly allies, which had defeated Germany.

Following the armistice, there was an urgent need for getting back to a peacetime economy, which meant the production of peacetime goods instead of munitions, the demobilization of millions of soldiers, and the absorption of these veterans into the business structure. But it was not easy to return to the prosperous world economy that had existed before 1914.

The conflict had brought about many changes in world trade. Europe in particular had suffered a serious decline in its share of the world's commerce because of war blockades, the reduction of consumer purchasing power, the loss of shipping, and the capture of overseas markets by the United States, Latin America, and Japan. These economic setbacks were felt keenly by Germany and Great Britain. Furthermore, the peace treaties had multiplied national boundaries, which soon became obstacles to the flow of goods.

Serious problems also existed in the domestic economies of the European nations. As a result of the war, the public debts of the participant nations zoomed, often accompanied by the circulation of paper money not backed by adequate reserves. Furthermore, the war left a legacy of tension between economic groups. Labor unions were determined not to give up wage gains acquired during the war.

For a brief period many of these economic problems were obscured by an artificial postwar boom. The peak of prosperity was reached in 1920, after which world trade and industrial activity diminished. Strikes, unemployment, and other industrial problems multiplied; and for the next five years the nations, particularly in Europe, tried to extricate themselves from this economic morass.

The inter-Allied debt problem. The most serious problem facing Europe as it strove to achieve a prosperous peace economy was the revolution in its financial position in relation to the rest of the world. In 1914 the United States had been a debtor nation, mostly to Europe, for the amount of $3.75 billion. The war reversed the situation, and in 1919 the United States was owed more than $10 billion by its fellow victors. This tremendous debt posed what economists call the transfer problem. Such international obligations could only be paid by the actual transfer of gold or by the sale of goods to the creditor country.

The various Allied powers in Europe had lent each other funds, with Britain acting as the chief banker. When their credits had been used up, they had turned to the United

States for financial help. Britain owed huge sums to the United States but was still a net creditor of $4 billion because of its European debtors. France, on the other hand, was a net debtor of $3.5 billion. Some of the former Allies argued that the inter-Allied debts were political, that all of them had in effect been poured into a common pool for victory, and that, with victory, all should be canceled.

In the summer of 1922 Great Britain proposed that it collect no more from its debtors —Allies and Germany alike—than the United States collected from Britain itself. It was becoming manifest to British statesmen that Germany would not be able to meet its reparation payments, and without them the payment of the inter-Allied debts—especially the debts owed to the United States— would be extremely difficult, if not impossible, to make.

Although the American government insisted that there was no connection between the inter-Allied debts and German reparations, negotiations were carried on, and debt payment plans were set up with thirteen nations. No reductions were made in principal, but in numerous instances the rate of interest was decreased. The total amount to be paid came to more than $22 billion.

France invades the Ruhr. It became apparent that the Allies had placed an impossibly

French soldiers and engineers man and guard a German locomotive during one of the numerous strikes that took place as a result of French occupation of the Ruhr, a rich industrial district of Germany.

heavy burden on Germany. In 1921 its total indemnities had been fixed at $32 billion. During the same year Germany made a payment of $250 million, which reacted disastrously upon its currency system. Upon the default of some of Germany's payments, French troops, supported by Belgian and Italian contingents, marched into the rich industrial German district of the Ruhr, undeterred by British and American opposition. Defying the French army, German workers went on strike. Many were imprisoned, and the French toyed with the idea of establishing a separate state in the Rhineland which would act as a buffer between Germany and France. While chaotic conditions in the Ruhr led to catastrophic inflation of German currency, the French gained little economic benefit from their occupation. Meanwhile, public opinion all over the world had been shocked by France's strong-arm tactics in the Ruhr.

Change for the better. Midway in 1923 the prospect of a tranquil and cooperative world seemed far off indeed. But while not apparent to the harassed statesmen of the period, the worst of the war's aftermath had run its course. The Franco-British quarrel, mainly over the Ruhr, was patched up, and French troops were evacuated from the Ruhr in 1924. In the same year a commission under the chairmanship of an American banker, Charles Dawes, formulated a more liberal reparations policy. Installments were reduced and extended over a longer period, and a large loan was floated to aid Germany's recovery. Reparations payments were now renewed, and the former Allies paid their debt installments to the United States on schedule.

There was also a spectacular development in international relations. At the Locarno Conference in 1925 Germany, Great Britain, Belgium, France, and Italy signed a treaty guaranteeing the existing frontiers along the Rhine, providing for a demilitarized German zone extending fifty kilometers east of the Rhine, and, in effect, pledging the signatories not to resort to aggression against each other. The Locarno Pact heralded a new era in European affairs. Germany accepted an invitation to join the League of Nations, and there were good grounds for believing that the hatreds of the past war were now on the wane.

Organization of the League of Nations. The League of Nations was the first ambitious attempt in world history to create an organization designed to prevent war and to promote international conciliation. Its main organs were a Council, an Assembly, and a Secretariat. The Council was the most important body, dominated by the great powers. It dealt with most of the emergencies arising in international affairs. The Assembly served as a platform from which all League members could express their views. It could make specific recommendations to the Council on specific issues; but all important decisions required the unanimous consent of its members, and every nation represented in the Assembly had one vote.

The Secretariat represented the civil service of the League. Numbering about seven hundred, the personnel of the Secretariat constituted the first example in history of an international civil service whose loyalty was pledged to no single nation but to the interests of all nations in common. All treaties made by members of the League had to be registered with the Secretariat; its fifteen departments had charge of the matters of administrative routine arising from the mandates and dealt with questions relating to disarmament, health problems, the protection of racial minorities, and any other problems which the League was considering.

In addition to the Council, the Assembly, and the Secretariat, two other important bodies were derived from the Covenant of the League. The first was the Permanent Court of International Justice, commonly referred to as the World Court. Its main purpose was to "interpret any disputed point in international law and determine when treaty obligations had been violated." It was also competent to give advisory opinions to the Council or Assembly when asked for them. (By 1937 forty-one nations had agreed to place before the World Court most basic international disputes to which they were a party.) The second international body affiliated with the League was the International Labor Organization. Pledged "to secure and maintain fair and humane conditions of labor for men, women, and children," this organization consisted of three divisions: a general conference, a governing body, and the International Labor Office.

The League as a peace agency. The record of the League from 1919 to 1929 was one neither of dismal failure nor of complete triumph. Restrained optimism was the mood of its supporters. Its greatest handicap was the refusal of the United States to become a member. Such threats to peace as disputes between Sweden and Finland, Poland and Germany, and Britain and Turkey were resolved. When a great power defied the League, as in the case of Fascist Italy's quarrel with Greece, the organization proved impotent. Little progress was made in the field of world disarmament. On one occasion, perhaps because of its relative military weakness, Russia proposed complete disarmament to League members. This proposal did not get very far because the British delegates were suspicious of the Russian government's sincerity. When this Russian proposal was made, one of the delegates replied:

If Mr. Litvinov [the Russian member] promises not to be angry I'll narrate a fable. . . . A conference of the beasts once discussed the question of disarmament. The lion spoke first and looking at the eagle suggested the abolition of wings. The eagle turning to the bull asked for the suppression of horns. The bull in his turn regarded the tiger and demanded the elimination of claws. It remained for the bear to speak and he proposed total abolition of every means of attack and defense so that he might take them all into his loving embrace.[8]

Other League activities. While the effectiveness of the League as a peace agency is debatable, certain of its activities deserve high praise. The League supervised the exchange and repatriation of thousands of prisoners of war and saved thousands of refugees from starvation. With its assistance, Austria, Bulgaria, and Hungary obtained badly needed loans, and the League rendered valuable service in administering the region of the Saar Basin and the Free City of Danzig. The League's efforts in the fields of health, humanitarianism, and intellectual activity were especially noteworthy. The League investigated the existence of slavery in certain sections of the world, sought to control the traffic in dangerous drugs, and stood ready to offer assistance when great disasters brought suffering and destruction to any portion of the world's population. It published books and periodicals dealing with national and international problems of all kinds and broadcast important information, particularly in the field of health, from its own radio station.

Naval disarmament. While little progress in the reduction of land armaments was made in the League, more encouraging success was registered outside its jurisdiction in naval reduction. The Washington Conference (1921-1922), called by the United States, reached agreement on the relative naval strength of the major naval powers. The United States, Britain, Japan, France, and Italy not only scrapped a large number of fighting craft but also agreed to a ten-year holiday in the construction of capital ships. Subsequent conferences at Geneva (1927) and London (1930), however, made little progress in limiting smaller naval craft, such as submarines and light cruisers.

Hopeful trends on the diplomatic front. Despite some serious initial crises and problems following World War I, the years from 1925 and 1929 seemed to indicate that a new era of international cooperation had commenced. Especially promising was a treaty to outlaw war, the Kellogg-Briand Pact (1928), pioneered by France and the United States. Within four years it had been signed by sixty-two nations. But while this pact renounced war as an instrument of national policy, it contained no provisions for enforcing the agreement.

Other attempts to improve international relations included further corrections of some of the worst abuses in the World War I treaties. In the field of reparations, a new schedule of payments, known as the Young Plan, was agreed upon in 1930. The total amount to be paid was greatly scaled down. It was also agreed that Allied occupation troops would be evacuated from the Rhineland five years in advance of the time stipulated by the Treaty of Versailles. In addition to these encouraging signs, there was a strong movement for European union at the end of the 1920's. Various congresses were held, and Aristide Briand, French minister of foreign affairs, prepared a comprehensive memorandum for a European Federal Union.

With these promising events in the background the League of Nations celebrated its tenth birthday in 1929. Speaking at Oxford about the first decade of the League, General Jan Smuts of South Africa, a founder of the international organization, declared:

Looked at in its true light, in the light of the age and of the time-honoured ideas and practice of mankind, we are beholding an amazing thing— we are witnessing one of the great miracles of history. . . . The League may be a difficult scheme to work, but the significant thing is that the Great Powers have pledged themselves to work it . . . [they have] bound themselves to what amounts in effect to a consultative parliament of the world. . . . The great choice is made, the great renunciation is over, and mankind has, as it were at one bound and in the short space of ten years, jumped from the old order to the new. . . .[9]

These noble and reassuring sentiments reflected what appeared to be an encouraging trend in international affairs after 1925. But what of the course of events within the major western nations? In particular, had democratic institutions in the 1920's held their own and lived up to the great promise envisaged by leading Allied statesmen during World War I? Lamentably, in the postwar era, the forces of democracy were confronted by dynamic new rivals, ideologies born of the extreme Left (Communism) and extreme Right (Fascism and Nazism) but united in their common denial of democratic values.

DICTATORSHIP OF THE PROLETARIAT IN RUSSIA

Prelude to revolution in Russia. Tsar Nicholas II and his subjects entered World War I in a buoyant mood of enthusiasm and patriotism. The weaknesses of the Russian economy, and the inefficiency and corruption in government, were hidden for a brief period under a cloak of fervent nationalism. By the middle of 1915, however, the impact of war was demoralizing the nation. Food and fuel were in short supply, war casualties were staggering, and inflation was mounting ominously. Strikes increased among the low-paid factory workers, and the peasants, who wanted land reforms, were restive. Confronted with these danger signals, the tsar showed little leadership.

Perhaps most serious was the fact that Nicholas and his empress were strongly influenced by a small clique of corrupt adventurers, notably the scandalous Rasputin. Sojourning briefly with a monastic sect notorious for its alternation of sexual orgies with spiritual raptures, Rasputin became a sham holy man who believed that "great sins made possible great repentances."[10] Despite his moral lapses, Rasputin gained wide recognition for supposed magical powers. This charlatan obtained tragic influence over the royal family, especially the empress, by claiming that his treatment of her only son protected him from his dread affliction of hemophilia.

In 1915 the tsar left his capital to assume command of the army at the battlefront, leaving the empress to administer the affairs of state. In effect, this allowed Rasputin a free hand in manipulating the empress to his own ends. Generals and ministers were cavalierly dismissed, the work of government departments seriously impaired, and military operations endangered. In December 1916 a group of patriotic Russian nobles, dismayed by Rasputin's malevolent power, assassinated him. The "mad monk" thus passed from the scene, but by this time the Romanov regime was beyond repair.

The revolution begins. On March 3, 1917, a strike occurred in a factory in Petrograd. Within a week nearly all the workers in the city were idle, and street fighting broke out. On March 11 the tsar dismissed the Duma and ordered the strikers to return to work. These orders precipitated the revolution. The Duma refused to disband, the strikers held mass meetings in defiance of the government, and the army openly sided with the workers. A few days later a provisional government headed by the moderate liberal, Prince Lvov, was named by the Duma, and the following day the tsar abdicated. There is little evidence to indicate that there was a calculated conspiracy behind the overthrow, which has been termed "one of the most leaderless, spontaneous, anonymous revolutions of all times."[11] Thus far the revolution had been, on the whole, peaceful.

Many historians have analyzed the complex background and causes of the revolution. Undoubtedly Rasputin was an important factor, but his role has generally been overemphasized; he was a symptom, not a cause. For a century or more the whole tsarist regime had become an anachronism, completely unable and unwilling to reform itself to meet the needs of its people. As an English historian has noted: "The complex revolutionary situation of 1917 was the accumulated deposit of Russian history, detonated by the explosion of war."[12]

Dominated by liberal middle-class representatives, the Duma hoped to achieve a political but not an economic revolution. Meanwhile the Marxian socialists in Petrograd had formed a soviet (council) of workers and soldiers' deputies to provide them the representation they lacked in the Duma. Determined that a thoroughgoing change should take place in accordance with Marxist teachings, the radical soviet cooperated with the provisional government for a few months.

In July, Lvov resigned and was succeeded by Aleksandr Kerenski, who was more progressive than his predecessor but not radical enough for the Bolsheviks. While Kerenski's government marked time, the Marxist soviet in Petrograd extended its organization all over the country by setting up local soviets. The new provisional government made a serious mistake when it decided to prosecute the war and honor its commitments to the Allies. Such a policy was increasingly unpopular with the masses, who were completely disillusioned by the heavy sacrifices demanded by the war effort.

Meanwhile Lenin, the exiled Marxist, who had been living in Switzerland, was anxious to return to Russia and transform the revolution according to his Bolshevik ideas. Hoping that widespread strife and chaos would cause Russia to withdraw from the war, Berlin helped Lenin return to Petrograd. A tumultuous reception by thousands of peasants, workers, and soldiers took place as Lenin's train rolled into the station. Lenin addressed the crowd with this message:

The people need peace; the people need bread; the people need land. And they give you—war, hunger, no bread; they leave the landlords on the land. . . . We must fight for social revolution, fight to the end, till the complete victory of the proletariat. Long live the worldwide Socialist revolution.[13]

Lenin's coup d'état. After many behind-the-scenes maneuvers, the soviets seized control of the government in November 1917, and drove Kerenski and his moderate provisional government into exile. This liberal and largely middle-class regime had lacked dynamism and forcefulness and could not cope with the complete ruthlessness of Bolshevik tactics. Lenin's coup d'état was an amazing feat. With audacity, careful organization, and astute propaganda, he had placed a party with a membership estimated at 30,000 in control of a nation of more than 170,000,000 people.

Lenin did not become a national hero overnight, however. In the free elections held to form a constituent assembly to frame a constitution, he and his followers were

In what has been termed "one of the most leaderless, spontaneous, anonymous revolutions of all times," Russian workers take their grievances to the streets of Petrograd during the revolution of 1917.

chagrined to receive just under 25 percent of the votes. When the assembly, which met in January 1918, refused to become a rubber stamp of the Bolsheviks, it was dissolved by the bayonets of Lenin's troops. It was Russia's last free parliament. With the dissolution of the constituent assembly, all vestiges of bourgeois democracy in Russia were removed. Moreover, this decisive step sealed the fate of the Mensheviks. Having ended the handicap of a democratic opposition, Lenin next freed his regime from the war problem by the harsh Treaty of Brest Litovsk (1918) with Germany, although with great sacrifice of Russian territory.

The Bolshevik fight for survival. The worst was yet to come. A powerful group of counterrevolutionaries termed White Russians began to make war on the Bolsheviks. At the same time the Allied powers sent several expeditionary armies to Russia to support the anti-Leninist forces. The Allies were fearful that the Bolsheviks were in a conspiracy with the Germans because of the Treaty of Brest Litovsk; they also hoped the White Russians might renew hostilities against Germany. In the fall of 1918 the Bolshevik regime was in a perilous condition, opposed by Russia's former allies and challenged by internal foes.

To counteract this ominous emergency, a ghastly reign of terror was begun within Russia as the Red Army and the Cheka (the secret police) destroyed all enemies of the revolution as well as those who were only lukewarm in their support of the revolution. The royal family, under arrest since the outbreak of the revolution, was made to pay for all the years of cruel and inept Romanov rule. In July 1918 they were herded into a cellar and shot. By 1920 all White Russian resistance had been crushed, the foreign armies had been evacuated, and about one million White Russian anti-Communist refugees were scattered over the earth.

After the surrender of the Central Powers in November 1918, Allied intervention in Russia ceased, and the Bolsheviks were able to concentrate their energies against the White Russians. Other factors contributing to the Bolshevik victory were the fanatical, do-or-die spirit of Lenin and his followers, the resentment against foreign intervention, and the lack of appeal of the White Russian movement, which sponsored no program of land and social reform.

Lenin's contribution to Marxist thought. As we previously noted in Chapter 30 V. I. (Nikolai) Lenin had made an important contribution to Marxist theory that set the pattern by which socialism in Russia would be guided. Opposing all democratic parliamentary procedures, such as an officially recognized opposition party, he believed that the new order should be established by a revolutionary "dictatorship of the proletariat" under Bolshevik leadership. The opposition group, the Mensheviks, charged that Lenin was confusing the dictatorship *of* the proletariat with the dictatorship *over* the proletariat, while they in turn were accused of having capitulated to gradualism by adopting a revisionist program. Both groups agreed, though, that the socialist revolution could be consummated in Russia only as part of a general uprising of the proletariat throughout Europe. As we have seen, the Bolshevik-Menshevik feud continued until the Revolution of 1917.

As a Marxist, Lenin accepted the two-revolutions sequence—that is, that the proletarian-socialist revolution must be preceded by a bourgeois-democratic revolution. He interpreted the toppling of the tsarist regime in March 1917 and its replacement by a provisional government of moderates and liberals as the first democratic revolution. His coup d'état in November 1917 engineered the second or proletarian-socialist revolution. Lenin justified the dissolving of the constituent assembly on the grounds that a higher form of the democratic principle had now been achieved which rendered a constituent assembly superfluous: the proletarian-socialist revolution had vested all power in the Russian republic in the people themselves, as expressed in their revolutionary committees or soviets.

The state: theory and practice. Many orthodox Marxists believed that once the dictatorship of the proletariat had liquidated the bourgeoisie, the way would be open for the progressive disappearance of the state and the abolition of the standing army and the bureaucracy, the two most characteristic institutions of the centralized bourgeois state. While Lenin thought that the state would eventually wither away, at the same time he believed that during the dictatorship of the proletariat the latter's power must be wielded by an "iron party" (the Bolsheviks). Ironically enough, the events which transpired between his coup d'état in 1917 and his death seven years later served not to weaken but to strengthen the role of the state in Russia.

In this period occurred three major developments relating to the Communist party. (The Bolsheviks were renamed Communists in 1918.) First, all other parties were eliminated. Second, the function of the Communist party was modified. No longer charged with the overthrow of existing institutions, the party now became the controlling element within the new governmental machinery of the state; the concentration of authority and power in the party was justified as "democratic centralism." Third, within the party itself authority was consolidated in the hands of a small elite group, the Politburo, which was composed of five members with Lenin as the chairman. The second major organ of the party was the Secretariat for the Central Committee.

The state was known as the Russian Socialist Federated Soviet Republic (R.S.F.S.R.). As the power of this government grew and the anti-Bolshevik forces were repelled, the jurisdiction of the R.S.F.S.R. expanded. In 1922 the Union of Soviet Socialist Republics (U.S.S.R.) was established, consisting of four constituent socialist republics: the original R.S.F.S.R., the Ukraine, White Russia, and Transcaucasia.

The constitution, adopted in 1924, established a federal system of government based on a succession of soviets which were set up in the villages, factories, and cities and in larger regions. This pyramid of soviets in each constituent republic culminated in the All-Union Congress of Soviets, which was at the apex of the federal government. But while it appeared that the congress exercised sovereign power, this body was actually governed by the Communist party, which in turn was controlled by the Politburo. So great did the authority of the Communist party become over the formation and administration of policy that before Lenin's death in 1924 it could be said without exaggeration that party and state were one. Consequently, whoever controlled the former must be master of the latter as well.

The period of war communism. One of Lenin's central beliefs was equalitarianism. He championed the program of "from each according to his ability; to each according to his needs" and believed in the principle of "maximum income," by which no state employee would receive a salary higher than a qualified worker. Following both Marx and Engels, Lenin subscribed to the ultimate goal of large-scale collective farming and the elimination of private ownership of land.

The period from the consolidation of the Bolshevik Revolution in 1918 until 1921 is known as the period of war communism, when the Bolsheviks sought to apply undiluted Marxist principles to the Soviet economy. Banks, railroads, and shipping were nationalized; the money economy was restricted; and private property was abolished.

Strong opposition to this program soon developed. The peasants wanted cash payments for their products and resented having to surrender their surplus grain to the government. Many laborers grumbled at being conscripted to work in the factories, and former business managers showed little enthusiasm for administering enterprises for the benefit of the state. This period was also a time of civil war, when the White Russians, aided by the Allies, were attempting the overthrow of the Communist regime.

The early months of 1920 brought the most dangerous crisis yet faced by the government. The years of civil strife had left Russia in a state of confusion and disruption. Total industrial production had been reduced to 13 percent of what it had been in 1913. Added to the misery caused by wartime dislocations and the shortages caused by inept or wasteful management in the recently nationalized industries was the suffering that followed the crop failures of 1920. Famine marched over the land, bringing more than twenty million people face to face with starvation.

In the meantime serious controversy developed between Poland and Russia over their boundaries. War followed in 1920, and after defeating Russia, Poland annexed a large slice of its territory, thereby sowing the seeds of later conflict. During these turbulent years other areas of Russia were chopped off to form Finland, Estonia, Latvia, and Lithuania. While the collapse of the first Marxist state seemed imminent, Lenin remained indomitable.

The NEP. Confronted with the collapse of the nation, Lenin beat a strategic retreat in spite of strenuous opposition from his colleagues. He felt that the new regime had run into difficulties because it had been too eager to change everything at once. A return to certain practices of the capitalistic system was recommended, and the New Economic Policy, or NEP, was inaugurated.

The retreat from war communism operated from 1921 to 1928. The peasants were freed from the onerous wholesale levies of grain; after paying a fixed tax, they were allowed to sell their surplus produce in open market. Factories employing less than twenty men were returned to private management, and a graduated wage scale was granted to the workers in the state industries. Commerce was stimulated by permitting private retail trading. Although simon-pure Communists criticized the wealthy peasants or *kulaks* who benefited from the new order of things and dubbed the private businessmen "Nepmen," such compromise proved highly beneficial and the economy revived. The NEP was designed as only a temporary strategic retreat from the former outright socialist system; the state continued to be responsible for banking, transportation, heavy industry, and public utilities.

The NEP was Lenin's last outstanding achievement. In spite of broken health, Lenin worked unceasingly until his death in January 1924. His tomb in Moscow's Red Square is a Mecca for thousands of followers who come to pay homage to the creator of the first Marxist state in history.

Stalin vs. Trotsky: the politician and the intellectual. Upon the death of the one man in the party who had possessed unchallenged authority and whose decrees were binding, a struggle for power broke out, and conflicts of policy and personality appeared. Two rivals who took different sides on most issues were Trotsky and Stalin.

Leon Trotsky (1879-1940), whose real name was Bronstein, had turned to Marxism in his early youth and, like Lenin, had known exile. During the revolution Trotsky had come to the forefront. He was a magnificent orator; and by his personal magnetism and his demonic energy, he had led the Red Army to victory. During his hectic career Trotsky wrote an amazing number of brilliant and provocative articles and books. A theorist and scholar, this intellectual, professor-like leader had personal defects of arrogance and egotism which contrasted with the peasant shrewdness and cunning of his less colorful but more calculating rival.

Stalin, born Joseph Dzugashvili in 1879 in the Georgian region of Transcaucasia, was the son of a poor shoemaker. Admitted to a seminary to be trained for the priesthood, young Stalin was later expelled for radical opinions. Before the revolution he engaged in much activity in the underground and was sent into exile four times. In 1922 *Pravda* carried a brief announcement that the Central Committee had confirmed Stalin as general secretary of the Secretariat—a decision that was to have momentous consequences after Lenin's death.

Trotsky, like Lenin, believed that the U.S.S.R. could not maintain itself indefinitely as a socialist island in a capitalist ocean and that it was therefore the duty of the Russian Communists to foster revolution elsewhere. Stalin, less the theorist than the political realist, viewed Trotsky's ideas of world revolution as premature. He noted that Marxism had made little headway outside of Russia, despite the existence of what from the Marxist standpoint were the most advantageous circumstances for revolution. The impoverished and war-disillusioned workers of Germany had not turned against the bourgeoisie, while in Italy socialist opposition had been crushed by Mussolini. Stalin advocated a new policy, which was to become known as "building up socialism in a single state."

In the struggle that ensued, Trotsky had the initial advantage of being one of the chief architects of the revolution and (second to Lenin) the best known Bolshevik in the Soviet Union. With his outstanding record and his mastery of ideological analysis, Trotsky not unnaturally expected to assume Lenin's mantle of leadership. But he reckoned without the political astuteness of Stalin, who had obtained a key administrative post in the party apparatus. Quietly and systematically, Stalin proceeded to shunt his rival aside. He placed his supporters in important posts in the government, assumed the powerful chairmanship of the Politburo, and by 1927 had brought about the expulsion of Trotsky and his followers from the party. Trotsky was exiled and led a hare-and-hounds existence until 1940, when he was struck down by the ax of an assassin in Mexico, probably on Stalin's orders.

With a well-organized governmental structure and an obedient bureaucracy and with the Trotskyites either exiled or rendered powerless, Stalin was ready by 1928 to put a daring new program into operation. The NEP was to be scrapped and replaced by a Five-Year Plan, which called for a highly ambitious program of heavy industrialization and the collectivization of agriculture. In spite of breakdowns and failures, the first Five-Year Plan achieved amazing results (see Chapter 33), mainly because of the heroic sacrifices of the common people. Russia, an inert sleeping giant before 1914, now became industrialized at an unbelievable speed, far surpassing Germany's pace of industrialization in the nineteenth century and Japan's early in the twentieth.

Changes in Soviet society. While the Russian economy was being transformed, the social life of the people underwent equally drastic changes. From the beginning of the revolution, the government attempted to weaken the importance of the family. A divorce required no court procedure; and to make women completely free of the responsibilities of childbearing, abortion was made legal. The policy of "emancipating" women had the practical objective of increasing the labor market. Girls were encouraged to secure an education and pursue a career in the factory or the office. Communal nurseries were set up for the care of small children; and efforts were made to shift the center of the people's social life from the home to educational and recreational groups, the soviet clubs.

Most observers in the 1920's credited the regime with abandoning the tsarist policy of persecuting national minorities in favor of a policy of tolerance toward the more than two hundred minority groups in the Soviet Union. Another feature of the regime that received praise was the extension of medical services. Campaigns were carried out against typhus, cholera, and malaria; the number of doctors was increased as rapidly as facilities and training would permit; and death and infant mortality rates steadily decreased.

Despite the seemingly confident exhortations of Lenin during the formative years of the Marxist state, Russia experienced grave hardships during the early 1920's due to civil strife and mismanagement of the state. Here former bourgeoisie women are forced to sell their dresses in the streets of Leningrad.

Coming under heavy fire in the West, however, were the Communist policies toward education and religion. Although education was made available to millions of children, the primary purpose of the school system was to indoctrinate the pupils with Communist precepts and values. There was also widespread religious persecution. Religious leaders were sentenced to concentration camps. Members of the party were forbidden to attend divine services. The Church was shorn of its powers over education, religious teaching was prohibited except in the home, and antireligious instruction was stressed in the schools.

Foreign relations in the 1920's. During the decade and a half following the Russian Revolution, the Soviet Union was not considered a member in good standing in the family of nations. From the beginning of the revolution, relations between the western democracies and the new Soviet regime had been cool. The Communists resented the intervention of Allied troops during the civil war, which they interpreted as a calculated capitalistic attempt to crush the Marxist revolution. For their part, the Allies were aroused over the separate peace Lenin made with Germany, the seizure of foreign property in Russia, and the repudiation of all foreign debts.

Probably the greatest barrier to friendship (or at least mutual tolerance) between the West and Soviet Russia was the Third Communist International, or Comintern, organized in 1919 and dedicated to the overthrow of capitalism the world over. Specific aims of the organization were to disseminate Communist propaganda, to establish Communist parties in all the important nations of the world, and to secure control of labor unions and other working-class groups wherever possible. In the 1920's the Comintern encouraged the organization of Communist parties by radicals who had broken off from moderate socialist groups all over the world. Communists of all countries became members of the Comintern, meeting in congresses held in Moscow and setting up committees to coordinate their activities. Thus the Communist party became basically different from all national political groups;

Under Stalin, the school became the mouthpiece of the new regime, as students were taught to conform, to love their country, and to believe in the infallibility of their leaders. These Russian schoolchildren were photographed under a poster of Stalin hugging a Siberian girl.

all Communists owed their allegiance to an international organization rather than to the nations in which they resided.

Another basic aim of the Comintern was to undermine colonialism. Lenin's beliefs against imperialism had been given wide publicity by many sources. But not so well known, however, was his idea that communism would be able to conquer Europe and America once it gained control of Asia. He is reported to have stated at one time that both London and New York could be conquered on the Yangtze.

RISE OF FASCISM IN ITALY

Problems in postwar Italy. During World War I the Italian armies had been badly mauled by their enemies, and Italy emerged from the peace conference a victor with only modest gains. The First World War aggravated the weaknesses of the Italian economy.

The lira fell to a third of its prewar value, unemployment rose, and severe food shortages developed. People refused to pay their rent, strikes broke out in industrial centers, and workers seized factories. Italy's economic plight invited agitation by extremists from both Right and Left.

Mussolini and the birth of Fascism. Within four years following the armistice in Italy, five incompetent premiers came and went. The situation seemed propitious for the appearance of a strong leader on the political stage. When he appeared, he was the jutting-jawed son of a blacksmith named Mussolini, and he bore the Christian name of Benito in honor of the Mexican revolutionary hero Benito Juárez.

Born in northern Italy, Benito Mussolini (1883-1945) had grown up in left-wing circles. Although he became editor of the influential Italian socialist newspaper *Avanti (Forward)* in 1912, he was far from consistent as regards his belief in socialism and its doctrinal opposition to "capitalist" wars. When a majority in the Italian Socialist party called for neutrality in World War I, Mussolini urged intervention. The *Avanti* was taken from his control and Mussolini was expelled. Undaunted, he founded his own paper *Il Popolo d'Italia (The People of Italy)*, in which he continued to advocate Italian intervention in the war on the side of the Allies. As part of his campaign for Italian participation in the war, Mussolini organized formerly leftist youths into bands called *fasci*, a name derived from the Latin *fasces*, the bundle of rods bound about an ax which was the symbol of authority in ancient Rome. When Italy entered the war, Mussolini volunteered for the army, saw active service at the front, and was wounded. After his return to civilian life, he reorganized the *fasci* into the *fasci di combattimento* ("fighting groups") to attract war veterans. The ultimate purpose of these groups was to capture the control of the national government.

The march on Rome. In the elections of 1919 the socialists capitalized on mass unemployment and hardship to emerge as the strongest party. Although the Fascists failed to elect a single candidate to the Chamber of Deputies, they succeeded in obtaining both approval and financial aid from industrial and landowning groups fearful of the triumph of Marxist socialism in Italy. Mussolini's black-shirted toughs broke up strikes and workers' demonstrations and, by beatings and overdoses of castor oil, "persuaded" political opponents of the error of their views. The central government remained virtually impotent during these outbreaks of violence.

Elections held in May 1921 resulted in a plurality for the liberal and democratic parties. A few Communists were elected to the Chamber of Deputies, and only thirty-five Fascists, among them Mussolini. But their leader had no intention of allowing the country to achieve economic recovery and political stability by following a liberal-democratic course. In November Mussolini established the National Fascist party.

Events in 1922 conspired to favor Mussolini's bid for power. The liberal-democratic government of the day was ineffective, and the socialists were divided among themselves, while the ranks of the Fascists had been strengthened by the enrollment of thousands of disaffected bourgeoisie, cynical and opportunistic intellectuals, and depression-weary workers. The general strike called in August by the trade unions in order to arouse the country to the menace of Fascism was smashed. On October 24 a huge crowd attending a Fascist rally at Naples shouted "On to Rome!" When some fifty thousand Fascist militiamen swarmed into the capital, King Victor Emmanuel III invited Mussolini to form a new government.

Mussolini organizes the Fascist state. Mussolini's first act as prime minister was the passage in 1923 of an enabling law which gave him dictatorial powers. By this means Mussolini acquired a temporary "legal" right to govern without democratic procedure. He quickly used his newly acquired power to dissolve all other political parties and thus completely eliminate opposition to his regime. The Fascist party was now in a position to recast the entire governmental apparatus.

The Fascist state was ruled by an elite in the party, which ruthlessly crushed all free expression and banished critics of the regime to penal settlements on islands off the southern Italian coast. Censorship of the press was established, and a tribunal for defense of the state was set up to punish any individuals not conforming to Fascist practices. Thus Fascist ideology was a continuation of the antirational, elitist cult of the leader or "great men" school prominent before 1914 and exemplified by such thinkers as Nietzsche. Fascism glorified force, accepting the tenets of social Darwinism. It was above all anti-democratic.

Parliamentary institutions of the pre-Fascist era were not destroyed overnight, however. The Senate continued to exist, even though completely dominated by Fascists; the Chamber of Deputies withered on the vine until the 1930's, when it was replaced by the Chamber of Fasces and Corporations. Meanwhile, all real power in the new state had been vested in the Fascist Grand Council, headed by Mussolini. The members of the council occupied the government's ministerial posts; in fact, at one time Mussolini himself held no less than eight offices. During 1925 and 1926 the Italian cities

Peter Blume's "The Eternal City" represents a young American artist's impressions of Italy ten years after Mussolini's march on Rome. A terrifying but flimsy jack-in-the-box of a Mussolini dominates a city of apathetic people living among the ruins of the past. But out of this nightmare emerges hope for the future; in the background, people climb out of the darkness into the sunlit forum, where others are already attempting to drag their Fascist masters from their mounts.

were deprived of self-government. With all units of local and provincial government welded into a unified structure dominated from Rome, the Fascist administrative system constituted the ultracentralization of government.

In 1929 Mussolini negotiated the Lateran Treaty with representatives of the Roman Catholic Church. By the terms of this agreement, Roman Catholicism was recognized as the state religion in Italy; and Vatican City, a new state of 108 acres located in Rome itself, was declared fully sovereign and independent. In addition, the Vatican was promised sums amounting to $91 million. Thus the long-standing controversy concerning the relationship of Church and state in Italy was settled amicably.

The corporate Fascist state. There is a marked difference in economic theory between Communist and Fascist states. The Communists are determined to destroy private capital and to liquidate the managerial-capitalist class. The Fascist system, some-

times defined as state capitalism, aims to abolish the class war through cooperation between capital and labor, by the compulsion of the state if need be. In Communist theory, labor is the state itself; in Fascism, labor and capital are both instruments of the state.

Mussolini based his ideas of economics on the views of the syndicalists, a movement which believed that industrial unions should be the cells of society and that a confederation of these unions, or syndicates, should constitute the state's governing body. Syndicalism was adapted to the objectives of Fascism, creating what is called the corporate state. Economically, Italy was divided into thirteen syndicates or corporations: six were formed from the ranks of labor, an equal number represented capital or management, and a thirteenth syndicate was established for the professions. Under the control of the government these bodies were to deal with labor disputes, guarantee adequate wage scales, control prices, and supervise working conditions. Strikes by workers and lockouts by employers were prohibited.

The corporate state also included the concept of economic functionalism—that is, the representation of all major national economic segments in the political process. In 1928, for example, a law set the membership of the Chamber of Deputies at four hundred. Eight hundred candidates were to be named by worker-employer groups and two hundred by various charitable and cultural organizations. From this master list the Grand Council then selected four hundred deputies. Mussolini liked to claim that the corporate state, embodying in theory a classless economic system together with economic functionalism, was one of Fascism's greatest contributions to political theory.

Economic goals of Fascist Italy. Some of the main economic goals of Fascism were to make Italy more self-sufficient, especially in the matter of food; to increase the power resources of the nation; and to expand foreign trade. A campaign called "the battle of the wheat" increased the home yield of this grain 70 percent. Extensive marshland was reclaimed and hydroelectric power resources increased. To some extent the intention to increase Italy's natural resources was commendable, but the drive was carried on to an extreme and uneconomic degree. Mussolini's desire to attain national self-sufficiency, a policy known in international economics as autarky, was primarily motivated not by the exigencies of economics but rather by those of war. In achieving this goal, much was accomplished, though often at a ruinous cost. Many projects were launched to provide for a home supply of materials which could be obtained much more cheaply from other nations.

Fascism's glorification of the state and war. The concept of the "inevitability" of war, added to the exaltation of the state and of its "destiny," created a supernationalism whose adherents tended to interpret the right of self-determination in terms of the expansion of the Fascist state at the expense of other nations. A foretaste of Mussolini's contempt for peace and his defiance of the League of Nations soon became apparent when he humiliated Greece in 1923 by the bombardment of Corfu. Mussolini warned the world that Italy intended to expand or explode, and his encouragement of a high birth rate in conjunction with meager territorial and natural resources pointed in only one direction—imperialism.

Fascism has been defined as "the cult of state worship." In the Italian totalitarian state the individual had no significance except as a member of the state. The Fascists were taught "to believe, to obey, and to fight" *(credere, obbedire, combattere)*. Fascist ideology governed the educational system. The first sentence pronounced by children at school was "Let us salute the flag in the Roman fashion; hail to Italy; hail to Mussolini." Textbooks emphasized the glorious past of the ancient Romans, the limitations imposed upon the present inhabitants by geography and western "plutocratic" nations, and the imperial destiny that awaited Italy's future development.

Mussolini provided the trappings of greatness while he talked of acquiring the substance. The ruins of imperial Rome were revered at the same time that new, ostentatious monuments, buildings, and official sculptures were erected. All public functions and displays of the state were clothed in propaganda, from the dedication of farm land salvaged from ancient swamps to the regime's vulgar displays of military might and its gigantic sports rallies.

As in the case of other dictatorial regimes, the Fascist social program had some commendable features, such as its slum clearance, its offensive against illiteracy, its campaign against malaria, and its system of child welfare clinics. To the casual observer the country seemed rejuvenated. For example, the notoriously erratic Italian trains now ran on time. But any positive achievements were more than outweighed by such nefarious results as the deification of war, excessive armaments budgets, and the fraudulent claim of the corporate state to protect the workers while it actually benefited the large landowners and industrialists. By 1930 Italy had the lowest standard of real wages in western Europe. The basic weakness and sham of Fascism, however, would not be exposed for another decade.

WEIMAR DEMOCRACY: THE REPUBLIC THAT FAILED

Revolution in Germany. Near the close of World War I, Woodrow Wilson had made it clear that the Allies would not enter into peace negotiations with the imperial government of Hohenzollerns. By November 1918, sick of the war and its privations, the German people were ready to do anything to bring the conflict to an end. The revolution that caused the kaiser to pack his bags and escape to Holland began in the navy. News of the revolt flashed like lightning through Germany, and the authority of the old government crumbled. On the same day that the chancellor turned over his authority to Friedrich Ebert—the leader of the majority socialist party, the Social Democrats—the republic was officially proclaimed.

The collapse of the imperial government provoked vigorous disagreement over the type of administration that was to replace it. The Communists wanted a complete social revolution as well as a political revolution, while Ebert's Social Democrats favored a democratic system in which the rights of private property would be safeguarded. In December 1918 and January 1919 the moderates and the radicals clashed violently; the Communists in Berlin were scattered and their leaders murdered. In a national election held to select a constitutional convention, the parties stressing moderation were triumphant, with the Social Democrats securing the most votes. The German revolution was democratic and bourgeois.

Problems of the Weimar Republic. The new constitution was adopted in midsummer of 1919 at Weimar, famous as the residence of Germany's greatest poet, Goethe. It provided for a president, a chancellor who was responsible to the Reichstag, and national referendums. The rights of labor were guaranteed, personal liberties were safeguarded, and compulsory education was planned for everyone up to the age of eighteen.

Parliamentary government in the Weimar Republic exhibited certain basic weaknesses, however. The principle of proportional rep-

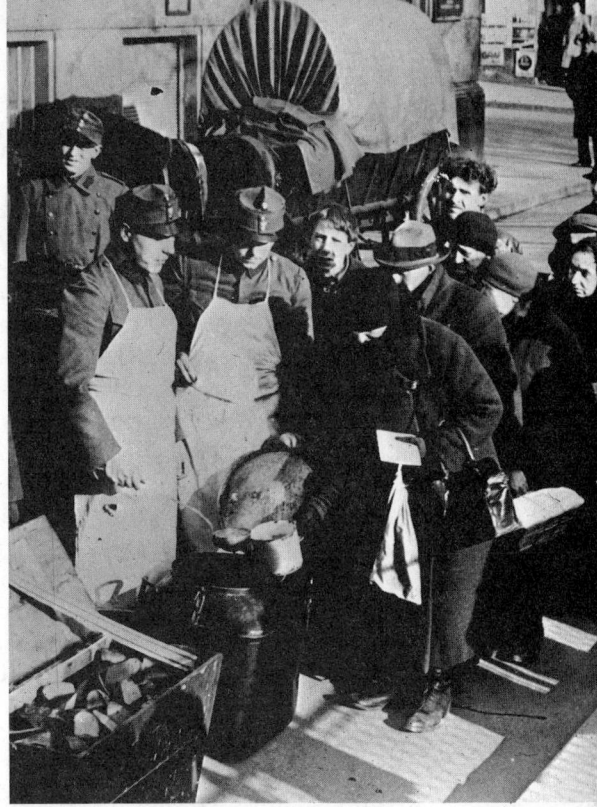

During the years of the Weimar Republic inflation destroyed the financial foundations of the German middle class, and continued economic depression gave added impetus to Hitler's rise in popularity. If formerly prosperous people were forced to stand in line for bread, they were also prone to listen to Hitler's promise of a higher standard of living.

resentation was carried so far that innumerable separate parties arose, and only the formation of coalitions enabled the government to function. Frequently unable to muster sufficient votes among a multiplicity of parties, the government was tempted to employ a constitutional provision that enabled the president to enact measures by decree in the event of disorder. By weakening the legislative process, such actions were bound to help discredit the parliamentary government in Germany.

In spite of difficulties and the opposition of Communists and monarchists, the Weimar Republic restored political stability to Germany and surmounted serious financial problems. (See Chapter 37 for its cultural accomplishments.) In 1923, when French and Belgian troops occupied the Ruhr, the wild inflation of the mark wiped out savings, especially of the middle class, and political moderates gradually lost their influence to ultranationalists and reactionaries. But after the French withdrew and the Dawes Plan enabled Germany to meet its schedule of reparation payments and to obtain large loans from abroad, the German economy took a turn for the better, and from 1925 to 1929 Germany enjoyed economic prosperity. Large public works projects were undertaken, industry was expanded, and Germany became the second largest industrial nation in the world. But disturbing forces were at work.

Factors favoring the growth of dictatorship. Germany in the late 1920's was a compound of numerous ingredients, many of which had been in existence for at least a century. With Prussia as their model, such men as Hegel and Treitschke had exalted the state at the expense of the individual; and the government of the kaisers had fostered despotism. Lack of experience in democratic government made the success of the Weimar Republic doubtful from the start. There were too many political parties; the army, which had never reconciled itself to the abolition of the empire, was not brought under effective civilian control; and the republic was too complacent and did not take the drastic measures essential to destroy the enemies of democracy. In short, "German democracy was utterly fair, legalistic, but not militant."[14]

Other difficulties threatening the new government stemmed from the resentments and frustrations engendered among the people by defeat in war. The powerful Prussian militaristic clique fanned the flames of discontent by fostering the legend that the German army had not been defeated on the field of battle but had been stabbed in the back by pacifist liberals and "decadent" democrats on the home front. The legend of the betrayal of the Fatherland was to be increasingly the refrain of those who came to favor Nazi militarism. The resurgence of strong feelings of nationalism was evidenced by the election to the presidency in 1925 of Field Marshal von Hindenburg, a stalwart Junker and hero of World War I.

The Treaty of Versailles embittered many Germans, and its use by the French to justify the invasion of the Ruhr sowed further seeds of hate. The so-called war guilt clause of the treaty, by which the Germans were forced to proclaim sole responsibilty for starting the war—which most impartial historians have been unable to assign to any single nation— was particularly rankling.

The ultranationalists made effective appeals to the industrialists and landowners, who were convinced that the republic could not effectively discourage the internal threat of communism. As a result of the war and the postwar inflation, professional people, white-collar workers, and skilled tradesmen feared the prospect of being dragged down to the level of the masses. Especially after the debacle of inflation, a deep sense of despair and futility fell upon the people. Blaming their elders for the catastrophe of 1918 and the humiliations that followed, German youth repudiated the past and sought a cause to redeem the Fatherland. They were vulnerable to the blandishments of any spellbinding would-be dictator.

Hitler's rise to prominence. The creator and high priest of German fascism was Adolf Hitler (1889-1945), the son of a minor customs official in Austria. An orphan at the age of seventeen, Hitler went to Vienna in 1908 hoping to become an architect or artist. While in the Austrian capital, he read pamphlets written by racists and proto-Fascists who championed such ideas as the leader concept and social Darwinism and became interested in Marxist socialism and Pan-Germanism. He experienced dire poverty in Vienna and a few years later moved to Munich, where he earned a scanty living by selling drawings.

When war broke out, Hitler joined a German regiment and was sent to France. The armistice of 1918 found him in a hospital. He said later that news of Germany's defeat caused him to turn his face to the wall and weep bitterly. Following his return from the war front, Hitler was hired by the authorities in Munich as a special agent to investigate Communist and other extremist movements. In the line of duty he was asked to check on a small organization called the German Worker's party. Hitler joined this group, whose fervently nationalistic doctrine was at once antidemocratic, anticapitalist, anti-Communist and anti-Semitic.

Before long the movement took the name

"National Socialist German Workers' party," and the words "National Socialist" (*Nationalsozialistische*) became abbreviated to "Nazi." In 1920 the party obtained a newspaper as a mouthpiece; soon thereafter the first of the paramilitary organizations, Storm Troops, or SA, was organized. Adopted as the emblem of the party was the swastika set against a red background signifying the community of German blood.

Hitler was now becoming better known. His remarkable oratorical gifts began to attract large crowds in Munich. With a kind of mystical exaltation, this charismatic leader had the uncanny ability to arouse and move mass audiences with his bombastic, passionate oratory. Likened to a "human phonograph," he has been termed the "greatest demagogue in history." Sometimes he would hire a dozen beer halls and dash from one to the other in an automobile, delivering fiery harangues at each. His initial political program called for land reform, the nationalization of trusts, abolition of all unearned incomes, and—in the field of foreign relations—a greater Germany to include all German-speaking peoples in Europe, the abrogation of the Versailles Treaty, and the restitution of Germany's prewar colonies. In 1923 Hitler staged his *Putsch*, or revolt, in Munich; coming prematurely, it failed, and he was sent to prison.

Mein Kampf. Before his release from prison in 1925, Hitler began to write *Mein Kampf (My Battle)*, at once an autobiography and a long-winded exposition of Nazi philosophy and objectives. In this work Hitler contends that history is fashioned by great races, of which the Aryan is the finest; that the noblest Aryans are the German people, who are destined to rule the world; that the Jews are the archcriminals of all time; that democracy is decadent and communism criminal; that foreign expansion into the Russian Ukraine and the destruction of Germany's prime enemy France are rightful courses for the German people; and that war and force are the proper instruments of the "strong." Again and again his sentences drip with acid as he fulminates against the Jews, Russia, and France. With his irrational creed and his ritualistic gestures, badges,

and uniforms, Hitler would one day surpass his predecessor Mussolini in Italy by becoming *Führer* (leader) of a new Germany based on despotism and terror.

DISILLUSIONMENT IN THE DEMOCRACIES

Democracy on the defensive. "In this autumn of 1919, in which I write, we are at the dead season of our fortunes. The reaction from the exertions, the fears, and the sufferings of the past five years is at its height. Our power of feeling or caring beyond the immediate questions of our own material well-being is temporarily eclipsed. The greatest events outside our own direct experience and the most dreadful anticipations cannot move us. . . . We have been moved already beyond endurance, and need rest."[15] Thus wrote the famed English economist John Maynard Keynes; his mood of apathy, disillusionment, and despair was shared by many people in the West.

The postwar period witnessed an inevitable reaction against wartime controls. In the English-speaking democracies, which were the chief bastions of laissez-faire economics, governmental controls were thrown off with all possible speed. The slogan "back to normalcy" in the United Stated indicated a desire to return to prewar economic habits and creeds. And halted throughout most of the democratic-capitalist world were the strong prewar movements to advance social welfare legislation and to regulate traditional laissez-faire economics. An unhealthy inertia resulted in the suspension of badly needed socioeconomic reforms.

The national mood and psychology prevailing in the democracies, whether long-established or newly created, differed basically from the mood and psychology in the rising dictatorships. The democracies drifted into listlessness and futility, while the totalitarian states exhibited resolution, dynamism, and purpose, even though of a ruthless variety. Hence the history of nations such as Britain and France was not so colorful and fascinating as that of the new dicator-

The coal mining regions of South Wales suffered severely during Britain's economic decline in the 1920's. Hampered by poor organization, old machinery, and inefficient methods, the coal industry was hard pressed to give either employment or compensation to the protesting miners.

ships. The attributes of democracy—tolerance, government by consensus, and protracted action—often seem rather unexciting. Furthermore, during the postwar period the democracies had no burning sense of national injustice as did Germany and, to some extent, Italy. After their herculean efforts for victory, they suffered a kind of national weariness. Because victory had not solved deep-seated problems, there was a feeling of disillusionment in western Europe. The inability of the democracies to measure up to the needs of the time gave the 1920's its characteristic mood and quality.

Unstable coalition governments in France. More than one million Frenchmen had been killed and some 13,000 square miles of French territory laid waste in the holocaust of World War I. Years later the nation would still feel the heavy loss of manpower and the economic devastation of a war that had been fought largely on French soil. While a commendable record was achieved in foreign affairs, especially the rapprochement with Germany, in internal affairs the country was plagued with inflation endangering the franc

and a spurious prosperity. In addition, parliamentary government was hindered by a multiparty system and by the brief tenure of unstable ministries. In sum, the story of the Third French Republic in the 1920's is a mixed plot of progress and setbacks, of successes and failures. Fundamentally, a national spirit and a sense of purpose were lacking. The war had sapped the vigor of the French nation, and the unhealthiness and lack of dynamism characteristic of the postwar mood were evident.

Evolutionary socialism comes to Britain. The 1920's were not a tranquil period for Britain. During these dismal years unemployment and bitter labor disputes disrupted the nation. In 1924 Ramsay MacDonald became Britain's first Labourite prime minister. The goal of the Labour party was to introduce socialism slowly and within a democratic framework. During four years of power the Labour government registered some successes in foreign affairs but at home generated little dynamism in solving Britain's critical economic problems. Following MacDonald's defeat at the polls in October 1924,

Britain was for the next five years led by a Conservative government under Stanley Baldwin, who was even less successful than his predecessor in providing vigorous leadership. Thus the decade following victory in 1918 saw an absence of forward-looking programs of economic development and reform and a seeming inability to measure up to the demands of a difficult new age. To many young English people, unemployed and maintained on a government pittance, the postwar period was aptly symbolized by a popular play of the time—*Love on the Dole.*

Change and ferment in the British empire. During this period serious tensions, mainly demands for home rule, were emerging in various parts of the British empire, mainly in India, Ceylon, Burma, and Egypt. An ominous trend was the growing antagonism between the Arab inhabitants of mandated Palestine and the Jewish Zionist immigrants (see Chapter 32). Happier developments were the attainment of home rule by the Irish Free State (the southern part of Ireland) in 1921 and Britain's recognition in 1931, in the Statute of Westminster, of a new national status for the dominions (Canada, Australia, New Zealand, and South Africa). Henceforth, the dominions and Great Britain were held together only by loyalty to the crown and by a common language, legal principles, tradition, and economic interests. Collectively these states were now known as the British Commonwealth of Nations.

Developments elsewhere in Europe. What had happened to the countries of southern Europe—Austria, Hungary, Bulgaria—which had been on the losing side in the war? For ten years after its creation, the new ministate of Austria wrestled with widespread unemployment, substantial opposition to its republican government, and the specter of bankruptcy. Little need be said about the depressing history of Hungary and Bulgaria. It immediately became evident in both these states that democracy did not have the slightest chance of taking firm root. Reactionary cliques blocked urgent reforms, anti-Semitism flourished, and Fascism attracted numerous adherents. Authoritarian regimes were the general rule in Europe by the early 1930's.

What were the chances for democracy in the states of Europe which had been created from the debris of the Austro-Hungarian empire and had never known democratic traditions? Among the most important of the succession states was Czechoslovakia. Four hundred years of Austrian rule had not diminished the patriotic zeal of the Czechs, and in November 1918, after the collapse of Austria, they joined with the Slovaks in establishing a republic, with Thomas Masaryk as president and Eduard Beneš as foreign minister. In addition to Czechs and Slovaks, the new republic included such minority groups as Germans in the Sudeten area, Ukrainians (Ruthenians), and Hungarians, constituting one third of the total population of fifteen million. Despite some tensions among these minorities, Czechoslovakia prospered, a large foreign trade was built up, and the government assisted small farmers by breaking up large estates. The people demonstrated that they were industrious and conscientious citizens. The country gave every indication of growing into a healthy democracy. Unlike Czechoslovakia, the neighboring succession states—Poland, Rumania, Yugoslavia—were the scenes of political instability, exploitation of the masses, and violence culminating in dictatorship.

In Finland and the Scandinavian countries (Norway, Sweden, and Denmark) representative government operated smoothly and economic prosperity was the general rule. During the 1920's democratic institutions together with relatively high living standards were also enjoyed in Switzerland, the Netherlands, and Belgium.

Prospects for democracy and enlightened rule were not so promising in the Iberian peninsula, where military and aristocratic privilege were still strongly in vogue, and where the peasants continued to live a drab and often miserable existence. In the 1920's the republic of Portugal was plagued by political instability. In 1928 Dr. Oliveira Salazar, a professor of economics, became the minister of finance and, in 1932, the leading figure in an outright dictatorship. He exercised his power unobtrusively, perhaps as befitted a professorial dictator. Spain witnessed the creation of a dictatorship in 1923, growing mass discontent, and the end of the monarchy with the declaration of a republic in 1931. At a time when many other countries were turning to dictatorship, it was heartening to witness the triumph of democracy in Spain. This triumph, however, was to be short-lived (see Chapter 33).

Growth of democratic ideals in Latin America. Across the seas in the lands to which Iberian culture had been transplanted, various nations were beginning to tackle their economic problems and were trying to make their governments democracies in more than name.

The huge wartime demands for Latin American products resulted in an economic boom; and though the end of the war brought about a familiar situation—a crisis in the economy—business expansion began again in the 1920's. However, a crucial weakness remained—the dependence of the economies of Latin America's twenty republics upon only a few products or, in some cases, upon a single product. Thus Brazil's prosperity depended on the world coffee market, which absorbed half its exports. Cuba depended on sugar; Bolivia, tin; Mexico, oil and silver; Venezuela, oil; Argentina, meat and wheat. Various Central American "banana republics" were equally dependent on the sale of bananas. Another weak spot was the land problem. On many large estates conditions resembled medieval serfdom. Because the Church was a great landowner, certain churchmen combined with the landed interests to oppose land reforms.

During the 1920's the movement for social reform in Latin America was spearheaded by Mexico, which came under a series of administrations, all claiming to be heir to the revolutionary spirit of the revolt of 1910. The government sought to exercise increasing control over the vast oil properties run by foreign investors; and the agrarian problem was partially solved at the expense of large landowners. These changes were accompanied by a wave of anticlericalism. Much Church property was seized, many churches were destroyed, and the priesthood had to go underground for a time.

Conditions in Mexico exerted a strong influence on other Latin American countries, and between 1919 and 1929 seven nations adopted new, liberal constitutions. In addition, there were growing demands for better economic and social opportunities, for a breakdown of the barriers that divided the few extremely rich from the many abysmally poor, and for improvements in health, education, and the status of women. Above all, there was an increasing desire for more stable political conditions.

Era of normalcy and big business in the United States. By 1919 wartime industrial expansion had won for the United States the supreme position in industrial equipment and wealth among the family of nations. Moreover, the nation had been transformed from a debtor nation to the world's greatest creditor. But while other nations increasingly looked to it for leadership, the United States turned away from the international scene. The wartime democratic idealism of President Wilson was shelved, the League of Nations was ignored, and isolationism triumphed over internationalism.

Internally, industrial strife and a wave of intolerance directed against immigrants, Catholics, Jews, and the League of Nations marked the postwar years. One important event was the ratification of the Eighteenth Amendment prohibiting the sale and possession of intoxicating liquors. However laudable its purpose, the law was broken by great numbers of citizens, and it strengthened the "bootleg" underworld and led to widespread violence and corruption.

In 1921 the inauguration of Warren G. Harding (1865-1923) as president on the platform of a "return to normalcy" ushered in a decade of Republican dominance. It soon became apparent that by "normalcy" the Harding administration meant resistance to pressure for such progressive measures as low tariffs and antitrust prosecutions. In foreign affairs the new president was bent upon isolationism and the repudiation of the League of Nations. In fact, the American ambassador in London was "instructed to inform the League's authorities that as the United States had not joined the League she was not in a position to answer letters from it."[16] Harding died suddenly in 1923, on the eve of the exposure of widespread corruption in his administration. The worst scandal concerned the leasing of government oil reserves at Teapot Dome, Wyoming, to private operators for $400,000.

Harding's vice president and successor, Calvin Coolidge (1872-1933), advocated high tariffs and reduction of taxes. His credo was summed up in these words: "The business of the United States is business." The Democrats tried in vain to raise the issue of corruption so rampant during Harding's regime, but under the glow of rising prosperity the voters in the 1924 presidential elections decided to "keep cool with Cal" and the Republicans won easily.

Little outstanding legislation was enacted during the second Coolidge administration. A difficult problem was agriculture. Although farm income continued to decline while the fixed payments for debts contracted during agriculture's wartime expansion had to be kept up, bills to ease the farmers' plight were repeatedly vetoed by Coolidge. Other segments of the national economy enjoyed what appeared to be dazzling prosperity in 1927 and 1928. Growing quantities of autos, radios, and refrigerators were purchased either with cash or, increasingly, on the installment plan. Stock speculation became a virtual mania. The stock market, mass production, high tariffs, large foreign loans, and installment buying—all seemed to be working together in harmony. These years marked the high tide of American big business and economic self-satisfaction.

In the 1928 presidential elections, Herbert Hoover (1874-1964), a successful mining engineer who had directed Belgian relief during the war, had as his Democratic opponent the governor of New York, Alfred E. Smith. A product of the "sidewalks of New York" and the first Catholic to obtain the presidential nomination, Smith as governor had sponsored progressive social legislation. In the election campaign he called for the repeal of prohibition because of the problems to which it had given rise, but Hoover won the the day on what one historian termed "prosperity, prohibition, and prejudice." When Hoover took office in 1929, he was supported by a Republican Congress and a nation enjoying unbounded industrial prosperity.

In retrospect the 1920's did little to enhance the national image and luster of the United States. After championing the first ambitious attempt to create an effective international organization, the League of Nations, the United States retreated into the comfortable cocoon of insular isolationism. Basic domestic issues were generally merely trifled with or ignored, and party dialogue in politics was seldom inspiring or informative. But most of the country enjoyed frenetic prosperity, whose unhealthy foundations were destined to crumble in the early 1930's.

SUMMARY

During the First World War various statesmen had uttered eloquent statements promising mankind a "world safe for democracy" and one progressively free of war. This anticipation was soon revealed as naively optimistic at the peace conference in Paris. Negotiations exposed the same old national rivalries and chauvinistic ambitions. The peace treaties, therefore, were neither fish nor fowl; they incorporated both the victor's traditional attitude of humiliating the vanquished and the concepts of a new international morality symbolized by the League of Nations.

Understandably the first five years after 1919 witnessed little but confusion and strife. The Germans balked at paying reparations, the French invaded the Ruhr, and numerous nations were agitated by civil strife and tensions with their neighbors. From 1925 to 1929, however, the feuds and discontent began to subside, giving way to peace and rising prosperity. The League of Nations registered encouraging, if not spectacular, progress.

While the western nations in the 1920's were striving to normalize and stabilize relations *between* themselves, significant developments were taking place *within* these various states. In the three great democracies —the United States, Great Britain, and France—this was in many ways a period of opportunities lost and important challenges ignored. The United States turned to isolationism, refusing to accept membership in the League of Nations, and at the same time engaged in a hectic economic boom compounded of stock market speculation, mass production, and the new installment buying. Britain "muddled" along prosaically with its traditional parliamentary institutions, even though they failed to cope adequately with the country's ills. France, under the Third Republic, presented a confusing spectacle of unstable and short-lived governments.

This chapter has emphasized the new totalitarian, antidemocratic systems because, unfortunately, in the postwar era they seemed the most vital and dynamic countries, destined to direct the course of history, no matter how tragic it was to be. A Communist, Marxist regime—both antidemocratic and anticapitalistic as well as implacably opposed to organized religion—was established in Russia over the debris of a discredited tsarist monarchy. The driving force behind this achievement was the audacity and leader-ship of Lenin. This founder's mission was further advanced in the late 1920's by Stalin, who inaugurated a ruthless program of industrialization. Another antidemocratic system was initiated in Italy by its high priest and leader, Benito Mussolini. Defined as the "cult of state worship," Italian Fascism glorified war and called for the rule of one party, which manipulated all economic power by means of the corporate state. Defeated Germany had entered the 1920's with a new government, the democratic Weimar Republic. Political inexperience, however, augmented by heavy economic burdens and a festering feeling of injustice spawned by the Versailles peace treaty, combined to discredit the government. Dispirited and frustrated, Germans began to turn to Adolf Hitler and his ultranationalist and racist movement of Nazism. This fanatic and his followers were intent upon destroying the established order and rectifying the "injustices" of Versailles.

SUGGESTIONS FOR READING

Stewart Hughes, **Contemporary Europe,** 4th ed. (Prentice-Hall, 1976) is an analysis of the happenings in the world since 1914. See also G. M. Gathorne-Hardy, **A Short History of International Affairs, 1920-1939** (Oxford); J. M. Keynes, **The Economic Consequences of the Peace*** (Torchbooks); H. U. Faulkner, **From Versailles to the New Deal,** Vol. 51 in **Chronicles of America** (U.S. Pubs.); and W. E. Leuchtenburg, **The Perils of Prosperity, 1914-1932** (Univ. of Chicago). A good account is Elmer Bendiner, **A Time for Angels: The Tragicomic History of the League of Nations** (Knopf, 1975).

E. Golob, **Isms: A History and Evaluation** (Books for Libs.) is a useful introduction to modern political and economic ideologies. See also C. J. Friedrich and Z. Brzezinski, **Totalitarian Dictatorship and Autocracy*** (Praeger); and H. Arendt, **The Origins of Totalitarianism*** (Harcourt Brace Jovanovich, 1973).

H. Seton-Watson, **From Lenin to Khrushchev*** (Praeger) is a history of the Communist movement in the twentieth century. The most useful single volume on Russian history in this century is D. Treadgold, **Twentieth-Century Russia** (Rand McNally, 1964). For the standard balanced history of the subject see W. H. Chamberlain, **The Russian Revolution, 1917-1921,*** 2 vols. (Grosset & Dunlap); and Adam B. Ulam, **In the Name of the People** (Viking, 1977). See also J. Reshetar, Jr., **A Concise History of the Communist Party of the Soviet Union*** (Praeger); and G. F. Kennan, **Russia and the West under Lenin and Stalin*** (Mentor).

S. W. Halperin, **Germany Tried Democracy*** (Norton) is the best short history of the Weimar Republic. For an insightful look at Versailles and the Weimar Republic see Richard M. Watt, **The Kings Depart: The Tragedy of Germany*** (Simon & Schuster); and W. Laqueur, **Weimar: A Cultural History** (Putnam, 1975). This should be supplemented by David Childs, **Germany Since 1918*** (Torchbooks); and G. Hilger and A. G. Meyer, **The Incompatible Allies: German-Soviet Relations, 1918-1941** (Hafner, 1971).

Three excellent critiques of Italian Fascism are A. Rossi, **The Rise of Italian Fascism** (Gordon Pr.); L. Fermi, **Mussolini*** (Phoenix); and E. Wiskemann, **Fascism and Italy,*** 2nd ed. (St. Martin's).

C. L. Mowat, **Britain Between the Wars, 1918-1940** (Univ. of Chicago) is an excellent treatment of the period. For a disquieting analysis of Britain's foreign policy up to the eve of Munich see R. W. Seton-Watson, **Britain and the Dictators** (Fertig, 1968). C. Barnett, **The Collapse of British Power** (Morrow, 1972) is a revisionist analysis of decline from 1914-1940. Interesting reading is Frances Donaldson, **Edward the Eighth*** (Ballantine, 1976).

Important works on individual states in the international scene are C. Macartney, **Hungary and Her Successors** (Aldine); M. Childs, **Sweden: The Middle Way*** (Yale); S. H. Thomson, **Czechoslovakia in European History** (Shoe String); O. Halecki, **History of Poland** (McKay, 1976); and L. Hanke, **Modern Latin America,*** 2 vols. (Anvil).

*Indicates a less expensive paperbound edition.

CHAPTER 32

Africa, the Middle East,
and India: 1914-1939;
China and Japan:
1914-1930;
Southeast Asia: 1914-1939

Africa and Asia Astir

INTRODUCTION. By the first decade of the twentieth century, after fifty years of aggressive expansion, the dynamic, highly industrialized, militarily invincible western powers had Europeanized much of the world. Both the powers themselves and the territories over which they gained control derived numerous benefits from this march of imperialism. Evils as well as benefits resulted from imperialistic control, however; sometimes the western powers brought enlightened rule, but all too often native peoples had to pay a heavy price—ruthless economic exploitation, racial discrimination, and harsh administrative controls—for whatever advantages they received.

The most significant achievement of imperialism was its transmission of revolutionary western political and social ideas to undeveloped societies. The explosive ideas of democracy, parliamentary government, and nationalism, in association with western science and technology, reawakened and revitalized the societies of the nonwestern world with their hundreds of millions of people. After World War I colonialism was never quite the same. The colonial peoples had heard and seen too much for them ever again to give the white man unquestioning obedience. Yet while the influence of World War I was revealed in the growth of nationalism in India and China and among the Arabs of the Middle East, the activities of many nationalist programs and anti-imperialist movements remained tentative and secret, attracting little attention. But over the years the forces of liberation gathered their strength; and with the impact of World War II, they exploded into action.

After the First World War a chapter in modern world history—the dominance of the West—began to draw to a close. In an-cient and medieval times—before Europe's amazing advances in knowledge, wealth, and power—East and West were in rough balance. After the Renaissance, the scientific and industrial revolutions, and the spread of democracy and nationalism, the West took a commanding lead. Springing from this imbalance, western imperialism should perhaps be regarded as an inevitable development. But the colonial system and the West's power monopoly could not last; from its height in 1919, western superiority went into a rapid decline, and by the 1930's it was becoming apparent that fundamental changes were taking place in the nonwestern world. We shall see how the tempo of these changes increased until the ferment in Africa and Asia created a critical challenge for the statesmen of the contemporary world.

NEW FORCES IN AFRICA

Pan-Africanism and Negro nationalism. In Africa opposition to imperialism grew during the war years, as democracy and self-determination of nations were so widely publicized by President Wilson. American Negro leaders demanded greater recognition of Negro rights, particularly in Africa. Dr. W. E. B. Du Bois (1868-1963), editor of the influential newspaper *Crisis*, believed that the Paris Peace Conference should help form an internationalized, free Africa. He proposed the nucleus for a state of some twenty million people, guided by an international organization. At the war's end, Du Bois and other American Negro leaders journeyed to Paris in order to present their ideas in person to the delegates at the peace conference. While in Paris, Du Bois was instrumental in convening a Pan-African Congress with representatives from fifteen countries; the gathering urged that the former German colonies be placed under an international agency, not under the rule of one of the victorious colonial powers such as Britain.

Complementing the sentiments expressed at the Pan-African Congress were the ideals of Negro nationalism. In a convention held in New York in 1920, the members issued the Declaration of Rights of the Negro Peoples of the World, a document which went on record against race discrimination in the United States and the "inhuman, unchristian, and uncivilized treatment" of the African in colonial empires.

The mandate system in Africa. As a result of the Pan-African movement—coupled with a growing liberal sentiment in various nations, especially Britain—all territories conquered by the Allies in World War I were declared to be mandates. Article XXII of the League Covenant stated that the "well-being and development" of backward colonial lands was a "sacred trust of civilization." In essence, the mandate system was a compromise between annexation of the spoils of war by the victors and establishment of an international trusteeship. Parts of the Cameroons, Togoland, and German East Africa (Tanganyika) went to Great Britain. The remaining portions of the Cameroons and Togoland became French mandates. Belgium received the mandate of Ruanda-Urundi (also a part of German East Africa), while the former German colony of Southwest Africa was allotted to the Union of South Africa.

Annual reports from the governments administering the mandates were subject to the scrutiny and evaluation of the Permanent Mandates Commission. While the commission had no effective power to rectify unsatisfactory conditions in a mandate, it could place the matter before the eyes of the world. On numerous occasions the suggestions and criticisms of the commission were heeded by the mandatory powers.

Judgments of the mandate system, a radically new concept in colonial administration, have differed widely. To many critics, international supervision was a unique invasion of national sovereignty. To others, the Permanent Mandates Commission did not have enough power, especially the right to send its own observers into the mandated areas.

Growth of African studies. Closely connected with Pan-Africanism and Negro nationalism was the movement among black intellectuals to rediscover the African past, to prove that Africa had known days of glory. One American writer maintained that the stirring cultural forces which had brought about the Renaissance in Europe had originated in Africa. He also declared that prior to the fifteenth century the cultural level in West Africa was equivalent to that in Europe.[1]

While this propaganda stemming from enthusiastic Negro nationalistic feelings was appearing, a more promising development was also taking place—a rising interest in African life and culture among some anthropologists, missionaries, and learned societies. Up to this time relatively little information was available concerning the religious systems, tribal organization, and agriculture of sub-Saharan Africa. Students of social anthropology, a new branch of the social sciences, undertook field trips to Africa; their findings made it clear that the backwardness of the African native was attributable in large part to disease and isolation. In 1926 the International Institute of African Languages and Cultures was organized. It was claimed with some justification that the project opened up a new era of international cooperation in the service of Africa. As an indication of the rising interest in this area,

new departments in the field of African studies were set up in various European universities, and a small number of Africanists began to be trained in the United States.

Impact of western colonial rule. The two decades following World War I witnessed the first massive and pervasive impact of European culture upon the African, which, to some degree, penetrated to all parts of the continent. While in some isolated bush areas tribesmen lived in Neolithic isolation, in the new cities many Africans led lives almost wholly European, at least in externals. Under colonial rule Africans now had to obey the laws and regulations of white administrators as well as those of their tribal councils and chiefs. To pay for better roads, public buildings, health and agricultural departments, taxes now had to be paid in cash, forcing many Africans to seek employment outside of their tribal areas in the towns, in the mines, in menial domestic or government service or on plantations run by Europeans. Habits of living changed, new modes of dress were adopted, new farming methods designed to produce cash crops were introduced, and a desire to buy enticing imported goods developed.

Contact with European modes of life rapidly undermined old faiths, customs, tribal loyalties, and social institutions—a process known as detribalization. But the African as yet belonged exclusively neither to his old tribal world nor to that of the white man. No longer bound by his tribe's laws, he was uneasy about the courts and the law of the Europeans; while accepting Christian doctrines, he secretly believed in the powers of his tribal deities. No matter what the benefits of imperial rule might be, it was paternal at its best and exploitive at its worst. Perhaps it was necessary and indeed desirable that Africa be brought into the mainstream of world forces; but it was a profoundly disrupting experience.

While colonial systems of administration varied, few Africans, outside of their tribal affairs, were allowed to participate in the important organs of colonial government. In British and French colonies a modicum of training in self-government was available to a small minority. Thus in 1922 in British

Nigeria, one of the most advanced colonies for African political participation, the Legislative Council of forty-six members included ten Africans, four of whom were elected. These were the first elected Africans in the legislatures of British tropical Africa.

New African leadership. The most significant consequence of colonial acculturation was the creation of a small nucleus of African intellectuals. Educational opportunities were generally meager. The great mass of Africans never attended school, and only an infinitesimal fraction was able to secure the equivalent of a high school education. But a few ambitious and competent young men did so manage and then continued advanced studies abroad, mainly in Britain, the United States, and France. It was largely from their ranks that the future leaders of independent Africa were recruited.

One of the first of these young students was Jomo Kenyatta, of the Kikuyu tribe, born in 1903 in what is now the independent state of Kenya and educated in a Scottish mission. Kenyatta became active in politics in the

In the rich gold mines of the Witwatersrand ("ridge of white waters") in Southern Transvaal, white laborers held relatively high-paying, skilled jobs, while native workers performed grueling tasks for miserable wages. Before the installation of modern air cooling, Africans endured temperatures of more than 100 degrees as they drilled the veins in cramped tunnels often more than a mile and a half below the surface of the earth.

early 1920's, and a pioneer nationalist, he published an African newspaper to disseminate his views. In 1929 he was a member of a delegation sent by the Kikuyu tribe to present a petition to the British Colonial Office regarding certain grievances. In 1931 he went to England again. After attending a small college and teaching Africans phonetics, Kenyatta studied anthropology at the London School of Economics. As a result he wrote a significant study, *Facing Mount Kenya*, which emphasized the disintegration of African tribal life following European colonial control. Kenyatta did not return to East Africa until 1946, and during his long sojourn abroad he traveled extensively in Europe and for a brief period attended Moscow University. After World War II Kenyatta became one of the most important and controversial African national leaders.

One of the earliest and most prominent young Africans to study abroad was Léopold Sédar Senghor. Born in 1916 in the French West African colony of Senegal, of a prosperous family, he attended a Catholic mission and then passed brilliantly from the *lycée* in Dakar. He pursued further studies in Paris, becoming the first African qualified to teach in a *lycée*. Senghor taught in several advanced institutions in France and carried on special studies in African cultures at the Sorbonne. In 1939, with the outbreak of war, he joined the French army. Taken prisoner, Senghor was approached by his German captors to desert the French cause, but he spurned these blandishments.

Senghor became one of the best educated African leaders. In the 1930's the young Senegalese's writings began to stress the beauty and complexity of African art, music, and psyche. Widely known as a gifted poet, Senghor exerted a strong influence upon the African intellectual revival after World War II. Interestingly he is a symbol of the psychological ambivalence often noted among African intellectuals. Married to a French lady, he probably is more at home in Paris than in Dakar. A master stylist in French, an ardent admirer of France and its contributions to world culture, Senghor yet belongs to the world of his ancestors. He became a vigorous champion of the traditions of his people and of the positive features of their indigenous culture.

Additional young Africans who studied abroad and became acquainted with western ideology could be mentioned, such as Kwame Nkrumah, from the Gold Coast (now Ghana), and Dr. Benjamin Azikiwe, from Nigeria. Both these students, who were later prominent in the new Africa, attended American universities. With these educational advantages they developed a renewed confidence in the destiny of Africa and a burning desire to have a part in ending colonial control. Thus, ironically, imperialism provided the essential dynamic for its eventual overthrow.

Segregation in the Union of South Africa. The most explosive area in the period between the First and Second World Wars was the Union of South Africa. Here the discontent of the African was the deepest, the confusing process of detribalization the most widespread.

South Africa is a plural society; that is, "a society comprising two or more elements or social orders which live side by side, yet without mingling, in one political unit."[2] The Dutch Europeans (the Boers) were rivals of the British settlers. Since 1902, when Britain defeated the two Boer republics, there had been bad blood between victors and vanquished. In 1909, through the union of the two former republics (the Transvaal and the Orange Free State) with the British colonies of Cape Colony and Natal, South Africa became a self-governing dominion in the British Commonwealth. But union did not bring cooperation. The Boers obtained official recognition for their language Afrikaans (developed mainly from seventeenth-century Dutch); they insisted upon their own flag and national anthem; and they talked about secession from the Commonwealth.

The rift between Briton and Boer was serious. More dangerous, however, was the increasing numerical gap between all Europeans on the one hand and the native population on the other. After World War I the Europeans began to eye the statistics nervously. The figures disclosed that there were 5,500,000 pure Africans in the Union and 1,800,000 whites, just under 50 percent of

them of British stock. In addition there were 200,000 Asiatics and 600,000 "coloured." Fearful of being overwhelmed by sheer numbers, many whites became convinced that the natives had to be kept separate from the European community socially and politically and that all political control must remain in the hands of the Europeans.

Segregation and the color bar spread rapidly in the 1930's. Africans were required to live on their tribal reserves. Only those who obtained special permission could work on farms owned by Europeans or in the cities; and in urban areas they were obliged to live in squalid, segregated "locations" and had to carry passes and identity cards under penalty of arrest and fine or imprisonment if found without them. Native labor unions were discouraged and strikes forbidden. In addition, governmental regulations or the white labor unions excluded Africans from certain skilled trades. Because of the enormous supply of unskilled native laborers, who would work for miserably low wages, uneducated Europeans—the "poor whites" —found it difficult to make a living. To favor this group, laws were passed earmarking certain jobs on the railroads and in city services for Europeans; wages for these jobs were raised, and the cost was paid by special subsidies. The practice was most discriminatory; the average wage for Europeans was just under four dollars a day, while that of the Africans was just over three dollars a week. In addition to the color bar in industry, the African was effectively barred from politics: he could not vote or hold office in any influential elective body or parliament outside his own tribal reserve.

African unrest was manifested in the increasing crime rate in the cities, in the formation of underground organizations, and in the determined efforts to secure political rights. Here and there in the back alleys and cellars of cities such as Johannesburg, young Africans ran their mimeograph machines, turning out handbills and papers advertising their grievances. One two-page sheet called the *African Liberator* declared:

Africa has come to the parting of the ways . . . Black South Africa has been bought and sold to some wolves in clothing of sheep who profess to be their friends. What does the African want? He wants liberty, equality, and opportunity. We demand our rights to have the same vote as Europeans, the same education, the same right to defend the country, the same right to sit in Parliament, Provincial Councils, and Town Councils. We do not want two nations in South Africa.[3]

Although the ferment of change and unrest began to be detected in other areas, only in the Union were African nationalist aspirations widespread. The unappeasable upsurge of nationalism was to wait until after World War II.

TENSIONS IN THE ARAB WORLD

Cultural links between Asia and Africa. The heart of the Arab world is the Middle East, a difficult region to define. The term is used most often in reference to the lands connecting Asia with Africa, the chief boundary markers being Cairo, Istanbul, Teheran, and the south coast of the Arabian peninsula. Nearly all the peoples of the Middle East are united in a common faith (Islam) and share common elements of Islamic culture and a common tongue, Arabic. Because of the unifying force of this heritage, Muslim North Africa (Morocco, Algeria, Tunisia) will be treated here as part of the Arab world.

With the exception of Morocco, North Africa at the beginning of the nineteenth century was nominally under the sovereignty of the Ottoman Turks, whose capital city was Constantinople. In practice, however, the various states in this area were self-governing. After 1815 all of North Africa from Casablanca in Morocco to Cairo in Egypt came under European imperialistic rule, while the other Arab lands in the Middle East continued under the despotic control of the sultans.

The Arab revolt. Just before the outbreak of the First World War, the Arabs within the Ottoman empire had reached the breaking point in their relations with the Turkish government. In 1913 an Arab Congress meeting in Paris demanded home rule and equality with the Turks in the empire. Because the Middle East was strategically important to Britain, the British government followed the rise of Arab discontent with great interest. During 1915 extensive correspondence was carried on between the British high commissioner in Cairo and Sherif Husein of Mecca (Husein ibn-Ali, 1856-1931), guardian of the holy places in the Hejaz. In the event of an Arab revolt, Great Britain would recognize Arab independence except in those regions of coastal Syria which were not wholly Arab—presumably excluding Palestine—and in those which might be claimed by France. But British commitments were purposely vague, and the whole correspondence has been described as a "monument of ambiguity."

In addition to the British alliance with the Arab nationalist movement, the indomitable desert warrior Abdul-Aziz ibn-Saud (1880-1953), sultan of Nejd in south-central Arabia, was induced to adopt a policy of benevolent neutrality toward Britain. The wooing of the Arabs thwarted the Turkish attempt to rouse the whole Muslim Middle East by preaching a *jihad*, or holy war, against the British.

Late in 1916 the Arab revolt began. Husein raised the standard of rebellion in the Hejaz, proclaimed independence from the Turks, and captured Mecca for his cause. In the fighting that followed, the Arab forces were commanded by the third son of the Sherif Husein, Emir Faisal (1885-1933), who was assisted by a remarkable English officer, Colonel T. E. Lawrence (1888-1935), later known as Lawrence of Arabia.

Under Lawrence, the Arabs took a decisive part in the last battle against the main Turkish forces in September 1918. When the war ended, Syria was occupied by the victorious Allied forces; a small French force was located along the coast of Lebanon; Emir Faisal and his Arab forces were in the interior, grouped around Damascus; and the British controlled Palestine.

The peace settlement. With Turkey defeated, the Arab leaders sought the independence they thought Britain had promised in the correspondence with Husein. When the peace conference met in Paris, it became painfully clear that the problem of political settlement in the Middle East was a jumble of conflicting promises and rivalries.

During the war years a number of important commitments had been made, starting with the British pledge in 1915 to Sherif Husein. In 1916, in the Sykes-Picot Agreement, Syria and Iraq had been divided into four zones, with Britain and France each controlling two. Palestine was to be placed under an international administration. The most important pronouncement bearing upon the postwar history of the Middle East was Britain's declaration to the Jewish Zionist organization in 1917.

Jewish aspirations to create a national home in Palestine had been rapidly growing after 1900. In 1903 a sympathetic British government had offered Theodore Herzl, the creator of the Zionist idea of a Jewish state, land in East Africa for a Jewish settlement. This proposal, however, had not been accepted. Following Herzl's death in 1904, the leadership of the Zionist movement had been assumed by Dr. Chaim Weizmann. Of Russian birth, Weizmann became a British subject and developed an intimate intellectual friendship with the English statesman Arthur James Balfour, who became keenly interested in the Zionist program. Balfour's admiration for Jewish religious and cultural contributions was profound; and he believed strongly that "Christian religion and civilization owed to Judaism a great debt and [one] shamefully repaid."[4]

During the course of World War I, the British government—strongly influenced by Balfour, then foreign secretary—became convinced that its support of a Zionist program in Palestine would not only be a humanitarian gesture but would also serve British imperial interests in the Middle East. Thus in November 1917 Britain issued the Balfour Declaration which stated:

His Majesty's Government view with favour the establishment in Palestine of a national home for the Jewish people, and will use their best endeavors to facilitate the achievement of this object, it being clearly understood that nothing shall be done which may prejudice the civil and religious rights of existing non-Jewish communities in Palestine. . . .

Zionists were disappointed that the Declaration did not unequivocally state that Palestine should be *the* national home for the Jewish people. In 1918 Great Britain made several declarations recognizing Arab national aspirations, and an Anglo-French pronouncement pledged the establishment of national governments "deriving their authority from the initiative and free choice of the indigenous populations."

At the Paris Peace Conference Emir Faisal, aided by Lawrence, pleaded the cause of Arab independence, but in vain. Faisal was still ruler in Damascus, and in March 1920, while the statesmen in Paris argued, a congress of Syrian leaders met and resolved

Shy and physically slight, Lawrence had roamed the Arab lands, studying the language and habits of the Muslims. In 1914 the British government engaged Lawrence to take part in the Arab guerrilla campaign against the Turks. Idolized by the Bedouin tribesmen he knew so well, Lawrence disrupted Turkish communication lines and destroyed so many locomotives that the Turks called him *El-Orens* ("destroyer of engines").

that he should be king of a united Syria, including Palestine and Lebanon. But in April the San Remo Conference of the Allied powers turned over all Arab territories formerly in the Ottoman empire to be administered as mandates. Syria and Lebanon were mandated to France; Iraq and Palestine, to Great Britain. To the Arabs the mandates were a poor substitute for independence and a flimsy disguise for imperialism.

From the Arabs' point of view, the peace settlement in the Middle East was a shabby piece of statesmanship compounded of ignorance, deception, and conflicting aims. Apologists for Britain and France point out that Britain made promises to France during the war because the British could hardly deny the requests of their most important ally, which had close missionary and educational ties in Syria. In 1916 Britain made its ambiguous pledge to Husein because of its desperate need for Arab friendship. Again, in the Balfour Declaration, Britain acted according to short-range interests; in order to swing the support of the world's Jews to the Allied cause and to maintain communications in the Middle East, Britain promised to open the Arab region of Palestine to Jewish settlement. It should be kept in mind that British statesmen sincerely believed that a Jewish national home could be reconciled with Arab interests; they had no idea of the massive influx of Jewish immigration during the 1930's. The plain fact remains, however, that the Allied statesmen at Paris were profoundly ignorant of the intensity of Arab nationalism.

The French in Syria and Lebanon. In 1920, following the San Remo Conference, a French army moved against Damascus and ejected Faisal from the throne. After this incident, France took over the mandate of Lebanon and Syria. Following a policy of divide and rule, the French attempted especially to woo the large Christian Arab groups in Lebanon. But they were not successful; the Arabs remained hostile. Strikes, demonstrations, and revolts were not uncommon.

Politically, French rule was a failure in Syria and Lebanon. At the outset a popular Arab king had been ejected, and for the next twenty years the French administration often suppressed personal and political liberties. Under French mandatory rule, however, the modernization of Syria-Lebanon proceeded: roads and public buildings were constructed, and the use of electricity and irrigation works was extended.

British policy in Iraq. Great Britain's vital interest in the mandate of Iraq was prompted largely by Iraq's rich oil resources, its growing importance in East-West air transportation, and its proximity to the Persian Gulf. But this interest did not prevent the British from taking steps to satisfy Iraqi nationalism after the outbreak of rebellion in June 1920. In March 1921 the Iraqi throne was offered to Faisal, who had lost his throne in Syria. A plebiscite strongly supported Faisal as ruler of the Iraqi, and a few months later he was proclaimed king. In 1922 Britain and Faisal's government signed a treaty which stipulated that Britain was to supervise the finances and military affairs of the new state. Three years later a constitution was adopted making the country a constitutional monarchy with a bicameral legislature. An Anglo-Iraqi treaty signed in June 1930 granted Iraq full independence, and in 1932 Iraq was admitted to the League of Nations. By these concessions Britain avoided the conflict that France experienced in Syria-Lebanon.

Arab-Jewish conflict in Palestine. Between the two world wars, Palestine was the most tempestuous area in all the Middle East, as Britain sought to protect its imperial interests and at the same time reconcile them with Zionism and Arab nationalism. Almost as soon as the mandate was set up, Arab riots broke out in Palestine. In 1919 the population was given at 700,000, with 568,000 Arabs, 58,000 Jews, and 74,000 others, mainly Christians. Realizing the apprehensions of the Arabs, the British sought to define the Balfour Declaration more precisely. While not repudiating Palestine as a national home for the Jews, the British government declared it "would never impose upon them [the Arabs] a policy which that people had reason to think was contrary to their religious, their political, and their economic interests."[5]

Such pronouncements and the fact that Jewish immigration was not large made possible a period of peace and progress from 1922 to 1929. As the Zionists reclaimed land, set up collective farms, harnessed the Jordan for power, and established many new factories, a veritable economic revolution took place. Tel-Aviv grew into a thriving modern city, an excellent university was founded at Jerusalem, and Palestine became the center of a Hebrew renaissance.

The era of peace ended in 1929 when serious disorders broke out, mainly Arab attacks on Jews. Violence continued to erupt in the early 1930's as the Nazi persecution of the Jews brought about a steep rise in immigration to Palestine and threatened the Arabs' predominant position in the area. In 1937 a British commission of inquiry recommended a tripartite division: Palestine would be divided into two independent states, one controlled by the Arabs and one by the Jews, with Britain holding a third portion, a small mandated area containing Jerusalem and Bethlehem. This recommendation satisfied no one and was not accepted.

Throughout the 1930's the "Palestine Question" was violently discussed in many parts of the world. Zionists argued that they had a historic right to the Holy Land, their original home, that Palestine had been promised to them in the Balfour Declaration and legalized by the League of Nations; that Jewish colonization constituted a democratic and progressive influence in the Middle East; and that Arab antipathy was mainly the work of a few wealthy effendis, since the mass of Arabs were profiting from the wealth being brought into Palestine. On the other hand, the Arabs argued that Palestine had been their country for more than a thousand years and declared that the Balfour Declaration did not bind them because they were not consulted in its formulation. They further insisted that much of Zionist economic development was not healthy because it depended upon subsidization of huge amounts by outside capital. Finally, they asked how could any people be expected to stand idly by and watch an alien immigrant group be transformed from a minority into a majority.

As war with the Axis powers loomed in 1939, Britain sought desperately to strengthen its position in the Middle East by attempts to regain Arab good will. A "white paper" was issued declaring that it was Britain's aim to have as an ally an independent Palestine established at the end of ten years, with guarantees for both the Arab and Jewish populations. During this ten-year period land sales were to be restricted. After the admission of 50,000 Jews, with the possibility of another 25,000 refugees from Nazi Germany, no more immigration would take place without the consent of the Arabs. The outbreak of World War II shelved the Zionist-Arab quarrel in Palestine; but after the war the controversy was to break out again with fatal virulence.

Emergence of Saudi Arabia. In the cradle of Islamic civilization—the Arabian peninsula—the various local rulers were largely outside the sphere of western control. The collapse of Ottoman rule in 1918 left several rival independent states such as Yemen, Hejaz, and Nejd to adjust their relations, plus a few British protectorates on the Arabian Sea and the Persian Gulf. Following hostilities between various contenders for leadership in the Arabian peninsula, ibn-Saud welded all tribal groups into a strong political unit. The new kingdom, Saudi Arabia, became endowed with enormous economic resources obtained from vast oil reserves discovered in 1932.

Riza Shah Pahlavi rules Iran. Persia, (or Iran as it came to be known in the 1920's), a land Muslim in religion but not Arabic in culture, had been the scene of strenuous British and Russian imperial rivalry before World War I. Following this conflict, a brilliant military officer, Riza Shah Pahlavi (1877-1944), seized the throne and established his own dynasty. A strongly nationalist reformer, Riza Shah abolished some of the special privileges enjoyed by foreigners —especially those of the Anglo-Iranian Oil Company. The army was modernized, education improved, trade and industry fostered, and important new railway lines constructed. But notwithstanding this impressive record, the Shah progressively developed the mind of a tyrant. Organs of government were relegated to puppetdom, and corruption increased. The decaying rule of Riza Shah was destined to collapse during World War II.

The problem of Egyptian sovereignty. While the Arabs in the mandates had been struggling for the right of self-determination, a parallel development was taking place in Egypt. When the British refused a delegation of Egyptian nationalists permission to attend the Paris Peace Conference and deported the spokesman of the group and his followers, the Nile valley rose in revolt.

After three years of disorder the government in London announced that Egypt was no longer a British protectorate. It was to be a sovereign state. Britain, however, was to remain responsible for the defense of the country, for the protection of foreign interests, and for communications vital to the British empire, above all the Suez Canal. Egypt grudgingly adapted itself to this declaration, made its sultan a king, and proclaimed a constitution in 1923. Anglo-Egyptian relations remained unsatisfactory, how-

Just as the Arabian garb of Lawrence, an Englishman, indicated his dedication to the Arab cause (see photo, p. 733), so the western dress of Kemal represents his attempt to westernize the Turkish nation. Under his leadership Turkey made more progress in the two decades after World War I than had been registered during the entire nineteenth century. In 1934 the people bestowed upon their leader the title of *Atatürk*, meaning "father of the Turks."

ever, and frequent negotiations between the two governments were fruitless.

Respite in the long record of Anglo-Egyptian acrimony came about through the threat of Italian Fascist aggression in Africa following Mussolini's conquest of Abyssinia (see Chapter 33). In 1936 Britain and Egypt arranged an alliance treaty. In case of war there was to be mutual assistance on a wide scale, and the status of the Sudan (theoretically under the dual sovereignty of Britain and Egypt but actually under British control) was to continue unaltered.

Aggressive nationalism in North Africa. Long before the outbreak of World War I, Algeria had become politically integrated with France; Tunisia had prospered under French rule and had maintained its native ruler, the bey; and the native sultan had also been retained in the protectorate France established in Morocco in 1911. Nevertheless, the storm signals of bitter nationalism had appeared, particularly in Morocco.

Following a revolt in 1912, the Moroccans in the 1920's vented their feeling against French rule on several occasions by riots and armed outbreaks. In the 1930's a modern nationalist movement began to function, but it was relatively weak. Tunisia, the most westernized area in French North Africa, also had a nationalist movement, but it was driven underground. In Algeria, which was part of metropolitan France, political agitation was slight. The growing desire of Muslims for French citizenship, strongly opposed by settlers from France, caused much resentment.

France deserves much credit for its colonial rule. Administration on the whole was just and efficient, the economy prospered, and living standards advanced. Nevertheless, a fundamental split existed between the privileged Christian minority and the overwhelming Muslim majority; the Arab populace admired examples of Arab assertiveness, as in Egypt and Morocco. Until 1939 the nationalist movement in North Africa was largely a monopoly of the relatively small intellectual groups and middle class. The mass of peasants remained quite apathetic.

Mustafa Kemal's rise to power in Turkey. We have seen in Chapter 28 how reform measures had been initiated by the Young Turks just before World War I. Defeat in the war, the revolt of the Arabs, and the impotence of the sultan's government convinced some patriots that only the most drastic measures could save the Turkish nation. In addition, they were embittered by the harsh terms of the Treaty of Sèvres (1920). It was bad enough to lose their empire, peopled by Arabs, but it was much worse to see their homeland, mainly Anatolia and the city of Smyrna, partitioned and invaded by the Greeks and Italians.

Imbued with a new spirit of nationalism, the patriots rallied around the military hero Mustafa Kemal Pasha (1880-1938), who had a brilliant record against the British at Gallipoli in World War I. An important figure in the Young Turks movement, Kemal was a born leader, thoroughly western in education and outlook. After the defeat of Turkey, he had been sent by the sultan to demobilize the Turkish troops in Asia Minor, but, disregarding his instructions, he had reorganized the troops and successfully defied the Allies. A new government was set up in Ankara, and Kemal was selected as president and commander in chief. Turkish patriotism was galvanized by the National Pact, a declaration of principles supported by Kemal. This document upheld the rule of self-determination for all people, including the Turks, and also proclaimed the abolition of the special rights heretofore enjoyed by foreigners in Turkey.

In 1921 Greek designs on Turkish territory were defeated by Kemal's armies. And in the following year the sultanate was abolished, followed by the establishment of a republic. The Allies agreed to a revision of Sèvres, and the Treaty of Lausanne, signed in 1923, returned to Turkey some Aegean islands and territory adjoining Constantinople. The heartland of Turkey—Anatolia—remained intact, and no reparations were demanded.

Kemal's reforms. The new constitution was democratic in form, but in reality Kemal was a dictator who brooked no interference with his plans. His dictatorship does not belong in the same category as those fashioned in Nazi Germany, or Fascist Italy, or Communist Russia, however. In the new Turkey there was little of the cult of the superior race; the brutal efficiency of the purge and the concentration camp was practically unknown. Dictatorship was regarded as the rough but essential highway to parliamentary government. Kemal envisioned a dictatorship as a necessary stage in raising his people to that level of education and social well-being which democratic government requires.

Under his rule the old institutions and customs of a backward oriental state were transformed or replaced within a few short years. In modern times such a wholesale adoption of new culture traits is duplicated nowhere except perhaps in Japan. The caliphate, the sultan's spiritual leadership of the Muslim world, was abolished. The courts of the Greek Orthodox Church were discontinued, and new law codes were promulgated. Education was taken out of the hands of the Orthodox Church, and school attendance was made compulsory to the age of sixteen. Use of the fez by men and the veil by women was forbidden. Polygamy was prohibited. In addition, the western Gregorian calendar and European numerals were introduced, and the Latin alphabet replaced the Arabic. Thus, Turkey was rejuvenated by its indefatigable leader, who created a new capital at Ankara.

INDIA SEEKS TO RULE ITSELF

Moves for self-government. Many observers had predicted that in the event of war Great Britain would find India a serious liability. But when hostilities began, nearly all unfriendly acts against Britain ceased. By 1917, however, it became apparent that the Indian people expected compensation in the way of more self-government. Parliament's reply indicated that the goal to be attained in India was the gradual development of self-government within the British empire.

The great leader of the Indian independence movement was Gandhi. He is shown here just after he arrived in England in 1931 to attend a round-table conference on the future of India.

In 1918 a British commission was sent to India to investigate the problem of Indian self-government. The result was a new constitution. The Government of India Act provided for a system of dyarchy, or double government, in the provinces, by which certain powers were reserved to the British while the provincial legislatures were accorded other, generally lesser powers. Thus the act represented only a step toward self-government.

Chances for India's acceptance of the act of 1919 were swept away by the outbreak of a struggle between the British and the Indian nationalists. In an ill-advised moment the British passed the Rowlatt Act (1919), which allowed the police and other officials extraordinary powers in ferreting out subversive activity. Although the act was never enforced, it was deeply resented as a token of repression. Disgruntled and disheartened, many nationalists demanded sweeping changes.

Gandhi and civil disobedience. The foremost nationalist leader in India was Mohandas K. Gandhi (1869-1948). Born of middle-class parents, Gandhi had been sent to London to study law; later he went to South Africa, where he built up a lucrative practice. During these years his standard of values changed completely. The new Gandhi repudiated wealth, practiced ascetic self-denial, condemned violence, and believed firmly that true happiness could be achieved only by service to one's fellow men.

Gandhi began his career as reformer and champion of his people in South Africa. The Indians there were subject to numerous restrictive laws which hampered their freedom of movement, prevented them from buying property, and imposed upon them special taxation. By the use of passive resistance, or noncooperation, Gandhi forced the government to remove some restrictions. Disdaining the use of violence, he believed that a just cause triumphs if its supporters attempt to convince those in power of injustices by practicing "civil disobedience." With Gandhi as their leader, the Indians in South Africa carried on various strikes, including hunger strikes; they refused work, held mass demonstrations, and marched into areas where their presence was forbidden by law.

When he returned to his native land shortly after the outbreak of World War I, Gandhi was welcomed as a hero. During the war he cooperated with the British government, but the Rowlatt Act and the disappointing concessions in the new constitution led him to announce his determination to force the British to give India self-rule.

In 1919 Gandhi introduced his campaign. A mass strike was declared in which all work was to cease and the population was to pray and fast. Contrary to Gandhi's plan, however, riots took place, Europeans were killed, and soldiers were sent to try to restore order. Although public gatherings were forbidden, a large body of unarmed Indians assembled at Amritsar. They were dispersed by gunfire, and several hundred were killed. All hope of cooperation between Indian and Briton was temporarily at an end. Arrested in 1922, Gandhi seemed to welcome being placed on trial; he assured the British magistrate that the only alternative to permitting him to continue his opposition was to imprison him. Sentenced to six years' imprisonment, Gandhi suffered a temporary eclipse.

There was little peace in India in the 1920's. During 1928 and 1929 a group of political experts from Great Britain, the Simon Commission, toured the country. The survey issued by the commission in 1930 suggested only a cautious advance in the direction of self-government. Meanwhile Gandhi initiated another campaign toward that goal.

British reform gestures. A promising road to conciliation opened in 1930, when a series of round-table conferences was arranged in London. A new scheme of government was hammered out, providing for a federal union which would bring the British provinces and the states of the princes into a central government. In the provinces the system of dyarchy was displaced by full autonomy, while in the federal government all powers were transferred to the Indians except defense and foreign affairs, which remained in the control of the British viceroy. From 1937, when this new Government of India Act came into operation, to 1939 the scheme of self-government worked smoothly. The possibility of federation, however, faded away as the native princes refused to enter the central government.

The Indian National Congress. The new system of government failed to satisfy the demands of the Indian nationalists, who continued to espouse the cause of complete independence for India. The chief element in the nationalist movement was the powerful Indian National Congress, which had become the organ of the militant nationalists. Membership, estimated at several million, was predominantly Hindu but also included many Muslims and members of other religious groups. Soon after the First World War, the Congress had come under the leadership of Gandhi, whose personal following among the people was the chief source of the party's tremendous influence. He transformed the Congress, which had been primarily a middle-class organization, into a mass movement including the peasants. Gandhi had other goals besides the

independence of India; he sought to end all drinking, to raise the status of women, to remove the stigma attached to the untouchables, and to bring about cooperation between Hindus and Muslims. Permeating all of Gandhi's ideas and actions was his belief in nonviolence; he was convinced that injustices and wrongs could be destroyed only through the forces of love, unselfishness, and patience.

In the 1930's Gandhi came to share his leadership with Jawaharlal Nehru (1889-1964), who came from a Brahmin family of ancient lineage. In his early youth Jawaharlal had all the advantages of wealth: English tutors, enrollment in the English public school of Harrow and later in Trinity College, Cambridge, where he obtained his B.A. in 1910 and was admitted to the bar in 1912. Upon his return to India, Nehru showed little interest in the law and gradually became completely absorbed in his country's fight for freedom.

Jawaharlal Nehru and Mohandas Gandhi, the beloved warriors of the fight for Indian independence, combined their skills, beliefs, and resources for the welfare of the masses of India.

A devoted friend and indeed a disciple of Gandhi, Nehru could not agree with the older leader's asceticism, mysticism, and his antagonism against western industrialism. At heart Nehru was a rationalist, an agnostic, an ardent believer in science, and a foe of all supernaturalism. Above all he was a blend of the cultures of both East and West, with perhaps the latter predominating. As he himself said: "I have become a queer mixture of the East and the West, out of place everywhere, at home nowhere. Perhaps my thoughts and approach to life are more akin to what is called Western than Eastern, but India calls to me."[6]

The Hindu-Muslim clash. India is a classic example of a plural society. The division in India was between the Hindus and Muslims and was known as the "communal problem." As Britain's imperial control over India began to show signs of ending, hostility between the two communities quickened. They were poles apart in culture and values. In a word, Islam and Hinduism represented a fundamental antithesis in nearly all facets of life. Many Muslims believed that in the event of independence they would be relegated to an ineffectual minority; in this sense the rivalry was a struggle for political power.

During the 1920's differences between Muslim and Hindu progressively developed. In the early 1930's the Muslim League, a political party, began to challenge the claim of the Indian National Congress to represent all of India. Its leader, Muhammad Ali Jinnah (1876-1948), originally a member of Congress and once dubbed by Indian nationalists as the "ambassador of Hindu-Muslim unity," had become alienated by what he considered the Hindu domination of Congress and its claim to be the sole agent of Indian nationalism. The Muslim League began to advance the "two-nation" theory, and in 1933 a group of Muslim students at Cambridge University circulated a pamphlet calling for the establishment of a new state to be known as Pakistan. This leaflet was a portent of momentous developments. In the fall of 1939 the Muslim League emphatically denounced any scheme of self-government that would mean majority Hindu rule.

NATIONALISM IN SOUTHEAST ASIA

Roots of decolonization. Southeast Asia underwent dramatic changes between World Wars I and II. Inspired by the Wilsonian ideal of "self-determination of peoples" or by the social revolutionary ideals of European socialism and the Russian Revolution, or by a combination of both, more and more Southeast Asian political, intellectual, and business leaders joined the anti-imperialist struggle, promoted national self-consciousness, and sought by one means or another the path to independence. The rise of Japan to the status of a world power indicated to Southeast Asian elites that the West was not alone in its ability to master technology and politics for purposes of national renewal. Furthermore, the spectacle of westerners barbarously slaughtering westerners in World War I gave birth to grave doubts concerning the validity of the West's claims of being a civilizing agent.

The imperialist powers continued to exploit their colonial possessions, apparently undaunted by the political ideals they had subscribed to during the First World War. But Southeast Asian populations grew dramatically. From 1930 to 1960 the populations of Siam, Malaya, and the Philippines increased by over 100 percent while the populations of Indonesia, Burma, and the states of Indochina all increased by well over 50 percent. Increased population pressures naturally contributed to unrest and the growth of nationalist movements.

Certain economic trends also characterized most of the region. The Chinese played a more and more important role as merchants and middlemen in the local economies. In Burma, Indians played the same role. European and Chinese capital investment brought about a rapid growth in the exploitation of natural resources, such as mines and forest products. In some countries, such as Siam and Indochina, rice production grew more rapidly than population, and they became rice-exporting economies. Imperialist exploitation coupled with an irregular world market, which crashed in 1929, led to the increasing impoverishment of large numbers of the population. This seemed to validate the Marxist-Leninist view of imperialism.

Throughout the area the elite became more assimilated to European culture as increasing numbers of young people went to the "mother countries" for education. The masses were hardly touched by this process, however, and the result was an increasing cultural and social dichotomy between the indigenous leadership and the people at large. With the exception of the United States in the Philippines and Great Britain in Burma and Ceylon, moreover, none of the imperialist powers undertook to prepare their colonies for self-government, as they had no intention of relinquishing them.

The Philippines. American civil government was established in the United States newly won Far Eastern possession on July 4, 1901, under William H. Taft. President McKinley declared that the primary American aim was to prepare the Filipinos for self-government. The first elections were held in 1907, and by 1913 Filipinos dominated both houses of the island legislature, while an American remained as governor-general or chief executive. By 1935, when the Philippine Commonwealth was inaugurated with a new constitution and the promise of independence in ten years, the islands had developed a complex political structure and a sophisticated political life.

Economic developments, however, decreased Philippine independence at the same time that the islands were being prepared for political independence. Before the outbreak of World War II, four fifths of Philippine exports went to the United States, and three fifths of its imports were American. Like most underdeveloped economies, the export trade was dominated by a very few products: hemp, sugar, coconuts, and tobacco. Independence, with its accompanying imposition of tariffs, would be economically difficult. Socially, the United States had prevented the development of a colonial-type plantation economy by forbidding non-Filipinos to own plantation lands. But native landlordism was rampant, and agrarian discontent manifested itself in brief uprising in the mid-thirties.

The Dutch East Indies. The growth of Indonesian self-consciousness and nationalism was paradoxically facilitated in the interwar period by the spread and increasing efficiency of Dutch rule. Stretched over 3100 miles of water, the numerous islands of Indonesia were integrated into political and communications systems by the Dutch. At the same time, the stringent limits put on the power and advancement of native elites led to bitterness and resentment. A Communist party was organized in 1920, and in late 1926 and early 1927 it attempted uprisings in Java and Sumatra, but they were unsuccessful. Police repression increased, and in 1930 the Dutch attempted to crush the Nationalist party by arresting one of its leaders, Sukarno, who became the first president of independent Indonesia after World War II. The colonial administration banned all discussions of any subject that might involve the concept of national independence. Even the name Indonesia was banned from official publications.

Burma and Malaya. India was the model for the development of Burmese nationalism and agitation for independence. The Indian Congress party stimulated Burmese political thought, but Buddhism provided the focus for organizational activity. In 1906 a Young Men's Buddhist Association was formed, and in 1921 it organized a General Council of Burmese Associations which gave organizational expression to nationalism on the village level. British promises to promote Indian self-government created a similar demand in Burma; in 1937 Burma was administratively split off from India, and a parliamentary system was inaugurated with a Burman prime minister under a British governor who was responsible for foreign relations, defense, and finance.

Malaya, in contrast to Burma, did not develop a strong nationalist movement. Perhaps the major reason for this was the existence of large ethnic groups that distrusted each other more than they felt the need to make common cause against the British. The Malays feared Chinese ethnic domination; eventually, the Chinese came to outnumber the Malays themselves. The Chinese were primarily interested in commerce and in developments in China, while the Indians, for the most part workers on plantations and in mines, looked toward India, rather than Malaya, as their homeland.

Indochina. The story of the Indochinese, and particularly the Vietnamese, struggle for independence is far too complex to be related here in anything but the most general terms. In fact, it has not yet ended. French rule in Indochina was in some ways the least enlightened of all the colonial regimes in Southeast Asia. In 1942, for instance, the colonial government had the highest proportion of Europeans in its service of any in the region, some 5100 French officials to 27,000 Indochinese.[7] Four fifths of the population was illiterate, and with over 21,000,000 people only about 500,000 children received any education at all, with only a few thousand receiving any higher education. French rule was characterized by political oppression, severe economic exploitation, and a rigid and stagnant traditional culture.

Revolution alone seemed the answer to Vietnam's problems. During World War I over 100,000 Vietnamese laborers and soldiers were sent to France, where many of them came into contact with liberal and radical thinking, which they then brought home. The Vietnam Nationalist party, patterned organizationally and intellectually on the Chinese Kuomintang, was denied any legal existence and, by the late 1920's, resorted to terrorism as the only form of political expression open to it. Communism rapidly became the major revolutionary ideology in the French colony. In 1920 a young Vietnamese calling himself Nguyen Ai Quoc ("Nguyen, the Patriot"), and later known to the world as Ho Chi Minh, participated actively in the formation of the Communist party in France. In 1930 he organized in Hong Kong what eventually became the Vietnamese (later Indochinese) Communist party. The 1930's in Vietnam were characterized by the spread of Communist ideas and organization, Vietnamese uprisings against French oppression, and strong repressive measures by the colonial government. As a result, the Communist party entered World War II as the major vehicle for the expression of Vietnamese nationalism.

Siam. In the interwar period Siam, which changed its name to Thailand in 1939, continued to modernize. Educational improvements, economic growth, and increasing political sophistication contrasted sharply, however, with the political and administrative domination of the country by the rather extensive royal family. In 1932 a French-trained law professor led a bloodless coup d'état, and a new constitution was promulgated with the agreement of the king, turning him into a reigning, but not ruling, monarch. Since then the country has been ruled by an alliance of army and oligarchy.

CHINA TRIES TO CHANGE

The end of the dynasty, the birth of the republic. During the course of the nineteenth century the once mighty Chinese empire increasingly felt the encroachments of the great imperialist powers. Loss of territory, the imposition of extraterritoriality, and foreign control of the tariff were symbols of China's impotence. But in the first decade of the twentieth century a strong nationalistic movement with liberal overtones emerged, determined to depose the Manchu dynasty, establish a republic, and modernize China. Only by these measures, it was felt, could China be saved.

Sun Yat-sen (1867-1925) emerged as the most important political leader of the new movement. Born near Canton, the son of a tenant farmer, he received a western education in Hawaii, was converted to Christianity, and in 1892 earned a diploma in medicine in Hong Kong. Shortly after, he became a leader in the Chinese nationalist movement, directing his energies toward the overthrow of the Manchus and the formation of a republic. Forced into exile in 1895, he traveled widely in Asia, Europe, and America, seeking political and financial aid from Chinese living abroad. During this period he organized the movement that eventually became the Kuomintang, or Nationalist party.

In 1911 a revolt broke out in China over a foreign loan to finance railways, and the outbreak spread like wildfire throughout the country. Yüan Shih-kai (1859-1916), an outstanding modernized military leader in North China and a confidant of the dowager empress Tzu Hsi, was able to persuade the imperial clan that the Manchu dynasty was doomed. In February 1912 the child emperor abdicated, and Yüan was asked to form a republican government. Although a few months earlier a revolutionary assembly in Nanking had elected Sun president of the new republic, he now stepped aside in the interest of national unity, and the Nanking assembly elected Yüan.

Dissension and warlordism. During the next decade and a half China went through a period quite similar to the dynastic interregnums that had punctuated all her previous history. It is impossible here to trace the confusion in Chinese politics in more than the barest outline.

In 1913 trouble broke out when Yüan negotiated a large loan with bankers from Britain, France, Germany, and Russia, thus giving these powers substantial influence in the government of the republic. The outcome was a new rebellion, endorsed by Sun. Yüan suppressed the revolt, and Sun fled to Japan. Now firmly entrenched, Yüan dismissed parliament and announced the imminent restoration of the monarchy with himself as emperor. Rebellion broke out again, Yüan's prestige evaporated, and in June 1916 the discredited dictator died.

China now entered a period of political anarchy. Warlords at the head of armies based on local power centers marched and countermarched across the country. The prize was the capital at Peking, possession of which apparently was thought to confirm the legitimacy of its occupier. The political picture was complicated by strained relations with Japan during the First World War and China's entry into the war. For a time the country was divided between two would-be governments, one in the north at Peking, the other in the south at Canton. Composed largely of those who had engineered the revolution of 1911-1912, the Canton government elected Sun as president in 1921.

The Three Principles of the People. Unable to obtain aid from the western powers to overcome the Peking government, Sun requested advisers from the Soviet Union. A military and political advisory group arrived, led by a brilliant Communist and international revolutionary, Michael Borodin. Under Borodin's guidance, the Kuomintang adopted many of the planks of the program subscribed to by the Communist party in the Soviet Union as well as its organizational structure.

Sun died in 1925. More skillful as a propagandist and revolutionist than as a political administrator, he had failed to reunite the Peking regime with his Kuomintang government. However, his social ideology had important results for the future. His most famous work, a series of lectures entitled *Three Principles of the People,* became the political manual of the Kuomintang. The three principles are: (1) nationalism—the liberation of China from foreign domination and the creation of a Chinese nation-state; (2) democracy—"government by the people and for the people"; (3) livelihood—economic security for all the people.

Chiang Kai-shek "unites" China. Sun's eventual successor as leader of the Kuomintang was the son of a petty landlord family, Chiang Kai-shek (1886-1975). Chiang studied at a military academy in Japan, was stirred by Sun's vision of a new China, and returned home to take an active part in the revolution. His obvious abilities attracted Sun's attention, and in 1923 he was sent to Russia for a brief period of indoctrination.

Under Chiang the armies of the Kuomintang began to drive northward in 1926. They encountered little opposition, and by early spring of the following year they reached the Yangtze valley and occupied Shanghai. But dissension broke out between radical and conservative elements in the Kuomintang, and a split became inevitable. The moderates under Chiang created a government at Nanking, and before the end of 1927, public opinion had crystallized behind this regime. Chiang used force against the leftist elements; the end of the Kuomintang alliance with the Communists was written in blood when a proletarian uprising in Canton was quelled with the loss of more than five thousand lives. Back to the Soviet Union went the Communist advisers; many radicals (including the widow of Sun Yat-sen) were driven into exile; and the Chinese Communists were scattered to the hills and mountains of south China, where they set up their own administrative units.

In retrospect, the split of 1927 stands out as a major event in modern Chinese history. Not only were Marxist radicals ousted, but moderate liberals also began to be eliminated. Nationalist strength lay with the city professional, banking, and merchant classes, and the Nanking government came to depend for financial support upon the foreign bankers at Shanghai. The regime began to take on a conservative character which hindered its leaders from understanding and dealing with the problems of the peasants.

With his government established at Nanking, Chiang's armies and his warlord allies again moved north and occupied Peking; China appeared once more to be united. Actually, however, China's unity was more appearance than fact. While large areas of the country had been conquered by Chiang's forces, other regions came under the Kuomintang by agreement between Chiang and local warlords. In theory the warlords were subordinate to Chiang, but they maintained power in their spheres of influence.

During the 1920's Chinese foreign relations improved. China's territorial integrity was guaranteed by the Nine-Power Treaty signed in 1922, and China was a member of the League of Nations. The Chinese government obtained the power to fix its own tariffs in 1929, and ten foreign powers gave up or lost the right of extraterritoriality. In addition, during this period Japan appeared relatively conciliatory toward its neighbor. But the sympathizers of the young republic could not overlook certain problem areas. In many regions the people were still tyrannized by bandits, and famine in the northwest cost the lives of millions.

A fervent patriot, Chiang nevertheless had little appreciation for the social and economic problems of his people. He placed much more store in their moral regeneration by traditional means. Strongly versed in Confucian teachings and at the same time a Christian, Chiang in the mid-thirties established the New Life Movement, which was a combination of Christian and Confucian ethics. He would have done better to appreciate the intellectual changes taking place in China and the social and economic aspirations of the peasants.

The New Culture Movement and Chinese communism. During World War I a Chinese intellectual revolution began at Peking University and then spread to students all over the country. Its first influential voice was the magazine *New Youth*. Returning from universities in the United States and Europe, students brought ideas of western science, liberalism, and democracy. In essence they sought to establish a new order and a new set of values to replace much of the discredited Confucian tradition.

Disillusionment with western values rapidly set in, however, following the Versailles peace treaty which tendered Chinese Shantung to Japan. Antiwestern sentiment was expressed in a violent student demonstration on May 4, 1919. A new ideological orientation now began in the New Culture Movement. Study groups were formed, especially at Peking University, where professors and students began to read Marx and Lenin and to apply their thought to the Chinese scene. Lenin's analysis and attack on imperialism struck a responsive chord. With some guidance from Russian Comintern agents, the First Congress of the Chinese Communist party was held in July 1921. A young student at Peking university named Mao Tse-tung was a delegate. About the same time, Chinese worker-students in France established the Young China Communist party in Paris. One of its leaders was Chou En-lai, later premier of Communist China.

Mao Tse-tung (1893-1976) was born in Hunan province, which was a traditional center of Chinese revolutionary activity. In 1918 he went to Peking University, where he worked as library assistant under Li Ta-chao, the founder of an important Marxist study group and one of the founders of the Chinese

Mao Tse-tung's belief that the revolution must be based on peasant uprisings was rejected by the early Chinese Communist party and was counter to the Marxian doctrine held by Moscow. Here a young Mao gives a speech at a meeting of Chinese Communists.

Communist party. Mao began to emerge as a distinctive leader with a new program for revolution when he wrote a report for the Communist party in 1927 about the peasant movement in Hunan. His belief that the revolution must base itself on peasant uprisings was condemned by the Central Committee of the Chinese Communist party, which adhered closely to the Moscow policy of basing the revolution on the urban proletariat. Nevertheless, Mao led a Hunanese peasant uprising that became known as the "Autumn Harvest Uprising." It was crushed, and in May 1928 Mao and other Communist leaders joined forces in the border region of Hunan and Kiangsi provinces. Acutely conscious of peasant needs, Mao organized the peasants in his region into a Chinese "soviet." Other Communist leaders did the same in other regions, and in 1931 delegates from the various local

soviets in China met and proclaimed the birth of the Chinese Soviet Republic. Meanwhile, Chiang Kai-shek's agents had destroyed the Shanghai apparatus of the Communist party. Within three years large Communist enclaves with a total population of about nine million existed in South China.

Mao Tse-tung's success as a Communist leader depended largely on his realization that it was the Chinese peasant, not the urban worker, who could be made the agent of revolution. Farmers' cooperatives were established and tax systems reformed. More drastic measures included the seizure and division of moderate-sized and large farms and the distribution of the goods taken from the landowners.

The Nationalists, who had neglected the countryside for the cities, were apprehensive of Mao's success. From 1931 to 1934 Chiang launched five military campaigns against the Communists, the last employing one million men and a German military staff. To escape annihilation, the Communists made their famous Long March two thousand miles to the northwest. Only a remnant of the original force reached Yenan, in Shensi province, where a new Communist stronghold was set up in 1935.

Changes in Chinese life. The changes that took place in Chinese life between the times of the Nationalist revolution and the beginning of World War II in the Far East were noteworthy. The number of Chinese receiving an education, though still small, increased remarkably. Chinese intellectuals championed the use of a new and simplified written language, while scholars labored for the adoption of Mandarin as a national speech so that men from all parts of China could speak together. Social customs were also considerably altered; in urban areas folkways and dress began to give way to occidental customs and fashions. Telephones, electric lights, modern water systems, and movie palaces appeared in the large cities.

Chinese commerce increased rapidly. Total foreign trade was seven times as great in 1929 as it had been in 1894. Nevertheless, civil warfare, currency insecurity, inefficient transportation systems, and national poverty all combined to keep China virtually an undeveloped nation. For the most part industry was controlled by foreign entrepreneurs, who raked in the profits. Because the impressive economic potentialities of China were not exploited for the advantage of the Chinese, the inhabitants of the republic continued to suffer.

JAPAN BECOMES A WORLD POWER

The Twenty-one Demands. As the twentieth century dawned, Japan had astonished the world by the tempo of its modernization. From a static, militarily weak, and dominantly agricultural nation, it was rapidly becoming a dynamic, militarily powerful, and highly industrialized state. There were serious problems ahead, however. The liberal statesmen of Japan sought means not only to support the rapidly increasing population but also to democratize the constitution. Unfortunately, Japan followed a path that led ultimately to aggression against its neighbors and to more, not less, dictatorial government at home.

When the First World War broke out in 1914, Japan ordered Germany to remove its warships from the Far East and to surrender the Kiaochow territory in China to Japan "with a view to the eventual restoration of the same to China." When Germany failed to reply to this request, the Japanese government declared war and seized the territory. Japan had not consulted China at all during this time, nor did the Japanese hesitate to violate Chinese neutrality.

In January 1915 Japan presented China with the notorious Twenty-one Demands, which startled the world by their frank disclosure of Japanese imperialistic designs on the Asian continent. Preoccupied as they were with the gigantic struggle in Europe, the European powers did little to hinder the Japanese, and indignant China had not the physical means to protest effectively. Under threats of coercion, the Chinese government acceded to the first sixteen demands in May; the remainder were reserved for later consideration. The intervention of the United States helped nullify the most dictatorial of the demands, which would have brought China completely under Japan's domination. China was forced, however, to acknowledge Japan's authority in Shantung province and to extend Japanese railway and land concessions in southern Manchuria.

In 1917 the Allied powers secretly agreed to support Japanese claims in the peace conference that would follow the First World War. While not a party to the agreement, the United States in the Lansing-Ishii agreement (1917) declared somewhat reluctantly that Japan deserved "special interest in China" owing to "territorial propinquity." Japan, in turn, agreed to respect the Open Door Policy in China. The Allies' position toward China was most embarrassing; China had entered the war on their side, chiefly to secure a spot during peace negotiations so that Japanese ambitions might be checked. China's only hope for preserving its independence lay in the growing tension between the United States and Japan.

Japanese foreign relations in the 1920's. Japan profited from its role in the war; in one way or another it controlled Shantung, Manchuria, southern Mongolia, and the German islands north of the equator, besides the territories and concessions it had wrested from China and Russia prior to the war. The increased power of Japan was particularly alarming to the United States and the British dominions in the Pacific. In 1921 Great Britain allowed its treaty with Japan, which Britain had renewed in 1911, to terminate without further renewal.

The growth of Japan's hold on China is revealed in a comparison of the investments by foreign powers in that country. In 1902 Japanese investment in China was negligible, but in 1914 it rivaled the investments of both Russia and Germany, and by 1931 it was second only to Great Britain's. In 1931 Japanese capital represented about 35 percent of all foreign investment in China. At the Washington Conference in 1921, the agreement by the three leading naval powers —Great Britain, the United States, and Japan—to reduce the tonnage of their capital ships in order to achieve a respective ratio

23. (preceding page) **Victor Horta: Hotel van Eetvelde, Brussels** (1899). The architects of the late nineteenth century sought to cast off the hidebound old "revival modes" which had weighed so heavily on nineteenth-century building. The art nouveau manner, portrayed here by Horta at the crest of its popularity, was intended to freshen the mainstream of western style, as well as to revivify a sense of craftsmanship which machine technology had greatly undermined. Oddly, Horta's imaginative use of iron did much to demonstrate the esthetic as well as practical possibilities of this most industrial of materials.

24. (left) **Paul Cézanne: "Still Life with Cherries and Peaches"** (1890's); **25. Oskar Kokoschka: "Die Windsbraut"** (1914). The still lifes of Cézanne are not so much pictures of peaches, cherries, and other memorabilia of the visible world as essays in pictorial architecture. Though he employed many Impressionist devices, such as direct color and bold brushwork, Cézanne replaced the breezy and casual composition of the Impressionists with a firmer, more calculated order. To create this soundness of structure, he positioned and modeled his forms with scrupulous care. Occasional distortions in symmetry were allowed in order to achieve a tighter, more dynamic organization. Post-Impressionism eventually helped foster modern Expressionism, whose essence was the expression of inner meaning through outer form, an expression of the power of emotion, the anguish, the joy, and deeply-felt sensitiveness to the inner qualities of man and nature. Kokoschka uses this form to give us a very personal and romantic account of his own love affair, in which the lovers are swept through a dream landscape of dimly moonlit mountains and valleys. True to the modern Expressionist tradition, Kokoschka's passionate search was for the exposure of an inner sensibility.

26. Wassily Kandinsky: "Improvisation with Green Center" (1913). Beginning around 1910, the innovative Russian artist Wassily Kandinsky completely abandoned representational forms in favor of a completely nonobjective, abstract style; a style that, by eliminating all resemblance to the physical world, gave a purely spiritual meaning to color and form. The results were kaleidoscopic creations that seem to demand a special insight and intuition on the part of the observer.

of 5-5-3 recognized the position of the Japanese navy as the third most powerful in the world.

In 1922 the Nine-Power Treaty was signed at Washington. All the signatories agreed to respect the independence, sovereignty, territoriality, and administrative integrity of China. Furthermore, they were to use their influence to preserve the Open Door Policy and "to refrain from taking advantage of conditions in China in order to seek special rights or privileges which would abridge the rights of subjects or citizens of friendly states, and from countenancing action inimical to the security of such states."[8] It is impossible to reconcile Japan's later acts in China after 1931 with the pact which it signed in 1922, just as it is difficult for the other signatories to excuse their apathy toward Japanese aggressions in China before they were themselves drawn into war against Japan.

The struggle for liberalism. From 1889, when Japan's new constitution was promulgated, to 1918, the government was mainly in the hands of an aristocratic oligarchy of elder statesmen called the *Genro*. By the end of World War I most of these political patriarchs had passed away, and the field of politics was now open for new blood, a fact signalized by the election to the post of prime minister of the first commoner ever to hold that office, Hara Takashi.

The period from 1918 to 1930 was of crucial importance. Japan seemed to be moving toward the establishment of a democratic, parliamentary government under its new liberal political leaders. There were serious obstacles to be overcome, however—not only the lack of a widespread popular liberal tradition and inexperience in parliamentary politics but also other factors. The concentration of wealth in the hands of a few fantastically rich families was not democratically healthy. Militarism, based on the revered *samurai* tradition which exalted war, was strong, and to this militaristic virus in the Japanese blood stream was added a strong authoritarian tradition, fostered by secret societies and the cult of Shintoism.

Many secret societies were connected with the army and were ultranationalistic and terroristic. Long a feature of Japanese life, they multiplied rapidly in membership after 1930. Originally a simple nature cult, Shinto by the end of the nineteenth century had been transformed into the cult of emperor worship and the deification of the state. Thus the Japanese were able to build a strong regime upon cults that already occupied an important position in the lives of the people, while the Nazis were forced to resurrect Teutonic cults that had been extinct for centuries in order to arouse national fervor.

It was with these serious handicaps that parliamentary government after 1918 sought to lead the nation away from excessive nationalism and militarism. Liberals in the Diet showed great promise and courage as they pressed reform and criticized the imperialistic intervention in Siberia of the Japanese army (along with other Allied forces) during the confused civil war following the Russian Revolution. Although liberalism suffered a serious setback in 1921 with the assassination of Prime Minister Hara, liberal strength returned in 1925 when the Universal Manhood Suffrage Bill was passed, granting the franchise to most males over twenty-five. However, liberal progress was often paid for with conservative legislation. Soon afterward a reactionary government came to power, advocating a stronger policy toward China; but this militaristic regime was in turn quickly succeeded by the most liberal government Japan had ever had. Led by Prime Minister Hamaguchi Yuko, this liberal regime assumed a policy of conciliation toward China, reduced army expenditures, and signed the London Naval Treaty.

Economic progress. In the economic sphere, Japan forged ahead rapidly. Thousands of factories were built, and Japanese manufacturers undersold foreign competitors in the world market, owing in part to the low Japanese wage standard and in part to the modern machine techniques which Japanese industrialists were swift to adopt. In textiles especially, Japan captured one market after another. Commerce and industry were controlled by a few giant concerns, in whose hands the greater part of the country's wealth was concentrated. By the 1930's Japan had become the first exporter in rayon, cotton textiles, matches, and raw silk.

Japanese economic prosperity was, however, more apparent than real. Serious economic weaknesses existed. The country lacked natural resources such as coal, iron, petroleum, timber, and cotton. The population was growing at an unbelievable rate. In 1920 the population was 56 million; in 1931 it had reached 65 million persons, crowded into a land area smaller than the state of California. In 1932 the annual increase reached 1,000,000. The Japanese economy needed to find 250,000 new jobs for young workers every year, to say nothing of feeding 1,000,000 additional mouths annually. Up to 1930 Japan had managed to pay its way by expanding its exports, which gave the nation foreign credits to buy raw materials and foodstuffs abroad. Should these exports suffer a substantial contraction, Japan would then be confronted with a serious national crisis. Just such a crisis occurred in the world depression which began in the 1930's.

Military fascism comes to Japan. Economic depression came to Japan with little warning and with shattering impact. Between 1929 and 1931, the Japanese export trade was cut almost in half. The sale of raw silk, which amounted to 40 percent of Japanese exports, rapidly plunged downward as the United States drastically reduced purchases. Unemployment, wage cuts, and strikes became common. As in Germany on the eve of Hitler's rise to power, frustration among the younger generation was widespread.

In 1929 and 1930 the liberal prime minister, Hamaguchi, sought with relatively little success to meet the depression. He also followed a conciliatory policy toward China and was willing to cooperate in disarmament proposals—aims bitterly opposed by the militaristic clique. Shot in November 1930, the prime minister died the following spring. This assassination was a tragedy from which Japanese liberalism never recovered in the decade before the Second World War.

A new group of ultranationalistic and militaristic leaders came into power. In contrast to the personal dictatorships in Nazi Germany and Fascist Italy, however, Japan was dominated by a military clique, which terrorized the civilian members of the government. Scoffing at democracy and peace, these leaders plotted to shelve parliamentary government in Tokyo and to use force on the mainland of China to secure essential raw materials and markets for goods, to spread the "superior" Japanese culture throughout Asia, and to find space for Japan's overcrowded population. This "beneficial mission" was known as the New Order in Asia.

SUMMARY

Between the two world wars imperialism went on the defensive before the rise of nationalism in the nonwestern world. The nationalistic stimulus in sub-Saharan Africa stemmed from the Pan-African movement of educated Negroes outside their homeland as well as from a very small educated class within the African states. This group sought to replace alien imperialistic control with self-government and to bring about the cultural resurgence of a people whose tribal way of life was slowly disintegrating as the black man came into contact with the numerous facets of western culture. The Pan-African movement did not affect the masses of the people in most areas, however; only in the troubled multiracial society of the Union of South Africa was there widespread unrest among Africans.

Nationalism was much stronger in the Arab world. In the lands formerly controlled by the Ottomans, Arab nationalists bitterly contested European control as set up in the mandate system; the British were ultimately forced to grant complete independence to Iraq, and outbreaks of violence occurred in the French mandate of Syria-Lebanon and especially in Palestine, where the Arabs resented the British attempt to set up a national home for the Jews. In Iran the nationalists threw off the influence of Britain and set up a government under the control of Riza Shah Pahlavi. Dissatisfaction with

French rule mounted in North Africa, and self-government was granted to Egypt by the British. In other areas of the Middle East Turkish nationalists under Mustafa Kemal built a new Turkey, while in the Arabian peninsula a new Arab power, Saudi Arabia, emerged under the dynamic leadership of ibn-Saud.

The strongest nationalism in all the colonial areas developed in India under the powerful leadership of Mahatma Gandhi. The effective use of nonviolence in his civil disobedience campaigns forced Britain to grant a substantial measure of self-government to the Indians.

In Southeast Asia nationalism began to rise steadily, although it did not as yet affect the majority of people. In Burma, Britain conceded some degree of self-government; unrest grew stronger in the French and Dutch colonies. In the Philippines nationalism was given ample opportunity to develop, and self-government was finally granted.

China was not, strictly speaking, a part of the colonial world, yet in many ways this vast and backward land was under the indirect influence of the great western powers. Faced with the prospect of virtual partition by these nations, Chinese nationalists, under the leadership of Sun Yat-sen, overthrew the Manchu dynasty and established a republic. After years of confusion and conflict between rival factions, power was consolidated under the Kuomintang and Chiang Kai-shek. The Chiang regime effected a gradual modernization of urban China, though agrarian reform was largely neglected.

Japanese history in the opening decades of the twentieth century was characterized by amazing progress in industrialization and by an attempt to introduce a democratic and responsible system of government. By 1919 the island kingdom had become one of the world's great powers. But its spectacular rise to greatness was also characterized by serious omens. There was disturbing evidence that military fascism was more potent than democracy and expansionist ambitions more powerful than love for peace.

SUGGESTIONS FOR READING

Barbara Ward, **The Interplay of East and West** (Norton) is a stimulating study of the interacting influences between East and West from ancient times to the present. P. Welty, **The Asians: Their Heritage and Their Destiny,** 4th ed. (Lippincott, 1973); and H. G. Matthew, ed., **Asia in the Modern World** (Mentor) are handy introductions. For valuable comparative studies see R. Emerson, **From Empire to Nation: The Rise of the Asian and African Peoples** (Beacon).

H. Kohn and W. Sokolsky, **African Nationalism in the Twentieth Century** (Anvil) is a summary of twentieth-century developments. Significant articles from the magazine, **Foreign Affairs,** can be found in P. W. Quigg, ed., **Africa: A Foreign Affairs Reader** (Klaus Repr.). Two astute observers survey Africa as it was before World War II: J. Huxley, **Africa View** (Greenwood); and John Hatch, **Africa Emergent** (Regnery, 1974). See also C. G. Segre, **Fourth Shore: The Italian Colonization of Libya** (Univ. of Chicago, 1975); Michael Crowder, **West Africa under Colonial Rule** (Northwestern, 1968); T. Hodgkin, **Nationalism in Colonial Africa** (New York Univ.); W. Cartey and M. Kilson, eds., **The Africa Reader,** Vol. I, **Colonial Africa** (Vintage, 1970).

G. Lenczowski, **The Middle East in World Affairs** (Cornell) is a first-rate survey. See also S. N. Fisher, **The Middle East: A History** (Knopf, 1968); Howard M. Sachar, **The Emergence of the Middle East** (Knopf); and W. C. Smith, **Islam in Modern History** (Mentor). A short history of the Jewish people is Abba Eban, **My Country** (Random House, 1972). See also B. Halpern, **The Idea of the Jewish State,** rev. ed. (Harvard, 1969). The Arab view of the political control of Palestine is presented in G. Antonius, **The Arab Awakening: The Story of the Arab National Movement** (Capricorn). On the impact of westernization in Turkey see D. E. Webster, **The Turkey of Ataturk: Social Process in the Turkish Reformation** (AMS Press). Other special studies are S. H. Longrigg, **Syria and Lebanon under French Mandate** (Octagon, 1972); and **Iraq, 1900 to 1950** (Verry, 1972).

T. W. Wallbank, **India in the New Era** (Scott, Foresman) is a useful and authoritative survey. For invaluable studies of the architects of Indian nationalism see K. Kripalani, **Gandhi: A Life** (Verry, 1968); E. Thomson, **Rabindranath Tagore** (Greenwood, 1975); and M. C. Rau, **Jawaharlal Nehru** (Interculture, 1975). See also B. R. Nanda, **Gokhale, Gandhi, and the Nehrus: Studies in Indian Nationalism** (St. Martin's, 1975).

J. Cady, **Southeast Asia: Its Historical Development** (McGraw-Hill) is a perceptive appraisal. See also C. Dubois, **Social Forces in Southeast Asia** (Harvard). R. S. Gupte, **A History of Modern China** (Verry, 1974) is an excellent account. For the basic study of the Kuomintang regime see C. Tuan-Sheng, **The Government and Politics of China** (Harvard). E. O. Reischauer, **Japan: The Story of a Nation** (Knopf, 1974) emphasizes the modern period. For a detailed description of how the military extremists undermined parliamentary government in Japan see Richard Storry, **The Double Patriots: A Story of Japanese Nationalism** (Greenwood, 1973).

*Indicates a less expensive paperbound edition.

CHAPTER 33

Depression and
World War II: 1930-1945

The Tragic Decade and Global Conflict

INTRODUCTION. On September 1, 1939, Hitler's legions marched into Poland, and the Second World War began. This outbreak of terrible violence marked the end of a tragic decade.

Ten years earlier the Wall Street stock market crash had ushered in a world-wide financial crisis—the Great Depression. Nation after nation fell victim to industrial decline, bank failures, deflated prices and profits, and commercial stagnation. People the world over suffered from lowered standards of living, unemployment, hunger, and fear of the future. In the western democracies the buoyant optimism of the 1920's was superseded by self-criticism and despair.

In desperation governments sought economic recovery by adopting restrictive autarkist policies—high tariffs, import quotas, and barter agreements—and by experimenting with new plans for their internal economies. The United States launched the New Deal, and Britain adopted far-reaching measures in the development of a planned national economy. In Nazi Germany economic recovery was pursued through rearmament, conscription, and public works programs, while in Italy Mussolini tightened the economic controls of his corporate state. Observers in many lands saw in the gigantic economic planning and state ownership of the Soviet Union what appeared to be a depression-proof economic system and a solution to the crisis in capitalism.

The economic malaise of the 1930's gave dictators their chance: Hitler took over control in Germany, and a militaristic clique grasped the reins of power in Japan. In 1931 the Japanese pounced upon Manchuria, and when the League of Nations proved powerless to interfere, war between Japan and China raged intermittently throughout the decade. While China was fighting for its national existence, Italy conquered Abyssinia, fascism emerged triumphant from the Spanish civil war, and by a series of "incidents" Hitler swelled the territory of the Third Reich and increased its power. Faced with blatant aggression by the Axis powers (Germany, Italy, Japan), England and France abandoned their faith in collective security and the League of Nations and adopted a policy of appeasement. Meanwhile, the Soviet Union played for time to build up its own defenses, and the United States detached itself from the increasing world tensions by maintaining its traditional policy of isolationism. Finally driven to the limit by the Axis, the European democracies and later the Soviet Union and United States took up arms to defend their independence and end the threat of world conquest.

Far more than World War I, World War II represented global conflict. Furthermore, the Second World War was a "total war" in that never before had civilian populations been so deeply involved. They were targets of the guns and falling bombs, and many were participants, often fighting beside the soldiers.

In many ways this was a new kind of war, not only in its enormous scope but also in its techniques and in its weapons. Technology made possible the mass bombing raids, the air-borne invasions, the amphibious assaults, the operations of carrier-based planes, the maneuvers of armored divisions, the coordinated efforts of the giant naval task force, and the mass murders of Nazi concentration camps; and science and technology combined to create the ultimate in efficiency and horror—the nuclear bomb. Yet World War II was also a war of men, fighting as men have fought throughout human history. After the weapons and techniques of modern technological warfare had done their worst, it was men who had to win or lose the battles. It was men who finally destroyed the Axis.

DEPRESSION THREATENS DEMOCRACY AND BREEDS TOTALITARIANISM

Phony prosperity of the "roaring twenties." In 1929 the world's most prosperous nation was the United States. President Hoover declared in his inaugural address:

Ours is a land rich in resources, stimulating in its glorious beauty, filled with millions of happy homes blessed with comfort and opportunity. . . . I have no fears for the future of our country. It is bright with hope.[1]

But despite the buoyant optimism in the United States and the apparent economic well-being in other countries, the world economy was in an unhealthy state. One by one, the cornerstones of the pre-1914 economic system—multilateral trade, the gold standard, and the interchangeability of currencies—were crumbling.

The desire for self-sufficiency, or autarky, led nations to manufacture goods or grow products at home, even though this policy was sometimes more expensive than importing what they needed. Then, to protect home products against competition from foreign imports, high tariff walls were raised. The United States led the movement toward higher tariffs. Other nations quickly retaliated with discriminatory tariffs against the United States and each other, American foreign trade seriously declined, and the volume of world trade steadily decreased.

The high tariffs had a crucial effect on the payment of war debts. As a result of America's high tariff, only a sort of economic ring-around-the-rosy kept the reparations and war-debt payments going. During the 1920's the former allies paid their war-debt installments to the United States chiefly with funds obtained from German reparations payments, and Germany was able to make these payments only because of large private loans from the United States and Britain. Similarly, American investments abroad provided the dollars which alone made it possible for foreign nations to buy American products. By 1931 the world was reeling from the worst depression of all time, and the entire structure of reparations and war debts collapsed.

Panic on Wall Street: the crash of 1929. In the postwar decade the activities of daring and often unscrupulous speculators made international finance a precarious and exciting world of its own. Operating on an international scale, the Swedish swindler Ivar Kreuger cornered the match market; in the United States, Samuel Insull's attempts to maintain a vast public-utilities empire helped push stock prices to dizzy heights; and an English speculator, Clarence Hatry, indirectly touched off the Wall Street crash. When Hatry's shaky companies failed, his English victims dumped their American securities to get ready cash. This in turn triggered a sickening slump in stock prices on Wall Street. The crash came in 1929, on October 24, "Black Thursday." "Prices fell farther and faster, and the ticker lagged more and more. By eleven o'clock the market had degenerated into a wild, mad scramble to sell. In the crowded boardrooms across the country the ticker told of a frightful collapse. . . . The uncertainty led more and more people to try to sell. . . . By eleven-thirty the market had surrendered to blind relentless fear. This, indeed, was panic."[2] Within a few weeks, stock prices had declined 40

percent. Fortunes were wiped out, business confidence was blasted, and the demand for goods plummeted. The growing paralysis in the American economy spread all over the world as the United States began to call in its foreign loans and decrease its imports.

In the face of impending world-wide disaster, President Hoover in 1931 succeeded in obtaining a moratorium of one year on all intergovernmental debts. At the Lausanne Conference (1932) German reparations payments were practically canceled in the hope that the American government also would make a substantial concession in reducing war debts, but the United States refused to concede that there was a logical connection between reparations and war debts. As the depression deepened, the debtors could not continue their payments. France refused outright in 1932; Great Britain and four other nations made token payments for a time, then stopped entirely in 1934; and only Finland continued to meet its schedule of payments. In the meantime, Germany had completely stopped paying reparations.

The depression begins. The effects of the depression were catastrophic the world over. Governments could not balance their budgets, factories shut down, and harvests rotted in the fields. The price of wheat fell to the lowest figure in more than three hundred years. The lives of the grower of cacao in the African Gold Coast, the coffee grower in Brazil, and the copra plantation worker in the Dutch East Indies were blighted, as were those of the factory worker in Pittsburgh, Sheffield, Lille, and Frankfurt. In the "land of plenty," one of the popular songs of the day was "Brother, Can You Spare a Dime?"

During the years following the crash most nations strengthened their resolve to employ autarky as their guiding economic principle. To increase exports and decrease imports, quota systems were put into operation, and tariffs were boosted to new highs. After almost a century of free trade, modified by a few protective duties levied during and after World War I, Great Britain enacted a high tariff in 1932 but allowed for the system of imperial preference, whereby lower tariffs were levied on members of the empire than on outside nations. The net effect was the increase of trade within the empire at the expense of trade with outside countries.

Another technique for increasing exports was to depreciate the currency, which meant reducing the value of a nation's money. When Japan depreciated the yen, an American dollar or a British pound could buy more Japanese goods. In effect, depreciating the yen lowered the price of Japanese exports. In most cases, however, devaluation brought only a temporary trade advantage; other countries could play the same game. In 1934 the United States reduced the amount of gold backing the dollar by about 40 percent.

The disturbances in the natural flow of world trade caused by the depression led nations to hoard their gold reserves—a trend strengthened by the fact that most nations had comparatively little gold, the United States, Great Britain, and France controlling three fourths of the world's supply. Many nations went off the gold standard, which meant that they would not pay foreign creditors in gold. Great Britain abandoned the gold standard in 1931; two years later the United States did likewise. Without gold as the medium of exchange between countries, barter became more and more prevalent in international trade.

The depression had profound implications for politics. The rash of democratic constitutions adopted after World War I had seemed to assure government by and for the common man, but in the tragic thirties democracy in many nations went into eclipse as unemployed and starving masses turned to dictators who promised jobs and bread. The hardships of the depression formed a dismal backdrop on a political stage where dictators seized the leading roles.

Considering the shattering impact of this world economic malaise, there has been relatively little research and comprehensive literature about its background and causes. Was it the inevitable consequence of unwise peace treaties; was it the result of the economic losses and disruption of trade suffered by the belligerents during World War I; or was it mainly caused by the United States tariff and reparations policies compounded by a fanatical fever of stock speculation? A

noted economist has called attention to a number of unhealthy conditions in the American economy: (1) the uneven distribution of income between the very rich and the extremely poor; (2) the lack of stability, honesty, and good management in the corporate structure; (3) an inherently unsound banking system; and (4) the lack of adequate economic intelligence available to businessmen.[3] Although all these factors existed to some degree in other national economies, the United States occupied such a central position in world finance that any substantial reverse or breakdown in its economy inevitably had world repercussions. As the dean of a noted American school of business administration has stated: "I can only repeat that I think it was primarily of American domestic origin, though with many complicating circumstances."[4]

The Five-Year Plans in the Soviet Union. The years from 1929 to 1939 comprised a dark decade in Russia—a period of massive industrialization and of convulsive inner struggles as Stalin established a personal dictatorship both total and terrible. While in the capitalist countries factories and mines were idle or running on reduced schedules and millions were unemployed, the Soviet people worked many hours a day, six days a week, in an all-out attempt to revolutionize Russia's economic structure. For the first time in history, a government controlled all economic activity.

In 1928 Stalin proposed a Five-Year Plan, the first of a number of such schemes aimed at the relatively swift accumulation of capital resources through the buildup of heavy industry, the collectivization of agriculture, and the restricted manufacture of consumers' goods. Although capitalism in the form of the NEP was abolished, citizens were permitted to own certain types of private property—houses, furniture, clothes, and personal effects. They could not, however, own property which could be utilized to make profits by hiring workers. The only employer was the state.

As part of the plan, the government took control of agriculture through the state farms. By the beginning of the Second World War 90 percent of the Russian land under cultivation was organized in one of two ways. The state farm (*sovkhoz*) was owned outright by the government and run by paid laborers. The collective farm (*kolkhoz*) was created from land given up by the peasants who accepted the government's decree to merge their holdings and from land taken from the *kulaks*—well-to-do farmers. The *kolkhoz* members worked the land under the management of a board of directors. At the end of the year the farm's net earnings were computed in cash and in kind, and the members were paid on the basis of the number of days they had worked.

A second Five-Year Plan, begun in 1933, sought to redress some of the mistakes of the first; greater emphasis was placed on improving the quality of industrial products and on manufacturing more consumers' goods. The year 1938 witnessed the initiation of the third Five-Year Plan, in which national defense became the major consideration. Industrial plants were shifted inland to the east, and efforts were made to develop new sources of oil and other important commodities. The world's largest tractor factory was erected in Chelyabinsk, the greatest electric power station in Dnepropetrovsk, and the largest automobile plant at Gorki.

The plans achieved remarkable results. Soviet authorities claimed in 1932 an increase of industrial output of 334 percent over 1914, and in 1937 a further increase of 180 percent over 1932. However, the high volume of production was often coupled with mediocre quality, and the achievements were secured only at an enormous cost in human life and suffering. At first a bare subsistence scale of living was imposed on the people by the burdensome expense of importing heavy machinery, tools, equipment, and finished steel from abroad. These purchases were paid for by the sale of food and raw materials in the world's markets at a time when the prices of such goods had drastically fallen. An even greater cost was the terrible loss of life brought about by the callous collectivization of agriculture. By a decree of February 1930, about one million *kulaks* were forced off their land and all their possessions confiscated. Many farmers consistently opposed regimentation by the state,

often slaughtering their herds when faced with the loss of their land. In some sections they revolted, and thousands were executed. A serious famine broke out and several million peasants died of starvation.

Another casualty of the Five-Year Plans was Lenin's basic concept of economic equalitarianism. In 1931 Stalin declared that equality in wages was "alien and detrimental to Soviet production" and a "petit-bourgeois deviation." So much propaganda was used to implant this ideological twist that the masses came to accept the new doctrine of the inequality of wages as a fundamental Communist principle. Piecework in industry became more prevalent, and bonuses and incentives were used to speed up production. It was indeed ironic that capitalistic practices were introduced to stimulate the growth of communism.

The great purges. While the Five-Year Plans were forging ahead, Stalin was establishing an all-powerful personal autocracy. From 1928 to 1931 and again from 1935 to 1938, Stalin settled his accounts with all his rivals through barbaric purges. The long arm of the secret police gathered in thousands of Soviet citizens to face the firing squad. Of the six original members of the 1920 Politburo who survived Lenin, all were purged by Stalin. Old Bolsheviks who had been loyal comrades of Lenin, high officers in the Red Army, and directors of industry were liquidated. It has been estimated that between 5 and 6 percent of the total population passed through the pretrial prisons of the secret police. The fitting climax to the purges came in 1940, when Stalin's archcritic Trotsky, living as an exile in Mexico, was murdered by a Soviet agent.

In 1936, notwithstanding the terror of his secret police, Stalin ostensibly turned to constitutionalism. A new constitution declared that: "All power in the U.S.S.R. belongs to the toilers of town and country as represented by the Soviets of Toilers' Deputies." On the surface many basic rights, such as free speech, secret ballot, and universal suffrage, were granted, together with a number of important economic and social rights. In practice, however, much of the new document was mere window dressing.

The people, however, were given some feeling of participation in their government by means of parades, rallies, and carefully supervised elections. The liberal features of the new constitution also improved Soviet Russia's image abroad. Nevertheless, the Communist party, with less than 1.5 percent of the population, still continued to dictate the government policy.

Crisis in Germany. World depression, accompanied by the cancellation of foreign loans to Germany and the withdrawal of foreign investments, was the culminating blow to the ill-fated Weimar Republic. In 1931 all banks were forced to close, and disorders broke out in many cities. A year later the number of unemployed had reached six million; and desperate, jobless workers roamed the streets shouting, "Give us bread." Night after night, police and military troops battled hungry mobs.

Up to this time the Nazi party had attracted only lukewarm support; there were but a handful of Nazi deputies in the Reichstag. By the summer of 1932, however, their number had swelled to 230, and the Nazis had become the largest political party. Hungry, frightened, and desperate, the impoverished masses turned to Hitler as a source of salvation. And, ironically enough, the rich also saw their salvation in Nazism. Alarmed at the growth of the German Communist movement, the great industrialists supported Hitler—a rabid anti-Communist—and his Nazi party as a shield against a proletarian revolution.

Once the Nazi movement began to gain popularity, Hitler and his master propagandist, Joseph Goebbels, utilized every type of persuasion to make the mass of the people permanent converts to Nazism. All over Germany huge meetings were organized. Then thousands of Storm Troopers marched into stadiums to form a great swastika, while martial music, the roll of drums, and the trumpeting of bugles filled the air. At first, no speaker was seen on the platform, starkly illuminated by a huge spotlight. Then, as the suspense became almost unbearable, into the beam of light stepped Goebbels or, on major occasions, Hitler himself. For hours the speaker poured forth a torrent of words.

With crusading zeal, Hitler used every type of propaganda to make the German people permanent converts to Nazism: huge meetings, parades, sporting events. Here, Hitler makes his entrance at the annual Nazi rally in Nuremberg, where he made some of his most virulent speeches.

"Germany is in ruins," "This is the result of reparations," "The Jews are behind all our woes," "It is only the Nazi party that can make Germany strong and prosperous, that will repudiate the reparations and make Germany's army and navy the fear of all Europe." Thrilled by these colossal displays and mesmerized by rituals and ranting speeches, the masses gave the Nazis increasing support.

Hitler becomes chancellor. For the Nazi party, 1932—when Hitler ran against the incumbent Paul von Hindenburg for the presidency of the German republic—was a crucial year. Although Hitler was defeated, Hindenburg asked the Nazi leader to join coalitions on two subsequent occasions. Hitler refused, demanding what was equivalent to dictatorial power.

It became increasingly difficult for the German ministries to carry on the government, and a second general election held in November was so costly to the Nazis that

On March 3, 1933—two days before a special election called by Hitler—fire broke out in twenty different places in the German Parliament House, called The Reichstag. According to police and the Nazis, the fire was started by Communists as a signal for a country-wide uprising, This photograph shows the smoldering blaze as it was being quelled.

the party treasury almost went bankrupt. Some observers believed that the Nazis had passed the crest of their power. At this point, however, a clique of aristocratic nationalists and powerful industrialists, fearful of a Communist revolution and the growing strength of the trade union movement, offered Hitler the chancellorship. In January 1933 a mixed cabinet of nationalists was created with Hitler at the head. Because he did not have a clear majority in the Reichstag, Hitler called a general election for March 5. During the campaign, radio broadcasts were monopolized by Nazi propaganda, and Storm Troopers bullied and coerced the voters. But many Germans became disgusted with the strong-arm methods, and the Nazis needed a dramatic incident to clear a majority in the election.

Just before the election, fire gutted the Reichstag building. The blaze was blamed on the Communists, though there was strong suspicion that the Nazis themselves had started it. When the votes were counted, Hitler controlled 44 percent of the deputies. The added support of the Nationalists (another 8 percent) gave the Nazis a bare majority. Quickly the Reichstag passed the Enabling Act, which granted Hitler the right to legislate by decree for the next four years. The Weimar constitution was never formally—only effectively—abolished; the Reichstag continued as a phantom legislature, but nearly all political power was exercised by one organization, the National Socialist party.

A dread intimation of things to come was Germany's withdrawal from the League of Nations in 1933. Two years later, in defiance of the Treaty of Versailles, Hitler introduced conscription. When President von Hindenburg died in 1934, Hitler became both chancellor and president; he was known as Führer (leader), and the new regime was described as the Third Reich.*

Persecution of the Jews. Hitler ruthlessly uprooted and smashed the democratic institutions by which he was brought to power. All rival political parties were disbanded by force, and individuals who had spoken out against Nazism mysteriously disappeared after midnight visits from the dreaded Gestapo—the Nazi secret police. Concentration camps were built to house thousands of prisoners. It has been estimated that in 1933 nineteen thousand Germans committed suicide and sixteen thousand more died from unexplained causes. Not until the end of World War II was the full horror of Nazi brutality revealed.

The doctrine of Aryan racial superiority was an integral part of Hitler's program, and the Jews bore the brunt of Nazi persecution. They were blamed for the Versailles Treaty, for all that was bad about capitalism, for revolutionary communism, for pacifism, and for internationalism—all represented as being facets of a Jewish plot to destroy Germany and seize control of the world. That such a fantastic tale was seriously believed by a considerable number of the citizens indicated the state of near psychosis into which Germany had fallen.

Once he was dictator, Hitler did everything to stifle and to destroy the Jews. They were prohibited from owning businesses, barred from public service, and deprived

*The First Reich was created by Otto the Great in 962; the Second by Bismarck in 1871.

of citizenship. Marriage between "Aryans" and "non-Aryans" was forbidden. Six million Jews were killed in extermination camps, where the Nazis used the most refined techniques of science to carry out loathsome mass murders. The German commandant of one of these camps has described its methods:

I used . . . a crystallized prussic acid dropped into the death chamber. It took from three to fifteen minutes to kill the people in the chamber, according to climatic conditions. We knew when the people were dead because their screaming stopped. We usually waited about half an hour before we opened the doors and removed the bodies. After the bodies were removed, our special commandos took off the rings and extracted the gold from the teeth of the corpses. . . . we built our gas chambers to accommodate two thousand people at one time. . . .[5]

Nazi propaganda and education. A Reich culture cabinet was set up to instill a single pattern of thought in literature, the press, broadcasting, drama, music, art, and movies. Forbidden books, including the works of some of Germany's most distinguished men of letters, were seized and destroyed in huge bonfires.

The school system was integrated with the German Youth Movement, which drilled and regimented boys and girls between the ages of ten and fourteen. The boys were taught above all else to be ready to fight and die for their Führer; the girls, to mother the many babies needed by the Third Reich. The German universities, once famous throughout the world for their academic freedom, became agencies for propagating such ideas as the racial myths of Nazism; and since Nazi doctrine elevated the state above all else, a movement was instigated to subordinate religion to the Hitler regime. Enrollment in the universities was limited to good Nazi material, and professors were dismissed by the score.

Public works and rearmament. In theory and in outward form, Nazism retained capitalism and private property. Business and labor, however, were rigidly controlled by the state. Labor unions were dissolved, and both workers and employers were enrolled in a new organization, the Labor Front. As in Mussolini's corporate state, the right of the workers to strike or of management to call a lockout was denied. Compulsory dues were taken from workers' wages to support Nazi organizations. As a sop, the government established the Strength Through Joy movement, which provided sports events musical festivals, plays, movies, and vacations at low cost.

The government's attempts to solve Germany's economic problems included levying a huge tax load on the middle class and increasing the national debt by one third in order to provide work for the unemployed. To create jobs, the first Four-Year Plan, established in 1933, initiated an extensive program of public works and rearmament. The unemployed were put to work on public projects (especially noteworthy was a great network of highways, or *Autobahnen*), in munitions factories, and in the army. The program led to the production of vast arma-

In "White Crucifixion" Marc Chagall takes as his theme the persecution of Jews during modern times. Note the burning synagogue, upper right, and the Jewish refugees throughout the picture. To give universality to his message and to symbolize man's ravaged innocence, Chagall focuses on the crucified figure of Christ.

ments and to their eventual utilization in aggression against other states.

Overlapping the first program, the second Four-Year Plan was initiated in 1936. The objective of this plan was to set up an autarkist state. In order to achieve self-sufficiency, quantities of substitute (*ersatz*) commodities —frequently both inferior in quality and more costly than those purchasable on the world market—were produced by German laboratories, factories, and mills. The standard of living continued to decline.

Nazism—Why? The rise and victory of the brutal, atavistic Nazi movement in such a culturally advanced nation as Germany must be regarded as one of the most momentous events of the twentieth century. How to account for this phenomenon and its leader, Hitler, constitutes one of the most complicated and fascinating problems in historical causation.

One school of thought has found the answer in the logical outcome of German history. Over the centuries national traditions had progressively united such elements as authoritarianism, submissiveness on the part of the individual, strains of unstable and explosive mysticism, anti-Semitism, and a belief in the superiority of the "Germanic-Nordic race." Other historians deny that a German national character had anything to to do with Nazism; they assert that it was the understandable result of the catastrophic impact of the Treaty of Versailles and the depression. Marxist explanations see Fascism coming to power in Germany because of the Communist menace and its threat to a crumbling capitalistic system. Such arguments naturally emphasize the financial assistance Hitler received from German big business. The role of the army has also received attention. The army had always been an important, influential, and respected force in public life, and the military chiefs, unhappy with their lot under the Republic, gladly turned their support to Hitler in 1933.

Social psychologists maintain that the key is to be found in the psychological mood of the German people. Generally the populace was in a condition of stress, insecurity, and frustration. The immediate post-1918 trends had had a painful effect upon all Germans, no matter what their social position. The depression, with its massive unemployment, political instability, and ineptitude of the leaders of the republic, left millions in a state of traumatic shock. "Hitler succeeded not because of a conspiracy of the few but because his movement gave high hope to the many of solving the pressing psychological demands of a people living under conditions of acute stress. Defeated by war and broken by inflation, the uprooted, humiliated, and insecure Germans were attracted to Nazism because they felt that their personal problems would be solved by a movement that promised to supply everything they lacked as individuals: dramatic action, a sense of purpose, a feeling of power."[6] Other nations, however, experienced shocks to their national lives, perhaps as traumatic as Germany's, and yet did not accept the extreme solution of Nazism. There were, then, certain elements in the German situation that were unique and conducive to a Nazi victory. Not least of these was the charismatic leadership of Hitler. Some observers maintain that there could have been no Third Reich without this perverted genius.

Depression under Italian Fascism. In 1933 the number of unemployed in Italy totaled more than one million, and the public debt reached an alarming figure. Italian wages were the lowest in Europe, and living standards had sunk to a level below that of 1914. To strengthen the Fascist economy, the nation was reorganized in 1934 into twenty-two government-controlled corporations, each consisting of syndicates of workers and employers. But in spite of a grandiose program of public works and the adoption of measures to increase agricultural output, Mussolini's corporate state continued to suffer from the depression.

In racial matters, the Fascist regime made half-hearted attempts to copy the Nazis. Italians were urged to be "race conscious," but the decrees issued against Jews were not rigidly enforced.

Parliamentary demoralization in France. The lack of vigorous leadership in the democratic nations and the mounting crisis in their capitalistic systems were best exemplified in France. Although the prosperity of the twenties carried over after other nations were engulfed in depression, in the early thirties France was faced with rising unemployment, budget deficits, the drying up of the lucrative tourist trade, and heavy military expenditures for security against a rearming Germany. Ministry after ministry was organized, only to collapse a few months later; citizens became more and more impatient with the government.

Disgust with the administration increased with the exposure of corruption in high places. It became known that many prominent politicians were involved in the machinations of Alexander Stavisky, who had cheated French investors out of some 600 million francs. When the ministry in power ignored public furor and refused to authorize an investigation, thousands of angry citizens thronged the streets of Paris on the evening of February 6, 1934, and tried to storm the Chamber of Deputies.

The outcome was a new government, the National Union, which ignored pleas for constitutional reform and for a grant of increased power to the prime minister. The agent of the wealthy and privileged classes, the National Union grew ultraconservative but continued to rule under a variety of prime ministers.

In 1936 emerged the Popular Front, a coalition composed of liberal parties united in opposition to the conservative elements in the government. In June the Popular Front won a national election; and Léon Blum (1872-1950), a noted lawyer and writer, became premier. The Popular Front endeavored to stem the influence of fascist ideas, to improve the country's finances, and to bring about certain fundamental economic reforms. In particular, the Popular Front promised to "break the power of the two hundred families who control the economic life of the nation."[7] In foreign policy the Popular Front was friendly to Great Britain and supported the League of Nations. This coalition faced numerous dilemmas. The central problem was how to cooperate with the Communists without being captured by them. Many Frenchmen were reluctant to support the Popular Front for fear it might commit France to fight against Germany for the benefit of the Soviet Union.

An epidemic of sit-down strikes embarrassed the new government, but gradually labor was conciliated by the passage of laws introducing a forty-hour week, higher wages, collective bargaining, and vacations with pay. Furthermore, the government extended its control over the Bank of France and initiated a public works program. Although the Blum government stood resolutely for the laborer and against monopoly and big business, it was equally against communist collectivism or fascist centralization. After only a year in office, however, Blum was forced to resign. Unfavorable trade balances, an enormous public debt, and an unbalanced budget proved too much for the Popular Front government. France swung back to conservatism. The forty-hour week was ended, and strikes were energetically suppressed.

The National Union and the Popular Front mirrored the widening chasm between the upper and lower classes. The working classes believed that the reforms of the Popular Front had been sabotaged and that a France ruled by a wealthy clique deserved little or no allegiance. On the other hand, some businessmen and financiers were horrified at the prospect of communism and flirted with fascism. The cleavage between classes was secretly encouraged by subtle propaganda from the totalitarian countries. While Frenchmen quarreled and France's economic strength was being sapped, Hitler's Germany, regimented and feverishly productive, was rapidly outstripping France in the manufacture of armaments. The ingredients for the tragic fall of France in the spring of 1940 had now been supplied.

Democracy in crisis elsewhere in Europe. Except in Finland and Czechoslovakia, a progressive weakening of parliamentary systems occurred in the smaller European states of eastern and Balkan Europe. These states retained a meaningless appearance of parliamentary forms. Behind the false front, however, a small clique—aided by secret police, censorship, and armed political supporters—stifled all opposition to the government in power.

"Muddling through" in Britain. It was inevitable that the depression would have catastrophic effects in the highly industrialized and heavily populated island of Britain. In two years exports and imports declined 35 percent, and three million unemployed roamed the streets.

A Labour administration, with James Ramsay MacDonald as prime minister, took office in 1929. Little was accomplished, and unemployment became more widespread as the depression deepened. When the Labour government fell, MacDonald retained his office by becoming the leader of a National Coalition government, which was primarily conservative. The bulk of the Labour party constituted the opposition.

Nothing spectacular was undertaken, but the country in typical British fashion did "muddle through." Unlike Germany, which gave up democracy, and France, which kept it but did not know what to do with it, Britain adhered strongly to its traditional parliamentary system. By 1937 a substantial measure of prosperity had been regained, and production registered a 20 percent increase over that of 1929. To achieve this comeback, much of what remained of laissez-faire policy was discarded. The government now regulated the currency, erected high tariffs, gave farmers subsidies, and imposed a heavy burden of taxation. The rich had a large proportion of their income taxed away, and what might be left at death was decimated by inheritance taxes. It was ruefully declared that the rich could hardly afford to live, much less to die.

Despite improvements in the economic picture, an increasing demand for the extension of the welfare state existed. There were pleas for expanded educational and health facilities, better accident and unemployment insurance, and more adequate pensions. A survey of Britain's social services, made in 1941 by the noted economist Sir William Beveridge, recommended a comprehensive system of social insurance. This plan served as the blueprint for Britain's post-World War II legislation that tried to give security "from the cradle to the grave."

The British Commonwealth weathers the storm. In common with the rest of the world, Britain's self-governing dominions were hard hit by the depression. Like Latin America, they were painfully susceptible to the effects of the world slump because they were primarily producers of basic materials, such as wheat, meat, lumber, and minerals. When prices of such products dropped to rock bottom, the dominions (which had borrowed heavily on outside capital) were able to avoid defaults on their obligations only by the most stringent economies. But democracy did not succumb; there were no violent overthrows in Australia, New Zealand, Canada, or South Africa, for parliamentary traditions were strong and natural resources were abundant.

Political instability in Latin America. The Latin American countries, which depended on the export of a few all-important raw materials for their prosperity, suffered serious economic crises as world prices collapsed. Largely as a result of the depression, six South American nations experienced revolutions in 1930.

Out of the increased industrialization and land reform resulting from the revolutions came the gradual development of a middle class, where before there had been only a small group of the extremely rich and great masses of the poor. Rising political, economic, and social standards promised better health and education for more people. The Catholic Church, accused by many of being the ally of the wealthy and powerful, was subject to growing anticlerical attacks, although the continent continued to be almost totally Catholic.

In 1933 the United States inaugurated the Good Neighbor Policy, whose beginnings can be traced back to the Hoover administration. By stimulating trade and formally agreeing that "no state has the right to intervene in the internal or external affairs of another," the United States demonstrated the sincerity of its overtures to the southern continent. In 1934 an Export-Import Bank was established in Washington to help finance foreign trade, especially with Latin America. It has been estimated that between 1934 and 1941 this institution created $560 million worth of American trade.[8] Rivalries among industrialized nations for the Latin

American market became very intense during the thirties. Nazi Germany concluded many barter agreements with Latin American customers and at the same time penetrated the countries politically by organizing German immigrants into pro-Nazi groups, fostering fascist politicians, and developing a formidable propaganda system. When war came and the chips were down, however, Latin America eventually lined up with the democracies.

The New Deal fights depression. In shocking contrast to the golden days of prosperity, the frenzied boom on the stock market, and the smug complacency of American businessmen in the 1920's was the economic paralysis which gripped the United States in 1930. By 1932, business failures numbered at least thirty thousand, and the number of unemployed was somewhere between twelve and fifteen million.

In the first few years after the crash President Hoover tried to prop up shaky businesses with government money in the hope that the benefits would filter down to the workers. Because the President believed that the government should not compete with private concerns, only a few public works projects were started. Hoover avoided federal relief, leaving to private charities and local governments the heavy responsibility for caring for the hungry. Toward the end of his term the depression steadily worsened, and thousands of people went hungry because they had no money for food.

The general dissatisfaction with the government was evidenced by the sweeping victory of Franklin D. Roosevelt (1882-1945), the Democratic standard-bearer, who was inaugurated in 1933. Under his leadership the New Deal, a sweeping program to cope with the national emergency, was put into operation. The three objectives of the New Deal were relief, recovery, and reform. Millions of dollars were appropriated for the relief of the unemployed, and vast sums were expended for the construction of public works in the belief that such activity would stimulate economic recovery. A combination work and relief program, the Civilian Conservation Corps, offered employment and education to thousands of young men. To

encourage building activity, the Federal Housing Administration offered liberal terms to finance new homes, especially for low-income families. Most significant was the Social Security Act, passed in 1935. For the first time in the history of the United States, a comprehensive scheme for unemployment insurance and a plan for old-age benefits were introduced.

To prevent a recurrence of the crash, measures were instituted to guarantee the savings deposits of small investors; and the sale of stocks and bonds was regulated by the Securities and Exchange Commission. The Tennessee Valley Authority was established to produce power at reasonable rates that would constitute a yardstick for public utilities. On the labor front, the National Labor Relations Board was designed to protect labor and give it the right to bargain collectively.

The measures and objectives of the New Deal aroused much controversy. Its opponents contended that it gave too much power to the labor unions, that it created a vast, irresponsible bureaucracy at Washington, D.C., that it spent public funds in a profligate fashion, and that it sought to destroy the capitalist system. Its supporters, on the other hand, maintained that the New Deal did not aim to destroy capitalism but rather to preserve it by adapting it to new circumstances, and that thus it represented a reasonable compromise between the discredited system of laissez faire with its unbridled opportunities for exploitation and, at the other extreme, the pervasive and all-powerful economic controls exercised by states under totalitarian regimes.

AGGRESSION AND APPEASEMENT

Japanese aggression in Manchuria. The first challenge to world peace occurred in September 1931, when Japan moved into Manchuria. Unable to cope with the invader, the Chinese appealed to the League of Nations, which appointed a committee of inquiry. The committee report condemned the aggression while trying not to affront Japan, which nevertheless resigned its League membership two years later. The significance of the Manchurian campaign was dreadfully clear. A demonstration that a great power could embark on aggression without any effective opposition from League members marked the beginning of the collapse of the League.

When the Chinese resorted to a nationwide boycott of Japanese goods, the Japanese attacked Shanghai and early in 1933 began to push deeper into northern China. To slow down the invasion and give themselves a chance to prepare for the inevitable struggle, the Chinese agreed to the Tang-ku Truce, which recognized Japanese conquests in Manchuria and northern China. The truce remained in effect for about four years, while the Japanese consolidated their position and the Chinese wrestled with internal threats.

The united front in China. In addition to the invaders, the Nationalist forces of Chiang Kai-shek had to contend with the Chinese Communists (see p. 745). The Chinese Com-

A band of Japanese soldiers triumphantly shout "Banzai!" as they return from a battle with the Chinese at Fengtai in 1937. Japan continued to play the role of an aggressor up to and during World War II, joining Italy and Germany in the formation of the Axis powers.

munists demanded a united front against the Japanese, stating that the first objective of all China should be whole-hearted resistance against foreign imperialism and aggression. In 1936 the Communists kidnaped Chiang and held him for two weeks. There was a great outcry from the Chinese people, and, influenced by the obvious national solidarity behind Chiang, the rebels asked him to lead a united China against the common enemy. In order to allay suspicion and achieve a united front, Mao Tse-tung agreed to end land confiscation and armed opposition to the Nanking government, to abandon the system of soviets, and to permit the incorporation of the Communist forces into the fight against Japan. Neither of the parties to the truce trusted each other, but they both feared the Japanese. China was unified just in time to meet the next Japanese thrust.

Japanese conquests continue. In 1937 fighting broke out again, this time around Peking. Farther south, Japanese troops captured Shanghai and advanced rapidly up the Yangtze valley to Nanking. The Chinese retreated westward, establishing a new capital at Chungking. In North China the Chinese armies were also forced to retreat, and the Japanese set up a government at Peking.

In 1938 Japan proclaimed the New Order in eastern Asia. Its objectives were the destruction of Chiang Kai-shek's regime, the expulsion of western interests in eastern Asia, and the establishment of a self-sufficient economic bloc to include Japan, Manchuria (which was renamed Manchukuo by the Japanese), and China.

The outbreak of war in Europe gave Japan its golden opportunity to extend the New Order in China and into the Asian colonies of the western powers. The year 1939 saw several strong but inconclusive offensives in China and the seizure of the island of Hainan, of strategic importance in relation to French Indochina, British Malaya, and the Dutch East Indies. After the fall of France in June 1940, the Vichy government allowed Japan to build naval and air bases in Indochina. Japanese pressure was also exerted on the Dutch East Indies and on British settlements in China. By the time Japan was actively engaged in the Second World War, the New Order was being rapidly expanded over much of Asia.

Of the three great powers which might have halted Japanese banditry in the 1930's, Britain was in the throes of an economic crisis, France suffered both political and economic paralysis, and the United States, feverishly occupied with its New Deal, was still isolationist, holding to the view "that foreign affairs are something not pleasant that happens to other people."[9]

Italy swallows up Abyssinia. Italian aggression in Abyssinia followed Japan's lead. As his first victim, Mussolini chose Abyssinia, the only important independent native state left in Africa and the nation which in 1896 had handed the Italians a humiliating defeat. Late in 1934 fighting broke out between the Abyssinians and the Italians, and in the following year the Italians made a wholesale invasion of Abyssinia. Emperor Haile Selassie appealed to the League, which tried to arrange for arbitration. Despite the Italian delegates' audacious argument that Abyssinia, not Italy, was the aggressor, the League voted to prohibit shipment of certain goods to Italy and denied it credit. But the effect of the sanctions was nullified because oil—without which no modern army or navy can fight—was not included in the list of prohibited articles. Apprehensive of alienating Italy, France and Britain were only lukewarm in their support of the sanctions; and since they were not League members, the United States and Germany largely ignored the prohibitions.

Using bombs, mustard gas, and tanks, the Italians advanced swiftly into Abyssinia and crushed the resistance of Haile Selassie's valiant soldiers. The whole sorry story ended in July 1936, when the sanctions were removed. Haile Selassie, an emperor without a country, went to live in England, the first of several royal exiles.

Germany marches into the Rhineland. The conflict over Abyssinia gave Hitler his first big opportunity to use the military force he had been building up. In March 1936, while the wrangle over the sanctions against Italy was taking place, German troops marched boldly into the Rhineland in defiance of the Treaty of Versailles and the Locarno agreements (see Reference Map 8). France immediately mobilized 150,000 troops, but Britain refused to support the use of force to compel Germany to withdraw. Many Englishmen thought it hardly worth while to risk war over Germany's demand to fortify its own territory. Others, however, recognized the danger in allowing Hitler to break an agreement with little or no protest.

Alliance of the Axis powers. Up until 1935 Germany had been diplomatically isolated in Europe, faced by the United Front of Great Britain, France, and Italy. But the Abyssinian incident and the imposition of sanctions broke up the United Front, and Italy became Germany's friend. In 1936 the friendship was formalized in the Rome-Berlin Axis, and one year later Mussolini followed Hitler's lead by withdrawing from the League.

Japan, the third major member of the Axis powers, joined forces with Germany in 1936 in the Anti-Comintern Pact. A year later Italy subscribed to the agreement. On the surface the agreement was directed against the international activities of communism; in reality the pact was aimed at Russia. The members of the Rome-Berlin-Tokyo Axis were preparing for expansion.

Dress rehearsal in Spain. In 1936 civil war broke out in Spain, shattering that country and threatening to involve all of Europe. The Spanish republic had been established five years earlier. Long overdue reforms were enacted: new schools were constructed, great estates were broken up, and the army was purged of its parasitic officers. But the republic brought neither prosperity nor stability to Spain. Reactionary groups tried to gain control of the government while left-wing groups resorted to terrorism. The middle-of-the-road reformist government became increasingly powerless to maintain order, and an uprising inspired by reactionary and military cliques began in July 1936.

The totalitarian powers—Italy and Germany—seized the opportunity to ensure a Fascist victory. Large numbers of Italian planes were made available to the Fascist insurgents, led by General Francisco Franco (1892-1975). Most of the regular army troops were faithful to Franco, and a quick victory was anticipated. But many groups stood by the Republic, and, as Communists gained increasing strength in the Republican government, the Soviet Union provided it with aid. Foreign Communists flocked to Spain, as did many idealistic anti-Fascists who were not Communists, including a number from Britain and the United States. The Republicans mustered stronger resistance than expected, and Franco's drive was checked at the outskirts of Madrid.

Instead of permitting arms to be sent to the recognized legal Loyalist government, which had the right under international law to purchase them in self-defense, Great Britain and France, fearful that the conflict would spread, set up a nonintervention system by which the nations of Europe agreed not to send arms to either side. France, Britain, the British Commonwealth, and the United States were the only nations that held to the agreement. Germany and Italy sent troops and equipment to the Fascists, while Russia sent matériel and personnel to the Loyalists at Madrid. Germany, Italy, and Russia tried out their new cannon and combat planes on Spanish battlefields. Internal dissensions weakened Russian assistance, which was not sufficient to offset German and Italian aid. In March 1939 Madrid fell, and the Spanish republic was no more. Franco, at the head of the new state, was endowed with absolute power. The Spanish civil war was not only a national catastrophe, which left permanent scars on a proud and gallant people, but also a dress rehearsal for the tragic global drama of World War II.

British appeasement and Allied weakness. Neville Chamberlain (1869-1940), whose name was to symbolize the policy of appeasement, had become the British prime minister in 1937. Determined to explore every possibility for reaching an equitable understanding with the dictators, Chamberlain persisted in trying to ease international tension despite snubs from those he wished to placate and also warnings from some of his colleagues and from experts in the British foreign office. Chamberlain's policies were strongly supported in England. Many Englishmen had a feeling of "peace guilt"—

namely, that Germany had been unfairly treated in the Treaty of Versailles. In other quarters, there was reluctant admiration for the Nazi regime and the belief that a strong Germany could serve as a buffer against Communist Russia. Most important, however, was the passionate and widespread desire for peace, arising from the war weariness and disillusionment suffered by the democratic peoples after World War I.

The world was uneasily aware of the growing weakness of the democracies and of the major shift in the European balance of power. The small states began to draw away from the impotent League of Nations. Some tried to make deals with Germany and Italy; others, such as the Scandinavian countries and Holland, ran for the dubious shelter of neutrality and "innocent isolation." Belgium gave up its alliance with France, and Poland signed a nonaggression pact with Germany. In the Little Entente of Czechoslovakia, Rumania, and Yugoslavia, only Czechoslovakia remained loyal to Paris. Hitler was fully aware of the pervading obsession for peace in Britain and of the decline of the French alliance system.

Hitler's Austrian coup. In announcing the military reoccupation of the Rhineland in the spring of 1936, Hitler had stated, "We have no territorial demands to make in Europe." The course of events was to belie this statement. By 1938 the German army had amazing strength, the *Luftwaffe* was at its peak, and Hitler was ready to embark on a daring program of expansion. His "territorial demands" were to prove limitless.

Hitler's first victim was his neighbor Austria. Previously, in 1934, Hitler had attempted to annex Austria; and the Austrian chancellor, Engelbert Dollfuss, had been murdered by Nazi agents. Partly because of Mussolini's opposition, this *Putsch* (coup) failed. Four years later, after Mussolini had become his ally, Hitler tried again.

The blow fell on Friday, March 11. American radio listeners were told at 2:15 P.M. that the Austrian chancellor had resigned, at 2:45 that German troops were crossing the frontier, and at 3:43 that the swastika had been hoisted over the Austrian chancellery. Meanwhile, Nazi agents in Austria took over the government; on Saturday German troops occupied most of the country.

Germany aspires to the Sudetenland. After the Austrian coup, Hitler moved on to his next objective, the annexation of the Sudetenland, an area in Czechoslovakia bordering on Germany and peopled mainly by Germans. In September 1938 the Führer bluntly informed Chamberlain that he was determined to secure self-determination for the Sudeten Germans. Chamberlain then persuaded Edouard Daladier, the French premier, that a sacrifice on the part of Czechoslovakia would save the peace. When France, previously counted as an ally by the Czechs, joined England in pressing for acceptance of the Nazi demands, Czechoslovakia had little choice but to agree. Chamberlain gave this news to Hitler, only to discover that the German demands had increased considerably. Hitler demanded that within one week the Czechs evacuate certain areas and that all military matériel, goods, and livestock in these areas be turned over to the Germans immediately. Astonished and embittered at the Führer's duplicity, the British prime minister refused to accept the new terms.

Munich seals the fate of Czechoslovakia. On September 28, 1938, the British House of Commons assembled to hear a report by the prime minister. As he neared the end of his address, a messenger delivered a note from Hitler inviting him to attend a conference at Munich. The following day Hitler, Mussolini, Daladier, and Chamberlain met at the Nazi headquarters in Munich and for thirteen hours worked out the details of the surrender of the Sudetenland. No Czech representative was present. Though an outspoken ally of Czechoslovakia, Russia was completely disregarded. (French and British statesmen distrusted Russia and presumably thought that Hitler's hatred of communism would not permit the attendance of a representative from Moscow.) Not only were all of Hitler's demands accepted, but Poland and Hungary also received slices of Czechoslovakia (see Reference Map 8).

Munich brought relief to millions of Europeans half-crazed with fear of war, but it was still a question whether this settlement would be followed by another crisis. Many hoped for the best but feared the worst. Immediately after Munich, Winston Churchill solemnly warned:

And do not suppose that this is the end. This is only the beginning of the reckoning. This is only the first sip, the first foretaste of a bitter cup which will be proffered to us year by year unless, by a supreme recovery of moral health and martial vigor, we arise again and take our stand for freedom as in the olden time.[10]

The mounting fears of French and British statesmen were confirmed in 1939. Early in March a bitter attack against the Czech government was inaugurated by the German press. Another coup was in the making. Hitler then summoned the Czech president, Emil Hacha, to Berlin. Subjected to all kinds of threats during an all-night session, Hacha finally capitulated and signed a document placing his country under the "protection" of Germany. His signature was a mere formality, however, for German troops were already crossing the Czech frontier. Not to be outdone, Mussolini seized Albania the following month, and the two dictators celebrated by signing a military alliance, the so-called Pact of Steel.

The shock of the final conquest of Czechoslovakia and Hitler's callous violation of pledges made at Munich ended the appeasement policy of France and Great Britain. For the first time in Britain's long history, the government authorized a peacetime draft. A tremendous arms program was launched. In Paris, Daladier obtained special emergency powers to push forward national defense.

Isolationism in the United States. The United States had been disillusioned by the results of the "war to make the world safe for democracy." Influential spokesmen asserted that World War I had been caused by the greed of munitions makers and stressed the centuries-old hatreds and rivalries in Europe; America, therefore, should insulate itself from these potent causes of international conflict. Reflecting this mood, Congress passed neutrality legislation between 1935 and 1937 which made it unlawful for any nation at war to obtain munitions from the United States.

As the Nazi and Fascist menace became apparent in the late 1930's, President Roosevelt and the state department worked strenuously to arouse the American people to the dangers of the world situation. In 1937, in his famous "quarantine speech," Roosevelt declared:

The peace, the freedom and the security of 90 per cent of the population of the world is being jeopardized by the remaining 10 per cent who are threatening a breakdown of all international order and law.

Surely the 90 per cent who want to live in peace under law and in accordance with moral standards that have received almost universal acceptance through the centuries can and must find some way to make their will prevail. . . . There must be positive endeavors to preserve peace.[11]

In May 1939 the president told leaders in the House of Representatives "that in case of war there was at least an even chance that Germans and Italians might win."[12] So strong was isolationist sentiment, however, that the warning went unheeded.

The Polish question and the Nazi-Soviet pact. It was Germany's aggression against Poland that precipitated the Second World War. The Treaty of Versailles had turned over West Prussia to Poland as a Polish Corridor to the sea (see map, p. 703). While 90 percent of the Corridor's population was Polish, the Baltic port city of Danzig was nearly all German. Late in March 1939 Hitler proposed to Poland that Danzig be ceded to Germany and that the Nazis be allowed to occupy a narrow strip of land connecting Germany with East Prussia. Chamberlain, with France concurring, warned the Nazi government that "in the event of any action which clearly threatened Polish independence," the British would "at once lend the Polish government all support in their power." In the months that followed the Allied warning, France and Britain competed with Germany for an alliance with Russia.

The Soviet Union had long been seriously concerned about the twin menaces of Nazi Germany and expansionist Japan. The Kremlin had supported the collective security system of the League and had supposedly called off the subversive activity of the Comintern (Chapter 31) in favor of popular-front governments to oppose the rising tide of Axis aggression. On the other hand, Soviet pledges to call off Comintern activity were openly violated; and the purge trials not only alienated public opinion in many parts of the world but seriously weakened the Red Army, whose leading officers had been removed.

As we have seen, Chamberlain and Daladier ignored the Soviet Union at Munich. Now, with the Polish question of paramount importance, Britain and France desperately needed Russia as an ally. But while British and French negotiators attempted to convince the Kremlin that their nations really desired an effective alliance against Nazi Germany, the Nazi and Soviet foreign secretaries were secretly working out the details of an agreement. On August 23, 1939, Russia and Germany signed a nonaggression pact, an utterly cynical arrangement between two inexorably antagonistic foes.

Through this agreement Stalin gave Hitler a free hand in Poland, thus precipitating war between Germany and Britain and France. Russian political strategy was that such a conflict would give the Soviet Union time to build up its armaments and would weaken the antagonists. With the pact in his pocket, Hitler could attack Poland without fear of intervention by his great rival to the east. Furthermore, he believed that Britain and France would not dare oppose his ambitions. But France and Britain at last understood that if they wished to stop Germany from dominating all of Europe, they must fight.

Basic causes of Hitler's war. Undoubtedly Germany nursed a sense of grievance over what were regarded as the injustices of Versailles. The most important cause of the war, however, was the ruthless ambition of an irrational dictator to gain control of Europe and as much of the rest of the world as he could master. Aiding and abetting his sinister ambition was the strong, even obsessive desire of the democracies for peace. Because Britain and France had long turned the other cheek, Hitler believed that they would not fight under any provocation. Hitler scoffed at the democracies: "Our enemies are little worms. I saw them at Munich."[13]

One of the great lessons of 1939 is that appeasement does not guarantee peace and that it does not take two equally belligerent sides to make a fight. Hitler was genuinely surprised to discover that he had pushed the democracies too far and that he had a real war on his hands. When he was handed the British ultimatum, he turned to Ribbentrop, his foreign minister, and asked: "Well, what now?" There was no reply, but Hermann Goering, the commander of the *Luftwaffe*, exclaimed: "Heaven help us, if we lose this war."[14] Unlike the controversy following World War I over the "war guilt" of the various nations, there has been virtually unanimous agreement that Nazi Germany was responsible for the war.

THE WORLD DIVIDED

Blitzkrieg in Poland. Without a declaration of war, Nazi troops crossed the Polish frontier early in the morning of September 1, 1939, and the *Luftwaffe* began to bomb Polish cities. On the morning of September 3, Chamberlain sent an ultimatum to Germany, demanding that the invasion be halted. The time limit was given as 11 A.M. of the same day. At 11:15 he announced on a radio broadcast that Britain was now at war. France also declared war, and after an interval of only twenty-one years since World War I Europe was again plunged into conflict.

For the first time the world had the opportunity to witness the awesome power of Nazi arms. Polish resistance crumbled, and at the same time Russian forces attacked from the east. In less than a month Poland had been partitioned by the Russo-German treaty. Britain and France did not try to breach the Siegfried line along the Rhine. With their blockade and mastery of the seas, they hoped to defeat Hitler by attrition.

Dunkirk. All seemed to be going according to this plan during the winter of 1939-1940. There was little fighting along the Franco-German frontier during this period of the "phony war," or *Sitzkrieg*. Russia, however, took advantage of the opportunity to force Finland to cede substantial territory, but only after unexpected stubborn resistance. In the late spring there were signs that the Nazi High Command was not prepared to accept a long war of attrition. Neutral Norway and Denmark were invaded and occupied. A month later, in May 1940, German armies overran neutral Holland and Belgium. From the latter, armored columns knifed into France through an undefended gap north of the Maginot line. German forces swept to the English Channel trapping an Anglo-French army of nearly 400,000 on the beach at Dunkirk.

The reverses in Norway and a military crisis in France led to Chamberlain's resignation, and Winston Churchill (1874-1965) became prime minister of Great Britain. While he had intermittently occupied high office during his long career in Parliament, which dated back to 1900, Churchill had suffered numerous frustrations and in the 1930's enjoyed little popular support. At that time he was described as "a might-have-been; a potentially great man flawed by flashiness, irresponsibility, unreliability, and inconsistency."[15] Yet in 1940 Churchill's qualities of leadership rose to match his nation's peril. During the next five years he was the voice and symbol of a defiant and indomitable Britain.

Confronted with the prospect of destruction of the British army at Dunkirk, Churchill refused to be dismayed. Appearing before Parliament as the new prime minister he announced, "I have nothing to offer but blood, toil, tears, and sweat," preparing the people for a long and desperate conflict. By herculean efforts hundreds of small craft, protected by an umbrella of the Royal Air Force, successfully evacuated some 335,000 soldiers. An army had been brought home, but all its heavy equipment had been lost.

The fall of France. After Dunkirk, the fall of France was inevitable. Anxious to be in on the kill, Mussolini declared war against France and Britain. Designated an "open city" by the French, Paris fell on June 14. As the German advance continued, the members of the French government who wished to continue resistance were voted down;

and Marshal Pétain, the eighty-four-year-old hero of Verdun in the First World War, became premier. Pétain immediately asked Hitler for an armistice, and in the same dining car in which the French had imposed armistice terms on the Germans in 1918, the Nazis and the French on June 22 signed the armistice agreement. France was split into two zones, occupied and unoccupied. In unoccupied France, Pétain's government at Vichy was supposedly free from interference, but in reality it was a puppet of the Nazis. And so the Third Republic, created in 1871 from the debris of defeat suffered at German hands, now came to an end because of a new blow from the same quarter. However, a remarkable patriot, General Charles de Gaulle (1890-1970), fled to London and organized a Free French government, which adopted as its symbol the red cross of Lorraine (flown by Joan of Arc in her fight to liberate France centuries earlier) and continued to aid the Allied cause throughout the war.

The crucial battle of Britain. With millions of Europeans already his captives and with millions more living in constant dread of his screaming dive bombers and clanking panzer

divisions, Hitler demanded that the British lay down their arms. But in the face of almost hopeless odds, they rallied to the support of their homeland. Churchill's eloquent defiance of Hitler stirred not only his own countrymen but all of the free world:

We shall go on to the end . . . . we shall defend our Island, whatever the cost may be, we shall fight on the beaches, we shall fight on the landing grounds, we shall fight in the fields and in the streets, we shall fight in the hills; we shall never surrender. . . .[16]

As a prelude to invasion, the Germans sought to gain control of the air over England. Their fighter and bomber squadrons crossed the Channel but were turned back with heavy losses by the R.A.F. All through the winter of 1940-1941, however, England continued to be racked by terrible raids. Night bombing destroyed block after block of England's cities; St. Paul's Cathedral in London stood as a solitary survivor in the midst of acres of desolation. Evacuating their children and old people and sleeping in air-raid shelters, Britain's people stood firm. Their air force retaliated in some

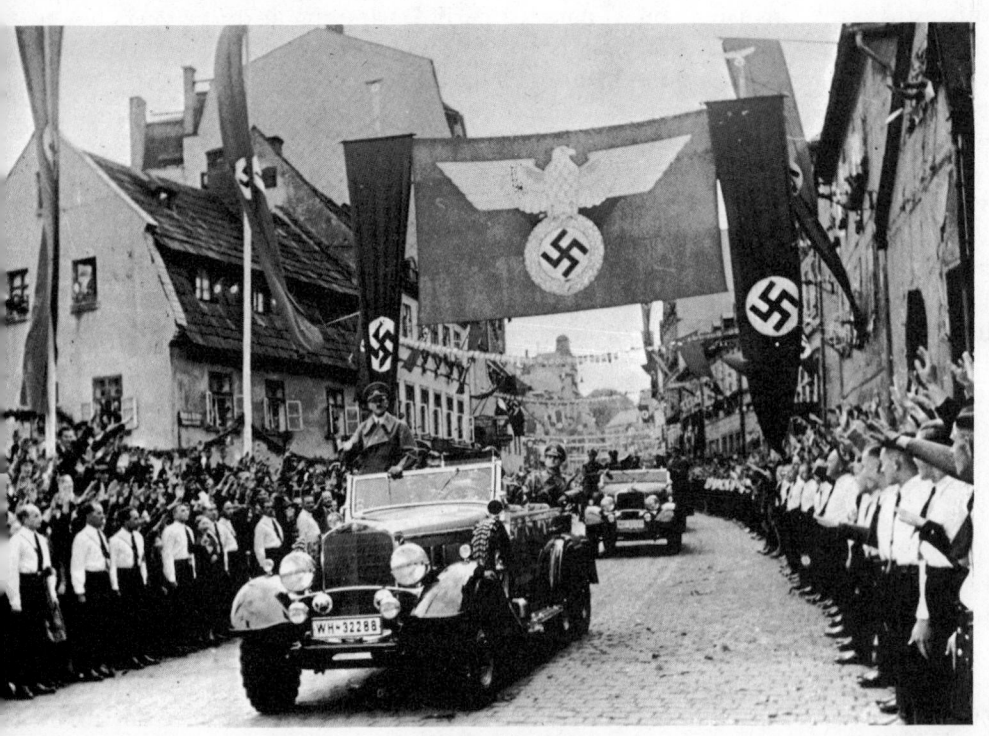

Hitler's victory in Czechoslovakia was only a prelude to the fear and aggression which many nations experienced under the force of Axis conquest. Once war was formally declared, the German, Italian, and Japanese armies proceeded to destroy the strongholds of the Allies, inflicting terrible losses. And like this Frenchman, people from many nations were forced to watch the Axis powers take over their country while their own forces either laid down their arms or escaped into exile. For a while, Axis victory indicated to the world that an Allied defeat was very possible.

measure by raiding the industrial cities of the Ruhr, and their naval forces remained on the offensive.

Italian failures and Nazi successes. Meanwhile, Mussolini was eager to share in the spoils. In October 1940 he invaded neutral Greece, but this thrust proved to be a costly failure. Other defeats were met in North Africa, and Abyssinia was recaptured by British forces. Hitler, on the other hand, continued to expand his domination over Europe. Rumania, Bulgaria, and Hungary became Nazi satellites. In the spring of 1941 Yugoslavia and Greece were overrun.

By the spring of 1941 nearly all of Europe had come under the iron heel of the Third Reich. Only Portugal, Switzerland, Sweden, and Turkey remained neutral. While ostensibly neutral, Spain under Franco was pro-Nazi. Britain, though still dangerous, was powerless to interfere on the Continent. The United States was profoundly disturbed over the Nazi successes but was still unprepared.

Hitler turns on the Soviet Union. Thwarted in his invasion plans of England, Hitler made the fatal decision to invade Russia. Stalin had no illusions about Nazi friendship. When he had signed the nonaggression pact with Hitler in 1939, Stalin had expected that in the event of war the antagonists would wear themselves out and suffer terrific losses. But now Hitler was master of western continental Europe. *Lebensraum* (living space) and badly needed raw materials could be had by expansion to the east.

In June 1941, without warning, a gigantic German attack was launched against Russia, even though many of Hitler's generals were apprehensive. Along a battlefront eighteen hundred miles long, nine million men became locked in struggle. At the outset, the Nazi armored panzer units were irresistible. Russian troops were killed or captured in enormous numbers. In October, Hitler's troops neared the suburbs of Moscow; Russia appeared to be on the verge of collapse. With the coming of winter, however, the Nazi offensive bogged down. Weapons froze, troops were inadequately clothed, and heavy snows blocked the roads. The German attack not only halted, but in the spring of 1942 the Russian army began to recover territory.

The "arsenal of democracy." Following the collapse of France and during the battle

THE CREST OF AXIS POWER

- Allies and areas they controlled
- Axis nations
- Area occupied by the Axis
- Vichy France
- Neutral nations

Battles:
- Allied victory ×
- Axis victory ⊗

Thrusts: →

ARCTIC OCEAN

Murmansk
WHITE SEA
Arkhangelsk
N. Dvina R.

Narvik

ATLANTIC OCEAN

FAEROE IS. (Den.)

NORWAY
Trondheim 1940 Apr.

FINLAND

Lake Onega

SHETLAND IS. (Br.)
ORKNEY IS.
Scapa Flow

SWEDEN

Bergen
Oslo

Helsinki

Lake Ladoga

SOVIET

Kazan

NORTH SEA

Goteborg

Stockholm
Tallinn

Leningrad

Gorki

GREAT
Glasgow
IRELAND
Dublin
Liverpool
BRITAIN
Birmingham
Air battle for Britain
July-Oct. 1940
London
Southampton Dunkirk
May-June 1940

DENMARK Apr. (1940)
Copenhagen

BALTIC SEA

ESTONIA
Pskov

LATVIA
Riga
W. Dvina R.

LITHUANIA
Kaunas

Moscow

UNION

Volga R.
Sarat

Hamburg

Danzig

Minsk

Smolensk

Voronezh

NETHERLANDS
May 1940
Hanover
Berlin
Elbe R.
Germany invaded Poland
Sept. 1, 1939

POLAND

Warsaw

Kiev
Dnieper R.

Kharkov

Don R.

BELGIUM 1940
Cologne
Dresden
Krakow
Lvov

GERMANY

La Havre
Lux.
Frankfurt
Prague
CZECHOSLOVAKIA
Mar. 1939

Rostov

Paris
Rhine R.

Munich

Vienna

Dniester R.

Sea of Azov

Nantes
Loire R.
FRANCE

AUSTRIA
Mar. 1938

Budapest
HUNGARY
Oct. 1940

RUMANIA
Nov. 1940

Odessa

Vichy
Lyons
SWITZERLAND
Milan
Venice
Trieste
YUGOSLAVIA
Apr. 1941
Belgrade
Bucharest
Danube R.

Sevastopol

BLACK SEA

Bordeaux

VICHY FRANCE

Marseilles

Genoa

BULGARIA
Mar. 1941
Sofia

Trabzon

SPAIN
Madrid

Barcelona

CORSICA

ITALY
Rome
Naples

ALBANIA
Apr. 1939

GREECE
Apr. 1941

Salonika

Istanbul
Ankara
Kizil R.

TURKEY

Valencia

BALEARIC IS.

SARDINIA

TYRRHENIAN SEA

ADRIATIC SEA

IONIAN SEA

Athens

AEGEAN SEA

Smyrna

Adana

Aleppo

SYR

Oran
Algiers
Bône
Tunis

SICILY
Palermo

MALTA
(Br.)

CRETE

CYPRUS
(Br.)

Beirut
Damascus

MEDITERRANEAN SEA

Jerusalem
PALESTINE

TRANSJORDAN

ALGERIA

TUNISIA

Tripoli

Bengasi

Alexandria

Suez Canal

SAUDI ARABIA

LIBYA

EGYPT

Cairo

Nile R.

RED SEA

of Britain, the American public began to understand the full implications of an Axis victory. After Dunkirk, arms were sent to Britain, a great rearmament program was undertaken, and compulsory military service was introduced. The Lend-Lease Act of 1941 empowered the president to make arms available to any country whose defense was thought vital to the national interest. Despite ideological differences, munitions were sent to Russia, Nazi Germany's new foe.

To define the moral purpose and principles of the struggle, Roosevelt and Churchill drafted the Atlantic Charter in August 1941. Meeting "somewhere in the Atlantic," the signatories pledged that after "the final destruction of Nazi tyranny," they hoped to see a peace in which "men in all the lands may live out their lives in freedom from fear and want." If the United States was not yet a belligerent in the fall of 1941, it was certainly not neutral.

Pearl Harbor draws the United States into war. It was Japan's expansionist policy which brought the United States directly into the conflict. Confronted with Japanese ambitions for the New Order in Asia, the United States froze Japanese funds and refused to sell it war matériel. In spite of this pressure, Japan made the fateful decision to continue its expansion; in October 1941, General Tojo, an avid militarist, became premier.

On Sunday, December 7, while special "peace" envoys from Tokyo were negotiating in Washington, ostensibly to restore harmony to Japanese-American relations, Japanese planes attacked Pearl Harbor, the American bastion in the Pacific. Half the United States fleet was crippled, and planes were wiped out on the ground. On the following day Congress declared war on Japan. In a few days Italy and Germany declared war on the United States; and Britain, together with the dominions, the refugee governments of Europe, and the Central American republics, ranged themselves with the United States against Japan. On January 2, 1942, the twenty-six nations which now stood arrayed against Germany, Italy, and Japan solemnly pledged themselves to uphold the principles of the Atlantic Charter and declared themselves united for the duration of the conflict.

High tide of the Axis. After Pearl Harbor, Japanese power expanded over the Pacific and into Southeast Asia (see map, next page). Hong Kong, Singapore, the Dutch East Indies, Malaya, Burma, and Indochina were all conquered. An American army was forced to cease its defense of the Philippines when it surrendered at Bataan. The Chinese, however, in their remote inland fortress-capital of Chungking, managed to hold off the Japanese. The summer of 1942 was an agonizing period for the foes of the Axis. A new German offensive pushed deeper into Russia, threatening the important city of Stalingrad. Egypt was placed in peril when the gifted German general, Rommel, inflicted a decisive defeat on the British army in Libya. All over the globe the Axis powers were in the ascendancy.

The road to victory for the Allies. Imminent defeat was suddenly and miraculously transformed to hope of victory in 1942. Further Japanese expansion in the Pacific was halted by two American naval victories —Coral Sea and Midway—and at Guadalcanal American marines began the conquest of Japanese-held islands. In November 1942 British and American troops landed in North Africa, and Axis forces were defeated by the British at Alamein. By May 1943 all Axis troops in North Africa had been destroyed or captured. Hitler fared no better in Russia, where in February 1943 an entire German army was surrounded and captured at Stalingrad. The next Allied thrust was against Italy; in July 1943 Sicily was captured. The whole edifice of Fascism now collapsed. Mussolini was stripped of his office and was later kidnapped by Nazi agents. A new Italian government signed an armistice as Allied forces landed in Italy. Rome was not captured until June 1944, and German resistance continued in northern Italy until the end of the war.

By the end of 1943 the initiative had definitely passed to the Allies. Russian divisions pushed into Poland and wheeled south into the Balkans. On D-Day, June 6, 1944, a vast armada of ships landed half a million men on the beaches of Normandy.

After violent fighting, British and American forces entered Germany in October. At the same time, Russian troops closed in from the east.

With victory in Europe in sight, Stalin, Roosevelt, and Churchill met at Yalta in the Crimea in February 1945 to discuss the peace arrangements. It was agreed that the Soviet Union could have a slice of Poland and territory and privileges in the Far East, a decision later severely criticized. It was also agreed that Russia would enter the war against Japan and that postwar Germany would be split into four zones. Yalta was the high point of the alliance. After this conference, relations between the Soviet Union and its allies quickly deteriorated.

As the Allied troops advanced through Germany, they uncovered the secret hell of Nazi inhumanity toward the people Hitler despised. In the concentration camps—Belsen, Buchenwald, Dachau, and others—they found the gas ovens which had de-stroyed millions of lives, the wasted bodies of slave laborers who had starved to death, and the living dead who had somehow survived torture and the cruel medical experiments to which they had been subjected. Between 1939 and 1945 the Jewish population in Nazi-occupied Europe had decreased from 9,739,200 to 3,505,800; and another 6,000,000 people—Poles, Czechs, Russians, and others—had also fallen victim to Nazi cruelty.

The Axis leaders did not live to see defeat. Mussolini, a cringing fugitive, was seized by anti-Fascist partisan fighters and shot to death; his mutilated body, with that of his mistress, was trussed up in the public square at Milan, an object of derision and hatred. While street fighting raged in Berlin, Hitler committed suicide. His body and that of the mistress he had just made his wife were doused with gasoline and set afire. Nor did the great wartime leader of the United States live to see the end of the war, although

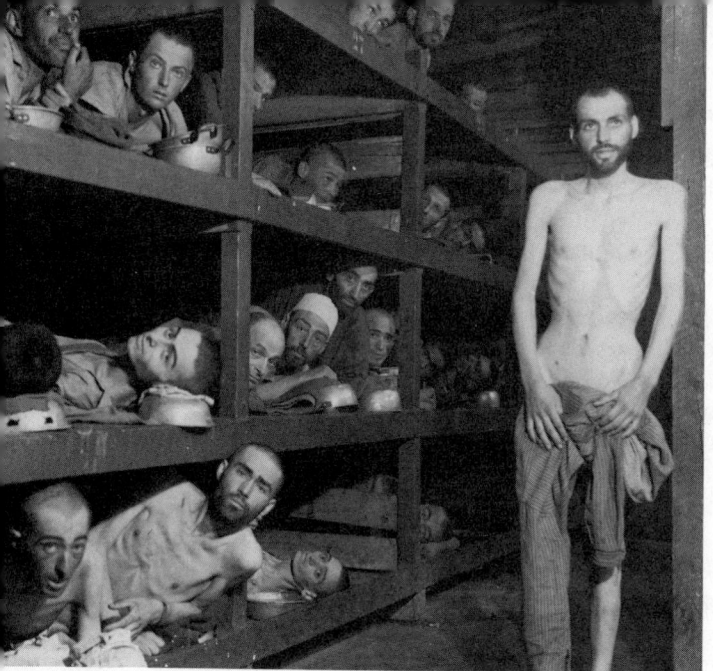

The world did not believe the rumors of the horrible atrocities that befell the Jews in Germany and other Nazi-occupied countries — did not believe, that is, until they actually saw. When the Allies finally broke into Germany in 1945, the world was sickened by the tortures and mass genocide that the Nazis had indeed accomplished. Above is a photograph of Jewish prisoners in the Buchenwald concentration camp.

he realized the imminence of victory. Franklin Roosevelt died suddenly in April 1945, less than a month before the German armies surrendered. The final surrender ceremony took place in Berlin on May 8, designated by President Harry Truman as V-E Day, Victory Day in Europe.

End of the war. While the Allied armies were finishing off the Germans, the Americans had been "island-hopping" their way to Japan, capturing in turn Tarawa, Kwajalein, and Saipan, after bloody struggles on the sandy beaches. In October 1944, with their victory in the battle for Leyte Gulf—the greatest naval engagement in all history—the Allies ended the threat of the Japanese fleet; and in January 1945 General MacArthur returned to the Philippines. The final phase of the war against Japan was unfolding. Only a few hundred miles from Japan, Iwo Jima and Okinawa were conquered; and from such advance bases, waves of American bombers rained destruction on Japanese cities. In the China-Burma-India theater, the Chinese, with American aid, were making inroads on areas previously captured by Japan.

From the Potsdam meeting of the Allied leaders in July-August 1945 came a warning to the Japanese that the war against them would take a new and angry turn. When Japan refused to surrender, an American bomber dropped the most terrible weapon yet invented by mankind—the atomic bomb—on Hiroshima. As the mushroom-shaped cloud rose over the city, only charred ruins were left beneath; an expanse of approximately three miles square—and 60 percent of the city—was almost completely obliterated. The Japanese government estimated that 60,000 people died, 100,000 were wounded, and 200,000 were left homeless. Whether or not the use of the bomb was justified is still a question for debate, but the new weapon achieved its purpose. A few days after the dropping of a second atomic bomb on Nagasaki, the Japanese sued for peace. The surrender ceremony took place September 2 on board the battleship *Missouri*, almost six years to the day after Hitler had plunged the world into the Second World War.

SUMMARY

From 1929 to 1945 the world was in turmoil. People were caught up in a bewildering procession of economic problems, of toppling governments, and of aggressions and finally in a world conflagration. As the focal point of the world's economy, the Wall Street crash of 1929 set off an international depression. To survive this economic earthquake, governments were forced to modify the capitalistic structure by increasing their controls, particularly in the United States and England.

The depression brought Hitler to power in Germany, and a chain of events leading to global conflict was set off. In the 1930's the Axis powers—Germany, Japan, and Italy—carried out a series of aggressions with little opposition. Manchuria, China, Abyssinia, Austria, and Czechoslovakia all heard the tramp of invading troops. By 1939 Hitler had thrown off his mask and revealed his real intentions: the expansion of Germany until much of the world was under the Nazi heel.

The Allied policy of appeasement ended abruptly with the invasion of Poland, and the Second World War was on.

This gigantic struggle can be divided into a series of stages. During 1939 and 1940 Germany virtually mastered Europe. Only Britain remained a defiant and lonely opponent. Following the fall of France, the United States made every effort to aid Britain and then Russia to forestall domination of the world by the Axis.

The totalitarian powers came perilously close to winning in the summer of 1942. After a sneak attack against the United States base at Pearl Harbor, the Japanese invaded island after island in the Pacific. Hitler marched through Russia up to the outskirts of Stalingrad. In North Africa British troops were pushed back into Egypt by General Rommel. By the end of 1942, however, the tide began to turn with an Allied victory in North Africa and a Nazi debacle in the icy streets of Stalingrad. Italy surrendered, the Germans were harassed out of Russia, the submarine menace so destructive to Allied shipping was brought under control in the Atlantic, and the Americans went on the offensive in the Pacific. Germany surrendered in May 1945; the Japanese in August.

In this titanic struggle there was no clear-cut ideological alignment. The exigencies of war helped conceal basic and even conflicting differences in ideology between Britain and the United States on the one hand and Russia on the other. At the same time, the explosion of two atomic bombs registered the awesome warning that world wars in the future would be suicidal for all concerned. Yet the world, numbed by its suffering and exhausted by its efforts, did not understand the danger inherent in the opposing aims of the two ideologies and the vital need to prevent their clash.

SUGGESTIONS FOR READING

J. K. Galbraith, **The Great Crash, 1929*** (Sentry) is a dramatic account of the onset of the depression in the United States. F. L. Allen, **Only Yesterday** (Harper & Row) is a lively social history of the 1930's. See also S. Adler, **The Isolationist Impulse*** (Collier); D. Perkins, **The New Age of Franklin Roosevelt: 1932-1945*** (Univ. of Chicago); and B. Mitchell, **Depression Decade: From New Era to New Deal** (Irvington).

W. L. Shirer, **The Rise and Fall of the Third Reich*** (Fawcett) is a full account by a journalist. Also notable are T. L. Jarman, **The Rise and Fall of Nazi Germany*** (Signet) and H. R. Trevor-Roper, **The Last Days of Hitler*** (Collier). A narrative with a unique portrait of Hitler is Albert Speer, **Inside the Third Reich*** (Avon, 1974); and J. C. Fest, **Hitler*** (Random House, 1975). John Toland, **Adolf Hitler** (Doubleday, 1976) contains much new information.

On the crisis in the West European democracies on the eve of World War II, the following are recommended: A Werth, **The Twilight of France, 1933-1940** (Fertig); J. F. Kennedy, **Why England Slept*** (Dolphin); and H. Thomas, **The Spanish Civil War*** (Harper & Row).

For various viewpoints on the war's origin see J. L. Snell, ed., **The Outbreak of the Second World War: Design or Blunder?** (Heath); A. J. P. Taylor, **The Origins of the Second World War*** (Premier); and L. Lafore, **The End of Glory** (Lippincott, 1970).

Winston Churchill, **The Second World War,*** 6 vols. (Bantam) is a brilliant panoramic survey. Good single-volume histories are L. L. Snyder, **The War: A Concise History*** (Dell); A. Werth, **Russia at War, 1941-1945*** (Avon); C. Wilmot, **The Struggle for Eu-** rope (Watts, 1974); D. D. Eisenhower, **Crusade in Europe*** (Dolphin); and G. Wright, **The Ordeal of Total War, 1939-1945*** (Torchbooks). Good discussions of wartime diplomacy are J. L. Snell, **Illusion and Necessity*** (Houghton Mifflin); H. Feis, **Churchill, Roosevelt, Stalin*** (Princeton Univ.); Joseph P. Lash, **Roosevelt and Churchill** (Norton, 1976); and C. E. Bohlen, **Witness to History*** (Norton, 1973). See also Averell Harriman and Elie Able, **Special Envoy to Stalin, 1941-1946** (Random House, 1975), a masterful personal narrative.

The amazing story of the initial German military triumphs is recounted in T. Taylor, **The March of Conquest*** (Simon & Schuster). R. Wheatley, **Operation Sea Lion*** (Oxford) is an absorbing account of Hitler's plans to invade Britain. Excellent works on other highlights of the war include H. E. Salisbury, **The Nine Hundred Days: The Siege of Leningrad*** (Harper & Row, 1975); C. Ryan, **The Longest Day: June 6, 1944*** (Popular Lib.), and **The Last Battle*** (Pocket Books); J. Toland, **Battle: The Story of the Bulge*** (Mentor); L. Collins and D. Lapierre, **Is Paris Burning?*** (Pocket Books); and W. L. Shirer, **The Collapse of the Third Republic*** (Simon & Schuster, 1971) which recounts a tragic period in France's history. See also J. Hersey, **Hiroshima*** (Bantam).

Excellent novels on World War II include Irwin Shaw, **The Young Lions*** (Signet); N. Mailer, **The Naked and the Dead*** (Signet); N. Monsarrat, **The Cruel Sea*** (Pocket Books); J. Hersey, **The War Lover*** (Bantam); and Herman Wouk, **The Winds of War** (Little, Brown).

*Indicates a less expensive paperbound edition.

A pilot in an airplane droning its way westward in the night sky over India in the early 1930's would occasionally see large splotches of bright lights as it passed over such cities as Madras, Hyderabad, and Bombay. Yet below in the countryside, shrouded in blackness, are thousands of villages. In these 650,000 hamlets live the overwhelming majority of the country's population of 388 million. The usual village consists of a few hundred acres supporting fifty to one hundred families. No paved roads connect it to other hamlets. Dirt paths which become impassable in the rainy season are its only means of communication with the outside world. The village is a confused pattern of narrow streets and lanes on which front one-story, single-room houses. They are made of mud with thatched roofs and have no chimneys or windows.

In such a village in northern India lives Ram Chand, a Hindu peasant, in a joint family. With him are his wife, his married son and daughter-in-law, and their two children. The older parents have lost three children in infancy and a daughter has married and left home. To accommodate these two families, their house has two rooms, instead of the usual one, although all cooking is done on a common hearth. In such a familial unit all wealth is held in common. If the younger couple should have additional children the joint family might split. Wealth in cattle and land would be divided as a new family unit was created. The floor of Ram Chand's family home is dirt smeared with a mixture of mud, water, and cow dung dried to a hard finish. Each room is incredibly bare: no furniture except a bench or perhaps a stringed *charpai* (bed), a few brass pots for cooking and holding water, and some large clay vessels for storing grain or vegetables. One corner is reserved for cooking; a few bricks covered with a small sheet of metal serve as a stove. The family usually sleeps on floor matting. Light, when needed, is provided by a mud saucer with an oil wick. Outside, garbage and filth litter the lanes. There is no running water and no sanitary facilities. Villagers go out into the open fields and children squat in the lanes. During the rainy season there are numerous smelly and noxious pools drawing flies and mosquitos.

The marriage of Ram Chand had been arranged by his parents with the aid of horoscopes, and he has done the same for his own son. Hindus regard marriage as both a social and religious necessity, as a son is needed to perform the funeral rites for his father. Ram Chand was married at the age of seventeen; his wife was two years younger. Traditionally girls are expected to be married before puberty. In the 1920's it was estimated that 40 percent of girls were married before fifteen and two million of them before the age of ten. Couples, however, did not live together immediately after betrothal. In 1930 marriage for a girl before age fourteen and, for a boy, before age eighteen was made a criminal offense. In Ram Chand's family, according to Hindu custom, he was the center of authority and expected his wife to defer to him, such as eating only after he finished. The authoritarian husband and docile wife were considered the ideal relationship by the village. But wives, as always, manage to manipulate many aspects of family life to their wishes. The situation of Indian women, however, caused much concern in enlightened circles. They married too early, had too many children, and had little chance for an education. Barely five percent were literate, and practically none in the villages could read or write. Moreover, their mortality rate was substantially higher than men's.

The social and economic organization of Ram Chand's village is incredibly complex. The caste system has been called "the cocoon of its environment." It dictates the vocation an individual would follow, the group from which a mate could be chosen, and the people one could associate with as friends. Superiority in the caste hierarchy ran from the Brahmins, followed by the traders, and then the occupational castes. These included the cultivators, and such trades as potters, barbers, carpenters, and blacksmiths. Each of these has its own caste rules dictating its social relations with other groups. The untouchables are the lowest in this hierarchy. They are scavengers and do the dirtiest work in the village. For all other Hindus, they cause religious pollution by touch and they defile food and drink. Usually they live in an area detached from the main village.

Peace and order are in the hands of a village council, the *panchayat*. It collects the land revenues, tries petty civil and criminal cases, and sees to the maintenance of minor roads and the village school. Less than three percent of the population of the country has the right to vote. Few peasants are allowed the vote and even fewer still trouble about politics outside their village.

Ram Chand and his fellows work long hours in the fields during seed time and harvest. Farming in India is a gamble — heavy monsoon rains come in a span of three months. While their husbands and sons are in the fields, the women are busy making trips to the village well, sweeping their homes, and spinning yarn. Children are often used to herd cattle. Very few attend the one-room village school; and in Ram Chand's village perhaps a dozen peasants out of the 200 adults are literate.

Wood and coal are too scarce and expensive to be used as household fuel. Women and children gather cattle manure, fashion it into patties, and dry it; this serves as the main fuel of the village. This practice denies the soil of a valuable source of humus.

The income of a peasant family, such as Ram Chand's, is pitifully small. He owns six acres of land broken up into various detached pieces. This fragmentation is widespread and it complicates farming. He owns two oxen for working the land and a buffalo cow gives his family milk. Ram Chand's income from crops is the equivalent of one hundred dollars. After supplying the family's needs, he will be able to sell what is left for about 39 dollars. A land tax of six dollars has to be paid thus leaving a paltry sum for clothing, house repairs, salt, and spices. Unfortunately Ram Chand also owes the moneylender, the *bania*, eighty dollars. The rate of interest is usurious and it is likely that his position would progressively get worse. Rural debt is one of the curses of Indian peasants. Debts incurred are not used for productive purposes but for marriage ceremonies and various religious rites. Peasants ruefully complain, ''The *bania* goes in like a needle and comes out like a sword.''

Low income and general poverty have much to do with deficiencies in diet. Hindus are usually vegetarians. They will not eat beef, although some will eat mutton and goat's flesh; but few ever eat meat because they cannot afford it and because caste restrictions do not permit it. Generally the diet is monotonous—it includes very little eggs, fruit, or milk. In the 1930's it is estimated that only 39 percent of the people are well-fed, about 40 percent are poorly nourished, and 20 percent are near starvation. While primitive herbal remedies might be obtained in the village, modern medical facilities are not usually available. Understandably life expectancy is very low: the average life span is only age 26. Malaria is a universal scourge, followed by tuberculosis, cholera, and typhoid.

The sanctity of life enjoyed by all animals, especially the cow, further contributes to the low level of living. Cow protection is one of the main tenets of Hinduism. Millions of aged and infirm cattle are permitted to live, eking out a miserable existence. Monkeys, rats, and other rodents roam the land unmolested, destroying vast amounts of farm products.

Despite low standards of living, Ram Chand and his fellows enjoy many simple pleasures. One of the favorite recreations is gossip and argument. Men brag about their sexual prowess while women clustering around the village well trade news about the marital squabbles of their neighbors. Prostitution is unknown but rumors of clandestine amours are often bandied about. Occasionally newspapers might be read by literate villagers to small groups. Going to nearby markets or shops in another village is always an exciting event. Throughout the year, the villagers enjoy numerous Hindu ceremonies: the celebration of the changing seasons, and special rites in a household for weddings, births, or the naming of a child. Itinerant entertainers, jugglers, and snake charmers bring the fun of magic to delighted peasants. The children play with homemade toys and kites. Little or no intoxicants are drunk but the slightly narcotic betel nut is universally chewed.

Traditionally, the thoughts and aspirations of Ram Chand and his fellow peasants seldom go beyond the confines of their village. Uppermost are the prospects of rainfall, family health, and the amount of the land tax. Occasionally some news might filter into the village from the outside but it is only vaguely understood. During the 1930's there are some faint signs of change beginning in rural India. Gandhi attacked the caste system and the miserable status of women. His campaigns against British rule attracted thousands of followers, some from the rural villages. Conditions in India's countryside can be duplicated to some degree in many parts of the rural world. During the next four decades its masses would become assertive. Forming what was to be known as the Third World, they would increasingly demand remedial attention.

PART EIGHT
Toward a New World

■ The shape of the world, political, economic, social, and technological, changed more dramatically in the three decades following World War II than in any comparable time period in human history. Since 1945 three major worlds have emerged, each with its distinctive way of life. The western world comprises most of the Americas, Australia and New Zealand, western Europe, and Japan. Stretching from Berlin through the Soviet Union to Peking is the communist world. The underdeveloped nations of Africa and parts of Asia make up the Third World. The conflicting interests of these three great human segments form much of the story of our times.

At the end of World War II, the great nations set about constructing a peace worthy of the sacrifice of millions of lives. An international organization, the United Nations, was created for this purpose. But almost overnight former allies became enemies, former antagonists became allies, and peace became the cold war. This confrontation between the United States and its allies and the Russian power bloc threatened world peace. While the UN on a number of occasions was able to dampen this rivalry, it was powerless to prevent war between these opposing systems. Twice the western and communist worlds came to the brink of conflict, over Berlin and Cuba. After 1972 there was some lessening of tensions. Complicated diplomatic maneuvers began, involving Russia, the United States, and China. The era of détente was initiated. Whether it would result in genuine disarmament and rapprochement remained to be seen.

Meanwhile significant changes were taking place within the western bloc and communist nations. The former enjoyed remarkable prosperity with the exception of Britain which proved unable to halt its alarming economic decline. In the United States involvement in the Vietnam War and scandals of the Nixon administration caused some decline in national will and purpose. Japan, defeated in war, became an ally of the West and enjoyed amazing economic growth. Notwithstanding some slight relaxations following the death of Stalin, the Soviet Union continued to be repressive. Every facet of life was controlled and no dissent was permitted.

Under Mao Tse-tung, the People's Republic of China became even more authoritarian than Russia. Its internal problems were many, especially how to feed its huge population. Mao, however, transformed his country into a great power. Following the death of this leader serious factionalism occurred in the government. The nature of its policies and how it might be transformed remained unclear in the late 1970's.

The course of events in the Third World was rapid and momentous. In little more than two decades the whole structure of colonialism collapsed. Dozens of new nations were created. Their new freedom was assailed by many problems, yet the people of Africa and Asia are determined that their road from dependence to independence is irreversible.

Political changes do not occur in a vacuum. Rather, they must be seen in relation to the other factors that shape society. Technology and economics on the one hand, and ideological systems on the other, play important roles; in addition the hopes and fears of society's members can be seen in the art, literature, and popular culture of the times. The twentieth century has been remarkable for the rapidity of developments on all these fronts.

History presents a continual change in the relation between human beings and the world around them. In the process not only the validity of particular cultures, but the nature of humanity itself is called into question. In this century three distinct conceptions of human nature and mankind's place in nature have dominated the scene: those of liberalism, socialism, and fascism. The liberal conception has stressed the timeless qualities and rights of individuals. The socialist (and especially the Marxist) conception has been that man is essentially a *social* being, and that his potentialities have evolved in a historical context. For the fascists, however, humans can only fulfill themselves through submission to the same natural laws that govern other living species—laws that are conceived of in terms of a ceaseless struggle for existence.

The record of the past decades, then, can be read not as a hodgepodge of unconnected events, but as part of a long story and debate. The forces of industrial development that had been centered in Europe not only have accelerated their pace, but have engulfed the entire globe. The international character of science and technology, of economic activity, of ideologies, of art and increasingly of life-styles, has signaled the beginning of a new phase in human history. The pattern is emerging, but the decisive aspects are not yet clear. The future remains an unfinished construction.

27. Northwestern University Library, Evanston, Illinois (1970). The magnitude of the revolution in modern architecture can be measured by the great diversity of forms it has engendered—not only structural forms, but functional forms as well. Many of the outward architectural structures of today, in fact, seem to take their shape only after the inward functional considerations of the structure are firmly set, unlike the architecture of the nineteenth century which was often more interested in the outward style manifestations of the building. Functional considerations played the primary role in the building of Northwestern's new $12-million library, which was ideally conceived "as a living, growing, developing intellectual program to enrich and transform the quality of life for the entire Northwestern academic community." The architects, Skidmore, Owings, and Merrill of Chicago, were challenged with the task of creating a building vast enough to accommodate all the material and space needed to serve the university population, as well as designing it to be adaptable to future change, especially technological change. The result is the above esthetic structure, situated on Lake Michigan's shore, which houses 1.7 million volumes, 1600 study carrels, 136 faculty study areas, 18 seminar rooms, numerous typing enclosures, and a computerized circulation system.

28. (opposite page) **Pablo Picasso: "Red Armchair"** (1931); **29. Hans Hofmann: "The Golden Wall"** (1961). With the turn of the twentieth century came an immense and colorful variety of expressive modes which have turned modern art into a kaleidoscope of styles and theories of art. Pablo Picasso, who deeply influenced most of the art movements of the twentieth century, broke with the western tradition of space in painting around 1905, creating in many of his works almost no sense of space or depth. Deeply affected by cubism, Picasso has, in this work, taken the woman and totally reconstructed her into elemental patches of brilliant color. Another cubist proponent, Hans Hofmann, has created works which range in expression from lyrical romanticism to precise geometry. His greatest concern lay in his concepts of pictorial structure on architectonic principles, an influence taken from early cubism. Both Picasso and Hofmann, with their bold splashes of color in abstract forms, had a large influence on a generation of younger artists.

30. (left) **Alexander Calder: "Red Petals"** (1942); **31.** (below) **Henry Moore: "Recumbent Figure"** (1938). In the twentieth century, sculpture—one of the oldest art forms—has tended to free itself from the extreme realism of the preceding period, and also from the long domination of the Greek ideal. Like the revolutions in painting, sculpture has gone through many expressive modes throughout its history, being shaped and molded to fit the innovative whims of a new creative era. The contemporary "mobile" sculpture of Alexander Calder introduced us to the new element of motion in three-dimensional art. Whether at rest or in motion, Calder's mobiles are an invigorating interpretation of balance in ever changing relationships among the parts. The work of Calder, perhaps the best known American sculptor before and after World War II, parallels the work of Henry Moore in era and influence. Moore, an Englishman, creates art on a monumental scale, equaling the old masters, but uses surreal elements in his work, like super-real forms with violent—yet sensitive—distortions. His favorite motifs are the reclining figure and the mother and child, two forms that result from natural processes of growth.

CHAPTER 34

The West and Communism Since 1945

War's Aftermath: The West and the Cold War

INTRODUCTION. With the end of global conflict a great longing to return to the pursuits of peace motivated most of humanity. Statesmen of the victorious Allied powers met to draft peace treaties, while in San Francisco they organized a new international institution, the United Nations, in order "to save succeeding generations from the scourge of war, which twice in our lifetime has brought untold sorrow to mankind."

For a brief period these arrangements concealed the more profound consequences of the war, chief of which was the emergence of two superpowers, the United States and the Soviet Union, which now superseded western Europe as centers of power. They created rival political and military blocs, thereby restructuring the postwar world into a bipolar configuration. The resulting confrontation came to be known as the cold war, a struggle that was neither war nor peace in the conventional sense but a constant maneuvering for advantage combined with incessant glowerings and threats. For a quarter of a century the world had to live with this cold war, which spasmodically threatened to burst into uncontrollable nuclear holocaust. An equilibrium of tension based on two military alliances in Europe—NATO and the Warsaw Pact—provided the basic structure of the world's power division, which was symbolized concretely by the Berlin Wall.

So widespread was the devastation of war that some observers in 1945 were asking, "Has Europe a future?" Extensive aid from the United States under the Marshall Plan and unremitting labor by the Europeans helped put recovery into high gear. The results were amazing. Rubble was removed, cities rebuilt, and factories restored. Postwar France labored under the stigma of defeat and costly colonial wars in Vietnam and Algeria. Its problems were surmounted under the masterful leadership of Charles de Gaulle. The economy progressed and France,

once again, became an important member of the western community of nations. What de Gaulle was to France Konrad Adenauer was to West Germany. Reviled because of its Hitlerian past, Adenauer dedicated his nation to democratic institutions and initiated its remarkable "economic miracle." Another defeated regime in Fascist Italy repudiated its past, and parliamentary government was established. Economic recovery was substantial but was accompanied by recurrent political instability. Of all the great European powers, Britain, victorious in war, ironically was unable to solve her economic problems. Labor and Conservative governments tried vainly to stem its economic decline. All of these war-torn countries in western Europe faced almost insuperable tasks with the restoration of peace.

THE WORLD AFTER THE LAST BATTLE

The ravages of conflict. With the surrender of Japan in September 1945, victory at last had been achieved and the world could now face the herculean task of tidying up the mess left after six years of conflict. From London to Tokyo large areas had been decimated by battle on the ground or bombing from the air. The misery and suffering of millions of people is difficult to comprehend: "None but a Dante could faithfully depict the terrors, the suffering, the anguish of heart and mind of the war period and its immediate aftermath."[1]

Much of former Nazi Germany lay in ruins, many of its major cities piles of rubble. Public utilities had ceased to function. Urban dwellers had no water or gas, electric and telephone wires had ceased to function. An American military official has given a graphic picture of defeated Germany: "The sight from the air of miles of gaunt chimneys in residential Berlin, the sight of old women dragging heavy wooden carts piled high with firewood from the *Grunewald* (forest) . . . the sight of a young man in a tattered *Luftwaffe* uniform staring dazedly at a wrecked plane in the woods near Frankfurt, . . . the statue

of William I hanging by one stirrup from an enormous bronze horse in Koblenz; trains so crowded that people were hanging on outside; the hundreds of notices pasted on bulletin boards asking for news of the whereabouts of a child, a parent, or a beloved . . ."[2] Twenty-five percent of German cities had been destroyed and human loss in dead ran to about one and a half million with two million unaccounted for. Italy, tied to the Nazis by Mussolini, suffered more desolation than any country in western Europe, excepting Germany. The privations suffered by the Italians were as bad, or even worse, as those endured by the Germans.

Thousands of miles to the east, the second major Axis power, Japan, also lay in ruins. Two million of its populace had been killed, 30 percent civilians. Nearly half of the area of its cities had been leveled by bombs. On the Asian mainland, China had been the victim of some fifteen years of Japanese aggression. The fighting there had not taken on the massive air bombardments and battle between huge heavily armored forces as in Europe. Much of it had been open warfare in the countryside, with the Chinese using hit-and-run guerrilla tactics. Thousands of villages had been destroyed with their peasants left to starve.

The victors survey their losses. The Second World War proved costly to the European victors, especially Russia. The number dead, half soldiers and the remainder civilians, was given officially as seven million. Probably it was much higher. Large tracts of farmland had been made useless, livestock decimated, towns and cities everywhere destroyed. While French losses in human lives were lower than in World War I, the material ruin was much greater. Harbors, bridges, railroad marshaling yards lay in ruins; a half-million buildings had been leveled. Across the Channel Britain counted the costs of war: the expenditure of twenty-five percent of its national wealth, the death of 64,000 civilians in the air blitz, and 300,000 lost in battle. Its merchant marine had lost half of its tonnage together with 35,000 seamen. Members of the anti-Fascist alliance, such as the United States, Canada, Australia, and New Zealand,

The bombing of Hiroshima on August 6, 1945, was followed three days later by the bombing of Nagasaki (aftermath shown). The destruction wrought by these two atomic bombs brought about a new awareness of humanity's ability to destroy itself. But the fact that only two bombs had killed 114,000 people did not deter nations from developing and stockpiling more sophisticated nuclear weapons.

whose homelands were remote from the main theaters of war suffered no material devastation. Their losses on the battlefield, however, were heavy. American combat dead, for example, was 389,000, nearly three times those in World War I.

The victors impose peace. Armies of the western allies and Russia fanned out to all parts of Germany. Four zones of occupation were established, one each for the French, British, Americans, and Russians. The capital of Berlin, located in the Russian zone, was divided into four parts, each sector occupied by one of the four powers. Free access was to be permitted by the Russians from the western zones to Berlin.

Amidst all the ruin and confusion in the occupation zones were millions of foreigners who had been seized by the Nazis to bolster home production. Estimates of these labor slaves ran at least to eight million. Some eight hundred Assembly Camps were set up by the British and American authorities to care for these unfortunate homeless, and by the end of 1945, five million displaced persons had been repatriated.

In the zones of occupation a policy of denazification and punishment of war criminals was carried out. Many were sentenced to prison. The most important action was the Nuremberg Trials of war criminals. A distinguished body of jurists conducted the proceedings. Of the leading Nazi officials, twelve were condemned to be hanged, seven were sent to prison, and three were acquitted. The trial was condemned by some critics as an act of vengeance, "a political act by the victors against the vanquished." In presenting the case for the prosecution it was stated that "the wrongs which we seek to condemn and punish have been so calculated, so malignant, and so devastating, that civilization cannot tolerate their being ignored because it cannot survive their being repeated."[3] It remained to be seen whether the Nuremberg Trials would serve as an adequate deterrent for future aggression.

In France as the German forces were ejected, underground groups began to take vigilante justice against those who had collaborated with the Germans. As many as 40,000 were summarily executed. Women who had been too friendly with the enemy were publicly humiliated and vilified. After the liberation, government courts were set up which sentenced more than 30,000 to prison terms and eight hundred to death. A large number of collaborators were discharged from government service.

Six peace treaties. At the Potsdam Conference in 1945, a Council of Ministers was set up to draft the peace treaties. After considerable bickering and wrangling, treaties were adopted in 1947 with Italy, Rumania, Bulgaria, Hungary, and Finland. The future of Austria remained uncertain until 1955 when a peace treaty was signed and occupation forces withdrawn. Serious differences, however, were encountered over the German peace settlement, with the western allies and Russia at complete odds. In 1951 a peace treaty was signed between Japan and the West which reestablished that country as a sovereign state.

HOPES AND PLANS FOR THE FUTURE

Designs for a better world. During the war when the western nations were undergoing devastation and privation, their peoples resolved that their sacrifices should earn them a better world. In 1941, the Atlantic Charter pledged the governments of Britain and the United States to support the "establishment of a wider and permanent system of general security" and "that men in all lands may live out their lives in freedom from fear and want." In Britain leaders of both major political parties were actively promising better conditions for their people after the war. In 1943 one declared: "Our people look to the government when victory has been won to accomplish four things: an enduring peace, based on the total disarmament of the enemy states; full employment; social security; and the physical reconstruction of our own country."

In the United States numerous organizations, especially from the churches and universities, as well as government agencies, gave thought to postwar planning. Emphasis

was upon economic security with better standards of living for all and a new international organization more effective than the League of Nations. The liberation of colonial peoples and the end of imperialism were also given much study. Allied leaders at Moscow in 1943 agreed on the necessity of establishing "a general international organization." Other conferences were held until the final details were worked out at Yalta in early 1945.

The United Nations — purposes and structure. The representatives of fifty governments met at San Francisco from April to June 1945 and drafted the Charter of a new organization, the United Nations. To achieve its purposes, the United Nations was equipped with six major organs: the Security Council, to maintain peace and order; the General Assembly, to function as a form of town meeting of the world; the Economic and Social Council, to improve living standards and promote fundamental human rights; the Trusteeship Council, to advance the interests of colonial peoples; the International Court of Justice, to resolve disputes between nations; and the Secretariat, headed by a secretary-general, to serve the needs of the other major organs. Much of the responsibility for improving the economic and social conditions of the world's people was entrusted to a dozen specialized agencies, such as the International Labor Organization, the Food and Agricultural and the World Health Organizations, and the UN Educational, Scientific, and Cultural Organization. The cornerstone of the permanent headquarters of the United Nations was laid in New York in October 1949. Though lacking the sovereign powers of its member states, the UN was a more wide-reaching instrument than its defunct predecessor, the League of Nations.

The most controversial issue at San Francisco was over the right of veto in the Security Council. The smaller countries held that it was undemocratic for certain governments to be privileged to block the wishes of the majority, but the Big Five — the United States, the Soviet Union, China, France, and Great Britain — maintained that singly and collectively they had special interests and responsibilities in maintaining global peace and security. The UN Charter, therefore, provided that the Security Council should consist of eleven members, five permanent members representing the great powers, and six elected by the General Assembly for a term of two years. On purely procedural matters any seven affirmative votes was sufficient; on matters of substance an affirmative vote was required including all those of the permanent members. In the years that followed this provision for veto power by any one of the great powers caused much acrimony and criticism; but realists recognized that given the actualities of power in 1945 peace could not be kept unless the five permanent members of the Council—in particular the Big Two—were willing to cooperate.

Problem of the ex-enemies. At the Potsdam conference in 1945 the Council of Foreign Ministers of the Big Five was set up to draft the peace treaties. Only minor difficulties were encountered in adopting treaties in 1947 with Italy, Rumania, Bulgaria, Hungary, and Finland. The future of Austria remained uncertain until 1955, when a peace treaty was signed and occupation forces withdrawn. What proved to be roadblocks to international cooperation were treaties with the major ex-enemies, Japan and Germany. Postwar Japan was given a new and more democratic constitution, the national economy was liberalized, workers were encouraged to join trade unions, and the great trusts were broken up. A peace treaty between Japan and the West, signed in 1951 over Soviet objections, reestablished that country as a sovereign state, while a Japanese-American security pact made allies of ex-enemies less than ten years after Pearl Harbor.

NOT PEACE, NOT WAR

Advent of the cold war. A world organization had been established and, despite some differences between members of the Grand Alliance, peace treaties had been drafted for five European nations. Peace arrangements for the countries of eastern Europe and Germany were a different matter. Here Allied and Soviet policies collided headlong. The ensuing controversy and confrontation between the western powers and Russia, known as the cold war, came as a grievous disappointment to many Americans.

During the war there had been wide admiration for the stout resistance put up by the Russians. President Roosevelt believed and Winston Churchill hoped that all members of the Grand Alliance would be able to cooperate in preserving the peace after victory. Between 1942 and 1945 there had been some disturbing evidence of what allied officials thought was the undue suspicions and secrecy of their Russian ally. Detailed information about allied strategy and weapons was made available to Moscow and Soviet experts were allowed to come freely to Britain and the United States. On the other hand little information could be obtained about Russian plans. Over twelve billion dollars of Lend-Lease supplies were sent to the Soviet Union but its extent and value was denigrated. "The jeep was widely regarded in the Soviet Union as a remarkable Russian invention."

Notwithstanding these disturbing omens the Grand Alliance seemed firm and united at the Yalta Conference in February 1945. Agreement was reached on the vexing problem of the future of liberated Europe. The great powers pledged to support the establishment of governments responsible to the will of the people through free elections. Yet in the next several months the Russians, supported by the armies of occupation, began to install communist puppet regimes in eastern Europe, especially Poland. On April 1, President Roosevelt sent a telegram of protest to Premier Stalin against the violation of Yalta pledges. Four weeks later Churchill sent a long message to Stalin in which he concluded: "There is not much comfort in looking into a future where you and the countries you dominate . . . are all on one side, and those who rally to the English speaking nations . . . are on the other . . . their quarrel would tear the world to pieces."[4] In spite of this plea, communist governments were forced not only on Poland, but also on Rumania, Hungary, and Bulgaria. In Yugoslavia and Albania independent native Communists seized power. It was these events that led Churchill to utter his famous warning: "From Stettin on the Baltic to Trieste in the Adriatic, an Iron Curtain has descended across the Continent."

Meanwhile in Germany there was continual controversy between the Russian and Allied occupation authorities. Agreements had been made whereby the country was to be considered a single economic unit. Agricultural products from the Russian zone were to be made available to the food deficit zones of the Allies. The Russians, however, closed their zone to western inspection and shipped large amounts of food and machinery home. In effect this policy faced the Allies with the necessity of purchasing food for their own areas. By May 1946 all reparations, mainly machinery, from the American zone to Russia were suspended; in the fall of this year Americans and British united their zones into one economic unit which came to be known as Bizonia. The French joined the union in 1948. Germany was now split into two divisions, one administered by the Allies, the other by Russia.

This bipolarization of Europe became increasingly apparent. In 1946 Soviet support of Communist guerrillas in Greece and its territorial demands upon Turkey revealed Russian designs in the eastern Mediterranean. Such expansionist aims did not go uncountered; President Harry S. Truman (1884-1972) announced in 1947 that the United States would support any country threatened by Communist aggression. This "Truman Doctrine" was followed by the dispatch of economic and military aid to Greece and Turkey—a move usually regarded as marking the start of the cold war. Meanwhile the sessions of the UN were marked by bitter exchanges between American and British representatives, on the one hand, and Russian on the other. The deliberations of the Security Council were constantly stymied by Soviet vetoes. An American program—the Baruch Plan—for the international control of atomic energy for peaceful purposes was rejected by Moscow in 1946.

This American initiative in aiding Greece and Turkey was followed by an offer, an-

nounced by Secretary of State George C. Marshall, to help Europe solve its dire economic problems. Western European nations eagerly accepted this American proposal, which was, however, rejected by the Soviet Union for itself and the countries of eastern Europe. Congress subsequently appropriated billions of dollars to implement the European Recovery Program—better known as the Marshall Plan—which proved so effective that within four years the industrial production of the recipient nations had climbed to 64 percent over 1947 levels and 41 percent over prewar figures.

To enable western Germany to participate in the Marshall Plan, the western Allies helped create the new Federal Republic of Germany, which comprised West Germany and West Berlin. Almost immediately the Soviet Union established the German Democratic Republic in East Germany and began to apply pressure to gain control over West Berlin as well. In 1948 all surface communication between Berlin and western Europe was suddenly cut off. American and British authorities met this blockade by organizing an airlift to supply food and fuel to the two million inhabitants of West Berlin. In 1949 the Soviet Union agreed to lift the blockade, a notable victory for the West in central Europe.

Until 1948 the Czechs maintained their traditional democratic institutions. Elections were free and uncontrolled. In a 1946 election Communists received only 38 percent of the votes and were losing support. Because of the deepening East-West conflict, Moscow resolved that it must control Czechoslovakia. In the spring of 1948, with the Red Army on its borders, the government was compelled to agree to a Communist-controlled regime.

Collective security by regional alliances. Deadlocks in the United Nations and its inability to guarantee international security, coupled with Soviet expansionism, led to the establishment of the North Atlantic Treaty Organization (NATO) in 1949. Composed of nations of western Europe (Great Britain, France, Belgium, Luxemburg, the Netherlands, Norway, Denmark, Portugal, and Italy) together with Iceland, the United States, and Canada, NATO was a regional al-

TERRITORIAL CHANGES
IN EUROPE AFTER
WORLD WAR II

- Annexed by the Soviet Union
- Annexed by Poland
- Annexed by Bulgaria
- Annexed by Yugoslavia

order "to repel the armed attacks and to restore international peace and security in the area." After three years of costly fighting—during which the United States carried the brunt of the burden in defending South Korea while Communist China dispatched "volunteers" to assist the North Koreans—an armistice was secured in July 1953. The status quo *ante bellum* was reestablished and South Korea's independence maintained. Although the peninsula had not been reunited, Communist expansion in the area had been contained.

A new era in American-Soviet rivalry. With the death of Stalin in 1953, Soviet foreign policy shifted from crude brinkmanship to a more sophisticated approach. Nikita Khrushchev (1894-1971), the new leader, realized that nuclear war would be suicidal to all concerned. By enunciating the doctrine of "peaceful coexistence," he repudiated the Stalinist view that war between socialist and capitalist worlds was inevitable. Rivalry between the two systems would continue, however, and Khrushchev boasted that in the near future the Soviet Union would overtake the United States economically, scientifically, and in the area of social justice. In his own words, "We shall bury you." Thus coexistence did not mean the end of tensions during Khrushchev's period of control in the Kremlin (1953-1964).

Meanwhile two Soviet technological triumphs appeared to affect the cold war. In 1957 Soviet scientists put the first artificial satellite in orbit and began producing intercontinental ballistic missiles (ICBM's). Following this scientific coup, Khrushchev took a tougher line in foreign policy, especially in regard to Berlin, which had long been a thorn in the Soviet side. West Berlin had become a showplace of freedom and affluence compared with East Berlin, and it was also a magnet for attracting manpower from East Germany. In 1958 Khrushchev demanded the withdrawal of all western forces and recognition of Berlin as a "free city," presumably seeking to bring the whole metropolis under Communist control. The United States refused to accede to this demand, its attitude strengthened by substantial advances in rocket power.

liance for mutual assistance in the North Atlantic area; in 1952 its territorial limits were extended to include Greece and Turkey. West Germany's entry into NATO in May 1955 was swiftly followed by the creation of the Warsaw Pact, which provided for a unified Communist military command in Soviet-dominated eastern Europe.

The Korean War. After Japan's surrender, Korea had been divided into American and Soviet zones of occupation. The departure of occupation forces left behind two hostile regimes, each claiming jurisdiction over the entire country. On June 25, 1950, North Korean troops crossed the 38th parallel into South Korea. Washington immediately called for a special meeting of the United Nations Security Council, whose members demanded a cease-fire and withdrawal of the invaders. (The Soviet delegate was boycotting the Council at the time and was not present to veto its action.) When the demand was ignored, the Council undertook to furnish assistance to the South Korean government in

The early years of the 1960's were marked by dangerous tensions that threatened to engulf the superpowers in a nuclear conflict. A summit meeting convened in Paris in 1960 broke up angrily, the situation exacerbated by an American U-2 reconnaissance plane having been discovered shot down over the Soviet Union. During the same year Khrushchev, speaking at the United Nations, demanded the resignation of the secretary-general, Dag Hammarskjöld, and denounced American foreign policy. The following year Moscow again demanded the withdrawal of Allied forces from West Berlin, and once more Washington refused to back down. President John F. Kennedy (1917-1963) declared that the Communists would not be permitted to gain control either gradually or by force, and the NATO alliance stood firm in the crisis. Backed by Moscow, the East German government erected a wall between East and West Berlin, thereby blocking the escape route formerly used by thousands.

The most serious crisis occurred in 1962 within ninety miles of the American mainland. Three years earlier Fidel Castro had wrested power from a right-wing dictatorship in Cuba and had begun to transform the island into a Communist state and to create a source for the diffusion of Marxist revolution directed against United States hegemony in Latin America. A setback to the administration of President Kennedy occurred when some Cuban exiles, trained under American auspices, invaded their homeland in April 1961 and were decisively defeated at the Bay of Pigs. The following year the Soviet Union sought to install rocket sites in Cuba. To the United States, these missiles represented a dangerous threat to the cold war balance of power. Kennedy ordered a naval blockade set up around Cuba and demanded that Moscow withdraw the offensive weapons. After a few days of "eyeball to eyeball" crisis, Khrushchev ordered the rockets removed after receiving assurances that the United States would respect Cuba's territorial integrity.

The Cuban imbroglio underscored the urgency of reducing the peril of atomic war. The result was a limited nuclear test ban treaty, signed in 1963 by Great Britain, the Soviet Union, and the United States, which outlawed the testing of nuclear devices in outer space, in the atmosphere, or under water. Although France, China, and India (now all nuclear powers) refused to sign, one hundred other states did. This test ban registered some lessening of tension, and relations between the superpowers improved in other ways. Scientific and agricultural exchanges were encouraged, and a "hot line" between the White House and the Kremlin was set up to prevent a communications breakdown and to facilitate understanding of their respective positions.

Thus in the early 1960's the era of the cold war had changed to one of peaceful coexistence. Much has been written on the causes and responsibility of the ominous confrontation. A group of revisionist American historians has argued that the cold war was mainly, and on the part of some, completely the responsibility of American policy. Such a thesis has not been generally accepted. While understanding the Russian desire to have friendly states on the western border, it has been pointed out:

> There is a world of difference between a friendly neighbor and a vassal state whose liberties have been subverted, whose parliamentary institutions (where they existed) have been swept aside, whose sovereignty has been subverted, and whose foreign policy is dictated by the Kremlin.[5]

Further, if the United States had determined to prevent Russian influences in central Europe its armies need not have stopped short of Berlin or Prague. Ruminating on the basic causes of the cold war, a historian of Soviet foreign policy has concluded: "Few things in history appear as inevitable as that there should have been tension between the U.S. and the U.S.S.R. following the conclusion of the war. The nature of both systems made it inevitable."[6]

GOVERNMENTS AND LEADERS IN WESTERN EUROPE

Britain's declining role. Great Britain emerged from World War II at the height of its prestige in the twentieth century. It had stood alone against Nazi tyranny and as a member of the Grand Alliance had contributed mightily to the final defeat of the Axis powers. But this acclaim and victory only concealed its dismal condition. The country in 1945 was in a near state of bankruptcy. In 1938 the balance between what Britain paid for imports and what was received for the sale of exports was a very small deficit more than made up by invisible exports, mainly interest and dividends on overseas investments. Unlike other industrial countries Britain had to import much of its food and huge amounts of raw materials needed for its factories. The only way to pay for these imports was by selling manufactured goods abroad. During the next three decades this problem continuously was to bedevil the British economy and influence every facet of policy, both foreign and domestic. As a result of the war Britain's investments had drastically declined; in addition, huge bills had been run up for the upkeep of British armies overseas. Massive credits and supplies had been made available by the United States. In addition when Lend-Lease had been terminated in the summer of 1945, a large loan was arranged by Britain with the American government.

After the wartime coalition government of Conservatives and Labour, the country held its first peacetime regular election in July 1945. To the amazement of many, Churchill was repudiated and Clement Attlee became prime minister. The new leader was not a dramatic personality but he was hard working and noted for his personal integrity. He came from a comfortable middle class background and was a graduate of Oxford. Some of his colleagues had risen from very humble circumstances. Ernest Bevin, his foreign secretary, had been the orphaned son of a poor agricultural worker and had to begin work at the age of eleven. By force of character and intellect he came to lead one of the largest unions in the world.

British socialism, unlike the Marxist variety, is not a foe of religion and has a strong religious basis. It does not advocate the nationalization of all industry but advocates a mix of state owned and privately operated companies. And above all, it believes in democratic government. With this philosophy the Labour government announced to parliament that we "will take up with energy the tasks of reconverting industry from the purposes of war to those of peace, of expanding our export trade and of securing by suitable control or by an extension of public ownership that our industries and services shall make their maximum contribution to the national well-being." Within two years the following industries were nationalized: coal mines, civil aviation, railways and road transport, overseas cable and wireless, and the Bank of England. In Britain's "mixed economy" eighty percent still were employed by private enterprise.

By 1951 the Labour government was running out of steam. Practically all of its objectives had been realized. The economy had improved and Marshall Plan aid had been terminated. Labor had been weakened, however, by factionalism. Its leftist wing was inclined to be anti-American and pro-Russian. This radical element was to continue to embarrass the Labour party which was essentially moderate in ideology. In 1951 the Conservatives won a general election which was to put them in power for thirteen years. Churchill became prime minister, an office he held until 1955, when he resigned and was followed by Anthony Eden.

During the 1950's, especially under the prime ministership of Harold Macmillan, economic conditions slowly improved. But in 1959 they rapidly deteriorated. Britain went badly in the red in its balance of payments. By the end of 1960 the economic outlook was dismal. The following year the government applied for membership in the Common Market. It was thought close economic association with Europe was urgently needed. In 1957 six states on the continent had formed the European Economic Community, a union of 169 million people. It registered important gains: tariffs were reduced 50 percent between its members, production mounted, and trade both within and outside the Common Market increased markedly. The issue of membership split both parties. During Britain's negotiations with the E.E.C. General de Gaulle suspended them. He continued to block British membership

Leader of the British Labour party Harold Wilson (left) and former Prime Minister Clement Attlee light up their pipes before starting their talks at Wilson's residence. Attlee, who had led the party in four general elections, apparently gave the right sort of advice to Wilson as the Labour party was victorious in the 1964 election for the first time in thirteen years.

as long as he was the head of the French state.

The long period of Conservative rule ended in 1964 with the election of a slim Labour majority. Harold Wilson became prime minister. The son of a pharmacist, he had won a scholarship to Oxford where he gained respect as a brilliant student. Entering parliament in 1945, in two years he became the youngest cabinet minister in some 150 years. Under his leadership important advances were made in education, slum clearance, and housing, but the old economic nemesis continued to plague the government. In 1967 it was forced to devalue the pound.

Various explanations have been offered for Britain's dismal economic record. Management, it is claimed, has been woefully slow to adopt new methods. Down to the 1960's there was not a single school of business administration or management in Britain. Much industrial equipment remained outdated. Another problem was that private capital was not being invested in industry because government spending, mainly on welfare services, was approaching 60 percent of the gross national product. Labor was also

partly to blame because of its failure to match per capita productivity with wage increases.

Notwithstanding these economic problems a high degree of security has been achieved for all. Both major parties are committed to the welfare state. In education seven new universities were established in the 1970's, technical colleges have been upgraded, and ample scholarships created for higher education. The status of working-class groups has been substantially improved, and the gap of incomes between rich and poor reduced. The progress in housing has been unprecedented, between 1945 and 1965 nearly five million houses or apartments were constructed. And nearly every home now has such "necessities" as a "telly," a car, and a "frig." It is apparent, however, that unless Britain can generate more dynamism in its economy, it will be difficult to maintain the present level of welfare services. In foreign policy, Britain, although reduced in power, has exerted a positive influence. It supported the U.S. action in Korea against Communist aggression; and successfully transformed its empire (see p. 830) into a commonwealth of independent nations. Firmly committed to NATO and, despite some troublesome differences, to a special tie to the United States, Britain has made a substantial contribution to world peace.

The lackluster performance of Labour in the late 1960's led to a conservative victory in the 1970 election under the banner of Edward Heath. The new leader had held several cabinet posts under Macmillan. While an effective debater, he was not a charismatic personality. His only significant achievement was to obtain British entry into the Common Market. During 1973 labor unrest and the Arab oil embargo (see p. 851) dealt a crippling blow to the British economy. In October the adverse balance of trade was $825 million. The following February the miners went out on strike against the government demanding a raise of more than 30 percent. The country went to the polls in 1974 giving Labour a slender majority. Wilson ended the miners' strike by acceding to their demands.

Continued industrial unrest, declining production, and alarming inflation led to significant changes in Britain's political leadership. Heath lost his position as head of the Conservatives in 1975. His successor was Margaret Thatcher who could become the first woman prime minister. The following year Wilson resigned his post to be succeeded by James Callaghan who had served in various cabinet positions and was regarded as a moderate in ideology. He warned the country: "We are still not earning the standard of living we are enjoying. We are only keeping up our standards by borrowing and this cannot go on indefinitely."

During 1976 Britain had to borrow $5.3 billion from ten other countries. Massive cuts were proposed for social services and for the armed forces. Many unions denounced this action but it seemed imperative, not only to Conservatives, but also to most leaders in Labour. "It has been said of the British that they are incapable of admitting defeat, which is why in the end they always win. But there can be no doubt that Britain faces the most serious challenge in her recent history as a liberal democracy."[7]

De Gaulle's France. During the hectic and tragic weeks in 1940 when German armies were overrunning France, a French officer, Charles de Gaulle, urged the government at Paris to move to North Africa in order to continue the struggle there protected by the French and British navies. As a youth de Gaulle was imbued with a passionate, even mystical, patriotism. Writing of his days as a young man in Paris he had mused: "Nothing struck me more than the symbols of our glories: night falling over Notre Dame, the majesty of evening at Versailles, the Arc de Triomphe in the sun."[8]

De Gaulle entered the French military college of Saint-Cyr, graduated in 1913, and joined the army. During World War I he was wounded and captured by the Germans. Following his release he continued his military career and in the 1930's wrote a prophetic work—*The Army of the Future*. The young strategist advocated tank divisions. The book sold badly in France, but was widely read in Nazi Germany.

When the French government decided in 1940 to capitulate to the German invaders, de Gaulle escaped to London in a British plane. Obtaining the support of Winston Churchill,

he became the symbol of French Resistance. In a famous broadcast to his people he declared: "Whatever happens, the flame of French resistance must not and shall not die. Must we abandon all hope? Is our defeat final and irremediable? To those questions I answer—No!"[9] A Free French National Committee was set up whose broadcasts had a huge clandestine audience. Military supplies were also smuggled to the Underground to support their sabotage and guerrilla tactics. By 1942 de Gaulle was accepted by the majority of Resistance groups as their leader.

In mid-August, 1944, a special Free French division drove the Germans out of Paris. On August 25 de Gaulle arrived in the capital. He led a huge exultant crowd down the great boulevard, the Champs-Elysees, and then was driven to Notre Dame cathedral where a service of thanksgiving was celebrated. This was one of the great moments in modern French history. "The immense enthusiasm of Paris that day was like one deep, unanimous sigh of relief at the thought that the German occupation was over; and de Gaulle was loved that day because he had come to symbolize the Liberation."[10]

The returning hero was proclaimed provisional president and for fourteen months was a virtual dictator by consent. Elections held in October 1945 confirmed that the people wanted a new constitution. Sharp differences, however, developed between de Gaulle and members of the government. The general resigned in January 1946 occupying himself with the writing of his memoirs. In the fall of that year the Fourth Republic was established. Unfortunately the old irresponsibilities of the Third Republic were repeated. There were too many parties, too little action, and too much bickering. The Fourth Republic had a mixed record during its dozen years of existence. In spite of its ignominious collapse in 1958 it was a period of substantial economic growth, population increased, and a national planning office was created. A possible Communist coup was thwarted and the agonizing involvement in Vietnam ended.

The collapse of the Fourth Republic came from Algeria. Revolt against the French connection had begun in 1954 and was a great drain on French resources. The French population, more than a million in number, insisted that Algeria be kept French. Army leaders supported them. Plots to overthrow the government in Paris were fomented. Faced by the prospect of civil war the ineffectual government referred to as that "regime of mediocrity and chloroform" resigned, naming de Gaulle as president. His new government was granted full power for six months.

De Gaulle had been fretting in his country home, writing his memoirs in elegant prose, but anxious to get into the political fray. Returning to Paris, a committee was created to draft a new constitution, this for the Fifth French Republic, which was overwhelmingly approved by referendum in September 1958. De Gaulle was named president for seven years and he proceeded to make this office the most important in the government. In the Fourth Republic, like its predecessor, the legislature was dominant; but now the president and his cabinet were the supreme power. During a crisis the executive could assume nearly total power. As de Gaulle com-

mented, "The assemblies debate, the ministers govern, the constitutent council thinks, the president of the Republic decides."

One of the priorities was to end the Algerian war. It dragged on, however, until 1962. After more revolts and plots against the president's life independence was finally arranged by de Gaulle. In this year he also strengthened the base of his authority by a decisive election victory. Released from the incubus of Algeria, de Gaulle concentrated on his foremost objective—to make France a great power, to give it grandeur. This obsession was eloquently described in his war memoirs: "All my life I have thought of France in a certain way. The emotional side of me tends to imagine France, like the princess in the fairy stories or the Madonna in the frescoes, as dedicated to an exalted, an exceptional destiny . . . In short, to my mind, France cannot be France without greatness."

For the next seven years he strove to make France the dominant power in Europe, a third force free of domination by either the United States or Russia. To this end he persisted in making France an independent nuclear power. In 1966 de Gaulle withdrew his military forces from participation in NATO although France remained a member of the alliance. Above all he was opposed to membership in any supranational agency. For this reason, while he tolerated the Common Market, he blocked any attempts to transform it into a political union. On the international front he recognized Communist China in 1964, became a critic of Israel while trying to strengthen ties with the Arab world, and renewed his veto in 1968 of Britain's membership in the Common Market. As a champion of Latin, especially French, culture, he aroused controversy during a visit to Canada when he supported separatist claims of its French Canadians. He also made state visits to two South American republics.

In 1965 de Gaulle, although seventy-five, ran for a second term as president. He had given his country stability, a new constitution, and enhanced international prestige. There were signs, however, that the nation was getting tired and irked with his masterful "reign." He won the election by a narrow

French Premier Charles de Gaulle (left) is the guest of West German Chancellor Konrad Adenauer on de Gaulle's first visit to Germany since World War II. The two leaders met to bolster French-German relations and in a communique agreed to defend "with vigor the maintenance of the status of Berlin."

margin and in the parliamentary elections of 1967 his legislative support was reduced to the slimmest margin. A serious upheaval of university students the next year supported by workers' strikes further weakened his authority. The next year he made a fatal error. A national referendum had been called to reorganize government on a regional basis. De Gaulle, unnecessarily, made it a vote of confidence. When the referendum failed, he resigned his office, retiring to his country estate. Here he died eighteen months later. Notwithstanding the manner of his final eclipse he was widely honored for his leadership in 1940, for establishing the stability of the Fifth Republic, and for ending the trauma of the Algerian war.

His successor was Georges Pompidou — an able administrator who gave evidence of vision in his leadership but who died prematurely in 1974. The country was moved away definitely from Gaullism with the election of Valéry Giscard d'Estaing as president. A Resistance hero and brilliant student, he had entered government service and was a high-ranking civil servant by the age of twenty-six. He had been Minister of Finance and Economic Affairs for a total of nine years. The new president initiated a series of important reforms relating to urban growth, real estate, divorce, and supported the vote to anyone over eighteen.

The recital of the political history of France since 1945 should not obscure its significant economic and social transformation. Its population has grown by twelve million. A massive exodus has taken place from country to city. The percentage of people living in towns of 2000 or more has doubled since the 1950's. The GNP advanced more quickly than that of either Britain or the United States. France has become a highly industrialized nation whose production rose by more than 70 percent between 1962 and 1972. Since 1969 the volume of its exports has risen yearly by 14 percent. France is also western Europe's leading agricultural country. The role of government in the economy is substantial, not only in planning, but it also controls a large segment of nationalized industry. Commendable progress has also been made in social services. In education, between 1958 and 1959, the national budget increased sevenfold. New universities have been established and the percentage of the young attending higher education institutions is the highest in Europe (about 600,000). A comprehensive system of social security provides medical care, old age pensions, and wage earners are entitled to an annual holiday of four weeks with pay. Adequate housing, largely because of the increase of population, has lagged behind. It is estimated that twenty-five percent of French families are poorly housed.

Resurgence in West Germany. The most important leader in Germany following World War II was Konrad Adenauer. His accomplishments were little short of amazing. "It was he who made possible an orderly transition from the Nazi regime to parliamentary government; he brought Germany out of an evil dictatorship, defeat, and burning chaos into the embrace of the democratic world. There had to be a bridge and Adenauer built it. On top of this he made Franco-German rapprochement a living fact for the first time in more than three hundred years, and brought West Germany into the community of civilized nations."[12]

This remarkable statesman was born in 1876 and had entered politics in 1906 as a member of the city council of Cologne. In 1917 he became its mayor until 1933 when he was dismissed by the Nazis. During Hitler's regime he was imprisoned twice but mostly lived in retirement at home cultivating his rose garden. After 1945 he entered German national politics becoming leader of the Christian Democratic party. With the blessing of the Allied occupation authorities a constitution was drafted by German representatives as the Basic Law of the German Federal Republic. Ratified by the German people in 1949, Adenauer at the age of seventy-three became chancellor.

The new government was democratic. Much had been learned from the weaknesses of the pre-Hitler Weimar Republic. The presidency was made weak and the real executive, the chancellor, was made strong with specific authority to determine "the fundamental policies of the government." This officer was responsible to the *Bundestag*, a popularly elected legislative body. One of the weaknesses of the Weimar Republic, the existence of small parties leading to multi-party coalitions, was eliminated. No party was recognized that did not win five percent of the total election votes.

Adenauer assumed leadership when Germany was still a moral outcast, its economy in ruins, the Allies still had important occupation rights limiting the nation's sovereignty, and the future of the new democratic institutions was uncertain. Adenauer, "this utterly sober, cool, frugal, practical man," had no interest in brooding about past Nazi crimes or his nation's defeat. His one driving obsession was to get his people to work.

Under the impelling force of his leadership, autocratic and domineering at times, Germany's economic miracle began. Cities and destroyed factories were rebuilt. Marshall Plan aid gave three billion dollars to this restoration. Some thirteen million refugees from Poland and Communist-controlled East Germany were resettled and supplied a needed additional work force. By the early 1960's the country had a gross national product of seventy billion dollars, its standard of living was fifty percent over that of 1939, and its gold reserves were the second largest in the world. As early as 1955 its national production exceeded the prewar figure with only fifty-three percent of its former territory. Providing the economic know-how for this recovery was Adenauer's Minister of Economics, Dr. Ludwig Erhard, a professional economist and a firm believer in laissez-faire economics. This economic advance was accompanied with little inflation, practically no unemployment, and little industrial unrest by labor.

As successful as Adenauer's leadership on the domestic front was his achievement in foreign affairs. Full sovereignty was gained in 1955 when Germany was admitted to NATO. Adenauer made the decision to align closely with the West and cultivate strong

An inspector checks completed automobile chassis at a Volkswagen assembly plant in Wolfsburg, West Germany. Volkswagenwerk is the sixth largest manufacturer located outside the United States. In 1977 they acquired a plant in New Stanton, Pennsylvania, in the hopes of boosting their United States sales.

ties with the United States. In 1963 he signed a treaty of friendship with France. The chancellor once remarked: "Today I regard myself primarily as a European and only in the second place as a German." It was natural that he brought his nation into Europe's new institutions: the European Coal and Steel Community, the Common Market, and the European Atomic Energy Community.

Adenauer's great frustration in foreign policy was his failure to achieve the reunification of West and East Germany. He might have been more successful if he had been less pro-western. But as a staunch Catholic and a foe of Communism he wanted no part of a deal with Russia leading to German unity if it meant breaking ties with the West. In 1963, after fourteen years in office, Adenauer retired and was succeeded by Ludwig Erhard as chancellor. The German people were ready for a new leadership and new policies. Following a term of office by Erhard and his successor, Kurt Kiesinger, the big change came in 1969 with the victory of the Social Democratic party. Only moderately socialistic, it had repudiated Marx and downgraded nationalization of industry. Its leader was Willy Brandt who became chancellor in 1969. A foe of the Nazis, he had fled to Norway where he became a member of the Resistance after Hitler's conquest. After the war he returned to Germany and became prominent in the Socialist party. In 1957 he became the popular and well-known mayor of West Berlin and in 1966 the Foreign Minister at Bonn.

Brandt was very active in foreign affairs. He was instrumental in getting Britain into the Common Market; and he strove to improve relations with communist eastern Europe and the Soviet Union by his policy of *Ostpolitik*. Journeys were made both to Moscow and Warsaw in 1970 in which he negotiated a treaty with Russia renouncing force and also an agreement with Poland recognizing its eastern border of the Oder and Neisse Rivers. A treaty was also signed with East Germany for improving contacts and reducing tensions. Germany, however, did not close the door to ultimate unification. In a note to the Soviet Union it stated: "This treaty does not stand in contradiction to the political aim of the Federal Republic of Ger-

many to work toward a condition of peace in Europe in which the German nation regains its unity in full self-determination." These negotiations paved the way for the two Germanys to enter the UN.

Brandt was primarily occupied with foreign affairs and after 1972 public opinion began to accuse him of neglecting domestic problems, such as inflation and rising unemployment. The policy of *Ostpolitik* was also attacked for there had been little improvement in the Berlin situation, symbolized by the nefarious wall dividing the city. A spy scandal also rocked Brandt's government and in the spring of 1974 he resigned. His successor was Helmut Schmidt who announced his intention to concentrate on domestic matters.

Italy: Economic advances with political uncertainty. Following the end of Mussolini's regime, Italy repudiated monarchy by a narrow margin. A new constitution was adopted in 1947 providing for a premier and a ministry responsible to the legislature. The Christian Democrats was the leading middle of the road party, strongly Catholic, pro-western, and anti-Communist. Its spokesman and leader was Alcide de Gasperi whose ministry governed the country from 1947 to 1953. Like Adenauer, de Gasperi was a strong adherent of democracy and supported European unity. In 1949 Italy joined NATO and became a member of the Common Market in 1957.

Within little more than a decade the Italian economy changed from predominantly agricultural to one based on industry. For a time, in the late 1950's and into the 1960's, industry advanced faster than in any other part of Europe. In 1960 the output of manufacturing tripled pre-1939 levels and in 1961 steel production was more than ten million tons. It was only one fifth of this figure in 1952. The Fiat company was a symbol of this economic resurgence. It employed 93,000 workers and had a yearly production of 650,000 cars. Another symbol of modernization was the spectacular motor freeway, the *Autostrada*, running from Milan to Naples. The most economic development occurred in North Italy around the thriving cities of Turin, Milan, and Bologna. Since World War II some ten million people migrated in Italy, from the country to the towns and from the South to the North. Southern Italy, however, has remained a kind of socioeconomic backwater: too many people, too few schools and roads, landlordism, and inefficient fragmented farms tilled by poor illiterate peasants. Much attention has been given the area by the government in the form of subsidies, tax concessions, and programs for flood control and better highways. Backward southern Italy remains a challenge and urgent problem to the government.

While the Italian economy gave grounds for some optimism the political story was not reassuring. After the retirement in 1953 of de Gasperi, politics became increasingly a series of cabinet crises, shaky coalitions, and government turnovers. By 1974 there had been thirty-six since the end of the Fascist regime. Corruption was widespread and government administration was hopelessly inefficient. The Christian Democrats had been the major party since 1947 but by the close of the 1960's it was increasingly ineffectual to cope with labor unrest, unemployment, and inflation. An epidemic of terrorism directed by leftists in the late 1970's menaced the very foundations of law and order in Italy.

TOWARDS A NEW EUROPE

Dictatorship's end in Portugal. As Europe moved into the late 1970's, it was amply evident that its general character had substantially altered in the past three decades. Some of the changes appeared all to the good, others possibly indicated serious problems ahead. In the field of politics a significant and hopeful change had emerged in southern Europe with the end of dictatorial regimes in Portugal, Spain, and Greece.

Portugal was an incredibly corrupt monarchy until 1910. The country then became a republic but maintained its record for internal turmoil. Between 1910 and 1920 there were twenty-one uprisings and forty-three cabinets. In the latter year the army ousted the politicians and took control of the government. Two years later the generals called

on Antonio de Oliveira Salazar to run the country. A professor of economics, a fervent Catholic, austere, he shunned social life, and was content to live on a very small salary. All of his time was devoted to running an authoritarian government. The press was censored, education neglected, and the masses had little voice in politics. Under Salazar, while some economic improvement took place, the people remained poor with a 67 percent illiteracy rate in 1941. In 1955 a five-year program to stimulate the economy was launched but its gains were cancelled out by an increase in population and by the enormous financial drain, 44 percent of the national budget, caused by Lisbon's colonial wars in its African territories.

Salazar, because of ill health, retired in 1968, and six years later a group of junior army officers overthrew the government. Serious divisions now appeared between the moderate liberal factions and the Communists. By the summer of 1976, however, elections confirmed the victory of the socialists. A new constitution was enacted establishing a democratic system. Yet the new government faced difficult problems. Six hundred thousand refugees from Africa had to be absorbed, unemployment was high, and runaway inflation was causing much hardship. A national spree after the revolution had led workers to seize many businesses, large farms, and hotels. In most instances private ownership had to be restored under efficient management.

Eclipse of Francoism. Spain emerged from its tragic civil war in 1937 bruised and almost ruined. One million people had been killed, cities and farmlands devastated, and thousands of its most vital citizens had fled abroad. General Franco emerged the unchallenged leader and dictator. The memory of the war's agonies was a source of strength to his regime, better Franco than a continuation of bloodshed. The supporters of the dictatorship were the army, rich landowners, businessmen, the clergy, and the *Falange*, the only legal political party. Censorship, the secret police, and the prohibition of unsponsored political parties and labor unions kept the populace quiescent.

Until the early 1950's Franco's regime was

regarded with disdain by the western democratic nations. After the advent of the cold war this attitude became somewhat tempered. The United States restored diplomatic relations and Spain became a member of the UN in 1955. The following year the Pact of Madrid provided naval and air bases to the United States; the agreement also provided for substantial American aid which by the 1960's had reached nearly two billion dollars. Widespread poverty and economic backwardness had long been characteristic of the Spanish scene. In the late 1950's the economy began to show marked improvement. American aid was a factor in this development.

By the 1950's a new generation, which knew little or nothing about the civil war, began to make itself heard. Student protests and workers' strikes indicated spreading unrest against authority. In 1974 the successful revolution in Portugal was an inspiration to opponents of the dictatorship. In the summer of 1975 Franco died. He had named his successor Prince Juan Carlos, thus indicating his wish that the monarchy be restored. The young royalist was inaugurated as king on November 22, 1975. In his speech of acceptance he promised to represent all Spaniards, recognizing that the people were asking for "profound improvements." In 1976 the government, somewhat modified on more liberal lines, announced amnesty for political prisoners, freedom of assembly, more freedom for labor unions, and plans for a general election in the spring of 1977. The post-Franco period was characterized by deep ideological divisions in society. Whether some kind of moderate consensus will emerge was the central question. The extreme leftist groups made excessive demands for change; the ultra-right conservatives wanted no change at all.

Democracy's trial in Greece. The legacy of political instability in Greece has been similar to that in Portugal and Spain. From 1821 to 1945 there were fifteen different types of government with 176 premiers, each averaging less than one year in office. Inefficiency in government, economic backwardness, and political crises continued to plague the Greek scene after 1945. In the spring of 1967 a group of army colonels seized power. A tyrannical

Townspeople in Valencia, Spain, gather to await the arrival of Franco's successor, King Juan Carlos I and Queen Sofia whose portraits decorate the town hall.

dictatorship was established which jailed many political figures and harshly crushed any criticism of its rule. Many prominent Greeks fled into exile. This military junta made a serious miscalculation in 1974 when it connived in the Cyprus crisis. This mistake led to its downfall. A new constitution was adopted which created a republic. Applying for membership in the Common Market in 1975, the new government stated its application was "based on our earnest desire to consolidate democracy in Greece within the broader democratic institutions of the European community to which Greece belongs." Whether or not the new leaders can guide their country into some permanent semblance of political stability remains to be seen.

Regionalism in the United Kingdom. The end of dictatorship in these nations was a positive indication of promise. But another development, that of regional nationalism, was more difficult to assess. During the past twenty-five years Europe has witnessed the steady growth of separatist tendencies, nationalistic and cultural, challenging the integrity of some of its nation states. Various groups, such as the Basques and Catalans of Spain, Irish, Welsh, and Scots in the United Kingdom, the Corsicans and Bretons in France, and various cultural-ethnic groups in Yugoslavia, have become conscious of their distinctive historic traditions and culture. They aggressively demand some form of home rule or even independence. The process of decolonization since World War II has helped stimulate regional nationalism. "Why refuse to the Basques what the inhabitants of (Africa) Rwanda have obtained."

Another important stimulus is the inequality of economic development of different regions within a country. Scotland is a case in point. When Britain had its empire and was still the workshop of the world there were many opportunities for less prosperous Scots to make a good livelihood in the colonies or migrate to industrial England. Since 1945 the empire has gone and economic conditions generally have deteriorated in the United Kingdom. Despite heavy subsidies voted by the British parliament for Scottish development, employment and wage rates have lagged behind those in England. In addition to the charge of economic

A bombed-out car blocks traffic in Londonderry, a largely Catholic city in Northern Ireland. The long history of religious turmoil is so deeply rooted that violence has become endemic to Northern Ireland's culture.

neglect, the Scots have a long history of pride in their national identity symbolized in their romantic attachment to the Gaelic language and the kilt. Scottish nationalism was not taken seriously until 1974 when the Scottish National party with its aim of independence won 30 percent of the Scottish votes in a national election, sending eleven members to the British parliament. This spectacular advance can be explained partially by discoveries of oil and gas in the North Sea. An independent Scotland could hope to claim much of these resources now in British territorial waters. Faced by rising Scottish demands, both major parties in Parliament agreed to "devolution," the creation of a degree of autonomy, in both Wales and Scotland, to be provided by regional assemblies. Planned for 1977, this has been described as the most sweeping constitutional change in Britain in the twentieth century.

Somewhat different from the separatist movement in Scotland is the vexing problem of Northern Ireland, or Ulster, an integral part of the United Kingdom. Since 1969 there has been an intensification of tensions between the Protestant majority and the Catholic minority. Mounting street fighting, sniping, and bombings caused the London government to abrogate the Stormont, Ulster's parliament, which to Catholics represented a legal-political weapon of the Protestant establishment. In 1974 a British-sponsored coalition government composed of moderate Protestants and Catholics lasted only five months before it folded under the pressure of a devastating general strike organized by uncompromising hard-line Protestants. Currently London is bending every effort to prevent a further deterioration of antagonisms into outright civil war.

The Common Market and economic integration. The most significant and promising development in Europe has been progress toward economic integration. Its first step was the creation of the European Coal and Steel Community in 1951 followed five years later by Euratom, the European Atomic Energy Community. The same six nations (West Germany, France, Italy, Belgium, the Netherlands, and Luxemburg) which had created these supranational agencies proceeded in

1957 to establish the European Economic Community, commonly termed the Common Market, with the avowed intention of building "the foundations of an enduring and closer union between European peoples." The new organization proceeded to reduce tariffs between its members; a great free trade union was created that became the fastest growing area in the western free world. From its headquarters in Brussels a staff of some three thousand experts administered the affairs of the Common Market. In the 1950's the income of its six members doubled; while the economic growth of the United States was 3.8 percent, that of France was 7.1 percent, Italy 8.4 percent, and West Germany 9.6 percent. During the above years trade nearly doubled between members of the Six. As their factories and power plants hummed with activity more than ten and a half million workers migrated, many with their families, from southern Europe and obtained employment. Lagging woefully behind these advances, Britain in 1973 became a member of the Common Market joined by Ireland and Denmark. The Six had now become the Nine. While no substantial progress had been made in transforming economic union into political integration various advances had been made toward adopting a common passport, a basic work week and holiday policy for all workers, and the equalizing of welfare benefits. The ultimate — a still distant goal — was a common foreign policy.

The Common Market helped bring spectacular changes in European life styles. The day of the common man has arrived and with it the lessening of class distinctions. While the population of rural areas has remained stationary or increased slowly, that of the cities has boomed. To service this new urban culture, supermarkets have become the vogue together with serve-yourself gas stations. Vending machines, juke boxes, and frozen foods are also plentiful. Americanization is a potent force among the young who drink Coca-Cola, chew gum, wear T-shirts and blue jeans. Families enjoy new gadgets such as refrigerators, washing machines, dishwashers, and vacuum cleaners. TV antennas intrude into the city skies. Above all is the automobile; during the 1950's its number doubled and by the early 1960's had reached thirty million. During the summer months hundreds of thousands of vacationers speed across Europe clogging the roads. Highway accidents have become horrendous with 14,000 fatalities in West Germany alone in one year.

Western Europe, unfortunately, was not to continue this socioeconomic transformation without interruption. By the early 1970's the economic boom began to slow down. The Middle East oil embargo together with subsequent major increases dealt heavy blows to the economy. "Stagflation" brought both inflation with rising unemployment. All members of the Common Market were affected, least in West Germany and most in Britain where the value of the pound fell in 1976 to $1.62, the lowest in history. By 1975 there were some shaky evidences that the depression was leveling out among members of the Common Market, except Britain. The timely discovery of oil and gas reserves in the North Sea, however, promised a badly needed economic windfall to Britain and to Norway. In the case of the former it is believed that this discovery should provide all its energy needs by 1980 plus a huge revenue for the government. For the latter by the 1980's it should provide ten times its energy needs together with a revenue of about two billion dollars a year. The economic prospects of western Europe were unclear in the late 1970's; but the North Sea discovery, and the development of sources other than petroleum, such as solar and nuclear power, should do much to solve Europe's energy problem, thus ensuring a renewal of economic progress.

LIFE AND POLITICS IN THE AMERICAS

The United States: progress and problems. The United States had emerged from World War II with its landscape unscathed and its economy the most powerful in history. The burgeoning of this industrial power made possible the vast number of global responsibilities undertaken by the American people after 1945: the expenditure of $128 billion (through 1967) for military and economic foreign aid; the maintenance of armed bases around the world; and the waging of two protracted wars in Asia. These developments abroad were accompanied by major domestic programs aimed at improving educational and economic opportunities and at extending benefits in such areas as unemployment insurance, public housing, urban renewal, social security, and medicare for the aged.

The administration of President Lyndon B. Johnson (1963-1968) was marked by notable reforms on a broad domestic front. However, various problems—including the reconstruction of urban "inner cores" and a vigorous attack against the accelerating pollution of the national environment—remained unsolved pending the termination of an unpopular Vietnamese war (see p. 853) which was costing the economy upwards of $30 billion annually. Meanwhile the problem of race relations became especially acute in the mid-1960's as the black minority sought to secure recognition of its civil rights, to improve its economic status and educational opportunities, and to be accepted fully into the mainstream of American life.

The 1960's found the United States involved in massive efforts to accord equal status, treatment, and opportunities to all its citizens. Since the 1954 decision of the Supreme Court calling for desegregation of public schools, the nation had sought to make the Constitution's provisions real and substantial for every American. Integration in schools and public facilities and equal voting rights for black Americans, who comprise one tenth of the nation's population, have been the dramatic objectives of the overall civil rights issue. By the middle of the decade those rights had been largely enacted into law, mainly because of pressures brought to bear by the civil rights movement, which in the fifties and early sixties was characterized by nonviolence. From 1965 to 1968, however, the nation was rocked by violence in the ghetto slums of cities as far apart as Los Angeles, New York, Detroit, and Washington. It had become apparent that the legal extension of guaranteed civil rights to the black population was not a sufficient answer to the social and racial problems of the nation.

The urban violence that characterized the middle of the decade was closely linked to the problem of continuing pockets of poverty in the world's wealthiest nation. The problem involves not only the black and the white sharecroppers of Alabama and Georgia and the Spanish Americans of the Southwest but the tenement dwellers of Harlem and Chicago; not only the unemployed of Appalachia but the school dropouts in Detroit who, as unskilled members of the labor force, are inevitably "the last hired, the first fired."

The domestic accomplishments of President Lyndon B. Johnson (1908-1973) were notable, but by the mid-1960's many observers felt that too little was being done too late to help the cities solve their social and economic problems. Congress was slow in providing the massive funds required to improve the living conditions of the ghetto dwellers. One of the reasons was budgetary: the rapidly escalating costs of the Vietnam War made Congress reluctant to vote funds for internal development if that meant an increase in taxes.

Consequently, the internal struggle for economic rights, which had largely supplanted the struggle for civil rights, became more and more linked with the war in Vietnam or, more precisely, the civil rights movement increasingly joined with the antiwar movement. Thus Dr. Martin Luther King, Jr., the Nobel laureate who had led the nonviolent civil rights movement, became a leader in the movement against the Vietnam War as well—until he fell victim to an assassin's bullet in 1968. Frustration with the slow pace of reform resulted in a more radical civil rights movement, and many younger Negro spokesmen began to demand political action and influence under the banner "Black Power." The more militant leaders, who also opposed the Vietnam War, emphasized that they were prepared, as they put it, to meet violence with violence in the attainment of their objectives of equal social, educational, and economic status for black Americans throughout the country.

The antiwar movement itself increased in importance as the war escalated. Beginning in the early 1960's with only a handful of urban and university intellectuals, by 1967 it included many of the most influential members of both houses of Congress from both political parties. On the nation's campuses and elsewhere, dissatisfaction with the draft laws and frustration at the slow progress being made in such fields as poverty legislation led to increasing disaffection with the government. Up to August 1973, when the United States withdrew from Vietnam, tens of thousands of young Americans sought refuge from military service in Canada.

Johnson did not seek reelection, and the 1968 and 1972 presidential contests were won by the Republican, Richard M. Nixon (1913-   ). Domestically, the Nixon administration showed a distinct shift toward a more conservative philosophy of government. To combat inflation, the administration did impose a wage-price freeze (August-November 1971) and wage-price controls (November 1971-January 1973) which were effective in reducing the rate of inflation from five percent to about three percent. But when the administration returned to a free-market ideology and began to decontrol the economy—the last few controls were allowed to expire in April 1974—prices began to accelerate, and during the first quarter of 1974 the rate of inflation reached twelve percent, with a six percent unemployment rate being projected for the year. The weakness of the American dollar among the world currencies led to its devaluation, which made this country's goods more competitive abroad. Protectionism also took the form of new import restrictions against foreign products. However, as of June 1974, the American balance-of-trade deficit continued to be a major problem.

In 1968, Nixon had made law and order a major campaign issue, but not only did the national incidence of crime increase thereafter, but the administration itself became tainted by scandal. Facing charges of bribery, extortion, and kickbacks dating from his days as a Maryland official, Vice-President Spiro Agnew resigned his office in October 1973, and was succeeded by Gerald R. Ford. At the same time the President himself was faced with the widely held belief that he had

participated in covering up the 1972 break-in at the Democratic National Committee's Watergate offices in Washington. Men connected with the President's reelection campaign were arrested and charged with the break-in and other campaign irregularities. Nixon withheld information concerning these activities from the special prosecutor, the grand jury, and the public on grounds of presidential confidentiality. By early 1974, the President had lost the confidence of most of the nation. In May 1974 the Judiciary Committee of the House of Representatives began impeachment proceedings and in July voted to recommend this action by a trial in the Senate. Repudiated and disgraced, Nixon resigned in August. His successor, Gerald R. Ford, granted him a full pardon observing: "I wanted to do all I can to shift our attention from the pursuit of a fallen president to the pursuit of the urgent needs of a rising nation."

In the wake of the Watergate scandal the Democrats increased their control of Congress substantially in the November 1974 elections. For the first time in decades the

Washington Post reporters Carl Bernstein (seated on chair) and Bob Woodward were the first to disclose the involvement of President Nixon's closest aides in the Watergate burglary and subsequent coverup. Here they watch Nixon in a televised denial of any knowledge in the affair. The aftermath of Watergate investigations eventually led to Nixon's resignation from office in August 1974.

legislative branch was likely to assume initiative on basic problems such as inflation, recession, unemployment, health insurance, and tax reform. At the end of 1974 inflation was still untamed and reached a double-digit figure, with more than eight million workers unemployed. While the economy showed some recuperation during 1976 from the worst slump since the Great Depression with a substantial rise of the GNP, unemployment still remained high with inflation a continuing problem. It was with this disturbing background that the presidential campaign opened in the fall of 1976 with Gerald Ford the Republican nominee and Jimmy Carter, former governor of Georgia, the Democratic aspirant.

Both candidates entered the election with some disadvantages. Ford was generally respected but labored under the incubus of Watergate. Carter had a scanty public record and was relatively unknown. While his roots were in a small Georgia town, Plains, he had graduated from Annapolis and served with distinction in the navy. His public career really began as governor of Georgia, from 1970 to 1974. Carter waged a vigorous campaign for the presidency, capitalizing on the widespread distrust and disillusionment with government. While the election was close, it was a victory for Carter and his running mate, Walter Mondale. For the first time since the Civil War, a man from the deep south had been elected to the White House. The new occupant was confronted in the international field with major problems: negotiation with Russian limitation of nuclear arms, the potential for renewed war in the Middle East, racial tensions in southern Africa, and delicate discussions with Panama over the canal. At home the new president was concerned with the need for government reorganization, tax and welfare reform, energy problems, and the urgent need for stimulating the economy.

Latin America: reform or revolt. The term *Latin America* comprises enormously different regions: Spanish- and Portuguese-speaking areas; homogeneous societies of European stock (Argentina, Uruguay, and Chile); dualistic Indian-Spanish societies (Peru, Bolivia, Ecuador, and Mexico); what

has been described as "melting-pot" societies in Brazil and Venezuela; industrially developed economies (Argentina, Mexico, and southern Brazil); and largely agricultural economies such as Ecuador and Paraguay. As a continent, Latin America shares many of the problems associated with the developing nations of the Third World. Nevertheless, for many observers, Latin America "has the greatest affinities, as regards both culture and institutions, with the Western world" and can be described "as a peripheral area of the industrialized West than as a component of the Third World."[13]

The period following World War II witnessed much political instability and rising social unrest in the region. The only countries with continuous elected governments from 1950 to 1966 were Chile, Mexico, Costa Rica, and Uruguay. Between these dates fourteen governments were toppled by force, and dictatorial rule was imposed on more than half of the Latin American population. Political instability and the seeds of social upheaval spring from appalling socio-economic disparities. Despite the region's great natural resources, the poverty of the average Latin American is cruel. Shanty towns on the edges of the large cities house thousands amid filth, disease, hunger, and vice. Life expectancy in Latin America is about forty; more than half of the adults are illiterate.

Some of the basic problems currently afflicting Latin American societies can be enumerated. First, agricultural productivity must be improved in order to lower food costs, increase supplies for both home consumption and export, and raise rural incomes. Second, the population explosion must be controlled; with a yearly increase of around 3 percent, Latin America has the fastest-growing population in the world. In the mid-1970's the region's population was estimated to be over 300 million; it is entirely possible that the figure will climb to 600 million by the year 2000. This great increase has led to a surge of poor peasants migrating to the cities. More than half of the population now live in urban centers. Mexico City, Buenos Aires, and São Paulo are among the world's largest. In twenty-five years it is estimated that eighty percent may live in cities. These peasant migrants live in atrocious conditions. In Lima, Peru, for example, which is a city of two million, 500,000 are squatters living in shanties without running water or sanitary facilities. More educational services are urgently needed, not only in the slum areas but throughout the various countries. In 1970 there were no schools for 52 percent of the children. High schools are found usually in the larger towns and cities. A survey in the 1960's revealed that of every one thousand children entering elementary school barely half finished the first few grades, of these only thirty went on to high school and graduated, and of these only two entered a university. The third of Latin America's basic problems is that national economies—especially those which are relatively developed—have suffered from inflation which has created far-reaching economic and social disturbances. Finally, Latin America must not only accelerate industrialization but also develop greater regional integration and better access to domestic and foreign markets.

These massive problems have made Latin America a battleground for opposing ideologies. Since 1948 the countries south of the Rio Grande have been aligned with the United States in the Organization of American States (OAS). Dominated by the United States, the "Colossus of the North," the OAS has sought to prevent Communist elements from acquiring control in Latin American countries. After 1959, when Castro was rapidly transforming Cuba into a Communist society, his attempts to export his brand of politics were countered by a boycott set up by the OAS. Under Castro, educational and health standards rose appreciably, as did living conditions among the peasantry, who comprised the great majority of the population. However, under this dictatorship, the professional and middle classes suffered losses in both living standards and personal liberties, and many thousands fled to the United States. The loss of these professional skills added to Castro's problems, and the most important being the dependence of Cuba's economy upon sugar and especially upon its export to other Communist coun-

An example of art featuring a revolutionary theme is on display in the Palacio de Bellas Artes in Havana, Cuba. The number "twenty-six" prominently displayed refers to the date of July 26, 1953, when Castro and his followers mounted an unsuccessful attack against the Moncada Army Barracks. Later, in exile, the rebels formed a revolutionary movement which was to invade Cuba and overthrow the Batista government in 1959. Seeking a name for this new movement, Fidel Castro decided to call it "The Twenty-Sixth of July."

tries. In the mid-1970's there was a growing movement to relax economic and diplomatic sanctions against Cuba. In 1975 sixteen members of the OAS voted to end the embargo and the U.S. also intimated a desire for détente. This last possibility was made remote with the intervention of thousands of Cuban troops in the Angola civil war (see Chapter 36).

In order to stimulate the economies and to prevent the further spread of communism from Cuba, President Kennedy initiated, in 1961, with Latin American cooperation, the Alliance for Progress. For the first decade, the United States pledged $20 billion, to which the recipients were to add $80 billion. It was thus hoped that democratic and economic reforms could eradicate those conditions against which communism's attack was chiefly directed.

Unfortunately, the Alliance did not make the progress originally expected. Although a number of agrarian and other reform laws have been enacted in different countries, implementation has proved tardy. Given the social traditions of paternalism and oligarchic rule, there has been little economic or political reform. Extreme inequalities exist in the distribution of income. According to a United Nations estimate for 1965, half of Latin America's population received only 14 percent of the region's total income, while 31.5 percent went to top income brackets comprising only 5 percent of the population. The annual per capita income averages $350, with Venezuela the highest at $950 and Haiti, with $65, the lowest. Latin America is far from reaching the point of economic takeoff. It is still in a race between reform and revolt.

As the 1960's ended there were signs that some positive changes were possible in Latin America. Observers went so far as to describe them as a "second revolution," the first being the revolt for independence in the nineteenth century. In the past, the main pillars of an entrenched oligarchy have been the Church, the landed aristocracy, and the military. The forces of the new reformist movement, termed Popular Nationalism, are liberal elements in the clergy, a new generation of urban intellectuals, and some social-minded young army officers. This military element is well-educated and dedicated to their country's progress and stability. They are critical of the past performances of professional politicians. These reformist groups are "demanding increased quicker participation in industrial and agricultural enterprises; more responsiveness of political institutions to popular needs; greater control by the central

September 11, 1973: Chilean infantry and tank units take up positions surrounding La Moneda, the presidential palace in Santiago. When President Salvador Allende refused to surrender after the army had staged its successful coup, the palace was bombed. Santiago police later reported that Allende had killed himself during the seige. Allende's vision of a democratically run Marxist government was replaced by the rule of a hard-line military junta.

government of traditional elites and foreign investment; and more rapid and effective economic growth."

Although the situation in Latin America is disturbing, there are some positive signs. It is beginning to shape its own destiny. Steps are being taken to protect fishing rights in off-shore waters, new restrictions have been placed on foreign investments, taxes and royalties have been raised on foreign enterprises, and in some cases sugar estates and mining and oil interests have been nationalized. In the late spring of 1969 a special Latin American committee formulated the *Consensus of Vina del Mar*. This eighteen-page document dealt with alleged external obstacles to Latin American economic growth such as tariff restrictions, regulations on foreign trade, and loan practices. It was largely a criticism of the United States.

The American economic presence in Latin America is massive. It employs about two million people in its various enterprises, pays twenty percent of the continent's taxes, and produces one third of its exports. The charge is continually made that it takes out more wealth than it puts in. Latin American frustrations and resentments were painfully visible when Nelson Rockefeller was sent on a fact-finding mission in 1969. Demonstrations, riots, and angry posters ("Yankee, Get Out") greeted this emissary in a number of cities. The role of the United States in Latin America has been mixed. It has an admirable record of numerous contributions, such as the Alliance for Progress, the health program of the Rockefeller Foundation, and programs for education, agriculture, and social improvements. On occasion, however, the U.S. has not been true to its proclaimed Good Neighbor Policy. A case in point was the revelation in 1974 that the CIA had used large sums to support the opponents of President Salvador Allende of Chile. This leader, an avowed Marxian socialist, had come to power by the elective process. In his hasty efforts to nationalize industry, both domestic and foreign-owned, and to redistribute land holdings, he had antagonized many of his own people. Allende's regime came to a bloody end in 1973. Military leaders ousted the president who died, perhaps a suicide,

during the fighting. The Chilean army seized power in a brutal fashion; there were numerous executions and imprisonments.

Another problem plaguing the image of the United States in Latin America has been its control of the Panama Canal. By the 1903 treaty (see p. 617) it administers a 550 square mile zone "in perpetuity." In the zone 3500 American employees run the canal and a force of 12,000 U.S. troops provide a defense contingent. In 1964 there was a serious outbreak of anti-Americanism in the Canal Zone. Panamanians accused the U.S. of inadequate payments for the use of their territory and claimed that the U.S. presence was a symbol of outdated colonialism. In short, Panama wanted to operate the canal and exercise sovereignty over the Canal Zone. Negotiations over these demands were spasmodic and unproductive between 1964 and 1974. In 1974 a treaty was signed in which it was agreed that the original 1903 treaty would be abrogated. It was to be superseded by a new agreement returning the Zone to Panamanian sovereignty. In turn the Republic of Panama would grant the United States the right to defend and operate the canal. In 1978 the Senate ratified two new Panama Canal Treaties; one guaranteed the canal's neutrality after the year 2000; the other pact governed U.S. operation and defense of the canal until it was handed over to Panama on the last day of 1999.

While occupied with the cold war, Vietnam, and the Middle East, the United States has not given much thought to its relations with its neighbors south of the Rio Grande.

It was obvious that "a new dialogue" was long overdue. In 1976 Secretary of State Kissinger made a tour of Latin American countries. In a major address in Venezuela he promised a continuation of U.S. aid (then running some $300 million annually). The pledge was also made that negotiations with Latin American countries would be "on the basis of parity and dignity." The secretary also stated that negotiations with Panama on the Canal would be renewed.

There was little doubt that Latin America in the late 1970's was moving but few cared to predict the ultimate direction. By 1976 eight of its countries were under military rule. Some regimes, as in Chile, acted too harshly in their seizure of power; others, as in Brazil, had achieved substantial economic progress but had neglected social programs. Mexico is in a class by itself. It has been stable and peaceful for forty years. It has had enviable economic growth. The government is dominated by one party which has had the support of the army. Problems remain: a rapidly growing population and a wide gap between the rich and the poor.

The next few decades would show whether authoritarian rule, usually associated with the military, could be progressive, a better instrument for positive change than the ineffectual pseudo-democratic regimes of the past.

SUMMARY

As history unfolds into the closing decades of the twentieth century its momentum for seismic change has accelerated. Boundaries change, power relations between nations are altered, and life styles are revolutionized by new mores and technology. And so it has been in western Europe since World War II. In the international field serious rivalry erupted between the Soviet Union and the European nations supported by the United States. This diplomatic tension, however, did not prevent Europe from repairing the damages of war and even surpassing the socioeconomic condition that existed before 1939. This was especially true of West Germany which in three decades became one of the richest and most productive countries in the world. This progress was also shared by a tariff union of nine members, the Common Market, which helped to bring a virtual economic boom to most of its members. Cities grew in population, families enjoyed an array of gadgets for the first time, and more recreation and entertainment was added to life by the proliferation of televisions and automobiles. The energy crisis in 1973 and 1974, and with it recession, had an adverse effect, but by 1975 there was some evidence that the economic picture was brightening.

Postwar America was in an enviable position. The cities and towns had escaped the devastation of war and the great industrial potential remained unscathed; now the United States was ready to produce the good things of peace. For nearly three decades prosperity was general and attention was concentrated on major reform programs in the fields of economic security, civil rights, and medical care. In the 1970's the enduring strength and fortitude of the American people were tested by tragic involvement in the Vietnam War, the scandal of Watergate leading to the disgrace and resignation of a president, and by the impact of a serious economic recession.

Latin America presented another problem. A huge continent endowed with rich resources, it still had to contend with widespread poverty, illiteracy, underdevelopment, and chronic political instability. The solution to these problems in the long run can only be provided by the people themselves. But the U.S. also has an important stake in their solution. It has, both for its own interests as well as for Latin America, the challenge to provide its good offices and resources. Above all, it should be ready to employ wise statesmanship to alleviate serious differences with its neighbors.

SUGGESTIONS FOR READING

J. Lukacs, **A New History of the Cold War,** 3rd ed. (Peter Smith); and N. Graebner, **Cold War Diplomacy*** (Anvil) are broad treatments of postwar international tensions. The United Nations is appraised in H. G. Nicholas, **The United Nations as a Political Institution,** 5th ed. (Galaxy, 1975).

The topic of American-Soviet relations is analyzed in Walter La Feber, **America, Russia, and the Cold War*** (Wiley, 1976); and P. Hammond, **Cold War and Détente: The American Foreign Policy Process Since 1945,*** rev. ed. (Harcourt Brace Jovanovich, 1975). See also L. Wittner, **Cold War America: From Hiroshima to Watergate*** (Praeger, 1974); C. Crabbe, Jr., **American Foreign Policy in the Nuclear Age,** 3rd ed. (Harper & Row, 1972); and J. C. Donovan, **The Cold Warriors: A Policy-Making Elite*** (Heath, 1974). Other important accounts include H. S. Dinerstein, **Soviet Foreign Policy Since the Missile Crisis** (Johns Hopkins, 1976); and M. Goldman, **Détente and Dollars: Doing Business with the Soviets** (Basic Books, 1975).

The resurgence of western Europe is dealt with in R. Mayne, **The Recovery of Europe: 1945-1973*** (Anchor, 1973); and M. Salvadori, **NATO: A Twentieth-Century Community of Nations*** (Peter Smith). See also Neil McInnes, **The Communist Parties of Western Europe** (Oxford, 1975); and T. Geiger, **The Fortunes of the West: The Future of the Atlantic Nations** (Indiana Univ., 1973).

Excellent accounts of the various countries in western Europe include David McKie and Chris Cooks, eds., **The Decade of Disillusion: Britain in the 1960's** (St. Martin's, 1973); Morris Fraser, **Children in Conflict** (Basic Books, 1977), covering the shattering effect of violence in Ulster; George Dangerfield, **The Damnable Question** (Little, Brown, 1976) is valuable on Anglo-Irish relations. See also P. A. Allum, **Italy: Republic Without Government?** (Norton, 1974); and Roy C. Macridis, **French Politics in Transition*** (Winthrop, 1975) on the aftermath of De Gaulle. Two outstanding biographies are Terence Prittie, **Willy Brandt: Portrait of a Statesman** (Schocken, 1974); and H. Pelling, **Winston Churchill** (Dutton, 1974). See Paul Preston, ed., **Spain in Crisis** (Barnes & Noble, 1976) which studies the evolution and decline of the Franco regime. Neil Bruce, **Portugal: The Last Empire** (Halsted, 1975) presents the background of the 1974 revolution.

Recent events in the United States are recounted in Geoffrey Hodgson, **America in our Time: From World War II to Nixon** (Doubleday, 1976), a perceptive picture by an English observer. Other important topics are R. Marcus and D. Burner, eds., **America Since 1945** (St. Martin's, 1972); and J. H. Franklin, **Racial Equality in America** (Univ. of Chicago, 1976). Recent domestic affairs are covered in Jim Heath, **Decade of Disillusionment: The Kennedy-Johnson Years** (Indiana Univ., 1975). On the fall of Richard Nixon see T. H. White, **Breach of Faith** (Atheneum, 1975); and Bob Woodward and Carl Bernstein, **All the President's Men** (Simon & Schuster, 1974); and **The Final Days** (Simon & Schuster, 1976).

The following sources illuminate the complex trends in Latin America: Julio Cotler and Richard Fagen, eds., **Latin America and the United States: The Changing Political Realities** (Stanford, 1974); S. Lindquist, **The Shadow: Latin America Faces the Seventies*** (Penguin, 1973); J. Lambert, **Latin America: Social Structures and Political Institutions*** (Univ. of California); Irwin Isenberg, ed., **South America: Problems and Prospects** (Wilson, 1975). On individual countries see R. E. Poppino, **Brazil: The Land and the People*** (Oxford, 1973); J. N. Goodsell, **Fidel Castro's Personal Revolution in Cuba*** (Knopf, 1973); and R. Feinberg, **The Triumph of Allende: Chile's Legal Revolution*** (Mentor).

*Indicates a less expensive paperbound edition.

CHAPTER 35

Russia, China, and Japan Since 1945

People and Politics: From Moscow to Peking to Tokyo

INTRODUCTION. The three decades following World War II witnessed startling new trends in western Europe and the Americas. Equally important changes took place in an area extending from East Germany through the Russian satellite states into the Soviet Union itself, eastward to the Pacific to Communist China and the islands of Japan.

Idealistic declarations made during World War II kindled hopes that dictatorships would wane with the advent of peace, especially in the case of Communist Russia. It soon became evident that its ruler, Stalin, had other intentions. Government controls were tightened and dissidents executed or imprisoned. Every aspect of life, in politics, thought, and art, had to extol the Soviet state. Minute precautions were taken to insulate the people from foreign ideas. All workers had to endure strict discipline. The right to strike was forbidden. While the masses were miserably housed and could buy only a pittance of consumer goods, the main thrust of economic activity under Stalin was geared to heavy industry and arms which grew at a hectic pace.

This system was continued until the death of Stalin in 1953 when a new leader, Nikita Khrushchev, succeeded to power. Somewhat more moderate in his brand of Communism than his predecessor, he introduced a kind of "thaw" even to the extent of denouncing Stalin for his crimes. There were some improvements for consumers and Soviet science made important advances with its first earth satellites. Mistakes in foreign policy and in his agricultural program led to the summary dismissal of Khrushchev in 1964. The new leaders, Leonid Brezhnev and Aleksei Kosygin, now took command. Efforts were made with some success to improve agriculture and increase the availability of consumer goods. In foreign affairs they were less adventurous and cooperated with the United States in the first steps of a diplomatic détente. There was, however, no letup in the Soviet arms program.

One of the most momentous happenings in world history in the last thirty years was the victory of Communism and its leader, Mao Tse-tung, in China. Politically, socially, and economically the face of China was changed. The country was cast into a tight Marxist mold. Farming was collectivized and all industry run by the state. Thought control and Communist indoctrination were even more drastic than in Russia. On two occasions, during the Great Leap Forward and the Cultural Revolution, the country was almost turned upside down as Mao sought to keep his people in a militant ideological mood. Mao died in 1976, one of the powerful leaders of his time, after having made his country a foremost power.

Defeated Japan took a different road than mainland China turning away dramatically from militarism and dictatorship to democratic institutions. Free enterprise was followed rather than Marxism. American military occupation was admirably administered; on the whole it was admired and respected by the Japanese. It ended in 1951 and the country began its energetic economic revival which by the 1960's had made it the third nation in the world in industrial productivity.

THE COMMUNIST WORLD AND JAPAN

The Soviet Union after World War II. The successful culmination of the Second World War in 1945 might well prove to have been the most glorious moment in the history of the Russian people. They had taken the greatest punishment from what had been thought to be the Nazis' invincible military machine, but in the end it was Russian soldiers who had battered down the gates of Berlin. While the terrible conflict had brought weakness and decline to such victor nations as France and Britain, and prostrate defeat to Japan, Germany, and Italy, Soviet Russia emerged from the war one of the two mightiest powers in the world. This victory, however, had been secured at staggering cost, both in human lives and in destruction of towns and cities. Since the first Five-Year Plan in 1928 and through the agony of war the Russian people had been working at feverish speed. What they desired above all was peace, repair of the damages of war, and an improvement in their standards of living.

Stalin, however, had different ideas. In 1946 a fourth Five-Year Plan was inaugurated. The Russian people looked forward to the production of more consumer goods. But Stalin and his Soviet planners decreed otherwise. The new Five-Year Plan, like its predecessors, concentrated upon heavy industry — especially the production of coal, steel, pig iron, and oil, which served the dual purpose of strengthening the country's potential and its military machine. With the onset of the cold war, Stalin and his Communist colleagues believed that Soviet Russia must prepare for war instigated by the capitalistic democracies. Great new industrial centers were erected far to the east where they would be less vulnerable to any foreign attack. By 1949 it was estimated that 80 percent of the industrial output came from an area east of a line drawn from Leningrad, through Moscow, and on to Stalingrad. Such an eastward move of industry necessitated a similar trek of population. There was first a mass deportation of people for security reasons, those whose complete loyalty to the Communist regime was suspect. Large numbers were also encouraged to move eastward to the new industrial towns. Many were transported to labor camps in the Arctic region. Thousands died from overwork, poor food, and the bitter cold. The horrible cruelties of a Stalinist labor camp have been depicted in the novel *One Day in the Life of Ivan Denisovich*, by Alexander Solzhenitsyn.

The government also set about completing its program of farm collectivization. The smaller farms were joined to make large agricultural units. The ultimate goal was to turn independent peasants into members of a kind of "farm-factory," working the soil but not a part of it. After 1950 this agricultural transformation was stepped up, but at the price of considerable discontent among the rural population.

Stalin not only drove his people to produce heavy industry and the sinews of war but his dictatorship was tightened. With a security police of half-a-million backed by the Red Army, no dissent or criticism was tolerated. Imprisonment, the labor camp, or a summary execution were the weapons of terror. After the war, more and more of the important posts in the Russian government were taken over by high-ranking members of the Communist party, so that "the whole tendency was to fuse more and more the supreme command of the Party with the supreme administration of the state."[1]

Meanwhile the discipline in the Communist party was tightened after the war. Entrance requirements were made more stringent, and membership swollen during the war was reduced. The party constituted less than four percent of the population, and its members came increasingly from the Communist intellectual and managerial class. A national election was held in 1946 for the Supreme Soviet. Its conduct and results illustrate how the Communist party controls the machinery of government. Nominations were made by trade unions and peasant groups, all party controlled, and these in turn were sent to the electoral committees which prepared the ballots. On these, voters were given only one choice, one name. It was reported that 99.7 percent of the people voted, and of this total less than one percent crossed out the name of an official candidate.

Soviet imperialism and eastern Europe. After 1945, while western powers were relinquishing control over their extensive colonial holdings, the Soviet Union staked out a colonial area of its own in eastern Europe. Throughout this large area, the Soviet Union effectively exercised political control, directed economic activities, and forbade any cultural or educational initiative that ran counter to Marxism-Leninism as interpreted by the Kremlin leadership.

Nevertheless, one Soviet satellite, Yugoslavia, broke Moscow's grip. Marshal Tito (1892-   ), a tough wartime resistance leader and top Communist in that country, at first went along with the Soviet "line." However, his national strength and geographical distance from Soviet forces enabled him to display a growing resentment of Russian interference. When Tito made a final political break with Soviet policy in 1948, he was encouraged by the western powers and held his ground despite Moscow's economic reprisals and threats of war.

While Tito remained a Communist and used western financial aid in such ideologically "correct" ventures as the build-up of heavy industry and the collectivization of agriculture, his successful defection stirred thoughts of rebellion in other satellites that wanted to regain some semblance of national independence.

Following the organization of the eastern zone of Germany into the German Democratic Republic, the East German regime proceeded to break up the large farms and expand heavy industry. As living standards stagnated, or in some instances declined, discontent mounted. Thousands of East Germans fled each week to West Germany; and in June 1953 severe food shortages, coupled with new decrees for longer working hours, touched off a workers' revolt which was quickly put down.

In Poland, as in Yugoslavia, communism

acquired a national coloration. Wladyslaw Gomulka, a formerly imprisoned national Communist, gained control of the Polish United Workers' (Communist) Party in 1956. Subsequently, he sent important Soviet officials back to Russia and permitted Polish workers considerable freedom of expression. He also extended greater autonomy to the Catholic Church (to which most Poles continued to belong). However, foreign observers ruled out any chance of Titoism in Warsaw for the foreseeable future.

Meanwhile national communism had been gaining ground in Hungary. The climax was reached in a widespread revolt in the fall of 1956, the creation of a popular government, and the withdrawal of Russian forces from Budapest. Reinforced Soviet troops, however, quickly returned to the capital where they stamped out the flames of national independence. Large numbers of freedom fighters died in the struggle, while more than 200,000 refugees fled to the West.

Life and work in Stalinist Russia. Following World War II the Soviet government erected an impenetrable wall around its frontiers. Travel abroad by its citizens was practically forbidden except for diplomats and members of special missions. In March 1947 a law was passed prohibiting the marriage of Soviet citizens with foreigners. In this same year a decree was passed prohibiting any Soviet citizen from discussing his work, no matter what kind, with a foreigner. Also the refusal of any person to return to his homeland from abroad was classed as treason. In addition, every precaution was taken to prevent books, periodicals, and news from the outside world getting into Russia. Radio programs beamed to eastern Europe and the Soviet Union were scientifically jammed and rendered unintelligible.

There were a number of reasons behind this action. There was the old Leninist suspicion and fear of the outside capitalist world so strong in the early 1920's. Much more important was the fact that complete isolation was essential if the Soviet government was to make the people believe that their lot, bad as it was, was much better than the economic plight of the "wage slaves" in capitalistic countries. Perhaps the most cogent reason for this Iron Curtain was to help Soviet leaders perpetuate the myth of foreign menace. Denied access to the rest of the world but exposed continuously to a propaganda of fear and suspicion about countries like Britain and the United States, the people of the Soviet Union lived in an atmosphere of crisis which made it easier for the government to impose new burdens on the masses.

Controls over art and thought. Not only was there this wall of isolation around Russia but a rigid pattern of conformity was imposed upon all its people. Up to 1928 there was considerable freedom for the intellectuals in Soviet Russia; but with the Five-Year Plans and the advent of Stalinism, art, science, and thought had to be mobilized for the Party's program and philosophy. From this time on to the outbreak of war with Germany there was a steady tightening of control over artists and scholars. During the conflict, all the national effort, including thought and art, was mobilized in the effort for victory. There was no need for government compulsion as musicians composed stirring war songs and patriotic symphonies, and novelists wrote of the truly epic resistance of the Russian people. With the removal of the Nazi menace in 1945 there was, as we have seen, a shift in Soviet foreign policy from lukewarm relations with the western democracies to outright hostility and what seemed, in the Fourth Five-Year Plan, to be preparation for inevitable war. With these developments in diplomacy and industrial mobilization, came a comparable conscription of all thought and culture. Regimentation of the artist now began with a degree of total control that is reminiscent of the powers exercised by the Reich Culture Chamber in Nazi Germany. In 1946 an attack began on writers who did not sufficiently support the Communist system in their works. They were told, "Soviet literature neither has nor can have any other interests except those of the people and of the state."

All writers were controlled by an agency called *Glavit* whose permission was essential for any author or artist to publish, speak, or exhibit in all the media of communication — the press, books, photographs, radio, public lectures, or art exhibits. In the unhappy event that any author was condemned for not being a "good Communist writer" he was barred from the Union of Soviet Writers and the door to all publishing houses—which were government owned and controlled—was closed. Even bourgeois-capitalistic dissonances, it seemed, were detected in Russian music and in 1948 a meeting of Russia's outstanding composers heard a bitter attack on their work. World-famous musicians, such as Prokofiev, Shostakovich, and Khachaturian were not spared. They were excoriated for their "vacuous music, lacking in ideological content and being remote from reality."[2] Following this warning all the composers admitted their sins and promised to write "Soviet music." The official Communist mouthpiece, *Izvestia*, then declared: "The composer strives sincerely to answer the demands of the party and the people, entering on the path of the ideal art of socialist realism."[3] Perhaps no one has better summed up the consequences of Stalinist thought control than André Gide, the French intellectual and winner of the Nobel prize for literature, when he observed:

In the Soviet Union it is accepted once and for all that on every subject—whatever may be the issue—there can only be one opinion, the right one. And each morning *Pravda* tells the people what they need to know, and must believe and think. . . . so that each time you speak with one Russian it is as if you had spoken with all.[4]

Inequalities in the economy. What was the lot of the common man in the years immediately following World War II? The whole justification for Marxism was its claim to be the instrument for raising the living standards of the masses. In studying the trend in standards on living, in real purchasing power, most western economists believe that in 1950 it was lower than it had been in 1928. Tremendous advances had been made in the production of coal, pig iron, steel, petroleum, electric power, chemicals, and armaments. Engineers, scientists, and all kinds of technicians have been trained in great numbers and have expertise on a level with the best in other countries. It was these Russian experts who were responsible for the perfection of the atomic bomb.

The average Russian worker, on farm or factory, was subject to a degree of control and reduced to a status of helplessness that could hardly be appreciated by members of a labor union in the United States. They could belong to unions but the function of these organizations is to ensure that the members are loyal and efficient, not to secure rights. Unions had nothing to do with collective bargaining and had no say in the determination of wage rates. All workers were subject to strict discipline. They could not strike. Punishment for lateness or absence was often forced labor for six months. Permission had to be obtained in order to change employment. Originally starting with the credo of "to each according to his need," Stalinist Communism practiced wage policies that did not differ in principle from those followed in the most capitalistic countries. In one industry, for example, sixty workers received from 1000 to 2500 rubles monthly, seventy-five from 900 to 1000, four hundred from 500 to 800, and one thousand received 125 rubles monthly.[5] The average range between the lowest and highest earnings was

Women factory workers at a television manufacturing plant in the Soviet Union are seen during their regular afternoon exercise session. Factory authorities believe that this daily exercise break helps remove fatigue, and in doing so, contributes to maintaining high production levels.

estimated to be as much as fifty to one. The politically favored, and the most efficient, constituted an elite class with a standard of living much above that of the masses. This minority lived in the best apartments, at times had a fine villa in the country, could have their vacations at special spas, and were provided with cars and chauffeurs. In contrast, in the average Russian city several families had to occupy one small apartment, each to one room and all sharing the bathroom and kitchen. Moscow had a population of five million with housing facilities for two million! An American authority on Soviet Russia wrote: "The Soviet economy and society of today are a far cry from the humanitarian visions of generations of socialist idealists. In the name of the working class, the Soviet State has fastened upon its workers chains so strong and so burdensome that they can only be compared with the worst abuses of peonage. No capitalist corporation in democratic western countries would ever dare treat its workers as the Soviet government, the world's greatest single employer, has treated those who operate its factories, railroads, and mines."[6]

The Khrushchev era. In the early 1950's Stalin's mind and temperament sank into a condition of paranoia. The aging dictator suspected everyone and his subordinates were dismissed or disgraced without apparent reason. For example, the director of national economic planning was removed from office in 1949 and subsequently executed. Late in 1952 there were signs that Stalin was planning a new purge. In January of the following year it was announced that a "doctors' plot" had been uncovered. These medical men served high Soviet officials and it was charged that they were planning to undermine the health of high military officials. Of the nine accused, seven were Jewish. Perhaps an anti-Zionist purge was in the making, but the purge did not materialize, for Stalin died suddenly in March 1953. He has been described as the most brutal and powerful tyrant in history. His regime has been summed up as combining "all the horrors of early industrialism, Victorian imperialism, political tyranny, and ideological infallibility into a single totalitarian whole."[7]

Following Stalin's death an official message was released urging the people to be vigilant against internal enemies which demands "the prevention of any kind of disorder and panic." Commenting on these words an authority on Russian affairs wrote: "The word 'panic' escaping the lips of the world's most powerful government betrays a fear that is ineradicably in their hearts: they fear the prostrate people whom they rule, they fear the outside world which they plan to conquer, and they fear each other."[8]

Stalin was buried with great pomp and praise, his embalmed body being placed next to Lenin's in the Kremlin mausoleum. Supreme power was now shared by three rivals: Lavrenti Beria, the head of the dreaded security police, Georgi Malenkov, a former right-hand party member of Stalin, and Vyacheslav Molotov, a specialist in foreign affairs. With the passing of Stalin Soviet dictatorship lessened somewhat. Known in Russia as the "thaw," mass terror was reduced, the doctors' plot charges were dropped, censorship was made less strict, and numerous releases were made from prison camps. The triumvirate of leaders did not remain intact long. The first casualty was Beria who, in 1953, was dismissed and executed. The Soviet press declared that this hatchet man for Stalin "had lost the face of a Communist and changed into a bourgeois renegade." In the same year Malenkov was demoted to be succeeded by a newcomer, Nikita Khrushchev (1894-1971), who in turn managed the ouster of Molotov and became the unchallenged leader of Soviet government in 1955.

Khrushchev was a self-made man, born of humble peasant parents. A shepherd at seven, later a miner, and then a worker in a factory, he joined the Communist party and quickly advanced in its ranks. On the way he managed to get the rudiments of a high-school education in a Party adult school. Becoming a loyal pro-Stalinist he defended the gruesome purges in the 1930's and after World War II belonged to Stalin's inner circle.

The new leader never lost his peasant heritage, being both tough and strong. He was outspoken, frequently lapsing into earthy and salty remarks. Notwithstanding his lack of formal education, he had a supple and penetrating mind. One of his main objectives was to get agriculture off dead center; farm production was one of the weakest elements in the Soviet economy. Khrushchev expanded the area under production, mainly in virgin, poor land, in desolate areas of Siberia and Central Asia. His most spectacular action was his denunciation of Stalin in 1956 at a Party Congress. In a speech he excoriated the dead leader as a barbarous tyrant, fully revealing the tragic record of Stalin's cruelties. This de-Stalinization led to the release of thousands of prisoners from labor camps. It also resulted in the removal of Stalin's body from the Lenin mausoleum to an insignificant grave.

Khrushchev was at the height of his power from 1958-1962. During these years he occupied center stage, both in domestic and international affairs. Industry continued to expand and there were some improvements for consumers. Soviet science made remarkable strides as Sputnik, the first earth satellite, was sent into space. Mistakes, both at

Wearing a jovial smile, Nikita Khrushchev warmly greets Cuban Premier Fidel Castro as the two world leaders meet on the floor of the United Nations. They both were in New York City for a 1960 General Assembly meeting.

home and abroad, mounted after 1962. The new farm policy was a costly failure. Khrushchev's promise that Soviet agriculture would soon surpass that of the United States proved an empty boast. After 1960 the dangerous dispute with Communist China came out in the open; and in 1962 the Cuban missile crisis brought the United States and Russia to the brink of war. These setbacks reduced the prestige of the U.S.S.R. throughout the Communist world. Criticism also increased at home against Khrushchev's risky policies in foreign affairs and for the extent of his de-Stalinization. While on a vacation in 1964, he was notified by party officials that he had been "released from his state duties"and must return to Moscow. The fallen leader now became a pensioned "un-person" under a mild form of house arrest living in a government compound outside Moscow. He was isolated from the public for the remaining eight years of his life. Khrushchev should be credited for ending capricious terror and for improving the living standards of the masses. In Moscow housing space was increased forty percent and workers obtained other improvements such as better pension rights, higher wages, and a shorter work week. While relaxing somewhat the tensions of the cold war with his "peaceful coexistence," too many of his actions in foreign affairs displayed crude threats and bluffs.

Russia and its empire after Khrushchev. The new leaders were Aleksei Kosygin as premier and Leonid Brezhnev as chief of the Communist party. The new leadership consisted of men who were accomplished bureaucratic politicians and technocrats. This change was mainly one of personnel, not of basic Soviet policy. The new team tried to improve agricultural production, a very weak element in the Russian economy. As an incentive, prices were raised for farm products and burdensome restrictions were lifted on the private plots of members of agricultural collectives. The amount of state capital invested in farming was substantially raised. It is difficult to run from the top a vast centralized economic system like that in Russia. The supply-demand mechanisms that control and guide production in capitalist countries are absent. A number of managers and economists called for some change in which decision-making would be in the hands of heads of factories and collective farms. While the Twenty-Third Congress of the Communist party of the Soviet Union, which met in 1966, retained centralized planning as the keystone of the country's socialist system, it also introduced more liberal regulations based on the principles of a free market. A price system reflecting supply and demand as well as distribution and production costs was widely considered. By the end of 1966 some four hundred economic enterprises were operating under the new system. These economic innovations, however, did not accomplish their expectations. While consumer goods were far more abundant in 1970 than a decade earlier, there were still serious problems: clothing was scarce and low in quality, as well as high in price; the demand for all kinds of consumer goods outstripped supply; and housing had a long way to go. The overall economic progress, however, achieved in the Soviet Union had been remarkable. Its GNP had reached the second highest in the world. But it had woefully neglected the wants of its citizens. Its major effort had been to supply the needs of its huge armaments economy. The Soviet GNP has been estimated to be about 62 percent that of America's; but its armaments' allocation runs about eleven percent, in contrast to just under eight percent in the United States.

Notwithstanding the harsh repression of the Hungarian revolt in 1956, the heavy hand of Soviet control over eastern Europe eased somewhat during the Khrushchev era. His successors allowed a moderate pace of liberalization to continue. By the 1970's all the satellites had cultural policies more liberal than those in Russia. The Catholic Church flourished in Poland, Hungary sold foreign books openly, and record albums of western rock music were widely sold in the stores of eastern Europe. Foreign travel became fairly common in most of the satellites; as many as 400,000 Hungarian tourists visited western countries in 1975. The consumer is also being courted. Increasingly, people are not interested in ideology but rather in personal comfort and success. In Poland, for example, the intellectuals and students have recognized

Shoppers throng the main arcade of the GUM Department Store in Moscow. The doorways shown are individual entrances to the various departments. With a staff of over 4000, GUM is Moscow's largest department store.

they must resign themselves to continued Communist government. At the same time, they have sought to reconcile this ideology with Polish interests, which include greater trade and cultural contacts with the West. In attempting to walk the razor's edge to satisfy both national aspirations and Soviet demands, Poland's leaders have permitted abstract art, blue jeans, and rock and roll. At the same time revisionist comment on the Communist regime in Warsaw is repressed.

While permitting changes in the socioeconomic spheres in the satellites in their policy of "relative autonomy" Russian leaders drew the line at substantial alterations in the area of politics. Governments must remain Communist in theory and practice accepting the basic rules laid down by the Kremlin. This unpalatable fact was learned by the Czechs in 1968. Reformist forces led by Alexander Dubcek had acquired power and proceeded to introduce programs aimed at liberalizing and revitalizing the economy primarily for the consumer, encouraging intellectual and commercial contacts with the West, and obtaining freedom of the press. Unhappily this move to realize a new vision of democratic socialism was crushed in August 1968 by an invasion of Soviet tanks and other armed forces obtained from the satellites. The reformist programs were abolished and Dubcek ousted. The Soviet government, in the so-called Brezhnev Doctrine, declared its right to intervene in any fellow communist country.

The forces of reaction had triumphed in Czechoslovakia, yet despite this setback, there is a question of how long Moscow can continue to control the lives of more than one hundred million east Europeans. Late in 1970 economic discontent erupted into rioting in Poland. Rumania has gone far in developing what in effect is its own foreign policy. Another disturbing problem for the Soviet hierarchy is restlessness among its minority populations. In the early 1960's about 55 percent of the total population was Russian. The remainder was a confusing mélange of different nationalities and faiths: Jews, Poles, Armenians, Tatars, Uzbeks, and others.

Since World War II there have been instances of unrest among these various non-Russian peoples, especially the Muslims in Central Asia and the Ukranians. The lot of the Jews has been especially harsh. Endless attacks are made against their faith and synagogues have been closed more widely than other churches. Few Jews get into universities and the government's harassment of those who wish to emigrate has aroused worldwide indignation.

Russian society in the late 1970's. Differences between Soviet and American society are many and deep but similarities exist. Russian women constitute about half the work force and 80 percent of working age are employed. Far more occupations are open to women than in the United States. Women do heavy manual work but they also constitute 75 percent of all physicians. Feminism for its own sake has many devotees in Russia; but the majority of married women are wage earners because of economic necessity. Child care centers are available for only about half of the working mothers and they still must do the usual house work in addition to their outside employment. Wage discrimination between the sexes has been abolished but in practice women usually earn less than men. Contrary to wide belief the Soviets are strongly committed to strengthening the

Protest against Communism took the overt form of a students' rebellion in Prague (left) against the invasion of Czechoslovakia by Soviet forces in August of 1968. In Moscow plainclothes policemen arrest two Jewish youths who were among those staging a demonstration after being denied permission to emigrate to Israel (right).

family, as an agent for inculcating the right social attitudes of obedience and self-discipline in children. During the past decade the government has been concerned over the low birth and high divorce rates. As in the United States, the family in Russia is undergoing stress. Parents often have little time for their children because both work. In addition children spend much of their day, and even night hours, in schools and youth organization activities. Inadequate housing also adds to family difficulties.

In both societies a heavy investment is made in education but for different purposes. American education has a large content of liberal and humanistic values; in Russia it is a tool for the purposes of the state. In its huge, centrally controlled system, students are worked very hard with the main emphasis upon science and mathematics. Primary and secondary education are free and open to all but entrance to universities is limited and controlled by a difficult examination. About 20 percent of high-school graduates are permitted to enter four-year institutions. Instruction is primarily utilitarian with more scientists and engineers being graduated than in the United States. The best of these are equal to any in the world. In addition to this comprehensive educational system, Russia, like the United States, provides widespread welfare benefits to all citizens. Pensions are given for old age, and payments from the state are available during sickness and pregnancy. Free medical treatment is also provided for all.

There has been a modest improvement in living standards for the masses in recent years but economic inequalities still exist. There were still wide gaps in wage scales. Standards of living, however, do not depend on pay alone. A small group of top politicians, industrial managers, scientists, and approved artists and intellectuals still continue to enjoy privileges denied the masses. Repression of reformist intellectuals, moreover, has progressively tightened since the Khrushchev period. An amazingly small group of courageous dissidents have continued to ask for more freedom. Among them were Boris Pasternak, the author of *Doctor Zhivago*, who was disgraced in 1958, and

Alexander Solzhenitsyn, world-famous Russian author, is reunited with his wife and children in Zurich, Switzerland. He was expelled from the Soviet Union in 1974 for his anti-Communist writings. Solzhenitsyn settled in Zurich but has since moved to Vermont.

more recently Alexander Solzhenitsyn, Russia's most famous living novelist, physicist Andrei Sakharov, and Andrei Amalrik and Roy Medyedev, noted social scientists. These and others have been dealt with harshly, the government using such punishments as labor camps, insane asylums, prison terms, exile abroad, and expulsion from the Union of Soviet Writers. These dissidents have little support from the masses. "For the majority of Soviet citizens the regime is simply a fact of life, like the weather. To them, a demonstration against the government must appear as unreasonable as a picket line to protest the cold Moscow weather."[9]

An interesting manifestation of dissent in the Soviet Union is the *Samizdat*, the underground press. Consisting usually of a few typewritten sheets, it is circulated clandestinely throughout the country. One *Samizdat*, "The Chronicle of Current Events," is a periodical published every two months. It carries on its masthead Article 19 of the UN's "Universal Declaration of Human Rights." A number of private agencies in the western countries obtain manuscripts of books from Russia, which are then printed and smuggled back into the Soviet Union. On occasion the works of famous Russian authors, denied publication in their own country, are printed in the West.

The Soviet Union celebrated the fiftieth anniversary of its Communist regime in 1967. The Kosygin-Brezhnev team seemed firmly in the saddle a decade later. This ruling group, with their colleagues, exhibited no internal conflict, but its members were getting old and would have to surrender their posts in the not too distant future. Whether this transfer would be peaceable or would repeat the vicious in-fighting that followed the demise of Stalin was a momentous question intriguing Kremlinologists.

COMMUNIST TRIUMPH IN CHINA

The worn-out Nationalist regime. At the end of World War II in 1945, the Chinese Nationalist government led by Chiang Kai-shek was really a defeated and worn-out regime. For ten years, from 1927 to 1937, it had possessed real vitality and had initiated many basic reforms which, if it had not been for the disruption of war, might have matured into a stable and progressive society. By 1944 Chiang's Kuomintang government had been sapped of its strength, its dynamism, and sense of mission. Above all, its administrative and military ranks were permeated with corruption. In contrast, the Communists came out of the war with greater popular support than ever, control of an area with ninety million people and an army of 500,000 disciplined and loyal men. While the Communists had not carried as heavy a burden as the Nationalist government during the war, the basic reasons for their strength were the devotion and self-abnegation of their leaders, the lack of corruption among the rank and file, and the appeal of land reform to the vast peasant population.

Civil war. Following V-J Day, American troops cooperated with Nationalist forces in reoccupying territory recently ruled by the Japanese, and facilities were provided to transport Chinese troops to strategic areas, such as Manchuria. Chiang had moved in the direction of trying to negotiate a settlement with Mao Tse-tung, but this effort was fruitless, and in October 1945 heavy fighting broke out between the two. Fully aware of the ominous implications of civil war, the American government endeavored to use its good offices to end the conflict. In December 1945, President Truman defined American policy by declaring that it regarded the Nationalist regime as the legal government of China, but since it was a one-party system, specified that full opportunity should be accorded to other groups to participate in a representative government, and that to encourage this result fighting should cease between the Nationalist government and the Chinese Communists.

The Marshall mission and report. It was to implement this policy and to act as friendly mediator that General George C. Marshall, Chief of Staff of the United States Army, was sent to China. His efforts at first achieved unexpected success, for in January he succeeded in getting a truce which stopped the fighting, and the convening of a conference attended by all parties. This body agreed on a plan for calling a national assembly to secure a democratic revision of the government and the unification of all armies in China under one authority. The leadership of Chiang Kai-shek was also recognized by all elements in the conference. This promising start, however, was quickly nullified as fighting broke out on several fronts in north China, and especially in Manchuria. Bitter fighting ensued with General Marshall vainly endeavoring to halt the hostilities.

Early in January 1947, General Marshall, having been appointed American secretary of state, returned home, his mission a failure. In a famous final report he excoriated the extremists in both the Nationalist and the Communist camps, and stated that the salvation of the country could only be found by the assumption of leadership by moderate liberals in both the Nationalist government and in the other parties, including the Communist. It is now clear that the admission of the latter in any coalition government would end in its destruction. On the other hand, Marshall was right when he believed that the Communists could not be defeated on the battlefield.

Communist victory. The tide quickly turned in favor of the forces of Mao Tse-tung during 1947. The bulk of Chiang's army was poorly equipped, miserably paid, and deficient in morale. The Communists now began capturing city after city, frequently after only token resistance. On the economic front there was a complete collapse. Chiang's government was utterly unable to control inflation. An American dollar was worth 93,000 Chinese dollars on the black market. Serious riots broke out, there was student unrest, and thousands of workers went out on strike in Shanghai.

This general collapse of the Nationalist regime and its loss of confidence of the Chinese people was naturally reflected in the military theater. By the end of 1947 the initial Nationalist momentum had halted and in 1948 its strength collapsed in Manchuria. The complete defeat of the Nationalist armies took place in 1949 with the Communist "People's Liberation Army" capturing the major cities of China. By the middle of 1950 Mao had become master of all China, with Chiang and a remnant of his forces fleeing to the island of Formosa. Following this debacle certain groups in the United States charged that Chiang's regime had been defeated because Communists or at least fellow travelers in the State Department and in other agencies of the United States government had used their influence to block aid being sent to the Nationalist government. This unfortunate witch-hunting crusade was led by the spectacular demagoguery of Senator Joseph McCarthy, who was finally completely discredited. It is pertinent to recall that American military aid to China during World War II totaled $845 million, and from 1945 to 1949 came to slightly more than two billion dollars. It is extremely doubtful whether additional American military aid poured into China would have affected the final outcome, for the bulk of the Nationalist forces did not have the will to fight; and large quantities of American arms actually sent to Nationalist China were turned over to the Communists by apathetic Nationalist leaders.

MAO'S CHINA ABOUT 1947

Area Controlled by Chinese Communists

CHINA UNDER MAO TSE-TUNG

A communist regime imposed: the People's Republic. Following their victory over Chiang's Nationalist government, Mao and his colleagues imposed a tightly centralized administration extending to Manchuria, Inner Mongolia, and Chinese Turkestan; in 1950 Red Chinese armies moved into Tibet. In order to cast China into a solid Marxist mold, intensive efforts were employed to redirect the whole course of society from traditional patterns, and all organized opposition to the regime was liquidated.

As in the Soviet system, all power was concentrated in the Communist party, governed by the People's Central Committee, whose members occupied the chief civilian and military posts. The day-to-day work of this committee was entrusted to a smaller Politburo headed by Mao, who was also chairman of the republic.

During his duel with the Nationalists, Mao Tse-tung had gained widespread support because of the popularity of his program expressed in the term the "New Democracy." This was in essence a mild program of reform calling for the confiscation of large farms, for state control of large business but for the protection of small private concerns; for rapid industrialization under state auspices; and for increased benefits to labor, such as social insurance. This program did much to gain for Mao the support of minor political parties, some businessmen and intellectuals.

Following their victory, the Communists energetically set about tackling China's economic problems. Corruption and inflation were brought under control. Since more than 70 percent of farm land was owned by 10 per-

Farmers clean string beans at a farm commune near Shanghai. The sign behind them features a quotation from Chairman Mao Tse-tung and has been placed in the field to stimulate the amount of work they do in the hopes of attaining increased production.

cent of the rich landlords, the government proceeded to confiscate the large holdings and distribute them to landless peasants. Landlords and wealthy peasants were stripped of their holdings and many were executed. In this way the traditional gentry elite were liquidated.

While land had been redistributed among the peasantry, the real objective of the Communist regime was to abolish individual, small holdings in favor of huge farm collectives. This new program began in 1953 and within three years practically all peasant farmers had become members of rural cooperatives, in which all labor, farm equipment, and land was communally pooled; but individual land ownership was still retained.

A first Five-Year Plan for economic development for agriculture and industry was begun in 1953. Impressive advances were made, mainly in heavy industry. This success led to the launching of a grandiose Second Five-Year Plan in 1958, in the so-called "Great Leap Forward." It called for a tremendous increase in the production of steel, electricity, and coal. Millions of urban and rural workers were galvanized into a frenzied effort. Thousands of small backyard furnaces were built to produce steel and coal. It was predicted that British industrial capacity would be passed in fifteen years. In addition to this program of industrialization, a new system of agricultural production was launched made up of People's Communes. Some 26,000 of these units were created, each averaging 5000 households with about 25,000 people. The heads of a Commune collected taxes, and ran schools, banks, child-care centers, dormitories, and communal kitchens. Even cemeteries came under their purview. All land, dwellings, and livestock belonged to the commune; farmers had become a rural proletariat paid in wages.

This "Great Leap Forward" with its crash industrialization and rural collectivization proved to be little short of disastrous. Errors were made in government planning, farm production declined, backyard steel and iron proved to be largely useless, and from 1959 to 1961 industry lacked essential raw materials and millions of people were without adequate food. Faced with this emergency the government radically changed its economic policy. The first priority was given to agricultural production. In the communes the centralization of control was lessened, inhuman regimentation was liberalized, hours of work reduced, and each peasant was given his own plot to till, free to keep or sell its produce. This modified communal system is still an essential part of China's economy. While its depersonalization and regimentation is abhorrent by western liberal standards, it offers some economic advantages. Its consolidation of large farm areas allows for more use of farm machinery; it also offers opportunities for some vocational specialization; and for the government it provides large centrally located reservoirs of manpower available for developmental projects. Between 1961 and 1964 industry staged a comeback. The discovery of petroleum provided a new source of energy. Big gains were made in light industry, mainly in consumer goods as well as in cotton production for clothing. A sign of technological progress was the perfection of a nuclear device in 1964 and the hydrogen bomb in 1967.

The Great Cultural Revolution. By the early 1960's it was evident that deep disagreements were developing within the leadership of China. After the failure of the Great Leap Forward, a division over policy became apparent; the moderates wanted to proceed slowly and pragmatically with social change and economic development; the radicals were impatient to effect a drastic restructuring of Chinese society. Mao believed his Communist party had lost its revolutionary zeal and was getting listless; he believed the masses should be kept in a state of fervor by mass meetings and propaganda. By the middle sixties a perplexed world could perceive the development of a gigantic ideological and political conflict in China. Mao and his supporters had organized a movement known as the Red Guards, composed chiefly of bands of high-school and college-age youths whose primary responsibility was to attack the radicals' liberal opponents, and to enforce a strict radical orthodoxy on party members and the populace. Placing political purification higher on the Chinese priority list than economic development, the Red Guards were permitted to interfere with economic production. Vast rallies and demonstrations were held; the entire educational system was closed from top to bottom to permit the ideological correction of texts and teachers, and those considered as carriers of outmoded ways of life and thought were often attacked in their homes and on the streets. Known as the Great Proletarian Cultural Revolution, this radicalization movement was based ideologically on what came to be known as "the thought of Mao Tse-tung," conveniently summarized in "the little red book" entitled *Quotations from Chairman Mao Tse-Tung*. This collection of excerpts from Mao's writings became the catechism of the Maoist movement, and memorization and repetition of quotations in speech and song were intended as an educational device to instill in everyone the essentials of Mao's thought.

By 1967 industrial production had declined and some areas in the country were approaching anarchy. The Red Guards had to be controlled and dispersed; and army detachments had to restore order in cities and provinces throughout the country. The excesses of the Cultural Revolution were halted and premier Chou En-lai set about repairing its damage. Industrial production was increased, schools were reopened, and the country returned to the prosaics of economic planning. Some purges took place, notably that of Lin Piao who had been named as Mao's successor in 1969, only to be disgraced two years later. Charged with plotting against Mao, it was reported that in trying to flee the country he had been killed in an airplane crash.

Life in Communist China. As one travels through the countryside of China, it is apparent that a tremendous amount of work has been done on the land. Millions of people, especially during the slack winter season, work at reforestation, on irrigation ditches, dikes, and terraces on the hills. Only 12 percent of Chinese territory is cultivable and every bit of earth must be utilized. Vast numbers of workers are recruited from communes and as many as forty million youths have been packed off to remote areas to live among the peasants and work the land. The government saw this rustication program as a means of solving unemployment and overpopulation in the cities. While some rural development has resulted, there has been much frustration and dissatisfaction among the displaced urban youths. Many try to return to the cities where they must live a precarious underground existence trying to avoid detection.

In the cities and communes the people look well-fed. There are no hungry people in China for the first time in its long history. Housing is poor and accommodations are crowded but no one sleeps on the streets. The masses are adequately clothed; men and women wear the same dress, padded pants and jacket. By western standards dress leaves something to be desired: "A Soviet dress was once described as a sack with a string tied around it. A Chinese dress has no string." Wages are usually low and differences between various rates are not as great as in Russia. They are supplemented by government price controls which keep other items low and by provision of accident insurance, medical coverage, child day-care centers, and maternity benefits. An effective national health program has also been created. The

The ideas of Mao Tse-tung reached into every corner of Chinese life and his presence was made known even in the privacy of people's homes. This is indicated by a working-class family eating their meal under a picture of Mao, along with other patriotic posters.

rural communes are served by the "barefoot doctors," who act as hygiene officials and paramedics; they are also agents for planned parenthood and distribute birth control devices and information. Serious health cases are sent to hospitals in the towns. A veritable crusade has been waged against filth and pests, as well as against epidemics and diseases. Smallpox, cholera, typhoid, and venereal diseases have nearly been eliminated.

Since 1949 major changes have been made in the status of women and consequently in that of the family. Traditional practices such as child marriage, sale of children, polygamy, discrimination against illegitimacy, and prohibition of remarriage for widows has been ended. While in Russia the solidarity of the family is regarded as essential, in China it is considered almost a necessary evil, a potential rival competing with loyalty to the state. Strong criticism has been directed at the concepts of familial solidarity, male supremacy, and parental authority. Divorce is also encouraged. Women are urged to work outside the home. In the communes they labor on the land, and also find employment in factories and in the professions. While not fully implemented, public policy is to pay equal wages for equal work. Women are also beginning to occupy posts in public affairs.

In addition to basic changes in the role of women, the educational system has been completely transformed. Before World War II barely 20 percent of the people were literate and only 75,000 could be classed as intellectuals and professionals. A crash program of schooling was undertaken by the Communists. "Spare time" schools, with half study and half work programs were set up for those who could not attend full time. Nearly all children were attending traditional elementary schools and enrollment in colleges and universities had increased fivefold. Texts and teaching materials were revised to inculcate Marxist doctrine and a considerable amount of time in communist ideology is spent at all educational levels. An essential part of educational theory insists that both teachers and students must engage in manual labor outside the classroom.

The passing of Mao Tse-tung. In the early 1970's, it was widely known that Mao's health was failing. While rival factions intrigued for power, Mao Tse-tung died in September 1976 at the age of 82. Huge nation-wide ceremonies were held to mark his passing. Called one of the titans of this century, he was one of the few leaders in recent times who left his mark on the world as well as dominating the lives and the thought of more than 800 million of his people. His "little red book" has been distributed by the millions in China and translated into many languages. He took his nation out of the Middle Ages into that of the nuclear era.

During the last months of his life the jockeying for power was relentless. Finally, after his death, the leaders of the most militant faction led by Mao's widow, Chiang Ching, were overthrown and disgraced. Mao's successor, as chairman of the Communist party and head of the Military Commission, was Hua Kuo-feng, a career party administrator. He was relatively unknown until the 1970's and was thought to be a compromise choice between the rival factions.

JAPAN: FROM DEFEAT TO ECONOMIC MIRACLE

The American occupation. On August 28, 1945, an advance party of 150 Americans landed on Japanese soil, the first contingent of a substantial army of occupation. Unlike the large military government set up in Germany, the existing Japanese officialdom was used as much as possible. Relatively small American groups planned occupation policy which was then passed on to Japanese officials for implementation. The people accepted the occupation, repudiating the militarism of the past, and becoming ardent pacifists. While the U.S. Supreme Commander, General Douglas MacArthur, is a somewhat controversial figure in American history, most experts give him high marks for his conduct of the occupation. He enjoyed the confidence and respect of the Japanese.

While willing to consider the views of other Allied powers, from the outset the United States played the dominant role. It stipulated that all territory outside the four main Japanese islands was to be taken away, that there was to be complete demilitarization, that aid would be given to Japan in building an adequate economy, and that democratic institutions should be encouraged both in the government and in the society at large. A purge of leaders in the military, the government, and some in business was carried out; and while there was some dismantling of industries to be used for reparations this practice soon halted.

During the first three years of occupation, the main emphasis was on reform. The school system was revamped based on the American pattern. Textbooks were rewritten for the deletion of militant nationalism, and the public school system was decentralized by the creation of locally elected school boards. Land reform was also carried out aimed at reducing tenancy and absentee landlordism. Unions were also given the right of collective bargaining and their membership grew rapidly. American reformers also sought to reduce the great concentration of wealth in the hands of monopolistic industries, the *zaibatsu*.

To cap all these changes a new constitution, largely the work of the occupation authorities, came into force in May 1947. It established a democratic parliamentary cabinet system in which sovereignty rested with the people, no longer with the emperor, who now was only "the symbol of the state." A bicameral legislature was created which selected the prime minister, and no limitation was placed on suffrage either for income or sex. A notable feature of the new constitution was its renunciation of war as a national policy and its prohibition of a standing army or navy.

By the end of the 1940's major reforms had been introduced by the occupation officials. The cold war in Europe and the invasion of South Korea by Communist forces led the United States to believe a new status should be given to Japan. Plans for a new constitution were drawn up but ran into Russian opposition. Finally without this power, a peace treaty was drafted and signed at a conference in San Francisco in 1951. The document came into force the following year in which Japan gained full sovereignty, it accepted the principles of the United Nations, and American occupation ended. A Security Pact was also signed with the United States giving it the right to station troops in Japan.

Challenge and response. With reforms and political questions out of the way, it became obvious that the country should concentrate on economic development. The population had grown substantially since the war to about 80 million. Because its non-mountainous farming area was very limited, Japan had to import 20 percent of its food. Natural resources were poor, requiring the importation of all its rubber, wool, and cotton; and 90 percent of its petroleum, 30 percent of its coking coal, and most of its iron ore, zinc, and salt. Notwithstanding these insuperable difficulties, the Japanese energetically set to work to build up their economy. The Korean War gave it an initial boost as large purchases had to be made for American forces. In 1950 the gross national product was ten billion dollars; by 1973 it had risen to three hundred billion. While Japan built half of the world's tonnage in shipping, it was also the biggest producer of motorcycles, bicycles, transistor radios, and sewing machines; it also ranked second in the manufacture of autos and TV sets.

Success in democratic government. Japan was equally successful in operating the new political system. Since the war the country consistently favored conservatism in politics, and with the exception of two brief periods, conservative parties have controlled the government. In 1955 two of these parties merged to form the Liberal Democratic party. It has been friendly to the West, favors modest rearmament, and backs the alliance with the United States. The Socialist party constitutes the major opposition demanding nationalization of industry, opposing the Security Treaty, and supports a neutralist stance in foreign affairs. The small Communist party has been ineffectual. The main support for the Liberal Democrats has come from rural areas; with the steady exodus from country to city this party has been steadily losing its dominance. In the last national election held in December 1976 it was definitely on the defensive. Some of its prominent members,

including a former prime minister, had been accused of taking bribes. Election results indicated a major change in Japanese political life. The popular vote of the Liberal Democratic party slipped to a little over 40 percent. Both the Socialist and Communist parties declined. Three splinter parties of the center gained substantially. The election marked the emergence of younger leaders but Japan continued to be conservative in its politics.

Japanese society changes. Massive economic progress brought about many changes in patterns of life, the most obvious being rapid urbanization. Rural areas lost population while that in the cities skyrocketed. Tokyo with more than eleven million became the largest urban area in the world. Three great centers of industry and population clustered around the three cities of Tokyo, Osaka, and Nagoya. With only one percent of the country's land area they have one third of its population—well over thirty-three million. "The chief impression given by the cities of Japan became one of vitality, gaiety, and unbounding vigor. All the arts, both native and western, flourished exuberantly. Intellectual life became more vigorous and prolific than ever. Literature and films bubbled with creativity. The pleasure districts of Tokyo, and with their night clubs, cabarets, bars, and fantastically variegated neon lights, became probably the biggest, gaudiest, and gayest in the world."[10] Cities also reflected the impact of Americanization with their rock music, American TV shows, hot dogs, coca cola, professional baseball, and beauty contests.

Within the home in cities, and to a lesser extent in rural areas, life styles reflect the new Japan. Per capita income has increased from $280 in 1958 to more than $1500 in 1970. There were few private cars in 1950, by 1970 there were seven million. Television began in 1952; by 1975 over 90 percent of homes had a TV set. Values and attitudes within the home changed along with the new gadgets. Parental authority declined as young marrieds, forsaking the traditional three-generation household, set up their own family unit. The loosening of family ties and the stresses and strains of urbanization have also been manifested in riots by radicalized students, and for the first time by the appearance of juvenile delinquency.

Before World War II there was little scope for Japanese women outside the family. Since 1945 they have been given the right to own property and sue for divorce. Educational opportunities have also been widened. In 1970 more than 20 percent of women students were attending post-high-school institutions. Nearly 40 percent of the country's work force now are women. But their role continues to be considered different from men's. While 70 percent of women, age twenty to twenty-four, are in the work force, with marriage they give up their jobs. "The main barriers are not legal but customs with roots that extend far back into Japan's past." While some of Japan's societal problems are disturbing, good progress has been made in dealing with the enormous pressure of people on the land. With an area about the size of California, the population had reached over 112 million in 1976; but there was evidence that the growth rate was declining. Birth control measures had reduced the birth rate from 30.8 per thousand in the 1930's to 18.6 in 1976.

From success to uncertainty. By the mid-1970's an economic miracle had been achieved and the experiment in democratic government proved remarkably successful. It was becoming abundantly clear, however, that a heavy price was being paid for the amazing expansion of industry. Housing in the burgeoning cities had been neglected, highways cluttered with dense traffic were a nightmare, and sewage disposal and sanitation facilities had become inadequate. The Japanese people began to talk about *Kogai*, "public hazard," a broader term than pollution. Smog enveloped the cities where policemen, directing traffic, had to wear masks and people complained of stinging eyes and sore throats. Children in schools were affected by respiratory ailments. An acrimonious dispute disturbed Tokyo over where its daily 13,000 tons of garbage should be dumped. Waters around industrial sites became so polluted that fishing was prohibited; and mysterious new diseases appeared caused by pollutants in the water. Numerous suits were brought against offending companies and

A scene on Tokyo's Ginza Street in present-day Japan details a mother traditionally dressed in a kimono and obi with her small son who is wearing a blazer and blue jeans. The great majority of Japanese now favor western-style dress.

Japanese firms belatedly began to realize the enormities of pollution by spending large sums on anti-*Kogai* equipment.

The realization of the urgent need for social engineering to improve the quality of life was followed in 1973 by the "oil shock." With the outbreak of the fourth Arab-Israeli war the Middle Eastern nations imposed an embargo on their oil exports. This action was followed by price increases of more than 400 percent by all the OPEC petroleum producers (see pp. 844). The impact of this action was felt in all the western industrialized nations but mostly in Japan. Inflation increased at an ominous rate, economic growth decreased, and in international trade the balance of payments became adverse. Some experts predicted dire economic difficulties ahead but the resourceful Japanese should be able to develop workable adjustments.

CHALLENGES STILL REMAIN

The Sino-Soviet split. Following World War II, a subtle interplay of diplomatic, military, and psychological relations between the great powers developed in the western Pacific. The 1950's had witnessed large-scale cooperation between Moscow and Peking and forms of Soviet assistance to China. These included cash loans, credits for industrialization, the training of thousands of Chinese students at Soviet universities and factories, and the dispatch of thousands of Soviet technicians to help build new factories, mines, and power plants in China. Throughout the 1950's the Soviet Union was China's principal source of machinery and other needed goods and its biggest customer.

On the other hand, during that same decade tensions were building up. Thus Mao made sure that the Russians abandoned the concessions they had acquired in Manchuria at the end of the nineteenth century (see p. 662). Moreover, both giants were competing in a prestige race to determine which one would be first to reach Marx's goal of pure communism and in the process could claim to be leader of the Communist world.

Like other European powers, Russia had gained territory when China was weak; now that the latter has acquired new strength — along with a thermonuclear capability — it seeks to regain as much of its former territory as possible. Territorial issues were raised publicly in 1963 when the Sino-Soviet split broke into the open, and since then tensions and armed conflict have intensified along the disputed borders as well as over the strategic western province of Sinkiang, which contains important sources of oil as well as China's nuclear installation sites.

The Sino-Soviet power struggle can be described in terms of two epithets: the charge of "adventurism" which Moscow hurls at Peking, and of "revisionism" with which the latter assails the Kremlin leadership. Each claims to represent Marxism-Leninism in its pure form and charges the other with betraying world communism. The Soviet leaders argue that in a thermonuclear age, when hydrogen bombs could destroy the whole world, communism must coexist with capitalism. In their view, the Chinese leadership either does not sufficiently understand the ecological risks of a nuclear conflict or expects that sufficient numbers of the huge Chinese population would survive to ensure Peking's primacy in any aftermath. In addition, Moscow charges Peking with substituting for Marx's teachings about labor-capital conflict the revisionist doctrine that pits peoples of the "countryside" (the underdeveloped nonwhites of Asia, Africa, and Latin America) against those of the "city" (the developed white populations of Europe, the Soviet Union, and North America).

For their part, the Chinese Communists charge Moscow with maintaining the international status quo of which, as a superpower, it is a major beneficiary. Hence, the Kremlin's leaders have abandoned Marxist revolution in favor of reaching a détente with Washington in order to ensure continued American-Soviet hegemony over the world. Soviet warnings about the dangers of nuclear warfare need not discourage Communist revolutions which can be prosecuted without

Each year on the first of October, Chinese citizens gather in Peking's T'ien An Men Square to commemorate the founding in 1949 of the People's Republic. In this parade the citizens warmly hail what the government calls "the establishment of revolutionary committees in every province, municipality, and region in China along with the victory of Chairman Mao's proletarian revolutionary line."

recourse to atomic weapons (as the Vietnam struggle attested). The present Kremlin leaders have revised Marxism to the point where they are reintroducing some elements of capitalism into the Soviet Union and its client states and are placing national interests before those of international communism.

Presently, no lessening of tensions—or of verbal abuse—between the two Communist giants has occurred. Meanwhile the Sino-Soviet split has served to accentuate centrifugal forces within the once monolithic Communist world, as various national governments have felt obliged to support one protagonist or another.

China turns to the United States. During the 1960's when China was at loggerheads with Russia it was also unfriendly to the United States. In the opening years of the 1970's, however, dramatic changes took place between these powers. The massive Soviet troop buildup along China's borders caused Peking to question the policy of opposition to both superpowers. Relations with the United States began to gradually improve as China saw Russia as her chief enemy. Thoughts of a détente with China also began to be aired in Washington. In July 1971, Henry Kissinger, Nixon's foreign-policy adviser, visited Peking to arrange for the first trip of a United States president to a country with which Washington had no diplomatic relations. It was also announced that the United States would not oppose the admission of mainland China to the United Nations which was gained in October 1971, while the representative of the Taiwan-based regime was expelled. The visit to China of President Nixon, in February 1972, was largely ceremonial. Agreements, however, were reached to increase scientific, cultural, and commercial changes. Liaison offices were opened in both signatory's capitals. The president's trip was expected ultimately to lead to the restoration of diplomatic relations. This détente improved China's "deterrence posture" against Russia. It also caused doubt in Moscow about the position of the United States in the event of a Soviet-Chinese war. Following the death of Mao Tse-tung, and the coming to power of new leaders, there was some conjecture about the future of Chinese foreign

Along with Chinese officials and their own entourage, President and Mrs. Nixon visit the Great Wall during their 1972 official visit to the People's Republic of China.

policy. As 1976 ended, however, there was no sign of a reorientation of Chinese policy based on closer ties with the Soviet Union.

American-Soviet détente. Coincidental with this rapprochement between China and the United States, the latter power also moved to improve relations with Russia. President Nixon visited Moscow in May 1972, where an important agreement was signed: the Strategic Arms Limitation Talks (SALT). To many observers this visit of an American president to Moscow signified the end of the cold war. Additional evidence of this growing détente were visits by the Soviet leader, Leonid Brezhnev, to Washington in 1973 and by President Nixon to Moscow again in 1974. Later that year the new American chief executive, Gerald Ford, visited Russia and signed a new ten-year pact on nuclear arms. In 1975 a Russian and an American spacecraft joined in orbit 138 miles over the earth. This was both a scientific achievement and a symbol of growing détente.

New diplomatic moves by Japan. Meanwhile Japan was watching the maneuvers of détente between America and Russia with some apprehension. Since 1947 a Security Treaty with Washington had guaranteed its defense. In effect Japan did not have a foreign policy of its own but had to go along with that of the United States, especially its continued impasse with mainland China. In the late 1960's considerable questioning had developed in Japan over the American defense alliance and especially the U.S. control of Okinawa which had been made into a great island fortress. In 1970 it was returned to Japan but the Defense Treaty was renewed, and with it, the retention of American armed forces. A year later the initiation of American détente with China caused consternation in Japan. Tokyo reacted by arranging normal diplomatic relations with China. It also recognized that Taiwan was an integral part of China.

By 1972 Japan had secured friendly relations with China and continued to depend upon the United States to protect its homeland islands and to protect its commerce on the ocean's sealanes. With Russia, its relations remained correct but chilly. No peace treaty had been arranged. A major obstacle has been the refusal of Moscow to return four small Japanese islands seized in the final days of World War I. For its part Russia would like to detach Japan, with its great industrial productivity, from its Security Treaty. At the same time the Soviets view the growing accord between Peking and Washington with suspicion. In the complicated jockeying for diplomatic advantage in the western Pacific, China has sought to use Japan in its rivalry with Russia by supporting her claim to the southern Kurile Islands.

Taiwan: uncertain future. Taiwan, with its nationalist regime established by the late Chiang Kai-shek, still continued to be a problem in Pacific power relations—especially to the United States. Under the security blanket provided by Washington, this small island of only 16 million people achieved amazing economic progress. Its foreign trade surpassed that of China, its giant neighbor; and it developed a productive capacity level higher than any other Asian country, excepting Japan. It is unlikely that the United States can secure full diplomatic ties with China

and continue its defense of Taiwan. Peking insists that it must be reunited with the mainland. Washington is reluctant at this time to sever its special relationship for several reasons: 1) It must maintain the credibility of its pledged word. 2) There is still the question of its considerable military importance, especially for the security of Japan and the Philippines.

Russia and the West: tensions of détente. While four powers, Russia, China, the United States, and Japan were involved in complicated and delicate diplomatic moves in the western Pacific, two of them were also concerned with the balance of strength and shifting political realities in eastern and western Europe. Both the United States and Russia were resolved to oppose any military intrusion into their respective spheres of interest: the NATO countries on the one hand and the Soviet Warsaw Pact nations on the other.

There had been an easing of tensions between these two power blocs from 1972 to 1975. The SALT agreement in 1972 gave some promise of a pause in the arms race. Another achievement was the Helsinki Conference on Security and Cooperation in Europe. In 1975 representatives of thirty European states, including Russia, and those from the United States, agreed to recognize the existing national frontiers as "inviable." The Conference also committed Russia to a number of liberal and humanitarian goals relating to the free movement of people and wider dissemination of information.

However, these promising signs of a real détente between East and West, between the United States and the Soviet Union, were followed by disillusionment after 1976. Soviet Russia continued to disregard its Helsinki pledges on human rights. Its intervention in Angola aroused fears about its intentions in Africa (see page 849). Most disturbing to the United States and its allies was the massive buildup of Soviet armed strength, especially in its navy. Moscow, having achieved rough parity in arms, now appeared to be striving for superiority with the United States. Negotiations in 1977 also bogged down in acrimony over SALT II, an attempt to reach agreement imposing new ceilings on nuclear weapons.

The United Nations, at thirty and after. In January 1946, the first sessions of a new international body, the United Nations, was held in London. The conclave met within sight of the rubble of bombed-out buildings. The delegates met in an atmosphere of euphoria and expectant idealism. They believed that conflict could be suppressed by the operation of collective security, by a concert of great powers acting in unison.

The United Nations was an improvement over the lamented League of Nations. In 1946 its members numbered 51; by 1977, there were 145, constituting a truly universal body. And during this existence the strength and tenacity of the organization had been demonstrated as it survived the buffeting of the cold war, the emergence of a new great power, China, the strains of massive decolonization, and four Arab-Israeli wars. It soon became apparent that the UN was powerless to coerce one of the great nuclear superpowers—Russia or the United States. It was the balance of nuclear terror, not collective security, that had become the major deterrent against a major war. The UN played a minor role in the dangerous crises over the Berlin blockade, the Cuban missile crisis, and the Soviet invasion of Hungary. It was also bypassed in the war in Vietnam and the invasion of East Pakistan by India. In one instance, the UN, largely with American support, was successful in halting Communist aggression against South Korea.

The UN, however, was able to develop a technique of international peacekeeping in which token forces were able to cope with brush-fire conflicts before they got out of hand. These contingents contained and defused conflicts in Kashmir, Indonesia, the Congo, Cyprus, and the Middle East. The most striking accomplishment of the UN was its success in helping to end colonialism, presiding over the creation of more than 70 newly independent nations.

One hears much about the diplomatic failures of the UN but little about the work of its specialized agencies which use some 80 percent of its resources and personnel. A great family of commissions, boards, and expert

Above is a general view of the United Nations Headquarters in New York City as seen from the west of the site which covers an eighteen-acre, six-block area. The buildings shown are the General Assembly on the left, the 39-story Secretariat in the center, and the Dag Hammarsjöld Library on the right.

groups have been diligently attacking economic, social, and cultural problems of humanity. Their program involves population studies, agricultural improvement, epidemic control, and protection of basic human rights. During the past decade the UN has given top priority to such matters as the peaceful exploitation of the oceans' seabeds, methods to counteract runaway increase of the world's population, and effective means to curb pollution of the human environment.

During the late 1960's and into the 1970's a considerable amount of criticism was directed against the UN. Little real progress had been made in the limitation of armaments, with nations spending a total of $300 billion annually. Unwise and even illegal resolutions were being passed by the General Assembly, such as the exclusion of Israel from UNESCO and denial of speaking and voting rights of South Africa. There were precedents in a supposedly international body of ominous potential danger. In 1967 the then Secretary-General, U Thant, felt impelled to say that the UN "has ten years to become effective or disappear." Certainly one can envisage a more efficient and smooth-working organization, but the UN can hardly be any better than the world it mirrors and represents with its welter of economic and political problems. As President Johnson once commented, the UN was "the best instrument yet devised to promote the peace of the world and to promote the well-being of mankind."

SUMMARY

In the three nations surveyed in this chapter there were significant changes in economic standards and ways of life. Soviet Russia continued to concentrate on heavy industry and arms to the detriment of the consumer. The growth of its navy was spectacular. Notwithstanding the pledges made at Helsinki to respect human rights, the Soviet Union continued to harass, imprison, and exile abroad some of its most gifted intellectuals. In Russian-dominated east Europe, considerable freedom came to be permitted in cultural and social activities but no shift was permitted from the official Kremlin ideology. This was attested by the invasion of Czechoslovakia in 1968 and the overthrow of its government.

Under Chinese Communism, individual freedoms were even more restricted than in the Soviet Union; thought control was completely pervasive. With more than 800 million people and a staggering annual increase, its leaders were confronted with an ominous race between population and resources. The consequence was a much more equilitarian and spartan life than in Russia. Life was bleak but practically all Chinese shared in the necessities and no one went hungry. The contrast in Japan was striking. This island nation, like China, had a population problem. But by incredible hard work, ingenuity, and drive, the scars of war were quickly removed. Industry boomed as its products were sold in many parts of the world. At home standards of living were dramatically raised. The average family enjoyed an income sufficient to provide it with a wide variety of consumer goods.

The western Pacific witnessed seismic changes in the relations between its interested powers following World War II. For more than three decades peace was threatened by the continued enmity between Soviet Russia and Communist China. At the same time, the latter power was hostile to the United States. However, America set in motion a diplomatic initiative that transformed the political atmosphere. It made a tentative détente with China and this in turn led to better relations with Russia, for this power had no wish to be confronted by an unfriendly China and America. Japan, meanwhile, played a muted role, content for the time being at least to follow the diplomatic lead of the United States and to accept its protective role.

These complicated power relations have been compared to a moving gyrating Calder mobile. "Two major elements today are America and the Soviet Union. China makes it a triangle. But Japan is there too. With the West European complex added, the interplay becomes more complicated."[11] That between the United States and Russia is of transcendent importance to the future of civilization. A conflict between them would likely spread from the Atlantic to the China Sea.

SUGGESTIONS FOR READING

Kurt London, ed., **The Soviet Union: A Half Century of Communism*** (Johns Hopkins, 1968); and I. Deutscher, **The Unfinished Revolution*** (Galaxy) both assess the first fifty years of Soviet history. An indispensable survey is Adam B. Ulam, **A History of Soviet Russia** (Praeger, 1976). For an analysis of the Khrushchev era see Roy A. and Z. A. Medvedev, **N. S. Khrushchev: The Years in Power** (Xerox, 1975); E. Crankshaw, **Khrushchev: A Career*** (Compass); and the Russian leader's own account of his career, **Khrushchev Remembers: The Last Testament*** (Bantam, 1976). See also A. Dallin and T. B. Larson, **Soviet Politics Since Khrushchev*** (Spectrum). A penetrating comparison is Paul Hollander, **Soviet and American Society: A Comparison** (Oxford, 1973).

The fragmentation of the Communist world is discussed in A. Gyorgy, ed., **Issues of World Communism*** (Van Nostrand Reinhold); and E. Crankshaw, **New Cold War: Moscow Versus Peking** (Books for Libraries). On the Communist bloc in eastern Europe see Z. Brzezinski, **The Soviet Bloc: Unity and Conflict,*** rev. ed. (Harvard); and H. G. Skilling, **Communism, National and International*** (Univ. of Toronto).

See Alexander I. Solzhenitsyn, **The Gulag Archipelago** (Harper & Row, 1975) for an account of the imprisonment and brutalization of Russian citizens. V. Voinovich, **The Life and Extraordinary Adventures of Private Ivan Chonkin** (Farrar, Straus, and Giroux, 1976) is a hilarious satire by a dissident.

The following titles are indispensable reading on post-1945 East Asia: Ralph N. Clough, **East Asia and U.S. Security*** (Brookings, 1975); J. A. Cohen, **Taiwan and American Foreign Policy*** (Praeger, 1971); H. C. Hinton, **Three-and-a-Half Powers: The New Balance in Asia*** (Indiana Univ., 1975); D. Lach and E. Wehrle, **International Politics in East Asia Since World War II*** (Praeger, 1975).

F. W. Houn, **A Short History of Chinese Communism*** (Prentice-Hall, 1973) is a brief basic account. R. Goldston, **The Rise of Red China*** (Premier, 1972); and J. Ch'en, **Mao and the Chinese Revolution*** (Galaxy) examine the rise of Mao's regime. See also R. Lifton, **Revolutionary Immortality: Mao Tse-tung and the Chinese Cultural Revolution*** (Random House); Edward F. Rice, **Mao's Way*** (Univ. of California, 1975); and F. Wakeman, Jr., **History and Will: Philosophical Perspectives of Mao Tse-tung's Thought*** (Univ. of California, 1975). A. D. Barnett, **Uncertain Passage*** (Brookings, 1974) covers the transition to the post-Mao period.

Edwin O. Reischauer, **Japan: The Story of a Nation** (Knopf, 1974) is especially valuable for the post-1945 period. See also K. Kawai, **Japan's American Interlude** (Univ. of Chicago, 1960); Z. Brzezinski, **The Fragile Blossom: Crisis and Change in Japan*** (Torchbooks); and R. P. Dore, **Land Reform in Japan*** (Univ. of California, nia).

*Indicates a less expensive paperbound edition.

Africa, Asia, and the Middle East Since 1945

New Nations in the Contemporary World

INTRODUCTION. One of the basic characteristics of the twentieth century has been change—change involving all aspects of man's life. Among these changes have been two vast world wars, the decline and fall of great monarchies, such as the Ottoman, the Hohenzollern, and the Romanov, the emergence of giant antidemocratic totalitarian systems, and amazing scientific and technological progress. Another basic transformation has been the eclipse of colonial systems. Imperial rule, at its height in Africa and Asia following World War I, molded and governed the lives of millions of subjects. Colonial control gave a certain static stability in large areas of the world; but it could not continue. It had, by the 1940's, outlived its dynamism and usefulness. Stability imposed by alien rule, despite some positive consequences, was an inadequate substitute for self-rule and with it the opportunity for people to try to solve their own problems.

World War II had a shattering effect upon colonialism. Such imperial powers as Britain and France no longer had the strength, nor indeed the moral will, to hold down their colonial wards. Equally important, the conflict generated and spread the ideology of self-determination and nationalism. These aspirations could not be denied. Within a period of two decades some five dozen African and Asian colonial areas became independent. Constituting what is usually referred to as the Third World—in contrast to the western and Communist worlds—these states are newly independent, generally economically underdeveloped, and diplomatically nonaligned; and they have sedulously sought to avoid entanglements in big-power rivalry.

This tripartite distinction is not completely clear-cut, however. There are marginal states, such as Afghanistan, Thailand, Iran, and Ethiopia, which are underdeveloped but not newly independent, and which have never, or only briefly, been under colonial control. Latin America is usually included as part of the western world. Although most of its nations have been independent for much more than a century and have at least the forms of democracy if not the reality, they can be classified as underdeveloped.

Undoubtedly the problems facing the nations of the Third World on the morrow of their independence were minimized. It is unnecessary, however, to ask whether the new nations would exchange their current condition, with all its problems, for their former colonial subjugation. A feeling of pride suffuses the leaders of the Third World and grows among its peoples. Colonialism was essentially a dead-end street. Independence, on the other hand, with its freedom of choice, gives people the opportunity to make their own destiny rather than having it imposed upon them.

This chapter outlines the untenable position of colonialism following World War II, describes the rapid process of decolonization, and discusses the basic problems of nation-making following independence. Attention is then given to the impact of the new Africa upon the United States. Finally, the chapter will describe the activities of Third World states in the United Nations and the problem of big-power intrusion into vacuum areas, notably in Vietnam, Africa, and the Middle East.

THE ECLIPSE OF EMPIRE

War's impact on imperialism. In 1945, European colonies, controlling more than one billion people, dotted the globe. Within the colonial powers there was a grudging realization that the days of Kipling and the domination by white men in Africa and Asia were drawing to a close. It was believed, however, that this liquidation would be a slow process. Actually it took just about two decades.

The war accelerated forces already in existence; in competition with these influences, imperialism could not endure. In areas once remote and untouched by modern change, westernized elites grew rapidly. The process of urbanization created professional and merchant classes imbued with western political ideology. The presence of European troops had a disturbing effect, sometimes exposing the vices of the white man and al-

lowing anticolonial European liberals to make secret contact with native leaders. Allied propaganda, with its emphasis upon a better postwar world and the crusade for democracy, tended to encourage Afro-Asian peoples to expect a "new deal" following the war. One of the most important anticolonial forces emanated from the United States. Various private organizations published programs for the postwar period, most of them calling for some reform or even abolition of the colonial system.

In the colonies the claim of European invincibility had been swept away by the impressive victories of Japanese arms at Pearl Harbor, Hong Kong, Singapore, and in Burma. These conquests led to the startling growth of nationalist movements in Asia—especially in Indonesia, French Indochina, Malaya, and Burma. Japanese occupation authorities carefully nourished anti-European sentiment. In India the western thrust of Japanese armies toward Bengal had caused the British government to make substantial concessions to Indian nationalist leaders. In 1942 the famous Cripps' Mission offered India independence within or without the British Commonwealth following the war. During World War II Africa remained generally tranquil. But the lessons of Allied defeats and echoes of anti-imperialism reached educated African circles.

New colonial policies. The various colonial powers were sensitive both to the demands of nationalism in the colonies and to the censure of world opinion against imperialism. In England, especially, a tired and perhaps more realistic younger generation no longer had any heart for empire. In fact, the British Labour party, which came into power in 1945, had always been anti-imperialistic. Toward the end of the war, however, the Labour party, supported by strong public opinion, realized the problems that would inevitably emerge with colonial independence and shifted its ground somewhat. For many of the colonies, particularly those in Africa, it announced a policy of gradual advances toward self-government in partnership with Britain, which would provide substantial financial and technical aid. The ultimate political aim was independence within a cooperative Commonwealth. Large sums, totaling $360 million by the end of 1956, were granted for colonial development.

During the war France also formulated a new program for its colonies. After 1945 large sums were earmarked for colonial development. In sub-Saharan Africa, for example, $700 million had been granted by 1955, plus large loans on very generous terms. France envisaged eventual self-government for its colonies but, unlike the British idea of Commonwealth, within a political structure dominated by Paris.

Belgium badly underestimated the force of nationalism in its huge African colony. Self-government in the Congo was ruled out as chimerical within the foreseeable future. What mattered was its economic development and the paternal treatment of Belgium's colonial wards. Portugal, on the other hand, had neither the resources nor the will to initiate a forward colonial policy. It denied that Angola and Mozambique were colonies, maintaining that they were integral units of the homeland and that all civilized Africans were therefore entitled to the same rights as citizens of Portugal. (Very few, however, had the opportunity to become educated and "civilized.") During the war the government of the Netherlands, an exile regime in England, issued statements indicating that following the reestablishment of peace, its empire would form a commonwealth, each part — especially the East Indies — having "complete self-reliance and freedom of conduct."

The chronicle of decolonization. These new colonial policies, based generally on programs of partnership between the imperial powers and their colonies, came too late. Nationalism would not be denied. Too much had happened during the war to undermine the traditional relationship of imperial overlordship and colonial subordination. The rapidity with which empires disappeared constitutes one of the great historic happenings of modern times. Their passing ended some four hundred years of what might be called the European phase of world history.

For a decade after 1945 it seemed that the new colonial policies might succeed, that independence might be gradually achieved. One of the first indications that the whole edifice of imperialism would quickly collapse came in the late 1940's when Indonesian nationalists demanded a complete break with the Netherlands. An ugly war ensued, and finally, in 1949, through UN mediation, the Dutch East Indies became Indonesia — a new nation. Largely with the help of the same international body, Libya, a former Italian colony, was tendered its freedom in 1951. Meanwhile, keeping its prewar promises, the United States had granted the Philippines independence in 1946. In the same part of the world France became embroiled in a tragic and costly war while trying to restore some semblance of its authority in Indochina (see p. 852).

In North Africa, France's two protectorates, Tunisia and Morocco, gained independence in 1956 relatively peacefully. The disagreement over the state of Algeria, however, became a veritable nightmare. France had poured millions of dollars into this territory, and by 1960 French immigrants numbered about one million, one tenth of the population. French enterprise had developed Algeria substantially, but the settlers dominated industry, agriculture, and the government, while the Muslim majority remained hopelessly poor.

Although Algeria was an integral part of France and sent representatives to Paris, resentment grew among the non-French population against French control of Algerian life. In the fall of 1954 violence broke out which, by 1958, had become a full-fledged revolution. A French army of 500,000 battled the insurgents who used guerrilla tactics — blowing up bridges, raiding towns, and ambushing French convoys. In this "dirty war" ruthless methods, including the use of torture, were employed by both sides. The agony of Algeria ended the Fourth Republic in 1958 and brought Charles de Gaulle to power as president in a new government. Although elements in the army and French civilians in Algeria were determined to keep it French, de Gaulle made plans for independence. This policy was supported by a plebiscite in France, but in Algeria it was challenged in 1961 by a revolt of French settlers backed by military units. This mutiny collapsed in a final orgy of atrocities by French diehards in both France and Algeria. In 1962 the country gained its independence after being tied to France for 132 years.

Seventy percent of the Europeans left, going to France or other countries such as Canada. The country was left scarred and battered. Well over 200,000 people had been killed, and the number of seriously wounded was even higher. It is one of the tragedies of our times that the understandable nationalism of the Muslim majority could not have been satisfied peacefully and have resulted in a friendly and cooperative relationship between France and Algeria.

While not renouncing its program of enlightened guidance for the colonies, Britain realized that an exception would have to be made in the case of India, which, during the war, had been given an unequivocal pledge of independence after the conflict. In 1947 this huge dependency gained its complete freedom as two nations: India and Pakistan. The following year the same status was granted to Burma and Ceylon. In the Middle East, Britain recognized the independence of Jordan in 1946 and two years later terminated its mandate of Palestine, an action that led to the creation of the state of Israel and a bitter war between this new nation and the Arab world.

Notwithstanding these cracks in the colonial structure, the new colonial programs appeared relatively successful, particularly in Africa. Appearances were deceptive, however, and mounting unrest in the West African colony of the Gold Coast forced Britain to give this colony independence as Ghana in 1957. In this same year Malaya became a sovereign state as Malaysia. Singapore, Malaya's major city and almost entirely Chinese in population, eventually broke away from Malaysia to become an independent member of the Commonwealth. It was now evident that nothing short of complete sovereignty could satisfy colonial nationalists. While on a tour of British Africa, Prime Minister Harold Macmillan acknowledged this fact when he declared:

The wind of change is blowing through this continent, and whether we like it or not this growth of national consciousness is a political fact and our national policies must take account of it.[1]

Africans rightly think of 1960 as their year. Eighteen new nations emerged, the most important being Nigeria and the Congo. France had enacted various reforms seeking to keep its African territories as autonomous republics under the jurisdiction of the French-directed Community. (Guinea, however, had elected to become completely independent in 1958.) This ingenious compromise, however, could not satisfy African aspirations. In 1960, therefore, all thirteen African republics within the French Community proclaimed their independence. While the old assimilationist dream of a great French imperial structure had ended, France did retain a unique status in its former colonies. Its culture persists in what can be called French-speaking Africa; and the new republics rely upon France for financial and technical aid.

During the years after 1960 further additions were made to the roster of new African nations. By 1977, fifty-one sovereign states could be identified, whereas in 1945 there had been only four. And in other parts of the world, colonies had practically disappeared from the map, with the exception of a few small oddments such as Gibraltar, Hong Kong, and various French islands in the South Pacific.

While not so spectacular as the triumphs of freedom in Africa or in South Asia, independence was achieved by various islands in the British West Indies, notably Jamaica, Trinidad and Tobago, and Barbados. The South American mainland colony of British Guiana also gained the same status as Guyana.

In retrospect, the eclipse of empires was an amazingly peaceful phenomenon. The British left India with warm words from Prime Minister Nehru: "It is rare in history that such a parting takes place not only peacefully but also with goodwill."[2] There had been bloodshed in the Dutch East Indies, post-independence riots between Hindus and Muslims in India and Pakistan, a tribal uprising of the Mau Mau in Kenya, tragic hostilities in the Congo, and a civil war in Angola. But considering the many territories and the millions of people involved, the transition from colonialism to statehood had been remarkably tranquil.

THE PROBLEM OF NATIONAL UNITY

In search of national unity. Many colonial peoples believed that the attainment of independence would usher in a golden age characterized by economic plenty, smooth-functioning governments, and proud national unity and purpose. There was euphoric optimism about the future following the exit of alien imperialists. Unfortunately, these hopes proved to be illusory. Nearly all the new nations were confronted by serious

problems, some challenging their very existence.

At the outset the new nations were confronted with the heavy costs of creating a diplomatic service and a military establishment. Economic and social development were urgently needed. In addition, there existed a desire for national prestige symbols, which led in some instances to showy non-productive facilities, such as uneconomic air lines and costly government buildings and hotels. But the most important problem was how to build and maintain national unity among disparate and sometimes antagonistic religious, cultural, and ethnic groups.

In many instances the new political entities in Africa and Asia are not the end result of a long historical process such as took place in medieval Europe, when small feudal principalities were hammered into homogeneous nation-states. The boundaries of numerous Third World states had been created by the imperial power that had ruled them. For example, Nigeria, which encompasses so many diverse and often hostile ethnic and tribal segments, was created by the force of British arms. It has been pointed out that the notoriously polyglot Hapsburg empire was more homogeneous than the Congo—formerly administered by Belgium—or the Sudan.

Tribalism and national unity in Africa. While the plural society (see p. 731) is found in various new nations of the Third World, it is almost universal in sub-Saharan Africa in the form of hundreds of tribes. The term *tribe* has been used extensively in the past but without precise definition. It can refer to a group of a few hundred people or one numbering several million. This term came into current use in the nineteenth century and generally referred to non-Europeans who were thought of as inferior and primitive, especially in their material and technological culture. In recent times anthropologists and especially African intellectuals have criticized the use of the term as unnecessarily degrading and disparaging. Until a more widely acceptable term is introduced however, *tribe*, rather than multi-ethnic societies, would seem to describe best the prevailing sociopolitical unit in Africa.

Tribalism is one of Africa's paramount

problems. It originated in the partition of this continent in the 1880's and after, when numerous tribes were placed in colonies willy-nilly, surrounded by completely artificial boundaries which had never existed before. On occasion tribes were arbitrarily divided, with one portion placed in one colony and the remainder in another. Such was the case of the Bakongo people who were located in the former Belgian Congo and in two neighboring colonies. The Somali were divided between Ethiopia, Kenya, and Somalia; and the famous lion-hunting Masai of East Africa found themselves in both former Tanganyika (now Tanzania) and Kenya.

African nationalists often deplore such tribal fragmentation. In general, however, the European-made colonies were larger and more economically viable than the hundreds of African tribal units they superseded. While there may ultimately be some rectification of these tribal separations, the urgent need in Africa is for the various tribes *within* the new nations to sublimate their traditional loyalties into a wider national allegiance. European colonialism has been referred to as "the glue that stuck these human [tribal] units together into a shape recognizable on an atlas and under a name like the Belgian Congo, Nigeria, Tanganyika, and so on."[3] Now that this foreign cohesive cement has gone, old tribal loyalties and rivalries are emerging to weaken national unity. The new elites and leaders think of themselves as Kenyans, Congolese, Ugandans, and Sierra Leonians, but the mass of people still continue to describe themselves as Kikuyu, Ibos, Hausa, or Masai. In too many instances African political parties are based on a particular tribe. This is an inducement to tribal rivalry and even civil war.

The reconciliation of tribal loyalties within the broader context of a national consciousness is a basic challenge in contemporary Africa. In the fairly stable and prosperous new nation of Zambia, its progressive president Kenneth Kaunda, commenting on a national election in 1967, declared:

We have canvassed so strongly and indeed viciously, along tribal, racial, and provincial lines, that one wonders whether we really have national or tribal and provincial leadership. I must admit publicly that I have never experienced, in the life of this young nation, such a spate of hate, based entirely on tribe, province, race, color and religion, which is the negation of all we stand for in this party and government.[4]

Tribal tensions in Kenya. The newly independent nation of Kenya has been torn by multitribal tensions. Its freedom had to be delayed because the two main tribes, the Kikuyu and Luo, were jockeying for power. Following independence, however, a single political party supported by both of these tribes became dominant and controlled the government. One of the members of its cabinet, Tom Mboya from the Luo tribe, became known internationally as a brilliant and promising statesman. It was thought he might ultimately assume the leadership upon the retirement of the venerable president Jomo Kenyatta. In 1969 this possibility was removed by the tragic assassination of Mboya by a disgruntled Kikuyu.

While rumblings of tribal tension continued in the early 1970's, Kenya is regarded as one of the most politically stable and economically sound of the new African states. It celebrated the tenth anniversary of its independence in 1973. Its president is highly regarded as a moderate and able leader. The capital, Nairobi, has also gained recognition and considerable prestige as the headquarters for important United Nations agencies and as a meeting place for African organizations.

Tribalism versus Congolese nationhood. Much world-wide publicity was given to the chaotic events following Belgium's granting of independence to the Congo in 1960 and the subsequent intervention of the United Nations. Possessing no ethnic or economic unity, this huge dependency, as large as western Europe, was carved out by the Belgian imperialist King Leopold I. Composed of some seventy major ethnic groups and divided into hundreds of tribes, the Congolese had been given practically no training in the art of self-government.

In 1959, however, confronted by general unrest and serious rioting, the Belgians precipitously promised independence. Meanwhile, the Congolese formed political parties

"Operation Tele-Niger," an experiment in teaching by television, has proven very successful in the West African nation of Niger. Children in villages within 900 miles of the capital of Niamey learn reading, writing, and other classroom subjects from these special programs which are beamed four times daily. A classroom teacher is present to aid the students in their study.

that were primarily tribal associations. As the date for independence approached in 1960, tribal war broke out, accompanied by looting and massacres. Following independence in the summer of 1960, workers' strikes, the mutiny of the native army, and attacks on Europeans brought virtual anarchy to the Congo. The crisis was intensified by the secession of the rich mining province of Katanga. Its leader, Moise Tshombe, apparently had no intention of providing revenues to support the rest of the Congo, now wracked by violence. This action was also supported by foreign mining interests which controlled the Katanga mines. At the request of the central government, United Nations forces intervened to restore order and ultimately to end the Katanga secession. Following severe fighting this objective was achieved, and the UN forces were withdrawn during the summer of 1964. Peace and stability did not follow, however. Terrorism and rebellion again

broke out in various parts of the Congo. The central government at Leopoldville (now renamed Kinshasa) was unable to restore order. During the emergency a rescue mission was organized to evacuate European hostages—but not before eighty of the prisoners had been massacred by the rebels. During 1965 a semblance of order was gained as the army took control of the civilian government in the person of its commander, Joseph Mobutu. Tribalism, regional revolts, and inexperience in self-government continued to harass the country; and as one authority observed, "It will be a miracle if the Congo at long last finds the stability it sorely needs."[5]

But by the mid-1970's, President Mobutu had succeeded in establishing his central government's authority over dissident, especially tribal, groups, and a remarkable degree of stability had been achieved. He had also enhanced the international status of his regime by making state visits to mainland China. Perhaps most interesting was the Congo's determination to eradicate all traces of colonialism by stressing its African heritage. Colonial monuments were torn down, the most notable being one of Henry Morton Stanley; the names of European streets, rivers, and newspapers were Africanized, and the country's name was changed to Zaire. This campaign was called "the return to authenticity."

Nigeria at war with itself. Nigeria has been called Africa's giant, its most populous country with some 57 million people. Nigeria's progress toward modernization has been rapid since World War II. Endowed with a variety of important natural resources, especially oil, it promised to be one of Africa's richest nations. When Nigeria became independent in 1960, it had several thousand well-trained civil servants, more than five hundred doctors, an equal number of lawyers, and a substantial body of engineers and other professional men. And, unlike the Belgian Congo, it had some forty years of training in self-government. Its constitution was the end result of a decade of constitutional experiment and continuous discussions with British officials.

Nigeria, however, is similar to the Congo

in its ethnic and tribal complexity. It has more than two hundred tribes and a dozen important languages. The three most important groups are the Yoruba, the Ibo, and the Hausa, each concentrated in one region. Living in western Nigeria, the Yoruba are a prosperous, sophisticated, urban people. One of their cities, Ibadan, has a population of more than half a million. The eastern region is the home of the Ibo. Crowded on poor soil, they have taken eagerly to western education, migrating in large numbers to other parts of the country to seek their fortune. These two groups, totaling at least sixteen million, are large enough to be called nations rather than tribes. The northern part of Nigeria is populated by the Hausa, a proud people numbering twenty million, who are Muslim in religion and way of life. Under British protection the four dozen Hausa rulers, the emirs, lived in palaces and followed the feudal traditions of their forefathers. Western education was disdained, and Arabic rather than English was taught in the schools.

While some tension and rivalry existed between the Ibo and the Yoruba, the main antipathy was between them and the northern Hausa. The latter were contemptuous of these non-Muslims, mainly Christian or pagan, who were aggressive in business and assertive in politics. Especially irritating to the Hausa were the more than one million Ibo in their midst. Outside their cities were the Strangers Settlements, inhabited by non-Muslim southerners, who filled such skilled positions as telegraph clerks, mechanics, station masters, and office employees. This situation led to ill-feeling, and in 1953 there were severe riots between the migrant community and the Hausa in one of the emirates.

Notwithstanding regional tensions and those stemming from the rivalry between progressive and traditional forces, Nigeria gained its independence in 1960 as a single national entity. This accomplishment was regarded as a model experiment in national integration. With its representative institutions based on British models, Nigeria was held up as democracy's best hope in Africa.

Military coups and civil war in Nigeria. This hope for Nigeria was shown to be tragically unrealistic. Danger signals began to flash only two years after independence. Each of the three main regions had its own political party, and none had a broad national base of support. Electioneering, therefore, took on the form of intense rivalry between the three regional peoples: the Hausa, Yoruba, and Ibo. The north, because of its population majority, enjoyed a dominant position in the central federal government. Between 1962 and 1965 a series of crises—disputed elections, quarrels over census figures, rampant corruption, and lawlessness—threatened to tear the new nation apart. In 1966 a group of young army officers, all Ibo, seized control of the federal government and in the process murdered prominent leaders, especially in the north. Apparently the coup had mixed motives, such as ending corruption and pushing modernization; but it also had implications of Ibo nationalism.

Power was given to an Ibo officer, General Johnson Aguiyi-Ironsi, who at the outset had a good chance to reconcile factions and clean up the government. Unfortunately his regime completely alienated the Muslim north. It did nothing to punish the perpetrators of the coup; it proceeded to strip the emirs in the north of their traditional functions; and, most important, it abolished the federation in favor of a unitary government in which the well-educated and enterprising Ibo might become dominant. The northerners now became fearful of the rising influence of the southerners.

In the spring and fall of 1966 rampaging mobs in the north, joined by soldiers, fell upon the hapless Ibos. Thousands were massacred and more than a million fled to their homeland in the eastern region. Meanwhile, a second coup had taken place; control over the central government was turned over to General Yakubu Gowon and Aguiyi-Ironsi was murdered.

The war for Biafran independence. After witnessing these events, the leader of the Ibos, Colonel Chukwuemka Ojukwu, in May 1967 proclaimed the secession of the Ibo from the federation as the state of Biafra. Hostilities between Biafra and the central government at Lagos began in July 1967. Outmanned and outgunned, the Ibo were encircled and

It was the children who were the most pathetic victims of the Biafran war. Although quantities of food supplies sent by relief agencies were stockpiled not far from the war zone, they were not allowed into the country until some time after the war's conclusion. Estimates of death by starvation ranged from twenty to fifty thousand; after a span of thirty months, the conflict ended in 1970.

driven into an area little more than sixty by forty miles by the summer of 1968. The conflict became a deadly siege in which six million civilians faced the prospect of starvation. Several thousand died daily, mainly young children. Public opinion in much of the world was shocked by the sufferings of Biafrans. Mercy flights carrying food to the starving Ibos were organized under great difficulty. By 1969, notwithstanding desperate resistance, the Biafran cause appeared hopeless. In January 1970 the secessionists laid down their arms, and thirty months of bitter fighting came to an end. Fortunately, reconciliation and stability developed rapidly. In the mid-1970's Nigeria, with more than seventy million people, emerged as the leading nation in black Africa. Its oil production reached two million

barrels a day, and it became a major factor in international trade.

Tribalism in retrospect. Tribalism and conflicting regional cultures and loyalties are serious impediments to national unity in Africa. There is the rivalry between one tribe and another, as in the case of the Luo and Kikuyu in Kenya, and the conflict between progressive, modernist groups who seek to create a single national unity and traditional, aristocratic elements, as in the case of the Congo. In Nigeria the Ibos aroused the resentment of the traditional and less westernized northern population. This tribal rivalry, largely fed by economic competition, led to tragic civil war. A special variety of tribalism has also led to civil war in the Sudan, where African tribes have opposed domination by the ethnically and culturally different

Arab ruling class. In Ethiopia, Muslims in its Eritrean province revolted against the central government.

Tribalism, or what is sometimes referred to as regionalism, will continue to be a serious obstacle to a sense of nationhood in the foreseeable future. One of the most distressing recent instances occurred in Burundi, in central Africa. Here the two most important tribes are the tall and aristocratic Tutsi, who have been the traditional rulers over their subject Hutu. There have been centuries of antagonism between these two ethnic groups. In 1972-1973 one of the worst tribal conflicts in African history erupted. Perhaps as many as 100,000 persons, mainly Hutu, were massacred by the Tutsi-controlled army.

Perspective on African nation-making. It is difficult to assess the prospects of nation-building in the Third World; too little time has elapsed to provide the necessary perspective. In attempting a balanced evaluation, one should keep in mind that numerous long-established western nations still have to contend with their "tribal tensions." One only has to refer to the smoldering antipathy between the Catholics and Protestants in northern Ireland which verged on civil war, the rancor between French and English Canadians in Quebec, and the rivalry in Belgium between the French-speaking Walloons and the Flemings speaking Dutch dialects. While the United States has been traditionally proud of its "melting pot," the plural basis of its society has been painfully manifest in recent demands of its Afro-American and Spanish-American (Latino) subcultures.

Regional tensions in India and Pakistan. During the heyday of western imperialism, India was the colony with the largest mass of people ruled by a foreign power. During its long history this subcontinent had only been partially united by the Mauryan emperor Ashoka and by the Mughul emperors. During the nineteenth century, however, its many linguistic and racial groups had been brought under a single British administration. Following World War II Britain stood ready to grant independence to India in accord with promises made during the conflict. Unfortunately, the chasm of suspicion between Hindus and Muslims had now widened to a menacing degree. Muhammad Ali Jinnah, leader of the Muslim League, demanded that India be partitioned, that Muslims not be included in an independent India dominated by its Hindu majority.

Confronted by the intransigence of the Muslim League and Gandhi's and Nehru's predominantly Hindu National Congress, Britain, fearful of civil war, persuaded both parties that partition was inevitable. Thus in 1947 the economic and geographical unity of the subcontinent was sundered. Pakistan, especially, was an artificial creation, consisting of two provinces separated by some one thousand miles of intervening Indian territory.

The immediate aftermath of partition was a rash of bloody riots between Hindus and Muslims that resulted in the murder of thousands. One of the victims was Mahatma Gandhi, who, because of his tolerance to-

PARTITION OF INDIA

ward Muslims, was assassinated by a Hindu in 1948. Another tragic sequel was the quarrel over the status of Kashmir. Predominantly Muslim in population, much of this territory came under the control of India, and a full-scale war with Pakistan was narrowly averted by the intervention of the United Nations in 1948. An uneasy truce and a cease-fire line were arranged, but in 1965 a short but inconclusive war broke out over the disputed territory. Tension over Kashmir still continues to poison Indo-Pakistan relations.

Partition has not guaranteed the unity of these two nations. India is not a single nation but consists of numerous different racial, linguistic, and cultural groups. "Nowhere do so many linguistically differentiated peoples, all of them so self-aware, all numbered in millions and tens of millions, confront each other within a single national body politic."[6] Without the binding force of British alien rule, ancient cultural and regional loyalties have emerged to challenge national unity. The Dravidian-speaking south is vehemently opposed to the expansion of northern Hindi as the official language, labeling it as Hindi imperialism. This southern nationalism has gone so far as to speak of the creation of a separate Dravidian state. Meanwhile, riots between the Muslim minority and the Hindu majority occur from time to time in various parts of India. It is understandable that one scholar has referred to the Indian republic as possessing a "facade of union, perilously uncemented."

Pakistan has been described as the impossible dream that failed: Regionalism was a major problem in Pakistan from the beginning. While its population was predominantly Muslim, its two main provinces differed widely in race, economic interests, and language. The Urdu-speaking western Pakistanis were better educated, had a higher standard of living, and were the dominant element in the civil service and the armed forces. The people in eastern Pakistan spoke Bengali, were generally backward economically and educationally, and complained of being exploited. They expressed their discontent in riots and threats of secession. Tensions and ill will between the two regions

increased rapidly in the 1960's. Eastern Pakistan in reality was a colony of the western region, which refused to treat it as an equal, politically or economically. With its population density of 1200 people per square mile, subject to recurrent famines and devastating floods East Pakistan was a desperately poor region that needed help to avoid catastrophe. Yet its civil servants were mainly from the western region and often seemed oblivious to the plight of the people they were supposed to serve. West Pakistan also had its economic problems, but the status of its people was substantially superior to that of the people in the eastern section. In 1970 a cyclone ravaged much of East Pakistan and caused 500,000 deaths. This disaster increased the enmity between the two regions as western bureaucrats seemed indifferent to the emergency.

Demands developed in East Pakistan for more self-government within the framework of a loose union with the western province. These demands were turned down by the central government controlled by a military dictator, who began moving troops into the eastern region. In March 1971 a reign of terror ensued in which thousands of civilians in the eastern province were massacred. The main targets were students and professional people. This mass terror led to a huge exodus of perhaps as many as eight million refugees into India. The influx of refugees created an intolerable burden for India, whose prime minister, Indira Gandhi, made plans to solve the problem. She signed a treaty of friendship with Soviet Russia in the summer of 1971. At the same time India covertly began to train guerrillas who were sent to harass the troops in East Pakistan. In December an Indian army invaded the eastern region, and in two weeks completely defeated the Pakistani forces and captured 90,000 troops.

This civil war created as many problems as it had solved. A new nation, called Bangladesh, had been created, but its land lay ravaged and despoiled. Several million refugees from India had to be resettled. Six million homes had been destroyed, and rail and water transport needed to be repaired. Large amounts of foreign aid were received, but the new country's future was uncertain. It

Suspected Pakistani collaborators are held prisoner by a group of Mukti Bahini guerrillas during the 1971 India-Pakistan war. The Mukti Bahini was a largely undisciplined militia of East Pakistan Bengalis trained in the use of weapons by Indian army instructors. At the war's end they turned into a lawless force, and it was only after concerted appeals for cooperation by Bangladesh's new prime minister that they voluntarily laid down their arms.

might survive as a client state of its helpful neighbor, but massive support from India was doubtful as this nation had serious problems of its own. Some observers asserted that for decades Bangladesh could only exist as an international basket case.

Defeat and dismemberment of their country shocked the people of West Pakistan and completely discredited their military dictatorship. A new civilian government was established, and under Prime Minister Zulfikar Ali Bhutto's vigorous leadership, a democratic constitution was adopted in 1973 and long needed reforms were planned. Relations with India were improved; most of the Pakistani P.O.W.'s were released; and mutual exchanges of civilians were carried out. Pakistan also recognized Bangladesh as an independent nation. An unexpected attack took place in 1974 when nationwide rioting

after an alleged rigged election broke out against Bhutto's government.

Only India emerged from the war with its image enhanced. It had humbled a troublesome rival and had become the major power in South Asia. This new status was further enhanced by its explosion of an atomic device in 1974.

Racial problems in Malaysia and Indonesia. Other new states in Asia lack the national unity that is made possible by a prevailing sentiment of common patriotism. The Federation of Malaysia, created in 1957, has a mixed population—51 percent Malays and 36 percent Chinese. In this plural society the Chinese, originally immigrants, came to hold a virtual monopoly of wealth and power. This dominance has led to resentment and strife. In 1969 and 1974 serious riots exploded. Systematic discrimination is now being practiced by the authorities, mainly of Malay origin, to reduce the wealth and the influence of the Chinese.

The huge archipelago of Indonesia, consisting of 3000 islands with a population of 110 million, has enjoyed little tranquillity since 1949, the year of its independence. A multi-ethnic state, it consists of a melange of many cultures, ranging from Stone Age to urban businessmen and sophisticated intellectuals. While some three hundred distinct ethnic groups have been identified, a major division exists between the Javanese and the non-Javanese in the Outer Islands. The two differ widely in economic interests, ways of life, and political outlook. Complicating the plural aspects of Indonesian society is the existence of a Chinese minority of some three million. Nearly all retail trading and moneylending is in Chinese hands. As in Malaysia, the native population resents this situation. There have been anti-Chinese outbursts and governmental attempts to restrict Chinese commercial activity; also a series of unsuccessful coups and revolts against the central authority in Java.

WHAT GOVERNMENT FOR THE NEW NATIONS

Requisites for western democracy. The colonial peoples' drive for freedom following World War II generally included democratic and equalitarian ideals. Educated to admire western liberal thought, their leaders felt they could make a stronger case for independence if this goal were based on imitation of the democratic philosophy of the colonial powers. Both the national leaders and the western imperial powers thought that, following the attainment of independence, most of the new states would enjoy the blessings of stable government, procured by efficient executives, responsible legislatures, free elections, and incorruptible courts — all in the western classical manner. It was not understood that successful democracies are not created full grown but develop, in some instances over hundreds of years.

It is generally conceded that for reasonable success democracy requires a high degree of the following requisites: (1) a literate electorate, (2) a high standard of living, (3) a substantial middle class, (4) a reasonable degree of social mobility, and (5) traditions of tolerance by which the majority in power will respect the rights of the minority. In general, only a few of the new nations possessed some of these requirements, none had all of them, and some were lacking in virtually all five criteria.

Repudiation of western models. Practically all the new nations began with parliamentary governments patterned after western models. But these soon gave way to military dictators or authoritarian one-party systems. In one year, 1958, generals took over in six countries: Iraq, Lebanon, the Sudan, Pakistan, Burma, and Thailand; Indonesia retained only the remnants of parliamentary government, while Egypt and Syria were already under authoritarian rule.

Within the first several years of Africa's experience with independence, twenty-seven states experienced forceful takeovers; and in four months in 1967 there were four military coups. Witnessing these events, an Africanist observed:

Coups, counter-coups, plots and conspiracies, assassination attempts, communal violence, and even armed rebellions now seem almost commonplace in Africa; in fact, the march of recent events on the continent has raised serious doubts about the viability of many of the new African states.[7]

Following most of these changes, the outward forms of parliamentary government have often been retained, but these have only camouflaged centralized control. In most of the new states, a charismatic leader — a magnetic, forceful personality with mass appeal and support — has become the head of the state, either as a dictator or as the representative and voice of the dominant, and usually unopposed, political party. Thus Gamal Abdel Nasser came to dominate affairs in Egypt, Julius Nyerere in Tanzania, Kwame Nkrumah in Ghana, Ayub Khan in Pakistan, Achmed Sukarno in Indonesia, and Sekou Toure in Guinea.

In essence these political transformations

demonstrate that what was tried was a graft of alien forms of government upon people whose institutions, traditions, and present conditions were utterly different from those in the West. Indonesia, Ghana, and Pakistan are cases in point, while India is a notable exception.

Sukarno's Indonesia. The biggest and richest nation in Southeast Asia is Indonesia. Yet for fifteen years after independence it was to experience declining exports, inflation, and food shortages. Its population problem had grown more acute and its economy more stagnant. The main responsibility for this debacle was Indonesia's flamboyant president, Achmed Sukarno (1901-1970). Following ruinous economic policies, he contracted huge Russian loans for arms, fought a costly guerrilla campaign against Malaysia, confiscated foreign businesses, and lavished money on costly, showy enterprises. At the same time he gathered all power into his own hands. Sukarno's only solution for his country's ills was to keep the masses in a continuous state of emotional nationalism. For a number of years he mesmerized huge audiences with a torrent of slogans. In 1965 a Communist plot to take over the country — partly made possible by his leftist policies — was unsuccessful, but thousands of Communist sympathizers were butchered. In 1967, appalled by the direction of national affairs, a military regime under General T. N. J. Suharto removed the discredited Sukarno and took command of the government. The new regime set about diligently to undo Sukarno's blunders but did not promise an early return to parliamentary institutions. In 1971, however, national elections were held. Under Suharto, Indonesia made impressive advances. Oil production was increased, and large amounts of foreign capital were obtained. Resentment against the Chinese minority continued to be a problem. In 1971 and 1974 there were serious racial outbursts during which thousands of students went on rampages, looting and damaging Chinese shops and homes.

During the mid-1970's, Suharto's government, essentially a military regime, faced serious problems. Some 30,000 political dissidents were in prison, there was annoying corruption in the civil service, and rural development of the peasants remained neglected. National elections were scheduled for May 1977 with Suharto promising new social and economic reforms.

Nkrumah's Ghana. Ghana was the first nation south of the Sahara to rise out of subservience to the white man in 1957. Kwame Nkrumah, its prime minister, was the idol of all African nationalists; and his newly freed nation was the symbol of liberalism and democracy in emergent Africa. But almost immediately Nkrumah began to muzzle the press and imprison the opposition. Quickly he developed into an outright dictator in the classic mold. At the same time he embarked on ruinous economic policies, such as showy projects and a large military establishment. Evidently enjoying his power, Nkrumah's controlled press represented him as the Great Redeemer and His Messianic Majesty. Ghana progressively slid downhill economically, saddled by a huge national debt and aided by much corruption on the part of Nkrumah's colleagues. In 1966 a group of army officers, embittered by Ghana's plight, seized control of the government. Anxious to speed economic recovery and to restore some semblance of political freedom, the army leaders permitted the return of parliamentary institutions in 1969. Ghana thus became the first African country to return to multi-party government after being a one-party state. This success was short lived. In 1972 another military junta seized power in a bloodless coup.

Oligarchic democracy in Pakistan. Pakistan, as already noted, was plagued by feuds between its eastern and western wings. At the same time, chronic corruption and the whole tenor of politics demonstrated the people's inability to operate parliamentary democracy. Shortly after independence the prime minister was assassinated; a number of short-lived governments followed, accompanied by intermittent rioting and states of emergency.

Finally, in 1958, General Ayub Khan seized power. At this time the country seemed to be falling apart. Parliament was dissolved, the constitution abrogated, the new regime moved against black marketeers, and corrupt politicians were barred from political activity. General Ayub had nothing but contempt for the politicians who had manipulated the votes of the masses and brought the country to the edge of ruin.

For ten years Ayub's system of enlightened despotism gave Pakistan reasonable stability and relief from irresponsible politicking. It also registered substantial economic progress. But the strength and popular support for his government rapidly waned after 1965. Corruption and concentration of wealth became widespread. Pent-up dissatisfaction burst in the closing weeks of 1968. Faced by what appeared to be a national revolt, the president resigned his office, turning it over to the leader of the armed forces, who proclaimed martial law. As we have seen, the tenure of this dictatorship was brief. In 1971, following defeat by India in the Bangladesh war, it was succeeded by a civilian government with a democratic constitution.

India, once the exception. In the long list of independent states few have retained genuine liberal regimes. Until 1975 the only outstanding exception was India which was called the world's largest democracy. After independence its parliamentary system functioned with little friction. This success was mainly due to Nehru, the country's first prime minister who was an ardent devotee of democratic government.

Following Nehru's death in 1964, his daughter, Mrs. Indira Gandhi, became prominent in politics and was named prime minister in 1966. Her popularity reached a peak with the defeat of Pakistan in 1971. Within two years, however, India was battered by serious harvest shortages, food riots, workers' strikes, and student unrest. Opposition to the government mounted. While in 1969, Indira Gandhi had declared: "Dictatorship is not necessary to fight hunger. Nor does dictatorship give people strength," she announced in June 1975 a state of emergency and the government's assumption of dictatorial powers. At least 10,000 of her critics were jailed, a rigid press censorship imposed, and fundamental civil rights in the constitution were suspended.

With all opposition muzzled, the people were exhorted to "work more and talk less." After a year, the new order claimed numerous gains, advances in productivity, a drop in inflation, curbs in the black market, and stepped-up birth control measures. Although Mrs. Gandhi claimed that her drastic measures were only temporary, some critics observed she may be moving "from dictatorship to dynasty." Early in 1977, however, there was some relaxation of authoritarianism. The government released many political prisoners and announced national elections would be held. The outcome of the election was that Mrs. Gandhi lost her seat in parliament and as a consequence resigned her post as prime minister. Authoritarianism has been repudiated but the road that India would now take remained in doubt.

Third World variants of western democracy. On the surface what has happened politically in the new nations might seem to add up to a discouraging record. But perhaps the process should be viewed rather as a search for a governmental system that is best designed to solve urgent problems—a system that is not merely derivative but is rooted in indigenous institutions, influenced somewhat by western ideas. During this experimental period many new nations have generally discarded what is regarded as too

Teaching of birth-control methods and practices has not met with much success in India which predicts a population of 800 million by the year 2000. A doctor at a family-planning clinic explains the method of contraception using the intrauterine device to a group of Indian women.

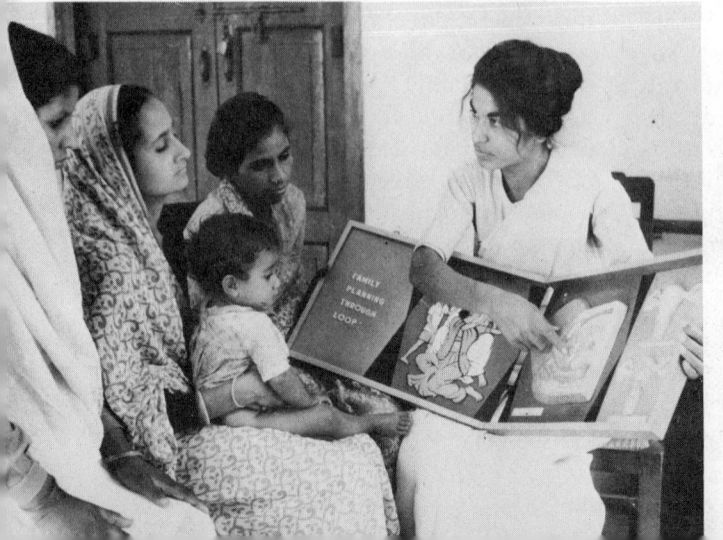

costly and time-consuming—the institution-alized western two-party system. Only a single political organization, therefore, exists to carry on an undivided attack on national problems. It is believed that basic decisions can be reached by consensus within the ruling party. While these new regimes present some authoritarian features, it is important to note that they generally make a significant commitment to the general ideology of democracy. Thus various leaders refer to their governments as Guided Democracy, Basic Democracy, or One-Party Democracy. In Egypt, where Nasser claimed that his military rule was democratic, it has been argued that the key to his concept of democracy was not so much the element of choice between candidates in elections as it was popular satisfaction with the individuals running the government and mass participation in implementing its progress.

Apologists for African one-party states were dismayed by the course of politics in the 1970's. In 1971 an uneducated army officer overthrew the regime in Uganda. General Idi Amin then proceeded to rule capriciously and by terror. Thousands were killed. There was also much political unrest in West Africa, as indicated by plots and army takeovers. Early in 1974 army mutinies, strikes, and student unrest convulsed Ethiopia. Thousands of deaths by famine and financial scandal involving the royal family provoked this unrest. In September 1974, the army deposed the emperor, Haile Selassie, and seized control of the government. Many of the former officials were summarily executed.

The economics of politics. Political stability and dynamism in the new nations are influenced by economic factors. It is impossible to separate economics from politics. Throughout the Third World there is a prevalent belief among the masses that their depressed economic condition can be improved. This "revolution of rising expectations" comes at a time when economic productivity is still insufficient to satisfy these aspirations. Mistakes and failures in economic development can lead to frustrations, unrest, and social conflict.

Two thirds of the world's population currently live in areas classified as underdeveloped, producing only one sixth of the world's income. Almost 60 percent of all people in the world live in areas where the per capita GNP is less than $200, whereas only 8 percent of the world's population live in areas where the GNP is over $3000.

The economic backwardness of Third World countries stems from such factors as undue dependence upon a single export commodity; the dominance of a peasant subsistence agricultural economy which is often inefficient; and lack of capital to provide funds for economic modernization and for educational facilities. Government revenues, especially in the African states, are often quite inadequate to provide for the needs of a modern nation.

Above all there is the appalling incubus of population pressure (see p. 890). Although India's national income increased 70 percent since 1950, two thirds of this growth was needed to take care of additional population, running more than twelve million annually. The eastern wing of Pakistan, which gained independence as Bangladesh, has a population of seventy-eight million jammed into an area not much larger than Arkansas. This area now has twice the population density of Japan and Holland with nothing remotely approaching their economic productivity. Until very recently Africa was thought to be a continent with reasonably good economic prospects, largely because of the absence of population pressure. The latest demographic studies, however, are disturbing. While Africa overall has a low average density, there are numerous pockets, as in Kenya and Tanzania, where the population pressure is acute. A distinguished Africanist observes: "Thus the entire continent is now, or soon will be, experiencing a population explosion of major proportions."[8]

At the beginning of the 1970's the nations of the Third World presented a spotty economic appearance. Some, notably in the Middle East, were profiting from tremendous oil revenues in what has been described as the greatest redistribution of wealth in history, resulting in one of the most incredible changes in world economics.

In the fall of 1973 the Organization of Petroleum Exporting Countries* raised oil prices some 400 percent. Their revenues jumped from $15 billion in 1972 to nearly $100 billion in 1974. By 1980, after spending all they can on domestic needs, the Arab Persian Gulf states, plus Iran, might possess nearly $300 billion, three quarters of the world's monetary reserves.

Much of the Third World has not enjoyed the heady prosperity of the oil-producing nations. While there have been substantial improvements in Thailand, Singapore, Malaysia, and Zaire, other nations have experienced disheartening conditions. In 1974 a four-year drought hit six West African countries and thousands of people died of starvation. The failure of the monsoon rains in India caused serious food shortages. Tragically, at a time when many Third World nations urgently need food, oil, fuels, and fertilizer, the rise in their cost makes their purchase almost impossible. The newly found wealth of the OPEC cartel side by side with desperate poverty has led to a new classification of the developing nations. "A Fourth World has precipitated out from the Third. Its members are those who lack major resources or economic power. The nations in this group are more dependent, more deprived, and more aware of it than any large segment of the world's population in history."[9] Given the current financial ills of Japan and the industrialized western nations, it is unlikely that they can contribute additionally, or even maintain, the level of their past foreign aid.

AMERICA
AND THE NEW AFRICA

American interest before World War II. During the nineteenth century American official interest in African affairs was minimal. The shaky independence of Liberia, which was founded in 1821 as a haven for freed slaves, was supported by the United States, but generally Washington assumed no addi-

*OPEC: Algeria, Ecuador, Gabon, Indonesia, Iran, Iraq, Kuwait, Libya, Nigeria, Qatar, Saudi Arabia, United Arab Emirates, Venezuela.

tional political responsibilities. While the slave trade was outlawed in 1807, the African squadron of the American navy accomplished little in intercepting slave ships. The main responsibility was assumed by Britain's permanent naval patrol along the west coast of Africa. With the abolition of slavery in 1863 in the United States and in Brazil, Cuba, and Puerto Rico in the 1870's and 1880's, the slave trade to the Americas dwindled to extinction.

In the closing decades of the nineteenth century American interest in Africa quickened somewhat. The government participated in the Berlin Conference (1884) which laid down general rules regulating the colonial partition of Africa. There was also increasing humanitarian and scientific interest in the "Dark Continent," and American missionary activity increased considerably. During the 1920's and 1930's, a high point in American isolationism, little thought was given to Africa.

World War II and Africa. World War II centered attention on Africa's strategic importance when lines of communication in the Mediterranean became precarious. The sea route around the Cape became vital and air transport to Egypt and surrounding areas were developed from South America to the western bulge of Africa. World War II also demonstrated the wealth of Africa's raw materials, especially uranium, copper, diamonds, gold, and cobalt. In the 1960's enormous petroleum production was developed in Algeria and Libya. For at least a decade, however, during the hectic initial years of the cold war, the United States was chiefly preoccupied with problems and crises in western Europe, the Middle East, and Asia.

The impact of African nationalism. These diplomatic concerns presented themselves at a time when nationalism was increasingly challenging colonial rule in Africa. Thus American policy-makers found themselves in a dilemma. In accordance with its traditional support of self-determination, the United States had subscribed to provisions in the United Nations Charter pledging ultimate freedom for all colonial people; but its strategy of containing communism regarded colonial rule—at least in the short run—as the best way to maintain stability in Africa. While the United States wanted a friendly Africa, at the same time it did not wish to offend the colonial powers, such as Britain and France, who were NATO allies. Moreover, the United States thought well of the new postwar colonial policies, especially of France and Britain, which sought time to build solid economic and political foundations for independence. Such considerations caused American policy to stress the dangers of premature independence. In the United Nations the United States abstained from voting on numerous resolutions, supported by Afro-Asian members, criticizing various facets of colonialism. Such lukewarm opposition to decolonization, together with hazy adherence to self-determination as an abstract and desirable principle, led many Afro-Asian leaders to consider the United States a supporter of colonialism.

The challenge of the New Africa. Following 1957 independence came with a rush to many African states. American relations were no longer with colonial powers but with the new African governments. With western control gone, the United States set about establishing new and closer avenues of communication. In 1958 a separate bureau of African affairs was created in the State Department. Foreign service personnel was increased in Africa. Economic aid reached a total of $407 million by 1968. During the next few years, however, the program of foreign aid was beset with difficulties. Economic productivity in the developing countries could not keep pace with population growth, there was world-wide inflation, and the post World War II optimism regarding the improvement of economic conditions in the Third World gave way to pessimism in the industrialized nations. In the United States domestic economic and political worries and the huge amount of money expended in Southeast Asia in the Vietnam War made Congress skeptical of foreign aid. In 1972, for example, assistance to African states was estimated to have been slightly more than $300 million.

United States race relations become international relations. Another objective of American policy, to cultivate friendship and warm diplomatic relations with African nations, was seriously jeopardized by racial discrimination in the United States. There is no doubt that the federal government's mounting offensive against discrimination can be explained not only by a sincere concern for civil rights for all but also by its desire to improve the American image in Third World countries.

In the early 1960's and 1970's issues of human rights continued to involve the United States in Africa as well as at home. In the UN it also has taken forthright positions opposing the white regime in Rhodesia, the policies of Portugal in Mozambique and Angola, and *apartheid* in South Africa. Nevertheless, despite African and some American criticism, the United States opposed the use of force against such regimes, and American business interests and commercial enterprises continued to be active. The successful drive for freedom in Africa also gave strong impetus to black Americans in their campaign for civil rights. The emergence of respected African statesmen did much to change an attitude of indifference towards Africa on the part of many American blacks to one of pride in their African heritage.

American interest in Africa's future. From lukewarm criticism of colonialism in Africa in the late 1940's and 1950's the United States, with the onset of President Carter's administration, adopted a policy of condemnation and opposition to any form of colonialism and racism in Africa. It cooperated with Britain in forming a solution to the Rhodesian problem, championed independence for Southwest Africa (Namibia), long under the control of South Africa, and sought to pressure this latter nation to end its policy of *apartheid*.

THE AFRO-ASIAN PRESENCE IN WORLD AFFAIRS

Into an uncertain world. As colonial empires disappeared, newly independent states entered the family of nations during one of the most unstable and troubled periods in world history. Nations such as Canada, Australia, and the United States had in their infancy been generally isolated from the tensions of big-power rivalry. The conclusion of global hostilities in 1945, however, brought neither peace nor actual war but almost continuous international crises as East and West probed and jockeyed for advantage in the so-called cold war.

Seeking to protect and insulate their newly found freedom, most of the new nations adopted a number of similar objectives. There was the universal desire to secure a voice in the councils of nations, especially the UN, and to receive recognition of their new sovereign status. Representatives of these new states were also extremely sensitive to slights and discriminations, particularly if they were based on color. In the nations of the Third World living conditions are, as we have seen, unbelievably low. And while some, such as India, Nigeria, and Indonesia, are potentially great powers by reason of size and population, others are so diminutive and poor as to promise little hope for eventual economic viability. The Republic of the Maldive Islands (see Reference Map 11), for example, a member of the United Nations, has an area of 115 square miles and a population of only 100,000.

To support ambitious development projects, governments have sought loans and technical assistance from the great powers. While seeking such aid, the emerging nations have sought to avoid domination by the major industrialized nations. The economic needs of the Third World states, however, make them vulnerable to foreign influences and pressures. Africans and Asians are especially sensitive to the dangers of "neocolonialism" made possible, if not always actual, by the necessary importation of business managers and technicians, dependence upon imported military supplies, and reliance upon set patterns of trade and outside sources of investment. Such factors can relegate a new nation to the status of a "client state."

Closely tied in with fear of "neocolonialism" has been the determination of Third World nations to avoid any involvement in superpower rivalry. Their diplomatic policy of nonalignment or neutralism regarded the

cold war as a tragic and frustrating facet of international affairs, obstructing the overriding task of consolidating fledgling regimes and their all-out attack on economic backwardness, poverty, and disease. Nonalignment holds that peaceful coexistence with all the great powers is both mandatory and possible.

Confronted with the same hopes and fears, the nations of the Third World have sought to cooperate with each other in various conferences and regional associations. The first such effort, the Asian Relations Conference, held in New Delhi in 1947, pledged support for all national movements against colonial rule and explored the basic problems of Asian peoples. Perhaps the most famous Third World conclave was the Afro-Asian conference at Bandung in 1955, attended by twenty-nine countries representing more than half the population of the world. As at New Delhi, anticolonialism, economic development, and cultural cooperation were the dominant topics. In the Middle East the new states established the Arab League in 1945, with a permanent secretariat in Cairo. While the League has pursued various objectives, its dominant posture has been its implacable opposition to the state of Israel. Africa has witnessed the establishment of various regional organizations, the most promising being the Organization of African Unity, created at Addis Ababa in 1963. Based on the full sovereignty of its members, it was in no sense a real African political union.

Until the establishment of the oil cartel, OPEC, attempts of Third World nations to achieve a semblance of unity did not fulfill expectations. Little agreement on important issues was obtained. The Arab League was torn by dissension between socialist-republican regimes, such as Egypt, and traditionalist-monarchical states, such as Saudi Arabia. While the OAU has witnessed some gains in African cooperation, its members have seemed primarily interested in pursuing their own national interests rather than those of continental dimensions.

Afro-Asians in the United Nations. The most spectacular impact of the new nations has been in the United Nations, where they have been instrumental in transforming its

The number of member nations in the Organization of African Unity has now reached forty-seven. Here representatives of these nations meet for a conference in Addis Ababa. The mural on the wall depicts the various leaders of the independent African nations.

membership and to a great extent its tone and purpose. Initially with a roster of 51 members, the General Assembly had increased to 145 by 1976. The dominance of western members had decreased to well below 40 percent of the membership, with Afro-Asian states holding the balance of power. In the 1970's the Third World nations became a potent force determining UN policies. With a substantial majority in the General Assembly, they voted to exclude South Africa from membership, ejected Israel from UNESCO, and adopted a resolution which asserted Zionism as a "form of racism and racial discrimination." Representatives of the new nations have also been vociferous in urging nuclear disarmament and supporting technical and economic assistance for underdeveloped areas. In 1974 Third World members were instrumental in securing approval of a Charter of Economic Rights and Duties of States. It made a series of demands: the prices of Third World commodities should be raised and tied to the cost of manufactured goods imported from western developed nations; foreign holdings could be nationalized on any terms the developing nations chose to set; outstanding debts of the poorer nations should be canceled or reduced; foreign aid should be increased. In response to these claims the United States made a number of proposals for helping developing nations. It also pointed out that the western advanced states also had a claim "for reliable supplies of energy, raw materials, and other products at a fair price."

Unfinished business in Africa. Meanwhile, southern Africa remains a potentially explosive area. The most significant event affecting southern Africa was the revolt of the Portuguese army in Lisbon in 1974. This coup ended nearly half a century of dictatorial rule. The military junta set about ending the thirteen years of costly revolt by black nationalists in its African territories: Angola, Mozambique, and Guinea-Bissau. Independence was granted to the last two with little difficulty. Freedom for Angola was complicated by the presence of half a million Europeans. Following the granting of independence in 1975 bloody strife broke out between three rival nationalist groups. With the onset of fighting hundreds of whites were evacuated by air to Lisbon and others sought asylum in South Africa and Rhodesia. Directly adjoining Mozambique with a common border is Rhodesia with some 250,000 whites and more than five million Africans. In 1965 this British colony, controlled by its small white minority, declared its independence from Great Britain which had insisted that such action could not be countenanced without the prior grant of full political rights to the African majority. Despite a crippling trade embargo imposed by Britain and economic sanctions levied by the United Nations, Rhodesia refused to accept Britain's conditions, labeled as NIBMAR (no independence before majority rule). In the fall of 1968 the British and Rhodesian prime ministers held a conference seeking some compromise solution, perhaps on a promise of "unimpeded progress toward majority rule." No settlement was reached, however, and in the spring of 1970 the final ties with Britain were severed when Rhodesia assumed the status of a republic. Meanwhile black nationalist guerrillas operating from Zambia and Mozambique continue to harass Rhodesia in hit-and-run forays. South Africa regards Rhodesia as a kind of bastion against black nationalism from the north, and its troops have actively joined local forces in

Students in Soweto, the township near Johannesburg where over one million blacks live, demonstrate near a truck that was looted and then set afire during disturbances which left over six hundred dead in 1976. On the first anniversary of the uprising violence again erupted.

seek-and-destroy missions against the guerrillas. Since 1974 the Rhodesian prime minister, Ian Smith, negotiated with black nationalist leaders—the issue being immediate black majority rule. By the spring of 1976 no settlement had been reached, and black guerrilla attacks from Mozambique became more frequent. In October 1976 the American secretary of state succeeded in obtaining what seemed to be a breakthrough in the Rhodesian impasse. Its prime minister agreed to black majority rule within two years. Black nationalist leaders and Ian Smith then met in Geneva to formalize agreements for the transfer of power. Unfortunately the discussions became deadlocked. Complicating the situation was the bitter rivalry between various black nationalist factions.

Directly to the south of Rhodesia is South Africa, the most economically advanced country on the continent. Booming cities, such as Johannesburg, rapidly growing industries, rich mining enterprises—especially gold—make South Africa a modern state except in its race relations. Observers the world over have been aware of the mounting strains within this republic, where the European minority has denied basic political and economic rights to the African majority by means of *apartheid*, a drastic policy of segregation and racial discrimination. How long the white community with less than 17 percent of the population could hold down the lid of this African boiler was problematical.

It was felt that a new approach should be tried. The South African government inaugurated a program of territorial segregation. Nine distinct and partially self-governing African states known as Bantustans were planned, each to be aided by substantial economic grants. The first to be established was the Transkei, with a Bantu population of 3.5 million. South Africa, however, still continued to depend upon a large African labor force domiciled and employed in European areas.

Although South Africa continued to enjoy an economic boom in 1973, there were disturbing indications of racial tensions. Bantustan leaders talked frequently of more political rights. There were massive strikes by African workers against their low wages, and the policy of *apartheid* was under fire from liberals, both white and black.

With the end of European control in Angola and Mozambique and the likelihood of a similar result in Rhodesia, the problem of maintaining the white minority regime became more problematical in the Republic of South Africa. Endeavoring to satisfy African political aspirations, independence was given to the Transkei in 1976. While the white government of South Africa will probably retain certain reserve powers in the Transkei, it remained to be seen whether this Bantustan program would be a solution to the country's racial problems or just provide time until more substantial changes are made. Serious riots, triggered by young black nationalists, periodically break out in the black townships near Johannesburg.

Big-power intrusion in the Third World. Internal conflicts, political instability, and dependence on outside sources for economic aid and military supplies invited major-power influence, and even interference, in the affairs of emerging nations in the Middle East, Africa, and Southeast Asia. During his first state visit to independent Africa, Chou En-lai, premier of Communist China, announced that the "area was ripe for revolution." Several African states have complained of Chinese support of plots to overthrow their governments. In the Nigerian civil war over the secession of Biafra, both Russia and Britain supplied the central government with arms, while France responded in kind for Biafra. All three powers were interested in strengthening their political and economic influence in Nigeria.

Big-power rivalry and intervention was also illustrated in the Congo following its independence from Belgium in 1960. The immediate aftermath was widespread chaos. This problem was referred to the United Nations, mainly on the initiative of the United States. The Soviet Union, however, sought to act independently by trying to circumvent the UN operation in the Congo. In effect this effort constituted a major cold war crisis. Supported by the great majority of its members, however, the United Nations successfully insulated the problem from big-power intervention. The most ominous instance of

big-power rivalry in Africa occurred in 1976-1977 when some ten thousand Cuban troops supported by Russian arms intervened in the Angolan civil war. The outcome was the victory of a pro-Russian faction.

The Middle East: after a fourth round. During the mid-1960's and into the 1970's world peace was ominously threatened by the Arab-Israeli conflict. In 1948 and again in 1956 Israel and the Arab countries had gone to war over their respective claims, including Israel's right to survival and free access to the Suez Canal. Continuous Arab terrorist attacks along Israel's borders, Arab refusal to recognize the existence of the state of Israel, and the refusal of both nations to provide some meaningful solution to the problem of Arab refugees from the wars of 1948 and 1956 were constant threats to the status quo.

Throughout late 1966 and the first half of 1967 tension, never really relaxed, began to increase rapidly. Finally, the Arabs mobilized their troops, requested the withdrawal of the United Nations peace-keeping forces, and blockaded the Gulf of Aqaba. War broke out on June 5. In seventy-two hours Israeli aircraft and tanks, with lightning speed, completely overwhelmed the combined Arab forces, and by the time a cease-fire was accepted on June 10, Israel occupied the entire Sinai peninsula including the east bank of the Suez Canal, the whole west bank of the Jordan River, Old Jerusalem, and border areas inside Syria commanding tactically important heights. Nothing, however, had been settled by the conflict. For the moment Israel felt secure, but the Arab states refused to enter into any direct negotiations aimed at removing the causes of hostility.

An uneasy peace. The superpowers have been deeply involved in the course of events in the Middle East. This area not only has the world's largest reserves of oil but strategically is a land bridge connecting three continents. Definitely pro-Arab, Russia hopes to become the major influence in the area, while United States policy is to prevent this domination. As the major supplier of arms and technicians to the Arab states, especially Egypt, Russia can pose as their benefactor and in turn expect to be the recipient of important favors. Heavily committed to the continued existence of Israel, the United States tried to discourage any substantial imbalance in the armed strength of Israel and its Arab neighbors, thus attempting to secure a stable Middle East in which all states could live in peace and not become the puppet of a single great power.

During the opening months of 1970 intermittent attacks by Arab guerrillas and regular army detachments across the Israeli border were countered by Israeli commando raids. Realizing the danger of Russo-American confrontation should a new round of war explode, Britain, France, the United States, and Russia carried on four-power talks to explore the possibilities of an overall settlement between the contending parties. The issues discussed related to the possibility of some retrocession of captured Arab territory, a solution of the long-festering refugee problem, and the internationalization of Jerusalem. Above all, the Jews insist upon the Arabs' unequivocal recognition of Israel as a sovereign state with a right to exist. While some hope of a settlement arose in the summer of 1970 when a cease-fire was accepted, the situation became charged with uncertainty a few months later with Israel's charge of cease-fire violations by Egypt and the sudden death of Nasser, the Arab leader.

In 1973, on October 6, the truce was broken by a coordinated Egyptian-Syrian attack on Israel. For the first few days the Arabs held the initiative, but Israeli forces counterattacked, crossing the Suez Canal into Egypt and driving to within twenty-five miles of Damascus, the capital of Syria. Some of the most desperate fighting since World War II took place with the destruction of 1800 tanks and 200 aircraft. During the conflict bigpower rivalry became ominous. The United States organized a large airlift of arms to Israel, and Russian intervention became a possibility. This danger passed when an initial cease-fire was secured by the initiative of the UN. In January 1974, a final pact was signed by Egypt and Israel providing for mutual troop withdrawals, the occupation of the east bank of the canal by Egypt, a UN buffer zone, and the return of prisoners. Fighting between Syrian and Israeli forces continued in the strategic Golan Heights area. A cease-fire agreement, however, was concluded the last week of May 1974, largely due to the skillful efforts of Dr. Henry Kissinger, American secretary of state. This agreement provided for the cession by Israel of some captured Syrian territory, a UN zone, and the return of prisoners.

Again in September 1975 a second agreement between Egypt and Israel was reached. It returned additional territory in the Sinai peninsula to Egypt and committed both sides not to resort to force. The United States agreed to provide up to 200 civilian technicians to service a precautionary warning system between the two sides. The U.S. also made commitments to provide additional arms and financial aid to Israel. By these agreements America strengthened its relationship with the Arab world at the expense of the Soviet Union.

New problems, however, continue to plague the Middle East. The Palestinian Liberation Organization (PLO) stepped up demands for the return of the west bank of the Jordan River and the Gaza Strip, both captured by Israel during the 1967 war. The object was the creation of an independent Palestinian state. Frequent Arab riots in this area harassed Israeli authorities.

Civil war also erupted in the Republic of Lebanon. This small nation's population, mainly Arab, was divided between Christians and Muslims. The influx of Palestinian refugees gave the latter a slight majority. Uneasy and long rivalry broke out into bitter fighting during 1975, centered in the capital city of Beirut. By the middle of the next year 25,000 people had been killed and many more wounded. The city had been gutted and burned. The once flourishing economy of the country was at a standstill with no early prospect of peace between the contending parties. As Arabs fought Arabs it was an embarrassing spectacle for the Muslims of the Middle East. The situation became more complicated when forces from Syria joined the fray. It then became apparent to neighboring states that the civil war could only bring harm to the Arab world. In October 1976, therefore, they agreed to impose a peaceful settlement. A security force, mainly Syrian, was set up to enforce a cease fire. By

A Lebanese boy poses for the camera in a bombed-out street in Beirut. In spite of the truce many of the children, like the adults, stay armed. After receiving training in Palestinian camps, youngsters ages twelve to fifteen roam the streets of Beirut while schools in the areas under Palestinian control remain empty.

The Arabs had also wielded for the first time a powerful weapon of their own—the oil embargo. In October 1973, angered by American support of Israel, ten Arab nations began cutting their oil production by five percent each month. Saudi Arabia cut production ten percent and then banned all oil exports to the United States. Libya, Algeria, and Abu Dhabi joined the embargo, which eventually included the Netherlands, Portugal, Rhodesia, and South Africa. The United States, which imported only eleven percent of its oil supplies from the Arabs, was not as badly affected as Japan and the western European nations which imported 82 and 72 percent respectively of their oil from the Middle East. By March 1974 when the embargo was ended, Arab oil production was fifteen percent lower than in October. The embargo had caused economic dislocations of varying severity throughout the world and had strained relations between the United States and its European allies who had refused to cooperate in the United States effort to supply arms to Israel. It had also caused numerous nations friendly to Israel to modify their policies in favor of the Arabs.

And what of the future? There still remain difficult problems, especially between Egypt and Israel. How much more of the occupied Sinai peninsula will Israel give back? (In 1977 the most militant Israeli party, who won the national election, pledged itself not to return any of its occupied lands.) What is to be the status of Jerusalem, so sacred to Jews, Muslims, and Christians? How can the demands of the displaced Palestinians for a state of their own on the west bank of the Jordan be met? And what will be the status of unhappy Lebanon?

year's end the country appeared to be returning to normal but the task of reconstruction would be long and costly.

Significance of the fourth Arab-Israeli war. The Middle East will never be quite the same because of the conflict. Its cost had been heavy to both sides, especially to Israel, which had spent five billion dollars and suffered five thousand casualties. Although Arab casualties were five times this number, morale among the Arab nations has mounted since the war. In contrast, the postwar mood of the Israelis has been somber and depressed. The war had made the fact clear that Egyptian and Syrian armies had learned to use sophisticated Russian weapons with determined skill and deadly effect.

WAR IN VIETNAM

The French war and the Geneva Conference. Following the end of hostilities in Indochina after World War II and the ejection of the Japanese forces, France sought to restore a semblance of its colonial authority. In

1946, however, it granted a measure of autonomy to Cambodia and Laos. The crucial problem was the status of Vietnam, where in 1945 a nationalist and pro-Communist movement led by Ho Chi Minh had established the independent Republic of Vietnam, usually referred to as the Vietminh regime. Negotiations led nowhere, and war broke out in December 1946. The struggle, at once anticolonial and ideological, lasted for nearly eight years and was characterized by cruel and violent tactics on both sides. The end came dramatically at Dien Bien Phu in 1954, when the French surrendered this massive stronghold along with 10,000 troops.

Later that year a conference was held at Geneva where agreements ended hostilities and established a truce line in the 17th parallel—the truce line being regarded as temporary, pending the holding of nationwide elections in July 1956 under international supervision. These elections were never held. Instead, a new political regime proclaimed the Republic of South Vietnam south of the truce line. Meanwhile, the split between the two geographical segments increased with the movement of refugees into South Vietnam and the progressive violation of the Geneva agreements by the introduction of military personnel and materials by the Communists on one hand and South Vietnam's allies on the other.

Washington had refused to sign the Geneva agreements; instead, it sponsored the establishment of the Southeast Asia Treaty Organization (SEATO) to combat the further spread of communism into Cambodia, Laos, and South Vietnam. In particular it sought to create a South Vietnamese regime capable of holding its own against the Vietminh and their fellow communists in South Vietnam.

America's involvement grows. At first the United States gave full support to Ngo Dinh Diem, the leading figure of the non-Communist regime in the south. He rejected Ho Chi Minh's requests for holding elections throughout all Vietnam under the Geneva agreements because he feared that the Saigon government would lose to the Hanoi regime. Unfortunately, despite Washington's urgings, the Diem government refused to carry out comprehensive land reforms, choosing instead to rely for support on the landlord class and the urban middle class.

At the same time, the Communists, thwarted in their aim of having North and South Vietnam united by a general election, began guerrilla operations against the Diem regime. This so-called Second Vietnamese War began in 1957. Disillusioned by Diem's failure to initiate urgently needed land reforms, many peasants tacitly or actively supported the local Communist guerrilla activity in the rural areas. In December 1960 the National Liberation Front (NLF)—popularly known as the Viet Cong—was established in the south and thenceforth received support from the Communist regime at Hanoi in its mounting guerrilla operations. Diem, in the face of a rising crisis, became more autocratic and less inclined to launch agrarian and other reforms. A coup and his assassination in 1963 did little to improve the situation as the NLF threatened to take over the entire country by force. Following a series of short-lived governments, President Nguyen Van Thieu took office in 1967.

In 1960 there were only 800 American military advisers in the country; four years later this figure had risen to 23,000. In August 1964, North Vietnamese torpedo boats were accused of attacking United States destroyers in international waters in the Gulf of Tonkin. Following President Johnson's request, Congress adopted, by a Senate vote of 88-2 and a House vote of 416-0, a joint resolution which approved the taking of "all necessary measures . . . to prevent further aggression" and authorized the President, at his discretion, to assist South Vietnam in its defense—using armed force if required. Thereafter the war became increasingly Americanized, until by 1968 there were more than 500,000 American troops in the country. During these years the United States assumed a progressively larger share of the burden of actual combat and in 1965 initiated an intensive air war against North Vietnam. This air war failed to produce the desired results and became a subject of bitter controversy on the American domestic front.

American intervention ends. By 1968 it was evident that victory in Vietnam was not

With the defeat of South Vietnam in 1975, the long years of conflict between North and South Vietnam had come to an end but the memories of the tremendous destruction and loss of life were not soon forgotten. A small South Vietnamese boy (left) cries over the grave of his father who was killed in combat. In the one-month period preceding the fall of the Saigon government the United States was able to evacuate thousands of South Vietnamese refugees. An American official (right) tries to dislodge a man who is attempting to climb aboard an already overloaded evacuation plane in Nha Trang.

in sight, and the antiwar ranks in the United States were growing steadily. American casualties mounted tragically, and the financial cost of the war was enormous. During the final months of President Johnson's administration, efforts were made to find an honorable solution to the conflict. The bombing of North Vietnam ended, and peace talks began in Paris with all interested parties. When President Nixon assumed office, he had an unmistakable mandate to end the war. There followed three years of frustrating negotiations until, in January 1973, the Paris Accord was signed. It provided for a cease-fire, the withdrawal of United States troops, and the release of all prisoners of war. There was, however, no provision for the withdrawal of North Vietnamese forces. Pending elections to be arranged later, the South Vietnamese government of President Thieu was to remain in power. An international commission was to be established to investigate cease-fire violations. This Accord did little more than end American intervention. The commission

was quite ineffectual, and the Vietnamese continued to fight among themselves. In early 1975 the North Vietnamese began a massive offensive. President Thieu's forces were indifferently led and put up little resistance. Saigon was captured in late April. Many South Vietnamese fled their homeland and some 140,000 obtained sanctuary in the United States. Communist takeovers also followed in Laos and Cambodia.

The United States legacy was 46,000 killed in action and a financial outlay of 146 billion dollars. At home the conflict left deep scars: the draft-age young had turned against their government, many had fled abroad, and the country had been convulsed with angry demonstrations between its hawks and doves.

Why had the United States made this massive military commitment on Asian soil? Notwithstanding official references to moral obligation, pledged word in various defense agreements, and the protection of a small and "democratic" nation against aggression, the basic reason for intervention—no matter how incorrectly construed—was the protection of the national interests of the United States. The "Domino theory" held that the fall of the South Vietnam regime would ". . . whet the Communists' appetite for aggression and widen the scope of their subversion. It would probably lead in the long run to a Communist takeover of . . . Laos and Cambodia, as well as Thailand, and trigger guerrilla explosions in Asia and throughout the underdeveloped world. It would strengthen the extreme Chinese 'line' throughout the Communist world, and perhaps undermine the more moderate trends seen in the Soviet Union and Eastern Europe."[10]

It will take the perspective of time for an objective evaluation to be made of American policy in Vietnam. Perhaps it will be seen that some positive lessons have been learned. But in the immediate aftermath of the conflict, it seemed that the price had been too high, the effort tragic and ill-advised.

SUMMARY

The explosion of anti-imperialism and the collapse of colonial systems came suddenly and unexpectedly in two short decades. This successful offensive of Afro-Asians, however, was not the sudden movement it appeared to be. Unobtrusively and gradually anti-imperialism had been developing for more than half a century. India—the forerunner—had witnessed the founding of the nationalist Congress party in 1885; and Gandhi's mass campaigns against British rule throughout the 1920's and 1930's were closely followed in other colonial areas. Emphasis upon Wilsonian self-determination during World War I and similar ideology during World War II kindled strong hopes and heady expectations among the world's colonial peoples. After 1945 they were sure not only that freedom would soon be won but that this new status would usher in a new and happier age of plenty and contentment for them.

Unfortunately, independence did not automatically solve age-old problems; indeed, in many instances, it added new ones. The consolidation of national unity proved especially precarious. India broke apart into three unfriendly states, and ethnic rivalries agitated both Malaysia and Indonesia. Tribal loyalties proved to be a major weakness in many African states, erupting tragically into civil war in Nigeria.

In addition to attacks on national unity, Third World nations have experienced difficulty in maintaining the traditional elements of western democracy. Within a few years, one-party states and military regimes became the prevailing political modes. In international affairs the new states have made a substantial impression. By 1970 they came to dominate the UN General Assembly. The overriding objective of this Afro-Asian majority was to end the last vestiges of racism and colonialism where they lingered in southern Africa. An interesting example of Third World influence in the international arena has been the new Africa's impact upon the United States. Its enhanced status caused the United States to give thought and action to strengthening its image and lines of communication in Africa. At the same time, black Americans tended to identify their struggle for civil rights and new dignity with the successful accomplishment of freedom in Africa.

The new nations have tried to present a united front in world affairs by the formation of such groups as the Arab League, the Bandung Conference, the OPEC oil cartel, and the Organization of African Unity. Such endeavors championed the principles of nonalignment in the cold war and opposition to any form of neocolonialism. Rivalries and instability in various areas of the Third World, however, notably in the Middle East and Vietnam, have invited big-power intrusion.

It is difficult to arrive at a balanced evaluation of the present and future of the emerging Afro-Asian states. Undoubtedly too much was expected from the winning of independence. It is likely, indeed inevitable, that in the immediate future there will be numerous instances of domestic turmoil; and in international affairs such confusion in "vacuum areas" may lead to big-power interference and ominous East-West confrontation. If the Third World can surmount these immediate dangers, it may, in the long-term future, gradually succeed in building stable nation-states administered by governments that are adequate for the tasks at hand and reasonably responsive to the will of the people.

Since their independence, the new nations have experienced reverses, some serious, and enjoyed achievements, some noteworthy. But generally their leaders are undaunted, facing the future with fortitude and hope.

SUGGESTIONS FOR READING

Some valuable surveys of modern India include: W. Norman Brown, **The United States and India, Pakistan, Bangladesh,** 3rd ed. (Harvard, 1972), the standard account; Durga Das, **India from Curzon to Nehru and After** (John Day, 1970), the reminiscences of a distinguished journalist; and Ved Mehta, **Portrait of India*** (Penguin). A solid biography is Z. Masani, **Indira Gandhi** (Crowell, 1976).

For studies of Southeast Asia see Michael Leifer, **The Foreign Relations of the New States*** (Longman, 1975); R. N. Kearney, **Politics and Modernization in South and Southeast Asia*** (Halsted, 1974); and R. Butwell, **Southeast Asia Today and Tomorrow*** (Praeger). For specific countries see Richard Allen, **A Short Introduction to the History and Politics of Southeast Asia*** (Oxford); W. T. Neill, **Twentieth Century Indonesia*** (Columbia Univ., 1973); and A. M. Taylor, **Indonesian Independence and the United Nations** (Greenwood, 1975).

On the Vietnam War see W. J. Duiker, **The Rise of Nationalism in Vietnam, 1900-1941** (Cornell) which gives the background during French rule. Thomas Powers, **The War at Home** (Grossman, 1973) covers the history of anti-Vietnam War movements in the United States. For personal assessments see J. Buttinger, **Vietnam: The Unforgettable Tragedy** (Horizon, 1976); A. M. Schlesinger, Jr., **The Bitter Heritage: Vietnam and American Democracy*** (Premier, 1972); C. Cooper, **The Lost Crusade: America in Vietnam*** (Premier, 1972); and F. FitzGerald, **Fire in the Lake*** (Vintage, 1973).

M. Halpern, **The Politics of Social Change in the Middle East and North Africa*** (Princeton) surveys the problems involved. See also T. C. Bose, **The Superpowers and the Middle East** (Asia, 1972) on the basic history of international rivalry since 1945. On the Arab point-of-view see W. R. Polk, **The United States and the Arab World,** 3rd ed. (Harvard, 1975), the standard work; Robert W. Stookey, **America and the Arab States: An Uneasy**

Encounter (Wiley, 1975); R. K. Ramazani, **The Persian Gulf: Iran's Role** (Univ. of Virginia, 1972). David Pryce-Jones, **The Face of Defeat: Palestinian Refugees and Guerrillas** (Holt, Rinehart and Winston, 1973), on the tragedy and drama of war victims. Jon D. Glassman, **Arms for Arabs: The Soviet Union and War in the Middle East** (Johns Hopkins, 1976) is the study of Soviet policy. The Arab-Israeli conflict is studied in R. and W. Churchill, **The Six Day War** (Houghton Mifflin, 1967); and Chaim Herzog, **The War of Atonement, October 1973** (Little, Brown, 1975). Two excellent biographies are Golda Meir, **My Life** (Putnam, 1975); and Avraham Avi-Hai, **Ben Gurion, State Builder** (Wiley, 1974). On the history of Israel see Howard M. Sachar, **A History of Israel** (Knopf, 1976); and W. Laqueur, **A History of Zionism** (Macmillan, 1968). Other topics of interest include G. M. Haddad, **Revolutions and Military Rule in the Middle East** (Speller, 1973); and W. Laqueur, **The Struggle for the Middle East*** (Penguin, 1972).

The difficulties facing the newly emerging nations in Africa are analyzed in George M. Daniels, ed., **Drums of War** (Third Press, 1974), a collection of primary sources on the Rhodesian problem; Larry W. Bowman, **Politics in Rhodesia: White Power in an African State** (Harvard, 1973); and Patrick Gilkes, **The Dying Lion** (St. Martin's 1975), covering Ethiopia on the eve of Haile Selassie's fall. Leonard Thompson and Jeffrey Butler, **Change in Contemporary South Africa*** (Univ. of California, 1975) is a superior collection of essays. Other subjects of interest are W. J. Hanna, *et al.*, **University Students and African Politics** (Africana, 1975); R. Emerson and M. Kilson, **The Political Awakening of Africa*** (Spectrum); and V. McKay, **Africa in World Politics** (Greenwood). Two interesting biographies are J. Murray-Brown, **Kenyatta** (Dutton, 1973); and Judith Listowel, **Amin** (Irish Univ.), a brief account.

*Indicates a less expensive paperbound edition.

CHAPTER 37

Intellectual and Cultural Ferment in the Twentieth Century

Society in Transformation

INTRODUCTION. "We feel that we actual men have suddenly been left alone on the earth. . . Any remains of the traditional spirit have evaporated. Models, norms, standards are no use to us. We have to solve our problems without any active collaboration of the past."[1] These words, written in 1930 by the Spanish philosopher José Ortega y Gasset (1883-1955), convey a viewpoint which has been shared by many writers, namely, that our century is divorced—even alienated—from previous periods of the western tradition. Advances in science and technology have revolutionized the lives of people throughout the world, and have created problems for which the past experience of humanity can provide neither precedent nor answers. From this viewpoint, the contemporary world with its four billion inhabitants is seen as undergoing a massive transformation—but towards what?

On the other hand, human history is also a continuum. On any given day innumerable births and deaths occur all over the planet, each birth a quantum of new life that merges into the pattern of the present like a thread woven into a tapestry or a dot of light on a television screen. In this sense, there are no breaks with history but only a gradual process of change in the planetary human pattern. Here we are reminded of the well-known maxim: "The more things change, the more they remain the same." Yet surely the converse is no less valid. History involves both evolutionary and revolutionary change—while some epochs tend to emphasize gradual processes at work, others are marked by relatively abrupt developments. To Ortega y Gasset and others, ours has been a century notable for its sudden, dramatic changes both of direction and of social structure and basic values. The thrust of this chapter is to test that proposition.

In the Prologue, we pointed out that human beings have always been interacting with their environment, and possess in common certain requirements: the physical necessities for life itself, social organization, security and order, knowledge and learning, self-expression, and religious or philosophical satisfaction. Together these form the basis of a "universal culture pattern" with all its segments intermeshing. Sometimes change occurs more rapidly in one segment than in another, thereby creating an imbalance within the society, or change may propel it from one stage of organization to another. Moreover, the particular "mix" of the contents of these segments makes every society unique, and provides it with its own specific world-view or overall ideology. (By "ideology" we mean a system of interdependent traditions, beliefs, myths, and principles held by a society and which serve to justify its behavior and values, and to defend its particular institutions and commitments.)

In the past two centuries, societies nurtured in the western tradition have developed their institutions and value systems in accordance with certain major social concepts. Three of these concepts were expressed in the French Revolution's slogan: Liberty, Equality, Fraternity. "Liberty" is associated largely with the rights of the individual and with the nation-state's claim to independence; it lies at the heart of liberalism, the ideology espoused by the middle class with its particular concern for representative government and free enterprise economy. "Equality" became the rallying cry of the proletariat, the factory workers and the Chartists, and it is ideologically expressed in Socialism, whether of the Christian, Fabian, or Marxist schools (see Chapter 24). "Fraternity," with its connotation of *community* which draws boundaries—cultural and geopolitical alike—between "us" and "them," expresses one of the most powerful and emotive ideologies of modern times, nationalism. In the last century, it redrew the maps of Europe and Latin America, and in our lifetime it has continued to redraw the maps of Asia and Africa.

In testing the proposition that we have been born into an era of fundamental transformation, we shall be searching for those segments of the universal culture pattern that seem to be especially involved in these changes. Also, we want to identify the major world-views and ideologies that have been prominent in our century. In what ways do they compete? To what extent do they affect, or in turn reflect, the contributions of scientists, writers, and artists? And are they likely to continue to diverge and compete, or are we also moving towards a new world-view, one that is global in dimension and allegiance?

THE SCIENTIFIC AND TECHNOLOGICAL REVOLUTIONS

"A new period in the history of mankind." We cannot pinpoint the precise time when one historical age gives way to another, for example, when the classical era in the West ceased and the Middle Ages appeared. The transformation was not neatly compartmentalized. Instead, a shift of social, economic, and political forces eventually tipped the scales of history, resulting in a very different outlook and set of guiding beliefs—a distinctly new "ethos" that came to dominate society in Europe. Similarly, the shift from the Middle Ages to the Renaissance was marked by yet another period of overlapping world-views and transition, one that was distinguished by a fundamental shift of man's perception about himself and his world. It set in motion the era known as early modern times, which was notable for the creation of such institutions as capitalism and the nation-state system, the advent of new inventions and science, the exploration of the world, and Europe's resulting subjugation of other continents. European hegemony reached its zenith in the century stretching from Waterloo to the First World War.

The period that opened in the wake of the galleons of Columbus and Da Gama has been replaced by a new set of historical developments dramatized by the blast-off of Sputnik and the landing of men on the moon. The far-flung colonial empires of European domination survived the holocaust of the First World War but have disappeared within a quarter of a century after the end of World War II. And whereas in 1939 capitalism and middle-class liberalism dominated the world's economic and political structures, while a socialist philosophy was in control of but one country, again dramatic changes have occurred to alter the world's ideological landscape and reduce the proportion of liberal, parliamentary-type member states in the United Nations to a seemingly permanent minority. A massive transformation has been at work in our century, inaugurating what one British historian has called "a new period in the history of mankind." Its "essential feature" is the unprecedented integration of the world's peoples, resulting from fundamental changes in the structure of national and international society:

It is a period of readjustment on a continental scale, and its emblem is the mushroom cloud high above Hiroshima and Nagasaki, the nuclear pile in which old certitudes were consumed forever. It is also a period which has experienced a break-through in scientific knowledge and achievement, and an alliance between science and technology, which has the power to change for all time the material basis of our lives on a scale inconceivable only fifty years ago, but which at the same time has brought us face to face with the possibility of self-extinction. It is, in short, a period of explosive new dimensions, in which we have been carried with breathtaking speed to the frontiers of human existence and deposited in a world with unparalleled potentialities but also with sinister undercurrents of violence, irrationality, and inhumanity.[2]

Since technology and science can serve any economic system or ideology, they have cut across all political boundaries and latitudes to irrevocably affect the life of everyone on this planet—whether it is the Eskimo working on an oil-rig in the Beaufort Sea, the once remote tribes of the upper Amazon valley watching their rainforest cover being penetrated by helicopters and highways, or a commune in Arizona constructing its vision of the new "city of man."

The Atomic Age. Humanity's ability to alter its relation with the biosphere is closely linked to its production and use of energy, that is, its use of "prime movers." Our paleolithic ancestors had to rely upon their own muscles, together with the controlled use of fire, to get things done. In later stone-age societies, men domesticated animals and thereby exploited more muscle power, while still later, ancient civilizations learned to harness nonbiological forms of energy—wind and water. The exploitation of steam as a prime mover had to await the Industrial Revolution, while the nineteenth century invented the means of generating electricity and utilizing the energy latent in petroleum. A direct relationship exists between stages of societal development and the consumption of energy. Among food-gatherers in East Africa about a million years ago, daily per capita consumption was about 2000 kilocalories. The rate rose to 12,000 kilocalories among farmers in 5000 B.C., whereas, around 1870, daily consumption reached the figure of 70,000. A century later, the average American was consuming some 230,000 kilocalories every day at his place of work, at home, and in his car.[3] In other words, a technological revolution has been transforming society which is currently confronted with shortages of fossil fuels; it must now obtain energy on a massive scale from the atom, and probably solar energy as well, in the next century.

Prior to World War I, physicists had been studying the structure of the atom and the nature of its energy. They came to understand that the atom has a positively charged nucleus around which negatively charged electrons revolve. Einstein's relativity theory suggested that the nucleus must contain enormous energy, because mass and energy are convertible and the amount of energy is equal to the mass multiplied by the square of the velocity of light. (This means that one pound of coal, if converted entirely into energy, would release as much energy as the combustion of one and a third million tons of coal.) But the atoms of radioactive elements, such as radium and uranium, disintegrated at their own speed, and physicists did not know how to speed up this process in order to release enough energy capable of being harnessed.

In the interwar years, however, the situation altered. In 1919, Ernest Rutherford was able to transmute one element into another by bombarding its nucleus with positively charged particles, while the discovery in 1932 of the neutron in the nucleus enabled Enrico Fermi and his associates to produce nuclear reactions. But as in Rutherford's case, more energy had to be expended than was in turn released from the bombarded nuclei. Just as a fire can continue to burn only because the combustion of each portion of fuel raises adjoining portions to the temperature of combustion, so an atomic "chain reaction" is required to split atoms in such a way as to produce more neutrons, which might then hit other atoms and cause them in turn to split and emit neutrons — and so on in continuous fashion. In January 1939, eight months before the outbreak of World War II, two German physicists found that the splitting of a uranium atom caused its nucleus to produce barium and also emit large amounts of energy. Subsequent studies in the United States and elsewhere confirmed that the neutrons released during such fission made a chain reaction possible. Thus was born the Atomic Age.

Just as in Greek mythology, when fire was acquired for mankind by Prometheus at a heavy price, so the Atomic Age ushered in its dual quota of promises and perils. Of the latter we are awesomely aware: the immolation of two Japanese cities in 1945 by relatively small atomic fission bombs, and the subsequent construction of thermonuclear weapons employing the principle of hydrogen fusion — which in turn can be projected to any point on the earth's surface by intercontinental ballistic missiles, each armed with a number of thermonuclear warheads. On the other side of the nuclear coin, the atom is being harnessed increasingly to generate energy, a development that is accelerating throughout the world. The existing known reserves of uranium might be exhausted by the end of the century; however, the use of fast breeder reactors could provide a virtually unlimited supply of atomic fuel. Given the fact that the world's consumption of energy from all sources just about doubles every decade, the major industrial countries in the late-1970's must invest huge sums in new energy-generating installations, and attention has been primarily concentrated upon nuclear plants, especially of the fast breeder type.

But here again, the promise of a seemingly limitless amount of atomic energy carries with it serious difficulties for the environment. Potentially dangerous accidents have occurred in a number of atomic installations, and a nuclear disaster apparently took place in the Soviet Union in 1958. In addition to guarding against nuclear accident, there is the problem, and cost, of providing suitable storage containers for radioactive waste and of maintaining them *indefinitely* in terms of equipment, energy, and military surveillance. In 1976, when the main issue in the Swedish national election centered on raising the number of nuclear reactors from five to thirteen by 1985, the voters defeated the Social Democrats (who had ruled for 44 years) in favor of a government pledged to a new energy strategy, including development of alternative forms of energy, such as wind, geothermal, and solar. Meanwhile, however, the Atomic Age had come to stay.

Peaceful use of the atom to generate energy is constantly increasing. This atomic reactor vessel at the Donald C. Cook Nuclear Plant, Bridgman, Michigan, is under construction.

Advances in biology and biochemistry. The twentieth century has also witnessed revolutionary accomplishments among the life sciences. By the time of World War I, the concept that chance variations in organisms alone accounted for evolution had been supplanted by an understanding of ordered systems of genes and chromosomes. Then, during the interwar years, scientists isolated the enzyme (an organic catalyst, usually a protein, which controls a cell's chemical reactions), and discovered its relationship to genes. The gene itself proved to be composed of deoxyribonucleic acid (DNA). In 1953, James D. Watson and Francis H. C. Crick provided a model of the structure of the DNA molecule. It is built like a "spiral staircase" in a double helix—and its components are mathematically "programmed" so that the order of these components along the double spiral comprises "the essential feature in determining the nature of the genes." It has been estimated that "one molecule of DNA in a human cell contains as much as several encyclopedia sets."[4] Since DNA is a fundamental genetic material, analysis of its structure is expected to provide us with far-reaching insights into the processes of heredity—and with knowledge capable per-

haps of shaping our own future as a species. This capability poses profound societal and ethical issues. To be able to predetermine gender could conceivably improve animal breeding and make food production more profitable, but what would it do to the present ratio of the sexes in human society? And if "genetic engineering" can be employed to eradicate undesirable traits in our existing hereditary makeup, what shall be the criteria for determining what is "undesirable," and who shall make the determination?

Meanwhile, biological and biochemical advances have proved invaluable in medical research and treatment. During the interwar years, various new synthetic drugs based on sulfanilamide successfully treated diseases due to streptococcus and pneumococcus infections. Similar success occurred in developing bacterial products derived from molds. In 1928, Alexander Fleming discovered that a species of fungus known as *Penicillium notatum* destroyed colonies of staphylococcus. From his discovery came the development of the first antibiotic, penicillin,

The era of genetic engineering has now become a reality. The organism that plays an important role in the process is *Escherichia coli*, a common bacteria. It can be engineered into reproducing a different set of genes through the DNA sequence; it was chosen because its own genetic structure is well documented. A scanning electron microscope photo of *E. coli* shows the bacteria magnified 25,000 times.

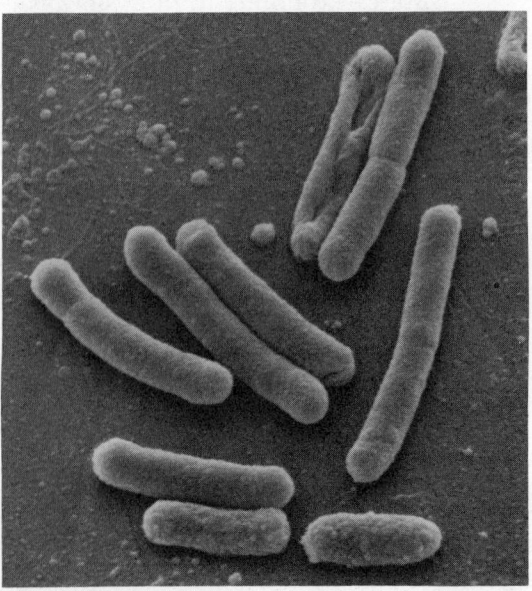

which with related drugs has proved the most effective means of treating certain types of pneumonia, syphilis, gonorrhea, and other infections. The result of such medical advances has been to lengthen our life span and to increase global population—the implications of which have become progressively apparent in the second half of the century.

The "Second Industrial Revolution." In the interwar years, important developments occurred in understanding the structure and behavior of the nervous system and the ways in which information is obtained and stored as memory. Studies led to the deduction that the firing sequence of neurons in the nervous system is predominantly circular, and that these circular cortical nets contain "trapped impulses" (called by neurologists a "reverberating circuit"), which have a persisting effect. These developments in neural and information theory made possible the construction of mechanical devices to store and retrieve data. World War II offered vast scope for the practical application of such studies. For example, the speed of moving targets required the intervention of devices capable of rapidly processing enormous amounts of information so as to make appropriate "decisions" and, in addition, function on the principle of self-correction:

Such a device compares its current state with some present "goal" state and adjusts its performance on the basis of the "observed" difference. Here, then, is a technological device which exhibits the "principle of equifinality" or "purposefulness" in a way which strikingly resembles the behavior of a living system. The postwar burgeoning growth of automation is a result of ever-widening application of this principle, and the science in which this principle is central has been called by Norbert Wiener *cybernetics* from the Greek *Kybernētes*—steersman.[5]

Wiener points out that the first industrial revolution was one of power; the second does not transform energy so much as it transmits information for purposes of control both within a given system and between systems. Basic to this changeover has been the invention of the vacuum tube and the computer, and the application of the principle of feedback in order to regulate the velocity and behavior of machines. The result has made possible the construction of automatic mechanisms of the most varied kinds. This development has been "reinforced by our new theoretical treatment of communication, which takes full cognizance of the possibilities of communication between machine and machine. It is this conjunction of circumstances which now renders possible the new automatic age."[6] The emerging era of electronic communications and decision-making can well be designated the "second industrial revolution"—leading to a "post-industrial age" that emphasizes "high technology" in the form of electronics, computers, cybernetics, and automation of the processes of mass production and distribution.

Other technological innovations and societal repercussions. The potency of this new high technology has already been marked by one of society's most spectacular accomplishments—the lift-off into outer space. The exploration of space began in the late 1950's; a decade later, astronauts had landed on the moon; while in 1976-1977, Mariner was transmitting pictures of remarkable resolution of the surface of Mars together with reports of that planet's chemical properties. We are well launched into the Space Age, and in the decades ahead—probably as an ongoing international program—we can expect to explore most or all of the planets of our solar system, and to plan "deep probes" further into our galaxy.

Meanwhile, "back on earth," the communications revolution has been transforming all contemporary societies by providing new knowledge and perspectives. Air travel and the automobile have given us unprecedented mobility. In an economically intermeshed world, the values that were sustained by cultural uniqueness are eroding. Technology has been altering traditional living patterns and values in still other ways. The first industrial revolution was centered in the West where advanced economies exploited their indigenous resources and also imported raw materials from the rest of the world, thereby creating a capitalist economy of global proportions. The second such revolution has already gone beyond its original location so as to start industrializing all parts of the world: petrochemical complexes in the Middle East, automated steel mills in India, hydroelectric installations in Africa, and the technological transformation of Japan and Soviet Asia. Today, we find a global network of highways, pipelines, railways, shipping and air lanes, as well as multinational corporations and publicly owned enterprises alike. Technology has in turn been transforming agriculture on a worldwide scale. Food-canning and refrigeration enable perishable foods to be shipped to all parts of the world together with the bulk movement of cereals. Food production is increased by plant genetics, new managerial methods, and large-scale

An aerial view of Rio de Janeiro details the modern section of the city divided by a band of forest from the *favelas*, the slums where the poorest citizens live. With a population of over 4.8 million, thirty percent of Rio's inhabitants still live in slum and squatter settlements.

farming businesses — while tractors and harvesters steadily reduce the number of farm workers.

The countryside needs fewer people to grow its food — and by the scores of millions the surplus has migrated to the towns in every continent. Whereas in 1900 there were 14 cities with a population of one million or more, of which six were in Europe and three in Asia, by the mid-1970's the figure had increased to 68 urban areas (cities and their surroundings) of over two million population, of which no less than 28 were in Asia and 8 in Latin America. Today, Shanghai and Tokyo are larger than New York or London, while in various parts of the world there are emerging massive urban corridors, such as in Japan and along the east coasts of the United States and Brazil. Urban sprawl gobbles up valuable agricultural land, and the cities of the developing countries are all too often ringed with "shanty towns" abounding in poverty, filth, disease, and social ferment. It used to be said that the world was being westernized. From a scientific and technological standpoint this would appear to be the case, although nonwestern societies are also attempting to rediscover and adapt their native cultures, as in the case of China, Mexico, and sub-Saharan Africa. But there can be little doubt that every continent today is in the throes of urbanization.

Changes in perspective and values. Our contemporary world is being transformed not only by technology but also by the philosophical implications of its scientific discoveries. As we have seen, Planck's quantum theory showed that energy is transmitted in discontinuous "packages" (*quanta*) of atomic particles. In 1927, Werner Heisenberg's "uncertainty principle" indicated that while the behavior of groups of atomic particles can be confidently predicted, no such certitude exists as regards any one particle. This factor of indeterminacy has given rise to speculation beyond the bounds of physics. The universe seems to be governed by statistical regularities which do not preclude elements of freedom of movement or choice for the individual. (It is on this dual basis of group predictability and individual unforeseeability that insurance companies and gambling casinos operate—profitably.) As in the case of quantum mechanics, Einstein's relativity theory has had an important "spillover" effect. Not only was the Newtonian model of the cosmos, based upon *absolute* space, time, and motion, replaced by a relativistic space-time continuum, but henceforth other thinkers began to ask whether absolutes necessarily existed in their own disciplines. Consequently, religion, philosophy, morals, and ethics have been subject to relativism.

Similarly, artistic standards have been affected. From the Renaissance to the end of the nineteenth century, spatial perspective constituted one of the most important factors in painting, and remained a constant element through all changes of style. The three-dimensional space of the Renaissance was the space of Euclidean geometry and was so deeply rooted in the minds of artists and laymen alike that no other form of perception, or perspective, could be imagined. But in modern physics, space is conceived of as relative to a moving point of reference, not as absolute and static. Breaking with traditional perspective, the Cubists and other artists have viewed objects relatively, from several points of view, with none of them possessing exclusive authority. Such a presentation of objects "introduces a principle which is intimately bound up with modern life—simultaneity."[7] Finally a new attitude is coming to be held about the role of science itself. It can no longer be conceived in terms of absolute standards of objectivity, or divorced from normative factors. Scientists are human beings immersed in, and reflecting, the perspectives and values of their own societies. Hence the questions they ask, and the answers they anticipate, are conditioned by their environmental training. It is precisely to these objectives that all world-views and ideologies must in turn address themselves.

WORLD-VIEWS IN COLLISION: 1918-1945

World War I: our century's first "watershed." Everyday life often proceeds with little disturbance for most people, and the effects of change become fully apparent only after many years. But we can now see that two global conflicts have comprised significant watersheds in this century. While science and technology were continually altering our relation with our environment, two world wars dramatically shifted human perspectives, and were both the causes and effects of changes in society. Those born before 1914 were bound to differ in values and outlook from those who had grown up after the end of the conflict—and similar differences occurred again between those who reached maturity in the interwar years and those whose life styles have been shaped by the decades following World War II. We are not dealing here simply with "generation gaps," i.e., the tensions that arise between parents and offspring, but with divisions that are more deeply rooted. Our century has spawned different social philosophies and attitudes between generations within a given society and also between major societies in turn. In short, we encounter watersheds that are both generational and ideological.

The First World War brought to an end a century of relative stability—one that believed in people's ability to "conquer" their environment and in a concept of progress that was seemingly inevitable. All this was shattered by a war intercontinental in scope and unprecedented in carnage. After 1918, politics, art, and social attitudes reflected widespread disillusionment with the old order—the world had obviously not been made "safe for democracy." In western democracies, where liberalism remained the dominant ideology, thinkers and artists questioned the traditional verities. In Russia, a new socialist movement set about to alter the very foundations of society and all segments of the culture pattern. And postwar Italian and German leaders were intent upon bending their people's traditional attitudes and values to conform to the ideology of nationalism in its most virulent form—fascism.

Experiment and debate in the Soviet Union. Nothing marked the new forces at work in the twentieth century so dramatically as the Russian Revolution, triggered off by World War I. Just as the French Revolution had sent shock waves across Europe more than a century before, so the impact of the Bolshevik revolution was to reverberate around the globe. Despite the fact that it soon became associated with the concept of "socialism in one country," Bolshevism was the leading wave of a creed that transcended national boundaries. As one historian has pointed out, it was no accident that the period of revolutionary advance in industrial technology, of the rise of mass society and the new conceptions of the state, also produced a new social philosophy. "It was an expression of the new forces which social and economic change had released, a doctrine defined to meet the needs of a new age."[8]

The specific development of Soviet society, however, was stamped by the crises of both internal and external origin that attended its birth and continued through the Second World War. The traditional Marxist scenario of the new socialist society emerging from the "womb" of a highly-developed capitalist society was altered, and the expectations of Lenin and his colleagues for successful revolutions in highly-developed capitalist countries such as Germany—from which the So-

viet Union would then be able to draw much-needed help—were not fulfilled. Socialist Russia, a premature baby, was left alone to fend for itself.

While the economic base of the Soviet Union was being overhauled during the 1920's, a vigorous debate was taking place over the kind of culture that should be encouraged for the Soviet masses. Should a specifically "proletarian" culture be promulgated, or were "bourgeois" forms to be tolerated? Lenin himself, before his death in 1924, sided with those who thought considerable freedom of expression should be permitted in cultural fields, and that there was much in prerevolutionary art and literature that could be of benefit to the masses. "Culture" was not something that could be imposed from the top, but had to develop through the participation of everyone in society.

The 1920's saw an explosion of creative endeavor in all fields of life. Some writers, like Maxim Gorky and the popular poet Vladimir Mayakovski, aligned themselves specifically with the revolution in their work. Others were less politically oriented, seeing

The cinema's rise to artistic prominence resulted from the influence of such great early directors as Sergei Eisenstein. He revolutionized film technique with his theories and practical application of montage—the juxtaposition of certain shots within a sequence in order to give greater impact to the content of a film. Pictured is a scene from the Odessa steps massacre sequence in *The Battleship Potemkin*, a powerful film still viewed today because of Eisenstein's notable use of nonprofessional actors and closeup shots.

in the revolution the opportunity for individual liberation and personal expression. The "Constructivist" artists were interested in practical design, and sought to integrate art with many aspects of everyday life. Soviet theater flourished under influential directors such as Vsevelod Meyerhold, and notable documentary and historical films were undertaken by Sergei Eisenstein and others.

Noteworthy, too, were reforms carried out at this time in the educational system. In place of the traditional division of curricula into separate and distinct subjects, the new "complex method" integrated schoolwork around a single large theme. Students and teachers were encouraged to work together, and students to participate as well in practical work outside the classroom; school programs now included visits to factories, museums, and theaters.

This period of experimentation did not survive the 1920's, however. With the desperate and painful rush to industrialize that began once Stalin was firmly in power, restrictions were clamped on many areas of life. A more orthodox school program returned. Divorce and abortion had been easy to obtain, but no longer. Experimental art and literature were discouraged, and things became difficult for those who did not conform. Yevgeny Zamyatin, for example, a well-known writer and one-time Bolshevik, felt it necessary to go into exile to pursue his literary career. The imposition of conformity was to give the concept of "socialist realism" a bad name in the West; yet those Soviet writers who sought in their work to come to grips with, and to give their audiences an insight into, the new forces shaping society were raising an important question about the artist's proper relation to society—a question that was not confined to the Soviet Union.

Not all Bolsheviks accepted without misgivings the growth of state power and control which became a feature of Soviet society under Stalin. In *State and Revolution* (1918), Lenin had affirmed his commitment to the Marxist concept that the state, after a necessary period of a "dictatorship of the proletariat," would wither away with the coming into being of a classless and democratic society. Yet despite Stalin's important

and controversial role in shaping the new form of the Soviet state, it would be wrong simply to attribute all developments here to the will of one person, or of any small group of leaders. Large-scale social forces, within and without the country, were at work during the interwar years and were carrying the Soviet Union forward along a path that few had envisaged.

Disillusionment in the West. Although the 1920's in the West are often portrayed nostalgically as an era of gaiety and triviality, the real picture is not so rosy or simple. The prewar liberal complacency about the direction of society was shattered by the holocaust of 1914-1918, and the standards of western society were inevitably challenged. The youths who had been promised that the war was to save the world for democracy emerged from the trenches only to become—if they were not already—bitterly disillusioned. The war did nothing to correct the inequalities of wealth and power in society, and labor unrest flared in numerous places.

This sense of disillusion was reflected in the arts. Until the First World War writers for the most part had contented themselves with themes and values familiar to the previous century. The majority continued to write as though theirs was the best of all possible worlds, because it was one in which "progress" seemed assured. Now the latest theories of physics and psychology were seized upon as starting points for literary vogues. Since according to the relativity theory nothing was "fixed" in the universe, why should not all customs, laws, and moral standards be considered equally relative? The behaviorists pictured man as a set of conditioned reflexes, while the psychoanalysts explained his conduct in terms of emotional drives and subconscious urgings, not of reason and free will. To many, individuals now appeared as irrational, puny bundles of viscera governed by forces beyond their control, and whose society was a thinly veneered savagery.

In 1922 the Anglo-American poet T. S. Eliot published *The Waste Land*, a long poem which expressed weariness with the ugliness and sterility of industrialized civilization, and which epitomized the atmosphere of skepticism and negation pervading the intellectual world in both Britain and the United States. Sinclair Lewis, in a series of novels, satirized the materialism and shallowness that he saw in much of American life. Other Americans expatriated themselves to Paris. The novels of F. Scott Fitzgerald, which are associated with the term "jazz age," look at problems of wealth and violence in the American scene. Another expatriate, Ernest Hemingway, rocketed to fame with vivid stories glorifying virility and action for its own sake—though in the crisis-torn thirties, he turned to another of his themes, the destructive impact of modern warfare, such as in *For Whom the Bell Tolls*.

The era also saw the appearance of a number of psychological studies. The English novelist D. H. Lawrence emphasized the significance of the sexual drive. In the multivolumed *Remembrance of Things Past*, the French writer Marcel Proust (1871-1922) explored psychological time, human relationships, and his own perceptions and mental processes by means of the stream-of-consciousness technique. This influential work recognized no lasting significance in the external world; one's own consciousness alone remains real. Also employing stream-of-consciousness, Irish-born James Joyce underscored the complexity and disorder of contemporary civilization in *Ulysses* (1922), a report on the experiences of a group of people during a single day in Dublin.

Freud's emphasis upon the unconscious and irrational states of the human mind made a strong impact on writers and artists alike. In the 1920's there emerged the Surrealists, who saw the subconscious mind as the vehicle that could free man from the shackles of modern society and lead him to freedom. They felt an affinity with "primitive" art and its close associations with magical and mythological themes, and they exalted the irrational and violent in human experience. Meanwhile, from a different perspective, the Cubists continued to expand their influence. Abstract, nonrepresentational painting was taken up by young artists all over the world—except in the Soviet Union where initial attempts at experimentation were aborted by ideological insistence upon "socialist realism." The interwar years saw Picasso modify his Cubist style; he developed a neo-classical style in the 1920's, while in the next decade he painted his famous *Guernica* mural, vividly depicting the destruction of a small Spanish town by fascist air forces in that country's civil war. This painting combines artistic autonomy with a direct relationship to contemporary world events.

"Guernica," named for a town destroyed in the Spanish civil war (1936-1939), reflects Picasso's horror and despair over a conflict he saw as the prelude to a still greater holocaust. Images of shattering force displace the austere Cubist precision that marked his earlier canvases.

The photographs of Dorothea Lange, one of a team of photographers employed by the Farm Security Administration from 1935 to 1942, chronicle life during the depression with vivid poignancy. In a masterpiece of photographic social commentary, a homeless farm family walks down an empty road in Oklahoma.

The revolt against traditional ways of thinking could also be discerned in the photographic arts. Still photography and motion pictures, whose basic principles had been developed in the previous century, became major vehicles of expression following World War I. Photographers and film directors explored the unique qualities of their media, in pursuit of new and vivid ways of *seeing*. True photo-reportage began in the mid-1920's when improved equipment and technical facilities enabled fleeting expressions and movements to be caught under varying lighting conditions. The film became the most popular, and universal, art form of the century. While most movies were made, and watched, for entertainment, the medium lent itself to the visual depiction of relationships and issues in contemporary society. Hence the innovation of documentary films, and of course social commentaries and satire by numerous actors, prominent among them Charlie Chaplin. And as books and mass-circulation magazines replaced art exhibits in acting as galleries for talented photographers, they also helped spur a preoccupation with everyday people and situations. During the depression, Dorothea Lange and other photographers working for federal agencies, notably the Farm Security Administration, employed their art as a powerful weapon in awakening Americans to the plight of their fellow citizens.

Writers were also spurred to social consciousness by the depression. In the United States, the poverty and ignorance of some parts of the South were portrayed by William Faulkner, while the plight of the "Okies" who trekked to California in search of economic survival was recounted by John Steinbeck in his moving novel, *The Grapes of Wrath* (1939). The depression was also notable for stimulating a new interest in folk songs of all kinds: regional, social, humorous, sad, but together projecting the vitality of a society determined to get on top of its problems. Perhaps the major interwar development in western popular music was jazz, an American form that originated with black musicians in New Orleans and in time spread over the continent and into Europe. Jazz musicians made use of both western and African cultural contributions, drawing upon brass band marches, French and Spanish songs and dances, and the spirituals and work songs of the American blacks. Jazz is yet another example of a cultural phenomenon of our times: the progressive universalization of taste, and the erosion of the double-standard in judging modern music; that is, between the traditional compartments labeled "classical" on the one hand, and "popular" on the other.

The Weimar period. Liberal and socialist forces were not absent from Germany after World War I, and they had their moment under the Weimar Republic, which seemed to embody all the various social forces of the era (see pp. 719). But while right-wing forces were growing in strength, those of the center and left were badly split. After the communist revolution so eagerly awaited by Lenin and many others was ruthlessly suppressed by government troops in 1919 and its leaders murdered, many Marxist socialists had little real sympathy for the Weimar government. In such an atmosphere, and with pressing economic difficulties, the Weimar Republic was living on borrowed time right from the start. Nonetheless, its brief life was notable for many important cultural developments.

The disillusion with old values that was for many the legacy of the war and its aftermath, together with new perspectives revealed by science and technology, was evident in the painting of the Expressionists, who employed distortion and clashing colors to break away from surface appearances and attempted to penetrate to the "essence" of things. Wassily Kandinsky (1866-1944) devoted his talents to abstract art, allowing viewers to derive their own interpretation and significance from the artist's arrangement of colors and form.

Two of the great art teachers at the Bauhaus were Wassily Kandinsky and Paul Klee. Kandinsky was the first to produce a work of abstract art free from figurative subject matter. Returning to his studio one evening, he found that one of his canvases had been placed upside down on the easel. It no longer portrayed anything, but seen in this way, it now appeared to him to be a beautiful composition—both fresh and dynamic. An example of a Kandinsky abstract (left) is "Improvisation #30 (Warlike Theme)." The paintings of Paul Klee as detailed in "Duke Leader Not Alone" (right) do not really fit in any of the accepted categories of contemporary art but utilize humorous, even simple and childlike, graphics along with a harmony of new forms and signs that emerge into a lyrical whole.

In his major work, *The Magic Mountain* (1924), novelist Thomas Mann presented at the same time a realistic story of life in a tuberculosis sanitarium in the Alps, and a symbolic evocation of European civilization on the eve of the war. In depicting the struggle between the promise of life and the lure of death, Mann was describing a conflict that occupied the spirit of many Germans; in having his hero finally choose life, Mann was reflecting his own personal commitment to the rational values symbolized by the Weimar Republic. The politically conscious playwright Bertolt Brecht, creator with Kurt Weill of *The Threepenny Opera* (1928), called for drama and literature that was popular and realistic, and committed to social progress. Realistic works, in Brecht's terms, were those that helped people understand the workings of society. Authors, he said, should not limit themselves to the realistic forms of the past, but should "make a lively use of all means, old and new, tried and untried, deriving from art and deriving from other sources, in order to put living reality in the hands of living people in such a way that it can be mastered."[9] But perhaps more indicative of the underlying currents of German society than the intellectual perspectives of Mann and Brecht was the extremely popular poetry of Rainer Maria Rilke (1875-1926). With his striking images and metaphorical language, Rilke painted a universe in which life, death, and all things were celebrated as elements of a single organic whole.

The functionalism which became an internationally accepted style of design in the interwar years had its most influential center in Germany's Bauhaus school, founded in 1918 by Walter Gropius. The center's staff included architects such as Ludwig Mies van der Rohe (1886-1959) and artist Paul Klee (1879-1940) along with Kandinsky. Teachers and students worked together in programs aimed at joining artistic expression and industry in order to reconcile contemporary man with his technologically altered environment. From architecture to pottery, from typography to home furnishings, the Bauhaus design for living reflected its members' belief that art and function should be synthesized. After Hitler closed down the school in 1933, many of its prominent members fled to other countries to carry on their work and spread the Bauhaus philosophy.

Another school destined for exile with the coming of the Nazis was the Frankfurt Institute for Social Research. Founded in 1923, it was committed to the Marxist proposition that the purpose of a critical understanding of society is to help effect social change. Among its members the Frankfurt school included Erich Fromm and Herbert Marcuse. Meanwhile, the universities in the Weimar period had their share of extreme right-wing and anti-Semitic exponents. One influential thinker was Oswald Spengler (1880-1936), who came to prominence in 1918 with the publication of *The Decline of the West*. He saw man's alienation from the natural world as responsible for the "tragedy" of human history. Western civilization was doomed to destruction through its own success; by creating an artificial world, we strangle ourselves in mechanical organization. Spengler also distinguished between two kinds of socialism: the materialist, Marxist version, which was alien to the German spirit, and the true Prussian kind, in which not class but blood and nation were important.

The fascist world-view. Although fascism first came to world attention in Italy (see pp. 715), it soon assumed its most extreme form in the German Nazi movement. Fascist ideology in Germany was a virulent form of social Darwinism, and took root in the decades preceding World War I in an atmosphere of German romanticism. This ideology served both as a nationalist force and an expression of reaction against the rapid industrialization that was cutting much of the populace adrift from traditional values.

Before the war, the chief exponent of Darwinism in the field of biology was Ernst Haeckel (1834-1919), who also tirelessly advocated that these principles be applied to society. Haeckel and the German "Monists" taught that the laws governing human life were the same as those governing the life of other species, and were to be found in the natural, not in the historical, world. The Monist League was hostile to the alienating and debilitating aspects of urban civilization; it extolled the virtues of rural life, and wanted a Germany rooted in strong peasant communities. This longing for roots and tradition was characteristic of the related "folkism" movement. Young people in particular were seeking an organic philosophy of life, and during the first three decades of the twentieth century youth organizations abounded, many of them expounding patriotism, love of nature, and idealizing the German past. Such thinking opposed mechanical civilization in favor of *Kultur*, which meant a type of society joining the German people in an intimate union with the forces of nature. Houston Stewart Chamberlain (1855-1927), a leading racist ideologist who had considerable influence on Hitler, claimed that the difference between *Kultur* and civilization could be summed up in the difference between the peasant and the factory worker: the former daily and subconsciously learned truth from living nature, from which the latter was alienated.

The Nazis, or "National Socialists," rejected both liberalism and Marxism. Proclaimed Joseph Goebbels, chief propagandist for the Nazi regime: "The Socialism that we want has nothing at all to do with the international-Marxist-Jewish leveling-out process. We want Socialism as the doctrine of the community. We want Socialism as the ancient German idea of destiny."[10] Central to the Nazi world-view was the tenet that human society must strictly obey the laws of the natural world; only by returning to nature could the atomistic and mechanical aspect of human society be done away with, for it was nature that was the source and repository of all life and consciousness. But the Nazis did not assume that nature was a place of harmony and "mutual aid," as had been taught by the anarchist philosopher Peter Kropotkin (1842-1921) and by certain socialists. Rather, it was a realm of dog-eat-dog struggle, where only the strong and ruthless was able to survive.

While adhering to a view of eternal struggle, the Nazis sought to avoid the ultimate defeat feared by Spengler by becoming not the foes but the agents of nature. Thus they opposed the faith in civilization and in human progress which they perceived in both liberalism and Marxism, and stood for that strain of German thought favoring the concept of *Kultur*. According to the Nazi world-view the universe possesses a mysterious, sacred essence which cannot be grasped by abstract intelligence. According to official Nazi "philosopher" Alfred Rosenberg, the characteristic German world-view took the form of a "mystic and cosmic vitalism." The individual has meaning only as part of his people *(Volk)*—an "organic totality"—but not as part of humanity in general, which is only an abstract concept, a conglomeration of many competing peoples and nations.

In line with his view of nature, Hitler saw marriage as "a mission in which it is the husband's task to fight for a livelihood and the wife's to manage the home in its capacity as the fortress from which the struggle for existence is waged." The woman's duty was to be, in order of importance: a mother; a wife; and/or a worker for the state. Since intellectual achievement was unnecessary in

Well-organized youth movements were an important key to the success of Nazism in Germany. Here a group of Hitler Girls walk through the woods on their way to lunch, to be followed by lessons in nature lore.

women, the Nazis fixed a quota for female students in higher education at 10 percent, and introduced a Domestic Service Year for girls leaving school, thus relieving pressure on the labor market and preparing them for their future domestic roles. The *Mutterkreuz* (Mother's Cross) was awarded to prolific mothers: bronze for producing four children, silver for six, gold for eight. But while the Nazis never stopped glorifying the virtues of womanhood, it was clearly to men that was entrusted the sacred duty of guiding society.

The Nazis' antipathy to modern art was plain. Shortly after they assumed power in Germany, various attempts were made to justify Expressionism by claiming it to be revolutionary and nationalist—but to no avail. Like the work of the Bauhaus, modern art was condemned as "cultural Bolshevism" and assigned to the rubbish heap. But at this point Hitler also condemned the cultural ideas of the "folkish" groups, ridiculing them as obsolete and backward-looking. From now on art was to reflect the spirit of a new, modern Germany, and was to advance Nazi politics. A notable example of such art was *The Triumph of the Will* (1937), a film tribute to the splendor and might of the new *Reich*.

After the Nazis came to power, the contradiction between the movement's origins and the realities of the modern world became increasingly apparent. To make Germany safe for small business, small farmers, and the small-town way of life, it was necessary to employ a strongly centralized state to exploit the resources of modern industry and advance the nation's cause in the international sphere. Under the Nazis the romantic German "will to power" no longer rejected industry and materialism but tried to assimilate them to its purposes. And as the requirements of big business and the military loomed ever larger in German life, those Germans who still longed for a sense of communion with nature and a return to traditional values were in for a rude shock. Hitler dreamed of a Reich that would endure "for a thousand years," but the *Kultur* that might have evolved from the Nazi world-view was immolated in a Berlin bunker in 1945.

NEW CULTURAL DIRECTIONS SINCE 1945

World War II: the second "watershed." The interwar years were marked by social upheaval, economic depression, disillusionment, and experimentation. They ended in the most inclusive and destructive conflict in history, climaxed by recourse to atomic bombs. We have lived in the shadow of their mushroom-shaped clouds ever since. Yet these were but the first of a number of "explosions" which have rocked the world since 1945; we speak about the population explosion, the information explosion, the urban explosion, and of course the spectacular disintegration of colonial empires continental in scale. In 1945, the United Nations Charter proclaimed a new era of equality among peoples, but the speed with which decolonization actually took place caught its framers unprepared and by surprise. It may well be that the Second World War ended one historical era marked by European hegemony, and that by the 1960's the world was clearly embarked upon a new era: one of global interaction of peoples, governments, economies, and resources. There is no going back to the other side of the watershed.

Some postwar cultural trends. The period from 1945 until the early 1960's represented something of a high tide in the liberal worldview. In contrast to the post-1918 period, when a general mood of disillusionment prevailed, the West—and especially the United States—emerged from World War II confident of its ability to remold the world. The boldness of Washington was apparent in its policies abroad where there was a determined effort to "contain" Soviet expansionism and establish American influence. As cold war tensions increased, anti-Communist feelings took on aspects of a crusade at home. A widespread view that the government, labor unions, and universities were infested with Communists and their sympathizers was reinforced by the attacks of Senator McCarthy and his followers. The Hollywood film industry was among the institutions hit by the campaign, and various actors, writers, and directors were "blacklisted"—prevented from working—or in other ways had their careers damaged.

For the most part, however, the 1950's gave the impression of being largely apolitical in the American domestic scene. What dissatisfaction there was tended to manifest itself in cynicism and the kind of personal retreat typified in the writings of J. D. Salinger—which appealed to the "silent generation" of students. Like the 1920's, this decade was preoccupied with postwar rebuilding and expansion. The West was busy constructing the consumer society, though new levels of economic prosperity also raised questions about the quality of life in industrial society. While for many Americans today, the "Eisenhower years" recall an interlude of peace and prosperity, for others they conjure up the flight to "suburbia" and its attendant conformity and homogenization of taste.

With a lessening of cold war confrontations, various liberal intellectuals proclaimed the "end of ideology." They argued that a basic consensus now existed among western policy formulators on such matters as acceptance of the welfare state, a mixed economy, and political pluralism. The problems of contemporary culture, including what was described as the "wasteland of television," lay outside the political sphere. Ideology, which had mobilized people on the basis of passionate commitment, was obsolete and about to be replaced by pragmatism. Utopian visions were out and piecemeal engineering was in. Western countries with their Keynesian economics had discovered the key to continuing progress. It was maintained by some that ideology was also losing its hold in the Soviet Union and eastern Europe; the dictates of modern technology were making all industrialized countries converge toward one basic path.

Yet not everyone greeted this prospect with enthusiasm. *The Technological Society* (1954) by Jacques Ellul painted a bleak picture of a world dominated by an "aristocracy of technicians," in which all moral values were being subordinated to the requirements of "technique," and human beings were increasingly mere appendages of technical processes. However, the 1960's were to show that not all social problems were amenable to simple technical solutions, and that the debate about fundamental values and the direction of society was far from over. Nor did all writers or artists share the prevailing liberal optimism. In *Waiting for Godot* (1955), for example, Irish playwright Samuel Beckett expressed the isolation and rejection felt by many in modern society. Manifesting itself in different ways, this sense of alienation has reflected a malaise pervading industrialized countries in recent decades.

One of the most widely read writers of the postwar period was Albert Camus (1913-1960), author of *The Stranger* and other works. Camus' belief in the absurdity of human existence was nonetheless combined with the concept of self-esteem and a certain joy in living. This attitude was made explicit in *The Myth of Sisyphus* (1942), in which he likened the human lot to that of the ancient Greek figure of Sisyphus, sentenced by the gods to push a rock to the top of a mountain, only to have it roll back down, and to have to repeat this task forever. Camus saw Sisyphus not only accepting this task with dignity, but finding satisfaction in his work. A liberal intellectual from French Algeria, Camus found himself during the period of the cold war and the struggle against colonialism in a rather uneasy position between the dictates of his philosophy of rebellion, and his allegiance to western European culture and values.

A more radical political position was adopted by Jean-Paul Sartre in his existentialist philosophy. His belief that human beings are "condemned to be free" was expounded at length in *Being and Nothingness* (1943), and reflected in his various plays and stories. After the war, Sartre recognized increasingly the constraints and responsibilities imposed on individual freedom by social forces—a move evident in his three *Roads to Freedom* novels. Sartre became one of the leading advocates of *littérature engagée* (committed literature), which claimed that since *all* writing is bound up with social life, the writer should be conscious of this fact and strive in his work to help readers understand the problems of society. By 1960 Sartre had produced a massive philosophical work, *Cri-*

tique of Dialectical Reason, in which he attempted to integrate existential insights into the situation of the individual with the historical perspective of Marxism.

Among Soviet writers to gain western admiration after the war were Mikhail Sholokhov and Boris Pasternak, both awarded Nobel prizes for their portrayals of life in revolutionary Russia. Pasternak's *Doctor Zhivago* (1958) did not find favor with Soviet authorities. On the other hand, Sholokhov was highly esteemed in his country for his epic novels of the people of the Don River region.

The Khrushchev era saw a certain amount of liberalization in the official attitude toward cultural affairs. Poetry is a highly popular art form in the Soviet Union, and during the 1960's various young poets — Yevgeny Yevtushenko being the best known in the West — were employing this medium to express their hopes for the future. Other figures, like Bulat Okudzhava (known for his satirical and antiwar lyrics) were using song to reach a wide audience. By the 1970's, however, a more restrictive official attitude had been reimposed, although a number of writers and artists, such as film director Andrei Tarkovsky, were attracting attention both at home and abroad.

The political debate within the Soviet Union among those who dissent from official policy is exemplified by three prominent figures. Novelist and Nobel laureate Alexander Solzhenitsyn, exiled from the country in 1974, rejected not only Soviet-style Marxism, but also modern liberalism which he felt lacked moral foundation. A fervid Russian nationalist, he called for a return to the traditional Russian values of village life and the Orthodox church. Nuclear physicist Andrei Sakharov, however, sought not to reject modern technological values but to liberalize Soviet society and open it to increased contact with the West. Then again, dissident Marxist historian, Roy Medvedev, felt that it was only through democratization that the Soviet Union could hope to realize its own professed ideals.

The 1960's and 1970's in the West. The civil rights movement in the United States and the Vietnam War provided focuses for a great outburst of political involvement and cultural ferment in the 1960's. Worldwide, students and other young people challenged the right to rule of those in power. Demonstrations sometimes met with violent reaction from authorities, with each side accusing the other of provoking the confrontation. Ideas and methods spanned national boundaries. Thus an uprising at Columbia University in April 1968 could be followed the next month by a worker-student rebellion in Paris which almost toppled the French government, both revolts sparked by local issues but involving certain shared assumptions about the nature of the political order.

The very nature of the New Left radicalism which developed at this time makes it hard to define with accuracy. In its passion for "participatory democracy," it was marked by factionalism and lack of any stable organizational structure on a large scale. Socialism, pacifism, and anarchism coexisted in varying degrees. With its emphasis upon decentralization, humanism, and cultural diversity, it differed from the more purely economic bias of the traditional Left.

One of the most important developments of the time was the women's liberation movement. Although *The Second Sex* (1949) by Simone de Beauvoir can be counted something of a landmark in focusing attention on the position of women in society, it was not until the 1960's that conditions were ripe for a mass women's movement in western countries. The whole range of assumptions about women's roles, and the relations between men and women, was sharply questioned, and many notable advances were made toward more equal rights. The women's movement raised the fundamental issue of how much of an individual's makeup is biologically determined and how much is culturally conditioned.

The political and social upheavals of the sixties were linked to the emergence of a "counterculture." This appealed for freer, more sensitive human relationships in place of an ethic that measured success in terms of material achievement and consumption. The individual was urged to develop his or her unique potential: imagination, spontaneity, and a heightened sense of feeling were

During a decade of ferment in the 1960's and beyond, various groups in the United States challenged the traditional view of their place in society, demanding an end to injustices and the right to take part in decisions affecting their lives. Encouraged by the gains of the black civil rights movement, college students (above, Kent State, 1970), Indians (below, Wounded Knee, 1973), and women called not only for legal rights but for the breakdown of social and cultural barriers to equality. If their protests and demonstrations were not always successful in effecting change, they at least provided a means for communicating their views to the public and for solidifying a sense of their own group identity.

Rock festivals, like the one at Woodstock in the summer of 1969, are an intrinsic part of what has come to be known as the rock culture. Replete with popular recording artists and elaborate sound equipment, they have provided a convenient meeting ground for young people, giving them a sense of community.

stressed. Whether or not they were a necessary ingredient of this new approach, there was an enormous increase in the use of marijuana and psychedelic drugs.

Popular music provided one of the mainstays of the counterculture. The folk music revival of the 1960's went hand in hand with the civil rights movement, where no rally was complete without its quota of inspirational songs; soon after, singers like Phil Ochs and Joan Baez became identified with the antiwar movement. Bob Dylan brought a new freedom to lyrics, whether his songs dealt with social problems or personal visions. Rock and roll, with Elvis Presley as its great idol, had emerged as the most popular music of the 1950's. Now there was a resurgence, led by The Beatles and The Rolling Stones, British groups who were ardent admirers of black rhythm-and-blues and the old rock and roll, but who brought their own style to the music scene. Rock music, now an

international phenomenon, entered its golden period in the late sixties with the fusion of these revitalized musical forms. By 1969, giant pop festivals, each attracting tens or even hundreds of thousands of spectators, had become the fashion.

If there were two conflicting tendencies in the 1960's — getting involved and dropping out — the second seemed to have dominated by the mid-1970's. This phenomenon was related to an anti-technology strain, a feeling on the part of many that things had become too big, too impersonal — that like the little man portrayed decades earlier in *Modern Times* by Charlie Chaplin, they had become caught in the machinery of mass society. On the one hand, this feeling led to a demand that the human dimension be more taken into account, and to the demand of the ecology movement that much more consideration be given to the effects of technology on the physical and social environments. Mean-

An immense curtain stretches for twenty-four miles starting north of California's Golden Gate Bridge and ending at the Pacific Ocean. It is constructed of 2050 panels of white woven nylon, attached to 90 miles of steel cable, and supported by 2200 steel poles. This project, which cost two million dollars, was allowed to remain intact for two weeks before it was scheduled to be torn down. It is the second such invention by the Bulgarian artist, Christo. An earlier curtain hung across a mountain pass in Colorado lasted only 28 hours before being shredded by the winds.

while, still others preferred to turn their backs on the values of rationality and technological progress. Mysticism and personal development was all the rage, as testified by the tremendous popularity of Carlos Castaneda's books about the Indian shaman Don Juan. As one commentator has written:

It is no secret that Americans have lost faith in politics. The retreat to purely personal satisfactions—such as they are—is one of the main themes of the seventies. A growing despair of changing society—even of understanding it—has generated on the one hand a revival of old-time religion, on the other a cult of expanded consciousness, health, and personal "growth". . . To live for the moment is the prevailing passion—to live for yourself, not for your predecessors or posterity. We are fast losing the sense of historical continuity, the sense of belonging to a succession of generations originating in the past and stretching into the future.[11]

Yet the trouble with the numerous therapies and cults of the 1970's, this writer points out, is not that they address trivial issues, but that they intensify the problem by obscuring the *social* origins of personal suffering and alienation.

NEW POLITIES AND OLD CULTURES

Négritude and African socialism. The rediscovery and reassertion of African values are epitomized in the term *Négritude*. It constitutes a rejection of western history and cultural standards and seeks to describe a uniquely African personality and culture on which new African societies can develop. The poetry of this cultural revolution was largely stimulated by two West Indians, Léon Damas and Aimé Césaire, and has perhaps reached its richest expression in the verse of Senegal's Léopold Senghor. He, too, has noted that the western philosophic and scientific tradition attempted to know objects by separating them from the observer, but that the more advanced philosophic and scientific thinking of this century has cast grave doubts upon such a method. The traditional African method of reasoning, on the other hand, is "intuitive by participation"; it holds that to know something one must experience it. This mixture of rejected western technological standards and rediscovered African values is found in Césaire's lines:

Listen to the white world
how it resents its great efforts
how their protest is broken under the rigid stars
how their steel blue is paralysed in the mystery of
the flesh.
Listen how their defeats sound from their victories.
Listen to the lamentable stumbling in the great alibis.
Mercy! mercy for our omniscient naïve conquerors.
Hurrah for those who never invented anything
hurrah for those who never explored anything
hurrah for those who never conquered anything
hurrah for joy
hurrah for love
hurrah for the pain of incarnate tears.[12]

As a part of this search for a sense of identity and viable culture, the African novel discloses an emphasis upon the following themes: reactions to the initial stages of colonization (such as Chinua Achebe's *Things Fall Apart* and *Arrow of God*); education and, in particular, the difficulties of adjusting to western education; the movement of Africans from rural areas to the cities; problems of nation-building both before and after independence (such as Peter Abrahams' *A Wreath for Udomo* or Achebe's *A Man of the People*); and problems of a more universal nature, including those of personality and psychology (examined in Ezekiel Mphahlele's *The Wanderers*).

The psychological damage that resulted to African peoples from the colonial experience was analyzed by Frantz Fanon (1925-1961), author of the widely-read book *The Wretched of the Earth*. According to Fanon, the colonizing force defines out of existence any reality in which black people can be accepted—by themselves or by others—as human beings with creative potential. The blacks are powerless because their experience has no validity in that realm which both they and others accept as "reality." Fanon took issue with the *Négritude* movement because he thought it futile to romanticize the African past, suspecting that such attempts reflect a deep inferiority complex when compared with European history. *Négritude* appeared to him more a *reaction* to the European challenge than a positive *action* to regain an authentic identity for the black.

By the beginning of the 1960's, a number of African leaders were proclaiming socialism as the path their newly independent countries should take to development. This socialism was to serve a double purpose: one economic, and the other psychological and cultural. Socialism is seen by its adherents as compatible with African societies in both these ways, since it is claimed that precolonial societies of sub-Saharan Africa exhibited a form of preindustrial socialism. They were based, it is argued, on equality and humanism. The extended family and the tribal community enjoined the concern of all for each. Decision was based on consensus, and the principle of unity was strongly cherished. Rather than attempt to make a clear break with the past, most African leaders have decided that modern African societies must evolve organically from the old.

Although there is in Africa today a conception of socialism that can legitimately be described as "African," it is probably too broad and too diverse to be described as a single ideology. In some countries, like Guinea, Mali, Ghana under Nkrumah, and recently, Mozambique and Angola, socialist thought has been more self-consciously revolutionary than in places like Senegal. Senegal's Senghor has placed special emphasis on the early, pre-1848 writings of Marx, with their attention to the problem of alienation. Here Senghor notes the role that Christianity and Islam have to play in building Senegalese socialism, for in its true form religion integrates man and universe. Lenin's ideas on party organization have been absorbed by the more "radical" socialist leaders, while his theory of imperialism has, in modified forms, been espoused by African leaders in general.

Both Senghor and Sékou Touré of Guinea, whose theoretical interpretations of Marxist socialism differ considerably, agree that European communism has too much in common with capitalism. Both these foreign systems place too much emphasis on material values; both employ the technical means of highly industrialized states, and as such are not necessarily applicable to under-industrialized Africa. In addition, most African leaders reject the Marxist concept of class struggle as it might apply to African states. Instead, they assert the need to build national unity.

The idea that independent African states are virtually classless societies which can proceed along the road to socialism with a minimum of internal conflict has not gone unchallenged. Fanon, for example, contended that there is generally an African bourgeoisie which takes power when the country gains independence, and then proceeds to demand enormous efforts from the industrial and agricultural workers in the name of national reconstruction. In fact, said Fanon, the true "proletariat" in a country like this is the great mass of poor peasants living in the countryside; together with the intellectuals and the outcasts and rootless fringe groups

Growing out of a new technological culture which made new forms and new functions possible through the use of such materials as steel, concrete, and glass, contemporary architecture may eventually be remembered as the most revolutionary of the visual arts in the twentieth century. Two architectural giants during the period were Mies van der Rohe and Le Corbusier, and the ongoing vitality of their individual approaches is evident in their continuing influence on other twentieth-century architects, who in turn are attempting to find their own particular style. The clean classical lines of Mies' 1921 project for a glass tower (top left) are reflected in many of the distinguished buildings being constructed today, such as Lake Point Tower (bottom left), a Chicago apartment building designed by Schipporeit-Heinrich, Inc. Similarly, the massive, sculptural grace of the entrance portico of the Assembly Building at Chandigarh (top right), one of three major government buildings Le Corbusier designed for the new capital of the Punjab in India, is echoed in the National Gymnasium in Tokyo by the Japanese architect Kenzo Tange (bottom right).

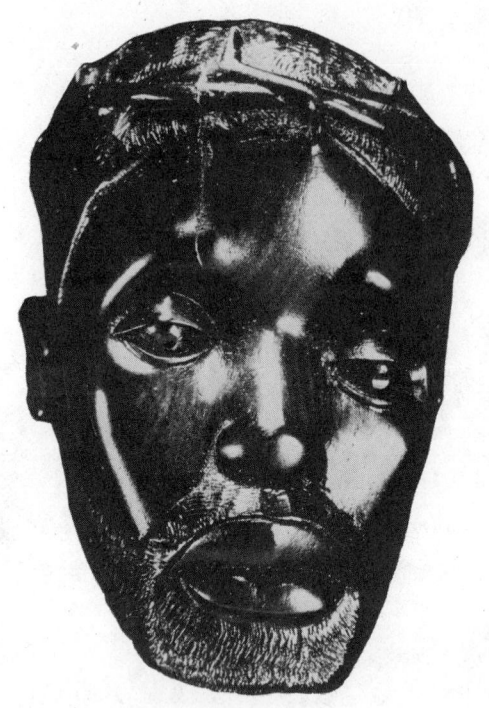

An extraordinary renaissance has taken place in African art in the past two decades. This woodcarving of Christ crowned with thorns is a powerful example of contemporary African sculpture.

living unemployed and destitute on the outskirts of the cities, the peasantry forms the real base of potential revolution.

One of the more interesting experiments in "African socialism" has been occurring in Tanzania. That country's leadership has stressed rural development. However, aware of the danger of class formation under the pressure of modernization, it has been decided that the socialist principles of harmony and equality must not be sacrificed to economic development; if necessary, Tanzania is to settle for a lower rate of economic development so as to preserve its non-economic ideals. An alternative to the normal pattern of large-scale modernization has been designed in the form of the *ujamaa* village program, where people are encouraged to cooperate in small groups and these small groups cooperate in turn for joint undertakings.

Ujamaa can be translated as "familyhood." Rural development, in the form chosen by the Tanzanian government, is consciously seen as an extension of traditional social patterns to meet modern needs.

Socialism in Africa firmly rejects the notion that it must reflect exactly socialist developments in other parts of the world. Julius Nyerere of Tanzania makes the point that the universality of socialism only exists if it can take account of people's differences, and be equally valid for all of them. "It is my contention that socialist societies in different parts of the world will differ in many respects even when they are fully developed instead of being, as now, at different stages on the road to socialism. The differences between these societies will reflect both the manner of their development, and their historical traditions."[13]

China: which road forward? The question of how the development of Chinese society would proceed was not clearly settled by the triumph of the revolution in 1949. Though there was now a determination to construct a communist society, the realization of such a goal was still a long way off. Mao Tse-tung and the more radical among the Chinese leadership became increasingly disenchanted with the Soviet model for building socialism, and eventually an open break occurred. Indeed, it was charged that the Soviet Union could not properly be called a socialist society at all, that it had reverted to the "capitalist road" and developed a new bureaucratic class structure.

Afraid that a similar trend was showing itself in China, Mao and his followers initiated the Cultural Revolution in 1966, and for two years life in the country underwent great upheaval (see pp. 817). The aim of the radicals, many of them students and young workers, was to reestablish the ideals of egalitarianism and greater participation by the masses in the political and cultural life of China. In particular, the objective in the wake of the Cultural Revolution was to break down the "three major differences" that were held to plague society and to be retarding progress toward a just social order: the difference between town and country, between worker and peasant, and between

The arts in China were importantly involved in Mao's Cultural Revolution. The Peking ballet troupe's performance of "Red Detachment of Women" (left) tells of an early Communist uprising against the Nationalist government when it was still in power. In a propaganda photo (right), peasants take time from their work in the fields to study a quotation from Chairman Mao which translates into "What really counts is conscientiousness and the Communist party is most particular about being conscientious."

mental and manual labor. The Communist party was expected to become more responsive to the needs of the masses. New emphasis was put on decentralization and self-reliance in many fields. Students were expected to combine study with practical work, and even bureaucrats and government officials were expected to engage in periodic stints of manual labor.

Classical Chinese culture was centered in the cities, and was the preserve of a small, sophisticated and literate ruling class. At the end of the First World War scholars like Chen Tu-hsiu and Hu Shih broke with classical traditions, substituting vernacular for literary Chinese in their own writings. They stressed the relation of contemporary thought to the life of the average Chinese, in contrast to the stereotyped and stilted subject matter of traditionalism. Vernacular literature spread rapidly during the interwar years and acquired a strongly social character. Lu Hsun (1881-1936), a writer much admired in China today, used satire to expose social evils in the 1920's and 1930's, and also translated many foreign works into Chinese.

The Cultural Revolution brought an increased emphasis on the visual arts, as part of an effort to reach all members of society. Literary culture, which stresses individual creativity, was downplayed in favor of cooperative art forms. Operas like *Taking Tiger Mountain by Strategy* and ballets like *Red Detachment of Women* were used to get political messages across to mass audiences. The radical line was to "put politics in command" in all areas of life, whether on the stage or in the factory. The revolution was an ongoing affair, it was claimed, and the final outcome could not be taken for granted:

Experience in class struggle tells us clearly that our socialist society is not "a jewelled palace in elfland's hills" but a society with classes, class contradictions and class struggle. The countryside after collectivization is not one without classes in which everything belongs to the public. A life-and-death struggle exists everywhere between the socialist road and the capitalist road.[14]

With the death of Mao Tse-tung in 1976 and the accession to the chairmanship of the Communist Party of Hua Kuo-feng, the radical cause appeared to suffer a setback. A more moderate course, both in politics and in cultural affairs, seemed in the offing—

though China's new direction at present is far from clear.

India's cultural revival. The centuries of British rule in India made a deep impression upon its institutions and values alike. The Indian intelligentsia was schooled in English educational forms, immersed in English literature, and prepared itself for the professions and civil service which in turn were British in structure and largely in content. Yet decades before independence, a cultural renaissance began. While a number of European scholars, such as Max Muller, were studying the intellectual treasures of the ancient Indian classics, some outstanding Indian philosophers, including Swami Vivekananda and Sri Aurobindo, began not only to reinterpret the Vedanta and other classical schools of thought but to place their teachings in a new relationship with western tradition as well. In addition, Indian culture produced a world-famous literary figure, Rabindranath Tagore (1861-1941), a poet, author, painter, and dramatist. Steeped in India's literary and philosophical traditions, Tagore described the *Vedas* as "the poetic testament of a people's collective reaction to the wonder and awe of existence." In his own works he sought in return to interpret afresh the contents of the *Vedas* and *Upanishads*, employing both English and Bengali as literary media. Though primarily a nationalist leader and politician, Jawaharlal Nehru (Chapter 36) also encouraged the Indian cultural revival by his own rediscovery of the subcontinent's variegated past. Nor is this national renaissance simply backward looking; rather it seeks to embody the cultural heritage and ethos in twentieth-century forms of expression so as to make Indian thought and art relevant to contemporary times and problems. In this connection, India has developed one of the largest, and most dynamic, film industries in the world, and the government employs this art form for purposes of entertainment and education alike.

Developments in Latin America. For some hundred and fifty years, the countries of Latin America have been politically independent, but it is during the present century that their quest for cultural independence and a recognizable self-identity has assumed major proportions. After World War I, Spanish American literature became progressively concerned with indigenous themes and problems. These included the environmental challenge, in particular the struggle with the jungle; the stresses confronting societies attempting to modernize and industrialize and to cope with the strains of urbanism; and above all, the social dilemmas confronting the Indians and blacks uprooted from their native culture patterns and seemingly condemned to subordination in a white man's world and value system.

Since World War II, this search for new cultural roots and an identity that differs from both Spanish and North American culture has accelerated. Thus we find the growth of a black art style in Brazil, which has a large African population, as well as the emergence of *Indianismo* with its rediscovery of pre-Columbian America. The famous National Museum of Anthropology in Mexico City is a monument to this search, as are the vivid frescoes of a brilliant coterie of Mexican painters, including José Clemente Orozco and Diego Rivera. So, too, are the novels of Miguel Angel Asturias of Guatemala and the

A section of a mural by José Orozco details Miguel Hidalgo, an early leader in the Mexican fight for independence, bearing a flaming sword and dominating a host of dying men.

poetry of Pablo Neruda of Chile, both Nobel prize winners. The convoluted, metaphysical fantasies of Argentina's Jorge Luis Borges have won him a worldwide audience, while the surreal tales of Colombia's Gabriel Garcia Márquez are in turn helping to mold a distinctive Latin American tradition. That tradition, according to one philosopher, is rooted in Spanish America's conviction that "tragedy, brutality, chaos, failure, and death, as well as triumph and compassion, aim at order, and earthly life, are an essential part of the glory of man."[15]

SUMMARY

The decades in the earlier part of this century witnessed the beginnings of a new explosion of technological innovation in the developed countries. The steel and chemical industries came into their own; electric lights, the internal combustion engine, new forms of transportation and communication, all made their appearance. Advances in medical science and biochemistry had profound demographic implications. Together with the technical side went great advances in scientific knowledge, such as the relativity theory, which affected human conceptions about the structure of the world.

At the same time, new social and political forces were stirring. Working class movements in Europe and North America were pressing for a more equitable distribution of wealth and power in society. World War I marked the beginning of the end of European dominance in world affairs, and triggered off great upheavals in the social order. In Russia the triumph of the Bolshevik revolution opened a great cultural debate, but the enthusiasm and experimentation of the 1920's gave way in the 1930's before the harsh realities of forced industrialization. Elsewhere in Europe and in North America the prevailing mood in the interwar years was one of disillusionment and frustration. In Italy and Germany fascist movements, preaching extreme forms of nationalism and

racism, promised to deliver the people from economic ruin. In Germany the artistic and intellectual achievements of the Weimar Republic were thrust aside by the social Darwinism of the Nazis, who aimed at overcoming the alienations of industrial society by reuniting humans with the forces of nature. The result was a complete rejection of the humanist principles of liberalism and Marxism, and led directly to the horrors of a new world war.

After 1945 the Soviet and United States-led blocs, each equipped with nuclear weapons confronted each other in a cold war. In the West a mood of alienation and rebellion manifested itself in the arts, in popular culture, and in existentialist philosophy. The 1960's were marked by youthful revolt, much of it centering on opposition to the U.S. role in Vietnam. New forms of dress and music and new life styles were in evidence. The struggle for women's liberation became an international movement. In the Soviet Union a less restrictive atmosphere prevailed from the mid-fifties to the mid-sixties, and many artists and intellectuals were asking more openly why the country had failed to live up to its ideals.

It was after 1945 that the underdeveloped countries began finally to assert themselves. Casting off colonial status, they confronted the problems of modernization. China, the world's most populous country, began the immense task of social transformation after the communist triumph of 1949, and in the 1960's underwent a further Cultural Revolution. African leaders sought to develop new African cultures by adapting modern ideologies to the special circumstances of their lands. Much of Latin America was oppressed by military dictatorship; the continent's writers and poets helped give voice to the aspirations and struggles of its peoples.

Meanwhile, still more rapid advances in technology and scientific knowledge have been helping transform human life. Computers, nuclear energy, space travel, genetic engineering, and more—all hold out both promise and danger. Technology is a powerful force for changing society, but a crucial role is still played by human values and the struggle for a more just world order.

SUGGESTIONS FOR READING

For an excellent introduction to political, technological, ideological, and cultural changes which mark the twentieth century as the onset of a new epoch in world history, see Geoffrey Barraclough, **An Introduction to Contemporary History*** (Penguin, 1975). That profound social changes have been taking place, such as a shift from a traditional emphasis upon individualism to mass democracy in a technological society, is the subject of J. Ortega y Gasset, **The Revolt of the Masses*** (Norton). The sociologists' prevailing theory that stability and equilibrium comprise the norms of society is challenged by W. F. Wetheim, **Evolution and Revolution*** (Penguin, 1974). A political revolution has been occurring in the passing dominance of the West and the emergence of new political entities and influence in former colonial areas; in this regard see K. M. Panikkar, **Asia and Western Dominance*** (Collier); J. Romein, **The Asian Century: A History of Modern Nationalism in Asia** (Univ. of California); and Colin Legum, **Pan-Africanism** (Greenwood, 1976).

The impact of science and technology upon contemporary society has stimulated a number of studies. The dangers inherent in a growing split in knowledge, perceptions, and values between the scientific and nonscientific segments of present-day industrial societies are examined by C. P. Snow, **Two Cultures: And a Second Look*** (Cambridge, 1969). The impact of technology upon overall social and economic planning is the subject of Daniel Bell, **The End of Ideology*** (Free Press, 1965). An optimistic view that technology can be put to humanity's service so as to reach new levels of learning and living alike is found in R. Buckminster Fuller, **Utopia or Oblivion: The Prospects for Humanity*** (Bantam, 1972); while Dennis Gabor, **Inventing the Future*** (Penguin, 1972) counts on our ability to overcome three great dangers: nuclear destruction, overpopulation, and the "Age of Leisure." On the other hand, various scholars warn against technology's impact on our physical environment and its adverse societal effects: see Barbara Ward and René Dubos, **Only One Earth: The Care and Maintenance of a Small Planet*** (Penguin, 1973); and Barbara Ward, **The Home of Man*** (Norton, 1976), a study of the problems of human settlement on a global dimension. The tendency of a technological society to adopt "bigness" or economies of scale as the most efficient and therefore "best" approach is challenged in E. F. Schumacher, **Small is Beautiful: Economics as if People Mattered*** (Harper & Row, 1973). Relating technology to human values and self-actualization is the theme of R. M. Pirsig, **Zen and the Art of Motorcycle Maintenance: An Inquiry into Values*** (Bantam, 1976).

The relationship of art and society has been viewed within a historical perspective in Raymond Williams, **Culture and Society, 1780-1950*** (Torchbooks). The problems of individual alienation and solitude as depicted in the literature of Rilke are analyzed in Erich Heller, **The Disinherited Mind: Essays in Modern German Literature and Thought*** (Harcourt Brace Jovanovich, 1975); and Peter Gay, **Weimar Culture*** (Torchbooks, 1970). Russian cultural trends are covered in J. P. Nettl, **The Soviet Achievement*** (Harcourt Brace Jovanovich); and Hedrick Smith, **The Russians** (Quadrangle, 1976). Contemporary trends in life and culture in China are analyzed in the Committee of Concerned Asian Scholars, **China! Inside the People's Republic*** (Bantam).

Trends in music are dealt with briefly in A. Einstein, **A Short History of Music*** (Vintage); and the visual arts in E. H. Gombrich, **The Story of Art,** 12th ed. (Phaidon, 1974). New concerns and social attitudes in a changing world which cannot rest content to employ traditional aesthetic canons are covered in E. Fischer, **The Necessity of Art*** (Penguin). For developments in Third World countries and regions, consult D. Keene, **Modern Japanese Literature*** (Grove); P. Henriquez-Urena, **Literary Currents in Hispanic America** (Russell); and G. Moore and U. Beier, eds., **Modern Poetry from Africa*** (Penguin).

*Indicates a less expensive paperbound edition.

EPILOGUE

Alternatives for the Future

INTRODUCTION. Probably every generation back to *Homo habilis* has felt that it had to endure "times that try men's souls." And because peoples everywhere have been visited by pestilence, famine, war, and death, there has long existed the millennial dream of a time when humanity would be freed from these miseries. Religions have traditionally sought to compensate for this world's suffering by the promise of heavenly happiness. In the western tradition, there also developed the concept that society can be improved by human endeavors as well. As we saw in earlier chapters, many outstanding minds conceived models of an ideal state, including Plato's *Republic*, Thomas More's *Utopia* (The Land of Nowhere), Francis Bacon's *New Atlantis,* and in modern times, Samuel Butler's *Erewhon.* It is a mark of our century's disillusionment with the disparity between societal principles and performance that it has produced some highly original "dystopias," that is, accounts of retrogressive societies whose aims and behavior denigrate human worth. One of the most provocative, and disturbing, dystopias is George Orwell's *Nineteen Eighty-Four.*

Published in 1949, the novel forecasts a society completely totalitarian in structure, methods, and values. No individual freedom exists in this society which for its part engages in continuous warfare to help ensure social cohesion and thought control. It is ruled by a party elite under the guidance of an omnipresent dictator called "Big Brother." Everywhere are posters with the caption: "Big Brother is watching you"; police patrols use helicopters to spy into highrise apartments; all rooms have telescreens that continuously receive and transmit information which in turn is recorded and filed in government dossiers. As a reaction to thought control and constant surveillance, people drastically modify their behavior. Whether Big Brother actually exists and will take action on the basis of a citizen's behavior is not crucial; the central point is that people believe that he does exist and will act against them, so they behave in order to be acceptable—and as a result invert their own values. It is a society governed by "double-think": this involves lies, the omission of facts which have become inconvenient, the simultaneous holding of two contradictory opinions, and the repudiation of morality while, at the same time, laying claim to it.

When *Nineteen Eighty-Four* first appeared, it was hailed for its imaginative rather than predictive qualities. However, now that we are within a few years of the author's date and in the midst of a "countdown to tomorrow," various social scientists and philosophers are asking whether we are moving toward this Orwellian world, and what is required to save our democratic way of life. Orwell foresaw that unless technology is made to serve humanistic values, it can become Dr. Frankenstein's twentieth-century monster capable of enslaving its creator. In fact, one could argue that Orwell failed to pay sufficient attention to the dynamic factor within the technological order itself. For example, his police state relied on physical surveillance, whereas the computer has now made possible an electronic surveillance that is far more effective and all-pervasive. Again, Orwell's state controlled all decision-making and weaponry. But today, technology has democratized the use of weapons: armed skyjackers, urban guerrillas, and self-proclaimed liberation armies have surfaced in a score of advanced and underdeveloped countries alike.

Of particular relevance to the subject matter which follows, Orwell did not address himself to a number of problems that can have repercussions as far-reaching as the factors which resulted in his totalitarian society. Perhaps he did not do so because these are environmental and societal problems which have mushroomed since the appearance of *Nineteen Eighty-Four*. They include the population explosion, the depletion of natural resources and the struggles which this process can trigger, and pollution's degradation of our environment. The manner in which these issues are handled could confront us with Orwellian versus humanitarian choices—choices which will have to be made because nothing less than global survival may be at stake. What is it to be—utopia or dystopia—or something in between? And do we really have alternative choices for our future? That is what we want to explore.

WHAT LIES AHEAD?

The visions projected by science fiction. Speculation about where humanity may be headed has often been presented in fictional form. But it was not until the nineteenth century that what was later to be known as science fiction became a popular literature. Mary Shelley's *Frankenstein, or The Modern Prometheus* (1818) was a seminal work that described vividly the dangers inherent in man's drive to impose his will on nature. The more optimistic stories of Jules Verne (1828-1905) reflected the prevalent Victorian attitude toward the role of technology in shaping the future. At the turn of the century, H. G. Wells (1866-1946) expressed a growing ambivalence toward the notion that science and technology would lead the way to a more humane existence. His belief that history was becoming "a race between education and catastrophe" was expressed in his "scientific romances," the more forceful of which spoke from his darker side, and showed his readers scientific nightmares—such as *The Island of Dr. Moreau*—or decadent humanity in the dim future of *The Time Machine*. And as we have noted, the realities of our century have spawned numerous anti-utopian works (or "dystopias"), such as those of Orwell and Yevgeny Zemyatin in *We*. By the same token, Aldous Huxley, in *Brave New World*, depicted a future in which genetic engineering, drugs, and mass entertainment are employed to keep the world pacified with an artificial happiness. In Ray Bradbury's *Fahrenheit 451* the population kills time by watching mindless programs on giant TV screens, while the job of firemen is not to stop fires but to start them—whenever they find a hoard of books.

But not all writers in this century have taken such gloomy views of the future. In the interwar years, American science-fiction magazines reflected technological optimism to a strong degree. Magazine illustrators conjured up technocratic dream-cities of gleaming towers and flying machines, where humans had become integrated with the environment they had created, and nature was all but banished. After World War II, Arthur C. Clarke best exemplified the optimistic strain in science fiction. Whether depicting the farming of oceans to feed the world of the near future (*The Deep Range*), or dealing with questions of immortality and human and alien intelligence in the far future (*The City and the Stars*), Clarke contemplated the universe and the vistas opened up by science with an almost mystical reverence. More recently, J. G. Ballard has explored "inner space" where technology and environment meet in the mind. In *Solaris*, the Polish author Stanislaw Lem speculates on the limitations of human knowledge while in amusing and satiric short "fables" he probes the ramifications of cybernetics.

The integration of humanity into a new emergent environment has been the subject matter of two contemporary American writers. Philip K. Dick has taken an essentially existentialist look at the perpetual dialectic between humans and the socio-technical worlds they construct, while Ursula K. Le Guin has brought the ancient Taoist philosophy to bear on the problem of the reconciliation of man and nature. Le Guin's *The Dispossessed* (1974) portrays an anarchist-communist society, supported by high technology and based on ecological principles.

While much science fiction is simply escapist entertainment, the more serious works help us to imagine life and society in a larger perspective—as part of an ongoing historical process. As such, they are part of the debate about the future: a debate that is more important today than ever before.

The need to think about the future. Given the many unknown variables involved, is it not foolhardy to try to make predictions about the shape of things to come? We would entirely agree if "prediction" were regarded in the sense of prophecy rather than of "forecasting" as that term is employed by meteorologists, for instance, who undertake to calculate future events on the basis of a rational analysis of existing data. In our view, sufficient evidence does exist to enable us to make some productive estimates about the direction of world events in the decades ahead. Moreover, given the factor of accelerating change, the need will increase to be as realistic as possible in planning for the last quarter of this century and be-

yond. Otherwise, our societal vessel may be overtaken, and possibly engulfed, by a tidal wave of catastrophic, but belatedly perceived, events. As we shall see, the human species is likely to be confronted with some of the most massive problems in its planetary existence. Failure to meet this challenge might well destroy the hard-won achievements of the past—whereas a successful response to new and untried circumstances could carry us to a more advanced plateau of creativity and well-being. The intertwined promise and perils center on three areas: the carrying capacity of the environment; the structure of society; and the ability of human beings to adapt or alter course.

The environmental balance-sheet. The entire universe may be regarded as a vast, unified energy system, responsible for all physical and biological manifestations alike. Matter and energy obey laws of cosmic proportion which hold galaxies and atoms alike in a dynamic, yet delicate counterbalance. Our planet in turn comprises an equilibrating ecosystem made up of innumerable subsystems which interact with one another so as to maintain an overall balance. When an imbalance occurs, the ecosystem has remarkable recuperative powers to right itself, like a ship rolling in heavy seas. But even as a towering wave may arc the careening vessel beyond the angle of return, so an overloading or misuse of our planetary ecosystem could conceivably damage it beyond remedy. We do not know where that point of no return lies, but we have need to be concerned. This is because "the two worlds of man—the biosphere of his inheritance, the technosphere of his creation—are out of balance, indeed, potentially in deep conflict. And man is the middle. This is the hinge of history at which we stand, the door of the future opening on to a crisis more sudden, more global, more inescapable and more bewildering than any ever encountered by the human species and one which will take decisive shape within the life span of children who are already born."[1]

Because of gigantic population increases, the food gap between developed and undeveloped countries has been increasing—with 40 percent of the latter (according to the Food and Agriculture Organization) having dietary deficiencies. The 1960's hailed the "Green Revolution" with its significant increase of food production—due to new varieties of rice and wheat, the development of new irrigation facilities, and reliance upon the massive use of fertilizers. Unfortunately, the Green Revolution has not affected the mass of peasants in the tropics. To be successful, it requires continued support by governments which, for their part, came to depend in the 1960's upon substantial aid from developed countries in the form of free grain. But in recent years, the situation has drastically altered. Europe, the Soviet Union, and Japan have greatly increased their meat consumption and now make large purchases of grain from exporting countries, which consequently no longer possess the former surpluses to assist the underdeveloped regions when weather fails and food supplies prove inadequate. The problem has been compounded by vast price increases of crude oil, wheat, and rice. Oil is involved in the manufacture of fertilizers, and countries like India have been confronted with a crisis which could go far to wipe out the gains of the Green Revolution, and even reduce grain output in the late-1970's by millions of tons. This kind of drop could one day cause famine—for millions of already undernourished Indians.

Beginning in 1973, western countries were faced by an unprecedented energy crisis as a result of unilateral decisions by OPEC, the Organization of Petroleum Exporting Countries (see Chapter 36). It took place at a time when the world's appetite for energy appeared insatiable. Because of a combined population explosion and demand for higher living standards throughout the world, some experts estimate that the global energy supply will have to triple by 2000 A.D. The "big five" of world energy are coal, petroleum, natural gas, uranium, and hydroelectric power. The last is an inexhaustible resource, coal and nuclear sources will be available for centuries, while petroleum and natural gas will probably be exhausted in a few decades. But the "big five" are distributed so unevenly as to create large concentrations of specific resources in certain regions—such as coal in the United States, uranium in Canada, and petroleum in the Middle East—while leaving other regions in a critical deficit situation. To what extent can this situation be remedied by national, regional, or global decisions? The peoples of the world are now aware that the energy crisis is not a temporary phenomenon. Can the planet's resources meet our increasing demands while still being conserved in amounts adequate for generations yet unborn? Earlier predictions of disaster have proved premature—yet it remains true that global resources are finite while demands upon them are outrunning the increase in population. In various critical areas, the United States has become a resource-deficit country. The richer domestic deposits of iron and other minerals have already been skimmed off, and the environment has deteriorated so far that the rising costs of preserving it must be added to those of resource exploitation. Moreover, OPEC has provided an example for developing countries with large deposits of critical resources—such as copper, tin, and bauxite, urgently required by the industrial nations. The struggle for resources in short supply must be expected to create new financial and political tensions in the years ahead.

The societal balance sheet. We have already alluded to the marked differences in demographic growth rates between the developed and underdeveloped regions. Presently, numerous countries in the First World are reaching steady-state, or no growth, in their populations, whereas a region like Latin America has a yearly increase of about three percent so that its population will probably climb from some 300 million in the 1970's to around 600 million in 2000 A.D. By that time, too, India will have at least 800 million people, and China well above a billion. How will the Fourth World in particular obtain sufficient food and shelter for its proliferating populations? Between 1950 and 1970, the urban population in the underdeveloped regions rose from 256 to 622 million—by 2000 A.D. this figure could increase threefold. Meanwhile, a third of the municipalities of Latin America have neither sewage systems nor running water, while the proportion in the Indian subcontinent and parts of Africa is still higher. "In village or town, in suburb or slum, men and women experience in their daily environment the fulfillment or frustration of all the drives and demands of aspiring modernity. Above all, it is in settlements that the physical consequences of the vast upheavals will reach their climax. Millions upon millions crowded in the exploding cities, all too often without the minimal provisions for urban cleanliness, offer man's most concentrated insult to the support systems of air, water, and soil upon whose integrity the survival of life itself depends."[2]

In this societal balance-sheet, we would suggest that two major forms of the "politics of energy resources" are present in the international environment. One of the forms makes use of fossil fuels, notably petroleum and natural gas; the second consists of food, in particular bulk grains. Translating these forms of energy into political counterparts, we can describe them respectively as "petro-power" and "agro-power"—terms which have been used by politicians. Possessing the lion's share of the world's oil resources, the OPEC countries are the foremost proponents of petro-power. Before their stocks run out, they seek to maximize returns and also buy into the highly diversified economies of the First World. And in advancing their own political interests in the Middle East, they have demonstrated their capacity to "turn off the tap" against those countries which they regard as pursuing policies favorable to Israel but hostile to their own. To counter this petro-power, some western exponents of *Realpolitik* advocate employing food as a political weapon in turn. As the chief exporter of surplus grain, the United States (it is argued) should concentrate upon selling most or all of its surpluses for hard cash in order to reduce substantially its current deficit on oil imports. Moreover, since various OPEC countries have poor physical resources for producing foodstuffs in amounts required by their burgeoning populations, the threat of withholding food can be employed as a weapon to discourage or halt the pursuit of policies deemed unfavorable to the national interests of various First World countries.

Seen within this perspective, the politics of energy resources might be able to attain some sort of global geopolitical equilibrium. But it has its price tag: one that has to be paid by those least able, the peoples of the Fourth World who need both fuel and food desperately but have little or no economic or political "clout" of their own. True, they do export raw materials, but the world prices for those products are set in the commodity markets of the First World. Meanwhile, finished goods cost more than raw materials, and the underdeveloped countries have to import most of their manufactured foods—and pay also the costs tacked on by worldwide inflation.

If a global societal balance is to be achieved, or even approximated, there will have to be a more equitable distribution of resources and technological skills. In order to overcome the fundamental obstacles to development, and thereby create a "new international economic order," the World Bank estimates that about $125,000 million will have to be invested in the poorer regions of the world over a ten-year period—in food and nutrition, rural and urban water supplies, urban housing and transport, and population and health programs. This would amount to $12,500 million a year—a massive sum, yet only one-twentieth of the amount annually being spent on armaments in the mid-1970's (and which represents more than the entire GNP in 1972 of all the world's poorer countries with their one-and-three-quarter thousand million people). "If we take the World Bank's estimate of basic needs, we reach the re-

markable conclusion that the entire proposed spending on the works of peace for an entire decade would amount to no more than half the world's *annual* bill for weapons. A yearly five percent transfer from arms spending to development would fund the entire World Bank program."[3] Will anything like that transfer be made? The prospects as of 1977 appeared unlikely, inasmuch as foreign aid from the developed countries has been steadily falling—from 0.6 percent of their GNP in 1960 to 0.3 percent in 1974, with the decline possibly dipping to 0.2 percent by 1980. Developmental programs for people have to take a very distant back seat to the development of programs for mutual destruction in the current armaments race, the costliest and most lethal in history.

As Heraclitus pointed out, change is the one constant in life—yet people are both enamored and repelled by it. This leads us to a fundamental question that has yet to be answered: Granted that society everywhere in the world—both rich and poor nations alike—is in the midst of profound transformation, just what does represent the most appropriate direction for us to take? And have we any say in the matter?

ROADS TO TOMORROW

Three alternative world-views. While soothsayers are peering into their cloudy crystal balls in an effort to discern the shape of the future, academics and others have been feeding data into computers and interpreting the printouts in terms of societal "scenarios" for the coming decades. Their versions are many and varied, perhaps a hopeful sign in view of the doomsday nature of some of the forecasts. For purposes of summary and discussion alike, we have attempted to cover the spectrum of forecasts by providing three alternative world-views of the future, and their accompanying societal strategies. We are *not* trying to indicate which one will prevail, for perhaps none of them will. Although we may have our personal preference at the starting-gate, favorites do not necessarily finish first (as track bettors are painfully aware). The three scenarios are all possible. Each is logical and has its exponents, and all deserve to be understood and assessed on their individual and comparative merits.

1. The Malthusian world-view. Named after Thomas Malthus, who asserted in 1798 that popu-

An Indian farmer, weak from hunger, sits on a desic-cated field. Drought and India's shortfall of nitrogen fertilizer led to a severe drop in grain production in the mid-seventies, threatening millions with the possibility of famine.

lation was bound to outstrip food production, this world-view paints a direful picture of society's future. But it may well be the prospect for the world's second most populous country, India. In 1974 a panel of Indian economists and social scientists issued a report designed to serve as a guide for national planning. It warned that unless drastic measures were quickly instituted, by 2000 A.D. about half the population could be homeless, food would be scarce, the fuel shortage so acute that the landscape itself might be denuded of trees, while the cities would keep proliferating. The coming crisis demanded "unorthodox and highly unconventional" solutions. As an alternative to complete disaster, the experts mapped a

scenario for the end of the century: "Population has been stabilized around 900 million, using compulsory methods. The energy needs are satisfied by successful tapping of solar energy. Such unconventional food as algae or manufactured proteins satisfies 50 percent of the nutritional requirements. In addition, pills that can supply nutritional requirements for the whole day are available free for those who cannot afford to buy the food." Car culture has now been transformed into a bus and cycle culture while, because of high population densities, Indians will live in "kibbutz-style communes" and use "community kitchens to reduce the requirements of construction materials per person."[4] Does this "doomsday" prognosis apply only to India, or could it involve all peoples in some degree of another?

The Malthusian world-view, or paradigm ("model" from the Greek word, *paradeiknynai*, meaning to show side by side) of reality, is primarily conservative in its philosophical outlook and attitude towards the nature of humanity. In regard to the traditional either/or argument as to whether "nature"—as represented by hereditary traits and the constraints of the physical environment—or, on the other hand, "nurture"—the capability of human society to alter man's relationship with nature in his own favor—is dominant, it comes down on the side of the former. Human nature is essentially fixed by genetic factors; the amount of natural resources is limited. And because the human species has been employing its science and technology to upset nature's age-old biospheric balance—such as by increasing its population and physical wants to the breaking point—disaster is bound to occur. The ecosystem's support mechanisms are overloaded, while human society is now so complex that it is becoming increasingly dysfunctional—witness the growing inefficiency of our cities' administrations and services. In effect, there are no longer sufficient resources to feed the world's burgeoning billions, and we are woefully mismanaging what we still possess. Malthus is being proven right: in the last analysis, nature "conquers" man.

We will recall that Darwin was strongly influenced by Malthus, and the evolutionary theory dramatized the concept of a struggle for existence among all species. This led in turn to social Darwinism with its emphasis upon "rugged individualism" in the marketplace and social hierarchy (as conferring rewards upon those most successful in life's struggle), while in the political sphere the doctrine of "survival of the fittest" was used to justify warfare and the imperialistic subjugation of "lesser breeds without the law."

The Lifeboat Ethic - A Valid Metaphor?

At stake in each of the three world-views is the issue of survival of our species—and though one of them is optimistic about the outcome, the other two are either cautious or downright pessimistic. In agreement with the Malthusian paradigm, Garrett Hardin propounds a closely reasoned thesis, entitled "The Ethics of a Lifeboat,"[1] employing a graphic metaphor to advance his arguments.

Each rich nation represents a lifeboat full of comparatively affluent people. Outside swim 100 persons, representing the poor of the world who would like to climb aboard. What should the passengers do? There are, say, 50 of them and the craft has a capacity for another 10. If they take aboard all of those swimming in the water, the boat will be swamped and everyone will drown. "Complete justice, complete catastrophe." If 10 swimmers are admitted, the safety factor is lost and the chances of total disaster are magnified. Moreover, *which* 10 are to be let in? The first 10? The best 10? The neediest 10? What is to be said of the 90 who are excluded? Or should no one be admitted aboard in order to maximize survival of the existing occupants? (For those passengers who feel guilty, the reply is simply: "Get out and yield your place to others"—thereby eliminating that sort of conscience and leaving the ethics of the lifeboat unchanged.)

In support of this long-term survival, Hardin argues that we must not devastate our environment for merely short-run humanitarian desires to save lives. If we do, posterity will suffer. We do not have the right to give away our heritage in this manner; it belongs no less to future generations. Population growth is so great that even if the world's resources were distributed equally, there would not be enough to support every person in any degree of dignity. The survival of the wealthiest nations depends upon keeping their surpluses for their own purposes; such surpluses are their safety factor in calculations of supply and demand. To share the surpluses would only worsen the population problem. Increasing the population by supplying more food would only increase hunger in turn, which would require still more aid—and thus continue a vicious spiral until total catastrophe resulted. Again, in the past the giving of aid by the wealthy nations to the poor has been accompanied, not by increased brotherhood, but by intensified animosity between the "haves" and "have-nots." Finally, the poor nations could, if they only wanted to badly enough or tried hard enough, do a better job of feeding and limiting their populations. The wealthy nations should not aid them because help will remove the incentive in the recipient countries to improve their own lot.

Counter-arguments have in turn been advanced.[2] 1) We are not yet in the "lifeboat" situation: the major food problem is not so much underproduction as poor distribution. Furthermore, it is technologically feasible to provide food for a world population several times the present size. 2) Hardin ignores or discounts the effects that an improved standard of living can have on population fertility in the developing countries, even as it flattened growth curves in Europe and North America earlier. 3) To share food with the poor countries should be only the initial step in an ongoing process of enabling them technologically and economically to become progressively self-sufficient. In any case, is it realistic to suppose that the poor nations will stand idly by and let the wealthy cut them off from the resources and information required for their survival?

Hardin's ultimate argument is based upon a utilitarian ethic as deserving a higher priority than an ethic based upon humanitarianism and justice: the greatest good for the greatest possible number of survivors requires that the wealthy keep their resources for themselves, because to ensure the survival of the species should be the primary goal of all individuals and certainly of all responsible governments. But what if his argument was adopted, and we learned subsequently that the predictions about the relationship of future population to existing fuel and food energy resources proved wrong, so that we let die unnecessarily thousands or millions of persons while we had the resources to save them? If error is possible, is it not incumbent upon our governments to err on the side of justice, on the side of those who are undeniably alive and hungry today? And pressed to the final point, why should the survival of the human species be regarded as the highest "good"—especially when it is purchased at such a price in political and moral behavior? Other species have become extinct without destroying the ecological balance. It may also be argued that without the retention of such uniquely human attributes as "justice" and "compassion," our species will not long remain fit or able to survive in any event:

FOOTNOTES

1. Hardin, Garrett, "The Ethics of a Lifeboat." Paper delivered before the American Association for the Advancement of Science, San Francisco, February 1974.
2. See, for example, Janet Besecker and Phil Elder, "Lifeboat Ethics: A Reply to Hardin," *Alternatives: Perspectives on Society and Environment*, Vol. 5, No. 1, December 1975.

Various futurist scenarios can be built upon the Malthusian world-view. Thus, exploding populations and the insatiable needs generated by the "revolution of rising expectations" in rich and poor countries alike will inevitably create conflicts both within and between nations, such as between the "haves" of the North and the "have-nots" of the South. As a variation of this scenario, the most powerful countries will reach an accommodation, or détente, to allocate between themselves spheres of political domination and economic exploitation. Countries like India are in any case doomed by Malthusian mechanisms to misery.

Another possible scenario for this world-view was provided by the much-debated initial report to the Club of Rome.[5] Its authors employed the computer to construct laboratory models of how global society can be expected to behave in the next hundred years, and they fed in massive amounts of data concerning such variables as population, non-replenishable resources, capital investment in industry and agriculture, and pollution. There is a growth factor in each of these variables — all of which are interlocked by feedback loops — and the statistical consequences of their interacting processes can be plotted in a time sequence. Given this continued growth factor, the computer was unable to come up with any combination of conventional responses that could provide enduring solutions. In fact, if exponential growth continued in the decades ahead, the printouts forecast a breakdown of the ecosystem and major regions alike with the next century.

Proposed solutions are drastic: an across-the-board reduction in population investment and resource usage that would create a steady-state world system. Just how drastic these proposals are can be appreciated when we recall that to shift from exponential growth to zero growth challenges the fundamental tenets of the ideology that has dominated the nation-state system. It is bound to have profound economic and psychological effects alike. For example, the replacement in the manufacturing industries of obsolescence and quick turnover by more durable goods would reduce the need for replenishment, and also reduce employment in our factories. Again, a no-growth situation would have the effect of maintaining existing disparities in living standards, and condemn the Fourth World's population to a permanent state of poverty and inequality. But if planetary stabilization is to be achieved, while permitting some growth in the underdeveloped regions, then a proportionately greater cutback would have to be accepted by the advantaged few in the rich countries.

2. The expansionist world-view. If pessimism is the keynote of the Malthusian model, optimism describes the mood of this second world-view. Its exponents have traditionally favored "nurture" over "nature"; they see humanity as capable of gaining progressive control over its ancient enemies of ignorance, pestilence, and famine. Logically, too, just as science and technology have carried our dominion of the environment to the poles and now into outer space, so genetic "engineering" should be able to expand not only human longevity but even intelligence — and perhaps improve human virtue as well. Human nature is regarded as pliable and subject ultimately to societal conditioning and values. Granted the biosphere and technosphere are currently out of balance — as evidenced by pollution and the numbers of endangered species — but it is well to remember that from the outset, man the tool-maker has always been tampering with the biosphere and disturbing its balance. Yet imbalances have been corrected in the past, and there is no reason to believe that this historical capability is about to be aborted. Consequently, the problems created by technology can be corrected by still better technology. In short it can be stated that man "conquers" nature.

This world-view has its philosophical roots in various western sources. One was Francis Bacon's advocacy of the inductive method as a means of acquiring knowledge and progressive mastery of the physical world. Another was the Protestant ethic and the effectiveness of work. A third was the Enlightenment's belief in the power of reason and rational behavior. Still another was the First Industrial Revolution which raised living standards dramatically, and helped to equate "progress" with the satisfaction of material wants. This paradigm — which has been dominant in the West from early modern times to recent decades — is historically associated with "growth." This includes growth of: knowledge and education; economic production and environmental control; the nation-state system and the ambitions of its members to expand both in power and territory; and industrialism, urbanism, and secularism. Little wonder, then, that such growth has been compatible with the theories of Adam Smith and Karl Marx alike (see Chapter 24). Industrialism, whether under capitalist or socialist direction, is geared to the exploitation of resources in order to create and satisfy mass markets, even as liberal and socialist regimes employ the techniques of managerial centralization to cater to mass culture and its ever-expanding demands and expectations.

With its commitment to exponential growth, the expansionist model abhors the goal of steady-state. Some of its exponents regard zero growth as flying in the face of evolution — and even depart from their advocacy of "nurture" to argue that it runs counter to "human nature" (as if "progress" were an innate trait and that "bigger" is to be equated with "better"). This argument itself is the product of historical experiences in the West. For example, in filling out their continental spaces, Americans and Canadians shared the assumption that "growth is to be correlated with progress, measurable in such terms as railway and road mileage, capital investment in industry, acreage under cultivation, population increase, and gross national product — in short, that the quantity and quality of life are mutually supportive, if not actually synonymous."[6]

Expansionism worked well in the past, and its exponents contend that it will continue to do so. They reject the Malthusian forecasts as both hysterical and historically inaccurate; for example, technology has so far increased food production to keep pace with biological reproduction. Again, earlier forecasts of resource depletion have proven premature. At present, no one knows accurately what the earth holds or can produce, or what uses may be made of new or recycled materials. Furthermore, the "high technology" of the Second Industrial Revolution accomplishes more with less physical resources; it is described by Buckminster Fuller as the "trend of comprehensive ephemeralization." This contemporary phenomenon of doing more with fewer "resource units of pounds, time, and energy" can bring to people everywhere the living standards enjoyed today by the advantaged minority, "all to be realized out of the earth's physical resources which are continually decreasing per each world man."[7] This means that growth can continue in the presently underdeveloped regions and enable them to move into the Industrial Age — while the technologically advanced economies are already moving into the Post-Industrial Age, in which the emphasis will be increasingly to provide services rather than simply physical goods.

Energy will be preeminently important in this Post-Industrial Age, and we are well embarked upon making a breakthrough to nuclear, thermonuclear, and even solar energy which can then provide humanity indefinitely with all the power it may need. Such limitless energy can be conceivably used to make synthetic metals, regenerate a degraded planetary environment, and fuel the technology for colonizing other planets — where the process of expansion will proceed anew. With such technological developments, it should prove possible to alleviate or even eliminate poverty — so that with the attainment of a new standard of living we can also envisage "the end of ideology." The post-industrial culture accompanying the post-industrial economy will enthrone science and technology along with technocratic values, yet cultural diversity will continue to flourish.

3. The ecological world-view. The keynote of this third paradigm is prudence — which means espousing neither pessimism or optimism. It could well adopt the motto of the Sierra Club: "Not blind opposition to progress, but opposition to blind progress." It regards human nature and intelligence quotients alike not as the sole expression of either "nature" or "nurture," but as the combined product of interacting hereditary and societal factors. This concept is integral to a world-view that regards the universe as a unified system, all of whose parts are connected and interacting. The advocates of this paradigm believe that because man himself cannot remain apart from nature, but on the contrary is an inseparable part of a vast ecosystem, it follows that he can never "conquer" his environment — but stands or falls with it because the universe is not dualistic but monistic.

The ecological world-view has different antecedents from the others. Some of the antecedents are nonwestern; they include the Upanishadic emphasis upon the oneness of life (see p. 95), and Taoism's message about the balance of nature and humanity's need to live in harmony with it (see p. 109). In the West, this world-view finds support from Christian and libertarian forms of socialism with their stress upon cooperation rather than conflict in the acquisition and use of resources, and again from Marx's objective of a classless society in which each member gives according to his or her ability and receives according to his or her needs. Anarchism is also involved. Peter Kropotkin in his *Mutual Aid* (1902) demonstrated that cooperation between members of the same species, and symbiosis between different species, seem to be just as essential as competition and struggle to the overall evolutionary process.

Again, the ecological world-view has a different sociopolitical and economic orientation from its counterparts. It is both conservative and socialist — in the sense of wanting to "conserve" the natural balance and resources for future generations and, at the same time, seeking to maximize the "social" allocation of current resources for all concerned. In this sense, it is allied with the findings and strategies of the various United Nations conferences on the environment, population, food, the seas, and human settlement. And where the expansionist paradigm tends to emphasize centralization (in the interests of economies of scale) and the homogenization of culture on a global scale, this world-view advocates a mixture of centralization and decentralization, as well as encouraging cultural diversity. Logically, it adopts this stance because the world itself is composed of both the simple and complex, the small and the large, and they coexist and interact. On this basis, the needs common to all—basic standards of nutrition, health, shelter, education—must be met on a global scale, and the resources required to meet these needs call in turn for international management and allocation—such as by the United Nations and its specialized agencies. At the same time, the *specific* uses to which these resources are put warrant decentralization of the decision-making process to the regional, national, and also local levels of society so as to take account of cultural and community uniqueness. Whereas the expansionist world-view places its faith primarily in the managers and experts, this paradigm calls into play the view as well of the "ordinary people" to redress technocratic values—because "small is beautiful."[8]

The ecological world-view has its own strategy. Unlike the Malthusian model, it does not call for total zero growth, nor on the other hand does it countenance continued exponential growth. It recognizes the ills of arbitrary and sudden cutoffs, which mean the loss of the social and psychological momentum that has sustained western societies over the past two centuries, and also the need of underdeveloped regions to continue to increase productivity and improve living standards. Growth, however, is to be selective. Hopefully, overall population growth would decrease in the Fourth World in the decades ahead, while the industrially advanced regions would plan to have a smaller output of nonrecyclable goods but those with a longer life expectancy, and a larger output of services. The desired objective would be a multivariable steady-state by the next century, one that recognized flexibility of approach and methods among the world's major regions.

There is involved here another kind of shift— from an emphasis upon material goods towards a new life-style, physically simpler but stressing qualitative factors. This calls in turn for a fundamental shift to values appropriate for meeting tomorrow's challenges. Some scholars, for example, have constructed their model of a "preferred world" upon the substantial realization of "four central values": 1) the minimization of large-scale collective violence; 2) the maximization of social and economic well-being; 3) the realization of fundamental human rights and conditions of political justice; 4) the rehabilitation and maintenance of environmental quality, including the conservation of resources.[9] At the same time, we cannot realistically expect to have these values implemented unless people everywhere perceive them as being fundamentally compatible with traditional values in the world's major cultures. Can disparate societies build upon their respective value systems in order to converge to a new ethical imperative? According to the third report to the Club of Rome, such an advance will be critical for the further evolution of human society.[10]

"WHERE THERE IS NO VISION . . ."

Some implications of the three world-views. Although the foregoing models provide different directions into the future, and advocate different strategies, they share a common concern about society's prospects, and they ask us in turn to become future-oriented in our own thinking. They may disagree about the effects of science and technology upon society and its traditional values, but they leave us in no doubt about the continuing crucial role which will be played by man the tool-maker in altering his physical and societal environments alike. Any solutions to the problems that afflict contemporary society will have to take account of the importance of technology and rational values in sustaining our civilization. In his book *Zen and the Art of Motorcycle Maintenance* (1974), Robert M. Pirsig has appealed for a new holistic outlook of life that would reconcile the dominant "classical" culture of our civilization with the "romantic" counterculture. The two cultures—the artistic one of feeling and immediate appearances and the scientific one of law and underlying form—must be integrated within a higher unity that stresses the ideal of *quality*. Significantly, each of these world-views cuts across the boundaries of traditional cultures and nation-states. Whether or not advances in electronic communication that could provide instantaneous person-to-person contact anywhere on earth are presently fashioning a "global village," or, again, that the problems which already beset us can be resolved only at a supranational level of organization and decision-making, there can be little question that the peoples of the Four Worlds are interdependent and vulnerable as never before in history.

But if the way ahead lies in the direction of some kind of international community, what is to become of the individual in such a structure, and what is to become of individual thought and life styles? Even in the small city-states of ancient Greece, men worried about the "tyranny of the majority," the subjugation of the one to the many. Are we to abolish war and poverty, only to replace them with mind-numbing uniformity? Will every African village have its piped-in Muzak, every polar community the same neon-lit supermarkets as Dallas and Bangkok? Will the great masses of humanity, freed at last from backbreaking toil, spend their endless vacations in front of wall-to-wall television screens, popping down pep pills or tranquilizers like candy? If we are to avoid an Orwellian world-order based upon a warfare totalitarianism, can we avoid in turn the pleasant meaninglessness of Aldous Huxley's *Brave New World?* What have the three world-views to offer in the way of scenarios here?

Religious faith in transition. In the past, societies were sustained by traditional religious, ethical, and moral values. But tomorrow's world will have to evolve new values as well in order to give meaning to the challenges posed by change. We have already some unprecedented questions to try to resolve. What are the implications posed by heart-transplant operations to prolong life in a recipient—are we now attempting to play God? Furthermore, who or what shall decide how much life would be good for the planet, and have we succeeded in resolving the basic question of the inherent worth, or sanctity, of the individual? The present generation is confronted with fundamental moral questions for which there is often no historical precedent and will have to search for new answers to new as well as to old questions.

Considering the changes in society, in technology and in scientific knowledge that have been taking place in recent years, it is hardly surprising that many people have been reassessing traditional concepts about the meaning of life and the ultimate nature of the universe. In the West institutionalized Christianity seems to have lost much of its general appeal; on the other hand there has been a great upsurge in the number and kinds of religious sects—some Christian, but many deriving inspiration from oriental sources. The growing influence of Taoism and Buddhism, for example, suggests that many people are receptive to views emphasizing the oneness of nature and the close relatedness of all forms of life—an essentially ecological view of universal processes. This implies, too, a shift away from seeing spirit, or God, in transcendent terms—as standing in some way outside or beyond our world—and toward seeing spirit as immanent in the world's processes. Such a shift may be reflected in new concern for the human predicament *here* and *now*—a concern apparent in the social consciousness of much of the Christian clergy today in Africa and Latin America.

Studying the future—its significance. Undoubtedly, there are more people thinking about society's future prospects and problems today than ever before in history. Why is this so? The answer is found in the complexity of contemporary civilization, and the accelerating speed at which it is changing. This brings us to the matter of "lead-time." For example, the energy crisis has forced numerous governments to take stock of their dwindling resources of oil and natural gas and to plan for producing alternative forms of energy, which in addition must meet still larger consumption demands in the decades ahead. But it will take time to construct new atomic installations, for example, while the option of using fast breeder reactors poses issues involving considerable efficiency and environmental risk alike (see p. 859). This is the kind of decision that has to be taken as early as possible on critical questions which for their part may not make a tangible impact on society for many years.

Even as we noted previously the problem of "demographic inertia," so we have to be concerned about what might be termed "sociocultural inertia." A large, complex society reminds one of a supertanker whose size and momentum prevent it from coming to a stop for many miles. To pursue this analogy, the futurologist has no intention of trying to halt society in its tracks—for even if that were possible, a sudden stoppage could prove catastrophic—but rather to assist society to be ready to change course. This not only requires the charting of viable alternative routes, but making sure that all concerned, including nearby traffic, are fully alerted to the need for a change of direction, and in turn accept the new destination.

The critical factors are *awareness* and *time*, because setting a new course—should that prove necessary—cannot wait for the storm that could engulf us if unprepared. We must develop contingency plans well in advance.

That is why so many are thinking these days about the future: scholars, institutions, governments, and international organizations. Some researchers work independently, often on specific problems such as ecological hazards, or the feasibility of developing alternative technologies for those in current use in, say, the developing countries. Other specialists collaborate on either national or global enterprises. One of these is the World Order Models Project (WOMP), composed of groups of scholars from a number of countries who are making a concerted study of the problem of eliminating war as a human institution. Various universities and research institutes have set up centers to assess more clearly the changes now occurring throughout the world and to develop options as various societies shift from exponential growth in the direction of steady-state. In the United States, we find such concentrations of effort at MIT, Stanford, and the Hudson Institute, with much of the initial impetus having been generated by a highly influential body of European origin, the Club of Rome.

A growing number of governments are now participating in the study of the future. This movement is illustrated in the case of Canada, where various federal departments have allocated resources to assess Canadian prospects and problems in the decades ahead, while the Canadian Senate has established a Commission on the Future. Sweden has probably been foremost among governments in initiating officially sponsored "future studies" (a term sometimes used synonymously with long-term planning). In 1973, a Secretariat for Future Studies was created and attached to the Swedish Cabinet Office. This Secretariat recognized that future studies differ from the ordinary run of official investigations in that they describe alternative trends within a longer time perspective. Its first four studies have dealt with energy and society in Sweden; resources and raw materials; Sweden in the world society; and working life in the future. The Secretariat has also been assessing the relationship of technology to Swedish society as a whole, and the future role and impact of communications systems. International organizations have in turn been getting involved. This is because future-oriented studies are also needed to guide the international community in its attempts to solve environmental and social problems. In this context, the United Nations Institute for Training and Research (UNITAR) has now set up its own Commission on the Future. One of its tasks, it has been suggested, should be to study how to adapt the decision-making process and administrative machinery of the United Nations system to the needs that will exist in the future for action at the international level."[11]

The futurologist makes no pretense at prophecy; avoiding the crystal ball and tarot cards, he employs a variety of methodological tools. As we have seen, the first two reports to the Club of Rome gathered massive quantities of facts and figures and fed them into the computer, which analyzed the data in terms of a systems model. For its part, the third report of the Club of Rome adopted not a quantitative but normative approach—it concentrated on analyzing the coexistence and interaction of the beliefs and value systems of the world's major cultures and what this process could portend for the future. In addition, many future studies are cast in the form of scenarios. Instead of forecasting what will probably happen, scenarios recognize the factor of uncertainty and consequently provide alternative images of the future. The images presented are considered plausible—some perhaps more than others—but they make different assumptions about the direction of trends. This methodology takes account of both objective and subjective conditions at work in the society for which goals and programs are devised—and it enables public policy planners "periodically to assess the manner in which trends are developing, to apply more recent data, and to reconstruct, with as much detail as is considered necessary, future scenarios."[12]

The relevance of world history for studying the future. In this book's Prologue, we stressed the Janus-like role of history: it permits us to view and appreciate the past as past, and in turn to visualize the past and present as prologue. We repeat that they conjoin to alert us to the need, not only to engage in new forms of planning for the years ahead, but no less to be willing to rethink our existing social goals and value systems. The historical evolution of humanity is open-ended, and far from being immutable, beliefs, values, and goals are continuously undergoing change. Here, the historical record becomes invaluable because it can provide us with what we shall continue to require: as long and accurate a perspective as possible from our global experience in order to make realistic analyses of what the Club of Rome calls the *"problématique humaine"* — the cluster of worldwide problems — and to take appropriate kinds of action to safeguard our planetary inheritance and improve our quality of life.

If, as every technological and social indicator seems to underscore, we are indeed moving towards a new type of civilization — one that is becoming progressively cross-cultural and transnational — we shall have special needs to present society's historical experience within a perspective that is itself global. Unless we can adopt such a perspective, our approach will continue to be ethnocentric and distorted, with all the attending misunderstandings and tensions. If we are moving towards a growing and accelerating convergence of once-compartmentalized social structures and value systems, we must think in new ways. Specifically, we shall have to regard the planet's peoples and societies not as a collection of disconnected historical entities, but as interconnected segments of a planetary system.

To shift from ideological and political confrontation to *détente* (a relaxation of tensions) has been a necessary step in moving away from a "cold war" mentality, but it is only the first step to entente — an international understanding providing for a common course of action; indeed, in the fullest sense of the phrase, to an *entente cordiale* among peoples of all continents. As the authors of the third report to the Club of Rome emphasize, this shift towards a global type of society calls for more than "coexistence" — it requires "interexistence":

In global society, coexistence is not enough; it merely condones the *status quo* and treats the world as a mosaic of still independent and mutually irresponsible states and societies. Continued adherence to it gives a new lease on life for outmoded beliefs and values, and permits the unfolding of the existing gaps and inequalities, and social and economic problems. But coexistence is an attitude rooted not in human nature but merely in the postwar period when, for a time, it had a positive function. Its fruitfulness is over. Yet this realization, rather than fuelling incipient wishes to detach oneself and one's society from the world, must lead to a new attitude of cooperative existence aiming at the self-determined integration of diverse nations and peoples in a humanistic world order. Hence in social humanism we move from the posture of coexistence to that of interexistence.[13]

Viewed from this perspective, our Epilogue becomes a Prologue to a new stage of human experience and societal attainment. Our Paleolithic ancestors found themselves in a single, undifferentiated planet. Since then, their descendants have spiraled through stages of progressive control of the environment and increasing complexity of economic activity, social organization, and political decision-making until, today, we find ourselves inhabiting once more a single — but now a highly differentiated and interrelated — planet. One species as ever, yet occupying innumerable ecological and cultural niches within a shared global ecosystem. A new chapter in our irreversible history is being written. The story line is not yet clear, and the plot will have its full share of surprises. But it should prove interesting . . .

SUGGESTIONS FOR READING

"Futurology" is creating a fast-growing literature. One of the first major works to question the traditional western belief in growth and to try to show the need for bringing the world of man into equilibrium with the forces of his environment is Jay W. Forrester, **World Dynamics,** 2nd ed. (Wright-Allen, 1973). This approach played a key role in the methodology employed in the first two Reports to the Club of Rome, namely, D. H. and D. L. Meadows *et al.*, **The Limits to Growth*** (Pan Books, 1974); and M. Mesarovic and E. Pestel, **Mankind at the Turning Point*** (Dutton, 1974). The third Report to the Club of Rome dealing with normative factors and issues is Ervin Laszlo *et al.*, **Goals for Mankind** (Dutton, 1977). A useful futures study prepared for the U.S. Government is found in D. S. Elgin, D. C. MacMichael, and P. Schwartz, **Alternative Futures for Environmental Policy Planning: 1975-2000** (Environmental Protection Agency, 1975).

Other books are relevant to an understanding of future studies. They include R. L. Heilbroner, **An Inquiry into the Human Prospect** (Norton, 1974), on the Malthusian world-view; and Daniel Bell, **The Coming of Post-Industrial Society*** (Basic Books, 1976), on the expansionist world-view. See also William Kuhns, **The Post-Industrial Prophets*** (Harper & Row); E. Laszlo, **A Strategy for the Future: The Systems Approach to World Order*** (Braziller, 1973); and **The World System: Models, Norms, Variations*** (Braziller, 1973); E. Jantsch and C. H. Waddington, eds., **Evolution and Consciousness: Human Systems in Transition*** (Addison-Wesley, 1976).

Recommended among the works published so far by the World Order Models Project (WOMP) is Richard A. Falk, **A Study for Future Worlds** (Free Press, 1975). This book challenges traditional, narrow approaches to the problems of an interdependent world, and offers its own design for a future world order together with a specific strategy for coping with the transitional period.

*Indicates a less expensive paperbound edition.

This profile depicts the life of a new generation of the Chand family in the Punjab region of India (see Family Profile 8). Nabin Chand, an infant in the 1930's, is now, some forty years later, head of the family. Although in many respects well-off by Indian peasant standards, the Chands of the 1970's still live under harsh conditions. Technological change is undermining traditional patterns of life, and the pressure of population growth is raising social and political questions.

The day begins early for ten-year-old Darshana Chand. She rises at five o'clock and makes tea for her father, then helps her sisters take grass and drinking water to the cattle. Before 7:30 she and her eight-year-old sister are off to school, which lasts until 1:30. After they return Darshana resumes her chores, which consist mainly of tending to the cattle.

Darshana's family—mother, father, the five children still at home, and a grandmother—devotes itself to making a living from its six acres of land. Father, together with seventeen-year-old Sohan, and Makan, the hired laborer, spends all day in the fields, not returning to the house until almost nine in the evening. The men's lunches are taken out to them—a walk of nearly a mile from the house—by Jagir, age fourteen, who is finished with her schooling and now spends her time helping her mother. She also looks after her younger brother, who at five is the only member of the family exempt from work. This is not to last, however; next year he not only will start school, but will be needed to help with household chores and tend the animals. Children are expected to be productive from an early age.

The family's eldest child, an eighteen-year-old daugher, has just left home after marrying a young man from a neighboring village—a marriage arranged between the parents of the two families involved. Already she is expecting her first child, and can look forward to a life much like that of her mother—one of many children and much hard work. Naturally, she is hoping her child will be a son, one who will grow up to work hard in the fields and help support his parents in their later years. The Chand family regrets the fact that they have only two boys—and one of them yet so young. Still, their eldest daughter was able to work from time to time in the fields, and now Jagir is old enough to take her place. A woman's place is said to be in the home, not outside, but with only one grown son, the Chands have little choice in the matter.

The Chands are among the four fifths of India's population of roughly 600 million that inhabits rural villages. The introduction of an improved variety of wheat in the late 1960's increased the land's productivity, but also meant a bigger workload for those farmers unable to mechanize their farms properly. It is true that the Chands have been able to purchase a tube well, a device for obtaining water from under the ground, for use in irrigation. They also employ chemical fertilizers and listen regularly to agricultural information programs on their transistor radio. But farming is still a labor-intensive occupation. Like the great majority of their neighbors, the Chands have neither the money to invest in a tractor, nor sufficient land to make such an investment economical in any case. It is only the well-to-do landowners with much greater holdings who have been able to take full advantage of the new strain of wheat and the new technology. Such men are increasingly becoming landlords and farm managers in charge of a labor force of hired wage earners.

The Chands are in no such position, however. The cost of the laborer they employ during sowing and harvest times puts a considerable strain on the family budget, and is a necessity forced on them by their need for help in the fields. As father never tires of saying, "Who in their right mind would pay two or three thousand rupees for a laborer if they had an extra son?" The Chands look forward to the time their second son will be able to take his place beside his father and older brother. They also hope that Sohan will be married soon, and that his wife will bear him many sons. Of course, more sons in the family increases the prospect of their small land holdings being further fragmented with the father's death (the daughters can be expected to marry and leave home). But with enough sons, enough work, and enough luck they may be able to purchase more land. That is the hope. The great fear is that they will not be able to make a go of things, and will all have to become agricultural laborers, working for someone else.

While technological change is making its impact felt at all levels of Indian society, it is not in itself the answer to the country's social problems. A gap is forming between the privileged minority—especially in the towns, but also in the countryside—who can afford to consume more or less as westerners do, and the poor majority of Indians. The Chands are not privileged, but they are relatively prosperous. They live in a two-story house of sun-dried bricks. In more than one sense, this puts them above those less fortunate villagers whose low mud houses are in danger of being destroyed in the heavy monsoon rains. Like the rest of the villagers, though, the Chands still have no indoor plumbing and must go out into the fields to relieve themselves.

Father is head of the household, and his word is

law. The children defer unhesitatingly to their parents. The family is a closely-knit unit, and each member has his or her particular tasks to perform to help promote the economic survival of all. Besides wheat, the family grows lentils, tomatoes, and other vegtables for their own consumption. Mother makes meals of wheat cakes, which she makes from flour, and perhaps a lentil curry, which she cooks over a fire fueled by cakes of dried cattle dung. Every day she washes the family's clothes by hand. Her whole life is devoted to caring for her family. Married at age seventeen, she is now about to become a grandmother at thirty-six. Even when she becomes too old to do the kind of heavy work she does now, she will be able to contribute to the household by spinning cotton into thread. Over the years there has been some improvement in the status of women: laws have been passed giving them freedom of marriage and divorce, and the right to own property. But practical considerations mean that most Indian women can hardly be considered liberated.

Although radio broadcasts have begun to make the villagers more aware of what is happening in the outside world, political and constitutional issues at the national level are generally of little interest to them. There is no police force or other official arm of outside authority in the village, and the villagers are wary of the government with good reason. They know that corruption is rampant at all levels of government; one incentive for obtaining an education for their children is to guard themselves against being cheated by moneylenders and landlords. Yet the great majority of Indian children under the age of fourteen are illiterate; the number in school is increasing, but not fast enough to keep pace with the exploding population—60,000 babies are born every day, and the country has an annual net increase of about fourteen million persons.

The announcement that the national government had declared a state of emergency due to India's political and economic situation did not make much of an impression on the villagers at first. A promise that land holdings in excess of eighteen acres would be redistributed to the landless met with some skepticism. Wealthy landowners have generally been able to escape previous half-hearted attempts at reform, and the plots of land handed out have usually been too small to be of much practical use. But now the government's new plans to limit family size are causing worry. In the past there have been birth-control workers in the village. The villagers would take the free contraceptive pills, agree to use them, and later throw them away. "We didn't want to hurt their feelings," explains Nabin Chand. "When they discovered we weren't using the pills, they thought it was because we were too ignorant to understand. But we did understand. We know that a small family means ruin—unless you have much land and much machinery and can hire other workers. But we are not rich people, so we threw the pills away."

Now the government is getting tough, and is launching a drive to sterilize parents who have had two or three children. The villagers are resisting. There are rumors that police have been rounding up men and taking them away in trucks to have vasectomies. Last week a couple of birth-control workers were beaten up in a neighboring village. "And if they come here there will be trouble too," says Nabin Chand.

The government's campaign to get people to work harder is incomprehensible to the Chands. Work is a full-time activity for the family—which generally means seven days a week, morning till night. "Leisure," in the sense of time free for private pursuits or idleness, does not exist—except perhaps when rain makes outside work impossible. Even time off for traditional religious festivals is rare these days. Bus lines now connect the village with other communities, but for the most part the family's traveling is limited to the occasional excursion by father or Sohan to the nearest market town to buy seed or for other business purposes.

The story of the Chands and their neighbors illustrates the fact that austerity measures and campaigns to limit population can have only a limited effect where most people live in poverty and the government is unwilling to undertake drastic reform to redistribute the nation's wealth. Even technological change is of ambiguous value in such a situation. For the Indian peasant, the road ahead looks to be a hard one.

Footnotes

PROLOGUE: PERSPECTIVE ON HUMANITY

1. David G. Mandelbaum, "Concepts of Civilization and Culture," *Encyclopaedia Britannica*, 1967 ed., Vol. 5, p. 831A.
2. See A. J. Toynbee, *Civilization on Trial* (New York: Oxford University Press, 1948), p. 11.
3. Quoted in *The New York Times* (July 15, 1973, Section 10), p. 16.
4. See P. Gardiner, *The Nature of Historical Explanation* (London: Oxford University Press, 1952), p. 98.

CHAPTER 1: ALONG THE BANKS OF RIVERS

1. R. E. F. Leakey, "Evidence for an Advanced Plio-Pleistocene Hominid from East Rudolph, Kenya," *Nature* (April 13, 1973), p. 449. See also "News and Views: More Questions Than Answers at East Rudolph," same source, p. 431.
2. R. Braidwood, *Prehistoric Men*, 7th ed., (Glenview, Ill.: Scott, Foresman and Co., 1967), p. 34.
3. G. S. Hawkins in collaboration with John B. White, *Stonehenge Decoded* (New York: Dell Publishing Co., 1966), pp. 117-118.
4. V. Gordon Childe, *New Light on the Most Ancient East* (London: Routledge & Kegan Paul Ltd., 1954), p. 114.
5. Tom B. Jones, *Ancient Civilization* (Chicago: Rand McNally & Co., 1960), p. 10.
6. V. Gordon Childe, *What Happened in History* (New York: Pelican Books, 1946), p. 74.
7. The ancient Mesopotamian chronology followed here is that presented in *The Cambridge Ancient History*, rev. ed. (1962) Vol. I, Ch. 6.
8. H. Frankfort, *The Birth of Civilization in the Near East* (London: Williams and Norgate, Ltd., 1951), p. 60.
9. "Les reformes d'Urukagina," trans. by M. Lambert in *Revue d'Assyriologie*, L (Paris, 1956), p. 183.
10. James B. Pritchard, ed., *Ancient Near Eastern Texts Relating to the Old Testament*, 2nd ed., trans. by E. A. Speiser (Princeton: Princeton University Press, 1955), p. 119.
11. *Sumerische und Akkadische Hymnen und Gebete*, trans. by A. Falkenstein and W. von Soden (Zurich: Artemis-Verlag, 1953), p. 188. For a partial translation and full discussion of this text, see S. N. Kramer, *From the Tablets of Sumer* (Indian Hills, Colo.: The Falcon's Wing Press, 1956), pp. 267-271.
12. H. de Genouillac, trans., in *Revue d'Assyriologie*, XXV (Paris, 1928), p. 148.
13. Quoted in Kramer, p. 50.
14. R. F. Harper, *The Code of Hammurabi* (Chicago: University of Chicago Press, 1904), p. 3.
15. *Ibid.*, p. 49.
16. *Ibid.*, p. 101.
17. From *Epic of Gilgamesh*, trans. by E. A. Speiser, in Pritchard, p. 90.
18. Nels Bailkey, ed., *Readings in Ancient History from Gilgamesh to Diocletian*, 2nd ed. (Lexington: D. C. Heath & Co., 1976), p. 27.
19. Quoted in *City Invincible: A Symposium on Urbanization and Cultural Development in the Ancient Near East*, ed. by Carl H. Kraeling and Robert McC. Adams (Chicago: University of Chicago Press, 1960), p. 163.
20. Quoted in M. A. Murray, *The Splendour That Was Egypt* (London: Sidgwick & Jackson, Ltd., 1949), p. 67.
21. Trans. by John A. Wilson, *The Burden of Egypt* (Chicago: University of Chicago Press, 1951), p. 117.
22. *Ibid.*, p. 164.
23. Adolf Erman, *The Literature of the Ancient Egyptians*, trans. by Aylward M. Blackman (London: Methuen & Co., Ltd., 1927), pp. 190, 196, 197.
24. From "The Instruction of Meri-ka-Re," trans. by John A. Wilson, *The Burden of Egypt*, p. 120.
25. *Ibid.*, p. 119.

26. Quoted in George Steindorff and George Hoyningen-Huene, *Egypt* (Locust Valley, N.Y.: J. J. Augustin Inc., 1943), p. 23.
27. Trans. by George Steindorff and Keith E. Seele, *When Egypt Ruled the East* (Chicago: University of Chicago Press, 1942), p. 125. Copyright 1942 by the University of Chicago Press.
28. Quoted in J. H. Breasted, *The Dawn of Conscience* (New York: Charles Scribner's Sons, 1939), p. 284.
29. Ezekiel 27:33-34. Revised Standard Version of the Bible.
30. B. W. Anderson, *Understanding the Old Testament* (Englewood Cliffs, N.J.: Prentice-Hall, Inc., 1957), p. 537.
31. I Samuel 8:6, 20. Revised Standard Version of the Bible.
32. I Kings 4:20 ff.; 10:14 ff. Revised Standard Version of the Bible.
33. II Kings 25:14. Revised Standard Version of the Bible.
34. Micah 6:8. Revised Standard Version of the Bible.
35. D. D. Luckenbill, *Ancient Records of Assyria and Babylonia*, I (Chicago: University of Chicago Press, 1926), p. 147.
36. Quoted in Georges Roux, *Ancient Iraq* (Baltimore: Penguin Books, Inc., 1966), p. 278.
37. Nahum 3:8. Revised Standard Version of the Bible.
38. Herodotus, *History*, I, 181; trans. by George Rawlinson.
39. Daniel 5:27. Revised Standard Version of the Bible.
40. Herodotus, IX, 122; trans. by A. R. Burn, *Persia and the West* (New York: St. Martin's Press, 1962), p. 61.
41. Herodotus, VIII, 98; trans. by Rawlinson.

CHAPTER 2: THE GLORY THAT WAS GREECE

1. Plutarch's *Lives*, II, trans. by Sir T. North (London: J. M. Dent & Sons Ltd., 1898), p. 144.
2. See Leonard R. Palmer, *Mycenaeans and Minoans: Aegean Prehistory in the Light of the Linear B Tablets* (New York: Alfred A. Knopf, Inc., and London: Faber and Faber, Ltd., 1961), Chapter 5, "The Last Days of Pylos."
3. Quoted in Werner Jaeger, *Paideia: The Ideals of Greek Culture*, I (New York: Oxford University Press, 1939), p. 70.
4. "Laws," V, 735; in *The Dialogues of Plato*, II, trans. by B. Jowett (New York: Random House, 1937), p. 503.
5. Plutarch's *Lives*, trans. by J. Dryden, rev. by A. H. Clough (New York: Modern Library, 1932), p. 107.
6. Trans. by A. R. Burn, *The Pelican History of Greece* (Baltimore: Penguin Books, Inc., 1966), p. 186.
7. C. E. Robinson, *Hellas: A Short History of Ancient Greece* (New York: Pantheon Books, 1948), p. 68.
8. From Thucydides, *The History of the Peloponnesian War*, II, 65, edited by Sir Richard Livingstone, by permission of the Oxford University Press, p. 130.
9. *Ibid.*, 37, 40, pp. 111,113.
10. Thucydides, II, edited by Sir Richard Livingstone, pp. 40-41.
11. *Ibid.*, I, 23, p. 46.
12. *Ibid.*, II, 65, p. 130.
13. *Ibid.*, V, 105, p. 270.
14. *Ibid.*, VI, 90, p. 325.
15. Herodotus, *History of the Persian Wars*, VII, p. 10.
16. Quoted in M. Cary and T. J. Haarhoff, *Life and Thought in the Greek and Roman World* (London: Methuen & Co., Ltd., 1951), p. 200.
17. "Apology," in *The Four Socratic Dialogues of Plato*, trans. by B. Jowett (Oxford: Clarendon Press, 1924), pp. 91-92.
18. "Phaedrus," 247; quoted in *The Greek World*, edited by Hugh Lloyd-Jones (Baltimore: Penguin Books, Inc., 1965), pp. 137-138.
19. Quoted in Cary and Haarhoff, p. 192.
20. Thucydides, I, 22, edited by Sir Richard Livingstone, pp. 44-45.
21. Trans. by Andrew Robert Burn, *The Lyric Age of Greece* (London: Edward Arnold (Publishers) Ltd. and New York: St. Martin's Press, 1960), pp. 166, 236.

22. *Ibid.*, p. 236.
23. From Agamemnon, trans. by Gilbert Murray in *Ten Greek Plays*, ed. by Lane Cooper (New York: Oxford University Press, 1929), p. 96. Reprinted by permission of George Allen & Unwin Ltd. for the Estate of Gilbert Murray.
24. Quoted in *The Cambridge Ancient History*, XI (Cambridge: The University Press, 1936), p. 696.
25. Moschus, *Idyl IX*, trans. by Ernest Myers in A. Lang, *Theocritus, Bion, and Moschus* (London: Macmillan and Co., Ltd., 1911), p. 210. Reprinted by permission of Macmillan London and Basingstoke.
26. G. Murray, *Hellenism and the Modern World* (Boston: Beacon Press, 1953), pp. 56-57.

CHAPTER 3: THE GRANDEUR THAT WAS ROME

1. Polybius, *Histories*, I, 10, trans. by Evelyn S. Shuckburgh (Bloomington: Indiana University Press, 1962), Vol. I, p. 10.
2. Livy, *Roman History*, XXXIII, 33, trans. by E. T. Sage in The Loeb Classical Library (Cambridge: Harvard University Press, 1945), Vol. IX, p. 367.
3. Plutarch's *Lives*, "Tiberius Gracchus," IX, 5, trans. by Bernadotte Perrin in The Loeb Classical Library (Cambridge: Harvard University Press, 1945), Vol. X, pp. 165, 167.
4. M. Hammond, *City-State and World State in Greek and Roman Political Theory Until Augustus* (Cambridge: Harvard University Press, 1951), p. 153.
5. Tacitus, *Annals*, XV, 44; trans. by Michael Grant (Baltimore: Penguin Books, Inc., 1959), p. 354.
6. Tertullian, *Concerning the Soul*, quoted in S. Katz, *The Decline of Rome and the Rise of Medieval Europe* (Ithaca, N.Y.: Cornell University Press, 1955), p. 7.
7. Virgil, *Aeneid*, VI, 847-853, in *Roman Civilization: Selected Readings*, II, ed. by Naphtali Lewis and Meyer Reinhold (New York: Columbia University Press, 1955), p. 23.
8. Aelius Aristides, *To Rome* (Oration XXVI), trans. by S. Levin (Glencoe, Ill.: The Free Press, 1950), p. 126.
9. R. C. Trevelyan, *Translations from Horace, Juvenal and Montaigne* (New York: Cambridge University Press, 1941), p. 129.
10. Quoted in Grant Showerman, *Century Readings in Ancient Classical Literature* (New York: The Century Co., 1925), p. 386.
11. Lucretius, *On the Nature of the Universe*, Book III, line 70, trans. by Ronald Latham (Baltimore: Penguin Books, Inc., 1951), p. 98.
12. Horace, *Odes*, III, 29 (in Part), translated by John Dryden.
13. From *Juvenal's Satires*, translated by William Gifford, revised by John Warrington. An Everyman's Library Edition (New York: E. P. Dutton & Co., Inc., 1954), p. 5. Reprinted by permission of the publishers, E. P. Dutton & Co., Inc. and J. M. Dent & Sons Ltd.
14. Lucretius, *On the Nature of Things*, Book III, lines 830 ff., translated by John Dryden.
15. Pliny, *Natural History*, II, xlv, 117-118; translated by H. Rackham, the Loeb Classical Library (Cambridge: Harvard University Press, 1938), Vol. I, pp. 259, 261.
16. Quoted in *Caesar and Christ* by Will Durant. (New York: Simon & Schuster, Inc., 1944), p. 506. Copyright 1944 by Will Durant, Copyright renewed © 1971 by Will Durant. Reprinted by permission of Simon & Schuster, Inc.

CHAPTER 4: THE ASIAN WAY OF LIFE

1. A. Coomaraswamy, *The Dance of Shiva* (Bombay: Asia Publishing House, 1948), p. 22.
2. W. T. de Bary, Jr., *et al.*, eds., *Sources of Indian Tradition* (New York: Columbia University Press, 1958), pp. 284-285. Reprinted by permission.
3. R. K. Mookerji, *Hindu Civilization* (London: Longmans, Green & Co., Ltd., 1936), p. 249.
4. N. Dutt, "Religion and Philosophy," in *The Age of Imperial Unity*, Vol. II of *The History and Culture of the Indian People*, ed. by R. C. Majumdar and A. D. Pusalker (Bombay: Bharatiya Vidya Bhavan, 1951), p. 371.
5. Cited in H. G. Rawlinson, *India: A Short Cultural History* (New York: D. Appleton-Century Co., Inc., 1938), pp. 51-52.
6. Quoted in H. G. Rawlinson, *Intercourse Between India and the Western World from the Earliest Times to the Fall of Rome* (New York: Cambridge University Press, 1926), p. 39.
7. R. K. Mookerji, "Asoka the Great," in *The Age of Imperial Unity*, Vol. II of *The History and Culture of the Indian People*, p. 92.
8. W. W. Tarn, *The Greeks in Bactria and India* (New York: Cambridge University Press, 1951), p. 181.
9. R. Grousset, *The Rise and Splendour of the Chinese Empire* (Berkeley and Los Angeles: University of California Press, 1953), p. 26.
10. W. T. de Bary, Jr., *et al.*, eds., *Sources of Chinese Tradition* (New York: Columbia University Press, 1960), pp. 63-64.
11. E. O. Reischauer and J. K. Fairbank, *East Asia: The Great Tradition* (Boston: Houghton Mifflin Co., 1958), p. 87.
12. See Hu Shih, "The Establishment of Confucianism as a State Religion During the Han Dynasty," *Journal of the North China Branch of the Royal Asiatic Society*, LX (Shanghai, 1929), pp. 34-35. See also J. K. Shyrock, *The Origin and Development of the State Cult of Confucius* (New York: Appleton-Century-Crofts, 1932).
13. See J. Needham, *History of Scientific Thought*, Vol. II of *Science and Civilisation in China* (New York: Cambridge University Press, 1956), p. 34.
14. Pliny, *Natural History*, trans. by H. Rackham (London: William Heinemann, Ltd., 1945), Book VI, I. 101, and Book XII, I. 84.
15. J. Needham, *Introductory Orientations*, Vol. I of *Science and Civilisation in China* (New York: Cambridge University Press, 1954), p. 239.

CHAPTER 5: THE CITY OF GOD

1. St. Jerome's *Commentary of Ezekiel*, I, Prologue.
2. E. Wilson, *The Scrolls from the Dead Sea* (New York: Oxford University Press, 1955), p. 60.
3. Frank M. Cross, Jr., *The Ancient Library of Qumran and Modern Biblical Studies*, rev. ed. (Garden City, N.Y.: Doubleday Anchor Books, 1961), p. 242.
4. John 18:33-38. From the *Good News Bible — New Testament*. Copyright © American Bible Society 1966, 1971, 1976, p. 258. Used by permission.
5. Acts 22:6-10. From the *Good News Bible — New Testament*, Copyright © American Bible Society 1966, 1971, 1976, p. 324. Used by permission.
6. Galatians 2:16, 3:28. From the *Good News Bible — New Testament*, pp. 421, 424.
7. Tertullian, *Apology*, Ch. 50, trans. by A. Souter (Cambridge: Cambridge University Press, 1917), p. 145.
8. Quoted in Henry Bettenson, ed., *Documents of the Christian Church* (London: Oxford University Press, 1943), p. 28.
9. *Ibid.*, p. 9.
10. Tacitus, *Germania*, Ch. 14, trans. by H. Mattingly. *Tacitus on Britain and Germany* (Harmondsworth: Penguin Books, Ltd., 1948), p. 112.
11. S. Katz, *The Decline of Rome and the Rise of Medieval Europe* (Ithaca, N.Y.: Cornell University Press, 1955), p. 7.
12. E. Gibbon, *The History of the Decline and Fall of the Roman Empire* (London: Methuen & Co., Ltd., 1896), Ch. XXXVIII, "General Observations on the Fall of the Roman Empire in the West."
13. A. E. R. Boak, *Manpower Shortage and the Fall of the Roman Empire in the West* (Ann Arbor: University of Michigan Press, 1955), p. 115.
14. Katz, p. 98.

CHAPTER 6: CITADEL AND CONQUEROR

1. Procopius, *History of the Wars*, Book I, trans. by H. B. Dewing (London: William Heinemann, Ltd., 1914), pp. 231, 233.
2. Geoffrey de Villehardouin, *The Conquest of Constantinople*, trans. by Sir Frank T. Marzials, Memoirs of the Crusades (New York: Everyman's Library, E. P. Dutton & Co., Inc., 1933), pp. 51, 65.
3. Quoted in J. F. C. Fuller, *A Military History of the Western World*, I (New York: Funk & Wagnalls, 1954), p. 522.
4. "The Book of the Prefect," trans. by A. E. R. Boak, *Journal of Economic and Business History*, I (1929), p. 600.

5. Quoted by C. Diehl, "Byzantine Art," in *Byzantium: Introduction to East Roman Civilization*, ed. by N. H. Baynes and H. St. L. B. Moss (New York: Oxford University Press, 1948), p. 166.
6. Procopius, *Buildings*, I, i, 33-34, trans. by H. B. Dewing (Cambridge: Harvard University Press, 1940), p. 17.
7. D. Talbot Rice, *Byzantine Art* (Harmondsworth: Penguin Books, Ltd., 1954), pp. 150-151.
8. Quoted in Alfred Guillaume, *Islam* (Harmondsworth: Penguin Books, Ltd., 1954), pp. 28-29.
9. See T. P. Hughes, *A Dictionary of Islam* (London: W. H. Allen and Co., 1885).
10. Quoted in E. H. Palmer, *Haroun Alraschid, Caliph of Bagdad* (London: Marcus Ward and Company, 1881), p. 76.
11. H. A. R. Gibb, "Literature," in *The Legacy of Islam*, ed. by T. W. Arnold and A. Guillaume (Oxford: Clarendon Press, 1931), p. 182.
12. *Rubáiyát of Omar Khayyám*, trans. by Edward Fitzgerald, Stanzas 12, 13, 71, 72.
13. Ibn Khaldun, *The Mugaddimah: An Introduction to History*, trans. by Franz Rosenthal, Vol. I (London: Routledge & Kegan Paul Ltd., 1958), p. 71.

CHAPTER 7: THE GUPTAS AND THE T'ANG: TWO GOLDEN AGES

1. Quoted in H. H. Gowen and J. W. Hall, *An Outline History of China* (New York: D. Appleton & Co., 1926), p. 117.
2. From *The Works of Li Po*, translated by Shigeyoshi Obata. Copyright, 1922, renewal, 1950, by E. P. Dutton & Co., and reprinted with their permission.
3. Quoted in Gowen and Hall, *An Outline History of China*, p. 127.
4. Obata, *The Works of Li Po*, p. 39.
5. Quoted in Gowen and Hall, *An Outline History of China*, p. 142.
6. K. S. Latourette, *The Chinese: Their History and Culture*, II (New York: The Macmillan Company, 1934), p. 264.
7. Quoted in I. Nitobé, *Bushido, the Soul of Japan* (Tokyo: Maruzen, 1935), p. 592.

CHAPTER 8: EUROPE'S SEARCH FOR STABILITY

1. Gregory of Tours, *History of the Franks*, II, 30; quoted in Eleanor S. Duckett, *The Gateway to the Middle Ages* (New York: The Macmillan Company, 1938), p. 231.
2. Quoted in C. Dawson, *The Making of Europe* (London: Sheed & Ward Ltd., 1932), p. 76.
3. Quoted in M. L. W. Laistner, *Thought and Letters in Western Europe, A.D. 500 to 900* (Ithaca, N.Y.: Cornell University Press, 1931), pp. 196-197.
4. *Ibid.*, p. 390.
5. *Piers the Plowman*, quoted in G. B. Adams, *Civilization During the Middle Ages* (New York: Charles Scribner's Sons, 1941), p. 222.
6. Quoted in E. M. Hulme, *History of the British People* (New York: Century Co., 1929), pp. 121-122.
7. Quoted in Sidney Painter, *French Chivalry: Chivalric Ideas and Practices in Medieval France* (Baltimore: Johns Hopkins Press, 1940), p. 169.

CHAPTER 9: THE WEST TAKES THE OFFENSIVE

1. Trans. by D. C. Munro, *Translations and Reprints from the Original Sources of European History*, Vol. I, No. 2 (Philadelphia: University of Pennsylvania Press, 1897), pp. 6-7.
2. Quoted in A. C. Krey, *The First Crusade* (Princeton: Princeton University Press, 1921), p. 261.
3. Quoted in R. H. C. Davis, *A History of Medieval Europe: From Constantine to Saint Louis* (London: Longmans, Green & Co., Ltd., 1957), p. 290.
4. E. P. Cheyney, *The Dawn of a New Era, 1250-1453* (New York: Harper & Bros., 1936), p. 132.

CHAPTER 10: NATIONS IN THE MAKING

1. Quoted in Dorothy Whitelock, *The Beginning of English Society* (Baltimore: Penguin Books, Inc., 1952), p. 66.
2. Quoted in E. P. Cheyney, *Readings in English History Drawn from the Original Sources* (Boston: Ginn and Co., 1908), p. 112.
3. D. C. Douglas and G. Greenaway, *English Historical Documents, 1042-1189* (New York: Oxford University Press, 1953), p. 200.
4. W. S. Churchill, *The Birth of Britain*, Vol. I of *A History of the English-Speaking Peoples* (New York: Dodd, Mead & Co., 1965), pp. 222-223.
5. Quoted in Churchill, I, p. 210.
6. Quoted in Cheyney, pp. 157-158.
7. Quoted in *ibid.*, pp. 183, 185.
8. Quoted in J. H. Robinson, *Readings in European History*, I (Boston: Ginn and Co., 1904), p. 202.
9. *Ibid.*, p. 204.
10. Jonathon F. Scott *et al.*, *Readings in Medieval History* (New York: F. S. Crofts and Company, 1933), pp. 464-465.
11. From *The Lay of the Cid*, trans. by Sheldon R. Rose and Leonard Bacon, pp. 25-26. Published in 1919 by The Regents of the University of California; reprinted by permission of the University of California Press.
12. R. H. C. Davis, *A History of Medieval Europe: From Constantine to Saint Louis* (London: Longmans, Green & Co., Ltd., 1957), p. 315.

CHAPTER 11: TO THE GLORY OF GOD

1. Quoted in R. H. C. Davis, *A History of Medieval Europe: From Constantine to Saint Louis* (London: Longmans, Green & Co., Ltd., 1957), p. 80.
2. Quoted in S. M. Brown, *Medieval Europe* (New York: Harcourt, Brace & Co., 1935), pp. 382-383.
3. Harry J. Carroll, Jr., *et al.*, *The Development of Civilization: A Documentary History of Politics, Society, and Thought*, I (Chicago: Scott, Foresman and Co., 1961), p. 304.
4. Henry Bettenson, ed., *Documents of the Christian Church* (London: Oxford University Press, 1943), p. 144.
5. Quoted in J. H. Robinson, *Readings in European History*, I (Boston: Ginn and Co., 1904), p. 283.
6. Quoted in S. R. Packard, *Europe and the Church Under Innocent III* (New York: Henry Holt & Co., 1927), p. 15.
7. Summerfield Baldwin, *The Organization of Medieval Christianity* (New York: Henry Holt & Co., 1929), p. 35.
8. From *The Portable Chaucer* edited by Theodore Morrison. Copyright 1949 by Theodore Morrison. Reprinted by permission of The Viking Press, Inc.
9. Quoted in J. Evans, *Life in Medieval France* (New York: Oxford University Press, 1925), p. 87.
10. From *A Catholic Dictionary*, 3rd ed., edited by Donald Attwater. Copyright 1931, 1949 and renewed 1959, 1977 by Macmillan Publishing Co., Inc. © Macmillan Publishing Co., Inc. 1958. Reprinted by permission of Macmillan Publishing Co., Inc. and Cassell & Collier Macmillan Ltd.
11. Luke 9:1-6. *Good News for Modern Man: The New Testament in Today's English* (New York: American Bible Society, 1966), p. 158.
12. Morrison, pp. 80-81.
13. Robert S. Lopez, *The Tenth Century: How Dark the Dark Ages?* (New York: Rinehart and Co., 1959), p. 1.
14. Quoted in Urban T. Holmes, Jr., "Transitions in European Education," in *Twelfth-Century Europe and the Foundations of Modern Society*, ed. by Marshall Clagett, Gaines Post, and Robert Reynolds (Madison: University of Wisconsin Press, 1961), p. 17.
15. *The Story of My Misfortunes: The Autobiography of Peter Abélard*, trans. by Henry Adams Bellows (Glencoe, Ill.: The Free Press, 1958), pp. 3, 10.
16. Quoted in *Introduction to Contemporary Civilization in the West: A Source Book*, I (New York: Columbia University Press, 1946), p. 85.
17. *An Encyclopedist of the Dark Ages: Isidore of Seville*, trans. by E. Brehaut (New York: Columbia University Press, 1912), pp. 218-219.
18. *The Art of Falconry . . . of Frederick II of Hohenstaufen*, trans. by Casey A. Wood and F. Marjorie Fyfe (Boston: Charles T. Branford Co., 1943), pp. 3-4.
19. Quoted in H. O. Taylor, *The Mediaeval Mind*, II (London: Macmillan & Co., Ltd., 1938), p. 524.

20. J. A. Symonds, *Wine, Women and Song* (New York: Oxford University Press, and London: Chatto & Windus Ltd., 1931), pp. 67-69.
21. From "Stabat Mater Dolorosa" quoted in Frederick B. Artz, *The Mind of the Middle Ages, A.D. 200-1500*, 2nd ed. (New York: Alfred A. Knopf, Inc., 1954), p. 332.
22. C. W. Hollister, *Medieval Europe: A Short History* (New York: John Wiley & Sons, Inc., 1964), p. 230.
23. Quoted in Amy Kelly, *Eleanor of Aquitaine and the Four Kings*, from F. J. M. Raynouard, *Choix des Poesies Originales des Troubadours*, Vol. III (Paris, 1816-1821), p. 86. Copyright 1952 by the President and Fellows of Harvard College. Reprinted by permission.
24. *L'Inferno*, Canto I, lines 1-3, trans. by Dorothy L. Sayers, *Dante, The Divine Comedy, I: Hell* (Harmondsworth: Penguin Books, Ltd., 1949), p. 71. Reprinted by permission of A. Watkins, Inc. as agents for the Estate of Dorothy L. Sayers and David Higham Associates Limited.
25. *Paradise*, Canto XXXIII, lines 121, 144 in Sayers, *Dante, The Divine Comedy*.
26. Geoffrey Chaucer, *Canterbury Tales*, trans. by J. U. Nicolson (New York: Crown Publishers, Inc., 1936), pp. 3-5.

CHAPTER 12: EUROPE IN TRANSITION
1. A. C. Flick, *Decline of the Medieval Church*, I (London: Kegan Paul, Trench, Trubner and Co., Ltd., 1930), p. 293.
2. R. H. Bainton, *The Reformation of the Sixteenth Century* (Boston: Beacon Press, 1952), p. 15.
3. Quoted in M. Cherniavsky, " 'Holy Russia': A Study in the History of an Idea," *The American Historical Review*, LXIII, No. 3 (April 1958), p. 625.
4. G. Barraclough, *History in a Changing World* (Oxford: Basil Blackwell, 1955), p. 134.

CHAPTER 13: MAN IS THE MEASURE
1. Quoted in J. Burckhardt, *The Civilization of the Renaissance in Italy*, trans. by S. G. C. Middlemore (London: George Allen & Unwin Ltd., 1921), p. 138.
2. William Shakespeare, *The Tempest*, Act V, Scene i.
3. Quoted in J. H. Randall, Jr., *The Making of the Modern Mind* (Boston: Houghton Mifflin Co., 1940), p. 213.
4. Quoted in F. B. Artz, *The Mind of the Middle Ages A.D., 200-1500*, 2nd ed. (New York: Alfred A. Knopf, Inc., 1954), p. 307.
5. *The Decameron of Giovanni Boccaccio*, trans. by Richard Aldington (New York: Garden City Publishing Co., 1949), p. 559.
6. F. B. Artz, *From the Renaissance to Romanticism: Trends in Style in Art, Literature, and Music, 1300-1830* (Chicago: University of Chicago Press, 1962), p. 102.
7. H. O. Taylor, *Thought and Expression in the Sixteenth Century*, I (New York: The Macmillan Company, 1920), p. 175.
8. Quoted in Randall, p. 118.
9. From the 1684 translation by Gilbert Burnet, in *Introduction to Contemporary Civilization in the West: A Source Book*, I (New York: Columbia University Press, 1946), p. 461.
10. *Ibid.*, p. 460.
11. Quoted in Taylor, pp. 328-329.
12. Montaigne, "Of the Education of Children," in *The Complete Works of Montaigne*, trans. by D. M. Frame (Stanford: Stanford University Press, 1957), p. 112.
13. *Ibid.*, p. 110.
14. J. van der Elst, *The Last Flowering of the Middle Ages* (New York: Doubleday & Co., Inc., 1946), p. 59.

CHAPTER 14: HERE I TAKE MY STAND
1. Quoted in R. H. Bainton, *Here I Stand: A Life of Martin Luther* (New York and Nashville: Abingdon-Cokesbury Press, 1950), p. 65. Copyright 1950.
2. *Ibid.*, pp. 66-67.
3. Quoted in R. H. Bainton, *The Reformation of the Sixteenth Century* (Boston: Beacon Press, 1952), p. 27.
4. Quoted in C. Hayes, *A Political and Cultural History of Modern Europe*, I (New York: The Macmillan Company, 1933), p. 154.
5. Quoted in H. Bettenson, ed., *Documents of the Christian Church* (London: Oxford University Press, 1943), p. 261 ff.

6. Quoted in P. Smith, *The Age of the Reformation* (New York: Henry Holt & Co., 1920), p. 69.
7. Quoted in George L. Mosse, *The Reformation*, 3rd ed. (New York: Holt, Rinehart and Winston, Inc., 1963), p. 31.
8. Quoted in Bainton, *The Reformation of the Sixteenth Century*, p. 58.
9. Quoted in Bettenson, pp. 282-283.
10. From *The Twelve Articles* in A. Schrier *et al.*, *Modern European Civilization: A Documentary History of Politics, Society, and Thought from the Renaissance to the Present* (Chicago: Scott, Foresman and Co., 1963), pp. 105-106.
11. Quoted in H. J. Grimm, *The Reformation Era, 1500-1650* (New York: The Macmillan Company, 1956), p. 175.
12. R. Fife, *The Revolt of Martin Luther* (New York: Columbia University Press, 1957), p. 693.
13. Bainton, *The Reformation of the Sixteenth Century*, p. 114.
14. Bettenson, p. 365.
15. Quoted in F. Eby and C. F. Arrowood, *The Development of Modern Education* (New York: Prentice-Hall, Inc., 1936), p. 91.
16. *Concerning Heretics . . . . An anonymous work attributed to Sebastian Castellio*, ed. by R. H. Bainton (New York: Columbia University Pess, 1935), pp. 122-123.
17. *Ibid.*, pp. 134-135.
18. Quoted in V. H. H. Green, *Luther and the Reformation* (New York: Capricorn Books, 1964), p. 141.
19. *Ibid.*, p. 142.
20. R. H. Tawney, *Religion and the Rise of Capitalism* (Baltimore: Penguin Books, Inc., 1947), p. 99.

CHAPTER 15: THE STRIFE OF STATES AND KINGS
1. Quoted in B. Reynolds, *Proponents of Limited Monarchy in Sixteenth Century France: Francis Holman and Jean Bodin* (New York: Columbia University Press, 1931), p. 182.
2. Quoted in G. Mattingly, *Renaissance Diplomacy* (London: Jonathan Cape, 1962), p. 239.
3. Quoted in M. Guizot, *The History of France from the Earliest Times to 1848*, II (New York: Thomas Y. Crowell & Co., n.d.), p. 428.
4. *Machiavelli: The Prince and Other Works*, trans. by A. H. Gilbert (Chicago: Packard and Co., 1941), p. 177 (Ch. 26).
5. *Ibid.*, p. 148 (Ch. 18).
6. *Ibid.*, p. 150 (Ch. 18).
7. *Ibid.*, p. 177 (Ch. 26).
8. Quoted in R. Ergang, *Europe from the Renaissance to Waterloo* (Boston: D. C. Heath & Co., 1954), p. 296.
9. *Ibid.*, p. 246.
10. Quoted in J. H. Elliott, *Imperial Spain, 1469-1716* (New York: St. Martin's Press, 1964), p. 282.
11. *Ibid.*, p. 283.
12. Quoted in P. Smith, *The Age of the Reformation* (New York: Henry Holt & Co., 1920), p. 215.
13. Quoted in Carl L. Becker, *Modern History* (Chicago: Silver Burdett Co., 1942), pp. 204, 205.
14. Carl J. Friedrich, *The Age of Baroque, 1610-1660* (New York: Harper & Bros., 1952), p. 129.
15. See "Grotius: *Law of War and Peace, Prolegomena*," in *The American Journal of International Law*, XXXV, No. 2 (April 1941), pp. 206, 217.

CHAPTER 16: OLD WORLDS BEYOND THE HORIZON
1. S. Lane-Poole, *Medieval India* (New York: G. P. Putnam's Sons, 1903), p. 271.

CHAPTER 17: BEFORE THE EUROPEAN IMPACT
1. Based on Joseph Greenberg, *The Languages of Africa*, 2nd ed., (Bloomington: Indiana University Press, 1966).
2. "Africa Speaks" in *The Horizon History of Africa* (New York: American Heritage, 1971), p. 80.
3. From David Killingray, *A Plague of Europeans* (New York: Penguin Books, Inc., 1973), p. 14.
4. *Ibid.*, p. 14.
5. Basil Davidson, *History of West Africa* (Garden City, N.Y.: Doubleday Anchor Books, 1966), p. 166.
6. Robert Rotberg, *A Political History of Tropical Africa* (New York: Harcourt Brace Jovanovich, 1965), p. 100.

7. *Ibid.*, pp. 85-86.
8. Killingray, p. 20.
9. See Phillip Curtin, *The Atlantic Slave Trade: A Census* (Madison: University of Wisconsin Press, 1969).
10. Cited in Basil Davidson, *The African Past: Chronicles* (Boston: Little, Brown and Company, 1965).

CHAPTER 18: SEEK OUT, DISCOVER, AND FIND
1. See H. Ingstad, "Vinland Ruins Prove Vikings Found the New World," *National Geographic Magazine*, Vol. 126, No. 5 (November 1964), pp. 708-734.
2. Quoted in Sir Percy Sykes, *A History of Exploration* (New York: Harper Torchbooks, Harper & Row, 1961), p. 108.
3. Quoted in H. H. Gowen, *An Outline History of Japan* (New York: D. Appleton Co., 1927), p. 255.
4. Quoted in H. Herring, *A History of Latin America*, 3rd ed. (New York: Alfred A. Knopf, Inc., 1968), p. 173.
5. Quoted in H. Robinson, *The Development of the British Empire* (Boston: Houghton Mifflin Co., 1922), p. 38.
6. Quoted in Sir George Clark, *The Seventeenth Century* (New York: Oxford University Press, 1961), p. 24.
7. Quoted in H. Heaton, *Economic History of Europe* (New York: Harper & Row, 1948), p. 315.
8. Quoted in *ibid.*, p. 238.
9. Quoted in J. B. Botsford, *English Society in the Eighteenth Century, As Influenced from Overseas* (New York: The Macmillan Company, 1924), p. 70.
10. Heaton, p. 239.
11. *Ibid.* (published in 1936), p. 363.

CHAPTER 19: NEW DIMENSIONS OF THE MIND
1. Quoted in *Introduction to Contemporary Civilization in the West*, I (New York: Columbia University Press, 1946), pp. 845-859.
2. F. Bacon, *The Works of Francis Bacon*, III, ed. by J. Spedding (London: Longman and Co., 1861), p. 156.
3. Quoted in J. H. Randall, Jr., *The Making of the Modern Mind*, rev. ed. (Boston: Houghton Mifflin Co., 1940), p. 221.
4. Quoted in *Introduction to Contemporary Civilization in the West*, I, p. 557.
5. Quoted in *Sir Isaac Newton's Mathematical Principles of Natural Philosophy and His System of the World*, ed. and trans. by F. Cajori (Berkeley: University of California Press, 1946).
6. H. Butterfield, *The Origins of Modern Science* (London: G. Bell and Sons, Ltd., 1949), p. 104.
7. See P. Hazard, *The European Mind: The Critical Years* (New Haven: Yale University Press, 1953).
8. A. Pope, "The Universal Prayer," in *The Poetical Works of Alexander Pope* (London: John James Chidley, 1846), p. 145.
9. W. L. Dorn, *Competition for Empire, 1740-1763* (New York: Harper & Bros., 1940), p. 181.
10. Quoted in F. E. Manuel, *The Age of Reason* (Ithaca, N.Y.: Cornell University Press, 1951), p. 39.
11. G. M. Trevelyan, *History of England* (London: Longmans, Green & Co., Ltd., 1937), p. 514.
12. Preserved Smith, *Origins of Modern Culture, 1543-1687* (New York: P. F. Collier, Inc., 1962), p. 484.
13. A. Pope, "Epistle to Dr. Arbuthnot," in *The Literature of England*, I, 5th ed., ed. by G. K. Anderson and W. E. Buckler (Glenview, Ill.: Scott, Foresman and Co., 1958), p. 1580.
14. A. Pope, "An Essay on Man," in *The Literature of England*, I, p. 1568.

CHAPTER 20: L'ÉTAT, C'EST MOI
1. Quoted in J. H. Robinson, *Readings in European History*, II (Boston: Ginn and Co., 1906), pp. 273-275.
2. Quoted in W. G. Crane *et al.*, *Twelve Hundred Years: The Literature of England*, I (New York: Stackpole and Heck, Inc., 1948), p. 572.
3. Quoted in A. F. Tyler, *The Modern World* (New York: Farrar and Rinehart, 1939), p. 186.
4. *Encyclopaedia Britannica*, VII, 1947 ed., p. 16.
5. Sir Ernest Barker *et al.*, *The European Inheritance*, II (London: Clarendon Press, 1954), p. 144.
6. Quoted in E. P. Cheyney, *Readings in English History Drawn from the Original Sources* (Boston: Ginn and Co., 1908), p. 426.
7. Quoted in *ibid.*, p. 503.
8. Quoted in P. Smith, *A History of Modern Culture*, I (London: George Routledge and Sons, Ltd., 1930), p. 226.
9. John Milton, "Areopagitica," in *The Literature of England*, I, 5th ed., ed. by G. K. Anderson and W. E. Buckler (Glenview, Ill.: Scott, Foresman and Co., 1966), p. 1182.
10. Quoted in G. B. Adams, *Constitutional History of England* (New York: Henry Holt & Co., 1934), p. 406.
11. Quoted in R. Ergang, *The Potsdam Führer, Frederick William I* (New York: Columbia University Press, 1941), p. 7.
12. W. L. Dorn, *Competition for Empire, 1740-1763* (New York: Harper & Bros., 1940), p. 9.
13. Quoted in *ibid.*, p. 139.
14. W. P. Hall and R. G. Albion, *A History of England and the British Empire, 1789-1914* (Boston: Ginn and Co., 1946), p. 453.
15. Quoted in Dorn, p. 314.
16. Quoted in P. Gaxotte, *Frederick the Great* (London: G. Bell & Sons, Ltd., 1941), p. 357.
17. Quoted in H. Robinson, *The Development of the British Empire* (Boston: Houghton Mifflin Co., 1922), p. 96.

CHAPTER 21: THE RIGHTS OF MAN
1. Thomas Mun, "England's Treasure by Foreign Trade" (1664), in *Introduction to Contemporary Civilization in the West: A Source Book*, I (New York: Columbia University Press, 1946), p. 641.
2. Adam Smith, *An Inquiry into the Nature and Causes of the Wealth of Nations*, Modern Library Edition (New York: The Macmillan Company, 1937), pp. 14, 421.
3. Quoted in G. R. Havens, *The Age of Ideas* (New York: Henry Holt & Co., 1955), pp. 105-106.
4. Quoted in J. E. Gillespie, *A History of Geographical Discovery, 1400-1800* (New York: Henry Holt & Co., 1933), p. 99.
5. J. J. Rousseau, *The Social Contract*, Book III, Chapter XVIII.
6. Quoted in J. H. Robinson and C. A. Beard, *Readings in Modern European History*, I (Boston: Ginn and Co., 1908), pp. 202-205.
7. Quoted in G. P. Gooch, *Frederick the Great; the Ruler, the Writer, the Man* (New York: Alfred A. Knopf, Inc., 1947), p. 109.
8. Quoted in C. Rossiter, *The First American Revolution* (New York: Harcourt, Brace & Co., 1956), prefatory note.
9. L. M. Larson, *History of England and the British Commonwealth* (New York: Henry Holt and Co., 1924), p. 529.
10. C. J. H. Hayes, *A Political and Cultural History of Modern Europe*, I (New York: The Macmillan Company, 1932), p. 614.
11. "The Declaration of the Rights of Man," in *The World in Literature*, III, rev. ed., ed. by R. Warnock and G. K. Anderson (Glenview, Ill.: Scott, Foresman and Co., 1967), pp. 288-289.
12. Quoted in J. E. Gillespie, *A History of Europe, 1500-1815* (New York: Alfred A. Knopf, Inc., 1928), p. 529.
13. Quoted in L. Madelin, *The French Revolution* (London: William Heinemann, Ltd., 1916), p. 323.
14. W. Wordsworth, "The Prelude; or, Growth of a Poet's Mind," Book XI, lines 108-112.
15. E. Burke, "Reflections on the Revolution in France," in *The Works of the Right Honorable Edmund Burke*, II (London: G. Bell & Sons, Ltd., 1886), p. 284.
16. Quoted in J. H. Randall, Jr., *The Making of the Modern Mind* (Boston: Houghton Mifflin Co., 1940), p. 433.
17. Quoted in Gillespie, p. 537.
18. Quoted in J. H. Rose, *The Life of Napoleon*, I (New York: The Macmillan Company, 1902), p. 264.
19. H. A. L. Fisher, *A History of Europe*, III (Boston: Houghton Mifflin Co., 1936; London: Eyre and Spottiswoode, Ltd.), p. 891.
20. George Rudé, *Revolutionary Europe, 1783-1815* (New York: Harper Torchbooks, 1966), p. 290.

CHAPTER 22: THE FOUNDATIONS FOR WORLD DOMINANCE
1. David S. Landes, *The Unbound Prometheus: Technological Change and Industrial Development in Western Europe from 1750 to the Present* (Cambridge: Cambridge University Press, 1969), p. 357.

2. I. Vyshnegradsky, quoted in William L. Blackwell, *The Industrialization of Russia: An Historical Perspective* (New York: Thomas Y. Crowell Company, 1970), p. 24.
3. Fernand Braudel, *Capitalism and Material Life: 1400-1800* (New York: Harper & Row, 1975), p. 11. William L. Langer, "Checks on Population Growth: 1750-1850," *Scientific American*, Vol. 226, No. 2, 1972, pp. 92-99.
4. Thomas R. Malthus, "An Essay on Population," in *Introduction to Contemporary Civilization in the West*, II (New York: Columbia University Press, 1955), p. 196.
5. Roger Price, *The Economic Modernisation of France* (New York-Toronto: John Wiley & Sons, 1975), p. ii.
6. Eugen Weber, *A Modern History of Europe* (New York: W. W. Norton & Company, 1971), p. 988.
7. J. D. Chambers, "Enclosures and the Labour Supply in the Industrial Revolution," *Economic History Review*, second series, V, 1953, pp. 318-343, as cited by Landes, p. 115.
8. Landes, p. 98.
9. Sidney Pollard, *European Economic Integration: 1815-1970* (New York: Harcourt Brace Jovanovich, Inc., 1974), pp. 56-62.
10. Quoted in F. A. Ogg and W. R. Sharp, *Economic Development of Europe* (New York: The Macmillan Company, 1926), p. 551.
11. Heinz Gollwitzer, *Europe in the Age of Imperialism: 1880-1914* (New York: Harcourt Brace Jovanovich, Inc., 1969), p. 20.
12. Charles Dickens, *Hard Times* (London: Thomas Nelson and Sons, Ltd., n.d.), p. 26.
13. J. H. Plumb, "The Victorians Unbuttoned," *Horizon*, Vol. 11, No. 4, 1969, pp. 16-25.
14. Landes, p. 233.
15. Pollard, pp. 74-78.

CHAPTER 23: CULTURAL RESPONSES TO THE CENTURY OF CHANGE
1. D. S. Mirsky, *A History of Russian Literature* (New York: Vintage Books, 1958), p. 102.
2. David Thomson, *England in the Nineteenth Century, 1815-1914* (Harmondsworth: Penguin Books, Ltd., 1950), p. 101.
3. Robert Schnerb, "Le XIXᵉ Siècle: L'Apogée de L'Expansion Européenne (1815-1914)," *Histoire Générale des Civilisations*, VI (Paris: Presses Universitaires de France, 1955), pp. 468-469.

CHAPTER 24: NEW IDEAS IN THE CHANGING EUROPEAN WORLD
1. W. Wordsworth, "Composed in the Valley near Dover, on the Day of Landing," in *English Poetry and Prose of the Romantic Movement*, ed. by G. B. Woods (Glenview, Ill.: Scott, Foresman and Co., 1950), p. 313.
2. W. Godwin, "Political Justice," in S. Hook, *Marx and the Marxists: The Ambiguous Legacy* (Princeton: D. Van Nostrand Co. Inc., 1955), p. 28.
3. Quoted in E. R. A. Seligman, ed., *Encyclopedia of the Social Sciences*, XIII (New York: The Macmillan Company, 1935), p. 510a.
4. Quoted in H. J. Laski, *Communist Manifesto: Socialist Landmark* (London: George Allen & Unwin, Ltd., 1948), p. 168.
5. C. Darwin, "The Origin of Species," in *Introduction to Contemporary Civilization in the West*, II (New York: Columbia University Press, 1955), pp. 453-454.

CHAPTER 25: POLITICAL RESPONSES TO CHANGING CONDITIONS: THE HALF CENTURY AFTER WATERLOO
1. Quoted in C. D. Hazen, *Europe Since 1815* (New York: Henry Holt and Co., 1910), p. 121.
2. Quoted in J. S. Schapiro, *Modern and Contemporary European History, 1815-1940* (Boston: Houghton Mifflin Company, 1940), p. 222.
3. Quoted in K. S. Pinson, *Modern Germany* (New York: The Macmillan Company, 1954), p. 116.
4. L. C. B. Seaman, *From Vienna to Versailles* (New York: Harper & Row, 1963), pp. 96-129.
5. G. N. Young, ed., *Selected Speeches by Lord Macaulay* (London: Oxford University Press, 1935), pp. 18-19.
6. M. T. Florinsky, *Russia: A History and Interpretation*, II (New York: The Macmillan Company, 1953), pp. 809-810.

CHAPTER 26: THE GROWTH AND DOMINANCE OF STATE POWER
1. Charles Tilly, "Reflections on the History of European State-Making," in *The Formation of National States in Western Europe*, ed. by Charles Tilly (Princeton: Princeton University Press, 1975), p. 15.
2. Edward H. Reisner, *Nationalism and Education Since 1789* (New York: The Macmillan Company, 1923), pp. 35, 145, and 211.
3. Robert Schnerb, "Le XIXᵉ Siècle: L'Apogée de L'Expansion Européenne (1815-1914)," *Histoire Générale des Civilisations*, VI (Paris: Presses Universitaires de France, 1955), p. 235.
4. Gabriel Ardant, "Financial Policy and Economic Infrastructure of Modern States and Nations," in *The Formation of National States in Western Europe* (Princeton: Princeton University Press, 1975), pp. 219-222.
5. J. E. Gillespie, *Europe in Perspective* (New York: Harcourt Brace Jovanovich, Inc., 1942), p. 253.
6. Quoted in F. Owen, *Tempestuous Journey: Lloyd George, His Life and Times* (London: Hutchinson & Co., Ltd., 1954), p. 186.
7. Quoted in C. G. Robinson, *Bismarck* (London: Constable and Co., Ltd., 1918), p. 472.
8. Quoted in Barbara Tuchman, *The Guns of August* (New York: Dell Publishing Co., Inc., 1962, p. 151.
9. Quoted in Basil Dmytryshyn, ed., *Imperial Russia: A Source Book, 1700-1917* (New York: Holt, Rinehart & Winston, Inc., 1967), p. 241.

CHAPTER 27: NEW EUROPES OVERSEAS
1. Quoted in J. Quincy, *Speeches Delivered in the Congress of the United States* (Boston: Little, Brown and Co, 1874).
2. Quoted in C. G. Sellers, Jr., *Jacksonian Democracy* (Washington, D.C.: Service Center for Teachers of History, 1958), p. 1.
3. C. Van Doren, ed., *The Literary Works of Abraham Lincoln* (New York: The Limited Editions Club, Inc., 1942), p. 65.
4. Quoted in F. R. Dulles, *America's Rise to World Power* (New York: Harper & Row, 1955), p. 4.
5. Quoted in *ibid.*, pp. 6-7.
6. H. S. Commager, *Documents of American History* (New York: Appleton-Century-Crofts, Inc., 1958), p. 170.
7. Quoted in H. C. Hockett and A. M. Schlesinger, *Land of the Free* (New York: The Macmillan Company, 1944), p. 482.
8. M. Ugarte, *The Destiny of a Continent* (New York: Alfred A. Knopf, Inc., 1925), p. 288.
9. Quoted in J. L. Mecham, "Conflicting Ideals of Pan-Americanism," *Current History*, XXXIII, No. 3 (December 1930), p. 402.
10. F. D. Scott, *Emigration and Immigration* (New York: The Macmillan Company, for the American Historical Association, 1963), p. 1.
11. S. E. Morison, *The Oxford History of the American People* (London: Oxford University Press, 1965), p. 793.
12. P. D. Curtin, *African History* (New York: The Macmillan Company, for the American Historical Association, 1964), p. 40.
13. Hubert Herring, *History of Latin America* (New York: Alfred A. Knopf, Inc.), p. 97.

CHAPTER 28: CULTURAL CLASHES OF IMPERIALISM: THE ISLAMIC WORLD AND AFRICA
1. Robert Schnerb, "Le XIXᵉ Siècle: L'Apogée de L'Expansion Européenne (1815-1914)," *Histoire Générale des Civilisations*, VI (Paris: Presses Universitaires de France, 1955), pp. 347-352.
2. L. S. Stavrianos, *The Balkans Since 1453* (New York: Holt, Rinehart & Winston, 1961), pp. 135-136.
3. Bernard Lewis, *The Emergence of Modern Turkey* (Oxford: Oxford University Press, 1968), pp. 1-17.
4. *Ibid.*, pp. 41-64.
5. Cited in Peter Fleming, *Bayonets to Lhasa* (New York: Harper & Row, 1961), p. 21.
6. Quoted in N. D. Harris, *Europe and the East* (Boston: Houghton Mifflin Company, 1926), p. 285.
7. A. Adu Boahen, "The Coming of the Europeans," *The Horizon History of Africa*, II (New York: American Heritage Publishing Co., Inc., 1971), pp. 305-327.

CHAPTER 29: EUROPEAN ADVANCE AND ASIAN ADAPTATION

1. Robert Schnerb, "Le XIXᵉ Siècle: L'Apogée de L'Expansion Européenne (1815-1914)," *Histoire Générale des Civilisations*, VI (Paris: Presses Universitaries de France, 1955), pp. 399-400.
2. P. Spear, *India, Pakistan, and the West* (London: Oxford University Press, 1958), pp. 109-177.
3. Quoted in T. A. Bailey, *The American Pageant* (Lexington, Mass.: D. C. Heath & Co., 1956), p. 630.
4. K. S. Latourette, *A Short History of the Far East* (New York: The Macmillan Company, 1947), p. 184.
5. Quoted in F. H. Michael and G. E. Taylor, *The Far East in the Modern World* (New York: Holt, Rinehart & Winston, 1956), p. 122.
6. Li Chien-nung, *The Political History of China, 1840-1928*, trans. by Sau-yu Teng and J. Ingalls (Princeton: D. Van Nostrand Co., Inc., 1956), p. 29.
7. Michael and Taylor, p. 183.
8. Quoted in Ch'u Chai and Winberg Chai, *The Changing Society of China* (New York: Mentor Books, 1962), p. 189.
9. Michael and Taylor, pp. 253-256.

CHAPTER 30: THE WANING OF THE EUROPEAN PRIMACY: WORLD WAR I

1. L. Fischer, *The Life of Lenin* (New York: Harper & Row, 1964), pp. 32-34.
2. Quoted in R. N. Carew Hunt, *The Theory and Practice of Communism* (London: Geoffrey Bles, 1950), p. 72.
3. Quoted by C. J. H. Hayes, *A Political and Cultural History of Modern Europe*, II (New York: The Macmillan Company, 1939), p. 572.
4. Viscount Grey of Fallodon, *Twenty-Five Years*, II (New York: Frederick A. Stokes Co., 1925), p. 20.
5. *The New Cambridge Modern History*, XII, 2nd ed., 1968, p. 191.
6. Quoted in F. P. Chambers, *The War Behind the War, 1914-1918* (New York: Harcourt Brace Jovanovich, Inc.), p. 473.
7. From "The Soldier," reprinted by permission of Dodd, Mead, & Company, Inc. from *The Collected Poems of Rupert Brooke*. Copyright 1915 by Dodd, Mead, & Company. Copyright renewed 1943 by Edward Marsh. Published in Canada by McClelland and Stewart Limited and in England by Sidgwick & Jackson Limited.
8. From "Anthem for Doomed Youth" by Wilfred Owen in *Collected Poems* (British title, *The Collected Poems of Wilfred Owen*: Edited by C. Day Lewis). Copyright Chatto & Windus, Ltd., 1946 © 1963. Reprinted by permission of New Directions Publishing Corporation, The Owen Estate, and Chatto & Windus, Ltd.
9. D. W. Treadgold, *Twentieth Century Russia* (Chicago: Rand McNally & Company, 1951), p. 154.
10. E. M. Remarque, *The Road Back*, trans. by A. W. Wheen (Boston: Little, Brown and Company, 1931), p. 25.

CHAPTER 31: NEW VISTAS AND OMINOUS FEARS

1. Quoted in L. M. Hacker and B. B. Kendrick, *The United States Since 1865* (New York: F. S. Crofts and Co., 1939), p. 520.
2. Quoted in F. P. Walters, *A History of the League of Nations*, I (London: Oxford University Press, 1952), p. 48.
3. Quoted in R. J. Sontag, *European Diplomatic History, 1871-1932* (New York: The Century Co., 1933), p. 275.
4. Quoted by E. Achorn, *European Civilization and Politics Since 1815* (New York: Harcourt, Brace & Co., 1938), p. 470.
5. Quoted in Sontag, p. 392.
6. J. M. Keynes, *The Economic Consequences of the Peace* (London: Macmillan and Co. Ltd., 1924), p. 211.
7. G. F. Kennan, *The Decision to Intervene* (Princeton: Princeton University Press, 1958), p. 471.
8. Quoted in A. G. Nazour, *Russia Past and Present* (New York: Van Nostrand Reinhold Co., 1951), p. 576.
9. Quoted in Walters, I, p. 213.
10. Sir Bernard Pares, "Rasputin and the Empress, Authors of the Russian Collapse," *Foreign Affairs*, VI, No. I (October 1927), p. 140.

11. W. H. Chamberlain, *The Russian Revolution, 1917-1921*, I (New York: The Macmillan Company, 1952), p. 73.
12. *The New Cambridge Modern History*, XII, 1960, p. 9.
13. E. Crankshaw, cited in "The Coup That Changed the World," *The New York Times Magazine* (February 19, 1967), p. 96.
14. Karl Lowenstein, in *Governments of Continental Europe*, ed. by J. T. Shotwell (New York: The Macmillan Company, 1940), p. 473.
15. Keynes, pp. 278-279.
16. Quoted in W. C. Langsam, *The World Since 1914* (New York: The Macmillan Company, 1943), p. 685.

CHAPTER 32: AFRICA AND ASIA ASTIR

1. W. E. B. Du Bois, *The World and Africa* (New York: Viking Press, 1947), pp. 148-163.
2. J. S. Furnivall, *Netherlands India* (Cambridge: Cambridge University Press, 1939), p. 446.
3. *African Liberator* (c. 1935). By permission of T. Walter Wallbank.
4. Blanche E. C. Dugdale, *Arthur James Balfour* (New York: G. P. Putnam's Sons, 1937), p. 325.
5. Quoted in H. Kohn, *Nationalism and Imperialism in the Hither East* (London: G. Routledge and Sons, Ltd., 1932), pp. 132-133.
6. J. Nehru, *Toward Freedom* (New York: John Day Co., 1942), p. 353.
7. E. O. Reischauer, J. K. Fairbank, and A. M. Craig, *East Asia, the Modern Transformation* (Boston: Houghton Mifflin Co., 1965), p. 751.
8. Compare F. W. Price and C. P. Barry, eds., *Collier's Encyclopedia*, V (New York: P. F. Collier and Son Corp., 1950), p. 180.

CHAPTER 33: THE TRAGIC DECADE AND GLOBAL CONFLICT

1. Quoted in F. P. Chambers, C. P. Grant, C. C. Bayley, *This Age of Conflict* (New York: Harcourt, Brace & Co., 1943), p. 495.
2. J. K. Galbraith, *The Great Crash, 1929* (Boston: Houghton Mifflin Co., 1955), p. 104.
3. *Ibid.*, Chapter X.
4. John H. Williams, "Economic Lessons of Two World Wars," in *An Age of Controversy*, ed. by G. Wright and A. Mejia, Jr. (New York: Dodd, Mead and Co., 1966), p. 239.
5. Quoted in A. Bullock, *Hitler: A Study in Tyranny* (London: Odhams Press, Ltd., 1952), pp. 642-643.
6. R. G. L. Waite, ed., *Hitler and Nazi Germany* (New York: Holt, Rinehart & Winston, Inc., 1965), p. 4.
7. Quoted in W. C. Langsam, *Major European and Asiatic Developments Since 1935* (New York: The Macmillan Company, 1938), p. 15.
8. W. C. Langsam, *The World Since 1914* (New York: The Macmillan Company, 1948), p. 214.
9. René Albrecht-Carrié, *France, Europe and the Two World Wars* (New York: Harper & Row, 1961), p. 56
10. W. S. Churchill, *Blood, Sweat and Tears* (New York: G. P. Putnam's Sons, 1941), p. 66.
11. F. D. Roosevelt, "Address at Chicago, October 5, 1937," in *The Literature of the United States*, II, ed. by W. Blair, T. Hornberger, and R. Stewart (Chicago: Scott, Foresman and Co., 1953), pp. 831-832.
12. Quoted in W. L. Langer and S. E. Gleason, *The Challenge to Isolation* (New York: Harper & Row, 1952), p. 138.
13. Quoted in *ibid.*, p. 181.
14. Quoted in *ibid.*, p. 200.
15. S. E. Ayling, *Portraits of Power* (New York: Barnes & Noble, Inc., 1963), p. 159.
16. Churchill, p. 297.

CHAPTER 34: WAR'S AFTERMATH: THE WEST AND THE COLD WAR

1. Arthur J. May, *Europe Since 1939* (New York: Holt, Rinehart & Winston, 1966), p. 157.
2. Marshall Dill, Jr., *Germany: A Modern History* (Ann Arbor: University of Michigan Press, 1961), p. 424.

3. Max Radin, "Justice at Nuremberg," *Foreign Affairs* (April 1946), p. 371.
4. Winston Churchill, *Triumph and Tragedy* (Boston: Houghton Mifflin Co., 1953), p. 497.
5. Thomas A. Bailey, *America Faces Russia* (Ithaca, N.Y.: Cornell University Press, 1950), p. 334.
6. Cited in Paul Y. Hammond, *Cold War and Détente* (New York: Harcourt Brace Jovanovich, 1975), p. 15.
7. Michael R. Hodges, "Britain Tomorrow: Business as Usual," *Current History* (March 1975), p. 138.
8. Charles de Gaulle, *The Call to Honor* (New York: Viking Press, 1955), p. 4.
9. *Ibid.*, p. 33.
10. Alexander Werth, *France, 1940-1955* (New York: Holt, Rinehart & Winston, 1956), p. 218.
11. De Gaulle, p. 3.
12. John Gunther, *Inside Europe Today* (New York: Harper & Row, 1961), p. 19.
13. Roberto de Oliveira Campos, "Gringos and Generals," *Interplay: The Magazine of International Affairs*, Vol. 3, No. 2 (August-September 1969), p. 5.

CHAPTER 35: PEOPLE AND POLITICS: FROM MOSCOW TO PEKING TO TOKYO

1. Quoted in *Britannica Yearbook* (Chicago: Encyclopaedia Britannica, 1947).
2. Anatole G. Mazour, *Russia Past and Present* (New York: Van Nostrand Reinhold Co., 1951), p. 409.
3. Quoted in *ibid.*, pp. 163-164.
4. Richard Crosman, ed., *The God That Failed* (Plainview, N.Y.: Books for Libraries, 1959), p. 163.
5. See Harry Schwartz, *Russia's Soviet Economy* (London: Jonathan Cape, 1951), pp. 457-468.
6. *Ibid.*, p. 536.
7. Hugh Seton-Watson, *From Lenin to Khrushchev* (New York: Praeger Publishers, Inc., 1960), p. 246.
8. Bertram D. Wolfe, "The Struggle for the Soviet Succession," *Foreign Affairs* (July 1953), p. 548.
9. Victor Baras, "Contemporary Soviet Society," *Current History* (October 1974), p. 183.
10. Edwin O Reischauer, *Japan: The Story of a Nation* (New York: Alfred A. Knopf, Inc., 1974), p. 251.
11. John Paton Davies, "America and East Asia," *Foreign Affairs* (January 1977), p. 394.

CHAPTER 36: NEW NATIONS IN THE CONTEMPORARY WORLD

1. From Prime Minister Harold Macmillan's speech, February 3, 1960, *Vital Speeches* (March 1, 1960).
2. Quoted in Earl Louis Mountbatten, *Time Only to Look Forward* (London: Nicholas Kaye, 1949), p. 74.
3. Elspeth Huxley, "Africa's First Loyalty," *The New York Times Magazine* (September 18, 1960), p. 4.
4. Quoted from address of Kenneth Kaunda in *Africa Report* (December 1967), p. 33.
5. Harry R. Rudin, "Political Rivalry in the Congo," *Current History* (March 1966), p. 179.
6. Selig Harrison, *India: The Most Dangerous Decades* (Princeton: Princeton University Press, 1960), p. 4.
7. Victor T. Le Vine, "Independent Africa in Trouble," *Africa Report* (December 1967), p. 19.
8. William A. Hance, "The Race Between Population and Resources," *Africa Report* (January 1968), p. 11.
9. Walter F. Mondale, "Beyond Détente: Toward International Economic Security," *Foreign Affairs* (October 1974), p. 5.
10. Denis Warner, "Vietnam," *Atlantic* (August 1969), p. 22.

CHAPTER 37: SOCIETY IN TRANSFORMATION

1. J. Ortega y Gasset, *The Revolt of the Masses* (New York: W. W. Norton & Co., Inc., 1961), pp. 27-28.
2. Geoffrey Barraclough, *An Introduction to Contemporary History* (New York: Penguin Books, Inc., 1975), p. 42.
3. See *Energy and Power* [*Scientific American*] (San Francisco: W. H. Freeman, 1971); especially W. B. Kemp, "The Flow of Energy in a Hunting Society"; R. A. Rappaport, "The Flow of

Energy in an Agricultural Society"; and E. Cook, "The Flow of Energy in an Industrial Society."
4. John Pfeiffer, *The Cell* [*Life Science Library*] (New York: Time-Life Books, 1964), p. 61.
5. Anatol Rappoport, "Foreword," in W. Buckley, ed., *Modern Systems Research for the Behavioral Scientist* (Chicago: Aldine Publishing Co., 1968), p. xix.
6. Norbert Wiener, *The Human Use of Human Beings: Cybernetics and Society*, 2nd rev. ed. (Garden City, N.Y.: Doubleday Anchor Books, 1954), p. 153.
7. S. Giedion, *Space, Time and Architecture* (Boston: Harvard University Press, 1962), pp. 431-432.
8. Barraclough, p. 201.
9. Bertolt Brecht, "The Popular and the Realistic," in D. Craig, ed., *Marxists of Literature* (Harmondsworth, England: Penguin Books Ltd., 1975), p. 423.
10. Joseph Goebbels, from a 1926 speech, "Lenin or Hitler?" in Z. A. B. Zeman, *Nazi Propaganda* (London: Oxford University Press, 1973), p. 206.
11. Christopher Lasch, "The Narcissist Society." *The New York Review of Books* (September 30, 1976), p. 5.
12. Quoted by Colin Legum, *Pan Africanism* (Westport, Conn.: Greenwood Press, 1962), p. 93. From a translation of Césaire's *Cahier d'un Retour au Pays Natal*.
13. Julius K. Nyerere, *Freedom and Socialism* (Dar es Salaam: Oxford University Press, 1968), p. 3.
14. Quoted in *China Reconstructs* (September 1976), p. 13.
15. F. S. C. Northrop, *The Meeting of East and West* (New York: Collier Books, 1966); see especially Chapter 2, "The Rich Cultures of Mexico."

EPILOGUE: ALTERNATIVES FOR THE FUTURE

1. Barbara Ward and Rene Dubos, *Only One Earth: The Care and Maintenance of a Small Planet* (New York: Penguin Books, Inc., 1973), p. 47.
2. Barbara Ward, *The Home of Man* (New York: W. W. Norton & Co., Inc., 1976), p. 9.
3. *Ibid.*, p. 270.
4. *New York Times Service*, reprinted in the *Kingston Whig-Standard* (January 20, 1974, pp. 1-2). See also the proposals of J. C. Kapur: *India in the Year 2000* (New Delhi: India International Centre, 1975), vii and 54 pp.
5. D. H. Meadows and D. L. Meadows, *The Limits to Growth* (New York: Universe Books, 1974); see also M. Mesarovic and E. Pestel, *Mankind at the Turning Point* [Second Report to the Club of Rome] (New York: E. P. Dutton & Co., Inc., 1974).
6. Alastair M. Taylor, "Some Political Implications of the Forrester World System Model," in Ervin Laszlo, ed., *The World System* (New York: George Braziller, Inc., 1973), p. 35.
7. R. Buckminster Fuller, *Utopia or Oblivion: The Prospects for Humanity* (New York: Penguin Books, Inc., 1972); see Chapter 1 and pp. 377-378.
8. For more on this thesis, see E. F. Schumacher, *Small Is Beautiful: Economics as if People Mattered* (New York: Harper & Row, 1973).
9. See Richard A. Falk, *A Study of Future Worlds* (New York: Free Press, 1975).
10. Ervin Laszlo et al., *Goals for Mankind: A Report to the Club of Rome on New Horizons of Global Community* (New York: E. P. Dutton & Co., Inc., 1977).
11. Inga Thorsson, "Memorandum Transmitted to UNITAR," *Future Studies in Sweden* (Stockholm: Secretariat for Future Studies, October 1974).
12. D. S. Elgin, D. C. MacMichael, P. Schwartz, *Alternative Futures for Environmental Policy Planning: 1975-2000.* (Prepared by the Stanford Research Institute, Center for the Study of Social Policy, for the Environmental Protection Agency, Washington, D.C., October 1975), p. 10.
13. Quoted in Laszlo.

List of Illustrations

LIST OF CHARTS AND DRAWINGS

LIST OF MAPS

Chronological Table 1

NEAR EAST AND EGYPT	INDIA AND CHINA

Neolithic revolution c. 7000

Sumerian city-states emerge c. 3500

B.C. 3000 Menes unites Egypt c. 3100

Old Sumerian period c. 2800-2370
Old Kingdom in Egypt c. 2700-2200

Akkadian empire c. 2370-2230
Neo-Sumerian period c. 2113-2006
Middle Kingdom in Egypt c. 2050-1800   Indus valley civilization c. 2300-1800—capitals at Mohenjo-Daro and
2000 Hittites enter Asia Minor c. 2000   Harappa

Hammurabi rules lower Mesopotamia 1760
Hittites sack Babylon 1595
New Kingdom or Empire in Egypt c. 1570-1090
1500 Thutmose III c. 1490-1436—the "Napoleon of Egypt"

Invasion of India by Aryans from Black and Caspian seas c. 1500
Vedic Age c. 1500-900—beginning of three pillars of Indian society; auton-
Hittite empire c. 1450-1200   omous village, caste system, joint-family
Akhenaton c. 1369-1353   *Vedas*—oldest Sanskrit literature
Era of small states 1200-700   Shang dynasty 1500-1027—China's first civilization
Phoenician and Aramean traders; the alphabet

Chou dynasty 1027-256—China's "classical age"—Mandate of Heaven
promulgated

Period of Decadence in Egypt c. 1090-332
1000 United Hebrew kingdom (1020-922): Saul, David, Solomon   Later Vedic Age in India c. 900-500—caste system becomes more complex:
Divided Hebrew kingdom: Israel (922-721); Judah (922-586)   priest, warrior, merchant, serf, "untouchable"
The great Hebrew prophets 750-550
Assyrian empire 745-612
Lydians and Medes   *Upanishads* 800-600—foundation of Hinduism
Chaldean empire (604-539): Nebuchadnezzar
Zoroaster, early 6th century
Persian empire (550-330): Cyrus; Darius (522-486)
End of the Babylonian Exile of the Jews 538   Guatama Buddha 563?-483—founder of Buddhism
500   Confucius 551-479—most famous and influential Chinese philosopher

Chinese poetry collected in *Shih Ching*, or *Book of Odes*
400   Two greatest Indian epics composed: the *Mahabharata* (including the
Bhagavad-Gita) and the *Ramayama*

Lao-tzu and Taoism—aim: intuitive approach to life; *Tao te Ching*
Mencius c. 372-289 links theory of Mandate of Heaven to democratic con-
cept of the will of the people in government
Alexander the Great crosses Indus valley 326
Conquests of Alexander the Great 334-331   Chandragupta Maurya founds Mauryan dynasty in India 322-c. 185
300 Death of Alexander (323); Ptolemy siezes Egypt; Seleucus rules Asia

Ashoka 273-232—"the first great royal patron of Buddhism"
Period of Warring States in China—Ch'in defeat Chou 221
China reunited under First Emperor, Shih Huang-ti 221-210
Han dynasty of China 202 B.C.-220 A.D.
200   Tamil kindgoms—Hindu states, chief trading area with the West
Mauryan empire falls 185; Bactrian rule extends to
India and Punjab; Graeco-Bactrian kingdom created
Maccabean revolt wins independence for Judea 142 (see Chapter 5)   Han emperor Wu Ti 141-87
100

Kushan empire in India (first century B.C.-220 A.D.)
Kanishka, Kushan ruler c. 78-128, sponsors *Mahayana*
Dead Sea Scrolls   ("Great Vehicle") school of Buddhism, which spreads north and east;
Pompey annexes Syria and Palestine 63   *Hinayana* ("Lesser Vehicle") Buddhism spreads south and east
Herod the Great, king of Judea 37-4
Jesus Christ c. 4 B.C.-30 A.D.
Paul (d. c. 65)
A.D. 100 Jews revolt from Rome (66-70)—end of the ancient Hebrew state

GREECE

ROME

3000 B.C.

Aegean civilization c. 2000-1200
Achaean Greeks invade Peloponnesus c. 2000

Indo-Europeans invade Italian peninsula 2000-1000; Latins settle in lower Tiber valley (Latium)

2000

Zenith of Minoan culture 1700-1450

Mycenaean Age 1450-1200

1500

Dorian invasion c. 1200

Greek Dark Ages c. 1150-750 and Homeric Age

Etruscans settle on Italy's west coast
Carthage founded in North Africa by Phoenicians c. 800
Rome founded 753
Greeks colonize southern Italy and Sicily

1000

Hellenic Age c. 750-338
Age of Oligarchy (c. 750-500): Hesiod; colonization
Athens—growth of democracy: Solon (594), Pisistratus (560), Cleisthenes (508)
Sparta—militaristic totalitarian state, Spartan League

Etruscans conquer Rome c. 600

Roman Republic established 509

500

Persian Wars (490-479): Marathon, Thermopylae
Delian League (478) and Athenian imperialism
Athen's Golden Age under Pericles (461-429)
Peloponnesian War (431-404)—Athens vs. Sparta

Plebeians vs. patricians (509-287)—tribunes and *Concilium Plebis*

Laws of the Twelve Tables c. 450

400

Philip II of Macedonia conquers Greece 338
Hellenic culture: Thales, Pythagoras, Democritus, Hippocrates, Socrates, Plato, Aristotle, Herodotus, Thycydides, Sappho, Aeschylus, Sophocles, Euripides, Aristophanes, Phidias, Praxiteles
Alexander the Great conquers Persia 331
Hellenistic Age 323-31—Ptolemaic Egypt, Seleucid Asia, Macedonia; Greek federal leagues

Roman expansion in Italy (338-270): Latins, Etruscans, Samnites, Greeks

300

Hellenistic culture: Epicurus, Zeno, Eratosthenes, Aristarchus, Euclid, Archimedes, Hipparchus, Polybius, Theocritus

Roman expansion in western Mediterranean 270-146—Punic wars: Hannibal

Roman expansion in eastern Mediterranean 200-133—wars with Macedonia and the Seleucids; Macedon and Greece annexed (146); first Roman province in Asia (133)
Reform movement of the Gracchi 133-121

200

Civil wars 88-30
Marius vs. Sulla (88-82): dictatorship of Sulla (82-79)
Pompey vs. Caesar (49-46): dictatorship of Julius Caesar (46-44)
Antony vs. Octavian (32-30)
Augustus' reconstruction—the Principate 30 B.C.-180 A.D.
Golden Age of literature: Cicero, Catullus, Lucretius, Virgil, Horace
Julio-Claudian and Flavian emperors 14 A.D.-96 A.D.
Antonine emperors (96-180): Hadrian, Marcus Aurelius
Silver Age of literature: Juvenal, Tacitus, Seneca, Plutarch

100

100 A.D.

Chronological Table 2

EUROPE

B.C. 100	
A.D. 1	
100	End of the *Pax Romana* 180-285—civil wars, economic decline, invasions
	Reconstruction by Diocletian (285-305)—the Dominate
300	Constantine (306-337)—Edict of Milan (313), Council of Nicaea (325), founding of Constantinople (330)
	Ulfilas (d. 383), missionary to the Goths
	Theodosius divides Roman Empire 395
	Battle of Adrianople (378)—German invasions begin
400	Alaric sacks Rome 410
	Western Church Fathers: Jerome, Ambrose, Augustine
	St. Patrick in Ireland c. 450
	Attila crosses the Rhine—battle near Troyes 451
	Pope Leo the Great (440-461)
	Odovacar deposes last western emperor 476
	Clovis (481-511) unites Franks, and rules Gaul
500	Theodoric (493-526) rules Italy; Cassiodorus and Boethius
	St. Benedict establishes Benedictine Order 529
	Lombards invade Italy 568
	Merovingian decline, sixth-seventh centuries
600	Pope Gregory the Great (590-604)
	Isidore of Seville (d. 636)—the *Etymologies*
700	Charles Martel (714-741) rules the Franks; defeats Muslims at Tours 732
	Bede (d. 735)
	St. Boniface (d. 755), "the apostle to the Germans"
	Pepin the Short (741-768) ends rule of Merovingian kings; "Donation of Pepin" to pope
	Charlemagne (768-814) revives Roman Empire in the West (800); fosters Carolingian Renaissance
800	Treaty of Verdun divides Carolingian empire into West Frankland, East Frankland, and Lorraine 843
	Magyar, Muslim, and Viking invasions terrorize Europe (ninth-tenth centuries)
	Alfred the Great (871-899) establishes strong Anglo-Saxon kingdom in England
	Kievan Russia emerges
900	Feudalism well established in France c. 900
	Henry I, the Fowler (919-936), founds Saxon dynasty in Germany
	Otto I, the Great (936-973)—alliance of crown and Church; routs Magyars at battle of Lechfeld 955; crowned emperor by pope 962
	Ethelred the Unready 978-1016—power of English government lags; invasion by Canute, Viking king
	Hugh Capet (987) founds Capetian dynasty
1000	Peace and Truce of God (eleventh century)
	Normans arrive in Italy 1016
	Yaroslav the Wise 1019-1054—peak of Kievan Russia; Byzantine influences in art and literature
	Salian House succeeds Saxon kings in Germany 1024
	College of Cardinals formed to elect pope 1059
	Pope Gregory VII (1073-1085) supports Cluniac religious reform; Investiture Struggle
	Norman Conquest of England 1066
	Fall of Bari to Normans 1071—last Byzantine stronghold in Italy
	The *Reconquista* gains Toledo from Muslims 1085
	First Crusade—Jerusalem captured; Latin kingdom of Jerusalem established 1099
1100	Renaissance of the twelfth century; revival of trade and towns
	Welf-Hohenstaufen rivalry (1106-1152) wrecks structure for a strong German State
	Louis the Fat 1108—first strong Capetian ruler in France
	Concordat of Worms 1122
	Second Crusade 1147
	Frederick Barbarossa (1152-1190)—centralized feudal monarchy; struggle with popes and Lombard League
	Henry II (1154-1189) reforms English judicial system; Thomas à Becket
	St. Dominic (1170-1221); St. Francis of Assisi (1182?-1226)
	Philip II Augustus (1180-1223) extends royal power
	Third Crusade 1189—the "Crusade of Kings"
	Frederick II 1194-1250—end of the medieval German empire
1200	Pope Innocent III 1198-1216—zenith of the medieval papacy
	Fourth Crusade 1202-1204—crusaders sack Constantinople
	King John of England signs Magna Carta 1215
	Kiev destroyed by Mongols 1240
	St. Thomas Aquinas (1225?-1274) reconciles faith and reason in *Summa Theologica*; zenith of scholasticism
	Louis IX (1226-1270) brings dignity to the French crown
	Edward I (1272-1307)—rise of Parliament; power of nobility curtailed
	Philip IV, the Fair (1285-1314), centralizes French government; humiliates Pope Boniface VIII
	Acre, last Christian stronghold in Holy Land, conquered by Muslims 1291
1300	Dante (d. 1321)
	Hundred Years' War between France and England 1337-1453
1400	Chaucer (d. 1400)

NEAR EAST AND BYZANTINE EMPIRE	INDIA, CHINA, AND JAPAN	
	Rule by Yamato clan in Japan	**100 B.**
(See also Chronological Table 1)	Kanishka ruler in India (c. 78-128)	**1 A.D.**
Christian missionaries	Expansion of Indian culture into Southeast Asia begins (second century)	**100**
	Fall of Han dynasty in China 220	
Eastern Church Fathers: Clement of Alexandria	Buddhism gains popularity in China (third century)	**300**
Council of Nicaea 325—Nicene Creed	Chandragupta I founds Gupta dynasty in India 320	
Constantine establishes New Rome (Constantinople) 330		
St. Basil (330-379) establishes Rule of St. Basil	Chandragupta II (c. 380-c. 413)—zenith of Gupta power	
	Kalidasa (c. 400-450), lyric poet, the "Indian Shakespeare"	**400**
	Buddhism enters Japan (sixth century)	**500**
Justinian (527-565)—reconquests; *Corpus Juris Civilis*; Hagia Sophia		
Muhammad 570-632—the Hijra	Harsha (606-647) rules northern India	**600**
Heraclius (610-641)—regains Syria, Palestine, Egypt from Persians	T'ang dynasty founded 618; golden era of China	
First four caliphs (632-661)—conquest of Syria, Iraq, most of Egypt and Persia	T'ai Tsung (627-650)—first great T'ang ruler	
	Taika reform in Japan 646; ruler considered divine	
Rise of the Shia	T'ang poets: Li Po and Tu Fu	**700**
Umayyad dynasty 661-750—expands in North Africa, Turkestan, Indus valley, Spain; defeated by Franks at Tours 732	Japanese court established at Nara 710	
Leo III (717-741) repulses Muslims 718; administrative and military reforms; iconoclastic controversy		
Abbasid dynasty 750-1258—end of Arab predominance; peak of Islamic power, civilization, and prosperity		
Harun-al-Rashid 768-809—relations with Charlemagne	Fujiwara period in Japan (857-1160); capital at Kyoto	**800**
Cyril and Methodius—missionaries to the Slavs	*Diamond Sutra* printed 868	
Golden age of Muslim learning 900-1100—advances in medicine, mathematics, literature, philosophy, architecture, decorative arts; geniuses of this period and later: Al-Razi, Avicenna, Alhazen, Al-Khwarizmi, Omar Khayyám, Averroës, ibn-Khaldun	T'ang dynasty falls 906	**900**
	Expansion of Indian culture into Southeast Asia ends (tenth century)	
	Sung dynasty founded in China 960	
Basil II (976-1025) defeats Bulgars	Gunpowder used by Sung c. 1000	**1000**
	Wang An-shih (1021 1086), Chinese socialist reformer	
Final separation of the churches 1054	Muslims invade India; Turks and Afghans annex Punjab 1022	
Seljuk Turks seize Persia and Iraq, conquer Baghdad (1055)		
Battle of Manzikert 1071—loss of Asia Minor to Seljuks		
Alexius Comnenus and the First Crusade 1096		
Kingdom of Jerusalem (1099-1291) and crusader states	Angkor Wat built c. 1100	**1100**
	China divided between empires of Sung (south) and Chin (north) 1127	
	Yoritomo (1147-1199) rules Japan as *shogun* from Kamakura 1192	
Saladin regains Jerusalem 1187	Genghis Khan (1162-1227) unites Mongols	
Fourth Crusade 1202-1204—Constantinople sacked	Hojo period in Japan 1199-1333	**1200**
Latin Empire 1204-1261	Delhi sultanate established 1206; Indian culture divided into Hindu and Muslim	
Fall of Abbasid dynasty—Baghdad conquered by Mongols 1258	Mongols conquer China 1234; *Pax Tatarica* links East and West via trade routes	
Michael Palaeologus regains Constantinople 1261	Kublai Khan (1260-1294), Yüan emperor of China	
	Marco Polo arrives at Kublai Khan's court c. 1275	
	"The Divine Wind" 1281	
Ottoman Turks invade Europe 1356	Kamakura destroyed 1333; Ashikaga shogunate founded in Japan 1338	**1300**
	Ming dynasty established in China 1368	
Constantinople falls to Ottoman Turks 1453	Tamerlane (Timur the Lame) destroys Delhi 1398	**1400**

Chronological Table 3

THE EUROPEAN SCENE

300

900

1000

1100

1200 Mongols conquer Kiev 1240
Transitional period in Italian art c. 1250-c. 1400—Giotto d. 1336
Rudolf of Hapsburg becomes Holy Roman emperor 1291
Pope Boniface VIII (1294-1303) feuds with Philip IV

1300 Avignon papacy 1309-1376
Hundred Years' War (1337-1453) begins
Golden Bull 1356
Petrarch 1304-1374
Great Schism 1378-1417
John Wycliffe d. 1384
Grand Prince of Moscow defeats Mongols at Kulikovo 1380

1400 The *quattrocento* (fifteenth century) of Italian Renaissance
Council of Constance 1414
Commercial Revolution 1450-1650
Gutenberg used movable type to print Bible 1454
Early Renaissance masters in Italy—Brunelleschi, Ghiberti, Donatello, Masaccio, Montegna, Botticelli
Wars of the Roses 1455-1485
Louis XI (the "universal spider") of France (1461-1483)
Ivan III (the Great) of Russia (1462-1505)
Ferdinand and Isabella begin joint rule in Spain 1479
Henry VII (1485-1509) founds Tudor dynasty in England
Reconquista ends with conquest of Granada 1492; unification of Spain completed
Maximilian I (1493-1519), Holy Roman emperor
Italian Wars (1494-1513) begin
Leonardo da Vinci 1452-1519

1500 Northern Renaissance (sixteenth century)—painters Jan van Eyck, Albrecht Dürer, Hans Holbein the Younger, Brueghel the Elder
Late Renaissance in Italy c. 1500-1530—Bramante, Michelangelo, Da Vinci, Raphael, Giogione, Titian, Castiglione, Cellini
Henry VIII of England 1509-1547
Luther posts ninety-five theses 1517; excommunicated, declared heretic at Diet of Worms 1521
Charles V elected Holy Roman emperor 1519
Suleiman rules the Turks 1520-1566
Peace of Augsburg 1555 ends Schmalkaldic Wars (1546-1555)
The Prince (1532) by Machiavelli
Henry VIII founds Anglican Church 1534
Loyola establishes Jesuit order 1534
John Calvin published *Institutes of the Christian Religion* 1536
Erasmus d. 1536
Council of Trent 1545-1563
Ivan IV (the Terrible) of Russia 1547-1584

1550 Mary Tudor reinstates Catholicism in England 1553-1558
Philip II of Spain 1556-1598
Era of Religious Wars (1556-1650) begins
Elizabeth of England 1558-1603
St. Bartholomew's Day Massacre 1572
Shakespeare 1564-1616
Battle of Lepanto 1571
Dutch United Provinces declare independence 1581
Time of Trouble in Russia 1584-1613
Spanish Armada 1588
Henry IV (1589-1610) founds Bourbon dynasty in France
Edict of Nantes 1598

1600 James I (1603-1625) founds Stuart dynasty in England
Bank of Amsterdam founded 1609
Thirty Years' War (1618-1648)—Peace of Westphalia 1648
De Jure Belli ac Pacis (1625) by Grotius
Colbert d. 1683
Lloyd's of London founded c. 1688
Bank of England chartered 1694

FAR EAST	AMERICAS AND AFRICA	
	Ghana empire in Africa c. 300-1200	**300**
	Mayan city-states in Yucatan peninsula 980-1200	**900**
	Eric the Red discovers Greenland c. 982	
Muslims invade India; Turks and Afghans annex Punjab 1022	Mali empire in Africa c. 1000-c. 1400	**1000**
	Zenj empire in Africa c. 1000-1497	
China divided into two empires: Sung and Chin 1127	Incas settle Cuzco valley in Andes (eleventh century)	**1100**
Yoritomo (1147-1199) rules Japan as *shogun* from Kamakura 1192	Ghana captured by Berbers 1076	
Hojo period in Japan 1199-1333	Toltecs dominate Mexican plateau (twelfth century)	
Delhi sultanate established 1206		**1200**
Mongols conquer China 1234	Fall of Ghana state 1240	
Kublai Khan 1260-1294—Marco Polo arrives at his court c. 1275		
	Aztec confederacy in Mexico (fourteenth century)	**1300**
Kamakura destroyed 1333; Ashikaga shogunate founded in Japan 1338		
Fall of Mongol China; Ming dynasty founded 1368		
Timur the Lame (Tamerlane) destroys Delhi 1398	Songhai empire in the African Sudan c. 1400-c. 1600	**1400**
Chinese naval expeditions to India, Near East, Africa (fifteenth century)	Atlantic slave trade begins (fifteenth century)	
	Zenith of Inca empire 1438-1532	
	Prince Henry the Navigator (1394-1460)	
	Diaz rounds Cape of Good Hope 1488	
	Columbus discovers New World 1492	
	Bull of Demarcation 1493; Treaty of Tordesillas 1494	
	North America claimed by Cabot for England 1497	
	Da Gama reaches India 1498	
Portuguese trade monopoly in Far East (sixteenth century)		**1500**
	Albuquerque captures Goa (1510) and Malacca (1511)	
Chinese edict bans foreign merchants in Chinese waters 1522	Balboa sights Pacific Ocean 1513	
Babur (the Tiger) defeats Delhi sultanate and Rajputs 1526-1527; founds	Cortés arrives in Mexico 1519; Aztec empire falls	
Mughul empire in India	Magellan rounds South America 1520	
Akbar (1556-1605) expands Mughul empire; promotes religious tolerance	*Conquistadores* in New World	**1550**
Portuguese granted right to trade with Chinese at Macao 1557	Jacques Cartier explores St. Lawrence River 1534	
Spanish use Philippines as trading stop c. 1565		
	Bartolomé de Las Casas c. 1560	
Japanese attempt invasion of China and Korea 1592		
Hideyoshi persecutes Christians in Japan 1592		
English East India Company incorporated 1600	Jamestown founded 1607; Quebec 1608	**1600**
Dutch East India Company formed 1602	Henry Hudson attempts to find shorter route to Far East 1609	
Tokugawa period begins in Japan 1603		
Foundations for Dutch East Indies laid by Coen 1618	Plymouth founded 1620	
Shah Jahan (1628-1658) promotes Muslim faith; height of Mughul empire	Dutch West India Company founds Manhattan 1624	
in India		
Europeans forbidden entry to Japan 1639	René La Salle takes possession of Louisiana territory for France 1681	
Manchu invade Ming China; establish Manchu dynasty 1644		
Aurangzeb (1658-1707); decline of Mughul power		

Chronological Table 4

SCIENCE AND TECHNOLOGY, THOUGHT AND ART

1500 Revolution in astronomy—Copernicus proposes heliocentric theory of universe, publishes *Concerning the Revolutions of Heavenly Spheres* 1543; Brahe attempts compromise between geocentric and heliocentric theories; Kepler coordinates Brahe's data; Galileo confirms Copernican theory

1550 Pioneers in medicine: Paracelsus experiments with new drugs; Vesalius, founder of modern anatomy; Harvey describes circulation of blood in *Anatomical Exercise on the Motion of the Heart and Blood* 1628
El Greco (1541?–1614), master of Mannerist style in painting

Francis Bacon (1561–1626) champions deductive method of philosophical inquiry; *Novum Organum* 1620; *New Atlantis* 1627

Descartes (1590–1650) proposes deductive method of philosophical inquiry; develops analytical geometry; proposes theory of philosophical dualism
1600 Gilbert's *De Magnete* 1600

Neoclassical dramatists in France—Corneille, Racine, Moliere
Inventions of seventeenth century: telescope, microscope, thermometer, pendulum clock, micrometer, barometer, air pump
Baroque style: Rubens, Velázquez, Vermeer, Hals, Rembrandt, Bernini; opera originates in Italy

1650 Defenders of absolutism—Hobbes of England, author of *Leviathan* 1651, and Bossuet of France

Scientific societies founded: Academy of Experiments at Florence 1657; Royal Society of London 1662; French Academy of Science at Paris 1666
Boyle's law is formulated 1660
Spinoza expresses his pantheistic philosophy; publishes *Ethics* 1663

Newton expounds theory of gravitation in *Philosophiae Naturalis Principia Mathematica* 1687

Locke, publishes *An Essay Concerning Human Understanding* 1690; advances doctrine of popular sovereignty as argument against absolutism in "Of Civil Government" 1690
Rococo style exemplified in works of Watteau; English portrait painting by Reynolds, Gainsborough

1700

Novel appears: Defoe's *Robinson Crusoe* 1719; Swift's *Gulliver's Travels* 1726; Richardson's *Pamela* 1740–1741; Fielding's *Tom Jones* 1749
Pope, foremost Neoclassical English poet, publishes *An Essay on Man* 1733
Hogarth's "The Rake's Progress" 1735;

Intellectuals adopt Deism, belief that God is creator of universe but cannot change laws of nature; Pietism develops to restore emotion and faith to religion, is later called Methodist movement under Wesley brothers in England 1738; Quietism is crushed in Catholic countries

Further experiments with electricity: Leyden Jar 1745; Franklin's experiment with kite 1752
Intellectual assault on absolutism led by *philosophes* Montesquieu (*The Spirit of Laws*, 1748) and Rousseau (*Social Contract*, 1762)
1750 Reaction on the Continent against Baroque and Rococo styles of architecture is manifested in Neoclassical style c. 1750
Formalism in music—Handel, Bach, Mozart, Haydn
Voltaire, prince of *philosophes*, publishes *Candide* 1759; Diderot spreads doctrines of rationalism and Deism, edits *Encyclopedie*
Great works of social sciences: Rousseau's *Emile* 1762; Beccaria's *Essay on Crimes and Punishments* 1764; Gibbon's *Decline and Fall of the Roman Empire* 1776–1788; Condorcet's *Progress of the Human Mind* 1794

Priestley isolates ammonia; discovers oxygen 1774; produces carbon monoxide gas 1799
Adam Smith's *An Inquiry into the Nature and Causes of the Wealth of Nations* defends laissez-faire economics 1776
Lavoisier discovers the law of the conservation of matter and formulates his combustion theory 1777
Kant's *Critique of Pure Reason* (1781)

Edmund Burke defends conservatism in *Reflections on the Revolution in France* 1790

Hutton's *Theory of the Earth* 1795—pioneer work in geology
Edward Jenner develops safe vaccination against smallpox c. 1798
1800 Volta discovers method for generating continuous flow of electricity 1800
Goya's "The Disasters of War" 1810

POLITICS

1500

1550

James of England (1603–1625) and successor Charles I antagonize Parliament; Petition of Right denies king's right of taxation with parliamentary consent 1628
Richelieu 1624–1642 becomes real authority behind French throne

1600

Frederick William, the Great Elector (1640–1688), makes Brandenburg the most important Protestant state in Germany
English Civil War (1642–1648); the Commonwealth and the Protectorate (1649–1660)
Mazarin (1643–1661) governs France during minority of Louis XIV; triumphs over enemies during civil war 1648–1653

1650

Restoration of Stuart kings in England—controversy between Charles II and Parliament 1660–1685; secret Treaty of Dover with Louis XIV 1670; Whig and Tory parties organized; Habeas Corpus Act 1679
Louis XIV (1661–1715) transforms French state into an absolute monarchy; invades Spanish Netherlands and German border districts 1667–1697; halted by William of Orange and allied nations
Peter the Great 1682–1725, absolutist tsar of Russia, attempts to westernize realm
James II of England (1685–1688) attempts to impose absolute rule
Louis XIV revokes Edict of Nantes 1685
Glorious Revolution—Whigs and Tories invite William of Orange to rule England; Bill of Rights passed; Parliament becomes dominant agency in government 1688

1700

Great Northern War 1700–1721—Charles XII of Sweden defeated by Peter the Great and allies
War of the Spanish Succession—English and allies renew struggle against French 1701; Treaty of Utrecht 1713
Frederick William I of Prussia (1713–1740) creates all-powerful central government; builds up army
George I initiates Hanoverian dynasty in England; beginning of creative cabinet government 1714
Robert Walpole becomes first prime minister of England 1721–1742

Frederick II, the Great (1740–1786), makes Prussia important power in European politics
War of the Austrian Succession 1740–1749—Frederick the Great invades Silesia 1740; France and England enter first stage of duel for world empire; Peace of Aix-la-Chapelle 1748

1750

Seven Years' War 1756–1763—Diplomatic Revolution aligns Austria and France against England and Prussia; struggle on Continent and in colonies; William Pitt's "system" brings English victories, such as battle of Plassey (1757) and battle of Quebec (1759); Treaty of Paris 1763
Catherine the Great (1762–1796) makes Russia major European power
George III of England (1770–1782) strives to destroy cabinet system; secures control of Parliament
Poland partitioned in three stages among Russia, Prussia, and Austria 1772–1795
American Revolution 1775–1783—Declaration of Independence 1776

American Articles of Confederation 1781; Constitutional Convention 1787; American Constitution adopted 1789
Pitt the Younger becomes prime minister 1783; restores cabinet government
French Revolution (first phase)—storming of Bastille; National Constituent Assembly draws up Declaration of the Rights of Man; formulates new constitution and government (Legislative Assembly) 1789–1791
French Revolution (second phase)—agitation by Jacobin movement led by Marat, Danton, and Robespierre; radical insurrection in Paris; National Convention proclaims the Republic; France repels invasion by Austria and Prussia 1792
Louis XVI executed 1793; Reign of Terror begins under Robespierre 1793; Robespierre executed; Directory assumes power 1795; Directory smashes First Coalition, except for England 1797
Napoleon establishes Consulate 1799; scatters Second Coalition forces 1799–1802; climaxes reforms with Civil Code, proclaims himself emperor 1804; destroys armies of Third Coalition; is defeated by British at Trafalgar, defeats Prussia 1805–1806; his invasion of Russia fails 1812

1800

English and allies defeat Napoleon at Leipzig 1813; Napoleon abdicates throne, goes to Elba 1814; returns to France and is defeated by Britain and Prussia at Waterloo; exiled to St. Helena 1815
Revolution in Latin America—Bolívar and San Martín gain independence for Spanish colonies in South America 1817–1825; Iturbide proclaims Mexican independence 1821; Pedro is crowned emperor of independent Brazil 1822

Chronological Table 5

POLITICS

1800

Congress of Vienna 1814–1815—Russia, Britain, France, Austria attempt to restore Old Regime; Quadruple (later Quintuple) Alliance formed
Louis XVIII of France establishes constitutional monarchy 1814–1824

Carlsbad Decrees temporarily discourage German nationalist youth movement 1819
Revolutions in Spain and Italy 1820–1821
Greeks rise against Turkish rule 1821–1827; Greek independence attained at Treaty of Adrianople 1829

Charles X, exponent of divine right, ascends French throne 1824
Tsar Nicholas I crushes Decembrist Revolt 1825; imposes reactionary repressive system
Catholic Emancipation Act in England 1829
Revolutions of 1830—July Revolution in Paris enthrones Louis Philippe; Belgians throw off Dutch rule; revolt unsuccessful in Poland
Mazzini initiates Italian *Risorgimento* c. 1830
Whigs end reactionary Tory rule 1830; Reform Bill 1832; slavery abolished 1833
Turkey becomes a protectorate of Russia 1831

Chartist movement for reform in England fails (1839, 1842, 1848)

Repeal of Corn Laws 1846
Revolution of 1848 in France—Louis Napoleon becomes president of Second Republic 1848
Revolution of 1848 in Germany—Frederick William IV of Prussia grants constitutional government; Frankfurt Assembly fails to establish new union; German Confederation restored at Olmütz 1850

1850

Cavour becomes prime minister of Italy 1852
Louis Napoleon proclaims himself Emperor Napoleon III 1852
Crimean War—Russia invades Turkey 1853; defeated at Sevastopol 1854–1855; Treaty of Paris 1856
Italy unified under Cavour—Austro-Italian War 1859; first Italian parliament 1861; Rome capital of united Italy 1871
Tsar Alexander II issues Emancipation Proclamation 1861; introduces reform 1864–1874
Bismarck appointed Prussian prime minister 1862
Polish insurrection crushed; policy of repression reimposed by Alexander II 1863
Germany unified under Bismarck—Prussia defeats Denmark (1864) and Austria (1866); wins Franco-Prussian War; William of Prussia proclaimed emperor of united Germany 1871
Ausgleich establishes Dual Monarchy of Austria-Hungary 1867
Gladstone and Disraeli alternate as English prime minister 1867–1880; Reform Bill of 1867 extends vote; Gladstone's Glorious Ministry 1868–1874
Parnell leads Irish Home Rulers; Gladstone introduces unsuccessful home rule bills 1886, 1893; third home rule bill passed 1919
Third Republic proclaimed in France 1870
Revolutionary Paris Commune 1871
Bismarck begins *Kulturkampf* 1872; forms Three Emperors' League with Russia and Austria-Hungary 1873; Triple Alliance with Austria and Italy 1882; Reinsurance Treaty with Russia 1887
Turkey crushes Bosnian and Bulgarian revolts, defeats Serbia, Montenegro 1875; Russia defeats Turkey 1877-1878; Treaty of San Stefano 1878
Congress of Berlin 1878
Abdul Hamid II imposes absolute rule over Ottoman empire 1878
Alexander II assassinated 1881; Alexander II revives system of repression, attempts policy of Russification 1881–1894
England approaches universal manhood suffrage 1884
Spirit of internationalism—annual Universal Peace Congresses begin 1889; first Pan-American Conference 1889; Hague Tribunal 1899
Emperor William II dismisses Birmarck 1890; allows Reinsurance Treaty to lapse; France forms Dual Alliance with Russia 1894
Dreyfus case 1894–1906
Nicholas II becomes tsar of Russia 1894
Herzl introduces Zionism; first Zionist congress meets 1897

1900

Social Democrats divide into moderate Mensheviks and radical Bolsheviks 1903; massacre of Bloody Sunday 1905; October Manifesto calls national Duma 1905
Britain forms alliance with Japan 1902; proclaims Entente Cordiale with France 1904; establishes Triple Entente with Russia and France 1907
Young Turks rebel 1908
Parliament Bill of 1911 curtails power of House of Lords
Diplomatic crises lead to World War I 1905–1914
Balkan Wars 1912–1913
Archduke Francis Ferdinand is assassinated 1914
World War I begins 1914

ECONOMICS AND SCIENCE

ARTS

Inventions revolutionize textile industry 1700's

Modern canal building in England begins 1759

Industrial use of Watt's steam engine 1785

Laissez-faire theory popularized—Malthus, Ricardo, Bentham, John Stuart Mill

First voyage of Fulton's steamship *Clermont* 1807

Atomic theory c. 1808

Industrial Revolution 1815–1870

Utopian socialists Saint-Simon, Fourier, Owen propose cooperative societies (early 1800's)

Lyell's *Principles of Geology* 1830–1833

Faraday's electric dynamo 1831

English social and economic reforms such as Factory Act of 1833 diminish doctrine of laissez faire

Penny post introduced in England 1840

Zollverein stimulates industry in German states

Morse perfects telegraph 1844

First law of thermodynamics stated 1847

Marx and Engels publish *Communist Manifesto* 1848

Proudhon founds anarchism

Christian socialists emphasize social aspects of Christ's teachings

Comte initiates science of sociology; Ranke founds school of scientific history

Bessemer improves smelting, refining of iron ore 1850's

Great Exhibition in London 1851

Darwin publishes *Origin of Species* 1859

Internal combustion engine 1860

Lister uses asepsis and antisepsis in surgery c. 1860

First International fails, anarchists under Bakunin oppose Marxist majority 1864–1873

Marx's scientific socialism expounded in *Das Kapital* 1867–1894

Mendeleyev classifies all known elements in periodic table 1869

Railroads cross North America 1869; Suez Canal 1869

New industrialism c. 1870–1914

Darwin's *Descent of Man* (1871)

Clerk-Maxwell advances electromagnetic theory of light 1873

Bell invents telephone 1876

Weismann distinguishes somatic and germ cells; Mendel formulates laws of heredity; Galton pioneers in eugenics

Pasteur and Koch prove germ theory of disease 1881

Hertz proves existence of electromagnetic waves 1886

Second International founded 1889; revisionism grows on Continent 1890's

Freud pioneers in psychoanalysis 1890's

Syndicalists emerge in France 1890's

Marconi devises wireless telegraphy 1895

X-ray discovered 1895

Electron theory formulated c. 1897

Pierre and Marie Curie discover radium 1898

Planck formulates quantum theory 1900

Pavlov advances study of conditioned reflexes 1900

Mendel's laws of heredity gain recognition c. 1900

Wright brothers' airplane 1903

Einstein produces equation $E=mc^2$, theory of relativity

Ford's Model T 1909

Rutherford's theory of positively charged atomic nucleus 1911

Einstein's general theory 1912

Preromantic writers—Rousseau, Schiller, Goethe **1800**

Goethe's *Faust*, Part I 1808

Romantic writers—Wordsworth, Coleridge, Shelley, Byron, Keats, Scott

Romanticist painters rebel against classical rules—Delacroix, Constable, Turner

Romanticism in music—Beethoven, Brahms, Tschaikovsky, Chopin; operas by Wagner and Verdi

Romantic nationalist writers—Hugo, Pushkin, Hegel; Michelet, Bancroft, Macaulay write national histories

Period of Gothic revival in architecture c. 1830

Goethe's *Faust*, Part II 1832

Victorian novelists—Thackeray, Dickens

Victorian poets—Tennyson, Browning **1850**

Social criticism—Arnold, Carlyle, Ruskin

Realistic painters Courbet and Daumier

Free and compulsory education becomes almost universal in western Europe 1870–1914

Impressionist painters Monet, Degas, Renoir; sculptor Rodin

Post-Impressionistic painters Cézanne, Van Gogh

Realist writers Tolstoy, Hardy, James, Clemens; naturalist Zola; Ibsen and Shaw write "problem plays"; symbolists represent reactions against extreme realism

Darwinian theory influences philosophers James (pragmatism) and Bergson (vitalism) **1900**

Music—Richard Strauss (post-Wagnerian), Debussy (impressionism), Stravinsky (polytonality), Schönberg (twelve-tone system)

Architecture—Sullivan, Wright, Gropius

Expressionism and Cubism

Chronological Table 6

U. S. AND LATIN AMERICA	BRITISH DOMINIONS
1750	
American Revolution 1775-1783	Peace of Paris—Canada becomes British possession 1763
	Canada's formative period 1763-1867—Quebec Act guarantees French custom and Catholicism in Canada 1774; division into Upper and Lower Canada 1791
Adoption of the United States Constitution 1789	Sydney, first English colony in Australia, established 1788
1800	
Louisiana Purchase 1803	
War of 1812—United States vs. Britain and Canada 1812-1814	
Missouri Compromise establishes boundaries of slave territory in United States 1820	
Brazil independence achieved 1822	
Monroe Doctrine 1823	
Andrew Jackson's presidency 1829-1837	
	British government assumes protection of New Zealand 1840
Pedro ii brings political liberty and economic and cultural progress to Brazil 1840-1889	
United States land area doubled by annexation of California, Texas, Oregon, the Southwest 1845-1860	
1850	Australian colonies achieve near self-government c. 1850; secret ballot in Australia 1855
Mexican dictator Santa Anna overthrown 1855; Juárez institutes anti-clerical *Reforma*; civil war ensues	Provinces of Canada form a federal union under British North America Act, and Canada becomes a Confederation 1867
American Civil War—the Federal Union preserved, slavery abolished 1861-1865	
Argentina becomes united republic 1862	
Napoleon iii invades Mexico, establishes brief empire under Maximilian 1863-1867	
United States occupies Midway Islands 1867	
Russia sells Alaska to United States 1867	
1870	
Porfirio Diaz, dictator, brings order without liberty to Mexico 1877-1880, 1884-1911	Treaty of Washington—Canada and United States arbitrate major differences 1871
First Pan-American Conference 1889	
Progressive movement in the United States initiates economic reform c. 1890-1914—trust-busting and regulation of transportation, foods, drugs under Theodore Roosevelt 1901-1909; Wilson's militant reform campaign, "New Freedom," initiates Federal Reserve Act 1913, Clayton Anti-Trust Act and Federal Trade Commission 1914	
"Dollar diplomacy"—United States exercises indirect controls in Latin America to protect investments 1890-1920's	Woman suffrage introduced in New Zealand 1893
Spanish-American War 1898; United States gains the Philippines, Guam, and Puerto Rico; Cuba becomes protectorate 1901	
United States annexes Hawaii 1898	
1900 Open Door Policy is declared 1900	
United States emerges as most powerful nation in the Western Hemisphere c. 1900	
Panama Canal begun under Theordore Roosevelt (1901-1909)	Commonwealth of Australia formed 1901
Era of Big Stick policy begins with the Roosevelt Corollary to the Monroe Doctrine 1904	
Madero defeats Diaz, rules Mexico 1911-1913	
Panama Canal opened 1914	

ASIA

AFRICA

1750

Battle of Plassey (1757) begins domination of India by British East India Company and England; Parliament takes control of East India Company 1773, appoints its highest official, the governor general of India 1784

1800

English acquire Ceylon 1796
Dutch government takes over East Indies; abolishes East India Company 1798

Cape Colony incorporated into British empire 1815

Boers establish Orange Free State and the Transvaal 1830's

China wars with England over opium and western exploitation 1839-1842; new ports opened to trade

1850

Taiping Rebellion—revolt against the Manchu 1850-1864; Manchu empress Tzu Hsi establishes national stability and furthers Chinese hatred of the West 1861-1908

Livingstone begins explorations in Central Africa 1853

Japan opens first ports to the West after Perry's visit 1854
English crush Indian Mutiny 1857, relieve East India Company of political responsibilities 1858
Russia penetrates land of the Caucasus, Turkestan c. 1860-1870

Britain makes treaties with Boers acknowledging their independence 1852, 1854; increased friction between Britons and Boers 1860-1885

Suez Canal completed 1869

The Meiji period—emperor made supreme authority; Japan modernized 1868-1912
Russia pushes south to Afghanistan and India c. 1870-1880

1870

Europe's golden age of imperialism 1870-1914: Belgium—Leopold II acquires Congo region 1876-1882; Leopold forced to turn over Congo Free State to Belgian government 1908. France—Egypt under joint financial control of Britain and France 1879; French obtain Tunisia 1881: Morocco made a French protectorate 1912. Britain—gains practical control of Suez Canal 1875; joint control of Egypt by British and French 1879; Lord Cromer assumes administration in Egypt 1883-1907; Somaliland is taken 1884; protectorate over Bechuanaland declared 1885; area developed for Britain by Rhodes' British South Africa Company named Rhodesia 1890; Anglo-Egyptian Sudan conquered 1898; Gambia, Sierra Leone, Gold Coast, and Nigeria gained through Royal Niger Company 1900. Germany—acquires Togoland, the Cameroons, German East Africa, German Southwest Africa 1880's; British and Germans settle dispute over territories in East Africa 1886, 1890. Italy—fails in attempted capture of Abyssinia 1896

Indian National Congress is formed 1885
Burma conquered by British c. 1885
French gain control over Indochina c. 1885
New constitution promulgated in Japan 1889

Gold discovered in Transvaal 1885

Japan defeats China in Sino-Japanese War 1894-1895
Filipinos rebel against American forces 1899-1902

Boer War 1899-1902—British defeat Dutch

1900

Boxer Rebellion—Chinese attack Europeans and are finally defeated by an international army 1900-1901
Open Door Policy calls for equal commercial rights in China for all nations 1900
Russo-Japanese War 1904-1905—Japan victorious
Anglo-Russian entente—Persia is put under dual control of Britain and Russia 1907
Japan annexes Korea 1910; accepted as first-class power
Republic of China proclaimed with Sun Yat-sen as president 1912

Boers and Britons join states and form Union of South Africa 1909

Italy wrests Tripoli from the Turks 1912

Chronological Table 7

1914 World War I 1914-1918

Armistice is signed 1918
Wilson presents Fourteen Points 1918

Czech republic established 1918

U.S. rejects membership in League of Nations 1919

Paris Peace Conference; League of Nations established 1919; Treaty of Versailles signed with Germany, Treaty of St. Germain with Austria, Treaty of Neuilly with Bulgaria 1919; Treaty of Sèvres with Ottoman empire, Treaty of Trianon with Hungary 1920
Little Entente formed 1920-1921; French allies include Belgium, Poland, Czechoslovakia, Rumania, Yugoslavia 1920-1927

Washington Conference—limited naval disarmament 1921-1922
Nine-Power Treaty—signatories agree to respect sovereignty of China 1922
Mussolini defies League of Nations in Corfu incident 1923
France invades German Ruhr, 1923
Dawes Plan eases German reparations, France evacuates Ruhr 1924
Locarno Pact 1925

Unstable coalition governments in France 1920's
Irish Free State created in southern Ireland 1921
Conservative Republican era in U.S. politics—Harding 1921-1923; Coolidge 1923-1929; Hoover 1929-1933
U.S. levies high tariffs, jeopardize war-debt payments, reparations
MacDonald, Britain's first Labourite prime minister 1924; Conservatives in power 1924-1929

Kellogg-Briand Pact renounces war 1928

1929

Young Plan scales down reparations payments 1930

Stock market crash in U.S. leads to world depression 1929
Labour party regains power in England 1929-1931
Revolutions in six South American nations 1930

Spain becomes republic 1931
National Coalition government in Britain begins 1931
Statute of Westminster creates constitution for British Commonwealth of Nations 1931

U.S. inaugurates Good Neighbor Policy 1933
Franklin D. Roosevelt becomes president of U.S. 1933; inaugurates New Deal

Mussolini conquers Abyssinia 1936

Popular Front gains power in France 1936

Rome-Berlin Axis formed, Japan and Germany form Anti-Comintern Pact 1936; Italy joins the Pact 1937
Spanish civil war 1936-1939

Conservatives regain control in France 1937
Neville Chamberlain, advocate of appeasement, becomes prime minister of England 1937

Hitler engineers coup in Austria 1938
Surrender of Sudetenland to Germany at Munich 1938; Hitler seizes Czechoslovakia, Mussolini seizes Albania 1939
1939 Russia, Germany sign nonaggression pact 1939
World War II—Germany invades Poland; France, Britain declare war 1939. *Sitzkrieg*; Russia defeats Finland 1939-1940. Hitler seizes Denmark, Norway, Low Countries, France 1940. Battle of Britain; Italian invasion of Greece and Africa fails; Hitler seizes Hungary, Balkans 1940-1941. Germany attacks Russia; Atlantic Charter signed; Pearl Harbor attack brings U.S. into war 1941. Japanese victories in Pacific 1941-1942. Battles of Midway and Coral Sea; Rommel victorious in Libya 1942. Soviets seize offensive in Russia; Axis surrender in Africa; Italy invaded; Allies launch second front; Normandy invasion, battle of Leyte 1944. Yalta agreements; Germany sur-
1945 renders; A-bomb dropped on Japan; Japanese surrender 1945.

Churchill becomes prime minister of England 1940
U.S. passes Lend-Lease Act 1941

RISE OF TOTALITARIANISM

ASIA AND AFRICA

Revolution in China 1911-1912; Manchu emperor abdicates, Yüan Shih-kai heads republic 1912-1916

1914

Japan presents China with the Twenty-one Demands 1915

Arabs revolt against Ottoman rule 1916-1918

Balfour Declaration 1917

Russian Revolution—Duma names provisional government, tsar abdicates, Bolsheviks under Lenin seize government 1917; Bolsheviks destroy White Russian resistance 1918-1920
Period of war communism 1918-1921
German revolution 1918; Weimar Republic set up 1919
Third Communist International (Comintern) formed 1919

Government of India Act of 1919 and Rowlatt Act passed, Gandhi begins campaign for independence 1919
French repress Arab nationalism in Morocco, Tunisia, Algeria, Syria-Lebanon 1919-1939
San Remo Conference—Allies overrule Arab nationalism, create mandates from Arab territories 1920
Communist party (1920), Indonesian Nationalist party (1927) oppose Dutch rule in East Indies
Sun Yat-sen controls Canton government in China 1921-1925
Riza Shah Pahlavi seizes Iran government 1921-1925

War between Russia, Poland 1920
NEP—Lenin restores some capitalistic practices 1921-1928
Mussolini establishes National Fascist party 1921; seizes Italian government in march on Rome 1922; divides Italian economy into government-controlled syndicates
Union of Soviet Socialist Republics established 1922
Hitler stages unsuccessful *Putsch* in Munich 1923; begins *Mein Kampf* 1925

Egypt becomes sovereign, with British restrictions 1923
Republic of Turkey set up with Mustafa Kemal Pasha as president, Treaty of Lausanne signed 1923
Ibn-Saud gains control of Arabian peninsula 1924-1925

Election of Hindenburg as president underlines rising German ultra-nationalism 1925
Trotsky loses bid for power to Stalin 1927
Stalin purges rivals 1928-1931, 1935-1938
Stalin inaugurates first Five Year Plan 1928

Universal Manhood Suffrage Bill passed in Japan 1925

Chiang Kai-shek purges Communists 1927; conquers Peking, unites China 1928

Hamaguchi's ministry peak of liberalism in Japan 1929; his assassination causes permanent liberal setback 1930

1929

Iraq gains full independence from Britain 1930
Round-table conferences on India 1930-1932
Arab violence in British mandate of Palestine 1930's
Segregation, unrest grow in Union of South Africa 1930's
Communists oppose French rule in Indochina 1930's
Japan invades Manchuria 1931
Chinese Communists proclaim Chinese Soviet Republic 1931; Chiang launches campaigns against Communists 1931-1934
Ibn-Saud's holdings renamed Saudi Arabia 1932

Republic in Portugal replaced by dictatorship of Salazar 1932
Russia begins second Five-Year Plan 1933
Hitler becomes dictator of Germany, Germany withdraws from League of Nations 1933; first Four-Year Plan established 1933, second 1936

Coup d'état in Siam (Thailand) 1932, new constitution promulgated
Japan withdraws from League of Nations, pushes into China 1933; T'ang-ku Truce 1933

Dictatorships formed in Albania, Bulgaria by 1935; in Greece 1936
Germans march into Rhineland 1936

Commonwealth of Philippines formed 1935
Government of India Act of 1935 goes into effect in British India 1937-1939; is rejected by native princes 1939

Italy withdraws from League of Nations 1937

British grant Burma restricted home rule 1937
War breaks out again between Japan and China 1937; Japan proclaims New Order in Asia 1938

Russia initiates third Five-Year Plan 1938

Fascist dictator Franco gains power, ends republic after Spanish civil war 1939

1939

Tojo becomes premier of Japan 1941

1945

Chronological Table 8

1945

Yalta Conference (Feb. 4-11)

Death of Roosevelt; Truman becomes president (Apr. 12)

Mussolini shot (Apr. 28); Hitler commits suicide (Apr. 30?)

V-E Day; surrender of Nazi Germany (May 8)

UN Charter signed at San Francisco (June 26)

Potsdam Conference (July 17-Aug. 2).

Atomic bomb dropped on Hiroshima (Aug. 6)

Unconditional surrender of Japan (Aug. 14)

1946

First General Assembly of the UN in London (Jan. 10)

Independence of the Philippines proclaimed (July 4)

New constitution establishes Fourth French Republic (Oct. 13)

Germany divided into Soviet, British, American, and French zones (Oct. 29)

1947

Truman asks aid for Greece and Turkey; Truman Doctrine (Mar. 12)

European Recovery Plan (Marshall Plan) introduced (June 5)

Dominions of India and Pakistan formed (Aug. 15)

1948

Gandhi assassinated (Jan. 30)

Communist coup in Czechoslovakia (Feb. 25)

Israel proclaimed state (May 14)

Berlin blockade (June 18, 1948-Sept. 30, 1949)

Defection of Tito from Cominform (June 28)

Republic of Korea proclaimed in Seoul (Aug. 15)

1949

North Atlantic Treaty (NATO) signed (Apr. 4)

German Federal Republic born in West Germany (May 23)

Soviets found German Democratic Republic (May 30)

Adenauer's Christian Democrats sweep West German elections (Aug. 14)

People's Republic of China established (Sept. 21)

Explosion of first Soviet atomic bomb announced (Sept. 23)

Chinese Nationalists abandon mainland for Formosa (Dec. 8)

Indonesia granted independence (Dec. 27)

1950

India becomes republic within British Commonwealth (Jan. 26)

U.S.S.R. and Red China sign thirty-year alliance (Feb. 14)

North Korean forces cross 38th parallel (June 25)

UN endorses Truman's request to send troops to South Korea (June 27)

1951

Chinese Communists attack UN forces in Korea (Jan. 1)

Japan signs peace treaty permitting U.S. troops to remain in Japan (Sept. 8)

Turkey and Greece join NATO (Sept. 20)

1952

Batista's coup d'état in Cuba (Mar. 10)

First U.S. H-bomb tested at Eniwetok (Nov. 1)

1953

Stalin dies; succeeded by Malenkov (Mar. 5)

Egypt declared a republic (June 18)

Korean armistice signed at Panmunjon (July 27)

1954

Nasser becomes premier of Egypt (Feb. 25)

U.S. Supreme Court outlaws racial segregation in public schools (May 17)

French defeated at Dien Bien Phu (May 7); Vietnam divided (July 21)

1955

Malenkov resigns; replaced by Bulganin and Khrushchev (Feb. 8)

Afro-Asian Conference at Bandung, Indonesia (Apr. 18-24)

West Germany admitted to NATO (May 9)

U.S.S.R. and eastern European satellites sign Warsaw Pact (May 14)

1956

Anglo-Egyptian Sudan becomes independent republic of Sudan (Jan. 1)

Egypt seizes Suez Canal; Nasser announces its nationalization (July 26)

Revolution in Hungary; crushed by Soviet army (Oct. 23-Nov. 30)

Israelis invade Sinai Peninsula; drive toward Suez Canal (Oct. 29)

1957

Gomulka's National Unity front wins Polish elections (Jan. 20)

Ghana becomes sovereign state in British Commonwealth (Mar. 6)

Creation of European Economic Community (Common Market) (Mar. 25)

Malaysia becomes independent state within British Commonwealth (Aug. 31)

Soviet Sputnik fired into orbit; space age begins (Oct. 4)

1958

Khrushchev becomes Soviet premier (Mar. 27)

First conference of independent African states, Accra, Ghana (Apr. 15)

De Gaulle becomes premier of France (June 1)

Guinea granted independence from France (Sept. 29)

Ayub Khan seizes power in Pakistan (Oct. 7)

1959

Cuban rebels under Castro overthrow Batista (Jan. 1)

Lunik I launched; first artificial planet to orbit the sun (Jan. 3)

1960

U.S. and Japan renew mutual security pact (Jan. 19)

Big Four Paris summit meeting collapses (May 16)

Belgian Congo declared independent republic of the Congo (June 30)

Nigeria granted independence (Oct. 1)

1961

UN Security Council authorizes peacekeeping force in Congo (Feb. 21)

U.S. supported Cuban expedition defeated at Bay of Pigs (Apr. 17)

Beginning of Berlin Wall (Aug. 13)

1962

New U.S. military command established in South Vietnam (Feb. 8)

Chinese Communists attack Indian Himalayan frontier (Oct. 20)

U.S.-Soviet crisis over missile bases in Cuba (Oct. 22-28)

1963

France vetoes British entry to Common Market (Jan. 29)

Signing of nuclear test ban treaty by U.S., Britain, and Russia (Aug. 5)

West German chancellor Adenauer resigns (Oct. 16)

U.S. President John F. Kennedy assassinated (Nov. 22)

Sino-Soviet rift splits leadership in Communist world

1964

Nehru dies; succeeded by Shastri (May 27)

U.S. adopts comprehensive Civil Rights Bill (July 2)

Khrushchev ousted; replaced by Brezhnev and Kosygin (Oct. 14)

Communist China explodes its first atomic bomb (Oct. 16)

1965

U.S. begins bombing North Vietnam (Feb. 7)

Rhodesia declares independence from Britain (Nov. 11)

1966

Indira Gandhi becomes prime minister of India (Jan. 19)

Army officers seize control of Ghana, ousting Nkrumah (Feb. 24)

French government announces withdrawal of its troops from NATO (March 9)

1967

Civil war begins between Nigerian federation and Biafra (May 30)

Six-day Arab-Israeli war (June 5-10)

1968

Nuclear nonproliferation treaty accepted by UN (June 10)

Soviet invasion of Czechoslovakia (Aug. 20)

President Johnson announces halt in bombing of North Vietnam (Oct. 31)

1969

De Gaulle resigns (Apr. 28); Pompidou elected premier of France (June 16)

Nixon announces policy of de-escalation of Vietnam conflict (June 9)

American astronauts land on the moon (July 20)

Willy Brandt elected chancellor of West Germany (Oct. 22)

1970

Biafran war ends (Jan. 13)

Rhodesia becomes a republic (March 2)

Nasser dies (Sept. 28); Anwar Sadat becomes premier of Egypt (Oct. 15)

1971

Bangladesh declares its independence from Pakistan (March 26)

Britain enters European Economic Community (May 13)

The People's Republic of China admitted to the UN (Dec. 3)

1972

Nixon visits Communist China (Feb. 17)

Nixon signs Strategic Arms Limitation Treaty in Moscow (May 26)

Break-in at the Democratic party's headquarters in the Watergate Hotel (June 17)

1973

Paris Accord ends American fighting in Vietnam (Jan. 27)

Allende overthrown in Chile (Sept. 11)

Egypt and Syria invade Israel (Oct. 6)

Arab oil embargo (Oct. 17)

1974

Arab oil embargo ended (April 18)

Portuguese army coup overthrows dictatorship in power since 1932 (April 25)

Brandt resigns (May 6); Schmidt becomes West German chancellor (May 16)

Giscard d'Estaing elected president of France (May 19)

Pro-Greek coup deposes government of Cyprus (July 15)

Nixon resigns and Gerald Ford becomes U.S. president (Aug. 9)

Pardon granted to Nixon by President Ford (Sept. 8)

1975

South Vietnam government surrenders to Communists; Cambodia and Laos fall (April 30)

Suez Canal, closed since 1967, reopened (June 5)

Mozambique becomes independent (June 25); Angola becomes independent (Nov. 11)

Israel and Egypt sign disengagement pact (Oct. 10)

Francisco Franco dies; succeeded by Juan Carlos I (Nov. 20)

1976

Syrian peacekeeping force enters Lebanon (June 21); ceasefire in Lebanon ends civil war (Oct. 21)

Viking lander I (July 20) and II (Sept. 3) successfully land on Mars

Death of Mao Tse-tung (Sept. 9), succeeded by Hua Kuo-feng (Oct. 12)

Rhodesia accepts British-U.S. plan for black majority rule (Sept. 24)

Jimmy Carter wins U.S. presidential election over Gerald Ford (Nov. 2)

Index

Suggested pronunciations for difficult or unusual words are respelled according to the table below, which is repeated in simplified form at the bottom of each right-hand page of the INDEX. The local pronunciations of many foreign words are too unusual for persons untrained in linguistics, and pronunciations given here are those commonly acceptable in unaffected, educated American speech.

a	hat, cap	j	jam, enjoy	u	cup, son	**FOREIGN SOUNDS**
ā	age, face	k	kind, seek	u̇	put, book	
ã	care, air	l	land, coal	ü	rule, move	Y as in French *lune*. Pronounce ē with the lips rounded as for English ü in *rule*.
ä	father, far	m	me, am	ū	use, music	
		n	no, in			
b	bad, rob	ng	long, bring			
ch	child, much					
d	did, red					
		o	hot, rock	v	very, save	Œ as in French *deux*. Pronounce ā with the lips rounded as for ō.
		ō	open, go	w	will, woman	
		ô	order, all	y	you, yet	
e	let, best	oi	oil, toy	z	zero, breeze	
ē	equal, see	ou	out, now	zh	measure, seizure	N *as in French bon.* The N is not pronounced, but shows that the vowel before it is nasal.
ėr	term, learn					
		p	pet, cup			
f	fat, if	r	run, try	ə	represents:	
g	go, bag	s	say, yes	a	in about	
h	he, how	sh	she, rush	e	in taken	H as in German *ach*. Pronounce *k* without closing the breath passage.
		t	tell, it	i	in pencil	
i	it, pin	th	thin, both	o	in lemon	
ī	ice, five	ŦH	then, smooth	u	in circus	

Abbasid (a bas′id) dynasty, 160–162, 164
Abdul-Hamid II, 640–641
Abélard (ab′ə lärd), Pierre, 251–252
Abraham, 29, 155
Abrahams, Peter, 877
Absolutism: assault on, 467–470; "enlightened," 469–470; in France, 443–447, 479; in Russia, 455–458; structure of, 442–443
Abu Bakr (ə bü′ bak′ėr), 155, 156, 158
Abu Dhabi, 851
Abyssinia, *see* Ethiopia
Achebe, Chinua, 877
Achilles, 42
Adams, John, 471–472, 611
Adams, Samuel, 472
Adelaide (Queen of Lombardy), 235
Adenauer, Konrad, 789–791
Advertising, 537, 538
Aeschylus, 54, 56
Afghanistan, 277, 639, 642, 643, 644, 654
Africa, 518, 824, 862, 888; anthropologists in, 832; Asante, 376, 377, 378, 380, 646; Axumite, 365–366; Bantu, 377; Belgium, 646, 648, 728, 830; contemporary, 877–878, 880; detribalization, 729–730, 731; early history, 361–362; England, 604, 646, 648–649, 728, 830; European impact on, 362, 372–373, 377, 378; France, 574, 645, 649, 728, 831–832; geography of, 361, 362–363, 367; Germany, 648; Holland, 377; imperialism in, 646–650, 728, 830; India, 371; intellectuals of, 730–731, 832, 877; Italy, 370, 602, 640, 645, 649, 678, 736; Kushite, 365–366; life-styles of, 363–364, 378, 379–380, 650, 729; mandate system in, 728–729; new nations of, 831–832; Ottoman, 644–645; peoples of, 363–364, 373, 377–380, 832–837; political unity in, 846; Portugal, 372, 373–374, 380, 395; prehistoric, 10–12, 364–365; Roman, 135, 366; slave trade in, 373–376, 398, 405, 406, 623, 631, 646, 844; sub-Saharan, 373, 377, 645–646, 729, 830, 832, 841, 862, 877;

trans-Sahara trade, 366, 369, 370, 371, 374, 376; Sudanic, 367–371, 378; trade with, 371–372, 374, 375–376, 396, 406; United States, 844–845, 848; wealth of, 649–650; pre-World War I, 675; post-World War I, 728–732; World War II, 771, 844; Zulu, 377. *See also* South Africa *and under individual nations and tribes*
Agamemnon, 41, 42, 54
Agnew, Spiro, 797
Agriculture: advances in, 497–498; Africa, 363, 364–365, 377; Byzantine, 148; Canada, 631; China, 104, 105, 106, 176, 349, 816, 817; culture system, 657; pre-Columbian, 381; Egypt, 21; England, 497–498; and food production, 887–888, 890, 891; France, 789; Germany, 498; India, 99, 888, 898a; irrigation, 21; Japan, 182; Latin America, 798; medieval, 199–200, 213, 215; Mesopotamia, 16; Muslim, 160, 161, 207–208; neolithic, 12, 15–16; in New World, 399–400; prehistoric, 1, 4; Rome, 72, 79, 130, 137; Russia, 498, 712, 713, 806, 810–811; Southeast Asia, 657; state subsidies to, 79; Sumeria, 15; technology of, 105, 106, 200, 213, 215, 364, 410, 862; United States, 725. *See also* Economy; Farming; Land distribution; Peasants
Aguiyi-Ironsi, Johnson, 835
Akbar (ak′bär), 343–344, 345
Akhenaton (ä′ke nä′tən), 22–23, 25, 26, 27, 28
Akkad (äk′äd), 15, 18
Alaric (al′ə rik), 135, 136
Alaska, 380, 657
al-Bakri, 367–368
Albania, 640, 641, 683, 781–782
Albigensians (al′bə jen′si ənz), 230, 248, 309
Albuquerque (al′bu kėrk), Afonso de, 395, 396
alcoholism, 118b, 386b, 511, 516
Alcuin (al′kwin), 193, 243
Alexander I (Russia), 487, 557, 561, 563, 565–566, 581–582
Alexander II (Russia), 583, 599, 603
Alexander III (Russia), 599, 675

hat, āge, cãre, fär; let, ēqual, tèrm; it, īce; hot, ōpen, ôrder, oil, out; cup, pùt, rüle, üse; ch, child; ng, long; th, thin; FH, then; zh, measure; ə represents *a* in *about, e* in *taken, i* in *pencil, o* in *lemon, u* in *circus.*

hat, āge, cãre, fär; let, ēqual, tèrm; it, īce; hot, ōpen, ôrder, oil,
out; cup, pùt, rüle, ūse; ch, child; ng, long; th, thin; ⊤H, then; zh,
measure; ə represents *a* in about, *e* in taken, *i* in pencil, *o* in lemon, *u* in circus.

---

hat, āge, cãre, fär; let, ēqual, tėrm; it, īce; hot, ōpen, ôrder, oil, out; cup, pu̇t, rüle, ūse; ch, child; ng, long; th, thin; ᴛʜ, then; zh, measure; ə represents *a* in *a*bout, *e* in tak*e*n, *i* in penc*i*l, *o* in lem*o*n, *u* in circ*u*s.

hat, āge, cãre, fär; let, ēqual, tẻrm; it, īce; hot, ōpen, ôrder, oil, out; cup, pủt, rüle, ūse; ch, child; ng, long; th, thin; ᴛʜ, then; zh, measure; ǝ represents *a* in *about*, *e* in *taken*, *i* in *pencil*, *o* in *lem-on*, *u* in *circus*.

hat, āge, cãre, fär; let, ēqual, tėrm; it, īce; hot, ōpen, ôrder, oil, out; cup, pút, rüle, ūse; ch, child; ng, long; th, thin; ŦH, then; zh, measure; ə represents *a* in about, *e* in taken, *i* in pencil, *o* in lemon, *u* in circus.

hat, āge, cãre, fär; let, ēqual, tèrm; it, īce; hot, ōpen, ôrder, oil; out; cup, pu̇t, rüle, ūse; ch, child; ng, long; th, thin; ᴛʜ, then; zh, measure; ə represents *a* in *about, e* in *taken, i* in *pencil, o* in *lemon, u* in *circus.*

---

hat, āge, cāre, fär; let, ēqual, tėrm; it, īce; hot, ōpen, ôrder, oil, out; cup, pŭt, rüle, ūse; ch, child; ng, long; th, thin; ᴛн, then; zh, measure; ə represents *a* in about, *e* in taken, *i* in pencil, *o* in lemon, *u* in circus.

hat, āge, cãre, fär; let, ēqual, tėrm; it, īce; hot, ōpen, ôrder, oil, out; cup, pùt, rüle, ūse; ch, child; ng, long; th, thin; ᴛʜ, then; zh, measure; ə represents *a* in *a*bout, *e* in tak*e*n, *i* in penc*i*l, *o* in lem-*o*n, *u* in circ*u*s.

hat, āge, cãre, fär; let, ēqual, tėrm; it, īce; hot, ōpen, ôrder, oil, out; cup, pút, rüle, ūse; ch, child; ng, long; th, thin; ᴛʜ, then; zh, measure; ə represents a in about, e in taken, i in pencil, o in lemon, u in circus.

Hat, āge, cãre, fär; let, ēqual, tėrm; it, īce; hot, ōpen, ôrder, oil, out; cup, pút, rüle, use; ch, child; ng, long; th, thin; ᴛʜ, then; zh, measure; ə represents *a* in *about*, *e* in *taken*, *i* in *pencil*, *o* in *lemon*, *u* in *circus*.

The Reference Maps

History accounts for man's activities in time, and maps depict them in space. Therefore, to understand mankind's experiences, knowledge of the planetary environment is essential. These reference maps show key areas at significant periods; they include basic physical features which affect man's attempts to control his environment as well as his fellow man.

Map 1: The Ancient Near East and Greece. In the area displayed we can trace the progressive expansion of man's environmental control resulting from his invention of new tools and social institutions. Thus the transition from food collecting to farming occurred in well-watered sites bordering the Syrian, Arabian, and Iranian deserts—such as at Jericho in the Great Rift Valley of the Jordan and at Jarmo in uplands to the east of the Tigris. The breakthrough from Neolithic barbarism to civilization, i.e., to societies sufficiently complex to permit the emergence of urban centers, occurred in two important river basins, the Tigris-Euphrates and the Nile—linked by a Fertile Crescent with minimal natural obstacles to impede the movement of peoples and goods.

Employing primitive craft, Neolithic seafarers had hugged the Mediterranean coasts and slowly pushed westward—as attested by Neolithic sites in Cyprus, Rhodes, and Crete. Improvements in maritime technology permitted the emergence of a splendid Aegean civilization centering at Knossos in Crete, and Pylos on the Greek mainland, and Troy in northwest Asia Minor. Civilization's center of gravity shifted progressively northward across the eastern basin of the Mediterranean, culminating in Hellas with its sea-oriented city-states: Corinth, Thebes, and, above all, Athens. Continued advances in maritime technology enabled the Greeks to master the eastern Mediterranean and Black seas and establish colonies, while the Phoenicians carried their mercantile ventures from their port cities of Tyre and Sidon along the North African coast. What the Tigris-Euphrates had been to the Babylonians, and the Nile to the Egyptians, the Mediterranean became to the Greeks, the Phoenicians, and eventually to the Romans—the "middle of the earth."

Map 2: The Roman Empire c. 117 A.D. This map underscores the importance of physical features in the creation of the Roman world-state. From its east-west maritime axis, the Roman *imperium* stretched into the hinterland, which was linked by rivers and roads to strategically located ports that provided transshipment to other parts of the empire.

The expansion of the Roman world followed a logical sequence. It began with Rome's conquest of the Italian peninsula and Great Greece (including Sicily). The Punic Wars opened up the entire western basin of the Mediterranean, while subsequent intrusion into the eastern basin made Rome mistress of the Hellenistic world. The first century B.C. saw the consolidation of Roman control in Asia Minor, the conquest of transalpine Gaul by Julius Caesar, and the annexation of Egypt, Numidia, and Cyrenaica. The territorial domain was rounded out later by the acquisition of Mauretania, Dacia, Armenia, and Mesopotamia.

Here we see the Roman world at its broadest expanse, encompassing almost 100 million diverse peoples and linked by the greatest communications network then devised. However, the world-state soon entered its time of troubles, attended by decline of population, of administrative efficiency, and of military power. The empire then found itself overextended and had to reduce its territorial perimeter. Armenia, Mesopotamia, and Dacia were abandoned, and eventually the Roman legions were recalled from Britain.

In the fourth century the once majestic Roman empire was polarized into two unequal segments—the western section administered from Rome and having the weaker but spatially larger area; and the eastern section controlled from New Rome (Constantinople) and having a larger population, more compact territory, and a stronger economy. At last the two segments, each centering on one of the major basins of the Mediterranean, were split asunder by the barbarian invasions. The classical world then gave way to the medieval world.

Map 3: The Ancient East. Here we encounter the homelands of the two major fluvial civilizations (societies originating in river basins) centering on the Indus-Gangetic and the Huang Ho drainage basins. The remarkable longevity of Indian and Chinese societies owes much to physical factors which inhibited alien intrusion. The Indian triangle was protected by the Indian Ocean and the Himalayas, though invasion was possible through the western passes; as for China, the obstacles posed by the Pacific Ocean, the forbidding Taklamakan and Gobi deserts, and a series of mountain ranges effectively limited entrance into the Huang Ho valley.

The map also shows the boundaries of three empires: the Han in China, the Mauryan in India, and the Parthian in western Asia. Note that they are contemporary with the Roman world-state at its zenith. After centuries of feudal fragmentation, China was reunited, and under Shih Huang-ti, the Great Wall was rebuilt and lengthened to keep the nomadic tribes in the north and west from pillaging the sedentary farmers tilling the "good earth" to the south. The centuries marked by the Han dynasty were stable and prosperous. So too were the centuries of Mauryan rule in India. Under Ashoka, a single administration extended from the Himalayas across the Narbada River and included the Deccan—leaving only the southernmost part of the subcontinent outside its rule. Meanwhile, to the northwest lay Bactria, where Hellenistic and Indian culture interfused, producing the Gandharran art found in Taxila.

This is the era, too, when the western and eastern segments of the Eurasian land mass were in commercial and cultural contact. Ships plied the Indian Ocean, taking advantage of the recently discovered monsoon mechanism while a tenuous but profitable Silk Route stretched from Ch'ang-an through Kashgar, Samarkand, and across Parthian lands to Ecbatana, Ctesiphon, and Seleucia. In addition, the movement of goods from both China and India westward enriched the "caravan cities" such as Palmyra (see Map 2).

Map 4: Medieval France, Spain, and the British Isles 1328. We can perceive here the emerging outlines of the national state system in western Europe. For example, in 1328 Edward II had to officially recognize Scotland as independent, while across the Channel, the extinction of the Capetian line set the stage for a protracted struggle over the succession to the French throne. Known as the Hundred Years' War (1337–1453), it was marked by the loss of large English holdings obtained in Plantagenet days. Meanwhile, ambitious French kings enlarged their domain from the Ile de France around Paris southward to the Mediterranean and then sought to expand their territory eastward at the expense of the feudal-fragmented Holy Roman Empire. The Iberian peninsula was also fragmented, but here the Christian kingdoms were girding to clear the peninsula of those Moors still entrenched in Granada.

Certain areas are noteworthy for their economic importance at this juncture: the Low Countries, where the textile industry enriched such towns as Bruges, Lille, Ghent, Ypres, and Cambrai; Champagne in northeastern France, where the most famous medieval fairs in all Europe were held; and southern France, with its thriving commercial centers at Narbonne and Marseille.

Note, too, that whereas in classical times urban centers predominated on the coast, in medieval Europe a large number of river-oriented towns were founded or acquired increasing importance. Roads were poor, and river transport was both economical and efficient. Rivers such as the Thames, Meuse, Seine, Loire, Rhone, Garonne, Tagus, Guadalquivir, and Po were being constantly utilized, while the Rhine and Danube, important as political and military boundaries in Roman times, were vital waterways throughout medieval times.

Map 5: Europe 1648. The year 1648 is a crucial one, for the Thirty Years' War, started as a religious conflict, ended with the victory of the national state which acknowledged no authority higher than its own sovereignty and interests. The map indicates the further territorial consolidation of the national state system (as compared with Map 4). Thus Scotland and England are now one political entity; the Iberian peninsula is demarcated as Spain and Portugal (though neither is any longer a first-class power); France has acquired bishoprics in Lorraine and a foothold in Alsace. The map also shows the emergence of Switzerland, the three Scandinavian countries, Poland, and Russia.

Germany and Italy remain territorially fragmented and politically unstable, as the Holy Roman Empire has vanished in everything but name and pretensions. The situation in the flat north European plain remains fluid; the boundaries of Brandenburg, Poland, and Russia were always subject to change on that plain, reflecting the fluctuating power relations of those states. Meanwhile, the Ottoman Turks continue to threaten central Europe despite their defeat at sea at Lepanto in 1571.

Map 6: European Empires c. 1700. With the age of exploration, western Europeans set out to explore the unmapped portions of the globe, spreading their religion, cultures, and languages wherever their questing galleons made a new landfall. In the wake of the explorer went the missionary, merchant, and musketeer so that in time Europeans controlled most, or all, of the land surface of every other continent. The age of exploration both intensified and territorially expanded European national rivalries.

This map has much to tell us. The European states bordering the Atlantic attempted to explore and colonize lands in the New World in latitudes roughly comparable to their own. Thus the Danes proceeded northwestward to Iceland and Greenland, the English and French competed for lands north of the Gulf of Mexico, and Spain and Portugal laid their claims in more southerly latitudes. Following Portuguese initiative, other Europeans sought out—and fought over—islands, coastal strips, and spheres of interest around the African and Indian coasts and in the archipelagoes of Southeast Asia.

The contrasting depths of European penetration of the New and Old Worlds at this juncture are significant. In the Americas, Europeans encountered either Stone Age Amerinds or pre-Columbian civilizations incapable of assimilating, much less fighting off, the newcomers. Consequently, the European acquisition of North and South America—and later of Australia—was complete. This resulted in the establishment of colonial empires in which the language, laws, religion, and cultural values of the respective metropolitan nations were brought *in toto* to the New World. In contrast, in sub-Saharan Africa as well as South and East Asia, the Europeans were invariably outnumbered. Hence, though they managed to establish trading settlements along the coast, and eventually acquire political ascendency in most of these regions, they did not succeed in replacing the indigenous culture patterns.

Map 7: Europe 1815. This map can best be examined by comparing it with Map 5—the European landscape 167 years earlier. The fewest territorial-political changes have occurred in western Europe, though some further consolidation has taken place. Thus Ireland is now part of the United Kingdom; Sweden has been allowed by the major powers to annex Norway (in compensation for its loss of Finland to Russia); while what had formerly been Holland and the Spanish Netherlands are now included in the Kingdom of the Netherlands. France, though deprived of some of Napoleon's earlier territorial conquests, has by this time acquired Alsace and Lorraine, and Franche Comté (to the immediate west of Switzerland).

A comparison of Maps 4 and 7 would seem to point to greater fragmentation of the defunct Holy Roman Empire. Actually the German people have now to give their allegiances to only thirty-nine states, as compared with some three hundred in the old Empire, and are loosely organized in a confederation. Most striking is the growth of Prussia from its nucleus in Brandenburg, due to its superb army, to dynastic inheritances, and to astute diplomacy. Italy remains highly fragmented; in Metternich's disdainful phrase, it is only a "geographical expression."

Further east, the political and territorial changes that occurred between 1648 and 1815 are more dramatic. The Austrian empire has expanded into northern Italy and also includes parts of Poland and territory formerly conquered by the Ottoman empire. Meanwhile, due to the partitions of 1772, 1793, and 1795, Poland has ceased to exist, while the corruption-ridden Turks are being forced back toward their home base in Asia Minor.

The most spectacular of all territorial gains has been registered by Russia, advancing westward toward the heart of Europe and southward in the general direction of Constantinople. Moscow has acquired Finland, Estonia, the bulk of Poland, the Ukraine, and Bessarabia.

Map 8: Europe August 1939. This map can be profitably compared with the map on page 687. The most noticeable changes result from the defeat of the Central Powers in World War I and also from alterations in what had formerly been tsarist Russia. Germany was shorn of its overseas colonies, while in Europe it lost Alsace-Lorraine, half of Schleswig, three western districts to Belgium, the Polish Corridor, and a zone in the Rhineland, which was demilitarized. The Austrian empire was dismembered; the nationalist movements of the Czechs, Poles, and Slavs achieved formal territorial recognition; and the remnant of the empire was converted into the separate states of Austria and Hungary. The Ottoman empire was in turn dissected: Greece obtained nearly all of European Turkey, Syria was mandated to France, Palestine and Iraq to Great Britain. After the Bolshevik Revolution, Russia lost much of its western territory, resulting in the establishment of Finland, Estonia, Latvia, and Lithuania, as well as the major portion of reconstituted Poland, while Bessarabia was ceded to Rumania.

Important changes also took place during the interwar years. Under Hitler, Nazi Germany reoccupied the Rhineland in 1936, seized Austria and occupied Sudetenland in 1938, and the following year seized other Czech territory as well as Memel. In 1939, too, Hungary annexed part of Slovakia, while Mussolini's Italy defeated and annexed Albania. The stage was also set for Russia to reannex territory lost after the Bolshevik Revolution.

Map 9: Africa 1914. Four major cultural environments of Africa, each with its unique historical development, may be partially explained by two physical features of the continent—the Sahara Desert and the Great Rift Valley, which runs from the Jordan Valley in Palestine to Western Tanzania. Separated from the rest of the continent by more than 1000 miles of the Sahara, most of the peoples of northwest Africa live close to the Mediterranean, which connects them with Europe from which has long come a flow of people, goods, and ideas. Northeast Africa, partly cut off from the rest of the continent by the Sahara, has long been linked with southwest Asia. Moreover, the Red Sea has always facilitated movement between northeast Africa and Arabia. Africa east of the Great Rift Valley has long been oriented to the Indian Ocean, to the Arab trader, and, since, the last century, to the European who has farmed the plateaus of Kenya, Uganda, and Tanzania.

The lands in the southern section of the Great Rift Valley also form part of sub-Saharan Africa. In this huge area the Sudanese savanna lands, equatorial rain forest, and the steppes and deserts of southern Africa succeed each other from north to south. In these lands occurred Europe's great scramble for empire in the nineteenth century.

Map 10: Africa. Profound political and territorial changes have occurred in Africa since 1914—undoubtedly the most spectacular to be found in any continent during the past half century. From being a vast collection of colonial holdings, Africa has emerged as an agglomeration of national states, virtually all having minimal political stability or economic viability. During the interwar years some major changes took place on the political landscape. German Togoland and the Cameroons were mandated to Great Britain and France; German East Africa was divided into two mandates: Ruanda-Urundi (Belgium) and Tanganyika (Great Britain); and German Southwest Africa was mandated to South Africa. Egypt became an independent kingdom, but Italy's possessions in East Africa were enlarged by the conquest of Abyssinia. Since World War II, however, a spectacular alteration has occurred. The entire continent has passed into indigenous political control, with the exception of Rhodesia, still under white minority control, and South Africa, where European domination remains entrenched.

Map 11: U.S.S.R. and Asia. Dominating Eurasia, the greatest land mass on earth, is the enormous area of the Soviet Union (more than 8 million square miles), extending on a west-east axis for 5000 miles. European Russia, largely a continuation of the north European plain, is drained by the Dvina, Dnieper, Don, and Volga, the last three flowing southward. East of the Urals virtually all rivers flow north to the Arctic, save the Amur,

which in its eastward journey also serves as a boundary with China. As the river pattern indicates, Soviet Asia tends to be separated from middle- and low-latitude Asia by physical obstacles, in this case steppes, deserts, mountains. The highest population and urban densities are found in Soviet Europe, while in Siberia, which is rapidly growing, the population is located along the major waterways or the Trans-Siberian Railroad.

As a result of their eastward expansion, the Russians had settled on the Pacific by 1649. In the next two centuries they penetrated east of the Caspian in what is now the Kazakh, Uzbek, and Turkmen Soviet Socialist Republics. In their expansion they collided with the Chinese in Sinkiang, Mongolia, and Manchuria. These border regions today constitute areas of tension and jockeying between the two major Communist powers.

For its part, China has continued to develop south of the Great Wall and Gobi Desert and east and north of such massive mountain ranges as the Tien Shan, Pamirs, and Himalayas. The vast majority of its estimated 750 million people live in the fertile Huang Ho and Yangtze basins or along the coast. Similarly, Indian society has continued to multiply within the confines of its triangular subcontinent, while influencing the culture patterns of neighboring lands to the east and south.

Southeast Asia has long been subject to recurrent cultural and military intrusions alike. Its highly indented coastline and physical terrain have contributed to a fragmentation of cultures and languages. Offshore in East and Southeast Asia are three archipelagoes: the Philippines; Japan, which is the most highly industrialized and prosperous of nonwestern countries; and Indonesia, whose estimated 110 million people make it the world's fifth largest country.

Map 12: Latin America. Latin America was first colonized by Southern Europeans, notably the Spaniards and Portuguese. Exploiting the mountain ranges, running the length of Central and South America, for their precious metals, the Spaniards increased their holdings until the close of the eighteenth century. They created several viceroyalties: New Spain, including Mexico and Central America; Peru, at first embracing all of Spanish South America; New Granada, in what is now Colombia and Venezuela; and La Plata, which subsequently became Bolivia, Paraguay, Uruguay, and Argentina. Brazil, discovered by the Portuguese Cabral in 1500, was made a viceroyalty in 1714.

In half a century (1776–1826) of colonial revolutions in the New World, Spanish and Portuguese

America became independent (except for Cuba and Puerto Rico which remained Spanish until 1898); but each of the Spanish viceroyalties split into more than one political entity.

The tropical regions of Latin America, including Mexico, Central America, and the lands drained by the Magdalena, Orinoco, and Amazon rivers, have predominantly Amerind populations. In contrast, temperate South America, comprising southern Brazil, Uruguay, Argentina, and Chile, finds Europeans in the majority. In 1960 Latin America had some 200 million people, roughly equivalent to the population of Anglo-America. But Latin America is the fastest-growing region in the world and within forty or fifty years may have a population of perhaps 600 million—or about double that of the United States and Canada.

Map 13: The Middle East. This region—segmented by deserts and seas, but with the latter providing interconnecting routes of travel—has long permitted maximal movement of peoples, goods, and ideas in virtually all directions. In this area, which is unique for the convergence of three continents, we find the birthplace of "civilization" and of three major religions, as well as a continuous succession of dynasties and empires. For centuries Islamic political authority and cultural vitality were bound up with the fortunes of the Ottoman empire, and when the latter was defeated by European powers, the Muslim peoples of this region were in turn subordinated in status and made to feel inferior. The twentieth century, however, has witnessed a resurgence of Islamic culture and political strength—attended by the creation of numerous independent states, including Morocco, Algeria, Libya, Egypt, Sudan, Syria, Lebanon, Jordan, Iraq, and Pakistan; and this resurgence has capitalized upon the strategic value of the region in the geopolitical programs of the superpowers, as well as upon its massive oil resources.

The region has also been in a state of continuous tension and intermittent conflict since the end of World War II, because of Arab-Israeli animosities. When the British mandate of Palestine was terminated in 1948, the area proclaimed itself the new state of Israel—a step sanctioned by the United Nations as well as both the United States and the Soviet Union. But the Arab states remained implacably opposed to any such recognition, and several campaigns were mounted in an effort to regain Palestine for the Muslim Arabs.

Two other Arab-Israeli conflicts occurred in 1967 and 1973. An Israeli victory resulted in occupation of the west bank of the Jordan River; the Sinai peninsula and east bank of the Suez Canal have since been returned to Egypt.

Map 14: Europe. This map can profitably be compared with Map 8 in order to obtain a clearer picture of territorial changes resulting from the outcome of World War II. As after World War I, defeated Germany and its allies were deprived of territory, with the Soviet Union emerging as the greatest single territorial beneficiary.

In 1945 Germany was stripped of East Prussia, while its eastern boundary was set at the Oder-Neisse rivers—the farthest line west achieved by the Slavs since the twelfth century. Moreover, postwar Germany was both ideologically and territorially split, its western segment associated in military and economic pacts with the western world, its eastern section integrated in the Communist world and a member of the Warsaw Pact. While faring better, defeated Italy lost its overseas colonies and Albania.

Conversely, the Soviet Union expanded westward, annexing part of Finland, all of Estonia, Latvia, and Lithuania, and the eastern portion of Poland, shifting that country's center of gravity westward at the expense of Germany. Stalinist policies and power also created a series of "people's democracies" from the Baltic to the Black seas, resulting in the iron curtain. Yet the region was to prove far from monolithic. Shortly after the war Tito declared Yugoslavia an independent Communist state, tiny Albania was later to ally itself with Peking in the great split within the Communist world, while the 1950's and 1960's also witnessed abortive attempts in Hungary and Czechoslovakia to gain greater freedom from Moscow's control.

The contemporary map of Europe differs markedly from earlier maps of the continent not only because of its ideological division but also because of the emergence of new economic groupings. To break down traditional trade barriers, the European Economic Community (the "Common Market") was formed. Another such community is the European Free Trade Association, or "Outer Seven." In an effort to keep pace, the Communist countries organized the Council of Mutual Economic Assistance. It will be interesting to watch the long-term effects of these economic groupings upon the traditional political forces —and boundaries—of Europe.

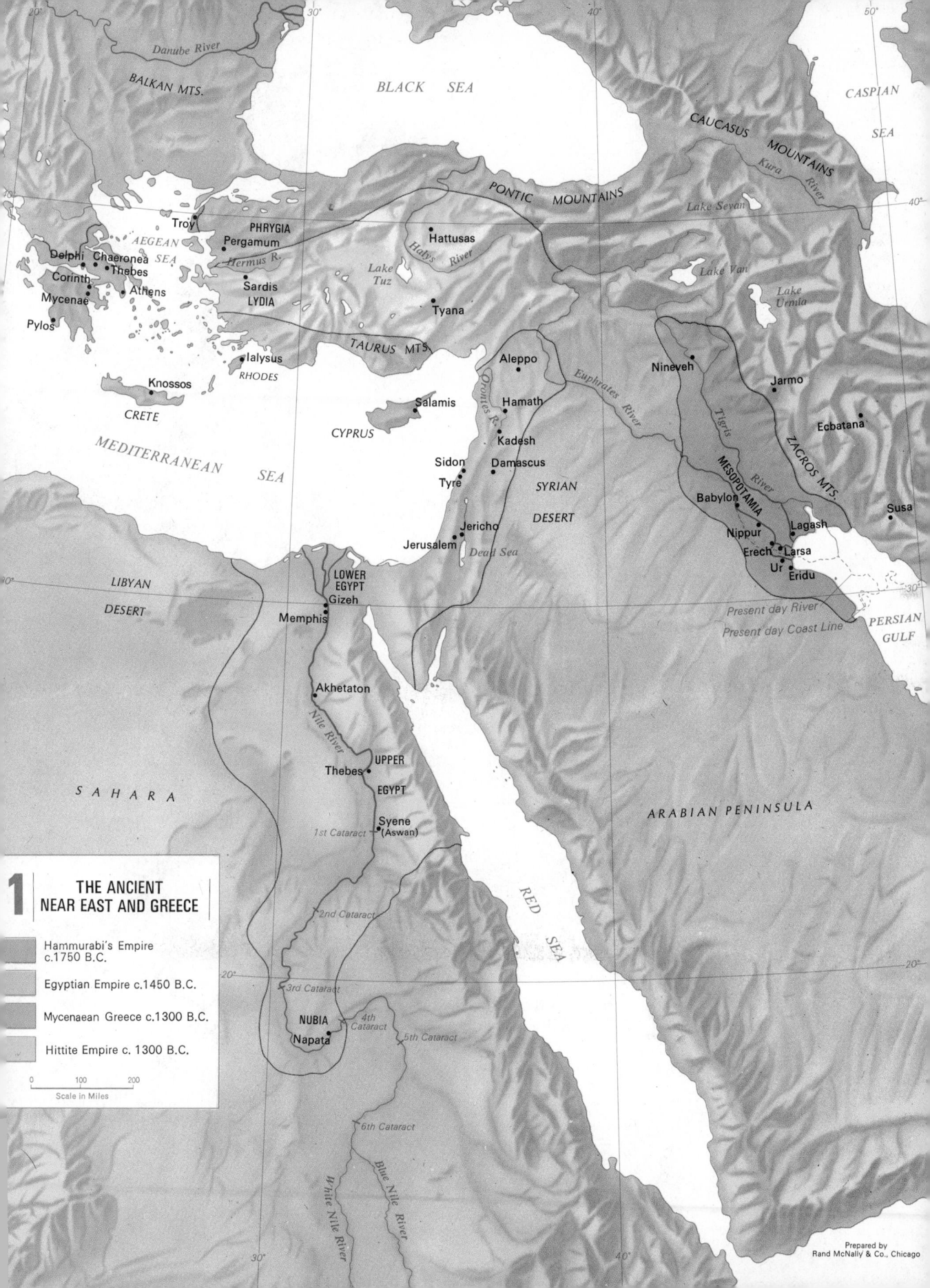

BALKAN MTS.

Danube River

BLACK SEA

CASPIAN SEA

CAUCASUS MOUNTAINS

Kura River

PONTIC MOUNTAINS

Lake Sevan

Troy

PHRYGIA
Pergamum

Hattusas

Halys River

Lake Van

Lake Urmia

Delphi Chaeronea
AEGEAN SEA
Thebes
Corinth
Mycenae   Athens
Sardis
LYDIA
Hermus R.

Lake Tuz

Tyana

Nineveh

Jarmo

Pylos

Ecbatana

ZAGROS MTS.

Ialysus
RHODES

TAURUS MTS.

Aleppo

Orontes R.

Euphrates River

Tigris River

MESOPOTAMIA

Knossos

CRETE

Salamis

Hamath

CYPRUS

Kadesh

Babylon

Susa

MEDITERRANEAN SEA

Sidon
Tyre

Damascus

SYRIAN DESERT

Nippur

Lagash
Erech Larsa
Ur Eridu

Jericho
Jerusalem

Dead Sea

LIBYAN DESERT

LOWER EGYPT
Gizeh
Memphis

Present day River
Present day Coast Line

PERSIAN GULF

Akhetaton

Nile River

SAHARA

UPPER EGYPT
Thebes

Syene
(Aswan)

1st Cataract

ARABIAN PENINSULA

RED SEA

2nd Cataract

1 **THE ANCIENT NEAR EAST AND GREECE**

Hammurabi's Empire c.1750 B.C.

Egyptian Empire c.1450 B.C.

Mycenaean Greece c.1300 B.C.

Hittite Empire c. 1300 B.C.

0   100   200
Scale in Miles

3rd Cataract

NUBIA   *4th Cataract*
Napata   *5th Cataract*

6th Cataract

Blue Nile River

White Nile River

Prepared by
Rand McNally & Co., Chicago

ATLANTIC

OCEAN

NORTH
SEA

IRELAND

IRISH
SEA

Antoninus' Wall
(C. 140 A.D.)

Hadrian's Wall
(C. 122 A.D.)

York
PENNINES
Chester • Lincoln
BRITAIN
Colchester
Bath • London
Thames R.

ENGLISH CHANNEL

GERMANIA

Elbe River

River

Cologne
BELGICA

Rhine River

Mainz

Paris
Seine

Meuse River

Saône R.

Danube

Loire River

GAUL

CENTRAL
MASSIF

ALPS
CISALPINE GAUL

Po River

BAY OF
BISCAY
Bordeaux
Garonne R.

CANTABRIAN MTS.
Douro River

Rhône R.

Lyons

Genoa
Ravenna

Pisa

ADRIATIC

PYRENEES

Marseilles

Tagus
Ebro River

Segovia
SPAIN
River

CORSICA

ITALY
APENNINES

Toledo

Rome

Guadiana River

Valencia

Saguntum

MADEIRA
ISLANDS

SIERRA MORENA
Cordova
Guadalquivir R.
Cádiz
SIERRA NEVADA
Strait of Gibraltar
Tangier • Pillars of Hercules

New
Carthage

BALEARIC
ISLANDS

SARDINIA

Naples
Pomp

MEDITERRA

TYRRHENIAN
SEA

Messina

SICILY
Syra

MAURETANIA
MOUNTAINS
Moulouya R.
ATLAS
Chélif R.
Medjerda R.
Utica
Carthage

MALTA

CANARY
ISLANDS

Chott
Djerid

NUMIDIA

Oea
Leptis
Magna

GRAND ERG OCCIDENTAL

GRAND ERG ORIENTAL

SAHARA

AHAGGAR
MOUNTAINS

2 | **THE ROMAN EMPIRE
C. 117 A.D.**

0   100   200   300
Scale in Miles

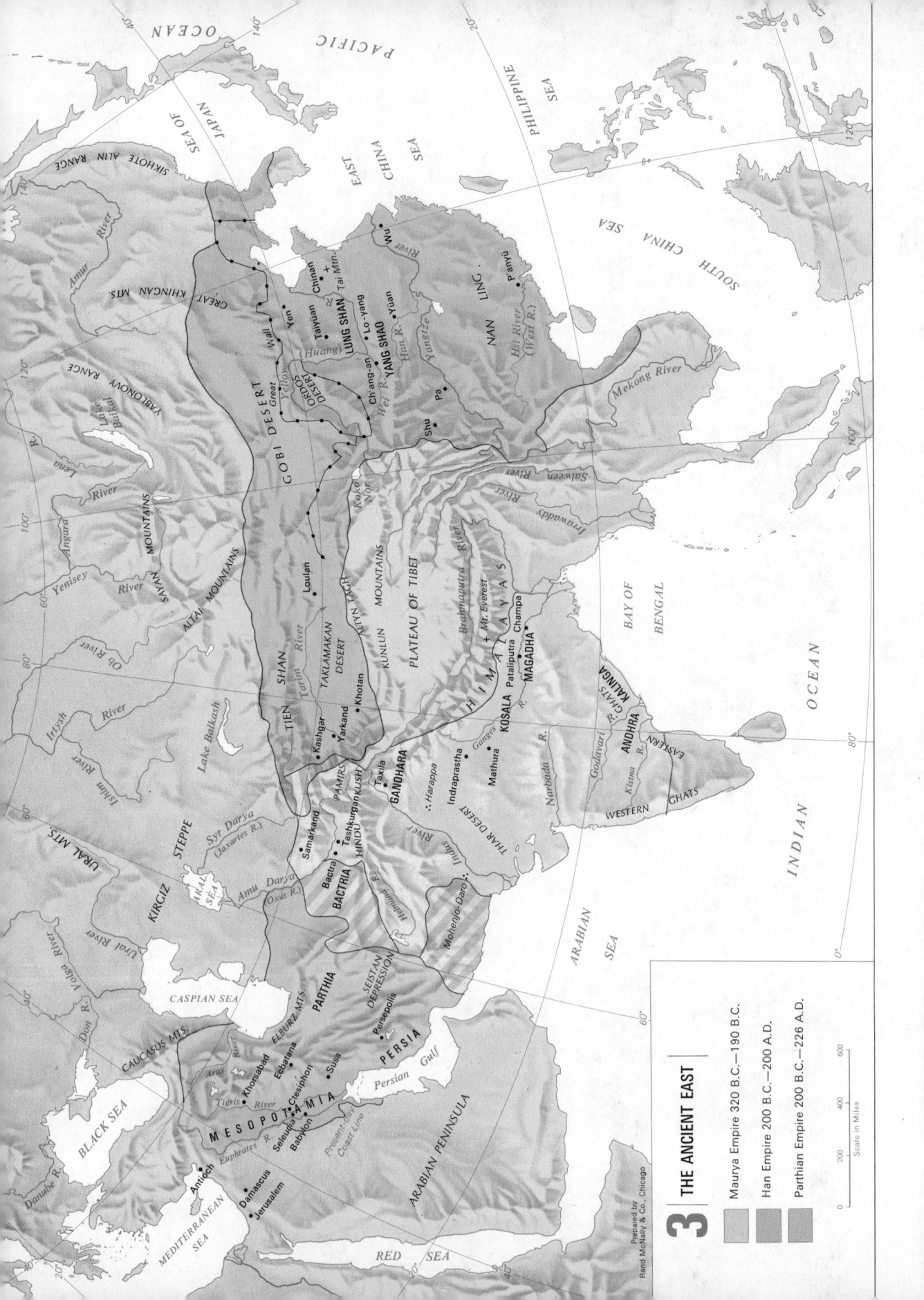

THE ANCIENT EAST

3

Maurya Empire 320 B.C.—190 B.C.

Han Empire 200 B.C.—200 A.D.

Parthian Empire 200 B.C.—226 A.D.

Scale in Miles
0   200   400   600

Prepared by
Rand McNally & Co., Chicago

PACIFIC OCEAN

SEA OF JAPAN

SIKHOTE ALIN RANGE

EAST CHINA SEA

PHILIPPINE SEA

SOUTH CHINA SEA

GREAT KHINGAN MTS.

Amur River

YABLONOW RANGE

Lake Baikal

SAYAN MOUNTAINS

Angara

Yenisey River

Lena River

Ob River

Irtysh River

Ishim River

ALTAI MOUNTAINS

Lake Balkash

URAL MTS.

STEPPE

KIRGIZ

Syr Darya (Jaxartes R.)

ARAL SEA

Amu Darya (Oxus R.)

Ural River

Volga River

Don R.

CAUCASUS MTS.

CASPIAN SEA

BLACK SEA

Danube R.

MEDITERRANEAN SEA

Antioch
Damascus
Jerusalem

RED SEA

ARABIAN PENINSULA

ARABIAN SEA

Aras
Tigris River
Euphrates R.
MESOPOTAMIA
Seleucia
Babylon
Ctesiphon
Khorsabad
Ecbatana
Susa
ELBURZ MTS.
Persian Gulf
PERSIA
Persepolis
SEISTAN DEPRESSION
PARTHIA
Present-day Coast Line

BACTRIA
Bactra
Samarkand
Tashkurgan
HINDU KUSH
PAMIRS
Kashgar
Yarkand
Khotan

TIEN SHAN
Tarim River
TAKLAMAKAN DESERT
Loulan
ALTYN TAGH
KUNLUN MOUNTAINS
PLATEAU OF TIBET

GOBI DESERT
ORDOS DESERT
Great Wall
Huang (Yellow) R.
Yen
Taiyuan
Chinan
Wei R.
Ch'ang-an
Lo-yang
LUNG SHAN
YANG SHAO
Tai Men
Shu
Pa

CHINA
Wu
River
Han R.
Yangtze
Hsi River (West R.)
P'anyü
NAN LING

Mekong River
Salween River
Irrawaddy River

HIMALAYAS
Mt. Everest
Brahmaputra River
Ganges R.
KOSALA
Pataliputra
MAGADHA
Champa
Indraprastha
Mathura
Taxila
GANDHARA
Harappa
Indus River
Jumna River
THAR DESERT
Mohenjo-Daro
Narbada R.
Godavari R.
Kistna R.
WESTERN GHATS
EASTERN GHATS
ANDHRA
KALINGA

BAY OF BENGAL

INDIAN OCEAN

NORWAY

SWEDEN

DENMARK

Copenhagen

ATLANTIC

Aberdeen

SCOTLAND

Glasgow

Edinburgh

NORTH

SEA

OCEAN

Durham

IRELAND

York

Galway

Dublin

Lincoln

Limerick

Chester

Elbe River

Wexford

Brandenburg

Shannon R.

Cork

Severn R.

ENGLAND

Haarlem

Amsterdam

Rotterdam

Weser River

St. David's

WALES

London

Rhine River

Bruges

Ghent

HOLY

Thames River

Bath

FLANDERS

Louvain

Winchester

Hastings

Ypres

Brussels

Agincourt

Lille

Cateau-

Meuse R.

ARDENNES

LUXEMBOURG

Crécy

Cambrai

Cambrésis

50°

ENGLISH CHANNEL

Amiens

Vervins

Rocroy

50°

Rouen

Soissons

Verdun

ROMAN

Compiègne

Paris

LORRAINE

Brest

NORMANDY

Chartres

CHAMPAGNE

Toul

ALSACE

Seine R.

Clairvaux

Danube River

Mont St. Michel

Champeaux

Luxeuil

BRITTANY

ANJOU

Orléans

Molesme

BURGUNDY

SWITZERLAND

Loire R.

Tours

Vézelay

ALPS

ROMAN

Carnac

Saône R.

VENICE

POITOU

FRANCE

Cluny

EMPIRE

BAY

Poitiers

Lyons

Po River

OF

CENTRAL

PAPAL

Cognac

STATES

BISCAY

AQUITAINE

MASSIF

Rhône R.

Dordogne

CORSICA

Bordeaux

Garonne River

Nîmes

THE CORNICHE

GASCONY

Marseilles

Santiago de

ASTURIAS

Toulouse

Toulon

Compostela

Oviedo

Roncesvalles

Carcassonne

Narbonne

Cave of

Pass

Covadonga

KINGDOM

Perpignan

SARDINIA

CANTABRIAN MTS

OF

Miño

León

Ebro

NAVARRE

PYRENEES

40°

Porto

Saragossa

Barcelona

Douro River

KINGDOM

PORTUGAL

Salamanca

OF

Cagliari

Segovia

ARAGON

KINGDOM OF

Madrid

40°

Toledo

Tagus River

Valencia

Palma

Lisbon

River

CASTILE AND

BALEARIC ISLANDS

Las Navas

SEA

de Tolosa

LEON

Segura R.

Guadiana River

Cordova

River

MEDITERRANEAN

Seville

Guadalquivir River

Granada

Cádiz

KINGDOM OF GRANADA

Strait of Gibraltar

Pillars of Hercules

MUSLIM   STATES

Tangier

Prepared by
Rand McNally & Co., Chicago

4 | MEDIEVAL FRANCE,
SPAIN, AND THE
BRITISH ISLES 1328

England and possessions

France

Kingdom of Navarre

Kingdom of Castile and Leon
and dependencies

Kingdom of Aragon
and dependencies

Kingdom of Granada

Portugal

0   100   200

Scale in Miles

EUROPE 1648

5

Prepared by
Rand McNally & Co., Chicago

URAL MOUNTAINS

KAZAKH

R U S S I A

PERSIA

ARABIA

SYRIA

CASPIAN SEA

CAUCASUS MTS.

Mt. Elbrus

L. Urmia

Tigris River

Euphrates River

Kura R.

L. Sevan

L. Van

PONTIC MOUNTAINS

Kizil River

TAURUS MTS.

L. Tuz

CYPRUS

EGYPT

Nile Delta

Alexandria

CYRENAICA

Bengasi

TRIPOLITANIA

Tripoli

MALTA

Ura River

Kama River

Vyschegda R.

Northern Dvina R.

Suchona River

Volga River

Don River

Sea of Azov

BLACK SEA

Constantinople

Bosphorus

Sea of Marmara

Dardanelles

AEGEAN SEA

RHODES

CRETE (Venice)

Athens

M E D I T E R R A N E A N   S E A

SALONICA

PINDUS MTS.

BALKAN MTS.

Bucharest

Danube R.

Dniester River

TRANSYLVANIA

Dnieper River

Moscow

Lake Onega

Lake Ladoga

Novgorod

Pskov

Peipus

VALDAI HILLS

Kiev

Western Dvina R.

INGRIA

ESTONIA

LIVONIA

Riga

Vilna

LITHUANIA

P O L A N D

Warsaw

Bug R.

Vistula River

O T T O M A N   E M P I R E

HUNGARY

Buda

Ragusa

A D R I A T I C   S E A

Naval Battle of Lepanto 1571

IONIAN SEA

TUNIS

Tunis

Bona (Fr.)

N O R W A Y

S W E D E N

F I N L A N D

Gulf of Bothnia

Gulf of Finland

Stockholm

GOTLAND

B A L T I C   S E A

L. Vatter

COURLAND

EAST PRUSSIA

Königsberg

Oslo

Copenhagen

DENMARK

Kattegat

Skagerrak

NORTH SEA

POMERANIA

BRANDENBURG

Berlin

SAXONY

Wittenberg

Prague

BOHEMIA

Vienna

AUSTRIA

CARINTHIAN ALPS

Venice

ITALIAN STATES

PAPAL STATES

Rome

Milan

Po R.

APENNINES

Tiber R.

Naples

NAPLES

SICILY

Palermo

Messina

TYRRHENIAN SEA

SARDINIA

CORSICA

Bona

Algiers

ALGIERS

FEZ AND MOROCCO

Oran (Sp.)

Melilla (Sp.)

Tangier (Sp.)

Strait of Gibraltar

Fez

GERMAN STATES

Hamburg

Bremen

HOLSTEIN

Osnabrück

Münster

Cologne

Elbe R.

Oder R.

BAVARIA

Munich

Augsburg

Stuttgart

Zurich

SWITZERLAND

Basel

Rhine R.

PALATINATE

Worms

Mainz

Trier

Metz

Verdun

Toul

Strasbourg

Mont + Bénac

Savoy

Turin

Genoa

Nice

Avignon

Marseilles

Rhône R.

Saône R.

HOLLAND

Amsterdam

NETHERLANDS

Brussels

Antwerp

SP. NETH.

FLANDERS

Paris

Seine R.

F R A N C E

Orléans

Loire R.

CENTRAL MASSIF

Toulouse

Garonne R.

Bordeaux

BAY OF BISCAY

Nantes

Brest

Bristol

Southampton

ENGLISH CHANNEL

London

Thames R.

ENGLAND

Edinburgh

SCOTLAND

PENNINES

Dublin

ULSTER

IRELAND

FAEROE IS. (Den.)

SHETLAND IS. (Scot.)

ORKNEY IS.

ATLANTIC OCEAN

P O R T U G A L

Lisbon

Oporto

Oviedo

CANTABRIA

S P A I N

Madrid

Salamanca

CASTILE

Barcelona

PYRENEES

Ebro River

Guadiana R.

Tagus R.

Douro R.

Guadalquivir R.

SIERRA MORENA

SIERRA NEVADA

Granada

Córdoba

Seville

Cádiz

Gibraltar

BALEARIC ISLANDS

Scale in Miles
0   100   200   300   400

	Austrian Hapsburgs		Islamic
	Spanish Hapsburgs		Lutheran
—	Holy Roman Empire		Roman Catholic
	Anglican		
	Calvinist		
	Greek Orthodox		

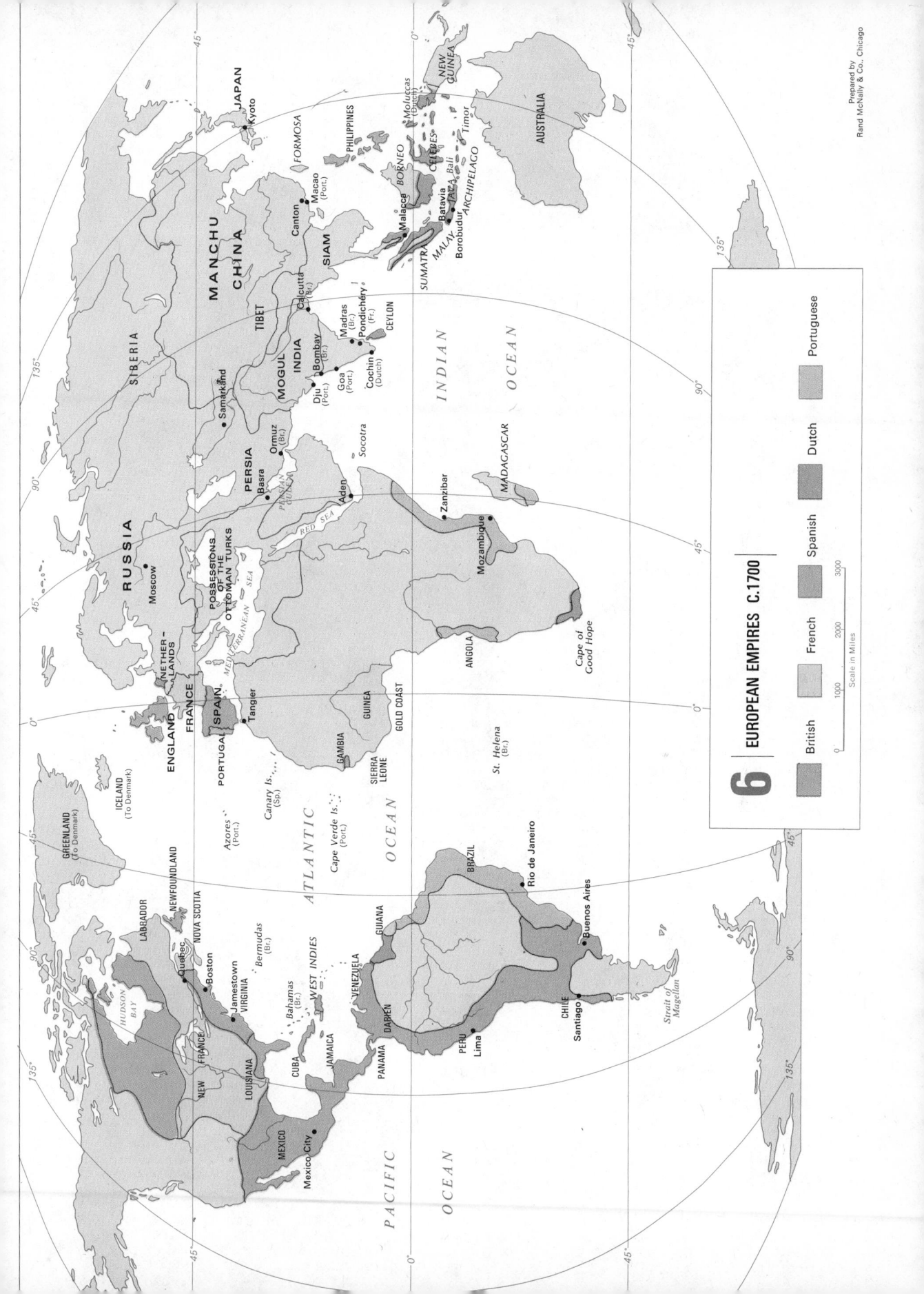

JAPAN
Kyoto

MANCHU CHINA

FORMOSA

Canton

Macao (Port.)

SIAM

PHILIPPINES

Moluccas (Dutch)

NEW GUINEA

CELEBES

BORNEO

Malacca

Batavia

JAVA Bali

Timor

AUSTRALIA

Borobudur

MALAY ARCHIPELAGO

SUMATRA

CEYLON

Calcutta (Br.)

TIBET

Madras (Br.)

Pondichéry (Fr.)

MOGUL INDIA

Bombay (Br.)

Goa (Port.)

Cochin (Dutch)

Dju (Port.)

SIBERIA

Samarkand

PERSIA

Basra

Ormuz (Br.)

Socotra

PERSIAN GULF

Aden

RED SEA

INDIAN OCEAN

Zanzibar

MADAGASCAR

Mozambique

RUSSIA

Moscow

POSSESSIONS OF THE OTTOMAN TURKS

MEDITERRANEAN SEA

ANGOLA

Cape of Good Hope

NETHER-LANDS

ENGLAND

FRANCE

SPAIN

PORTUGAL

Tanger

GUINEA

GOLD COAST

GAMBIA

SIERRA LEONE

St. Helena (Br.)

ICELAND (To Denmark)

GREENLAND (To Denmark)

Azores (Port.)

Canary Is. (Sp.)

Cape Verde Is. (Port.)

ATLANTIC OCEAN

BRAZIL

Rio de Janeiro

Buenos Aires

GUIANA

VENEZUELA

DARIEN

CHILE

Santiago

PERU

Lima

PANAMA

LABRADOR

NEWFOUNDLAND

NOVA SCOTIA

Quebec

Boston

Jamestown

VIRGINIA

Bermudas (Br.)

WEST INDIES

Bahamas (Br.)

CUBA

JAMAICA

NEW FRANCE

LOUISIANA

MEXICO

Mexico City

HUDSON BAY

Strait of Magellan

PACIFIC OCEAN

Prepared by
Rand McNally & Co., Chicago

6 EUROPEAN EMPIRES C.1700

British   French   Spanish   Dutch   Portuguese

Scale in Miles

0   1000   2000   3000

URAL MOUNTAINS

Tavda R.
Tura R.
Ishim R.
Tobol R.

RUSSIAN EMPIRE

CASPIAN SEA

PERSIA

Ural River

L. Urma
Kura River
CAUCASUS MTS.
Mt. Elbrus
CIRCASSIA
PONTIC MOUNTAINS
Van
L. Tuz
TAURUS MTS.
SYRIA
Jerusalem
Beirut
Euphrates River
Tigris River
Ankara
Smyrna
CYPRUS
Alexandria

Arkhangelsk

White Sea
L. Onega
L. Ladoga
St. Petersburg
Narva
Novgorod
L. Ilmen
L. Peipus
Reval
Riga
Moscow
Tsaritsyn
Kharkov
Poltava
Azov
Sea of Azov
CRIMEA
Sevastopol
Odessa
Kiev
BLACK SEA
Constantinople
San Stefano
Adrianople
Bosporus
BALKAN MTS.
Dardanelles
Sea of Marmara
AEGEAN SEA
GREECE
Athens
Navarino
IONIAN ISLANDS (Br.)
CRETE

FINLAND
Nystad
Helsinki
Stockholm
Aland Is.
Gotland
Oland
BALTIC SEA
Königsberg
Danzig
LITHUANIA
Tilsit
Warsaw
POLAND
Vistula R.
Bug R.
Niemen R.
Western Dvina R.
Northern Dvina R.
Sukhona R.

Volga River
Don River
Dnieper River
Dniester River

BESSARABIA
MOLDAVIA
CARPATHIANS
TRANSYLVANIAN ALPS
TRANSYLVANIA
HUNGARY
WALLACHIA
RUMANIA
Bucharest
BULGARIA
SERBIA
Belgrade
Karlowitz
MONTE NEGRO
ALBANIA
HERZEGOVINA
BOSNIA
DALMATIA
CROATIA
SLAVONIA

EMPIRE OF AUSTRIA
BOHEMIA
Prague
Carlsbad
Austerlitz
Sadowa
Troppau
Breslau
Buda
Pest
KINGDOM OF HUNGARY
Vienna
Laibach
Venice
VENETIA
LOMBARDY
Verona

PRUSSIA
BRANDENBURG
Berlin
SAXONY
Leipzig
Frankfurt
BERG
Cologne
Aix-la-Chapelle
HANOVER
Bremen
Hamburg
MECKLENBURG

KINGDOM OF NORWAY AND SWEDEN
Bergen
Oslo
Göteborg
L. Vänern
L. Vättern
Skagerrak
Kattegat
Copenhagen
KINGDOM OF DENMARK
SCHLESWIG
HOLSTEIN
NORTH SEA

KINGDOM OF THE NETHERLANDS
Amsterdam
The Hague
Utrecht
BELGIUM
Brussels
Antwerp
Waterloo
Sedan
LUXEMBOURG

THE UNITED KINGDOM OF GREAT BRITAIN AND IRELAND
Edinburgh
Glasgow
Liverpool
Manchester
Birmingham
London
Dublin
IRISH SEA
ENGLISH CHANNEL
Dover
Le Havre
Paris
Versailles
Valmy
Seine River
Nantes
Lorient
La Rochelle
Bordeaux
BAY OF BISCAY

FRANCE
ALSACE
Strasbourg
BADEN
WÜRTTEMBERG
Ulm
BAVARIA
Munich
Augsburg
SWITZERLAND
Geneva
NEUCHATEL
Verdun
Sedan
SAVOY
Nice
MONACO
PIEDMONT
Genoa
Milan
PARMA
LUCCA
TUSCANY
Florence
SAN MARINO
PAPAL STATES
Rome
CORSICA (Fr.)
Elba
LIECHTENSTEIN

KINGDOM OF SARDINIA

Marseilles
Rhône River
Loire River
Saône River
Rhine River
Central Massif
Garonne River

PYRENEES
ANDORRA
Barcelona
BALEARIC ISLANDS

SPAIN
Madrid
CANTABRIAN MTS.
Duero River
Ebro River
Tagus River
SIERRA MORENA
SIERRA NEVADA
Oran
Algiers

PORTUGAL
Lisbon
Cádiz
Cape Trafalgar
Gibraltar (Br.)
Strait of Gibraltar
Ceuta (Sp.)
Melilla (Sp.)
MOROCCO
Casablanca

ATLANTIC OCEAN

FAEROE IS. (Den.)
SHETLAND IS. (Br.)
ORKNEY IS. (Br.)

KINGDOM OF NAPLES AND SICILY
Naples
Palermo
Tyrrhenian Sea
MALTA (Br.)
Adriatic Sea
Ionian Sea
APENNINES

MEDITERRANEAN SEA

Tunis
TUNIS
ALGERIA
ATLAS MOUNTAINS

Tripoli
TRIPOLITANIA

Bengasi

OTTOMAN EMPIRE

Prepared by Rand McNally & Co., Chicago

7 EUROPE 1815

───── Boundary of German Confederation

▨ Small German States

Scale of Miles
0   100   200   300   400

8 | EUROPE AUGUST 1939

German aggression

- Military reoccupation of the Rhineland 1936
- Seizure of Austria 1938
- Seizure of Memel 1939
- Occupation of Sudetenland 1938
- Seizure of other Czech territory 1939
- Other territorial aggressions
- Czech territory annexed by Hungary 1938-1939
- Italian seizure of Albania 1939

Prepared by Uni-Map, Inc. Palatine, Ill.

ATLANTIC

OCEAN

London
Amsterdam • Berlin
• Brussels • Warsaw
Paris
Vienna
Budapest
Belgrade
Rome
Constantinople
Athens
BLACK SEA
CASPIAN SEA
Aral Sea

Madrid
Lisbon
Tehran
MEDITERRANEAN
Damascus
Baghdad
Tangier • SP. Algiers
Casablanca MOROCCO Tunis
ATLAS MOUNTAINS TUNISIA
MOROCCO ALGERIA Tripoli
IFNI Bengasi
Jerusalem
SEA
Alexandria
Suez Canal
Cairo
MADEIRA IS.
(Port.)
CANARY IS.
(Br.)

RIO DE ORO
LIBYA
EGYPT
LIBYAN
DESERT
ARABIAN

Villa
Cisneros
S A H A R A
Aswan
AHAGGAR MTS.
Mecca PENINSULA

TIBESTI
MASSIF
NUBIAN
DESERT
ANGLO-
ERITREA
Aden

FRENCH WEST AFRICA
S U D A N
Omdurman
Khartoum
Asmara
Gulf of Aden

Dakar
SENEGAL
Timbuktu
Niger R.
L. Chad CHAD
EGYPTIAN
L. Tana
FR. SOM.
Djibouti
Berbera
BR. SOM.

GAMBIA
Bissau PORT.
GUINEA
Bamako
Kano
Ft. Lamy
Shari
SUDAN
Addis
Ababa
ABYSSINIA
(ETHIOPIA)

FRENCH GUINEA
SIERRA
LEONE
IVORY
COAST
GOLD
COAST
TOGO
DAHOMEY
NIGERIA
Benue R.
ITALIAN SOMALILAND

Freetown
Monrovia
LIBERIA
Lagos
Lome
Accra
CAMEROONS
Douala
EQUATORIAL
AFRICA
UBANGI-SHARI
Bomu R.
Uele R.
CONGO
Congo
BASIN
Stanleyville
Entebbe
L. Albert
UGANDA
KENYA
(BR. EAST AFR.)
L. Rudolf
Mogadishu

GULF OF
GUINEA
FERNANDO PO
(Sp.)
PRINCIPE
(Port.)
SAO TOME
(Port.)
ANNOBÓN
(Sp.)
RIO
MUNI
Libreville
GABON
FRENCH
Brazzaville
Léopoldville
CABINDA
BELGIAN
CONGO
Lake
Victoria
Mt. Kilimanjaro
Tabora
GERMAN
EAST
AFRICA
Nairobi
Mombasa
ZANZIBAR (Br.)
Dar-es-Salaam

INDIAN
OCEAN

ALDABRA IS.
(Br.)

Luanda
Lake
Tanganyika
COMORO IS.
(Fr.)

ANGOLA
(PORT. WEST AFR.)
NORTHERN
RHODESIA
Lake
Nyasa
NYASALAND
Blantyre

Benguela
Livingstone
Salisbury
SOUTHERN
RHODESIA
Zambezi
Victoria
Falls
Beira
MOZAMBIQUE
(PORT. EAST AFR.)

GERMAN
SOUTHWEST
AFRICA
KALAHARI
DESERT
BECHUANALAND
Windhoek
Walvis Bay
NAMIB DESERT
MADAGASCAR
Tamatave
Tananarive

Lüderitz
Mafeking
Pretoria
Johannesburg
SWAZILAND
Lourenço Marques
BASUTOLAND
Orange R.
UNION OF
Durban
Limpopo R.

SOUTH AFRICA
East London
Cape Town
Port Elizabeth
Cape of Good Hope

9 | AFRICA 1914

British
French
German
Belgian
Portuguese
Italian
Spanish

0   400   800
Scale in Miles

Prepared by Uni-Map, Inc. Palatine,

ATLANTIC

OCEAN

Azores .. (Port.)

Madeira Is. (Port.)

Canary Is. (Sp.)

NORTH SEA

BALTIC SEA

EUROPE

•Dublin

•London

•Amsterdam •Berlin •Warsaw

•Brussels

•Paris •Bern •Prague •Vienna •Budapest

•Bucharest

•Belgrade *Danube R.*

Dnieper R.

Volga

•Moscow

Aral Sea

ALPS

Rhine

BLACK SEA

CAUCASUS MTS.

•Baku

CASPIAN SEA

•Lisbon •Madrid •Rome

MEDITERRANEAN

•Algiers •Tunis

CRÈTE SEA

•Istanbul

•Ankara

•Athens

CYPRUS

•Beirut

•Tel Aviv •Damascus •Amman

•Jerusalem

•Baghdad

Euphrates R. *Tigris R.*

•Tehran

ASIA

PERSIAN GULF

•Tangier •Rabat

ATLAS MOUNTAINS

MOROCCO

•Casablanca

•Agadir

IFNI (Sp.) •Sidi Ifni

•Aiún

•Tripoli

•Bengasi •Alexandria

Suez Canal

•Cairo

—Israeli – occupied area June, 1967

ARABIAN

•Riyadh

ALGERIA

LIBYA

EGYPT

LIBYAN DESERT

S A H A R A

TIBESTI MASSIF

NUBIAN DESERT

RED SEA

•Mecca

PENINSULA

MAURITANIA

•Nouakchott

MALI

NIGER

CHAD

•Sana

•Aden *Gulf of Aden*

•Dakar

GAMBIA •Banjul

JINEA- SSAU •Bissau

GUINEA

•Conakry •Freetown

SIERRA LEONE

•Monrovia

LIBERIA

Cape Palmas

SENEGAL

Senegal R.

Gambia R.

•Bamako

S U D A N

•Niamey

•Ouagadougou

UPPER VOLTA

Niger R.

•Kano

NIGERIA

•Khartoum

SUDAN

L. Chad

•Fort-Lamy

Benue R.

White Nile

Blue Nile

L. Tana

ERITREA •Asmara

AFARS AND ISSAS (Fr.) •Djibouti

AMHARA

•Addis Ababa

PLATEAU

ETHIOPIA

IVORY COAST

GHANA

TOGO

BENIN

•Lomé •Lagos •Accra •Porto- Novo

•Abidjan

CAMEROON

•Santa Isabel

EQUATORIAL GUINEA

Principe

São Tomé

CENTRAL AFRICAN REPUBLIC

•Bangui

•Yaoundé

Ubangi R.

Uélé

Bomu R.

CONGO BASIN

•Kisangani (Stanleyville)

Congo R.

L. Albert

Mountain Nile

UGANDA

•Kampala

L. Rudolf

KENYA

+Mt. Kenya •Nairobi

•Mogadishu

SOMALIA

ATLANTIC

OCEAN

Ascension (Br.)

GABON

•Libreville

CONGO

•Brassaville

Congo R.

Kasai R.

ZAIRE

•Kinshasa (Léopoldville)

Kwango R.

RWANDA •Kigali

BURUNDI •Bujumbura

Lake Victoria

Kilimanjaro +

•Dar es Salaam

L. Tanganyika

•Zanzibar

INDIAN

OCEAN

•Luanda

St. Helena (Br.)

•Benguela

ANGOLA

Cunene

Zambezi

ZAMBIA

•Lusaka

MALAWI

L. Nyasa

TANZANIA

Ruvuma R.

Aldabra Is. (Br.)

Comoro Is. (Fr.)

MOZAMBIQUE

CHANNEL

MADAGASCAR

•Tananarive

NAMIBIA

•Windhoek

•Walvis Bay (S. Africa)

(S. W. Africa)

NAMIB DESERT

KALAHARI DESERT

BOTSWANA

•Serowe

•Gaberone

•Mafeking

•Pretoria

•Johannesburg

SOUTH

•Maseru

LESOTHO

Zambezi R.

•Zamba

Victoria Falls

Kariba Lake

•Salisbury

RHODESIA

•Zimbabwe

DRAKENSBERG

•Mbabane

SWAZILAND

BOPHUTHATSWANA

•Durban

MOZAMBIQUE

•Lourenço Marques

Orange R.

AFRICA

TRANSKEI

•Cape Town

Cape of Good Hope

•Port Elizabeth

INDIAN

OCEAN

10 | AFRICA

Map information based upon data available August **1978**

0   400   800

Scale in Miles

Prepared by
Rand McNally & Co., Chicago

OCEAN

NEW SIBERIAN ISLANDS

180°

Wrangel I.

ANADYR RANGE

BERING SEA

CHERSKIY MTS.

VERKHOYANSK

Lena River

Zhigansk

Verkhoyansk

MOUNTAINS

Kolyma R.

Markovo

Seymchan

Vilyuy River

Yakutsk

LIST   REPUBLIC

Aldan River

Magadan

60°

KAMCHATKA PENINSULA

SEA OF OKHOTSK

Petropavlovsk

Aleutian Islands

180°

PUBLICS

Lake Baikal

Irkutsk

Amur River

Aleksandrovsk

SAKHALIN

Ulan-Ude

Chita

YABLONOVY RANGE

Khabarovsk

Korsakov

Kuril Islands

GREAT KHINGAN MTS.

HOKKAIDO

MONGOLIA

Ulan Bator

Harbin

Vladivostok

SEA OF JAPAN

GOBI DESERT

Paotow

Kalgan

Peking (Peiping)

Mukden

NORTH KOREA

JAPAN

HONSHU

NAN SHAN

Koko Nor

Tientsin

Port Arthur

Pyongyang

Seoul

SOUTH KOREA

Osaka

Tokyo

PACIFIC

N MOUNTAINS

Lanchow

Sian

Yellow (Huang) River

KOREA

Pusan

Kitakyushu

KYUSHU

SHIKOKU

TIBET

CHINA

Wuhan

Yangtze River

Shanghai

YELLOW SEA

EAST CHINA SEA

30°

Lhasa

MALAYAS

SIKKIM

BHUTAN

Chungking

Hsi River

Foochow

OCEAN

Brahmaputra R.

NAN LING

Taipei

Ryukyu Islands

Dacca

PAK

Kunming

Canton

Kowloon

TAIWAN (FORMOSA)

Calcutta

BURMA

Hanoi

Macao (Port.)

Victoria

HONG KONG (Br.)

NORTH VIETNAM

HAINAN

Rangoon

Vientiane

LAOS

VIETNAM

SOUTH CHINA SEA

LUZON

Guam I. (U.S.)

BAY OF BENGAL

THAILAND

Bangkok

SOUTH VIETNAM

Quezon City

Manila

PHILIPPINES

PHILIPPINE SEA

CAMBODIA

Phnom Penh

Saigon

CHINA SEA

Celebes Sea

YLON

bo

MINDANAO

MALAYSIA

BRUNEI (Br.)

SABAH

MALAYA

Kuala Lumpur

SARAWAK

SINGAPORE

BORNEO

CELEBES

MOLUCCA ISLANDS

0°

Sukarnapura

NEW IRELAND

WEST IRIAN (Indo.)

NEW GUINEA

TERRITORY OF NEW GUINEA (Austl.)

SUMATRA

Djakarta

Surabaja

JAVA

INDONESIA

FLORES

Dili

PORT. TIMOR

PAPUA (Austl.)

NEW BRITAIN

OCEAN

OCUSSI (Port. Timor)

TIMOR

AUSTRALIA

Port Moresby

90°

120°

150°

Great
Salt Lake

ROCKY MOUNTAINS

Chicago

New York

Washington

ATLANTIC

OCEAN

Denver

St. Louis

UNITED STATES

Colorado R.

Bermuda Is.
(Br.)

Dallas

Mississippi R.

New
Orleans

MEXICO

Laredo

Miami

GULF OF

MEXICO

BAHAMA ISLANDS
(Br.)

Monterrey

Havana

SIERRA MADRE OCCIDENTAL

GULF OF CALIFORNIA

Tampico

CUBA

Rio Grande

SIERRA MADRE ORIENTAL

DOMINICAN
REPUBLIC

Guadalajara

Mérida

WEST

PUERTO
RICO
(U.S.)

Guadeloupe
(Fr.)

Sta. Maria R.

Mexico
City

Chapultepec

Veracruz

Chichen Itza

JAMAICA

Port-
au-Prince

HAITI

Santo
Domingo

Uxmal

Kingston

Acapulco

Oaxaca

Balsas R.

BELIZE

BRITISH
HONDURAS

INDIES

Martinique
(Fr.)

Conchos R.

CARIBBEAN SEA

BARBADOS

GUATEMALA
Guatemala

HONDURAS
Tegucigalpa

NICARAGUA

TRINIDAD AND TOBAGO
Port-of-Spain

San Salvador

EL
SALVADOR

Managua

Barranquilla

Lake
Maracaibo

Caracas

Orinoco R.

COSTA RICA
San José

CANAL
ZONE

Colón

Panama

U.S.

PANAMA

VENEZUELA

Georgetown

GUYANA

SURINAM
(Neth.)

Paramaribo

FRENCH GUIANA

Cayenne

Bogotá

COLOMBIA

Buenaventura

Magdalena R.

GUIANA HIGHLANDS

Frontera

Rio Negro

Japurá R.

Manaus

Belém

Quito

ECUADOR

Guayaquil

GALÁPAGOS IS.
(Ec.)

Iquitos

Marañón R.

Amazon R.

Purús R.

Madeira River

Tapajós R.

Xingú River

Tocantins R.

Recife

PACIFIC

PERU

Lima

Ucayali R.

ANDES

Guaporé R.

Mamoré R.

BRAZIL

PLATEAU OF
MATO GROSSO

São Francisco R.

BRAZILIAN

HIGHLANDS

Salvador

Arequipa

Lake
Titicaca

La Paz

BOLIVIA

Sucre

OCEAN

Rio Grande

Bello
Horizonte

Brasília

ATACAMA DESERT

PARAGUAY

Pilcomayo R.

São Paulo

Rio de Janeiro

Santos

Antofagasta

GRAN CHACO

Asunción

Salado R.

Iguassu
Falls

Paraná River

Uruguay R.

Tucumán

MTS.

Mt.
Aconcagua

Córdoba

Santa Fé

Rosário

URUGUAY

Montevideo

Valparaiso

Santiago

Mendoza

ARGENTINA

Buenos
Aires

Rio de la Plata

ATLANTIC

Colorado R.

PAMPAS

CHILE

ANDES

Valdivia

PATAGONIA

Bahía Blanca

Chubut R.

OCEAN

Punta Arenas

FALKLAND IS.
(Br.)

TIERRA DEL FUEGO

Cape Horn

SOUTH GEORGIA
(Br.)

Drake Passage

SOUTH
ORKNEY IS.
(Br.)

ANTARCTICA

12 LATIN AMERICA

Map information based upon
data available August 1968

0   400   800

Scale in Miles

Prepared by
Rand McNally & Co., Chicago

THE MIDDLE EAST

13

Scale in Miles
0   100   200   300   400

Prepared by
Rand McNally & Co., Chicago

URAL MOUNTAINS
Sverdlovsk
Tura R.
Orenburg
Kuybyshev
Perm
Ufa
Ural River
Kotlas

Kuybyshev Res.
River
Gурьev
Kama

CASPIAN
SEA
Baku

IRAN
Tabriz
L. Urmia

IRAQ
Baghdad
Tigris River
Euphrates
SYRIAN DESERT

UNION
Penza
Volgograd
Astrakhan
Gorki
Moscow
Don R.
Rybinsk Res.

OF
Volga River
Don River
Rostov
Sochi
Batumi
CAUCASUS MTS.
Mt. Elbrus
PONTIC MOUNTAINS
Tbilisi
L. Sevan

SOVIET
Orel
Kharkov
Kiev
Poltava
Sea of Azov
CRIMEA
Sevastopol
Yalta
Odessa

SOCIALIST
Smolensk
Minsk
Dnieper River
Dniester River
Bug R.

REPUBLICS
Leningrad
VALDAI HILLS
Lake Onega
Lake Ladoga
White Sea

Arkhangelsk
Northern Dvina R.
Sukhona River

SYRIA
Damascus
Amman
Dead Sea
LEBANON
Beirut
ISRAEL
Jerusalem
Suez C.
CYPRUS
Nicosia

TURKEY
Ankara
Istanbul
Sea of Marmara
Dardanelles
Bosporus
TAURUS MTS.

BLACK SEA
Varna
Bucharest

FINLAND
Helsinki
Turku
Gulf of Finland
Tallinn
Vilna
Riga
Kaliningrad
L. Peipus
Western Dvina R.

SWEDEN
NORWAY
Oslo
Bergen
Stavanger
Lulea
GULF OF BOTHNIA
Gotland
Oland
Stockholm
Gotland
L. Vaner
L. Vater
BALTIC SEA

DENMARK
Copenhagen
Kattegat
Skagerrak

POLAND
Warsaw
Gdańsk
Szczecin
Wroclaw
Cracow
Vistula
Oder R.

EAST GERMANY
Berlin
Brest
Lvov

RUMANIA
TRANSYLVANIAN ALPS
CARPATHIANS
Danube R.

BULGARIA
Sofia
BALKAN MTS.
Salonika
GREECE
Athens
PINDUS MTS.

AEGEAN SEA
RHODES
Candia
CRETE

CZECHOSLOVAKIA
Prague
Bratislava
SUDETES

HUNGARY
Budapest
Vienna

AUSTRIA
ALPS

YUGOSLAVIA
Belgrade
Sarajevo
ALBANIA
Tirana
ADRIATIC SEA

WEST GERMANY
Hamburg
Bremen
Cologne
Bonn
Frankfurt
Stuttgart
Munich
Rhine R.
Elbe R.

ITALY
APENNINES
SAN MARINO
Venice
Milan
Turin
Florence
Rome
Naples
Palermo
SICILY
Tiber R.
Po R.

NETHERLANDS
Amsterdam
The Hague
Rotterdam
BELGIUM
Antwerp
Brussels
LUX.
Luxembourg
LIECH.
MONACO
Nice
Monte Carlo

SWITZERLAND
Bern
Geneva
Mont Blanc
Trieste

UNITED KINGDOM
SCOTLAND
Aberdeen
Edinburgh
Glasgow
ENGLAND
Newcastle
Manchester
Liverpool
London
Thames R.
WALES
NORTHERN IRELAND
Belfast
IRELAND
Dublin
IRISH SEA
NORTH SEA

FRANCE
Paris
Lyons
Marseilles
Strasbourg
Bordeaux
Brest
Nantes
Seine R.
Loire R.
Rhône R.
Garonne R.
CENTRAL MASSIF
PYRENEES

CORSICA
Ajaccio
SARDINIA
Cagliari
TYRRHENIAN SEA

MALTA
TUNISIA
Tunis
LIBYA
Tripoli
Bengasi

MEDITERRANEAN SEA

SPAIN
Madrid
Barcelona
Valencia
Bilbao
SIERRA NEVADA
SIERRA MORENA
Guadalquivir R.
Douro R.
Tagus R.
Ebro River
CANTABRIAN MTS.
BALEARIC IS.
Palma

PORTUGAL
Lisbon
Oporto

MOROCCO
Rabat
Tangier
Ceuta (Sp.)
ATLAS MOUNTAINS
ALGERIA
Algiers
Oran
Strait of Gibraltar
Gibraltar (Br.)
ANDORRA
BAY OF BISCAY

ATLANTIC OCEAN
Faeroe Is. (Den.)
Shetland Is.

14 | EUROPE

Map information based upon data available November 1966

Scale in Miles
0   100   200   300   400